THE POLITICS OF CHINA

Third Edition

Thirty years ago, China was emerging from one of the most traumatic periods in its history. The Chinese people had been ravaged by long years of domestic struggle, terrible famine, and economic and political isolation. Today, China has the world's second-largest economy and is a major player in global diplomacy. This volume, written by some of the leading experts in the field, tracks China's extraordinary transformation from the establishment of the People's Republic of China in 1949; through the Great Leap Forward, the Cultural Revolution, and the death of Chairman Mao; to its dynamic rise as a superpower in the twenty-first century. This latest edition of the book includes a new introduction and a seventh chapter that focuses on the legacy of Deng Xiaoping, the godfather of China's transformation, and his successors Jiang Zemin and Hu Jintao. Under Mao, China challenged the outside world ideologically and militarily. Today China's challenge as an economic and diplomatic superpower may prove even more formidable. As a comprehensive and authoritative appraisal of China's last sixty years, this book will be invaluable for professionals working in the region and for students assessing what China will mean for their futures.

Roderick MacFarquhar is the Leroy B. Williams Professor of History and Political Science and Professor of Government at Harvard University. He has had an illustrious career. He was Director of the Fairbank Center for East Asian Research at Harvard University, the founding editor of *The China Quarterly*, and a member of Parliament. His publications include *Mao's Last Revolution* (2006), co-authored with Michael Schoenhals, and *The Origins of the Cultural Revolution* (3 vols., 1974, 1983, 1997). He is also co-editor, with the late John K. Fairbank, of volumes 14 and 15 of *The Cambridge History of China* (1987, 1991).

THE POLITICS OF CHINA

CHINA

Sixty Years of the People's Republic of China

Third Edition

Edited by

RODERICK MACFARQUHAR

Harvard University

CAMBRIDGE UNIVERSITY PRESS
Cambridge, New York, Melbourne, Madrid, Cape Town,
Singapore, São Paulo, Delhi, Tokyo, Mexico City

Cambridge University Press
32 Avenue of the Americas, New York, NY 10013-2473, USA

www.cambridge.org
Information on this title: www.cambridge.org/9780521145312

First published 1994
Second edition published 1997
Third edition published 2011

Printed in the United States of America

A catalog record for this publication is available from the British Library.

Library of Congress Cataloging in Publication data

The politics of China : sixty years of the people's republic of China / [edited by] Roderick
MacFarquhar. – 3rd ed.
p.   cm.
Includes bibliographical references and index.
ISBN 978-0-521-19693-2 (hardback) – ISBN 978-0-521-14531-2 (paperback)
1. China – Politics and government – 1949–   I. MacFarquhar, Roderick.   II. Title.
DS777.75.P64   2011
320.951–dc20   2011001976

ISBN 978-0-521-19693-2 Hardback
ISBN 978-0-521-14531-2 Paperback

CONTENTS

Tables and maps   *page* vii

Preface   ix

Abbreviations   xi

Introduction   1
by RODERICK MACFARQUHAR, *Leroy B. Williams Professor
of History and Political Science, Harvard University*

1 The establishment and consolidation of the new regime,
   1949–1957   6
   by FREDERICK C. TEIWES, *Professor of Government, The
   University of Sydney*

2 The Great Leap Forward and the split in the Yan'an leadership,
   1958–1965   87
   by KENNETH LIEBERTHAL, *Professor of Political Science, The
   University of Michigan*

3 The Chinese state in crisis, 1966–1969   147
   by HARRY HARDING, *Professor of International Affairs, The
   George Washington University*

4 The succession to Mao and the end of Maoism, 1969–1982   246
   by RODERICK MACFARQUHAR, *Leroy B. Williams Professor
   of History and Political Science, Harvard University*

5   The road to Tiananmen: Chinese politics in the 1980s   337
    by RICHARD BAUM, *Professor of Political Science, The University
    of California, Los Angeles*

6   Reaction, resurgence, and succession: Chinese politics since
    Tiananmen   468
    by JOSEPH FEWSMITH, *Professor of International Relations and
    Political Science, Boston University*

7   Dilemmas of globalization and governance   528
    by ALICE MILLER, *Research Fellow, Hoover Institution at
    Stanford University*

Appendix: Leaders and Meetings   601

References   607

Index   651

TABLES AND MAPS

TABLES

1	Agricultural cooperatives: Development and targets	*page* 59
2	Politburo named after CCP's Ninth Congress, April 1969	249
3	Lin Biao's team: Allies and conspirators	267
4	Leadership changes, April 1969–August 1973	282
5	The political complexion of the Politburo after the death of Zhou Enlai	297

MAPS

| 1 | PRC: political (*pinyin* romanization) | 8 |
| 2 | Administrative regions, 1949–54 | 31 |

PREFACE

The aim of this book is to provide a comprehensive account of sixty years of the politics of the People's Republic of China, 1949 to 2009. The first four chapters, covering the years of the Mao era and its immediate aftermath, 1949–1982, are drawn from Volumes 14 and 15 of the *Cambridge History of China* (*CHOC*). The fifth and sixth were commissioned for the first and second editions of this book to cover the Deng Xiaoping era. The seventh chapter was commissioned for this third edition to cover the final years of this cycle of Cathay.

The chapters drawn from *CHOC* were part of an integrated schema that included chapters on economics, education, culture, society, and foreign policy, but since "politics took command" of everything in Mao's China, these chapters on politics touch on those other topics as well.

In the passage of time since the publication of the first edition of this book, some of our contributors have moved on: Frederick Teiwes is now Emeritus Professor at the University of Sydney; Kenneth Lieberthal has joined the Brookings Institution as a Senior Fellow and is Director of the John L. Thornton China Center; in 2009, Harry Harding became the founding Dean of the Batten School of Leadership and Public Policy at the University of Virginia; and Joseph Fewsmith is now Professor of International Relations and Director of the Center for the Study of Asia at Boston University. But we have thought it appropriate to retain in the contents the titles they held when they wrote their chapters.

The John King Fairbank Center for East Asian Research has been renamed the Fairbank Center for Chinese Studies, but Nancy Hearst is still its librarian, and she painstakingly undertook the time-consuming tasks of proofreading the seventh chapter, preparing its bibliography for integration into the main one, and updating the appendixes at the end of the volume.

This third edition is again dedicated to the memory of John King Fairbank, the organizing genius behind the six *CHOC* volumes on modern China.

ABBREVIATIONS

AF	Air Force
alt	alternate
APC	Agricultural Producers' Cooperative
APC	armored personnel carrier [chap. 5]
BSAF	Beijing Students' Autonomous Federation
CAC	Central Advisory Commission
CASS	Chinese Academy of Social Sciences
CC	Central Committee
CCP	Chinese Communist Party
CDIC	Central Discipline Investigation Commission
CITIC	China International Trust and Investment Corporation
CMC	Central Military Commission
CO	commanding officer
CPPCC	Chinese People's Political Consultative Conference
CPSU	Communist Party of the Soviet Union
CRG	Cultural Revolution Group
CUST	Chinese University of Science and Technology
f	female
FYP	Five-Year Plan
GLF	Great Leap Forward
GPCR	Great Proletarian Cultural Revolution
HQ	headquarters
KMT	(Kuomintang) Guomindang
MAC	Military Affairs Commission
MAT	Mutual Aid Teams
MR	Military Region
NCNA	New China News Agency
NEP	New Economic Policy
NKVD	*Narodnyi Komissariat Vnutrennikh Del*

NPC	National People's Congress
PAP	People's Armed Police Force
PKI	Communist Party of Indonesia
PLA	People's Liberation Army
PRC	People's Republic of China
PSC	Politburo Standing Committee
Rev Comm.	Revolutionary Committee
SARS	Severe Acute Respiratory Syndrome
SASAC	State-owned Assets Supervision and Administration Commission
SC	Standing Committee
SEC	State Economic Commission
SEZ	Special Economic Zone
SPC	State Planning Commission
TVE	township and village enterprise
USSR	Union of Soviet Socialist Republics
VC	vice-chairman
WHO	World Health Organization
WTO	World Trade Organization

INTRODUCTION

RODERICK MacFARQUHAR

Sixty years is a long life-span for a revolutionary regime to survive and remain vigorous.[1] The celebration in 2009 of the 60th anniversary of the Chinese communist conquest of power and the creation of the People's Republic of China (PRC) was in stark contrast to the fate of its erstwhile Soviet "elder brother." Despite suffering terrible human tragedies and political upheavals – notably, the great famine of 1959–61 and the Cultural Revolution of 1966–76[2] – the PRC had emerged as a powerful and dynamic country. The purpose of this volume is to chronicle how that came about. The purpose of this introduction is to proffer a hypothesis, based on that chronicle, to explain the Chinese success.

One factor was surely the longevity of the revolutionary leadership.[3] Despite the enormous problems of revolutionary nation-building described in the first two chapters of this volume covering the period from 1949 to 1965, the seven members of the ruling Politburo Standing Committee (PSC) remained in place for seventeen years until Mao purged colleagues whom he no longer trusted

---

1 The English Revolution of the 17th Century – the Protectorate – lasted only slightly more than a decade from the execution of King Charles I in January 1649 to the restoration of his son as King Charles II in 1660. If one takes the storming of the Bastille on 14 July 1789 as the symbolic start of the French Revolution, it was only fifteen years until Napoleon was crowned emperor in 1804. If one dates it from the execution of Louis XVI in 1793, the revolutionary era lasted barely a decade. The Soviet regime lasted seventy-four years, but by the 60th anniversary of the Bolshevik Revolution in 1977, the Soviet Union was wallowing in the stagnation and corruption of the Brezhnev era, and the efforts of Gorbachev to revive it in the late 1980s with *perestroika* and *glasnost* only brought about its demise. Despite the loss of its Soviet benefactor and the U.S. embargo, the Cuban revolutionary regime celebrated its 50th anniversary in 2009 under the continuing aegis of the Castro brothers. The communist revolution in Vietnam – partially a liberation struggle – was finally victorious in 1975, and a strong regime has been in power for thirty-six years.

2 For the famine, see below, Chapter 2, and, for more detail, Frank Dikötter, *Mao's Great Famine: The history of China's most devastating catastrophe, 1958–1962* (London: Bloomsbury, 2010); for the Cultural Revolution, see below, Chapters 3 and 4, and Roderick MacFarquhar and Michael Schoenhals, *Mao's last revolution* (Cambridge, Mass.: Harvard Belknap Press, 2006).

3 The English Protectorate collapsed two years after the death of Oliver Cromwell, the Lord Protector. Robespierre, Danton, and other prominent French revolutionary leaders were guillotined in 1794, only a year after the execution of Louis XVI and Marie Antoinette. Stalin made sure that all leaders of the Bolshevik Revolution had been executed long before he himself died.

during the Cultural Revolution.[4] Even so, two members of the pre-Cultural Revolution PSC, Deng Xiaoping and Chen Yun, as well as other senior leaders, survived that political upheaval, and Deng emerged in 1978 and used his revolutionary prestige to lead the post-Mao recovery. Living into his early 90s, Deng was able to put his stamp upon China's reform (*gaige*) and opening up (*kaifang*) and to see a successor leadership firmly in place before dying in 1997.

A second factor was control of the military, which determines whether or not a revolutionary leader has the ultimate means to enforce his will. Mao Zedong headed the Party's Military Affairs Commission through the Civil War and until the day he died and, after the 1949 Revolution, allowed only one civilian colleague, Deng, to be a member. This increased Deng's legitimacy in the eyes of the People's Liberation Army (PLA). He had been chief political commissar of one of the great field armies that had won China from Chiang Kai-shek's Nationalists in the Civil War, and in the 1970s and 1980s, he twice served as PLA chief-of-staff, the only civilian ever to do so. This career experience and prestige enabled him to dislodge the PLA from the positions of political power it had taken over from the disrupted Communist Party during the chaos of the Cultural Revolution, described in Chapters 3 and 4. It meant, too, that in the crisis of 1989 over how to deal with the students in Tiananmen Square,the PLA would obey orders emanating from Deng to expel the demonstrators, with deadly force where needed.[5]

A third factor may have been readiness to rule. Unlike the Soviet leaders who were mainly exiled intellectuals engaged in ideological disputes before 1917, the Chinese communists had had many years experience in governance during their time in Yan'an and other base areas prior to the success of the revolution. The Party had been honed into a formidable instrument of power. And, again unlike the Soviets, the Chinese communists fought and won their Civil War before they took power. Thus, after three years of economic recovery, Mao felt able to abandon New Democracy, his version of Lenin's "liberal" New Economic Policy (NEP) of the early 1920s, and initiate the collectivization of agriculture and the nationalization of industry. He completed the program by 1956, without the catastrophic disruption caused by Stalin's bloody collectivization and First Five-Year Plan (FYP) (1928–32), which dealt a lasting blow to Soviet agriculture. Those long years of governing experience

4 Unlike Stalin, Mao seems never to have ordered the execution of his colleagues, although he was prepared, as in the case of PRC president, Liu Shaoqi, to allow them to die of neglect in custody.
5 By contrast, in the English Revolution Richard Cromwell lacked authority after the death of his father, and this left power in the hands of General Monck, who brokered the return of Charles II. In France the executions of the French civilian revolutionary leaders enabled Brigadier General Napoleon Bonaparte to fill the vacuum after rising rapidly during France's revolutionary wars. Trotsky and, later and more brutally, Stalin disciplined the Soviet Red Army and its top brass to accept strict civilian control. Gorbachev was the only general secretary to face a revolt by his generals. Their coup was a failure perhaps because Soviet generals were unused to this role, but it led inexorably to Gorbachev's downfall, underlining the importance of control of the military to the leader of a revolutionary regime.

both before and after 1949 meant that the Chinese Communist Party (CCP) emerged from the ten-year battering of the Cultural Revolution damaged but not destroyed.

A fourth factor may have been the length and impact of the revolutionary high tide.[6] By the time the Soviet Union collapsed, rural collectivization and the command economy with its Five-Year Plans had lasted over sixty years. No Russian remembered pre-World War I capitalist industrialization. The NEP was a distant memory in Soviet history books. During the Brezhnev era, entrepreneurship involved corruption and the black market, a fitting background for the rise of the oligarchs who looted the economy of post-Soviet Russia. The new nation became heavily dependent on its mineral wealth.

The relative ease with which the rural-savvy CCP pushed through collectivization,[7] and later herded the peasants into ultra-collectivist communes, was a triumph that confounded their Soviet brethren. But almost certainly the peasants joined these new rural organizations as a result of the unrelenting pressure by CCP cadres rather than because they were converts to socialism. For in the wake of the great famine, it became clear that the unfamiliar tenets of collectivization had not been sufficiently inculcated into the minds of the peasants; even some of Mao's senior colleagues effectively favored decollectivization. And in the aftermath of the Cultural Revolution, in the late 1970s, the peasants of the two provinces worst hit by the famine, Anhui and Sichuan, spearheaded a return to family farming.[8] Decollectivized agriculture along with township and village enterprises (TVEs) were the springboard for the Chinese economic miracle. The socialist high tide had not lasted long enough to undermine traditional Chinese rural entrepreneurship.

A fifth factor was probably nationalism.[9] Few of the recruits to the CCP in the 1920s, including Mao, were well schooled in Marxism-Leninism. But the

6 The English Civil War involved fighting in all parts of the British Isles, and Cromwell had little time to institutionalize a strong civilian order before his death. The French revolutionaries established a new calendar, but they had no time to found a new order before they fell victim to the Reign of Terror. On the other hand, the Stalinist command economy based on rural collectivization and state-owned industry lasted over fifty years to the end of the Soviet period, inhibiting the rise of a dynamic new economy in the post-Soviet era, but leaving openings for the emergence of a new breed of unscrupulous economic oligarchs.

7 Mao Zedong, Liu Shaoqi, Zhu De, and Deng Xiaoping all came from rural backgrounds (of varying degrees of wealth), and even the few leaders who were not from peasant families would have learned a great deal about the countryside during their sojourns in the base areas before 1949.

8 Zhao Ziyang, later prime minister, later still the General Secretary dismissed at the time of the 1989 Tiananmen events, was the Sichuan first Party secretary who godfathered the reforms in Sichuan; see Chapter 5. His counterpart in Anhui was Wan Li, later chairman of the standing committee of the National People's Congress at the time of Tiananmen.

9 For Lenin and the early Soviet leaders, the revolution was all: the Russian Civil War was fought to defend the revolution and the belief was that the Bolshevik Revolution would be safe only when revolutions had taken place in countries like Germany and Britain. When those revolutions failed to appear, Stalin's "socialism in one country" policy was designed to safeguard the revolution by strengthening the Soviet Union. But probably not till the Nazi invasion and, after World War II, during the Cold War against the West was Soviet patriotism actively cultivated.

Bolshevik Revolution and Lenin's excoriation of imperialism suggested that the CCP would be a better alternative to Sun Yat-sen's Nationalist Party as an instrument for patriotic young intellectuals intent on capturing power, expelling imperialists, and restoring China to its erstwhile greatness. Of course, under Comintern tutelage and with Stalin's example they went with the socialist program as an essential part of self-strengthening. In power, Mao carried his socialist and egalitarian convictions to the limit, first in the Great Leap Forward, then in the Socialist Education Campaign (Chapter 2), and to an even greater extreme in the Cultural Revolution, when he plunged China into political and economic chaos in an endeavor to plant socialism firmly in the hearts and minds of his countrymen.

Mao's effort was counterproductive. His colleagues who survived the Cultural Revolution, notably Deng, realized that twenty years of leftist excesses had subverted the original purpose of the revolution to build a strong modern China. The purpose of the Deng reform program was to reorient the Party and nation toward economic development and to eschew ideological excess. The rapid pace of change during three decades of reform (Chapters 5, 6, & 7) has shown how much time was wasted during the Maoist era. But the challenge for China's current leaders is to modify the extremes of wealth the reforms have encouraged – "to get rich is glorious" – and to steer the nation back toward a more equal society, although not to the extremes espoused by Mao.

But underlying these social and economic challenges are political issues. Despite the enormously important reform program that he bequeathed, Deng Xiaoping did not leave behind a fully institutionalized polity (Chapter 6). Jiang Zemin and his successor Hu Jintao managed to surmount serious domestic shocks – Falungong, the SARS epidemic, the contaminated milk scandal, the deaths of thousands of children in the shoddily built schools leveled during the Sichuan earthquake, ethnic unrest in Tibet and Xinjiang, along with tens of thousands of protest demonstrations across China each year – without apparent threat to Party rule. The Chinese leadership has become a self-perpetuating oligarchy (Chapter 7). To broaden the oligarchy's appeal, Jiang opened the doors of the Party to professionals and even private entrepreneurs, discarding the traditional recruitment only from the ranks of peasants, workers, soldiers and cadres. It remains to be seen if this was the equivalent of letting the fox into the chicken coop; surely, it will further dilute the Party's "serve-the-people" ethos and likely increase the already widespread intra-Party corruption.

With the effective jettisoning of Marxism-Leninism-Mao Zedong Thought as an explanation of the world and a guide to action and losing thus the justification for its practitioners to run China, with no rule of law and a tenuous rule by law, the Party is dependent on economic success and national prestige for its legitimacy. The Beijing Olympics, the 60th anniversary parade, and the Shanghai Expo must have occasioned patriotic pride. But Chinese society is increasingly modernized, increasingly sophisticated, and increasingly more demanding, as the unquenchable "blogosphere" daily demonstrates. Yet, the Chinese leadership tries to control that society of 1.3 billion people from one center by employing a secretive system devised over a hundred years ago for conspiratorial activities against the government of the day. Can this be the guarantee of another sixty years of Party rule, another cycle of Cathay? Perhaps a further edition of this work will tell.

CHAPTER 1

THE ESTABLISHMENT AND CONSOLIDATION OF THE NEW REGIME, 1949–1957

FREDERICK C. TEIWES

AN OVERVIEW

When the People's Republic of China (PRC) was formally established on 1 October 1949 the nation's new leaders faced daunting problems. Society and polity were fragmented, public order and morale had decayed, a war-torn economy suffered from severe inflation and unemployment, and China's fundamental economic and military backwardness created monumental impediments to the elite's goals of national wealth and power. Yet by 1957 the leaders of the Chinese Communist Party (CCP) could look back on the period since 1949 with considerable satisfaction. A strong centralized state had been established after decades of disunity, China's national pride and international prestige had grown significantly as a result of fighting the world's greatest power to a stalemate in Korea, the country had taken major steps on the road to industrialization and achieved an impressive rate of economic growth, the living standards of its people had made noticeable if modest progress, and the nation's social system had been transformed according to Marxist precepts in relatively smooth fashion.

Moreover, all this had been accomplished with only limited divisions within the Party elite. Thus Chairman Mao Zedong could convincingly claim at the Eighth CCP Congress in September 1956 that "we . . . have gained a decisive victory in the socialist revolution [and] our Party is now more united, more consolidated than at any time in the past."[1] A year later, intervening events and persistent problems set the stage for considerably enhanced elite conflict as the CCP began to evolve the bold new developmental strategy of the Great Leap Forward (GLF); yet Mao reaffirmed that the socialist revolution had been achieved,[2] while his leading colleague Liu Shaoqi, plausibly argued that Party

[1] "Opening address at the Eighth National Congress of the Communist Party of China" (15 September 1956), in *Eighth National Congress of the Communist Party of China*, 1.7.
[2] In his "Talk at a meeting with Chinese students and trainees in Moscow" (17 November 1957), in *CB*, 891.26, Mao declared that the victory represented by the change of ownership systems in 1956 had not

6

unity remained firm.[3] As China began to move in uncertain directions, the official judgment of the PRC's first eight years as a period of achievement and cohesion was still fully credible.

What explains the achievements of this initial period? To a considerable degree, the unity of leadership sustained throughout 1949–57 was the bedrock upon which other successes were built. The extent of this unity was remarkable in view of not only the drastic purges and bitter conflicts that marked the history of the Communist Party of the Soviet Union, but also the factional cleavages that had afflicted the inner Party life of the CCP in the 1920s and 1930s. Only one major purge – that of Gao Gang and Rao Shushi in 1954–5 – affected the top elite; as we shall see, even this conflict had a relatively limited impact on Party cohesion. Even more significantly, nearly all the surviving Central Committee (CC) members chosen at the Seventh Party Congress in 1945 were reelected in 1956. In addition, elite stability was reflected in the largely undisturbed pecking order within the higher reaches of the regime. Although subtle shifts of rank and influence inevitably occurred, dramatic rises such as that of Deng Xiaoping who vaulted from the relatively low twenty-fifth position on the 1945 CC to Politburo status in 1955 and then to the Party's General Secretaryship in 1956, were rare indeed. And apart from the very small number actually dropped from the CC in this period, key figures who suffered losses of power and influence were generally restored to equal status after relatively short periods of penance.

Such leadership was an enormous political asset. With a strong elite commitment to maintaining both clearly defined power relations and the principle of Party unity, policy issues could be vigorously debated within official forums without danger to the regime. Since personal maneuvering for advantage was kept to a minimum under such circumstances – indeed, too blatant maneuvering would be counterproductive – relatively unfettered debate maximized the likelihood of balanced and flexible decisions. Once a decision was made, the commitment to unity as well as formal norms of Leninist discipline usually guaranteed prompt implementation by responsible leaders of the various hierarchies of the PRC. More broadly, the aura of authority and confidence generated by a united leadership served to impress ordinary officials and the populace and thus facilitate their enthusiasm for or acquiescence in Party programs.

The sources of leadership unity were varied. The victory of 1949 against considerable odds was obviously a crucial factor. This victory, which

been conclusive but "genuine success in the socialist revolution" had been achieved as a result of political and ideological movements in 1957.

3 After various debates in 1957, Liu in December told visiting Indian Communists: "Our Party has guarded its unity at all times, there's been no split . . . ; no one has gone his own way." Cited in MacFarquhar, *The origins of the Cultural Revolution*, 1.311.

Map 1. PRC: political (*pinyin* romanization)

represented both the culmination of a protracted revolutionary struggle and
an opportunity for national renewal, greatly enhanced the authority of the top
leaders who had developed the Party's successful strategy. At a more prosaic
level, revolutionary success provided the spoils of power that were widely
shared within the elite. Individuals and groups from the many pre-1949 CCP
civilian and military organizations, leaders whose revolutionary credentials
were linked to particular episodes such as the Nanchang uprising of 1927,
which marked the founding of the Red Army, or the December 9 movement
of Beijing students against Japan in 1935, and various personal networks
within the leadership, all benefited from the parceling out of positions and
influence. Although the Long Marchers who were closest to Mao tended to
predominate in the highest bodies overall, no major revolutionary group was
discriminated against except those leaders who had challenged Mao before
he achieved unquestioned preeminence, and even those figures received some
symbolic positions and tangible power. Thus there were few groups with
immediate grievances that threatened unity.

After 1949, moreover, shared ideological commitment to Marxism and
a broad consensus on ambitious industrialization and social transformation
further contributed to elite cohesion. Although ideological movements are
notorious for splits and infighting – phenomena the CCP would experience
in later years – and broad agreement on goals does not necessarily prevent
bitter conflict over means and priorities, circumstances operated to inhibit
such developments in the early and mid-1950s. To a substantial degree, this
resulted from the mutually reinforcing interplay of Party unity and policy
success throughout the period. Unity contributed to effective solutions to
problems; success in solving problems further deepened leadership solidarity.
Success also served to mask or diminish any latent conflict over goals. As long
as rapid rates of economic growth were attained, any unpalatable byproducts of
modernization would hardly give cause for a fundamental challenge to existing
policy. Another vitally important element was the existence of a model that
specified not only goals but means as well: the experience of the Soviet Union
in building socialism. A wide consensus existed on following the Soviet model,
which served to focus policy debate on incremental modifications rather than
on fundamental approaches, and thus lower the stakes of any conflict.

The high level of unity from 1949 to 1957 did not mean an absence of
leadership cleavages but simply that they remained latent in comparison with
later periods. One potential source of division was the diversity of revolutionary careers among the Party elite. Although unified by the larger struggle,
at the same time participants in different revolutionary events and organizations developed their own personal networks and group identities. During
the Cultural Revolution after 1965, such groupings would become critically

important: For example, those who had engaged in "white area" or under-ground work under the leadership of Liu Shaoqi generally shared the fate of their leader during the troubled 1966–7 period. From 1949 to 1957, however, contrasting pre-1949 experiences normally did not disrupt the larger lead-ership cohesion. The one major attempt to use such differences for political gain, the Gao Gang–Rao Shushi affair, was ultimately a failure.

Another source of tension carried over from revolutionary days was the inevitable friction among various personalities at the apex of the CCP elite. A clear example was the prickly relationship between Mao and one of his leading generals, Peng Dehuai, which reportedly led Peng to complain in 1953 that "The Chairman doesn't like me [nor] does he hold me in esteem."[4] Such personal conflict would arguably contribute to Peng's dismissal as minister of defense in 1959, yet in the early years of the PRC it was basically submerged as Peng's talents were utilized in key military roles and on the supreme policy-making body, the Party Politburo.

Other cleavages arose from the circumstances of the early years themselves. Inevitably the large agenda of policy issues facing the new elite produced different views and thus conflict among various advocates. One recurring cause of conflict was the question of how quickly to push economic development and social transformation. On any given question some voices would be heard for pressing ahead to achieve the desired goals, whereas others could be raised in warning against disruption due to too rapid a pace. Yet differences among various approaches were relatively narrow; furthermore, the positions of top leaders were not rigidly linked to one or another tendency but shifted according to the issue and circumstances. As a result, leadership polarization did not occur as it did in later periods, when conflicting policy views were much more fundamental.

A related source of limited, nonpolarized conflict was the increasing iden-tification of individual leaders with institutions and departments they headed as the new system took shape and became increasingly bureaucratized by the mid-1950s. Thus, for example, Premier Zhou Enlai undoubtedly had an inter-est in developing the roles and powers of the government apparatus as distinct from the Party organization, which was more the direct concern of Liu Shaoqi and Deng Xiaoping, whereas while army leaders such as Peng Dehuai had a natural concern with maximizing military resources. From 1949 to 1957, however, such conflicting bureaucratic interests were largely accommodated in the pursuit of larger goals, and direct institutional clashes such as that of Party and army during the Cultural Revolution were avoided. Despite an increasing

4 As quoted in a Red Guard publication, *Mass criticism and repudiation bulletin* (Guangzhou), 5 October 1967, trans. in URI, *The case of Peng Teh-huai 1959–1968*, 123.

tendency to approach issues from the perspectives of the departments they led, individual leaders still placed priority on the overall Party line and the consensus of the Politburo collective.

In sum, important cleavages and tensions existed within the CCP elite, including the Politburo, throughout the early and mid-1950s, but they did not seriously disrupt the predominantly consensual mode of leadership. Ultimately it was not the lack of tensions but the willingness of Mao and his colleagues to minimize the tensions that did exist that created the unusual unity of these early years. Such willingness, however, was inseparable from the circumstances examined in this chapter. When these circumstances no longer prevailed – when the Soviet model no longer commanded general agreement and official policies produced major disasters rather than a string of successes – latent cleavages became manifest and Party unity was eroded and then shattered. Throughout this drama the character of Mao Zedong's leadership was a central factor. We turn now to Mao's crucial role in sustaining the unity of 1949–57.

The role of Mao Zedong

Mao Zedong was clearly the unchallenged leader of the CCP throughout the 1949–57 period. Mao's preeminent position within the Party was already indisputable by the mid-1940s. Not only was Mao the subject of a major personality cult, but by 1943 his leading colleagues ceased voicing subtle doubts about his theoretical capabilities and in 1945 "the thought of Mao Zedong" was enshrined in the CCP's new constitution. Moreover, despite the emphasis of Party rules on collective leadership, Mao was granted formal powers to act unilaterally in certain instances.[5] The basis of Mao's burgeoning power was the success of Party strategies and policies after the onset of the Sino-Japanese War in 1937, which he had shaped more than any other leader; the conclusive success of these strategies and policies from 1945 to 1949 further bolstered his ultimate authority. Much as the victory of 1949 deepened Party unity generally, it also solidified Mao's authority. By virtue of that victory, Mao approximated the ideal charismatic leader whose exceptional abilities were acknowledged as the key to success, as well as the ideal founder of a new dynasty, with all the implications of obedience that role carried in traditional culture.

Mao's authority was further enhanced by his major initiatives in the 1949–57 period, instances where his individual judgment clashed with that of key

5 According to a recent inner Party report by Liao Kai-lung, "Historical experiences and our road of development" (25 October 1980), in *Issues & Studies*, November 1981, 92, in March 1943 a Politburo decision appointed a Secretariat of Mao, Liu Shaoqi, and Ren Bishi to handle day-to-day work, but granted Mao individually the power to make final decisions concerning matters before the Secretariat.

colleagues and/or broader elite opinion. The Chairman apparently took such initiatives on only three occasions during these years. The first, in October 1950, concerned China's response to the northward march of American forces in Korea. On that occasion Mao seemingly overrode reservations of the great majority of his associates concerning costs and dangers, secured their acquiescence, and ordered the involvement of Chinese troops in the war.[6] Although the costs of the PRC's Korean venture were indeed high, the benefits achieved in security and international peace were widely perceived as outweighing these costs and thus reinforced Mao's reputation for political wisdom. The second instance, which will be examined in more detail later, was the Chairman's initiative to speed up the pace of agricultural cooperativization in mid-1955 despite an official decision a few months earlier to temper the rate of growth. The resultant basic achievement of collectivization by the end of 1956, far in advance of the most optimistic projections, once again seemed to demonstrate Mao's insight.

The final initiative, Mao's efforts in the face of substantial reservations within the elite to promote intellectual criticism of the Party through the Hundred Flowers movement in 1956–57 (also analyzed later), was less successful. However, the damage to his prestige was minimized by his abrupt shift of position in mid-1957.

On balance, both the broader achievements of the initial period and the specific successes of Korea and collectivization left Mao's position at the end of 1957 as strong as ever despite the setback of the Hundred Flowers. The Chairman's strength was reflected in his moves, apparently dating from 1953, developed at the Eighth Party Congress, and reaffirmed in early 1958, to divide the leadership into two "fronts." Under these arrangements Mao would retreat to the "second front," where he could contemplate matters of theory and overall policy while divorced from daily operations. Such steps indicated not only great confidence that his ultimate authority was secure but considerable faith in his leading colleagues as well.

The fact of Mao's unchallenged authority was the linchpin of the entire edifice of elite stability. Apart from the decisive initiatives described previously, Mao served as the final arbiter of policy disputes when his associates were unable to reach a consensus. Under these circumstances, policy advocacy to a substantial degree was aimed at winning the Chairman's approval rather than functioning as a tool in the pursuit of supreme power, as in the Soviet Union after the deaths of Lenin and Stalin. With all groups within the leadership

---

6 In addition to Cultural Revolution sources, this version of the Korea decision is supported by the excerpts from the recollections of Peng Dehuai published in 1981, *Peng Dehuai zishu* (Peng Dehuai's own account), 257–8.

owing loyalty to Mao, any latent tensions among them were largely kept in check.

Although Mao's authority made leadership unity possible, it by no means guaranteed cohesion. Stalin had amply demonstrated how a supreme leader could consciously create disunity among his subordinates, and in later years Mao's erratic behavior would exacerbate existing elite tensions. In the 1949–57 period, however, Mao sought to enhance elite solidarity by generally adhering to official Party norms of collective leadership and democratic discussion and more broadly by emphasizing ability and achievement as criteria for leadership. Unlike Stalin, Mao did not set his colleagues at each other's throats; nor did he demand that they have close factional links to himself. Instead, the ranking members of the ruling elite were men of talent and major figures in the history of the CCP in their own right. Liu Shaoqi had a quite distinct career involving work in the so-called white areas behind enemy lines, while Zhou Enlai, the third-ranking figure and leading government administrator, had even opposed Mao in the early 1930s. Red Army leader Zhu De and economic specialist Chen Yun had been more closely associated with Mao but were still individuals of independent prestige, and only Deng Xiaoping of the inner core of the 1950s could be considered a member of Mao's long-standing personal faction. With his own power secure, Mao chose to utilize the considerable talents of such leaders and mold them into a cooperative team. Thus, in addition to there being no advantage in challenging the Chairman, there was little gain in exaggerating policy differences to outmaneuver potential rivals because of Mao's commitment to solidarity.

Closely linked to this commitment was Mao's willingness to observe, by and large, the formal rules of collective leadership. Although Mao obviously reserved the right to insist on his own way in matters of prime concern and collective leadership in fact did not mean simple majority rule,[7] his general practice in the early and mid-1950s was to arrive at policies through wide-ranging discussions where the opinions of all relevant officials were valued for the contributions they could make to informed decisions. More-over, again with some lapses, Mao chose to observe the principle of minority rights, whereby dissenters within the leadership could retain their views and even reiterate them at a future date without fear of punishment. This rela-tively democratic style served Mao well by encouraging debate on key issues,

---

7 Mao acknowledged this in 1962 when he defined his adherence to democratic centralism in the following terms: "[W]hen I say something, no matter whether it is correct or incorrect, *provided that everyone disagrees with me*, I will accede to their point of view because they are the majority" (emphasis added). "Talk at an enlarged central work conference" (30 January 1962), in Stuart Schram, ed., *Mao Tse-tung unrehearsed: Talks and utters: 1956–71*, 165.

deepening elite commitment to the relatively open policy process generally, and thus reinforcing the overall sense of leadership solidarity.

Mao's contributions to effective decision making and Party unity were further enhanced by the nature of his main political concerns during the 1949–57 period. In these years Mao tended to limit his interventions largely to those areas he knew best – agriculture and revolution above all else. The Chairman clearly considered himself an expert on the peasantry after years of leading a rural-based revolution, and in the 1950s he continued to spend considerable amounts of time in the countryside. By "revolution" Mao meant overall strategies for extending CCP power and furthering the process of socialist transformation, concerns well suited to his experience in the pre-1949 period.

In addition, together with Zhou Enlai, Mao was the architect of China's foreign policy, as befitted someone who had dealt with major international actors during the anti-Japanese and civil wars. Finally, as the author of the CCP's basic policy on literature and the arts in 1942, Mao continued to take a keen if sometimes idiosyncratic interest in this sphere and the affairs of higher intellectuals generally. As a result, with the possible exception of the cultural sphere, in all these areas Mao possessed credentials his colleagues respected; his assertions of authority regarding them could not be regarded as arbitrary or ill-informed. Equally important was the fact that the Chairman generally restricted his role in areas he was not familiar with to the synthesis of and arbitration among the opinions of his more specialist colleagues. This was particularly the case in one of the most crucial policy areas of the period – economic construction. Thus both Mao's prestige and elite solidarity were reinforced by the hesitancy to impose his views in matters where, by his own admission, he lacked understanding. In contrast to later periods, Mao's *substantive* policy impact was relatively limited throughout 1949–57; his contribution to Party unity came from actively performing the role of ultimate arbiter while keeping dramatic personal initiatives to a minimum.

Finally, leadership unity was also bolstered by the fact that Mao's intellectual position in these years was on the whole orthodox and mainstream. In good Marxist fashion his notion of social change centered on the transformation of ownership patterns, and in good Stalinist manner he gave high priority to rapid industrialization. In most matters he shared with his colleagues a deep commitment to economic and technical advance, a keen awareness of objective limits to Party policies, and a determination to steer a course between "leftist" excesses and "rightist" timidity. Thus when debate did occur, generally Mao's relatively centrist position served to ameliorate conflict and build a consensus rather than polarize differences within the leadership. The Chairman's intellectual position, then, aided his pursuit of consensus politics. But both Mao's orientation and his consensual politics depended to a substantial degree on the existence of the Soviet experience of building socialism.

The Soviet model

In the 1949–57 period, broad agreement existed within the CCP leadership on adopting the Soviet model of socialism. This model provided patterns of state organization, an urban-oriented developmental strategy, modern military techniques, and policies and methods in a wide variety of specialized areas. As already suggested, given the consensus on following the Soviet path, policy debate was shifted from the fundamental to the incremental level. In contrast to the bitter disputes of Bolshevik politics in the 1920s due to basic differences over both the ultimate shape of and the means to achieve socialism, with an established model of socialism already in existence, Chinese policy debates by and large dealt with matters of nuance and degree.

The basic issues were these: Precisely what were the positive and negative features of the Soviet model? How should the CCP adapt the model to suit Chinese conditions? How fast should the Soviet path be followed? Although such questions did result in spirited debate, they were hardly the types of issues to split the Party. In addition, the presence of an existing and ostensibly successful socialist system in the Soviet Union served to bolster the confidence of the Chinese elite and society generally in official policies, since the broad outlines of both process and outcome were presumed to be known.

Various aspects of the Soviet model and Chinese adaptations will be analyzed in both this and later chapters. Here it suffices to say that CCP leaders never adopted a position of uncritical borrowing from the Soviet experience. The essence of Mao's program for revolution before 1949 had been the need to address Chinese realities, and he was not about to disown that principle during the stage of building socialism. Moreover, Mao's strong nationalism had led in the early 1940s to a clear declaration of independence from any Soviet control over CCP affairs, and this too militated against unthinking imitation.

Nevertheless, the willingness to alter the model varied considerably from sphere to sphere and over time. Where the Party had its own established competence, as in rural policy, distinctive Chinese approaches were common – although even in such areas the Soviet model remained relevant. In contrast, where the CCP was without experience, its creativity was limited. As Mao put it after the fact: "In the early stages of nationwide liberation we lacked the experience to administer the economy of the entire country. Therefore, during the First Five-Year Plan (FYP) we could only imitate the methods of the Soviet Union."[8] Yet CCP leaders gained confidence with time, and by 1956 they began to modify Soviet experience regarding the economy and other key areas. It would only be with the GLF of 1958, however, that a fundamental break with the Soviet model would take place.

Why was the Soviet model adopted so decisively by the Chinese leadership after 1949? To a certain extent this was a logical corollary of the decision to "lean to one side" in foreign policy. Whatever the possibilities might have been for a more balanced international posture had American diplomacy been less hostile to the CCP during the civil war, in 1949 the PRC found the Soviet Union the only available source of military and economic aid. Following the Soviet precedent was a least in part a price that had to be paid for securing that aid. More fundamental, however, was a long-term ideological orientation toward Soviet Russia. This not only involved a sense of being part of a common movement against international capitalism and imperialism but was also reflected in basic organizational principles and practices. Despite unique emphases and Mao's insistence on independence, in a fundamental sense the CCP had been following the Soviet model since its earliest days, when Leninist organizational principles and methods were infused into the fledgling Party by agents of the Communist International.

Moreover, even though Mao continued to insist on a degree of ideological distinctiveness in the immediate post-1949 period, there was still a sense in which the Soviet Union remained an authority on basic ideological questions. This was perhaps most graphically demonstrated by Mao's nocturnal visits to the residence of Soviet Ambassador Yudin to thrash out theoretical issues – sessions that may have contributed to doctrinal adjustments in the Chairman's *Selected works* when they appeared in 1951.[9] Given the acceptance of Soviet ideological authority in the broadest sense, Russian pronouncements on building socialism were sure to carry weight.

Although international factors and general ideological orientation undoubtedly made CCP leaders receptive to the Soviet model, the crucial factor was their deep commitment to socialist modernization. The men who led the CCP to victory in 1949 were not mere agrarian revolutionaries; they were both Marxists seeking a socialist future and modernizers striving to realize the dream of a "rich and powerful" China. They were acutely aware of their own inexperience with developmental problems. As Mao declared in mid-1949: "We shall soon put aside some of the things we know well and

8 "Reading notes on the Soviet Union's *Political economics*" (1960–62?), in *Miscellany of Mao Tse-tung Thought* (hereafter cited as *Miscellany*), 2.310.

9 Khrushchev reported Mao's visits to Yudin in *Khrushchev remembers*, 464–5; see also *Khrushchev remembers: The last testament*, 242.

be compelled to do things we don't know well."[10] Given both the desire for development and the fact that the Soviet Union was the only existing example of a state that both was socialist and had achieved rapid growth on a backward economic base, the decision to follow the Soviet path was all but inevitable.

The decision was further facilitated by the fact that as good Marxists the CCP leaders accepted the transition to urban-oriented developmental strategies as a natural consequence of revolutionary success. Although CCP leaders were proud of their revolutionary traditions and concerned about the corrupting tendencies of the cities, there is little to indicate that Mao or anyone else initially saw any fundamental contradictions between the revolutionary experience of Yan'an and the Soviet model. The predominant feeling, rather, was one of desirable progression to a higher stage. Mao had regarded guerrilla warfare never as an end in itself but rather as a necessary stage of struggle forced on the CCP by its relative weakness; when the time came for large-scale operations by massed troops, the more advanced military style was pressed enthusiastically.

Similarly, the whole rural phase of the revolution had been necessary but was always seen as a prelude to the capture of the cities. At the moment of victory, Party leaders were eager to get on with the task of nation building and showed little awareness that the imported Soviet strategies might clash with CCP traditions. And even when that awareness developed in the mid-1950s, they expected that any contradictions would be, in Mao's terms, "nonantagonistic" and thus safely handled by adjustments within the overall framework of the Soviet model.

In conclusion, a few general remarks about the Soviet model are in order. First, no single Soviet model in fact existed. Although the basic institutional and economic pattern to be followed was that of the Stalinist system as it developed after the mid-1950s, CCP leaders had a whole range of periods and practices in Soviet history to choose from. During agricultural cooperativization, for example, the CCP looked for guidelines more to the principles articulated by Stalin in 1927–9 during his debate with Bukharin than to Stalinist collectivization practice after 1929. Second, even where a strong desire to institute Soviet methods on a broad scale may have existed, lack of requisite technical resources could severely inhibit their adoption. Another consideration is that in altering specific Soviet practices, the CCP was not necessarily rejecting Soviet advice. Throughout the 1949–57 period, Soviet leaders and specialists considered their mistakes as lessons the Chinese could and should benefit from. In particular, the Russian's own criticisms of Stalinist

10 Mao, SW, 4.422.

practice after the dictator's death often influenced CCP thinking on the need to alter existing approaches.

Finally, it is important to emphasize that Soviet influence had a wide impact beyond the attitudes of top policy makers. Although key leaders were always, albeit in fluctuating degrees, aware of the need to adapt Soviet experiences to Chinese realities, ordinary officials and the general populace were often overwhelmed by the public emphasis on advanced Soviet experience. Propaganda treatment of the Soviet Union as a respected "elder brother" and such slogans as "The Soviet Union of today is our tomorrow" hardly encouraged critical emulation, with the result that mindless copying did occur in many fields. In still another sense, the positive image of the Soviet Union allowed elements of China's intelligentsia to pick up some less orthodox tendencies of Russian intellectuals despite the disapproval of both Soviet and Chinese officialdom. All in all, throughout the 1949–57 period Soviet influences affected both CCP policy and Chinese society in a variety of complex ways. In some senses the process was beyond the control of Party leaders, but more fundamentally it reflected their conscious choice. And when those leaders – or a dominant group of them – saw the need to break away from the Soviet path after 1957, it was well within their capabilities to do so, even though many Soviet influences inevitably remained.

CONSOLIDATION AND RECONSTRUCTION, 1949–52

In 1949, victory came with startling suddenness. The traditional northern capital, Beijing fell by negotiated surrender in January. The People's Liberation Army (PLA) crossed the Yangtze and quickly seized Shanghai in April and the central China urban complex of Wuhan in May. Thereafter the PLA met little sustained military resistance. It took the southern commercial center of Guangzhou in October shortly after the formal establishment of the PRC, and finally reached the southwest city of Chengdu in December. At the end of the year only Tibet and Taiwan were beyond reach of the new leadership in Beijing. The Tibetan situation would be rectified by 1951 through a combination of military action and negotiation with the local authorities, whereas the Taiwan question would remain a major item of unfinished national business over three decades later.

To a significant degree, the military victories of 1949 solved one of the major problems of the preceding forty years – the lack of national unity. This very fact was a substantial asset for CCP leaders as they grappled with still unresolved questions. The national unity that was necessary to restore China's greatness was a heartfelt goal for all patriotic Chinese. Mao expressed their sentiments in September 1949 by declaring, "Ours will no longer be a nation subject to insult and humiliation. We have stood up."[11]

But although the achievement of national unity considerably legitimized the new regime in the eyes of the educated elite, to secure the deeper political control required for both social transformation and modernization, it would have to confront the parochialism that had dominated Chinese society from time immemorial. Although the CCP had attained some success in broadening horizons in the North China villages that the Party controlled during the revolutionary period, in most rural areas the awareness and interests of the peasants were limited to events in their villages and nearby areas. Even in China's cities, the lives of ordinary people were bound by small social groups and involved little consciousness of developments at either the municipal or national level.

An integrated national political system would, therefore, require the state's penetration of society in a way that had never been attempted by previous regimes, and such penetration in turn would necessitate both the careful development of organizational resources and intense mass mobilization to jar various sections of society out of their narrow frames of reference. By reaching deep into society, the CCP could tap new sources for support. At the same time, it ran the risk of alienating affected groups. The new leaders also faced tasks arising from the more immediate legacy of a dozen years of large-scale warfare – the need to overcome continued resistance by elements that had long struggled against the CCP, to rehabilitate a severely damaged economy, and to restore orderly governmental operations. All of this would tax CCP resources and ingenuity. But at the same time, the situation created a substantial reservoir of backing from a war-weary populace longing for peace and order.

In the early days of the PRC, Mao and his colleagues spoke of a three-year period to restore China's production to prewar levels and establish the political control and organizational capacity needed before socialist construction and transformation could be undertaken in earnest. The projection proved remarkably close to the mark.

This recovery period inevitably saw conflicting emphases. On the one hand, the initial needs of economic revival and political acceptance argued for reassuring key groups in society and making tangible concessions to their interests. The policy of reassurance, however, was in tension with the imperative of establishing firm organizational control as a prelude to planned development. Although this contradiction was always present and the subject of debate within the leadership, a marked shift in emphasis occurred in late 1950. From

11 Mao, *SW*, 5.17.

that time, roughly corresponding with the Chinese entry into the Korean War, the CCP's social programs intensified, mass movements were launched, and the regime penetrated society in a much more thorough manner than initially. But in the first year or so of power, the stress was on reassurance in view of both the fragility of the situation and the limited resources the Party had at its disposal.

Initial problems and policies

The problems encountered in 1949 by the new leaders and the policies they designed for dealing with them varied enormously over the vast face of China. Differences in economic and cultural levels, agricultural patterns, local customs, and ethnic composition all required suitably varied responses. The crucial difference, however, was the degree of CCP presence in various areas before 1949. Although the gradations in this regard are quite complex, in broad terms three types of areas manifested fundamental differences. First were the "old liberated areas" of North China, the Northeast, and parts of the Northwest and East China containing about one-quarter of the nation's population, where the CCP had basically established its power in the countryside by 1947–8 and often much earlier. These were the areas where the revolution was essentially won; as Mao put it in 1950: "It was the victory of the agrarian reform [in the old liberated areas] that made possible our victory in overthrowing Chiang Kai-shek."[12] Here the CCP had created an organizational presence down to the grass roots, drawn substantial numbers of peasants into the Party, basically eliminated organized resistance, and made substantial progress in social reform programs that generated considerable mass support among the poorer sections of rural society. As Mao indicated, it was from this base that the CCP launched its classic strategy of the "countryside surrounding the cities" as the conclusive battles of the civil war were fought in 1947–8. By 1949 the main tasks in these areas were to extend political control and begin land reform in those pockets where the Party had not ruled, and to check up on the results of land reform and develop low-level forms of cooperative agriculture elsewhere. By mid-1950 land reform was declared complete in the old liberated areas, and in that year something like one-third peasant households in these areas had been organized into mutual aid teams (MAT), the first step on the road to collectivization.

In sharp contrast to the old liberated areas stood the "new liberated areas," consisting of much of East and Central China, the overwhelming portion of the Northwest, and the vast expanse of territory south of the Yangtze.

12 Ibid., 33.

Here, apart from some scattered revolutionary bases left over from the rural revolution of the 1920s and 1930s (plus some underground Communists in the cities), the Party lacked organizational resources or mass support. Unlike the protracted revolutionary struggle in the north, victory in the new areas came by military conquest from without by what were to a substantial extent alien armies. Rather than the countryside surrounding the cities, the pattern was the opposite one of first seizing cities and then extending control outward to the rural areas.

A corollary of the absence of a CCP presence was the strength of anti-Communist groups even after basic military victory. In its most extreme form, continued armed resistance was offered by remnant Kuomintang (KMT; Guomindang) military units and the forces of secret societies, ethnic minorities, and other locally organized self-defense groups. Even in mid-1950 Mao spoke of more than 400,000 "bandits" scattered in remote regions of the new liberated areas that had not yet been wiped out, and PLA mopping-up actions continued against such forces, especially in the Northwest, as late as 1954. Most areas, however, were reported clear by mid-1951. Although such armed resistance obviously prolonged the process of establishing control, more significant was the political and social influence of local elites whose interest was in maintaining the status quo. To counter this influences, thorough land reform would be required, and it would have to start from scratch.

Finally, all the tasks that faced cities in the old liberated areas – establishing public order, restoring production, curbing inflation, and checking unemployment – also had to be dealt with in the urban centers of the new areas from a more precarious position, given the unsettled state of the surrounding countryside. Although the more advantageous rural conditions in the old liberated areas allowed cities there to achieve the goals of urban reconstruction considerably more quickly than those in the new areas, China's urban centers, containing some 50 million people, can be considered a separate category from both the old and new areas.

With the exception of a few small and medium-sized cities in North and Northeast China, the CCP had not held urban centers before late 1948, and its hold over those seized was often tenuous and short-lived. The vast majority of cities before 1949 were centers of anti-Communist power where CCP presence was limited to relatively weak underground forces, albeit much weaker in the south than the north. These forces could play only an auxiliary role in the takeover of the cities, and Party cadres from the liberated areas were often scornful of underground Communists who, in their eyes, had contributed so little to success. This attitude was further reflected in the new regimes established in the cities in which underground workers were given clearly secondary roles, whereas power gravitated to the outsiders whose careers had been made in the PLA and rural areas.

As the CCP moved into China's major cities, it held substantial assets, but it also suffered from major inadequacies. Ironically, in some senses the problems encountered in 1949 were exacerbated by the very rapidity of a final victory that considerably exceeded the expectations of Party leaders. At the start of the civil war in 19465 many top leaders such as Zhou Enlai anticipated a struggle of up to twenty years before the Communists could achieve ultimate success, and even in the spring of 1948, when the tide of battle in North China had turned in favor of the CCP, Mao predicted that another three years would be required for victory.[13] The sudden and vast expansion of the areas under Communist control left the Party acutely short of the personnel and skills needed for nationwide rule.

One solution was the rapid recruitment of new Party members as the CCP extended its geographical control; in the period from 1948 to the end of 1950, CCP membership increased from about 2.8 million to 5.8 million. Such a vast influx at a time of revolutionary struggle and then the multiplying demands of rule could not be carefully regulated. At the 1956 CCP Congress, Deng Xiaoping criticized the "undue speed [of Party growth during] the two years just before and after liberation [where] in certain areas [the CCP] grew practically without guidance and without plan."[14] Given such uncontrolled growth and the lack of systematic training, the predominantly peasant new Party members often lacked even rudimentary knowledge of Marxist ideology or basic skills of literacy. An additional problem was that most new recruits had entered the fold under circumstances where eventual success was clear. As a result, Party leaders could not be sure whether such individuals joined out of genuine commitment or out of opportunism. Thus although the rapid Party expansion around the time of takeover was undoubtedly necessary, it was only a partial answer at best to personnel and skill shortages.

Inadequacies of manpower, skills, and experience affected the countryside of the new liberated areas but were most sharply felt in the cities. We have already noted the Party leadership's acute sense of inexperience when it came to the modern sector. In terms of personnel, the CCP had at its disposal some 720,000 qualified individuals to serve as civilian cadres in government administration where more than 2 million posts had been filled under the KMT.[15] But although the CCP's inadequacies and shortages were pronounced, it must be

13 Zhou's views are reported in *The New York Times*, 25 September 1946. Mao's prediction is in Mao, *SW*, 4.225.

14 Teng Hsiao-p'ing, "Report on the revision of the constitution of the Communist Party of China" (16 September 1956), in *Eighth National Congress*, 1.215.

15 The CCP figure is given by An Tzu-wen, "Training the people's civil servants," *People's China*, 1 January 1953. The KMT figure is estimated by Yi-maw Kau, "Governmental bureaucracy and cadres in urban

emphasized that the skills and experience the Communists brought with them from the rural base areas were considerable and relevant. Although the base areas were far less complex than the cities, the administration of more than 100 million people had obviously nurtured a whole range of governmental skills.

Similarly, despite the egalitarian ethos that marked the Yan'an years, the CCP was already developing specialized career lines with cadres versed in finance, commerce, and education, as well as agriculture and military affairs. In addition, the CCP's control of cities as early as 1945–6, however restricted, had provided direct experience in consolidating urban control, dealing with the bourgeoisie, and actually running urban enterprises. Indeed, when the major cities fell in 1949, the CCP possessed sufficient cadres trained in economic management to take immediate control of the 2,700 large enterprises that dominated the modern sector. The radical of the Party's earliest urban experience, moreover, facilitated the development of a more moderate policy in 1947–8 that became the basis of programs fully articulated in 1949.

But perhaps the most valuable asset the Party possessed was the attitude of its leaders that the urban phase of the revolution was to be eagerly welcomed. When Mao declared in early 1949 that "[t]he period 'from the city to the village' and of the city leading the village has now begun,"[16] he expressed not only a willingness to give priority to urban affairs but also a recognition that urban modes were most progressive and the only path to modernization. This was reflected in many ways, such as the 1950 decision to emphasize the recruitment of workers into the Party, a measure that had the bonus of bringing the CCP more into line with Soviet orthodoxy. The overriding effects of the leadership's orientation were to ensure that urban problems were dealt with on their own terms and to discredit the "charming but useless" notion of "urbanizing the countryside [while] ruralizing the towns."[17] The key to CCP success in the base areas of North China had been the insistence on focusing on the actual problems of the villages, and the achievements of the initial period of urban rule would similarly flow from a preoccupation with the tasks at hand there.

These assets notwithstanding, the shortage of skills and personnel clearly left the Party unable to assume total operational control of the cities in 1949. In these circumstances, two strategies were adopted. One was to limit Party involvement to critical areas while allowing other segments of society to carry on as before; the second was to tap additional sources of personnel to ensure the orderly functioning of government and public utilities. One of the earliest

China under communist rule, 1949–1965," 237, on the basis of data from the 1948 statistical yearbook of the Republic of China.

16 Mao, SW, 4.363.

17 From a 1949 CCP pamphlet cited in Suzanne Pepper, Civil war in China: The political struggle, 1945–1949, 379.

acts of the occupying authorities was to call on existing personnel to remain at their posts. Only a small number of people with close ties to the KMT were detained; the great bulk of officials continued to work in the same jobs and at the same salaries as before. Communist cadres were dispatched to the various administrative organs and key economic enterprises to assume political control and gain an understanding of operations, but actual administration and management to a substantial extent remained in the hands of the "retained personnel" from KMT days.

A second major source of personnel was the recruitment of "new cadres" (not necessarily new Party members) from the ranks of students and other literate urban youth. These intellectual youths possessed skills lacked by many "old cadres" from the base areas who had accompanied the PLA to the cities. Although the inclusion of these additional groups was absolutely necessary, it led to considerable tensions within the hastily thrown together official class. Many old cadres considered themselves tested by years of revolutionary struggle and looked down upon new cadres and retained personnel as untrustworthy. In particular, they deeply resented the choice posts obtained by young intellectuals by virtue of their abilities and the fact that retained personnel continued to receive salaries while they received only daily necessities under the revolutionary supply system. New cadres and retained personnel, for their part, resented the domineering attitude of old cadres, who they felt received preferential treatment on the basis of past political services. In the short term, Party leaders coped with the resultant problems by urging the various groups to lay aside their grievances and strive for amicable relations. In the longer term, from 1951 on, measures included transferring old cadres lacking the necessary skills for urban work back to the countryside, stepping up political and professional training of new cadres while at the same time weeding out those who were judged unreliable, and ousting retained personnel from official positions as newly recruited cadres became available.

While expanding its personnel resources, the Party initially limited its scope of activities. Given that many functions were beyond the new government's immediate capabilities, various private groups were allowed or even encouraged to provide services to the public. For example, the government mobilized traditional benefit societies to provide relief for the needy, and in 1950 private and religious bodies still controlled nearly 40 percent of China's higher educational institutions. This approach flowed from a decision taken early on not merely to limit but actually to contract the scope of Party activities. Despite warnings from the highest CCP authorities not to import the methods of rural class struggle to the cities, in late 1948 and early 1949 many of the cadres entering the newly liberated cities still clung to leftist notions of mobilizing the downtrodden and sought to do so on a broad basis. They spread their limited resources thinly and in uncoordinated fashion through-out residential areas and small-scale enterprises. This practice was reversed by measures initiated by Liu Shaoqi in Tianjin in April and May 1949 and subsequently adopted in other urban centers. Liu centralized political organization and reallocated cadres to the modern economic sector, the educational sphere, and government administration while leaving the traditional sector to its own devices. The net effect was to enhance the CCP's capacity to shape the future course of events by giving it control of the institutions and forces that really mattered.

Liu's Tianjin interlude also enabled the Party to come to terms with the key economic problem that Mao had only shortly before singled out as the primary focus of urban work – the restoration of production, especially industrial production. Here again the enthusiasm of recently arrived cadres was proving an obstacle. Given both the Party's earlier official encouragement of workers' demands under KMT rule and the continuing labor unrest, such cadres backed the workers against management, with the result that many factories did not function, owing to industrial strife. This, Liu argued, was a leftist deviation preventing economic recovery. He instituted policies calling for labor discipline, managerial authority to limit wages and fire excess personnel, and "reasonable" settlements of disputes. The interests of workers regarding wages and conditions were far from ignored, but the emphasis was to restrict their demands and appeal to them to make short-term sacrifices in the interest of long-term gains.

These policies succeeded in restoring production; on a national basis, pre-war peaks were achieved in many spheres by 1952. As a result, major inroads were made in alleviating serious urban unemployment. Moreover, the revival of industrial production, together with the opening of supply routes from the hinterland, helped bring under control the severe inflation that had discredited the KMT. These developments – together with such measures as removing money from circulation by taxes, bonds, and forced savings; curbing government expenditures; controlling key commodities through state trading companies; and severe punishment of speculation – succeeded in reducing the astronomical levels of KMT inflation to the manageable rate of about 15 percent by 1951.

Meanwhile, the CCP was able to combine economic recovery with an increasing capacity to control the private sector, Whereas capitalists saw Communist-controlled trade unions as a useful device for securing labor concessions, the unions, together with labor laws, provided the CCP with potent devices for enforcing its demands as well as modestly improving the lot of urban workers. In addition, the leading economic role of the large national-ized enterprises, state trading companies, and banks provided potent external controls over capitalist enterprises through loans, contracts to purchase products and supply raw materials, designated selling agents, and officially determined prices. As a result, the process of economic recovery not only secured broad public support for the CCP, but further added to the Party's capabilities for determining subsequent developments.

United front and democratic dictatorship

One of the keys to the CCP's initial success in consolidating control was its ability to maximize support and minimize fears. A number of factors worked in the Party's favor. As previously indicated, the very fact of unification resulted in the patriotic support of educated elites and broader public relief that peace had been restored. This also had a traditional aspect, since the PRC was widely accepted as a new dynasty that had the right to establish its own orthodoxy. Another favorable circumstance was the near-total discrediting of the KMT, especially among urban middle classes. The Communists were welcomed even by groups such as the industrial bourgeoisie that had good reason to fear their ultimate aims. The hopes and receptiveness of the population, in the cities at least, were not simply a product of circumstances; they reflected sustained CCP efforts to reassure key groups and the public as a whole. As we have seen, civil servants were kept at their posts and capitalists were assisted in reviving their enterprises. Meanwhile, the populace as a whole was impressed by the generally impeccable behavior of the occupying troops – in sharp contrast to the performance of KMT forces when they returned to the cities in 1945.

These and other measures, it must be stressed, were not improvisations. Rather, they reflected one of the characteristic features of Mao's strategy – the united front. To a significant degree, revolutionary success was built on the principle of gathering a wide collection of allies by setting relatively limited goals and defining enemies as narrowly as possible. It was this united front practice that was now applied to the postliberation situation.

The approach was reflected in the general program and institutional arrangements proclaimed at the founding of the PRC. A key element was the effort to seek the broadest base of legitimacy by linking the new regime to the past. In theory, the temporary supreme organ of state power pending the establishment of a system of people's congresses was designated as the Chinese People's Political Consultative Conference (CPPCC), a body that drew its lineage from the Political Consultative Conference convened by the KMT in early 1946 as a multiparty body ostensible, seeking to avoid civil war. Similarly, the united front itself was traced back to the founder of the KMT, Sun Yat-sen.

Into the united front and CPPCC were drawn the so-called democratic parties, the small middle-class and intelligentsia-based groups that had futilely attempted to become a third force during the struggle between the KMT and CCP. Not only did delegates from these parties vastly outnumber those formally assigned the CCP, but more significantly, eleven of the twenty-four ministers appointed in the new government were minor party representatives or unaffiliated "democratic personages." Although political power clearly rested in the hands of the CCP, these positions were not mere formalities. More broadly, the advice of prestigious non-Communist figures was genuinely sought throughout the early years of the PRC.

Equally significant was the moderate, conciliatory nature of the CCP blueprint for the future: the Common Program. The hallmark of this document was gradualism. Although longer-term objectives, particularly in the economic sphere, were included, the emphasis was on immediate tasks. In Zhou Enlai's words, the ultimate goals of socialism and communism were "not put . . . in writing for the time being [although] we do not deny [them]."[18] Mao even more strongly emphasized the gradual nature of the Party's program in mid-1950 when he declared, "The view . . . that it is possible to eliminate capitalism and realize socialism at an early date is wrong [and] does not tally with our national conditions."[19]

In addition to gradualism, the Common Program adopted the classic united front tactic of narrowly defining enemies as "imperialism, feudalism and bureaucratic capitalism." Policies for reasserting China's national rights and squeezing out Western enterprises were genuinely popular, although this patriotic appeal was somewhat undercut by the decision to align with the Soviet Union. "Bureaucratic capital" – the limited number of large enterprises that had been run by figures closely connected with the KMT and were now confiscated by the new state – was also a popular target, particularly among private capitalists (the "national bourgeoisie") who had suffered grievously from KMT favoritism toward well-connected firms. Finally, feudal forces were defined as landlords, who made up only 3 to 5 percent of the rural population. Not only were rich peasants excluded from the list of enemies, but the need to maintain the "rich peasant economy" became a key aspect of CCP rural policies. This approach further served, as Mao elaborated in early 1950, to "isolate the landlords, protect the middle peasants [and] set at rest the minds of the national bourgeoisie," which was closely tied up with the land problem.[20]

The united front was also enshrined at the level of Marxist theory. A "new democratic state" was established that was not an orthodox dictatorship of the proletariat but, instead, a "people's democratic dictatorship" in which the peasantry, petty bourgeoisie, and national bourgeoisie joined the working class

18 *Selected works of Zhou Enlai*, 1.406.   19 Mao, *SW*, 5.30.
20 Ibid., 24–5.

as ruling classes. In adopting this concept, the CCP broke with current Soviet orthodoxy on state forms. Although Soviet theoreticians had also accepted the bourgeoisie as part of the state apparatus in the East European "people's democracies" before 1948, that stand had been reserved in conjunction with the split with Tito, and the Russians now refused to acknowledge Chinese claims. By persisting in their position until 1953–4, when CCP writers began to acknowledge the fundamental similarity of the proletarian and people's democratic dictatorships, Party leaders indicated not only the importance they attached to the united front tactic but a determination to insist on ideological as well as political independence where circumstances warranted.

Such assertions of independence notwithstanding, the Soviet influence in the general theoretical as well as specific policy sense was considerable. Various Soviet theoretical texts were widely studied in China and Lenin's New Economic Policy served as a reference for the gradualism of the new democratic economy. And in the larger political sense that state form was, of course, identical to that of the Soviet Union – the dictatorship was ultimately that of the Communist Party. For as the theory of the people's democratic dictatorship made clear, the classes making up the state were not an alliance of equals. The alliance was led by the working class – that is, its vanguard, the Party – and the other members were to be educated by the proletariat. In the case of the national bourgeoisie – a bone of contention with the Soviets – this education could be harsh indeed, since that class was described as vacillating and having an exploitative side. Initially the united front approach emphasized the role of the bourgeoisie and the vast majority of the population in building the new China, but the democratic dictatorship could always quickly redefine the political status of any segment of the "people."

Military and regional rule

The situation in 1949 guaranteed that in the first instance Communist rule would be military and decentralized. Since the newly liberated areas fell to the PLA and the task of eliminating bandit opposition remained, Military Control Commissions were initially established as the supreme local authority. These, however, were explicitly temporary. According to the Common Program, the duration of military control would be determined strictly according to local conditions, and it would give way to civilian authority as soon as this was feasible. Similarly, the great variations from area to area required decentralized administration because no uniform policy could apply to the whole nation. But this too was seen as transitional from the outset. For this function China was divided into six large regions (excluding Inner Mongolia and Tibet, which were administered separately). Reflecting the conditions of the period, four of these regions – the Central-South, East China, the Northwest, and the Southwest – were run by military-administrative committees, whereas North China and the Northeast were given people's governments to indicate the successful completion of the military tasks. These regional administrations, with some changes in nomenclature, remained in existence until 1954, but their powers were gradually transferred to the center as conditions allowed. Party regional bureaus and military regions existed on the same geographical bases, but these were too phased out in 1954–5.

The shift from military to civilian rule was remarkably smooth. Although the Military Control Commissions initially exercised wide powers over governmental and Party organs, their personnel were soon absorbed into the units they were sent to control. Within a matter of months the commission became a coordinating and supervisory body whose offices were largely empty of staff as administrative functions were increasingly undertaken directly by the new governments. By 1951, its functions were largely reduced to security and garrison matters as local governments now issued decrees alone. The fact that close relations had been built up between political and military figures during the prolonged revolutionary struggle undoubtedly goes far to explain the smoothness of the shift to civilian rule. But at least equally important was the clear distinction between civilian and military authority that Mao articulated in 1938: "Our principle is that the Party commands the gun, and the gun must never be allowed to command the Party."[21] This principle was reflected in appointments to the large regions; the key position of Party first secretary was held by political figures in every region except the Central-South, where Lin Biao, one of the PLA's most successful commanders and a long-standing favorite of Mao's, occupied the post. Moreover, the relatively limited degree of differentiation of political and military roles was to be significantly widened. The Common Program called for military modernization, including the formation of an air force and navy, and the Korean War provided the impetus for modernization in earnest with the help of substantial Soviet aid. Although many PLA commanders adopted civilian roles, the great bulk found ample career opportunities in an increasingly professionalized military.

Meanwhile, the powers of the regional administrations remained considerable over the 1949–52 period. This was not apparent in the strict legal sense, since they were placed directly under the Government Administrative Council or cabinet in Beijing, with no autonomous rights of their own. In fact, however, given that the fledgling governmental structure was finding its legs and had only rudimentary planning and statistical capabilities, much

Map 2. Administrative regions, 1949–54 (Note: By the end of 1952, Chahar had been divided between Inner Mongolia, Shanxi and Hebei; and Pingyuan between Henan and Shandong. In 1954, when the administrative regions were abolished, Songjiang was incorporated into Heilongjiang; Liaodong and Liaoxi were combined to form Liaoning. Suiyuan was merged with Inner Mongolia, and Ningxia became part of Gansu. In 1955, Sikang was divided between Sichuan and Tibet, and Jehol was divided between Inner Mongolia, Liaoning and Hebei. Ningxia reappeared as the Ningxia-Hui Autonomous Region in 1958)

was necessarily left to the regions. In addition, given the vast differences in conditions and problems from area to area, central leaders remained uncertain as to exactly how much regional authority was required and allowed considerable local experimentation. The overall pattern was for the center to lay down policies in fairly general form and leave to the regions the issues of pace and means of implementation. For example, in mid-1950 the Beijing authorities passed an agrarian reform law but apparently did not establish any central monitoring body; the process of implementation was placed in the hands of land reform committees set up in each regional administration.

The powers of the regions were also reflected in the fact that initially some of the CCP's most powerful figures headed military-administrative committees and people's governments. Looking at the top elite broadly, some two-thirds of the Central Committee served outside Beijing in these years. One key sign of change was the gradual transfer of such leaders to the center as the period wore on. By 1952 the most powerful regional figures had assumed important duties in Beijing, even if they generally still continued to exercise their local powers on a concurrent basis. Moreover, as the capacities of the central bureaucracies increased and conditions in the regions became more uniform, specific powers were transferred to Beijing. Thus in March 1950 the Government Administrative Council enacted a decision unifying national financial and economic work, but in other cases, such as a November 1951 decision increasing the appointment powers of the regions, the continued need for decentralized administration was acknowledged.

Decentralized administration, of course, gave scope for the "localist" deviation of ignoring the spirit of central directives in order to further some parochial interest. Perhaps the clearest case of this in the 1949–52 period occurred with regard to land reform in the southern province of Guangdong. There local cadres carried out a milder and slower process of reform than elsewhere, resulting in higher-level criticism and eventually the displacement of key figures by new leaders sent in from the outside. But what is significant about this episode is that the main antagonists of the local cadres were less the central authorities in Beijing than the leaders of the Central-South military-administrative committee in Wuhan. Indeed, there is little evidence to suggest regional resistance to central authority in these years, although the inevitable "errors" of the regions were criticized in Beijing. The variations that did occur were accepted by the central leaders as not only necessary but desirable under the circumstances. Basically, this meant that programs were initiated first in North and Northeast China, where conditions were more stable and organizational resources more plentiful, and extended south only as the situation allowed. The Northwest and Southwest in particular lagged in the implementation of programs, but unlike the Guangdong case this was accepted by Beijing as logical given the strong resistance of bandit forces in these regions.

The outstanding case of regional particularity was the Northeast. This had little to do with later distorted charges that Gao Gang had established an "independent kingdom" there (to be discussed later). Rather, it reflected the fact that the Northeast was the most advanced region and served as a bellwether for the rest of the country for a number of reasons. First, having benefited from industrialization under Japanese rule, the Northeast had the most developed economic base. It provided 34 percent of China's industrial output in 1949 and 52 percent in 1952. Second, by virtue of being the first region totally liberated, the Northeast could move more quickly toward comprehensive policies and was able to begin regional planning by 1950. And finally, proximity to the Soviet Union and Soviet holdings in the regional railroads and the port of Luta (Port Arthur–Dalian) combined to provide easy access to Soviet aid and influence. Thus the Northeast instituted Soviet methods of economic management, albeit with difficulty due to shortages of skilled personnel, and these methods were generally endorsed by the central leadership in Beijing for extension to China as a whole.

The model role of the Northeast, whereby policies were tested and refined there before being popularized on a nationwide basis, was not limited to the advanced industrial sector. In youth work the region in general and Harbin in particular were held up for emulation, and one of the critical mass movements of the period, the Three Antis Campaign focusing on urban corruption, was first carried out on a trial basis in the Northeast. The attitude of the central leadership toward the Northeast was summed up in an article recording impressions of the region by Song Qingling, Sun Yat-sen's widow and a leading united front figure in Peking. According to Song, China had a bright future and "our Northeast is leading the way."[22] Beijing encouraged the Northeast's trailblazing role while at the same time viewing the Northwest and Southwest as backward areas where far different policies were needed and proper.

Land reform

The crucial task for the new liberated areas generally was land reform. To this task the CCP brought experience and personnel that were often lacking for the more complex conditions of the cities. The Party, after all, had been engaging in rural revolution for over two decades by the time the PLA crossed the Yangtze. In that time Party leaders had attempted a variety of approaches and refined a set of methods for peasant mobilization. Yet in some senses the

---

22 *Renmin ribao* (People's daily, hereafter *RMRB*), 1 May 1951.

job facing the Communists in the vast rural areas was even more difficult than that undertaken in the cities. For one thing, it was not totally clear even to top Party leaders just how applicable past experience was to the new situation. Mao called attention to the altered circumstances in early 1950: "[T]he agrarian reform in the north was carried out in wartime, with the atmosphere of war prevailing over that of agrarian reform, but now, with the fighting practically over, the agrarian reform stands out in sharp relief, and the shock to society will be particularly great!"[23]

Even more significant was the vastness of the territories now seized. Even if the CCP could have miraculously dispatched all its 4.5 million members in 1949 to these areas, the resultant cadre force would still have been inadequate for penetrating the widely dispersed peasant population. Moreover, the Communists came to the villages of the new liberated areas as outsiders with little knowledge of local conditions, carrying ideas based on quite different agricultural and ownership patterns, and often not even speaking the native dialect. Given both the sparseness of personnel and their alien status, the success of the CCP in completing land reform in areas occupied by over 90 percent of the rural population by fall 1952 is testimony to the relevance of its earlier experience and particularly to the determination of Party leaders.

The initial penetration of the countryside came in the form of PLA units that fanned out from the cities to the rural market towns and then to the villages. These troops, apart from bandit suppression, generally limited themselves to disarming the local population, carrying out security functions, and organizing village militias. In the wake of the PLA, small groups or somewhat larger work teams of cadres came to the village. Only a small proportion, perhaps 10 percent at most, were old cadres with experience in the northern agrarian struggle. The bulk was made up of students and other urban intellectuals, young rural intellectuals with family ties to landlords and rich peasants, urban unemployed, and, where available, local Communist underground workers. Extreme youth as well as questionable class backgrounds often characterized these political workers.

One of their earliest tasks was, with the aid of the PLA, to collect taxes to support the new regime. This undertaking was bound to create friction between cadres and peasants, as suggested by the fact that more than 3,000 cadres were killed in the first year after takeover trying to collect the grain tax. As it became apparent that the new policies were shifting the burden away from the poor to the rich, however, support was generated for the new order. Other measures undertaken by the cadres in this initial period included the organization of peasant associations, carrying out a program of rent and interest

23 Mao, SW, 5.24.

reduction, and conducting struggles against "despots" or "local bullies," in other words, the most oppressive elements of the old elite. None of these efforts went without a hitch. Despots were sometimes arbitrarily designated; peasants frequently returned rent money to landlords in secret; and by the fall of 1950 in many areas only about 20 percent of the hastily organized peasant associations were judged reliable. Indeed, in these later stages of land reform, programs often had to be repeated two or three times before success was achieved. The limitations of the entire effort were further revealed by surveys at the end of land reform showing that only 40 percent of the peasants in some areas belonged to peasant associations.

All these measures were preparatory for the main work of agrarian reform – the confiscation and redistribution of landlord land. In June 1950 the central authorities promulgated the agrarian reform law to guide this work. Reflecting Mao's views on the differences of the current situation from the wartime land reform of North China and the policy of maintaining the "rich peasant economy," the new law and Liu Shaoqi's report on it advanced an explicitly economic rationale for the program. Thus the view that land reform's main function was to relieve the poor was rejected, and "freeing the rural productive forces" and "paving the way for industrialization" were emphasized. Moreover, the law was sanguine about the ease with which landlord opposition could be overcome under peacetime conditions and insisted on political order as a prerequisite for implementation.

This analysis was, however, already being undercut by difficulties encountered in preparations for land reform in the villages of the new liberated areas. One factor was peasant uncertainty as to how far the CCP program would go, especially the concern that redistribution would affect the land of rich peasants and even middle peasants. More ominous from the CCP's perspective was the traditional power and influence of the landlords over the peasantry generally. Ordinary peasants were simply afraid to oppose the forces that had been dominant on the local scene for so long, because they had little confidence that Communist rule was irreversible. A particularly difficult problem was the blurring of class lines in the traditional village. The distinction between various better-off peasant strata and landlords was often clearer to work teams of outsiders than to local poor peasants. Also, social tensions were mitigated by traditional obligations of landlords toward peasants in hard times, as well as particularistic ties of family, local residence, and clan. All these links could be and were used by landlords to subvert the peasant associations, conceal land and other wealth, and maintain the existing power structure through secret societies and other devices.

As reports indicating the entrenched power of the existing rural social order came to the attention of responsible Party leaders in the late summer of 1950, policy began to be reconsidered. The shift to a more radical line came definitively in November and December, shortly after the Chinese intervention in Korea. Some official statements cited the Korean conflict as a justification, and certainly increased social tension and rumors of the return of the KMT were a factor. Nevertheless, the fundamental reason for the change was the great difficulties the relatively moderate program had already encountered.

As a result, the new land reform program of stepped-up implementation, an emphasis on class struggle, and mass mobilization even at the risk of some social disorder was in sharp contrast to the principles of the agrarian reform law. When Deng Zihui, a leading Central-South official who would soon become the CCP's top agricultural specialist, attacked peaceful land reform and asserted that politics must come before economics, he was in effect criticizing the official line of six months earlier. It is important to note that even so substantial a policy shift had little political fallout, as Liu Shaoqi and others who had articulated the earlier line retained their prominence. Undoubtedly this was partially due to the fact that the milder policy had been Mao's own, but it also reflected the willingness of all concerned to treat program changes as necessary adjustments in the light of new evidence rather than as issues for political advantage.

Under the new line, land reform proper was launched. The major steps were a class identification of all village inhabitants, followed by the confiscation and redistribution of landlord land and other productive property, A leading role in the process was played by work teams dispatched by county-level land reform committees, and one of their main functions was to purify the peasant associations and select activists from their midst for local leadership positions. This new leadership was predominantly drawn from the poor peasants, although official policy reserved one-third of the leading peasant association posts for middle peasants. In many areas, by virtue of their skills, middle peasants were able to dominate. In addition, the work teams sought to mobilize the entire village against the landlords through such devices as "speak bitterness" meetings and mass trials. These methods subjected the landlords to public humiliation, and the trials also resulted in the execution of members of this class on a significant scale, perhaps 1 to 2 million individuals.[24] Moreover, under the new guideline of "not correcting excesses prematurely," the aroused

24 In the absence of official statistics it is impossible to know the numbers involved, but it appears clear that early 1950s estimates by anti-Communist sources of 14 to 15 million deaths are far too high. For a careful review of the evidence and a cautious estimate of 200,000 to 800,000 executions, see Benedict Stavis, *The politics of agricultural mechanization in China*, 25–30. A larger number is suggested by reports based on refugee interviews of a "policy to choose at least one landlord, and usually several, in virtually every village for public execution." A. Doak Barnett with Ezra Vogel, *Cadres, bureaucracy and political power in communist China*, 228.

masses frequently engaged in unchecked outbreaks of violence and brutality against landlords that resulted in additional deaths. Although reports of peaceful land reform persisted throughout the movement, it appears that continued efforts to draw class lines and generate antagonism had a considerable effect.

As an economic reform program, land reform succeeded in redistributing about 43 percent of China's cultivated land to about 60 percent of the rural population. Poor peasants substantially increased their holdings, but middle peasants actually benefited most because of their stronger initial position. It remains debatable how much of a contribution land reform made to overall agricultural productivity. In any case, the main achievement of the movement was political. The old elite was stripped of its economic assets, some of its members were killed, and as a class it had been humiliated. The crucial fact was the old order proved powerless, and peasants could now confidently support the new system. The old village institutions of clan, temple, and secret society had been displaced by the new, which assumed their educational, mediatory and economic functions. And a new elite of village cadres from the ranks of poor and middle peasants whose horizons had been broadened by the class-oriented perspective of the CCP.

In achieving this rural revolution, the Party had used both coercive and persuasive methods. Constant propaganda on the evils of the old system and benefits of the new was undoubtedly a significant factor in winning the peasants to the CCP program, but the force used against the landlords was crucial in convincing the entire rural population where power lay. Yet as important as coercion were the tangible rewards Party policies provided for the poorer elements in the villages. A more equitable tax burden, reduced rents, and finally land – in addition to leading posts for the most active – did much to convince the peasant masses of the rightness of the Party's cause. By demonstrating its credibility during land reform as both a force to be feared and a provider of a better life, the CCP greatly enhanced its future persuasive capabilities among the peasants.

Urban mass movements

Although land reform radically altered life in China's countryside, a series of urban mass movements left an indelible impact on the cities. The most important of these were the campaign to suppress counterrevolutionaries that was launched in February 1951 and lasted into 1953, and from fall 1951 to summer-fall 1952 the Three Antis Campaign against corrupt cadres, the Five Antis drive against the hitherto respected national bourgeoisie, and the thought reform campaign aimed at the intellectuals. All these movements were extremely intense and generated considerable tension and apprehension in society. As in the countryside, official violence was used on a substantial scale, particularly in the counterrevolutionaries campaign and to a far lesser degree in the Three and Five Antis campaigns.[25] In addition, intense psychological pressure was brought to bear by various measures, including forced confessions in small groups and mass trials attended by tens of thousand (and broadcast to millions). This not only fostered a climate of distrust that broke down established personal relationships, it also resulted in large numbers of suicides – possibly on the order of several hundred thousand.[26] These campaigns indicated to broad sections of society the full extent of the Party's aims for social transformation. As the emphasis shifted from reassurance to tightening control, many groups that had hitherto been left basically alone were now drawn into the vortex of directed struggle. By the end of 1952 the CCP had become, for the majority of China's urban population, a force to be reckoned with.

All these campaigns were launched after the Chinese entry into the Korean War in late 1950, and their intensity was undoubtedly linked to Korea. Party leaders saw a genuine need for vigilance, given not only the danger of American attack but also the possibility of KMT efforts to return to the mainland. In any case, KMT sabotage operations were real, and dissident elements were encouraged by the potential opportunities created by the Korean involvement. The general level of social tension was further raised by a campaign directed at all groups to "resist America and aid Korea" launched in late fall 1950. The shift in leadership attitudes at the time of the Korean intervention is indicated in Mao's comments on counter-revolutionaries. In late September 1950, shortly before the decision to intervene, Mao declared, "It is imperative that we do not kill even a single agent"; by the start of 1951 he argued that "we must firmly kill all those reactionary elements who deserve to be killed."[27]

But although the Korean War undoubtedly contributed to the change in attitude and probably made the various campaigns harsher than they would

25 Again, in the absence of precise official statistics, the number of executions cannot be known. But the primarily urban campaign against counterrevolutionaries may have resulted in as many as 500,000 to 800,000 deaths (see Stavis, *The politics of agricultural mechanization*, 29). The matter is obscure, since these figures are based on a 1957 reference by Mao to counterrevolutionaries who had been liquidated, but from the context it is impossible to tell whether the people in question were the targets of this particular campaign or a more general category including the victims of land reform and other movements.

26 The main sources of the scope of suicides are refugee accounts. Chow Ching-wen, *Ten yean of storm: The true story of the communist regime in China*, 115, 133, estimates that more than 500,000 people committed suicide during the suppression of counterrevolutionaries and another 200,000 plus during the Three and Five Antis movements. Although these estimates may be exaggerated, it is clear from official sources that suicides were a significant phenomenon.

27 "Comments on the work of suppressing and liquidating counterrevolutionaries" (1950–1), in *Miscellany*, 1.6.

have been otherwise, in another sense Party leaders used the Korean situation to press ahead on tasks that would have been undertaken anyway. Measures to deal with counterrevolutionaries had been drafted before Korea, and the vacillating bourgeoisie and Western-oriented intellectuals had clearly been targeted for ideological transformation. Indeed, the most significant campaigns started in the fall of 1951, a year after the Korean involvement, and Mao subsequently indicated that internal considerations were primary by observing that only "after the completion of agrarian reform [were we] able to launch the 'Three Antis' and 'Five Antis' campaigns."[28]

The suppression of counterrevolutionaries movement was aimed at spies and others engaged in active resistance to the new regime. High on the list of those under attack were former members of the KMT and KMT-linked organizations, as well as secret society leaders. The definition of "counterrevolutionary," however, was extremely broad, and in implementing the campaign it appears that not only active opponents but also genuinely popular local figures who had the potential to become alternative leaders were affected. In the conduct of the movement, the CCP displayed a conscious effort to avoid Soviet methods of public security work. Although in many respects the drive was a classic police effort marked by midnight arrests, Mao's directives emphasized a uniquely Chinese approach. First, there was an effort to secure mass participation in the process of uncovering counterrevolutionaries and a sensitivity to the need to avoid offending public opinion by excesses; to this end non-Party personages were invited to participate on committees overseeing the movement. Even more important was Mao's insistence on Party committee authority over all public security work. In direct contrast to Stalinist practice, where the secret police were virtually an independent hierarchy capable of terrorizing the Party, Mao emphasized precise control over counterrevolutionary matters by higher-level Party organs.

The general public seemingly found the counterrevolutionaries campaign, frightening but understandable, especially at a time of external threat. The tree interrelated campaigns of 1951–2, however, came as a rude awakening to groups who had up to then received mild and even supportive treatment from the CCR. The key targets of the Three Antis Campaign were urban cadres, especially those in financial and economic departments, who had become involved in corruption as a result of their dealings with the bourgeoisie. Although these individuals included some relatively high-ranking Communists (although no one of Central Committee or ministerial rank), the vast majority were either retained personnel or new cadres whose commitment to

28 "Summing-up speech at 6th expanded plenum of 7th CCP Central Committee" (September 1955), in *Miscellany*, 1.16.

the Communist cause had always been suspect. The Five Antis Campaign was directed explicitly at lawbreaking capitalists, particularly large capitalists, who allegedly engaged in a whole range of economic crimes and defrauded the state and public, but its larger target was the national bourgeoisie as a class. And although thought reform focused on higher-level intellectuals who assertedly aided "American cultural imperialism," the more general objective was to weaken the influence of all intellectual currents that strayed from the CCP's version of Marxism-Leninism.

What was being attacked in the largest sense was a whole complex of urban non-Communist values that had hitherto been tolerated. Many cadres, taking their lead from official policy encouraging the bourgeoisie, had come to regard capitalists as progressive and capable members of society. Capitalists, for their part, hoped to continue both their business practices and well-to-do style of life. Finally, leading intellectuals valued independent thinking and resisted being pushed into a Marxist straitjacket.

The overall effect of the three movements was to bring these elements to heel. This had several aspects. Direct punishment of the most serious offenders plus the enormous psychological pressures brought to bear destroyed the self-confidence of the concerned groups. Moreover, these pressures undermined existing patterns of social relations; *quanxi* – that is, personal relations based on family, school, or workplace ties – could no longer guarantee protection against the demands of the state. Related to this was the success of the Party in discrediting these groups in the eyes of others who traditionally had had submissive attitudes toward them. Thus workers in small enterprises who had previously accepted the paternalism of their employers now began to adopt official class struggle attitudes.

Organizationally, the control of the bourgeoisie over their enterprises was weakened by both the establishment of new trade union organs and the purging of existing unions that had often been run by friends and relations of the capitalists. Of critical importance was the recruitment of a new elite for lower-level positions in economic enterprises and government. As retained personnel and tainted new cadres were weeded out, their positions and others opened up by economic expansion were filled by worker activists who had emerged in the course of the Three and Five Antis campaigns or earlier. To a substantial degree, the attack on retained personnel was made possible by the availability of workers trained for administrative tasks in the preceding year who were now promoted to more responsible posts, and the campaign itself generated large numbers of new cadres ostensibly loyal to the CCP program. Given the continuing need for the managerial and intellectual skills of existing groups, the change was not as dramatic as in the countryside, but China's cities as well as villages saw the emergence of new elite elements in these years.

Finally, the Three and Five Antis campaigns had an important economic impact. Apart from generating substantial funds for investment and development through fines and back taxes, the movements greatly enhanced state control over private enterprises through new loans and government contracts that capitalists found necessary in their financially weakened state. Moreover, these toughened external controls were now accompanied by internal controls. A key measure was that businesses with heavy fines to pay would meet their obligations by selling stock to the state and creating joint public-private enterprises – a process that resulted in sending state cadres to assume leading positions in the concerned firms. Together with the strengthened trade unions, the setting up of Party branches in many large and medium-sized enterprises, and especially the vast amounts of information gathered during the investigation of capitalists' "crimes," this now gave the authorities a much greater knowledge of the internal workings of the private economic sphere. As a result, CCP leaders had achieved a position where planned economic development was genuinely feasible.

SOCIALIST CONSTRUCTION AND TRANSFORMATION, 1953–6

On the basis of the substantially increased political control resulting from the various mass campaigns in rural and urban areas, the PRC entered a new phase of socialist construction and transformation in 1953. In that year, nationwide economic planning began. At first, due to China's primitive planning and statistical capabilities, the demands of the Korean War, and apparent delays in negotiations with the Soviet Union for economic aid, only annual plans were possible. But with the Korean War and Soviet aid negotiations both concluded in mid-1953, more comprehensive planning could be started. Finally, in mid-1955 a first FYP for the entire 1953–7 period was approved.

With planned construction went socialist transformation – the change from private to state and collective ownership in agriculture, handicrafts, and capitalist industry and commerce. A new emphasis on transformation came with the formulation of the "general line for the transition to socialism" in mid-1953 and its public announcement in October. In some respects this general line reflected continuity with the preceding period. First, its hall-mark was gradualism; both industrialization and transformation would take place over a fairly long period of about fifteen years in a step-by-step manner. Also, the practice of the general line was still within the framework of the united front. The national bourgeoisie in particular would continue to play a vital role. The initial stage of transition would be "state capitalism," where the private sector was increasingly linked to the state sector, but capitalists would still retain about one-quarter of the profits from their enterprises. Given the nature of the

CCP's united front policies, however, the process of transformation naturally contained threatening aspects for the bourgeoisie, albeit in muted form. As Liu Shaoqi put it in September 1954, "The idea that there is no longer class struggle in our country is completely wrong [but] the aim [of restricting capitalist exploitation] can be achieved by peaceful means."[29]

Despite its continuities, the general line meant a somewhat more radical policy, reflected in the concept of a transition to socialism rather than New Democracy. The politics of its adoption in 1953, furthermore, indicated differences within the leadership going back several years over precisely how much emphasis to place on reassuring key groups in society and how much on controlling and transforming them. Although Mao does not appear to have taken quite so individual an initiative as in the Korean War, agricultural cooperativization, and Hundred Flowers decisions, the Chairman now played a major role in shifting the emphasis more decisively to the side of transformation. At an important financial and economic work conference in summer 1953, Mao addressed a number of issues, including concessions to rich peasants and hesitations in developing socialized agriculture. But the sharpest issue, which became entangled in the Gao Gang affair (discussed later), was the new tax system introduced by Minister of Finance Bo Yibo in December 1952 that lightened the tax load on private capitalists. This, Mao declared, was based on "bourgeois ideas which are favorable to capitalism and harmful to socialism."[30]

The attack on Bo served to warn others of like views of the need to step up the process of change. This warning was effective without being disruptive, since the policy shift called for was relatively moderate, and the Chairman emphasized the need to guard against left as well as right deviations. Moreover, the handling of Bo's case was an instance of limiting elite conflict in the interests of Party unity. At the conference Mao declared that Bo's error was not a mistake in line and appealed for unity. And although Bo stepped down as minister of finance, in little more than a year he was again appointed to one of the PRC's leading economic posts.

By 1953 the CCP had amassed substantial resources on the basis of which socialist construction and transformation could begin. In economic terms, 70 to 80 percent of heavy industry and 40 percent of light industry were state owned in late 1952. State trading agencies and cooperatives handled more than 50 percent of total business turnover, and government leverage over the remaining sectors had increased due to the development of joint firms and revamped trade unions. Organizationally, in addition to the large numbers of cadres and activists who had emerged from training programs and mass

29 Collected works of Liu Shao-ch'i 1945–1957, 292–3.   30 Mao, SW, 5.104.

movements, the CCP had been strengthed as a result of a "Party rectification and Party building" movement begun in 1951 that would conclude in early 1954. This campaign for reform and recruitment weeded out about 10 percent of CCP members (some 580,000 individuals) who were either tainted by ties to enemy classes or simply lacked commitment to or understanding of Party programs, and at the same time in relatively cautious manner recruited about 1.28 million new members, to bring total membership to 6.5 million at the end of 1953.

In another organizational move, by late 1952 the CCP had expanded its network to cover most elements of the urban population and part of the peasantry as well. In addition to the impact made by the campaigns of 1951–2, the Party extended its control to the urban grass roots by developing residents' committees on a street-by-street basis, a process that was finally formalized in 1954. At the same time, the articulation of bureaucratic "units" (*danwei*) further enhanced the CCP's organizational sway in the cities. The *danwei* became a potent force for political control both by providing the framework for work, residence, and social intercourse for most employees in official organizations and by establishing regular political rituals involving all unit members in directed activities such as the study of documents and mutual criticism in small groups.

Moreover, "mass organizations" originally organized as national bodies in 1949 to educate and mobilize major population groups had taken on substantial proportions. By 1953, the New Democratic Youth League had grown to 9 million members, the trade unions numbered 12 million, and the women's federation at least formally enrolled 76 million. Although these and other mass organizations were often passive in their actual activities, they nevertheless represented an impressive framework for providing contact with Party policies and some sense of popular participation. Such organizational scope with "the great majority . . . belong[ing] to some organization," Mao noted in 1955, had never happened in thousands of years. But as a result, he claimed, it had changed the oft-lamented Chinese condition of "being like loose sand" into national unity.[31]

In focusing these resources on economic development, the CCP won genuine support from a people attracted by the promise of both improved living conditions and national glory. Within leadership circles there was unanimity that *planned* construction was the only acceptable method – not only ideologically preferred but more efficient than "chaotic" capitalist development. One important consequence of the emphasis on planning was that it created a critical link between economic objectives and social transformation.

31 Ibid., 173–74.

The projected change in ownership patterns not only expropriated suspect classes, it gave the state the direct control over economic resources without which planning would be ineffective. Thus, although arguments often raged over the precise nature of that link, there was fundamental consensus on socializing not only the modern sector but also agriculture, since, in the words of the Chairman of the State Planning Commission, Li Fuchun: "Socialism cannot be built on the basis of a small peasant economy; it must have a foundation of large scale industry and large scale collective farming."[32] Clearly there was no basic contradiction between economic and political objectives for CCP leaders as the first FYP unfolded.

Another consequence of the planning ethos was the push for regularization in all spheres of life. At the overall institutional level this was manifested in the 1953–4 elections for a National People's Congress and the adoption by that Congress when it met in September 1954 of a formal state constitution. Administratively, regularization meant centralization. As the State Planning Commission and new economic ministries were created in the latter half of 1952, various regional powers were reduced and others placed directly under central authority. Then, in 1954–5 the regional administrations and parallel Party and military bodies were abolished on the grounds of incompatibility with the needs of planned construction. Given the long buildup of increased central control, this explanation is convincing, although there are indications that the timing may have been influenced by the Gao Gang affair. More broadly, regularization affected a whole spate of efforts to codify administrative practice, organizational structures, and cadre recruitment, training, and wages. By 1955, new tables of organization appeared to standardize previously diverse administrative demarcations, staff offices were created to coordinate the work of related bureaus, new record-keeping and accounting practices were introduced to provide a basis for comprehensive planning, cadre recruitment procedures completed the transition from ad hoc training classes and personal introductions to reliance on the regular school system and formalized assessments, and the previous uncoordinated mix of cash wages and supplies gave way to fixed, highly articulated salary scales for various categories of state employees. A particularly significant development was a series of military professionalization measures in 1955, including the introduction of insignia, ranks, and wage scales that significantly altered the informal and egalitarian traditions of the PLA. Clearly the new planned society contained elements at variance with the CCP's revolutionary history, but there is little evidence that

---

32 "Report on the First Five-Year Plan for development of the national economy of the People's Republic of China in 1953–1957" (5–6 July 1955), in *Communist China 1955–1959: Policy documents with analysis*, 47.

in those days of high expectations Party leaders were particularly concerned about the discrepancies.

The start of planned economic construction also deepened the impact of the Soviet model; as Mao put it in early 1953: "There must be a great nation-wide upsurge of learning from the Soviet Union to build our country."[33] The emulation of Soviet methods, study of Soviet theory, placing Soviet experts in key ministerial, enterprise, military, and scientific and educational advisory posts, dispatching Chinese students and specialists to Russia, and publication of large numbers of translated Soviet texts had been part of the Chinese scene since 1949–50 or earlier, but the arrival of even primitive central planning significantly enhanced the importance of these features. The crucial element, of course, was the Stalinist economic strategy of high rates of reinvestment, emphasis on capital-intensive high-technology projects, agriculture as a major source of funds for industrial growth, and priority investment in heavy indus-try. Although there were continual debates over the details of the plan and allocation of resouces within it, when the first FYP was belatedly formulated in 1955, it closely followed the Soviet model in principle. Also of great impor-tance was Soviet financial and technical aid for the large-scale modern plants that were the core of the plan.

The great weight of the model and the assistance of the Soviet govern-ment, however, did not eliminate independent thinking in China. Some min-istries discussed problems caused by too hastily adopting the Soviet model, and in areas where Chinese officials felt particularly competent they were known to reject Soviet advice. Nevertheless, the trend was the other way among many PRC administrators and specialists dealing with the modern sector. As Mao complained subsequently: "'Dogmatism' took hold in many fields: It didn't matter whether [a Soviet] article was correct or not, the Chi-nese listened all the same and respectfully obeyed."[34] In the 1953–5 period, however, there was little sign of effort from the top to correct this state of affairs.

The Gao Gang affair

Soon after socialist construction and transformation were launched, the CCP suffered its only major leadership purge of the 1949–57 period, The ousting of Gao Gang and Rao Shushi from key Party and state posts in early 1954, followed by their formal expulsion from the CCP a year later, marked not only the most serious high-level conflict of the period but one different in character

---

33 "Closing speech of the fourth session of the [C]PPCC" (7 February 1953), in K. Fan, ed., *Mao Tse-tung and Lin Piao: Post-revolutionary writings*, 102.
34 "Talks at the Chengtu conference" (March 1958), in Schram, ed., *Mao unrehearsed*, 98.

from other instances of elite friction. The principals were among the most powerful in the regime: Gao was a Politburo member, head of the State Planning Commission, and the top Party, government, and military official of the Northeast region; Rao was director of the Central Committee's organization department, which controlled high-level appointments, a Planning Commission member, and the leading Party and government figure in East China. Seven lesser officials from the Northeast and East China were denounced with them, and Cultural Revolution sources linked about a dozen high-ranking central and local leaders to the affair with varying degrees of credibility.

The Gao–Rao affair has long been one of the most obscure chapters in CCP history. Contemporary sources were relatively limited in number and content, and the case received only minor attention during the Cultural Revolution. In the absence of extensive information, various analysts have advanced speculative interpretations emphasizing such factors as possible policy differences, regionalism, Gao's alleged ties to the Soviet Union, and Mao's health.[35] Although all these explanations have some relevance, none is adequate. Fortunately, new data have become available in the post-Mao period that allow a more detailed and accurate understanding of the political maneuvering that briefly threatened the Party's hardwon unity.[36]

The essence of the Gao–Rao affair was their attempt to oust Liu Shaoqi and Zhou Enlai from the number two and number three positions in the CCP. The primary target was Liu, who as the generally acknowledged successor to Mao, was the main obstacle to Gao's ambitions. Although there were maneuvers at formal Party meetings, Gao and Rao basically operated outside established bodies and conducted private negotiations with some of the regime's highest figures. As the 1955 official verdict on the case declared, their activities could fairly be described as "conspiratorial" and as an "unprincipled" effort to grasp enhanced personal power.

The immediate context for these activities, which were primarily carried out from June to December 1953, included both the process of centralization

---

35 The most comprehensive account of the Gao–Rao case is Frederick C. Teiwes, *Politics and purges in China: Rectification and the decline of Party norms 1950–1965*, ch. 5, which emphasizes Mao's deteriorating health as the key circumstantial factor influencing Gao Gang. Other interpretations include: Franz Schurmann, *Ideology and organization in communist China*, ch. 4 (on policy differences); John W. Lewis, *Chinese Communist Party leadership and the succession to Mao Tse-tung: An appraisal of tensions* (on regionalism); and Mineo Nakajima, "The Kao Kang affair and Sino-Soviet relations," *Review*, March 1977 (on the Soviet connection).

36 The major post-Mao sources relied on in the following interpretation are: Chen Shihui, "Guanyu fandui Gao Gang, Rao Shushi fandang yinmo huodong de wenti" (Questions concerning opposition to the anti-Party conspiratorial activities of Gao Gang and Rao Shushi); Zhengzhi xueyuan Zhonggong dangshi jiaoyanshi (Political academy CCP history teaching and research office), *Zhongguo gongchandang liushinian dashi jianjie* (Brief introduction to major events in the CCP's sixty years), 297–400, 405–9; *Deng Xiaoping wenxuan* (Selected works of Deng Xiaoping), 257–58; Liao Kai-lung, "Historical experiences," *Issues & Studies*, October 1981, 79; and discussions with Chinese officials and scholars.

and regularization then underway and the debates surrounding the implementation of the new general line. The former consideration involved changes of institutional structure, and thus of personnel to staff new structures, to meet the needs of planned economic construction. In addition to a new state structure, consideration was being given to holding an Eighth Party Congress, which would require electing a new Party leadership. The possibilities for reallocation of power inherent in this situation were intensified by the end of the year when Mao, who wished to lighten his responsibilities, raised the question of dividing the leadership into two fronts, with others taking over some of his duties. The second matter, debates relating to the general line, meant that policy discussions were taking place in a potentially divisive political climate. Although the policy issues were in fact comparatively narrow, the opportunity was there for ambitious politicians to attempt to enlarge differences into questions of line.

If these circumstances opened up the possibility of conflict, the key factor in Gao Gang's bid for power was his assessment of Mao's attitude. Although Gao was reportedly reluctant to leave his regional power base,[37] when he arrived in Beijing in late 1952 he both assumed impressive new powers as head of the Planning Commission and resumed his close personal relationship with Mao. Gao had been on friendly terms with the Chairman in Yan'an. Mao respected Gao as a founder of the Northwest revolutionary base area and felt he was a local cadre with a good grasp of grass-roots reality. The two also hit it off personally. After 1949, Mao was further impressed by Gao's achievements in the Northeast and considered him a capable leader who could strengthen the work of the CC. This favorable disposition toward Gao coincided with a certain dissatisfaction toward the work of Liu and Zhou – especially their advocacy of greater caution in both economic construction and the development of agricultural cooperatives than Mao desired. Mao expressed this dissatisfaction in several private talks with Gao in the first part of 1953. Whatever the Chairman's intentions, Gao took this as a sign of trust and an opportunity to move against Liu and Zhou.

Another factor apparently feeding Gao's ambitions was the initial outcome of the post-Stalin succession in the Soviet Union, where the relatively youthful Malenkov assumed the reins of leadership despite the claims of the more

---

37 The monopoly of regional power is the key to the official charge that Gao had set up an "independent kingdom" in the Northeast. Gao reportedly sought to place all power in the region in the hands of his close personal followers and deny real authority to other officials such as the second-ranking Party secretary, Lin Feng. This did not mean that the Northeast took an independent policy line from the center; in fact, the Northeast vigorously implemented central directives and was in turn repeatedly praised for its trailblazing efforts in carrying out new policies. The prompt implementation of central policy notwithstanding, Mao later cited Gao's exploitation of shortcomings in regional administration as one reason for subsequently abolishing the regions. Mao, *SW*, 5. 293–4. See Teiwes, *Politics and purges*, 184–91, for further analysis of the regionalism issue.

senior Molotov and Kaganovich. By analogy, Gao seemingly reasoned, he could supersede Liu and Zhou, who represented a slightly older generation of CCP leaders. By this point Gao had already gained the support of Rao Shushi, who became persuaded that Gao's rising status was a prelude to his supplanting Liu as successor. Rao did not want to back the wrong horse, despite his own historical links to Liu. In fact, historical connections enhanced Rao's receptiveness to Gao's blandishments, since Rao's deputy in the Central Committee organization department, An Ziwen, had much closer ties to Liu than he had. Rao apparently felt he was not in full control of his new post, and this facilitated his willingness to make common cause with Gao Gang against Liu Shaoqi.

Although the official verdict in both 1955 and the post-Mao period claimed that the Gao–Rao conspiracy lacked any policy content, this was not strictly the case. Gao and Rao did not present any comprehensive policy program of their own, but they did use the debates surrounding the new general line to attack the policies of others. The key instance was the attack on Bo Yibo's tax policies at the June–August 1953 finance and economic conference. Gao Gang initiated the attack by likening Bo's policies to Bukharin's peaceful transformation. Mao seemingly was impressed with Gao's theoretical sophistication and joined the criticism. The Chairman, however, was unwilling to press the case to the extremes implied by Gao and by the end of the conference concluded that there was no mistake in line and that it was imperative to safeguard Party unity. It is unclear, however, whether Mao at this stage realized the full implications of Gao's activities. By attacking Bo, much as was the case when Rao attacked An Ziwen at the subsequent September–October organization work conference, Gao was actually aiming at his patron, Liu Shaoqi. In any case, Mao seems to have contented himself with the appeal to unity and did not directly criticize Gao Gang.

Gao Gang also sought to bolster his position by cultivating good relations with the Soviet Union. As Party leader in the Northeast Gao naturally had close working relations with Soviet personnel, but these extended into gray areas. He apparently developed particularly close ties with Soviet consular personnel in the Northeast and with Kosygin, who was dispatched on business from Moscow. In discussions with these people, Gao pictured Liu and Zhou as anti-Soviet in contrast to himself, Subsequently, once he had already been defeated politically, revelations of these links were used to build opinion against Gao. But although his relations were regarded as abnormal, they were not seen as equivalent to working for the Soviet Union. Contrary to some Western interpretations, which saw Gao as Stalin's agent in the Northeast, Gao apparently was attempting to bank on Soviet support in any fluid situation that might arise during his bid for enhanced power. Given the economic, political, and ideological ties with the Soviet Union in this period, a favorable attitude on Moscow's part could be a political plus. But it was a dubious game given the strong commitment to national independence among CCP leaders – a commitment none felt stronger than Mao. In the event, Gao's cultivation of the Soviets did not play a minor part in his conspiratorial activities or his fall, but it was nevertheless part of the overall design.

More important than criticism of the performance of Liu, Zhou, and their allies or the pursuit of Soviet support was Gao's effort to win backing for his cause by promising posts in a new Gao regime to high-level leaders, and by fanning resentment on the part of leaders whose revolutionary careers had centered in the Red Army or rural base areas against specialists in white area work behind enemy lines, such as Liu and Zhou. The latter consideration seemingly had considerable force in the context of the forthcoming realloca-tion of posts. The opportunity was presented to Gao by a draft list for the new Politburo prepared by An Ziwen, supposedly without the knowledge of Liu Shaoqi, which shortchanged military leaders and gave disproportionate prominence to white area figures. The key distortion, from the point of view of military cadres, was that An's list included his white area colleague Bo Yibo's but not the great military leader Lin Biao. Although such cadres could accept Liu Shaoqi's position as number two, given his many contributions to the revolutionary cause, they were disgruntled at the prominence given to Peng Zhen and Bo at the expense of leading PLA figures.

Armed with this issue, Gao Gang headed south on summer holidays to recruit additional adherents to his cause. Already having secured East China through Rao Shushi, as well as his own Northeast, he calculated he could win over all of the six large administrative regions except North China, where Peng Zhen and Bo Yibo ruled. In his approaches Gao apparently claimed that he had Mao's blessing and this – together with the resentment generated by An's list paid dividends. Both Lin Biao of the Central-South and Peng Dehuai of the Northwest expressed agreement with Gao's views on reorganizing the Party and state and reallocating leading positions, although this apparently was the extent of their involvement. Gao was less successful in his dealings with two other key leaders, Deng Xiaoping and Chen Yun. Although Deng, the key figure in the Southwest, apparently found Gao's entreaties compelling enough to enter "formal negotiations" (*zhengshi tanpan*), he ultimately rejected them on the basis that Liu's role in the Party "was the outcome of historical development,"[38] Chen Yun, the center's economic overlord who was offered a Party vice chairmanship upon Gao's return to Beijing seemingly was even less receptive than Deng.

38 *Deng Xiaoping wenxuan*, 257.

The turning point came when Chen and Deng, apparently operating independently, brought Gao's actions to Mao's attention. Whatever the Chairman's intentions had been in his personal conversations with Gao at the start of the year, he now expressed anger at Gao's "underground activities." The culmination of the affair came at a December Politburo meeting when Mao proposed that he go on holiday and that, in accord with existing practice, Liu would take charge in his absence. Mao had been planning a holiday before Gao's maneuvers had been revealed to him for several reasons – poor health, a desire to reflect on the new state constitution, and depression over the death of one of his sons in Korea. But at the Politburo meeting he drew out Gao, who now proposed leadership by rotation rather than entrusting power to Liu and indicated his own desire to be Party vice chairman, general secretary, or premier. Mao then did what he had failed to do at the finance and economic conference – he criticized Gao sharply. This, together with carrying out his holiday plans and entrusting Liu with the organization of the February 1954 plenum, which would emphasize the theme of Party unity, effectively squashed the plans of Gao Gang and Rao Shushi.

Unity was indeed emphasized in the winding up of the affair. Mao apparently hoped Gao could be saved for important future duties, but Gao attempted suicide during the February plenum and eventually succeeded in August 1954. Lin Biao and Peng Dehuai were not punished for their complicity; instead, their assertions that they had been deceived by Gao into believing he had Mao's support was deemed sufficient explanation.[39] Moreover, the need to repair the damage to unity which had been created by An Ziwen's list was recognized and Lin Biao, along with Deng Xiaoping, was raised to Politburo status in 1955.

Several lessons can be drawn from the Gao–Rao affair that at once indicate the importance and the fragility of Party unity. In political terms, Gao Gang could not expect to match the enormous strength of Liu and Zhou. These leaders could not be easily categorized as white area figures; their careers intertwined with crucial experiences throughout the entire history of the CCP, including armed struggle in base areas. Indeed, Liu and particularly Zhou had substantially broader contacts among PLA leaders than Gao Gang, who had played no role in the pre-1935 southern phase of the revolution. Yet this inherent weakness notwithstanding, Gao managed to win the support of four of China's six large administrative areas. Party unity started to fray at the possibility of the military being shortchanged in the new leadership structure. The commitment to Party unity on the part of Chen Yun and Deng Xiaoping,

---

39 Tensions continued to linger under the surface, however. A major reason for Liu Shaoqi's strong support of Mao against Peng Dehuai at Lushan in 1959 was Liu's bitterness over Peng's role in the Gao–Rao affair.

on the other hand, played a crucial role in derailing Gao's plans. These men valued the Party rules, which rejected secret factional activities of the type engaged in by Gao and Rao, and they feared the damage to the Party if those activities succeeded.

But undoubtedly the greatest lesson of the affair was the crucial role of Mao. The Chairman's private statements to Gao, whatever their intent, fueled Gao's ambitions and launched his activities. The claim that Mao supported his initiatives was enough to give pause to or gain support from those approached by Gao Gang. Finally, when Mao confronted Gao, the conspiracy collapsed with virtually no resistance. Mao emerged from the Gao Gang–Rao Shushi case as the crucial support of leadership stability. But the overall course of the affair also indicated his potential to threaten Party unity.

The constitutional and institutional pattern

In September 1954 the PRC replaced the temporary arrangements made in 1949 by adopting a state constitution. Strictly speaking, this was not a permanent constitution; it was designed to meet the needs of the period of transition to socialism. But given the long-term nature of that period, it was expected to last many years. Continuity with the past was explicitly asserted: "This constitution is based on the Common Program of the CPPCC of 1949, and this is an advance upon it."[40] In addition to the united front stance of the Common Program, there were some basic structural similarities with the institutional arrangements laid down in 1949 by the Organic law of the Central People's Government. Those arrangements, however, had been comparatively skimpy, and the constitution laid out a much more articulated state structure. The major changes reflected the difference between the unsettled conditions of 1949 and the new period of planned development. The system of people's congresses promised in 1949, theoretically the highest organs of state power, was now formally established.

Of greater political significance, the shift from military to civilian rule that had taken place in the first few years was also formalized. Thus under the Organic Law, the military, in the form of the People's Revolutionary Military Council, had stood equal to the cabinet and directly under the Central People's Government Council, Now, however, a Ministry of Defense was established and placed under the new cabinet, the State Council, on a par with thirty-four other ministries and commissions.

Although Mao claimed in mid-1954 that the constitution was "based mainly on our own experience but has drawn upon what is good in the

40 "Constitution of the People's Republic of China" (20 September 1954), in Harold C. Hinton, ed., *The People's Republic of China, 1949–1979: A documentary survey*, 1.99.

constitutions of the Soviet Union and the [East European] People's
Democracies,"[41] in fact the document basically followed the pattern of the
Stalin constitution of 1936. The basic structure consisted of "elected" congresses from the local to national levels, which theoretically appointed government administrative bodies at each level. These administrative organs were
legally responsible to the congresses that appointed them and to higher-level
administrative organs. In addition, an ostensibly independent judicial system
of courts and people's procurators was set up.

All of this, as well as a similar list of citizens' rights and duties, was found in
the 1936 Soviet document. Of the differences that did exist, some – such as the
Chinese failure to guarantee the universal, equal, and direct suffrage by secret
ballot of the Soviet electoral system – were attributed to the fact that conditions lagged behind those in Russia and, indeed, often reflected provisions of
the earlier 1924 Soviet constitution. In a few major instances, however, Chinese leaders clearly rejected Soviet practice as unsuitable. For example, a few
state bodies and offices had no Soviet counterpart. The most significant was
the creation of a clearly separate and highly visible state chairman – in the
event, Mao – rather than simply relying on top officials of the congress system
(the Supreme Soviet in the USSR) to perform the functions of a head of state.
In this CCP leaders were adopting imperial practice and, like the KMT before
them, clearly felt that Chinese tradition required such an office.

Another area where the new constitution deliberately parted from Soviet
precedent was in discarding the fiction that ethnic minority areas could secede.
The PRC was declared a "unified multinational state" where "autonomous"
minority regions were inalienable parts of the national territory. In the Soviet
Union, the "right" to secede went back to the postrevolutionary civil war,
when it was a useful weapon against White and foreign forces who temporarily held most minority areas. In addition, the fact that over the following
decades minorities grew to half of the Soviet population undoubtedly made
any withdrawal of the right unseemly as well as unnecessary. In China, the
problem is intrinsically less threatening, since minorities make up only 6
percent of the population. But it is a key issue, nevertheless, since minority
areas occupy 60 percent of national territory, including most strategic border-
lands, contain extensive mineral and pastoral resources, and had been a major
preoccupation of successive pre-Communist regimes.

Historically, the Han (ethnic Chinese) had explained their sphere of control outward from the North China plain by absorbing or pushing back the
minority "barbarian" peoples that stood in their path. How to deal with these
barbarians thus became an important question of imperial policy. The thrust

41 Mao, SW, 5.143.

of this policy was minimal control; it aimed at little more than nonaggression and securing a vague commitment of loyalty to the imperial court while interfering as little as possible in local ways of life. In contrast, the KMT regime, influenced by Western concepts of nationalism, followed a much more assimilationist approach denying minority autonomy, but the inherent weakness of that regime forced it to compromise or resulted in policies that alienated minorities without being able to impose domination.

When the CCP came to power, it had an incentive to avoid the counterproductive practices of the KMT, but its long-term goals required more than the minimal imperial policies. As in other matters, CCP leaders saw Soviet practice as the appropriate model. Although the right to secede was not taken over (indeed, it had been discarded as early as 1938, probably in response to the minority hostility that the Communists encountered on the Long March and the encouragement of independence movements by foreign powers), the basic Soviet institutional device of autonomous areas became the basis of Chinese policy. Administrative subdivisions from the provincial to autonomous village (*xiang*) level were given autonomous status, often using traditional minority nomenclature; native languages and cultures were developed in these autonomous areas; and minority figures were placed in official positions, although ultimate power remained with the normally Han Party leaders.

Although the autonomy principle has been a constant of the Soviet model, the content given it by the CCP reflected more the benign Soviet approach of the 1920s than the assimilationist approach of the Stalinist period after 1929. Thus the emphasis was on "nationalization" – a process that involved not only the adoption of national minority forms but also the recruitment of minority cadres, efforts to train Han cadres in local ways, and genuine cooperation with the "patriotic upper strata" – traditional leaders who had both local prestige and expertise and thus could guarantee smooth relations with the populace.

These policies were linked to others that sought gradually to deepen CCP control – the development of transport and communications links with Han areas, Han emigration to some but not all minority areas, modest efforts to improve economic conditions without disrupting local customs, the development of new administrative organs to replace traditional structures, political education emphasizing that minorities were part of the larger Chinese motherland, and social reforms in most nationality regions patterned on developments in Han areas but implemented more slowly in light of local conditions. Overall, CCP policies sought to draw the minorities gradually into the Chinese mainstream; they aimed at fundamental transformation but at a pace and in a manner sensitive to local customs and avoiding unnecessary disruption.

The CCP, using these policies, had considerable success in bringing the far-flung minority areas under central control and beginning the process of social transformation, but such efforts in areas traditionally hostile to the Han and possessing "backward" social structures inevitably produced tensions. Despite the relatively moderate approach, throughout the early 1950s reports surfaced of "Han chauvinism" as Han cadres alienated local populations by applying Chinese practices mechanically. During the relaxation begun in 1956 and extended during the Hundred Flowers movement in 1957 (see Chapter 5), official efforts to promote criticism of Party shortcomings led to a flood of attacks on Han cadre misbehavior and more fundamentally on the limitations of autonomy, and even resulted in separatist demands. The most extreme manifestation of minority alienation was a 1956 revolt in the Tibetan areas of Sichuan against the introduction of reforms. One consequence was the emigration to Tibet proper of a significant number of refugees who later became an important factor in the major 1959 Tibetan rebellion (see Chapter 2). Clearly, even the skillfully modulated policies of 1949–57 had not eliminated resistance to Chinese control; but on balance, the PRC had gained a much firmer foothold in minority areas than any previous regime.

As suggested by the minorities question, the actual institutional pattern in operation was more significant than the constitutional prescription, and here too there were similarities to but also major differences from Soviet practice. Basically, this was a system of parallel Party and state hierarchies, with the Party, unmentioned in the constitution, the ultimate locus of authority. In this the Chinese system was patterned more on the formal relationships in the Soviet Union than on actual Stalinist practice. For Stalin the Party, although theoretically supreme, was merely one of several hierarchies, including the virtually independent secret police, which he could personally manipulate to guarantee his dominance. In China, true to Leninist principles, Party leadership had a more concrete reality. Ultimate policymaking power rested with central Party bodies, especially the Politburo and Secretariat, and at local levels Party committees were more powerful than people's governments. Party control was also ensured by the wearing of dual hats: Leading Party secretaries also held key administrative posts, a practice at variance with the more distinct Soviet hierarchies even after Stalin. Indeed, as the institutional pattern for planned construction was taking hold in China, the Soviet Party was only gradually reasserting its dominance in post-Stalin Russia.

In another regard, however, institutional relationships were fundamentally influenced by the Soviet pattern. The Soviet-style command economy required a set of centralized administrative practices that enhanced the relative position of the state structure. Although there was no question of ultimate Party authority over policy, a vast number of administrative decisions related to economic management fell to the State Council and its subordinate bodies. The dominant administrative pattern was that of vertical rule – units in the modern sector were placed directly under central ministries, thus bypassing local Party committees. Mao accurately captured the situation when he declared, "The major powers grasped by the Central Committee consist only of revolution and agriculture. The rest are in the hands of the State Council."[42] At the central level, operational decisions increasingly flowed to the specialists required by the capital- and technology-intensive Soviet model, and these administrators exercised direct control over skilled personnel at each subordinate level. This bolstered not only the position of Premier Zhou Enlai but also those of such key economic officials as Chen Yun, Li Fuchun, Li Xiannian and Bo Yibo.

At the basic level in the modern sector, the industrial enterprise, this often left the Party organization in a fairly peripheral role. After an initial period of considerable confusion and variation in the roles of factory Party committees, by 1953 the trend was toward restricting their functions to education and propaganda, and the factory manager assumed control of overall operations. This situation, as we shall see, was changed by 1956, but in the early days of the first FYP, factory Party committees were often simply another functional organization within the enterprise. Overall the Party remained supreme, but throughout the 1953–7 period the state's powers frequently eclipsed those of specific Party organizations.

Another key part of the state apparatus, the "political and legal work system" of courts, procurators (public prosecutors), and police, was deeply influenced by the Soviet model, although it departed from Stalinist practice in crucial respects. As in the Soviet Union, not only were courts and procurators declared constitutionally independent, but by 1954 they had adopted Soviet-style administrative practices that granted a substantial degree of functional autonomy. As part of the overall emphasis on regularization and professional-ization in the mid-1950s, these bodies, as well as the police who theoretically were an integral part of the government under the Ministry of Public Security, increasingly handled individual cases without interference from local Party committees or government councils. Ultimately, of course, political and legal departments were subject to CCP authority in the basic policies were laid down by central Party bodies and closely coordinated with the overall goals of the official line. Moreover, local Party committees maintained general oversight over this sensitive area, which sometimes led to friction with the departments as they attempted to assert the autonomy sanctioned by state policy.

The police were clearly the most important of the political and legal depart-ments. Although there are huge gaps in hard information about the public security apparatus, it obviously played a crucial role from the founding of the PRC as an instrument of public order and control. In addition to ordinary police functions and its obscure role as a political police, the public security force administers a large penal system, including labor camps whose inmates undoubtedly number in the millions and provide significant economic resources for the state.[43] With such resources at its disposal, the police had required firm Party control. As already indicated, Mao, unlike Stalin, moved to ensure that the police did not operate as an independent coercive apparatus capable of destroying the integrity of Party and state organizations. In the 1955 campaign against counterrevolutionaries, as in the earlier 1951–3 effort, strict oversight by Party bodies was again imposed. Day-to-day control over the police was exerted by Minister of Public Security Luo Ruiqing, a Party official of high rank but below Politburo status. Luo reported directly to Mao and also to Peng Zhen, the Politburo member most heavily involved in political and legal work.[44] Although guidance of the public security apparatus undoubtedly provided individual figures with a potentially potent instrument for inner elite conflict, under the conditions of the 1950s it was a resource of strictly limited utility.

Although the Party and state hierarchies were clearly crucial, an important auxiliary role was played by the various mass organizations. These bodies were designed according to Lenin's concept of "transmission belts." Although transmission belts performed the role of representing the views of their members to leading Party authorities, their primary function in both Leninist and Stalinist practice was to act as purveyors of Party policies to the masses they represented. In the initial period after liberation there was a significant debate as to the relative weight of these two roles in the most significant mass organization, the All-China Federation of Trade Unions, but the issue was settled by the end of 1951 in favor of orthodox Soviet practice.

In this debate many in the trade unions, apparently led by Li Lisan, argued that unions had become too subservient to management in both privately owned and state-run enterprises and as a result had alienated the workers. These cadres held that the basic task of the unions was to uphold workers'

---

43 Although remarkably little firm data are available on the PRC's labor reform system, useful descriptions are found in A, Doak Barnett, *Communist China: The early years, 1949–55*, 60–7; and the firsthand account in Bao Ruo-wang (jean Pasqualini) and Rudolph Chelminski, *Prisoner of Mao*. Both sources speculatively estimate a labor camp population in the millions, with Bao and Chelminski (p, 10n) suggesting a likely number well in excess of 10 million.

44 Foreign observers have speculated that Kang Sheng, a Politburo member heavily involved in security work in the 1930s and early 1940s, continued to control the police after 1949, but this was not the case. Kang was relieved of security duties after the Seventh Party Congress in 1945 and subsequently went on sick leave in 1949, allegedly out of pique that Rao Shushi was given the top regional post in East China. Kang reemerged after the Gao–Rao affair but concentrated on theoretical work. It was only in the Cultural Revolution that he again became involved with coercive instruments of rule. See Zhong Kan, *Kang Sheng pingzhuan* (Critical biography of Kang Sheng), 83, 96, 106–12, 114, 191, 284.

interests, and to accomplish this aim some degree of operational autonomy was necessary. At the end of 1951 Party leaders intervened to denounce these views as "economism" and "denying Party leadership of the trade unions," and in a top-level reshuffle of union personnel in 1952, Li Lisan was replaced as trade union chief. Although Li's personal setback was limited – he retained his posts as minister of labor and Central Committee member – and was perhaps related to the fact that he had been one of Mao's main opponents in the early 1930s, the net effect of the affair was firmly to subordinate the union structure to Party leadership. This standard Soviet role also applied to all other mass organizations, and it became even more pronounced in the first FYP period, when virtually all bodies centered their activities on plan fulfillment.

Agricultural cooperativization

The successful completion of agricultural cooperativization by the end of 1956 was one of the most significant developments of the entire first FYP period in a number of senses. First, it was an enormous achievement of social and institutional transformation to bring the great bulk of the Chinese people under socialist forms of organization – a task fundamentally more difficult than the socialization of the modern sector – and one that on this ground alone demands detailed examination. Second, although Soviet collectivization more than twenty years was relevant experience in a number of ways, CCP leaders developed their own approach and methods, which resulted in a far less disruptive process than had occurred in Russia. Moreover, as a policy issue, cooperativization was a hotly debated question within the leadership, although these debates did not fundamentally erode Party unity. Finally, the resolution of this issue came as a result of Mao's personal initiative in calling for a stepped-up pace of building agricultural cooperatives in mid-1955.

As Vice-Premier Chen Yi put it, Mao's intervention "settled the debate of the past three years."[45] Subsequently cooperativization was accomplished far more quickly than had been previously thought possible, although the pace also greatly exceeded Mao's expectations and the methods often violated his guidelines. In any case, the achievement of an almost totally socialized agricultural sector by late 1956 was widely seen as both a great success for the Party and a vindication of Mao personally. (For a more specifically economic analysis of this development, see *CHOC* 14, Chapter 3.)

Moves toward socialized agriculture had begun even before nationwide liberation with the development of mutual aid teams (MATs) – arrangements for pooling peasant labor – in the base areas of North China. Mutual aid was

45 *RMRB*, 13 November 1955.

developed after 1949 in both old and new liberated areas, so that by the end of 1952 about 40 percent of all peasant households were in MATs. Meanwhile, experimental Agricultural Producers' Cooperatives (APCs) were established, but it was only in 1952–3 that they appeared in substantial numbers. From 1952 until Mao's intervention in 1955, the rate of cooperativization intensified and relaxed several times. As Table 1 demonstrates, in the winters of 1952–3 and 1954–5 sharp increases were registered in the number of cooperatives, but in each following spring the rate of growth was reduced and some cooperatives were disbanded. This pattern was clearly linked to the ongoing debate, but it also reflected the problems of disorganization and planning confusion, harsh cadre methods, and the alienation of better-off peasants that resulted from hasty implementation of the program. After Mao's intervention, in contrast, not only did the movement surge forward at a stepped-up tempo, but the following spring of 1956 saw the reorganization of the cooperatives into so-called higher-stage or fully collectivized bodies instead of a new period of consolidation.

Chinese policy contained several major modifications of the Soviet experience. First, cooperativization was designed as a gradual, stage-by-stage process, rather than the sudden and chaotic pattern of the Soviet Union. CCP policy envisioned a three-step process: first MATs, where labor was pooled but ownership rights over land and other productive factors were retained by individual peasants; then the lower stage APC, where productive property was now controlled by the collective but each peasant received a dividend according to his relative contribution of land, tools, and animals; and finally the higher-stage APC (or full collective), where the dividend was abolished and payment was strictly according to labor.

Another important difference was the policy of restricting rather than liquidating rich peasants. In contrast to the forced deportation and killing of Russian *kulaks*, Chinese rich peasants saw their economic position eroded by various means and were used as a target for political mobilization until the latter stages of the movement, when they were allowed into the APCs. Thus although the rich peasants were still objects of class struggle, their comparatively mild treatment limited the disorder and destruction of economic resources that marked the Soviet campaign.

A third feature, which also ameliorated the rural situation, was CCP avoidance of Stalin's single-minded stress on extracting agricultural surplus to support industrialization. China's first FYP also relied heavily on agriculture supporting industry, but CCP leaders realized that China's countryside had far less surplus to extract than Russia's. As a result, throughout the first FYP, official policy aimed at increasing agricultural production so that *both* the industrial development plans of the state would be met and peasant living

TABLE I
Agricultural cooperatives: Development and targets

	Existing APCs	1954–5 target	1956 target	1957–8 target
Fall 1952	3,644ᵃ (0.1 %)ᵇ			
Spring 1953	5,800 reduced to 3,645 in Hebei province			
Mao 11/53	ca. 15,000 (0.2%)			700,000–1 million (ca. 15–22%) "by 1957"
Central Committee 12/53	14,900 (0.2%)	35,800 (ca. 0.5%) fall 1954		800,000 (ca. 18%) "by 1957"
Deng Zihui 7/54 (Head of CCP Rural Work Department)	ca 114,000 (2%)	600,000 (ca. 12–13%) spring 1955	1.5 million (ca. 33%) "by 1956"	3 million (ca. 66%) "by 1957"
Central Committee 10/54	ca. 230,000 (4.7%)	600,000 (ca. 12–13%) spring 1955		
February–March 1955	670,000 reduced to 633,000 (14.2%)			
Central Committee Rural Work Department spring (May?) 1955	ca. 633,000 (14.2%)		1 million (ca. 22%) October	
June 1955	634,000 (14.2%)			
First FYP 7/30/55	650,000 (ca. 14.3%)			33% "by 1957"
Mao 7/31/55	650,000 (ca. 14.3%)		1.3 million (ca. 29%) October	50% spring 1958
Average 17–20 provinces 9/55	?		37.7% spring	60.3% 1957
Central Committee 10/55	1.277 million (32%)			70–80% in advanced areas, spring 1957; 70–80% overall, spring 1958
21 provinces 11/55	1.583 million (41.4%)	70–80% in advanced areas, end 1955	70–80% overall, end 1956	
Mao 12/55	1.905 million (63.3%) (4% hi APCs)ᶜ		70–80% end 1956	
Agricultural draft program 1/56	1.53 million (80.3%) (30.7% hi APCs)		85% "in 1956"	"hi APCs practically complete by 1958"
March 1956	1.088 million (88,9%) (54.9%; hi APCs)			
June 1956	994,000 (91.9%) (63.2% hi APCs)			
December 1956	756,000 (96.3%) (87.8% hi APCs)			

ᵃNumber of APCs; lower-stage APCs until December 1955, thereafter divided into lower-and higher-stage APCs as indicated. Number of APCs declines throughout 1956 owing to larger size of higher APCs.
ᵇ(%) = peasant households in APCs.
ᶜhi = higher stage.
Sources: Shi Jingtang et al., eds., *Zhongguo nongye hezuohua yundong shiliao* (Historical materials on China's agricultural cooperativization movement), 989–91; "Agricultural cooperativization in Communist China," *CB*, 373; Mao, *SW*, 5.139–40; and *Communist China 1955–1959*, 120.

standards would rise. Although it remains uncertain just how consistently this objective was realized, the Party concern for peasants' livelihood served to reduce resistance as well as build support. Finally, a more strictly economic and technical modification was the emergence by mid-1954 of a policy that in view of China's backward industrial base, collectivization should precede the mechanization of agriculture rather than be developed in tandem.

These substantial changes from the Soviet pattern did not mean total rejection of the Soviet experience, however. On the contrary, not only were various Soviet writings studied to bolster the official case for cooperatives, but the developed Soviet collective as laid down in the model *kolkhoz* (collective) rules of 1935 was the concrete form of higher-stage APC that the CCP basically adopted. In terms of process, moreover, the Soviet experience provided lessons and sources of support for all sides of the debate within the CCP. Those who argued against rapid expansion cited Stalin's warning against being "dizzy with success" when excesses threatened the Soviet program. But others, like Mao in July 1955, could argue that the Soviet experience showed it was possible to correct errors quickly and accomplish cooperativization according to a more optimistic schedule.

Some aspects of the crucial stage of the debate during the first seven months of 1955 are clear, including Mao's decisive role and the nature of the arguments, but the precise political contours are less certain.[46] As we have seen, there was undoubted consensus in early 1955 on the desirability of cooperativization for economic as well as social and political goals; promulgation of the first FYP in July reemphasized the importance of building APCs for planned economic growth. There was also the relatively recent agreement on collectivization before mechanization, although differences remained over precisely how far ahead of mechanization the socialization process should develop. Moreover, a shared awareness of the problems facing the CCP existed. Socially and politically, there was broad agreement that the continued existence of small peasant production engendered rural capitalism and thus threatened the consolidation of socialism. Economically, all participants believed that the failure of agricultural growth to keep pace with the planned rate of industrialization threatened

---

46 The following account differs somewhat from interpretations which, drawing on Cultural Revolution sources, emphasize differences between Mao on the one hand and a whole array of central officials on the other. See, for example, Parris H. Chang, *Power and policy in China*, 9–17. "Agricultural cooperativization in communist China," *CB*, 373; Kenneth R. Walker, "Collectivisation in retrospect: The 'socialist high tide' of autumn 1955–spring 1956," *CQ*, 26 (1966); and particularly documents in the post-Mao internal publication, *Dangshi yanjiu*. 2.1 (1981), (Research on Party history), 28 February 1981, namely, Deng Zihui, "Zai quanguo disanci nongcun gongzuo huiyi shang de kaimu ci" (Inaugural speech at the third national rural work conference) (21 April 1955) 1981.1, 2–9; and Qiang Yuangan and Lin Bangguang, "Shilun yi jiu wu wu nian dangnei guanyu nongye hezuohua wenti de zhenglun" (A discussion of the debate within the Party in 1955 concerning the issue of agricultural cooperativization).

the entire first FYP, since agricultural production substantially determined industrial growth rates.

Since there is little indication of any key policy maker advocating a substantial scaling down of industrial targets, how to increase farm production became a key concern. The central issue was the pace of setting up APCs. Throughout these months a cautious approach was advanced primarily by the Central Committee's Rural Work Department and its head, Deng Zihui, in conjunction with the Politburo's leading economic specialist, Chen Yun. This approach was initially endorsed not only by Liu Shaoqi but also by Mao himself. Deng emphasized the overambitious planning, cadre excesses, and disillusionment of the more productive peasants that had accompanied the rapid expansion of APCs in 1954 and early 1955. In this view, a careful consolidation of existing APCs and a modest rate of future growth aiming for a million cooperatives by fall 1956 was called for if peasant hostility was not seriously to damage agricultural production. In pursuing this policy, Deng ordered the dissolution of 20,000 newly established but badly organized APCs. Against this approach were those advocating a more expansionary policy on the grounds that APCs had a demonstrated capacity for increasing production, could more easily obtain the agricultural surplus for the state, and would also check tendencies to rural class polarization that seemed to be growing with agriculture still overwhelmingly private.

As indicated earlier, Mao initially supported Deng's policies. In March the Chairman proposed the slogan "halt, shrink, develop," which reflected the importance of consolidation before new advances. In mid-May, however, Mao shifted his position to one of dissatisfaction with the pace of cooperativization, and a sharp debate with Deng ensued. While Deng upheld the rural work department's target of 1 million APCs by October 1956, Mao warned against a passive approach and argued for a goal of 1.3 million.[47] In retrospect, it appears that Mao's initiative in the latter part of May, and not his 31 July speech on cooperativization normally cited by scholars,[48] was decisive in producing policy change. Not only were the number of APCs again expanding in June and July, but May also saw the decision to launch a new campaign

47 Mao's target was laid down in his 31 July speech on cooperativization but was apparently argued during the May debate with Deng. See Mao, *SW*, 5.187; and Qiang Yuangan and Lin Bangguang, "Shilun dangnei zhenglun," 13.
48 Analysts writing without benefit of post-Mao information on the Chairman's May activities often stressed the suddenness and decisiveness of Mao's July speech because of its apparently more radical targets than those incorporated in the first FYP published the day before Mao spoke. See, for example, Stuart R. Schram, "Introduction: The Cultural Revolution in historical perspective," in Schram, ed., *Authority, participation and cultural change in China*, 39. Such analyses, however, overlook the fact that the first FYP target of one-third of all peasant households in APCs "by 1957" was not necessarily more conservative than Mao's target of 50 percent by *spring 1958*, since the winter season of 1957–8 would surely be a period of significant growth.

against counterrevolutionaries – a major aim of which was to silence opposition to collectivization within society at large. Moreover, owing to conviction, conversion, or calculation, in the days before Mao's speech such leading officials as Minister of Agriculture Liao Luyan and Deng's erstwhile ally Chen Yun spoke out sharply in defense of collectivization.

Mao's intervention starting in May 1955 and culminating in his July speech was less significant as policy innovation than as a decisive political act. In policy terms, although doubling the number of APCs to be established over the next fourteen months was a significant intensification of the campaign, Mao's program was not overly radical. It called for careful preparations for new APCs, allowed peasants to withdraw or even dissolve unsatisfactory cooperatives, and warned against rashness as well as timidity in cooperativization. Moreover, even though Mao's targets substantially raised those earlier decided on by the rural work department, the rate of increase was less than that achieved in the year from early 1954 to early 1955, and the absolute numbers inolved were only slightly larger. Indeed, Mao's targets for 1956–7 were more conservative than the projection made by Deng Zihui in mid-1954.

But if the Chairman's program was not excessively radical, its political impact was. Mao ended the hesitation of the previous months by indicating that expansion was the only ideologically correct course. He began his July speech with a criticism of "some of our comrades [who are] tottering like a woman with bound feet,"[49] and throughout this period he applied the "right deviationist" label to Deng, who continued to express reservations. In the face of Mao's sharpened political definition of the issue, few officials held out; vigorous implementation of cooperativization unfolded.

Mao's success was undoubtedly due in the first instance to his unchallenged role as leader, but several other factors were working in his favor. One was the comparatively moderate nature of his program and the argumentation behind it. Although the political tone of the July speech was ultimately decisive, the marshaling of survey data and careful reasoning carried considerable weight, Also aiding Mao was the fact that his program at least came to grips with the serious problems facing the rural sector, although the more conservative approach held little promise of a breakthrough. Politically, the fact that Mao was not speaking alone but expressing the views of a significant segment of the elite gave his recommendations an important boost, as did the fact that even those opposed to rapid increases shared a belief in the desirability of APC's on both economic and social grounds. Although in later years objections would be voiced to using the "rightist" label against Deng Zihui, at the time the traditional mild approach to inner elite dissent also contributed to closing ranks behind Mao. Deng was required only to make a self-criticism and temporarily suffered a reduction in power, but he never lost his posts. Finally, as the campaign picked up steam, the overfulfillment of the Chaiman's targets seemed to discredit contrary views.

Indeed, the nearly complete establishment of fully collectivized APCs by the end of 1956 was due more to the zealous implementation of the campaign by the Party apparatus than to Mao's program. Cadres throughout rural China, reacting to the pressures created by Mao's speech and the campaign against counterrevolutionaries, concluded that it was "better to err to the left than the right." From the time of the July speech until the end of 1955, China went through a cycle of Mao and the Party center setting goals, the provinces outstripping those goals, the center revising its targets upward, and the provinces once again overfulfilling central targets. Even at the end of the year, Mao estimated it would take another three to four years basically to complete the higher-stage APCs. But in 1956 the localities yet again greatly outstripped his targets. In the process, however, the policy of advancing by stages that the Chairman had carefully advocated in 1955 was discarded. More than a quarter of all peasant families joined APCs without prior organization into MATs, and a widespread tendency to skip the lower-stage APCs altogether appeared. Although Mao continued to warn against leftist excesses in the fall and winter of 1955–6, he was fundamentally elated by the rapid progress. This breakneck speed would cause serious problems of adjustment in 1956–7, but the basic organizational breakthrough had been achieved.

In comparative terms, Chinese cooperativization was accomplished in a considerably smoother manner than its Soviet counterpart, but outright revolts apart, nearly all forms of peasant resistance that had occurred in Russia – withdrawing from cooperatives, reducing levels of productive investment and activity, slaughtering livestock, spreading rumors – appeared in China, albeit to a lesser degree.

Various factors explain the easier passage. The conscious adaptation of Soviet practice in the direction of gradualism and reduced social tensions were, of course, of major significance. Also crucial was the disciplined Party apparatus in the countryside, an organizational force that had been far weaker or even nonexistent in the Soviet case. Strong Party committees at the county level were able to organized large numbers of work teams and guide fundamental change in villages. Particularly important was the CCP's presence in the villages themselves. Seventy percent of all *xiang* had Party branches by the start of 1955, and 90 percent had them by the end of the year.

The basis of this rural elite was the cadres who had emerged during land reform. Added to this base were new recruits drawn from activists during the cooperativization movement itself, a process that intensified and increasingly focused on poorer peasants in 1955, and demobilized soldiers who became available as the PLA stepped up modernization measures in 1954–5. Equally important were repeated training programs and indoctrination of this rural cadre force in socialist principles. Although there were pronounced tendencies for cadres to seek a life of independent farming at the end of land reform, such tendencies were checked by constant reinforcement that sought to relate all official tasks to the concept of socialist transformation. At no time did the rural leadership structure fall completely under the sway of small peasant production, as had happened in the Soviet Union in the 1920s.

Another major reason for the relative success of the Chinese program was the CCP's carefully constructed rural economic policies, which not only provided benefits for a majority of the peasants but also gave the peasantry as a whole little choice but to cooperate. Credit cooperatives, supply and marketing cooperatives, and the planned marketing of grain and other key commodities all increasingly restricted the private economic opportunities of rich peasants and channeled economic resources preferentially to the cooperative sector, thus increasing the attractiveness of joining the APCs.

Policies were explicitly framed with an eye to protecting the interests of the relatively well-off and productive middle peasants who before mid-1955 often had a dominant role in APCs. Beyond this, the basic propaganda appeal emphasizing better living standards and the general ability of official policies to at least avoid a decline in standards despite fair to poor harvest conditions in 1953 and 1954 gave the peasants some reason to expect tangible results from the APCs. When the "high tide" of cooperativization was launched in the context of a bumper harvest in mid-1955, the regime's economic credibility, which had been established during land reform, was still working for it.

The potent combination of administrative pressures, normative appeals, coercion, and tangible results that had achieved remarkable success in land reform and the initial period of cooperativization now came into play during the high tide. The situation differed markedly from the immediately preceding stage in that tangible benefits were now increasingly focused on the poorer peasants, to the detriment of better-off middle peasants. The cancellation of the land dividend in the higher-stage APCs represented a direct transfer of economic resources between the two groups, and given the numerical dominance of the poorer elements – estimated at 60 to 70 percent of the peasantry – a powerful interest group for the change was created. Normative appeals, which continued to be heavily laced with the promise of prosperity, as a result were especially potent for the poor, although even within this group, those who hesitated were with some frequency forcefully herded into APCs. Pressure often bordering on coercion was applied to the better-off middle peasants, and outright coercion in the form of arrests and mass struggle was used against counterrevolutionaries, including some rich peasants.

In all of this, the cadres continued to be a driving force that responded to a similar set of pressures. Increasingly drawn from the poor peasants by the recruiting measures of late 1955, village leaders were at once the prime target of educational efforts, the direct recipients of administrative pressures with coercive overtones, and the main beneficiaries of local transformation. The switch to higher-stage APCs not only benefited cadres as it did less well-off peasants, it also eased their administrative tasks because they no longer had to calculate the divisive land dividend. And it cemented their political dominance by weakening the middle peasants. With this key group highly motivated, the majority of peasants having reason to anticipate material gains, and disadvantaged groups under tight control but not threatened with liquidation, the momentum for rapid collectivization proved irresistible.

Transforming the modern sector and the first leap forward

By fall 1955 the mounting evidence of a breakthrough in cooperativization allowed Mao and his colleagues to turn some of their attention to the transformation of industry and commerce. The Three and Five Antis campaigns had been launched only after the basic success of land reform. Similarly, with the vast, difficult to control countryside now advancing rapidly toward socialism, Party leaders felt the time had come to use their great leverage in the modern sector. Earlier debates on the speed of the socialist transformation of industry and commerce had paralleled those over the rate of building APCs.

Some saw the need for pushing ahead in order to facilitate central planning, whereas others urged caution on the grounds that conditions were not yet ripe and that overly hasty socialization would disrupt production and overwhelm the state's nascent planning capabilities. In the fall of 1955, however, there was general agreement that socialization of the modern sector would have to keep pace with cooperativization. Although socialized industry and commerce were well in advance of cooperativization in mid-1955, first FYP goals were modest in calling for only "the greater part" of privately owned businesses to adopt some form of state capitalism by the end of the Five-Year-Plan period.

From the end of October 1955 to January 1956, however, Mao and other leaders met with prominent capitalists to impress upon them the need for a stepped-up pace of transformation while ostensibly soliciting their views. In these encounters Mao, as he had with agricultural cooperatives, warned against excessive rashness and even declared himself more cautious than Chen Yun, but the invited businessmen did not fail to pick up the essential message and quickly pledged support for an accelerated program. On the basis of these pledges, a new target of completing transformation into joint state-private enterprises by the end of 1957 was laid down.

What followed paralleled the overfulfillment of APC targets but in even more startling form. Chen Yun organized meetings of provincial leaders to press for the new target but was quickly overtaken by the actions of another Politburo member, Beijing mayor Peng Zhen. In December Peng set the end of 1956 as the target date for Beijing, and in January the actual transformation was completed in the first ten days of the month. Other cities did not want to appear laggard, and by the end of January the process had been basically completed in all major urban centers. Obviously such an extremely rapid transformation was superficial. Instead of the prescribed process of careful preparatory work that allowed the state to take operational control, it amounted to a formal declaration of a change in ownership without any change in personnel or internal organization. To avoid disrupting production, the State Council in early February ordered that existing operations be unchanged for six months following transformation. The actual work of taking inventories and economic reorganization was done gradually and was heavily dependent on the private capitalists whose skills were still required in a modern sector where the shortage of cadres remained acute.

Although the extension of rapid socialization from agriculture to industry and commerce was to be expected, a less predictable development occurred as Mao sought a "leap forward" in economic construction. In December Mao attacked "right conservative thinking" in a wide range of work: "The problem today . . . lies in agricultural production; industrial production; . . . handicraft production; the scale and speed of capital construction in industry, communications and transport; the coordination of commerce with other branches of the economy; the coordination of the work in science, culture, education and health. . . . In all these fields there is an underestimation of the situation, a shortcoming which must be criticized and corrected."[50] In late 1955 and early 1956 Mao apparently saw an opportunity to attack China's economic and cultural backwardness in much the same way as he had the socialist transformation. Despite continued warnings against "left adventurism" as well as "right conservatism," Mao's thought underwent a subtle shift in the direction of radicalism in the period between his July speech and the end of 1955.[51] This was particularly apparent in his commentary on a volume dealing with cooperativization, where he claimed that "a raging tidal wave [is] sweeping away all demons and monsters" and if "600 million 'paupers' . . . take

50 Ibid., 5.240.
51 See the 1980 report of Liao, "Historical experiences," November 1981, 88, which traces the origins of Mao's leftist thinking to his late 1955 prefaces to *Socialist upsurge in China's countryside*.

their destiny into their own hands . . . they can overcome any difficulty on earth."[52]

Mao would soon retreat from this highly optimistic view in the face of mounting problems, but at the time there was little to indicate significant opposition within top leadership circles. Whether because of genuine enthusiasm over the advances in socialization or an unwillingness to challenge a determined Chairman, other leaders joined in the effort to push China's first leap forward.

In terms of concrete policies, in November 1955 Mao proposed a number of long-term measures to boost agricultural production that were expanded and approved in January as a twelve-year draft program for agricultural development over the 1956–67 period. This program laid down ambitious goals, including 100 to 140 percent increases in grain yields, something Mao had expressed doubts over as recently as the previous fall. To accomplish this, the mass mobilization of peasant labor and rural financial resources was assigned a central role. But the program also place a heavy emphasis on scientific and technical inputs and material incentives. In implementing the program, the same phenomena occurred as with regard to socialist transformation – lower-level units significantly increased the targets of the draft program and began to implement its measures in a blind, disruptive manner. Similarly, spurred on by Mao's slogan demanding "more, faster, better, and more economical" results, officials at all levels raised short-term targets for both industrial and agricultural production in an effort to reach first FYP goals a year ahead of schedule. Various industrial ministries increased their 1956 targets by 25 percent or more; Zhou Enlai set a 9 percent growth in grain output as a minimum goal for the year; and some *xiang* leaders called for 40 percent increases in grain production. This too led to economic dislocations as the administrative system had again proved itself too responsive to pressures from above. These dislocations and the other problems arising from the high tide and leap forward soon forced their attention on the leadership, and dealing with them became a major feature of the period of adjustment that followed.

ADJUSTING THE NEW SOCIALIST SYSTEM, 1956–7

The new course that emerged in early 1956 was built on a basic reassessment of conditions in China. According to Mao in January, the high tide of socialist transformation had resulted in a "fundamental change in the political situation."[53] This view, which would be modified by the latter part of 1957,

---

52 Mao, *SW*, 5.244, 250.
53 "Speech to Supreme State Conference" (January 1956), in Helene Carrère d'Encausse and Stuart R. Schram, comps., *Marxism and Asia*, 292.

reflected the orthodox Marxist concern with the relations of production – that is, ownership. With the means of production now largely in the hands of the state or collective units, the victory of socialism over capitalism had been basically decided.

A number of related propositions flowed from this analysis. First, although class struggle was by no means eliminated, in the new situation where enemies of socialism no longer had significant economic means at their disposal, class conflict would markedly attenuate so that, as Mao would put it a year later: "The large scale, turbulent class struggles . . . characteristic of . . . revolution have in the main come to an end. . . ."[54] Second, this situation called for a fundamental shift in Party priorities to economic development. Mao outlined this new direction while promoting the leap forward in January: "The object of the socialist revolution [is] to set free the productive forces [and] wipe out China's economic, scientific and cultural backwardness within a few decades."[55] But the new priority was not simply a product of the economic push; later in the year, after the leap forward was discarded, the Eighth Party Congress identified economic backwardness as the heart of the "main contradiction."

A third proposition was that the broadest range of social forces could now be rallied behind the developmental effort in a new adaptation of the united front. Under the slogan of "mobilize all positive factors," the leadership sought not simply to win the backing of dubious sections of society but to encourage creative inputs by all groups, especially China's intellectuals, who had skills urgently required for modernization. Finally, the victory of socialism meant the establishment of a new system that inevitably had its shortcomings and conflicts – what Mao termed "contradictions among the people." In this view, tensions in society were predominantly manifestations of legitimate divergences of interest, and the task of the Party became one of mediating the claims of different economic sectors and social groups while performing the new institutions of socialism.

A key innovation in these circumstances was a new policy toward intellectuals. In 1955, steps were taken to win intellectual support through forums addressing their problems and awards for top scientists, but these measures were compromised by attacks on such figures as the literary theorist Hu Feng in the context of the campaign against counterrevolutionaries. In 1956, however, the approach to the intellectuals was pursued in a more relaxed political atmosphere influenced in part by the thaw in Soviet treatment of its intelligentsia begun in late 1955, but more fundamentally by the assumption of the weakening of class struggle after socialist transformation.

54 Mao, *SW*, 5.395.   55 "Speech to Supreme State Conference" (January 1956), 292–3.

A major statement of the new policy was made by Zhou Enlai in January 1956 in the context of promoting the leap forward in the economy, and a further step came in a May speech by the head of the Central Committee's propaganda department, Lu Dingyi. Zhou advocated improved salaries and living conditions, the provision of better working conditions and resources, and more rapid promotions and easier admission into the CCP, and Lu explained Mao's new slogan "Let a hundred flowers bloom, let a hundred schools contend." According to Lu, free discussion and independent thinking were necessary to avoid academic stagnation, and the imposition of dogmatic restrictions on intellectual life was hostile to true Marxism-Leninism.

A further measure was an effort to bolster the status of the small democratic parties that had been drawn into the united front in 1949. Under the slogan of "long-term coexistence and mutual supervision," these parties of intellectuals, one-time KMT officials, and businessmen were urged to criticize the performance of the government and build up their own memberships and organizations. Despite the more relaxed atmosphere, all these measures were circumscribed by reassertions of the principle of Party leadership, calls for the continuing ideological remolding of intellectuals, and assertions that the handling of such dissidents as Hu Feng had been entirely correct. As a result, throughout 1956 most Intellectuals responded cautiously, although there were enough sharp criticisms to cause a substantial number of cadres to adopt an obstructionist attitude despite efforts by the top leadership to push the new program.

Although the new policies toward intellectuals continued to mid-1957, the economic leap forward, together with the rapid pace of socialist transformation, created a set of problems necessitating institutional adjustments and policy reversals by late spring 1956. By this time central officials were becoming aware of the imbalances and planning chaos in the overall economy, plus peasant disillusion with both wasteful efforts to realize the draft agricultural program and the rigidities of the new APCs. Starting in April 1956 and continuing into the summer of 1957, measures to deal with these problems were undertaken under a program that became known as "opposing rash advance" – measures including insistence on realistic targets, emphasis on coordination in planning and quality in output, increasing the scope of peasants' private production within the APC framework, reestablishing a limited rural free market, reducing the size of APCs, and heavy criticism of coercive leadership methods by APC cadres. The major architects of this program were Zhou Enlai and Chen Yun, and broad support by the Party's leading economic officials quickly formed.

Mao was far from enthusiastic. Although he surely agreed with some aspects of the program, particularly those increasing material incentives for the peasants, and initially accepted the need to curb excesses, by mid-1956 he was clearly distressed by retrenchment measures that had ended the leap forward in production. Nevertheless, Mao did not attempt to challenge the new program but, instead, accepted the views of his colleagues in an area where, by his own admission, he lacked competence. In so doing the Chairman adhered to the consensual style he normally followed in the 1949–57 period, but he also harbored doubts and regrets that would play a key role in the launching of the GLF.

Adapting the Soviet model

As CCP leaders developed policies for the new situation, they began to examine the Soviet model in a more self-consciously critical manner. Previously Mao and his associates had made significant alterations in the Soviet pattern and called in a general way for adapting Soviet experiences to Chinese conditions, but they had not dwelled on Russian shortcomings or CCP innovations in public or internal statements. Indeed, as late as January 1956 Mao could still profess to believe that the CCP had merely elaborated on Soviet achievements and "since the October Revolution there have been no new things of note."[56] By this time, however, a systematic review of the Soviet model was already underway that would soon lead to explicit and sharp criticisms of defects in the Russian system.

All this would develop within the context of strains in Sino-Soviet relations following the Twentieth Soviet Party Congress in February 1956, but such strains were not a fundamental cause of the reexamination of the model. In any case, throughout 1956 and most of 1957, the emphasis was still on learning from the Soviet Union, but in a highly selective fashion that rejected backward aspects of Soviet practice.

A growing realization that the Soviet Union had begun from a much higher industrial base than the PRC, yet had only achieved a pace of growth that seemed somewhat slow, apparently set the stage for the reevaluation of the model. This involved Politburo discussions with leading personnel from thirty-four central economic departments and led to one of Mao's most significant speeches, the April 1956 "Ten great relationships." As Mao later observed, this talk, which drew general conclusions based upon the previous months' discussions and thus represented more than Mao's personal view, "made a start in proposing our own line for construction [that] was similar to

---

56 "Zai Zhonggong zhongyang zhaokai de guanyu zhishi fenzi wenti huiyi shang de jianghua" (Speech at the conference on the question of intellectuals convened by the CCP Central Committee) (20 January 1956), in *Wansui* (1969), 33.

that of the Soviet Union in principle, but had our own content,"[57] Although references to Soviet shortcomings covered a wide scope, in many areas such as agriculture Chinese practice had long been distinctive. Where Mao called for adjustments in existing practices, the changes suggested were modest and left the basic Soviet-style institutional structure and economic strategy in place.

A central question was the ratio of investment between heavy industry on the one had and light industry and agriculture on the other. Mao attacked Soviet overemphasis on heavy industry but reaffirmed its primary claim for investment funds, asking only that "the proportion for agriculture and light industry must be somewhat increased."[58] This was indeed done in June 1956, when the ration of heavy industry to light industry investment was marginally reduced from 8:1 to 7:1; and in September proposals for the second FYP slightly increased agricultural investment from 7 to 10 percent in comparison to the first FYP.

Another key concern of the "Ten great relationships" was economic administration: "We must not follow the example of the Soviet Union in concentrating everything in the hands of the central authorities, shackling the local authorities and denying them the right to independent action."[59] Here too Mao was cautious, calling for greater consultation with the localities, the enlargement of their powers "to some extent" within the framework of unified central leadership, and further investigation of the problem. What was envisioned here was a move away from vertical ministerial control to a form of "dual rule" where powers were shared between the ministries and regional authorities, but there was no clarity as to method.

The State Council subsequently held a series of meetings on how to curb excessive centralization, and the proposals for the second FYP assigned more construction projects to local authorities. Moreover, other approaches to combating overcentralization were advocated that emphasized indirect planning (norms for reference only) and the use of market mechanisms. Proposals in this regard were made by Chen Yun in September 1956 at the Eighth Party Congress, and in the following months experiments with methods of enhancing enterprise autonomy and selective purchasing on the market were carried out. In January 1957, however, the State Council decided that the basic pattern of planned allocation would continue for the year because of the complex administrative problems any change would require, and undoubtedly also because of the opposition of many economic planners. Similarly, despite intense debate in economic journals over methods of decentralization throughout 1957, until the fall of the year no major decision had been taken.

57 "Talks at the Chengtu conference" (March 1958), in Schram, ed., *Mao unrehearsed*, 101.
58 Mao, *SW*, 5.286.   59 Ibid., 292.

Throughout this debate on how to modify Soviet-style administration, it is important to note, contemporary Soviet developments were a contributing factor. The Soviet Union had undertaken decentralization measures of its own in mid-1955, and views of Soviet economists on the need to overcome the rigidities of central planning had made a significant impact on leading participants in the Chinese debates. Indeed, even in areas where the CCP was far less beholden to the Soviet model than in economic planning, Soviet reforms played an influential role. Thus Party leaders had initially adopted the Soviet machine tractor station as the method for spreading the mechanization of agriculture. These stations, which were separate entities contracting their services to APCs, had many inefficiencies and often worked at cross-purposes with the cooperatives. Criticism of their faults in the Soviet Union and Eastern Europe and Soviet experiments with placing tractors under the direct control of collectives were already underway in spring 1956 when Politburo member Kang Sheng represented the CCP at the East German Party Congress. The problem was discussed extensively at this Congress, and upon his return Kang conducted an investigation in China. This resulted in a critical report in November, experiments with alternatives in 1957, and finally the decision to place agricultural machinery directly in the hands of the APCs in 1958, the same year the machine tractor station was abolished in the Soviet Union.

Additional aspects of modifying the Soviet model are illustrated by another issue raised in the spring 1956 Politburo discussions – the system of factory management. In the early 1950s the Soviet system of "one-man management," which placed ultimate authority in the hands of the factory manager, had been widely introduced in the Northeast. This system had been recommended, but not ordered, for the entire country in early 1953. Beginning in 1954, criticisms of the system were increasingly aired but defenses were also published, and during 1954 – 6 it continued to be allowed as one variant of enterprise management pending a Politburo decision. One of the factors at work in this case was that the PRC simply lacked sufficient numbers of competent personnel to make one-man management work. The system not only never predominated in China as a whole but was only partially implemented even in the Northeast. In addition, there was significant resistance from Party cadres who objected to restrictions on their powers and resented the authority the system vested in managers from suspect class backgrounds.

Moreover, these cadres raised the potent charge that the system violated CCP traditions of Party control and collective decision making, that it was "only centralism and no democracy." Such arguments, in conjunction with the inadequate resources for one-man management and the increasing number of Party cadres who had been recruited and trained in industry in the preceding years, were crucial when the leadership decided on a new system upgrading the powers of the factory Party committee above those of the factory manager. In announcing this decision to the Eighth Party Congress, the Party official responsible for industry, Li Xuefeng, emphasized the importance of Party traditions. This change, however, was far from a rejection of Soviet industrial methods. Indeed, in the same period Soviet-style piecework wage systems were being extended throughout most of China.

Another area where CCP traditions became a central issue in adapting the Soviet model was modernizing the PLA. By 1956, Party leaders clearly felt that political traditions were being eroded by the Soviet-aided modernization effort and began a series of measures to check this trend. These included intensified political education for officers, a strengthening of the Party committee structure within the PLA, attacks on overspecialization and excessive emphasis on ranks and titles, increased PLA participation in production, salary cuts for higher-ranking officers, and an emphasis on democratic relations between officers and men. By such measures Party leaders sought, in the words of Tan Zheng, deputy director of the PLA's political department, to ensure that "no amount of modernization will change the fact that ours is a people's army."[60] This, however, in no way implied a downgrading of military modernization. Thus Tan criticized the "guerrilla" tendencies of those who refused to adjust to the needs of modern warfare; the need to assimilate Soviet military experiences, albeit in an undogmatic manner, continued to be emphasized; modernization measures continued unabated; and at the end of 1957 a program was unveiled for professionalizing all officers within five years. The basic aim of the 1956–7 adjustments was still to modernize, but within the context of PLA traditions. This would cause some strains within the officer corps, but Party and army leaders saw no inherent incompatibility in the effort.

Other policy shifts in 1956–7 represented modifications of the Soviet model. Particularly in 1957, there was increasing attention to small- and medium-scale industry, in contrast to the Soviet emphasis on large, capital-intensive plants. Similarly, in education, the expansion of elite specialized institutions that were the core of the Soviet approach slowed down, and a renewed emphasis on small community-run schools appeared (see *CHOC* 14, Chapter 4). Thus a second low-technology leg was gaining increased prominence, but it would become a major feature of Chinese developmental strategies only under the "walk on two legs" slogan of the Great Leap Forward. For the time being, such programs were clearly auxiliary and did not challenge the continued predominance of the modern, large-scale sector. Finally, the reexamination of the Soviet model meant a new receptiveness to alternative foreign sources of ideas, including not only Communist Yugoslavia but also the advanced capitalist

60 "Speech by Comrade T'an Cheng" (18 September 1956), in *Eighth National Congress*, 2.265.

states of the West. But there was, in fact, little of such eclectic borrowing, and the Soviet-style structures and strategy remained fundamentally in place until late 1957.

The Eighth Party Congress

When the Party Congress convened in September 1956 for the first time in eleven years, the occasion was marked by an outpouring of both self-congratulation and self-criticism. There was indeed much reason for congratulation over both the victory of 1949 and the success of socialist transformation in 1955–6. Moreover, the Party had grown during the period of transformation into a mammoth organization of 10.7 million members that now penetrated most aspects of social, economic, and political life. But Party leaders also recognized that many tasks remained and many faults existed within the new system, and the Congress was marked by a remarkably frank yet ultimately self-confident analysis of the problems facing the regime.

The main task, as affirmed by the political resolution of the Congress, was getting on with the job of economic development. The policy line for this task elaborated the "opposing rash advance" theme, although (perhaps with a view to Mao's sensibilities) right conservatism received pride of place in the official listing of deviations to be avoided. The proposals for the second FYP announced by Zhou Enlai reflected balance, moderation, and realism, but they still called for a slight increase in the rate of reinvestment compared with the first FYR Overall, the program of the Congress was not one of retreat, but the emphasis was decidedly on *steady* advance.

In many ways the 1956 Party Congress was less of a personal triumph for Mao than its predecessor in 1945, which had put the seal on his leadership of the Party. On the surface, several developments diminished Mao's role: The reference to his thought as part of the CCP's guiding ideology was deleted from the new Party constitution, and the Congress placed heavy stress on collective leadership. In 1956, however, there were a number of factors operating against any outpourings of adulation, although fundamentally Mao's position remained unchallenged.[61] One consideration arose from external events – Khrushchev's denunciation of Stalin's "personality cult" at the Soviet Party Congress in February. Under these circumstances, any lavish praise of the Chinese leader would have been unseemly, and Mao later stated that he fully concurred in the decision to delete his thought from the constitution.

---

61 This analysis (cf. Teiwes, *Politics and purges*, 226–30) differs from interpretations seeing "Mao in eclipse" at the Congress (e.g., Chang, *Power and policy*, 29ff.) and those emphasizing conflicts between Mao and other leaders (e.g., MacFarquhar, *Origins*, 1, part 2).

A second consideration, one that suggests both Mao's self-assurance and his confidence in his associates, was the need to arrange for an orderly succession. Mao's subsequent statements indicate that he took several concrete steps at the Eighth Congress for his eventual retirement to the second front – removed from operational decisions – so that his colleagues could gain sufficient prestige to ensure a smooth transition after his death and thus avoid the strife that marked Soviet politics after Stalin. The post of honorary Party Chairman was created for Mao's eventual retirement; Liu Shaoqi's status as heir apparent was bolstered by entrusting him with the presentation of the political report (a role Mao filled in 1945); and strong collective organs were established in the Politburo Standing Committee and an enlarged Party Secretariat. None of this meant Mao was abdicating real power. As he put it in early 1958, when proposing new measures for his retreat to the second front, " 'Whenever the nation is urgently in need . . . I will shoulder this leadership task once again."[62]

Linked to Mao's continued dominance was a much broader pattern of leadership stability. This stability was reflected not only in the reelection of virtually all CC members but in personnel arrangements at all levels. The new Politburo Standing Committee consisted of the same five men who had made up the old Secretariat, formerly the inner core of leadership, plus the rapidly promoted Deng Xiaoping, The size of the full Politburo was nearly doubled to take in all pre-Congress members plus most PLA marshals who were not already included and all vice-premiers except Deng Zihui, who apparently was made to pay for his views on cooperativization. Within this top body there were some alterations in the pecking order, but apart from the significant rise of Deng Xiaoping and the dropping of Zhang Wentian (an old opponent of Mao's in the 1930s) and Kang Sheng to alternate status, these were relatively minor.

Similarly, the more than doubled ranks of full Central Committee members included not only nearly all former full members but also all but three alternates, who were promoted en masse. In addition, over 100 new individuals were added to the new CC – roughly one-third as full members and the remainder as alternates – yet the background characteristics of the 170-person body were remarkably similar to the 1945 CC.

The new central bodies also reflected the PRC's emerging institutional pattern. The expansion of the Politburo and CC was essentially accomplished by coopting the key figures in the regime's various hierarchies. As a result, the broader elite tendency toward specialization was carried into the highest

62 "Sixty points on working methods" (19 February 1958), in Jerome Ch'en ed., *Mao papers: Anthology and bibliography*, 75.

bodies, guaranteeing that the views and interests of each major sector would be represented. Particularly important at the Politburo level was the selection of three key officials responsible for the economy – Li Fuchun, chairman of the State Planning Commission, Finance Minister Li Xiannian, and the chairman of the State Economic Commission Bo Yibo (as an alternate) – who now joined Chen Yun on the vital policy-making organ. The appointments further demonstrated the centralized nature of the system under the first FYP, since nearly three times as many CC members served in Beijing as in the provinces. Finally, the composition of the new top elite also reflected the post-1949 shift to civilian rule and the central role of the Party in the system. Full-time civilian Party and government officials outnumbered PLA leaders by 2 to 1 on the Politburo and nearly 3 to 1 on the CC while the ratio of full-time Party, government, and military leaders was something on the order of 6:5:4.

The institutional representation on the new CC was a manifestation of the substantial degree to which Chinese politics had become bureaucratized. Party leaders had long been critical of various bureaucratic practices – red tape, organizational proliferation, decisions made in offices without firsthand knowledge of actual conditions – and by the mid-1950s were increasingly aware of the constraints placed on their options by the ever more specialized administrative machine they had created. Despite measures to reassert control, including transfers of Party cadres to key ministerial posts, strengthening the role of Party committees within government agencies, and attacks on excessive professionalization, leaders at all levels found their perspectives increasingly dominated by the organizations in which they served. Even the top decision-making generalists were trapped; as Mao complained in early 1958: "The Politburo has become a voting machine,... you give it a perfect document and it has to be passed."[63] The qualms of Mao and others notwithstanding, in ways besides the composition of the new ruling bodies, the proceedings of the Eighth Party Congress represented a full flowering of bureaucratic politics.

With the period of revolutionary transformations ostensibly past and economic development the main task, the Congress heard a long series of speeches by leaders articulating their departments' opinions on how to accomplish the broader goal. Similarly, the need to adjust the institutions of the new socialist system generated proposals advancing the interests of specific organizations. In some cases a degree of restraint was required when decisions had already gone against the institution concerned, but even her bureaucratic interests were expressed. Thus Minister of Defense Peng Dehuai could not explicitly call for more resources, since the decision had been made to cut defense spending from 32 to 20 percent of budgetary expenditure in the second FYP, but

---

63 "Talks at the Nanning conference" (11–12 January 1958), *Miscellany*, 1.80.

he still emphasized the need to press ahead with military modernization and to strengthen defense.

Where policies were still undecided, however, appeals for organizational interests were often blatant. This was especially the case in speeches by provincial Party leaders who sought favorable consideration from the central authorities over resources and policy guidelines. For example, Shandong's Tan Qilong hoped that "the central Ministry of Water Conservancy . . . will give us support with regard to technology, investments, and similar problems," and also asked "the relevant central ministries when settling sowing plans . . . not to be too rigid [and] enable us to make a reasonable apportionment in accordance with . . . actual conditions of the area."[64] Given the relaxed political atmosphere and the specialized nature of the job at hand, the Eighth Congress was a fitting occasion for articulating the views and interests of a vast array of bureaucratic organizations.

Party rectification and the Hundred Flowers

The criticisms of shortcomings in the system that had marked not only the Eighth Congress but much official commentary since spring 1956 foreshadowed a more systematic effort to overcome faults through a Party rectification movement. Initially, this campaign was to be patterned on the great Yan'an rectification of 1942–4, an effort to combat by relatively persuasive means dangerous ideological and political tendencies within the Party so that it could more successfully pursue the struggle against the Japanese and KMT. Now, with new problems and opportunities arising in the socialist era, the Party would again be reformed in an even more low-key manner, like a "gentle breeze and mild rain," to make it a more effective force for economic construction.

A major target of the reform effort was "subjectivism," the backward ideological state where unfamiliarity with changing conditions caused Party officials to apply unsuited concepts and methods arbitrarily to current problems. A particularly significant manifestation criticized at this juncture was the dogmatic copying of foreign (Soviet) experiences, and the recommended cure was to raise the general level of Marxist-Leninist theory in the Party, develop knowledge of specialized fields, and carry out research into actual conditions.

Closely linked to subjectivism was the sin of "bureaucratism," the drifting away of officials from the masses and social reality and toward becoming a privileged elite. This was particularly dangerous because as a part of a ruling organization, Party members were in a position to seek their own advantage

---

64 Cited in Roderick MacFarquhar, "Aspects of the CCP's Eighth Congress (first session)," paper presented to the University Seminar on Modern East Asia: China, Columbia University, 19 February 1969, 10, 13.

and ignore the interests of the people. Various forms of supervision were required to prevent such abuses.

The third main evil attacked was "sectarianism," the tendency of Party members to feel superior to non-Party people and discriminate against them in organizational life. This was a problem of critical importance regarding the skilled intellectuals, and the Hundred Flowers and mutual supervision policies were aimed at overcoming it.

Concrete steps indicating a Party reform movement began in mid-1956 with a program for the study of rectification documents, but at the Eighth Congress rectification was still a relatively low-priority item despite frequent attacks on the three evils. External events – the Polish October and the abortive Hungarian revolt – forced a higher priority for rectification. Mao subsequently claimed that the danger of letting problems fester, revealed by Hungary and Poland, convinced him of the need to handle "contradictions among the people" correctly, and at a November 1956 CC plenary meeting the Chairman announced a mild rectification campaign for "next year."

The lessons of Eastern Europe, however, were ambiguous. On the one hand, restiveness of the population as a result of bureaucratic perversions – a situation manifested to a more limited degree in China by a significant number of industrial strikes in 1956 – argued for dealing with such deviations before matters got out of control and thus enhanced the significance of rectification. On the other hand, the situation in Eastern Europe exploded in large part because political controls had been eroded, and the official CCP analysis of these events cited "revisionism" – the challenge to orthodox Party rule – as the main danger. This position argued for caution regarding Party reform, and in January a decision for full-scale rectification was announced for 1958, not 1957.

Mao clearly contributed to this more cautious approach with warnings against an "antisocialist tide" that allegedly had appeared in the latter half of 1956, but it is equally clear that he did not want a total halt to reform efforts or a return to arbitrary methods of dealing with intellectuals. In winter 1956–7, however, many middle- to upper-echelon officials and ordinary cadres attempted to do just that as a decidedly more restrictive atmosphere emerged.

By February, Mao concluded that bold action was required if Party reform was not to be totally eroded, and he intervened with two major speeches. In them Mao reverted to the fundamentally confident view of 1956. Victory had been achieved, and the main task was attending to flaws in the system. The intellectuals were a basically loyal force that could make great contributions to economic and cultural development. Now the nation was united as never before, and shortcomings could be overcome in a nondisruptive fashion. The Chairman, however, when revealing that rectification was once again scheduled for 1957, also introduced some novel and unsettling ideas concerning reform methods. Not only would Marxism-Leninism not be stipulated as the guiding ideology for criticism, but intellectuals would be invited to play a key role in offering criticism of the Party. Thus the Hundred Flowers was converted from an encouragement of academic debate to a method of conducting rectification. Mao sought to reassure cadres that intellectuals' criticism would be helpful and that rectification would still be according to "gentle breeze and mild rain" methods. But the prospect of CCP members being directly criticized by bourgeois intellectuals was enough to send shudders of concern throughout the Party elite.

There was considerable resistance to Mao's innovative approach, although the precise contours of opposition remain unclear.[65] Mao himself claimed in April that 90 percent of "Party comrades" had a negative attitude toward the refurbished Hundred Flowers and added that "I have no mass base."[66] Indeed, there does appear to have been widespread opposition among lower- and middle-rank cadres charged with controlling intellectuals on a day-to-day basis. These officials, whose immediate powers and prerogatives were at stake, had a different perspective from the more removed top leadership. Fearing that the process would get out of hand, such cadres failed to encourage the "blooming and contending" of intellectuals, but instead indiscriminately attacked their critical opinions.

At higher levels, there is good reason to believe that some leaders in the Party propaganda apparatus responsible for both publicizing the Hundred Flowers and organizing many of the conferences of intellectuals where blooming and contending took place were less than enthusiastic about the new policy. Clearly the CC's newspaper, the *People's Daily*, was laggard in responding to Mao's initiative and was sharply criticized by the Chairman as a result. This apparent resistance can be explained in essentially similar terms to the opposition of lower-ranking cadres: As officials responsible for the daily management of intellectuals, they probably felt the dangers of the new approach outweighed any possible benefits.

Conflict within the Politburo itself over rectification remains uncertain, despite some scholarly analysis that sees Mao seriously at loggerheads with his colleagues.[67] Certainly it is likely that such a novel policy, which exposed the Party of the proletariat to rebukes by intellectuals from bourgeois

65 The following analysis and that for the subsequent section on the Anti-Rightist Campaign is drawn from Teiwes, *Politics and purges*, chs. 6–7. For contrasting interpretations, see the sources cited in note 67.
66 "Talk at the Hangchow conference of the Shanghai bureau" (April 1957), in *Miscellany*, 1.67.
67 Major analyses holding that both the rectification and subsequent Anti-Rightist campaigns were occasions for major dissension within the top leadership are: MacFarquhar, *Origins*, 1, parts 3 and 4; and Richard H. Solomon, *Mao's revolution and the Chinese political culture*, ch. 17. This interpretation is also adopted in Chapter 2 of this volume.

backgrounds, caused debate within the highest circles. Some information claims opposition to Mao on this issue by Liu Shaoqi and Peng Zhen, but the total pattern of evidence is inconclusive. Peng in particular was a vigorous supporter of blooming and contending in his publicized statements, and Liu, although silent in public, nevertheless toured the provinces and advanced views consistent with Mao's to closed Party meetings. In any case, if reservations were expressed behind the closed doors of the Politburo, they did not sharply polarize the leadership. The combination of Mao's power and the general leadership's commitment to free debate within Party councils but disciplined implementation outside undoubtedly were the crucial factors in dampening any divisions. Other factors were also at work – the broad consensus on the nature of the new situation; the fact that Mao had not over a long period consistently pushed radical rectification methods that might have crystallized opposition but instead had changed his position according to altered circumstances; and finally, the fact that the initial response of the intellectuals to Mao's invitation was restrained and thus did not pose a dramatic threat to Party rule.

The at first tepid response of the intellectuals was understandable, given the ideological remolding they had been subjected to since the thought reform campaign of 1951–2. Despite anxiety that relaxation would be followed by renewed pressure, they finally reacted to repeated official prodding and to the fact that throughout May 1957 those who were bold enough to speak out were not punished with an outpouring of countercriticism. In one sense, the intellectuals' criticism by and large was not threatening to Party rule. The bulk of it dealt with problems and conflicts directly related to their roles and functions. Moreover, in the overwhelming number of cases, the criticisms advanced were similar to strictures directed at subjectivism, bureaucratism, and sectarianism in the official media since 1956. Even proposals for institutional change, such as the idea of turning the CPPCC into an upper house of the National People's Congress, reflected ideas that had been advanced by the highest Party leaders.

In another sense, however, the attacks were deeply unsettling. This was due less to some suggestions that deviations might be somehow intrinsic to the system or even the few extreme sentiments calling for the Party's demise than to the cumulative vehemence of complaints concerning intellectuals' daily confrontations with Party authority and the depth of discontent they reflected. The strength of feeling was particularly apparent in the views and actions of students, who even took to the streets to articulate their grievances. By focusing on the shortcomings of Party cadres in the everyday affairs of their work units, intellectuals were in effect raising the issue of the Party's competence to guide China in the new peiod of socialist construction. Yet it must be emphasized that this did not amount to a rejection of the system. Even some of the most outspoken student critics still supported public ownership, hailed Mao as "the revolutionary leader who saved China," and expressed a loyal if ambivalent attitude toward the CCP: "We want Party leadership, but we are resolutely opposed to the Party alone making decisions."[68] The results of blooming and contending suggested continuing support for the broad outlines of the system and for the CCP program of building a new China, but at the same time a deep alienation among skilled groups from the concrete manifestations of Party rule. By mid-May the Party leadership was dismayed at what had unfolded. The extent of discontent among intellectuals who had been assigned such a key role in development, and especially among students who had been raised in the PRC, was deeply distressing. Moreover, cadre morale had suffered a severe jolt as a result of being required to endure the critical onslaught.

Why did the Hundred Flowers experiment fail? Essentially the failure was due to some fundamental misconceptions concerning the new situation in China. Assuming that the intellectuals essentially stood on the side of socialism and had no fundamental clashes of interest with the system, Mao concluded that they could make positive contributions even to so sensitive an affair as Party rectification. This did not take into account the facts that bourgeois intellectuals as a group had often been subjected severe pressure since the early days of the PRC, that their interests as they conceived them had often been grievously violated, and that their relations with Party cadres were marked by mutual mistrust. When Mao thrust the intellectuals into the forefront of rectification, he in effect asked them to perform an impossible task: to criticize boldly Party authorities they often feared and loathed, yet to do so in the spirit of a gentle breeze and mild rain.

Party cadres too were placed in an unprecedented position. In effect, they were being asked to redefine Party leadership in ways that were never precisely stipulated to take into account the views and talents of non-Party intellectuals. Moreover, they were themselves subject to the criticism by these individuals of suspect class origins and backward ideology, something that seemed most unjust. Given the underlying tensions between cadres and intellectuals, any effort that exacerbated those tensions, however unwittingly, was bound to get out of control. (For further discussion, see *CHOC* 14, Chapter 5.)

The Anti-Rightist Campaign

Although a direct counterattack was launched only in early June 1957, by mid-May top CCP leaders decided that unchecked blooming and contending was

---

68 From a Beijing student pamphlet translated in Dennis J. Doolin, *Communist China: The politics of student opposition*, 50, 55.

unacceptably weakening Party control over the intellectuals. Mao was in the forefront of this effort despite his earlier championing of the Hundred Flowers. Not only did the Chairman undertake the key initiatives that began the policy shift, but throughout the summer of 1957 Party policies toward "rightists," as the non-Party critics were dubbed, all bore his imprint. Mao, moreover, was not shy about reversing himself on a whole series of specific issues. For example, in April Mao hailed the non-Party Shanghai paper *Wenhui bao* for publicizing critical opinions. In July he bitterly attacked the same newspaper as a rightist organ. In February he proposed a review of counterrevolutionary cases, but in October he denounce the democratic Party leader Luo Longji for a similar proposal.

Whatever the reasons for so unscrupulous an about-face in these and other instances, the net effect was to remove any differences that may have existed between the Chairman and other leaders. With his illusions about the intellectuals shattered, Mao came down strongly on the side of firm Party control.

The counterattack on the critics took the form of an Anti-Rightist Campaign. This campaign was defensive in tone. It attempted to refute critical arguments advanced by intellectuals in the spring and restore Party dominance in the urban organizations where blooming and contending had been primarily conducted. Ironically, given the intellectuals' criticism of heavy-handed Party methods, organizational measures taken in conjunction with the Anti-Rightist Campaign – particularly the transfer of reliable Party cadres to leadership positions in educational and cultural units – resulted in a substantial increase in Party control compared with the situation before the Hundred Flowers. The main focus of the movement itself was initially on leading members of democratic parties who were singled out as the core of rightist groups. These individuals had quite accurately been disparaged by student critics as "cautious old men" for the moderate views they advanced in the spring, yet now they were charged with plotting the overthrow of the regime. They were subjected to violent press attacks and large-scale struggle meetings and forced into abject confessions; yet by late 1958–9 most were restored to posts in the democratic parties, indicating that the harshest accusations against them were not taken seriously.

Nevertheless, they served as useful symbols to set the tone for the campaign, which spread to rightists generally within intellectual organizations from mid-July. Although non-Party intellectuals were the key targets, Party intellectuals who had spoken out for their professional rather than their Party interests in the spring also suffered on a smaller scale. The total impact on China's intellectuals was devastating: Altogether some 550,000 were labeled rightists, the psychological pressures of struggle sessions resulted in a significant number of suicides, and reform through labor was apparently meted out on a large scale. In the post-Mao period the severity of the campaign has been regarded as a major mistake of "enlarging the scope of class struggle," with perhaps 98 percent of all rightist labels wrongly applied.[69] (For further discussion, see *CHOC* 14, Chapter 5.)

The harshness of the movement should not obscure the fact that the leadership's attitude toward intellectuals did not become totally negative in mid-1957. In an effort to avoid complete alienation, official guidelines for the campaign held that only a small number of intellectuals were rightists and advocated a lenient overall approach. This reflected a continuing belief that intellectuals had an important role to play in China's modernization despite their ideological backwardness.

Mao expressed the leadership's ambivalence in July by attacking intellectuals as unwilling to submit to the Party but, nevertheless, citing the need to win over individual "great intellectuals [who are] useful to us."[70] The Hundred Flowers fiasco had demonstrated that intellectuals could not be relied on politically, but it did not settle the issue of their role in economic and cultural development. As the Anti-Rightist Campaign unfolded in the summer of 1957, overall economic policy initially remained on the same moderate course as in 1956, an approach requiring a major role for professional expertise. Thus it was still quite possible that once Party control was reestablished, a policy of concessions to intellectuals short of a leading role in Party rectification could have been adopted. The severity of the Anti-Rightist Campaign, however, undoubtedly damaged the enthusiasm of intellectuals for the Party's developmental goals. The leadership, moreover, now had reason to doubt a strategy that placed wavering intellectuals in so central a role.

Other factors were also at work. The general attempt to deal with grievances in society by political relaxation had adverse social effects with important economic ramifications. Of particular significance was the situation in the countryside. The critical atmosphere toward APC abuses officially encouraged in 1956 led to what subsequently was called a "small typhoon" including substantial peasant withdrawals from the cooperatives in the winter of 1956–7. The Hundred Flowers led to further deterioration of the situation as disgruntled peasants, reportedly encouraged by press and radio reports of urban blooming and contending, challenged the rural cadre structure and increasingly engaged in such "spontaneous capitalist" activities as decentralizing APC

---

69 The 98 percent assessment, and also the 550,000 figure for rightists, appears in the 1980 report by Liao, "Historical experiences," October 1981, 80–1. The 1981 official *Resolution on certain questions in the history of our Party since the founding of the People's Republic of China* {27 June 1981}, NCNA, 30 June 1981, trans. in *FBIS Daily Report: China*, 1 July 1981, K1–38. more cautiously affirmed the correctness of counterattacking rightists but held that the scope of attack was too broad.

70 "Zai Shanghai shi gejie renshi huiyi shang de jianghua" (Speech at the conference of all circles in Shanghai municipality), (8 July 1957) in *Wansui* (1969), 121.

responsibility to individual peasant households, demanding more money and grain from the state while selling less surplus to it, and speculative activities.

Particularly disturbing was the fact that some cadres participated in capitalist behavior and conspired with peasants to conceal or underestimate grain output. This, together with another poor crop whereby food output lagged behind the rate of population increase, resulted in a severe grain supply crisis. Party leaders responded with a summer 1957 decision to clamp down on the rural free market and launch a rural socialist education movement. This movement conducted propaganda on the claimed superiority of socialism among the peasants generally, arrested offending former landlords and rich peasants, carried out a limited purge of rural Party members who engaged in irregular practices, and as a result of bolstering the collective sector, restored overall cadre authority vis-à-vis the peasantry. Once again the combination of persuasive and coercive methods, together with a direct appeal to the interests of the new rural elite, was successful in achieving Party objectives.

Added to such social and political problems were related economic ones. The unsatisfactory performance of the agricultural sector was underlined by consecutive below-par years in 1956 and 1957. Not only had the new cooperative structure failed to provide a production spurt, but the subsequent emphasis on material incentives within the APC framework had also been unsuccessful. The lag in agriculture had its impact on industrial growth, and Zhou Enlai announced a 20 percent cut in capital construction in June 1957. Following the logic of the "Ten great relationships," the leadership modestly increased total state investment in agriculture in 1957, but this promised no breakthrough. With the Soviet economic strategy called into question, one possible alternative was to focus on gradually increasing agricultural output while accepting a reduced rate of overall growth. But since Party leaders viewed a high rate of growth as a key goal, such as alternative was an unlikely long-term strategy.

Thus by fall 1957 a number of pressures were converging for change in developmental strategy: perceived deficiencies of the Soviet model, the questionable reliability of the intellectuals, the socially disruptive consequences of political relaxation, and a sluggish economy. Moreover, the cautious marginal adjustments that had been made to the Soviet model – greater awareness of the key economic role of agriculture, moves toward administrative decentralization, and more emphasis on smaller-scale industrial projects and locally supported education – provided outlooks and programs that could be developed into a grander innovative strategy. Finally, Mao and some of his leadership colleagues could look back from the latter part of 1957 over the events of the preceding two years and draw some dubious but nevertheless influential conclusions.

On the positive side, Mao decided that although his initial view on the decisive victory of socialist transformation in 1956 had been premature, as success had been limited to the ownership front, the rectification and Anti-Rightist campaigns had achieved that fundamental victory on the political and ideological fronts. Therefore, the Chinese people were ready as never before to carry out an economic and technical revolution. From a more negative perspective, Mao declared that the "opposing rash advance" policies had been a serious mistake that not only caused economic losses by dampening the enthusiasm of the masses but also encouraged the rightists to launch their political assault. The lesson to be drawn was that the leap forward approach of early 1956 must be pushed without reservation in order to sustain the ardor of the workers and peasants. These ideas began to become dominant during the plenary meeting of the Central Committee in September – October 1957, and by the end of the year China was well on the road to the Great Leap Forward.

Conclusions

Although major problems faced Party leaders in late 1957, the overall performance of the PRC since 1949 had been remarkably successful. Despite resentment of particular features of CCP rule, the regime had obtained far-reaching popular support as a result of achievements in securing social order, launching economic development, improving living conditions, and restoring national pride. At the same time it had accomplished a basic social and institutional transformation, so that by 1956 China had entered the socialist stage.

The reasons for these successes varied. As emphasized throughout this analysis, the Soviet model and leadership unity were critical factors, factors, that would be removed or weakened with the Great Leap Forward. In particular, with the model providing clear goals and unity producing strong commitment to official programs, conditions were optimal for utilizing to full advantage the disciplined Party apparatus that had played a central role in revolutionary victory. Although hardly immune to organizational and political shortcomings, the Party organization generally proved responsive to major initiatives and policies – sometimes overzealously so. In the 1949–57 period, with brief exception of the Hundred Flowers experiment, CCP programs reinforced the authority of this disciplined apparatus and thus enhanced the regime's capabilities for development and transformation.

Success was also due to CCP leaders' skillfully combining persuasive, coercive, and tangible appeals in securing compliance. Constant efforts to convince the populace of the Party's view persuaded many individuals and groups of the correctness of Communist policies and made even more people aware of

acceptable modes of behavior. Coercion was used both to break the opposition of hostile groups and to impress the majority that the Party was a force
that could not be resisted. And programs designed to further the tangible
interests of key social groups – especially poorer peasants and the burgeoning
cadre elite – provided crucial support for the CCP on the basis of perceived
self-interest.

Another important factor was the applicability of strategies and methods
that had served so well during the revolutionary period. The mass mobilization
techniques developed in the rural base areas of North China proved adaptable
to land reform and agricultural cooperativization throughout China after 1949.
Also, notwithstanding the miscalculations of 1956–7, the united front tactic
that had been effective against the Japanese and KMT generally succeeded in
narrowing active resistance, neutralizing wavering elements, and maximizing
support under conditions of CCP rule. Especially important was the fact that
the pre-1949 realism and careful marshaling of resources largely prevailed
between 1949 and 1957. Although the ambitious programs of this initial
period often stretched organizational resources, they rarely overextended them
to the point where official hierarchies could no longer effectively guide social
and economic change. And when this did occur in early 1956, it was corrected
in a matter of months.

Finally, the accomplishments of the first eight years were due in large
measure to the absence of any perceived incompatibility among the goals
pursued or methods used by the CCP. Social goals and economic objectives
were regarded as mutually reinforcing. Agricultural cooperatives were the
accepted solution to production problems as well as ideologically desirable, and
socialization of the modern sector both eliminated capitalism and facilitated
planned economic growth. Similarly, institutionalization and mass campaigns
were both accepted as appropriate means for socialist ends. Campaigns were
suited to major efforts at social transformation, and strong institutions were
needed to guide planned development and manage a socialist society. Even
where tensions were acknowledged, as between military modernization and
PLA traditions, it was assumed that contradictions could be resolved without
damage to any important goal. In later years, as Mao and other Party leaders
increasingly realized that economic objectives had major social costs, that
strong institutions could threaten some values while safeguarding others, and
that the very content of socialism was uncertain, the potential for conflict grew
and the relatively smooth advances of the formative period became increasingly
difficult to sustain.

CHAPTER 2

THE GREAT LEAP FORWARD AND THE SPLIT IN THE YAN'AN LEADERSHIP 1958–1965

KENNETH LIEBERTHAL

AN OVERVIEW

The year 1958 began with the Chinese Communist leaders optimistic about their ability to lead the country up the path of rapid economic development and social progress. To be sure, not all Politburo members agreed on the best methods to use to accomplish these great tasks, but overall confidence was high and the degree of underlying unity clearly sufficient to enable the Chinese Communist Party (CCP) to act in a consistent and decisive manner. Seven years later, deep fissures had rent this leadership to the point where Mao Zedong himself stood on the verge of launching a devastating attack against many of the colleagues with whom he had worked for more than three decades. That attack would, in turn, launch China into a decade so tumultuous that even in the early 1980s leaders in Beijing would look back to the eve of the 1958–65 era wistfully as the time when the Party's power, prestige, and unity had reached pinnacles. The eight years between 1958 and 1965 were a period of major transition in the Chinese revolution.

To be sure, not all had gone smoothly for the Chinese Communists after 1949. There had been significant disagreement among the leaders over the pace and contours of the development effort. During 1953, for example, Finance Minister Bo Yibo had come under sharp criticism for advocating tax policies that would, Mao felt, slow down the development of the public sector of the economy. In 1955, Mao openly disagreed with his colleagues over the pace of the proposed collectivization of agriculture and effectively overturned the program they had adopted. His efforts in 1957 to encourage non-Party intellectuals to criticize the Party had brought bitter disagreement at the highest levels. And throughout this period there were repeated efforts to rectify what were seen as unhealthy tendencies in the Party and government bureaucracies as the new system of political power became consolidated.

The key point about the 1949–57 period, however, is that the conflicts were handled in a way that managed to preserve basic unity among the elite and maintain the élan of the revolutionary movement. Similarly, although many citizens dissented bitterly from the CCP's policies of this period, the overall prestige of the Party and of the new system remained high. The Communists could rightly proclaim that their policies were making China stronger and wealthier, even if they were forced to "break some eggs" to make their national omelette. It was precisely this prestige that the CCP lost during the 1958–65 period, with virtually catastrophic consequences. It is ironic that this period proved on balance to be so destructive, for it began with the Great Leap Forward (GLF), a program based on almost utopian optimism about what the Party, with its methods of mass mobilization, could accomplish.

During the spring and summer of 1958 Mao and his colleagues pushed the Great Leap idea as an alternative to the development strategy that had been imported from the Soviet Union for the first Five-Year Plan (FYP) of 1953–7. Needing some way to overcome bottlenecks that appeared to preclude a simple repetition of the first FYP strategy, the Chinese leaders settled on an approach that utilized the mass mobilization skills they had honed to a fine edge during the Anti-Japanese War years in Yan'an. This new strategy (with its various component parts, including communization of the countryside), threw the country into a frenzy of production activity that lasted into 1959. Key elements in this strategy, however, ultimately made the production upsurge a prelude to economic disaster rather than to the anticipated time of plenty.

The Great Leap strategy entailed significant changes in the political situation. It stripped considerable power from the central government bureaucracy and transferred it in many cases to local Party cadres. It shunted technical specialists aside in production units and replaced them with political generalists good at firing up the enthusiasm of the workers. It raised the pervasiveness of political demands in all fields to a new level, as superhuman work motivated by political zeal was key to the successful implementation of this new developmental approach. And it introduced important new strains into Sino-Soviet relations, as it de facto decreased the authority of the many Soviet advisers in China and implicitly challenged the previously sacrosanct Soviet model.

Given the extent of these changes, serious problems naturally arose when the Great Leap began to falter. By the end of 1958 Mao and others were aware that extremism in the name of the Leap was already causing some damage, and they made appropriate modifications in targets and policies to keep the movement on track. But information about the actual results of state grain procurement in early 1959 revealed that the situation was worse than was previously thought, and during that spring Mao led the effort to bring greater rationality and efficiency to the program. The movement proved difficult to bring under control, however, as those who had inherited greater power during 1958 continued to resist any retreat from the policies of that year.

During the summer of 1959 this problem of bringing the GLF under control became entangled in elite politics in a very damaging way. Peng Dehuai, a leading military man who had long had a stormy relationship with Mao, returned from a trip to the Soviet Union and Eastern Europe in June and shortly thereafter made a biting critique of the "petty-bourgeois fanaticism" of the Great Leap at a major Party work conference convened at Lushan. The rationale for Peng's actions at Lushan remains uncertain, but Mao chose to interpret it as a direct attack on his personal leadership and responded sharply. Mao demanded that Peng and his supporters be removed from power, and he suggested that the Soviet Union had become involved in Peng's challenge. The immediate results were twofold: The purge of Peng swamped the efforts to rein in the Great Leap and produced a second upsurge in radical policies lasting into 1960, and relations between China and the Soviet Union became more strained.

Both these results bore bitter fruit in 1960. The Leap upsurge caused enormous further damage to the economy, to the extent that by late 1960 famine was stalking the land. Relations with Moscow continued to deteriorate to the point that in the summer of 1960 the Soviets suddenly withdrew all their assistance from China. Soviet aid was at that time still sufficiently crucial to a number of key industrial development projects that this action produced grave economic consequences in the People's Republic of China (PRC). It also distracted Beijing's attention from the economic disaster that was looming in the countryside, thus delaying timely measures to salvage the situation there.

By the end of 1960, therefore, the GLF had produced economic disaster in the hinterland, and during 1961 this fundamental economic malaise spread through the cities. Beijing now recognized the full gravity of the problem and drafted a series of programmatic documents to deal with the situation. During this year of crisis, there is every indication that Mao supported the far-reaching retreat from the GLF that his colleagues devised. Indeed, in June 1961 Mao made a self-criticism at a key Party meeting in Beijing,[1] and the Party as a whole adopted policies of retrenchment as official doctrine.

Once the crisis began to ease, however, tensions among the leaders ros~ Mao sought to regain his position as the person who defined th- ' the moment. His power and image had eroded as a (misjudgments during the GLF, and his concern abo his influence had increased. He had reached the concl

---

1 Since not full text of this confession is available, it is unfortunately no
  either thorough or perfunctory.

in the Soviet Union had demonstrated that under improper leadership, a Communist state could actually degenerate into a highly exploitative system. Substantively, Mao concluded that the GLF had discredited the notion of making phenomenal economic progress by relying on mass mobilization, but he still firmly believed in the importance of mass mobilization for preventing the bureaucratic degeneration of the revolution that had occurred in the Soviet Union.

Those of Mao's colleagues in direct control of the CCP apparatus disagreed with this latter judgment. They were anxious to restore internal CCP discipline and to pursue a path of economic development that made appropriate use of specialists and technical expertise. Although they shared many of Mao's goals, therefore, they shied away from some of his methods. Given the distribution of executive power in the wake of the Great Leap, they probably would have carried the day – implementing Mao's basic agenda but modifying it in ways that made it compatible with their more bureaucratic approach – had Mao not found some key allies to boost his strength.

These allies were his wife, Jiang Qing; the man he had put in to replace Peng Dehuai, Lin Biao; and a key member of the security system, Kang Sheng, who joined forces with the Chairman and his former secretary, Chen Boda, to overthrow the system that had emerged in the wake of the GLF. The gradual formation of this coalition between 1962 and 1965 will be detailed further on. Each member had personal reasons for joining the coalition, and all agreed on the desirability of changing the succession so that Liu Shaoqi (or someone else like Liu) would not eventually take over full power from Mao. The period thus became tangled up with coalition politics and intrigues over the succession.

The specific issues in contention, of course, changed over the years. During the early part of 1962 there was a significant disagreement over the degree of recovery that had already taken place in the countryside. Mao felt that recovery had gone far enough to permit Beijing again to seize the initiative and reassert its authority. Liu Shaoqi, Deng Xiaoping, Chen Yun, and others disagreed, arguing that the Party must continue to implement emergency measures to salvage the situation. The question of rehabilitating those who in 1959 had warned about the dangers inherent in the Leap also arose then. Mao agreed that many of these "rightists" should now be rehabilitated, but he drew the line at bringing back Peng Dehuai, to the chagrin of many of his colleagues (but not of Lin Biao).

By the fall of 1962 Mao had carried the day on the issue of the degree of recovery from the GLF, and the question now shifted to the best means to restore the regime's power and prestige in the country. Mao advocated a policy of building the Party in the countryside using means that entailed extensive mobilization of the peasantry. His colleagues subsequently tried to achieve rural Party rectification through internal bureaucratic means instead. In his frustration with the bureaucratic biases of other Politburo leaders, Mao adopted two measures to enhance the role of his brand of politics in the system.

Starting in 1963, the Chairman increasingly promoted the People's Liberation Army (PLA) as the model organization for Chinese to follow. The PLA had, under Lin Biao, acquitted itself well in technical military tasks, from progress toward building an atom bomb (the first Chinese atom bomb test took place in October 1964) to achieving an impressive series of victories in the border war with Indian forces in the fall of 1962. At the same time, Lin had promoted political work among the troops, centered on the study of Mao Zedong's thoughts as condensed and dogmatized in the *Quotations from Chairman Mao*. The PLA in Mao's eyes became an organization that had achieved the optimum synthesis of technique and politics, and Mao sought to expand its role in the political system. Lin Biao strongly encouraged this development – and the power of the Chairman on whom it depended.

Also beginning in 1963, Mao supervised the drafting of nine "letters" from the Central Committee (CC) of the CCP to the CC of the Communist Party of the Soviet Union (CPSU). These polemical documents spelled out Mao's contention that the Soviet Union had degenerated into a nonsocialist political system, a development Mao called going down the path of "revisionism." Mao used these letters to give wide publicity in China to the issue of revisionism and, essentially, to make his case (somewhat obliquely) against the policies of colleagues whom he opposed.

Between 1963 and 1965 Liu Shaoqi and the other Party leaders who later were to become the key initial targets of the Cultural Revolution carried out a very impressive program of economic recovery, bringing production in 1965 back up to the levels achieved on the eve of the GLF in almost every sector (and, of course, ahead of these levels in some sectors). As noted, these leaders appear to have tried to accommodate many of Mao's demands while channeling them so as to make them less disruptive to the bureaucratic system they had reconstructed. The available documentation suggests that these leaders were not oblivious of the dangers lurking in the machinations of Lin Biao, Jiang Qing, Kang Sheng, and their followers, but there appears little reason to believe that before 1965 they saw these dangers as threatening in a fundamental sense.

Liu Shaoqi, Deng Xiaoping, and their colleagues of like mind seem to have regarded the situation as difficult but not impossible to manage. They were ultimately proved disastrously wrong in this evaluation. They had tried to meet Mao partway and to limit as much as possible the leverage of his eventual coalition partners in the system. Thus, for example, the attempt to enhance the power of the army by establishing military-type political departments in the civilian governing organs starting in 1964 met strong resistance, as did Jiang Qing's repeated efforts to acquire authority over cultural policy. But as the middle of the decade approached, Mao himself saw this ongoing give-and-take less as the inevitable frictions of national politics and more in terms of a Manichean struggle of good against evil. This new perspective, of course, raised the stakes enormously, and an increasingly disturbed and restless Mao began to take the fateful steps that led to unleashing the Cultural Revolution in 1966.

This brief overview captures the highlights of a period in which four fundamental transitions took place: from a basically united leadership to one that was deeply divided; from a wholly legitimate CCP rule to one far less readily accepted; from a relatively disciplined and spirited CCP membership to one demoralized and uncertain; and from agreed-upon ways of handling intra-Party conflicts to disagreement over basic norms for resolving such tensions. In short, during 1958–65 the Chinese Communist movement lost some of its key political assets, both in terms of the organizational weapon it possessed in the Party and in terms of its reservoir of legitimacy among the population. These losses contributed to the deep divisions that led in turn to the Cultural Revolution. In greater detail, this story unfolded as follows.

ORIGINS OF THE GLF

Many forces contributed to the decision to adopt the policies collectively known as the GLF. Among these, the most fundamental were the problems produced by the first FYP, modeled after the Soviet Union's development strategy. These problems were political, social, and economic, with the economic issues at their heart.

The Soviet strategy developed by Stalin and adopted by the PRC demanded two conditions: that a planning mechanism channel resources overwhelmingly into the development of heavy industry, with the metallurgical industry receiving first priority; and that the rural areas be starved for funds and exploited as needed to provide resources to permit the growth of heavy industry in particular and of the urban sector in general. The Chinese copied their planning apparatus so successfully from the Soviets that during their respective first FYPs, the Chinese managed to devote nearly 48 percent of their public capital investment to industrial development, whereas the comparable Soviet figure was under 42 percent. The problem arose in the other part of the equation – the exploitation of the rural areas to support this urban industrial policy.

The Soviet Union had used agriculture during the first FYP both as a source of exports that would enable the government to import machinery and technology for industry and as a source of food for the rapidly expanding urban working force. Peasant deaths in the millions occurred either directly from Moscow's harsh imposition of the collective farm system or less directly from the resulting famine when the government maintained constant levels of agricultural procurement even as agricultural production fell more than 25 percent from 1929 to 1932–3, This approach assumed that there was a real surplus in agriculture and sought a way to make that surplus serve the goals of the political leadership.

The Chinese case differed in two fundamental respects from that of the Soviet Union. First and more important, per capita output in China in 1957 was only half that of the Soviet Union in 1928 in the production of grain (290 vs. 566 kg per person) and vegetable oils (1.7 vs. 3.0 kg per person). Thus, whereas the Soviets could debate how best to secure control over a consistent rural surplus, the Chinese had to develop a means first to create and enhance that surplus and then to gain control over its distribution. Second, whereas Soviet Party membership was more than 70 percent urban, the CCP was more than 70 percent rural in social composition. These differences in the social compositions of the two parties presumably made the CCP somewhat more reluctant to adopt a strategy premised on the misery of the countryside and the starvation of millions of country dwellers. Thus, in late 1957 China groped for a strategy that would enhance agricultural output while still permitting the rapid growth of capital-intensive heavy industry. The different elements of such a strategy, especially with regard to agriculture, were hotly debated at the Third Plenum of the Eighth CC in September and early October 1957.

The problem in agriculture was how to persuade the peasants to increase their output and marketings while Beijing devoted state investment to the heavy industrial sector. There was clear recognition among the leaders that the formula followed up to then would not solve the problem. Mao Zedong wanted to utilize political and organizational tools to boost peasant output. Chen Yun, the fifth-ranking member of the Party and the highest-ranking economic specialist, however, premised his recommended solution on the assumption that the peasants would respond only to increased material incentives and not to either coercion or ideological exhortation. Material incentives required not only that the peasants receive good prices for their products but also that they have consumer goods available to purchase with the money they earned. State investment would, therefore, have to shift somewhat in the direction of light industry in order to provide the consumer goods necessary to make this rural strategy work. The light industrial sector would also produce relatively quick turnover on capital with a substantial profit rate, thus providing over time an adequate capital pool for the speedy development of heavy industry.

In this balanced approach, therefore, Chen argued essentially that each sector could help the others and that the Chinese need not view trade-offs among sectors as a zero-sum game. He also pointed out the impossibility of feeding the large numbers of highly paid urban industrial workers if his advice were to be ignored (as, in fact, it was). In many ways, Chen Yun's policies in 1957 paralleled those of Nikolai Bukharin in the Soviet Union in 1927–8; and as Bukharin was brushed aside by Stalin, Chen was pushed from center stage by Mao.

Chen's policy recommendations, which amounted to the most comprehensive developmental alternative put forward in the China of the 1950s, were defeated in part by simple impatience. Chen himself readily admitted that his formula for balanced growth would not produce any developmental miracles in the next few years. But the explanation for Chen's defeat is in fact more complex. His strategy presumed that the Chinese government, as distinct from the CCP, would continue to play the central role in running the economy. The system established under the first FYP placed enormous power in the central government ministries. Although these were, like all bodies, under overall Party control, the greatest concentration of non-Communist experts was employed in the staffs of these ministries.

Ministerial work inevitably placed a premium on literacy, statistical skills, and the ability to deal in abstractions – all skills far more prevalent among the urban intelligentsia than among the peasant mass that had contributed so many stalwarts to the Party during the years in the wilderness. But the Hundred Flowers movement and the resulting Anti-Rightist Campaign in 1957 had largely discredited the urban intelligentsia and any development strategy that depended centrally on their contributions. Indeed, the harsh penalties exacted of the rightists in the wake of this campaign literally reduced the numbers of intellectuals outside of prison camps and thus changed the parameters of human capital that would inevitably shape the development strategy the government adopted.

The more radical, anti-intellectual atmosphere spread from the urban to the rural areas during the late summer and fall of 1957. In the countryside the Anti-Rightist Campaign was directed against those who had voiced doubts about the efficacy of the rapid cooperativization (essentially, collectivization) of agriculture that had swept China during the previous two years. Collectivization at China's low level of agricultural development and mechanization had itself been a policy signifying the primacy of human organizational factors in the country's economic growth. Thus, the Anti-Rightist Campaign in both urban and rural areas bolstered the position of those who believed that proper mobilization of the populace could accomplish tasks that the "bourgeois experts" dismissed as impossible. As such, the Anti-Rightist Campaign in the countryside facilitate the adoption of a policy of mass mobilization to build irrigation facilities during the winter of 1957–8. This policy proved highly successful, but it also highlighted several problems inherent in the rural organizational structure at that time.

First, a lack of appropriate organizational units to marshal people and resources hampered large-scale mobilization. Second, there was an absolute shortage of labor if the peasants were to put in millions of man-days at nonagricultural tasks such as dam building. Third, there was a continuing problem over establishing a good fit between basic-level government units and the economic units in the countryside. In 1956 the government had abolished the districts (*qu*) and amalgamated the administrative villages (*xiang*), but this had led to a series of escalating organizational problems that had not been resolved by the winter of 1957–8. The upshot of these issues was pressure in the countryside to devise a bigger unit that would be able to control large labor resources and also to fit neatly into the government administrative hierarchy.

The solution devised after some experimentation in early 1958 was the People's Commune (*renmin gongshe*), which itself then underwent major organizational changes between 1958 and 1962. The initial communes were huge, centralized units embracing several standard marketing areas.[2] They served both as the basic-level government organs and the key economic units. Their size permitted them to take control over not only agricultural production but also local industry, commerce, education, and the militia. Under commune direction, moreover, the organization of agricultural labor changed dramatically, with many peasants now assigned to specialized work teams that traveled from one village to another to perform particular tasks.

These initial communes proved too large to manage, and their attempt to base members' incomes on the total production of units that embraced tens of thousands of peasants provided too few incentives for individual effort. Therefore, in a series of stages from 1959 to 1962, the effective level of collective organization became smaller. Within the communes, this evolution entailed the formation first of brigades and then of smaller units called "teams," with the income of individual peasants depending on the total output of these successively smaller units. Also, by 1962 the communes themselves had been reduced in size, with the total number of communes increasing from the original 25,000 to 75,000. By 1962 these changes made many communes

2 The standard marketing area included the villages that traditionally marketed their goods at the same periodic market. These areas had social as well as economic identities, as marriages often took place between peasants of different villages within the same SMA. See G. William Skinner, "Marketing and social structure of rural China," *JAS* (November 1964, February 1965, and May 1965). A June 1961 CC decision had mandated that communes be reduced to the size of former *xiang* or amalgamated *xiang*: Fang Weizhong, ed., *Zhonghua renmin gongheguo jingji dashiji* (Record of major economic events in the PRC), 306.

conform roughly to the former standard marketing areas and made the most important economic unit within the commune, the team, coincide with either small villages themselves or with socially relatively cohesive neighborhoods within larger villages.

The shift from expertise toward mobilization in both urban and rural areas as of the conclusion of the Anti-Rightist Campaign meant that the apparatus best suited to mobilization efforts – the CCP – would assume a relatively greater role than it had under the Soviet-style strategy followed since 1953. This expansion in the span of control of the CCP would inevitably come at the cost of the government bureaucracy. Some administrative decentralization would strip power from central ministries. An important result of the discrimination against expertise would be the dismantling of the state statistical system, the bulwark of a development strategy that depended on expert calculation of possibilities and optimalities. And at the highest levels, the CCP apparatus directed by the Politburo and the Secretariat (headed by Deng Xiaoping) would play a far more important role, with the functions of the premier and the State Council reduced accordingly.

Two more sets of issues fed into the development of the Great Leap strategy. On a social level, the first FYP had adopted the Soviet approach to material and status differentials, with the result that Chinese urban society was becoming increasingly stratified by the mid-1950s. This stratification extended into the government bureaucracies, where the free supply system was replace by a complex system of civil service grades in 1955. Similar grading systems were applied to various sectors of industry, commerce, and the educational system. The natural results were increasing status consciousness among the Chinese and encouragement of the type of careerism that was good for economic growth but rubbed against Mao Zedong's revolutionary grain. A strategy that relied more on ideological and coercive than on economic and status incentives might upset this unwanted social spinoff of the first FYP.

Second, Mao's own position in the system would be affected by the type of economic development strategy pursued. The Chairman's personal political strengths lay in the areas of foreign policy (especially toward the great powers), rural policy, and issues of revolutionary change (essentially, defining how rapidly change could be carried out, given the prevailing mood and conditions in the country). Urban economics, and especially the technicalities of finance and planning, were subjects about which he knew very little. Thus, Mao complained bitterly at the Nanning Conference in January 1958 that the Finance Ministry had for several years been sending the Politburo position papers so technical and complex that he simply had to sign them without even reading them. This situation naturally limited Mao's role in the system, and he determined to change it by forcing through a strategy of development that shifted the action from the areas in which he lacked strength to those where he felt more confident.

On the most fundamental level, finally, the motivations producing the GLF strategy drew from very deep currents in the history of the Chinese Communist movement. Once before, when the revolution faced seemingly intractable odds, a creative set of military and political policies centered on mobilizing a wide range of forces had saved the day. The CCP had entered Yan'an as a bedraggled remnant of what it had been in the mid-1950s. By the end of World War II the CCP and its army had vastly increased in size, strength, and vigor, even though the intervening years had witnessed almost constant military challenges from the Guomindang or the Japanese. The CCP quite naturally tended in later years to idealize this time in the wilderness, seeing it as a period when the Party was truly close to the masses, when bureaucratism and social stratification did not tarnish revolutionary idealism, and when well-motivated leaders and their followers overcame seemingly insuperable odds to survive and eventually conquer. Given Mao's disgust with the sociopolitical results of the first FYP and the fundamental agricultural bottleneck that seemed to threaten the chances for the rapid industrial development that he craved, Mao and much of the rest of the top leadership seem to have harkened back to the Yan'an spirit (and methods) as the source of their hope. Mass mobilization, social leveling, attacks on bureaucratism, disdain for material obstacles – these approaches would again save the Chinese revolution for its founders.

Thus, a broad range of forces pushed the leadership, and Mao in particular, toward adoption of a Great Leap strategy in 1958. A developmental dilemma, combined with dissatisfaction over the social consequences of the Soviet model, produced the search for a mobilizational alternative to previous practice. Organizational tensions between the Party and state apparatuses and between basic-level governmental and economic units in the countryside added to the stresses. Finally, beginning at the Qingdao Conference in July 1957 and continuing through the following year, Mao began advocating a radically new approach toward making China strong and wealthy. This strategy, which was fleshed out during a series of meetings (at the Third Plenum in September–October, the Hangzhou and Manning conferences in January 1958, and the Chengdu Conference in March), called for use of organizational and mobilizational techniques to bring about simultaneous rapid development of agriculture and industry. The logical next step, the GLF, was formally adopted at the Second Session of the Eighth Party Congress in May 1958. One of its most prominent features, the communization of agriculture, became official policy at the Beidaihe Conference in August of that year.

The GLF strategy

Briefly, the strategy of the GLF had four key elements:[3]

1. To make up for a lack of capital in both industry and agriculture by fully mobilizing underemployed labor power, This approach would be especially important in the rural sector, where mass mobilization would produce essentially self-financed development that would solve the agricultural stumbling block to rapid overall growth and would provide inputs (especially food) for urban industrial growth. This, in turn, would allow China to accomplish the simultaneous development of industry and agriculture.
2. To carry out "planning" by setting ambitious goals for China's leading economic sectors and in essence simply encouraging any type of innovation necessary to permit the other sectors to catch up with these key sectors. "Bottlenecks be damned" captures the spirit of this approach.
3. In industry, to rely on both modern and traditional methods to enhance output. Thus, for example, major steel complexes would receive substantial new investment at the same time that "backyard" steel would be smelted by any group capable of doing so. Overall, the traditional sectors were to feed inputs into the modern sector while taking virtually nothing back in return.
4. In all areas, to disregard technical norms (and the specialists who stressed them) in favor of, in the lexicon of the times, achieving "more, faster, better, and more economical results." In practice the "more and faster" overwhelmed the "better and more economical."

This seemingly know-nothing approach appeared to work for a while. To an extent, of course, the appearances were false – the virtual destruction of the statistical system combined with tremendous pressure on cadres down the line to produce astonishing results. The not too surprising consequence was that an enormous amount of false reporting seriously misled the leadership as to the actual state of affairs in the country. Two elements did combine to make 1958 a year of substantial real economic achievements, however, and thus to lend some credibility to the Great Leap strategy.

First, the 1958 weather was exceptionally good, with the result that agricultural performance was better, other things being equal, than would normally have been the ease. The organizational confusion attendant on the rapid formation of communes undoubtedly decreased agricultural yields, but the underlying weather conditions were sufficiently favorable to give at least the appearance of abundance throughout most of that fateful year.

3 The economic strategy of the GLF is analyzed in *CHOC*, 14, Chapter 8.

Second, in the industrial sector many of the major projects that had been begun during the first FYP began to come on stream during 1958, producing impressive growth in industrial output. Again, objective conditions made it possible for a leadership that wanted to believe in the efficacy of the radical Great Leap strategy to find some support for its faith.

These various factors produced a rising crescendo of support for the GLF, both within the CCP and among the general populace, through the early and middle months of 1958. Foreign observers were astonished at the fervor of the popular efforts to leap into Communism by performing shock-force work tasks. Groups of peasants put in incredibly long hours with virtually no rest and sustained this grueling pace for weeks on end. The leadership's claims for the efficacy of these efforts grew as the fervor built. In some areas, the newly formed communes began to do away with money as a medium of exchange, and by the fall the common assumption that the country's perennial food problem had been solved led to free supplies of food for many commune dwellers. In carrying out this mass mobilization strategy, the CCP cadres took over an increasing portion of the work from their government counterparts, and at the center the Party Secretariat under Deng Xiaoping assumed unprecedented power and authority. Had the GLF produced even a substantial portion of what was hoped, undoubtedly it would have further knit together the already impressive solidarity of the central leadership. But things did not turn out that way.

Politics of the GLF

The record makes clear that Liu Shaoqi, Deng Xiaoping, and most other leaders supported the GLF strategy wholeheartedly throughout 1958. Indeed, the only obvious civilian dissenters at the Politburo level that year were Premier Zhou Enlai and the top economic administrator, Chen Yun. Within the military, many army leaders did not like the new obligations to support the militia and to participate in civilian work that the GLF imposed on the PLA. Perhaps the most prominent among these military dissenters was Defense Minister Marshal Peng Dehuai.

Liu Shaoqi and Deng Xiaoping had much to gain from the GLE. Both worked primarily in Party affairs and, as noted earlier, the CCP apparatus as a whole greatly expanded its power under the Leap. Deng personally had played a prominent role in the Anti-Rightist Campaign in 1957, and going back to the 1930s he could be considered to have been a part of Mao Zedong's personal clique in the Party. The GLF was primarily a Maoist alternative to the Soviet development strategy, and Deng identified himself closely with the success of this effort. He played a key role in managing the GLF via his position as head of the CCP Secretariat.

Liu Shaoqi had greater personal independence from Mao, but Liu also had to consider the succession. In the mid-1950's Mao had proposed that he should step back to the "second line," and by the beginning of 1958 he indicated that he would relinquish his position as head of state and remove himself from much of the day-to-day work in the Party leadership. In that way he could both determine the line of succession and devote himself more fully to working on the future direction of the Chinese revolution. During 1958 Liu Shaoqi probably had the succession very much on his mind, and personal support for Mao's plans would have been important in his strategy for obtaining the Chairman's blessing as the next in line.[4] Not surprisingly, therefore, Liu gave the keynote address on the GLF to the Second Session of the Eighth Party Congress, the meeting that formally adopted a Great Leap strategy for China. And in fact Liu did replace Mao as head of state when Mao relinquished that position in April 1959. In addition, of course, insofar as the GLF set China on the path of rapid progress toward Communism, it would create an enviable situation for a successor to inherit. There is no indication that during 1958 Liu Shaoqi felt it would do anything other than this.

The concerns of the other three leaders mentioned earlier are easily understood. Chen Yun's opposition centered on strongly held views about the proper development strategy for China to pursue, views that differed fundamentally from the core elements of the leap. Zhou Enlai certainly must have resented having his own organization – the State Council – assume a diminished position in China's development strategy, and Zhou may very well in addition have believed in a strategy closer to that advocated by Chen Yun. Peng Dehuai had differed with Mao over many issues since the 1940s. Peng had taken charge of the Hundred Regiments campaign against the Japanese then and was subsequently sharply criticized by Mao for the conception and conduct of this offensive. Peng Dehuai had led the Chinese troops in Korea, and under his command Mao's son was lost when his plane was shot down. At the conclusion of the Korean War, relations between Mao and Peng worsened. For these personal reasons alone, Peng may well have opposed a strategy so closely identified with Mao as was the GLF.

But Peng's opposition had stronger grounds than personal animosity. Peng wanted a strong, modernized, professional military organization, and he believed the Soviet Union was the only possible source of the necessary weapons, equipment, technology, and aid. Peng sought good relations with Moscow and, not surprisingly, modeled the PLA after the Red Army. Given his view of the importance of Soviet military aid, he could do little else. Mao,

---

4 Liu had formally obtained this in 1945, but that probably was not sufficient to make him fully confident as of 1958–9.

however, disagreed on all these counts. He felt that military spending had to be curtailed and that the best way to accomplish this would be to have the PLA enhance its capacity to wage guerilla war (to defend against invasion and prolonged occupation of the country) while at the same time developing an indigenous nuclear weapons capability. The latter would discourage the type of nuclear blackmail to which the PRC might otherwise be susceptible. The nuclear component of this strategy certainly put a premium on Soviet cooperation, but the conventional side suggested that China should develop its own military manuals and materials rather than rely on the Soviet model.

As noted earlier, Mao conceived of the GLF as a way to break out of the Soviet economic development model's constraints, given China's very different factor endowments. On the military side too, Mao now sought to cast off the Soviet model, and he made this clear at a prolonged enlarged meeting of the Military Affairs Commission (MAC). It met directly after the Great leap strategy was adopted by the Second Session of the Eighth Party Congress in May and continued until July 1958. Khrushchev had been supportive of Mao's desire for nuclear aid (for reasons having more to do with Communist bloc affairs than with Sino-Soviet relations), but this switch in China's conventional military strategy increased the already rapidly growing strains in Sino-Soviet relations.[5] To add insult to injury from Peng's perspective, the guerrilla conception of the role of the PLA demanded that the army create closer working relationships with the civilian population, a task that cut into military training and put the army in charge of the development and management of an enormous militia force.

Finally, at just this time Mao moved Lin Biao, long a close supporter on one of China's finest military tacticians, into a position on the Politburo that gave Lin a higher CCP rank than Peng. The implications must have been clear – to both Lin and Peng. During 1958 these tensions paled beside the overall enthusiasm of the bulk of the leadership for the GLF strategy; but when the Great Leap began to encounter serious problems, they rose to the surface to cause great resentment and prevent a timely shift in tactics for management of the GLF itself, ultimately producing a political and economic disaster of the first magnitude.

Inspection trips by the leaders during the fall of 1958 indicated that problems were brewing. In some places, peasant stories of food shortages belied the official statistics that showed abundance almost everywhere. In other areas, the excellent crops were not harvested fully and on time because too many workers had been shifted into local industry or had left to join the large state-run factories in the cities. Indeed, urban population growth sky-rocketed during

---

5 On Sino-Soviet relations during this period, see *CHOC*, 14, Chapter II.

1958. At the same time, the performance of the steel sector made it clear that the original utopian goal of producing 30 million tons of steel in 1959 (1957 production had been 5.35 million tons!) could not be reached. Thus, by late 1958 Mao realized that adjustments were necessary, although he still felt the basic GLF strategy was sound.

Mao began to advocate these adjustments at the First Zhengzhou Conference in November and then followed this up at the Wuchang Central Work Conference and at the Sixth Plenum that followed it in November–December 1958. He called for the 1959 steel target to be reduced from 30 million to 20 million tons, and he suggested that the government publicize grain production statistics that were lower than the highest internal estimates of the time. Mao himself characterized his approach in this period as having combined the revolutionary fervor of the August Beidaihe Meeting with a practical spirit.[6] But soon the practical spirit – spurred on by alarming findings about the actual state procurement of grain at the end of 1958 – forced the Chairman to take stronger measures to rein in the increasingly obvious excesses of the GLF.

By the time the Chinese leadership gathered to map out strategy for 1959 at the Second Zhengzhou meeting in late February, Mao had decided that strong words were necessary to prevent the Leap from becoming a disaster. Focusing on problems in the rural communes, Mao declared himself in favor of "right opportunism." Essentially, he demanded that the level of communization be decreased, with more ownership rights being vested below the commune level itself. He called for a less cavalier attitude toward the interests of the basic-level cadres and peasants and threatened (for dramatic effect) to resign from the Party if appropriate reforms were not adopted. One senses here that Mao still fully believed in the correctness of the basic Great Leap strategy but that he worried that "leftist" errors among cadres carrying out the policy would produce a catastrophe that would do great harm both to China and to the Chairman's own position. During this same period, Mao invited Chen Yun to assume an active role in devising appropriate industrial targets and implementing related measures to make the Great Leap more rational and effective.

Events of the following few months made it clear that Mao was having trouble bringing middle-level cadres to heel in rectifying the errors of 1958. Some of the early stalwarts of the Leap, such as Wu Zhipu in Henan and Li Jinquan in Sichuan, showed little inclination to pull back on their earlier positions now. Ke Qingshi, the First Party Secretary in Shanghai and one of the key supporters of the backyard steel production drive, was reluctant to admit the problems of this effort. And more generally, sentiment in favor of

6 Mao, *Wansui* (1969), 258.

going all out seemed to remain strong at the provincial through commune levels of the Party apparatus.

It is not completely clear just why this should have been the case. It may have reflected in part the fact that these cadres had won increased power and influence as a result of the Great Leap strategy and yet had not worked at the basic levels, where they would feel more acutely the personal tensions the policy was creating. Also, the greater concentration of peasant cadres at the provincial through commune levels may partially explain this phenomenon, as the Great Leap had some of the atmosphere of a millenarian movement that would free the countryside from the chains of the cities and free the peasant cadres from the scrutiny of the urban-bred experts. In any case, all evidence suggests that Mao devoted much attention throughout the remainder of the spring of 1959 to reining in the excesses of the Great Leap in order to make his basic development strategy work.

The Tibetan revolt broke this concentration on development problems during the spring of 1959. This border region, whose society was so vastly different from the socialist community the Chinese sought to establish, had been smoldering for some time. Although a truce of sorts had been worked out that had kept things calm in Tibet through the promised postponement of significant reforms, news of the Great Leap that came in from elsewhere significantly raised tensions. There had been revolts by Tibetans living in Sichuan in 1956 and in Gansu and Qinghai provinces in 1958, with refugees from these areas living in Lhasa and contributing to the unease there. Some specific actions and missteps by Han soldiers and civilians in Tibet in early 1959 sparked an actual revolt in this tense atmosphere, and the Dalai Lama fled to India for safety.

The revolt evidently took the Chinese by surprise, and additional troops had to be sent in from outside the region to quell it. Although the main body of the revolt was put down with relative ease, the issue of how to handle the diplomatic and security fallout continued to trouble the leadership into the summer.[7] There is, however, no evidence suggesting that the leadership was divided over how to deal with this issue at the time.

THE LUSHAN CONFERENCE, JULY 1959

By July, when the top leadership gathered at the mountain resort of Lushan, the Tibetan revolt had been suppressed militarily, even if its diplomatic repercussions were just beginning. Mao and his colleagues now turned their attention

---

7 Peng Dehuai subsequently recollected that he had the Tibetan question very much in mind as the Lushan Conference of July got under way: *Peng Dehuai zishu* (Peng Dehuai's own account), 267.

back to reviewing the economic situation and mapping out a new strategy. Mao, at least, seems to have felt fairly well satisfied that his efforts at reining in the excesses of the Great Leap were achieving adequate results.

The Lushan Conference, however, lasted for almost the entire month of July and proved to be one of the most fateful in the history of the PRC. By the end of the meeting, Mao had launched a ferocious attack against Peng Dehuai, China's defense minister and one of the ten marshals in the PLA, and had set in motion the effort necessary to replace Peng with Marshal Lin Biao. While still indicating that consolidation rather than expansion of the Great Leap was the order of the day, Mao had also launched an Anti-Right Opportunist Campaign that swamped the consolidation effort and itself produced a "second leap," with disastrous consequences. An enormous amount of data have been made available on the Lushan Conference over the years, but key questions about personal motivations and individual strategies still remain unanswered.

Indeed, the problems of interpretation extend back to before the conference itself. Peng had traveled to several Warsaw Pact countries and returned to Beijing on 12 June 1959. He had met with Khrushchev on this trip and may well have voiced his general consternation at the commune program and its effects on, among other things, the army and Sino-Soviet relations. In any case, almost immediately after Peng's return to Beijing, Khrushchev suddenly canceled the agreement under which Moscow was providing Beijing with the nuclear aid so valued by Mao and launched a public attack on the commune idea, the first such public criticism of the Chinese effort by the Soviet leader.

When Mao unleashed his counterattack against Peng, he tried to suggest that Khrushchev and Peng had colluded in a strategy that had Khrushchev pressure the Chinese over the Great Leap at the same time that Peng attacked the policy privately at Lushan. To add further mystery to the situation, one of Peng's close collaborators in his activities at Lushan was Zhang Wentian, a vice-minister of foreign affairs who had long had close ties with the Soviet Union. MacFarquhar suggests, indeed, that it was Zhang who put Peng up to his critique of the GLF at Lushan.[8]

In any case, at Lushan itself Peng Dehuai first voiced some criticisms of the Great Leap during small group discussions that overall seemed in keeping with the types of remarks Mao himself had been making during the previous few months. The one exception lay in a comment to the effect that Mao may not have fully understood what was going on in his own home village, as it appeared that the people there had received far more state aid than Mao had realized (an explosive assertion, given Mao's implicit claim that *he* understood China's rural situation better than any other leader).

---

8 Roderick MacFarquhar, *Origins of the Cultural Revolution*, 2. 204–6.

On 14 July Peng wrote a letter to Mao that summed up his feelings about the problems of the GLF. Peng may have decided to take this action as a result of what he perceived to be a disturbing and continuing air of unreality at Lushan, or he may have been incited by Zhang Wentian. Indeed, it is possible that Peng's object was to embarrass Mao and possibly to upset the succession to Liu Shaoqi that Mao had set in train. Under interrogation during the Cultural Revolution, Peng claimed that he had intended the letter as a heartfelt and respectful communication to the Chairman for the latter's eyes only.[9] Much to his surprise, however, the Chairman had the letter printed and circulated to all participants at Lushan and gave it the rather formal sounding title of "Peng Dehuai's letter of opinion" (*Peng Dehuai de yijian shu*).

On 23 July Mao responded to the letter with a vengeance. Intervening comments by Zhang Wentian and probably by others at the meeting may have convinced the Chairman he had a snowballing problem on his hands that he had better deal with quickly and decisively. Alternatively, it is possible that Mao had essentially set up Peng once he had received the marshal's letter, using his actions as an excuse to replace Peng with his own favorite, Lin Biao. If the latter is true, the Khrushchev's open criticism of the communes in a speech in Eastern Europe on 18 July played right into Mao's hands.

In any case, Mao's counterattack on 23 July drew a sharp line between permissible criticism and Peng's "right opportunist" remarks. He claimed that Peng sought to attack the Chairman rather than simply give advice on how to run the GLF better. He asked sarcastically why Peng had not expressed his views at meetings earlier in the spring, since Peng by then had already carried out the investigations that had led him to his negative conclusions. Mao reminded his audience that he himself had been sharply critical of the methods used in the GLF, but Peng had held his silence. Now, at a major meeting designed to set the tone for policy over the coming months leading up to the tenth anniversary of the victory of the revolution in October, Peng had chosen to launch an attack out of the blue, and evidently with substantial support from some quarters. The fact that Peng lived in the house next to Mao's in the Zhongnanhai compound in Beijing must have added to the Chairman's sense of chagrin and betrayal. Mao's conclusion was clear – Peng had so grossly violated permissible behavior that he and his "clique" would have to undergo rectification. Khrushchev's criticism of the commune movement opened Peng to the accusation that he had taken his criticisms to the Soviet leader to enlist his help before he had made them known to his fellow members of the Politburo.

9 For Peng's recollections of Lushan while under interrogation and the only authorized version of the letter to be published in China, see *Peng Dehuai zishu*, 265–87.

Mao's biting presentation shocked his audience. Peng himself did not sleep for nights afterward, reportedly being caught totally unawares by Mao's response. Given that much of what Peng had to say had in fact been the type of language Mao himself had encouraged during the previous few months, others were evidently baffled by the vehemence of the Chairman's position. As noted, Mao did have a legitimate complaint about Peng's previous silence. Also, some of Peng's comments in the letter to Mao seemed in a subtle way to be direct and serious criticisms of the Chairman personally rather than simply of the policies the Chairman had encouraged (and about which Peng had remained largely silent). Yet Mao's reaction was so contrary to normal practice that there may well have been some additional considerations at stake.

First, Peng belonged to the group of marshals that in general had been disgruntled over the distribution of top posts after the Communist victory in 1949. During the several decades of struggle for power, most of the key CCP leaders had been in the base areas, but some had spent much of their time either running the underground networks in China's cities (as had Liu Shaoqi) or doing formal liaison work with the Guomindang (as had Zhou Enlai). After 1949, the latter groups took a disproportionate share of top posts. The shadowy Gao Gang affair in 1954–5, the only Politburo-level purge before the Lushan meeting, seems to have involved a challenge by some of the former base area leaders (principally to Zhou Enlai and Liu Shaoqi) for leading posts in the new regime. Peng Dehuai was allegedly involved in that affair, but the desire to limit the damage produced a decision to hold the resulting purge to the smallest possible number of people. Peng's actions at Lushan may, therefore, have been seen by Mao as his second attempt to position himself for higher office. The fact that Mao had recently moved Peng's rival, Lin Biao into a higher-ranking CCP post than Peng's suggests that the Chairman had, by contrast, in fact been looking for a way to ease Peng out of power. Peng's criticism at Lushan may have provided an opportunity for Mao, with circulation of Peng's letter as the first step in this maneuver.

Several months before Lushan, Liu Shaoqi had assumed the post that Mao relinquished as Chairman of the PRC. This reaffirmed Liu's claim to be the successor to Mao, and Liu's practice began for the first time to be given equal status with that of Mao in public displays. This transition may well have heightened the implicit contention over the succession issue and sparked Peng to undertake more serious action than he otherwise might have taken. It may also have increased Mao's own sensitivities to the succession dimension of the issue and made him see Peng's criticism more readily in terms of a bid to weaken Mao's power (and Mao's ability to designate his own successor).

Zhang Wentian also plays into this scenario. Zhang had become the General Secretary of the Party during the Long March but was later eased out by Mao in Yan'an. A highly educated and articulate man, Zhang had been demoted bit by bit since 1949. His close ties with the Soviet Union made him the natural choice for Beijing's first ambassador to Moscow, but when he returned from that post he languished as a vice-minister of foreign affairs. Perhaps more important, he was demoted from full to alternate member status on the Politburo at the Eighth Party Congress in 1956 (he was formally removed from the Politburo altogether in 1961). Zhang may well have viewed his rightful position as more exalted than the one to which he was being consigned, and with the tensions over the GLF and over the succession in 1959 he may have decided to act. His private conversations with Peng Dehuai at Lushan could have sharpened his sense of opportunity, and he may have manipulated the less sophisticated Peng into making the comments that the latter put forward. Through Peng, Zhang may have felt he could ally his personal ambitions with those of many of the old marshals. Also, Peng was held in close affection among many top leaders, and Zhang was not. In this scenario, then, Peng may have been more a stooge than a plotter, used by Zhang to create the atmosphere at Lushan that would justify Zhang's own eloquent critique of the GLF. Zhang delivered such a critique at length at the meeting on 20 July.[10]

Mao would probably have been highly sensitive to this type of maneuvering by Zhang, and this may have determined the framework in which the Chairman viewed Peng's criticism. This would also help explain the fact that Mao waited nine days after receipt of Peng's letter before making a counterattack. Alternatively, of course, Mao may simply have wanted to circulate Peng's letter and allow enough time for any sympathizers to show themselves in subsequent discussions before the Chairman made his own strong views plain. Should Mao have accepted the "Zhang Wentian as instigator, Peng Dehuai as stooge" scenario, the Chairman could still have decided to counterattack by aiming primarily at Peng, for several reasons: his general desire to downgrade Peng and promote Lin Biao; his need for a more well-known scapegoat; or Peng's own discussions with Khrushchev, which may have made him the more vulnerable of the two.

One last possibility is that Peng's challenge was implicitly more dangerous to Mao than Zhang's. Unlike Zhang, Peng had close ties to a key constituency, the old marshals. Also, unlike Zhang's, Peng's position as minister of defense gave him unique access to information to understand the views of two key groups that Mao was anxious to keep firmly under his own aegis: China's peasants (whose views Peng learned via military mail and other sources, as almost all conscripts in the PLA were from the countryside); and the PLA

10 MacFarquhar presents the strongest case for the scenario involving Zhang Wentian as a principal instigator: MacFarquhar, *Origins*, 2. 204–6.

itself. Thus Mao may have felt it was imperative to train his fire on Peng, even if Zhang was the key figure behind the criticisms at Lushan.

The confrontation at the Lushan conference was then played out during the Lushan Plenum (the Eighth Plenum of the Eighth Central Committee) in August and an Enlarged MAC meeting in September. During the latter, Peng formally lost his defense portfolio and was told to engage in study for several years. Zhang Wentian and two others (Huang Kecheng, chief of staff of the PLA, and Zhou Xiaozhou, first secretary of Mao's home province of Hunan) were similarly purged as members of a (seemingly misnamed)[11] "military clique."

The consequences of Lushan

As suggested previously, the long-term consequences of the Lushan Conference and the Peng Dehuai affair were profound. One of the most significant was that Mao seems at Lushan to have broken the unwritten rules that had governed debate among the top leadership to that point. Before Lushan, it was accepted that any leader could freely voice his opinions at a Party gathering, and debate could be heated. Nobody would be taken to task subsequently for what he said, as long as he formally accepted and acted in accord with the final decision reached. But Mao's actions at Lushan can be interpreted as having changed all that.

First, Mao labeled internal criticism by a top colleague "unprincipled factional activity." He then demanded that others choose between himself and his adversary and that the loser be punished. At a minimum, this stance would hinder future free discussion among Politburo members. Given the fact that it required almost all other top leaders to take a stance,[12] it undoubtedly sowed some personal bitterness that would later bear fruit. There is no evidence that any top-ranking leader voted against Mao after the Chairman had drawn the line at Lushan.

The Peng Dehuai affair also produced some personnel changes of both short- and long-term significance. The most immediate result was Lin Biao's promotion to minister of defense. Lin, as noted, was a long-time follower of Mao's, and his new position gave Mao perhaps more secure control over the PLA than had previously been the case. Lin, in turn, was determined to keep Peng from staging a political comeback that would threaten Lin's own

---

11 Peng several years later still expressed befuddlement as to why the four of them were called a military clique. Aside from Peng's denial that any clique existed, two of the four were not connected with the military. But Peng recalled that his detractors had been absolutely adamant in giving them this label. See *Peng Dehuai zishu*, 278–9.
12 Some, like Deng Xiaoping and Chen Yun, were absent from Lushan for different reasons.

power.[13] As will be seen later, this issue continued to fester in Chinese politics throughout the early 1960s.

Other personnel shifts took place in connection with Lushan. Luo Ruiqing yielded his position as minister of public security to become PLA chief of staff. A more obscure change elevated Hua Guofeng to a higher post in Hunan province than he had previously held. Hua's promotion may have stemmed from an act of loyalty to Mao during the Chairman's time of need at Lushan. If so, Hua's service probably consisted of supporting Mao's version of developments in his home village of Shaoshan against the charges of Peng Dehuai, backed up by Hua's superior, Hunan First Secretary Zhou Xiaozhou. Hua's willingness to undercut a long-time mentor in service to Mao stood him in good stead more than a decade later, when Mao again needed loyal subordinates to ferret out opposition in the wake of the Lin Biao affair.

Finally, as noted earlier, the dynamics of the Lushan meetings and the campaign against right opportunism that followed cut short the rectification and consolidation efforts Mao had set in motion during the previous half year. Opposition to opportunism swept the country during the fall of 1959, removing all those who had expressed doubts about the efficacy of the GLF policies during the previous months. Not surprisingly, this campaign effectively terminated the spring 1959 effort to rectify and consolidate the communes, and by early 1960 a new Great Leap was under way. Mao encouraged this development through, for example, his March 1960 endorsement of a new "constitution" for the Anshan Iron and Steel Works that replaced the previous management approach there (modeled after the steel workers at Magnitogorsk) with one that put primary emphasis on politics. In April, the National People's Congress (NPC) formally adopted the Chairman's twelve-year agricultural program (a prominent feature of the brief "little" leap in the first half of 1956), and at the same NPC Mao's close supporter, Tan Zhenlin, again endorsed the commune program. Indeed, these spring 1960 months witnessed an attempt to organize urban communes and a renewal of the effort to "send down" (*xiafang*) cadres. It is not clear what occurred – other than the attack by Peng Dehuai – that made Mao abandon his analysis of early 1959 in favor of renewed faith in a Great Leap strategy. The fact that during the first half of 1960 the leaders focused their attention primarily on Sino-Soviet relations permitted this leap strategy to mushroom to disastrous proportions.

The second Great Leap failed with a vengeance. According to figures released in 1981, agricultural output in 1960 was only 75.5 percent of that in 1958

---

13 Peng in fact was designated to head the effort to develop a "third front" in Southwest China in 1965 in response to Mao's increasing sense of a security threat from the United States. But the Cultural Revolution cut short Peng's effort. Peng was summoned to Beijing, where he endured Red Guard criticism, beatings, and incarceration until his death in 1974.

(1961 output went down another 2.4 percent). Light industry uses primarily agricultural products as inputs, and thus light industrial shifts tend to lag one year behind those in agricultural output. In 1960, light industrial output decreased by 9.8 percent. It then declined by 21.6 percent in 1961 and by another 8.4 percent in 1962. The cumulative impact was to produce a serious goods famine to match the food shortages. Heavy industrial output also declined sharply, going down 46.6 percent in 1961 compared with 1960, and another 22.2 percent in 1962 over 1961.[14]

Overall, this renewed leap in late 1959 and 1960 produced the most devastating famine of the twentieth century in China (and probably in the world). The fundamental cause of this mass starvation was political, in that mistaken policies (such as insisting that the peasants leave land fallow in 1959 to avoid losses from not having enough storage facilities to handle the anticipated surplus) led inevitably to serious food shortfalls. These shortfalls were exacerbated enormously by the regime's blindness to the problem, to the extent that high agricultural procurement quotas continued to drain the countryside of available supplies into 1961. Bad weather and the mid-1960 withdrawal of Soviet technicians added to the difficulties, but neither of these latter two elements would have produced the more than 20 million "excess" deaths (deaths over and above the normal death rate) that occurred during 1959–61.[15]

The terrible consequences of the renewed Great Leap and the rancor over the purge of Peng Dehuai combined to unravel the political consensus that had held the Yan'an leadership together through its days in the wilderness and its first decade in power. This process of political deterioration developed through a range of issues, any one of which in itself might have been manageable. But taken together they set the stage for the final split of the Yan'an leadership: the Great Proletarian Cultural Revolution (GPCR). Six different strands were woven into this tapestry of political decay during the early 1960s.

First, Khrushchev's decision to try to bring a halt to the GLF and demonstrate to China the great importance of its Soviet connection by swiftly withdrawing Soviet advisors and aid at the height of the 1960 crisis had the unintended effort of shocking Mao into a fundamental reevaluation of the development of the Russian Revolution. To be sure, Mao had previously found much to fault in the evolution of the Soviet Union and the actions of its leaders, but the Chairman had not previously thought in terms of a fundamental degeneration of the Soviet system. Khrushchev's crude pressure tactics

14 Figures from an article by Ma Hong in *RMRB*, 29 December 1981, 5, trans. in *FBIS*, 8 January 1982, 11–12. Ma Hong does not indicate how his percentages are calculated; presumably he used gross value of output each year.
15 From 1959 to 1961 the total size of China's population fell by 13.5 million. The number of excess deaths was, of course, far higher. State Statistical Bureau, comp., *Statistical yearbook of China, 1984*, 81. For a further discussion, see *CHOC*, 14, Chapter 8, notes 27 and 28.

raised this possibility, and the thought was frightening. By implication, if the Soviet revolution could change from socialist to fascist (or social imperialist), then any socialist revolution was in theory reversible. Given Mao's very much weakened position in Beijing as a result of the Great Leap fiasco, he evidently began to fear that his life's work in China might have laid the basis ultimately not for the most just society in the world but, rather, for an extremely exploitative system.

Mao thus began to devote a large portion of his energy to dealing with the Soviet issue, and he brought Kang Sheng, who had training in Marxism-Leninism and understood Soviet affairs well, to center stage to help him wrestle with Sino-Soviet relations. When within several years Mao began to have very serious doubts about the course his own successors were following, he then used the struggle with "Soviet revisionism" to give publicity in China to what amounted in reality to a critique of the policies of his own colleagues. Relatedly, Kang Sheng had learned his approach to political infighting in the Soviet Union of the mid-1930s, and Kang's ascendancy in Beijing in the early 1960s therefore increased the tendency in the Forbidden City to wage struggles by Stalinist rather than more traditionally Maoist rules of the game.

Second, Mao's own prestige in the highest levels of the CCP suffered badly because of the GLF fiasco. Indeed, the Chairman made some form of self-criticism at a CCP Central Work Conference in Beijing in June 1961. As noted earlier, Mao had in any case planned to retreat to the second line in the Politburo as of 1959 so that he could devote more time to major issues and be less involved in daily administrative affairs. But once the disasters of 1960–1 became fully evident, Mao found himself pushed more effectively out of day-to-day affairs than he would have liked. At the same time, some of his previous key supporters, such as Deng Xiaoping, no longer paid him the deference he felt was his due (Lin Biao proved to be the notable exception). Thus, for example, Mao complained during the Cultural Revolution that Deng had not listened to him since 1959. Deng had, as noted earlier, previously been a key supporter of Mao's. But when it came time to pick up the pieces from the GLF catastrophe, Deng played a central role via his stewardship of the CCP Secretariat, and he did not fully agree with the Chairman over the proper remedies and the lessons to be drawn.

The third strand is precisely the fact that different leaders drew different conclusions from the utter failure of the GLF. Mao personally recognized, as his subsequent actions showed, that political mobilization cannot itself produce rapid economic growth, and thus the Chairman did not proclaim major production increases as a goal of the Cultural Revolution. But as the GPCR also illustrates, Mao retained his faith in the efficacy of political mobilization to produce changes in outlook, values, and the distribution of political power.

Most of Mao's supporters against Peng Dehuai at Lushan, by contrast, concluded after their investigations of the situation in 1960–2 that large-scale political campaigns and the entire Yan'an style of "high tide" politics had become counterproductive in virtually every way. Thus, although Mao no longer saw political movements as the basis for economic growth, many of his colleagues wanted to eschew campaign politics altogether.

Fourth, the CCP itself had taken charge of running the GLF, and the CCP suffered in prestige and organizational competence as a result of the failure of this monumental effort. The demoralization of the lower ranks of the CCP became still more acute as the country slowly pulled out of the Great Leap because in the end the cadres who had supported the second Leap were now purged for their "leftism," while Mao's own responsibility was carefully shielded to protect his legitimacy. For example, Mao's June 1961 self-criticism was never circulated to lower levels of the Party. Given the enormous strains on basic-level CCP cadres during 1960–2, it is not surprising that many lost their sense of revolutionary élan, thus giving the CCP apparatus to an extent feet of clay. The question of how best to rectify the basic-level CCP organs caused additional dissension in the upper levels, as various leaders proposed their own somewhat different methods of dealing with this important issue.

A fifth problem concerned disagreement over just how quickly China was recovering from the depredations of the GLF. Different assessments naturally justified different measures for bringing about a more normal situation. Mao tended to be more optimistic than many of his colleagues as this issue was debated in 1962, and indeed the Chairman seems to have begun to suspect that the pessimists were trying to limit his own flexibility and room for maneuver in the system. As Mao became more concerned with revisionism, this set of issues assumed increasing importance for him.

Finally, whatever one's views about the speed of China's recovery, there was no doubt about the extraordinary extent of the damage that the GLF (and especially its second stage) had done. In other words, the events of 1959–61 essentially vindicated what Peng Dehuai had said and written at Lushan. To add insult to injury, Peng carried out fairly extensive rural investigations during 1962, and that August he summarized his findings and submitted an 80,000-character document to the Central Committee justifying his rehabilitation on the grounds that his principled criticism at Lushan had been correct. But Lin Biao could not tolerate Peng's rehabilitation, and Mao did not want it either. In addition, by 1962 Mao may already have been thinking about the need to rely increasingly on Lin and the PLA as his concerns about his other colleagues grew. Thus, Mao blocked Peng's rehabilitation – and in so doing did further damage to the norms that had governed relations among the leaders to that date.

AFTER THE LEAP: THE LIU-DENG PROGRAM

In sum, the failure of the GLF left a full menu of problems on the plates of the central leaders. These varied from interpersonal relations among the top people, to frayed institutional capabilities, to the relation of foreign to domestic policy. Basic political methods as well as immediate economic and other goals were at issue. All these concerns, moreover, interacted in a way that tended to heighten Mao's suspicions and make it more difficult to find agreed-upon solutions. In more detail, these issues arose as follows:

The leadership began to turn its attention to coping with the Great Leap disaster during a meeting at Beidaihe in July–August 1960. The termination of all Soviet aid to China that June forced Beijing to think in terms of a self-reliant development effort and to take stock of the deteriorating situation in the countryside. Several types of initiatives flowed out of Beidaihe and subsequent deliberations over the following few months, as the magnitude of the summer crop failure became evident. First, the second Great Leap was formally terminated, and the guiding policy now became one of "agriculture as the base, industry as the leading factor," with "readjustment, consolidation, filling out, and raising standards" replacing the previous formula of "more, faster, better, and more economical results." Mao had first put forward the "agriculture as the base" formula in 1959, but it was not implemented until the fall of 1960. It became official CCP policy at the Ninth Plenum in January 1961.

Second, the CCP center sought to increase its control over its badly damaged nationwide apparatus through the re-creation of six regional bodies. (The parallel regional government bodies that had existed in the early postliberation years were not established.) Relatedly, efforts were made to salvage the situation in the countryside through moving back toward a system that provided greater material incentives. The disastrous fall harvest drove home the magnitude of the problem to the extent that in November Zhou Enlai presided over the drafting of an emergency measure on rural policy, called the Twelve Articles of Peoples Communes. This stopgap document essentially permitted great decentralization within the communes. Indeed, in Byung-joon Ahn's words, with the implementation of the Twelve Articles, "the GLF simply collapsed."[16]

Taking the pressure off cadres to implement GLF policies did not, however, make clear where the CCP should go from there. The specific reasons for the failure of the Great Leap remained unclear, and the CCP had not yet devised appropriate responses to put the country back on a long-term path of

---

16 Byung-joon Ahn, *Chinese politics and the Cultural Revolution*, 47.

development. Rather, during the spring of 1961, local leaders were in general given great leeway to implement whatever measures – even including, in many places, a de facto dissolution of the communes – they felt were necessary to alleviate the famine that was devastating China. On a policy level, two types of responses were adopted. The first, initiated by Lin Biao and focused on the military, stressed renewed study of politics as a way to boost morale and increase discipline. The second, led by Liu Shaoqi and Deng Xiaoping, produced a series of investigations that provided the material used for programmatic policy documents in major spheres of work.

In the military, in September 1960, Lin called for a program of concentrated study of Mao's works. Famine in the countryside had produced considerable demoralization among the soldiers, and Lin felt it important to revive political work to combat it. Since this effort was directed in general toward barely educated peasant recruits, it inevitably involved a simplification and dogmatization of Mao's Thought. The attempt to make Mao's Thought comprehensible to simple soldiers eventually produced the *Quotations from Chairman Mao Zedong*, the "little red book," which would become the Bible of the Red Guards during the Cultural Revolution. During 1960–3, however, those responsible for work in urban China disparaged the idea that Lin's dogmatic exegesis of Mao's writing could serve any useful purpose outside the military.

Liu and Deng supervised the investigation and drafting process that culminated in a series of programmatic documents that are generally known by the number of articles in each. During 1961–2 the following major policy papers were produced: Sixty Articles on People's Communes; Seventy Articles on Industry; Fourteen Articles on Science; Thirty-five Articles on Handicraft Trades; Six Articles on Finance; Eight Articles on Literature and Art; Sixty Articles on Higher Education; and Forty Articles on Commercial Work. Although, of course, the specifics concerning the drafting process varied for each of these policy papers, all shared some elements. In each case a Party leader took charge of the drafting process. Thus, Mao oversaw the drafting of the Sixty Points, Bo Yibo supervised the Seventy Articles on Industry (after preliminary work under the aegis of Li Fuchun), Li Xiannian covered finance, Zhou Yang and Lu Dingyi managed literature and art, Peng Zhen handled education, and so forth.

In addition, three broad policy groups were established under the Secretariat to oversee and coordinate policy toward major issue areas: Li Fuchun and Chen Yun's group reviewed economic policies, Peng Zhen's took charge of cultural and educational affairs, and Deng Xiaoping's covered political and legal work. This mode of operation thus had Chen Yun, for example, make significant policy reports and pronouncements in the following areas in 1961: fertilizer production, foreign trade, urban population growth, agricultural policy, and coal production. In early 1962, as will be noted, Chen became centrally involved in the overall evaluation of China's conditions and the policies to be pursued in the future.[17]

In drafting the various program documents, the person in charge typically first ascertained the actual situation and problems through carrying out on-the-spot investigations, often including (where appropriate) visits to units or locales with which he had ties from the past. In addition, meetings were convened with the experts or practitioners involved so as to mobilize their support and solicit their opinions. These documents went through a number of drafts, most of which reflected additional consultation both within the Party and among the non-Party experts. This presumption that experts could make valuable contributions conflicted sharply with the approach Lin Biao was taking at the very time in the military. To Lin, Mao's Thought contained both the answers and the source of any necessary inspiration. The division among top leaders in the wake of the GLF disaster thus went beyond personal political likes and dislikes and included fundamental aspects of policy process and political calculation.

The substance of the policies developed by the apparatus under Liu Shaoqi and Deng Xiaoping also struck at the heart of the assumptions that underlay the GLF. In fertilizer production, for example, Chen Yun called for construction of fourteen additional plants, each with a 50,000-ton-per-year capacity for production of synthetic ammonia. These plants would be large and modern, supplanting the inefficient small-scale chemical fertilizer production that had become so popular during the GLF. They would also require substantial imports of key components from abroad, moving China away from its previous policy of self-reliance. Bo Yibo's Seventy Articles on Industry placed renewed stress on the role of experts and on the use of material incentives – almost directly contradicting the Anshan Iron and Steel Constitution that Mao had promulgated the previous year. The Eight Articles on Literature and Art promised the reintroduction of traditional art forms and permitted a broader range of topics to be explored by artists. The Sixty Articles on Education stressed quality of education and undercut many of the locally run (*minban*) schools that had been opened as a part of the GLF strategy. And the Sixty Articles on People's Communes articulated a detailed set of regulations that fixed the team as the basic accounting unit, made provision for private plots,

---

17 The precise institutional roles of various CCP and state organs in this process are not clear. The Secretariat under Deng Xiaoping seems to have assumed overall charge of the drafting of these documents. But key individuals involved, including Bo Yibo. Zhou Yang, Lu Dingyi (until 1962), and Chen Yun did not themselves serve on the Secretariat. Evidently the Secretariat tapped the resources of a range of organs, including the pertinent State Council staff offices, to develop the policies noted. The role of the State Council in this drafting process remains unclear. It did, of course, become involved in the implementation of these policies once they had been approved by the Politburo.

and in general tried to shift agricultural production toward a system that provided greater material incentives for peasant labor.

These policies overall marked a dramatic shift from the priorities of the GLF. They brought experts and expertise back to center stage, produced greater reliance on modern inputs to achieve growth, reimposed central bureaucratic controls over various spheres of activity, and appealed to the masses more on the basis of material self-interest than of ideological mobilization. There is no evidence that Mao Zedong objected to these trends during 1961. Indeed, Mao himself had actively participated in drafting the Sixty Articles on Peoples Communes and had called for serious investigations to be carried out at the Guangzhou meeting in March 1961. In June the Chairman had made a self-criticism at a central work conference in Beijing. But as these investigations and consultations yielded to policy programs, Mao evidently became increasingly disconcerted – and he was not alone.

The Seven Thousand Cadres Conference, January–February 1962

The situation erupted during 1962, when basic disagreement arose as to how quickly the country was recovering and, therefore, over what future goals and time frames should be. In January–February a Seven Thousand Cadres Work Conference convened to review methods of leadership and to sum up the situation. There was more agreement on the former than on the latter. Liu Shaoqi made the key report and several other speeches to this conference, and he called for greater use of democratic centralism and less personal command by key individuals. In addresses on 26 and 27 January, he blamed much of the recent trouble on the Party center and stressed the importance of avoiding the brutal purges and counterpurges that had racked the Party during the twists and turns of the previous few years. Liu specifically criticized the vehemence of the attack on right opportunism in the wake of the Lushan Conference, and he is reported to have called for the rehabilitation of Peng Dehuai, among other rightists. Mao's own talk to the conference on 30 January generally endorsed these themes, and Mao informed the cadres in the audience that he himself had made a self-criticism the previous June (he also warned them to be prepared to do the same). Thus, this conference in general helped to patch up the rather tattered decision-making apparatus within the Party.

But in other areas the conference failed to produce a consensus. In terms of what had caused the Great Leap disaster, Liu argued that wrong political decisions accounted for 70 percent, with the Soviet withdrawal of aid and the several years of bad weather accounting for the other 30 percent. Mao felt this stood the true situation on its head. Liu also felt that the economy still remained in a crisis and would take a long time to put back into shape.

Mao argued, by contrast, that things had now largely returned to normal. Perhaps Mao meant his evaluation to apply only to the political and not the economic situation. Liu, in any case, appears to have harbored a far gloomier assessment of the general situation than Mao at this time. His more pessimistic evaluation would, in turn, provide a rationale for more far-reaching measures to salvage the situation.

Interestingly, Zhou Enlai supported Mao at this meeting and seems to have given an overall positive assessment of the GLF. On substantive issues later in 1962, by contrast, Zhou strongly backed Liu Shaoqi and Chen Yun. Thus, the premier's performance at the Seven Thousand Cadres Conference evidently reflected his operational practice of siding with Mao whenever there was an open clash more than his substantive agreement with the Chairman's position. Zhou is often compared by Chinese to a "willow branch," and his actions during the spring of 1962 reconfirm the appropriateness of a characterization that includes both strength and a graceful ability to bend with the wind. Not surprisingly, Mao also received strong verbal backing from Lin Biao at the conference.

Three other leaders were less clear in their positions. Deng Xiaoping reiterated the correctness of Mao Zedong's Thought but then supported Liu Shaoqi on substantive issues such as the rehabilitation of rightists. Chen Yun had been asked to present a report on the situation in finance and trade, but he demurred on the basis that he had not yet fully clarified the situation in that sphere. Perhaps, however, Peng Zhen's performance sums up most clearly the difficult and uncertain position in which Politburo members found themselves in January 1962.

Peng had ordered his subordinates in the Beijing municipal hierarchy to investigate the real causes of the GLF disaster and prepare a report for him. It is not clear whether he did this on his own or as an integral part of a broader leadership effort to determine the lessons that should be drawn from the GLF. In any case, the initial investigation started in late May 1961, and in November Peng issued a second order that all central directives between 1958 and 1961 should be reviewed as part of this effort. Deng Tuo, a Beijing Party secretary who had edited the *People's Daily* until 1957, assumed charge of this investigation. After convening a meeting at the Changguanlou in December 1961, Deng Tuo reported on the group's findings to Peng Zhen.

The report they made placed the blame for the disaster directly on the mobilizational politics of the GLF strategy. The center had approved and circulated too many false reports, had issued too many conflicting directives, and had virtually totally ignored economic reality in its calls for action by local cadres. In short, the GLF disaster must be laid largely at the doorstep of the Politburo. Given Mao's headstrong leadership of that body since 1958, there is little question that the Changguanlou report in fact amounted to a severe critique of the Chairman's own work.

Peng reportedly went to the Seven Thousand Cadres Conference in January 1962 prepared to spell out the case made in the Changguanlou report. When he grasped the tenor of the meeting, however, he hesitated and in fact did not criticize the Chairman's leadership at this major conference. Peng by then fully recognized the magnitude of the GLF catastrophe and certainly would not support that type of mobilizational effort again in the future. At the same time, he could not bring himself to confront Mao on the issue directly. This kind of lingering ambivalence meant, in turn, that even after the searing experiences of 1961, a current in support of GLF-type policies would remain strong within the Party throughout 1962 and thereafter.

Given the enormity of the problems engendered by the GLF, it is a tribute to Mao's inherent authority that he could still shape the outcome of conclaves such as the Seven Thousand Cadres Conference in 1962. This reflects the unique position that the Chairman had assumed within the Chinese Party after 1949. Unlike other Communist parties in power, the Chinese created distinctive roles for the First Secretary (or General Secretary) and the Chairman. The former role was an integral part of the organizational hierarchy of the Party. The latter position stood apart from and above that hierarchy. It was a position whose formal authority evolved somewhat during successive Party constitutions but whose real power derived from the stature of the incumbent, who was regarded as virtually a philosopher-king. In the eyes of his colleagues, Mao had conceptualized the Chinese revolution itself. Although people recognized that he could make serious mistakes and thus might try to vitiate his initiatives through bureaucratic devices, none had the courage (or gall) to question directly Mao's fundamental evaluation of the current situation and the priority tasks of the Party. There were, in short, no effective institutional curbs on Mao's power, and the Chairman used this advantage with great skill when he felt challenged or threatened.

Unfortunately, insufficient documentation is available from the Seven Thousand Cadres Conference to specify the dynamics of the discussions or the details of the final consensus at the meeting. It appears that on balance the conference left many issues only partly resolved. Indeed, the major issues with which it grappled continued to engender disagreement and tension among the leaders throughout the remaining years before the Cultural Revolution. These issues included the following. The rehabilitation of rightists: This meeting split the difference by agreeing that many should be brought back but that Peng Dehuai and some other leading rightists should remain under a cloud. An evaluation of the current situation: This conference did not reach an agreement that would hold for more than a month or two. Mao seems to have forced a reasonably optimistic perspective on the conference, but this was challenged almost immediately and subsequently remained a contentious issue. Party rectification: Although this conference made some progress toward accomplishing the vitally necessary task of reconstructing a disciplined and responsive Party apparatus, the issue of how best to carry out this task would continue to sow discord among the leaders. Thus, the January–February 1962 conference marked an uncertain transition from the desperation of 1961 to a more positive effort to shape events in 1962 and afterward. While the meeting reflected the fact that Beijing was again ready to begin to seize the initiative, it also revealed the fissures within the central leadership that the traumatic previous three years had produced.

These fissures cracked open a bit wider under the strain of a Ministry of Finance projection, made available to Chen Yun just after the Seven Thousand Cadres Conferences in February 1962, that the central government would face a budget deficit on 2 to 3 billion *yuan* that year under current plans and projections. Chen, always sensitive to the inflationary pressures budget deficits produced, prepared a wide-ranging report that cast the overall situation in gloomy terms and called for appropriate changes in plans. This included a significant scaling down of the production targets discussed during the previous month. Chen feared a deteriorating food situation and suggested emergency measures to increase marginally the supplies of fish and soybeans. He also argued that the poor agrarian situation demanded a revision of the recently adopted plans for recovery. This would entail designating 1962–5 as a period of recovery, where energies would remain focused on rural production, and growth in the metallurgical and machine-building industries would necessarily be held back.

With Mao in Wuhan, Liu Shaoqi had assumed charge of day-to-day affairs of the Politburo. He called the Xilou Conference, named for the building in Beijing in which it was convened on 21–3 February, to discuss Chen's views. The Xilou meeting strongly endorsed Chen's sober assessments which in any case seems to have come close to the picture that Liu himself had painted at the recently concluded Seven Thousand Cadres Conference. In addition, at Xilou both Liu and Deng Xiaoping endorsed the various systems of "individual responsibility" in agriculture (a de facto partial decollectivization) that had been tried in hard-hit provinces such as Anhui. These endorsements reflected a belief that the agricultural situation still not "bottomed out" as of the time of the conference. Also, at Xilou Li Xiannian admitted the accuracy of Liu Shaoqi's criticism of recent state financial work.

The Xilou Conference decided to convene a meeting of Party core groups in the State Council to discuss this new assessment. They met on 26 February and, enthusiastically endorsing Chen's analysis, passed the issue to the Secretariat.

Liu Shaoqi urged the Secretariat to circulate Chen's report as a CC document, with an attached comment by the Standing Committee of the Politburo. Since (unnamed) people objected to the tone of the proposed document, Liu, Deng, and Zhou traveled to Wuhan to report to Mao on its contents and background. Mao reportedly approved circulation of the document. After this, Chen had the Central Finance and Economics Small Group discuss the document and a related report on commercial work that also reflected Chen's views.

Following the Central Finance and Economics Small Group meeting, Zhou Enlai took charge of this key body. Reportedly, Chen had to pull back from day-to-day involvement due to illness, although he evidently remained an influential counselor behind the scenes.[18] The Ministry of Metallurgy refused to accept Chen's analysis and continued to hold out for a larger steel target – placed at 25 to 30 million tons by 1970 – as the core of the new Five-Year Plan. Chen stressed instead the need for a recovery period followed by balanced growth. In early summer 1962 Zhou Enlai brought together the secretaries of the six regional Party bureaus, along with members of the Politburo, to focus on Chen's ideas, which Zhou put forward as the correct framework for CCP planning. Ke Qingshi, the Maoist stalwart from Shanghai who had been a key force in the backyard steel furnace drive of 1958, objected to Zhou's position on the ground that the premier was characterizing the situation in terms far worse than those used at the Seven Thousand Cadres Conference. Zhou countered that the budget deficit that sparked this revision became known only after the conference had been adjourned. Zhou's speech was then circulated to a wider audience, evidently over Ke's strong objections.

Thus, two significantly different assessments of the situation emerged during the first half of 1962. Mao Zedong, supported at least by some provincial officials, by Lin Biao in the military and by people in the heavy-industry sector,[19] argued that the country was well on the way to recovery and thus that the time had come to begin to exercise some initiative in moving China farther along a socialist path. Mao thus opposed further decollectivization in agriculture and backtracking in other areas, such as culture. Mao's ruminations on the development of the Soviet revolution were spurring his concern over trends in China during these months, but overall he seems to have spent most of the time from February 1962 until the August Beidaihe Central Work Conference in partial seclusion in central China.

18 In 1966 Liu Shaoqi "confessed" that during 1962 he had been overly influenced by Chen's views. Chen also seems to have attended the Tenth Plenum in September 1962, even though no other public appearances by him were recorded before the Cultural Revolution.
19 Mao's support almost certainly also came from others, such as Tan Zhenlin in agriculture, but the documentation to support this conclusion is lacking.

Liu Shaoqi, Deng Xiaoping, Chen Yun, and others, by contrast, had concluded by late February that the situation remained almost desperately bad and that a significant recovery period would be necessary before Beijing could again really assume the initiative. The grim rural situation demanded further concessions to peasant material interests in the form of official endorsement of speculative activities by the peasants and the type of decollectivization referred to as "going it alone" (*dan gan*). The general social demoralization demanded that the regime yield to popular tastes in cultural fare, permitting the staging of old operas and plays and the composition of other works that played down revolutionary politics in favor of traditional favorite themes and characters. The desperate economic situation also demanded that the regime woo former capitalists and the technical intelligentsia into active efforts to revive the urban economy. Thus, whereas Mao felt the general situation permitted renewed efforts to move the country again toward his socialist ideals, many of his colleagues demurred. They thought the regime would have to retreat further and nurse its institutional capabilities back to health before a more active strategy would be feasible.

The Beidaihe Conference and the Tenth Plenum

The clash between these two approaches came at the August 1962 Beidaihe meeting.[20] Liu and his confreres came to this meeting having spent the preceding months actively pursuing the policy implications of Chen Yun's analysis of China's situation. Thus, for example, in February they convened a National Conference on Scientific and Technological Work in Guangzhou, and a month later they brought together a National Conference for the Creation of Dramas and Operas in the same city. Both meetings tried to mobilize support by yielding to the preferences of the groups of non-Party participants. As of early August, a related conference on short novels about the countryside was in session in Dalian. In the interim, Deng Xiaoping convened a meeting of the Secretariat to review the data on individual farming (*dan gan*), at which he pronounced his subsequently famous dictum "It does not matter whether a cat is black or white, so long as it catches mice." And, of course, the already recounted succession of events around Chen Yun's assessment was unfolding.

20 This work conference began on 6 August and continued until the latter part of that month. These major summer central work conferences were more than simply business meetings. Although they were extremely important in policy formulation, in addition, they were social gatherings, with wives frequently in attendance, evening entertainment provided, and time allowed for side trips and diversions. Key leaders might miss significant parts of the conferences, presumably reading the stenographic record to keep posted on the deliberations. Thus, conferences often appeared to drag on for one to two months and may even, as here, have shifted location partway through. Since these conferences generally were not covered in the press at the time, it is often impossible to establish precise dates for their opening and closing.

Mao Zedong approached this meeting in another frame of mind. He evidently felt increasingly isolated from the mainstream of decision making, even thought his signature continued to be sougt on CC documents before they were disseminated. Mao reportedly had ceased sitting in on Politburo meetings as of January 1958.²¹ Originally, this had probably reflected his assumption of more independent decision-making authority at the start of the Great Leap; or it may have been part of a genuine effort to retire to the second line and give his colleagues more prestige. But over time it may well have taken on other significance for him, making him feel increasingly isolated and neglected by his colleagues. Mao clearly began in 1962 to search for ways to reassert himself in the system, and one of the most interesting dimensions of the politics of the period 1962–5 is the putting together of the coalition that would enable the aging Party Chairman to break into a position of dominance in 1966.

This search coincided with the development of the independent political ambitions of three key individuals – Jiang Qing, Lin Biao, and Kang Sheng. Others hovered in the background, at times playing important roles. Chen Boda, always the Maoist loyalist, was willing to encourage any move that would enhance the role of his patron. Wang Dongxing, a former bodyguard of Mao's, became involved in the byzantine palace security dimension. Zhou Enlai played the political game cautiously, always keeping his lines open to both the Chairman and other members of the Politburo. At the crucial moment in 1966, however, Zhou put himself squarely on Mao's side, enabling the Chairman to complete the coalition necessary to launch the Cultural Revolution.

As Mao faced the Central Work Conference at Beidaihe in the late summer of 1962, however, he had yet to formulate fully either the challenge or his strategy. He was highly troubled by the events of the months since the Seven Thousand Cadres Conference, though, and he listened to the reports during the first days of the Beidaihe meeting with chagrin. Zhu De, one of the most respected of the old marshals, called for expansion of the individual responsibility system in agriculture and for other measures that put him solidly with Liu's and Deng's evaluation of the problems in the countryside. Chen Yun reiterated his position on the rural situation and tasks. Other Politburo members reported on major issue areas,²² but unfortunately no information is available on either the timing or the substance of their remarks. The timing is important, because on 9 August, Mao addressed the meeting, employing such biting sarcasm that his talk probably seriously affected the tone of the entire proceedings.

21 *Yomiuri Shimbun*, 25 January 1981, trans. in *FBIS/PRC* Annex, 13 March 1981, 7.
22 Chen Boda, only an alternate Politburo member at the time, reported on agriculture; Li Xiannian on commerce; Li Fuchun (possibly with Bo Yibo) on industry and planning; and Chen Yi on the international situation. Liu Shaoqi also addressed this meeting.

Mao bitterly attacked the Ministry of Finance, whose budget deficit projection had provided the basis for Chen Yun's February report and all that had followed from it. He then stressed the fact that China still faced the need for class struggle, and it was obvious that he felt the continuing retreat from socialist policies simply exacerbated the dangers in this sphere. He attacked directly the adoption of an individual responsibility system in farming and called for a campaign of "socialist education" to rectify the Party apparatus in the rural areas. And he warned against the possibility of capitalist or even feudal restoration in the PRC. Jiang Qing subsequently revealed that she had been working on the Chairman to sensitize him to the "degeneration" of the arts and culture since 1959, and her proddings had found a reflection in Mao's stress on the need for proletarian ideology in his address to the Beidaihe meeting.[23]

Mao thus succeeded in turning the agenda around so that at least in part it reflected his own priorities. His commanding presence was most easily brought to bear at these central conclaves, and he took full advantage of his political resources there. Liu Shaoqi evidently challenged the Chairman's priorities in at least some respects at this meeting, as Liu subsequently commented that he had "inclined to the right" at Beidaihe and had not begun to correct himself until the Tenth Plenum that convened on 24–27 September. What emerged was a patchwork compromise in an atmosphere of somewhat heightened political tension.

The Tenth Plenum revealed all the cleavages and contradictions that had boiled up at the Beidaihe meeting. Mao presided over this meeting, and his speech to the participants closely linked the degeneration of the Soviet Union to the fact that class struggle would still exist in China for decades to come. Mao was persuaded by Liu and others at this meeting, however, to make clear that the issue of class struggle should not be allowed to swamp other policy decisions coming out of the Tenth Plenum, as had happened after the Eighth Plenum at Lushan in 1959.[24]

Mao's general concern with class struggle reflected a more basic fear of his that the Chinese revolution was beginning to head down the path of revisionism. A cynic might note that revisionism to Mao seemed to be anything that he disliked, but dismissing the term on this level would in fact be misleading. Mao was very concerned to shepherd the revolution along collectivist and relatively egalitarian paths. He distrusted urban-based bureaucracies and China's intellectuals as a whole. Even though many of his concrete policy proposals

23 Roxane Witke, *Comrade Chiang Ch'ing*, 304–5. Witke places this speech on 6 August, whereas other documentary sources give the 9 August date used in the text.
24 *RMRB*, 15 January 1982, 5, trans. in *FBIS/PRC*, 25 January 1982, K-22. A partial text of Mao's speech is available in *Chinese law and government*, 1.4 (Winter 1968–9), 85–93.

had the effect of exploiting the countryside to develop urban-based industry, he nevertheless seems genuinely to have thought of himself as a representative of China's poor peasants. Although Mao believed in the efficacy of technological progress, he nevertheless distrusted the high culture and its carriers that were essential for nurturing technical development.

In the aftermath of the GLF tragedy, Mao could not argue as of 1962 that mass mobilization could restore the country's productive capacities. He therefore continued to yield to the entreaties that the Party make full use of material incentives and technical expertise to recoup the situation. But Mao also, as of the Tenth Plenum, decided to draw the line. He resolutely opposed decollectivization in agriculture and insisted that the communes remain intact (or be restored where they had been abandoned). He also recognized that current policies would increase the strength of the groups in society that he trusted least – the former landlords and rich peasants in the countryside, former capitalists, technical specialists, and intellectuals in the cities. He also feared that a period of normality would nurture tendencies toward sluggish bureaucratism among the many middle-level cadres that had shown themselves so prone to this evil in the past. Thus, Mao called for measures to bring political issues onto the agenda (but without disrupting normal work). He also strengthened the organs responsible for handling those who slip into counterrevolution – the Public Security Ministry and the CCP Control Commission.

The Tenth Plenum embraced Mao's overall analysis in theory but in its concrete provisions kept close to the methods that had been worked out during 1961–2 to bring about a recovery from the GLF. This compromise produced a communiqué that in some paragraphs echoed Mao's rhetoric and in others drove home the logic that Liu, Deng, and Chen had put forward. That this compromise was not put together easily is confirmed by reports that at this plenum Liu Shaoqi, Li Xiannian, Deng Zihui, and Xi Zhongxun made self-criticisms. A subtheme that continued to rankle at this meeting was the Peng Dehuai affair. As noted, Peng wrote and circulated an 80,000-character self-justifying report to provide a basis for his full rehabilitation. Mao demurred, agreeing only to assign Peng some low-level work in the future. The Chairman argued that only those who fully recognized their errors would be rehabilitated – evidently unwilling to admit that in Peng's case, the error was Mao's.

Much Chinese and Western historiography has portrayed 1963–5 as a time of two-line struggle between a Maoist camp, on the one hand, and a Liu–Deng headquarters, on the other. The real situation, though, was not so simple. The group that helped Mao launch the Cultural Revolution in 1966 consisted of diverse elements that had joined together for different reasons. Thus, one important desideratum of these years concerns how the various components of the Maoist coalition formed, and the impact each had on the politics of this era. The other key dimension is the evolution of Mao's own thinking as he came to grips both with his potential coalition partners and with the policies that Liu Shaoqi and his colleagues were implementing. The two key coalition groups were those headed by Lin Biao and Jiang Qing. After analyzing these, we turn to Mao's direct attempts to deal with the major policy initiatives of Liu and company during 1963–5.

THE RISE OF LIN BIAO

Lin Biao faced two tasks after he became minister of defense in September 1959. One was to consolidate his position in the PLA; the other was to solidify his relationship with Mao Zedong and help Mao to enhance his own power in the Chinese political system. Lin executed a complex strategy for accomplishing these related tasks, one that eventually put him in a key position to help Mao launch and sustain the Cultural Revolution.

Lin began his reform of the PLA by bringing back into prominence the Military Affairs Commission (MAC) of the Party. This body had existed nominally throughout the period of Peng Dehuai's stewardship, but in reality its role seems to have diminished with the increasing estrangement of Peng and Mao. Lin revived the MAC, appointing to its standing committee seven of China's ten marshals (leaving out Peng Dehuai and Zhu De, who allegedly supported Peng in 1959).

Little is known about the composition of the MAC, as the Chinese have never published a full list of its members or details on its staff.[25] Before 1976, though, all individuals identified as being MAC members were uniformed members of the military, with the sole exception of Mao Zedong, its chairman. The MAC is formally a Party body and is the command vehicle through which the Party exercises control over the professional military. Party leaders such as Zhou Enlai in fact addressed major meetings of the MAC. But the day-to-day leadership of this body generally resided in the Minister of Defense. And, given that Mao was the only civilian identified as a MAC member, it appears that this body's real purpose was to give the Chairman of the CCP[26] a special place in military decision making. Thus, the revival of the MAC should perhaps more accurately be viewed as a reassertion of Mao's close association with the uniformed military command.

---

25 The most complete account of the MAC available in the secondary literature is in Harvey Nelsen, *The Chinese military system*.

26 The chairmen of the CCP have been ex officio chairmen of the MAC until Deng Xiaoping stopped this practice during Hua Guofeng's tenure in these positions.

Lin not only moved the MAC to center stage, he also made personnel changes to ensure his control over the Ministry of Defense. He quickly dropped three of the seven vice-ministers in office as of the time of his appointment and appointed six new vice-ministers of his own. Relatedly, he made virtually a clean sweep of the Chinese high command, recognizing the former seven departments into three and appointing to each people who appeared to be his supporters (including Luo Ruiqing, the head of the Public Security apparatus until the showdown at Lushan). These personnel changes in the ministry were probably linked to the revival of the MAC: The MAC formally makes all high-level appointments in the Ministry of Defense.

At about this time, Lin began, as noted, to stress the use of Mao Zedong Thought in the military. Many others in the PLA disagreed with this approach, but Lin made it a centerpiece of his reign as minister of defense. Lin's approach became official policy at the conclusion of the enlarged meeting of the MAC in September–October 1960. This occurred just as the fourth volume of Mao Zedong's *Selected Works* was being published. Whether or not the two were linked in planning and execution, there is little doubt that Lin's tack further endeared him to an increasingly beleaguered Chairman Mao.

Indeed, the fact that the propagation of the works of specific leaders was seen as an important political question is highlighted by the plans for publication of the *Selected Works of Liu Shaoqi* and a collection of essays by Chen Yun, both of which were being put together in 1962. Neither appeared, reportedly because Liu himself objected to the publication of his works, and Mao essentially pigeonholed the Chen volume.[27] The question of the relative treatment of Mao and Liu had become a sensitive political issue after Liu took over the chairmanship of the PRC from Mao in April 1959.

Lin Biao then took a series of initiatives to enhance the role of the PLA in CCP affairs. He quickly began to increase the number of Party members in the military, perhaps because that would give him a greater say in national CCP affairs. During 1963–5, moreover, he worked to expand the PLA's organizational responsibilities, blurring at some points the boundaries between Party and military. These years saw the heads of the various military districts become secretaries in five of the six regional Party bureaus that had been formed in the wake of the GLE. At the same time, at least half of the provincial Party first secretaries became political commissars in the military districts, putting them at least partially into the chain of command of the General Political Department of the PLA. This multiple officeholding in Party and Army could, in theory, have been used to increase Party control over the PLA,

27 On Liu, see *RMRB*, 15 January 1982, trans. in *FBIS/PRC*, 25 January 1982, K 19–22. On Chen, see Deng Liqun, *Xiang Chen Yun tongzhi xuexi zuo jingji gongzuo* (Study how to do economic work from comrade Chen Yun), 8–9.

but experience indicates that the real effect was very much the opposite. These were essentially predatory moves by the PLA to increase its power vis-à-vis the Party. The PLA under Lin was also increasing its control over the civilian population. Mao in 1962 ordered the formation of a civilian militia under military control, and the implementation of this order enhanced the military's contacts with the civilian sector.

Given these activities by the army, Mao increasingly pointed to the PLA as the type of organization that could successfully integrate politics and expertise – that could, in the terminology of the time, be both Red and expert. For during these same years Lin was bolstering the professional training and discipline in the ranks, and the military was heading the effort to develop China's atomic bomb. Also, in October 1962 the PLA acquitted itself well in the brief border war with India, thus adding to its prowess and prestige.

During 1963 the PLA generated several models of political rectitude, including a selfless soldier (Lei Feng) who had died in an accident and an outstanding military company, the Good Eighth Company of Nanjing Road. Following initiatives to have people emulate these military models, in December 1963 Mao issued a general call for people to "learn from the PLA," a startling slogan given that the Party was supposedly the fount of all wisdom. In the Chairman's eyes, the problems with the first FYP had essentially demonstrated the inadequacies of the government administration, and the Great Leap catastrophe had substantially discredited the CCP. Thus, Mao began to look toward the military as the type of organization that might achieve the balance of political virtue and technical/organizational expertise that he regarded as vital for the PRC.

Soon Mao went from hortatory campaigns to learn from the PLA to a far more direct approach to increasing the military's leverage within the government and Party. In 1964, at Mao's direction, government units – and subsequently some CCP organs also – began to form political departments within the units. These were modeled after the political system within the army, and a number of the people who staffed them either went through training courses run by the military for this purpose or were themselves recently demobilized army personnel. These departments never became solidly established – partly because of resistance in the government and Party, partly because they could not define clearly their role, and partly because there were constant skirmishes over who would be the personnel to staff them. But the whole exercise again reflected the increasingly aggressive posture of the PLA vis-à-vis the Party and government – and Mao's encouragement of this trend.

In May 1965 Lin Biao took the unusual measure of having all ranks in the PLA abolished. This initiative again made the military appear to be the most advanced politically, since it alone was acting to implement the egalitarian ideals of the revolution. From the point of view of political power, moreover, this measure may in some degree have strengthened Lin's hand within the PLA. It meant, essentially, that a former officer's power now derived solely from his actual operational assignment. He would no longer have rank that could itself convey certain rights and privileges. Given that Lin held the top operational position within the army, the independent power of the other eight marshals (Luo Ronghuan had died in 1963) and of the officer corps itself should have been weakened somewhat by this measure.

Also in 1965 the PLA took direct control over the Public Security forces. Luo Ruiqing, former minister of public security and a man with extremely strong ties in its apparatus, was at the time the chief of staff of the PLA. As we shall see later, Lin turned against Luo in December 1965 and by May 1966 had him purged and vilified. One effect of the purge was to leave Lin in a better position to marshal the resources of the public security apparatus – one of the most powerful organizations in the country – to support Mao and Lin himself. He appears to have used these resources well once the Cultural Revolution began.[28]

The conflict with Luo Ruiqing was broader than the issue of control over the public security forces, however. The year 1965 was a very bad one for China's foreign policy. Zhou Enlai had hoped to put together an Afro-Asian Conference that would take an anti-Soviet line in the spring, but this effort failed. The PRC also tried unsuccessfully to influence the outcome of the August–September Indo-Pakistani war, and the Soviet Union proved in the final analysis to be able to play a constructive mediating role in that conflict. And the PRC's careful cultivation of the Communist Party of Indonesia (PKI) ended in disaster when in September 1965 the PKI supported a coup attempt against the military that failed. All these missteps produced a growing feeling of isolation and seige in Beijing, just as the United States began to increase substantially its involvement in Vietnam, posing the possibility of a direct U.S. attack on southern China in the near future.

Within this troubling international context, Beijing's leaders debated options and strategy. Luo Ruiqing appears to have preferred an approach that would relieve some of the tension on China by seeking better relations with the Soviet Union – based on joint efforts to combat the United States in Vietnam. Luo recommended the Soviet strategy of the eve of World War II, a strategy of projecting conventional force to engage the enemy well outside of the country's boundaries. This strategy demanded, in turn, that China maximize the output of its military-related heavy industry, striving for efficient industrial production as a high priority goal. Given the logistical demands

28 As will be noted, Kang Sheng played a significant role vis-à-vis the Public Security apparatus, too.

of this strategy, it also presumed that China's cities would serve as the key production bases for the effort and that Soviet help would be available to supplement the PRC's inadequate industrial base.

Lin Biao, by contrast, argued that Vietnam should basically fight the war itself, with indirect Chinese support but no direct intervention. He lauded the CCP's strategy against the Japanese, a strategy that required luring the enemy deep into the country and then wearing him down through guerrilla war techniques. This in turn demanded the dispersal of industry, a policy of regional basic self-sufficiency, playing up the role of the militia and of unconventional forces rather than of the regular army and whipping up high political fervor among the population. It did not demand – and indeed it argued against – a strategy of rapprochement with the post-Khrushchev leadership of the Soviet Union. Lin laced his argument with quotations from Mao Zedong, and the strategy he advocated dovetailed neatly with a whole series of civilian, foreign policy, and military policy preferences of the Chairman's. Liu Shaoqi and Deng Xiaoping seem to have been opposed to many of these.

Thus, while building up his position in the military and enhancing the role of the PLA vis-à-vis the Party and government, Lin also carefully cultivated Mao and tried to support the Chairman's policy preferences in the system. In general terms, the Mao cult in the army redounded to the Chairman's overall political benefit. Indeed, starting in 1964, the book of Mao quotations that had been developed for use in the army was distributed among model youth to reward their accomplishments. On a more specific level also, as indicated by his wide-ranging strategic recommendations about Vietnam, Lin injected himself directly into the increasingly fractious relations that Mao had with Liu, Deng, and company. In some cases, his main purpose seems, indeed, to have been precisely to exacerbate tensions between Mao and his Politburo colleagues.

For example, at the September 1959 enlarged meeting of the MAC that formally stripped Peng Dehuai of his post as minister of defense, Lin's attack on Peng and his characterization of the latter's errors were far harsher than those of Mao. Lin, trying to solidify his own newly acquired position, argued that Peng was virtually irredeemable and the Mao Zedong Thought was the quintessence of Marxism-Leninism. Lin's position, finally accepted by Mao, helped to drive a wedge between the Chairman and the other members of the Politburo more sympathetic to Peng. At the Seven Thousand Cadres Conference in January–February 1962, Lin leaped to Mao's defense (and that of the GLF itself) when debate occurred over the causes of the difficulties in which China found itself. Lin not only strongly supported Mao and the Three Red Banners (the GLF, the People's Communes, and the general line), but he also called on all present to study Mao Zedong

Thought. Although documentary evidence is lacking to spell out Lin's role in other meetings involving the Party elite, it seems that he had continued to try both to build up the Chairman and to exacerbate Mao's relations with other leaders. For example, in May 1966 Lin spoke darkly about the chances of a coup against Mao and the need for the Chairman to protect himself against such a threat.

These activities indicate that Lin Biao was an ambitious man who had developed a clear political strategy soon after taking office as defense minister in 1959. That strategy was to link his fortune with that of Mao, and the disastrous effects of the Great Leap then required that Lin use his resources to bolster Mao's position in the system, in addition to simply solidifying his own position in the Chairman's eyes. Taken together, Lin's initiatives show that he was more than simply a puppet of the Chairman. Rather, although his interests overlapped with those of Mao, he also seems to have worked hard to prevent any improvement in relations between Mao and his colleagues on the Politburo. By the very nature of the situation, what were probably Lin's most effective efforts in this endeavor would remain known only to the few prinicipal participants themselves.

Mao, it should be noted, never became fully a captive of Lin's initiatives. As noted elsewhere, for example, Mao perceived a major national security threat to China growing out of the potential escalation of the Vietnam War after the Gulf of Tonkin incident in 1964. In response, the Chairman undercut the original strategy for the third FYP and called instead for devotion of major investment resources to building a "third line" of industries in the remote hinterland of Southwest China. Mao created an informal State Planning Commission headed by Yu Qiuli to oversee this new strategy. The body consisted basically of the people who in the 1970s would become known as the "petroleum clique," and during the Cultural Revolution it essentially merged with and superseded the formal State Planning Commission. The plan advocated by this group was the same one Lin Biao espoused for dealing with Vietnam. But Mao assigned Peng Dehuai, Lin's nemesis, to take charge of the Sichuan-based headquarters for constructing the third line.

Culture: Jiang Qing

A second key component of the coalition that formed to launch the Cultural Revolution was Mao's wife, Jiang Qing, and the group she put together in the cultural sphere. Indeed, in February 1966 Lin Biao and Jiang Qing clearly linked up when Lin invited Jiang to stage a Forum on Literature and Art for Troops and made her the official cultural adviser to the military. This for the first time gave Jiang an official position that she could use as a base for pursuing her political goals.[29] But she obtained that help from Lin only because she had spent considerable effort over the preceding years building up her own resources in the cultural realm and winning her husband to her point of view.

Jiang Qing had long held strong views about the directions in which cultural policy should move, and for an equally long time she had nursed hatreds against the Communist cultural establishment that kept her at arm's length. When Jiang Qing had gone to Yan'an and won Mao's heart, she replaced Mao's popular second wife, He Zizhen, who had suffered terribly as one of the very few women on the Long March. Mao's colleagues obtained the Chairman's agreement that he would keep Jiang Qing out of politics if they would not object to his having Jiang replace He in his bedroom.

Even in Yan'an Jiang Qing had advocated developing a new type of revolutionary cultural repertoire, and she had been active in the development of revolutionary plays during those years. A very bright, astute, and ambitious woman, she evidently felt acutely the ostracism imposed on her by the male-dominated cultural and propaganda apparatus. After 1949, Jiang remained very much in the background, owing in part to her continuing health problems and in part to the unwillingness of the cultural establishment to listen to her or give her an official place in the system. Jiang does, however, seem to some extent to have served the Chairman as an informal political confidante. For example, she flew to Lushan when Mao informed her that trouble had erupted at the Lushan conference in July 1959. On that occasion Mao asked her not to come, but he evidently did not forbid her to participate, and indeed he called her from the meeting to discuss with her his response to Peng's challenge.

The year 1959 seems to have been the start of a turning point in Jiang's health, and as her physical well-being became more assured, her energy for participating in politics and cultural affairs also grew. After the Lushan meeting, Jiang went to Shanghai to rest, and while there she had gone to a number of theaters. She was appalled at the content of the productions, finding that "old" themes and styles were very much in vogue and feeling that this should be rectified. Jiang gradually began to put together a faction of people who would help her carry out her plans to revolutionize Beijing Opera and other aspects of Chinese culture.

Mao, of course, was central to Jiang's efforts, and she herself claims that by 1962 she had convinced him that the cultural sphere needed attention. Indeed, Mao instructed her in the spring of 1962 to draft a policy statement for the CC on policy toward culture. Jiang's effort provided some of the

29 Jiang had held a minor position in cultural affairs in the early 1950s.

background for Mao's call at the August 1962 Beidaihe meeting to promote "proletarian" culture. But Jiang's position paper did not become official policy until May 1966, when a considerably revised draft of it became one of the basic documents that led to the Cultural Revolution.

Jiang Qing and Kang Sheng

Jiang found a natural conjoining of interests with two others with whom she had ties from prerevolutionary days: Kang Sheng and Ke Qingshi. Kang Sheng came from Jiang's home town of Zhucheng in Shandong province, and the two of them had known each other before Jiang went to Yan'an. Kang specialized in three areas of work: liaison with other Communist parties, public security, and higher education. What brought them all together was Kang's evidently fairly sophisticated training in Marxism-Leninism while he was learning the finer points of police work from the NKVD in the Soviet Union in the mid-1930s, and his ongoing involvement with the issues of revisionism and counterrevolution.

Kang had had major responsibility in public security affairs prior to the 1950s, and as a result took some of the blame when Khrushchev made his de-Stalinization speech to the Soviet Twentieth Party Congress. Kang was dropped from full membership in the Politburo in September 1956, at the same time that the Party dropped Mao Zedong Thought as part of the guiding ideology specified in the CCP constitution. As of the early 1960s, however, things were moving in a direction potentially favorable to Kang. With the Sino-Soviet dispute having reached a critical stage, Mao – who remained the dominant figure in handling the dispute on the Chinese side – needed a theorist with Kang's knowledge to help him draft the CCP CC's attacks on "Khrushchev revisionism." At the same time, Kang – probably through his long friendship with Jiang Qing – learned that Mao was planning to push for the proletarianization of Chinese culture. Kang could play a useful role in that effort, especially if he could link it to counterrevolutionary activities to justify his involvement.

Kang effected this linkage at the Tenth Plenum in September 1962, where he launched an attack on Xi Zhongxun for the latter's involvement in the production of a purportedly counterrevolutionary novel about Liu Zhidan, one of the early Communist guerrilla fighters in Shaanxi who had died in 1936. Claiming that the novel about Liu in fact vilified Mao, Kang argued that using novels for purposes of contemporary political criticism was a new invention. He thus established an intellectual link with Jiang Qing, who was trying to call Mao's attention to the political attacks against the Chairman that she had seen in the writings of intellectuals during the previous few years.

Kang subsequently served as a bridge between Jiang Qing and some of the radical intellectuals she brought to the fore in the early stage of the Cultural Revolution. Kang's work in higher education gave him entrée to major educational units, and he took advantage of this to cultivate key individuals. The most prominent among these turned out to be Guan Feng and Qi Benyu of the Research Institute of Philosophy of the Academy of Sciences, Nie Yuanzi of the Philosophy Department of Peking University, and several people at the Higher Party School.[30] Kang, like Lin Biao, was willing to foment trouble if need be to attain his purposes. For example, in the Higher Party School he attacked Yang Xianzhens's theory of "two combine into one" as an anti-Maoist negation of the Chairman's philosophical premise that "one divides into two." Through such theoretical skulduggery, Kang managed to purge Yang and to increase the influence of his followers in the Higher Party School. As of mid-1964, Kang also heavily and personally involved himself in Jiang Qing's efforts to revolutionize Beijing Opera.[31]

Ke Qingshi, Shanghai's mayor, was an old friend of Jiang Qing's. Ke had in 1958 been one of the most vociferous supporters of the GLF and especially of the backyard steel furnace campaign. He was made a full member of the Politburo in the spring of 1958, and Shanghai became a major beneficiary of the Leap strategy.[32] As noted earlier, even in mid-1962 Ke had continued to support a Maoist interpretation of the current situation as opposed to the more pessimistic views of Chen Yun and others. Ke, then, like Kang Sheng, Lin Biao, and Jiang Qing, had good reason to want to bolster Mao's standing.

In late 1962 Kang Sheng spoke with Ke about the need to have literature and art portray heroes drawn from the ranks of people who had emerged over the thirteen years since 1949, a line very much in tune with Jiang Qing's own thinking. Ke during the GLF had already sided with Shanghai's "worker-writers" against the professional authors.[33] In January 1963 Ke made just such an appeal in Shanghai, calling on the local intelligentsia to abandon old repertoires, adopt the class struggle of the Tenth Plenum, and stage new dramas with heroes drawn from the ranks of post-1949 workers, peasants, and soldiers. Mao soon chimed in with support, calling the Ministry of Culture a "ministry of emperors and princes, generals and ministers, gifted scholars and beauties."

Jiang Qing had been in touch with Ke in 1959 about cultural matters in Shanghai, and she remained in contact with him throughout the early 1960s (Ke died in 1965) on this issue. Through Ke, Jiang linked up with Zhang

30 *Zhengming* (Hong Kong), 34 (August 1980), 45.   31 Ibid.
32 See Christopher Howe's contribution to Christoper Howe, ed., *Shanghai: Revolution and development in an Asian metropolis*, 173–9.
33 See Ragvald contribution to Howe, ed. *Shanghai*, 316.

Chunqiao (who was in the cultural apparatus in Shanghai) and Yao Wenyuan, a Shanghai critic. Yao, in turn, had cultivated good ties among the newly developing "proletartian writers" – workers who had taken up the pen during the 1950s – in Shanghai.[34]

Thus, Jiang Qing during the early 1960s worked on her husband and began to put together her own coterie of advocates of a "revolutionization" of China's culture. The Ministries of Culture and Education and the Propaganda Department of the CCP, all manned by old opponents of Jiang's, paid her no heed and scoffed at her efforts. Clashes occurred at national meetings dealing with culture such as the June–July 1964 Festival of Beijing Opera on Contemporary Themes. Jiang had been developing her own model plays in Shanghai and through Mao kept up pressure to reform the cultural fare offered the Chinese people. Finally, in about June 1964 the Party Secretariat formed a Five-Man Group to coordinate efforts toward cultural reform. Peng Zhen, who conceivably was being considered by Mao as a potential replacement for Liu Shaoqi as the Party Chairman's successor, took charge of the group. Kang Sheng was the member, however, who most clearly was loyal to Mao and Jiang Qing, rather than to Liu Shaoqi or Deng Xiaoping.

To Jiang Qing, the Five-Man Group proved more a hindrance than a force for positive changes in cultural policy. The group generally followed the preferences of the Beijing cultural establishment (represented on the group by Lu Dingyi, the head of the Propaganda Department of the CCP). Jiang continued to seek other avenues for putting her priorities in the cultural and political spheres on the national agenda. The approach she adopted that eventually proved to have the greatest impact on national politics was to focus on the issue that Kang Sheng had raised at the Tenth Plenum in 1962 – that novels and plays could be used for political purposes. Jiang particularly pointed to the play *Hat Rui dismissed from office*, written by Wu Han. This play concerned the upright actions of a Ming official in the face of unfair attacks from his political enemies, and Jiang argued to Mao that the play in fact represented a veiled defense of Peng Dehuai. Chiang's specific accusation is plausible but probably wrong – Wu Han had begun work on a play about Hai Rui before the Lushan Conference, and he did so at the specific request of one of Mao's current secretaries, Hu Qiaomu.[35] Nonetheless, in the increasingly suspicion-charged atmosphere of 1965, Jiang persuaded Mao to have Yao Wenyuan write a critique of the play that raised the hidden political issues supposedly involved.

34 See ibid., 309–23.
35 For an early examination of this problem, see MacFarquhar, *Origins of the Cultural Revolution*, 2. 207–12.

Yao's critique, published in November 1965, was important for three reasons. It cast the issue of cultural reform as a political rather than a purely academic matter, thus raising the possibility that the regime would again carry out a major political campaign against the intellectuals. It attacked a play written by a subordinate and close friend of Peng Zhen's, thus putting Peng to the test as to whether he would protect Wu Han or side with Mao.[36] And it came from Shanghai (where Mao was then residing), symbolizing Mao's decision that the leaders in Beijing had moved so far away from his preferred positions that he would have to launch an attack on them that relied primarily on forces outside the central political apparatus. Jiang Qing's group provided important resources for this effort.

But Jiang's contacts as of 1965, other than Kang Sheng, were among radical intellectuals and people at lower levels of the system. Thus, when Jiang joined in the coalition to launch the Cultural Revolution, she brought in people unsympathetic to the bureaucratic values and practices that had developed since 1949. These were the people of ideas, not the people of organizational skills. Not surprisingly, therefore, they would prove themselves adept at manipulating ideas but disastrously inadequate at managing the economy.

The fact that Jiang's coalition included Kang Sheng proved important for the politics of the 1960s. Kang was ruthless and more than willing to destroy those who stood in his way. His movement toward the center of the political stage in and after 1962 permitted him to build on the bitterness of the Peng Dehuai affair, with its damage to previous norms of intra-Party struggle, and contribute to changing completely the way the Party leaders dealt with each other in political disputes. The radical intelligentsia in Jiangs entourage had never been schooled in these intra-Party norms, and thus easily joined in wholesale violations of previous practice. Zhang Chunqiao was the only one in this group as of the mid-1960s who had enjoyed an extensive career as a bureaucrat outside secret police work. Not surprisingly, Zhang also became the person in this group most sensitively attuned to the need to preserve order, build authority, and secure a bureaucratic base as the group acquired power.

Overall, Jiang Qing wanted to change Chinese culture and to avenge the many years of slights she had suffered at the hands of Lu Dingyi and other leaders of the cultural establishment. Her coalition included people who were willing to wage ruthless struggles in order to destroy the Party establishment Lin Biao had a more careful bureaucratic game to play, one that w⌐ ˙

---

36 Actually, Peng would lose either way. If he protected Wu Han (as he subse⸤ himself vulnerable by that act. If he attacked Wu Han, however, he would ⸤ the acknowledgement that he had permitted an anti-Maoist to achieve high ⸜ municipal apparatus. Given the likely negative effect of this episode on Peng like to know more about the real background to Yao Wenyuan's article.

to his replacing Liu Shaoqi as Mao's successor. For this, he could utilize the destructive power of Jiang Qing (and her ability to cultivate Mao's worst instincts), and thus in February 1966, as noted previously, Lin cemented a coalition with Jiang by appointing her cultural adviser to the army. Jiang then used this position as a platform from which to make a wide-ranging attack against those who opposed her views on culture, whether related to the military or not.

RECTIFICATION

Let us now shift our focus from Mao's eventual coalition partners to the Chairman himself. As of 1962 Mao saw the revolution threatened by adverse forces at both the apex and the base of the political system. At the apex, his colleagues wanted to continue policies that Mao felt would simply strengthen the hands of the anti-Communist forces in the society. At the base, the Chairman recognized that the damage that the GLF had done to basic-level Party units, especially in the countryside, had been enormous. He determined, as Harry Harding has written,[37] to use rectification campaigns to remedy both problems. Rectification essentially allowed Mao to order the formation of a new hierarchy of temporary organs that would deal with the established institutions to remedy a problem. It was an ideal tool for Mao to use to enhance his leverage in the system.

Mao highlighted the need for Party rectification at the August 1962 Beidaihe meeting and at the CC's Tenth Plenum that September. There was little argument over the need for rectification, but subsequent events would prove that there could be significant disagreement over the tools to be used. Experiments in rural rectification were carried out in selected spots following the Tenth Plenum, and the results of these provided the basis for the initial programmatic document of the rural rectification effort, the Socialist Education Campaign.

Mao personally played a determining role in drafting this document at central work conferences in February and May 1963. The resulting Former Ten Points called into being "poor and lower middle peasants' associations" to serve as a vehicle for exercising supervision over the erring basic level cadres. The problem, it turned out, was that poor and lower middle peasants had also suffered badly during the GLF, and many of them by 1963 were either disillusioned or corrupt. As this became evident during the course of the year, new measures (the Later Ten Points) were drafted by Deng Xiaoping and Peng Zhen and promulgated in September 1963.

---

37 Harry Harding, *Organizing China*, 196.

The Later Ten Points recognized the problems in the poor and lower middle peasants' associations and called for stricter recruitment criteria for them. More significantly, this document worked on the assumption that they were by nature unable to supervise adequately the commune and brigade committees. It therefore called for the formation of urban-based work teams to carry out this rectification campaign. It further asserted that these teams should first take care of problems at the provincial, prefectural, and county levels before dealing with the basic-level cadres. Since these higher-level organs were located in cities, the document initiated an urban Five Antis Campaign to rectify the higher levels and lay an appropriate groundwork for follow-up work at the basic levels.[38] The effect of these shifts was to leave the peasants' associations essentially without a significant task to perform. Rectification had been shifted to a purely internal Party matter. Mao, however, had seen mobilization of non-Party people as one of the benefits of the rectification process, and in June 1964 the Chairman indicated his concern that the implementation of the Socialist Education Campaign was not involving sufficient mobilization of the poor and lower middle peasants.

During the first part of 1964, high-level cadres went down to the basic levels to carry out investigations of the conditions there. This method of acquiring data harkened back to the work style of the Yan'an period and reflected the fact that the leaders knew they could not rely on the reporting that came up through normal channels. Thus, for example, Liu Shaoqi went to Henan province for eighteen days – the province that had been a pacesetter during the Great Leap and had ended in a parlous state at the conclusion of the movement. Liu's wife, Wang Guangmei, spent five months incognito at the Taoyuan Brigade near her native city of Tianjin.

The Lius' findings made them deeply pessimistic about the situation in the rural areas. They ascertained that corruption was widespread and that many basic-level cadres opposed the Party (as did a large percentage of the peasants). As they came back from these trips, they felt that counterrevolution had a grip on a large portion of rural China and that draconian measures would be necessary to rescue the situation. Mao may well have agreed with this diagnosis – but he subsequently disagreed strongly with the measures taken to effect a cure.

The Revised Later Ten Points were drafted in September 1964 and reflected Liu's approach to the rectification campaign. They called for large work teams to go to selected communes and virtually take over the communes and shake them to the foundations in order to put them into shape. A work team would

38 This Five Antis Campaign should not be confused with the other campaign of the same name that peaked in early 1952. See Chapter 1.

stay in one locale for appproximately six months and would deal harshly with those cadres who were found to have become lax and corrupt. While in the communes, these work teams would also carry out a new class categorization in the countryside – the first such effort since land reform at the beginning of the 1950s. The whole Socialist Education movement would, according to the calendar of the Revised Later Ten Points, take five to six years to carry out throughout the country.

Mao Zedong had three complaints about the implementation of the Revised Later Ten Points. First, they narrowed the target of attack from revisionism to corruption. Second, they imposed penalties that were too harsh on the cadres. And third, they involved the imposition of massive work teams on the communes rather than mobilizing the masses themselves to carry out the campaign. In short, the Socialist Education movement had been twisted around to the point where it no longer served as a vehicle for propagating Mao's ideas about revisionism but, rather, had become a relatively savage effort to reimpose discipline in the rural Party organs.

Mao's response to this set of trends was to seize the initiative with his own new program document for the Socialist Education movement. Issued in January 1965, Mao's Twenty-three Articles reoriented the campaign so that it would become a general educational effort on the evils of revisionism at all levels of the Party. In the rural areas, this meant that the work teams pulled back, and many of the former cadres who had been severely punished by them were now rehabilitated – and their replacements removed. This simply increased the divisions among cadre ranks in the countryside on the eve of the Cultural Revolution.

Mao's efforts to use rectification as a means of forcing his political agenda on the society, then, proved only partially successful. As in his attempt to bring his version of politics more directly to bear through the formation of political departments in government and Party organs starting in 1964, the ruling bureaucracies proved capable of protecting their right to handle their own organizational affairs themselves. The Revised Later Ten Points were harsh, but they were also an approach that kept the rectification problem within the Party and precluded large-scale use of non-Party bodies to rectify the CCP. But it was precisely Mao's growing concern about the directions of policy within the CCP – a concern nurtured by Jiang Qing, Kang Sheng, and Lin Biao (along with Chen Boda and others) – that made the Chairman increasingly determined to enhance his leverage over this core political organization.

A changing Mao

Mao personally did not share the sense of personal insult that haunted Jiang Qing, and there is no reason to believe that he felt comfortable with the notion of Lin Biao as his successor at any point before the late 1960s, if then.[39] It appears, in fact, that during 1963–5 Mao had been toying with the notion of building up Peng Zhen as the replacement for Liu as his successor. Thus, as suggested earlier, Mao gradually put into place a coalition of partners to launch the Cultural Revolution, but he fully shared the goals and perspectives of none of them. How, then did the Chairman himself arrive at the conclusion that it was necessary to launch a frontal assault on his colleagues in the Politburo?

Three elements appear crucial to understanding Mao's psychological evolution during the critical years of 1959–66: his changing understanding of the potential evolution of the Chinese revolution; his continuing concern with the problem of succession; and his related sense of impending death. All of these intertwined in a way that escalated his fear that his life's work had produced a political system that would, in the final analysis, turn away from his values and prove as exploitative as the one it had replaced.

Mao's concerns about the future of the revolution cannot be separated from his evolving analysis of the degeneration of the Soviet political system. To be sure, Mao had spent much of his career fighting Soviet influences in the CCP, and in both substance and style he was the least Soviet of the Chinese leaders. During the mid-1950s he had launched concerted efforts to move China away from the Soviet model of development, and starting in 1958 he had included the military and military doctrine in this effort. But whereas before 1959 Mao had felt that the Soviet leaders had often been overbearing and lacking in understanding of the Chinese situation, after 1959 he began to wrestle with the question of whether the Soviet revolution itself had not gone fundamentally astray and changed its nature.

Essentially, as the Soviet Union began to try to interfere in Chinese internal affairs, to declare that its own revolutionary era was over, and to seek a more stable accommodation with the United States, Mao began to wonder whether the victory of socialism in a country ensured that there could not be a resurgence of capitalism in that society. Many things contributed to this intellectual shift. Mao thought he saw Khrushchev attempt to establish leverage over the Chinese navy in 1958, and perceived another attempt by Khrushchev to interfere in Chinese affairs via cancellation of the nuclear sharing agreement and collusion with Peng Dehuai in 1959. In that year also, Mao saw Khrushchev's declaration that the Soviet Union had become a "state of the whole people" rather than a "dictatorship of the proletariat";[40] his Camp David summit with the United States and the related effort to achieve

---

39 Indeed, at the height of Mao's reliance on Lin during 1966, he is said to have written to Jiang expressing his distrust of Lin.

40 By calling the Soviet Union a state of the whole people, Khrushchev indicated that the exploiting classes had been destroyed and class struggle had ended in the Soviet Union. A dictatorship of the proletariat, by contrast, is the form of dictatorship used by a Communist Party in power to wage class struggle against the remnants of the exploiting classes.

peaceful coexistence with the West; Moscow's seeming neutrality in the 1959 border tensions between Beijing and New Delhi; and the Soviet withdrawal of advisers from China in mid-1960. These were but a few examples.

Growing out of this new concern, Mao began a period of study of Soviet political economy, and he concluded that even Stalin had made some fundamental errors in this central theoretical sphere. He instructed Chinese delegations to debate the Soviets on the issues on which there was disagreement, and the Soviet responses increased his concerns. Jiang Qing noted that the swift withdrawal of Soviet advisers in 1960 had "shaken" Mao,[41] and probably from that point on he determined that, at a minimum, Khrushchev himself must be ousted in order to put the Soviet system back on solid ground. The refusal of the Soviet leadership to remove Khrushchev simply increased Mao's anxiety.

Having waged struggles with Khrushchev at meetings since 1958, Mao in 1963 decided that it was time to make the polemics open. On this central ideological plane, his Politburo colleagues evidently could not deny him the lead. Thus, during 1963–4 Mao supervised the writing of nine polemics, each of which was given wide publicity in China. As noted previously, Mao enlisted Kang Sheng's talents in writing these pieces, at a time when Kang had already become involved in the struggle against revisionism in the cultural arena at home.

It appears in retrospect that Mao used the nine polemics as a device for giving publicity to his political thinking within China. These polemics raised all the issues on which Mao in fact disagreed with his colleagues on the Politburo, and they provided a vehicle for identifying the Chairman's political views with the anti-Soviet struggle then being waged. This linkage of Chinese nationalism with Mao's political critique of revisionism proved a potent mixture – so potent, in fact, that Mao subsequently had the Chinese media attack Liu Shaoqi during the Cultural Revolution simply as "China's Khrushchev."

But beyond the shrewd politics in this approach there lay a human tragedy. There is no reason to suspect that Mao himself did not believe what he was saying about the degeneration of the Soviet revolution. He evidently could see the same forces underway in China, where his colleagues now argued (as they had in 1956) that class struggle must be subsumed under the overriding importance of the struggle for production. Inevitably, if these trends were allowed to continue, the younger generation would grow up with a revisionist perspective. Undoubtedly, history would then prove to be as unkind to Mao as it had been to Stalin after his death. Mao was a man with a keen sense of China's history, who compared himself in 1965 with the country's greatest

41 Witke, *Comrade Chiang Ch'ing*, 304.

emperors. He could now see the possibility of being remembered as a man who had in fact led the country astray. Equally disconcerting, his legacy to China might be a political system that exploited his beloved countryside and colluded with imperialism. Thus, Mao's observations of the evolution of the Soviet revolution significantly raised the stakes for him as he saw the trends in China during the first half of the 1960s.[42]

Mao's changing role in the Chinese political process also contributed to his sense of urgency. As noted previously, the Chairman reportedly had stopped his regular attendance at Politburo meetings in January 1958.[43] After that, he still received reports on Politburo discussions, and he had to approve all documents issued in the name of the CC before they could be circulated as official documents.[44] The same stricture evidently did not, however, apply to the documents issued by the Party Secretariat headed by Deng Xiaoping, and the Secretariat assumed a major role in the policy process of the first half of the 1960s. Mao subsequently complained, as noted earlier, that Deng did not consult with him on policy matters after 1959. Although this complaint may well have been exaggerated for effect, the sense of grievance undoubtedly was there.

More fundamentally, when Mao had pulled back from regular participation in Politburo meetings, it in fact marked the beginning of a period in which he dominated the political system more than at any time previously. Mao at that point indicated also that he would like to give up his role as head of state so that he could concentrate on the larger issues of the development of the revolution. On both the Party and state sides, therefore, in 1958 Mao saw himself as moving to a somewhat more Olympian role, in firm control over the central directions of policy while at the same time moving into place successors in whom he would have confidence. The greater responsibilities acquired by Liu Shaoqi, Deng Xiaoping, and Lin Biao in 1958–9 reflect the implementation of this strategy.

But after the collapse of the GLF, Mao found that in 1962 he was not able to assume full control of the basic directions of policy again. Rather, Liu and Deng now appeared to restrict his access to the policy flow and to twist the meaning of his directives, such as those on rectification. Thus, although Mao had wanted to step back to the second line in 1958–9, he was dismayed as that

---

42 Parenthetically, the fact that the Soviet leadership did not change Moscow's position on the issues in dispute with China in the wake of Khrushchev's ouster in October 1964 confirmed to Mao that it was the system and not simply an individual that had degenerated. This also helps to explain the vehemence of Mao's opposition to Luo Ruiqing's suggestion in the spring of 1965, noted earlier, that China cooperate with the Soviet Union to oppose the escalating U.S. commitment in Vietnam.

43 After that date, Mao attended only those Politburo meetings that he wanted to address. Otherwise, he relied on reports of what had happened at the meetings.

44 Documents issued by the Politburo were said to be issued by the Central Committee, so this rule in fact enabled the Chairman to ride herd on all official documents set out by the Politburo.

changed its meaning in the wake of the GLF. He then began to test his proposed
successors to determine whether they would support the general policies he
believed to be central to the future of the revolution. The more he tested, the
more they (with the exception of Lin Biao) demonstrated their inadequacy.

The heart of this growing disparity between Mao's priorities and those of
his successors lay in the different lessons they drew from the GLF. Mao, as
noted earlier, learned that mass mobilization is not the key to rapid economic
development. But at the same time, he retained his faith in mass mobilization
as an instrument of ideological renewal, social change, and rectification. Mass
mobilization was not, however, a policy that could be carried out by central
ministries in Beijing. Rather, by its very nature, it relied on the skills of CCP
generalists, rather than technical specialists, and demanded tolerance of sufficient decentralization to permit the flexibility this strategy inevitably entailed.
Thus mass mobilization was to an extent an inherently anti-intellectual and
anti-bureaucratic approach, although it could be implemented without totally
dismantling a centralized, specialist-dominated political system.

Liu Shaoqi and his colleagues concluded from the Great Leap that China
had progressed beyond the point where mass mobilization was any longer a
useful tool of policy. Given the parlous state of the country's economy and
political institutions in 1962, they felt that strong measures must be taken
to put control over the economy back in the hands of experts in the central
ministries and commissions, and that related efforts must be made to rebuild
disciplined Party and state organizations that would link the center to the
basic levels. The high tide politics inherent in major political campaigns
could only disrupt the effort they were making to salvage what they could
from a bad situation. The campaign approach had served the CCP well in the
days in Yan'an and the early 1950s, but it was no longer suited to the complex
task of governing the country in the 1960s.

Mao tried to nudge the system back toward his own priorities through
a series of measures. Some, like the use of rectification campaigns to bring
mass mobilization back into the system, have already been detailed. Aside
from these, the Chairman periodically indicated specific policy preferences
in various fields that had the effect of attacking the urban orientation and
technical premises of the Liu–Deng strategy. In culture, egged on by his wife
and Kang Sheng, he demanded that writers and artists go to the grass roots
in order to understand life through living with average people, especially in
the countryside. In medicine, he leveled a series of blasts at the Ministry of
Health and demanded that the best doctors of the country leave the cities and
practice in the rural areas.[45] In education, he advocated a shorter curriculum,

45 For details, see David Lampton, *The politics of medicine in China*, 129–92.

more concentration on applied studies rather than theory, and the integration of manual labor with the academic curriculum in a significant way. He also wanted school textbooks rewritten to take better account of local needs and conditions.[46] In all these areas, the Chairman's recommendations would have the effect of undercutting the control exercised by the authorities in the relevant ministries in Beijing.

Mao also objected to the economic centralization and specialization inherent in the program of forming specialized national companies to run major sectors of the economy. Calling these companies "trusts," Mao argued instead for greater regional self-sufficiency. As noted earlier, this approach also tied in neatly with Mao's preferred strategy for coping with the escalating threat from the United States in Vietnam in 1965.[47]

The results in virtually every area were largely the same. In each case, Liu Shaoqi and others accepted the general thrust of Mao's critique of current policy and took some measures to implement his ideas. But at the same time, these measures fell far short of the drastic restructuring of the system Mao had in mind. As a result, Mao increasingly saw his colleagues as running a bureaucratic leviathan that gobbled up his pressing demands and turned them into relatively innocuous reforms that did little to affect the basic functions and trends of the system.

Finally, Mao's concerns about these issues grew rapidly in 1964–5 because, as his available speeches and interviews indicate, he began to focus on his own mortality. Beginning in 1964, he made repeated references to "going to see Karl Marx" and the inevitable mortality of any man. He also revealed these concerns in startling fashion in an interview with André Malraux in early 1965. Although it is impossible to be precise about Mao's mental state at the time, it seems reasonable to conjecture, as Robert Lifton has, that the Chairman increasingly saw his physical life coming to a close and his fundamental identity as defined by the fate of the revolution he had fathered. In other words, Mao thought he could achieve immortality only through the continuation of his revolution along proper paths,[48] but what the Chairman saw as he looked around him was the subversion of that revolution through the revisionism of his chosen successors. The psychological and political stakes for him thus became so high that he felt compelled eventually to launch a brutal frontal assault on the Party he had spent his life creating.

46 For details, see Peter Seybolt, ed., *Revolutionary education in China*, Introduction and 5–62.
47 On trusts, see Ahn, *Chinese politics and the Cultural Revolution*, 139–44.
48 Robert Lifton, *Revolutionary immortality*.

The split in the Yan'an leadership

This analysis has focused on the different components that came together to launch the Cultural Revolution in 1966. It has said relatively little about the targets of that major campaign. Much could be written about the policies and developments of 1962–5, a time of impressive economic recovery and policy initiatives in a range of areas related to the economy. But the economic side of this analysis belongs in another chapter, and on a political level it appears that the leaders tried to reestablish the system that had developed by late 1956: a system of clear division of responsibility, with a powerful Secretariat serving the needs of the Politburo, with extensive ministerial direction of the government and the use of wide-ranging State Council commissions to prevent the system from becoming too fractionated along functional lines, and so forth.[49]

It seems too that the leaders of this system did not see themselves as approaching a showdown with Mao. They continued to respect him and tried to accommodate what they must have felt were his somewhat misguided policy demands. But they were concerned overwhelmingly with putting the country back on its feet after the GLF and recapturing the initiative in their dealing with Chinese society. In this, as noted, they disagreed with Mao's more optimistic assessment of the situation as of 1962 – and probably thereafter. And they were almost certainly aware of the potential dangers of allowing Mao's future coalition partners to realize their ambitions. Thus, as noted, they tried to limit the PLA penetration of other organs and attempted to keep Jiang Qing out of power in the cultural arena. Unfortunately, too little data are available to specify what, if any, measures were taken against Kang Sheng's growing power.

Indeed, so much of our information on the period from the Great Leap to the Cultural Revolution comes from the polemical literature of 1966–76 (and the often almost equally biased material from after 1976) that it is important to bear in mind the issues that remain in doubt about the history of these eight years. The key unknowns or areas of significant doubt are the following:

First, what did the various members of the leadership who did not join the Cultural Revolution coalition think about the Chairman and his policy preferences during these years? The record presented during the Cultural Revolution is almost wholly negative, but it is also highly selective. For example, although the propaganda apparatus purportedly tried to play down Mao's preferences, in point of fact the official media of the day gave enormous

---

49 As of 1965, the number of State Council ministries and major commissions stood at fifty-five, the same number as existed at the height of the first Five-Year Plan, before the streamlining of the government during the GLF.

prominence to the cult of Mao and the critique of revisionism. Also, even though a range of indicators suggests that throughout much of the later part of this period Mao was purposely elevating Peng Zhen, virtually every quotation from Peng made available during the Cultural Revolution had him disparaging Mao's health policies, Jiang Qing's attempts to reform opera, and the like. Indeed, on substantive issues it appears that the leaders around Liu always tried to meet Mao more than halfway (although they were understandably less tolerant of Jiang Qing and more wary of Kang Sheng[50] and Lin Biao). By about 1964 Mao may, therefore, have begun to distort reality quite seriously in his own mind, his suspicions fed by his wife and others who hoped to gain by a reordering of the leading organs. Although Liu and colleagues clearly did not fully share Mao's sense of priorities and methods, the Chairman's changing mental state and concerns about his mortality may have cause him to turn normal types of policy disagreements into a moral struggle between the forces of good and evil.

Second, one important dimension of this story – the role of the public security apparatus and of Mao's personal security forces – is unfortunately too well hidden from public view to be told. Both Kang Sheng and Luo Ruiqing, as noted, had been key figures in the public security system. When Luo left the Ministry of Public Security to move into the PLA in the wake of Lushan, he was replaced by Xie Fuzhi, who in turn rocketed to political power during the early part of the Cultural Revolution. Xie's meteoric rise in 1966–7 suggests that the Ministry of Public Security played a key part in the conflicts leading to the Cultural Revolution, but the details are not available. The former head of the CCP's General Office, Yang Shangkun, was formally purged in 1966, and he was said to have planted listening devices in Mao's private quarters. Once Yang was out of the way, Mao's personal security force (the 8341 Division, which also provided security for other ranking leaders), under the Chairman's long-time bodyguard Wang Dongxing, moved quickly to take over the former functions of the General Office. This same unit assumed charge of the detention of ranking leaders during the Cultural Revolution. But little concrete can be said about the role of Wang Dongxing and the entire security apparatus during the years before 1966.

Third, the role of Zhou Enlai remains somewhat obscure, even though the premier maintained a high profile throughout these years. Zhou's entire career suggested that he would lean toward Liu Shaoqi's preferences on policy issues during 1962–5, and yet in the summer of 1966 Zhou's support proved crucial to Mao's launching of the Cultural Revolution. Zhou's 1966 performance, in

---

50 For example, Wang Jiaxiang prevented Kang Sheng from gaining full access to the materials on the CCP's relations with other Communist Parties: *Gongren ribao* (Worker's daily), 4 February 1981, trans. in *FBIS/PRC*, 26 February 1981, L-9.

turn, raises questions about his real role during the previous years. Did he himself begin to think of replacing Liu Shaoqi as Mao's successor? If so, did he quietly contribute to the Chairman's distrust of his colleagues? Perhaps Zhou simply adhered to a rule that he would support Mao in any showdown, even though he might try to curtail some of the Chairman's policy thrusts with which he disagreed. Unfortunately, Zhou is such an important figure that the different hypotheses about him support considerably different interpretations of these crucial years – and the data necessary to discriminate among them are missing.

In sum, for all the years that have passed and the data that have become available, the period from the GLF to the Cultural Revolution remains at best partially understood and will be so for some time to come. Much more can be pieced together now that the "moderates" are having their chance to contribute to the literature, but these additions to the record leave uncomfortably large gaps. On the basis of what can be learned at this point, however, there is a clear answer to the question "What caused the split in the Yan'an leadership?" The answer is that it was a combination of three factors: different lessons drawn from the catastrophic consequences of the GLF; the tensions arising from the issue of the succession to Mao, which was constantly on the agenda after 1958; and the growing fears of an aging and possibly increasingly senile leader. Too much information is missing, though, to enable us to judge the relative weight and influence of each of these factors.

CHAPTER 3

THE CHINESE STATE IN CRISIS, 1966–1969

HARRY HARDING

The Great Proletarian Cultural Revolution, which by official Chinese reckoning lasted from the beginning of 1966 to the death of Mao Zedong some ten years later, was one of the most extraordinary events of this century. The images of the Cultural Revolution remain vivid: the young Red Guards, in military uniform, filling the vast Tiananmen Square in Beijing, many weeping in rapture at the sight of their Great Helmsman standing atop the Gate of Heavenly Peace; veteran Communist officials, wearing dunce caps and placards defiling them as "monsters" and "freaks," herded in the backs of open-bed trucks, and driven through the streets of major cities by youth only one-third their age; the wall posters, often many sheets of newsprint in size, filled with vitriolic condemnations of the "revisionist" or "counterrevolutionary" acts of senior leaders. The little red book carried by the Red Guards – a plastic-bound volume containing selected quotations from Chairman Mao – remains a symbol of the revolt of the young against adult authority.

From a purely narrative perspective, the Cultural Revolution can best be understood as a tragedy, both for the individual who launched it and for the society that endured it. The movement was largely the result of the decisions of a single man, Mao Zedong. Mao's restless quest for revolutionary purity in a postrevolutionary age provided the motivation for the Cultural Revolution, his unique charismatic standing in the Chinese Communist movement gave him the resources to get it underway, and his populist faith in the value of mass mobilization lent the movement its form. Mao's breadth of vision and his ability to shape the destiny of 800 million Chinese are the elements of myth, producing a man who appears larger than life.

But, as in classical tragedy, these seemingly heroic elements were, in the end, fatally flawed. Mao's quest for revolutionary purity led him to exaggerate and misappraise the political and social problems confronting China in the mid-1960s. His personal authority gave him enough power to unleash potent social forces but not enough power to control them. And his confidence that the masses, once mobilized, would be the salvation of the country proved woefully misplaced as the mass movement degenerated into violence, factionalism, and chaos. The Cultural Revolution, which Mao hoped would be his most significant and most enduring contribution to China and to Marxism–Leninism, instead became the monumental error of his latter years.

Because of Mao's ability to move China, what was a tragedy for the man became simultaneously a tragedy for the nation. China's leaders now describe the Cultural Revolution as nothing less than a calamity for their country. Although the economic damage done by the Cultural Revolution was not as severe as that produced by the Great Leap Forward (GLF), and although the human costs were not as devastating as those of the Taiping Rebellion, the Japanese invasion, or the Communist revolution itself, the effects of the Cultural Revolution in terms of careers disrupted, spirits broken, and lives lost were ruinous indeed. The impact of the movement on Chinese politics and society may take decades finally to erase. What is more, these costs of the Cultural Revolution were largely the predictable consequences of Mao's perception that China was on the brink of the restoration of capitalism, and of his prescription that the mobilization of urban youth was the best way to prevent it.

From a different point of view, that of political analysis, the Cultural Revolution is equally intriguing. Political scientists have become accustomed to speaking of "crises" of political development, during which established political institutions are challenged and shaken by the pressures of economic transformation, intellectual ferment, political mobilization, and social change.[1] Unless effective reforms can be undertaken, political crises can produce violence and disorder, and even revolt and revolution. In this sense, the Cultural Revolution appears at first glance to have been similar to crises of political modernization experienced by many other developing countries in the twentieth century. The Chinese Communist Party (CCP) faced high levels of urban protest, rooted in widespread dissatisfaction with a variety of social, economic, and organizational policies. It proved unable either to suppress the dissent or to accommodate it effectively. The result of these circumstances, in China as elsewhere, was chaos and anarchy, until the military intervened to restore order and begin the reconstruction of political institutions.

What is unique about the Cultural Revolution, however, is that this political crisis was deliberately induced by the leader of the regime itself. It was Mao who called into question the legitimacy of the CCP. It was Mao who mobilized

---

[1] Leonard Binder et al., *Crises and sequences in political development.*

the social forces that would undermine his own government. And it was Mao who provided the political and ideological vocabulary for protest and dissent. The man who had undertaken a revolution against China's old regime now sought to launch a revolt against the new political establishment that he himself had created.

But Mao's victory in his first revolution was not matched by comparable success in the second. Successful revolutions are, as Mao himself recognized, acts of construction as well as destruction: They build a new order even as they destroy an old one. Mao's first revolution was guided not only by a critique of the existing system but also by a relatively coherent image of a new economic and political order. Similarly, the first revolution not only mobilized mass discontent but also produced a disciplined revolutionary organization, the CCP, that could govern effectively after the seizure of power. Mao's second revolution, in contrast, had no clear guiding vision and produced no unified organization to implement a new set of programs and policies. It toppled the old regime but left only chaos and disorder in its place.

This chapter is a history and analysis of the first three and a half years of the Cultural Revolution, from its initial stirrings in late 1965 to the convocation of the Ninth National Congress of the CCP in April 1969. This is the period that some have described as the Red Guard phase of the Cultural Revolution and others as its manic stage. It is the period in which the political crisis induced by Mao was the deepest, the chaos the greatest, and the human costs the highest.

These three and a half years encompass several shorter periods, each of which is dealt with in turn in this chapter. First, there was the growing confrontation between Mao and the Party establishment from the fall of 1965 to the summer of the following year. During that period, Mao began to develop a power base with which to confront those leaders in the Party whom he regarded as revisionists. Using his political resources, Mao secured the dismissal or demotion of selected officials within the armed forces, the cultural establishment, the Beijing municipal government, and the Politburo itself. Then, at the Eleventh Plenum in August 1966, Mao obtained the formal endorsement of the Party's Central Committee (CC) for a criticism of revisionism on an even broader scale.

The second period, from the Eleventh Plenum through the end of 1966, was one in which Mao's assault on the Party establishment spread across the country, with the Red Guards now its major instrument. The outcome of this period was not, however, what Mao had intended. He had apparently hoped that the Red Guards would form a unified mass movement, that officials would accept criticism from these ad hoc organizations in a sincere and open manner, and that the Party would therefore emerge from the Cultural

Revolution with its orientation corrected and its authority intact. In fact, none of these developments occurred. The Red Guards split into competing organizations, with some attacking the Party establishment and others defending it. Party leaders at the provincial and municipal levels sought first to suppress the mass movement, then to coopt it, and finally to evade it. The escalation of conflict, both between competing Red Guard organizations and between the mass movement and the Party establishment, served not to strengthen the authority of the Party but to weaken it. By the end of 1966, the political institutions in many of China's most important cities were in total collapse.

During the third period, from January 1967 until mid-1968, Mao ordered that political power be seized from the discredited Party establishment. After a few weeks of uncertainty as to the procedures by which this would be done, Mao decided that political power would be shared, at the provincial and municipal levels, by coalitions of three forces; the mass organizations that had emerged during the Cultural Revolution, those cadres who were able to survive the movement, and the People's Liberation Army (PLA). The problem was that none of these groups was completely reliable. The mass organizations were prone to violence and anarchy, and the cadres and the PLA, particularly at the provincial and municipal levels, tended to work together to suppress the most obstreperous of the Red Guard activists. Unable completely to control the forces he had unleashed, Mao's only recourse was to play one against another. Once again, the result was near chaos, and Mao ultimately concluded that the only way to prevent collapse was to demobilize the Red Guards and allow the PLA to restore order.

This decision marked the beginning of the final stage under consideration in this chapter: the reconstruction of the Chinese political system. This process culminated with the Ninth Party Congress in April 1969, which elected a new CC, approved a new Politburo, and adopted a new Party constitution. Given the preeminent role of the Chinese military during this period, it should not be surprising that army officers occupied the plurality of the leadership positions filled at the Ninth Congress, or that Minister of Defense Lin Biao secured anointment as Mao's successor. But even the growing power of the military in civilian affairs was not sufficient to restore political stability. Power remained divided among the radical intellectuals who had mobilized the Red Guards, the veteran officials who had survived their assault, and the military who had finally suppressed them. As the next chapter in this volume will reveal, the legacy of the Red Guard stage of the Cultural Revolution was chronic instability that was ultimately to be removed only by the death of Mao Zedong, the purge of the radicals, and the emergence of Deng Xiaoping as China's preeminent leader.

THE CHINESE STATE IN CRISIS 151

TOWARD A CONFRONTATION

Sources of political conflict

Mao Zedong surveyed the political scene in China in the early 1960s with increasing dissatisfaction. On issue after issue, the Party had adopted policies that Mao regarded as unnecessary or unacceptable: a return to private farming in agriculture, the resurrection of material incentives in industry, a concentration on urban medicine in public health, the development of a two-track system in education, and the reappearance of traditional themes and styles in literature and the arts. Most of these policies had been advanced by their proponents as ways of restoring social cohesion and economic productivity after the Anti-Rightist Campaign and the GLF. In Mao's view, however, these measures were creating a degree of inequality, specialization, hierarchy, and dissent that was incompatible with his vision of a socialist society.[2]

Mao's dissatisfaction with Party policies was exacerbated by growing personal tensions between the Chairman and some of his chief lieutenants. There were, to begin with, an increasing number of incidents that Mao chose to regard as acts of *lèse-majesté*. Although Mao had supposedly withdrawn voluntarily from day-to-day leadership in late 1958, he increasingly resented the way in which some leaders, particularly the Party's secretary-general, Deng Xiaoping, failed to consult with him before making decisions on major issues. In October 1966, for example, Mao would complain that "Whenever we are at a meeting together, [Deng] sits far away from me. For six years, since 1959, he has not made a general report of work to me."[3] In March 1961, when he discovered that Deng had made some major decisions on agricultural reorganization without consulting him, Mao asked sarcastically, "Which Emperor decided these?"[4] Mao was irritated by the allegorical criticisms of his leadership that began to appear in Chinese literature and journalism in the early 1960s, and must have been even more angered that officials responsible for intellectual matters, including Peng Zhen and Lu Dingyi, were doing nothing to bring the offending writers to task.

In addition, Mao became increasingly frustrated by his inability to bend the bureaucracy to his will. Between 1962 and 1965 he tried, in five areas of long-standing personal interest, to alter the policies that the Party had adopted in the immediate post-Leap period. Mao attempted to halt trends

2 On the emerging conflict between Mao and his colleagues in the early 1960s, see Byung-joon Ahn, *Chinese politics and the Cultural Revolution: Dynamics of policy processes;* Harry Harding, *Organizing China: The problem of bureaucracy, 1949–1976*, ch. 7; Roderick MacFarquhar, *The origins of the Cultural Revolution. 2. The Great Leap Forward 1938–60;* and Chapter 2 of this volume.
3 Jerome Ch'en, ed., *Mao papers: Anthology and bibliography*, 40.
4 Parris H. Chang, *Power and policy in China* (rev. ed.), 131.

toward private farming in agriculture, proposed reform of the curriculum and examination system in higher education, criticized the concentration of public health facilities in urban areas, proposed the creation of peasant organizations to uncover corruption and inefficiency among rural Party and commune cadres, and denounced the reappearance of traditional themes and revisionist theories in intellectual affairs.

Although the Party establishment ultimately responded to each of these initiatives, it did so in a way that Mao justifiably believed to be half-hearted and unenthusiastic. In part, this was because many senior leaders continued to support the policies that had been adopted in the post-Leap period and were reluctant to alter them at Mao's behest. In part, too, the sluggishness in responding to Mao's wishes reflected the normal attempt of bureaucracies to act gradually and incrementally, preserving as much of existing routines as possible even while undertaking some of the new initiatives that Mao proposed. Moreover, Mao's intentions were often expressed in vague and ambiguous language, with the Chairman better able to criticize emphatically tendencies he disliked than to suggest concrete alternatives.

In any event, Mao's conclusion was that the sluggishness of the bureaucracy, the emergence of traditional and "bourgeois" ideas in intellectual life, and the emphasis on efficiency in national economic strategy together created the danger that revisionism – a fundamental departure from a genuinely socialist path of development – was emerging in China. At first, Mao voiced these concerns in a rather low-keyed manner. In 1962, for instance, he called on the Party to overcome revisionism, but said that this task should not "interfere with our [routine] work . . . or be placed in a very prominent position."[5] Equally important, Mao initially attempted to overcome revisionist tendencies in the Party through rather modest and traditional means: the launching of campaigns within the bureaucracy to study Marxist–Leninist doctrine and to emulate model leaders.

But as the ineffectiveness of these measures became apparent, Mao's warnings became more pointed. He ultimately concluded that revisionism was more widespread than he had anticipated and that the highest leaders of the Party, because of their reluctance to cope with the problem effectively, were possibly guilty of revisionist thinking themselves. At a work conference in September 1965, Mao asked his colleagues, "If revisionism appears in the Central Committee, what are you going to do? It is probable that it will appear, and this is a great danger. "[6]

5 Stuart R. Schram, ed., *Chairman Mao talks to the people: Talks and letters, 1956–1971*, 193–5.
6 Ch'en, *Mao papers*, 102.

It was only gradually that these warnings about revisionism were transformed into a systematic theory justifying a Cultural Revolution. Significantly, in fact, the movement itself was launched before a full theoretical justification was provided for it. But two editorials published in 1967 have been identified by the Chinese as laying out in fullest form Mao's emerging theory of "continuing the revolution under the dictatorship of the proletariat."[7] Although these essays were not written by Mao himself, there is little reason to doubt that the ideas expressed in them reflected the Chairman's views.

Taken together, the editorials conclude that, in Mao's eyes, the greatest danger to a successful socialist revolution is not the threat of attack from abroad, but rather the restoration of capitalism at home. Mao believed that the experience of the Soviet Union after the death of Stalin proved that the restoration of capitalism could occur if "revisionists" usurped power within the ruling Communist Party. To prevent this, it would be necessary to wage continuing class struggle against those "Party persons in authority" who might attempt to follow the capitalist road. Indeed, this would be the major form of class struggle in socialist society after the nationalization of industry and the collectivization of agriculture. The method for waging this class struggle would be to "boldly arouse the masses from below" in a Cultural Revolution, in order to criticize not only revisionist power holders within the Party but also the selfish and liberal tendencies within their own minds. Because the problem of revisionism was thus rooted in human selfishness, it would be necessary to have a succession of Cultural Revolutions over many decades to preserve the purity of purpose of a socialist society.

Forging Mao's power base

By 1964, the basis began to be created for such an assault on the Party establishment. The elements of this power base were created initially in a piecemeal and seemingly uncoordinated manner. One element was produced by the impersonal operation of social and economic policy, which created disadvantaged and disenchanted groups in society, particularly among the urban young. A second, under the guidance of Mao's wife, Jiang Qing, began to emerge in the intellectual and cultural spheres. A third was produced, within the army, by Minister of Defense Lin Biao. Between 1964 and 1966, these three elements were more systematically assembled into a

---

7 Editorial department of *Renmin ribao* and *Hongqi*, "A great historic document," 18 May 1967, in *PR*, 19 May 1967, 10–12; and editorial departments of *Renmin ribao, Hongqi*, and *Jiefangjun bao*, "Advance along the road opened up by the October socialist revolution," 6 November 1967, in *PR*, 10 November 1967, 9–11, 14–16. Recent accounts have revealed that the latter essay was drafted under the supervision of Chen Boda and Yao Wenyuan. See Sun Dunfan et al., eds., *Zhongguo gongchandang lishi jiangyi* (Teaching materials on the history of the Chinese Communist Party), 2.268. (Hereafter *Lishi jiangyi*.)

political coalition that, under Mao's leadership, was powerful enough to conduct the Great Proletarian Cultural Revolution against even an entrenched
Party apparatus.

The PLA

The most crucial element in Mao's power base, given its control of organized
armed force in China, was the PLA under the leadership of Lin Biao.[8] After
succeeding Peng Dehuai as minister of defense at the Lushan Plenum in 1959,
Lin had devoted particular attention to reviving political work in the military
apparatus – a policy intended both to ensure the loyalty of the armed forces to
Maoist leadership and to bolster his own reputation in Mao's eyes. Lin rebuilt
the Party branches at the basic levels of the PLA, resurrected the network
of political departments that had deteriorated under Peng's stewardship, and
tightened the control of the Party's Military Affairs Commission (MAC) over
military matters. Lin intensified the army's program of political education,
basing it in large part on a new compilation of quotations from Mao Zedong,
a collection that would serve as the model for the little red book later used by
the Red Guards.

At the same time, Lin sought to restore some of the military traditions of the
revolutionary period. In the 1950s, the organizational and tactical principles
of guerrilla warfare as practiced in the 1930s and 1940s had been set aside in
favor of those characteristic of more regularized armed forces. A formal system
of ranks and insignia had been instituted. The militia had been deemphasized,
with Peng Dehuai proposing that it be supplanted by a more formal system of
military reserves. Greater priority had been placed on hierarchy and discipline,
as against the "military democracy" of earlier years. Soviet military doctrine,
with its stress on positional warfare and modern ordnance, replaced the Maoist
doctrine of mobile warfare using primitive weapons.

A reaction against the abandonment of the PLA's revolutionary heritage
in favor of these "foreign doctrines" was apparent as early as the mid-1950s.
Accordingly, some attempts to redress the balance were undertaken in the latter part of the decade, while Peng Dehuai still served as minister of defense. But
the process of "rerevolutionization" accelerated under Lin Biao's leadership.
New military manuals stressed such traditional concepts as joint command
by political commissars and line officers, the importance of political work
in maintaining the loyalty and morale of the troops, close ties between the

---

8 On the PLA in the early 1960s, see John Gittings, "The Chinese army's role in the Cultural Revolution,"
   Pacific Affairs, 39.3–4 (Fall-Winter 1966–7), 269–89; John Gittings, *The role of the Chinese army*, ch. 12;
   Ellis Joffe, "The Chinese army under Lin Piao: Prelude to political intervention," in John M, H. Lindbeck,
   ed., *China: Management of a revolutionary society*, 343–74; and Ellis Joffe, *Party and army: Professionalism
   and political control in the Chinese officer corps, 1949–1964*.

army and civilian society, and egalitarian relations between officers and men. Military strategy once again emphasized the infantry (as opposed to specialized services), the militia (as opposed to the regular forces), and small-unit tactics (as opposed to maneuvers by larger, multiservice forces). Finally, in a step with enormous symbolic significance, military ranks were abolished in 1965, and officers removed the Soviet-style uniforms and insignia they had worn since the mid-1950s and returned to the unadorned olive-drab uniforms of the Yan'an years.

And yet, Lin Biao never allowed this policy framework to weaken the military prowess of the PLA. Even as he proclaimed that men were more important than weapons in ensuing military victory, Lin simultaneously sponsored the modernization of the air force and the development of China's nuclear capability. He said that political education should have the highest priority in military training, but he saw to it that the troops actually devoted more time to military exercises than to ideological study. Lin reassured the PLA's adherence to the principle of people's war, but the level of militia activity declined from the heights reached during the GLF, and rural militia units devoted more attention to agricultural production and internal security than to military affairs.

Thus, during the early 1960s, Lin presided not only over the revitalization of the political structure in the armed forces and the restoration of some traditional military concepts, but also over the successful border campaign against India in 1962 and the detonation of China's first atomic bomb two years later. These achievements indicated that the "redness" of the PLA did not come at the expense of its military expertise.

The successful performance of the PLA in the early 1960s contrasted with the widely perceived decay of the Party and state agencies during the same period. It is little wonder, therefore, that Mao came to see Lin Biao as a more effective organizational manager and a more loyal lieutenant than either Liu Shaoqi or Deng Xiaoping, and began to identify the PLA as a model for civilian bureaucracies to emulate. To that end, a nationwide campaign to "Learn from the PLA" was launched in February 1964. As part of that movement, the government bureaucracy was ordered to form political departments, modeled on those in the PLA, that would be responsible for the regular political education of civilian officials. Between 30 and 40 percent of the positions created in those new political departments were held by demobilized PLA cadres or by officers seconded from the armed forces.[9]

9 On the campaign to learn from the PLA, see Ahn, *Chinese politics*, ch. 6; John Gittings, "The 'Learn from the army' campaign," *CQ*, 18 (April–June 1964), 153–9; Harding, *Organizing China*, 217–23; and Ralph L. Powell, "Commissars in the economy: The 'Learn from the PLA' movement in China," *Asian Survey*, 5.3 (March 1965), 125–38.

Lin Biao was hardly reluctant to see the army assume this new role. It is quite likely, in fact, that Lin suggested the formation of political departments in state agencies in the first place; and it is even possible that he proposed they be placed under the supervision of the General Political Department of the armed forces. If adopted, such a recommendation simultaneously would have dramatically increased the influence of the PLA in civilian affairs and would have made significant inroads into the traditional responsibilities of the Party organization. Although Liu Shaoqi accepted Mao's decision to establish political departments within government bureaus, he allgedly insisted that they be placed under the jurisdiction of the Party agencies responsible for economic work, rather than under the PLA's political apparatus.[10]

Even so, the initiation of the "Learn from the PLA" Campaign and the creation of the political departments in the government bureaucracy gave the PLA and Lin Biao more influence over civilian affairs than at any time since the early 1950s. In February 1966, the PLA held a conference on cultural matters that, although nominally dealing only with literature and art in the armed forces, had great impact on civilian cultural circles as well.[11] And in March 1966, Lin wrote a letter to a work conference on industrial and commercial affairs advocating that economic administrators be more active in the study of Maoism – a relatively innocuous message, but one that symbolized Lin's growing ability to speak out on matters concerning national economic policy.[12]

The radical intellectuals

The second element in the nascent Maoist coalition was a group of radical intellectuals who, by mid-1966, would come to serve as the doctrinal arbiters and mass mobilizers of the Cultural Revolution. The key person in assembling these leftist propagandists and writers was Mao's wife, Jiang Qing, who quickly realized that the emerging tensions between Mao and the Party establishment gave her an unusual opportunity to realize her own political ambitions.

Before traveling to Yan'an to join the Communist movement in 1937, Jiang Qing had been a second-string actress and an active participant in Shanghai's artistic and political demimonde. Her liaison with Mao in 1938 seemed at first to offer this ambitious woman the chance to switch from the theater to politics. But, given Jiang Qing's rather checkered background, her marriage to the Chairman was bitterly opposed by many other senior Party leaders and may have been accepted only after she agreed to refrain from political activity for

10 Radio Peking, 16 December 1967, cited in John Gittings, "Army-Party relations in the light of the Cultural Revolution," in John Wilson Lewis, ed., *Party leadership and revolutionary power in China*, 395.
11 Kenneth Lieberthal, *A research guide to central Party and government meetings in China 1949–1975*, 238–9.
12 Michael Y. M. Kau, ed., *The Lin Piao affair: Power politics and military coup*, 321–2.

thirty years.[13] Ill health forced her to keep the bargain throughout the 1950s; but in the early 1960s, with her health if not her temperament somewhat improved, she undertook a new project: the reform of Chinese culture. This was a task for which her earlier theatrical career had given her some minimal credentials, and for which Mao's growing impatience with "revisionism" in culture provided substantial encouragement and support.

Jiang's initial efforts to reform traditional Beijing Opera encountered the disdain of established performers, the opposition of officials responsible for cultural affairs, and thus the neglect of the press.[14] Faced with these obstacles, Jiang turned to a group of young, relatively radical intellectuals in Beijing and Shanghai. Compared with more prestigious members of China's urban intelligentsia, these were younger men, lower in rank, less cosmopolitan in outlook, and more steeped in Marxist intellectual traditions. Many had taken, out of a combination of conviction and careerism, relatively radical positions on academic and cultural matters ever since the Anti-Rightist Campaign of 1957 and had been engaged in an ongoing debate with their more liberal seniors throughout the cultural relaxation of the early 1960s.[15]

Jiang Qing developed contacts with two main groups of these radical intellectuals: One was centered in the Institute of Philosophy and Social Science of the Chinese Academy of Sciences in Beijing (including Guan Feng, Qi Benyu, and Lin Jie), and another was centered in the Municipal Propaganda Department in Shanghai (including Zhang Chunqiao, the director of the bureau, and Yao Wenyuan). The former group, more academic in character, specialized in history and philosophy. The Shanghai group, in contrast, was more experienced in journalistic criticism and more knowledgeable about the creative arts. Jiang's entree to these groups was facilitated, in the case of Beijing, by Chen Boda, who for years had served as Mao Zedong's personal secretary and theoretician; and, in the case of Shanghai, by Ke Qingshi, the Party chief for the East China region, who, unlike many Party leaders, remained close to Mao even after the debacle of the GLF.

Between 1963 and 1966, Jiang Qing and her coterie of intellectuals focused principally on cultural and artistic matters, particularly on her interest in the reform of Beijing Opera and other performing arts. (In this undertaking another regional Party secretary, Tao Zhu of the Central-South region, also proved supportive of Jiang Qing.) Gradually, however, as the confrontation between Mao and the Party establishment grew more intense, the radical

---

13 Ross Terrill, *The white-boned demon: A biography of Madame Mao Zedong*, 154.

14 On Jiang Qing's role in this period and her relationship with young, radical intellectuals, see Merle Goldman, *China's intellectuals: Advise and dissent*, ch. 3; and Roxane Witke, *Comrade Chiang Ch'ing*, 321–2.

15 The distinction between the Shanghai and Beijing groups is drawn from Goldman, *China's intellectuals*, ch. 3.

intellectuals began to turn to more overtly political themes, providing, as we shall see, both the criticism of Mao's rivals and the ideological rationale for the Cultural Revolution.

This second element in the Maoist coalition, to use Lowell Dittmer's apposite expression, played the role of "imperial favorites."[16] The radical intellectuals had narrow careers, rather dogmatic and idealistic political positions, and little political standing independent of their association, through Jiang Qing, with Mao. They had little stake in the established political order in China and perceived clearly that their own careers would be advanced more rapidly through opposition to the system than through patient accommodation. But their power would increase as Mao found that their loyalty to him, their skills at propaganda, and their mastery of radical doctrine made them useful tools in his assault on the Party establishment.

A mass base

The final element in the Maoist coalition, latent until the middle and latter parts of 1966, was a mass base, composed of those elements of urban Chinese society that regarded themselves as disadvantaged. Paradoxically, social tensions in Chinese cities had been substantially increased by two policies, adopted under Mao's prodding, that were supposed to create a more egalitarian society: the reemphasis on class background in educational recruitment and job assignment, and a program of part-time industrial employment for suburban peasants.

The most active in Mao's mass base were China's high school and college students. Their participation in the Red Guard movement of the Cultural Revolution can be explained in large part by the normal idealism of the young, which made them ready to share Mao's indignation at the elitism, inequality, and bureaucratic stagnation that seemed to be plaguing China in the mid-1960s. China's student population doubtless also welcomed the sense of importance and power provided by their involvement in Mao's campaign against revisionism.

In addition, the educational policies of the early 1960s had produced serious cleavages and grievances among China's students. While opportunities for primary and junior middle school education were expanding, enrollment at both senior middle schools and universities declined sharply from the levels attained during the GLF, as the state sought to retrench overextended budgets during a period of serious economic recession. There was a sharper differentiation between elite middle schools, whose graduates had a good

16 Lowell Dittmer, "Bases of power in Chinese politics: A theory and an analysis of the fall of the 'Gang of Four,'" *World Politics*, 31.1 (October 1978), 42.

chance to go to college, and lesser institutions, whose graduates had little prospect for higher education. By 1964–5, furthermore, in a program foreshadowing the mass rustification policies of later years, middle school students who had not been placed in universities or industrial enterprises were being sent, in large numbers, to frontier and rural areas.[17]

These declining opportunities for upward mobility – and the real danger of a permanent transfer to the countryside – focused student concern on the standards for advancement. Formally, three criteria were important in assigning students to elite middle schools, universities, and the most desirable jobs: class background, academic achievement, and political behavior. But the relative weight of the criteria was changing in the mid-1960s, with class background and political behavior becoming more important and academic achievement becoming less so. By the eve of the Cultural Revolution, the most fortunate students were thus those from cadre or military families. These students' academic records were not always superior, but they were increasingly benefiting from the new emphasis on class background as a criterion for enrollment in senior middle schools, universities, and the Communist Youth League. Next came students from worker and peasant families, whose good class background now offered some compensation for what was often mediocre classroom performance. At the bottom were students from bourgeois or intellectual families, who often enjoyed superior academic records but whose bad or middling class background was becoming an ever greater obstacle to advancement.[18]

Just as students were divided by the politics of the early 1960s, so too were urban workers. The economic policies of the 1950s had already produced cleavages between permanent workers and apprentices, between skilled and unskilled laborers, and between workers at large state factories and employees of smaller collective enterprises. In each case, the former received substantially higher salaries and job benefits than did the latter.

These divisions, the result of the application of the Soviet model to China, were widened by the implementation of the "worker-peasant system" of industrial employment in 1964. Under this policy, industrial workers were hired from suburban communes on a temporary or part-time basis, as required by specific factories and enterprises. The system was officially justified as an effort to reduce the social and economic disparities between city and countryside by producing a class of people who were simultaneously workers and peasants. In practice, however, the principal appeal of the worker-peasant system was

17 On educational policy in the early 1960s, see John Gardner, "Educated youth and urban–rural inequalities, 1958–66," in John Wilson Lewis, ed., *The city in communist China*, 235–86; and Donald J. Munro, "Egalitarian ideal and educational fact in communist China," in Lindbeck, *China*, 256–301.
18 This categorization of Chinese students is based on Hong Yung Lee, *The politics of the Chinese Cultural Revolution: A case study*; and Stanley Rosen, *Red Guard factionalism and the Cultural Revolution in Guangzhou (Canton)*.

much less noble: Factories welcomed the opportunity to hire temporary contract workers who were paid lower wages, who were ineligible for the pensions
or medical benefits that state enterprises were required to provide to permanent employees, and who could be fired for poor performance.[19]

The consequence of the worker-peasant system, therefore, was to exacerbate
social tensions rather than to ameliorate them. This employment policy not
only produced an underclass of dissatisfied workers, who received less remuneration and less job security for the same work than did permanent employees,
but also raised the specter of downward mobility for many more. The tendency in many state enterprises was to reassign positions from the permanent
payroll to the more flexible worker-peasant system. Thus, apprentices saw the
opportunities for advancement drying up, and even permanent workers faced
the danger that they would find themselves transferred to the countryside to
become contract employees.

When the Cultural Revolution broke out in mid-1966 and when mass
protest was officially encouraged, many of these collective resentments, as
well as individual grievances, formed the emotional fuel for the Red Guard
movement. As in any complex social movement, there was only a loose cor-
relation between one's socioeconomic standing in the mid-1960s and one's
political orientation during the Cultural Revolution. But a common pattern
in the Red Guard movement was the anger against the Party establishment by
students from bad or middling classes, who felt that their chances for upward
mobility were steadily declining, and by those workers who occupied lower
positions on the ladder of economic specialization.[20]

The emerging crisis

The issues and tensions just discussed came to a head between the fall of 1965
and the summer of 1966 as Chinese leaders engaged in heated controversies
over Chinese military policy, strategy toward Vietnam, policy toward the
literary community, and the rectification of the Party. These debates enabled
Lin Biao and Jiang Qing, with Mao's backing, to push potential rivals aside,
extend their control over China's military and cultural establishments, and
thus strengthen Mao's political base. In the case of the PLA, a dispute over
China's response to the escalating conflict in Vietnam provided the occasion
for the purge of the chief of staff, Luo Ruiqing, who was potentially able
to challenge Lin's control over the armed forces. In the cultural realm, an
early skirmish over a historical drama that was allegedly critical of Mao

19 Lee, *Politics of the Cultural Revolution*, 129–39.
20 Marc J. Blecher and Gordon White, *Micropolitics in contemporary China: A technical unit during and after
the Cultural Revolution.*

led ultimately to the dismissal of the first Party secretary in Beijing, the reorganization of the Party's Propaganda Department, and the appointment of Chen Boda, Jiang Qing, and Kang Sheng – a longtime public security specialist with close ties to Mao – as leaders of the unfolding campaign against revisionism. Within a few months, Mao had broken decisively with Liu Shaoqi over the way to extend that campaign from the cultural community into the universities and the bureaucracy.

The spring of 1966 also witnessed the gradual melding of the three elements of Mao's political base – the army, the radical intellectuals, and the disenchanted youth – into a relatively coherent coalition that could spearhead the Cultural Revolution. A linkage between Jiang Qing and Lin Biao was forged at a forum on literature and art in the armed forces in February 1966, at which Jiang Qing, who had little connection with the PLA in the past, came to assume a leading role in the military's cultural activities. Within the next few months, the radical civilian and military leaders surrounding Mao Zedong began to mobilize support among disenchanted sectors in urban China. During June and July, the Cultural Revolution Group under Chen Boda, Jiang Qing, and Kang Sheng started to build connections with radical students and faculty in key universities in Beijing, and encouraged them to launch intense criticism of university, Party, and government leaders. By the end of July, the PLA had begun to provide supplies and logistical support to the leftist organizations that were springing up on major campuses.

Finally, in August 1966, the CC of the CCP held a rump session in Beijing. Attended by little more than half the members of the CC and packed with Red Guards, the plenum adopted a resolution authorizing the mobilization of China's urban population to criticize "those persons in authority who are taking the capitalist road." It was this decision that authorized what, by year's end, had become an all-out assault by Mao and his lieutenants against the Party establishment. With it, the Cultural Revolution entered its most chaotic and destructive period.

Luo Ruiqing

The military policies of Lin Biao had not gone unchallenged in the high command of the PLA. Lin's principal rival was the chief of staff, Luo Ruiqing, who came to question the appropriateness of Lin's military policies in 1964–5, as the escalation of American involvement in the war in Vietnam presented China with an unexpected threat on its southern borders.[21]

---

21 On the Luo Ruiqing affair, see Harry Harding and Melvin Gurtov, *The purge of Lo Jui-ch'ing: The politics of Chinese strategic planning;* and Michael Yahuda, "Kremlinology and the Chinese strategic debate, 1965–66," *CQ,* 49 (January–March 1972), 32–75.

In retrospect, Luo Ruiqing's challenge to Lin Biao still appears somewhat surprising. Luo had been a political commissar throughout much of his pre-1949 career and had served as minister of public security (rather than a troop commander) during the 1950s. There was little reason, therefore, to suspect that Luo would have opposed the emphasis on ideological indoctrination and political loyalty that characterized Lin's service as minister of defense. What is more, Lin and Luo had had a close personal relationship during the Communist revolution. Luo had served under Lin in the First Corps of the Red Army in the early 1930s, and had been Lin's deputy at both the Red Army College and Kangda (the Resist-Japan Military and Political University in Yan'an). When Lin Biao became minister of defense in 1959, Luo was promoted to the position of chief of staff. If Luo's appointment was not at Lin's initiative, it was at least with his approval.

Lin Biao had, since the early 1950s, been a victim of chronic illness – variously described as a war wound, stomach difficulties, tuberculosis, or a combination – that periodically forced him to curtail his physical and political activities. The recurrence of these physical ailments in the early 1960s apparently created serious tensions between Lin and Luo Ruiqing. At a minimum, Luo may have wished, in light of Lin's illness, to be granted greater operational authority over the armed forces; or, alternatively, Luo may have hoped that Lin would resign as minister of defense in his favor. According to one dramatic account, Luo actually told Lin to his face that "a sick man should give his place to the worthy! Don't meddle! Don't block the way!"[22]

The growing participation of American forces in the Vietnam War – a step Chinese leaders had apparently not anticipated – also strained the relationship between the two men. Luo began to propose more intensive military preparations, in case the United States should decide to carry the war to China. As Luo put it in May 1965:

> It makes a world of difference whether or not one is prepared once a war breaks out. . . . Moreover, these preparations must be made for the most difficult and worst situations that may possibly arise. Preparations must be made not only against any small-scale warfare but also against any medium- or large-scale warfare that imperialism may launch. These preparations must envisage the use by the imperialists of nuclear weapons as well as of conventional weapons.

Moreover, Luo argued that if war did come to China, the PLA should be prepared to defend the country from prepared positions and then counterattack across China's borders to destroy the enemy "in its own lair."[23]

---

22 Harding and Gurtov, *Lo jui-ch'ing*, 10.
23 [Luo Ruiqing] Lo Jui-ch'ing, "Commemorate the victory over German facscism! Carry the struggle against U.S. imperialism through to the end!" *PR*, 20 (14 May 1965), 7–15.

Luo's recommendations, which may have reflected the views of China's professional military planners, proved unacceptable to Lin Biao. For one thing, the strategy of linear defense that Luo proposed contradicted the principles of people's war, according to which the Chinese Army would attempt to lure an invader deep inside China so as to overextend his supply lines and destroy him piecemeal. What is more, Luo's insistence that, as he put it in September 1965, there were "a thousand and one things to do" before China was ready for war[24] implied that the PLA should reorder its priorities, at least temporarily, so as to place greater stress on military preparation. Of these two considerations, it was the second that was probably the more controversial. The PLA was playing an ever larger role in civilian society and was becoming a critically important part of Mao's power base in his emerging confrontation with the Party establishment. If adopted, Luo's proposals would have reversed this process: They would have drawn the army from political affairs, and thus largely removed it from the Maoist coalition.

The controversy between Lin Biao and Luo Ruiqing reached its climax in early September, when the two men published articles on the twentieth anniversary of the surrender of Japan at the end of World War II that contained very different implications for Chinese defense policy.[25] Luo argued that China "certainly must have sufficient plans and certainly must complete preparations" in case the United States attacked China. Lin, in contrast, implied that the Americans were unlikely to be so rash, and that even if they were, there would be ample time to mobilize "the vast ocean of several hundred million Chinese people in arms." This was to be Luo's last major public utterance, and by the end of November, he dropped from public view altogether. Lin Biao began assembling a bill of particulars against his colleague, which he presented to a CC conference in Shanghai on 8 December. The conference appointed a seven-man team, headed by Marshal Ye Jianying, to examine Lin's case against Luo.

The investigation soon took an inquisitorial turn. The team, accompanied by representatives from various branches of the military, engaged in what was later described as "face-to-face" struggle against Luo in March 1966. After Luo's self-criticism was rejected as inadequate, he tried unsuccessfully to commit suicide by leaping from the building in which he was confined. On 8 April, the investigation team concluded its work by recommending to the CC that Luo be dismissed from all his posts in the PLA, as well as from his duties as a vice-premier and a member of the Party Secretariat. That report, in turn, was approved by an enlarged meeting of the Politburo in early May.

---

24 [Luo Ruiqing] Lo Jui-ch'ing, "The people defeated Japanese fascism and they can certainly defeat U.S. imperialism too," CB, 770 (14 September 1965), 1–12.
25 Lo, "The people defeated fascism"; Lin Piao, Long live the victory of People's War.

There is some reason to believe that Peng Zhen, a Politburo member serving concurrently as first Party secretary in Beijing, defended Luo during the course of the investigatory process, but his views were rejected.[26]

The Luo Ruiqing affair was important for two reasons. It provided persuasive evidence that Mao and Lin had the will and the ability to secure the dismissal of officials who disagreed with their policies and who challenged their personal standing. It also enabled the two to increase their control over two key elements in the coercive apparatus of China. The dismissal of Luo as chief of staff, and his replacement somewhat later by Yang Chengwu, gave Lin further influence over the main forces of the PLA. In addition, the purge of Luo was followed by the dismissal of some of his former lieutenants in the Ministry of Public Security, thus enabling Kang Sheng to strengthen his control over the state security apparatus.

Wu Han and Peng Zhen

At the same time as Luo Ruiqing was coming under serious attack, Mao turned his attention to the problem of dissent among the intellectuals.[27] He focused his fire on *Hai Rui dismissed from office (Hai Rui ba guan)*, a play by Wu Han, an author and scholar who served concurrently as a deputy mayor of Beijing. The Chairman charged that this historical drama, which nominally depicted an upright Ming dynasty official unjustly dismissed by the emperor, Jiaqing, was actually an allegorical criticism of Mao's purge of Peng Dehuai at the Lushan Plenum in 1959. That Mao may well have encouraged Wu to write the play in the first place did not affect the Chairman's judgment of the final product.

In dealing with Wu Han and *Hai Rui*, Mao took a two-pronged approach. Initially, he assigned the responsibility of criticizing Wu Han's play to a Five-Man Group on revolution in culture (*wenhua geming wuren xiaozu*), headed by Peng Zhen, which had been established in 1964. This put Peng in a difficult position, for, as first Party secretary of Beijing municipality, he was responsible for the actions of one of his own deputy mayors. Perhaps because of his personal connections with Wu Han, as well as his more general beliefs about the best way to handle policy toward intellectuals, Peng soon made clear what his approach would be: to focus on the historical issues raised by Wu Han's play rather than on its possible allegorical content, and to discuss those issues in an open way in which "everyone is equal before the truth."[28]

26 On the fate of Luo, see Ahn, *Chinese politics*, 203–4; and Lieberthal, *Research guide*, 248–9.
27 On the Wu Han affair, see Ahn, *Chinese politics*, 195–213; Goldman, *China's intellectuals*, ch. 5; Jack Gray and Patrick Cavendish, *Chinese communism in crisis: Maoism and the Cultural Revolution*, ch. 4; Lee, *Politics of the Cultural Revolution*, ch. 1; and James R. Pusey, *Wu Han: Attacking the present through the past*.
28 "The Great Proletarian Cultural Revolution – a record of major events: September 1965 to December 1966," *JPRS*, 42, 349. *Translations on Communist China: Political and sociological information* (25 August 1967), 3.

Aware of Peng's predilections on the case, Mao decided simultaneously to take a second tack. He asked Yao Wenyuan, one of the Shanghai intellectuals associated with Jiang Qing, to prepare his own criticism of Wu Han's play. Mao emphasized that Yao's article should address what he considered to be the crucial issue: that Wu Han had intended Hai Rui to be a historical analogue for Peng Dehuai. The extent of Mao's personal interest and involvement in this matter is suggested by his reviewing Yao's essay three times before agreeing that it was ready for publication.[29]

Yao's article – a harsh direct attack on Wu Han – was published in Shanghai in early November, before the Five-Man Group in Beijing had taken any formal action on the Wu Han case. Peng Zhen's reaction was one of outrage, not merely because his subordinate was being criticized so strongly, but also because he believed that publication of such an article, without the formal approval of the responsible Party organs, was a violation of the principles of inner-Party struggle. Together with Lu Dingyi, director of the Party Propaganda Department and a member of the Five-Man Group, Peng succeeded in blocking republication of Yao's essay in any central or Beijing municipal newspapers. It was only after the personal intervention of Zhou Enlai, apparently acting as Mao's behest, that the article appeared in newspapers with wider circulation – first in the *Jiefangjun bao* with a laudatory editorial note, and then in the *Renmin ribao* (People's Daily) with a skeptical introduction.

Even though he had lost the battle to suppress the publication of the Yao Wenyuan essay, Peng still vigorously attempted to keep criticism of intellectuals on what he considered to be the proper course. With a working majority on the Five-Man Group (of whose members only Kang Sheng was a firm supporter of Mao's position), Peng continued to obstruct the publication of further articles by radical writers such as Qi Benyu that he considered to be excessively critical of Wu Han. He stuck to this position despite direct criticism from Mao toward the end of December, when the Chairman accused Peng of ignoring the possible analogy between Hai Rui and Peng Dehuai. Peng defended himself on the somewhat narrow grounds that there had been no personal contact between Peng and Wu, and that Wu Han was therefore innocent of any factionalist behavior. But Peng promised Mao that the Five-Man Group would reach a final decision on the issue within two months.

The Five-Man Group held at least two crucial meetings on the subject: the first on 2 January 1966 and the second on 4 February. Despite all the evidence that Mao would be dissatisfied with their report – evidence provided not only by Mao's conversations with Peng in December but also by warnings from

---

29 Yao Wen-yuan, "On the new historical play *Dismissal of Hai Rui*," reprinted in *Jiefangjun bao*, 10 November 1965, trans. in *CB*, 783 (21 March 1966), 1–18.

Kang Sheng – the group decided to stick with the approach Peng Zhen had originally adopted. On 3 February, two deputy directors of the Propaganda Department, Yao Zhen and Xu Liqun, drafted a statement summarizing the views of the majority of the Five-Man Group.

This document, known as the "February Outline" (*eryue tigang*), acknowledged the problem of bourgeois tendencies in culture but emphasized the desirability of focusing on the academic issues involved.[30] Implicitly, the outline distinguished two different approaches to the problem of "people like Wu Han." The first approach would treat such problems as a political issue, would characterize dissenting views or unorthodox approaches as antisocialist or counterrevolutionary, and would use administrative means to suppress them. The second approach, in contrast, would treat such matters as serious academic issues that should be "reasoned out," under the principle of "seeking truth from facts."

The outline opted decisively for the second approach, declaring that the Party's policy toward intellectuals should continue to be guided by the principle of "letting one hundred schools of thought contend." The goal should be to overcome dissidence and unorthodoxy through superior academic work, not by "beating them [dissident intellectuals] politically." The process should be a lenient one, and critics should not "behave like scholar-tyrants who are always acting arbitrarily and trying to overwhelm people with their power." Above all, the outline proposed that the struggle against bourgeois ideology be conducted "under leadership," "prudently," and over a "prolonged period of time,"

The February Outline departed decisively in two significant ways from the views of Mao Zedong and the radicals around Jiang Qing. It pointedly avoided any conclusion as to whether Wu Han had intended *Hai Rui* as an indirect criticism of Mao's dismissal of Peng Dehuai, and thus evaded the responsibility that Mao had explicitly assigned it. What is more, the outline criticized the radical intellectuals exemplified by Yao Wenyuan as much as the allegedly revisionist scholars such as Wu Han. The Five-Man Group refrained from criticizing any radical writers by name. But it warned that some "revolutionary Leftists" were acting like "scholar-tyrants," and even called for the "rectification" of the incorrect ideas among the left.

The February Outline was discussed and approved by the Standing Committee of the Politburo, chaired by Liu Shaoqi, on 5 February. Peng Zhen and others then traveled to Wuhan to discuss the matter with Mao. As expected, Mao apparently objected to the harsh treatment of the radicals in the outline

---

30 "Outline report concerning the current academic discussion of the Group of Five in charge of the Cultural Revolution," in URI, *CCP documents of the Great Proletarian Cultural Revolution, 1966–1967*, 7–12.

report and its failure to issue a decisive criticism of Wu Han. Nonetheless, Peng returned to Beijing claiming that Mao had approved the February Outline, and the document was circulated under the imprimatur of the CC on 12 February.

In the fall of 1965, Yao Wenyuan's direct criticism of Wu Han had stood in sharp counterpoint to the milder approach favored by Peng Zhen and the Party Propaganda Department. Now, in February 1966, the outline issued by the Five-Man Group would stand in contrast to another document prepared under the joint auspices of Lin Biao and Jiang Qing. The document was the summary of the meeting on literary and art work in the armed forces, held in Shanghai on 2–20 February 1966 that forged the political alliance between Jiang Qing and Lin Biao.[31] Like Yao Wenyuan's earlier article, the Forum Summary (known in Chinese as the February Summary, or *eryue jiyao*) was drawn up under Mao's personal supervision and was reportedly revised by Mao three times before it was circulated through inner-Party channels.

The Forum Summary took a position on intellectual problems that was diametrically opposed to that of the February Outline. It not only described China's cultural life as having been characterized by "sixteen years of sharp class struggle" between the revolutionary and revisionist perspectives, but also claimed that cultural affairs were now under the "dictatorship of a black anti-Party and anti-socialist line" – a sharp attack on the leadership provided by the Propaganda Department and the Five-Man Group. The Forum Summary called for active mass criticism of these tendencies rather than the more lenient and scholarly kind of criticism envisioned by the February Outline.

The Forum Summary ignored the case of Wu Han and *Hai Rui* altogether. This was because the issue at this point was no longer Wu Han but, rather, the behavior of Peng Zhen, the Party Propaganda Department under Lu Dingyi, and the Five-Man Group they controlled. At a Central Work Conference at the end of March, Mao Zedong harshly attacked Peng Zhen, Wu Han, and the February Outline; and threatened to disband the Five-Man Group, the Beijing Municipal Party Committee, and the CC's Propaganda Department. As he said to Kang Sheng, using vivid imagery drawn from ancient Chinese mythology:

> The central Party Propaganda Department is the palace of the Prince of Hell. It is necessary to overthrow the palace of the Prince of Hell and liberate the Little Devil.... The local areas must produce several more [Monkey Kings] to vigorously create a disturbance at the palace of the King of Heaven. If P'eng

31 "Summary of the forum on the work in literature and art in the armed forces with which Comrade Lin Piao entrusted Comrade Chiang Ch'ing," *PR*, 10.23 (2 June 1967), 10–16.

Chen, the Peking Municipal Party Committee, and the central Propaganda Department again protect the bad people, then it will be necessary to dissolve the Peking Municipal Committee, and it will be necessary to dissolve the Five-Man Group. Last September, I asked some of the comrades what should be done if revisionism emerged in the central government. This is very possible.[32]

After the work conference, Peng Zhen apparently realized that further defiance of Mao would be useless. In a desperate attempt to preserve his own position, he encouraged the Beijing Party Committee to intensify its criticism of Wu Han, began an attack against Deng Tuo, another Beijing Party official who had written veiled criticisms of Mao's leadership, and even began to prepare his own self-criticism. In early April, according to one Red Guard account, Peng called a joint meeting of the Five-Man Group, the leadership of the Propaganda Department, and members of the Beijing Municipal Party Committee at his residence. With deep emotion, he acknowledged that he had made serious mistakes in his handling of the revolution in culture but insisted that the rest of his political record was exemplary. He pleaded for the support of his colleagues; "As the old saying goes, we depend on [our] parents' protection at home but depend on [our] friends' kind help outside. I am now looking forward to your help."[33]

But it was too late. At a meeting of the Party Secretariat between 9 and 12 April, Peng found himself the target of criticism not only by Kang Sheng and Chen Boda, but also by Deng Xiaoping and Zhou Enlai. The Secretariat decided to disband Peng Zhen's Five-Man Group and to propose to the Politburo the establishment of a new leading group for cultural reform that would be more sympathetic to Mao's concerns.[34] During many of these dramatic developments, Liu Shaoqi was away from Beijing on an ill-timed visit to Pakistan, Afghanistan, and Burma, and was thus unable to lead a defense of Peng Zhen and Lu Dingyi.

The May Politburo meeting

The final fates of the two principal targets thus far – Luo Ruiqing and Peng Zhen – were decided together at an enlarged meeting of the Politburo between 4 and 18 May. The highlight of the meeting was an impromptu speech by Lin Biao, much of the data for which, it was later charged, had been provided by Zhang Chunqiao.[35] In it, Lin linked the question of Luo Ruiqing with that of Peng Zhen and Lu Dingyi by accusing the three men of planning,

32 *Miscellany of Mae Tse-tung Thought*, 2.382.   33 Ahn, *Chinese politics*, 207.
34 Lieberthal, *Research guide*, 246–7; "Record of major events," 10–11.
35 Lieberthal, *Research guide*, 248–9; Kau, *Lin Piao*, 326–45; *RMRB*, 18 May 1978, in *FBIS Daily Report: China*, 24 May 1978, E2–11.

in conspiracy with Yang Shangkun, the director of the Secretariat of the CC, a military coup against Mao and the radicals. "You may have smelled it – gunpowder," Lin told the Politburo melodramatically.

Lin supported these fantastic charges with a detailed discussion of the role of military force in acquiring political power. He emphasized the prevalence of military coups in both Chinese and contemporary world history, chronicling assassinations and usurpations in nearly every major dynasty and noting that there had been an "average of eleven coups per year" in the Third World since 1960. Although these facts were intended to make his case against Luo, Peng, Lu, and Yang more plausible, they also reflected Lin's fascination with the use of military force to pursue political goals. And he revealed that he had already put this historical lesson into practice: Acting under Mao's orders, Lin said, loyal troops had been sent into radio broadcasting stations, military installations, and public security offices in Beijing to prevent further attempts at "internal subversion and counterrevolutionary coups d'état."

Equally interesting was Lin's sycophantic portrait of Mao. Accusing Luo, Peng, Lu, and Yang of being "opposed to Chairman Mao and opposed to Mao Zedong Thought," Lin went on to extol Mao's genius, and to identify loyalty to Mao as a key criterion for holding Party or government office. "Chairman Mao has experienced much more than Marx, Engels, and Lenin. . . . He is unparalleled in the present world. . . . Chairman Mao's sayings, works, and revolutionary practice have shown that he is a great proletarian genius. . . . Every sentence of Chairman Mao's works is a truth; one single sentence of his surpasses ten thousand of ours. . . . Whoever is against him shall be punished by the entire Party and the whole country."

The enlarged meeting of the Politburo received, and approved, the report of the work group that had investigated Luo Ruiqing and instructed that it be circulated within the Party and the armed forces. It also issued a circular on 16 May, which Jiang Qing later claimed to have drafted, on problems in cultural affairs.[36] The 16 May Circular (*wuyiliu tongzhi*) revoked the February Outline, charging that it tried to "turn the movement to the Right" by obscuring the contemporary political issues that were being discussed within the intellectual community, and that it attempted to "direct the spearhead against the Left" by criticizing the emergence of "scholar-tyrants." The circular blamed Peng Zhen for the February Outline, dissolved the Group of Five, and established a new Cultural Revolution Group (*wenhua geming xiaozu*) (CRG) that would report directly to the Standing Committee of the Politburo

36 "Circular of the Central Committee of Communist Party of China," in "Collection of documents concerning the Great Proletarian Cultural Revolution," *CB*, 852 (6 May 1968), 2–6. On Jiang Qing's role, see Witke, *Chiang Ch'ing*, 320.

(i.e., to Mao) rather than to the Party Secretariat (i.e., to Deng Xiaoping and Liu Shaoqi), as had its predecessor. Whereas a majority of the Five-Man Group had opposed Mao's views on the handling of the Cultural Revolution, the new Cultural Revolution Group was dominated by Mao's personal supporters and the radical intellectuals surrounding Jiang Qing. The group was headed by Chen Boda, with Kang Sheng as an adviser, and with Jiang Qing, Zhang Chunqiao, Yao Wenyuan, Qi Benyu, Wang Li, and Guan Feng as members.

Although the principal purpose of the new Cultural Revolution Group was to continue the criticism of bourgeois ideas in the cultural sphere, the 16 May Circular also warned that ranking Party and state officials might well suffer the same fate as Peng Zhen and Luo Ruiqing. It was necessary, the circular said, to eliminate the

> representatives of the bourgeoisie who have sneaked into the Party, the government, and the army. When conditions are ripe, they would seize power and turn the dictatorship of the proletariat into a dictatorship of the bourgeoisie. Some of them we have already seen through, others we have not. Some we still trust and are training as our successors. There are, for example, people of the Khrushchev brand still nestling in our midst.

In this way, the circular presented a major escalation of Mao's drive against revisionism: from a movement directed principally at intellectuals, to one aimed at the Party as a whole.

The May Politburo meeting set the stage for the reorganization of the Beijing Municipal Party Committee, the Party Propaganda Department, and the Party Secretariat, which was announced in early June. Peng Zhen was replaced as Beijing's first secretary by Li Xuefeng, then the first secretary of the North China Bureau; Lu Dingyi was replaced as head of the Propaganda Department by Tao Zhu, previously first secretary of the Party's Central-South Bureau; and Yang Shangkun was replaced as staff director of the Party Secretariat by Wang Dongxing, a vice-minister of public security who concurrently commanded the elite guards unit in the capital.

The dismissals of men of such rank in late May and early June showed that Mao was determined to have his way on issues that were of importance to him, and that he was able to secure the replacement of officials who did not comply with his wishes. Moreover, each reorganization – of the General Staff Department of the PLA, of the group responsible for cultural reform, of the Beijing Municipal Party Committee, of the Party Propaganda Department, of the Party Secretariat – strengthened Mao's coalition and weakened those who would resist or oppose him. Rather than appeasing Mao, in other words, each purge simply made it easier for him to escalate his assault on revisionism in the Party.

The Fifty Days

By warning of "representatives of the bourgeoisie" who had "sneaked into the Party, the government, and the army," the 16 May Circular indicated that Mao wanted a thoroughgoing purge of revisionism throughout China, not just in the cultural sphere but throughout the bureaucracy. Still away from Beijing, in relative seclusion in Central China, Mao left the conduct of this effort in the hands of Liu Shaoqi, a man whom he would later say he already suspected of revisionism, and who other radicals would claim was one of the officials referred to indirectly in the 16 May Circular as "people of the Khrushchev brand" being trained as Mao's successors.

Whether or not Liu was fully aware of Mao's suspicions, he did face a serious dilemma in June 1966. On the one hand, if he were to have any hope of survival, he would have to show enthusiasm and efficiency in combating revisionism. On the other, he had to do so in a way that preserved central control over a rapid process of political mobilization, particularly on college campuses, and that protected what was left of his eroding political base. Liu's attempts to resolve this dilemma were reflected in his actions during a fifty-day period in June and early July 1966, during which, in Mao's absence from Beijing, he was principally responsible for the day-to-day affairs of the Party.

By this time, radical students and teachers, particularly in Beijing, were well aware of the debate over cultural reform and of Mao's views about the February Outline. In part, this was simply because younger professors who were members of the Party had access to the documents on the subject, such as the 16 May Circular, that were being circulated within the Party organization. But it was also because the leaders of the newly established CRG were sending representatives to major college and university campuses in Beijing to mobilize mass support.[37]

On 25 May, a group of radical professors and teaching assistants at Peking University (Beida) led by Nie Yuanzi, a teaching assistant in the philosophy department, wrote a large-character wall poster (*dazibao*) criticizing the university's leadership for having supported the liberal policies of the February Outline and for having prevented mass discussion of the political issues raised by the *Hai Rui* affair. According to accounts published well after the Cultural Revolution, Nie received direct encouragement from a "theoretical investigation group from the central authorities," led by Kang Sheng's wife, Cao Yiou, which had arrived at Beida under orders to "kindle the flames and spread the fire to upper levels."[38]

---

37 Sun, *Lishi jiangyi*, 2.247.
38 The events at Beida are drawn from *HQ*, 19 (October 1980), 32–6.

The university administration, not surprisingly, took prompt action to suppress this kind of dissent. In this they were supported by Zhou Enlai, who sent a second central work group to criticize Nie's wall poster the night it was displayed at Beida, But, having learned of the contents of the *dazibao*, Mao Zedong ordered that it be broadcast and published nationally, with favorable commentary, on 1 June. This decision, followed presently by the announcement that the entire Peking University leadership was being reorganized, served to legitimate spontaneous mass protest as part of the campaign against revisionist officials. So, too, did increasingly inflammatory editorials that began to appear in *Renmin ribao* after the newly reorganized central Propaganda Department had undertaken a restaffing of the central news media.

With this encouragement, wall posters written by students and faculty began to appear at university campuses and in middle schools throughout China. Most probably focused on educational issues – the admissions process, course examinations, and curricula were the questions of greatest concern – but some accused university leaders and higher-level officials of supporting revisionist policies. As at Beida, it is very likely that much of this explosion of dissent was encouraged and coordinated by the new CRG under Chen Boda, Jiang Qing, and Kang Sheng. In short order, the authority of university leaders on other campuses collapsed, and discipline among students and faculty quickly eroded.

It was this rapid process of political decay – the rise of dissent and the collapse of authority – that must have been of particular concern to Liu Shaoqi.[39] Operating without clear instructions from Mao, he decided on several measures he hoped would simultaneously demonstrate his willingness to combat revisionism and bring the student movement under Party leadership. To begin with, he ordered the suspension of university enrollment for half a year to permit a thorough reconsideration and reform of the examination system and the university curriculum. At the same time, he organized a large number of work teams – perhaps 400 teams with more than 10,000 members in all – and dispatched them to universities and high schools and to bureaucratic agencies responsible for finance, trade, industry, and communications. Given the frequent use of work teams in past Party rectification campaigns, Liu doubtless considered his decision to be routine, appropriate, and noncontroversial.

What was ultimately Liu's undoing was less the principle of dispatching work teams than the instructions under which they operated. They apparently were told that large numbers of ordinary bureaucratic officials and university

39 On the fifty days, see Ahn, *Chinese politics*, ch. 9; Jean Daubier, *A history of the Chinese Cultural Revolution*, ch. 1; Lowell Dittmer, *Liu Shao-ch'i and the Chinese Cultural Revolution: The politics of mass criticism*, 78–94; and Harding, *Organizing China*, 225–9.

faculty were to be subject to criticism and possibly dismissal. In the Ministry of Finance, for example, 90 percent of the cadres reportedly were criticized; in the Ministry of Culture, work teams were authorized to dismiss two-thirds of the ministry's officials, In universities, large numbers of administrators and faculty came under attack, beginning a reign of terror that would last for a decade.

The work teams were also told to reestablish Party leadership over the student movement in the nation's major universities and high schools. A Politburo conference on 13 July, after reviewing the Cultural Revolution in Beijing's middle schools, concluded that the most important task on each campus was to "restore the leading role of the Party branch" and to "strengthen the work teams."[40] Putting the same point in somewhat blunter language, the first Party secretary of Anhui province announced that, "for units where the leadership is not in our hands, work teams must be sent immediately to win it back."[41]

The reassertion of Party leadership over the student movement implied the demobilization of the radical students and their faculty supporters. National policy was still to permit student demonstrations, rallies, and wall posters as long as they were confined to campus. But many local Party committees and work teams, in their zeal to impose control over the student movement, took a stricter approach. In some places, *dazibao* and rallies were banned altogether, and in others they were allowed only if permission had been obtained from the work team. Some radical students were expelled from the Communist Youth League, others were subjected to struggle meetings, and still others were sent to the countryside for a stint of labor reform. As a result of such stringent measures, the work teams were able to restore a modicum of normality to many universities.

But although some students were persuaded to cease political activity, the restrictions imposed by the work teams drove others into deeper opposition. Secret student organizations, some of which took on the name "Red Guards" (*hongweibing*), formed to resist the activities of the work teams, despite Liu Shaoqi's ruling that such organizations were "secret and [therefore] illegal."[42] Other student groups were organized at the behest of the work teams to provide them with support. The result, in other words, was not only the partial demobilization of the student movement but also the polarization of the remaining activists.

The work teams' suppression of the radicals soon became a matter of considerable controversy at the highest levels of the Party. In early July, the case

40 Sun, *Lishi jiangyi*, 2.250.   41 Radio Hefei, 16 July 1966.
42 "Record of major events," 25.

of Kuai Dafu, one of the leading radical students at Qinghua University, who had been criticized by the work teams sent there, was the subject of a high-level Party meeting in Beijing. In that meeting, Liu Shaoqi attacked Kuai as a troublemaker, and Kang Sheng defended his right to criticize revisionism in the Party. It was by this time common knowledge that activists such as Kuai Dafu had direct connections with the central CRG advised by Kang Sheng, whereas the work teams with which Kuai had come into conflict had been dispatched on the order of Liu Shaoqi. What gave this particular case special poignancy was the fact that the leader of the work team sent to Qinghua was none other than Liu Shaoqi's wife, Wang Guangmei.[43] In this way, Liu's political future had become inextricably intertwined with the performance of the work teams.

As Mao Zedong saw it, the work teams repeated the same mistakes that Liu Shaoqi had committed during the rural Socialist Education Campaign earlier in the 1960s.[44] In that campaign, directed against corruption and "capitalist tendencies" among rural cadres, Liu's approach had been to dispatch large numbers of work teams to grass-roots Party organizations, restrict peasant participation in cadre rectification, criticize large numbers of commune officials, and downplay the responsibility of higher-level Party leaders. In Mao's eyes, Liu's conduct of the rectification of the universities and the urban bureaucracy in mid-1966 was guilty of similar errors. Once again, large numbers of lower-level officials were being attacked and mass involvement was being restricted, without any recognition that the ultimate cause of revisionism lay in the sympathetic attitudes of higher officials.

The Eleventh Plenum

Thus, in mid-July, angered at Liu Shaoqi's conduct of the campaign against revisionism in the bureaucracy and his management of the radical student movement, Mao abruptly ended his stay in Hangzhou and headed for Beijing. On the way back to the capital, Mao stopped for a swim in the Yangtze River — an act intended to demonstrate that he had the physical vigor needed for the political battles ahead. Although Mao had been active behind the scenes in Hangzhou, this was his first public appearance in many months, and it received unprecedentedly syncophantic coverage in the Chinese media. The official report of the event carried by the New China News Agency began with the sentence "The water of the river seemed to be smiling that day" and went on

43 Ahn, Chinese politics, 218.
44 On the Socialist Education Movement, see Ahn, Chinese politics, eh, 5; Richard Baum, Prelude to revolution: Mao, the Party, and the peasant question, 1962–66; and Harding, Organizing China, ch. 7.

to tell of a militiaman from the Hankou Thermal Power Plant who "became so excited when he saw Chairman Mao that he forgot he was in the water. Raising both hands, he shouted: 'Long live Chairman Mao! Long live Chairman Mao!' He leapt into the air, but soon sank into the river again. He gulped several mouthfuls, but the water tasted especially sweet." Thereafter, the president of the World Professional Marathon Swimming Federation invited Mao to take part in two forthcoming races, for the Chairman's speed, as reported by the New China News Agency dispatch, was nearly four times the world record.[45]

Upon his arrival at the capital, Mao called a meeting of regional Party secretaries and members of the CRG where he demanded the withdrawal of the work teams dispatched by Liu Shaoqi. "The work teams know nothing. Some work teams have even created trouble. . . . Work teams only hinder the movement. [Affairs in the schools] have to be dealt with by the forces in the schools themselves, not by the work teams, you, me, or the provincial committees."[46] The Beijing Municipal Party Committee immediately announced that work teams would be withdrawn from all universities and high schools in the city, and would be replaced by "Cultural Revolution small groups" to be elected by the teachers, students, and staff at each school.[47]

But Mao was not mollified by the Beijing Party Committee's quick capitulation. He began preparations for a CC plenum, the first since 1962, that would endorse the measures already undertaken and legitimate his vision of a revolution against revisionism in China. The session, which convened in early August, was probably attended only by about half of the full and alternate members of the CC – a reflection of both the depth of division within the Party and the haste with which the meeting had been called. The plenum was packed, not only by Party officials who were not members of the CC but also by "representatives of revolutionary teachers and students from the institutions of higher learning in Peking."[48] In addition, Lin Biao apparently reinforced military control over key installations in the capital area – thus tightening the grip over the city that he had first announced at the enlarged Politburo meeting in May. Even so, Mao himself later admitted that he received the support of a bare majority of those attending the meeting.[49]

This rump session of the CC made decisions in three principal areas. On personnel matters, it agreed to the promotion of several of Mao's principal supporters and the demotion of those who had resisted him or who had misread his intentions over the past several months. The plenum endorsed

45 "Quarterly chronicle and documentation," *CQ*, 28 (October–December 1966), 149–52.
46 Ch'en, *Mao papers*, 26–30. 47 Sun, *Lishi jiangyi*, 2.250.
48 Lieberthal, *Research guide*, 255–7. 49 *Miscellany of Mao Tse-tung Though*, 2.457–8.

the May Politburo decisions concerning the dismissals of Peng Zhen, Luo Ruiqing, Lu Dingyi, and Yang Shangkun, and dropped Peng and Lu from the Politburo. For his mishandling of the "Fifty Days" Campaign, Liu Shaoqi was stripped from his Party vice-chairmanship and demoted from the second to the eighth position in the Party hierarchy. Lin Biao succeeded Liu as second in command and was made sole Party vice-chairman, thus replacing Liu as Mao's heir apparent. Chen Boda and Kang Sheng, leaders of the new CRG, were promoted from alternate membership on the Politburo to full membership. And Minister of Public Security Xie Fuzhi, who came to form a rather close association with the CRG, was appointed an alternate member of the Politburo and named the member of the Party Secretariat responsible for all political and legal matters, the position formerly held by Peng Zhen.

Not all the new appointments to the Politburo were close associates of Lin Biao or Jiang Qing. Other personnel decisions made at the Eleventh Plenum seemed to reflect compromises that Mao, Lin Biao, and the Cultural Revolution Group made with the Party and military establishments. A number of veteran civilian and military officials, not closely associated with Jiang Qing, Chen Boda, or Lin Biao, were added to the Cultural Revolution Group. Four senior provincial leaders – Tao Zhu, the new director of the Propaganda Department; Li Xuefeng, the new first Party secretary in Beijing; and regional Party secretaries Song Renqiong and Liu Lantao – received appointments as Politburo members. And three more PLA marshals – Ye Jianying, Xu Xiangqian, and Nie Rongzhen – were also added to the Politburo, perhaps as a way of counterbalancing Lin Biao's growing political influence.

On policy matters, the formal political report given by Liu Shaoqi was overshadowed by the text of Lin's May talk on coups d'état and by a friendly letter sent by Mao to a group of Qinghua Middle School Red Guards in late July, both of which were circulated among the delegates to the plenum.[50] In reviewing the crucial issues of the early 1960s, the plenum's communiqué endorsed all the positions associated with Mao Zedong and indirectly criticized some of those taken by Liu Shaoqi. Mao's approach to the Socialist Education Campaign, as embodied in the Former Ten Points of May 1963 and the Twenty-three Articles of January 1965, was said to be the correct way of dealing with organizational problems in the countryside. The plenum cited with approval Mao's concern with promoting revolutionary successors and his theory that class struggle continues in socialist society. It also noted favorably his calls to learn from such model units and organizations as the Dazhai ⁻duction brigade, the Daqing oil field, and the PLA.

50 Sun, *Lishi jiangyi*, 2.251.

Finally, the plenum adopted a Sixteen Point Decision on the Cultural Revolution (*wenge shiliu tiao*), laying out Mao's vision for the movement.[51] The principal goal was nothing less than to "change the mental outlook of the whole of society." It was to

> struggle against and overthrow those persons in authority who are taking the capitalist road, to criticize and repudiate the reactionary bourgeois academic "authorities" and the ideology of the bourgeoisie and all other exploiting classes, and to transform education, literature and art, and all other parts of the superstructure not in correspondence with the socialist economic base.

The principal mechanism was to be the mobilization of "the masses of the workers, peasants, soldiers, revolutionary intellectuals, and revolutionary cadres." Even though they could be expected to make mistakes, the Decision proclaimed, the key to success in the Cultural Revolution was "whether or not the Party leadership dares boldly to arouse the masses." It was improper either to resist the movement, or even to attempt to control it.

The Sixteen Points, reflecting serious differences within the CC, were highly ambiguous on the question of the degree of disorder that would be tolerated during the Cultural Revolution. On the one hand, the Decision acknowledged approvingly that there were likely to be "disturbances" in the course of the Cultural Revolution. It cited Mao's remarks in his 1927 report on the Hunan peasant movement that revolutions cannot be "so very refined, so gentle, so temperate, kind, courteous, restrained and magnanimous." It also set a sweeping goal for the movement: the "dissmiss[al] from their leading posts [of] all those in authority who are taking the capitalist road [so as to] make possible the recapture of the leadership for the proletarian revolutionaries." And it prohibited any reprisals against students in high schools or universities who participated in the movement.

On the other hand, reportedly at the instigation of Zhou Enlai and Tao Zhu, the Decision contained several specific provisions that were clearly intended to moderate the conduct of the Cultural Revolution.[52] It emphasized the possibility of uniting "ninety-five per cent of the cadres" and prohibited the use of coercion or force. It largely exempted ordinary scientists, technicians, cadres, and Party and government agencies in the countryside from the full force of the movement. It insisted that the Cultural. Revolution not be allowed to hamper economic production. And it stipulated that although "bourgeois academic 'authorities'" and revisionists in the Party should be criticized, they

---

51 "Decision of the Central Committee of the Chinese Communist Party concerning the Great Proletarian Cultural Revolution," in "Collection of documents Concerning the Great Proletarian Cultural Revolution."

52 *RMRB*, 5 January 1986, in *FBIS Daily Report; China*, 24 January 1986, K12–22.

should not be attacked by name in the press without the approval of the cognizant Party committee.

Even so, the general tone of the Eleventh Plenum was significantly different from what these formal caveats might suggest. Even as the plenum was in session, Mao wrote his own *dazibao*, which he posted outside the CC's meeting room, in which he accused "some leading comrades" – the reference was clearly to Liu Shaoqi and Deng Xiaoping – of "adopting the reactionary stand of the bourgeoisie" by sending out work teams to college campuses and government offices during the Fifty Days.[53] And the plenum itself endorsed the decision to dismiss or demote three of the twenty-one members of its Politburo. Together, these two developments symbolized the broad significance of the Eleventh Plenum: to legitimate a broad attack on the Party establishment and the intellectual community, at the personal initiative of Mao Zedong, that would entail a high degree of mass mobilization and an intense degree of political struggle.

THE COLLAPSE OF AUTHORITY

The emergence of the Red Guards

The Eleventh Plenum endorsed Mao's vision of the Cultural Revolution as the "arousal of the masses" to criticize revisionist tendencies in "all . . . parts of the superstructure not in correspondence with the socialist economic base." In so doing, it brought together two themes that had been present in Mao's thinking since the early 1960s: first, that the Party establishment itself had been responsible for the emergence of revisionism in China since the GLF and, second, that the best way to combat revisionism was to mobilize the ordinary citizenry of China – and especially China's young people – against it.

The Sixteen Point Decision of the Eleventh Plenum on the Cultural Revolution envisioned a mechanism for popular participation that survived for only a few weeks. The plan was to establish popularly elected Cultural Revolution committees (*wenhua geming weiyuanhui*) in grass-roots units from factories and communes to universities and government organs. These organizations were to be modeled after the Paris Commune of 1871 in that their members were to be selected through a system of general election and were to be subject to criticism and recall by their constituents at any time. They were, in short, to be broadly representative of the organization in which they were formed.

Significantly, however, the Cultural Revolution committees were not expected to replace the Party committees or the administrative structure.

53 Ch'en, *Mao papers*, 117.

Instead, the Decision of the Eleventh Plenum described them somewhat ambivalently as a "bridge to keep our Party in close contact with the masses." On the one hand, the committees were supposed to be permanent organizations for criticizing revisionism and struggling against "old ideas, culture, customs, and habits." But on the other, the Decision specified that they were to remain "under the leadership of the Communist Party."

The problem, from a Maoist perspective, is that this conception of the Cultural Revolution committees had inherent flaws that stripped them of their effectiveness. To begin with, the stipulation that the committees accept Party leadership made it possible for the local Party committees to coopt or control them by ensuring that the masses "elected" committee members who were relatively conservative in outlook. And the provision that the committees be elected virtually ensured, in the universities at least, that they be divided in reflection of the increasingly polarized student body. In many cases, the Cultural Revolution committees were dominated by the children of high-level cadres, not only because children from cadre families had come to constitute the largest single group among university students, but also because higher-level Party committees were likely to favor their colleagues' children as leaders of the mass movement. What is more, the Cultural Revolution committees were preoccupied with the problems of their particular units rather than with the broader questions of national policy that the Maoists intended should be the more important focus of the Cultural Revolution.

But another model of popular participation was immediately available: that of the Red Guards. Just before the Eleventh Plenum approved the concept of Cultural Revolution committees, Mao Zedong wrote a letter to a group of Red Guards at the Qinghua Middle School in Beijing that tacitly endorsed that alternative form of organization. Although the Eleventh Plenum's Decision on the Cultural Revolution did not even mention the Red Guards by name, Red Guard representatives were present in the meeting room. Compared to the Cultural Revolution committees, the Red Guards must have appeared to be a way of lifting the Cultural Revolution out of an exclusive concern with the affairs of grass-roots units and toward the consideration of broader issues and criticism of higher-level leaders. Whereas the Cultural Revolution committees seemed likely to fall under the control of the Party apparatus, the Red Guards could more readily be manipulated by the Cultural Revolution Group.[54]

Thus, within a week after the close of the Eleventh Plenum, a series of massive Red Guard rallies began in Beijing. Although the Cultural Revolution committees were never repudiated, and even received sporadic attention in the

---

54 On the interplay of these two models of organization, see Harding, *Organizing China*, ch. 8.

press for the rest of the year, it was clear nevertheless that they had been eclipsed by the Red Guards. The eight rallies, organized with the logistical support of the PLA, brought together 13 million Red Guards from all over China in the three months between 18 August and 26 November 1966.[55] Films of the events present vivid images of these enraptured young middle school students: some chanting revolutionary slogans, tears streaming down their faces; others waving their copies of Mao's quotations at the distant deity reviewing them on the Gate of Heavenly Peace. The Red Guard organizations bore such martial names as the "Red Flag Battalion," the "Three Red Banners Group," and the "Thorough Revolution Corps." Many Red Guards wore military uniforms, and Mao himself put on a Red Guard armband, thus conveying the clear message that the Red Guards had the support of both Mao and the PLA. Directives issued by the CRG in the name of the CC gave the Red Guards the right to organize parades and demonstrations, use printing presses and publish newspapers, and post *dazibao* criticizing Party committees at all levels.

The Red Guard movement drew on many of the socioeconomic cleav-ages and grievances discussed earlier in this chapter, particularly the tension between class background and academic performance as criteria for success in China's educational system. Beyond this, the mobilization of Red Guards was facilitated by several other factors: a sense of excitement at being called upon by the leader of their country to become involved in national affairs; a sense of opportunity that one's future would be fundamentally affected by involvement in the Cultural Revolution; the suspension of classes and admissions exami-nations, which relieved millions of middle school and university students of academic responsibility; and, above all, the provision of free railway trans-portation to Red Guards seeking to travel around the country to "exchange revolutionary experiences." The Red Guard organizations drew not only on urban youth but also on the large numbers of young people who had been sent down to the countryside in the early 1960s and who now took advantage of the disorder of the time to return to the cities.

But the Red Guard movement did not, in the fall of 1966, achieve the goals that Mao had foreseen for it. To begin with, the Red Guards remained fascinated with what the Chairman must have regarded as secondary, even trivial, issues. Taking seriously the injunction of the Eleventh Plenum to combat the "four olds" – old ideas, old culture, old customs, and old habits – the Red Guards took to the streets looking for evidence of bourgeois culture. Young men and women wearing long hair were stopped on the streets and shorn on the spot. Women wearing tight slacks were subjected to the "ink bottle test": If a bottle of ink placed inside the waistband could not slip

---

55 Sun, *Lishi jiangyi*, 2.254.

freely to the ground, the pants would be slashed to shreds. Shopkeepers were forced to take down signboards bearing traditional store names and to replace them with more revolutionary labels. Red Guards themselves often changed the names of streets, occasionally arguing among themselves over which new name would be the more progressive. One group of Red Guards proposed that the menaing of traffic signals be changed so that red, the color of revolution, would signify "go" rather than "stop."

Another Red Guard organization from a middle school in Beijing drew up a list of 100 examples for "smashing the old and establishing the new," which give some flavor of this aspect of the Cultural Revolution. They told "rascals and teddy boys" to "shave away your long hair" and "remove your rocket-shaped shoes." They insisted that people should stop drinking, desist from smoking, and give up the "bourgeois habits of keeping crickets, fish, cats, and dogs." Laundries, they said, should refuse to launder the clothing of "bourgeois families," and "bath houses must as a rule discontinue serving those bourgeois sons of bitches, and stop doing massage for them." This group of Red Guards also demanded that their own school change its name from the "No. 26 Middle School" to the "School of Mao Zedong's Doctrine."[56]

Some Red Guard activities were much less amusing. Teachers and school administrators were often regarded as principal representatives of the "bourgeois" class in China, and untold numbers were harrassed, beaten, or tortured at the hands of their own students – often to death. Homes of former industrialists or landlords were invaded and ransacked, in a search for "contraband materials" or hidden wealth. Art objects were confiscated, ornate furniture smashed or painted red, and walls covered with quotations from Mao Zedong. Members of the pariah classes, such as landlords, were rounded up and forcibly deported from major cities. At Peking University alone, 100 homes of faculty and staff were searched, books and other personal effects seized, and 260 persons forced to work under "supervision" with placards around their necks listing their "crimes."[57] The descent into often mindless violence and brutality simply continued and intensified, albeit under less official auspices, the reign of terror against China's bourgeois classes, particularly intellectuals, that had begun under Party leadership during the Fifty Days earlier the same year.

From the outset, the Red Guard movement was plagued with serious factionalism, with the main issue under dispute being the identity of the principal targets of the Cultural Revolution. To a very large degree, the divisions among the students occurred along the fault lines created by the educational

---

56 *SCMM*, 566 (6 March 1967), 12–20.
57 For descriptions of Red Guard violence, see Gordon A. Bennett and Ronald N. Montaperto, *Red Guard: The political biography of Dai Hsiao-ai;* Ken Ling, *The revenge of heaven: Journal of a young Chinese;* and *HQ*, 19 (October 1980), 32–6.

policies of the early 1960s.[58] Students from cadre or military families usually insisted that the Red Guard movement remain under Party leadership, and tried to moderate the criticism leveled at the Party establishment. Instead, they sought to direct the spearhead of the movement against a different set of targets: intellectuals, scholars, former industrialists and landlords, and signs of bourgeois culture in China's urban society.

Students from bourgeois backgrounds, in contrast, saw the Cultural Revolution as an opportunity to overcome the discrimination they had experienced in the early 1960s, when the growing emphasis on class background had put them at a disadvantage in university admissions, Yough League and Party recruitment, and job assignments. From their perspective, the Red Guard movement offered an unparalleled chance to demonstrate a degree of revolutionary conduct that would outweigh their undesirable family origins and a legitimate opportunity to vent their grievances against the Party establishment. Maoist sympathizers who had been suppressed and persecuted during the Fifty Days now saw the possibility of reversing the verdicts that had been imposed on them by the work teams. They argued that their resistance to the teams had been an act of rebellion against "incorrect" Party leadership – a right now guaranteed them by the Sixteen Points adopted at the Eleventh Plenum.

The divisions within the student movement have been captured in a number of detailed case studies of Red Guard organizations in Beijing and Guangzhou. One reveals that, in a sample of nearly 2,200 middle school students in Guangzhou, the overwhelming majority of students from cadre families (73 percent) joined organizations that defended the Party establishment, while a slightly smaller majority of students from intellectual backgrounds (61 percent) and a plurality of students from other bourgeois families (40 percent) joined rebel organizations. Analyzed somewhat differently, the same data show that the "loyalist" organizations drew the bulk of their membership (82 percent) from children from cadre and worker backgrounds, whereas the "rebel" organizations recruited their members principally from families of intellectuals (45 percent).[59]

From a Maoist perspective, this was an irony of the highest order in that the most radical students in a revolutionary campaign against reivsionism were representatives not of the proletariat, as the rhetoric of the day insisted, but rather of the bourgeoisie itself. From a less ideological point of view, however, the divisions within the student movement are much more understandable. Those who criticized the Party most vehemently were those who had

58 On cleavages within the Red Guard movement, see Lee, *Politics of she Cultural Revolution;* Rosen, *Red Guard factionalism;* and Anita Chan, "Images of China's social structure: The changing perspective of Canton students," *World Politics,* 34.3 (April 1982), 295–323.

59 Chan, "Images of China's social structure," 314, Table 2.

gained the least from the Party's educational policies and whose families had been the principal victims of the Party's "class line," whereas those who supported the Party against attack were the children of Party officials and were those who had benefited the most from the prevailing system of Party recruitment, university admissions, and job assignments.

The reaction of the Party establishment

The failure of the Red Guard movement to follow the course that Mao had intended, and its descent into disorder, factionalism, and violence, can be attributed to a number of causes. In part, it was because the restraints on the mass movement contained in the Sixteen Points were not strong enough to counterbalance the inflammatory rhetoric of that same document, of the official Party press, and of the leaders of the Cultural Revolution Group. In part, it was because the Cultural Revolution was conducted in a way that significantly departed from the original vision embodied in the Eleventh Plenum in that the movement was implemented not by Cultural Revolution committees under Party leadership, but rather by Red Guard organizations that took as their right and obligation the rejection of Party authority. Perhaps most important, it was the result of a decision to mobilize millions of immature young people in a highly charged political atmosphere, to encourage them to engage in "revolutionary struggle" against vaguely defined targets, and to denounce as "suppression of the masses" any attempt to bring them under leadership or control.

Another reason for the difficulties of the Red Guard movement can be found in the opposition of the Party establishment itself. Officials could only have been bewildered by the notion that their records were to be evaluated by loosely organized groups of high school and university students, wearing military uniforms and waving small red books of Mao's quotations. But it was clear that their jobs were at stake. The Eleventh Plenum Decision had spoken of dismissing Party people in authority taking the capitalist road. And, in a speech to the plenum, Lin Biao had discussed the same matter in even blunter terms. The Cultural Revolution, he said, would involve "an overall examination and overall readjustment of cadres" according to three political criteria: whether they "hold high the red banner of Mao Zedong Thought," whether they "engage in political and ideological work," and whether they are "enthusiastic about the revolution." Those who met the criteria were to be promoted or retained in office; those who did not were to be dismissed so as to "break the stalemate" between those who supported Mao's programs an those who opposed them.[60]

---

60 Kau, *Lin Piao*, 346–50.

Even more alarming, it was rapidly becoming apparent that more than careers were involved. As already mentioned, an untold number of teachers and principals had by this time been beaten, tortured, and even murdered by their own students. And Party cadres were by no means exempt from similar forms of violence. In the first few months of the Red Guard movement alone, at least one Party official – the first secretary of Tianjin municipality – died as a result of a struggle meeting with radical students, and another – Pan Fusheng of Heilongjiang – was hospitalized after being denied food for four days.[61]

In some places, officials may have heeded the Party's injunctions to submit themselves freely to interrogation and criticism by the Red Guards. But the overall pattern was one in which officials tried to delay, divert, or disrupt the movement.[62] Initially, some attempted to ban the Red Guard organizations outright on the grounds that they had not been officially sanctioned by the Eleventh Plenum. Another tactic was to permit the formation of Red Guard organizations but then to place their activities under tight restrictions, similar to those imposed by the work teams during the Fifty Days, that prohibited them from holding parades or demonstrations, posting wall posters, or printing their own newspapers.

The convocation of the huge Red Guard rallies in Beijing, and the publication of laudatory editorials in the central press, however, soon made it impossible to deny the legitimacy of the Red Guard organizations. Consequently, local officials began to employ a more subtle approach. Some tried to sacrifice a few subordinates (in an analogy with chess, the Chinese used the phrase "sacrificing the knights to save the king" to describe this tactic) as a way of demonstrating sincerity without placing themselves in jeopardy. Some staged "great debates" to discuss whether or not their Party committee had exercised truly "revolutionary" leadership but manipulated the meetings so as to ensure the correct outcome. Some sought to prevent Red Guards from posting wall posters by covering blank walls with quotations from Mao Zedong, in the confident belief that covering such sayings with *dazibao* would ʿe tantamount to sacrilege. Still others tried to evade the Red Guards by ʿring their offices to local military compounds, which the radical students ʿot enter.

ʿncipal tactic, however, was for provincial and local cadres to encour-
ʿation of conservative mass organizations to defend them against

ʿ, 132.
ʿ officials to the Red Guard movement, see Parris H. Chang, "Provincial Party
ʿval during the Cultural Revolution," in Robert A. Scalapino, ed., *Elites in*
ʿo1–39; and Richard Baum, "Elite behavior under conditions of stress:
ʿn p'ai' in the Cultural Revolution," in Scalapino, *Elites*, 540–74.

criticism by the radicals. Working through the Party organization and the Youth League within each university and middle school, it was possible to organize students who had a stake in maintaining the status quo and to portray more radical Red Guard groups as being members of bourgeois families seeking revenge on the Party. Working through the trade unions, the local leaders also organized more conservative workers into "Scarlet Guards" (*chiweidui*) to defend Party and government buildings against assaults by radical Red Guards. As a result of such maneuvers, the Red Guard movement, which had originally been based on college and middle school campuses, began to move outward into the ranks of the industrial work force.

This tactic was facilitated by a set of central regulations that, ironically, favored the Party establishment over the CRG. Central policy at first restricted membership in Red Guard organizations to students from what were called "five red" family backgrounds – workers, peasants, soldiers, cadres, or revolutionary martyrs – and prohibited students from bourgeois backgrounds from participating in the Red Guard movement. This not only limited the size of the student movement – only 15 to 35 percent of middle school and university students belonged to the original Red Guard organizations in the late summer and early fall of 1966[63] – but it also paradoxically restricted membership in the Red Guards to precisely those students who were more likely to defend the Party establishment.

Why did officials resist the Red Guard movement in all these ways? Part of the answer lies in their desire for self-preservation in the face of a movement they must have regarded as anarchic and uncontrolled. But local and provincial officials must have also believed that they had support in Beijing, and that their best strategy would be to try to ride out the worst of the campaign and hope that it would soon be brought to an end. After all, neither Liu Shaoqi, Deng Xiaoping, nor Zhou Enlai had been dismissed from the Politburo by the Eleventh Plenum. Liu, to be sure, had been demoted in rank, but he remained president of the People's Republic. Deng and Zhou retained their positions as secretary general of the Party and prime minister of the State Council. And Tao Zhu, the former head of the Party's Central-South regional bureau, who had been named director of the Party Propaganda Department in early June, was also attempting to prevent the Red Guard movement from claiming too many victims. All these central leaders, in their speeches, actively supported efforts to restrict membership in the Red Guards to students from five red backgrounds, to maintain unity and discipline of Red Guard organizations, and to use the principle of majority rule to subordinate the radical minority to the more conservative majority.

---

63 Lee, *Politics of the Cultural Revolution*, 85.

The response of the Maoists

By the end of September, therefore, it was becoming clear to Mao, Lin, and the CRG that the Cultural Revolution was not proceeding as originally intended. There had been much criticism of the four olds but little criticism of leading officials. Only a few lower-level cadres had been forced to resign. The main trend was for the Party establishment to evade, subvert, and coopt the movement.

Accordingly, early October saw a substantial radicalization of the Cultural Revolution and the strengthening of the CRG at the expense of the Party establishment. This development was first reflected in a series of speeches and editorials, most of which were written by members of the CRG on the occasion of China's National Day on 1 October. These statements criticized Party cadres for their resistance to the Cultural Revolution, reiterated that the Red Guards had the right to rebel against the Party organization, and emphasized that the main target of the Cultural Revolution was revisionists in the Party and not, as conservative organizations had argued, the four olds. Perhaps most important, they announced that the restrictions on membership in Red Guard organizations would be overturned so that radical students from bad class backgrounds could legally join the mass movement.

Moreover, between 9 and 28 October a central work conference was held in Beijing to assess the Cultural Revolution's progress thus far, and to find ways of overcoming the obstacles it had encountered.[64] At first, Mao and Lin sought to gain the delegates' support for the Cultural Revolution by reassuring them about the movement's purposes. They promised that most cadres would be able to "pass the test" of the Cultural Revolution, if only they would welcome, instead of trying to evade, mass criticism. "If [cadres] have made mistakes," Mao said, "they can probably correct them! When they have corrected them, it will be all right, and they should be allowed to come back and go to work with a fresh spirit." Mao even submitted his own self-criticism, in which he acknowledged that the emergence of revisionist policies in the early 1960s was partly the result of his own choice to retire to a "second line" of leadership and relinquish responsibility for day-to-day decisions. What is more, Mao admitted, he had not anticipated the "big trouble" that was created by the mobilization of the Red Guards.[65]

But the delegates to the work conference were still not mollified. What was originally expected to be a three-day meeting stretched on to more than two weeks, and what was supposed to have been a conciliatory atmosphere

---

64 Lieberthal, *Research guide*, 259–62. The dates, which differ somewhat from those given by Lieberthal, are from Sun, *Lishi jiangyi*, 2.255.
65 Ch'en, *Mao papers*, 40–5; and Jerome Ch'en, ed., *Mao*, 91–7.

gradually became more and more acrimonious.[66] Chen Boda gave a report charging that the struggle between the "proletarian" and "bourgeois" lines that had been evident in the early 1960s was now being reflected in the conduct of the Cultural Revolution. Mao Zedong and Lin Biao stopped giving reassurances to worried cadres and now vehemently attacked officials who tried to check or elude the movement. Mao complained that "only a very few people firmly place the word 'revolt' in front of other words. Most people put the word 'fear' in first place." Lin attributed the resistance of the Party to the obstruction of some central officials, and he named Liu Shaoqi and Deng Xiaoping as the probable culprits. Both men were compelled to submit self-criticisms to the conference.

The effect of these developments in October 1966 was greatly to reduce the influence of conservative mass organizations.[67] Late in the year, some loyalist organizations in Beijing did engage in a last stand, attacking radical Red Guard groups, criticizing Lin Biao, defending Liu Shaoqi, and insisting that the proper course was to "kick away the CRG to make revolution on our own." But their power was clearly on the wane. Some conservative organizations submitted self-criticisms, some were taken over by radical students, and others collapsed as their leaders were arrested by public security forces.

The CRG was also able in late 1966 to intensify the mass assault on the Party establishment. Easing restrictions on membership in mass organizations quickly increased the size of the radical factions. At the same time, the CRG strengthened its liaison with those organizations that it considered to be most sympathetic, and urged them to amalgamate into larger, more effective bodies. In November and December, Red Guards were allowed to enter factories and communes, and workers were authorized to form their own "revolutionary rebel" organizations, thus breaking the effective monopoly previously enjoyed by the Party establishment in organizing workers and peasants. Free transportation to Beijing was ended so as to encourage Red Guards to end their "revolutionary tourism" and return to their home cities and provinces to "make revolution" against local Party committees.

Most important of all, the CRG began to identify high-ranking officials for the mass organizations to attack and provided friendly Red Guards with information that could be used as the basis for their criticisms. Red Guard delegations were sent from Beijing to major provincial capitals with specific instructions as to which local officials should be put to the test. Radical Red Guard organizations were informed that Liu Shaoqi and Deng Xiaoping

66 Sun, *Lishi jiangyi*, 2.255.
67 On events following the October work conference, see Daubier, *History of the Cultural Revolution*, ch. 3; Dittmer, *Liu Shao-ch'i*, ch. 5; Lee, *Politics of she Cultural Revolution*, 118–29. The escalation is also reflected in the central directives issued during the period, in "Collection of documents."

had opposed Mao Zedong and could be subjected to criticism. The CRG provided the Red Guards with copies of Liu's and Deng's self-criticisms at the October work conference, and wall posters attacking the two men began to appear in greater numbers in November and December. According to evidence presented at the trial of the "Gang of Four" in 1980–1, Zhang Chunqiao met with the Qinghua student radical Kuai Dafu at Zhongnanhai on 18 December and told him to discredit Liu and Deng publicly. "Make their very names stink," Zhang is alleged to have said. "Don't stop halfway."[68] And, toward the end of the year, Tao Zhu was dismissed from the directorship of the Propaganda Department, for attempting to shield provincial officials and central propaganda and cultural affairs cadres from criticism, and for allegedly seeking to strip control over the movement from the Cultural Revolution Group. Five other important central officials – Yang Shangkun, Luo Ruiqing, Lu Dingyi, Peng Zhen, and He Long – were forced to attend mass rallies in Beijing, where they were denounced and abused for hours on end.

The message of these developments was clear: No one in China, save Mao Zedong himself, was to be exempt from criticism, and the methods of criticism could be harsh indeed.

The collapse of provincial authority

The result of the escalation of the Cultural Revolution in the last three months of 1966 differed from one part of China to another. In more remote provinces, where the mobilization of radical students was difficult, provincial leaders remained well entrenched. But where mobilization did occur, the consequence was not the rectification of local officials, as Mao had hoped, but rather the nearly complete collapse of provincial authority.

Shanghai provides the best example of this latter process.[69] The inflammation of central rhetoric in October encouraged the formation of the first radical, citywide workers' organization, the "Workers' Headquarters," early the following month, This organization, composed primarily of such under-privileged workers as apprentices and temporary contract laborers, was apparently formed by some lower-level cadres (such as Wang Hongwen of the No. 17 State Cotton Mill, who would rise to national prominence later in the Cultural Revolution) with the assistance of radical students. The mayor of Shanghai, Cao Diqiu, had by some accounts been willing to comply, albeit

---

68 *A great trial in Chinese history: The trial of the Lin Biao and Jiang Qing counter-revolutionary cliques,* Nov. 1980–Jan. 1981, 35.

69 Accounts of events in Shanghai in this period can be found in Neale Hunter, *Shanghai journal: An eyewitness account of the Cultural Revolution;* and Andrew G. Walder, *Chang Ch'un-ch'iao and Shanghai's January Revolution.*

reluctantly, with the central directives on the Cultural Revolution. But he resisted the formation of the Workers' Headquarters, on the grounds that the creation of independent workers' organizations had not yet been sanctioned by central directives, and that the formation of such groups would almost certainly interfere with production.

When the Workers' Headquarters approached Cao, seeking official recognition and material support, he therefore denied their request. Angered, the leaders of the Headquarters commandeered a train and left for Beijing to present their case to the central leadership. Cao ordered the train sidetracked at a suburban station outside Shanghai, where his representatives again tried to explain his position.

At first the central CRG supported Cao's stand. But when the workers still refused to return to their factories, the radical leaders in Beijing sent Zhang Chunqiao to negotiate with them. Zhang undercut Cao Diqiu by agreeing to recognize the Workers' Headquarters, on the condition that their Cultural Revolutionary activities not be permitted to interefere with their normal production assignments – a decision that Cao had no alternative but to endorse.

The city government's position was further weakened by the arrival, in Shanghai, of Nie Yuanzi, apparently with instructions to expose the head of the city's education department as a revisionist and to accuse Cao Diqiu of shielding him. In the aftermath of her arrival, a group of radicals took over the local newspaper, the *Jiefang ribao*, demanding that it distribute copies of Nie's address. Several days later, the government capitulated.

The collapse of Cao's authority, however, was not primarily the result of these actions by radical workers and intellectuals. It was, instead, the result of a countermobilization, at least partly spontaneous, by more conservative Shanghai citizens. During the occupation of the *Jiefang ribao*, groups of Scarlet Guards and other supporters attempted to storm the building to retake it from the radicals. Postal workers refused to distribute copies of the tabloid containing Nie's speech. The Scarlet Guards issued demands that Cao repudiate his "capitulation" to the radicals, and that he not concede anything further to them.

Cao's response to this process of polarization was, according to the careful study by Andrew Walder, to "sign any and all demands that were made to his office" by either faction.[70] The result was a torrent of requests by disadvantaged sectors of society for economic benefits. Workers who had been transformed into temporary laborers, and contract workers who had been laid off, demanded reinstatement and back pay. Permanent workers lobbied for higher wages and

70 Walder, *Chang Ch'un-ch'iao*, 36.

for increases in benefits, and charged that the disruption of production by the radicals would cause a reduction in their own bonuses.

Fights and riots broke out between the conservative and radical factions, and after one in which eight conservatives were reportedly killed, the Scarlet Guards called a general strike. This, coupled with the strategy of the besieged municipal government – to meet the demands of all factions – led to the collapse of the Shanghai economy: runs on banks, hoarding of supplies, disruption of electricity and transportation. By the end of December, China's largest city was in chaos.

The "January Revolution"

The situation in Shanghai was, in extreme form, representative of what had happened in much of urban China by the end of 1966. Essentially, three processes were at work, which taken together caused the collapse of Party authority. First of all, there was the mobilization of large sectors of Chinese society, who were making ever greater demands on the Party bureaucracy. The process had begun as a deliberate attempt by the Maoists in Beijing to organize a force to criticize the Party. But once it began, the process fed on itself, with mobilization by the Maoists engendering a form of countermobilization – some spontaneous, some highly organized – in support of the Party establishment.

Accordingly, the process of mass mobilization produced a high degree of polarization in Chinese society, mirroring the intense factionalism that already existed at the highest levels of the Party leadership. In calling on the students (and later the workers) of China to criticize revisionism in the Party, Mao seems to have naively believed that they would act as a relatively unified force – that the "great union of the popular masses," of which he had spoken and written since the mid-1920s, would form in the course of the Cultural Revolution.[71] What happened was precisely the opposite. Mass mobilization aggravated deep cleavages within Chinese society, particularly those separating students of cadre families from those with bourgeois backgrounds, and those separating skilled permanent workers from less skilled and temporary employees.

Third, mobilization and polarization were accompanied by the delegitimization of Party authority. By authorizing the Red Guards to rebel against revisionists in the Party, and by asserting that people should obey only those

---

71 On this tendency in Mao's thinking, see Stuart R. Schram, "From the 'Great Union of the Popular Masses' to the Great Alliance," *CQ*. 49 (January–March 1972), 88–105.

Party directives that corresponded with Mao Zedong Thought, the Maoists in effect stripped the Party of unconditional legitimacy without providing any alternative structure of authority in its place. At the same time, the delegitimation from above was reinforced by a withdrawal of legitimacy from below. As beleaguered Party organizations sought to cope with the explosion of popular demands by trying to please everyone, they ultimately pleased no one. The Shanghai experience vividly illustrates the authority crisis that occurs when a regime loses control over an escalating process of mobilization and countermobilization.

Mao's response to the collapse of authority was, in effect, to authorize radical groups to push aside the discredited (or recalcitrant) Party committees and constitute new organs of political power in their place. Once again, Shanghai was the frontrunner in this stage of the Cultural Revolution.[72] On 6 January 1967, a mass rally in Shanghai confirmed officially what had already occurred in fact: It dismissed Cao Diqiu and other municipal officials from their posts. On that same day, Zhang Chunqiao, as a representative of the CRG, returned to Shanghai from Beijing to establish a new municipal government to replace the overthrown Party committee. With his encouragement, and with the support of the CRG, constituent organizations of the radical Workers' Headquarters issued demands for the restoration of social order and economic production: demands that the economic grievances of workers be shelved until a "later stage" of the Cultural Revolution, that workers remain at their posts, and that enterprise and bank funds be frozen. At the same time, rebel organizations, backed by units of the PLA, began taking over factories, docks, newspapers, and other economic enterprises. From these beginnings, it was only a short time before the ultimate step was taken: The radical organizations announced the formation of a new organ of political power in Shanghai that would assume the political and administrative functions of the old Party committee and municipal government.

In the latter part of the month, this sort of power seizure was authorized for all of China. On 22 January, a vitriolic editorial in *Renmin ribao* encouraged radical organizations throughout the country to rise up and take power away from the Party committees:

> Of all the important things, the possession of power is the most important. Such being the case, the revolutionary masses, with a deep hatred for the class enemy, make up their mind to unite, form a great alliance, [and] seize power! Seize power!! Seize power!!! All the Party power, political power, and financial power usurped by the counterrevolutionary revisionists and those

---

72 On events in Shanghai, see Wilder, *Chang Ch'un-ch'iao*, ch. 7. A similar seizure of power took place in Shanxi.

diehards who persistently cling to the bourgeois reactionary line must be recaptured![73]

The following day, a formal CC directive repeated *Renmin ribao's* call for a mass seizure of power from "those in authority who are taking the cpitalist road." It described the Cultural Revolution not simply as a criticism of bourgeois and revisionist tendencies in China, as had the Decision of the Eleventh Plenum, but rather as "a great revolution in which one class overthrows another."[74]

The radicalization of the goals of the Cultural Revolution was accompanied by a radicalization of the composition of the CRG. In January and February 1967, all the representatives of the PLA and the regional and provincial Party organizations that had been appointed to the group the previous year were removed – along, of course, with Tao Zhu, who lost membership in the group when he was purged as director of the Propaganda Department in December. This meant that, once again, the CRG reflected solely the interests of the radical intellectuals associated with Jiang Qing, Kang Sheng, and Chen Boda. No longer was their viewpoint moderated by the more conservative outlooks of senior Party and army officials.

The CC's 23 January directive also initiated an escalation of the Cultural Revolution along a second dimension. Through the latter half of 1966, the PLA had played a somewhat aloof and ambivalent role in the Cultural Revolution. In some ways, to be sure, it had been actively involved on the side of the Maoists: by providing a forum for Jiang Qing's assault on the prevailing line in literature and art; by providing, through the *Jiefangjun bao*, a mouthpiece for radical viewpoints in the spring of 1966; by securing Beijing during such crucial meetings as the May 1966 central work conference and the Eleventh Plenum, in August; and by providing logistical support for the Red Guards. In other ways, however, it had stood on the sidelines or even taken a hostile position. The Decision of the Eleventh Plenum had specifically exempted the army from the jurisdiction of the Cultural Revolution Group, and other directives had apparently ordered military units to take a posture of noninvolvement in the confrontation among mass organizations and between radical groups and the Party establishment. And in many areas, the PLA had served as an "air raid shelter," providing sanctuary for local and provincial Party officials and a force for suppressing radical organizations.

Until 23 January, then, the most active elements in the Maoist coalition had been the radical brain trust, as symbolized by the CRG, and the mass base, as typified by the radical Red Guard and revolutionary rebel organizations.

---

73 *RMRB*, 22 January 1967, in *PR*, 10.5 (27 January 1967), 7–9.

74 "Decision of the CCP Central Committee, the State Council, the Military Commission of the Central Committee, and the Cultural Revolution Group under the Central Committee on resolute support for the revolutionary masses of the left," 23 January 1967, in "Collection of documents," 49–50.

Now, in light of the general stalemate that had occurred throughout the fall, and the collapse of authority that had begun to appear around the turn of the year, Mao decided to throw the army – the third element of his power base – more fully into the fray. The 23 January directive, citing a recent directive from the Chairman that "the PLA should support the broad masses of the Left," ordered that the armed forces drop any pretense of noninvolvement, stop serving as an "air raid shelter for the handful of Party power holders taking the capitalist road," give "active support . . . to the broad masses of revolutionary Leftists in their struggle to seize power," and "resolutely suppress" any "counterrevolutionaries or counterrevolutionary organizations" that offered resistance.

Once the decision had been taken to authorize the seizure of power, however, other equally important decisions remained. Who should seize power? Who should exercise it? Through what organizational forms? Perhaps the most pressing issue in this regard was whether or not the masses could really assume the role that had been assigned to them. The language of the 22 January *Renmin ribao* editorial and the CC's directive of the following day suggested a kind of Marxist jacquerie: a mass uprising to depose those who had usurped power and departed from correct policies. But the masses of China were deeply divided into competing interests and largely ignorant of the details of political administration, rather than a unified political force that could provide an effective alternate government.

Both these problems were reflected in the wave of power seizures across the country in late January. In some places, competing mass organizations each claimed to have seized power, and appealed to Beijing for support. In other places, Party officials used friendly mass organizations to stage what were later described as "sham" seizures of power. In still other localities, mass representatives entered Party or government offices, demanded the seals with which official documents were "chopped," and then walked out, in the belief that the capture of the symbols of power meant that power itself had somehow been seized. As Zhou Enlai himself put it, power was "surrendered" by the Party but was not effectively "retained" by the Red Guards.[75]

The extent of these difficulties was indicated by the fact that China's central news media acknowledged and endorsed only four of the thirteen power seizures that occurred across the country at the end of January. An important editorial published on 1 February in *Hongqi* (Red Flag), the Party's theoretical journal, tacitly admitted that the concept of a Marxist jacquerie was unworkable. Instead, the editorial stipulated that power should be seized not simply

75 Philip Bridgham, "Mao's Cultural Revolution: The struggle to seize power," *CQ*, 34 (April–June 1968), 7.

by a "great alliance" of mass organizations, but rather by a "three-in-one combination" (*sanjiehe*) of representatives of the "revolutionary masses," local military officers, and Party and government officials whose attitude was judged to be sufficiently "revolutionary." The presence of mass representatives would reflect the original populist ethos of the Cultural Revolution. But, as the editorial admitted, "it will not do to rely solely on the representatives of these revolutionary mass organizations." Without the other two components of the "three-in-one combination," "the proletarian revolutionaries will not be able to solve the problem of seizing and wielding power in their struggle. . . . , nor can they consolidate power even if they seize it." Cadres were necessary because of their administrative experience and their knowledge of the details of policy and programs; military representatives, who became, as we will see, the most important part of the three-in-one combination, would be able to ensure discipline and suppress any opposition to the seizure of power.[76]

With this issue resolved, the second problem taken up by the Maoist center was the form that the new organs of power would assume. For a brief period, the Maoists flirted with the idea of reorganizing China around the principles of the Paris Commune: All officials would be drawn from the ranks of ordinary citizens, be chosen by general election, be paid the same salaries as ordinary workers, report regularly to their constituents, and be subject to recall at any time. These principles, which imply a form of government completely different from that of classic bureaucracy, had been endorsed by Marx, Engels, and the pre-1917 Lenin as the form of political institutions that the dictatorship of the proletariat would introduce, replacing the bureaucracies that, in Lenin's words, were "peculiar to bourgeois society."[77]

The model of the Paris Commune had been fashionable among Chinese radicals in 1966, the ninety-fifth anniversary of the Commune's short existence. A long article in the February issue of *Hongqi*, well before the Eleventh Plenum, had recounted the history of the Commune and advocated that its principles be applied to China. The plenum itself, in authorizing the formation of Cultural Revolution committees, had provided that these new organizations embody the principles of the Commune, even though it simultaneously stipulated that the committees would supplement, and not supplant, the more bureaucratic Party and state organizations.[78]

With this as background, it was not surprising that radical Chinese would again turn to the model of the Paris Commune once the decision had been

76 *HQ*, 3 (1 February 1967), in JPRS, 40,086, *Translations from Red Flag* (1 March 1967), 12–21.
77 Vladimir I. Lenin, "The state and revolution," in Henry M. Christman, ed., *Essential works of Lenin*, 290.
78 *HQ*, 4 (15 February 1966), in JPRS, 35,137, *Translations from Red Flag* (21 April 1966), 5–22; *Decision*, sec. 9. On the use of the Paris Commune as a model in this period, see John Bryan Starr, "Revolution in retrospect: The Paris Commune through Chinese eyes," *CQ*, 49 (January–March 1972), 106–25.

taken to seize power from the Party and state bureaucracies in January 1967. Implicitly echoing comments by Marx a century earlier that the proletariat could not simply take over the state machinery of the bourgeoisie but would have to create new forms of organization, the *Hongqi* editorial of 1 February argued that the revolutionary rebels of China could not merely seize power in the existing Party and government agencies, but would have to create completely new organizational forms. Although it provided no clear guidelines as to what these new forms should be, the editorial strongly implied that they should be patterned after the Paris Commune. In keeping with this suggestion, many of the new provincial and municipal governments formed in late January announced that, in line with the principles of the Commune, their officials would be selected through mass elections and would be subject to supervision and recall. Some, such as Shanghai and Harbin, actually proclaimed themselves to be "people's communes."

In the situation prevailing in early 1967, however, such a step was as unrealistic as had been the earlier call for a mass uprising to seize power. The situation in Shanghai, for example, in no way reflected the exercise of immediate democracy, Paris Commune style. In organizing the Commune, Zhang Chunqiao had ignored the principle of direct election, promising only that such elections might be held at some future point "when conditions become ripe." In fact, the formation of the Shanghai Commune immediately produced grumblings that Zhang had favored representatives of the Workers' Headquarters at the expense of other groups and that he was using the PLA to suppress opposition. Some people complained that he was ignoring the economic demands raised by workers in late December, and that he himself, as a former director of the municipal Propaganda Department and a current member of the central CRG was hardly an "ordinary citizen." As Andrew Walder has pointed out, "Despite the utopian images conjured up by the commune . . . , the Shanghai Commune was probably supported by less than one-fourth of Shanghai's politically active working population and relied heavily upon the PLA for its very survival."[79]

Realizing that talk of "people's communes" raised expectations of immediate democracy that could not possibly be realized in a highly mobilized and polarized setting, Mao Zedong called Zhang Chunqiao and Yao Wenyuan back to Beijing to persuade them to change the name of the Shanghai Commune. Mao's concern was that a faithful implementation of the Paris Commune model would produce a further collapse of political authority, the exclusion of cadres and military representatives from the three-in-one combination, an inability to restore order and suppress counterrevolutionaries, and problems

79 Walder, *Chang Ch'un-ch'iao*, 61.

in finding a role for a reconstituted CCP later on. All these tendencies the Chairman labeled "most reactionary."[80]

Thus on 19 February, the day after Mao's meetings with Zhang and Yao, the CC banned the use of the term "people's commune" at the national, provincial, or municipal levels.[81] (It retained its original meaning, of course, as the name of the largest level of joint economic and political administration in the countryside.) Instead, the CC resurrected a term from revolutionary days – "revolutionary committee" (geming wenyuanhui) – to describe the "revolutionary, responsible, and proletarian provisional power structures" formed as a result of the seizure of power. The historical reference was particularly apt, for the revolutionary committees of the 1940s had also been three-in-one combinations of mass representatives, Party cadres, and military personnel, formed as provincial governments in areas recently "liberated" by the Red Army. But the use of the term in 1967 also underlined a key point: Like their predecessors of the Yan'an years, the revolutionary committees of the Cultural Revolution were now regarded only as provisional governments, pending the organization of something more permanent. Already, it seemed, Mao was envisioning ways of reducing the high level of mass mobilization that the Cultural Revolution had produced.

The third issue at stake in early 1967 was the process by which these revolutionary committees would be formed. With the notion of general elections discarded and the Party apparatus in shambles, the only element of the three-in-one combination that was in a position to organize the revolutionary committees on a nationwide basis was the PLA. Thus, the procedure authorized by Beijing was that, after the overthrow of the local Party committees, the local military garrison (for cities) or military district command (for provinces) would form a "military control committee" (junshi guanzhi weiyuanhui), responsible for restoring order, maintaining production, and beginning the selection of the mass representatives, cadres, and military officers to serve on the revolutionary committee. In essence, the army became a national work team, with responsibility for deciding not only which cadres would survive the Cultural Revolution, but also which mass organizations deserved representation on the revolutionary committees.[82]

The overthrow of the Party committees in early 1967 has been described by the Chinese themselves as the "January Revolution" (yiyue geming) and has been described outside the country as tantamount to a military seizure of

---

80 For the texts of Mao's remarks, see Miscellany of Mao Tse-tung Thought, 2.451–5; and JPRS, 49,826, Translations on Communist China (12 February 1970), 44–5.

81 "CCP Central Committee's notification on the question of propagandizing and reporting on the struggle to seize power," 19 February 1967, in "Collection of documents," 89; Ch'en, Mao papers, 136–7.

82 Harding, Organizing China, 253.

power. But neither the analogy of a mass revolution nor that of a military coup is an adequate way of understanding this period. It is true that the January Revolution involved a level of popular dissent, mass organization, and political protest unknown since 1949. But official rhetoric notwithstanding, the main purpose of the seizure of power in January was less to overthrow authority than to restore order. Granted, too, that the main beneficiary of the seizure of power was the PLA, as the country fell under military rule. But military intervention in Chinese politics in early 1967 occurred at the behest of civilian authorities in Beijing, not in defiance of them. If the events of January 1967 in China amounted to a revolution, in other words, it was a revolution from above; and if they resulted in military rule, then that outcome reflected the decision by one civilian faction to use military force to overthrow another, rather than a military coup against civilian authority.

The main participants in the three-in-one combination

The establishment of the three-in-one combination as the official framework for the creation of revolutionary committees defined the principal issue for the next ten months. In how many administrative units and at what levels of government should power be seized? What balance should be struck among the three components of the three-in-one combination as each revolutionary committee was formed?

The principle of the three-in-one combination also illustrated quite clearly the main lines of cleavage in Chinese politics produced by the Cultural Revolution. At the provincial and municipal levels, cadres, mass organizations, and military units all competed for representation on the revolutionary committees. In Beijing, in turn, each component of the three-in-one combination had its sponsors at the highest levels of Party leadership: Zhou Enlai and other senior civilian leaders represented the interests of cadres; the CRG, under Jiang Qing, Chen Boda, and Kang Sheng, represented the interests of the radical mass organizations; and Lin Biao and his associates in the MAC of the Party sponsored the interests of the armed forces.

But it would be incorrect to imply that these three vertical networks were internally unified, Just as there was conflict within the mass movement among radical and conservative Red Guard organizations, so too were there cleavages inside the armed forces between those sympathetic to Lin Biao and those who opposed him, and divisions between those cadres who were willing to accommodate to the Cultural Revolution and those who chose to resist it. And, significantly, none of the three organizational networks, or their elite sponsors in Beijing, was able to secure or maintain the unqualified support of Mao Zedong.

An understanding of the events of the remainder of 1967 and the first half of 1968 can therefore be facilitated by a brief analysis of the interests and behavior of each of these three vertical networks in Cultural Revolutionary China, beginning with what remained of the Party and state bureaucracy. By the end of January 1967, it was clear that every government and Party official in China was subject to criticism, dismissal, and even physical assault by radical organizations. Some cadres had already fallen from power, including the early targets of the Cultural Revolution, such as Peng Zhen, Lu Dingyi, and Luo Ruiqing; and the victims of the radicalization of the Red Guard movement in late 1966 and the first power seizures in January 1967, such as Tao Zhu and Cao Diqiu. Still others, such as Liu Shaoqi and Deng Xiaoping, and Zhou Enlai and his vice-premiers, had come under heavy criticism but had not actually been dismissed. Elsewhere, the fate of the vast majority of cadres was still uncertain. Leaders at each level waited to see whether they could secure appointment to the revolutionary committees that were now being formed under military sponsorship, while their subordinates remained in office with their authority weakened but not completely eliminated.

The interest of the cadres, as symbolized by Zhou Enlai, was primarily to moderate the impact of the Cultural Revolution on the state and Party bureaucracy. Zhou's goals throughout the movement were, to the greatest degree possible (1) to exempt the most important agencies of the Party and government from the most disruptive Cultural Revolutionary activities, (2) to prevent mass organizations from seizing power without authorization from a higher level, (3) to limit the geographic scope of operation of any particular mass organization, and (4) to ensure the maintenance of normal production and administrative work.[83] In addition, Zhou sought to protect a number of high-level officials from Red Guard attack. In January, he reportedly invited between twenty and thirty cabinet ministers to take turns living in the guarded leadership compound in Zhongnanhai, and enabled the first Party secretaries from a number of regions, provinces, and major cities to move to Beijing, where they would be free from harassment or criticism by local Red Guards.[84]

Despite the common interests of cadres in limiting the scope of the Cultural Revolution, there were differences of outlook within the ranks of Chinese officialdom. Some cadres, particularly those of lower ranks, saw the Cultural Revolution as an opportunity for more rapid advancement or for revenge against colleagues with whom they had poor personal relations. In some provinces and municipalities, therefore, a pattern emerged by which lower-echelon officials joined with radical mass organizations in seizing power from

83 On Zhou Enlai's role in the Cultural Revolution, see Thomas W. Robinson, "Chou En-lai and the Cultural Revolution," in Thomas W. Robinson, ed., The Cultural Revolution in China, 165–312.
84 Sun, Lishi jiangyi, 2.260–1.

their superiors. Important examples include Hua Guofeng, a secretary of the provincial Party committee in Hunan; Ji Dengkui, an alternate secretary in Henan; and, of course, Zhang Chunqiao of Shanghai – all of whom rose to positions of even greater prominence in their provinces as a direct result of the Cultural Revolution. This would be the basis for later controversy as those cadres who benefited from the Cultural Revolution in this way came into confrontation in the latter half of the 1970s with those who had been its principal victims.

The second main vertical network was that of the CRG and the radical mass organizations it mobilized, protected, and to some degree directed. The main interests of the CRG appear to have been to discredit as many cadres as possible, to give mass organizations the greatest scope and autonomy in their activities, and to maximize the participation of mass representatives on revolutionary committees. To this end, the CRG began, as early as August 1966 but on a wider scale late in 1967 and in 1968, to draw up lists of CC members, provincial Party and state leaders, and members of the National People's Congress and Chinese People's Political Consultative Conference whom they considered to have been "capitulationists" during the revolutionary period or "revisionists" after 1949. By August 1968, for example, Kang Sheng had allegedly compiled a list of more than 100 members of the CC and 37 members of the Party's central disciplinary apparatus whom he wanted to see expelled from the Party.[85] In addition, the CRG used friendly Red Guard organizations to organize mass demonstrations and criticism against Party and government officials, to seize compromising materials from their homes, and to obtain useful information through detention and torture of suspected revisionists and, in some cases, members of their families, their servants, or their office staff.[86]

These activities brought the CRG into conflict with both of the other two vertical networks active in the Cultural Revolution. The CRG tried to expand the scope of political struggle to include virtually all officials at all levels of the bureaucracy, whereas the cadres obviously sought to narrow the targets of the Cultural Revolution to a smaller number. The CRG wished to grant radical mass organizations greater autonomy to seize power from Party committees and government agencies, whereas civilian officials such as Zhou Enlai attempted to place power seizures under the control of higher authorities and to restrict mass organizations to supervisory rather than administrative functions.

In addition, the CRG came into increasing conflict with the PLA over the military's role in the Cultural Revolution. In January 1967, when the seizure of

85 Ibid., 2.271.   86 *A Great trial*, passim.

power first got underway, Chen Boda contrasted the Cultural Revolution with the final stages of the revolution in China in the 1940s. Then, he said, the Red Army seized power, "exercised military control, and issued orders from top to bottom." During the Cultural Revolution, he said, it would be the masses, and not the military, "who take over."[87] The role that Mao granted to the PLA in overthrowing the Party establishment and organizing revolutionary committees was thus far greater than the CRG would have preferred. Even worse, the local military forces did not always appoint mass representatives to revolutionary committees in the numbers that the CRG wanted or from the mass organizations that it supported. The formation of revolutionary committees inevitably led, therefore, to attacks on local military headquarters by some dissatisfied Red Guard organizations, and thus to tensions between the PLA and the CRG in Beijing.

This leads to the third vertical network active in the Cultural Revolution: the PLA itself. The role of the army, as we have seen, escalated steadily throughout 1966 and 1967. Now, once the Cultural Revolution entered the stage of the seizure of power, the military played an even greater part in Chinese politics. Its job was not only to help seize power from the Party establishment, as it was ordered to do on 23 January, but also to ensure thereafter that order was maintained. This second purpose was served by military occupation of key warehouses, banks, broadcasting stations, and factories; military supervision of spring planting; military management of civil aviation; and establishment of military control commissions in major administrative jurisdictions where power had been seized.[88] Altogether, 2 million officers and troops of the PLA participated in civilian affairs during the Cultural Revolution.[89]

In general, the military appears to have had a single major interest during the Cultural Revolution: to maintain order and stability, prevent the collapse of the Chinese social and political fabric, and thus avoid a situation in which China would be vulnerable to foreign invasion. In addition, some military officers had a related interest in maximizing their own influence on the new revolutionary committees, increasing the number of military representatives, and protecting the military against attacks by Red Guards.

Beyond these common interests, however, the divisions within the military during the Cultural Revolution appear to have been every bit as great as those within ranks of the cadres or among the country's mass organizations.[90]

87 *Huo-ch'e-t'ou*, 7 (February 1967), in *SCMP*, 3898 (14 March 1967), 4–7.
88 The escalation of military involvement can be traced through the central directives in "Collection of documents."
89 Edgar Snow, *The long resolution*, 103.
90 See Jürgen Domes, "The Cultural Revolution and the army," *Asian Survey*, 8.5 (May 1968), 349–63; Jürgen Domes, "The role of the military in the formation of revolutionary committees, 1967–68," *CQ*, 44 (October–December 1970), 112–45; Harvey W. Nelsen, "Military forces in the Cultural

Some of the cleavages were structural, resulting largely from the division of the PLA into local and main forces. The main forces – including the navy, air force, and the elite elements of the ground forces – were better equipped and directly subordinated to central command. The local forces, in contrast, were composed of lightly equipped infantry forces, commanded by military districts (corresponding in virtually all cases to provinces) and military regions (comprising several neighboring provinces), and responsible for a wide range of civilian activities.

During the Cultural Revolution, it was the main forces that remained more faithful to central directives from Lin Biao, not only because they came directly under the command of a General Staff and a MAC that he had packed with his own supporters, but also because they were the main beneficiaries of the program of military modernization that Lin had undertaken in the early 1960s. In contrast, the local forces, whose commanders often had close ties with local Party officials, often acted in conservative fashion as defenders of the provincial and municipal Party establishments. A study by Jürgen Domes, for example, has suggested that, of the twenty-nine military district commanders at the outset of the Cultural Revolution, only five gave the movement their backing, eight gave it nominal support only after they had brought local mass organizations under their control, and sixteen were unsupportive.[91]

A second set of cleavages within the military formed around personal factions. During the latter part of the Communist revolution, the Red Army had been divided into five great "field armies," each responsible for liberating a different part of the country. The personal associations established during this period formed the basis for factional networks of officers far after 1949. It was widely believed that Lin Biao, in seeking to consolidate his control over the PLA after his appointment as minister of national defense in 1959, had favored officers from the field army he had commanded (the Fourth) over officers from other factions.[92] After his purge, Lin was accused of having assembled derogatory materials about ranking officers from other field armies, particularly Nie Rongzhen, Xu Xiangqian, He Long, and Ye Jianying, who might have thwarted his attempt to establish exclusive personal control over the armed forces.[93]

Revolution," *CQ*, 51 (July–September 1972), 444–74; and Harvey W. Nelsen, "Military bureaucracy in the Cultural Revolution," *Asian Survey*, 14.4 (April 1974), 372–95.

91 Domes, "Role of the military."

92 The *locus classicus* for an analysis of the importance of field armies in Chinese military politics is William W. Whitson with Chen-hsia Huang, *The Chinese high command: A history of communist military politics, 1927–71*. See also Chien Yu-shen, *China's fading revolution: Army dissent and military divisions, 1967–68;* and William L. Parish, "Factions in Chinese military politics," *CQ*, 56 (October–December 1973), 667–99.

93 *A great trial*, 82–9.

As a final element in this assessment of the major participants in the three-in-one combination, it is important to underscore the tensions and conflicts that emerged from time to time between Mao and each of these three vertical networks. Mao's main differences were obviously with the Party and state cadres, for it was they whom he suspected of revisionism and against whom he directed the Cultural Revolution. On the other hand, Mao seems to have acknowledged the need for trained administrators to serve on the revolutionary committees. He claimed to hope that the cadres would be able to "pass the test" of the Cultural Revolution ("Who wants to knock you down? I don't," he told the central work conference in October 1966),[94] and he protected a few ranking civilian officials, particularly Zhou Enlai, from Red Guard criticism.

But Mao also had his differences with both Lin Biao and the CRG. Although Mao had selected Lin to head the Ministry of Defense in 1959 and chose him as his heir apparent at the Eleventh Plenum in 1966, the Chairman apparently questioned many of Lin's views on questions of history and ideology. In a letter to Jiang Qing in early July 1966, he criticized Lin for overstating the importance of military coups and military power in the history of China and the history of developing countries, and for exaggerating Mao's own personality cult. "I have never believed that those several booklets of mine possessed so much magic," Mao wrote to his wife. "This is the first time in my life that I have involuntarily agreed with others on an issue of major significance."[95]

Much of Mao's criticism of Lin could simultaneously be read as a criticism of the CRG, for the encomiums to Mao Zedong Thought in mid-1966 and the sycophantic treatment of Mao in the Chinese press were as much its responsibility as that of the PLA. Some of Mao's statements in January about the Shanghai Commune suggest that Mao was concerned about anarchistic tendencies among the Cultural Revolution Group and about their desire to overthrow all of the country's cadres.[96] There is no evidence to suggest that Mao was ever willing to authorize the use of armed force by mass organizations, as Jiang Qing and her colleagues on the Cultural Revolution Group were sometimes prepared to do.

Mao had a variety of resources and strategies to employ against any of these three networks should they prove insubordinate or recalcitrant. The cadres were the most easily controlled, as they had the weakest power base at the time. As a general instrument, Mao could allow the central Cultural Revolution Group to intensify its criticism of Party and government officials, confident that this would be promptly reflected in the actions of radical

94 Ch'en, Mao papers, 45.   95 CLG, 6.2 (Summer 1973), 96–9.
96 Miscellany of Mao Tse-tung Thought, 2.451–5; and JPRS, 49,826, Translations on Communist China (12 February 1970), 44–5.

mass organizations. More specifically, Mao could identify particular cadres for exclusion from revolutionary committees, for punishment, or for protection.

The PLA, in contrast, had much more power than civilian officials, for army officers controlled the organized armed force that now was essential to the stability of the regime. But the army could be controlled – in part by increasing the leeway given to radical mass organizations to criticize army officials and in part by disciplining errant officers through the military chain of command. Thus, commanders unsympathetic to the Cultural Revolution were removed or transferred in five military regions and six military districts in the spring of 1967, and about eight more district commanders met similar fates later that year. In extreme situations, as we shall see, Mao and Lin could dispatch main force units into provinces where local comanders had been particularly obdurate.

Mao also had a variety of mechanisms for controlling the mass organizations. He could tighten restrictions on radical mass activities, giving Red Guard and revolutionary rebels less leeway to criticize civilian and military officials when their tendencies toward fragmentation and violence seemed to get out of hand. In addition, Mao and his representatives could label particular organizations as either "revolutionary" or "counterrevolutionary," depending on their subservience to central directives, and could give local military units the authority to suppress and disband mass organizations that had been deemed counterrevolutionary.

The shifting balance

Given these cleavages – within each vertical system, among the three organizational networks, and between each vertical system and Mao Zedong – the formation of revolutionary committees in 1967–8 was thus an exceedingly complicated task. In only a few places – Heilongjiang, Shanghai, Guizhou, and Shandong – were revolutionary committees formed smoothly in the first two months of 1967. Here the key was the existence of alternative leadership, usually from the pre-Cultural Revolution provincial or municipal Party establishment, which was able quickly to fill the collapse of authority that occurred in January. In other provinces, where the existing military and civilian leadership was divided and the mass organizations were deeply fragmented, the formation of revolutionary committees was a much more protracted process, involving continued conflict and competition.

The twenty months during which the revolutionary committees were selected, March 1967 to October 1968, were essentially a period of shifting balances among the three competing organizational networks in which each would periodically gain or lose power relative to the others. Throughout the period, Mao retained the ability to determine the balance of power among the three vertical networks, although his decisions were clearly made in response to the actions of the cadres, the military, and the mass organizations, and although he never controlled the situation completely. The dynamics of the period can best be understood by examining four key turning points: the "February Adverse Current" of February–March 1967: the Wuhan Incident of late July 1967, the purge of a so-called "516" Group of radicals in early September, and the dismissal of Chief of Staff Yang Chengwu and the disbanding of the Red Guards in the summer of 1968.

Each of these turning points is important both for its origins and for its consequences. Each episode emerged from the tensions within and among the three key vertical networks already discussed. Each reflected, from Mao Zedong's perspective, the unreliability of one or more of the three organizational systems: The February Adverse Current showed that senior Party leaders still resisted the Cultural Revolution and the Red Guard movement; the Wuhan Incident demonstrated that high-ranking military commanders, particularly at the regional level, tended to side with conservative mass organizations against their radical opponents; and the 516 affair and the disbanding of the Red Guards in mid-1968 reflected the proclivities of the mass movement and, indeed, of the leaders of the Cultural Revolution Group itself, toward violence and disorder.

Together, the three episodes also produced a shift in the balance of power among the three organizational systems that dominated Chinese politics during this period. Although the three networks had begun, at least in theory, as equal participants in the three-in-one combination, by the end of 1967 it was evident that the PLA was well on its way to establishing predominance over both the civilian cadres and the mass organizations. The disbanding of the Red Guards in mid-1968, and the transfer of millions of young people to the countryside, removed these participants from the Chinese political stage altogether.

The February Adverse Current

The Decision on the Cultural Revolution adopted by the Eleventh Plenum in August 1966 had envisioned a mass movement that would be sweeping yet controlled. The emphasis on mass mobilization and mass criticism – particularly on the part of young people – promised to make life much more complex for the nation's Party and government officials. But significant limits were imposed in three areas. First, the cadre policy outlined in the Sixteen Points involved strict criticism but lenient treatment. The Eleventh Plenum had stipulated that most cadres were "good" or "relatively good," and had implied that they could remain at or return to their posts once they had made "serious self-criticism" and "accepted the criticism of the masses." Second, the movement was undertaken in the name of the Party and was to be conducted under the leadership of the CC, if not of the Party apparatus at lower levels. And third, Cultural Revolutionary activities within the PLA were to be insulated from those in the rest of society and placed under the leadership of the Party's MAC rather than that of the Cultural Revolution Group.

By the end of January 1967, however, it was abundantly clear that the Cultural Revolution was overstepping each of these boundaries. A number of ranking cadres, including Peng Zhen and Luo Ruiqing, had been "detained," without any warrant or other legal sanction, by radical mass organizations. Others were paraded through the streets of China's cities, with dunce caps on their heads and placards around their necks listing their "counterrevolutionary offenses." At least one member of the State Council, Minister of Coal Industry Zhang Linzhi, had been beaten to deaths and other high-ranking officials had been physically abused. Liu Shaoqi and Deng Xiaoping had come under virulent verbal attack.

The authorization to mass organizations to "seize power," and the creation of Shanghai Commune, suggested that even the principle of Party leadership was being abandoned, for, as Mao himself pointed out, there was no room for a vanguard Party within the structure of a Paris Commune. What is more, the turmoil of the Cultural Revolution now threatened to spread into the ranks of the armed forces, as the PLA was ordered to intervene in civilian politics in support of the left. And Lin Biao himself seemed eager to incite his followers within the armed forces to criticize, in Red Guard style, those senior marshals, such as Zhu De, He Long, and Ye Jianying, who might challenge Lin's control over the armed forces.[97]

To cope with these problems, the central authorities issued a series of directives and statements throughout the month of February that were intended to limit the chaos being produced by the Cultural Revolution. The attempts at political stabilization proceeded along four tracks. First, as we have already seen, the model of the Paris Commune, which promised direct democracy without Party leadership but would have delivered little but factionalism and disorder, was repudiated by Mao personally. It was replaced by the model of the revolutionary committee and the directives to the PLA to intervene in the Cultural Revolution to support the left – both of which measures were intended to provide an organizational framework for restoring order and discipline to the country. As part of the implementation of the three-in-one combination, the central media began a campaign to publicize Mao's policy

97 "Collection of documents," 19–20, 21; A Great trial, 160, 164.

of relative leniency toward cadres who had "committed errors" either before the onset, or during the early months, of the Cultural Revolution.

Second, Mao intervened to limit the use of force and violence by Red Guard organizations. Writing to Zhou Enlai on 1 February, Mao criticized the tendency to force cadres under criticism to "wear dunce caps, to paint their faces, and to parade them in the streets." Describing such actions as "a form of armed struggle," Mao declared that "we definitely must hold to struggle by reason, bring out the facts, emphasize rationality, and use persuasion.... Anyone involved in beating others should be dealt with in accordance with the law."[98] Similar injunctions against the use of force were contained in a directive issued by the MAC on 28 January, a document said to have been drafted under the sponsorship of such senior military officials as Ye Jianying, Xu Xiangqian, and Nie Rongzhen and then approved by Mao. The directive declared: "Arresting people at will without orders is not permitted; ransacking of homes and sealing of doors at will is not permitted. It is not permitted to carry out corporal punishment or disguised corporal punishment, such as making people wear tall caps and black placards, parading them in streets, forcing them to kneel, etc. Earnestly promote civil struggle, resolutely oppose struggle by brute force."[99]

Third, attempts were made to limit the impact of the Cultural Revolution on those state and military organizations that were crucial to the maintenance of economic production and political order. In February, outside mass organizations were ordered to leave all central party departments and those central state ministries and bureaus responsible for national defense, economic planning, foreign affairs, public security, finance and banking, and propaganda; power seizures in the armed forces were limited to such peripheral organizations as academies, schools, cultural organs, and hospitals; and all Cultural Revolution activities of any kind were "postponed" in seven crucial military regions.[100] In addition, the CC and the State Council issued a further directive attempting to preserve the confidentiality of all secret documents and files, including the personnel dossiers of Party and state cadres, which had been the source of much of the evidence used by mass organizations in their criticism of leading officials.[101]

Finally, central directives tried to narrow the scope of activity allowed to mass organizations, to the point that, if these directives had been implemented, the Red Guard movement would have been brought to an end. Mass organizations were told to stop traveling about the country to "exchange revolutionary experiences," and were ordered to return to their native cities

98 JPRS, 49,826, *Translations on Communist China* (12 February 1970), 22.
99 "Collection of documents," 54–5. See also Dittmer, *Liu Shao-ch'i*, 152–3.
100 "Collection of documents," 56, 61, 66, 71–2, 78–9, and 89.   101 Ibid., 84.

and towns. Middle school students were told to return to school, resume classes, and "attend their lessons on the one hand and make revolution on the other." National alliances of Red Guard organizations, which had begun to form spontaneously (or with encouragement from the CRG) during the January Revolution and which potentially threatened to become so powerful that they could not be controlled, were described as "counterrevolutionary organizations" and were ordered to disband immediately. Disgruntled elements of the work force, notably contract workers, temporary laborers, and workers who had been transferred to jobs in border regions, were told that they should stay at their posts and that their demands would be dealt with at a later stage of the Cultural Revolution.[102]

Encouraged by these developments, a group of senior Party leaders from both the civilian and military spheres began to launch an attack on the whole concept of the Cultural Revolution.[103] These officials included Marshals Ye Jianying, Nie Rongzhen, and Xu Xiangqian, and Vice-Premiers Chen Yi, Li Fuchun, Li Xiannian, and Tan Zhenlin. They used the occasion of a series of meetings on "grasping revolution and promoting production" that were convened by Premier Zhou Enlai in mid-February to express their criticism of the Cultural Revolution. These veteran cadres apparently raised four principal issues: whether it was proper to separate the mass movement from the leadership of the Party; whether it was correct to attack so many senior officials; whether it was justified to produce disorder in the armed forces; and, on that basis, whether the Cultural Revolution should be continued or, as these officials clearly believed, be brought to a rapid end.

The most dramatic of these meetings occurred in Huairen Hall, inside the Zhongnanhai complex in Beijing, on an afternoon in mid-February. At this meeting, the contending groups were literally arrayed along two sides of a long table, with Zhou Enlai sitting at one end. To Zhou's left were Chen Boda, Kang Sheng, Xie Fuzhi, and other members of the Cultural Revolution Group; to the prime minister's right were the three marshalls, the five vice-premiers, and State Council officials Yu Qiuli and Gu Mu. The meeting soon turned into a shouting match between the two sides, with Tan Zhenlin, the vice-premier responsible for agricultural work, at one point rising from the table and declaring his intention to resign, only to be restrained by Chen Yi and Zhou Enlai.

An account of the proceedings – distorted, it was later charged – was soon relayed to Mao Zedong by members of the Cultural Revolution Group.

102 Ibid., 72, 82, 83, 85, 87–8.
103 This account of the February Adverse Current is based on RMRB, 26 February 1979, in FBIS Daily Report: China, 28 February 1979, E7–20; and the recollections of Nie Rongzhen, in Xinhua ribao, 21 and 22 October 1984, in FBIS Daily Report: China, 6 November 1984, K21–4. See also Lee, Politics of the Cultural Revolution, ch. 6; Daubier, History of the Cultural Revolution, ch. 5.

Mao was furious at some of the opinions expressed at the meeting, which he considered to be a repudiation of his leadership. Aware of Mao's anger, the radicals soon described these meetings as a "February Adverse Current" (*eryue niliu*) and used them as evidence in their mounting campaign to purge all surviving senior cadres from office.

In some ways, therefore, the result of the meetings in Zhongnanhai was similar to that of the Lushan Conference of the summer of 1959, during the GLF. On both occasions, China was in the midst of a tumultuous mass movement launched by Mao Zedong. In both cases, the disruptive consequences of the campaign had already become apparent, and efforts were underway to limit them. But on both occasions, some senior officials not only criticized the excesses of the campaigns but also expressed some opposition to the movement as a whole. In both cases, Mao took the criticisms as a challenge to his personal leadership. As a result, not only did the two movements continue long after their adverse consequences had become clear, but some of the measures originally intended to remedy those consequences were canceled or postponed.

Thus, the February Advent Current had the effect of reradicalizing the Cultural Revolution by discrediting the attempts that had been made earlier that month to restore order. One manifestation of this development was the decision to move criticism of Liu Shaoqi and Deng Xiaoping from Red Guard wall posters and tabloids into the official Party press, albeit through the use of such epithets as "China's Khrushchev" and "The Number Two Party Person in Authority Taking the Capitalist Road." Given the fact that Liu and Deng served, respectively, as president of the Republic and the general secretary of the Party, this step removed any remaining doubts that all cadres throughout the country were legitimate targets of attack. In a related measure, the 16 May Circular of 1966, with its harsh attack on "representatives of the bourgeoisie" in the Party, government, and army, appeared in the public media on the first anniversary of its adoption.

Emboldened by these developments, radical mass organizations issued stronger and more frequent criticisms of a number of surviving civilian officials throughout the spring of 1967. A prominent target was Tan Zhenlin, who had been one of the most active participants in the February Adverse Current and whose outspokenness made him a favorite quarry of the radicals. At the climactic meeting at Huairen Hall, Tan had described Kuai Dafu, the Qinghua University radical who was then one of the darlings of the CRG, as a "counterrevolutionary clown." Tan allegedly sent several written reports to Mao and the CC urging an end to the Cultural Revolution, in one of which he called Jiang Qing a "latter-day Empress Wu Zetian." According to accounts sympathetic to the radicals, Tan had also attempted to reinstate Ministry of Agriculture officials who had been overthrown during the January Revolution.

Another goal of the radicals was the dismissal of Foreign Minister Chen Yi, who like Tan Zhenlin, made no attempt to hide his acerbic attitude toward the Cultural Revolution and the Red Guard movmeent. In one widely circulated although possibly apocryphal account, Chen Yi responded to an unpleasant encounter with one group of Red Guards by waving his own copy of the little red book, the *Quotations from Chairman Mao Zedong*, and saying: "Now it's my turn. Allow me to quote for you from Chairman Mao, page 320. Chairman Mao has said: 'Chen Yi is a good and faithful comrade.'" It was up to the Red Guards to discover that the Chinese edition of the *Quotations* had no such page.[104]

But the ultimate target of many of the radical mass organizations, and possibly the CRG was Zhou Enlai, who was regarded by the radicals as the "backstage supporter" of the February Adverse Current and the protector of officials such as Tan and Chen. In Beijing, a number of wall posters were displayed that began as attacks on Tan and Chen but ended with criticisms of Zhou Enlai.

In this way, the February Adverse Current placed senior cadres in an increasingly vulnerable and passive position. To be sure, there were still periodic interventions by Mao, reasserting his conviction that 95 percent of China's cadres could be redeemed. Mao and Zhou also attempted to save some cadres from public criticism and physical assault, at least for a time. Zhou himself was protected by Mao, and Zhou worked to protect such officials as Liao Chengzhi, Chen Yi, Li Fuchun, and Li Xiannian. It was at this point that a number of provincial and municipal officials were brought to Beijing, so that their physical safety could be ensured.

But such measures did not protect everyone or prevent the progressive weakening of the political positions of veteran civilian officials. Liu Shaoqi and Deng Xiaoping were placed under house arrest sometime in the summer of 1967. The central CRG came to assume many of the powers of the Politburo and the State Council. And the radicals continued to use the February Adverse Current as evidence that senior cadres opposed the Cultural Revolution, the CRG, and Mao's leadership. Of the three vertical networks in the Cultural Revolution, the veteran officials were now in by far the weakest position.

The Wuhan Incident

Three of the most significant developments in China in mid-1967 were the serious divisions that emerged between radical and conservative mass organizations, between conservative and radical forces within the PLA itself, and between the CRG and the armed forces. The Wuhan Incident of 20 July

104 Daubier, *History of the Cultural Revolution*, 220.

(referred to in Chinese as the "7/20 Incident," the *qierling shijian*, after the date on which it occurred) provides the best example of the development and implications of these cleavages.[105]

When the PLA was ordered to supervise the formation of revolutionary committees at the provincial and municipal levels across the country, that task was assigned principally to the military regions and to the local and garrison forces under their command. Many regional commanders had close personal associations with the Party officials in the provinces, which disposed them to side with the more conservative mass organizations to protect the Party establishment. Similarly, the PLA's proclivity for maintaining order and discipline placed it in conflict with more radical mass organizations that sought to overthrow all officials and disregarded economic production for the sake of making revolution.

During the month of February, therefore, many regional commanders, using as justification the restrictions on the Cultural Revolution that had recently been issued by the central authorities, began to clamp down on the most obstreperous radical organizations. In the Wuhan Military Region, this involved decisions by the commander, Chen Zaidao, first to dissociate himself from, and then to order the disbanding of, a coalition of radical organizations known as the "Workers' General Headquarters" on the grounds that they were persistently engaging in disruptive activities that endangered both social order and economic stability.

The criticism of the February Adverse Current gave radicals in both Beijing and the provinces the opportunity to protest the "suppression" of leftist mass organizations by the PLA. On 2 April, *Renmin ribao* published an editorial calling for "proper treatment of the Young Generals" (i.e., the Red Guards) that was based on information supplied by disgruntled radicals in the Wuhan and Chengdu military regions. The same week, the CC and the MAC published separate directives that greatly reduced the PLA's ability to suppress radical mass organizations.[106] The directives stripped the armed forces of the authority to declare any mass organization to be counterrevolutionary, to suppress those who criticized military leadership, or to make mass arrests. Henceforth, the power to classify mass organizations was to be made by Beijing alone, and those who had been labeled as counterrevolutionaries by regional military commanders were to be pardoned. The directives were reportedly the result of joint efforts by Lin Biao and members of the CRG, which suggests that, at

---

105 This discussion of the Wuhan Incident is drawn from Chen Zaidao, "Wuhan 'qierling shijian' shimo" (The beginning and end of the "July 20th Incident" in Wuhan), *Gemingshi ziliao*, 2 (September 1981), 7–45; and Thomas W. Robinson, "The Wuhan Incident: Local strife and provincial rebellion during the Cultural Revolution," *CQ*, 47 (July–September 1971), 413–38.

106 "Collection of documents," 111–12, 115–16.

this point at least, there was still a high degree of cooperation between these two elements of the Maoist coalition.

Because these directives greatly reduced the PLA's ability to restore order, they also significantly increased the degree of conflict between conservative and radical mass organizations. Radicals began to seize weapons from military armories and, in southern China, from shipments of munitions intended for North Vietnam. In some places, the PLA responded by supplying weapons to more conservative organizations. The incidence of armed struggle vastly increased, exacting a toll not only in human lives but also in economic production. In Wuhan, the principal consequence was that the radicals launched a series of protests and demonstrations calling for a reversal of the "adverse currents" in the city. These activities apparently received Jiang Qing's personal endorsement.

Because the directives of early April had provided that only the central authorities would have the right to decide on the political orientation of competing mass organizations, Chen Zaidao requested a meeting with Zhou Enlai and the CRG to discuss the situation in Wuhan. According to Chen's own account, the meeting concluded that the behavior of the Wuhan Military Region had been basically correct, and that the radicals in the city should be told to stop attacking it. Unfortunately for Chen, word of this agreement leaked out in Wuhan before it had been officially announced in Beijing, thus leading Jiang Qing to charge that Chen was taking undue advantage of his success, and emboldening her to try to undo the agreement.

Meantime, the struggle among mass organizations in Wuhan intensified. In mid-May there came into existence a conservative umbrella organization known as the "Million Heroes," which took as its program the defense of the military region and the majority of veteran cadres. According to Chen Zaidao, the Million Heroes counted among their membership about 85 percent of the Party members in Wuhan and enjoyed at least the tacit support of most of the local armed forces. Chen claimed that the military region command officially took a neutral position between the competing mass organizations and called for unity between them. But it is likely that the true preferences of Chen and his subordinates were clear to all those involved.

Thus a second series of meetings was held, this time in Wuhan in mid-July, to try again to resolve the problems in the city. Participating in the meetings from Beijing were Zhou Enlai, two representatives of the central military command (Li Zuopeng and Yang Chengwu), two members of the Cultural Revolution Group (Wang Li and Xie Fuzhi), and, for some of the meetings, Mao himself. Both Mao and Zhou now criticized Chen for his disbanding of the Workers' General Headquarters in February and ordered that that organization be reinstated. But Mao apparently urged unity of the competing mass organizations and disclaimed any intention of "knocking down" Chen Zaidao.

Zhou then returned to Beijing, leaving Xie and Wang to convey the results of the meetings to all parties in Wuhan. Fairly or not, the two men presented Mao's and Zhou's instructions as a repudiation of the military region command, a criticism of the Million Heroes, and an endorsement of the city's radical mass organizations. Angered by this development, representatives of the Million Heroes stormed the hotel where Xie and Wang were staying, and then a group of soldiers from the local garrison seized Wang Li, detained him, and possibly beat him. Xie was spared only by his formal position as a vice-premier and minister of public security.

This insurgency was suppressed by dispatching Zhou back to Wuhan to secure Wang Li's release and by mobilizing substantial numbers of naval and airborne forces to seize control of Wuhan. Wang, Xie, and Chen Zaidao all flew off to Beijing, the first two to receive a hero's welcome, the latter to undergo criticism and interrogation.

As in the case of the February Adverse Current, the immediate results of the Wuhan Incident were remarkably limited. Like Tan Zhenlin, Chen Zaidao received much less punishment than one might have expected for his act of disloyalty – for what in Chen's case was portrayed by the radicals as an act of mutiny. He was dismissed as military region commander but was otherwise treated relatively leniently and was rehabilitated less than two years after the fall of Lin Biao. Chen himself has attributed this to the goodwill of Mao and Zhou Enlai, but one also wonders about the degree to which Lin Biao would have welcomed the complete humiliation of a regional commander, even a recalcitrant one, at the hands of the CRG.

The purge of the 516 Group

Although the Wuhan Incident had relatively slight effects on its principal participants, its broader consequences were devastating. Radicals, including members of the CRG, took the occasion to call for a further assault against conservatives and revisionists in both Beijing and the provinces. On 22 July, only two days after the Wuhan Incident, Jiang Qing introduced the slogan "Attack with words, defend with force" (*wengong wuwei*).[107] This was the first time a leader of her rank had endorsed the armed struggles that were sweeping the country, and her statement only complicated any efforts to restore order.

The targets of this upsurge of radicalism included foreign diplomats in China, the Ministry of Foreign Affairs, and Zhou Enlai. Diplomats from a

---

107 *SCMP, Supplement*, 198 (August 1967), 8.

number of countries were harassed, and the British legation was burned to the ground. A young diplomat named Yao Dengshan, who had formerly been stationed in Indonesia, engineered a power seizure in the Foreign Ministry, directed not only against Chen Yi but also, by implication, against Zhou Enlai, who had attempted to protect Chen.[108] Radical wall posters written during this period called for the downfall of the "old government," for the criticism of the "backstage boss of Chen Zaidao," and for dragging out "another Liu Shaoqi, one who has stood guarantee for the greatest number of people."[109] Zhou was apparently detained in his office for two and a half days by radical Red Guards, who wanted to drag him out for "struggle."

The most important target this time was not Zhou Enlai, however, but the PLA itself. An editorial in *Hongqi* in early August called on radicals to strike down the "handful of military leaders taking the capitalist road,"[110] That there might be revisionists in the PLA was hardly an unprecedented notion: It had been contained in the 16 May Circular of 1966, as well as numerous editorials in the first half of 1967. But in the aftermath of the Wuhan Incident, such a slogan was explosive and had immediate consequences. Regional commanders, including some closely associated with Lin Biao, came under attack: Huang Yongsheng, commander of the Guangzhou Military Region and an ally of the defense minister, was described as the "Tan Zhenlin of Guangzhou" by radical Red Guards.[111] If not checked, such a formula threatened the ability of the armed forces to maintain any kind of order in China.

Mao, Zhou, and Lin all had common cause for opposing this escalation by the CRG: Lin because it threatened the unity and legitimacy of the armed forces; Zhou, because it threatened his control over foreign affairs and the State Council and brought his own political position under attack; and Mao, because it moved China even further away from the elusive goal of unity that he appeared to seek.

In late August, therefore, the Cultural Revolution Group was reorganized. Four of its most radical members – Wang Li, Mu Xin, Lin Jie, and Guan Feng – were dismissed, and a fifth, Qi Benyu, fell from power four months later. The Party's theoretical journal *Hongqi*, which, under the editorship of Chen Boda, had been the mouthpiece of the Cultural Revolution Group, was forced to suspend publication. This 516 Group (*wuyiliu bingtuan*) – named after the 16 May Circular of 1966 – was accused of using the February Adverse Current

---

108 On the struggles in the Ministry of Foreign Affairs during this period, see Melvin Gurtov, "The Foreign Ministry and foreign affairs in the Chinese Cultural Revolution," in Robinson, *Cultural Revolution*, 313–66.
109 On the renewed surge of radicalism in this period, see Lee, *Politics of the Cultural Revolution*, ch. 8, and Daubier, *History of the Cultural Revolution*, ch. 8.
110 *HQ*, 12 (August 1967), 43–7.   111 Daubier, *History of the Cultural Revolution*, 207.

as a pretext for criticizing first Yu Qiuli, then Li Xiannian, Li Fuchun, and Chen Yi, all with the ultimate goal of overthrowing Zhou Enlai, himself. The radicals were assigned responsibility for the wall posters attacking Zhou Enlai in August.[112]

On 5 September, all four of the central authorities in China – the CC, the MAC, the State Council, and the CRG – issued a joint directive attempting to end armed struggle in the country and to revive the tattered authority of the PLA. Red Guard organizations were forbidden to seize arms from the armed forces, and the army was forbidden to transfer arms to mass organizations without central authorization. The PLA was now allowed to use armed force, as a last resort, against mass organizations that resisted its attempts to restore order."[113]

That same day, in a rambling extemporaneous speech to a Red Guard rally in Beijing, Jiang Qing sought to distance herself and the survivors of the CRG from the four who had been dismissed. Without referring to them by name, she described the 516 Group as a small number of "extreme leftists" who had attempted to seize control of the mass movement. She repudiated the call to "drag out a handful from the PLA" as a "trap" set by these ultra-leftists to bring China into chaos. While still defending her own formulation "attack with words, defend with force," she now argued that the situation in China did not warrant the use of force in any circumstance. Despite doing her utmost to deny any personal responsibility for the 516 Group, Jiang Qing had in fact been forced into making a statement that amounted to self-criticism.[114]

The chaos of August and the 516 affair had important implications for the course of the Cultural Revolution. First, as we will see, it shifted the focus of the Cultural Revolution from the destruction of the old political order to the creation of a new one. In September, Mao Zedong revealed his "great strategic plan" for the rest of the Cultural Revolution, based on his travels across the country throughout the summer. In essence, this called for an end to disorder and the most rapid possible progress toward the formation of revolutionary committees in the twenty-two provincial-level units in which they had not yet been organized.

As that process got underway toward the end of 1967, it appeared that the events of the summer had also readjusted the balance between the radical mass organizations and the regional military commanders in favor of the latter. In the spring of 1968, as we shall see shortly, there was a final resurgence of

---

112 On the fall of the "516" Group, see *CB*, 844 (10 January 1968); and Barry Burton, "The Cultural Revolution's ultraleft conspiracy: The 'May 16 Group,'" *Asian Survey*, 11.11 (November 1971), 1029–53.

113 *SCMP*, 4026 (22 September 1967), 1–2.   114 Ibid., 4069 (29 November 1967), 1–9.

radicalism, but it never reached the high water mark set in August 1967. When forced to choose between the mass movement and the PLA – between continued disorder and the only hope for political stability – Mao selected the latter. As a result, the military was now able to move relatively steadily toward institutionalizing its dominant position in the new provincial revolutionary committees.

The 516 affair also changed the pattern of alignment among the central leadership in Beijing. Of all the leading members of the CRG, the one most closely associated with the victims of the 516 purge, and thus the one most seriously weakened by it, was Chen Boda. All five victims of the 516 affair had apparently served as deputy chief editors of *Hongqi* directly under Chen; all had been closely associated with Chen in the radical intellectual and journalistic establishment in Beijing in the early 1960s; and the closing of *Hongqi* could only be interpreted as a repudiation of Chen's editorial policies. Realizing that his position was weakening, Chen Boda now sought new sources of political support. He appears to have chosen Lin Biao. This was a marriage of political convenience that offered advantages to both parties. Chen could offer Lin the ideological and theoretical trappings that had been noticeably lacking in Lin's own public pronouncements. In turn, Lin could grant Chen the backing of the vertical network – the PLA – that now seemed certain to emerge from the Cultural Revolution in the strongest position. It is highly plausible that Chen Boda began to work more closely with Lin Biao in late 1967, offering the ghostwriting services he had earlier provided to Mao and the CRG.

The purge of Yang Chengwu and the suppression of the Red Guards

The 516 affair notwithstanding, there was one final resurgence of radical mass activity in the spring and early summer of 1968. This brief radical revival was made possible by a still mysterious leadership shuffle within the PLA: the dismissal, in March 1968, of Acting Chief of Staff Yang Chengwu, along with the political commissar of the air force and the commander of the Beijing Military Region.[115]

The purge of Yang Chengwu appears to have been a prototypical example of the cleavages produced by the Cultural Revolution: the divisions between radicals and conservatives in the provinces, the conflict betweeen Zhou Enlai and the CRG, and the tensions within the PLA among representatives of

---

115 Accounts of the dismissal of Yang Chengwu by participants in the event include those by Lin Biao, in Kau, *Lin Piao*, 488–50; by Nie Rongzhen, in *Xinhua ribao* (9 and 10 October 1984), in *FBIS Daily Report: China*, 5 November 1984, K18–21; and by Fu Chongbi, in *Beijing wanbao*, 12 April 1985, in ibid., 1 May 1985, K9–10. See also Harvey W. Nelsen, *The Chinese military system: An organizational study of the Chinese People's Liberation Army*, 97–101.

different field army factions. All of these conflicts seem to have played their part in Yang's sudden fall from grace.

Toward the end of 1967, Yang had been responsible for resolving a number of provincial disputes, just as he had accompanied Mao to Wuhan on a similar assignment in July. In both Shanxi and Hebei, Yang supported the conservative factions against their more radical opponents. In Shanxi, Yang refused to back the radical chairman of the provincial revolutionary committee against a challenge from more conservative military officers in the province; and in Hebei, Yang supported a coalition of conservative military units and mass organizations against a similar coalition of radicals that had been endorsed by Xie Fuzhi.

What is more, Yang Chengwu and Fu Chongbi, the commander of the Beijing Military Region, took Zhou Enlai's side in the premier's dispute with the CRG and radical mass organizations. It was apparently Yang and Fu who provided military protection for a number of civilian and military leaders close to Zhou. And after the dismissal of Qi Benyu, Yang encouraged Fu Chongbi to send a small force of soldiers to the offices of the CRG, nominally to arrest Qi's followers and to search through the files looking for evidence of wrongdoing. Whatever Yang's ultimate intentions, it was not unreasonable for the remaining members of the CRG, including Jiang Qing and Xie Fuzhi, to believe that Yang was looking for materials that might incriminate them.

Finally, Yang was also involved in internecine struggles within the armed forces. Although Yang had some historical ties to Lin Biao, he had served in the final years of the revolution in the Fifth Field Army, not the Fourth. Yang's relations with Lin's closest lieutenants, including Air Force Commander Wu Faxian, were quite strained, and Lin apparently came to doubt Yang's loyalty. At the same time, Lin could use the purge of Yang Chengwu as a way of attacking his own rivals Nie Rongzhen and Xu Xiangqian, who had served as Yang's superiors in the Fifth Field Army.

Yang Chengwu was therefore accused of having supported a second February Adverse Current, which, like the first, had as its intention the protection of conservative forces, particularly senior cadres, against attack by the radicals. The immediate effect of his dismissal was twofold. First, it enabled Lin Biao to strengthen his control over the Administrative Office of the Party's MAC, which exercised day-to-day control over the armed forces. Lin was now in a position to staff this crucial body with five people personally loyal to him: Wu Faxian, Huang Yongsheng, the commander of the Guangzhou Military Region who now replaced Yang Chengwu as chief of staff; Li Zuopeng, the political commissar of the navy; Qiu Huizuo, the head of military logistics; and Ye Qun, Lin's own wife.[116]

---

116 Sun, *Lishi jiangyi*, 2.270–1.

The second consequence of the Yang Chengwu affair was to legitimate a resurgence of activity by radical mass organizations in protest against their alleged underrepresentation on the new revolutionary committees. Violence was particularly widespread in Shanxi, Hebei, Shandong, and Guangdong. At Beijing's Qinghua University, rival factions barricaded themselves in campus buildings behind cement barricades and wire fences, and used catapults to launch chunks of brick and concrete against their adversaries.

In provinces such as Guangxi, where the revolutionary committee had not yet been formed, factional violence flared to even greater proportions. Competing organizations stole weapons from trains carrying military supplies to Vietnam and fought each other with machine guns, bazookas, and even antiaircraft weapons. The victims of the violence, often bound and trussed, floated down the Pearl River, to be discovered in the waters off Hong Kong.

It was the violence at Qinghua University that caused the final suppression of the mass movement and the demobilization of the Red Guards. Mao ordered troops from Unit 8341, the elite security force protecting central Party leaders, together with workers from a knitwear mill and a printing plant in Beijing, to enter Qinghua in late July. A few days later, on the night of 28 July, Mao met with student leaders from both Qinghua and Peking universities. Noting that Kuai Dafu had complained that a "black hand" had sent workers to the universities to suppress the Red Guards, Mao declared: "The black hand is still not captured. The black hand is nobody else but me." Mao complained that the Red Guards were engaged in factional armed struggle, instead of carrying out the Cultural Revolution in a principled way:

> In the first place, you are not struggling; in the second place, you are not criticizing; in the third place, you are not transforming. Yes, you are struggling, but it is armed struggle. The people are not happy. The workers are not happy. The peasants are not happy. Peking residents are not happy. The students in most of the schools are not happy. Most students in your school are also not happy. Even within the faction that supports you there are people who are unhappy. Can you unite the whole country this way?[117]

Unless the Red Guards could shape up, Mao warned, "we may resort to military control [of the schools], and ask Lin Piao to take command."

Shortly thereafter, just as Mao had threatened, "worker-peasant Mao Zedong Thought propaganda teams," supervised by military officers, began to enter China's major universities. On 5 August, Mao sent some mangoes, which he had received from a group of Pakistani visitors, to the propaganda team at Qinghua as a personal endorsement of their activities. Mao justified the suppression of the Red Guards by arguing that the leadership of the Cultural

117 *Miscellany of Mao Tse-tung Thought*, 2.470.

Revolution should be in the hands of the "working class" rather than students. In the middle of the month, Mao issued a directive declaring that "it is essential to bring into full play the leading role of the working class in the Great Cultural Revolution." A few weeks later he ordered that the "masses of the workers," in cooperation with "Liberation Army fighters," should take the lead in the "proletarian revolution in education."[118]

Toward the end of August, Yao Wenyuan, whose article on Hai Rui had launched the Cultural Revolution, now wrote another essay, which, in essence, brought the Red Guard stage of the movement to an abrupt end. Entitled "The working class must exercise leadership in everything," Yao's article was a scathing critique of the excesses of the mass movement, written by a man who had ridden to power on its back. The anarchism and factionalism of the Red Guard movement were ascribed to the "petty-bourgeois" outlook of its participants. "The facts show," Yao stated, "that under [the] circumstances it is impossible for the students and intellectuals by themselves alone to fulfill the task of struggle-criticism-transformation and a whole number of other tasks on the intellectual front; workers and People's Liberation Army fighters must take part, and it is essential to have strong leadership by the working class."[119] Under such leadership, the remaining mass organizations were disbanded and Red Guard newspapers and periodicals ceased publication.

By the end of the year, the demobilization of the Red Guard organizations had been accompanied by the physical removal of millions of youths from the cities to the countryside. In December, Mao issued yet another directive that deemed it "very necessary for educated young people to go to the countryside to be reeducated by the poor and lower-middle peasants. Cadres and other city people should be persuaded to send their sons and daughters who have finished junior or senior middle school, college, or university to the countryside." By the end of 1970, about 5.4 million youths had been transferred to rural areas, mostly in their home provinces, but often to remote border and frontier regions. Few had any hope that they would ever be able to return to their homes.[120]

THE RECONSTRUCTION OF THE POLITICAL SYSTEM

With the purge of the 516 Group in late August 1967 and the demobilization of the Red Guards the following spring, the emphasis of the Cultural Revolution shifted from the destruction of the old order to the creation of a new one – from what the Chinese called a period of "struggle and criticism" (*doupi*)

---

118 Ch'en, *Mao papers*, 105.   119 *PR*, 11.35 (30 August 1968), 3–6.
120 Thomas P. Bernstein, *Up to the mountains and down to the villages: The transfer of youth from urban to rural China*, 57–8.

to one of "criticism and transformation" (*pigai*). Reconstructing the political system involved two principal elements: the completion of the organization of revolutionary committees and the rehabilitation of the Party itself.

What is particularly noteworthy about this period is that the formal structure of China's "new" political order differed very little from that which existed on the eve of the Cultural Revolution.[121] The movement began with Utopian rhetoric about "overthrowing" bureaucracy and establishing direct democracy along the lines of the Paris Commune. But when the work of political reconstruction actually got underway, the blueprint that was followed was much less visionary. Officials were "reeducated" in "May 7 cadre schools" (*wuqi ganxiao*) where, through physical labor and political study, they were supposed to cultivate a more selfless and efficient style of work. The revolutionary committees, and the bureaucracies they supervised, were supposed to be smaller, more capable, and more committed to Maoist values than their predecessors. And because they contained a small number of mass representatives, they were presumed to be more responsive to popular concerns. Still, the organizational policies of the period of reconstruction made it clear that government institutions would still be structured along bureaucratic lines, and that the CCP would remain a Leninist organization that would guide the work of the revolutionary committees.

What distinguished the new political system from its predecessor was less its structure than its staffing. Military officers played a much more important role, particularly at higher levels, than at any time since the early 1950s. Veteran civilian officials were pushed aside in favor of men and women who were less experienced, less educated, less cosmopolitan, and less qualified – although not necessarily any younger. Party recruitment was resumed and emphasized the absorption of large numbers of mass activists from the Red Guard movement. Moreover, Party and state organizations were plagued by serious factionalism as a result of the unresolved conflicts among the victims, activists, and bystanders of the Cultural Revolution.

Mao's "strategic plan"

In September 1967, Mao Zedong devised what was described as his "great strategic plan" for concluding the Cultural Revolution. While defending the disorder of the previous twenty months ("Don't be afraid of making trouble. The bigger the trouble we make, the better"), Mao acknowledged that this troublemaking had served its purpose and should now be brought

---

121 For a description and evaluation of organizational changes wrought by the Cultural Revolution, see Harding, *Organizing China*, chs. 8 and 9, passim.

expenditiously to an end. "The car will overturn if it is driven too fast," Mao warned. "It is therefore necessary to be cautious."[122]

The immediate task, as Mao saw it, was to complete the formation of China's twenty-nine provincial revolutionary committees. Up to then, the process had been agonizingly slow: Only six revolutionary committees had been established at the provincial level between January 1967 and the end of July. "What we must principally accomplish now," Mao instructed, "is the great alliance and the three-in-one combination." This Mao hoped could be done by January 1968.

Mao appears to have believed that two guidelines would facilitate the formation of the remaining revolutionary committees. To begin with, Mao was now prepared to see the PLA dominate the process, in fact if not in name, and was therefore willing to testify to the army's authority and loyalty and to forgive its occasional failures. As he put it in late summer, "The army's prestige must be resolutely safeguarded. There can be no doubt whatsoever about that." In a rather magnanimous reference to the Wuhan Incident, Mao continued: "It was unavoidable that the army should have made mistakes in tackling for the first time the large scale fighting tasks of supporting the left, supporting industry and agriculture, and carrying out military control and military training. The chief danger at the moment is that some people want to beat down the PLA."[123] The importance Mao assigned to the army was reflected in his reluctance to see the PLA become a target of general criticism after the dismissal of Yang Chengwu the following spring.[124]

As a second guideline, Mao recognized that the formation of revolutionary committees could be accelerated if their mass representatives were drawn from a broad spectrum of mass organizations rather than solely from those that had been endorsed by local military commanders. This concept of inclusiveness was embodied in an instruction that the PLA should "support the left, but no particular faction," and in Mao's directive that "the working class has absolutely no reason to split into two hostile factional organizations."[125] The promulgation of Mao's ideal of national unity was accompanied in late 1967 by increasingly virulent press attacks against factionalism and anarchism, both of which were now described as manifestations of petty bourgeois ideology.

The completion of the formation of revolutionary committees occurred in two stages after Mao's tour of China in the summer of 1967. Between August 1967 and July 1968, committees were formed in eighteen provincial-level

122 *CLG*, 2.1 (Spring 1969), 3–12.   123 Nelsen, *Chinese military system*, 83.
124 Philip Bridgham, "Mao's Cultural Revolution: The struggle to consolidate power," *CQ*, 41 (January–March 1970), 5.
125 *Jiefangjun bao*, 28 January 1968, in *PR*, 11.5 (2 February 1968), 8–9; and Ch'en, *Mao papers*, 146.

units. The last five, in such deeply divided provinces as Fujian and Guangxi, and in such sensitive border areas as Xinjiang and Tibet, were created after the final suppression of the Red Guard movement in July. In general, the committees were produced in a series of negotiated settlements, in which local military commanders and Beijing leaders sought to impose unity on competing mass organizations.

Because of Mao's stipulation that they should be broadly representative of a wide range of viewpoints, the revolutionary committees were generally large and unwieldy organs, composed of between 100 and 250 members each.[126] The standing committees of the revolutionary committees, however, was more manageable bodies, often smaller than the comparable Party and state leadership groups that had existed before the Cultural Revolution. The composition of the standing committees varied with the trends of the times, with more mass representatives appointed in more radical periods and fewer named in more moderate phases. Although mass representatives secured a reasonable number of places on the revoultionary committees formed during this period (61 of the 182 chairmen and vice-chairmen), effective power was concentrated in military hands. Of the twenty-three chairmen, twelve were troop commanders and five were professional commissars. Of the first vice-chairmen, fourteen were commanders and five were commissars. All the rest were Party officials; not one was a mass representative.[127]

Over the longer term, Mao also foresaw the reconstruction of the Party once the revolutionary committees had been established as provisional governments in all China's provinces. From the beginning, the Chairman had seen the Cultural Revoultion as a movement to purify the Party, not to destroy it. The purpose of the Cultural Revolution committees, as described in the Sixteen Points of the Eleventh Plenum, had been to serve as a bridge linking the Party to the masses, not to act as a replacement for the Party. Similarly, the purpose of the Red Guards had been to overthrow "capitalist readers" in the Party but not the Party as an organization. Mao's principal objection to applying the model of the Paris Commune to China in early 1967, it will be recalled, was that there was no clear role for the Party in such a structure. "If everything were changed into a commune, then what about the Party? Where would we place the Party? . . . There must be a party somehow! There must be a nucleus, no matter what we call it. Be it called the Communist Party, or Social Democratic Party, or Kuomintang, or I-kuan-tao, there must be a party."[128]

126 Frederick C. Teiwes, *Provincial leadership in China; The Cultural Revolution and its aftermath*, 27, 29.
127 These data are based upon those in Richard Baum, "China: year of the mangoes," *Asian Survey*, 9.1 (January 1969), 1–17.
128 *Miscellany of Mao Tse-tung Thought*, 2.453–4. The Yiguandao, in Communist historiography, was a reactionary secret society during the Nationalist period.

If the Party had been set aside by the Red Guards and the revolutionary committees, that was a temporary phenomenon, not an ultimate goal of the Cultural Revolution.

Now, in September 1967, Mao believed that the time had come to think about the reestablishment of the Party. "The party organization must be restored," Mao said, and "party congresses at all levels should be convened." Mao was optimistic that this could be accomplished relatively quickly: "I see that it will be about this time next year [i.e., September 1968] that the Ninth Party Congress is convened."[129] Mao assigned the task of rebuilding the Party to Zhang Chunqiao and Yao Wenyuan, with Xie Fuzhi, who was responsible for political and legal affairs during the Cultural Revolution, also playing an active role. On 10 October, Yao presented a preliminary report that laid out some basic principles for Party reconstruction.[130] Yao's report envisioned a top-down process, which would begin with the convocation of a national Party Congress to select a new CC and to adopt a new Party constitution. The delegates to the Congress would be appointed by the central authorities after "negotiation" with the provinces. After the conclusion of the Party Congress, the rebuilding of the Party at lower levels could begin. New Party committees at each level would embody, according to Yao's report, no fewer than three three-in-one combinations: Each would be a combination of the old, the middle-aged, and the young; of workers, peasants, and soldiers; and of masses, army officers, and cadres.

On the basis of Yao's report, the CC issued, on 27 November, a "Notice on the opinions about convening the Ninth Party Congress" and then, on 2 December, a further document "On the opinions regarding the rectification, restoration, and reconstruction of the Party structure." These documents followed the outlines of Yao's report, with two important amendments. First, the "Notice" added a decision that had been implicit from the beginning of the Cultural Revolution: that Lin Biao was now to become Mao's successor. "A great many comrades suggest," the "Notice" declared, "that the Ninth Party Congress vigorously propagandize the fact that Vice-Chairman Lin is Chairman Mao's close comrade-in-arms and successor, and that this be written down into the Ninth Party Congress's reports and resolutions so as to further enhance Vice-Chairman Lin's high prestige."

Second, the CC documents announced the resumption of "Party life" at the basic levels. Provisional Party branches, often called "Party core groups," were formed within revolutionary committees to guide the rectification of the Party at the basic levels. Their task was to begin a "purification of the ranks"

129 *CLG*, 2.1 (Spring 1969), 3–12.
130 On Yao's report and the two subsequent Party documents, see Lee, *Politics of the Cultural Revolution*, 296–301.

of Party members, expelling those who had been shown to be revisionist, and absorbing "fresh blood" from the activists of the Cultural Revolution.

The Twelfth Plenum

Although the reconstruction of the Party was thus anticipated in the fall of 1967, the process did not really get underway until the formation of the last provincial-level revolutionary committees in September 1968. Once that crucial task had been accomplished, however, the surviving central leadership quickly convened the Twelfth Plenum of the CC, which was held in Beijing between 13 and 31 October.

Like the Eleventh Plenum, in August 1966, the Twelfth Plenum was a rump session of the Party's CC. Only fifty-six full members of the CC attended the meeting, representing a bare quorum of the surviving members of the body.[131] Furthermore, like its predecessor, the Twelfth Plenum was packed with people who were not CC members. But where the additional observers in 1966 had been the "revolutionary students and teachers" from the Red Guard movement, in 1968 the extra participants were members of the CRG, representatives of the provincial revolutionary committees, and "principal responsible comrades of the Chinese People's Liberation Army" – the officials, in other words, who were now the survivors and beneficiaries of the Cultural Revolution.[132]

The radicals entered the meeting with ambitious goals: to win endorsement of the events of the preceding two years and to complete the purge of the highest levels of the Party establishment. They were more successful in achieving the first objective than the second. The plenum's final communiqué praised the accomplishments of the Cultural Revolution, lauded Mao's theory of "continuing the revolution under the dictatorship of the proletariat," held that Mao's "important instructions" and Lin's "many speeches" given during the movement were "all correct," and described the CRG as having "played an important role in the struggle to carry out Chairman Mao's proletarian revolutionary line." It endorsed Mao's assessment that the Cultural Revolution was "absolutely necessary and most timely for consolidating the dictatorship of the proletariat, preventing capitalist restoration, and building socialism." It declared that "this momentous Cultural Revolution has won [a] great and

---

131 On the participants in the Twelfth Plenum, see Hu Yaobang, "Lilun gongzuo wuxu hui yinyan" in *Zhonggong shiyijie sanzhong quanhui yilai zhongyang shouyao jianghua ji wenjian xuanbian* (Introduction to theoretical work conference), in (Compilation of major central speeches and documents since the Third Plenum of the Eleventh Central Committee), 2.55; and Deng Xiaoping, "Remarks on successive drafts of the 'Resolution on certain questions in the history of our Party since the founding of the People's Republic of China,'" in *Selected works of Deng Xiaoping* (1975–1982), 290.

132 For the communiqué of the Twelfth Plenum, see *PR*, 11.44 (1 November 1968), supplement, v–viii.

decisive victory." And, with an eye to the future, the plenum adopted a new draft Party constitution and announced that the Ninth Party Congress would be held "at an appropriate time."[133]

In perhaps its most important decision, the plenum announced that Liu Shaoqi was being dismissed from all his government and Party positions, and was being expelled from the party "once and for all." The plenum's resolution on the subject – the first time Liu had been criticized by name in an official public document during the Cultural Revolution – disparaged Liu in inflammatory language. He was described as a "renegade, traitor, and scab hiding in the Party," as "a lackey of imperialism, modern revisionism, and the Guomindang reactionaries," and as having "committed innumerable counterrevolutionary crimes." And yet, the supporting documents circulated after the plenum (at least those available in the West) dealt principally with Liu's activities in 1925, 1927, and 1939, during the early stages of the revolution, and said little about his behavior after the establishment of the Peoples Republic.[134] This would suggest that the plenum was unable to agree on how to characterize Liu's post-1949 activities.

During the small group sessions surrounding the meeting of the CC, the CRG and Lin Biao launched a vigorous attack upon the February Adverse Current of 1967. Curiously, Mao's closing speech to the plenum took a more conciliatory view of that episode than he had in the past. The Chairman now described the infamous meeting in Huairen Hall as an occasion for members of the Politburo to exercise their right to express their opinions on critical political issues. Nonetheless, Mao did nothing to prevent the plenum's communiqué from denouncing the February Adverse Current as an attack on the "proletarian headquarters with Chairman Mao as its leader and Vice Chairman Lin as its deputy leader."

But despite their best efforts, the radicals were unable to secure the removal from the CC of any of the most active participants in the February Adverse Current, save for Tan Zhenlin, who had already been purged the previous year. Li Fuchun, Li Xiannian, Chen Yi, Ye Jianying, Xu Xiangqian, and Nie Rongzhen all remained on the CC. Above all, the CRG's proposal that Deng Xiaoping not only be removed from the CC but also be expelled from the Party altogether, along with Liu Shaoqi, was rejected after a personal intervention by Mao Zedong.[135]

133 The text of the draft Party constitution is in Union Research Institute, *Documents of the Chinese Communist Party Central Committee, September 1956–April 1969*, 235–42.

134 The indictment of Liu Shaoqi, entitled "Report on the examination of the crimes of the renegade, traitor, and scab Liu Shao-ch'i," is in URI, *Documents of the Central Committee*, 243–50.

135 For these aspects of the Twelfth Plenum, see Sun, *Lishi jiangyi*, 2.274; and the recollections of Nie Rongzhen, in *Xinhua ribao*, 23 October 1984, in *FBIS Daily Report: China*, 7 November 1984, K20–1.

Beyond these points, the Twelfth Plenum made few important policy decisions. It spoke vaguely of a "revolution in education" that would be undertaken under the leadership of the workers' propaganda teams but did not indicate what specific new programs would be adopted. Similarly, it described the Cultural Revolution as "promoting the emergence of a new leap in our socialist construction" but announced no new economic plans. The Cultural Revolution may have been intended to repudiate some of the economic and social policies of the early 1960s that Mao regarded as revisionist, but the plenum indicated that no new revolutionary policies had yet been established to replace them.

The Ninth Party Congress

The Ninth Party Congress, convened in April 1969, reflected many of these same trends. Much of the political report, delivered to the Congress by Lin Biao, was an attempt to justify the Cultural Revolution as a "new and great contribution to the theory and practice of Marxism-Leninism."[136] Lin praised both the army and the CRG for their achievements since 1966 and, in a veiled reference to surviving senior civilian cadres, again criticized the February Adverse Current (here described as an "adverse current lasting from the winter of 1966 through the spring of 1967") as a "frenzied counterattack" on the Cultural Revolution that was intended to "reverse the verdict on the bourgeois reactionary line."

On matters of domestic policy, Lin's political report – like the communiqué of the Twelfth Plenum – said virtually nothing. It simply noted that the economic situation was good – that there had been "good harvests," "a thriving situation in industrial production," a "flourishing market," and "stable prices" in the preceding years – and concluded that it was "certain that the great victory of the Great Proletarian Cultural Revolution will continue to bring about new leaps forward on the economic front." It also claimed that the seizure of power in "departments of culture, art, education, the press, health, etc." would end the domination of these sectors by "intellectuals" and "persons of power taking the capitalist road," but it did not indicate what new policies would result. The report also referred at some length to the expulsion of old members from the Party and the recruitment of new ones, but it did not provide any fresh clues as to the process by which this would occur.

136 Lin Biao's report is in *PR*, 12.18 (30 April 1969), 16–35. The drafting of this report is subject to various interpretations. Zhou Enlai reported at the Tenth National Congress in 1973 that the first draft had been written by Lin Biao and Chen Boda but was "rejected by the Central Committee." See *The Tenth National Congress of the Communist Party of China (Documents)*, 5. More recently, Hu Yaobang has claimed that the report was written by Kang Sheng and Zhang Chunqiao. See Hu, "Lilun gongzuo wuxu hui yinyan," 57.

The contribution of the Ninth Party Congress to China's political reconstruction, then, lay in the decisions it took about the new Party constitution and central Party leaders. Compared to the previous Party constitution, adopted by the Eighth Party Congress in 1956, the new document stressed the guiding role of Mao Zedong Thought and the importance of continued class struggle – neither of which concepts had appeared in the earlier version.[137] In addition, opportunities for membership in the Party were now offered only to those who had the proper class background. The 1956 constitution had opened the doors of the Party to anyone who "works and does not exploit the labor of others" and who accepted the responsibilities of Party membership. The 1969 constitution, in contrast, restricted Party membership principally to those from worker, poor and lower-middle peasant, and military backgrounds.

The most important feature of the new constitution, however, was its brevity and lack of precision. Containing merely twelve articles, the new document was only about one-fifth as long as the 1956 constitution. The new constitution contained no reference to the rights of Party members. No attempt was made to specify in any detail the structure and powers of Party committees and various levels, the procedures for disciplining Party members, or the relation between the Party and the state – all of which had been important features of the earlier constitution. Eliminated from the Party structure were the Secretariat, which had supervised the central Party apparatus; the office of the general secretary, who had overseen day-to-day Party functions; and the entire network of control commissions, which had been responsible for inner-Party discipline. Thus, the organizational structure for the Party that emerged from the Ninth Party Congress was significantly more flexible, less institutionalized, and therefore more open to manipulation by elements of the top leadership, than had been the case before the Cultural Revolution.

The Ninth Party Congress also selected a new central leadership not only for post-Cultural Revolution China but, it appeared, for the post-Mao era as well. Lin Biao's position as sole vice-chairman and as "Comrade Mao Zedong's close comrade-in-arms and successor" was established as a formal provision of the new Party constitution. Only 54 of the 167 members of the previous CC were reelected at the Ninth Party Congress. Those who were removed from the Party elite at this point included a large number of provincial and regional Party leaders who had not been appointed to revolutionary committees, as well as important economic specialists, such as Bo Yibo and Yao Yilin, who had previously served in the State Council. After a protracted campaign by the

137 The 1969 Party constitution is in *PR*, 12.18 (30 April 1969), 36–9. The 1956 constitution is in URI, *Documents of tie Central Committee*, 1–30.

radicals, most of the veteran civilian and military officials connected with the February Adverse Current lost their positions on the Politburo, although they retained their memberships in the CC. The most prominent victim of the Ninth Party Congress was Deng Xiaoping, who was dropped from the CC but who still was not criticized by name in the official Congress documents.

The delegates to the Congress, and the CC it elected, gave plain evidence of the effects of the Cultural Revolution on the Chinese political system. First, they illustrated the preeminence of the military. An analysis of the films of the Congress revealed that approximately two-thirds of the 1,500 delegates appeared in military uniforms. Of the CC, 45 percent were military representatives, compared with 19 percent of the CC elected at the Eighth Party Congress in 1956.[138] The rise of the military came at the expense of both civilian officials, who were the main targets of the Cultural Revolution, and mass representatives, who might have been expected to be its principal beneficiaries. Mass representation on the new central Party organs was minimal. To be sure, 19 percent of the CC members were "of the masses," but they tended to be older workers and peasants rather than the younger mass activists who had emerged during the Cultural Revolution. Greater representation of military officers also meant a decline in representation of civilian officials, particularly from the State Council, who fell to about a third of CC membership. Given the differences in education and career path between the PLA and those government leaders, this change in the composition of the CC was correlated with a decline in the level of education and amount of experience in foreign countries.

Second, and equally important, the Congress demonstrated the decentralization of power that had been produced during the Cultural Revolution. In 1956, about 38 percent of the CC held provincial offices, and the rest occupied positions in the central military, Party, and government agencies. In 1969, in contrast, fully two-thirds of the CC members were provincial representatives. This trend was not, however, so clearly reflected on the Politburo. Only three of the members of the Politburo on the eve of the Cultural Revolution could be classified as provincial or regional representatives. By comparison, two civilian officials with exclusively provincial responsibilities (Ji Dengkui and Li Xuefeng) and three local military commanders (Chen Xilian, Xu Shiyou, and Li Desheng) were elected to the Politburo at the Ninth Party Congress.

Third, the Ninth CC saw a shift of power to a more junior generation of leaders, although not to a younger one. Indeed, "inexperience without youth"

138 For analyses of the composition of the Ninth Central Committee, and comparisons with its predecessor, see Gordon A. Bennett, *China's Eighth, Ninth, and Tenth Congresses, Constitutions, and Central Committees: An institutional overview and comparison;* and Robert A, Scalapino, "The transition in Chinese Party leadership: A comparison of the Eighth and Ninth Central Committees," in Scalapino, *Elites,* 67–148.

is one way of characterizing the CC produced by the Ninth Party Congress. Of the 170 full members of the Committee, 136 (and 225 of the 279 full members and alternates) had not served on the CC before the Cultural Revolution. But, with an average age of about sixty, the Ninth CC was only slightly younger than the one it replaced and was substantially older than the Eighth CC had been at its election in 1956. Furthermore, the Ninth CC was of distinctly lower rank than its predecessor because of the influx of regional military leaders, second-echelon provincial officials, and mass representatives into CC membership.

In a final development, the Politburo approved by the CC illustrated the continued fragmentation of power at the highest levels in Beijing. The twenty-five full and alternate members of the Politburo included, in addition to Mao and Lin, five central military officials closely linked to Lin, six people associated with the CRG, three regional and provincial military commanders not closely tied to Lin, two senior civilian officials attacked during the Cultural Revolution, one other PLA marshal to counterbalance Lin Biao, three mid-level Party officials who had risen to power as a result of the Cultural Revolution, and three veteran Party leaders well past their prime. The composition on the Politburo thereby reflected the divisions among the victims, survivors, and beneficiaries of the Cultural Revolution; between the military and the civilian radicals who had come to power during the movement; between Lin Biao and his rivals in the central military leadership; and between the central military establishment and the regional commanders.

In short, despite the successful attempts to end the violence of the Red Guard movement and the preliminary efforts to begin the reconstruction of the Chinese political system, the Ninth Party Congress left the country with a volatile political situation. The outlines of post–Cultural Revolution policy were undecided; power was divided among groups with noticeably different interests; and the structure of the Party and state was vague and uninstitutionalized. Although he was the nominal successor to Mao Zedong, Lin Biao's power base was highly fragile. Over the next two years, Lin would attempt to strengthen it by perpetuating military dominance of civilian affairs and by putting forward a policy platform that he believed would have wide appeal. These efforts, however, ultimately led to Lin's physical demise, as well as his political downfall.

CONCLUSIONS

How can we fairly judge the origins and development, consequences, and significance of this first stage of the Great Proletarian Cultural Revolution in China? The task is an unusually difficult one, bedeviled by the complexity of the events, the uncertain reliability of the information contained in the Red Guard press, and the lack of clear historical perspective on events that, as of this writing, took place less than twenty years ago.

The job of analysis is also entangled in the extreme and changing evaluations of the Cultural Revolution that have appeared in both China and the West since the Ninth Party Congress. During the late 1960s and early 1970s, the Chinese described the Red Guard movement as a creative and effective way, in Mao Zedong's words, "to arouse the broad masses to expose our dark aspect openly, in an all-round way, and from below." In the official interpretation of the day, the Cultural Revolution enabled the Chinese working classes to "smash revisionism, seize back that portion of power usurped by the bourgeoisie," and thereby "ensure that our country continues to advance in giant strides along the road of socialism."[139] As late as 1977, even after the purge of the Gang of Four, Chinese leaders continued to portray the Cultural Revolution in glowing terms. "Beyond any doubt," Hua Guofeng declared at the Eleventh Party Congress, "it will go down in the history of the proletariat as a momentous innovation which will shine with increasing splendor with the passage of time." Indeed, Hua promised that further Cultural Revoultions "will take place many times in the future" as a way of continuing the struggle against bourgeois and capitalist influences within the Party.[140]

Within two years, however, the official Chinese line had completely changed. In mid-1979, Ye Jianying described the Cultural Revolution as "an appalling catastrophe suffered by all our people." The interpretation that has prevailed more recently is that China was never in danger of a capitalist restoration, that Mao's diagnosis of China's political situation in 1966 "ran counter to reality," that the programs produced in the latter stages of the Cultural Revolution were impractical and Utopian, and that the Red Guards were naive and impressionable youth led by "careerists, adventurists, opportunists, political degenerates, and the hooligan dregs of society."[141] An official resolution on Party history, adopted in 1981, condemned the Cultural Revolution as causing "the most severe setback and the heaviest losses suffered by the party, the state, and the people since the founding of the People's Republic."[142]

The reassessment of the Cultural Revolution in China has been fully replicated in the West. During the 1970s, the Cultural Revolution was described by many Americans as a worthy example of Mao's desire to preserve communitarian, egalitarian, and populist values in the course of economic development

---

139 These quotations are drawn from Lin Biao's report to the Ninth Party Congress, in *PR*, 12.18 (30 April 1969), 21.

140 *The Eleventh National Congress of the Communist Party of China (Documents)*, 51–2.

141 *Beijing Review*, 5 October 1979, 15, 18, 19.

142 "Resolution on certain questions in the history of our party since the founding of the People's Republic of China," *FBIS Daily Report: China*, 1 July 1981, K14.

and of his conviction that "bureaucracy and modernization do not necessarily lead to an improved quality of life." The origins of the movement were said to lie in Mao's "noble vision" of a society in which "the division involving domination and subjection will be blurred, the leaders will be less distinguishable from the led . . . ,and the led will take part more directly in the policy-making process." It was believed that the Cultural Revolution would devise socioeconomic programs that would prevent China from "ossifying in the morass of bureaucratism and statism."[143]

As the Chinese have become more critical of the Cultural Revolution, so too have Western observers. Mao's "fanaticism" has been compared to that of Hitler and Stalin, and the Cultural Revolution has been likened to the Inquisition and the Holocaust. The origins of the movement are traced not to a noble vision, but to a perverted perception of China's social and poitical problems in the mid-1960s. The decade from 1966 to 1976 is portrayed as a period of "chaos and destruction" that produced "one of the worst totalitarian regimes the ancient land had ever seen." By "destroy[ing] the intellectuals, wip[ing] out the universities, and . . . wreck[ing] what there was of China's economy, the Cultural Revolution set back China's modernization for at least a decade."[144]

These rapidly changing interpretations of the Cultural Revolution shoud raise doubts about our abilities to portray accurately and fairly the tumultuous events of the late 1960s. Nonetheless, what is now known about the Cultural Revolution suggests the following assessment of the origins and consequences of the movement.

Origins

The ultimate responsibility for the Cultural Revolution rests squarely with Mao's diagnosis of the problems confronting Chinese society in the early and mid-1960s. It cannot be denied that many of the shortcomings Mao identified were indeed rooted in observable reality. Local Party organizations, particularly in the countryside, had become seriously corrupt and ineffective. Higher-level administrative agencies, both state and Party, were overstaffed, underskilled, and enmeshed in bureaucratic routine. The social and economic policies introduced in the aftermath of the GLF were reviving industrial and agricultural performance, but at the cost of growing inequality between skilled and unskilled workers, between communes blessed with fertile

143 These quotations are drawn from Harry Harding, "Reappraising the Cultural Revolution," *The Wilson Quarterly*, 4.4 (Autumn 1980), 132–41.
144 These quotations are taken from Harry Harding, "From China, with disdain: New trends in the study of China," *Asian Survey*, 22.10 (October 1982), 934–58.

land and those to whom nature had been less kind, between bright students and their more mediocre classmates, and between urban dwellers and rural folk.

But Mao characterized these problems in extreme form. He chose to interpret the emergence of bureaucratism and inequality as signs that China was proceeding along a revisionist course, and to trace their origins to the presence of disguised "capitalists" and "bourgeois elements" at the highest levels of Party leadership. In so doing, Mao brought his lifelong concern with class struggle in China to its logical conclusion. For most of the first two-thirds of his life, Mao had waged revolution against those whom he considered to be the enemies of the Chinese people. For a short period in the mid-1950s, after the unexpectedly successful collectivization of agriculture and nationalization of industry, Mao briefly considered the notion that class struggle in his country might now basically be over. But it was difficult for him to hold to such a conclusion for long. By the time of the Anti-Rightist Campaign in late 1957, he had developed the view that the struggle between antagonistic classes continued to be the principal political contradiction in the socialist period, just as it had been in China's presocialist years. And if not by the Lushan Plenum of 1959, then certainly by the Tenth Plenum in January 1962, Mao had come to the conclusion that the focal point of this class struggle was inside the leadership of the Party itself.

Thus, contemporary Chinese leaders and intellectuals are correct in saying that Mao was accustomed to seek the "class origins" (*jieji genyuan*) of problems in Chinese society and to interpret differences of opinion inside the Party as evidence of class struggle. As one Chinese historian has concisely put it, "Mao thought that inequalities and shortcomings in society were a sign that class struggle had not been handled well."[145]

Mao was also strongly influenced by developments in the Soviet Union in the late 1950s and early 1960s. Confronted with evidence of Moscow's attempts to manipulate China's foreign policy and to control its economy, and concerned by signs of growing inequality and stagnation inside the Soviet Union, Mao reasoned that the great-power chauvinism and revisionism apparent in Soviet foreign and domestic policy could only reflect the degeneration of the leadership of the Communist Party of the Soviet Union (CPSU). Once having reached this conclusion, Mao logically inferred that the risk of a similar retrogression existed in China as well.

145 Shao Huaze, "Guanyu 'wenhua. da geming' de jige wenti" (On several questions concerning the "Great Cultural Revolution"), in Quanguo dangshi ziliao zhengji gongzuo huiyi he jinian Zhongguo gongchandang liushi zhounian xueshu taolun hui mishu chu (Secretariat of the National Work Conference on Party Historical Materials and the Academic Conference in Commemoration of the Sixtieth Anniversary of the Chinese Communist Party), ed., *Dangshi huiyi baogao ji* (Collected reports from the Conference on Party History), 252.

In his analysis of the Soviet Union, Mao stressed the consequences of the political succession from Stalin to Khrushchev. Although Mao had been quick to criticize Stalin's shortcomings, he was still persuaded that Stalin remained, on balance, a great Marxist revolutionary. Concerning Khrushchev, the Chairman reached the opposite conclusion. From the Twentieth Congress of the CPSU on, Mao appears to have become ever more persuaded that Stalin's successor was himself a revisionist, whose rise to power had made possible nothing less than the restoration of capitalism in the birthplace of the October Revolution. Given Mao's own advanced years in the mid-1960s, the lesson was poignant. As he said to Ho Chi Minh in June 1966, "We are both more than seventy, and will be called by Marx someday. Who our successors will be – Bernstein, Kautsky, or Khrushchev – we can't know. But there's still time to prepare."[146]

Mao's strategy for dealing with the emergence of revisionism in the course of succession is also of crucial importance in understanding the origins and outcomes of the Cultural Revolution. Mao's approach was to call on the country's university and middle school students to criticize capitalist tendencies in China, first on their own campuses and then at higher levels of the Party bureaucracy. Paradoxically, however, Mao's view of Chinese youth in the mid-1960s was tinged with large doses of skepticism. In 1965, he told Edgar Snow that since the young people of China had not yet personally experienced their own revolution, they might "make peace with imperialism, bring the remnants of the Chiang Kai-shek clique back to the mainland, and take a stand beside the small precentage of counter-revolutionaries still in the country."[147] But Mao seemed confident – unwarrantedly so, as later developments would prove – that relying on the youth would serve to temper them as well as to purify the Party. In this sense, the Cultural Revolution was to provide a revolutionary experience for an entire new generation of Chinese, even as it offered a means of testing the revolutionary commitment of an older generation of Party officials.

The strategy was characteristically Maoist in at least two regards. First, it embodied long-standing populist elements in his thinking: his conviction that even the vanguard Party needed to be rectified and reformed through criticism from the people it led, and his belief that the masses of China should be encouraged to become involved in even the highest affairs of state. In the fall of 1967, in evaluating the results of the Cultural Revolution, Mao would stress the degree to which this populist ideal had been realized: "The important feature of this excellent situation is the full mobilization of the

---

146 Shao, "Guanyu . . . jige wenti," 356.   147 Mao is quoted in Snow, *Long revolution*, 221–2.

masses. Never before in any mass movement have the masses been mobilized so broadly and deeply this one."[148]

Second, Mao's strategy for the Cultural Revolution reflected his tendency to rely on the unreliable in uncovering the darker side of Party leadership. For Mao deliberately to seek criticism of the Party from those very groups that lacked firm commitment to socialism was not unprecedented. In the mid-1950s, he had done so from intellectuals during the Hundred Flowers Campaign, During the Socialist Education Campaign of the early 1960s he had mobilized the peasantry to purify the rural Party organization, although he simultaneously acknowledged the existence of spontaneous capitalist tendencies even among the poorer peasants. And now, in the mid-1960s, he mobilized millions of students – at best naive and immature; at worst, in Mao's own words, ready to "negate the revolution" – to attack revisionism in the Party.[149]

Although this strategy was characteristic of Mao, it was still highly unorthodox for the Party. As Frederick Teiwes has demonstrated, the mobilization of students to criticize "Party persons in authority taking the capitalist road" ran counter to at least three major Party traditions: that Party leaders should not be penalized for their views on matters of policy, and should be allowed to retain their opinions even if they were in the minority; that Party rectification campaigns should result in mild sanctions rather than "merciless blows"; and that mass participation in Party rectification, if allowed at all, should be under the firm leadership either of the regular Party apparatus or ad hoc Party work teams.[150] What is more, by launching the Cultural Revolution through irregular procedures, in the face of reluctance or opposition from the greater part of the central Party leadership, Mao simultaneously violated a fourth norm as well: that of collective leadership and majority rule.

Only a leader with Mao's unique authority within the Chinese Communist movement could have successfully abandoned all these simultaneously. It is no exaggeration, therefore, to conclude that the principal responsibility for the Cultural Revolution – a movement that affected tens of millions of Chinese – rests with one man. Without a Mao, there could not have been a Cultural Revolution.

But if Mao was a necessary condition for the Cultural Revolution, he was not a sufficient one. To begin with, Mao had, as we have seen, crucial political resources in addition to personal legitimacy. These included, first, a sizable popular base. This mass support included both the sincere and the

148 Stuart R. Schram, *The political thought of Mao Tse-tung*, rev. ed. 370.
149 Snow, *Long revolution*, 223.
150 Frederick C. Teiwes, *Leadership, legitimacy, and conflict in China: From a charismatic Mao to the politics of succession*, ch. 3.

opportunistic, both the enthusiastic and the acquiescent. Some participated out of personal devotion to Mao, the man who had liberated their country from imperialism and warlordism. Others joined the Cultural Revolution for the same reason that so many supported reform in the 1980s: their concern that a Soviet model of development would take China down the road of ossification, inequality, and authoritarianism. Still others became Red Guards and revolutionary rebels because of specific grievances against particular cadres. As a former Red Guard has put it, Chinese used the Cultural Revolution to "get back at their superiors for everything from tiny insults to major abuse of policy."[151]

Over time, this mass base began to dissipate as many of those who participated in the Cultural Revolution became disillusioned with the violence and chaos it engendered. Nonetheless, Mao was able to mobilize enough mass support in late 1966 and early 1967 to shake the CCP to its very foundations. And for this, the Chinese people themselves must bear some accountability.

Mao also relied on political support within China's national leadership. As we have repeatedly emphasized in this chapter, Mao's resources included a group of ambitious political ideologues and organizers in both Beijing and Shanghai who could develop more systematically his rather inchoate observations about the dangers of revisionism in China, enhance Mao's personal charisma through the manipulation of the mass media, mobilize the disenchanted sectors of urban society, and, to a degree, direct the activities of the mass movement. At the same time, Mao enjoyed the support of important elements of the PLA, particularly Lin Biao and major figures in the high command, who provided political support to the Chairman in early 1966, gave logistical assistance to the Red Guard movement later that year, overthrew the Party establishment in early 1967, and then undertook the restoration of order between mid-1967 and mid-1969.

But responsibility must also be assigned to the rest of the Party establishment for not resisting Mao more vigorously. The official Chinese version of the Cultural Revolution now places great stress on the opposition to Mao, at both central and local levels, that emerged after January 1967. The February Adverse Current of 1967 is singled out for particular credit as an example of "unceasing struggle" carried out by the Party against the Cultural Revolution. But by this time the Cultural Revolution had already received the formal endorsement of the Eleventh Plenum of the CO. The forces of mobilization, conflict, and chaos were already irreversible.

The Party establishment might have been able to stop the Cultural Revolution if, earlier, it had acted in a more unified way to oppose Mao rather

151 Liang Heng and Judith Shapiro, *Son of the revolution*, 47.

than acceded to his decisions. Of particular importance was Zhou Enlai's assistance in securing the wider publication of Yao Wenyuan's article on Hai Rui in November 1965, his involvement in the criticism of Peng Zhen in April 1966, his defense of radical students such as Kuai Dafu in September and of the CRG as late as December 1966, and his failure to associate himself unambiguously with the February Adverse Current of February 1967. Of special interest is the revelation that Zhou was the author of one of the most vitriolic denunciations of bureaucracy to come out of the Cultural Revolution, a document previously attributed to Mao Zedong.[152] This suggests that Zhou may have genuinely believed that the danger of bureaucratic rigidification required drastic measures. Alternatively, Zhou may have supported Mao for reasons of personal loyalty or self-preservation. In either event, Deng Xiaoping later acknowledged that Zhou had done things during the Cultural Revolution for which he later had been "forgiven" by the Chinese people.[153]

But Zhou should not be singled out for blame. Ye Jianying and Yang Chengwu were involved in drafting the report justifying the purge of Luo Ruiqing.[154] Deng Xiaoping appears to have joined Zhou in the criticism of Peng Zhen in April 1966. And, more generally, the entire Politburo consented to the dismissal of Luo Ruiqing, the reshuffling of the Beijing municipal Party committee, and the purge of the Party Secretariat and Propaganda Department in May 1966, and to the adoption of the Sixteen Points on the Cultural Revolution at the Eleventh Plenum in August.

On the complexity of the Party leadership in the early stages of Mao's assault against it, the official resolution on Party history is silent. But Chinese historians have been more forthcoming. As one has put it, the Politburo may have adopted such measures as the 16 May Circular without believing in them, or even because it felt compelled to do so; but it endorsed Mao's decisions nonetheless, and must therefore "bear some responsibility" for the Cultural Revolution.[155]

In explaining the acquiescence of the Party establishment in the spring and summer of 1966, the Chinese have emphasized the importance of Mao's personal authority over the rest of his colleagues on the Politburo and the CC. This implies that Mao enjoyed charistmatic standing among the Party leadership, as well as among the Chinese masses. It further suggests that his

---

152 *RMRB*, 29 August 1984, in *FBIS Daily Report: China*, 31 August 1984, K1–4.
153 Deng Xiaoping, "Answers to the Italian journalist Oriana Fallaci," in *Selected works of Deng Xiaoping*, 329–30.
154 Lieberthal, *Research guide*, 243, 249.
155 Jin Chunming, "'Wenhua da geming' de shinian(The decade of the "Great Cultural Revolution"), in Zhonggong dangshi yanjiuhui, (Research Society on the History of the Chinese Communist Party), ed., *Xuexi lishi jueyi zhuanji* (Special publication on studying the resolution on history), 159–60, and Shao, "Guanyu . . . jige wenti," 378.

ability to lead the CCP to victory against enormous odds in the late 1930s and 1940s had given him an air of infallibility that had been only slightly tarnished by the disaster of the GLF.

Recent Chinese accounts have also revealed that Mao was, in effect, presenting the Party with a choice between Lin Biao and Liu Shaoqi as his successor, and that many Party leaders initially agreed that Lin was the better man. In the words of Deng Liqun, a man who was Liu Shaoqi's secretary before the Cultural Revolution and who was responsible for propaganda work in the early 1980s, Mao's preference for Lin "could not be said to have been without support within the Party." This was because, compared to Liu Shaoqi, Lin was more loyal to Mao, appeared to have a deeper commitment to ideology, and certainly had a better understanding of military matters. At a time when China was faced with the escalation of American involvement in the Vietnam conflict and a deepening military confrontation with the Soviet Union, many senior Party leaders apparently were persuaded by the argument that "to run a country and a Party like ours well, it won't do only to know politics and not military matters."[156]

Just as Mao can be held accountable for the origins of the Cultural Revolution, so too must he bear much of the blame for its outcomes. Many of the most devastating consequences of the movement – particularly the violence, disorder, and loss of life – can be considered the predictable, if not inevitable, results of the strategy that Mao employed. In mobilizing the masses, Mao sanctioned the use of highly inflammatory rhetoric, casting the movement as nothing less than a Manichaean struggle between the forces of revolution and counterrevolution in China. He brought to the surface deep cleavages and grievances within Chinese society without creating any mechanisms for organizing or directing the social forces he unleashed. He seems to have envisioned a self-disciplined revolutionary movement, but he produced a divided and factionalized force over which he, the CRG, and even the army could exercise only limited control. He expected Party cadres to welcome and support mass criticism of their own leadership, and he reacted in disappointment and outrage when, not surprisingly, they attempted to suppress or manipulate the mass movement in order to preserve their own positions.

The flaw in Mao's strategy, in other words, was that he waged only half a revolution between 1966 and 1969. He failed to design a viable and enduring alternative political order to replace the one he sought to overthrow, or to transform the political resources he had mobilized from a destructive force into a constructive one. In this sense, the Cultural Revolution was the second

---

156 Deng Liqun, "Xuexi 'Guanyu jianguo yilai dangde ruogan lishi wend de jueyi' de wenti he huida" (Questions and answers in studying the "Resolution on certain historical questions since the founding of the state").

unsuccessful Chinese revolution of the twentieth century. In 1911, Sun Yatsen had succeeded in overthrowing the Manchu dynasty; but he was unable to create effective republican institutions to replace the fallen monarchy, and China fell under military rule. In the late 1960s, Mao succeeded in seizing power from the Party establishment, but he was unable to design effective populist institutions to replace the Leninist Party-state. Once again, political power fell into the hands of the Chinese military.

In Mao's defense, perhaps the most that can be said is that at the height of the Cultural Revolution, he did try to moderate its destructive impact on the Party apparatus and on society as a whole. Mao attempted to prevent armed struggle and physical persecution, as is apparent in a number of central directives that he authorized forbidding beating, house raiding, looting, incarceration, and destruction of personal property.[157] He criticized the factionalism that had plagued the mass movement and called on revolutionary committees to include representatives of all competing mass organizations. Mao not only repeatedly emphasized that the majority of cadres were good, but he was also personally responsible for protecting a number of high-ranking officials, the most important of whom was Zhou Enlai, against attack.[158]

The problem was that these interventions were not completely successful in controlling the factionalism and violence of the Cultural Revolution. In the final analysis, the only way in which Mao could have regained control over the movement would have been to repudiate it completely. And this he refused to do. He never abandoned the concept of the Cultural Revolution, the theory behind it, or the strategy it reflected. Nor did Mao repudiate his own lieutenants who were responsible for much of the violence. To the end of his life, he continued to believe that the Cultural Revolution was a timely, necessary, and appropriate device for ensuring that China would follow a truly revolutionary course after his death.

Consequences

There is a certain all-or-nothing quality to the Cultural Revolution between 1966 and 1969. Important sectors of Chinese society were affected in a thorough manner, whereas other equally important parts of the country were hardly touched at all. Similarly, some of the consequences of the Cultural Revolution have already proved ephemeral, whereas others will continue to affect China for decades to come.

---

157 See, in particular, the 6 June 1967 directive prohibiting "armed struggle, illegal arrest, looting, and sabotage," in CCP documents of the Great Proletarian Cultural Revolution, 463–4. Recent Chinese accounts attribute this directive to Mao personally. See Jin, "'Wenhua da geming' de shinian," 164.

158 Witke, Comrade Chiang Ch'ing, 363.

The Cultural Revolution largely spared rural China and the 620 million people who lived there in the late 1960s. The exceptions were a relatively small number of communes close to large and medium-sized cities, especially those in suburban counties located within municipal boundaries. These suburban areas did experience some Cultural Revolutionary activities as peasants engaged in struggles for power at the commune and brigade levels and participated in mass protest in the neighboring cities. In his careful study of the Cultural Revolution in the Chinese countryside, Richard Baum has identified 231 places in which rural disorder was reported by the Chinese press between July 1966 and December 1968. Of these, 42 percent were in suburban counties, especially around Beijing, Shanghai, and Guangzhou; and another 22 percent were within 50 kilometers of large of medium-sized cities. Less than 15 percent, in contrast, were more than 100 kilometers away from an urban place. Baum's findings do not imply, of course, that only 231 communes were directly involved in the Cultural Revolution. But his data do suggest that the Red Guard stage of the Cultural Revolution did not have a deep impact far beyond the major cities of China. It was, instead, principally an urban movement.[159]

If the countryside was touched lightly, relatively few urban residents remained unaffected by the Cultural Revolution, since the movement was conducted in virtually every high school, factory, university, office, and shop in China. In an interview with Yugoslav journalists in 1980, Hu Yaobang estimated that 100 million people – roughly half the urban population and virtually all those of working age – were treated "unjustly" during the Anti-Rightist Campaign, the Cultural Revolution, and other Maoist movements. Allowing for a bit of exaggeration, we can regard Hu's figure as a reasonably accurate indication of the comprehensive impact of the Cultural Revolution on urban China.[160]

Economically, China suffered surprisingly little from the Red Guard phase of the Cultural Revolution. Grain production rose in both 1966 and 1967, fell substantially in 1968, but then regained 1966 levels in 1969. The poor performance registered in 1968 may have been partly related to the political turmoil of that year, but it also reflected the fact that the weather in 1968 was significantly worse than in 1967. Moreover, the rapid recovery of grain production the following year suggests that the Cultural Revolution had only limited and temporary effects on agricultural output.

---

159 Richard Baum, "The Cultural Revolution in the countryside: Anatomy of a limited rebellion," in Robinson, *Cultural Revolution*, 367–476.
160 Tanjug, 21 June 1980, in *FBIS Daily Report: China*, 23 June 1980, L1. Some Western accounts mistakenly assign responsibility for these 100 million victims to the Cultural Revolution alone; see, for example, *Washington Post*, 8 June 1980.

A similar pattern was evident in industry. Industrial output fell some 13 percent in 1967 as a result of the disruption of the normal work of both factories and transportation lines. As a result, state revenues, state expenditures, and investment in state-owned enterprises also fell precipitously in 1967 and 1968. But the industrial economy quickly revived. Industrial output in 1969 once again exceeded the level of 1966, and state revenues, expenditure, and investment followed suit the following year.[161] By the beginning of 1971, according to Western estimates, industrial production had achieved full recovery, regaining the levels that would have been projected from the growth rates of the early 1960s.[162]

Thus the effects of this phase of the Cultural Revolution on the Chinese economy were limited in extent and duration; they were certainly far less severe than those of the GLF one decade earlier. But the consequences of the Cultural Revolution for cultural and educational affairs were much greater.[163] The Chinese stage and screen stopped presenting any work of art other than a handful of "revolutionary" films, operas, and ballets written under the sponsorship of Jiang Qing. The sale of traditional and foreign literature was halted, and libraries and museums were closed. Universities were shut down in the summer of 1966, and middle schools suspended instruction in the fall, so that their students could participate in the Cultural Revolution. Although middle school education was resumed the following spring, college classrooms remained dark for the next four years. It was only in the summer of 1970 that the first new class of university students was recruited, and even that process was limited to a fraction of China's institutions of higher learning.

From a strictly curricular perspective, the damage of the early phase of the Cultural Revolution to the Chinese educational system was only moderate. More detrimental were policies implemented after 1969 that politicized the curriculum, reduced the length of training, required lengthy doses of physical labor, and selected students on the basis of class background rather than academic promise. On the other hand, many cultural and educational institutions sustained serious physical damage. The collections of many libraries and museums were damaged, disrupted, or dispersed. Red Guards defaced or destroyed numerous historical sites, religious structures, and cultural artifacts.

161 Data on industrial and agricultural output are drawn from Arthur G. Ashbrook, Jr., "China: Economic modernization and long-term performance," in U.S. Congress, [97th], Joint Economic Committee, *China under the Four Modernizations*, 1.104. Data on state revenues, expenditures, and investment are from *Beijing Review*, 19 March 1984, 27–8.

162 Robert Michael Field, Kathleen M. McGlynn, and William B. Abnett, "Political conflict and industrial growth in China: 1965–1977," in U.S. Congress, [95th], Joint Economic Committee, *Chinese economy post-Mao*, 1.239–83.

163 This discussion of the effects of the Cultural Revolution on the educational system draws upon Marianne Bastid, "Economic necessity and political ideals in educational reform during the Cultural Revolution," *CQ*, 42 (April–June 1970), 16–45.

And the military, once it had been sent into the universities to restore order, requisitioned many campus buildings for its own use. Many of these effects were not fully remedied until well after the death of Mao Zedong in 1976.

The most serious impact of the Cultural Revolution on the cultural and educational spheres was on scholars, writers, and intellectuals. No precise figures are yet available on the persecution and harassment suffered by cultural circles between 1966 and 1969, but the trial of the Gang of Four in 1980–1 has provided some illustrative data. The indictment in that trial claimed that 2,600 people in literary and art circles, 142,000 cadres and teachers in units under the Ministry of Education, 53,000 scientists and technicians in research institutes, and 500 professors and associate professors in the medical colleges and institutes under the Ministry of Public Health were all "falsely charged and persecuted," and that an unspecified number of them died as a result.[164] Most suffered at the hands of relatively autonomous Red Guard organizations in their own units, but a minority were victimized by Jiang Qing personally. Concerned that damaging information about her career in Shanghai in the 1930s might be released by her opponents, Jiang Qing organized groups to search the homes of writers and artists in Shanghai to confiscate letters and photos relating to her past.

The persecution of intellectuals was fully matched by the maltreatment of Party and government leaders. The rate of political purge was extremely high. It reached 70–80 percent at the regional and provincial levels, where four of six regional Party first secretaries and twenty-three of twenty-nine provincial Party first secretaries fell victim to the Cultural Revolution. In the central organs of the Party, the purge rate was about 60–70 percent. Only 9 Politburo members out of 23, 4 secretariat members out of 13, and 54 CC members out of 167 survived the Cultural Revolution with their political positions intact. Only about half of the fifteen vice-premiers and forty-eight cabinet ministers remained on the State Council at the end of the movement.[165]

The rates of purge were not, of course, uniform throughout the bureaucracy.[166] Studies of the organizational impact of the Cultural Revolution have suggested chat the turnover was higher in some functional areas (especially agriculture, industry, planning, and culture and education) than in others (such as national defense, and finance and trade); that, predictably, the higher one's rank, the more likely one was to fall victim to the Cultural

164 A great trial, 182–3.
165 On the rates of purge, see Bennett, China's Eighth, Ninth, and Tenth Congresses, Constitutions, and Central Committees; Donald W. Klein and Lois B. Hager, "The Ninth Central Committee," CQ, 45 (January-March 1971), 37–56; Scalapino, "The transition in Chinese Party leadership"; and Teiwes, Provincial leadership in China.
166 Richard K. Diao, "The impact of the Cultural Revolution on China's economic elite," CQ, 42 (April-June 1970), 65–87.

Revolution: and that, somewhat ironically, non-Party cadres suffered somewhat less from the Cultural Revolution than did officials who were Party members. All told, the level of purge can be estimated in a rough manner by reference to a Chinese claim that some 3 million cadres who had been labeled as revisionists, counterrevolutionaries, or "Party persons in authority taking the capitalist road" were rehabilitated in the late 1970s. This may have represented as much as 20 percent of a bureaucracy of 15 to 20 million officials.

The Cultural Revolution was not characterized by the great purge trials and mass executions of the Stalin period. Most victims of the Cultural Revolution survived the movement and secured their political rehabilitation after the death of Mao and the purge of the Gang of Four. But the experience for China's bureaucracy was still not pleasant. A large number – again perhaps as many as 3 million – were sent to May 7 cadre schools, usually in rural areas, to engage in physical labor, conduct intense ideological study, and forge "close ties" with neighboring peasants. Although some officials, especially those younger in years, found the experience to be rewarding in ways, the May 7 schools represented a true physical hardship for older cadres, especially those who remained in the schools, separated from their families, for a long period of time.

Other officials experienced fates worse than a stint in the May 7 cadre schools. Some were placed in isolation in their own work units, where they underwent severe psychological harassment aimed at inducing confessions of political malfeasance. An unknown number were beaten and tortured. Some were killed, some died in confinement, and others committed suicide. Liu Shaoqi was placed under house arrest in 1967, beaten by Red Guards later that year, and died in prison in 1969. He Long, a marshal in the Chinese armed forces, was hospitalized for the malnutrition he suffered while under house arrest and then died after glucose injections complicated his diabetic condition.[167] Other ranking officials known to have died during the Cultural Revolution include Peng Dehuai and Tao Zhu, both members of the Politburo; two Beijing municipal Party secretaries, Liu Ren and Deng Tuo; Wu Han, the author of Hai Rui, who was concurrently a deputy mayor of Beijing; Shanghai's Mayor Cao Diqiu and Deputy Mayor Jin Zhenghuan; and Vice-Minister of Public Security Xu Zirong. Luo Ruiqing, the former chief of staff, attempted suicide.

The children of leading officials also suffered political persecution and physical torture. Some, like Deng Xiaoping's daughter, joined their parents in internal exile. Others, like Deng's son, were crippled for life at the hands of

---

167 David Bonavia, *Verdict in Peking: The trial of the Gang of Four*, passim.

Red Guards. An adopted daughter of Zhou Enlai's was allegedly tortured by Red Guards. And others were subject to intense criticism and abuse because they were the sons and daughters of their parents.

The total number of deaths attributable to the Cultural Revolution is not known with certainty. Of the 729,511 people named in the indictment of the Gang of Four as having been deliberately "framed and persecuted" by them and their associates, 34,800 are said to have been persecuted to death. These include nearly 3,000 people in Hebei, 14,000 in Yunnan, 16,000 in Inner Mongolia, and more than 1,000 in the PLA.[168] Fox Butterfield attributes to a well-informed Chinese the estimate that 400,000 people died during the Cultural Revolution.[169] Extrapolations based on deaths in particular provinces, such as Fujian and Guangdong, are somewhat higher, ranging between 700,000 and 850,000, but these figures are based on provinces that experienced higher than the average level of violence and disorder. It might not be unreasonable to estimate that approximately half a million Chinese, out of an urban population of around 135 million in 1967, died as a direct result of the Cultural Revolution.

Beyond the immediate effects just considered, the events of 1966–9 also had longer-term consequences. To begin with, the Red Guard years produced an explosive combination of a deeply fragmented leadership and weak political institutions. Leadership at the central and provincial levels was divided among veteran Party officials, regional and main force military commanders, mass representatives, and lower-level cadres who had risen to power as a result of the Cultural Revolution. The authority of the Party itself had been brought into serious question, but the institutions that had taken the place of the Party, the revolutionary committees, were described as only temporary organs of government. The Cultural Revolution had discredited the socioeconomic policies and organizational norms of the early 1960s, but the new leadership had not yet come to any consensus on what should replace them.

This fragmentation of power established the patterns that dominated Chinese politics for the next seven and a half years, until the death of Mao Zedong in September 1976. There was, first, a struggle between civilian and military leaders over the role of the armed forces in post–Cultural Revolution China. Lin Biao's unsuccessful effort to institutionalize military dominance of civilian poiltics was followed, after his death in the fall of 1971, by more effective attempts to disengage the PLA from civilian affairs. The events of the late 1960s also produced a struggle over the definition of post–Cultural Revolution programs, pitting more conservative officials, who sought to resurrect the policies of the early 1960s, against radical leaders, who wished to formulate

168 A great trial, 21.   169 Fox Butterfield, China: Alive in the bitter sea. 348.

a set of more egalitarian and populist programs in industry, agriculture, and intellectual life. And the fragmentation of power so evident in the Politburo selected at the Ninth Party Congress led ineluctably to a serious struggle to succeed Mao Zedong among the officials (like Deng Xiaoping) who had been victims of the Cultural Revolution, the ideologues and organizers (like Jiang Qing) who had led it, the military leaders (like Lin Biao) who had ended it, and the middle-level cadres (like Hua Guofeng) who had survived it. In short, the "manic phase" of the Cultural Revolution from 1966 to 1969 produced seven or eight years of lesser turmoil, resolved only by the purge of the Gang of Four in October 1976 and the emergence of Deng Xiaoping's reform program in December 1978.

The restoration of order in 1976, and the initiation of economic and political reform in 1978, did not, however, mark the final elimination of the effects of the Cultural Revolution. Two enduring consequences remained very much in evidence as China entered the mid-1980s. One was a deep-seated factionalism infecting almost every government agency, industrial and commercial enterprise, and Party committee. Factional conflict was created by the struggle for power at the height of the Cultural Revolution, was preserved by the insistence on broad consensus and representation in the formation of revolutionary committees, and was strengthened by the rehabilitation of large numbers of victims of the Cultural Revoultion during the mid-1970s. Such conflict seriously reduced the effectiveness of political institutions by making both policy decisions and personnel appointments captives of factional considerations.

Second, the events of the late 1960s created a serious crisis of confidence among the young people of China. For the more than 4 million high school and university students – many of them former Red Guards – who were relocated to the countryside in 1968 and 1969, the suspension of normal patterns of schooling meant a dramatic and often devastating change in their future prospects. Although almost all were able to return to their homes by the end of the 1970s, the fact that most were unable to complete their education meant that their career paths and life chances had changed for the worse. The fact that so calamitous an event was launched in the name of Marxism served to undermine their faith in ideology, and the inability of the Party to prevent the Cultural Revolution served to weaken their confidence in the existing political system.

The process of disillusionment occurred for different youth at different times. For some, the turning point was the restriction and eventual demobilization of the Red Guards after the January Revolution, a clear sign that those who had once been told that they were the leaders of the movement were now to be made its scapegoats. For others, the critical event was the discovery of the poverty of the Chinese countryside, whether during the exchange of revolutionary experiences in 1966–7 or during the notification programs of later months. One former Red Guard, who experienced both of these awakenings, spoke for an entire generation when he vented his rage and frustration in an interview with American scholars after his escape to Hong Kong in 1967:

> Nothing can describe my anger at the way the situation had developed in March [1967]. Those sons of bitches (the PLA and the military training platoon in his middle school) had thrown us all out the window. . . . We had virtually succeeded in seizing power, in making a true revolution. Now the bastards had thrown it all away.
>
> [My time in the countryside] was another eye-opening experience. [The peasants] ceaselessly complained about their hard life. They said they had little food to eat, even in good crop years. . . . Times had been better, they felt, even under the Kuomintang, when a man could work, save some money, invest it, and improve himself. . . . They also preferred Liu Shao-ch'i to Mao because they identified Liu with the private plots which gave them the chance to put some savings [away] and move up the ladder. . . . I had thought that only capitalist roaders and counterrevolutionaries had such thoughts. But I had just heard them from the mouth of a revolutionary poor peasant who had worked for the Party for more than twenty years. . . . In ten short days, my world outlook had been challenged by the reality of peasant life and attitudes.[170]

The effects of that disillusionment also varied from individual to individual. For some young people, China's so-called Lost Generation, the consequences were political cynicism, a passivity and lack of initiative in work, and a growing materialism and acquisitiveness. This crisis of confidence among youth, coupled with the decline in the rule of law during the Cultural Revolution, is widely believed to have contributed to a rise in crime and antisocial activities in the late 1970s. For others, especially those who had received some college education before 1966, time in the countryside provided an opportunity for reading, reflection, and debate about the future of their country. Many of these former Red Guards later constituted a group of younger intellectuals who, in the late 1970s and early 1980s, helped to formulate the general principles and specific policies for the economic reforms of the post-Mao era.

As of the late 1980s, in fact, it appeared that, paradoxically, the chaos of the Cultural Revolution had been an important condition for the reforms of the post-Mao era. The fact that so many senior cadres had suffered so greatly during the Cultural Revolution, and yet had survived it, helped create the leadership for economic and political liberalization once the movement had come to an end. The disillusionment of thousands of educated youth and intellectuals during the Red Guard movement stimulated many of the radical ideas that would later be translated into concrete reforms. And the

170 Bennett and Montaperto, *Red Guard*, 214–17 and 222–4, passim.

devastating impact of the Cultural Revolution on the CCP, all in the name of preventing revisionism, weakened the Party's ability to resist a restructuring of the political and economic order that went far beyond that which Mao had found so objectionable in the Soviet Union. In short, had there been no Cultural Revolution, it is unlikely that reform in the post-Mao period would have gone as far or as fast.

But the long-term consequences of the Cultural Revolution remain uncertain. It is not yet clear whether the Cultural Revolution served as a precedent for, or immunization against, the recurrence of similar undertakings in the future. From the vantage point of the 1980s, of course, the inoculatory effects of the Cultural Revolution appeared to be greater. The damage done by the Red Guards, without any countervailing accomplishments, warns strongly against launching a similar "open door" rectification soon. Over time, however, it remains possible that memories will dim, and that the Cultural Revolution will appear more noble and salutary in retrospect than it does today. If so, the Cultural Revolution could still serve as a prototype for another struggle for political power in China or another attempt to purify the country of inequality, corruption, and elitism through mass mobilization. The issue is whether the post-Mao reforms will create sufficient political institutionalization, economic prosperity, social stability, and cultural modernization such that the Cultural Revolution will have little appeal even after the inoculatory effects have worn off.

CHAPTER 4

THE SUCCESSION TO MAO AND THE END OF MAOISM, 1969–1982

RODERICK MacFARQUHAR

INTRODUCTION

The Great Proletarian Cultural Revolution was an attempt to shape the future of China. Its method was to change the nature of the Chinese people. It was to be a "great revolution that touches people to their very souls."[1] The masses were to liberate themselves by class struggle against the main target, "those within the Party who are in authority and are taking the capitalist road,"[2] These so-called Soviet-style revisionists were alleged to be seeking to corrupt the masses by using old ideas to restore capitalism. By transforming the ideological realm – education, literature, the arts – and embracing Mao Zedong Thought, the Chinese people were to inoculate themselves against poisonous contagion.

Mao's objective was a China that was pure though poor, more egalitarian and less privileged, more collectivist but less bureaucratic, a society in which all worked as one, not so much because they were led by the Communist Party (CCP) as because an inner compass – Mao Zedong Thought – pointed them toward the magnetic pole of true communism.

The goal of the Cultural Revolution was to provide the right answer to the question, After Mao, what? But success would depend on the answer to an earlier question, After Mao, who? If alleged capitalist-roaders like head of state Liu Shaoqi survived the Chairman in positions of power, then China would "change its color." China must not only be guided by the correct line and policies, but had to "train and bring up millions of successors who will carry on the cause of proletarian revolution."[3] In the storm of the Cultural

The author is grateful to Thomas Bernstein, John Fairbank, Merle Goldman, Kenneth Lieberthal, and Michael Schoenhals for comments and suggestions on drafts of this chapter.

1 "Decision of the Central Committee of the Chinese Communist Party concerning the Great Proletarian Cultural Revolution," URI, *CCP documents of the Great Proletarian Cultural Revolution, 1966–1967*, 42.
2 Ibid., 45, 46.
3 "On Khrushchev's phoney communism and its historical lessons for the world," *The polemic on the general line of the international communist movement*, 477. This is the last and most important of the nine polemics

Revolution, new leaders were to emerge, steeled in struggle, "proletarian" in outlook, in whose hands the Maoist brand of socialism would one day burn fiercely.

In the interim, Mao had to cleanse the top ranks of the CCP and install a new successor whom he could trust implicitly to preserve his vision and hand it down. Hence the internecine struggle and purges described in Chapter 3. Mao's victory in that battle was heralded at the CCP's Ninth Congress in the spring of 1969, which rubber-stamped his personal choice as heir, Defense Minister Lin Biao. But this produced a new conundrum, After Mao, which? Was it the demoralized and decimated Party that would run China, or the army, a body with equally revolutionary credentials, which had emerged after three years of Cultural Revolution as the master of the country? This was an institutional issue of supreme importance, with momentous implications for hundreds of millions of Chinese, But for the most part it was fought out between small coteries of leaders, plotting in their residences, clashing at central meetings, with the liquidation of one clique or the other finally emerging as the only viable solution.

THE MILITARIZATION OF CHINESE POLITICS

The CCP's Ninth Congress in April 1969 was a triumph for Lin Biao individually and for the People's Liberation Army (PLA) institutionally. Defense Minister Lin's position as second only to Mao, first achieved at the Eleventh Plenum of the Central Committee (CC) in August 1966, was confirmed. The new Party constitution formally designated him Mao's successor, the first time a comrade-in-arms of the Chairman had achieved that distinction.[4] Lin's military colleagues, as Chapter 3 pointed out, were very prominent at the

---

issued by the CCP against the revisionism of the CPSU in 1963–4. These documents are crucial for understanding Mao's concerns on the eve of the Cultural Revolution.

4 Indeed, the only time any Communist Party has ever taken such a step. Lin Biao's new status was attested to by the extravagant praise lavished on him by Zhou Enlai in his speech to the CCP's Ninth Congress; Zhou's address is included in a sixteen-page unpublished collection of speeches to the Congress, and has been translated and annotated for publication by Michael Schoenhals.

A Party historian has stated that when the presidium for the Ninth Congress was being appointed, Mao suggested that Lin should chair it and that he, Mao, should be vice-chairman, only to be interrupted by a loud shout of "Long live Chairman Mao" from Lin Biao.

The same historian has suggested that Mao indicated his preference for Lin Biao as his successor as early as 1956. It seems that when votes were cast for Party Chairman at the first plenum after the CCP's Eighth Congress in September that year, Mao was one vote short of unanimous approval. It was established that Mao had not voted for himself, nor for his number two, Liu Shaoqi, but for Lin Biao? See Tan Zongji, "Lin Biao fangeming jituan de jueqi jige fumie," (The sudden rise of the Lin Biao counterrevolutionary clique and its destruction), in *Jiaoxue cankao: quanguo dangxiao xitong Zhonggong dangshi xueshu taolun hui, xia* (Reference for teaching and study: national Party school system's academic conference on CCP history, vol. a) (hereafter *Jiaoxue cankao, xia*), 40, 42. The author is grateful to Michael Schoenhals for sharing both these items with him.

congress; PLA representation on the CC rose from 19 to 45 percent.[5] At the First Plenum of the new CC after the Congress, the number of active-service soldiers appointed to the Politburo rose dramatically.[6]

The rise of Lin Biao and the military was in some ways a logical culmination of the Chinese revolution and indeed conformed to a pattern familiar from Chinese history. Whenever political control broke down, often under the impact of economic disaster, uprisings took place. Force was met with force, and a process of militarization of the upper levels of the polity took place. Eventually some more able and ambitious rebel leader, sometimes a peasant, more often an aristocrat, would seize the chance to overthrow the dynasty by force, eliminating other aspirant rebel chiefs in the process. The generals who had backed the founding emperor in his struggle for power would assume powerful positions under the new dynasty.[7]

This process of replacement of one dynasty by another normally took many decades, a period of warfare disguised by the neat traditional assignment of a single year as the moment of passage of the mandate of heaven. This is particularly evident in the long-drawn-out decline and fall of the Qing dynasty and the subsequent struggle for power between aspirant successor regimes, culminating in the CCP victory in 1949.

During the decades that followed the defeat of the Qing by the British in the first Opium War (1839–42), the Manchus were beset by both foreign invaders and domestic rebels. The dynasty's initial response was to rearm on traditional lines, but this proved ineffective. Regional loyalists had to set up their own forces to supplement hapless imperial armies.[8] Finally, the dynasty embarked upon defense modernization, with sufficient success to ensure that the creator of the new army, Yuan Shikai, emerged as both the power broker who arranged the abdication of the last emperor in 1912 and the power holder who dominated early republican politics.[9] The era of the general as political leader had begun.

After the collapse of Yuan Shikai's ill-judged attempt to set up a new dynasty and the death of the would-be emperor himself shortly thereafter, China

---

5 See Chapter 3. In view of the participation of virtually every older member of the CCP leadership in armed struggle at some point in his career, the calculation of military representation on the CC is often a question of definition. The "Quarterly Chronicle" of the *CQ* (39. [July–Sept. 1969], 145) estimated it at about 40 percent, Ying-mao Kau (*CLG* [Fall–Winter 1972–3], 8) at 38 percent. Domes, on the other hand, has estimated PLA representation as 40.3 percent at the Eighth Congress and 50 percent at the Ninth; see Jürgen Domes, *The internal politics of China, 1949–1972*, 210.

6 See Table 2.

7 For the Qin-Han transition, see *CHOC*, 1.110–27; for the Sui-Tang one, see *CHOC*, 3. 143–68; for the Yuan-Ming, see *CHOC*, 7.44–106.

8 See *CHOC*, 11, ch. 4, and Philip A Kuhn, *Rebellion and its enemies in late imperial China: Militarization and social structure, 1796–1864*.

9 See *CHOC*, 11.383–8, 529–34, and *CHOC*, 12, ch. 4.

TABLE 2

Politburo named after CCP's Ninth Congress, April 1969

(Leaders named to the Politburo after the two sessions of the Eighth Congress in 1956 and 1958 appear in ordinary type; those added at the CC's Eleventh Plenum in 1966 appear in caps; those added after the Ninth Congress are in boldface.)

Standing committee: ranked	
Mao Zedong	Chairman
Lin Biao	Vice-chairman
Standing committee: unranked	
Chen Boda	Chair, CRG[a]
Zhou Enlai	Premier
Kang Sheng	Adviser, CRG
Full members: unranked	
Ye Qun	PLA
YE JIANYING	Marshal
Liu Bocheng	Marshal
Jiang Qing	Vice-chair, CRG
Zhu De	Marshal
Xu Shiyou	Gen.; CO Nanjing MR[a]; Chair, Jiangsu RevCom[a]
Chen Xilian	Gen.; CO Shenyang MR; Chair, Liaoning RevCom
Li Xiannian	Vice-premier
Li Zuopeng	Gen.; Navy Political Commissar
Wu Faxian	Gen.; Air Force CO
Zhang Chunqiao	Vice-chair, CRG; Chair, Shanghai RevCom
Qiu Huizuo	Gen.; Head, PLA Logistics
Yao Wenyuan	Member, CRG; Vice-chair, Shanghai RevCom
Huang Yongsheng	Gen.; PLA chief of staff
Dong Biwu	Vice-head of state
XIE FUZHI	Min. Public Security; Chair, Beijing RevCom
Alternates: unranked	
Ji Dengkui	Vice-chair, Henan RevCom
LI XUEFENG	Chair, Hebei RevCom
Li Desheng	Gen.; Chair, Anhui RevCom
Wang Dongxing	CO Central Bodyguard
Actual ranking[b]	
Mao Zedong	
Lin Biao	
Zhou Enlai	
Chen Boda	
Kang Sheng	
Jiang Qing	
Zhang Chunqiao	
Yao Wenyuan	

Note: (1) Of twenty-three members of the pre-GPCR Politburo, fourteen dropped. (2) Of sixteen new members since the GPCR started, ten = military. (3) Of twenty-five members of the new Politburo, twelve = military; of these, ten were on active service. This compares with seven out of twenty-six in the 1956–8 Politburo, of whom only two were on active service. Eighth CC: civil = 76.3%, PLA = 23.7%; ninth CC: civil = 52.5%, PLA = 47.5%. (4) Three men with provincial jobs in the pre-GPCR Politburo, eight in this one. Provincials in eighth CC = 37%; ninth CC = 58.6%.
[a] CRG = Cultural Revolution Group; MR = Military Region; RevCom – Revolutionary Committee.
[b] Derived from picture in *Zhongguo gongchandang dijiuci quanguo daibiao da hui (huace)* (Ninth Congress of the Chinese Communist Party [picture volume]).

entered the warlord era (1916–28), during which none of Yuan's erstwhile subordinates and rivals proved sufficiently powerful to take over his role.[10] But as control of China's nominal government in Beijing passed from one warlord to another, it became clear to the revolutionaries who had conspired to overthrow the Qing dynasty and then been thrust aside by Yuan that without military power of their own, they would remain helpless or beholden to the unreliable favors of a warlord. It was then that Sun Yat-sen turned to Moscow, and in 1924 his military aide, Chiang Kai-shek, set up the Whampoa Military Academy with Soviet advisers, in order to train officers for a revolutionary army loyal to the KMT (Guomindang).[11]

Had Sun lived longer, perhaps the reshaped KMT would have emerged as a powerful political organization able to subordinate its army to its purposes. But his death in 1925 unleashed a struggle for the succession, which was soon won by Chiang Kai-shek because of his military power base. Although the KMT played an important role when Chiang set up the Nationalist government in 1928, the army remained the ultimate source of power within his regime.[12]

On Moscow's orders, the newborn CCP collaborated with the KMT, and Communist officers and cadres served in the Northern Expedition that enabled Chiang to triumph over the warlords. But when Chiang turned on the CCP in 1927, it became clear to Mao Zedong, as it had become clear to Sun before him, that without its own military force, there was no future for a political movement in China. Political power grew out of the barrel of a gun.[13] On Jinggangshan and in the Jiangxi Soviet, he and his colleagues created the forces and developed the strategy that brought victory in the civil war with the KMT two decades later.[14]

There was a fundamental difference between what the CCP later called the People's Liberation Army (PLA) and Chiang Kai-shek's forces. Mao insisted that the Party should command the gun and that the gun must never be allowed to command the Party.[15] The PLA was not to be just another warlord army, or even a military-dominated party-army amalgam on the KMT model, but a revolutionary force led by the CCP in the service of a cause delineated by it.

But it was never quite that simple. Theoretical princples of Party control may be hard to enforce in the heat of battle when life or death rests on the decision of the military commander.[16] Military subordination may be

---

10 See CHOC, 12, ch. 6.   11 See CHOC, 12.540.
12 See Lloyd E. Eastman, The abortive revolution: China under Nationalist rule, 1927–1937.
13 Mao, SW, 2.224.   14 See CHOC, 13, ch. 4.   15 Mao, SW, 2.224.
16 During the anti-Japanese war, Peng Dehuai launched the Hundred Regiments campaign in clear defiance of the principles laid down by Mao on avoiding major offensives that carried no certainty of victory. In his memoirs, Peng admitted mistakes with respect to this campaign, including launching the offensive early without consulting the CC's MAC, but he cited a telegram from Mao as indicative of

impolitic to insist on if, like Mao, you rely on the support of the generals for your rise to power.[17] Mao's personal political power did indeed grow out of the barrel of the gun; his way of ensuring political control of the army was to retain his chairmanship of the CC's Military Affairs Commission (MAC) from 1935 until his death more than four decades later.

Moreover, when political triumph has been engineered by generals can they be denied the fruits of power? Not with impunity. When Gao Gang made his bid to be recognized as Mao's successor in the mid-1950s, he sought and found support from generals who, he argued, had been short-changed in the post-Liberation distribution of posts.[18] Although Gao Gang lost out, the Party leadership got the message. Lin Biao, one of the military men who seems to have been attracted by Gao's arguments, was quickly raised to the Politburo, and after the CCP's Eighth Congress in 1956, seven of the PLA's ten marshals emerged as members of that body.[19]

The importance of the military within the polity was further demonstrated at the Lushan Conference in 1959, when then Defense Minister Peng Dehuai implicitly challenged Mao's handling of the Great Leap Forward (GLF). Peng's willingness to stick his neck out can be attributed to a number of factors, but its significance is that only the current head of the military establishment had the institutional base from which to initiate an attack that impugned the Chairman's competence and thus his authority. The extent to which Mao felt threatened and outraged by an assault from within what he had always considered his stronghold can be gauged from the bitterness of his rebuttal; only by portraying the issue as a choice between himself and the turbulent defense minister did he force the other marshals to accept Peng's dismissal.[20]

Ironically, Peng Dehuai's disgrace led to an increase in the PLA's status within the polity. Peng's replacement as defense minister by Lin Biao, Mao's disciple from the early 1930s, gave the Chairman greater confidence in the military's loyalty to himself and his ideas. As Lin promoted the study of Mao

the Chairman's approval. In view of the shrill attacks made on Peng over this issue during the Cultural Revolution after the passage of a quarter of a century, it seems possible that this campaign may have been launched against Mao's wishes or at least against his better judgment, and that his approval had been forthcoming only to preserve a facade of unity. For Mao's views on strategy in the anti-Japanese war, see Mao, *SW*, 2.180–3, 227–32; for Peng Dehuai's version, see his *Memoirs of a Chinese Marshal*, 434–47.

17 See Raymond F. Wylie, *The emergence of Maoism: Mao Tse-tung, Ch'en Po-ta and the search for Chinese theory, 1935–1945*, 68–71.

18 See *CHOC*, 14.97–103.

19 The founder of the Ming dynasty, Zhu Yuanzhang, who came to power after long military campaigns, was careful to award noble titles to all his principal generals shortly after his proclamation as emperor; see *CHOC*, 7.105.

20 See *CHOC*, 14.311–22. The Kangxi emperor was not so fortunate; he had to fight an eight-year-long civil war to subdue the dynasty's three most powerful generals before consolidating the Qing regime in the late seventeenth century; Lawrence D. Kessler, *K'ang-hsi and the consolidation of Ch'ing rule, 1661–1684*, 74–90.

Zedong Thought and issued the first edition of the "little red book" of Mao quotations to the armed forces, the PLA was designated the exemplar even to the CCP.[21]

Thus when Mao launched his assault on the Party leadership at the outset of the Cultural Revolution, he could be confident that the other major revolutionary institution would support him. Later, when the Red Guards found the overthrow of provincial leaders harder than expected, Mao was able to call on the PLA to support the left. When the triumphant Red Guards fell to internecine warfare and many cities of China were the scenes of armed clashes, it was a general – Chen Zaidao in Wuhan in the summer of 1967 – who blew the whistle. Although Chen himself was disciplined, ultra-leftist cadres were also purged, and a year later Mao authorized the rustication of the Red Guards. The mass base of the Central Cultural Revolution Group was dissolved. The way was clear for the triumph of Lin Biao and his generals at the Ninth Congress.[22]

For Mao the issue must have seemed stark, even though among his colleagues he dismissed Soviet attacks on Chinas "military bureaucractic dictatorship" as not worth refuting.[23] All his life he had insisted on the primacy of the Party over the army; after his death, the prospect was that the army would dominate the Party. The CCP might go the way of the KMT. Could he accept this?

THE FALL OF LIN BIAO

The CCP's Ninth Congress should have signaled a return to some semblance of normalcy: Mao's "proletarian revolutionary line" reigned unchallenged, his enemies had been defeated, a new leadership was in place, and civil strife had been suppressed. Mao had heralded a "great victory" as early as October 1968, and in his political report to the Congress, Lin Biao proclaimed: "The victory of the Great Proletarian Cultural Revolution is very great indeed."[24] When discussing the future, Lin Biao talked of "continuing the revolution in the realm of the superstructure,"[25] that is, building the new society for which the Cultural Revolution had been launched. For the victors, if not for the victims when they were finally able to rewrite the histories, the Cultural Revolution was over. The year 1969 was meant to mark a new beginning after revolution, like the Liberation twenty years earlier.

But if this had been a "Congress of Victors," the calm it should have presaged was as short-lived as that after the CPSU's Seventeenth Congress in 1934 for

---

21 See *CHOC*, 14.335–42.   22 See Chapter 3.
23 At the First Plenum of the Ninth CC; see Wang Nianyi, *1949–1989 nian de Zhongguo: da dongluan de niandai* (China from 1949 to 1989: decade of great upheaval), 395.
24 *CB*, 880 (9 May 1969), 37.   25 Ibid., 34.

which that appellation was coined. Insofar as the Cultural Revolution meant a struggle for power among the elite to determine who had the right to shape the future, it was far from over, and indeed was soon to take an even more dangerous turn. There were three arenas: the reconstruction of the Party, the rebuilding of the state structure, and foreign affairs. Underlying all three was the specter of Bonapartism conjured up by Lin Biao's rise to power.

The reconstruction of the Party

In the absence of any properly constituted lower-level Party committees, delegates to the Ninth Congress had supposedly been chosen either by "consultation" between revolutionary committees and local "rebel" groups[26] or simply by directive from the higher levels.[27] Because the PLA dominated the revolutionary committees,[28] it was hardly surprising that the military were so much in evidence at the Congress. With the Congress resulting in many promotions for PLA officers, it was even less surprising that the process of provincial party construction reflected the prevailing power realities.

Mao had begun to call for the reconstruction of the Party as early as October 1967 with his "fifty character policy" statement, directing that party organs should be formed from advanced elements of the proletariat. At the new CC's First Plenum after the Ninth Congress, he repeated his call to revive the Party, But although the declared hope of the leadership was to rebuild from the bottom up, and in 1970 the CC publicized the party construction experience of Peking University, Beijing No. 27 Rolling Stock Plant, and the No. 17 State Cotton Mill in Shanghai as models,[29] Party branches proved difficult to set up.

By late 1969, the major effort had been transferred upward to the counties and municipalities, but even at this level progress was slow. In the year between November 1969 and November 1970, only 45 of the nation's 2,185 counties had set up Party committees. Presumably recognizing the futility of proceeding on these lines, the central leadership authorized the prior formation of provincial-level committees. The first was formed in Mao's home province, Hunan, in December 1970, with one Hua Guofeng as its first secretary, and by mid-August 1971 all twenty-nine provincial-level units were similarly

---

26 These were the organizations of blue-collar workers, the Red Guard groups having been disbanded.

27 Teaching and Research Office for CCP History of the [PLA] Political Academy, ed., *Zhongguo gongchandang liushi nian dashi jianjie* (A summary of the principal events in the 60 years of the Chinese Communist Party), 559.

28 Of twenty-nine provincial revolutionary committees, twenty-one were headed by PLA officers; Domes, *The internal politics of China*, 205.

29 Hao Mengbi and Duan Haoran, eds., *Zhongguo gongchandang liushi nian, xia* (Sixty years of the Chinese Communist Party, part 2), 610.

endowed, with the PLA well in evidence. The military had supplied twenty-two of the twenty-nine first secretaries and 62 percent of the cadres running the provincial secretariats.[30]

According to post–Cultural Revolution accounts, Party rebuilding resulted in the induction of many disruptive rebel elements and the exclusion of old officials. Although a prime focus of the continuing "purify the class ranks" campaign launched in May 1968 had been to exclude ultra-leftist elements, allegedly the net was cast far wider and the campaign was used against blameless cadres.[31] This in itself probably displeased Mao, who appears to have wanted to reeducate, rehabilitate, and reemploy experienced cadres as part of an effort to restore stability and unity. But the more pressing issue was the clear failure of Lin Biao and the PLA to accept his injunctions to help rebuild a civilian Party that would reestablish its control over army and nation.[32] Well before the formation of the last provincial Party committees, it must have been obvious that the PLA would dominate them as it dominated the provincial revolutionary committees. Moreover, Lin Biao was giving evidence of wanting to dominate the state structure at the center as well as in the provinces.

Rebuilding the state structure

On 8 March 1970, Mao gave his opinions on rebuilding the state structure. He advocated convening the Fourth National People's Congress, at which a revised state constitution would be agreed upon. The constitution would abolish the position of head of state. The following day the Politburo endorsed Mao's opinion, and on 16 March it formulated some principles regarding the NPC session and the constitution, which were submitted to the Chairman and endorsed by him. On 17 March, a central work conference met to flesh out what had been agreed on. But Lin Biao soon joined issue on the question of the office of head of state. On 11 April, he proposed in writing that Mao should resume the office of head of state, which he had ceded to the late Liu Shaoqi in 1959, otherwise "it would not be in accord with the psychology [*xinli zhuangtai*] of the people." The Chairman summarily rejected this suggestion, telling the Politburo on 12 April: "I cannot do this job again; this suggestion is inappropriate." At a Politburo conference toward the end of the month, Mao used a historical analogy from the period of the Three Kingdoms in the third century A.D. when stating for the third time that he would not take on the state chairmanship and that the post should be abolished.

30 See Domes, *The internal politics of China*, 215.
31 Hao and Duan, *Zhongguo gongchandang liushi nian, xia*, 608–11.
32 Philip Bridgham, "The fall of Lin Piao," *CQ*, 35 (July–September 1973), 429–30.

Yet Lin Biao persisted. Two of his military allies in the Politburo were on the constitution-drafting group: Wu Faxian, the air force head, and Li Zuopeng, the navy's chief commissar. In mid-May, Lin asked them to include a clause on the post of head of state, and despite a fourth disclaimer by Mao in mid-July that one should not create a post for the sake of a person, behind the scenes Lin Biao's wife, Ye Qun, kept promoting the idea with Lin's supporters. Ye asked Wu Faxian plaintively what Lin Biao would do if the state chairmanship were not reestablished, an indication of Lin's own interest in the post if Mao continued to decline it.[33]

Why would the Chairman's formally anointed successor in the Party press this issue in the teeth of Mao's opposition? Why would he want a ceremonial post with no more prestige than its occupant's status within the Party? Philip Bridgham has argued that Lin was dismayed that the new constitution would leave him junior in governmental status to Premier Zhou Enlai, in whose cabinet he was a vice-premier and minister of defense, and at the implication that the Chairman was now contemplating a joint leadership of Lin and Zhou to succeed him.[34] It can also be argued that Mao's tenure in the state chairmanship had conferred a certain aura on it, certainly a status senior to the premier's, and that Liu Shaoqi's tenure in the post before the Cultural Revolution had shown that it guaranteed considerable publicity, as well as exposure in the international arena.

The key to Lin Biao's behavior in this matter, however, is almost certainly a deep sense of insecurity, probably exacerbated by the relative isolation to which illness and temperament confined him.[35] He had emerged as Mao's principal colleague as early as 1966, but he still required the reassurance, never granted to Liu Shaoqi, of being named successor in the Party constitution. Now he sought the further reassurance of being named head of state. Personal psychology aside, this insecurity probably stemmed in part from an uneasy consciousness that the manner in which he had risen to power was illegitimate and was bitterly resented by survivors of the Cultural Revolution among his generation of leaders. Even this would have mattered little had he had total confidence in Mao's backing. He was surely unnerved by Mao's suggestion

---

33 Wang, *Da dongluan de niandai*, 392–4; Hao and Duan, *Zhongguo gongchandang liushi nian*, 613.

34 Bridgham, "The fall of Lin Piao," 432–3.

35 See Zhang Yunsheng, *Maojiawan jishi* (An on-the-spot report on Maojiawan), passim. Zhang was one of Lin Biao's secretaries from 19 August 1966 until 17 November 1970. Lin apparently feared light, wind, water, and cold and hated to sweat. He did not take baths and did not eat fruit. He insisted that his accommodation should be kept at a constant 21°C (about 70°F), with no greater variation than half a degree. (Ye Qun liked her room temperature to be 18°C!) But probably the most debilitating aspect of Lin's condition, as far as carrying out his duties was concerned, was his inability or refusal to read documents, with the result that his secretaries had to select and summarize from the mass of paper that reached his office as much as they could read to him in 30 minutes. Ibid., 8–12; Wang, *Da dongluan de niandai*, 373–5, 377.

to him that since he (Lin) was also old, he, too, should have a successor, and that Zhang Chunqiao would be a good candidate;[36] and as the documents circulated after Lin's fall indicate, he seems to have viewed Mao as someone always ready to knife his closest associates in the back:

> Today he uses sweet words and honeyed talk to those whom he entices, and tomorrow puts them to death for fabricated crimes.... Looking back at the history of the past few decades, [do you see] anyone whom he had supported initially who has not finally been handed a political death sentence?... His former secretaries have either committed suicide or been arrested. His few close comrades-in-arms or trusted aides have also been sent to prison by him.[37]

Why, then, did Lin Biao defy Mao so blatantly? Possibly he felt that the Chairman might relent; possibly he wanted to use the issue as a litmus test of Mao's attitude toward himself. Or possibly, with his military colleagues grouped around him, he now felt strong enough to force Mao to concede; after all, Mao had been dependent upon the PLA for the success of the Red Guards, and later the generals' anxieties had helped compel Mao to suppress them. Could not the dominant role of generals within the Politburo be used to promote the defense minister's interests?

Moreover, Lin Biao had another important ally in his quest for status: Chen Boda, Mao's longtime ideological adviser and onetime political secretary.[38] Chen had headed the Central Cultural Revolution Group from its creation in the spring of 1966, a confirmation of his closeness to the Chairman, and he soon rose to the fourth position in the leadership under Mao, Lin, and Zhou Enlai, a ranking confirmed by pictures taken at the Ninth Congress. Yet, a year later, Chen, after years of loyal service to Mao, had chosen to support Lin Biao in defiance of the Chairman's repeatedly stated views.

One explanation is that the dissolution of the Cultural Revolution Group in late 1969 had deprived Chen of a starring role in the post–Ninth Congress constellation, and that he may have felt threatened by the campaign against ultra-leftism.[39] Equally, the crumbling of the original coalition that backed Mao at the outset of the Cultural Revolution under the impact of events of 1966–9 may have left Chen feeling isolated. The Shanghai leftists Zhang Chunqiao and Yao Wenyuan were linked through Jiang Qing (Madame Mao) to the Chairman; indeed, the youthful Yao seemed to have replaced Chen Boda as the favored bearer of Mao's message. Yet, at the outset of the Cultural

36 Ibid., 387–8.
37 Michael Y. M. Kau, *The Lin Piao affair: Power politics and military coup*, 87. These words were probably written by Lin Biao's son, but they clearly reflect the knowledge and experience of the older man.
38 For Mao's indebtedness to Chen Boda, see Wylie, *The emergence of Maoism*, passim.
39 Bridgham, "The fall of Lin Piao," 432.

Revolution, Zhang, Yao, and even Jiang Qing had been Chen's subordinates in the Cultural Revolution Group. In preparation for the Ninth Congress, Chen had originally been chosen as the principal drafter of Lin Biao's political report, with Zhang and Yao as his aides; but when Chen proved unable to produce a satisfactory draft in time, Zhang and Yao took over the task, under the supervision of Kang Sheng. Kang, Mao's longtime aide in the internal security field, also had close ties to his fellow provincial Jiang Qing, and Chen appears to have been jealous of Kang's connections.[40]

Lin Biao, on the other hand, had consolidated his position on a PLA base and no longer seemed to need the support of the leftists. Indeed, Lin and his followers and Jiang Qing and hers were increasingly divided into rival camps; and whereas Lin may have had long-term worries about the security of his role, he seems to have had excessive confidence that in the short run he could dominate Jiang's clique. Perhaps Chen Boda agreed and, looking to the future, thought his best prospect was to offer to perform for Lin Biao the same role he had previously performed for Mao.[41] The decision was to prove disastrous for Chen's career.

The struggle over the state chairmanship came to a head at the Ninth CC's Second Plenum, held at the ill-starred Lushan mountain resort from 23 August to 6 September 1970. Once again, Mao was locked in struggle with a defense minister, although this time he was not sure enough of his own strength or the minister's discipline to risk a direct confrontation at this stage.

On the eve of the plenum, 22 August, the Politburo Standing Committee, consisting of Mao, Lin Biao, Zhou Enlai, Chen Boda, and Kang Sheng, met to agree on the main themes of the plenum. Mao pointedly stressed the need for unity and the avoidance of factionalism, his habitual device when seeking to undercut opposition.[42] But Lin Biao and Chen Boda again proposed the retention of the state chairmanship and urged Mao to assume it. Mao refused once more but pointedly added that whoever wanted to take on the job should do so.[43]

40 See Zhong Kan, *Kang Sheng pingzhuan* (A critical biography of Kang Sheng), 15–16, 146–7. For Chen Boda's jealousy of Kang Sheng, see Zhang, *Maojiawan jishi*, 190–2; for Chen's problems with the report for the Ninth Congress, see ibid., 210–11, and "Wang, *Da dongluan de niandai* 387. According to the latter source, Chen Boda, miffed, continued working on his own draft, but it was the Zhang–Yao one that Mao, after several revisions, eventually approved. Lin Biao was apparently interested only in Mao's input and the final version of the report.

41 At his trial in the winter of 1980–1, Chen Boda said only that "after he learned of the power struggle between Lin Biao and Jiang Qing, he sympathized with Lin Biao"; see *A great trial in Chinese history*, 116. For the development of rival camps and the confidence of Lin's side, see Zhang, *Maojiawan jishi*, 382–9, and Wang, *Da dongluan de niandai*, 382–8.

42 See Mao's behavior at the 1959 Lushan Conference; see Roderick MacFarquhar, *The origins of the Cultural Revolution*, 2.220.

43 Hao and Duan, *Zhongguo gongchandang liushi nian*, 613–14.

The plenum was opened the next day by Zhou Enlai, who listed the agenda as the revision of the state constitution, the national economic plan, and war preparedness. Unexpectedly, and without clearing his remarks with Mao in advance,[44] Lin Biao intervened to express his conviction that it was extremely important for the new constitution to express Mao's role as the great leader, head of state (*guojia yuanshou*), and supreme commander, as well as the guiding role of Mao Zedong Thought as the national ideology. Implicitly, he was threatening the opponents of retaining the state chairmanship with accusations of being anti-Mao.[45]

As in the past, Lin was stressing Mao's transcendent genius and role in order to display his own devotion and thus achieve his own ends, a strategy that Mao appears to have been aware of and uncomfortable with even from the beginning of the Cultural Revolution.[46] But for most of the 255 CC members present who were not in the know, Lin Biao was giving the opening, keynote address on behalf of the central leadership, and they were hardly likely to express opposition. His wife, Ye Qun, sought to press home this advantage, urging Lin's PLA allies Wu Faxian, Li Zuopeng, and Qiu Huizuo, the chief of logistics, to speak up in support and to lobby CC members from their own arm of the services. Another PLA supporter, Chief of Staff Huang Yongsheng, was telephoned in Beijing and informed of Lin's demarche.[47] At a Politburo meeting held that evening to discuss the economic plan, Wu Faxian proposed revising the following day's arrangements so that the plenary session could listen to a tape recording of Lin's speech and discuss it. That night, without formal authorization, Chen Boda was busy drafting a clause on the state chairmanship for the constitution and collecting quotations on the theory of genius.[48]

It is not clear whether Mao attended the Politburo session on the evening of 23 August – presumably not – but Wu Faxian's proposal was accepted and the plenum listened to the Lin Biao tape the following morning. On the afternoon of 24 August, after agreeing on their plan of action, Chen Boda, Ye Qun, Wu Faxian, Li Zuopeng, and Qiu Huizuo divided up and spoke in favor of the Lin line at the sessions of the North China, Central-South, Southwest, and Northwest regional groups. They distributed a selection of quotations from Engels, Lenin, and Mao on the theory of genius to bolster Lin's position, and

44 Gao Gao and Yan Jiaqi, *"Wenhua da geming" shinian shi*, 1966–1976 (A history of the ten years of the "Great Cultural Revolution," 1966–1976), 348.
45 Ibid., 614.
46 See Mao's letter of 8 July 1966 to Jiang Qing in *CLG*, 6.2 (Summer 1973), 96–9. Later that year, in a speech to the Military Academy devoted to the theme of raising the study of Mao's writings to a new stage, Lin Biao praised the Chairman as the "greatest talent of the present era" and urged everyone studying Marxism–Leninism to devote 99 percent of their effort to his works; see *I&S*, 8.6 (March 1972), 75–9.
47 Hao and Duan, *Zhongguo gongchandang liushi nian*, 614.
48 Teaching and Research Office for CCP History, *Zhongguo gongchandang lishi nian dashi jianjie*, 561–2.

Chen Boda told the North China group that anyone opposing Mao's assumption of the state chairmanship was opposing the concept of Mao as a genius. Reports of their remarks were printed in the group bulletins and distributed. No one at the group meetings suggested Lin Biao for head of state.[49]

Mao, it was later claimed, was well aware that Lin's tactic was for the CC to agree that the new constitution should retain the state chairmanship and then to take the position himself if Mao persisted in refusing it.[50] If so, then Mao's remark at the Politburo Standing Committee meeting on the eve of the plenum was perhaps a provocation, designed to suggest to Lin that Mao's real objection was not to the post but to occupying it himself. Thus Lin and his supporters would be encouraged to promote the state chairmanship proposal and, given enough rope, would hang themselves.

Certainly Mao acted speedily when the speeches of Lin's supporters in the regional groups were brought to his attention by Jiang Qing and Zhang Chunqiao on 25 August, an action Mao later described as his wife's meritorious service against Lin. Jiang and Zhang, whose political base outside Shanghai had crumbled with the rustication of the Red Guards and the suppression of civil strife, presumably had no wish to see Lin Biao's already formidable power and status increased further. Indeed, by now, their own hopes of inheriting any portions of Mao's mantle clearly depended on the erosion of Lin Biao's position, and Zhang Chunqiao had earlier clashed with Wu Faxian on the Lin program in a group discussion.[51]

Mao must have realized that Lin's supporters were moving so fast that the plenum might be jockeyed into supporting the state chairmanship proposal if he did not declare himself. Even Wang Hongwen, a close follower of Zhang Chunqiao and the latter's deputy in Shanghai, was sufficiently enthused or naive to trumpet the praises of Lin Biao's keynote speech in the Shanghai caucus and was preparing to repeat the performance before the East China group.[52] In the key North China group, a man as close to Mao as Wang Dongxing was persuaded by Chen Boda's rhetoric. So, later on 25 August, Mao called the Politburo Standing Committee into session, an expanded meeting, presumably in order to allow the Chairman to pack it with additional supporters such as his wife and Zhang Chunqiao. was decided that discussion of Lin Biao's speech in the group sessions should cease forthwith, and the

49 Hu Hua, ed., *Zhongguo shehuizhuyi geming he jianshe shi jiangyi* (Teaching materials on the history of China's socialist revolution and construction), 300; Teaching and Research Office for CCP History, *Zhongguo gongchandang liushi nian dashi jianjie*, 562; Gao and Yan, "*Wenhua da geming*" *shinian shi*, 348; Hao and Duan, *Zhongguo gongchandang liushi nian*, 614. For quotations from these speeches, see ibid., 614–15, n. 1; Wang, *Da dongluan de niandai*, 398–9.

50 Hao and Duan, *Zhongguo gongchandang liushi nian*, 615–16.

51 Ibid., 616; Wang, *Da dongluan de niandai*, 402.

52 Gao and Yan, "*Wenhua da geming*" *shinian shi*, 349. After Mao's intervention, Wang hastily changed his speech of approval into a criticism of Chen Boda!

bulletin of the North China group with Chen Boda's offending remarks was recalled. Chen was ordered to make a self-criticism.[53]

Mao set the tone for a counterattack by circulating, on 31 August, "A few of my opinions," a document in which he exposed his erstwhile ideological adviser's "bourgeois idealism" and accused him of rumor-mongering and sophistry. Mao's broadside provided ammunition for the criticism of Chen, Wu Faxian, and Lin's other supporters in group sessions.[54] Only Chen Boda, however, was hounded out of office, perhaps because he could be credibly accused of being the fount of Lin's theoretical position. Probably more important, his disgrace did not threaten Lin directly, as the dismissal of one of his PLA allies would have done. Mao knew Lin Biao's power and, as he later admitted, he was not yet ready to confront him. He spoke privately to Lin but told other leaders that his deputy had to be protected.[55]

Even so, Lin Biao had got the real message. In a brief two and a half days,[56] Lin's attempt to obtain the state chairmanship had been defeated, an awesome reminder of Mao's power to manipulate the Party elite. Before leaving Lushan after the close of the plenum on 6 September, Lin summed up the lesson he had learned to Wu Faxian: "Doing things in the civilian manner didn't work; using armed force will work."[57]

Disagreement over foreign policy

The issues of Party building and the reconstruction of state institutions basically were about power. There also seems to have been one issue of policy dividing Mao and Lin, although it is given less attention in Chinese sources: the opening to America. This is dealt with in detail in CHOC 15,[58] and it will only be sketched here.

The origins of the startling turnabout in Sino-American relations that brought President Nixon to China in February 1972 are well known. The bloody reverse sustained by the Chinese in a frontier clash with Soviet troops on Zhenbao (Damansky) Island in the Ussuri River in March 1969 clearly aroused concern in Beijing that Moscow was going to escalate what had hitherto been a series of minor confrontations. There was subsequently a series of clashes on the northwestern frontier, a particularly serious one occurring in Xinjiang in August, and rumors began to emanate from Eastern European

53 Teaching and Research Office for CCP History, *Zhongguo gongchandang lishi nian dashi jianjie*, 562.
54 Hao and Duan, *Zhongguo gongchandang liushi nian*, 616; a full text of Mao's remarks is in Wang, *Da dongluan de niandai*, 403–4.
55 Gao and Yan, *"Wenhua da geming" shinian shi*, 349–50.
56 That is, from 23 August through noon on 23 August; ibid., 349.
57 *"Gao wenti buxing, gao wuti xing;* see Hu, *Zhongguo shehuizhuyi geming he jianshe shi jiangyi*, 302.
58 See *CHOC*, 15, Chapter 5.

sources that the Russians were sounding out their allies about a "surgical strike" against Chinese nuclear weapons installations.

The immediate tension was somewhat defused by the brief meeting between Premier Kosygin and Premier Zhou Enlai at Beijing airport on 11 September, but the Chinese clearly continued to take the danger very seriously. In the aftermath of the Ussuri River clash, the Beijing press had already drawn an analogy with the Soviet invasion of Czechoslovakia in the summer of 1968, a move the Russians had subsequently justified with the "Brezhnev doctrine," which effectively allowed the Soviet Union to overthrow any Communist government of which it did not approve. The question for the Chinese leadership was how to achieve national security in these new circumstances.

It is conceivable that the clash on Zhenbao Island began with an ambush by the Chinese, and that this was intended by Lin Biao to provoke a frontier flare-up in order to impress upon delegates to the CCP's Ninth Congress the importance of the heroic PLA, and so justify the role it was assuming within the Party.[59] Whether or not this is correct, the lesson learned by Mao and Zhou Enlai from the clashes of 1969 was almost certainly the opposite: The Soviet Union was embarked on a far tougher line on the border,[60] and, however determined in border clashes, the PLA probably would be incapable of defending China effectively if the Soviet Union were to launch a major attack. Hence the receptivity of Beijing to the overtures of the Nixon administration. An opening to Washington could undermine the calculations of the Russians as to the impunity with which they could attack China. Indeed, even before the forging of the Sino-American link, the Nixon administration had indicated that Moscow could not assume its benevolent neutrality in the event of Soviet aggression.[61] The original Sino-Soviet rift derived in large measure from Chinese anger at Soviet-American détente; Chinese denunciations of the revisionism of the CPSU leadership began after the Russians and the Americans had signed the partial test ban treaty; the Cultural Revolution had been launched in order to prevent the emergence of similar revisionism in China. It is hardly surprising, therefore, that the breakthrough in Sino-American relations would require a great deal of explanation for Chinese nurtured on a diet of ideological principle rather than realpolitik.[62]

59 A twenty-nine-year-old commander involved in the Zhenbao clash, Sun Yuguo, was introduced to the Ninth Congress by PLA Chief of Staff Huang Yongsheng, and was given an emotional welcome by Mao; see Mao's brief remarks in a collection of major speeches to the Ninth Congress available in the library of Harvard's Fairbank Center.

60 See, for instance, the estimate of a Chinese officer involved in the clashes as reported in Neville Maxwell, "The Chinese account of the 1969 fighting at Chenpao," *CQ*, 56 (October–December 1973), 734. See also *CHOC*, 15, ch. 3.

61 Henry Kissinger, *White House years*, 184.

62 See, for instance, the documents circulated within the Kunming Military Region in *Chinese Communist internal politics and foreign policy*, 115–45.

Lin Biao may well have felt revulsion at what looked like an Asian equivalent of the Nazi–Soviet pact. He may have reasoned that if China really could
not stand alone if threatened by both superpowers simultaneously, would it
not be better to come to terms with a revisionist Soviet Union rather than an
imperialist United States? Lin's position on this issue has never been fully clarified. He was later accused of "isolationism" and "great nation chauvinism,"[63]
which suggests that he opposed any link-up with the United States or the
Soviet Union[64] and argued that China was strong enough to protect itself.
Mao told Nixon and other foreign visitors that Lin Biao had opposed contacts
with America.[65]

If Mao were reporting accurately, it is easy to understand his motives. The
PLA would loom larger than ever in a China isolated and menaced. And
under conditions of national peril, the right of one of the great revolutionary
marshals to inherit the mantle of Mao could not be disputed. The arts of peace
and diplomacy, the province of Zhou Enlai, would seem less important.

Unfortunately for Lin, Mao felt he had to buy time with diplomacy, and on
7 October the New China News Agency (NCNA) announced that Sino-Soviet
border negotiations were about to begin. Yet Mao remained suspicious of
the Russians, and in mid-October the Politburo decided to heighten vigilance
immediately. On 17 October 1969, apparently acting on Mao's somber analysis
of the world situation, Lin issued his "Order No. 1," putting the PLA on
emergency alert and ordering the evacuation of cities.

Lin was resting in Suzhou at the time, in a house once owned by Madame
Chiang Kai-shek. According to the secretary who transmitted Lin's order
to Chief of Staff Huang Yongsheng in Beijing, the defense minister's concern was that the Russians might be preparing a surprise attack when the
PRC's guard was down because of the arrival of the Soviet negotiating mission. Mao was apparently sent a copy of the order for approval two hours
before Huang was sent his copy and evidently did not countermand it. Later
condemnation of Lin's order was probably at least partly due to contemporary
concern about the sharp reactions to it by the Russians, the Americans, and the
Taiwan regime; so obvious a preparation for war might have been used by the
Russians as an excuse for further military action on the border. After Lin was
disgraced, Mao was able to blame him for an action that was clearly sparked by
himself.[66]

63 Ibid., 132.   64 See CHOC, 15, ch. 3.
65 Kissinger, White House Years, 1061; NYT, 28 July 1972, quoted in Bridgham, "The fall of Lin Piao,"
    441–2. See also CHOC 15, ch. 5. Yet Lin Biao's secretary testifies that his late chief took virtually no
    interest in foreign affairs; Zhang, Maojiawan jishi, 329–33.
66 Ibid., 316–23; Zhonggong dangshi dashi nianbiao (A chronological table of major events in the history
    of the Chinese Communist Party), 372. Zhang's account gives a sobering revelation of how hurriedly
    members of the Chinese leadership took steps that might have resulted in war.

The border negotiations began on 20 October without mishap. Simultaneously, the Chinese and the Americans were initiating what Henry Kissinger later called an "intricate minuet"[67] as they cautiously probed through twenty years of hostility and suspicion. By the end of 1969, it was clear to the Americans that their signals, messages, and hints had borne fruit. Throughout 1970, as Lin Biao was campaigning to become head of state, Sino-American contacts grew. By 21 April 1971, when Zhou Enlai invited Kissinger to visit Beijing,[68] Lin's civilian route to more power had proved a dead end, and he was launched upon a more perilous course.

"Throwing stones, mixing in sand, and digging up the cornerstone"

Lin Biao's decision to seize power by force was almost certainly triggered by his political rebuff at the Lushan Plenum, but its timing was probably determined by the relentless campaign that Mao waged against his associates after that meeting. During the autumn and winter of 1970–1, it must have become clear to the defense minister that if he did not act soon, he would be finished. Mao's actions seem almost provocative, as if he wanted to force Lin Biao to make a false move. If he did, he would court death.

The postplenum campaign against Chen Boda took a number of forms. First, there was the denigration of Chen himself, the gradual buildup of a campaign from November 1970 through April 1971 and beyond, which started from the premise that he was anti-Party and a sham Marxist. Simultaneously, senior cadres were told to study Marxism–Leninism and prescribed six books by Marx, Engels, and Lenin and five articles by Mao, the proclaimed objective being to enable them to distinguish materialism and idealism. In fact, Mao was hitting at Lin Biao, who had advocated shelving the study of the Marxist–Leninist classics and reducing the study of Mao's Thought to the recitation of quotations. Chen's crimes were investigated by Ye Jianying, who visited

---

The evacuation order probably had an additional advantage, if not motivation: to get senior cadres, potential threats to Lin Biao's power, out of Beijing. A number of marshals were dispersed along the Beijing–Guangzhou railway line: Chen Yi at Shijiazhuang, Nie Rongzhen at Handan, Xu Xiangqian at Kaifeng, Ye Jianying at Changsha, Liu Bocheng at Hankou, Zhu De and former chief planner Li Fuchun in Conghua county in greater Guangzhou. Some had probably lined up against Lin Biao at the recent Lushan plenum; all but Li were potential obstacles if he wanted to use military means to achieve power. For the dispersal process, see Nie Rongzhen, *Nie Rongzhen huiyi lu, xia* (The memoirs of Nie Rongzhen, part 3), 861–4. Ye Jianying was soon back in harness investigating Chen Boda; see the later discussion. The NCNA report on the Sino-Soviet negotiations is quoted in Kissinger, *White House years*, 186. See also *CHOC*, 15, ch. 3.

67 Kissinger, *White House years*, 187.
68 Ibid., 193, 684–703, 714. Kissinger speculates that an attempt by PRC fighter planes to intercept an American intelligence-gathering aircraft a hundred miles off the Chinese coast on 2 July, at a time when diplomatic relations were improving, may have been a reflection of an internal power struggle in Beijing; ibid., 697. In view of Lin Biao's close relationship with PLA Air Force Chief Wu Faxian, this seems a reasonable speculation.

Fujian, Guangdong, and Guangxi to look into his activities, and were made the excuse for a rectification campaign clearly designed to wean cadres from loyalty to Lin.[69]

Mao later described his tactics against Lin Biao and his followers as "throwing stones, mixing in sand, and digging up the cornerstone."[70] "Throwing stones" meant sniping at Lin's allies. At Lushan, Zhou Enlai had privately told Wu Faxian, Li Zuopeng, and Qiu Huizuo that they should make self-criticism to the CC. The day after the plenum ended, at Jiujiang airport at the foot of Lushan, Lin Biao posed for a souvenir snapshot with them and Huang Yongsheng, and discussed tactics with them and his wife. It was agreed that Wu's position had to be restored, Lin and Huang had to be protected, and that in response to Zhou's order, false self-criticisms would be made.[71]

But when the written self-criticisms appeared on Mao's desk the following month, he scribbled dissatisfied comments all over them. When the MAC called a conference of 143 officers on 9 January 1971, and Lin's allies neither criticized Chen Boda nor self-criticized despite Mao's repeated strictures, the Chairman expressed his displeasure by ordering the proceedings of the conference to be ignored. Finally, on 29 April, at a central meeting called to discuss progress in the anti–Chen Boda rectification campaign, Zhou Enlai accused Huang Yongsheng, Wu Faxian, Ye Qun, Li Zuopeng, and Qiu Huizuo of mistakes in political line and factionalism.[72]

"Mixing in sand" meant adding Mao loyalists to bodies otherwise dominated by Lin's people. Ji Dengkui, elected to alternate membership of the Politburo at the Ninth Congress, and a general, Zhang Caiqian, were appointed to the MAC's administrative group on 7 April 1971, to offset the power there of Huang Yongsheng and Wu Faxian. Mao had already taken other organizational measures to ensure his control of personnel and propaganda. On 6 November 1970, a new Central Organization and Propaganda Group, reporting directly to the Politburo, was set up to oversee the CC's Organization Department, the Central Party School, the *People's Daily*, the theoretical journal *Hongqi* (Red flag), the New China News Agency, the Central Broadcasting Bureau, the

69 The CC's first anti-Chen document, issued on 16 November 1970, already set out the main accusations against him: anti-Party, sham Marxist, careerist, and plotter. On 26 January 1971, the CC issued a collection of materials to document Chen's "crimes" throughout his career. Two CC notifications, on 21 February and 29 April, detailed how the movement to criticize Chen should be carried out. See Hao and Duan, *Zhongguo gongchandang liushi nian*, 617–18; Wang, *Da dongluan de niandai*, 406–9. For Ye's investigation, see *Yingsi lu: huainian Ye Jianying* (A record of contemplation: remembering Ye Jianying), 265, 294, 301–4.

70 "*Shuai shitou, shan shazi, wa qiangjiao*"; *CLG*, 5.5–4 (Fall–Winter 1972–3), 38; Hu, *Zhongguo shehuiyizhuyi he jianshe shi jiangyi*, 302.

71 Gao and Yan, "*Wenhua da geming*" *shinian shi*, 349–50. The photograph at Jiujiang is reproduced in Yao Ming-le, *The conspiracy and murder of Mao's heir*, 57.

72 Hao and Duan, *Zhongguo gongchandang liushi nian*, 619–20, Hu, *Zhongguo shehuizhuyi geming he jianshe shi jiangyi*, 302; *CLG*, 5.3–4 (Fall–Winter 1972–3), 38.

Guangming Daily, and a number of other organs. The group head was Kang Sheng, and its members were Jiang Qing, Zhang Chunqiao, Yao Wenyuan, Ji Dengkui, and a general, Li Desheng. Kang Sheng soon cried off because of illness and Li Desheng became first secretary of the new Anhui provincial Party committee in January 1971. Mao's wife and her Shanghai colleagues were left in charge, taking over what had once been Chen Boda's media empire,[73] thereby achieving a major national power base for the first time since the end of the Red Guard movement.[74]

"Digging up the cornerstone" meant reorganizing the Beijing Military Region. In an increasingly tense confrontation with his minister of defense, Mao had to be sure that the troops in charge of the capital were loyal to himself and not Lin Biao. On 16 December 1970, he called for a conference to explain why the Party committees of the North China region and the North China Military Region had allowed Chen Boda to become their backstage boss (*taishang huang*) when he had not been given the appropriate powers by the CC. Insofar as there may have been any justice in the accusation – and it is easier to picture the bookish Chen Boda as a surrogate for Lin Biao than as the *éminence grise* of a military unit – it probably only reflected the normal deference any sensible party official would pay to a member of the Politburo Standing Committee; it is hard to imagine so lofty an individual being quizzed about his credentials. No matter: For Mao, who himself disdained going through channels, any credible infraction of organizational discipline was grist to his mill.

Zhou Enlai called a North China conference on 22 December 1970, ostensibly to criticize Chen Boda's crimes and those of his imitators in the region. During the course of the month-long conference, the leadership of the Beijing Military Region was reorganized: Lin Biao's followers, the commander and the second political commissar, were reassigned, and the Thirty-eighth Army, thought to be loyal to the defense minister, transferred out.[75]

"571"; Lin Biao's abortive coup

According to subsequent testimonies, Lin Biao authorized the preparation of plans for a possible coup during a visit to Suzhou with his wife and son in February 1971. The planning for the coup was to be conducted by a small band of relatively junior officers led by his son, Lin Liguo, from his base in the air force. The precipitating events were presumably Mao's rebuff to Lin

73 *A great trial in Chinese history*, 226.
74 Hao and Duan, *Zhongguo gongchandang liushi nian*, 618.
75 Ibid., 618; Hu, *Zhongguo shehuizhuyi geming he jianshe shi jiangyi*, 302; Ying-mao Kau, "Introduction: The case against Lin Piao," *CLG*, 5.3–4 (Fall–Winter 1972–3), 12.

Biao's allies' stand at the recent MAC meeting and the reorganization of the PLA in the capital. How was Lin to respond? He evidently opted for attack as the only method of defense.

Perhaps the most extraordinary aspect of Lin's bid for power, apart from its ineptitude, was his demonstrated weakness in his own bailiwick. Despite his position as minister of defense, he did not rely on his Politburo allies at the head of various arms of the PLA. According to the evidence brought out at the trial of Lin Biao's surviving supporters in 1980–1, whatever else they did, Huang Yongsheng, Wu Faxian, Li Zuopeng, and Qiu Huizuo were not involved in any plot to assassinate Mao.[76]

Lin Liguo's formal position in the air force, which he owed to his father's influence, was deputy director of the General Office – a key bureau through which all paper flowed – and concurrently deputy chief of operations. According to the evidence of his chief, Wu Faxian, at his trial in 1980, from 6 July 1970, "everything concerning the Air Force was to be reported to Lin Liguo and everything of the Air Force should be put at his disposal and command."[77]

Lin Liguo formed his group of conspirators (see Table 3), known as the "joint fleet," from an investigation team Wu Faxian had authorized him to set up. Most members were thus officers of the PLA Air Force. (AF). Lin Liguo's "command unit" was drawn, apart from himself, mainly from the Nanjing Military Region, which controlled East China.

In February 1971, Lin Liguo picked up Yu Xinye, a deputy section chief in the PLA AF HQ, in Hangzhou, summoned a deputy director of the PLA AF HQ's general office, Zhou Yuchi, from Beijing to Shanghai, where between 20 and 24 March he plotted with them and Li Weixin, a deputy director of the Political Department of the PLA's Fourth Group in Nanjing, on the basis of his father's orders.

The discussions of the conspirators indicate an assessment of the political situation by the Lin family that the moment to strike was almost nigh, and that delay in a time of stability could allow civilian leaders to strengthen their positions; Mao was engaged in his habitual playing off of factions, building up Zhang Chunqiao to offset the defense minister.[78] Yet a peaceful transition to power seems not to have been ruled out even at this stage. A second possibility

---

76 See A great trial in Chinese history, 117–23. The following account of Lin Biao's plot has been put together from a number of sources, but virtually all are official or semiofficial versions, written by the victors or based on their evidence. In events so momentous as the demise of an heir apparent, there are many reasons why evidence should be doctored, and there can be no guarantee that if the CC's innermost archives are one day opened, another version will not emerge. It still seems worthwhile to spell out in detail the currently most believable version of the Lin Biao affair in order to depict the nature of Chinese politics of the time. Any revised version is likely only to underline the way in which the fate of China was settled by the ambitions and intrigues of a very small group of desperate leaders and their families.

77 Ibid., 93.   78 Kau, The Lin Piao affair, 90–1.

TABLE 3
Lin Biao's team: Allies and conspirators

Lin Biao[a]
Ye Qun[a]
Allies

Politburo members
Huang Yongsheng, PLA chief of staff[b]
Wu Faxian, PLA AF CO[b]
Li Zuopeng, PLA Navy, 1st political commissar[b]
Qiu Huizuo, director, PLA logistics, dept.[b]
Others
Zheng Weishan, acting CO, Beijing MR?)

Conspirators

"Joint Fleet"
Lin Liguo, deputy director, PLA AF General Office[a]
Wang Weiguo, political commissar, PLA AF 4th Group, Nanjing
Chen Liyun, political commissar, PLA AF 5th Group, Zhejiang
Zhou Jianping, deputy CO, PLA AF Nanjing units
Jiang Tengjiao, former political commissar, PLA AF, Nanjing[b]
Zhou Yuchi, deputy director, general office PLA AF, Beijing[c]
Hu Ping, deputy chief of staff, PLA AF, Beijing
Guan Guanglie, political commissar, PLA unit 0190
Li Weixin, deputy director, PLA AF 4th Group political Dept.
Liu Beifeng, PLA AF HQ CCP office[a]
Lu Min, director, PLA AF Operations Dept., Beijing
Wang Fei, deputy chief of staff, PLA AF, Beijing
Yu Xinye, deputy section chief, PLA AF HQ, Beijing[a]

[a] Killed in an air crash in Mongolia.
[b] Tried in 1980–1.
[c] Committed suicide after the failure of 571.

was that Lin would be thrown out. Again, surprisingly, in view of events at the Second Plenum and since, some conspirators felt this was unlikely in the next three years. But Lin Liguo at least knew the perils of such forecasts; "Nothing is predictable. The Chairman commands such high prestige that he need only utter one sentence to remove anybody he chooses." When Yu Xinye objected that Lin Biao had been Mao's personal choice, Lin Liguo reminded him dryly that Liu Shaoqi had been accorded the same honor.[79]

The third option for Lin Biao was to assume power "ahead of time." Two alternative scenarios were discussed: to get rid of his rivals, principally Zhang Chunqiao, and to get rid of Mao himself. The conspirators expressed no qualms about the latter act but were concerned as to how it could be presented to the nation without negative repercussions. Zhou Yuchi suggested that the blame for Mao's murder could be put on others, even Jiang Qing, but added that politically, Lin "would pay a very high price for resorting to this alternative." So the decision was taken to strive for Lin's peaceful transition to power, but to make preparations for a coup.[80]

Lin Liguo decided to code-name the plot "571," because the Chinese words for these numbers (*wuqiyi*) are a homonym for armed uprising (*wu [zhuang] qiyi*). Mao was referred to as "B-52." As initially discussed, the plot involved only arresting Zhang Chunqiao and Yao Wenyuan. The idea of assassinating Mao seems to have been devised by Yu Xinye late in the day,[81] perhaps in response to the Chairman's activities in southern China.

No actions of the Chairman could have been better calculated to have alarmed Lin Biao than the comments Mao made during his whistle-stop tour from mid-August to mid-September 1971. His principal visits were to Wuhan, Changsha, and Nanchang, and he met Party and PLA officials from Hubei, Henan, Hunan, Guangdong, Guangxi, Jiangsu, and Fujian.[82] Talking to them, he described the activities of Lin Biao's allies at the Second Plenum as a "two-line struggle," thus equating it with the cases of Liu Shaoqi, Peng Dehuai, Gao Gang, and other anathematized former leaders.

At first, refraining from blaming Lin Biao by name, Mao accused his henchmen of "planned, organized, and programmed" "surprise attacks and underground activities" at the Second Plenum. However, no one could have failed to realize his real target when he remarked: "A certain person was very anxious to become state chairman, to split the Party, and to seize power." When he finally mentioned Lin's name it was more in sorrow than in anger, but the defense minister could not have been deceived: "This time, to protect Vice-Chairman Lin, no conclusions concerning individuals were reached. But, of course, he must take some of the responsibility. What should we do with these people?"[83]

Mao's likely answer to his own question could not have been in doubt in the Lin household. Equally interesting, however, was the clear indication in the Chairman's remarks of why he was pursuing his struggle against his anointed successor. At one point he criticized the practice of local Party committees taking their decisions to PLA Party committees for approval. At another, he modified his own earlier slogan that "the whole country should learn from the PLA" by adding on "the PLA should learn from the people of the whole nation."[84] It was the threat of military domination of the polity that moved Mao.

The Chairman must have known and intended that his remarks would soon reach Lin Biao. They were, in fact, reported to Navy Commissar Li Zuopeng, who informed Chief of Staff Huang Yongsheng and Logistics Director Qiu Huizuo on 6 September. Huang immediately telephoned Ye Qun, who was

---

80 Ibid., 92–3.   81 Ibid., 93–5.
82 Hao and Duan, *Zhongguo gongchandang liushi nian*, 621.
83 Kau, *The Lin Piao affair*, 57–61.   84 Ibid, 64.

with her husband and son at the seaside resort Beidaihe. Two days later, Lin Biao issued Lin Liguo with what was allegedly his authorization to activate the plan for a coup: "Expect you to act according to the order transmitted by Comrades Liguo [Lin Liguo] and Yuchi [Zhou Yuchi]." The same day, Lin Liguo left for Beijing to make the final arrangements for Mao's assassination.[85]

From 8 to 11 September, Lin Liguo and members of his joint fleet discussed a number of methods for killing Mao as his special train journeyed north back to the capital: attacking the train with flame throwers, 40-mm rocket guns, or 100-mm antiaircraft guns; dynamiting a bridge the train had to cross; bombing the train from the air; or, less dramatic but perhaps surer, face-to-face assassination by pistol.[86]

All these plans were to prove fruitless. While the conspirators were learning about Mao's activities, the Chairman had got wind in Nanchang at the end of August that Lin Biao might be up to no good.[87] On his return journey, therefore, Mao made sudden departures and curtailed stopovers, leaving Shanghai far sooner than expected, heading back to Beijing on 11 September, passing through the places where his special train might have been intercepted before the plotters were ready.[88] On the afternoon of 12 September, he stopped the train at Fengtai station just outside Beijing and held a two-hour conference with senior military and civilian officials based in the capital, before pulling into the main station later that evening.[89] There is no indication that Mao's precipitate action was triggered by any knowledge of a specific plot, let alone its details. Possibly he had acted on an instinct for survival honed by long years of guerrilla warfare. Whatever the motives, his run for cover precipitated the crisis the Chinese now refer to as the "13 September Incident" (jiuyisan shijian).

The 13 September Incident

When Lin Liguo learned the Chairman had escaped death, he immediately put into high gear a plan to set up a rival regime in Guangdong, which Lin

---

85 A great trial in Chinese history, 96–97. According to a much later account based on an interview with Lin Biao's daughter, Lin Doudou; Huang telephoned on 5 September, but since she was not in Beidaihe when the call came through and the trial version tells of telephone logs, 6 September seems the more likely date for Huang's call; see "Lin Doudou who lives in the shadow of history," Huaqiao ribao (Overseas Chinese news), 15 June 1988, 3. However, one recent mainland history states that Lin Liguo was informed directly by one of the participants in Mao's meetings late on the night of 5 September; see Hao and Duan, Zhongguo gongchandang liushi nian, 621.

86 A great trial in Chinese history, 97.

87 Hao and Duan, Zhongguo gongchandang liushi nian, 622; "Lin Doudou who lives in the shadow of history."

88 Gao and Yan, "Wenhua da geming" shinian shi, 379–80.

89 Hu Hua, Zhongguo shehuizhuyi geming he jianshe shi jiangyi, 309.

Biao and Ye Qun had been considering for some time; it had been prepared simultaneously with the assassination plot. It was agreed that Lin and Ye would fly south on 13 September, leaving Beidaihe at 8:00 A.M., and expect to rendezvous in Guangzhou with Lin's top military allies – Huang Yongsheng, Wu Faxian, Li Zuopeng, and Qiu Huizuo – and Lin Liguo's coconspirators. After completing arrangements in Beijing, Lin Liguo flew to Shanhaiguan, the airport for Beidaihe, in one of China's few British-built Tridents, secretly commandeered through his network of air force supporters, to supervise the evacuation of his parents.[90] He would perhaps have succeeded, but for the intervention of his sister, Lin Liheng.

Lin Liheng was better known by her nickname Doudou (Bean Curd) which her father had given her because of his fondness for that food. Doudou was very close to Lin Biao but was treated brutally by her mother Ye Qun, whom both she and her brother called "Director Ye!"[91] Driven to distraction, Doudou began to believe that Ye Qun could not possibly be her real mother, and the doctor who had delivered her in Yan'an had to be summoned to testify that Ye was.[92] On one occasion, Doudou had tried to commit suicide. Director Ye's reaction was "Let her die"; Doudou's father was not told.[93]

On 6 September, Lin Doudou had been summoned to Beidaihe from Beijing by her brother on the pretext that her father was ill. When she arrived, Lin Liguo had informed her of Mao's activities in southern China, indicated that Lin Biao's back was against the wall and candidly revealed the three options being considered: to kill Mao; to set up a rival government in Guangdong; or to flee to the Soviet Union. Doudou argued with her brother for two days, rejecting all three courses, suggesting that Lin Biao should simply retire from the political limelight like China's senior soldier, Zhu De.[94]

According to her account, Doudou's sole concern was her fathers safety. She encouraged the servants to eavesdrop on Lin Biao, Ye Qun, and Lin Liguo to find out what they were up to; on 8 September, after her brother had left

---

90 Gao and Yan, "*Wenhua da geming*" *shinian shi*, 381–3.

91 "Lin Doudou who lives in the shadow of history," *Huaqiao ribao*, 14 June 1988. According to one admittedly suspect source, Lin Doudou was born in 1941 in the Soviet Union. This would have been toward the end of Lin Biao's three-year period of hospitalization there; see Yao, *The conspiracy and murder of Mao's heir*, 130.

92 "Lin Doudou who lives in the shadow of history," *Huaqiao ribao*, 14 June 1988. It may have been this story that was the ultimate source for the assertions by Jaap van Ginneken that Doudou was the child of Lin Biao's first wife, Liu Ximing, and that Ye and Lin Biao were not married until 1960; van Ginnekan, Jaap, *The rise and fall of Lin Piao*, 263, 272. The date of Ye's marriage so Lin Biao is uncertain; see Klein and Clark, *A biographic dictionary of Chinese communism, 1921–1965*, 1. 567; but one resident of Yan'an in the mid-1940s has confirmed that they were married then (private communication). For a longer account of Doudou's unhappy position in the Lin–Ye household, see Zhang, *Maojiawan jishi*, 256–92, 429. Despite Zhang's critical account of Ye's activities, he asserts that working for her was slightly better than working for Jiang Qing; ibid., 429.

93 *Huaqiao ribao*, 15 June 1988.   94 Ibid.

for Beijing, she got word to the detachment of PLA Unit 8341 – the guards regiment assigned to CCP leaders – stationed by her parents' house, to be sure to protect Lin Biao whatever happened.[95] Despite Doudou's agitated behavior, no one had the courage to intervene, especially because Ye Qun had been putting it about that her daughter was distraught because she was in love; indeed, she was on the verge of becoming formally engaged.[96]

The engagement celebrations took place on the afternoon of 12 September, beginning before Lin Liguo's return from Beijing. On his arrival, he told his sister he had come especially for the occasion, but aroused her suspicions by immediately hurrying off to confer with his parents. At about 10:20 P.M. Doudou went personally to alert the CO of Unit 8341. This time the commander telephoned Beijing.[97]

When the report reached Premier Zhou Enlai at about 10:30 P.M., he was chairing a meeting at the Great Hall of the People to discuss his government report to the Fourth NPC session. He immediately telephoned Wu Faxian and Li Zuopeng to check whether or not there was a Trident at Shanhaiguan airfield.

While all this was going on, Ye Qun had spent a quiet hour gossiping on the telephone with Madame Qiu Huizuo. Alerted via Lin Liguo's network to Zhou's inquiries, Ye decided to try to disarm suspicion. At 11:30 P.M. she telephoned the premier to tell him of the Lin family's interest in leaving Beidaihe to go to a hot-springs resort. In response to the premier's queries, she said they wanted to go by air rather than rail, but had not arranged a plane. Zhou warned that the weather was currently bad and that he would discuss the Lins' proposed air journey with Wu Faxian.[98]

Once Ye was off the line, Zhou again called Wu Faxian and Li Zuopeng, who, as senior naval officer, was in charge of the Shanhaiguan naval air base, and ordered that the Trident was not to be allowed to take off unless permission was jointly given by Zhou, Li, Huang Yongsheng, and Wu Faxian. In Beidaihe, Ye sprang into action. With Lin Liguo, she aroused Lin Biao, who had taken a sleeping pill, telling him that people were coming to arrest him. Papers were burned, and the family got into their car and left for the airport. The Unit 8341

---

95 Ibid., 15 and 16 June 1988.   96 Gao and Yan, "*Wenhua da geming*" *shinian shi*, 384.

97 Ibid., 384–5. Another account says that Doudou approached the guard commander at about 8:30 P.M.; see "Lin Doudou who lives in the shadow of history," "*Huaqiao ribao*, 16 June 1988. Wang, *Da dongluan de niandai*, 427–30, has an account of the events of 11 and 12 September as seen by Lin Liguo's fiancée, Zhang Ning.

98 Yu Nan, "Zhou zongli chuzhi '9.13' Lin Biao pantao shijian de yixie qingkuang" (Some of the circumstances regarding Premier Zhou's management of the 13 September incident when Lin Biao committed treachery and fled), *Dangshi yanjiu* (Research on Party history), 3 (1981), 59; Wang, *Da dongluan de niandai*, 431; Hao and Duan, *Zhongguo gongchandang liushi nian*, 622; Gao and Yan, "*Wenhua da geming*" *shinian shi*, 386; *Huaqiao ribao*, 16 June 1988. The latter account says that it was Zhou who telephoned Ye.

guards were too timid to stop them. Fortunately for the fugitives, Li Zuopeng had distorted Zhou Enlai's instructions and had told the Shanhaiguan base authorities that the Trident could take off if just one of the four men named gave permission, which Li did. At 12:32 A.M., Lin Biao, with his wife and son, took off.[99]

Zhou had been informed at about midnight that the Lins had fled their compound. On hearing the news, Zhou ordered Wu Faxian to ground all aircraft in China, and then sent an aide to Wu's headquarters to keep an eye on him.[100] Zhou then drove to Mao's residence in the Zhongnanhai to brief him personally. When radar indicated the Trident would be crossing into Mongolian territory, Wu Faxian telephoned to ask whether the plane should be shot down. Zhou asked Mao for his orders. Mao is quoted as replying philosophically: "Rain has to fall, women have to marry, these things are immutable; let them go."[101] Zhou, not knowing the details of Lin's activities and wanting to prevent any threat to Mao's safety, got the Chairman to leave his residence and move to the Great Hall.

Only now did Mao order Zhou to summon senior officials there for a Politburo conference, the clearest indication of how China was ruled. The meeting convened after 3:00 A.M., but Mao did not attend, whether for security reasons or out of embarrassment at the defection of his personally chosen heir is uncertain. Zhou informed his Politburo colleagues of Mao's return to the capital the previous afternoon and of Lin Biao's flight. He warned them to be prepared for anything.[102] It was not until the afternoon of 14 September that Zhou learned from the PRC embassy in Ulan Bator that Lin Biao's Trident had crashed at approximately 2:30 A.M. on 13 September near Undur Khan in Mongolia, killing the eight men and one woman on board.[103]

A more recent, unofficial account throws doubt on this description of events by focusing on the main question it prompts: Why did the Lins not fly south as arranged? The new account suggests that the Lin family did not immediately abandon their original plan to set up a rival regime in Guangdong, a plan that, after all, they would have had to advance by only about eight hours. This

99 *Huaqiao ribao*, loc. cit., 16, 17 June 1988; Hao and Duan, *Zhongguo gongchandang liushi nian*, 622; A great trial in Chinese history, 99; Gao and Yan, *"Wenhua da geming" shinian shi*, 387–91. According to Wang, *Da dongluan de niandai*, 432, Mao's imprimatur had also to be obtained.

100 Yu, "Zhou zongli," 59. The Air Force CO failed to prevent some of Lin Liguo's collaborators from trying to escape by helicopter; A great trial in Chinese history, 99–100.

101 *"Tian yao xiayu, niang yao jiaren, dou shi meiyou fazi de shi; you tamen chu ba."* See Hao and Duan, *Zhongguo gongchandang liushi nian*, 623.

102 Yu, "Zhou zongli," 59, This account was written partly to dispel rumors that Zhou had withheld the news of the flight from Mao until just before the plane was about to cross the frontier. A more hard-nosed view preferred by some scholars to explain Mao's apparent relaxed attitude toward Lin Biao's escape is the the PLA Air Force's night-fighter capability was too limited to permit it to bring down the fleeing plane.

103 Ibid.

version argues that the Trident was in the air for almost two hours, whereas the flying time to Undur Khan for such a plane should have been less than an hour. It claims that the Trident in fact first flew south for about ten minutes and then returned to Shanhaiguan, but found the air base closed, as Zhou Enlai had instructed. Why the Lins should have abandoned their southern strategy is not explained, but the implication of the story is that Zhou refused to let Lin land to force the latter to flee to the Soviet Union, thus putting himself beyond the pale as a national traitor.[104] Whatever the truth, the most dangerous threat to Mao's power and person since the Liberation was over. The specter of Bonapartism had been exorcised for the time being.

The impact of the fall of Lin Biao

The death of Lin Biao enabled Mao and Zhou Enlai to purge the Politburo of the central military leaders who had been his allies, if not his coconspirators. On the morning of 24 September, Zhou Enlai summoned PLA Chief of Staff Huang Yongsheng, PLA AF head Wu Faxian, PLA Navy Political Commissar Li Zuopeng, and PLA Logistics Director Qiu Huizuo to the Great Hall to tell them that they were dismissed and had to make thorough self-examinations. Each left under arrest, and each would eventually stand trial. The survivors among Lin Liguo's group of young turks in the PLA AF were also swept away.

But although the PLA had lost its most powerful figures in the civilian leadership and its high-profile role had been diminished, it was far from the end of PLA institutional dominance within the civilian polity. A major military presence in Party and government remained. Ye Jianying, one of China's ten marshals and a longtime ally of Zhou Enlai, took charge of a revamped MAC, directed the investigation into Lin Biao's activities within the major military units,[105] and played an increasingly important political role. His loyalty to Mao and the premier could be assumed, but he was nevertheless a representative of the military establishment.[106] Wang Dongxing, the CO of the central

---

104 See *Huaqiao ribao*, 17 June 1988. An alternative explanation could be that the Trident did not fly a straight course toward Mongolia but zigzagged to avoid interception. Another version retailed by a former public security official to a China scholar was that Premier Zhou managed to talk the pilot into flying back into Chinese air space, but that the latter was then shot down by Lin Liguo, who took over the controls. Lin proved unable to handle the plane and it crashed. An even more sensational, supposedly "insider" account of the demise of Lin Biao, discounted by many scholars as fabricated, alleges that he was killed on Mao's orders in a rocket attack when driving home after a banquet at the Chairman's villa outside Beijing on 12 September. See Yao, *The conspiracy and murder of Mao's heir*, ch. 16.

105 Hao and Duan, *Zhongguo gongchandang liushi nian*, 624; *Yingsi lu*, 305–8, 346. For the dismissal of Lin's senior military allies, see Yu, "Zhou zongli," 59.

106 Among Mao's remarks during his southern tour in the summer of 1971 is an admonition on 28 August to respect Ye Jianying because of his firmness in crisis, as demonstrated by his loyalty to the future Chairman during the latter's struggle with Zhang Guotao in 1935. This comment, which occurs

bodyguard, PLA Unit 8341, was even more committed to the Chairman and was a public security official rather than part of the military mainstream,[107] but he was certainly not a civilian cadre. These men, in contrast to Lin Biao, would faithfully support Mao in his continuing efforts to recivilianize the polity.

The continuing power of PLA cadres in the provinces was symbolized by the continuing presence within the Politburo of three generals with top provincial responsibilities: Xu Shiyou, chairman of the Jiangsu Revolutionary Committee and CO of the Nanjing Military Region; Chen Xilian, chairman of the Liaoning Revolutionary Committee and CO of the Shenyang Military Region; and alternate member Li Desheng, chairman of the Anhui Revolutionary Committee and CO of the Anhui Military District. All of them had kept on the right side of Mao during the Cultural Revolution.

What is less easy to assess is the impact of Lin's fall on Mao. Liu Shaoqi had been axed in the heat of the Cultural Revolution, at a time when Mao had generated enough momentum to gain widespread support for the need to change leaders. Even Liu's former secretary, Deng Liqun, later admitted that in 1966 he had felt it was probably right that Mao's successor should be someone able to handle military as well as Party affairs, and he testified that this was a common opinion within the CCR.[108] Lin Biao was an authentic revolutionary hero and unquestionably a longtime Mao loyalist. The Chairman's assessment that Lin was a better bet than Liu may have been resented by the latter's followers in the Party machine, but it was probably accepted unquestioningly within the broader political world.

Now the "best pupil" had not merely been found wanting but, as Zhou Enlai would reveal at the CCP's Tenth Congress in 1973,[109] had even attempted to assassinate the Chairman himself. How could Mao have been so wrong for so long? His letter to Jiang Qing in 1966 expressing concern about Lin

---

in what appears to be an unexpurgated manuscript version of Mao's remarks available in Harvard's Fairbank Center Library, illustrates both the importance of Ye to Mao in his dealings with the military at this time, as well as how the Chairman never forgot a favor or a slight. I am grateful to Michael Schoenhals for bringing this remark to my attention.

107 Wang Dongxing is not listed among the senior officers named "Wang" whose biographies are given in volumes 1 and 2 of the official, *Zhongguo renmin jiefangjun jiangshuai minglu* (The names and records of marshals and generals of the Chinese People's Liberation Army).

108 See Deng Liqun, "Xuexi 'Guanyu jianguo yilai dangde ruogan lishi wenti de jueyi' de wenti he huida" (Questions and answers in studying the 'Resolution on certain historical questions since the founding of the state'), in *Dangshi huiyi baogao ji* (Collection of reports to the Party history conference), 153. Confirmation that Deng Liqun was not exceptional in this regard is in Tan Zongji, "Lin Biao fangeming jituan de jueqi jiqi fumie," 42, 43. According to this latter source, when Liu Shaoqi was criticized at the Eleventh Plenum and a new number two had to be found from the PSC, Deng Xiaoping was ruled out because he, too, was under fire; Chen Yun, because he was rightist; Zhu De, because he was too old; and Zhou Enlai, because Mao was not satisfied with him and Zhou himself had often said that he was not able to assume command (*wo zhege ren shi buneng guashuaide*). That left only Lin Biao; ibid., 42.

109 *The Tenth National Congress of the Communist Party of China (Documents)*, 5–6.

Biao's activities was quickly circulated within the Party,[110] but it underlined rather than explained away Mao's failure to prevent this dangerous man from emerging as his officially anointed successor. Was the Chairman unable to detect traitors and sham Marxists among men who had been close to him for decades?

Perhaps equally damaging was the revelation of how the top ranks of the CCP were riddled with treachery and intrigue worthy of the palace politics of the old imperial Chinese court, with plenty of obvious equivalents for the traditional panoply of empresses and eunuchs, officials and generals. Was this the purified politics the Cultural Revolution should have produced? While the turbulence and purges of the early years of the Cultural Revolution probably disillusioned most of Mao's closest colleagues, the fall of Lin Biao almost certainly spread that disillusionment among a far wider group[111] and would be a source of political malaise when Mao's successors tried to rebuild after his death.

THE RISE AND FALL OF THE GANG OF FOUR

The succession problem

For the moment, Mao's main problem was to reconstruct the top leadership and, in particular, to select a credible successor. He had destroyed the very procedures by which he had hoped to spare China the succession struggles experienced by other totalitarian states, notably the Soviet Union after the death of Stalin. His "two fronts" system had been devised in the 1950s to give his colleagues experience and exposure in the front line while he monitored them from the second line. Liu's takeover from Mao of the post of head of state had been part of that process, but it did not outlast Liu himself. Similarly, the "best pupil" model could not outlast Lin Biao.[112] How was the Chairman to

---

110 Hao and Duan, *Zhongguo gongchandang liushi nian*, 625–6; also see n. 43. This letter was so convenient for Mao to be able to circulate after the death of Lin Biao that post–Cultural Revolution Party historians seem to have questioned its authenticity. In response, one senior historian recounted the following episode: Lin Biao had been most agitated when he had learned about Mao's letter in 1966, so much so that Mao decided not to have it circulated and indeed ordered it burned. When the burning ceremony took place, the leftist propagandist Qi Benyu protested to Zhou Enlai that Mao's words were too precious to be destroyed in this way; the premier reassured him that he had ordered Tao Zhu, then director of propaganda, to make a copy! It was copies of this copy that had to be circulated after Lin's death, thus presumably giving rise to doubts about its authenticity. See Tan Zongji's account, "Lin Biao fangeming jituan." This fascinating anecdote, which tells as much about Zhou Enlai as about Lin Biao, was first noticed by Michael Schoenhals.

111 Hao and Duan, *Zhongguo gongchandang liushi nian*, 624. This argument has also been made to the author by Chinese friends who experienced this disillusionment at that time.

112 For a longer discussion of the problem of succession under Mao and Deng Xiaoping, see Roderick MacFarquhar, "Passing the baton in Beijing," *New York Review of Books*, 35.2 (18 February 1988), 21–2.

solve the problem of "After Mao, who?" and the even more crucial question "After Mao, what?"

Three groups began to emerge in the Politburo in the wake of Lin: radicals, survivors, and beneficiaries of the Cultural Revolution. The radicals were the rump of the original ultra-leftist coalition that had formed around Mao to launch the Cultural Revolution. By 1967, the interests of Lin Biao and the Cultural Revolution Group had already begun to diverge sharply, but they remained on the same side in important ways. With the disappearance of Lin Biao and his allies, the former coalition was reduced to Kang Sheng, Jiang Qing, Zhang Chunqiao, Yao Wenyuan, and Xie Fuzhi, who had not originally been a member of the core group but had made himself extremely useful to it as the Cultural Revolution got underway from his vantage point as minister of public security. Kang Sheng, however, appears to have played an increasingly nominal role owing to failing health, and Xie died in 1972, leaving a rump of Jiang, Zhang, and Yao.

The survivors were those senior officials who had collaborated with Mao, even though they almost certainly opposed the main thrust of the Cultural Revolution: Premier Zhou Enlai, Vice-Premier Li Xiannian, acting head of state Dong Biwu, and three old marshals: Zhu De, Liu Bocheng, and Ye Jianying. Of these, only Zhou, Li, and Ye were active politically; the other three had survived in the Politburo because their loyalty to Mao could be relied upon under almost any circumstances. Indeed, Liu Bocheng's continued membership was essentially a courtesy to a great revolutionary warrior, who was apparently mentally competent but physically blind and politically inert.

After the shock of the Lin Biao affair, Mao seems to have felt it expedient to reinforce his ties to this group by agreeing to rehabilitate a number of senior officials whose fall could credibly be blamed on Lin Biao. Those early critics of the Cultural Revolution known as the "February adverse current" were restored to grace if not to their old offices. When one of them, former Foreign Minister Chen Yi, died in January 1972, Mao unexpectedly attended the memorial ceremony and gave a high appraisal of the old marshal.[113]

One rehabilitation would profoundly affect China's history: that of "the number two Party person in authority taking the capitalist road," former CCP General Secretary Deng Xiaoping. Deng and some of his family were in Jiangsi province, where they had been moved from Beijing as a result of Lin Biao's evacuation order in October 1969. Deng worked a half day as a

---

113 Hao and Duan, *Zhongguo gongchandang liushi nian*, 624. For a description of Mao's last-minute decision to attend the Chen Yi memorial ceremony on 10 January 1972, at which he told Prince Sihanouk of Cambodia that Chen had supported him, whereas Lin Biao had opposed him, see the series of eleven articles by Zhang Yufeng, "Anecdotes of Mao Zedong and Zhou Enlai in their later years," in *GMRB*, 26 December 1988–6 January 1989, translated in *FBIS Daily Report: China*, 27 January 1989, 16–19, and 31 January 1989, 30–7. This was the last such ceremony that Mao was able to attend.

fitter in a country tractor plant. When Lin Biao fell, he wrote twice to Mao, in November 1971 and August 1972, asking to be allowed to work once more for the Party and nation. After receiving the second letter, Mao made approving comments on Deng's revolutionary record, although it was not until March 1973 that the formalities for his return to Beijing were completed.[114] The reasons for Deng's second coming and its results will be explored later in the chapter.

The beneficiaries of the Cultural Revolution were those officials who had risen as a result of the purge of their seniors, as well as through their own ability to manipulate the turbulent politics of the late 1960s and early 1970s. In the immediate aftermath of the fall of Lin Biao, these were principally military figures: Xu Shiyou, Chen Xilian, Li Desheng, and Wang Dongxing; but they also included a civilian cadre, Ji Dengkui, who was involved in the post-Lin cleanup and would achieve increasing prominence.[115]

The problem for Mao now was that there was no obvious successor among the three groups likely to preserve the gains of the Cultural Revolution. Zhou Enlai was, without question, the highest-ranking official under Mao. If the Chairman had considered him an appropriate successor, he could have appointed him long since, to widespread approval. But Mao was not prepared to entrust his ultra-leftist program to any of the survivors. Anyway, Zhou could not be assumed to outlive Mao, for in May 1972, in the course of a regular checkup, he was found to have cancer at an early stage.[116]

The rump of the old Cultural Revolution Group was the obvious place for Mao to look for a like-minded successor. The Chairman must have been aware, however, that the PLA was unlikely to accept as supreme leader anyone who had done so much to stir up violence, bloodshed, and disorder as Jiang Qing or Zhang Chunqiao. Nor, apparently, did any beneficiary of the Cultural

---

114 See Gao and Yan, *"Wenhua da geming" shinian shi*, 328–30; Hao and Duan, *Zhongguo gongchandang liushi nian*, 624. For a more detailed account of Deng's sojourn in Jiangxi, see Qiu Zhizhuo, "Deng Xiaoping zai 1969–1972" (Deng Xiaoping in 1969–1972), *Xinhua wenzhai* (New China digest), 112 (April 1988), 133–55. A copy of Deng's letter of 3 August 1972 is available in the library of Harvard's Fairbank Center. In it, he expresses his support for the Cultural Revolution, without whose "incomparably immense monster-revealing mirror" (*wubi juda de zhaoyaojing*) men like Lin Biao and Chen Boda would not have been exposed. The letter, which Michael Schoenhals drew to my attention, is a combination of flattery, self-abasement, and an account of Deng's own opinions about and experience of Lin and Chen.

115 For Ji's role in the post-Lin cleanup, see *Huaqiao ribao*, 18 June 1988. For an explanation of Ji's promotion under Mao's aegis, see Wang Lingshu, "Ji Dengkui on Mao Zedong," *Liaowang* (Observer), overseas edition, 6–13 February 1989, translated in *FBIS, Daily Report: China*, 14 February 1989, 22–6.

116 For the claim that the cancer was discovered in May, see Gao and Yan, *"Wenhua da geming" shinian shi*, 474. *Bujin de sinian* (Inexhaustible memories), 583, provides the information that the cancer was in its early stages and tells how Mao ordered a special group to be set up to supervise Zhou's treatment. Curiously, *Zhou zongli shengping dashiji* (Major events in the life of Premier Zhou), 494, only gives the year, though it provides a month-by-month chronology.

Revolution yet have the stature to attract broad-based support and the Chairman's endorsement.

In these difficult circumstances, Mao took an extraordinary step. He catapulted a junior radical into the very apex of the leadership. Wang Hongwen, aged only thirty-six at the time of Lin Biao's demise, had risen during Shanghai's January Revolution from a humble position as a Shanghai factory security chief to a workers' leader in support of Zhang Chunqiao and Yao Wenyuan. By this time he was the effective boss of China's most populous city and leftist stronghold, as well as political commissar of its PLA garrison.[117] In the autumn of 1972, Wang was transferred to Beijing, appearing in public there for the first time in October at the celebration of the fiftieth birthday of Prince Sihanouk in the Great Hall of the People, to the bewilderment of junior Chinese officials.[118] At Mao's direction, Wang was effectively inducted into the Politburo in May 1973, along with two beneficiaries of the Cultural Revolution: Hua Guofeng, the Hunan first secretary, who seems to have distinguished himself in the post–Lin Biao investigations,[119] and Wu De, the Beijing first secretary.[120]

The rise of Wang Hongwen was clearly designed to provide a more acceptable image for the radical faction. Wang, at thirty-seven, was good-looking and personable, and symbolized two constituencies critically important in the Cultural Revolution: youth and the workers. Through Wang, the radicals may have hoped to rekindle the youthful enthusiasm that had been dampened by the disbanding of the Red Guards. Wang's proletarian credentials could also be expected to attract the support of the urban workers. And whatever Wang's role in Shanghai, no general could blame him for the nationwide urban anarchy in 1967 and 1968.

After the CCP's Tenth Party Congress in August 1973, Wang was thrust into the Party's number three position and was named a vice-chairman and member of the Politburo Standing Committee.[121] The fourth member of what

117 For Wang Hongwen's life, see Ting Wang, *Wang Hongwen, Zhang Chunqiao pingzhuan* (Biographies of Wang Hongwen and Zhang Chunqiao), 49–134. See also Gao and Yan, *"Wenhua da geming" shinian shi*, 442–8. Neale Hunter, *Shanghai Journal: An eyewitness account of the Cultural Revolution*, and Andrew G. Walder, *Chang Ch'un-ch'iao and Shanghai's January Revolution*, which cover the period of Wang Hongwen's emergence, but with little mention of Wang himself.
118 The present author witnessed officials' inability to explain what Wang Hongwen was doing in Beijing, shaking hands with the assembled VIPs along with elders and betters like Zhou Enlai, Li Xiannian, and Foreign Minister Ji Pengfei. Curiously, a banquet given for Prince Sihanouk was made the occasion for another equally amazing first appearance in Beijing: the return of Deng Xiaoping to public life on 12 April 1973; see John Gardner, *Chinese politics and the succession to Mao*, 62.
119 See Ting Wang, *Chairman Hua: Leader of the Chinese Communists*, 77–80.
120 Hao and Duan, *Zhongguo gongchandang liushi nian*, 628.
121 The consternation in China at Wang's meteoric rise can be guessed at when one remembers the disbelief with which American politicians and press reacted during the 1988 presidential campaign to then Vice-President Bush's choice of an unknown forty-one-year-old senator, Dan Quayle, as his running mate, a position that, unlike Wang's, conferred only potential power.

would later be known as the Gang of Four was now in place, outranked only by Mao and Zhou Enlai. With only six years' experience of revolutionary struggle and politics, he was expected to keep up with and contend against men like the premier, who had survived six decades of revolutions, civil wars, foreign invasion, and Party infighting. It was a grossly unequal contest, another Maoist gamble that would fail.

Zhou Enlai's anti-leftist offensive

When Wang Hongwen arrived in Beijing, his radical colleagues, Jiang Qing, Zhang Chunqiao, and Yao Wenyuan, were on the defensive. They had benefited from the fall of Lin Biao and his military clique, which removed a major obstacle to their inheriting Mao's mantle, but Lin Biao's actions had tarnished the leftist cause. Some of the dishonor he had incurred inevitably rubbed off on his erstwhile allies from the Cultural Revolution Group.

Zhou Enlai took advantage of the radicals' disarray in the wake of the 13 September Incident to renew his year-old campaign to stabilize administration and encourage production. In December 1971, he lectured officials of the State Planning Commission (SPC) on the need to restore order and responsibility to an anarchic industrial management system. Intimidated by leftist threats, plant directors were afraid to maintain discipline. The guidelines produce by the SPC as a result of Zhou's prodding were vetoed by Zhang Chunqiao and thus could not be distributed as formal documents. It was claimed that they nonetheless had a salutary effect on industrial production, although the figures do not bear this out.[122]

In agriculture, Zhou ordered that the egalitarianism of the Dazhai brigade should be imitated only when local circumstances permitted.[123] One such manifestation of egalitarianism had been a tendency to shift the accounting unit from production team to production brigade. During the grim famine years after the GLF when incentives for the peasants were vital to stimulate production, the Party had made the production team into the unit for accounting. The team was the smallest, lowest-level organization in the three-tier setup

122 Hao and Duan, *Zhongguo gongchandang liushi nian*, 626; *Guanyu jianguo yilai dangde ruogan lishi wenti de jueyi zhushi ben (xiuding)* (hereafter *Zhushi ben*) (Revised annotated edition of the Resolution on certain questions in the history of our party since the founding of the People's Republic), 414–16. According to the PRC State Statistical Bureau, *Zhongguo tongji nianjian, 1981* (Chinese statistical yearbook, 1981), 233, steel production figures for these years were as follows (m. = million): 1969 – 13.3 m. tons; 1970 – 17.7 m. tons; 1971 – 21.3 m. tons; 1972 – 23.3 m. tons; 1973 – 25.2 m. tons; i.e., bigger increases in the years up to and including Lin Biao's fall than thereafter. See also Yan Fangming and Wang Yaping, "Qishi niandai chuqi woguo jingji jianshe de maojin ji qi tiaozheng," (The blind advance in our national economic construction in the early 1970s and its correction), *Dangshi yanjiu*, 5 (1985), 55–60. For an analysis of the relative lightness of the effect of the Cultural Revolution industry after the anarchy of 1967–8, see *CHOC*, 15, Chapter 6.

123 *Zhushi ben*, 416.

of the rural communes, and accounting at the team level meant that income was distributed within the most cohesive and homogeneous rural collective entity. When the right to act as the accounting unit was ceded by a group of teams to the production brigade, of which they were part, it entailed redistributing income from richer to poorer teams. This aroused great resentment. The radicals had encouraged a movement toward brigade accounting starting in 1968, but this had already been checked in 1970, before Zhou Enlai's counterattack.[124] Another indicator of rural radicalism was the tolerance accorded peasants' private plots. Here, too, leftism seemed to be on the retreat as early as 1970, well before the fall of Lin Biao.[125] Nor do grain output figures suggest a general boost in agricultural production after 13 September 1971.[126]

Nevertheless, 1972 could be called Zhou Enlai's year. There was relaxation in the cultural sphere. With the premier's encouragement, a call for a restoration of educational standards and scientific research was published by a leading academic, albeit not in the *People's Daily*, which was controlled by the radicals, and not without a counterattack by Zhang Chunqiao and Yao Wenyuan.[127] At a major conference of more than 300 senior central and provincial officials held in Beijing from 20 May to late June 1972, Zhou deepened the attack on Lin Biao and won a ringing personal endorsement from the Chairman.[128] Yet the premier was unable to liquidate the leftist positions because, in the last analysis, the radicals were still backed by Mao. By December 1972, the Chairman had decided that the antileftist tide had gone too far. In response to the urgings of Zhang and Yao, he decreed that Lin Biao had not been an ultra-leftist after all, but an ultra-rightist![129] The radicals resumed their offensive.

---

124 See David Zweig, *Agrarian radicalism in China, 1968–1981*, 57–60 and ch. 5; also Zweig. "Strategies of policy implementation: policy 'winds' and brigade accounting in rural China, 1966–1978," *World Politics*, 37.2 (January 1985), 267–93.

125 Zweig, *Agrarian radicalism in China*, 57–60 and ch. 6.

126 The grain output figures are as follows: 1969 – 210.9 m. tons; 1970 – 239.9 m. tons; 1971 – 250.1 m. tons; 1972 – 240.4 m. tons; 1973 – 264.9 m. tons; see State Statistical Bureau, *Zhongguo tongji nianjian, 1983*, 158.

127 That 1972 was the year of Zhou Enlai is the assessment of Laszlo Ladany, *The Communist Party of China and Marxism, 1921–1985: A self-portrait*, 355–6, who deals with the issues to be covered. Zhou took the opportunity to try to rebut decisively an allegation that he had betrayed the CCP in 1932, which had apparently been discreetly encouraged by Kang Sheng and Jiang Qing in 1967. But although he circulated a brief statement from Mao that exonerated him, the Gang of Four continued to use the charge against him almost until his death; see "Guanyu Guomindang zaoyao wumie de dengzai suowei 'Wu Hao Qishi' wenti de wenjian" (Document on the problem of the Guomindang maliciously concocting and publishing the so-called 'Wu Hao notice'), *Dangshi yanjiu*, I, (1980), 8; 'Wu Hao' was one of Zhou Enlai's aliases at that time. See Hao and Duan, *Zhongguo gongchandang liushi nian*, 626–7, for a discussion of the article on educational reform by Zhou Peiyuan; and Merle Goldman, *China's lectuals: Advise and dissent*, 162–6, for a general discussion of the attempt to revive science. For inability to control the *People's Daily*, see Jin Chunming, "'Wenhua da geming' de shinian" of the Great Cultural Revolution), 203–4.

Zhongguo gongchandang liushi nian, 625–6.

is politically necessary but ideologically bizarre redefinition, see a series of ten entitled "Cong pi 'zuo' daoxiang fanyou de yici geren jingli" (The experience

The Tenth Party Congress

Wang Hongwen, Zhang Chunqiao, and Yao Wenyuan were put in charge of preparing the three main documents for the Tenth Party Congress, held in Beijing from 24 to 28 August 1973, striking proof that they had recaptured the ideological high ground. The documents were the political report, which was delivered by Zhou Enlai; the report on the revision of the Party constitution, delivered by Wang; and the draft new constitution.[130]

Not surprisingly, the reports and the constitution reflected the line of the Ninth Congress, despite the dramatic developments within the Chinese leadership since then. In Wang Hongwen's words, "Practice over the past four years and more has fully proved that both the political line and organizational line of the Ninth Congress are correct."[131] Naturally, Lin Biao's name was excised from the new constitution, but the radicals would not have wanted to discard a document that reflected the ideals and achievements of the first three years of the Cultural Revolution. Instead they reaffirmed the concept of the Cultural Revolution, inserting into the general program of the new constitution the words: "Revolutions like this will have to be carried out many times in the future."[132] There is no way of knowing if they attempted to make Zhou Enlai say something similar, but no such assertion appears in his report.[133]

Other additions to the constitution reflected other major concerns of the radicals: criticizing revisionism; going against the tide; the need to train revolutionary successors; the inviolability of Party leadership over other institutions, most importantly the PLA; the impermissibility of suppressing criticism.[134]

The new central leadership of the CCP, chosen at the postcongress CC plenum, reflected the resurgence of the radicals. The Politburo Standing Committee was greatly enlarged, nine members compared with five in 1969. Of those nine, Mao, Wang Hongwen, Kang Sheng, and Zhang Chunqiao could be regarded as strong supporters of the goals of the Cultural Revolution; Zhu De (age eighty-six) and Dong Biwu (age eighty-seven) were grand old men with little remaining political clout, whose presence might have comforted a few nostalgic senior officials, but who (if consulted) would almost certainly back

---

of one individual of the reversal from criticizing 'leftism' to opposing rightism), in *Huaqiao ribao*, 12–21 March 1989.

130 Hao and Duan, *Zhongguo gongchandang liushi nian*, 628.

131 *The Tenth National Congress of the Communist Party of China (Documents)*, 42. Zhou Enlai used virtually the same words; ibid., 9–10.

132 Ibid., 45.

133 William A. Joseph has argued that Zhou's report contains subtle hints that Lin Biao really was a leftist not a rightist; see his *The critique of ultra-leftism in China, 1958–1981*, 138–9. If so, then Zhou presumably modified the draft after Wang and Zhang submitted it to him.

134 *The Tenth National Congress (Documents)*, 47, 48, 50, 52, 55.

TABLE 4

Leadership changes, April 1969–August 1973

(Names in boldface are of new entrants into the Politburo; names in capital letters represent promotions within the Politburo as of the Ninth Congress. At both congresses, only the chairman and vice-chairmen were ranked; the rest were given in order of the number of strokes in the characters of their surnames. The order of the post–Ninth Congress Politburo has been juggled to make it easier to note the changes between 1969 and 1973.)

Ninth Congress		Tenth Congress	
Mao Zedong	PSC	Mao Zedong	PSC
Lin Biao	PSC		
Zhou Enlai	PSC	Zhou Enlai	PSC VC
Chen Boda	PSC		
		Wang Hongwen	PSC VC
Kang Sheng	PSC	Kang Sheng	PSC VC
Ye Jianying		YE JIANYING	PSC VC
Li Desheng	(alt)	LI DESHENG	PSC VC
Zhu De		ZHU DE	PSC VC
Zhang Chunqiao		ZHANG CHUNQIAO	PSC
Dong Biwu		DONG BIWU	PSC
Jiang Qing (f)		Jiang Qing (f)	
Ye Qun (f)			
Liu Bocheng		Liu Bocheng	
Xu Shiyou		Xu Shiyou	
Chen Xilian		Chen Xilian	
Li Xiannian		Li Xiannian	
Li Zuopeng			
Wu Faxian			
Qiu Huizuo			
Yao Wenyuan		Yao Wenyuan	
Huang Yongsheng			
Xie Fuzhi			
Ji Dengkui	(alt)	JI DENGKUI	
Li Xuefeng	(alt)		
Wang Dongxing	(alt)	WANG DONGXING	
		Wei Guoqing	
		Hua Guofeng	
		Wu De	
		Chen Yonggui	
		Wu Guixian	(alt)
		Su Zhenhua	(alt)
		Ni Zhifu	(alt)
		Saifudin	(alt)

Notes: PSC = Politburo Standing Committee; VC = vice-chairman; alt = alternate member; (f) = female.

Mao; Li Desheng, a dark-horse entrant soon to become CO of the Shenyang Military Region, had shown himself sensitive to radical demands during the early years of the Cultural Revolution and could be counted as an opportunistic supporter of the radicals. This left only Zhou Enlai and Ye Jianying as effective voices of moderation.

New entrants to the Politburo like Hua Guofeng, Wu De, and Chen Yong-gui (the peasant Stakhanovite who headed the party committee of the Dazhai Brigade) were nearly all beneficiaries of the Cultural Revolution who could presumably be expected to support its goals. Senior cadres like Li Jingquan and Tan Zhenlin, whom Zhou had managed to get rehabilitated during the antileftist Interlude, made it onto the CC but failed to return to the Politburo.

In the aftermath of their success, the radicals dipped their brushes in vitriol as they prepared to denounce their most formidable opponent: Premier Zhou Enlai himself.

"Pi Lin, pi Kong"

On 18 January 1974, with Mao's approval, the party center circulated a document prepared under the direction of Jiang Qing entitled "The doctrines of Lin Biao, Confucius and Mencius."[135] According to one account, the original authorization for this bizarre-seeming linkage was a comment by Mao to a Qinghua University study group in August 1973 that Lin and Confucius could be criticized together.[136] But the Qinghua inquiry itself must have been sparked by Mao's remark in March 1973 at a central work conference called to criticize Lin Biao that it was also necessary to criticize Confucius. Mao reinforced his message in a couple of poems written in May and August criticizing China's senior intellectual, Guo Moruo, for praising the Confucians and reviling their principal tormentor, China's First Emperor, Qin Shihuangdi.[137] It was not inapposite that Mao himself was often seen by his countrymen as a founding emperor similar to Qin Shihuangdi,[138] a ruler excoriated as a tyrant by generations of Chinese historians.

By August, Mao's words must have been widely known among the political cognoscenti. That month, the People's Daily, controlled by the radicals, carried an article by a Guangzhou professor that laid out some of the major themes of the subsequent campaign, including the one most relevant to current politics. The Confucian Analects were quoted as saying: "Revive states that have been extinguished, restore families whose line of succession has been broken and call to office those who have retired to obscurity." This was an oblique but

---

135 "Lin Biao yu Kong-Meng zhidao"; see Hu, Zhongguo shehuizhuyi geming he jianshe shi jiangyi, 316.
136 Yue Daiyun and Carolyn Wakeman, To she storm: The odyssey of a revolutionary Chinese woman, 323.
137 Teaching and Research Office for CCP History, Zhongguo gongchandang liushi nian dashi jianjie, 568. Mao pursued his comparison of Confucius and Qin Shihuangdi in conversation with a doubtless mystified visiting Egyptian leader; ibid. I have been unable to trace the poems referred to in this source. Mao was accustomed to using Guo Moruo' s poems as a foil for his own; see, for instance, Chinese Literature, 4 (1976), 43–4, 48–50. But there is no indication in Moruo shici xuan (Selected poems of Moruo) of any recent poems of Guo's to which Mao might have been replying.
138 Union Research Institute, The cast of Peng Teh-huai, 36.

unmistakable critique of Zhou's rehabilitation of senior cadres, particularly clear to those who knew that this passage referred to the actions of Zhou's namesake, the great statesman of the twelfth century B.C. the Duke of Zhou.[139]

While this article was being debated up and down China, Jiang Qing got Qinghua to form a group to provide the intellectual ammunition for a full-scale and credible official campaign.[140] The group was led by Chi Qun, formerly head of the propaganda section of the political department of the central guards, PLA Unit 8341, but by this time the chairman of the Qinghua University Revolutionary Committee, with responsibility also for educational reform at the capital's other major institution of higher education, Peking University. His second-in-command was Xie Jingyi, also originally from PLA Unit 8341, a woman who was very close to Mao and Jiang Qing, possibly serving as the latter's secretary before moving to Qinghua to become Chi Qun's deputy chairman.[141]

In autumn 1973, these two recruited twelve scholars (a number later increased to thirty-two) from Qinghua and Peking universities to do the research and writing needed to link Lin Biao and Confucius and, presumably, to pinpoint the historical analogies that could be used for more urgent current purposes. This ideological hit team was designated the Beida-Qinghua Two Schools Big Criticism Group, and known as *Liang Xiao* (Two Schools) for short. Its members were moved into special accommodation, given special food, and taken on fact-finding missions, often in the company of Jiang Qing.[142] They became the core of a network of followers that the Gang established up and down the country.[143] The document circulated on 18 January 1974 was *Liang Xiao's* first major product.

This marked the formal start of the official campaign to "Criticize Lin Biao, criticize Confucius" (*pi Lin, pi Kong*), masterminded by Jiang Qing and Wang Hongwen, and foreshadowed by the 1974 New Year's Day joint editorial in the *People's Daily, Hongqi*, and the *Liberation Army News*.[144] This might have seemed like an amplification of the ongoing drive to weed out supporters of Lin Biao in the Party and the PLA. Indeed, it was later alleged that a

---

139 "Quarterly chronicle and documentation," *CQ*, 57 (January–March 1974), 207–10. The fact that the remarks by Zhou Enlai on foreign affairs, a field he had made very much his own, were criticized by the Politburo in November 1973 at Mao's suggestion, of course encouraged the Gang of Four to believe their moment was coming; Wang, *Da dongluan de niandai*, 417.

140 Yue and Wakeman, *To the storm*, 323. The key role of Qinghua in the launching of the *Pi Lin, pi Kong* campaign, and Jiang Qing's links with that institution, suggests that she may have prompted its original submission to Mao.

141 Ibid., 303. For a transcript of discussions between Jiang Qing and these two, see Wang, *Da dongluan de niandai*, 479–89.

142 Yue and Wakeman, *To the storm*, 323–6. Yue Daiyun's knowledge of this group is extensive because her husband, Tang Yijie, was one of the twelve scholars.

143 Jin, "*Wenhua da geming*," 194.   144 Gao and Yan, "*Wenhua da geming*" *shinian shi*, 495.

"Book-reading Group" (*dushu ban*) headed by Wang Hongwen attempted to gain control in military units. But its real purpose, formulated by Kang Sheng, was to undermine Zhou Enlai, as had been clear from the first salvo the previous August.[145]

On 24 January, allegedly without permission but probably with Mao's consent, Jiang Qing held a *pi Lin, pi Kong* rally for the Beijing garrison; the following day she held a similar one for central Party and government cadres, at which she, Yao Wenyuan, Chi Qun, and Xie Jingyi made speeches.[146] Thereafter, she and her team traveled far and wide, penetrating even high-security military establishments, making speeches, or "lighting fires," as their activities were later described.[147] The campaign flooded the media and dominated the political activities of units in town and country.[148]

The unjustified restoration of old families was one theme. It was emphasized that there was an ongoing battle between those who wanted to go forward and those whose desire was to turn back the wheel of history.[149] Another was the contrast between the Confucians and the Legalist scholar-statesmen who worked for Qin Shihuangdi.[150] It was the Legalists who had convinced the Qin dynasty of a ruler's need to impose stern discipline and harsh punishments, an analogy perhaps intended to elevate class struggle over rehabilitation. The misdeeds of the Duke of Zhou figured largely in speeches and articles.[151]

Whatever the psychological impact of this historical onslaught on the living Zhou, the premier was increasingly incapacitated by his cancer, having to cut engagements, and finally to agree to surgery.[152] He left his office in the Zhongnanhai complex on 1 June 1974 and moved into the Capital Hospital, which became his base for the remaining eighteen months of his life.[153] He left the hospital only occasionally, mainly to make sorties for important political

---

145 Hu, *Zhongguo shehuizhuyi geming he jianshe shi jiangyi*, 316. See *Yingsi lu*, 295–6, for the allegation about the reason for the *dushu ban*; Michael Schoenhals has brought to my attention a reference to these study groups in *Zhonggong zhongyang dangxiao nianjian, 1984*, 4, which suggests that they had less ambitious aims. For Kang Sheng's role, see Zhong, *Kang Sheng pingzhuan*, 310–11. Merle Goldman argues that Zhou Enlai was able partly to diffuse the campaign, in *China's intellectuals*, 166–76. A leading member of the *Liang Xiao* group has since claimed that at no time were articles authored or supervised by him aimed consciously at Zhou.

146 Goldman, *China's intellectuals*, 166–76; Hao and Duan, *Zhongguo gongchandang liushi nian*, 634; Wang, *Da dongluan de niandai*, 489–94.

147 Yue and Wakeman, *To the storm*, 324–7; Gao and Yan, *"Wenhua da geming" shinian shi*, 496–7; Hao and Duan, *Zhongguo gongchandang liushi nian*, 634.

148 "Quarterly chronicle," *CQ*, 58 (April–May 1974), 407; ibid., 59 (July–September 1974), 627–30.

149 Ibid., 58 (April–May 1974), 407–8.   150 Ibid., 408.

151 Teaching and Research Office for CCP History, *Zhongguo gongchandang liushi nian dashi jianjie*, 569.

152 Zhou always insisted on getting Mao's permission before submitting to surgery; see *Bujin de sinian*, 583. For his letter to Mao reporting in detail on his condition and asking permission for his third operation in March 1975, see *Zhou Enlai shuxin xuanji* (Zhou Enlai's selected letters), 633–5.

153 *Zhou zongli shengping dashiji*, 504; *Huainian Zhou Enlai* (Longing for Zhou Enlai), 585–6.

purposes.[154] But if the radicals had cause to rejoice that a foe whom they had so far failed to topple was weakening, their satisfaction was short-lived. The terminal illness of Zhou Enlai posed Mao a major political problem, and he solved it in a manner repugnant to his radical followers.

The return of Deng Xiaoping

Mao had to find someone to take Zhou Enlai's place, to oversee the day-to-day running of the country. Although the Chairman evidently considered it nationally therapeutic and probably also personally exhilarating to encourage upheaval, he was well aware of the need for a stabilizing force to prevent total chaos. During the early years of the Cultural Revolution, and on earlier occasions like the GLF, too, Zhou had played that role. Although he could still rise to (or rather, for) the occasion – most notably, leaving the hospital to deliver the report on the work of the government at the first session of the Fourth NPC on 13 January 1975 – it was no longer possible for him to work the long hours needed to supervise every major national concern.

Unfortunately for Mao, Wang Hongwen turned out not to have the political skills that the Chairman presumably thought he had detected in the young man when he was operating in Shanghai.[155] More important: Despite his senior ranking, Wang had proved to be little more than a cat's-paw in the hands of Jiang Qing and Zhang Chunqiao,[156] thus destroying his credibility as an independent new force. Although post-Cultural Revolution historians have axes to grind, there seems little reason to doubt their evidence that during the *Pi Lin, pi Kong* campaign, Wang Hongwen had collaborated so closely with Jiang and Zhang as to force Mao to realize he was not a viable replacement for Zhou. By the time Mao started warning Wang against allying with Jiang, it was already too late.[157]

Quite apart from her activities on Mao's behalf earlier in the Cultural Revolution, Jiang Qing was barred from power by the prejudices built into the political culture by two millennia of Chinese male historiography. Mao recognized that, as a woman, Jiang Qing was a political liability. Female rulers were traditionally denounced by male historians for their disruption of the Confucian patrilinear succession system and for their alleged misdeeds. From 1974, Jiang Qing tried belatedly to revise the negative historical images of

154 Zhou also made at least one sortie for sentimental reasons when in September 1975 he paid his last visit to his barber of twenty years in the Beijing Hotel; see Percy Jucheng Fang and Lucy Guinong J. Fang, *Zhou Enlai: A profile*, 184.
155 Wang Hongwen's most spectacular failure, his inability to restore order to strife-torn Hangzhou in 1975, was still to come; see Gardner, *Chinese politics and the succession to Mao*, 74.
156 Jin, "*Wenhua da geming*," 187.   157 Hao and Duan, *Zhongguo gongchandang liushi nian*, 638.

the Empress Lü of Han and Empress Wu of Tang,[158] who were, along with the Empress Dowager of the late Qing, the historians' main bêtes noires.

What is less easy to understand about this period is Mao's periodic dissociation from Jiang Qing and her Shanghai followers while they remained so important to the promotion and preservation of his Cultural Revolution goals. Marital conflict is a possible explanation. According to Terrill's account, in 1975 Jiang Qing moved out of the Zhongnanhai compound, where China's leaders lived, and took up residence in the Diaoyutai guest house complex. This source implies that political difficulties may have been the cause rather than the result of the rift.[159] Mao certainly chose to give that impression, telling her on 21 March 1974: "It's better not to see each other. You have not carried out what I've been telling you for many years; what's the good of seeing each other anymore. You have books by Marx and Lenin and you have my books; you stubbornly refused to study them." It was at a Politburo meeting in July 1974 that the Chairman first criticized his wife's political actions in front of their colleagues, and referred to her and her allies as a "Gang of Four." Jiang Qing, he told people, represented "only herself," had "wild ambitions," wanting "to become chairman of the Communist Party."[160] But a story widespread in Chinese political circles is that Jiang Qing moved because she was outraged by Mao's liaison with a young railway car attendant whom he had introduced into his household.[161] Yet another version is that Jiang Qing, whatever her views of Mao's amours, had in fact moved out of his house long before the Cultural Revolution. What does seem certain is that politically Mao and Jiang Qing still needed each other, and it is significant that whatever his strictures, he usually maintained that her errors were corrigible,[162] lending some credence to one Chinese view that Mao's attacks on the Gang of Four were part of an elaborate smoke screen designed to disarm their foes by implying he had deserted their cause. If so, then his principal dupe was Deng Xiaoping.

On 4 October 1974, no longer able to ignore the implications of Zhou Enlai's illness, Mao proposed that Deng Xiaoping should take the premier's place in charge of the government with the title of first vice-premier. One of Mao's two principal victims at the onset of the Cultural Revolution was to

158 Gao and Yan, "Wenhua da geming" shinian shi, 513–17. For Kang Sheng's role in this campaign, see Zhong, Kang Sheng pingzhuan, 315. See also Roxane Witke, Comrade Chiang Ch'ing, 464–66, 473; Ross Terrill, The white-boned demon: A biography of Madame Mao Zedong, 308–11; History Writing Group of the CCP Kwangtung Provincial Committee, "The ghost of Empress Lü and Chiang Ch'ing's empress dream," Chinese Studies its history, 12.1 (Fall 1978), 37–54; Yuan Ssu, "Bankruptcy of Empress Lü's dream," Chinese Studies in History, 12.2 (Winter 1978–9), 66–73.
159 Terrill, The white-boned demon.
160 Ibid., 324–5; Witke, Comrade Chiang Ch'ing, 476; Hao and Duan, Zhongguo gongchandang liushi man, 637–80.
161 Terrill recounts this story in The white-boned demon, 317.   162 Jin, "Wenhua da geming," 210.

return to run China. The meteoric rise of Wang Hongwen had been extraordinary enough, but this was an even more astonishing appointment. Yet it had been clear since the end of the previous year that Deng's star was again in the ascendant and why. The issue was the PLA's role in the polity.

Mao had told a Politburo conference on 12 December 1973 that he wanted the COs of the military regions reshuffled, clearly to deprive them of their long-standing PLA commands and connections and their recently acquired Party and government posts. He complained that the Politburo did not deal with politics and that the MAC did not deal with military affairs, a not very subtle hint to the military to get out of politics. To lessen the anxiety of the generals at the implications of these proposals, Mao did two things: He suggested that Deng Xiaoping should enter the MAC and take on the job of chief of staff, and he criticized himself for being taken in by Lin Biao's denunciation and harsh treatment of the PLA's revolutionary heroes. Whether this explanation deceived the generals as to the ultimate responsibility for the mistreatment of their colleagues is doubtful, but it was at least an apology, coupled with a plea to let bygones be bygones.

Mao got his way: The MAC promulgated the reshuffle of eight COS of military regions, and on the same day the CC authorized Deng's return to a major political role in the MAC and a place on the Politburo. The elements of the bargain were clear. In return for giving up political power, the generals were promised that it would be put into the responsible hands of a trusted old comrade. Deng later commented approvingly, perhaps even wonderingly, that all eight COs reported for duty at their new posts within ten days.[163] To the disgust of the Gang, Deng was chosen to lead the Chinese delegation to a special session of the United Nations in April 1974 and deliver a speech introducing Mao's theory of the three worlds to a global audience.

The Gang of Four could at least console themselves that by rehabilitating Deng, Mao had weakened their strongest potential opponents, the military. But when in October Mao revealed his intention of putting Deng in charge of the country, the Gang of Four were spurred into furious activity to try to deflect the Chairman from his purpose. Wang Hongwen flew secretly to see him in Changsha on 18 October.[164] Through Wang and other emissaries, the Gang alleged that Zhou was shamming illness and secretly plotting in the

---

163 *Zhonggong dangshi dashi nianbiao*, 386; "Quarterly chronicle and documentation," *CQ*, 58 (April–May 1974), 410; for an analysis of the regional reshuffle, sec ibid., 57 (January–March 1974), 206–7; for Deng's comment, see *Selected works of Deng Xiaoping (1975–1982)*, 97.
164 For a description of Wang Hongwen's visit to Mao, see Zhou Ming, *Lishi zai zheli chensi* (History is reflected here), 2. 196–203.

hospital with Deng, and the atmosphere in the capital had the flavor of the 1970 Lushan Conference. Mao rejected their protests, praising Deng's ability. When Zhou, disregarding his illness, flew with Wang Hongwen to Changsha on 23 December, the Chairman reaffirmed his commitment to Deng, and proposed to implement his earlier suggestion that Deng be made a vice-chairman of the MAC and PLA chief of staff. Political balance was preserved by the appointment of Zhang Chunqiao as director of the PLA's General Political Department and second-ranking vice-premier. At a CC plenum in Beijing from 8 to 10 January 1975, presided over by the ever vigilant Zhou Enlai, these appointments were formally agreed upon, along with the even more striking decision that Deng should return to the Politburo Standing Committee as a vice-chairman of the Party.[165] The stage was set for the last great campaign of Mao's career.

Deng Xiaoping's year in charge

Deng Xiaoping has not revealed his thoughts on assuming day-to-day control of both Party and government in January 1975.[166] Did he believe that the Chairman had turned his back on the Cultural Revolution and had licensed him to revive the more rational policies that had been pursued on its eve?

There were some encouraging signs: the rehabilitation if not reinstatement of men like himself; Zhou Enlai's speech to the Fourth NPC promoting, with Mao's support, long-term economic planning and what later became known as the "four modernizations" – of agriculture, industry, defense, and science and technology;[167] most important, there was Mao's call for stability and unity and his criticism of the factional activities of the Gang of Four. Mao also seemed to wish to turn back the clock to more permissive policies in the cultural sphere, advocating the restoration to office of former officials

---

165 Hao and Duan, *Zhongguo gongchandang liushi nian*, 637–9; Gao and Yan, *"Wenhua da geming" shinian shi*, 530–7. Recent mainland historians are coy about how Zhang Chunqiao's appointment was brought about, presumably because they wish to avoid clouding their image of Mao playing a strongly positive role in the restoration of Deng at this time. An alternative or an additional explanation for Mao's recall of Deng, still current in China, is that he wanted to use him to displace Zhou Enlai. According to this scenario, Mao worried that Zhou might outlast him; the premier had cancer, but the Chairman allegedly had a serious stroke in late 1972, which could have convinced him that he might still die first. Mao's preference for Deng may have been partly because he considered him a less formidable opponent for the Gang of Four; it might also have had to do with his close earlier relation with him – Deng had remained loyal to Mao when the latter's back was up against the wall; for the Mao-Deng relationship, see MacFarquhar, *Origins*, 1.140–5.

166 Hao and Duan, *Zhongguo gongchandang liushi nian*, 639–40.

167 When Zhou had first called for the four modernizations in 1964, he had not cited Mao in his support; see Gardner, *Chinese politics and the succession to Mao*, 67.

like Zhou Yang, and telling Deng Xiaoping that a hundred flowers should bloom again in all branches of the arts. Encouraged, perhaps led on, by the Chairman, Deng Xiaoping and his principal supporters, Ye Jianying and Li Xiannian, criticized the Gang at Politburo meetings in May and June for their allegations that an eleventh "line struggle" was in progress and that the new leadership was guilty of pragmatism. Ever a weather vane, Wang Hongwen made a self-criticism, thereafter retiring to Shanghai for a few months, but his three comrades remained stubbornly silent.[168]

Deng energetically tackled pressing problems:[169] first, the military issue, which was a prime motive for Mao to recall him to office. Of Deng's eight speeches made in 1975 republished in his *Selected works*, three dealt with military affairs. Less than three weeks after he had formally assumed his military offices, Deng was attacking the bloated size and budget of the PLA, its inefficiency and lack of discipline, and the factionalism endemic among its officer corps. He stressed the need for PLA obedience to Party policies. In a later speech, he added conceit and inertia to his list of PLA faults.[170]

A more urgent problem was labor unrest, most notably the strikes and sabotage by railway workers at Xuzhou, Nanjing, Nanchang, and elsewhere, apparently resulting from leftist rabble-rousing during the *Pi Lin, pi Kong* campaign. Communications had been disrupted on four major trunk lines, causing massive economic dislocation. Deng restored order by a mixture of threats and conciliation, and the reinstatement of central control.[171] Wang Hongwen had been unable to settle leftist-fomented strife in Hangzhou. Deng simply sent in the PLA and arrested the troublemakers.[172]

In search of solutions to deep-seated, longer-term problems relating to the economy, Deng called conferences and launched a number of initiatives. Three major policy documents were produced: "Some problems in accelerating industrial development" on 18 August, prepared by the State Planning Commission: "Outline report on the work of the Academy of Sciences" on

168 Hao and Duan, *Zhongguo gongchandang liushi nian*, 645–7; Fang Weizhong, ed., *Zhonghua renmin gongheguo jingji dashiji (1949–1980)* (A record of the major economic events of the PRC [1949–1980]), 544–5; Jin, "*Wenhua da geming*," 212. A struggle over the political line was, of course, the most serious type of intra-Party dispute: the Lin Biao affair had been numbered the tenth such struggle, the Liu Shaoqi purge the ninth.
169 For a summary of Deng Xiaoping's activities from January through October 1975, at which point he was no longer able to exercise effective power, see Hao and Duan, *Zhongguo gongchandang liushi nian*, 640–1.
170 *Selected works of Deng Xiaoping (1975–1982)*, 11–13, 27–42.
171 Jürgen Domes, *The government and the politics of the PRC: A time of transition*, 127; Fang, ed., *Zhonghua renmin gongheguo jingji dashiji (1949–1980)*, 541–3. The trunk lines were: Tianjin–Pukou; Beijing–Guangzhou; the Longhai (Lianyungang–Tianshui) line, a major east–west artery linking coastal Jiangsu with Gansu in the northwest; and the Zhe-Gan line joining Hangzhou and Nanchang.
172 Gardner, *Chinese politics and the succession to Mao*, 74.

26 September, prepared by Hu Yaobang, Hu Qiaomu, and others;[173] and "On the general program of work for the whole Party and nation" in mid-October, written by Deng Liqun.[174]

The industry document dealt with the roots of a wave of strikes that broke out in the middle of the year in Central and South China in response to leftist agitation for a more egalitarian wage system.[175] The document talked of "a handful of bad people sabotaging the work under the banner of 'rebellion' and 'going against the tide'"; of management being "in chaos"; of low productivity, low quality, expensive maintenance, high costs, and frequent breakdowns; and of the particularly serious problems in the raw materials, fuel, and power industries.[176] In his comments when the document was presented to the State Council, Deng stressed the need to support agriculture, introduce foreign technology, strengthen industrial research, bring order to management, put "quality first," enforce rules and regulations, and restore material incentives.[177] A month later, in the discussions of the report on the Academy of Sciences, Deng pressed for better training, higher educational standards, more expert leadership, and more time to be spent on science (and by implication, less on politics).[178]

But it was the document formulating a general program for Party and nation that struck at the leftists most broadly, copiously quoting from early Mao writings to drive home the point that revolution could not be stressed to the detriment of production: "It is purely nonsense to say that a certain place of work or unit is carrying out revolution very well when production is fouled up. The view that once revolution is grasped, production will increase naturally and without spending any effort is believed only by those who indulge in fairy tales."[179] No wonder Jiang Qing denounced these documents as "three great weeds" and characterized this one as a "political manifesto for the restoration of capitalism."[180]

Jiang Qing joined battle with Deng also on the issue of agriculture. At the First National Conference on Learning from Dazhai [brigade] in Agriculture, which brought together 3,700 delegates from 15 September to 19 October, she called for a return to the commune ideal of the height of the Great Leap Forward in 1958, with an emphasis on egalitarianism and class struggle. Deng,

173 For an analysis of these two documents, see Kenneth Lieberthal, *Central documents and Politburo politics in China*, 33–49.

174 Fang, ed., *Zhonghua renmin gongheguo jingji dashiji* (1949–1980), 550–5; translations exist in Chi Hsin, *The case of the Gang of Four*, 203–86.

175 Domes, *The government and politics of the PRC*, 128.

176 Chi, *The case of the Gang of Four*, 246, 247, 257.

177 Selected works of Deng Xiaoping, 43–6; Fang, ed., *Zhonghua renmin gongheguo jingji dashiji* (1949–1980), 550–2.

178 Chi, *The case of the Gang of Four*, 287–95.   179 Ibid., 227.

180 Teaching and Research Office for CCP History, *Zhongguo gongchandang liushi nian dashi jianjie*, 576.

on the other hand, looked back to the early 1960s, and the various incentives used then to encourage peasant initiative.[181]

In another bizarre example of invoking historical or literary texts for contemporary political purposes, Jiang Qing used her Dazhai speech to get at Deng Xiaoping by excoriating the hero of a famous old novel, the *Shuihu zhuan* (Water margin). She asserted that "this book must be read carefully to see the features of this renegade.... That man Song Jiang had many double-dealing tricks![182] ... Song Jiang made a figurehead of Chao Gai; aren't there people just now who are trying to make a figurehead of the Chairman? I think there are some."[183] Typically, the *Shuihu zhuan* analogy was not her idea but stemmed from criticism by Mao of Song Jiang's capitulationism or revisionism, a theme immediately pounced on by the Gang's sophisticated polemicist, Yao Wenyuan.[184]

Mao's behavior throughout Deng Xiaoping's year in power was contradictory.[185] He backed Deng's measures and defended them from attacks by the Gang of Four, but he simultaneously propounded his own leftist views and allowed Zhang Chunqiao and Yao Wenyuan to publicize theirs. He bemoaned wage differentials, payment according to work, and commodity exchange; in those respects, he said, the PRC did not differ much from pre-1949 China; only the system of ownership had changed. Encouraged by Mao's statements, Zhang Chunqiao and Yao Wenyuan published in the *People's Daily* a set of thirty-three quotations from Marx, Engels, and Lenin on the theory of proletarian dictatorship, carefully choosing comments that lent credence to their own position.[186] With the Chairman's permission, Zhang and Yao both wrote major theoretical exegeses to justify their own views and his: on the overriding importance of class struggle and the proletarian dictatorship; on the danger of commodity exchange undermining the socialist planned economy; on the worrying emergence of new bourgeois elements encouraged by material incentives; on the urgency of pressing forward to higher stages of collective ownership and then to state ownership; and on the continuing danger of China turning revisionist.[187]

Mao's ambivalence may have reflected indecision, a genuine conflict between head and heart. It may also have been a manifestation of his increasing

---

181 Domes, *The government and politics of the PRC*, 129–30; Fang, ed., *Zhonghua renmin gongheguo jingji dashiji (1949–1980)*, 552–3.

182 History Writing Group, "The ghost of Empress Lü," 55.

183 Teaching and Research Office for CCP History, *Zhongguo gongchandang liushi nian dashi jianjie*, 574.

184 Ibid., 573–4. For a detailed discussion of the *Shuihu zhuan* affair, see Goldman, *China's intellectuals*, 201–13.

185 Hao and Duan, *Zhongguo gongchandang liushi nian*, 648.   186 Ibid., 644–45.

187 Yao Wen-yuan, "On the social basis of the Lin Piao anti-Party clique," and Chang Ch'un-ch'iao, "On exercising all-round dictatorship over the bourgeoisie," are translated in Raymond Lotta, *And Mao makes 5: Mao Tse-tung's last great battle*, 196–220.

infirmity. From early 1974 until August 1975, when he had an operation to remove one of two cataracts in his eyes, he was unable to read; with his confidential secretary terminally ill in hospital, Mao was forced to depend on his young female companion, Zhang Yufeng, to read official documents and newspapers to him. By the end of 1975, Parkinson's disease was rendering him literally speechless, even in some of his meetings with foreign VIPs, able to communicate only by writing or by grunts comprehensible only to his attendants. According to Zhang:

> Having trouble speaking, he could only utter some mumbled words and phrases. Having worked around him for a long time, I could manage to understand what he said. Whenever the Chairman talked with other leading comrades, I had to be present to repeat his words. But when his speech and pronunciation became extremely unclear, all I could do was to lipread or guess from his expression. When his speech was at its worst, he could only write down his thoughts with a pen. Later, the Chairman had a great difficulty getting about. He could not walk on his own; he could not even move a step without help.[188]

Mao's leftist nephew, Mao Yuanxin, seems to have been transferred from the Northeast in late September 1975 to act as the Chairman's liaison officer with the Politburo. He, too, weighed in against Deng. Iago-like, Mao Yuanxin slanted his reports and poured doubts about Deng's loyalty to the Cultural Revolution into the Chairman's ear. He found a sympathetic listener.[189]

All these factors may have helped shape Mao's attitude. But in the light of Mao's long acquaintance with Deng, it seems unlikely that, in 1973, the Chairman was so naive as to think that the onetime number two capitalist-roader had changed his spots. The more likely hypothesis is that Mao's elevation of Deng Xiaoping was a tactic designed partly to hoodwink the military in order to deal more effectively with the problem "After Mao, which?" and partly to buy time while he sought a solution to the problem "After Mao, who?" The views he expressed during 1975 give no indication that he had changed his long-cherished ideas on the correct answer to "After Mao, what?"

The death of Zhou and the fall of Deng

Even before the death of Zhou Enlai on 8 January 1976, there was a rising tide of criticism of Deng Xiaoping's policies. Probably the Gang of Four

---

188 Zhang, "Anecdotes of Mao Zedong and Zhou Enlai in their later years." Ross Terrill in *Mao*, 395–7, 400–1, 411–13, 417–18, traces the Chairman's deteriorating health as manifested at his meetings with successive foreign visitors through the summer of 1976.

189 Hu, *Zhongguo shehuizhuyi geming he jianshe shi jiangyi*, 326; Hao and Duan, *Zhongguo gongchandang liushi nian*, 648–49. One report suggests that Mao Yuanxin was only with his uncle until November 1975, but other indications are that he remained in Beijing at the Chairman's side until his death.

realized that the Chairman's tolerance of Deng was wearing thin and decided to move in for the kill. As at the start of the Cultural Revolution, the initial battleground was the intellectual sphere.

A Qinghua University Party official, perhaps instigated by Deng's supporters, had written twice to Mao, complaining of the ideas and lifestyle of the Gang's loyal followers there, Chi Qun and Xie Jingyi. Mao took this as an attack on the Cultural Revolution, and his reply in support of Chi and Xie was publicized by them on 3 November as the opening salvo of a campaign to "repulse the right deviationist wind to reverse the verdicts."[190] They also seized their chance to attack the minister of education, Zhou Rongxin, who at Deng's request had been pressing for a restoration of educational standards.[191] At stake for Mao and the Gang of Four was one of the surviving legacies of the Cultural Revolution, or "new socialist things," an egalitarian education system emphasizing simpler and more practical courses that would be more easily accessible to worker-peasant-soldier entrants to universities.[192]

Toward the end of November, at Mao's orders, the Politburo called a notification conference, at which Hua Guofeng read out a summary of a speech by the Chairman, thereafter circulated to senior Party officials in the provinces. The burden of the Mao text and subsequent supportive central documents was that from July through September, political rumors had been rife, attempts had been made to split the top leadership, and attacks had been made on the Cultural Revolution in an effort to reverse its verdicts.[193] Effectively Mao had withdrawn his mandate from Deng and reshaped the current campaign into a drive to "criticize Deng and repulse the right-deviationist wind to reverse the verdicts."

It was at this point that Zhou Enlai died, precipitating a political crisis that would reverberate through China during the rest of the year. Zhou had been relatively inactive for months, but while he still lived, he symbolized rationality and restraint, a guarantee that however chaotic the country became, somewhere, someone was attempting to restore order and to protect people from the worst effects of the Cultural Revolution. Deng Xiaoping, who had been a worker-student with him in Paris in the early 1920s, probably summed up the general attitude to Zhou in an interview four years later:

190 *"Fanji youqing fan'an feng"*; see Hao and Duan, *Zhongguo gongchandang liushi nian*, 649.
191 Gardner, *Chinese politics and the succession to Mao*, 75–6. For a detailed analysis of educational developments during the Cultural Revolution, see *CHOC*, 15, Chapter 7.
192 Other new socialist things included Jiang Qing's revolutionary operas; the rural "barefoot doctor" or paramedic system; the May 7 cadre schools where officials spent months, sometimes years, performing manual labor; emulation of the collectivism of Dazhai brigade. See "Nothing is hard in this world if you dare to scale the heights," *RMRB, HQ, JFJB* Joint editorial, 1 January 1976, translated in "Quarterly chronicle and documentation," *CQ*, 66 (June 1976), 412.
193 Hao and Duan, *Zhongguo gongchandang liushi nian*, 649.

Premier Zhou was a man who worked hard and uncomplainingly all his life. He worked 12 hours a day, and sometimes 16 hours or more, throughout his life.... Fortunately he survived during the "Cultural Revolution" when we were knocked down. He was in an extremely difficult position then, and he said and did many things that he would have wished not to. But the people forgave him because, had he not done and said those things, he himself would not have been able to survive and play the neutralising role he did, which reduced losses. He succeeded in protecting quite a number of people.[194]

Zhou held the office of premier until the day he died. Now the choice of his successor could no longer be put off Deng was the obvious candidate. His selection would have signaled a continuing willingness to retain a moderating figure at the helm. Despite the mounting tide of leftist criticism of his restorationist policies, Deng had not yet suffered any public humiliation, and was allowed to give the memorial address at Zhou Enlai's funeral.[195]

But Mao must have calculated that to allow Deng to inherit Zhou's mantle would make him virtually immovable, certainly after his own death. Deng had to be struck down now or he would eventually remove those who sincerely sought to preserve the Maoist vision and the achievements of the Cultural Revolution. The same argument militated against the succession of other leading survivors like Ye Jianying and Li Xiannian.

The likeliest radical candidate for the premiership was the most capable member of the Gang of Four, the second-ranking vice-premier under Deng Xiaoping, Zhang Chunqiao. But Mao had almost certainly decided long since that a radical would not be a viable successor to Zhou. Far from being able to preserve Maoism, a radical premier would precipitate a backlash that would remove both person and program.

So Mao had to choose a beneficiary of the Cultural Revolution, presumably on the shrewd assumption that such a person would be sufficiently indebted to Mao and committed to the Cultural Revolution to try to tread the same path. A beneficiary might also want to preserve a radical element in the leadership to balance any threat to his own position from the old guard. Thus the pure Maoist torch would be kept alight within the Politburo, even if not at its very apex.

Mao chose Hua Guofeng, for reasons that are still not known; perhaps the Chairman simply made another mistake in selecting an appropriate heir. Hua's work as an official in Mao's home province had brought him early to

194 "Answers to the Italian journalist Oriana Fallaci," in *Selected works of Deng Xiaoping (1975–1982)*, 329–30. For a suggestion that at the outset of the Cultural Revolution, Zhou Enlai took a positive view of it, see Zhou, *Lishi zai zheli chensi*, 1. 57–8.
195 Deng's speech is in "Quarterly chronicle and documentation," *CQ*, 66 (June 1976), 420–4.

the Chairman's favorable attention.[196] It has also been suggested that Hua played a key role in the post–Lin Biao cleanup, but so did Ji Dengkui, another potential candidate as successor. Hua's position as minister of public security, assumed at the Fourth NPC a year earlier, gave him a power base that Mao may have thought an untested successor would need. On 21 and 28 January, he conveyed to the Politburo that Hua should be made acting premier and take over from Deng the control of the Party's daily work.[197] Mao also ordered that Deng's ally, Ye Jianying, be replaced as head of the MAC by a military beneficiary of the Cultural Revolution, Chen Xilian, presumably to prevent Hua being outflanked.[198] The covert campaign against Deng was stepped up.

The Gang of Four's strategy

The Gang of Four were furious at the elevation of Hua Guofeng, especially Zhang Chunqiao, who had apparently long coveted the premiership.[199] This led them to commit a major strategic error that probably cost them whatever slim hope they might have had of retaining power after Mao's death. Instead of collaborating with potential allies, they went all out for power.

The political complexion of the Politburo at this time was not unfavorable to the Gang. (See Table 5.) The survivors from among the pre-Cultural Revolution old guard were on the defensive and weak in active members. With Deng and Ye Jianying neutralized on the sidelines, Wang Hongwen and Zhang Chunqiao could have worked with Hua Guofeng to dominate the Party from their vantage point within the Politburo Standing Committee. Hua would presumably have welcomed such support at this critical time, especially since it would have come with Mao's blessing. The Gang's natural allies were

---

196 See Michel Oksenberg and Sai-cheung Yeung, "Hua Kuo-feng's pre–Cultural Revolution Hunan years, 1949–1966: The making of a political generalist," CQ, 69 (March 1977), 29–34.

197 Why "acting?" Conceivably for protocol reasons: Hua could not formally be named premier until so appointed by the NPC; but when he did obtain the full title in April, it was not as a result of some constitutional process. Possibly Mao, conscious of the error he had made in elevating an untried Wang Hongwen to a top slot, put Hua on probation to minimize the damage if he proved equally incompetent. Or possibly he wished to diminish opposition from among his old comrades by implying that Deng had not been permanently displaced but only temporarily set aside. The latter hypothesis might also serve to explain why Mao, in his attacks on Deng, was careful to say that the latter's sins were contradictions among the people and could be resolved; see Hao and Duan, Zhongguo gongchandang liushi nian, 650.

198 Fang, ed., Zhonghua renmin gongheguo jingji dashiji (1949–1980), 559. According to this account, Chen Xilian was to replace Ye Jianying while the latter was sick, but since no other account I have seen (e.g., Hao and Duan, Zhongguo gongchandang liushi nian, 649; Gao and Yan, "Wenhua da geming" shinian shi, 575) mentions this as a motive, one must assume that this was a political illness brought on by anger at Mao's decision about Hua. Certainly Ye had been well enough to attend Zhou's memorial service on 15 January.

199 For Zhang Chunqiao's reactions to his personal setback, see Gao and Yan, "Wenhua da geming" shinian shi, 575–6.

TABLE 5

The political complexion of the Politburo after the death of Zhou Enlai

(Names in boldface are of members of the Standing Committee; those in capitals are of full members, others are of alternate members. A name in parentheses means the person probably was politically dormant owing to age or illness.[a])

Radicals	Beneficiaries	Survivors
Mao Zedong	**Hua Guofeng**	**Deng Xiaoping**
Wang Hongwen		**Ye Jianying**
Zhang Chunqiao		**(Zhu De)**
JIANG QING	LI DESHENG[b]	LI XIANNIAN
YAO WENYUAN	CHEN XILIAN	(LIU BOCHENG)
	JI DENGKUI	XU SHIYOU
	WANG DONGXING	WEI GUOQING
	WU DE	
	CHEN YONGGUI	
	Wu Guixian	Su Zhenhua
	Ni Zhifu	Saifudin

[a] Kang Sheng and Dong Biwu died in 1975.

[b] For reasons that are not clear, Li Desheng "asked to be relieved of" his vice-chairmanship of the CCP and membership of the PSC when Deng Xiaoping took over the running of the country in January 1975; see *Zhonggong dangshi dashi nianbiao*, 391. Li had been a commander in the Second Field Army led by Liu Bocheng and Deng Xiaoping during the Civil War. In 1982, he wrote the preface to one of the many accounts of their military exploits: see Yang Guoyu, et al., eds., *Liu Deng da jun zhengzhanji* (A record of the great military campaigns of Liu [Bocheng] and Deng [Xiaoping]), 1.1–4.

beneficiaries like Hua. They were relatively young and active; and, as Mao probably sensed, because of the manner in which they had risen to power, they would be suspected by and suspicious of the survivors. Moreover, the beneficiaries included key military and political figures who could be important allies in any showdown: Chen Xilian, the commander of the Beijing Military Region; Wang Dongxing, the commander of the leaders' guards, PLA Unit 8341; Wu De, the party boss of the capital.[200]

But without Mao in firm daily control, the Gang brooked no compromise, instead allowing their naturally combative attitudes free rein. Accustomed until recently to acting as the Chairman's gatekeeper and representative.[201] Jiang Qing was not about to play second fiddle to a political upstart. As early as the Dazhai conference the previous autumn, she had begun sniping at the timidity with which the rising Hua Guofeng, whom she described as a "nice gentleman of Malenkov's ilk," sought to pursue their shared goals.[202] Now, instead of reassessing their position in the wake of Hua's appointment,

200 The suitability of these men as allies of the radicals is underlined by the fact that Deng Xiaoping insisted on their removal when he returned to power after the death of Mao. These three, together with Ji Dengkui, were nicknamed the "little gang of four."

201 Jin, "*Wenhua da geming*," 191–2.   202 Domes, *The government and politics of the PRC*, 130.

the Gang stepped up their campaign against him,[203] thus ensuring he would eventually have to turn to the survivors for support. Yet the reality of interdependence was about to be dramatically demonstrated.

Not content with pursuing Deng and undermining Hua, the Gang recklessly flouted what they must have known was popular sentiment about Zhou Enlai. When the premier died, no announcement was made that he would be cremated or where and when the ceremony would take place. But the news got out, and an estimated 1 million people lined the route from Tiananmen Square to the Babaoshan Cemetery, many clutching white paper chrysanthemums to symbolize their mourning. At one point, the crowd surged forward and stopped the cortege to demand that Zhou be buried, which would be in accordance with the Chinese custom; only after Zhou's widow, Deng Yingchao, got out of her car and assured the crowd that cremation had been the premier's wish was the cortege allowed to continue.[204] In the weeks that followed there was evidence from all around the country of the popularity of Zhou and the unpopularity of his enemies.[205]

The Gang's reaction was not to lie low for a time, but rather to confront Zhou's memory. Their control of the media enabled them to restrict the public airing of grief and to sanction blatant attacks on his policies, although he was not denounced by name.[206] They finally overstepped the mark on 25 March, when the Wenhui bao, a major Shanghai newspaper controlled by them, printed a front-page article in which Zhou Enlai was unmistakably referred to as a "capitalist-roader." In Nanjing, there were strong student-led protests against the Gang, which were not covered by the media. But the news reached Beijing and other cities because students, using tar, wrote slogans on the outside of railway carriages.[207] This "Nanjing incident" was the prelude to a far more dramatic demonstration of support for Zhou and Deng and hatred for the Gang of Four in the heart of the capital, right in front of the large portrait of Mao on the Gate of Heavenly Peace, the Tiananmen.

The Tiananmen incident, 1976

It was the time of the traditional Qing Ming Festival when ancestors were remembered and their graves swept. In an effort to stamp out "superstition" years earlier, the CCP had attempted to transform this festival into a time for remembering revolutionary heroes. Now the people of Beijing seized this

203 Gao and Yan, "Wenhua da geming" shinian shi, 576–7.
204 Roger Garside, Coming alive!: China after Mao, 8–9.
205 Gao and Yan, "Wenhua da geming" shinian shi, 582–6.   206 Ibid., 581–2.
207 Ibid., 586–97; Hao and Duan, Zhongguo gongchandang liushi nian, 652; Garside, Coming alive! 110–14.

opportunity to commemorate one of the greatest of all the CCP's heroes and to express their views on the current political situation.

Pupils of Beijing's Cow Lane Primary School placed the first wreath by the Heroes' Monument in the center of Tiananmen Square on 19 March. Four days later, a man from Anhui province laid another one, with a dedication to Zhou Enlai's memory. Both were swiftly removed by the police. The head of the capital's public security bureau muttered darkly about a "serious class struggle at the back of the wreaths." At dawn on 25 March, a middle school left its wreath, and shortly thereafter some workers left their memorial board beside it. On 30 March, the first group of soldiers left theirs. These tributes were not removed, and they had a galvanizing effect on the city's population.[208]

From 30 March on, the laying of wreaths at the monument escalated rapidly, in defiance of the orders of the city authorities. Column after column, dozens of units, thousands of people, marched to the square to place their wreaths, declaim their tributes, and read those of others. On the festival day, 4 April, a Sunday holiday, an estimated 2 million people visited the square.

The bottom part of the Heroes' Monument was buried in wreaths. Surrounding it, an army of wreaths mounted on stands marched outward toward the sides of the square. A typical wreath was homemade of paper flowers, usually in mourning white, with a picture of Zhou Enlai in its center, and two ribbons of white silk hanging from it, inscribed with a memorial tribute. Many had eulogies or poems pinned to them; other poems were pasted on the monument. It was these tributes that became the focus of attention of the crowds, packed tight but eager to find out to what degree others shared their feelings.[209]

Some eulogies simply commemorated the premier:

> He left no inheritance, he had no children, he has no grave, he left no remains. His ashes were scattered over the mountains and rivers of our land. It seems he left us nothing, but he will live forever in our hearts. The whole land is his, he has hundreds of millions of children and grandchildren and all China's soil is his tomb. So he left us everything. He will live in our hearts for all time. Who is he? Who is he? He is our Premier![210]

---

208 Gao and Yan, *"Wenhua da geming" shinian shi*, 598–9.

209 Garside, *Coming alive!* 115–36. Garside, a Chinese-speaking British foreign service officer who had been posted back to the British embassy in Beijing in January 1976, gives an elegiac eyewitness account of these events. The fullest and most vivid Chinese account is probably that in Gao and Yan, *"Wenhua da geming" shinian shi*, 598–637; the estimate of the numbers in the square on 4 April is in this source, 611. The present author was in Beijing from 1 to 4 April, but this account relies heavily on these two sources.

210 Quoted in Garside, *Coming alive!* 117.

Such sentiments were widely shared, but it was the attacks on the Gang of Four that were most keenly read. Some were hidden behind veils of allusion. Others were totally transparent:

> You must be mad
> To want to be an empress!
> Here's a mirror to look at yourself
> And see what you really are.
> You've got together a little gang
> To stir up trouble all the time,
> Hoodwinking the people, capering about.
> But your days are numbered. . . .
> Whoever dares oppose our Premier
> Is like a mad dog barking at the sun –
> Wake up to reality![211]

In the face of this verbal onslaught, the Gang of Four temporarily woke up to reality. They collaborated with the beneficiaries in the Politburo to take strong action. The Politburo had already met on 1 April to agree that the Nanjing incident had been splittist and supportive of Deng Xiaoping. On the basis of that negative assessment, the Beijing police had begun to take action in Tiananmen Square on 2 and 3 April, trying to inhibit the mourners, removing some wreaths.[212]

On the evening of 4 April, as the Qing Ming Festival drew to a close, the Politburo met again to assess the situation in Tiananmen Square. Prominent members of the old guard – Zhu De, Ye Jianying, Li Xiannian, and the general Xu Shiyou, who had supported them – were not present;[213] Deng Xiaoping could not have been there either. The beneficiaries and the Gang of Four appeared to be in total command. Hua Guofeng blamed provocateurs for what was happening in Tiananmen Square and opined that some poems were vicious direct attacks on the Chairman and many others in the central leadership. Another beneficiary, the Beijing Party first secretary, Wu De, detected coordinated activity and attributed it directly to preparations made by Deng during 1974–5. He said, "The nature of [the activity] is clear. It's a counterrevolutionary incident."[214] Jiang Qing asked if the safety of the central leadership was guaranteed and why their opponents had not been arrested.[215]

---

211 Xiao Lan, *The Tiananmen poems*, 29–30. This set of English translations comprises only a small fraction of the poems and eulogies pasted up in the square at this time. See, for instance, *Geming shichao* (A transcript of revolutionary poems), an two volumes, republished later as Tong Huaizhou, ed., *Tiananmen shiwen ji* (Poems from the Gate of Heavenly Peace).
212 Hao and Duan, *Zhongguo gongchandang liushi nian*, 652.   213 Ibid.
214 Hu, *Zhongguo shehuizhuyi geming he jianshe shi jiangyi*, 331.
215 Gao and Yan, "*Wenhua da geming*" *shinian shi*, 619.

The basis for continued collaboration between the Gang of Four and the beneficiaries became clear during the meeting. Both groups felt threatened. What they stood for was being rejected. If Hua were correct in asserting that Mao personally was a target of some of the mourning verses, then even the ultimate basis of their shared power was being questioned.[216] If that could happen while the Chairman was still alive, what about when his backing was only posthumous? At the very least, this massive and unprecedented upsurge of support for Zhou meant that the Chinese people now rejected Mao as the unique and godlike guide to their future. There was an alternate path, and they preferred it. They rejected, too, Mao's choice of successor. The implication of their homage to Zhou was that they wanted Deng Xiaoping back as his rightful heir. Everyone at the Politburo meeting that night knew that his return would spell disaster for them.

It was thus necessary to act swiftly and firmly. Mao Yuanxin relayed the conclusions of the meeting to his uncle, and when the Chairman sent back his agreement, the police were ordered into action. By 4:00 A.M. on 5 April, the square had been totally cleared of wreaths and writings; people who stayed late to read the verses or stand guard over the memorials were arrested.[217] By about 5:00 A.M., Wang Hongwen was instructing the police on how to behave when day came.[218]

News of the authorities' action spread rapidly, and people began converging on the square from all over the city, this time as individuals rather than in groups. But one group, ten middle school students, did turn up just after 6:00 A.M. to lay their tribute, only to find their way barred by soldiers and workers' militia who surrounded the monument, explaining that it had to be cleaned.[219] A foreign eyewitness who arrived at 8:00 A.M. reported that already there were 10,000 people in the square. Facing the Great Hall of the People on the west side of the square, they shouted, "Give back our wreaths! Give back our comrades-in-arms!"[220] Ordered to disperse but given no explanation for the removal of the wreaths, the crowd lost its temper. A police van was overturned and its occupants forced to apologize for alleging that the crowd was being led astray by "class enemies." A radical and presumably rehearsed Qinghua student who had the temerity to criticize wreath laying on behalf of the "biggest capitalist-roader in the Party" was

---

216 One clear dig at Mao and his "feudal-style" cult came in a reference to the emperor Qin Shihuangdi, to whom the Chairman was often implicitly compared: "China is no longer the China of the past, And the people are no longer wrapped in utter ignorance, Gone for good is Qin Shi Huang's feudal society." Quoted in Garside, *Coming alive!*, 127.

217 Hu, *Zhongguo shehuizhuyi geming he jianshe shi jiangyi*, 331.

218 Gao and Yan, *"Wenhua da geming" shinian shi*, 621. 219 Ibid.

220 *"Huan wo huaquan, huan wo zhanyou"; Zhonggong dangshi dashi nianbiao*, 401; Garside, *Coming alive!* 129.

roughed up and forced to retreat. By the early afternoon, several police vehicles had been burned, and a police command post had been stormed and set on fire.[221]

At 6:30 P.M., Wu De broadcast an appeal through the square's loudspeaker system, calling on people to disperse.[222] Most did, all but a few hundred, according to Chinese accounts.[223] Then, at 9:35 P.M., the square was suddenly flooded with light. Martial music was played over the loudspeakers. Members of the militia, the public security forces, and the Beijing garrison troops, who had been assembled in the Forbidden City behind the Tiananmen, appeared on the square, armed with sticks, and began beating people. By 9:45 P.M., the carnage was over and the wounded members of the "masses" were taken away for interrogation.[224]

Meeting that evening, the Politburo concluded that this "incident" had been a "counterrevolutionary riot." On 7 April, informed of the events by Mao Yuanxin, the Chairman ordered the publication of the *People's Daily's* version of what had happened together with the text of Wu De's appeal. Deng was to be relieved of all his posts, but allowed to retain his Party membership in case he reformed; what else might have befallen him is unclear, for on the same day he is said to have been spirited away to safety in the south by the PLA, where his allies on the Politburo, Xu Shiyou and Wei Guoqing, controlled the local armed forces.[225]

In perhaps his most important decision on 7 April, Mao ordered that Hua Guofeng should be immediately elevated to the premiership and first deputy chairmanship of the CCP.[226] Either the situation was too dangerous to delay longer or Hua had met whatever test Mao had set him; at any rate, the Chairman had made his final choice of successor. Three weeks later, on the evening of 30 April, after the new first deputy chairman reported to him on the state of the country, Mao used the legitimating words that Hua would later brandish as a talisman: "With you in charge, I'm at ease."[227] In fact, Hua was to prove no more viable than any of his three predecessors. But Mao would never know.

221 Garside, *Coming alive!* 129–39.

222 The text is Gao and Yan, *"Wenhua da geming" shinian shi*, 629–30.

223 Ibid, 633, Hao and Duan, *Zhongguo gongchandang liushi nian*, 653, specifies 388 arrests. Garside, *Coming alive!* 132, says that 4,000 remained in the square after Wu De's speech, but this was on the basis of estimates rather than police records.

224 Hao and Duan, *Zhongguo gongchandang liushi nian*, 653; Gao and Yan, *"Wenhua da geming shinian shi*, 634–5. Garside cites contemporary noncommunist reports of too killed; *Coming alive!* 132.

225 Domes, *The government and politics of the PRC*, 132. I am unaware of any Chinese source that has admitted that this was how Deng's safety was preserved, and many Chinese analysts believe he remained in the capital.

226 Hao and Duan, *Zhongguo gongchandang liushi nian*, 653.

227 *"Ni ban shi, wo fangxin";* Gao and Yan, *"Wenhua da geming" shinian shi*, 699.

The death of Mao

For superstitious or tradition-minded Chinese, which probably meant the majority of the nation, the year 1976 was replete with omens of disaster. The death of Zhou in January was followed in July by the death at eighty-nine of the grand old soldier of the revolution, Zhu De, the general whose loyalty to Mao during the early years in the wilderness had ensured military subservience to the Party. Three weeks later, a massive earthquake hit the area of the North China coal-mining city of Tangshan, killing more than 242,000 people and leaving more than 164,000 seriously injured.[228]

Throughout the country there was unrest, sparked on the one hand by leftist agitation against Deng Xiaoping and on the other by popular anger over the way he had been purged. There were stoppages again on the railways. Steel production was 1.23 million tons below target in the first five months of 1976. The production of chemical fertilizer, cotton yarn, and other key industrial goods fell precipitously, causing a drop of 2 billion yuan in national financial receipts. Targets for the annual plan had to be scaled back.[229]

At this time of natural disaster, political turmoil, and economic disruption, it became clear to the elite that Mao's life was drawing to a close.[230] With Deng down but not yet out, it would clearly have been sensible for the Gang of Four to solidify the alliance forged with the Politburo beneficiaries during the Tiananmen riot in order to be sure of weathering the critical weeks ahead. But they threw away their last opportunity by attacking Hua Guofeng at a national planning conference in July. They had evidently decided to confront the beneficiaries by military force if necessary, and in August, as the Chairman's life was ebbing away, they began to put the Shanghai militia, which they had been building up since 1967, into a state of readiness.[231]

The generals, too, were preparing. As the senior marshal by virtue of his place on the Politburo, Ye Jianying was lobbied by General Wang Zhen to move against the Gang of Four. Ye's fellow marshal Nie Rongzhen and General Yang Chengwu also had frequent strategy sessions with him. Ye was having consultations with members of the Politburo, presumably including Hua Guofeng and other beneficiaries whom the Gang had spurned. He also

228 Fang, ed., *Zhonghua renmin gongheguo jingji dashiji (1949–1986)*, 568.
229 Ibid., 567. For reports of pro-Deng poular unrest, see Gao and Yan, *"Wenhua da geming" shinian shi*, 641–59; for an analysis of leftist agitation, see ibid., 662–76.
230 For an account of Mao's parlous condition at the time of the annual Spring Festival, see Zhang, "Anecdotes of Mao Zedong and Zhou Enlai in their later years."
231 Hao and Duan, *Zhongguo gengchandang liushi nian*, 654–5; Gao and Yan, *"Wenhua da geming" shinian shi*, 678–9. In early September, Jiang Qing was revisiting the Dazhai brigade when an urgent message came from Beijing saying that the Chairman was sinking fast. She allegedly went on playing poker with her guards and medical attendants for some time before leaving for the capital; Ibid., 691.

traveled to his native Guangdong, where he reportedly found Deng Xiaoping in a combative mood:

> Either we accept the fate of being slaughtered and let the Party and the country degenerate, let the country which was founded with the heart and soul of our proletarian revolutionaries of the old generation be destroyed by those four people, and let history retrogress one hundred years, or we should struggle against them as long as there is still any life in our body. If we win, everything can be solved. If we lose, we can take to the mountains as long as we live or we can find a shield in other countries, to wait for another opportunity. At present, we can use at least the strength of the Canton Military Region, the Fuchou Military Region, and the Nanking Military Region to fight against them. Any procrastination and we will risk losing this, our only capital.[232]

But Ye wanted to wait. He indicated to Wang Zhen that he did not think it appropriate to move before Mao's death;[233] he justified procrastinating with the phrase "Spare the rat to save the dishes" (*tou shu ji qi*),[234] implying that he did not want to humiliate Mao by arresting his wife as a counterrevolutionary while he was still alive. When Mao died at ten minutes past midnight on 9 September, Ye Jianying was ready to act.[235]

The arrest of the Gang of Four

The strategic mistake of the Gang of Four had been to fail to make common cause with the beneficiaries. Their tactical error was for all of them to remain in Beijing after Mao's death. Lin Biao's plan to set up a rival CC in Guangdong, Deng's – indeed, the whole history of the Chinese revolution – should have taught them the critical importance of relocating to a secure base area when faced with potentially superior force. They ignored those lessons.

Jiang Qing and her colleagues were clearly affected by hubris. They had risen to power rapidly and easily by virtue of Mao's support, and they had exercised that power in an imperious manner with his acquiescence. All of them had luxuriated in a degree of privilege that the CCP had launched a revolution to eliminate but that, as Milovan Djilas has pointed out, is an inevitable

232 Quoted in Garside, *Coming alive!* 140–1; the source of the quotation is unclear. Garside does not explore the implications of Deng's remark about finding "a shield in other countries."
233 Xue Yesheng, ed., *Ye Jianying guanghui de yisheng* (Ye Jianying's glorious life), 342–3. Formally, Ye and Nie were ex-marshals, as military ranks had been abolished under Lin Biao before the Cultural Revolution.
234 Wang Nianyi, "'Wenhua da geming' cuowu fazhan mailuo" (Analysis of the development of the errors of the 'Great Cultural Revolution,') *Dangshi tongxun* (Party history newsletter), October 1986.
235 At some point during Mao's last days (hours?) of life, all members of the Politburo were brought in one by one to pay their final farewell; see Fan Shuo, "The tempestuous October – a chronicle of the complete collapse of the 'Gang of Four,'" *Yangcheng wanbao*, 10 February 1989, translated in *FBIS Daily Report: China*, 14 February 1989, 17.

companion of bureaucratic dictatorship.[236] In an earlier century, they would have been a court cabal, presuming upon their closeness to the emperor, insufficiently acquainted with the realities of power outside his penumbra.

Unlike most such cabals, the Gang of Four had a considerable regional power base in Shanghai to which they could have temporarily retreated. Instead, they apparently assumed that the combination of their relationship to Mao, membership in the Politburo Standing Committee, and control of the media had equipped them to take power in the capital, and they bent all their efforts to that goal. At the predawn Politburo meeting just after Mao's death, Jiang Qing appeared to be more interested in securing the immediate expulsion of Deng Xiaoping from the CCP than in settling the funeral arrangements.[237]

The Gang seem to have had a three-pronged plan of action: to assert their right to Mao's ideological mantle; to attempt to gain control of the Central Party apparatus; and to prepare for armed confrontation. Under Yao Wen-yuan's direction, the main media organs were soon trumpeting the importance of Mao's alleged deathbed injunction (*linzhong zhufu*): "Act according to the principles laid down" (*An jiding fangzhen ban*). Not to do so would be to "betray Marxism, socialism, and the great theory of continuing the revolution under the dictatorship of the proletariat."[238] Clearly the objective was to head off any attempt either to reverse the current campaign against Deng Xiaoping or, even more threatening, to disavow the Cultural Revolution.

By creating an appropriate ideological climate through the press, the Gang could sway lower-ranking cadres' judgment of the balance of forces in the capital.[239] But this was not tantamount to taking over the reins of power. Shortly after Mao's death, the Gang attempted to assert a right of leadership over provincial organs. Wang Hongwen set up his own "duty office" in the Zhongnanhai, sending a message to provincial committees in the name of the CC's General Office ordering all major problems to be referred to himself.[240]

---

236 Milovan Djilas, *The New Class: An analysis of the communist system*, 42–7. Terrill devotes much space to a discussion of Jiang Qing's privileged lifestyle, and to a comparison of her and outstanding Chinese empresses; see Terrill, *The white-boned demon*, esp. 317–23.

237 Xue, ed., *Ye Jianying guanghui de yisheng*, 342.

238 Hao and Duan, *Zhongguo gongchandang liushi nian*, 656. According to post-Cultural Revolution accounts, Mao actually said to Hua Guofeng on 30 April 1976, "Act according to past principles" (*Zhao guoqu fangzhen ban*); see Gao and Yan, "*Wenhua da geming*" *shinian shi*, 699. One analysis of the difference between the formulations argues that the Gang of Four's version suggests obedience to specific policies that they had been promoting on Mao's behalf or that they might claim to have documentary proof of in the Chairman's papers, whereas the Hua Guofeng version advocates no more than a vague continuity. See Gardner, *Chinese politics and the succession to Mao*, 111–13.

239 Provincial papers immediately began repeating Mao's alleged deathbed injunction; see Hu, *Zhongguo shehuizhuyi geming he jianshe shi jiangyi*, 335.

240 Whether in doing this Wang exceeded his authority as a member of the Politburo Standing Committee as afterward alleged must remain uncertain. Two years earlier, Wang had apparently attempted to insert Shanghai cadres in central CCP and government organs, though with what success is unclear; see Zhong, *Kang Sheng pingzhuan*, 316.

From 12 September, the Gang promoted a write-in campaign to pressure the Politburo to appoint Jiang Qing chairman in Mao's place.[241] Pictures published on the occasion of the obsequies for the late Chairman were designed to accustom the public to the idea of Jiang Qing emerging as his successor.[242]

The Gang pressed for a swift decision. On 19 September, Jiang Qing demanded that the Politburo Standing Committee – at this point consisting of Hua Guofeng, Wang Hongwen, Ye Jianying, and Zhang Chunqiao – hold an emergency conference and that she and Mao Yuanxin should attend, but Ye should not. At the meeting, Jiang proposed the Mao Yuanxin should be entrusted with sorting through his uncle's papers, presumably with a view to his discovering, or at least "discovering," a last will favoring her takeover. The vote went in favor of keeping the Chairman's papers locked up in the CC's General Office.[243]

On 29 September, at another Politburo conference, Jiang Qing and Zhang Chunqiao tried to force the issue of her future role. They rejected a proposal from Ye Jianying and Li Xiannian that Mao Yuanxin should return to his job in Liaoning province, countering with a suggestion that he should be entrusted with preparing the political report for the next CC plenum.[244] The Gang were outvoted, however: Mao Yuanxin was ordered back to Liaoning, and the leadership question was shelved.[245]

The Gang's third measure was to prepare for confrontation. The militia in Shanghai, perhaps 100,000 strong, was issued with weapons and arms, and warned to be ready for a fight. Secret contacts were established with Ding Sheng, the CO of the Nanjing Military Region. Wang Hongwen and the others breathed fire in speeches before friendly audiences.[246]

Mao Yuanxin caused a momentary panic on 2 October when he ordered an armored division to move to Beijing, but a telephone call to Ye Jianying from the Military Region headquarters elicited an immediate countermanding order.[247] Despite, or perhaps because of, the vicissitudes of the Cultural Revolution, the military chain-of-command loyalty was firmly in place, and the Gang and their adherents were not part of it.

---

241 Ibid., 334–35; *Zhonggong dangshi dashi nianbiao*, 403.
242 Ladany, *The Communist Party of China and Marxism, 1921–1985*, 385. For an eyewitness account of the memorial service on 18 September, see Garside, *Coming alive!* 147–49. In late September, a mimeographed copy of Mao's purported last wishes reached Hong Kong; according to it, Mao had asked a group of leaders in June to help Jiang Qing in "hoisting the Red Flag" after he was dead. See Ting, *Chairman Hua*, 112.
243 Jin, "*Wenhua da geming*," 214–15. Another version has Jiang Qing and Mao Yuanxin bullying Mao's secretary into handing over some documents, which were only returned after Hua Guofeng's intervention; see Ting, *Chairman Hua*, 111.
244 Jin, "*Wenhua da geming*," 214–15.   245 Xue, ed., *Ye Jianying guanghui de yisheng*, 345.
246 Hao and Duan, *Zhongguo gongchandang liushi nian*, 655–66; Jin, "*Wenhua da geming*," 214–15.
247 Gao and Yan, "*Wenhua da geming*" *shinian shi*, 699.

Post–Cultural Revolution historians may well have exaggerated the extent to which the Gang were bent on a military coup. Even in their wildest fantasies, they could not have believed that their Shanghai militia could prevail over the likely opposition of most of the PLA. Shanghai could perhaps be a last-ditch stronghold, but not a Yan'an-style springboard for victory. Indeed, by remaining in Beijing, Jiang Qing and her colleagues gave every impression of having deluded themselves into thinking that even after Mao, it would be politics as usual. The struggle would go on, but under Cultural Revolution rules that had always brought the Gang out on top. But their patron was dead, and they were up against men who had fought long years to win China, and had made a revolution by disregarding the rules and taking swift and ruthless action when need be.

Sooner or later, such action was inevitable, for the reasons Deng Xiaoping had given. Ye Jianying apparently felt that Hua Guofeng had to play a key role because of his positions as the CCP's first deputy chairman and premier. Ye found Hua indecisive. Hua had originally wanted to convene a CC plenum to settle the leadership dispute with the Gang of Four, but after the Politburo confrontation on 29 September, and after Ye had promised him the support of the old comrades if he stood up and fought, Hua became convinced that the time for formal procedures was long past.[248]

An ideologically uncompromising article in the *Guangming ribao* on 4 October, following provocative speeches by Jiang Qing and Wang Hongwen, finally triggered the coup against the Gang, according to one account.[249] There were worrying indications that the Gang were planning some sort of action, for their followers were told to expect good news by 9 October. Alarmed, Ye Jianying went into hiding in the capital. Then, on 5 October, Hua Guofeng, Ye Jianying, and Li Xiannian held a Politburo conference at the PLA General Staff HQ in the Western Hills outside Beijing, to which the Gang were not invited. It was unanimously agreed that Jiang Qing, Wang Hongwen, Zhang Chunqiao, Yao Wenyuan, Mao Yuanxin, and their principal supporters had to be seized. Wang Dongxing and PLA Unit 8341 were ordered to carry out this decision. They did so on 6 October. When Jiang Qing was arrested at her residence, her servant spat on her. The Cultural Revolution was over.[250]

---

248 Xue, ed., *Ye Jianying guanghui de yisheng*, 344–5.

249 This article was prepared by two members of the *Liang Xiao* group, apparently at the urging of the editors of the *GMRB*. According to one of the authors, the article was dashed off with no prior consultation with members of the Gang of Four. Nevertheless, it was sufficiently disquieting for Politburo member Chen Xilian to return immediately to Beijing from Tangshan to consult with Ye Jianying.

250 There is some disagreement as to the precise manner and moment of the arrest of the Gang of Four. According to Fan, "The tempestuous October," 21, a meeting of the Politburo Standing Committee was called (presumably by Hua Guofeng) to discuss the final proofs of the fifth volume of Mao's *Selected works* and to study the proposals for the Mao mausoleum to be built in Tiananmen Square. In

INTERREGNUM

In the immediate aftermath of the death of Mao and the purge of the Gang of Four, the urgent national need was for calm and stability. The Party, the PLA, and the people had to be reassured that the era of upheaval was over and that the country was under firm but moderate leadership. A somewhat contradictory image of change combined with continuity had to be conveyed.

A priority was to settle the question that had rent the leadership since the outset of the Cultural Revolution: "After Mao, who?" The leading survivors, Ye Jianying and Li Xiannian, presumably decided that this was no time for renewed struggle within the rump of the Politburo, already reduced by death and defeat to sixteen of the twenty-five appointed at the Tenth Congress only three years earlier. Whatever his merits, Hua Guofeng wore the mantle of legitimacy and had the rights of occupancy. He had been the Chairman's choice, he was in place, and he had led the beneficiaries into the anti-Gang camp. On 7 October, his assumption of Mao's posts as chairman of both the Party and its MAC was announced. Because he retained the premiership, Hua was now formally the heir of both Mao and Zhou Enlai. By combining the roles of both men, he seemed to have been placed in an impregnable position. He would discover that position conferred prestige and privilege, but power had deeper roots.

Simultaneously with agreeing on a new leader, the Politburo had to neutralize the country's one radical bastion. Fortunately Shanghai turned out to be a paper tiger. Deprived of their national leaders, the Gang's deputies there vacillated, allowed themselves to be lured to Beijing by transparent stratagems, and finally collapsed without fulfilling any of their threats of a fight to the finish. In the event, there was a week of light armed resistance. The Politburo dispatched two of their alternative members, Su Zhenhua, and Ni Zhifu, to take control; Xu Shiyou temporarily reassumed his old command of the Nanjing Military Region, displacing the unreliable Ding Sheng, to provide the

addition to Wang Hongwen and Zhang Chunqiao, who would come to the 8:00 P.M. meeting in the Huairentang in the Zhongnanhai complex as of right, Yao Wenyuan was also invited under the pretext that as the nation's leading propagandist, he would be the obvious person to carry out any last-minute revisions or polishing for the Mao volume. When each arrived, Hua Guofeng read out an agreed statement: "The central authorities maintain that you have committed unforgivable crimes, and have made a decision on investigating your case. You are prohibited from having access to the outside world during the investigation." Thereupon, Wang Dongxing's personnel escorted the prisoners away. Simultaneously, Jiang Qing and Mao Yuanxin were being arrested in their residences elsewhere in the Zhongnanhai. See also Wang, *Da dongluan de niandai*, 607–9; Xue, ed., *Ye Jianying guanghui de yisheng*, 345–6; *Yingsi lu*, 74–5. According to Gao and Yan, "*Wenhua da geming*" *shinian shi*, 700–3, however, the Gang of Four were all arrested in their residences in the Diaoyutai in the early hours of 6 October.

politicians with any necessary military backup.[251] With Shanghai reclaimed, it was now up to Hua Guofeng to provide the country with leadership.

Hua Guofeng's dilemma

From the outset, Hua Guofeng's leadership was hamstrung by an insoluble dilemma, symbolized by the contradictory heritages of Mao and Zhou that he had been bequeathed. On the one hand, there was no doubt that Mao wanted the goals and gains of the Cultural Revolution to be maintained. To disavow the Cultural Revolution would be to undermine the position of the man who had chosen him as his successor, and indeed to negate the whole period whose upheavals had permitted Hua to rise from relative obscurity to his current eminence. Hua's only claim to legitimacy was Mao's blessing, and he moved swiftly to ensure that only he had control of Mao's legacy. On 8 October, it was announced that a fifth volume of the late Chairman's selected works would be published under the editorial control of Hua Guofeng. A simultaneous decision was to erect a mausoleum for Mao in Tiananmen Square, in defiance of a twenty-seven-year-old rule agreed to by the Chairman and his colleagues not to emulate the Soviet pattern of honoring leaders by erecting tombs and renaming cities and streets.[252] Hua had no doubt of Mao's continuing significance for himself; he, and presumably his fellow beneficiaries, wanted to try to ensure that Mao's continuing significance for the country would be set in marble.

Hua's personal amulet was Mao's now oft-echoed sentence "With you in charge, I'm at ease." But it was necessary to coin a slogan that would convey in the ideological realm the symbolism enshrined in the mausoleum: The Chairman is forever with us. Appropriately, Hua approved a formula proposed by Wang Dongxing that seemed to set Mao Zedong Thought in concrete: "Whatever policy Chairman Mao decided upon, we shall resolutely defend; whatever directives Chairman Mao issued, we shall steadfastly obey." Their aim was to head off questioning of the actions of the later Mao, which had helped to bring them and other members of what came to be known as the "whatever faction" to power.[253] Moreover, the preservation of the Mao cult provided a basis and a justification for the burgeoning cult of Hua Guofeng

251 Gao and Yan, "*Wenhua da geming,*" *shinian shi,* 703–8; Hao and Duan, *Zhongguo gongchandang liushi nian,* 657; *Zhonggong dangshi dashi nianbiao,* 405. Domes's account suggests greater bloodshed – *The government and politics of the PRC,* 138.

252 *Zhonggong dangshi dashi nianbiao,* 405.

253 First divulged in a joint editorial of *RMRB, HQ,* and the *Jiefangjun bao* on 7 February 1977; *Zhonggong dangshi dashi nianbiao,* 406–7; Hao and Duan, *Zhongguo gongchandang liushi nian,* 670.

himself, badly needed if this unknown successor was to establish a position among Party and people.[254]

But the attempt of Hua and the whatever faction to don Mao's protective mantle had already been challenged by Deng Xiaoping's protectors in the south. In a letter to Hua, Xu Shiyou and Wei Guoqing queried the advisability of hushing up Mao's shortcomings, which were known to all; indicated that Mao's blessing of Hua as successor was insufficient legitimation and that it had to be confirmed by a CC plenum; and hinted broadly of a challenge to Hua at such a plenum if Mao's incorrect verdict on Deng were not reversed.[255]

Hua fought back. At the central work conference held from 10 to 22 March to discuss progress on the anti-Gang campaign, he reaffirmed the "two whatevers," repeated formulas from the Cultural Revolution, maintained that the Tiananmen incident was counterrevolutionary, and asserted that the campaign against Deng and the right-opportunist wind to reverse the verdicts had been correct. He even denounced the Gang of Four as extreme rightists (the tactic *they* had used in the aftermath of the Lin Biao affair) in an effort to defend the continuation of leftist policies.

Hua came under fire from Party veterans, notably Chen Yun, who had been a member of the Politburo Standing Committee and its predecessor for more than two decades up to the Cultural Revolution. Chen and another critic, Wang Zhen, focused on the linked questions of the assessment of the Tiananmen incident and the need for a second rehabilitation of Deng Xiaoping, which they claimed was universally demanded. Hua must have wondered if this was the support of veteran cadres that Ye Jianying had promised him in return for taking a lead against the Gang of Four. At any rate, he rejected the demands of Chen and Wang and even refused to allow their speeches to be printed in the conference record.[256]

There is no suggestion in Chinese accounts of this work conference that Ye Jianying or Li Xiannian joined in their old comrades' criticisms of Hua's position. Almost certainly their feelings must have been mixed. Formally, it would have been unusual for a member of the Politburo Standing Committee

254 Ibid. Books and pamphlets about Hua were churned out by the presses. According to Stuart R. Schram, writing in 1984, the card index in the Library of Peking University contained approximately 300 entries of books and pamphlets contributing to the Hua cult, a small fraction, in his judgment, of those published around the country; Stuart R. Schram, "'Economics in command?' Ideology and policy since the Third Plenum, 1978–84," CQ, 99 (September 1984), 417, n. 1. A favorite publicity photograph of Hua at this time was of him with Mao, supposedly at the moment when the late Chairman had uttered the magic words of benediction. Some observers claimed to detect that Hua changed his hairstyle to make him resemble Mao.
255 Domes, *The government and politics of the PRC*, 146–7.
256 Hao and Duan, *Zhongguo gongchandang liushi nian*, 670–1; *Zhonggong dangshi dashi nianbiao*, 407–8. The gist of Chen Yun's speech is to be found in *Chen Yun wenxuan (1956–1985)* (Selected works of Chen Yun [1956–85]), 207.

like Ye to criticize another member of that select body in front of a large gathering of more junior Party officials. More importantly, Ye and Li owed a certain loyalty to Hua, who was now in a sense their creation as well as Mao's. And while Ye and Li had doubtless supported everything Deng had tried to do during 1975, they must have been ambivalent about him returning in 1977. With Deng absent, they dominated the political picture as elder statesmen guiding Hua; with Deng back, they would at the very least have to cede part of that role to him. And what would be Deng's attitude toward them? Would he not feel that they, like Zhou, had done and said things they regretted in order to survive the Cultural Revolution? And if so, would he forgive the living as well as the dead?

Yet Ye and Li would have appreciated the strength of sentiment within the Party and PLA and realized that with Mao gone it would be difficult to hold the line against Deng's return. They must have known, too, that Deng was more likely than Hua to be able to engineer the post-Cultural Revolution turnaround that most desired. Political confusion, factional battles, and indiscipline encouraged by years of leftist agitation were once again damaging the economy. There were widespread reports of strikes, sabotage, and renewed disruption of rail traffic. The 1976 plan results, affected in part by the Tangshan earthquake, had been considerably below target, and the estimated losses over the last three years of the Cultural Revolution, 1974–6, were 28 million tons of steel, 100 billion yuan in value of industrial production, and 40 billion yuan in state revenues.[257] Hua Guofeng had called for a return to "great order," but Deng was more likely to bring it about.

After the work conference, Ye and Li must have advised Hua that to resist the Deng tide could be politically disastrous for him. The most that could be done was to obtain a guarantee from Deng that he would let bygones be bygones. On 10 April, Deng wrote to the CC condemning the two whatevers, and proposed instead the use of "genuine Mao Zedong Thought taken as an integral whole." He was subsequently visited by two "leading comrades" of the CC's General Office, one presumably its director, Wang Dongxing, seeking to negotiate a deal before the beneficiaries, now the whatever faction, agreed to his return. Deng, to judge from his own account, was not in a mood for compromise, pointing out that if the two whatevers were correct, there could be no justification for his rehabilitation or reversing the verdict on the Tiananmen incident. Even Mao himself had never claimed that whatever he said was correct, nor had Marx or Lenin.[258]

257 Fang, ed., *Zhonghua renmin gongheguo jingji dashiji* (1949–1980), 573–4; Domes, *The government and politics of the PRC*, 140–2.
258 *Selected works of Deng Xiaoping* (1975–1982), 51–2; Hao and Duan, *Zhongguo gongchandang liushi nian*, 671.

Deng's letter has never been released, so it is uncertain whether in it or an earlier communication he indicated, as rumored, his willingness to support Hua Guofeng's continued leadership of the Party.[259] Some such undertaking seems likely, or there would have been no reason for the whatever faction to agree to his return. If it were given, that could be why the letter was not included in Deng's *Selected works:* It would have contrasted sharply with Hua Guofeng's eventual fate.

Whatever the understanding, it enabled Deng Xiaoping to attend the Tenth CC's Third Plenum from 16 to 21 July and be reinstated in all his offices: Party vice-chairman and member of the Politburo Standing Committee; vice-chairman of the MAC; vice-premier; and PLA chief of staff. Hua Guofeng had his positions formally endorsed, and stubbornly maintained his support for the two whatevers and the Cultural Revolution. The available text of Deng's speech *indicates* that he repeated his advocacy of an integrated view of Mao Zedong Thought, but was discreet enough not to attack the two whatevers frontally at this time; he had to prepare the ground before his next attack. Instead, he promoted an old slogan of Mao's that was to become the essence of Deng Xiaoping's post-Mao policies: "Seek truth from facts."[260]

On the basis of the compromise cemented at the plenum, the CCP was able to hold its Eleventh Congress in August. On this occasion, it was Hua's turn to be discreet, not reasserting the two whatevers or repeating his estimation of the Tiananmen incident as counterrevolutionary. But he clearly felt unable to criticize Mao or disavow the Cultural Revolution without undermining his own position. Instead, he opened with a long and effusive eulogy of the late Chairman, went on to reaffirm the necessity for and success of the Cultural Revolution, the correctness of the line of the Tenth Congress (at which he entered the Politburo), and the need to persist with class struggle and continue the revolution under the proletarian dictatorship; and he observed chillingly that "Political revolutions in the nature of the Cultural Revolution will take place many times in the future."[261]

Deng Xiaoping emerged at the Congress as the CCP's third-ranking leader, after Hua and Ye Jianying (who reported on the new Party constitution). Deng's brief closing speech was the only other address to be accorded publicity. He referred to Hua as "our wise leader" but did not emulate his wisdom by praising the Cultural Revolution. He avoided controversy by calling for a

259 Garside, *Coming alive!* 174. For Deng's expression of support in conversation with Hua Guofeng, see the manuscript minutes of Hua's visit to Deng and Liu Bocheng in a hospital on 26 October 1976, available in Harvard's Fairbank Center Library. I am grateful to Michael Schoenhals for drawing my attention to this source.
260 The slogan *shishi qiushi* dates back to the Han period; *Selected works of Deng Xiaoping,* 55–60; *Zhonggong dangshi dashi nianbiao,* 409–10.
261 *The Eleventh National Congress of the Communist Party of China (Documents),* 52.

return to honesty and hard work, modesty and prudence, plain living and hard struggle, and, of course, seeking truth from facts. But he, too, had to compromise and express support for the current line to "grasp the key link of class struggle" and "continue the revolution under the dictatorship of the proletariat," dogmas of the Eleventh Congress later condemned by Chinese Party historians.[262] No wonder Deng chose not to include this speech in his *Selected works*, despite the importance for him and the CCP of the occasion on which it was given.

Out of this Congress there emerged a leadership that was purged of the left but that did not particularly favor the left's victims. One third of the CC elected at the Tenth Congress disappeared, which included more than 75 percent of its representatives from mass organizations, presumably for leftist sympathies. Another category of probable leftists, the more recent entrants into the Party, also suffered heavily, being reduced by more than 70 percent.

The Politburo was also a compromise, but weighted in favor of survivors and beneficiaries of the Cultural Revolution, with only six of twenty-six members drawn from the ranks of the victims. One man who would later help spearhead Deng's reform program secured a toehold as an alternate member: Zhao Ziyang. In the new five-man Politburo Standing Committee, Deng was the only one who would later emerge as a strong critic of Hua and the whatever faction. Hua was now buttressed by his key supporter in that grouping, Wang Dongxing, who was presumably being recognized both for his service against the Gang and for the power he wielded as head of PLA Unit 8341. Ye Jianying was joined by his joint guarantor of Hua's position, Li Xiannian.[263]

Hua's "great leap"

Insofar as Hua Guofeng had a vision of "After Mao, what?" it seems to have been an unlikely combination of mid-1960s radicalism and mid-1950s economics. Certainly, the more generally acceptable part of Hua's dual heritage was Zhou Enlai's commitment of China to the four modernizations. Here was a goal around which all except the most rabid leftists could unite. And surely Hua visualized a successful development program as providing the answer to the many who were asking themselves what right he had to be at the top.

262 Ibid., 191–5; Hao and Duan, *Zhongguo gongchandang liushi nian*, 674. One report has it that Deng was originally scheduled to deliver a speech on seeking truth from facts, written by Hu Qiaomu, but that when Deng was assigned the closing address, Nie Rongzhen gave the Hu text, which was later published in *Red Flag*, though no longer described as a Congress speech; I am indebted to Michael Schoenhals for this information.

263 *The Eleventh National Congress of the Communist Party of China (Documents)*, 227–36. For a more detailed breakdown of the composition of the new CC and Politburo, see Domes, *The government and politics of the PRC*, 150–1.

An unexceptionable but also unexceptional bureaucratic career in the provinces before the Cultural Revolution; junior enough not to have been in the first group of provincial officials to be targeted by the Red Guards; the luck still to be around when the tide turned and experienced cadres were once again in demand; senior enough to be transferred to the capital when the Lin Biao affair left large gaps in the leadership; competent enough and leftist enough to have been acceptable to Mao when Wang Hongwen failed him – no one could blame Hua for being lucky, but was his record justification enough for him to try to lead China after Mao and Zhou when his elders and betters were available? Probably not, in many people's eyes, and hence Hua's need to prove himself.

Unfortunately for Hua, his need to deliver the goods outstripped China's ability to produce them. At the first session of the new (Fifth) NPC in February–March 1978, Premier Hua unveiled his grandiose version of the original Ten-Year Plan (1976–85) foreshadowed by Zhou in his last NPC speech in 1975. The plan target for steel output in 1985 was 60 million tons (1977: 23.7 m. tons), for oil, 350 million tons (1977: 93.6 m. tons). For the remaining eight years, Hua called for the construction of 120 major projects, 14 major heavy industrial bases, and capital investment equivalent to that expended in the previous twenty-eight years. The plan failed to take account of the lessons of the 1960s and the economic damage of the 1970s.[264] As is explained in *CHOC* 15, Chapter 6, the plan could not have reflected any careful thought or accurate data: The oil fields on which expanded production would supposedly be based were a pipe dream; the foreign exchange costs would have been enormous, because what came to be known as Hua's "great leap outward" placed heavy reliance on machinery imports. Instead of picking up Zhou's torch, Hua had mimicked Mao's grandiose visions. Instead of covering himself with glory, he had pointed China toward another economic disaster. This, too, would be used against him.

The Third Plenum

The manner in which Deng Xiaoping turned the tables on Hua and the whatever faction is an illustration of the mysterious nature of power in the PRC. Hua was supreme leader in all branches of Party and state, Deng was not. The whatever faction was in power; Deng's supporters were not. Yet, in the relatively short period between the Third Plenum of the Tenth CC, in July 1977, and the Third Plenum of the Eleventh CC, in December 1978, those

264 Fang, ed., *Zhonghua renmin gongheguo jingji dashiji*, (1949–1980), 595–6.

power relations had been turned around. The method appears to have been mobilization of elite opinion through the press.

On 11 May 1978, the *Guangming ribao* published a pseudonymous article entitled "Practice is the sole criterion for testing truth," which became a second rallying cry for the Deng forces. The author of the article, Hu Fuming, was then vice-chairman of the Philosophy Department of Nanjing University and a Party member. He later claimed he had submitted the article for publication in the autumn of 1977 in opposition to the two whatevers entirely on his own initiative, because he felt that without rebutting that doctrine there was no hope of Deng's returning to power.[265] Self-generated it may have been, but the article that appeared had undergone considerable revision and strengthening on the basis of the ideas of two theoreticians working at the Central Party School under Hu Yaobang.[266] It struck at the roots of Cultural Revolution doctrine, which, whether expressed by Lin Biao, Jiang Qing, or Hua Guofeng, held that Mao's writings and statements were eternal verities that should not be tampered with, whatever the circumstances.

To the annoyance of Hua Guofeng and Wang Dongxing, the article was quickly republished in the *People's Daily* and the *Liberation Army News* and was the spark that lit a prairie fire of nationwide debate.[267] Deng Xiaoping himself joined in the fray in a speech to a PLA political work conference in June, when he reasserted the need to "seek truth from facts."[268] Astutely, he used quotations from Mao's works to prove that this principle did not mean rejecting him but, on the contrary, represented a return to the best traditions and practice of the Chairman himself,[269] and concluded with a rhetorical flourish:

> Comrades, let's think it over: Isn't it true that seeking truth from facts, proceeding from reality and integrating theory with practice form the fundamental principle of Mao Zedong Thought? Is this fundamental principle

265 See Stuart R. Schram's report of his interview with Hu in his "'Economics in command?'" 417–19.
266 For instance, Hu Fuming's original title had been "Practice is a criterion of truth," which was then revised to read "Practice is the criterion of all truths" before finally appearing as "Practice is the sole criterion of truth." The genesis of this article has been minutely investigated by Michael Schoenhals, who presented a seminar paper on the subject at Harvard's Fairbank Center on 3 February 1989.
267 Hao and Duan, *Zhongguo gongchandang liushi nian*, 680–3; Domes, *The government and politics of China*, 187. On hearing of the negative reaction of leading politicians, Hu Fuming, according to Schoenhals, got so worried that he dissociated himself from the article (which was noted in internal bulletins) on the grounds that it had been changed beyond recognition. A follow-up article, by one of Hu Yaobang's two acolytes, was published in the *Liberation Army News* as a result of the intervention of Luo Ruiqing; this was Luo's last major political act before his death in August 1978.
268 *Selected works of Deng Xiaoping*, 127–32. Hu Jiwei, the editor of *RMRB*, had been reprimanded by his former chief at the paper, Wu Lengxi, for republishing the article, and Hu Qiaomu rebuked Hu Yaobang for the activities of his subordinates. Deng's intervention was thus a crucial development and was given big play by Hu Jiwei in *RMRB;* Schoenhals seminar.
269 Schram, "'Economics in command?'" 419.

outdated? Will it ever become outdated? How can we be true to Marxism-Leninism and Mao Zedong Thought if we are against seeking truth from facts, proceeding from reality and integrating theory with practice? Where would that lead us? Obviously, only to idealism and metaphysics, and thus to the failure of our work and of our revolution.[270]

At this stage the battle was far from won. Earlier at this PLA conference, Hua Guofeng and Ye Jianying had both spoken, but neither had saluted Deng's banner of truth.[271] Yet on 24 June, the *Liberation Army News* published an article supporting Deng, immediately republished in the *People's Daily*, which had been prepared under the direction of Luo Ruiqing.[272] Luo had been dismissed as chief of staff on the eve of the Cultural Revolution but had rejoined the CC at the Eleventh Congress; if his authorship were widely known within the elite, it would doubtless have influenced a lot of senior officers to throw their weight to Deng's side. Certainly, from this point on the debate heated up, and by mid-September, when Deng returned to the attack on the two whatevers in a speech in the Northeast,[273] something he had eschewed in Hua's and Ye's presence in June, conferences in ten provinces had supported his position.[274] Perhaps as dispiriting for the whatever faction, that quintessential survivor, Li Xiannian, had hinted that he was prepared to abandon Hua and back the new line. By November, leading officials in all provinces and military regions had thrown their weight on Deng's side. It was at this point that a central work conference, originally proposed by Deng two months earlier, convened in Beijing on 10 November.[275]

The principal elements on the agenda were how to reinvigorate agriculture and settling the 1980 economic plan. But Chen Yun again took a lead in quickly transforming the meeting into a full-scale debate on the errors of the Cultural Revolution. He wanted retrospective justice to be done to Bo Yibo, whose revolutionary record had been besmirched, and posthumous justice done to Tao Zhu, who had fallen at the end of 1966, and Peng Dehuai, who had been dismissed in 1959 and then been publicly denounced during the late 1960s. Kang Sheng's grave errors should be acknowledged. But Chen's most provocative proposal for the whatever faction was his insistence that the positive nature of the Tiananmen incident be affirmed.[276]

Chen Yun's speech triggered a wave of supporting speeches, notably from Tan Zhenlin, demanding that a whole series of incidents during the Cultural

270 *Selected works of Deng Xiaoping*, 132.   271 Domes, *The government and politics of the PRC*, 156.
272 Hao and Duan, *Zhongguo gongchandang liushi nian*, 682. Michael Schoenhals tells me that the *Liberation Army News* article was the first to criticize the two whatevers.
273 *Selected works of Deng Xiaoping*, 141.   274 Domes, *The government and politics of the PRC*, 157.
275 Hao and Duan, *Zhongguo gongchandang liushi nian*, 682–3, 686–7. Deng was touring in Southeast Asia issed the opening of the conference.
Yun wenxuan (1956–1985), 208–10.

Revolution should be reassessed.[277] Hua Guofeng had evidently anticipated this onslaught, or moved very quickly to accommodate himself to it. On 15 November, it was announced that the Beijing Party committee had reassesed the Tiananmen incident as "completely revolutionary," and the following day that Hua himself had written an inscription for the first officially approved anthology of Tiananmen poems. Similar reassessments of similar incidents in Nanjing, Hangzhou, and Zhengzhou had been announced earlier.[278] With that position conceded, it was less surprising that the whatever faction were also prepared to accept the rehabilitation of a large number of victims of the Cultural Revolution, most of whose fates were not directly attributable to themselves.

A far more dangerous setback for Hua Guofeng and the whatever faction was the entry of a group of victims into the Politburo at the CC's Third Plenum, held 18–22 December to formalize the results of the work conference, large enough to tip the balance of the leadership in Deng's favor. Chen Yun was restored to his old position as a CCP vice-chairman and a member of the Politburo Standing Committee, and made first secretary of a new body, the Discipline Inspection Commission, which set out to purify the Party ranks of Cultural Revolution leftists.[279] Three other Deng supporters, Hu Yaobang, Wang Zhen, Deng Yingchao, Zhou Enlai's widow, joined the Politburo. In addition, nine senior victims were made full CC members. At a Politburo meeting summoned on 25 December, an embryo central secretariat was re-created, with Hu Yaobang at its head; Wang Dongxing was simultaneously sacked from his leadership of the CC General Office, which had functioned as a secretariat during the Cultural Revolution.[280] Wang and other members of the whatever faction maintained their positions on the Politburo, but the writing was now on the wall for them.

Their predicament was underlined by the decisive swing away from leftism, even of their variety, that the conference and plenum represented. The two whatevers were rejected. Class struggle was no longer to be the "key link"; the four modernizations were to take precedence. The theory of "continuing the

277 Hao and Duan, *Zhongguo gongchandang liushi nian*, 689.

278 Garside, *Coming alive!* 200–201; the text of the Beijing Party announcement is in "Quarterly chronicle and documentation," *CQ*, 77 (March 1979), 659.

279 Deng Xiaoping made clear in his speech to the plenum that the kind of people whom he detested were those who had engaged in "beating, smashing and looting, who have been obsessed by factionalist ideas, who have sold their souls by framing innocent comrades, or who disregard the Party's vital interests. Nor can we lightly trust persons who sail with the wind, curry favour with those in power and ignore the Party's principles"; *Selected works of Deng Xiaoping*, 160.

280 For a full summary of the results of the work conference and the Third Plenum, as well as some of the events leading up to them, see Materials Group of the Party History Teaching and Research Office of the CCP Central Party School, *Zhongguo gongchandang lici zhongyao huiyi ji, xia* (Collection of various important conferences of the CCP), 274–80.

revolution under the proletarian dictatorship" was abandoned. Deng indicated in his speech to the plenum that the time had not yet come for an overall appraisal of the Cultural Revolution and Mao himself.[281] But the policies adopted by the plenum represented a radical turn from the previous decade.

First and foremost, the Third Plenum took the first steps away from agricultural collectivization so strongly maintained by Hua Guofeng. As already indicated, where rural socialism was concerned, Hua differed only in pace and not in goal from the Gang of Four. Even after the latter had been purged, he pressed forward with policies for greater egalitarianism, such as promoting brigade accounting and curbing private plots and rural fairs. By mid-1978, reflecting Hua's weakening position, those policies were beginning to be attacked.[282] The Third Plenum rejected Hua's program and the Dazhai model. To unleash the "socialist enthusiasm" of the peasantry, the plenum returned to the policies of the early 1960s and established a framework that proved to be only the beginning of a radical restructuring of rural China:

> The right of ownership by the people's communes, production brigades and production teams and their power of decision must be protected effectively by the laws of the state; it is not permitted to commandeer the manpower, funds, products and material of any production team; the economic organizations at various levels of the people's commune must conscientiously implement the socialist principle of "to each according to his work," work out payment in accordance with the amount and quality of work done, and overcome equalitarianism; small plots of land for private use by commune members, their domestic side-occupations, and village fairs are necessary adjuncts of the socialist economy, and must not be interfered with; the people's communes must resolutely implement the system of three levels of ownership with the production team as the basic accounting unit, and this should remain unchanged.[283]

Not even in the industrial sphere was Hua's program endorsed. His Ten-year Plan went conspicuously unmentioned. Instead, Chen Yun's influence was again clearly visible in the plenum's call for more balanced and steadier growth, rather than the massive investment in heavy industry preferred by Hua.[284] When he addressed the annual session of the NPC in June, he had to announce that rather than press ahead at the hectic speed he had espoused a year earlier, reassessment by the State Council since the Third Plenum had led to a decision to dedicate the years 1979–81 to "readjusting, restructuring, consolidating and improving" the economy.[285]

---

281 *Selected works of Deng Xiaoping*, 160–1.
282 Domes, *The government and politics of the PRC*, 163–4.
283 Quoted in "Quarterly chronicle and documentation," CQ, 77 (March 1979), 170.
284 Ibid., 169.   285 Ibid., CQ, 79 (September 1979), 647.

Democracy Wall

The defeat of Hua and the whatever faction at the Third Plenum was mainly the product of successful mobilization by Deng Xiaoping and his supporters of the "silent majority" of cadres and officers who had always opposed the Cultural Revolution. But the work conference and plenum took place against a backdrop of vigorous public support in the capital for Deng's line that could not but have influenced a leadership with vivid memories of the impact of the Tiananmen incident.

That incident had demonstrated the degree to which national discipline, so strikingly instilled in the early 1950s, had been weakened by the Cultural Revolution. "To rebel is justified," Mao had proclaimed, and on 5 April 1976, thousands in the capital had rebelled against the political leadership and the economic and social program that the Chairman was attempting to set in place for after his demise. The strikes, slowdowns, and simple hooliganism taking place in various parts of China in the mid-1970s underlined that it was not simply the politically aware inhabitants of the capital who understood that the authority of the CCP had been gravely undermined.

The death of Mao, and the gradual reemergence of leaders who wished to disavow the whole Cultural Revolution, triggered a new outburst of public activity in the capital designed to help that process along. The Tiananmen incident had been Act 1 in the popular struggle to rehabilitate Deng and what he stood for. The entr'acte had been the replacement of Mayor Wu De, heavily responsible for the repression of the Tiananmen protesters, in October 1978 after eighteen months of veiled attacks in the press and open attacks in posters.[286] Democracy Wall was supposed to be Act 2. But this time the curtain was rung down early, and by Deng himself.

A week after the beginning of the central work conference, the first posters went up on a stretch of wall along the Chang'an dajie, the wide avenue that passes the Tiananmen, not far from the square.[287] The very first, put up by a mechanic, criticized Mao by name for supporting the Gang of Four and dismissing Deng Xiaoping. Another early one called Deng "the living Zhou Enlai" and denounced the authorities' handling of the Tiananmen incident. A third attacked a "small group of highly place people," clearly the whatever faction, for preventing a reassessment of the alleged counterrevolutionary nature of the incident.

286 Garside, *Coming alive!* 194–96.
287 This following brief summary of Democracy Wall is based principally on the eyewitness reports of Garside, *Coming alive!* 212–98, and Canadian journalist John Fraser's *The Chinese: Portrait of a people*, 203–71, and the analysis and poems contained in David S. G. Goodman, *Beijing street voices: The poetry and politics of China's democracy movement*. Both Garside and Fraser made many contacts with participants in the "democracy movement."

These themes of support for Deng, antagonism toward the whatever faction, and criticism of Mao characterized many of the posters. They must have given Deng and his supporters at the work conference a feeling of satisfaction that at this critical juncture they could claim popular backing. But the poster writers did not stop there. Soon they were putting out pamphlets, papers, and magazines and setting up discussion groups such as the Human Rights Alliance and the Enlightenment Society. Within a week of the first poster's going up, people at Democracy Wall were no longer content simply to read each other's posters, but were actively debating issues, and even with foreigners. On 26 November, the American syndicated columnist Robert Novak was given questions to ask Deng Xiaoping when he interviewed him the following day. When, on the evening of the 27th, Novak's colleague John Fraser, the Toronto *Globe and Mail*'s Beijing correspondent, relayed to a mass audience the fact chat Deng had told Novak that Democracy Wall was a good thing, "pandemonium broke out"; but Eraser's excited auditors sobered up when they heard that Deng, in a foretaste of things to come, had said that not all the things written up at the wall were correct.[288]

Democracy Wall was a more profound phenomenon than the Tiananmen incident. The latter was a brief burst of anger against Mao and the Gang of Four; most of the poems mourned Zhou Enlai or excoriated Jiang Qing. At Democracy Wall, on the other hand, young Chinese, mainly blue collar with a junior high or high school education,[289] explored a wide range of political and social problems and, though often displaying a considerable degree of naiveté, were clearly enthused with the possibility of China embracing the "fifth modernization," democracy:

> The 5th National People's Congress opens red flowers,
> Drawing up the people's new constitution.
> Eight hundred million people joyously sing together,
> Of one heart to establish a new nation.

> The fresh blood of the revolutionary martyrs is sprinkled,
> In exchange for today's new constitution.
> Protect democracy, protect people's rights,
> Advance the Four Modernizations.[290]

As his interview with Novak illustrated, Deng Xiaoping's first reactions to the democracy movement were broadly positive. The day before that interview, Deng had told a leading Japanese politician: "The writing of big-character posters is permitted by our constitution. We have no right to negate or criticize

288 Fraser, *The Chinese*, 245.
289 This is the analysis of a Chinese participant quoted by Goodman, *Beijing street voices*, 141. This person, who was arrested in May 1979, blamed the "arrogance" of the intellectuals for their lack of participation.
290 From Li Hong Kuan, "Ode to the constitution," quoted in Goodman, *Beijing street voices*, 70.

the masses for promoting democracy. . . . The masses should be allowed to vent their grievances!"[291] Unfortunately for the movement, Deng Xiaoping quickly perceived contradictions between democracy and the four modernizations and, whatever his earliest reactions, soon found Democracy Wall more of an embarrassment than an advantage in his current political struggles.

The contradiction was that widespread political debate could get out of hand and undermine the stability and unity that he proclaimed as vital for China's economic advance. He surely remembered that it was when young people went on the rampage in the early Cultural Revolution that China's cities were thrown into chaos and the Chinese economy suffered its worst setbacks of that decade. The embarrassment was that the silent majority of old cadres and senior PLA officers upon whose support he relied in his struggle with the whatever faction were not happy at a new threat to their authority and position. They had not welcomed the overthrow of the Gang of Four just to allow some new form of Cultural Revolution to spring up.

Nothing could be done for fear of adverse publicity before Deng's visit to the United States from 28 January to 4 February. But despite that overseas triumph, Deng's position thereafter may have been weakened temporarily as a result of the inability of the PLA to teach Vietnam a convincing military lesson during the border war from mid-February to mid-March, a cause that was close to Deng's heart. One report suggests that as late as mid-March, Deng was telling senior colleagues that suppressing the democracy movement would have unfavorable results: "Counter-revolution can be suppressed, sabotage can be restricted, but to walk back down the old road of suppressing differing opinion and not listening to criticism will make the trust and support of the masses disappear."[292] But he agreed to abide by majority opinion, and at the end of March he proclaimed that the four modernizations demanded that the country adhere to the "four cardinal principles": the socialist road; the dictatorship of the proletariat; the leadership of the CCP; and Marxism–Leninism and Mao Zedong Thought.[293] In justifying the introduction of criteria highly reminiscent of Mao's action at the outset of the Anti-Rightist Campaign in 1957, Deng said that

> certain bad elements have raised sundry demands that cannot be met at present or are altogether unreasonable. They have provoked or tricked some of the masses into raiding Party and government organizations, occupying offices, holding sit-down and hunger strikes and obstructing traffic, thereby seriously disrupting production, other work and public order. Moreover, they have raised such sensational slogans as "Oppose hunger" and "Give us human rights," inciting people to hold demonstrations and deliberately

291 Quoted in Garside, *Coming alive!* 247–8.   292 Quote in ibid., 256.
293 *Selected works of Deng Xiaoping*, 172.

trying to get foreigners to give worldwide publicity to their words and deeds. There is a so-called China Human Rights Group which has gone so far as to put up big-character posters requesting the President of the United States to "show concern" for human rights in China. Can we permit such an open call for intervention in China's internal affairs?[294]

Wei Jingsheng, the editor of the journal *Exploration* and a prominent figure in the democracy movement, condemned Deng for laying aside "the mask of protector of democracy." Three days later the Beijing authorities issued regulations to curb the democracy movement, and the following day Wei was arrested. At his trial in October 1979, he was given a fifteen-year jail term.[295] On the basis of a CC Plenum decision in February 1980, at the 1980 NPC session, the clause in the state constitution guaranteeing citizens free speech and the right of assembly was shorn of the commitment so dear to Mao: the right to engage in great debate and to put up big-character posters.[296] For the moment, the democracy movement had been shut down.

The fall of Hua Guofeng

The Third Plenum is rightly appraised by Chinese Party historians as a major turning point in post-1949 history. Had Hua Guofeng been adept or swift enough, he might have made common cause with the old cadres against Deng on the issue of the democracy movement. Perhaps it was concern that this could happen that led Deng to move so fast. But in fact, Hua and the whatever faction were too mired in the Cultural Revolution for such an alliance to have had more than temporary success.

In the event, Hua watched helplessly as an anti-whatever coalition was inexorably built up within the top leadership. At the CC's Fourth Plenum from 25 to 28 September 1979, Zhao Ziyang was promoted to full membership of the Politburo. The rehabilitated Peng Zhen, the former Beijing first secretary who, after Deng and Liu Shaoqi, had been the most senior victim at the start of the Cultural Revolution, returned to the Politburo. Eleven other prominent old cadres were readmitted to the CC.

A bigger breakthrough for Deng occurred at the Fifth Plenum from 23 to 29 February 1980, when Hua's supporters in the whatever faction – Wang Dongxing, Ji Dengkui, Wu De, and Chen Xilian (the "little gang of four") – were relieved of all their Party and state posts. Chen Yonggui, the model peasant leader from Dazhai, who was regarded as incompetent rather than malevolent, was simply allowed to drop out of Politburo activities. Hu Yaobang and Zhao

294 Ibid., 181.   295 Garside, *Coming alive!* 256–7, 262.
296 *Zhonghua renmin gongheguo diwujie quanguo renmin daibiao dahui disanci huiyi wenjian* (Documents of the third session of the fifth NPC of the PRC), 169.

Ziyang were elevated to the Politburo Standing Committee. Hu, a Deng loy-alist who had been leader of the Youth League in the 1950s, was made the CCP general secretary, a job that had been vacant since Deng was removed from it early in the Cultural Revolution. The newly reconstituted secretariat was staffed almost exclusively with Deng's supporters. Finally, it was agreed that all the charges against the Cultural Revolution's number one capitalist roader, Liu Shaoqi, were false and that he should be rehabilitated.[297]

Deng's next step was to eradicate the influence of the whatever faction from the State Council. Vice-premiers Chen Xilian and Ji Dengkui were removed in April 1980 as a consequence of the decisions at the Fifth Plenum, but ousting Hua Guofeng from the premiership proved more difficult. Deng advocated separating the functions of Party and government, and proposed that in addition to Hua, a number of other old cadres including himself would resign as vice-premiers, thus also permitting the rejuvenation of the State Council. Although Deng's desire to eliminate overlapping of the two institutions was genuine, this device could have deceived nobody, least of all Hua. Hua may well have tried to use his chairmanship of the MAC to seek succor from the PLA; a brief report of his speech to a PLA political work conference in May 1980 suggested that he might have hoped to forge bonds of loyalty on the basis of shared Maoist values.[298] But even if PLA generals were beginning to get restive about some of Deng's policies, it was highly unlikely that they would select Hua as their champion.

After a Politburo conference in August (and a postponement of the annual NPC session until the very end of the month), the top leadership agreed that Hua should be replaced as premier by Zhao Ziyang. Deng, Li Xiannian, Chen Yun, and three other senior cadres duly resigned as vice-premiers, and Chen Yonggui was also relieved of that duty.[299] Three new vice-premiers were appointed, including Foreign Minister Huang Hua, leaving the State Council purged of all beneficiaries of the Cultural Revolution and comprising only survivors and victims.[300]

The stage was now set for the shredding of Hua's reputation and his eviction from his remaining posts. At a Politburo meeting in November–December, at the request of a large number of high-ranking cadres, Hua's record was submitted to pitiless scrutiny. He was accorded merit for helping to get rid

297 Materials Group, *Zhongguo gongchandang lici zhongyao huiyi ji, xia*, 281–9.
298 Hua stressed moral values alongside material incentives; see "Quarterly chronicle and documentation," *CQ*, 83 (September 1980), 615.
299 The announcement of the resignations of Deng and the five other senior cadres was made separately from that of Chen Yonggui, and in slightly different terminology, to indicate that Chen was going in disgrace rather than in honorable retirement; see *Zhonghua renmin gongheguo diwujie quanguo renmin daibiao dahui disanci huiyi wenjian*, 175–6.
300 Domes, *The government and politics of the PRC*, 173–5; Hao and Duan, *Zhongguo gongchandang liushi nian*, 705–9.

of the Gang of Four but was censured for serious erros and failure to correct himself on a number of issues of principle. Even the mistakes he had apparently corrected were brought up again.

He had persisted with the slogans of the Cultural Revolution; he had not taken the initiative in repairing the damage caused by it. Here he was again being attacked for pursuing the anti-Deng campaign after the Cultural Revolution and refusing to reverse verdicts on the Tiananmen incident. He was held responsible for rushing a decision to create the Mao mausoleum and to publish the fifth volume of the Chairman's works, both of which had presumably been agreed to by Ye Jianying and Li Xiannian. He was also blamed for hindering the rehabilitation of victims of the Cultural Revolution. He had been "pragmatic" [sic] in his attitude toward the Mao problem and hence his support for the two whatevers. He was held largely responsible for the blind advance and the resulting serious losses to the economy in the previous two years.[301] In sum, the meeting agreed that Hua "lacks the political and organizational ability to be the chairman of the Party. That he should never have been appointed chairman of the Military Commission, everybody knows."[302]

Totally humiliated, Hua asked to be relieved of all his posts, but in the interests of protocol and perhaps of saving Ye Jianying's face,[303] he was not accorded the merciful release of a coup de grace. He would not be removed from the chairmanship of the Party or the MAC until a formal decision could be made by the CC's Sixth Plenum. But although he would thus retain his titles until the end of June 1981, at which point he would be demoted to a vice-chairmanship of the Party, his jobs were immediately taken over: the party chairmanship by Hu Yaobang, and the MAC chairmanship by Deng himself – the person everyone knew should have been appointed chairman of the MAC!

In the end, because of delays in holding the CCP's Twelfth Congress,[304] Hua remained a titular member of the Chinese top leadership for perhaps

301 Hao and Duan, Zhongguo gongchandang liushi nian, 709–10; Zhonggong dangshi nianbiao, 438–9; Materials Group, Zhongguo gongchandang lici zhongyao huiyi ji, 290–1.
302 Quoted in Domes, The government and politics of the PRC, 176.
303 As was already argued, Ye bore a certain responsibility for Hua's retention of the leadership after the purge of the Gang of Four in 1976 and for persuading him to readmit Deng to the leadership in 1977. When the Sixth Plenum did meet in June 1981, Ye Jianying was absent, apparently ill, but sent a letter agreeing to the personnel changes and the criticisms of Hua Guofeng. That an official Party account thought it necessary to publish extracts from this letter suggests concern lest his absence be misinterpreted. See Materials Group, Zhongguo gongchandang lici zhongyao huiyi ji, 293.
304 Domes points out that the Fifth Plenum in February 1980 had decided to call the CCP's Twelfth Congress ahead of time, i.e., before the Eleventh Congress's five-year term expired in 1982. He suggests that the hoped-for date was early in 1981, but that disagreement over the assessment of Mao and administrative reforms forced a delay, so that the Eleventh Congress ran its full term; see The government and politics of the PRC, 183.

eighteen months longer than had been intended. But in September 1982, Hua Guofeng was reduced to membership of the CC. His erstwhile collaborator Wang Dongxing scraped into the bottom place among the CC alternates. The Hua interregnum had formally ended.

DENG XIAOPING'S PROGRAM

After Mao, who?

At the time of the Third Plenum in December 1978, it became clear that Hua Guofeng, however imposing his titles, was only a stopgap heir and that Mao's real successor would be Deng Xiaoping. Ironically, Deng's eventual triumph was due in large part to Mao's own actions. If Mao had not recalled Deng to office as Zhou sickened, Deng could not have emerged as the obvious man to run China in absence of the premier. If Mao had not purged him again after Zhou's death, Deng would not have become the symbol of a new political order to replace that of the Cultural Revolution. Certainly, the triumvirate of Hua Guofeng, Ye Jianying, and Li Xiannian would have been in a stronger position to keep the angry victims of the Cultural Revolution at bay.

What is striking about Deng's ascendancy was the way in which, from the very start, he shunned titular confirmation of his power. He insisted on ranking himself below Ye Jianying in the list of CCP vice-chairmen long after Ye's role as post-Mao power broker had ended.[305] At no time was there any suggestion that Deng contemplated taking over the Party chairmanship, the general secretaryship, or the premiership. Instead, he quickly gathered around him the men he wished to succeed him, giving them posts and responsibilities so that they could gain experience and respect. This was the successor-training operation that Mao had talked about but never really implemented.

A principal reason for Deng's self-denial was his determination to avoid appearing to covet a Mao-like role. Indeed, the chairmanship was dropped from the Party constitution at the Twelfth Congress in order to prevent anyone from attempting to assume Mao's mantle. Another preventive measure was the Party's long-expected reappraisal of Mao. The object was to demystify his godlike image by coolly assessing his achievements and his errors, especially during the Cultural Revolution. The CCP was better placed to be courageous than the CPSU had been with Stalin. When Mao's faults came to be listed, Deng, a victim, had no reason to fear the question reportedly shouted at

---

305 In his letter to the Sixth Plenum (n. 304), Ye suggested that the order of the top three members of the Politburo Standing Committee should be Hu Yaobang, Deng Xiaoping, and Ye Jianying, thus reversing the standings of himself and Deng. This was perhaps politeness, perhaps realism in the wake of the fall of Ye's protégé Hua, but Deng ensured that Ye retained his senior ranking.

Khrushchev, an accomplice, when he made his secret speech denouncing Stalin in 1956: "And where were you, comrade, when all this was going on?"

Nevertheless, Deng also had more reason to be cautious than Khruschchev had a quarter of a century earlier. However intemperate the Chinese may have considered the latter's secret speech, Khrushchev always knew that the CPSU had the untarnished image of Lenin on which to fall back. For the CCP, Mao was both Lenin and Stalin, and if an assessment were not carefully handled, both images might be damaged, with incalculable effect on the Party's legitimacy.

Moreover, even among chose who deplored the Cultural Revolution, there were many who wanted Mao protected and some of his actions upheld as correct. PLA generals in particular did not want excessive condemnation either of the man who led them to victory or of their role in the Cultural Revolution. One device was to blame as much as possible on Lin Biao and the Gang of Four, and from 20 November 1980 to 25 January 1981, the regime staged a Nuremberg-style trial of the surviving leaders of the Cultural Revolution.

The trial did publicize considerable evidence of their misdeeds. The claim was made that almost 730,000 people had been framed and persecuted and that nearly 35,000 of them had been "persecuted to death." Most of the accused meekly admitted their guilt and cooperated with the court. Zhang Chunqiao, on the other hand, chose to remain silent throughout the proceedings, and Jiang Qing defended herself forcefully, repeatedly insisting that she had only done what Chairman Mao had told her.[306]

The trial was an effective means of allowing victims to see that their persecutors had been humiliated and punished and of enabling some even to denounce them in public. But Jiang Qing's testimony served to underline that the ultimate guilt was Mao's and that the Party would have to find some means of coming to terms with that fact while steering clear of a root-and-branch condemnation that would be too damaging even for the survivors. Early indications that Mao would be accused of "crimes" during the Cultural Revolution did not materialize. Some PLA behavior in that period was assessed positively. Deng made sure that armchair historians would not undermine his important constituency in the PLA.[307]

306 *A great trial in Chinese history*, 102–3; the figures for the numbers of victims are on 20–1. A good analysis of the trial, with extracts, is contained in David Bonavia, *Verdict in Peking: The trial of the Gang of Four*. The full official text of the proceedings is in Research Office of the Supreme People's Court, ed., *Zhonghua renmin gongheguo zuigao renmin fayuan tebie fating shenpan Lin Biao, Jiang Qing fangeming jituan an zhufan jishi* (A record of the trial by the Special Tribunal of the PRC's Supreme People's Court of the principal criminals of the Lin Biao and Jiang Qing revolutionary cliques); Jiang Qing's appearances are covered on 117–21, 194–9, 227–41, 296–302, 341–7, 399–414.
307 Domes, *The government and politics of the PRC*, 180–2.

Thus, in his earliest comments to the drafters of what eventually emerged as the "Resolution on certain questions in the history of our Party since the founding of the PRC," Deng insisted that the first and most essential point to be covered was

> affirmation of the historical role of Comrade Mao Zedong and explanation of the necessity to uphold and develop Mao Zedong Thought. . . . We must hold high the banner of Mao Zedong Thought not only today but in the future. . . . The first [point] is the most important, the most fundamental, the most crucial.[308]

Three months later, when he found the latest draft inadequate on this issue, he called it "no good" and demanded rewriting. The tone of the draft was "too depressing"; criticizing Mao's personal mistakes alone would not solve problems.[309] In a later comment, he underlined how politically sensitive the issue was. Without an appropriate evaluation of Mao's merits and faults, "the old workers will not feel satisfied, nor will the poor and lower-middle peasants of the period of land reform, nor the many cadres who have close ties with them." He hinted at potential PLA dissatisfaction.[310]

After more than a year of discussions among thousands of officials and historians, the Resolution was adopted by the Sixth Plenum in time for the sixtieth anniversary of the founding of the CCP, on 1 July 1981. It placed the blame for the Cultural Revolution squarely on Mao: "The 'cultural revolution,' which lasted from May 1966 to October 1976, was responsible for the most severe setback and the heaviest losses suffered by the Party, the state and the people since the founding of the People's Republic. It was initiated and led by Comrade Mao Zedong."[311] After an analysis of all the crimes and errors of the period, the Resolution supplied the balance that Deng had insisted on. It described Mao's leftist error in the Cultural Revolution as, after all, "the error of a proletarian revolutionary." In his later years, Mao had confused right and wrong and mistakenly believed that his leftist theories were Marxist. "Herein lies his tragedy."[312] Even during the Cultural Revolution, he could be praised for protecting some cadres, fighting Lin Biao, exposing Jiang Qing,

---

308 *Selected works of Deng Xiaoping*, 276, 278.   309 Ibid., 282, 283.

310 He did this by referring to PLA soldiers' approval when they read what he had said about Mao in an interview with a foreign journalist, i.e., PLA troops were keenly concerned with what was said publicly about Mao.

311 *Resolution on CPC history (1949–81)*, 32.

312 The description of Mao as a tragic hero was a repetition of the formula the CCP had suggested for Stalin in the aftermath of Khrushchev's secret speech in 1956. The concept was, in fact, a breakthrough. Hitherto, in both the Soviet Union and the PRC, there had been a Manichean insistence on the simple juxtaposition of good and evil, black and white, with no allowance made for shades of gray. If one committed an error, one either purged oneself of it totally or was condemned as a reactionary or a counterrevolutionary. The model of the flawed leader had implications for politics and literature.

and pursuing a successful foreign policy.[313] The Resolution concluded that although it was true that Mao had made "gross mistakes" during the Cultural Revolution, "if we judge his activities as a whole, his contributions to the Chinese revolution far outweigh his mistakes."[314]

The Resolution achieved the balance Deng had wanted while also explaining why Mao had gone wrong. As his prestige had increased, he had become arrogant and put himself above the CC. His colleagues failed to take preventive action, and collective leadership was undermined. Intra-Party democracy was not institutionalized; relevant laws lacked authority. The Stalinist model of leadership had had its impact, as had centuries of Chinese "feudal autocracy."[315] The assessment of Mao sounded right, but Deng's Resolution succeeded no better than Khrushchev's secret speech in explaining how democracy could be institutionalized or laws respected under a system of proletarian dictatorship and CCP rule.

If Deng would not reject the system he had helped create, he personally would attempt to learn the negative lessons of Mao's leadership. Yet his rejection of Mao's titles and cult failed to deal with tendencies deep in the "feudal" political culture. Deng had taught Hua that position did not confer power or authority. Now he himself had to come to terms with the corollary: Power and authority could not be wished away simply by refusing titles; the imperial tradition could not be exorcised by Party resolution. No matter how loudly he protested that he participated in only one or two key decisions a year, he was regarded by both supporters and opponents as the court of last resort.

Partly this was a matter of generations. In sharp contrast to post-Stalin Russia, in which only survivors and beneficiaries remained, in post-Mao China many of the leader's victims, who were also fellow Long Marchers, were still alive.[316] They could return to power untarnished by his errors and garlanded still with their revolutionary achievements. It was impossible for men like Hu Yaobang and Zhao Ziyang, whom Deng picked out as his successors to match the legitimacy he could claim as of right.

Partly it was a question of relationships, *guanxi*, Deng had a network of friends, colleagues, and contacts in both the Party and the army who could be vital to the successful promotion of a policy. Hu Yaobang and, to a lesser extent, Zhao Ziyang had their networks, too, but they were not comparable in power and prestige as allies for governing China.

Partly it was a question of emergent factionalism. In the initial post-Mao era, all the returning victims could agree on the urgent tasks of removing

313 *Resolution on CPC history (1949–81)*, 41–2.   314 Ibid., 56.   315 Ibid., 48–9.
316 Had Bukharin been allowed to survive, he would have been only sixty-four on Stalin's death. Deng was seventy-four at the time of the Third Plenum.

the beneficiaries of the Cultural Revolution and liquidating the policies of that era. As that task neared completion, the original coalition began to split over where to go next. Deng did not always see eye to eye with Chen Yun or Peng Zhen, to name the two most prestigious returned victims besides Deng himself. Had Deng been able to retire and take with him his whole revolutionary cohort, leaving Hu and Zhao to cope with their own generation, the succession process would have been easier to manage. But since Deng's old comrades-in-arms evinced no desire to leave the stage, Deng had to stay on to prevent them from using *their* superior credentials to derail his protégés.

Partly it was a question of talent. Deng Xiaoping was clearly an exceptional leader even among an extraordinary array of revolutionary veterans. Neither Hu Yaobang nor Zhao Ziyang was able to prove himself an equally outstanding successor.

Partly it was a reflection of an only partially solved question: Which would dominate, Party or PLA?

After Mao, which?

When the Politburo summed up Hua's shortcomings in late 1980, it was far more contemptuous about his right to be chairman of the MAC than about his right to lead the CCP. Yet in a state where the Party commanded the gun, any leader whom the Party chose should automatically have received the respect of the generals. Clearly that was never accorded to Hua. He became MAC chairman in 1976 presumably because the obvious available candidate, Marshal Ye Jianying, insisted on it and stood by Hua to lend him authority. When Deng returned as vice-chairman of the MAC and chief of staff of the PLA in mid-1977, the generals probably took little further account of Hua. When Deng effectively took over the chairmanship in late 1980, their world seemed correctly ordered again.

Deng may have felt he had no option but to assume this one of Mao's titles, but his action caused as many problems as it solved. It confirmed to the PLA generals that they had a right to be commanded only by the person with supreme authority in the country; that they had a direct line to the top, without interruption by layers of bureaucracy; that although the minister of defense was responsible to the premier, who in turn was responsible to the Party, none of this mattered, because all important issues would be thrashed out in the MAC. It thus confirmed what everyone knew – that the PLA was an institution apart – just when the generals needed to be brought back into line.

Deng's objective was to restore PLA discipline and end its unwillingness to obey orders or to implement Party policies laid down by the CC. As we have seen, he had brought up these problems in 1975, but he now admitted that they had not been solved then.[317] He may well have thought that only he could bring the PLA to heel. Given the difficulties even he experienced, perhaps he was right. The problems were both political and institutional.

The rehabilitation of Liu Shaoqi in May 1980 was one major political issue. That action had undermined a major justification for the Cultural Revolution and was thus a direct repudiation of Mao, whose reputation the generals had consistently wanted to safeguard. Ye Jianying, and even Xu Shiyou, Deng's protector in 1976, evinced disapproval by failing to show up for the memorial meeting at which this symbolically important act took place.[318] The generals were also angry at two successive rounds of severe military budget cuts in late 1980 and early 1981; it may have been partly in retaliation for these that the PLA initiated a drive for ideological discipline. But probably the more important reason was the generals' desire to counter the more relaxed political atmosphere that Deng and the reformers were trying to encourage but that had produced many attacks on military privilege. An army writer, Bai Hua, was made the exemplary target to stand for all critical intellectuals.

In the face of evident PLA anger, Deng must have decided to excise from the Resolution on Party history any criticisms of the role of the PLA in the Cultural Revolution. But even this failed to appease the generals, for on the eve of the CCP's Twelfth Congress, in September 1982, an article in the *Liberation Army News* attacked "some responsible comrades in cultural fields" for supporting bourgeois liberal points of view. Deng's reaction to this gross breach of military and political discipline was swift. Immediately after the Congress, the director of the PLA's General Political Department, Wei Guoqing (another Deng protector in 1976), and the head of the navy were both dismissed.[319]

Deng evidently realized the institutional problem in the relationship between the PLA and the CCP, but his efforts to remedy it failed. In the new state constitution promulgated at the Fifth Session of the Fifth NPC in late 1982, an important institutional innovation was included: the creation of a Central Military Commission, responsible to the NPC, to direct the PLA. According to the explanation given by Peng Zhen in his speech to the NPC, "The leadership by the Chinese Communist Party over the armed forces will not change with the establishment of the state Central Military Commission. The Party's leading role in the life of the state, which is explicitly affirmed

317 *Selected works of Deng Xiaoping*, 29–30, 97–8.
318 Domes, *The government and politics of the PRC*, 171–2. Domes argues that in the case of Xu, personal pique at not being made defense minister or chief of staff may have been another motive for his action on this occasion.
319 Ibid., 178–82, 185.

in the Preamble, naturally includes its leadership over the armed forces."[320] What Peng Zhen conspicuously failed to mention was that the preamble made no mention of the Party's MAC as the instrument of that leadership. What then was to be the relationship of the MAC to the new body?

An article in a Party journal gave a strong hint of what was in the wind. It detailed the history of the Central Military Commission, showing how at some times it had been a Party organ and at other times a state organ. Both types of military commission had been legitimate. Referring to the creation of the new state body, the writer affirmed that the MAC would continue to exist as a Party organ. Yet the implication was that the time had come to sever the direct CCP–PLA link and make the PLA simply a part of the state structure, as in most other countries. The history of the PLA showed that this had been normal practice from time to time and therefore nothing to be feared.[321] For double reassurance, Deng Xiaoping legitimated the new body at the NPC by taking on its chairmanship in addition to his chairmanship of the MAC.

If Deng's objective was to prepare the ground for the abolition of the MAC, he did not achieve it. The new commission raised the profile of the PLA in the state structure by subordinating it no longer to a mere State Council ministry but to an NPC commission, but no general seems to have been ready to accept it as a substitute for the MAC. Instead, just when Deng and his colleagues were urging a general retrenchment of the bureaucracy, the country was saddled with two identical military commissions, both led by Deng Xiaoping and Yang Shangkun (as executive vice-chairman).

Even when Deng would finally manage to resign from the Politburo at the CCP's Thirteenth Congress in 1987, taking all his old comrades with him, he still could not retire from his MAC chairmanship, The CCP constitution stipulated that the MAC chairman had to be a member of the Politburo Standing Committee, so Deng endorsed a constitutional revision that permitted him to stay on.[322] He installed the new CCP general secretary, Zhao Ziyang, as first vice-chairman of the MAC, which suggested that the MAC would be preserved and that the NPC equivalent had been set up in vain.

The recent history of the MAC has confirmed the tenacity with which the PLA has maintained its institutional position within the CCP over the years. Under Deng's leadership, civilian control of the PLA would be gradually reinstated, especially after he engineered the exodus of virtually all remaining generals from the Politburo and sharply reduced PLA representation in the

---

320 *Fifth session of the Fifth National People's Congress*, 94.
321 Yan Jingtang, "Zhongyang junwei yange gaikuang" (Survey of the evolution of the Central Military Commission), in Zhu Chengjia, ed., *Zhonggong dangshi yanjiu lunwen xuan, xia* (Selection of research papers on the history of the CCP), 3. 367–87.
322 *Documents of the Thirteenth National Congress of the Communist Party of China (1987)*, 85.

CC during the major central meetings held in September 1985. But the MAC issue illustrated that civilian control was still on the PLA's terms: that it must be asserted through the MAC, and the MAC must be headed by Deng as long as possible. Perhaps when the PLA is further denuded of revolutionary generals and colonels by retirements and deaths, and the Long March is history not memory, the post-Deng generation of CCP leaders will be able to assert its primacy over the military and assign to it a more conventional role in the state system. Until then it can be assumed that the PLA, the agent of victory during the revolution and the repository of power during the Cultural Revolution,[323] will remain a major factor in the polity. As the above account has indicated, how its political influence will be utilized will depend on the CCP's program and policies.

After Mao, what?

The conservatism of the PLA generals was a factor that Deng Xiaoping had to take into account in his drive to revitalize China. For Deng's reform program challenged not merely the ultra-leftist Maoism of the Cultural Revolution, but also what might be called the "Sinified Stalinist" line pursued by Mao and his colleagues when copying the Soviet model in the 1950s. Moreover, the reforms relaxed central control and allowed more freedom of thought and action, a permissiveness unlikely to commend itself to the ultimate guardians of law and order in the wake of the upheavals of the Cultural Revolution.

The economic reforms and their impact are covered in detail in *CHOC* 15, Chapter 6.[324] Deng turned back the clock, dismantling the commune system set up during the GLF in 1958, returning control over production to the farm family for the first time since land reform in the early 1950s. The regime might claim that no ideological change had taken place because the land was formally still owned by the collective; it was only contracted back to the peasantry. Peasants might worry that their newly granted freedom to plan their own cropping patterns, hire labor to assist them, and sell part of the harvest in rural free markets[325] would suddenly be snatched back in yet another 180-degree

---

323 During the discussions of the resolution on Party history, Deng got quite angry at the suggestion that the Ninth Congress should be declared illegitimate or that the Party should be considered to have ceased to exist during the Cultural Revolution. Perhaps it was partly because he realized that to say that would constitute a formal admission that the PLA had been the only functioning revolutionary organization during that turbulent decade, that it had survived whereas the CCP had not, and that it had run most of the country while the CCP had not; *Selected works of Deng Xiaoping*, 290–1.

324 See the following discussion. For details about the various forms of rural reform in the early stages, see also Kathleen Hartford, "Socialist agriculture is dead; long live socialist agriculture!: Organizational transformations in rural China," in Elizabeth J. Perry and Christine Wong, eds., *The political economy of reform in post-Mao China*, 31–61.

325 See Terry Sicular, "Rural marketing and exchange in the wake of recent reforms," in Perry and Wong, eds., *The political economy of reform in post-Mao China*, 83–109.

policy shift. But in fact, private farming had been reinstated, even in cases where the peasants were reluctant to forfeit the security of the collective.[326]

This second liberation of the peasantry, bolstered by higher procurement prices, had a massive impact on production and on rural incomes, as *CHOC* 15, Chapter 6 shows. The political implications were also of enormous significance. A majority of the 800 million peasants had been given a major stake in the reform program, and they trembled when conservative ideological winds blew coldly from Beijing. But even Chinese neoconservatives like Chen Yun had welcomed the short-lived experiments with agricultural responsibility systems in the early 1960s, and it eventually became clear that no Beijing politician would challenge the rural new deal, unless either its economic justification declined drastically or its impact on rural and regional equity became so negative as to carry grave dangers of renewed class struggle.

Rural cadres were initially unhappy about their new tasks and diminished control.[327] But as they began to use their political skills and connections to preserve their status and increase their incomes by assuming brokering roles, the cadres realized that the new deal could benefit them too.[328] From a long-term perspective, the initial distrust of aging cadres was less important than the implications of the reforms for the CCP. Dynamic rich peasants (often former cadres) were held up as models, and their recruitment to the Party was mandated. In some cases this aroused envy.[329] But provided that the recruitment policy was maintained, the prospect was the transformation of a poor peasant party into a rich peasant one, with considerable implications for class attitudes and ideological predilections. The "serve the people" ethos of the CCP was bound to be adulterated by the new slogan "To get rich is glorious." This, in turn, would almost certainly ensure that the CCP would continue to eschew class struggle and focus on economic development as its prime goal.

The complexities of industrial restructuring and market reform posed far greater problems for Deng Xiaoping and his colleagues, as Dwight Perkins shows in *CHOC* 15, Chapter 6. There was no single step, like decollectivization, capable of generating an economic breakthrough that could not be gainsaid. On the contrary, many people stood to lose by urban reform: bureaucrats who forfeited power as greater independence was ceded to managers of state enterprises; managers of state enterprises who envied the even greater freedom accorded collective and private companies; workers in state

---

326 Hartford suggests that not all peasants w$$ the destruction of the commune system; ibid., 138–9.

327 See Richard J. Latham, "The implications of rural reforms for grass-roots cadres," in ibid., 57–73.

328 This comment is based on the author's own observations and conversations in China, along with those of others.

329 For a discussion, see Elizabeth J. Perry, "Social ferment: grumbling amidst growth," in John S. Major, ed., *China briefing, 1985*, 39–41, 45–6.

enterprises who feared harder work and job insecurity in the search for efficiency, and who envied the rising incomes of workers in the nonstate sector and peasants in the countryside; and every urban dweller, including intellectuals and students, who was hurt by the higher prices accompanying the reforms.

The reform program also implied a fundamental if dimly perceived threat to the legitimacy of the CCP. Party cadres were told to "seek truth from facts" and told that "practice is the sole criterion of truth." They were instructed to acquire knowledge that would equip them for the new era. The longstanding tension within the CCP between the demand for "redness" (political fervor) and the demand for "expertise" (professional skills), which formerly had been resolved in favor of the *yang* of redness, now seemed to have been settled in favor of the *yin* of expertise.

This was a potential blow to the roughly 50 percent of Party cadres who had been recruited during the Cultural Revolution, for their strengths were presumably in the field of political agitation. But it also placed a question mark over the role of the Party itself. The claim of the CCP to its vanguard role, like that of the CPSU and other parties, was rooted in its ideology. The premise was that its mastery of the ever correct ideology of Marxism–Leninism–Mao Zedong Thought enabled it to understand the present and plan for the future with a sureness inaccessible to non-Marxists. But if correctness was now to be found in practice or facts, what was the function of ideology?

Ideology had already been greatly devalued by the hyperbole of the Cultural Revolution and the attribution of almost supernatural powers to Mao Zedong Thought.[330] The new emphasis on practice was a very grave blow. Deng Xiaoping's declaration that Marxism–Leninism–Mao Zedong Thought was one of four cardinal principles that could not be questioned did little to soften it.[331] CCP rule, although itself one of the four cardinal principles, now appeared to be justifiable only by competence and success, shaky foundations in view of the problems facing post-Mao China. At risk was the deep-rooted attachment in the Chinese political culture to the concept of an elite bureaucracy sanctioned simply by its commitment to and mastery of a totalist ideology that claimed to explain the world and man's place in it.

The increasing irrelevance of the Party was underlined by reformers' attempts to separate its functions from those of the government.[332] The declared aim was to free Party cadres to concentrate on overall questions

---

330 See George Urban, ed., *The miracles of Chairman Mao: A compendium of devotional literature*, 1966–70, 1–27.

331 See "Uphold the four cardinal principles," *Selected works of Deng Xiaoping*, 172–4, 179–81. The other three were the socialist road, the dictatorship of the proletariat, and the leadership of the CCP.

332 "On the reform of the system of Party and state leadership," ibid., 303.

of principle and line. Local government functionaries and managers who were not all CCP members were to be granted greater leeway to get on with their jobs regardless of ideological considerations.

But in a state in which virtually all top government officials were senior Party members and participated in the discussions of the Politburo or the CC, it was not clear what should be the role of the "pure" Party official. Of course, he had to run the Party machine, but its role, too, was unclear in an era when class struggle and movement politics had given way to economic development.[333] During his tenure as CCP general secretary, Hu Yaobang ignored the separation of roles, seeming to want to assert a right as China's top leader to make pronouncements on all spheres of national life. He made a number of overseas trips as if he were head of state or government.[334]

The Party's powers were further restricted by the provision in its new constitution passed at the Twelfth Congress in 1982 that "the Party must conduct its activities within the limits permitted by the Constitution and the laws of the state." As Hu Yaobang explained this "most important principle" in his report, it was now formally "impermissible for any Party organization or member, from the Central Committee down to the grass roots, to act in contravention of the Constitution and laws."[335] A constitutional provision by itself was hardly a guarantee. But the emphasis on legality after the Third Plenum, in reaction to the anarchy of the Cultural Revolution when the elite had suffered most, together with the passage of various legal codes for the first time, at least signified an understanding that the unbridled power of the Party ultimately threatened everyone.[336]

Such formal restrictions on the Party were accompanied by concrete attempts to diminish "bureaucratism," whose harmful manifestations included

> standing high above the masses; abusing power; divorcing oneself from real-
> ity and the masses; spending a lot of time and effort to put up an impressive
> front; indulging in empty talk; sticking to a rigid way of thinking; being

333 The dilemma may be loosely compared to that of party officials in the Western European democracies. During periods of opposition, the life of the party qua party looms large, for it is the instrument of agitation with which class war is waged in the country at large in order to oust the government of the day. If the strategy is successful and party leaders become government ministers in their turn, the role of the party greatly diminishes as its leaders occupy themselves with running the country and ensuring its economic prosperity. Purely party officials from then on take a subordinate role and rarely interfere with government policy, but are expected, rather, to ensure the loyalty of the party rank and file to whatever the government does.

334 There was perhaps some justification for this during Hu's brief period as CCP chairman, after the Sixth Plenum of the Eleventh CC in June 1981, but none after the Twelfth Congress in September 1982 when the chairmanship was abolished and the newly supreme post of general secretary became his only job. I use the term "formal" because, of course, ultimate power rested with Deng Xiaoping, whatever his nominal title.

335 *The Twelfth National Congress of the CPC*, 49.

336 For a discussion of some of the issues involved in the new emphasis on legality in the PRC, see R. Randle Edwards, Louis Henkin, Andrew J. Nathan, *Human rights in contemporary China*.

hidebound by convention; overstaffing administrative organs; being dilatory, inefficient, and irresponsible; failing to keep one's word; circulating documents endlessly without solving problems; shifting responsibility to others; and even assuming the airs of a mandarin, reprimanding other people at every turn, vindictively attacking others, suppressing democracy, deceiving superiors and subordinates, being arbitrary and despotic, practising favouritism, offering bribes, participating in corrupt practices in violation of the law.

According to Deng, such practices had reached "intolerable dimensions both in our domestic affairs and in our contacts with other countries."[337]

Attacks on bureaucratism were nothing new within the CCP, dating back at least to the Rectification Campaign in Yan'an in the early 1940s. The Cultural Revolution itself could in part be explained as Mao's final and most devastating attempt to destroy bureaucratism in order to unleash the pure revolutionary fervor of the masses. Deng's methods were less devastating, but he, too, wished to unleash the masses, though to create wealth rather than make revolution. Here again, Party cadres were being pushed to one side.

Despite these limits on the authority of the Party, the average peasant, worker, manager, or intellectual continued to behave circumspectly in the presence of its officials. Habits of obedience and memories of suffering inhibited any attempt to test the new permissiveness too far. The bureaucracy might be on the defensive, but it was still enormously powerful.

That may be the historians' final verdict on the Cultural Revolution. By the CCP's Twelfth Congress, in 1982, the erosion of the Party's authority as a result of the Cultural Revolution, the subsequent moves to restrain arbitrary use of power, the decline in the force of ideology, the unleashing of the peasant and the attempt to free up the urban economy all carried the potential for a role for society vis-à-vis the state possibly greater than at any previous time when China was united under a strong central government. Mao had always stressed that out of bad things came good things. Those burgeoning social forces would finally challenge the bonds of state authority in the Tiananmen demonstrations of 1989.

337 "On the reform of the system of Party and state leadership," *Selected works of Deng Xiaoping*, 310.

CHAPTER 5

THE ROAD TO TIANANMEN: CHINESE POLITICS IN THE 1980s

RICHARD BAUM

INTRODUCTION

By the time the Twelfth Party Congress met in September 1982, China's new leaders had done much to overcome the post-Mao crisis of confidence. They had repudiated Mao's Cultural Revolution, renounced his economic theories, and reinstated his purged opponents. But acknowledging past mistakes was one thing; charting a viable course for the future was quite another. Although members of the reform coalition forged by Deng Xiaoping could agree among themselves, in principle, on the need for economic reform and opening up to the outside world, they differed over just how far and how fast to move toward revamping the basic ideology and institutions of Chinese socialism. Most important, they differed over precisely how much "bourgeois liberalization," if any, could be countenanced in a society that continued to call itself Marxist–Leninist.

Sometimes, disagreement took the form of arcane academic debates over such issues as the special characteristics of China's "spiritual civilization" or the relevance to China of such foreign concepts as "universal humanism" and "alienation." As often as not, academic debates served to mask highly contentious policy disputes – for example, over the tolerable limits of free market activity and private accumulation of wealth, the severity of the problem of "spiritual pollution" posed by the influx of Western cultural influences, and the proper boundaries of free expression for artists, writers, and other creative intellectuals whose contributions were deemed essential to the success of China's modernization drive.

Research for this chapter was completed in the autumn of 1990 at the Sinology Institute, University of Leiden. I would like to express my deep appreciation to the director, staff, and students of the Institute for giving so unselfishly of their time and energy during my term as a visiting scholar. Special thanks are due to Tony Saich and Geor Hintzen for their valuable insights and comments on earlier drafts of this chapter.

Just beneath the surface of these debates lay the potent issue of stability versus chaos. Throughout the decade, China's top leaders repeatedly tempered their expressed desire for modernization and reform with a deep concern for maintaining political order and discipline. Wanting to enjoy the fruits of modernity without the destabilizing effects of spontaneous, uncontrolled social mobilization, they tended to follow each new round of reform with an attempt to retain or regain control. Letting go (*fang*) with one hand, they instinctively tightened up (*shou*) with the other.

As early as the spring of 1979, with the closure of the Xidan democracy wall and the concurrent issuance of Deng Xiaoping's inviolable "four cardinal principles" – adherence to the socialist road, the people's democratic dictatorship, Communist Party leadership, and Marxism–Leninism–Mao Zedong Thought – this ambivalent pattern of relaxation and control, *fang* and *shou*, began to display recurrent, periodic fluctuations and phase changes. The result was a distinctive *fang–shou cycle*, characterized by an initial increase in the scope of economic or political reform (in the form, e.g., of price deregulation or intellectual liberalization), followed by a rapid release of pent-up social demand (e.g., panic buying or student demonstrations); the resulting "disorder" would set off a backlash among party traditionalists, who would then move to reassert control. A conservative retrenchment would follow, marked by an ideological assault on "liberal" tendencies and an attempt to halt (or even to reverse) the initial reform. The ensuing freeze would serve, in turn, to exacerbate existing internal contradictions and stresses, leading to the generation of renewed pressures for relaxation and reform – and so on.[1]

Three complete repetitions of the multiphase *fang–shou* cycle occurred in the 1980s. Although the cycles were broadly recursive, over time there occurred a discernible intensification of their underlying antinomies as each new swing of the pendulum served to amplify existing socioeconomic tensions and evoke more intense political reactions. As the amplitude of the oscillations increased, so too did the polarization of forces; as a result, what began as a series of nonantagonistic debates over the ends and means, scope and magnitude, consequences and limits of reform escalated steadily from the realm of philosophic discourse to become, by the spring of 1989, an acute struggle for survival among mutually antagonistic political forces.

---

1 For variations on the theme of *fang–shou* cycles in post-Mao China, see Tang Tsou, "Political change and reform: The middle course," in Tang Tsou, ed., *The cultural revolution and post-Mao reforms: A historical perspective*, 219–58; also Thomas B. Gold, "Party-state versus society in China," in Joyce K. Kallgren, ed., *Building a nation-state: China at forty years*, 125–52; also Harry Harding, *China's second revolution: Reform after Mao*, Chapter 4; and Lowell Dittmer, "Patterns of elite strife and succession in Chinese politics," *China Quarterly* (hereafter, *CQ*) 123 (September 1990), 405–30. The *locus classicus* for analysis of cyclical phenomena in modern Chinese politics remains G. William Skinner and Edwin A. Winckler, "Compliance succession in rural communist China: A cyclical theory," in Amitai Etzioni, ed., *Complex organizations: A sociological reader* (second edition).

Throughout all the polarizing vicissitudes of the 1980s, one figure loomed larger than all others: "senior leader" Deng Xiaoping. Deng personally embodied all the complex antinomies of *fang* and *shou*. He believed that China could have both market competition *and* a monistic political order; socioeconomic modernity *and* a "socialist spiritual civilization"; a vigorous, creative intelligentsia *and* a high degree of ideological conformity. As the decade wore on, however, and as these goals began to oscillate rather than to converge, Deng found it increasingly difficult to steer a middle course between *fang* and *shou*. He (and China) began to swerve, first one way and then the other, as he searched in vain for a viable, coherent center.

For the better part of a decade, Deng, who turned eighty in 1984, tried to reform China's inefficient command economy, create a rationalized governmental structure, and effect an orderly political succession. Twice he supported a major overhaul of China's patriarchal leadership system; in both cases, the ensuing polarization of forces compelled him to abort the project. Twice he tried to leave the political stage, designating pragmatic, reform-oriented heirs apparent to succeed him; both times his choices were eventually rejected, as first Hu Yaobang and then Zhao Ziyang ran afoul of Party conservatives. Twice he backed wide-ranging structural reforms in China's urban economy; both times a rising tide of inflation, corruption, and resultant social unrest forced him to retreat.

With the middle ground of orderly, institutionalized reform becoming more elusive, Deng was increasingly forced to rely upon his personal prestige and authority to preserve a semblance of political stability and unity. Unable to create a viable structure of authority that combined both *fang* and *shou*, and unable to locate a successor acceptable to all major factions, he was unable to retire from active leadership. Consequently, his personal authority became more, rather than less, critical to the coherence, indeed the very survival, of the regime. Yet the more he intervened in the decision process *ex cathedra*, the more elusive became his quest for a rationalized political order. Therein, perhaps, lay the supreme paradox of Deng's political stewardship: In his quest to lead China out of the "feudal autocracy" of the Maoist era toward modernity and rule by law, Deng increasingly resorted to highly personalized instruments of control – instruments that were the very antithesis of the system he sought to create.[2]

With fundamental institutional reform blocked, Deng was forced to improvise as he went along, introducing a series of ad hoc, piecemeal measures designed to promote the objective of orderly change. In the early 1980s, for example, when old guard Party leaders proved reluctant to retire, Deng gave

2 This theme is explored in Stuart R. Schram, "China after the 13th congress," *CQ* 114 (June 1988), 177–97.

them their very own Central Advisory Commission (CAC) to help ease them into inactivity. Yet many still refused to leave the stage voluntarily, and Deng could not (or would not) force them off. Consequently, the temporary became permanent: The CAC became a virtual shadow cabinet, parallel and powerful. Still active in the late 1980s, this "sitting committee," as it was popularly (and derisively) known, played a key role in fashioning the June 1989 military crackdown at Tiananmen Square.

In similar fashion, as part of his campaign to modernize and professionalize China's outmoded Maoist military establishment, Deng tried to move the People's Liberation Army (PLA) out from under CCP control (as had been the traditional practice), placing it directly under the jurisdiction of the central government. But since outright abolition of the Party's powerful Military Affairs Commission (MAC) would have alienated China's conservative old guard, Deng improvised once again. He created a parallel governmental MAC alongside the existing CCP organ, which was allowed to remain wholly intact. He then proceeded to staff the new body with exactly the same Party veterans who controlled the existing MAC, thereby ensuring the redundancy – and virtual impotence – of the new government commission. When PLA troops were called to Beijing to put down student protests in May–June 1989, it was the Party's MAC that gave the orders.

When China's urban consumers balked at the prospect of reform-induced commodity price hikes in the late 1980s, Deng once again offered an expedient compromise: He slowed down the decontrol of prices and granted city dwellers a series of temporary food and housing subsidies to help ease the pain of transition to market-regulated pricing. Shortly thereafter, a combination of consumer panic buying and conservative criticism forced the government to halt price decontrol altogether; as a result, the temporary once again became semipermanent as China limped along with a semireformed, two-tier price structure that retained many of the worst irrationalities of the old system while perpetuating the costly transitional subsidies of the new one. More than one observer likened the government's indecisive, start-and-stop approach to price reform to an attempt to leap across the Grand Canyon serially in several jumps.

In each of the preceding examples, an *ad hoc* policy improvisation, originally intended to serve as a bridge or stepping stone to fundamental structural reform, was frozen in place due to a conservative backlash, becoming in the process an impediment to further systemic change. Cumulatively, the effect was to exacerbate existing structural tensions and stresses rather than to resolve them.[3]

3 The paradoxical consequences of partial reform are discussed in David Zweig, "Dilemmas of partial reform," in Bruce Reynolds, ed., *Chinese economic policy*, 13–40; Susan Shirk, *The political logic of economic*

Notwithstanding the increasing turbulence and frequent policy improvisations of the 1980s, for a brief period in late 1987 and 1988 it appeared that a viable developmental formula might, after all, be found. Under Zhao Ziyang, a new path for China's political development was sketched out, one that was neither totalitarian nor democratic, but that contained the first ideological and institutional sprouts of emergent social pluralism. This was the "new authoritarianism" (*xin quanwei zhuyi*), a hybrid system that purported to combine the economic vitality of *fang* with the centralized political authority of *shou*. The proposed system was characterized by continued one-party tutelage and a "consultative" structure of limited political participation, on the one hand, and a state-induced shift toward market regulation of the economy and the recognition of diverse, pluralistic societal aspirations and interests, on the other.[4]

Unhappily for China, the new formula was never adequately tested. Mounting consumer unrest over surging inflation, made worse by rumors of impending price decontrol and rendered politically volatile by deepening public resentment over flagrant official profiteering, triggered a wave of urban consumer panic in the summer of 1988. CCP conservatives, afraid of incipient political instability, instinctively reacted by halting price deregulation, freezing structural reform, and reasserting centralized control over the economy.

By the spring of 1989, reform-related stresses had reached critical levels. With the economy and society stalled midway between plan and market, between bureaucrats and entrepreneurs, between *shou* and *fang*, China continued to suffer from the worst distortions of the old system without enjoying the anticipated benefits of the new. It was truly a "crisis of incomplete reform."[5] Following the unexpected death of Hu Yaobang in mid-April, the political center began to crumble as a student-led, inflation-bred, corruption-fed protest movement in Beijing brought the Chinese capital to the very brink of governmental paralysis. Faced with a mounting urban revolt against a government whose authority was being openly challenged by its citizens, in early June a group of elderly, semiretired Party conservatives, supported now by a clearly exasperated Deng Xiaoping, reentered the political arena with a vengeance and played their trump card, the PLA.

reform; and Richard Baum, "The perils of partial reform," in Richard Baum, ed., *Reform and reaction in post-Mao China: The road to Tiananmen,* 1–17.

4 The concept of "new authoritarianism" is discussed in *Jiushi niandai* (hereafter, *JSND*), April 1989, 82–4. See also Mark Petracca and Mong Xiong, "The concept of Chinese neo-authoritarianism: An exploration and democratic critique," *Asian Survey* (hereafter, *AS*) 30.11 (November 1990), 1099–1117; Ma Shu Yun, "The rise and fall of neo-authoritarianism in China," *China Information* (hereafter, *CI*) 5.3 (Winter 1990–1), 1–19; and "The debate on the new authoritarianism," *Chinese Sociology and Anthropology* 23.2 (Winter 1990–1), passim. For further analysis, see the subsections "Political reform: Toward 'neoauthoritarianism' and "Zhao's neoauthoritarian counteroffensive."

5 The term is borrowed from Lowell Dittmer, "China in 1989: The crisis of incomplete reform," *AS* 30.1 (January 1990).

The bloody crackdown and repression that followed put an end, at least temporarily, to the developmental dynamism of the 1980s. With the massacre of several hundred – perhaps more than a thousand – civilians in the streets of Beijing, Deng Xiaoping appeared on the verge of losing his biggest gamble: that modernization and socioeconomic reform could be achieved without undermining the country's political stability. Under the cumulative stresses engendered by a decade of reform-induced sociopolitical mobilization, Deng's carefully crafted coalition came unglued. Zhao Ziyang was dismissed and placed under house arrest for aiding and abetting a "counter-revolutionary rebellion"; a number of his more liberal supporters were sacked, arrested, or driven into exile; and a new wave of repression, recrimination, and regimentation spread throughout China. Though energetic efforts were made by Party leaders to keep up the appearance of political unity and consensus, the subsequent rigidity and paralysis of government policy be-spoke the existence of deep, painful political wounds that mere words of self-assurance could not assuage. This chapter seeks to describe and analyze how – and why – the reform decade ended so disastrously for China, belying the greatly elevated hopes and aspirations of the early 1980s.

FIRST CYCLE: LIBERALIZATION AND RESTRAINT

The Twelfth Party Congress

There were few, if any, signs of the debilitating trauma to come when the Twelfth CCP Congress met in September 1982. In his opening address to the Congress, Deng Xiaoping struck a moderate note, declaring that the Party's principal domestic task for the remainder of the decade was "to intensify socialist modernization . . . [with] economic construction at the core." In line with this objective, Deng carefully balanced his call for the further deepening of reform with an injunction to build a new "spiritual civilization" to ensure that China's modernization would maintain its socialist orientation.[6]

On the political side, the Twelfth Congress emphasized the twin tasks of rejuvenating the Party's leadership and creating a more highly institutionalized, collectively responsible structure of command and control. A formidable obstacle to the realization of the former objective was the absence of any regular mechanism of retirement for superannuated Party cadres. Historically, there had been two principal avenues of exit from political life in the

---

6 The text of Deng's speech is translated in BBC, *Summary of World Broadcasts/Far East* (hereafter, *SWB/FE*) 7120 (2 September, 1982). For analysis of the Twelfth Party Congress, see Lowell Dittmer, "The 12th congress of the Chinese Communist Party," *CQ* 93 (March 1983), 108–24; and *Issues and Studies* (hereafter, *I&S*) 18. 11 (November 1982), 14–62.

People's Republic of China (PRC): death (or disability) and purgation.[7] In an effort to create a more appealing third alternative, the Twelfth Party Congress created the CAC, one of Deng's previously mentioned "temporary" innovations, to serve as a way station en route to full retirement for senior Party leaders with more than forty years of service to the revolution. Members of this council of elders would be entitled to retain their full salaries, ranks, and perks, and would continue to be regularly consulted by Party leaders on matters of importance; but they would cease serving on the Party's regular decision-making bodies, thus making room for younger, more vigorous, and technically proficient cadres.

On the eve of the Twelfth Congress it had been widely speculated that with the creation of the CAC, a substantial number of eligible Party veterans would choose to retire from active duty.[8] In the event, such expectations proved overly optimistic, as at least fourteen top-level veterans, most notably Politburo Standing Committee members Ye Jianying (eighty-six), Chen Yun (seventy-seven), and Li Xiannian (seventy-three), chose not to exercise the retirement option.[9] Through an adroit parliamentary maneuver, Deng Xiaoping (seventy-seven) managed to finesse the question of his own retirement: As newly elected chairman of the CAC, he was constitutionally mandated to serve, *ex officio*, as a voting member of the Politburo's Standing Committee.

Defending his own decision not to retire, Chen Yun argued that "there aren't many young cadres qualified to take over leadership posts. . . . Some [of us] still have to stay on the front line." Chen's Standing Committee colleague, Ye Jianying, was even more blunt in his refusal to step down: "I'll [continue to] perform my duties with all my energy . . . and stop only when I die" (which he finally did in 1986).[10]

---

7 See Michel Oksenberg, "The exit pattern from Chinese politics and its implications," *CQ* 67 (September 1976), 501–18.

8 See, for example, the statement by vice-premier Wan Li in *SWB/FE* 7109 (20 August 1982).

9 Other veteran Politburo members who declined to retire at the Twelfth Congress included Nie Rongzhen (eighty-three), Xu Xiangqian (eighty-three), Deng Yingchao (eighty-one), Peng Zhen (eighty), Ulanfu (seventy-seven), Wang Zhen (seventy-four), Song Renqiong (seventy-three), Liao Chengzhi (seventy-three), and Yang Dezhi (seventy-two). In preliminary discussions of the proposal to establish the CAC prior to the Twelfth Congress, it had been the stated intent of the commission's designers (including Deng Xiaoping, who first proposed the idea in an August 1980 address on leadership reform) to make the CAC independent of, and coequal with, the CC in power and authority. A third leading party body, the newly established Central Discipline Inspection Commission (CDIC), had also been slated to enjoy coequal status with the CC and the CAC. The idea of three-way parity was rejected at the Twelfth Congress, however, and the two new party commissions were given a reduced role in policymaking – a fact that may have contributed to the last-minute decision of several elderly Politburo members to put off their retirement. Over time, the CAC gained de facto veto power over important Politburo decisions, making it in effect a shadow CC (see the subsections "Combatting bourgeois liberalism," "Toward reform and renewal: The Thirteenth Party Congress," "Reenter the gerontocrats," and "Waging moral warfare: Gorbachev, the media, and the hunger strike."

10 *Renmin ribao* (hereafter, *RMRB*), 7 September 1982.

As an added retirement sweetener for recalcitrant veteran cadres, the new Party constitution, ratified by the Twelfth Congress, stipulated that all members of the CAC were entitled to attend plenary meetings of the Central Committee (CC) in a nonvoting capacity; at the same time, the several vice-chairmen of the CAC were granted the statutory right on nonvoting participation in plenary sessions of the Politburo.[11] Such provisions apparently helped take the sting out of retirement, as a group of sixty-five CC members over the age of seventy (including fourteen alternates) relinquished their seats and accepted appointment to the new commission. In addition to these 65 voluntary retirees, another group of 131 incumbent members and alternates of the Eleventh CC (elected in 1977) failed to gain reelection to the Twelfth CC. The majority of the unseated cadres were erstwhile "leftists" and "whateverists" who had risen to prominence during the Cultural Revolution or the Hua Guofeng interregnum, and who were now being systematically weeded out by Deng's followers.

Despite the obvious reluctance of some of China's most senior leaders to leave the political stage, in the end a rather substantial turnover in Party leadership did take place below the level of the Politburo. Fully 60 percent of the 341 CC members and alternates elected by the Twelfth Congress were newcomers. The average age of these first-timers was fifty-eight; the youngest new member was thirty-eight; many had received a college education. While applauding this overall rejuvenation of the Party's leadership, official Chinese accounts of the proceedings of the Twelfth Congress conveniently ignored the fact that on average, the twenty-five members of the new Politburo were actually *older*, at seventy-two, than their predecessors.[12]

If cadre retirement proved a difficult hurdle, so too did the task of institutionalizing the Party's command structure. During the late Maoist period, the CCP had come under the putative influence of "feudal autocracy" and the "cult of personality," leading to an "over-concentration of power" in the hands of Mao and a small group of his lieutenants.[13] To help remedy this problem and to strengthen the norm of collective leadership, the Twelfth Congress formally abolished the posts of CC chairman and vice-chairmen, supplanting them with a revitalized Central Party Secretariat, an organ that had been abolished during the Cultural Revolution. Under the revised party *nomenklatura* that governed high-level personnel appointments and ranks, the general secretary of the Central Secretariat nominally became the top-ranking

11 See "Constitution of the Communist Party of China," *Beijing Review* (hereafter, *BR*) 25.38 (20 September 1982), 14–16.

12 The six-member Politburo Standing Committee (Deng, Hu Yaobang, Ye Jianying, Zhao Ziyang, Li Xiannian, and Chen Yun) was older still, averaging seventy-four years – just one year younger than the average age of the retirees on the CAC.

13 See the earlier discussion by Roderick MacFarquhar.

party leader, though his autonomy was constrained by a new constitutional provision that held that "no party member, whatever his position, is allowed to stand above the law or . . . make decisions on major issues on his own."[14]

Unlike the Politburo, which continued to be dominated by elderly revolutionaries of the first (i.e., Long March) generation, the Central Secretariat, under the direction of newly elected general secretary Hu Yaobang (sixty-seven), was staffed with a number of younger, better-educated cadres, including members of both the second (anti–Japanese war) and third (civil war) generations of Party leaders. The average age of the twelve full and alternate members of the new Secretariat was sixty-three, almost a full decade younger than their Politburo counterparts.[15]

BUILDING "SOCIALIST SPIRITUAL CIVILIZATION"

A final programmatic theme raised at the Twelfth Party Congress was the call to create a "socialist spiritual civilization" that would offer CCP members effective moral protection against the corrosive effects of "bourgeois liberalization" and other unwanted by-products of China's structural reform and opening to the outside world. In his address to the Congress, General Secretary Hu Yaobang asserted that the successful construction of a socialist material civilization in China ultimately depended on the prior attainment of a high level of spiritual civilization. In postulating such a causal relationship between spirit and matter, Hu tacitly reversed the priorities established at the time of the Third Plenum in December 1978, when the development of society's productive forces had been elevated to the position of summum bonum.

The reason for the reversal was clear: A wind of bourgeois liberalization had blown across China since the Third Plenum. In such a situation, Hu Yaobang asserted, "capitalist forces and other forces hostile to our socialist cause will seek to corrupt us and harm our country." Confronted with such a challenge, he continued, "it will not be possible to prevent in all cases the degeneration of some members of our society and party or block the emergence of a few exploiting and hostile elements." To minimize the effects of such degeneration,

---

14 See "Constitution of the Communist Party." It was reported at the time that the main reason Party leaders favored a general secretary over a chairman was that the former, as part of a collective leading body, would merely be first among equals, thus reducing the likelihood of the emergence of a potentially overbearing dictator. For analysis of the Party constitution, see Tony Saich. "The People's Republic of China," in W. B. Simons and S. White, eds., *The party statutes of the communist world*, 83–113.

15 On generational change in China's leadership in the early 1980s, see Hong Yung Lee, "China's 12th central committee," *AS* 23.6 (June 1983), 673–91; also William de B. Mills, "Generational change in China," *Problems of Communism* (hereafter, *POC*) 32.6 (November–December 1983), 16–35.

CCP members were called upon to hold firmly to the Party's established ideals, moral values, and organizational discipline.[16]

In raising the specter of renewed disturbances by capitalist forces, Hu Yaobang was ostensibly bowing to the demands of Party traditionalists rather than expressing his own deeply felt convictions.[17] Consequently, he hedged his warnings against the dangers of ideological degeneration, couching them in relatively restrained, nonmilitant language. While acceding to the traditionalists' claim that class struggle "still exists," for example, he added two significant caveats: It existed only "within certain limits," and it no longer constituted the "principal contradiction."[18] Finally, in announcing the leadership's intention to launch a comprehensive three-year Party consolidation and rectification drive in the latter half of 1983, Hu Yaobang went out of his way to stress that Maoist-style methods of mass mobilization and struggle would not be employed in the new campaign.[19]

In sum, the Twelfth Congress took an ambivalent stance on China's most pressing developmental issues, seeking thereby to minimize conflict among contending leadership factions and constituencies. While pragmatically stressing the need to further deepen the process of economic reform and opening up to the outside world, Party spokesmen simultaneously intensified their warnings of spiritual degeneration; by the same token, while declaring class struggle in the main to be over, they held out the clear possibility (made explicit in the new CCP constitution) that class struggle could become even sharper in the future. Although the Twelfth Congress thus split the difference on a number of troublesome issues of ideological and political orientation, the resulting compromises left considerable room for future discord.

Constitutional reform: Strengthening socialist legality

In the aftermath of the Twelfth Congress, political attention was focused on the newly revised PRC state constitution, approved by the National People's Congress (NPC) on 4 December. Two years in the making, the new constitution reflected a clear rejection of the ultra-left political philosophy of the Cultural Revolution and a reversion to a more routinized form of "socialist legality,"

---

16 Hu Yaobang's speech is translated in *SWB/FE* 7125 (8 September 1982).

17 Party leaders in China are frequently called upon publicly to express consensual positions that may differ from their own personal views. This is a major feature of Party discipline under "democratic centralism"; for this reason, it is sometimes difficult to sort out what is personal and discretionary from what is consensual and obligatory in the formal speeches and reports of Party leaders.

18 The idea that class struggle continues to exist "within certain limits" was first officially formulated in the CCP's 1981 *Resolution on CPC history, (1949–81)*.

19 *SWB/FE* 7125 (8 September 1982). No details were given in Hu's speech concerning the forthcoming Party consolidation movement.

closely akin to the system originally imported from the Soviet Union in 1954.[20]

Echoing a theme raised at the Twelfth Congress, the new constitution emphasized the creation of orderly, accountable, legally regulated governmental institutions and procedures. Toward this end, the legislative functions and powers of the NPC and its Standing Committee (SC) were augmented; tenure in office for government leaders was limited to two consecutive five-year terms; and new prohibitions were added against certain officials serving concurrently in more than one leadership post. Such measures were ostensibly intended to create a "clear division of power" and to ensure a "strict system of responsibility in implementing laws."[21]

The 1982 constitution sought to strike a careful balance between civil liberties and civic duties. Although a number of new citizens' rights and safeguards were incorporated into the document, including the right to personal dignity, sanctity of the home, and protection against deliberate frame-up, false accusation, and libel, the practical effects of this constitutional innovation were sharply reduced by a series of explicit caveats and qualifiers. For example, the right of citizens to enjoy "freedom and privacy of correspondence" was subject to the proviso, "except in cases involving state security or criminal investigation." Equally limiting was a clause that held that "The exercise by citizens . . . of their freedoms and rights may not infringe upon the interests of the state, of society, and of the collective, or upon the lawful freedoms and rights of other citizens."[22] Finally, the 1982 constitution reaffirmed the Party's four cardinal principles, though it did so in watered-down language that appeared to give virtually equal emphasis to the importance of strengthening China's socialist democracy and legal system.[23]

On the whole, China's new constitution represented a careful attempt to balance the inherently conflicting imperatives of *fang* and *shou*. Relatively tolerant and permissive compared to previous charters, the document reflected

20 The text of the 1982 state constitution appears in *BR* 25.52 (27 December 1982), 10–18. For analysis, see Tony Saich, "The fourth constitution of the People's Republic of China," *Review of Socialist Law* 9.2 (1983), 113–24; and Richard Baum, "Modernization and legal reform in post-Mao China: The rebirth of socialist legality," *Studies in Comparative Communism* (hereafter, *SICC*) 19.2 (Summer 1986), 69–103.

21 See Peng Zhen, "Report on the draft of a revised constitution of the PRC," *BR* 25.50 (13 December 1982), 9–20.

22 Similar language had been invoked by China's top leaders in the spring of 1979, when the government closed down the democracy wall and arrested human rights activist Wei Jingsheng. See the earlier discussion by MacFarquhar.

23 The relevant passage (in the preamble to the constitution) stated that "Under the leadership of the CCP and the guidance of Marxism–Leninism–Mao Zedong Thought, the Chinese people will . . . continue to adhere to the people's democratic dictatorship and follow the socialist road, steadily improve socialist institutions, develop socialist democracy, improve the socialist legal system, and work hard . . . to turn China into a socialist country with a high level of culture and democracy."

a clear break from the political philosophy of the Cultural Revolution. At the same time, however, it fell far short of institutionalizing the pluralistic rule of law, resembling instead a rationalized variant of neoclassical Leninist rule *by* law.[24]

From socialist legality to socialist humanism

After almost two years of relative quiescence brought on by the spring 1981 conservative literary attack against PLA writer Bai Hua,[25] China's critical intellectuals became markedly bolder in the months following the constitutional reform of December 1982. In the early winter of 1982–3, a vigorous academic debate unfolded in Beijing on the question of the contemporary relevance of such concepts as "alienation" (*yihua*) and "humanism" (*rendao zhuyi*) in socialist society. Among the more prominent participants in this debate were Wang Ruoshui, deputy editor-in-chief of the *People's Daily*, and Ru Xin, vice-president of the Chinese Academy of Social Sciences (CASS).[26]

The debate began to heat up in mid-January 1983 with the publication of Wang Ruoshui's controversial essay "In defense of humanism." In this essay Wang noted that certain "well-meaning comrades" in the party disapproved of humanist values, regarding them as anti-Marxist heresy. "They set Marxism and humanism in total opposition to one another," he wrote; hence they are unable to see any universal relevance in the idea of "human worth." Rejecting this view on the grounds that it erroneously equated the concept of human worth with *bourgeois* humanism, Wang proposed an entirely different type of humanism:

> *Socialist* humanism implies resolutely abandoning the "total dictatorship" and merciless struggle of the ten years of chaos, abandoning the deification

24 Following Jowitt's typology of the stages of development of postrevolutionary Leninist regimes, H. C. Kuan has characterized China's 1982 constitution as "inclusionary" in nature, reflecting the Party's desire to coopt the active support of intellectuals and other relevant social forces. See his "New departures in China's constitution," *SICC* 17.1 (Spring 1984), 53–68. On the distinction between rule *of* law and rule *by* law, see Jerome A. Cohen, *The criminal process in the People's Republic of China, 1949–63: An introduction*, 5ff.

25 Bai Hua's controversial screenplay, *Ku Lian (Bitter Love)*, was attacked by conservatives for being too negative and pessimistic about China's recent past, in particular about the damage inflicted by CCP policies during the Great Leap Forward and the Cultural Revolution. The Bai Hua affair is discussed in Tsou, "Political change and reform," 227–31; see also Richard Kraus, "Bai Hua: The political authority of a writer," in Carol Lee Hamrin and Timothy Cheek, eds., *China's establishment intellectuals*, 201–11.

26 Along with a handful of other liberal critics of dogmatic Marxism, Wang and Ru had begun writing essays on the relationship between socialism and humanism as early as 1980. See David A. Kelly, "The emergence of humanism: Wang Ruoshui and the critique of socialist alienation," in Merle Goldman with Timothy Cheek and Carol Lee Hamrin, eds., *China's intellectuals and the state: In search of a new relationship*, 159–82. For further analysis of the origins and development of the debate over socialist humanism, see Stuart Schram, "'Economics in command?': Ideology and policy since the Third Plenum, 1978–84," *CQ* 99 (September 1984), 433ff.

of one individual . . . , upholding the equality of all before truth and the law, and seeing that the personal freedoms and human dignity of citizens are not infringed upon. . . . Why should this sort of socialist humanism be treated as a strange, alien, or evil thing?[27]

Academic advocacy of humanist values reached a high water mark in the spring of 1983. In March, at a Beijing symposium marking the centenary of Karl Marx's death, a leading Communist literary cadre and one-time guardian of Maoist intellectual orthodoxy, Zhou Yang, presented a paper pointedly upholding the contemporary relevance and utility of socialist humanism. Defending the controversial notion that alienation could arise under socialism, Zhou suggested that China's previous lack of democracy and sound legal norms had given rise to a situation wherein the people's servants had become their masters. This, he said, was a relevant example of political alienation. Economic alienation also existed, averred Zhou, because of China's critical "lack of understanding and experience" of socialist construction. As a result, he charged, "we did many stupid things" and "ate our own bitter fruit." Arguing that economic and political alienation existed objectively, he concluded that it was "pointless" for people to be alarmed by such terms.[28]

Adding another strong critical voice to the flourishing debate on socialist humanism and alienation, senior party theoretician Su Shaozhi, in a paper delivered at the Beijing centenary symposium on Marxism, affirmed that a "crisis of Marxism" existed. Calling the crisis "our punishment for having treated Marxism in a dogmatic fashion," Su argued that the bitter legacy of Cultural Revolution dogmatism had led "some people" to deny completely the contemporary relevance of Marxism. While carefully avoiding personal concurrence in such negative assessments, Su concluded that "only by creatively developing Marxism can we truly uphold [it]."[29]

For a brief period in the spring of 1983, even the conservative wing of the CCP appeared to accept the propriety (if not the validity) of such arguments. At a meeting on "Marx and Man" held in early April, for example, Deng Liqun, head of the CC's propaganda department and a leading Party traditionalist, grudgingly conceded that the debate on socialist humanism and alienation

27 Wang Ruoshui, "Wei rendaozhuyi bianhu" (In defense of humanism), *Wenhui bao* (hereafter, *WHB*) (Shanghai), 17 January 1983. A partial translation appears in *Inside China Mainland* (hereafter, *ICM*), June 1983, Supplement 7–8.
28 Zhou Yang, "Inquiry into some theoretical problems of Marxism," *RMRB*, 16 March 1983.
29 Su Shaozhi, "Develop Marxism under contemporary conditions," *Selected Studies on Marxism* 2 (February 1983), 1–39. See also Schram," 'Economics in command?' . . . ," 434–7.

contained "many good points" and would contribute to the vigorous development of the Party's "double hundred" policy toward intellectuals.[30]

After more than three months of free-flowing blooming and contending,
official tolerance for the ongoing debate over socialist norms and values began
to diminish noticeably. Social critics like Wang Ruoshui and Su Shaozhi had
come uncomfortably, if only elliptically, close to denying the Party's doctrinal
and political legitimacy, and such defenders of the faith as Deng Liqun were
finding it increasingly difficult to refrain from calling them to account. By the
end of May, the humanism–alienation debate was no longer being reported,
benignly or otherwise, in the Party media; and by early June a new term had
been coined to describe the heterodox ideas ostensibly being propagated by
Wang, Su, and other members of the humanist school: "spiritual pollution"
(*jingshen wuran*.)[31]

Straws in the wind: The Sixth NPC

The first significant public hint of a shift in the prevailing political wind
was contained in Zhao Ziyang's "Report on the work of the government,"
delivered in early June to the opening session of the Sixth NPC. While
defending the Party's established policies of economic reform, opening up to
the outside world, and intellectual blooming and contending, Zhao added a
fresh warning against the growing tendency of bourgeois liberalism in the
ideological and cultural spheres. Examples were said to include writers and
artists who "disregard the social consequences of their work" and who "view
their work as a means to grab fame and fortune." Such behavior, said Zhao, was
symptomatic of "decadent ideology" and was "incompatible with the policy
of serving the people and socialism."[32] Although no concrete measures were
called for beyond a general exhortation to criticize such trends, Zhao's remarks
proved worrisome to China's oft-burned critical intellectuals.

Also of concern to careful readers of Zhao's report was the premier's use of
strong language on the subject of law and order. Speaking of shortcomings in
public security work, Zhao noted that a rising tide of serious crime, including a wave of violent offenses such as hijacking, murder, robbery, rape, and

---

30 *RMRB*, 12 April 1983. The term "double hundred" refers to the policy "Let a hundred flowers bloom,
    let a hundred schools of thought contend," first enunciated by Mao in 1956. Schram, "'Economics in
    command?'" notes that Deng Liqun's remarks were published under a provocative headline supplied
    not by Deng himself but by the liberal-leaning editors *of People's Daily*, Hu Jiwei and Wang Ruoshui.
    The headline read, "To discuss humanism and the theory of human nature is an excellent thing."
    Hu and Wang were later criticized by Deng Liqun and "transferred" from their jobs for promoting
    "spiritual pollution." See the subsection "Combatting humanism and 'spiritual pollution.'"
31 The term was first used by Deng Liqun in a 4 June 1983 speech to the Central Party School in Beijing.
    See *Zhengming* (hereafter, *ZM*) 76 (1 February 1984), 6–11.
32 Zhao Ziyang, "Report on the work of the government," *BR* 26.25 (4 July 1983), XVIII–XIX.

larceny, had begun to pose a definite problem in China. At the same time, he acknowledged a pronounced upsurge in the incidence of nonviolent economic crime and corruption on the part of government cadres who "seek personal gain by abusing [their] position and power." Attributing the breakdown in social order to the "intolerable political and ideological apathy" allegedly displayed by certain public security arid law enforcement personnel, Zhao Ziyang stressed that it was necessary to "suppress counterrevolutionary activities" and "deal powerful blows" to criminals in all spheres.[33]

In the wake of the premier's call for enhanced law and order, a draconian crackdown on crime was launched in the summer of 1983. Marked by the suspension of certain constitutional and statutory rights of criminal defendants, the campaign witnessed a flurry of mass trials, hasty verdicts, truncated appeals, and summary executions.[34] Although not necessarily unpopular with China's increasingly crime-weary citizens, the anticrime campaign gave further impetus to the ideological chill that was beginning to envelop China. More important, it gave Party traditionalists a potent issue, law and order, and a viable pretext, the need to combat crime at its putative source, for launching a new offensive against ideological corrosion.

The offensive took shape at the end of the summer. Beginning in mid-September, there was a pronounced increase in the stridency of articles published in certain bellweather journals. The editors of *Red Flag* (*Hongqi*), for example, now pointedly criticized "some people in cultural circles" who had been "taken in" by "the allure of abstract humanity and humanism" to the point where "social and class nature have been abandoned." Calling this an erroneous viewpoint that reflected a "serious antagonistic struggle in the political sphere," the article stressed that since class struggle still existed, it was necessary to strengthen the organs of people's democratic dictatorship in order to combat harmful views.[35] In a subsequent article, *Red Flag's* editors went even further, claiming a presumptive link between the influence of bourgeois mentality, on the one hand, and the severity of China's recent crime wave, on the other:

33 Ibid., XX–XXI.
34 A resolution adopted by the NPC Standing Committee in early September served to suspend a number of statutory provisions governing the handling of criminal cases – including provisions setting time limits for the delivery of indictments, the issuance of subpoenas, and the right to appeal convictions. The stated purpose of the suspension was to "promptly punish criminals who seriously jeopardize social order" (*Xinhua* [hereafter, *XH*], 2 September 1983). According to various sources, between 6,000 and 10,000 convicted lawbreakers were executed in the second half of 1983. See *Far Eastern Economic Review* (hereafter, *FEER*), 10 November 1983 and 16 February 1984; also Amnesty International, *China: Violations of human rights*, 54–5. For a collection of media reports concerning implementation of the 1983 anticrime campaign, see *ICM*, October 1983.
35 *Hongqi* (hereafter, *HQ*) 18 (16 September 1983).

Although our country has already abolished the system of exploitation and
established a socialist society, . . . all kinds of elements hostile to the socialist
system and to the people still exist. *Various kinds of crime are bound to occur
where the influence of bourgeois extreme individualism . . . is still present.* We must
see that these serious offenders are detestable in the extreme. . . . If we let
them get away with [their] crimes . . . and fail to suppress them, *if we speak
of "mercy" and "humanism," it will be a grave dereliction of our duty . . . to the cause
of socialism.*[36]

Combatting humanism and "spiritual pollution"

Under mounting pressure from Party traditionalists, the uneasy ideological
compromise crafted by Party leaders a year earlier now began to show signs
of stress. The fault lines in Deng Xiaoping's coalition were clearly evident at
the Second Plenum of the Twelfth Party Congress, held on 11–12 October
1983. In his speech to the plenum, Deng steered a middle course between the
increasingly polarized factions of his reform coalition. First, he addressed the
principal concerns of the Party's moderate-to-liberal wing, led by Hu Yaobang
and Zhao Ziyang. Speaking of the need to continue combatting remnant leftist
influences from the Cultural Revolution, he noted that "three kinds of people"
(*sanzhong ren*) were continuing to undermine Party unity and discipline from
the left: those who rose to power in the Cultural Revolution on the coattails of
the Lin Biao and Jiang Qing cliques; those who engaged in factional activities,
rumor mongering, and various other forms of "subversive" partisan behavior;
and those guilty of "looting, smashing, and grabbing" during China's ten
years of chaos. Such people, said Deng, should be firmly disciplined, including
expulsion from the Party where necessary. To accomplish this task, he said, the
forthcoming Party consolidation movement would concentrate on exposing
and rectifying the "three kinds of people."[37]

After thus addressing the main concerns of his centrist and liberal constituencies, Deng shifted his focus almost 180 degrees to launch a sharp,
three-pronged attack on abstract humanism, the theory of socialist alienation,
and spiritual pollution. Sardonically observing that a considerable number
of Party theorists preferred to indulge in abstract contemplation of human
nature rather than attempting to understand and resolve concrete problems

---

36 *HQ* 17 (1 September 1983) (emphasis added). As early as 1982, Party conservatives had begun to
    attribute China's rising crime rate to an influx of corrosive foreign ideas under the open door policy.
    One internal (*neibu*) Chinese publication thus stated that "since [initiating] the policy of opening
    to the outside world, encroachments by bourgeois ideology from abroad [and] infiltration by hostile
    foreign influences [have] directly or indirectly [contributed to] criminal activities in society. This is
    the objective reason [why the situation of public security] has not taken a basic turn for the better."
    (*Look* Monthly, September 1983, trans. in *ICM*, October 1983, 7).
37 An unofficial transcript of Deng's address appears in *I&S* 20.4 (April 1984), 99–111.

encountered by real people, Deng tersely dismissed abstract humanism as "un-Marxist; it leads youth astray." On the related issue of the possibility of alienation occurring under socialism, Deng sharply rebutted the viewpoint advanced by Zhou Yang and others in the spring of 1983:

> A number of comrades . . . say that alienation exists in socialist society . . . in the spheres of economics, politics, and ideology. . . . Such talk cannot help people gain a correct understanding . . . of the many problems which have appeared in socialist society. . . . In fact, this can only lead people to criticize, mistrust, and negate socialism, to lose confidence in the future of socialism and communism. . . . [38]

Turning to questions of political orientation, Deng noted that a number of unhealthy ideas had recently become fashionable among party theoreticians, including "the abstract concept of democracy," advocacy of "free speech for counterrevolutionaries," and "doubts about the four cardinal principles."[39] Such ideas "run counter to Marxist common sense," said Deng; in addition, they discredit the Party's proletarian character and engender doubts about the future of socialism, thereby sowing confusion among Party members. Displaying contempt for writers and artists who "dwell eagerly on the gloomy and the pessimistic," Deng called on Party workers in literature and the arts to eulogize the CCP's revolutionary history, the four cardinal principles, and the heroic achievements of the Chinese people under socialism.[40]

Continuing in this vein, Deng next decried a growing attitude of "doing anything for money" among writers and performing artists, many of whom "run around everywhere, . . . indiscriminately giving performances . . . using low and vulgar form and content to turn an easy profit." Such people are guilty of "pandering to the low tastes of a section of their audiences," Deng continued; they "commercialize spiritual productions" and thus "occupy an unworthy place in the world of art." Pointedly labeling such phenomena "spiritual pollution," Deng called for a vigorous ideological struggle to "resolutely overcome weakness, laxity, and liberal attitudes."[41]

Although the effects of spiritual pollution were said to have seriously affected only a minority of Party theoreticians and ideological workers, Deng warned of dire consequences if firm steps were not taken to combat the problem. "Don't imagine," he warned, "that a little spiritual pollution doesn't amount to very much and is not worth making a fuss over. . . . If we do not immediately . . . curb these phenomena, . . . the consequences could be extremely serious."[42]

38 Ibid.
39 Some liberal intellectuals, including *People's Daily* deputy editor Wang Ruoshui, among others, had openly expressed doubts about Deng's four principles as early as 1979.
40 *I&S*, 20.4 (April 1984). 41 Ibid. 42 Ibid.

Having thus addressed the principal concerns of his coalition's liberal and conservative wings, Deng instructed his comrades to avoid going to extremes to rectify ideological problems of the right or the left. In the forthcoming Party consolidation movement, he urged, comrades must at all times "seek truth from facts" (*shishi qiushi*) and resist the temptation to employ the "crude and extreme" methods adopted in the past, characterized by "cruel struggle and merciless attacks." It was essential, he concluded, to adopt a kindly attitude toward comrades who had committed mistakes, resisting the temptation to "take every bush and tree for an enemy."[43]

At the conclusion of its brief two-day plenum, the CC adopted twin resolutions on Party consolidation and rectification. Responding to Deng Xiaoping's injunction to avoid crude and extreme methods, the resolutions hewed closely to the ideological midline, denouncing with equal vigor the three kinds of people on the left and spiritual polluters on the right.[44] Under the guidance of the CCPs newly created Central Discipline Inspection Commission (CDIC), headed by Chen Yun and Bo Yibo, the consolidation drive was to be carried out in two stages over a period of three years. Although no specific targets or quotas were announced, diplomatic sources in Beijing reported that some 3 million Party members, principally young leftists who had been recruited during the ten years of chaos, were initially targeted for rectification.[45]

Whatever Deng Xiaoping's original intent, the 1983 Party consolidation movement quickly veered off the tracks and out of control. No sooner had the Second Plenum ended than a barrage of newspaper articles appeared, canonizing the four cardinal principles, condemning spiritual pollution, and vigorously denouncing abstract humanism and the theory of socialist alienation.[46] By early November, a number of leading CCP traditionalists, including Deng Liqun, Wang Zhen, Peng Zhen, and Chen Yun, had weighed in on the dangers

---

43 Ibid.

44 The text of she resolution on Party consolidation appears in *XH* (Chinese and English), 12 October 1983.

45 *Asiaweek* 43 (28 October 1983), 13; *ICM*, February 1985, 20–1. Thomas Gold has argued that Deng Xiaoping's denunciation of spiritual pollution at the Second Plenum was a "tactical feint" designed to gain conservative support for his real objective, which was said to be to rid the Party of residual ultraleftists. (Gold, "'Just in Time!' China battles spiritual pollution on the eve of 1984," *AS* 24.9 [September 1984], 952.) After earlier sharing Gold's view, I am now inclined to believe (in light of Deng Xiaoping's subsequent behavior in 1986 and 1989, to be examined later) that Deng was being entirely candid in his denunciations of rightist dangers at the Second Plenum but that he wished to avoid giving leftists an excuse to reverse his hard-won economic reforms. For other views on this controversy, see Schram, "'Economics in command?' . . ."; Tony Saich, "Party consolidation and spiritual pollution in the People's Republic of China," *Communist Affairs* 3.3 (July 1984), 283–9; and Colin Mackerras, "'Party consolidation' and the attack of spiritual pollution," *Australian Journal of Chinese Affairs* (hereafter, *AJCA*) 11 (January 1984), 178.

46 See, for example, *RMRB*, 20, 23, 25, 31 October and 2 November 1983.

of liberal ideological corrosion, explicitly invoking Deng Xiaoping's remarks at the Second Plenum to support their arguments.[47]

Deng Liqun (no relation to Deng Xiaoping) was the conservatives' primary hatchet man. According to reports subsequently circulated in Hong Kong, Deng Liqun's leading role in the early attack on spiritual pollution was motivated by two main considerations: his own strong traditionalist values and an equally strong desire to undermine the growing prestige of Hu Yaobang. Deng's antipathy to Hu was said to stem from envy kindled when he (Deng) was passed over for the post of CCP general secretary prior to the Twelfth Party Congress in 1982. Armed with the potent issue of spiritual pollution, an issue on which Hu Yaobang was believed to be vulnerable, Deng Liqun now set out to undermine his rival.[48]

In the ensuing storm, a wide variety of social phenomena were singled out as manifestations of spiritual pollution. These included, inter alia, the "worship of individualism"; the proliferation of pornographic films and videotapes; the attitude of "looking to make money in everything"; the revival of "clan feuds" and "superstitious practices" in rural areas; and even the wearing of Western-style hairdos and high-heeled shoes by female college students.[49] In some areas, vigilantes reportedly harassed people whose hair was unusually long or who wore flared trousers. In other places, factory workers were organized to search for "yellow" (pornographic) audiotapes and books. And in the city of Lanzhou, provincial police headquarters reportedly organized local gendarmes to "read good books and sing revolutionary songs" as an antidote to such

---

47 Chen Yun was somewhat enigmatic in his early response to the problem of spiritual pollution. At a CC meeting in May 1983, for example, Chen reportedly displayed considerable restraint in criticizing intellectuals who had strayed from the path of socialism and patriotism, arguing that "we must not [overreact]; we must not drag in too many people on account of some small matters." He also conceded that the much-criticized PLA writer Bai Hua was a "genius," and he recommended that his CC comrades should "see and welcome" Bai's banned screenplay, "Bitter Love." Chen's speech is unofficially reported in *ICM*, March 1984, 15–16.

48 Although the "sibling rivalry" theory of Deng's antagonism toward Hu Yaobang is based largely on circumstance, it nevertheless squares nicely with a number of known facts. For one thing, Deng Liqun and Hu Yaobang were among Deng Xiaoping's strongest supporters and closest confidants in the later years of the Maoist era. Hu had been Deng Xiaoping's pre–Cultural Revolution bridge partner and protégé, and Deng Liqun, who once served as personal secretary to Mao Zedong's one-time heir apparent, Liu Shaoqi, played a key role in defending Deng Xiaoping at a critical juncture in 1975 when the latter was under attack by the Gang of Four for having put forward the controversial idea of "taking the three directives as the key link" (*ZM* 78 [1 April 1984]). Whatever the truth of the sibling rivalry theory, it is clear that from the outset of the spiritual pollution campaign in 1983 until Hu Yaobang was finally ousted from power in January 1987, Deng Liqun wasted no opportunity to embarrass Hu and erode his base of support. For a detailed account of the growing rivalry between Deng and Hu, see *ZM* 76 (1 February 1984).

49 See, e.g., *RMRB*, 29 October and 5 November 1983; *Jingji ribao* (hereafter, *JJRB*), 1 November 1983; *Hubei people's broadcasting station*, 20 October 1983; and *Heilongjiang people's broadcasting station*, 2 November 1983.

putative evils as "wearing mustaches and whiskers, singing unhealthy songs, being undisciplined, and not keeping one's mind on work."[50]

In addition to denouncing various social manifestations of spiritual pollution, China's cultural watchdogs attacked a number of alleged high-level purveyors of ideological corrosion. Wang Ruoshui and Zhou Yang were singled out for particularly strong criticism, as was Hu Jiwei, Wang Ruoshui's boss and chief editor of the *People's Daily*, who had been a key supporter of Hu Yaobang.[51]

At an enlarged Politburo conference held in November, Hu Yaobang and Zhao Ziyang fought back, claiming that the spiritual pollution campaign had gone too far and that ultra-leftists had taken advantage of the ideological cover provided by the campaign to sabotage the "correct line" of the Eleventh CC's Third Plenum, negating economic reform (particularly in rural areas) and opposing China's opening to the outside world. Calling the attack on spiritual pollution a "false show of force," Hu and Zhao argued that the main focus on Party consolidation and rectification should be the elimination of the three kinds of people.[52]

A short while later, at a meeting of the Central Party Secretariat, Hu and Zhao were reportedly assailed by an unidentified speaker (said to be Deng Liqun) who "shouted at the top of his voice that 'spiritual pollution threatens the life of the party.'" At that point, Zhao Ziyang played his trump card. Noting that "Japanese capitalists are postponing agreements with us ... because they are frightened by the ... movement to eliminate spiritual pollution," Zhao threatened to resign: "If things go on like this," he warned, "I shall be Prime Minister no longer."[53]

In the end, fearing disruption of his hard-won economic reform and open-door policies, Deng Xiaoping intervened on the side of Hu and Zhao to bring the campaign to a halt.[54] The two reform leaders did not emerge entirely unscathed, however; in return for securing the conservatives' agreement to

---

50 See *RMRB*, 16 and 17 November 1983; *Foreign Broadcast Information Service* – China, *Daily Report* (hereafter, *FBIS*), 3 November 1983, Q2, T7; Gold, "'Just in time!' ... ," 956–8.

51 *ZM* 78, (1 April 1984). The attack on Zhou Yang was spearheaded by veteran party theoretician Hu Qiaomu, another member of Deng Liqun's anti–spiritual pollution coalition. Hu Qiaomu's lengthy critique of the abstract humanism-alienation school appears in *RMRB*, 27 January 1984. Under pressure from Hu Qiaomu and others, Zhou Yang made a series of self-criticisms in October and November 1983 in which he retracted many of his earlier statements on the subject of humanism and socialist alienation and accepted blame for spreading spiritual pollution in the cultural arena (*RMRB*, 11 November 1983; *BR* 26.50 [12 December 1983], 11–12; *XH*, 11 October 1983, reported in *ICM*, December 1983, 4–5). At around the same time, Hu Jiwei reportedly got into trouble because, among other reasons, he had tried to suppress publication of Wang Zhen's 23 October speech attacking Wang Ruoshui's theory of humanism (*Qishi niandai* [hereafter, *QSND*] 12 [December 1983], 57–8).

52 *ZM* 76 (1 February 1984), 6–11, in *FBIS*, 7 February 1984, W1–11.

53 *ZM* 78 (1 April 1984), in *FBIS*, 6 April 1984, W1–8.

54 In has been reported that Deng Xiaoping's son, Deng Pufang, warned his father that if the campaign was pursued too vigorously, it could undermine the reform program and thus erode Deng's own

end the campaign, Hu Yaobang was reportedly pressured into accepting the dismissal, technically labeled a "reassignment," of Wang Ruoshui and Hu Jiwei, his two top supporters at the *People's Daily*.[55] With the deal thus done, by early December the spiritual pollution storm began to abate; by the turn of the new year, 1984, all that remained were a few occasional squalls and a number of embittered feelings.[56]

Although Deng Liqun managed to secure the reassignment of two leading liberal media critics, he clearly emerged from the clash over spiritual pollution as the big loser. Not only did his own preferred policies fail to carry the day, but beginning in December 1983, he was placed in the unenviable position of having publicly to defend policies with which he strongly disagreed. In a series of press statements and interviews with visiting foreigners, the veteran propagandist now spoke approvingly (if reservedly) about economic reform and opening up to the outside world and less stridently about the dangers of ideological degeneration. Perforce, his antagonism toward Hu Yaobang remained undiminished by the experience.[57]

SECOND CYCLE: LIBERALIZATION AND REBUFFS

In the wake of the spiritual pollution campaign, China's reformers found themselves faced with a new set of problems on the economic policy front. Though the conservative ideological offensive was nipped in the bud, it had struck a raw nerve in many parts of the country where economic reform had at best brought only mixed blessings. In some rural districts, for example, village officials, resentful of the newfound prosperity of local entrepreneurs, had taken advantage of the antipollution drive to restrict the free-market activities of peasants and impose a variety of discriminatory taxes and fees on newly affluent "specialized households."[58] In China's less developed interior provinces, renewed opposition to Deng Xiaoping's preferential coastal development strategy (a key element of his open policy) also began to crystalize in this period. Throughout the country, those localities, groups, and individuals most highly disadvantaged by reform, or simply afflicted with envy of others more successful than themselves, a condition known in China as "redeye

prestige. See Ian Wilson and You Ji. "Leadership by 'lines'; China's unresolved succession," *POC* 39.1 (January–February 1990), 34.

55 *FBIS*, 14 November 1983, K1; *ICM*, December 1983, 2.

56 One early tipoff that Hu Yaobang and Zhao Ziyang were winning their confrontation with Deng Liqun came when both the general secretary and the premier wore Western-style suits and ties on their separate trips to Japan and America in late November and early January, respectively.

57 Deng Liqun's retreat is documented in Schram," Economics in command?' . . . ," 453ff.; see also Gold, "'Just in time!' . . . ," 961–2.

58 On the increasing incidence of such phenomena in the 1980s, see Jean Oi, *State and peasant in contemporary China*.

disease" (*hongyanbing*), took advantage of the antipollution campaign to disparage the high costs and adverse side effects of reform. The result was a revival of leftism, which was especially pronounced in the rural hinterland.

Confronting a potentially serious economic backlash, leaders of the reform coalition, most prominently Deng Xiaoping himself, now evinced renewed concern over the leftist challenge.[59] With Deng's support, Hu Yaobang began to speak out more forcefully on the need to reaffirm and strengthen economic reforms. At the end of February 1984, Hu instructed the editorial department of the *People's Daily* to draft for publication a series of hard-hitting commentaries favorable to renewed reform. After the articles were drafted, supporters of Deng Liqun reportedly tried to have them quashed, without success.[60]

Throughout the late winter and spring of 1984, editorials in official newspapers reinforced the impression that the Hu–Zhao group had regained the initiative. Five main themes were stressed: (1) the principal danger at the present time is leftism; (2) market reforms and responsibility systems in rural areas must be further expanded and perfected; (3) a key objective of economic reform is to "enable people to get rich"; (4) intellectuals are a precious national asset to be nurtured and cherished; and (5) the open policy and coastal development strategy are long-term policies to be further enriched and extended.[61]

The Party's shifting stance was fully revealed in a *People's Daily* editorial on 1 April. Based on a talk by Hu Yaobang, the article stated unequivocally that leftism, rather than bourgeois liberalism, was the principal source of ideological "weakness and laxity" at the present time.[62] Reviewing past damage inflicted on China by ultra-leftist ideas, the editorial called for the complete elimination of Cultural Revolution influences, which were said to have "penetrated very deeply."

The anti-leftist trend was quickly incorporated into the CCP's ongoing consolidation–rectification campaign, which entered its second phase in

59 See, the series of important editorials in *RMRB*, 20 February, 15 March, 1 April, and 23 April 1984.
60 One of the articles in question contained a sardonic echo of the ultra-leftist Cultural Revolution slogan "Boldly smash the old and create the new." According to reports out of Hong Kong, it was language such as this, now being used by Hu Yaobang's supporters to promote economic reform, that aroused the ire of Hu Qiaomu, Deng Liqun, and other traditionalists in the Party's central propaganda department. See *ZM* 78 (1 April 1984).
61 A major expansion of the open policy was announced in April, when fourteen coastal cities, including Shanghai, Tianjin, and Guangzhou, were added to the four existing special economic zones as preferred locations for foreign investment and technology transfer. See *China Daily* (hereafter, *CD*), 13 April 1984.
62 Deng Xiaoping himself had issued some of the strongest earlier warnings against liberal-induced ideological weakness and laxity; see his address to the Second Plenum of October 1983. Now Hu Yaobang clearly reversed the direction of the main threat. It is presumed that he did so with Deng Xiaoping's approval, since in a 1984 interview with foreign journalists Hu indicated that although he and Zhao Ziyang handled routine matters by themselves, on "important matters in foreign and domestic affairs" Deng Xiaoping alone decided things. See *Mingbao* (hereafter, *MB*), 6 December 1984, in *ICM*, March 1985, 2.

March 1984.[63] Throughout the spring, two themes dominated media discussions of Party rectification: admonitions to stamp out leftist "factionalism" and exhortations to promote young, technically competent members of the "third echelon" (*disan tidui*) to positions of responsibility in the Party and government.[64]

It was hardly coincidental that the Party consolidation drive should now focus on the search for talented younger leaders: Many of the harshest attacks on spiritual pollution in the fall of 1983 had come from veteran cadres who were at or near, and in some cases well beyond, the age of retirement, including such Politburo holdouts as Chen Yun, Peng Zhen, and Wang Zhen. Nor was it entirely coincidental that the man placed in charge of the Party's third-echelon executive head hunt, veteran CCP organizer and Mao biographer Li Rui, should use a literary review of Chen Yun's *Selected works* as the vehicle for launching the new youth movement.[65] Whatever the ironic intent behind Li's choice of venues, the media now published a number of articles praising the talents of younger intellectuals, technocrats, and other well-educated third-echelon leaders who had made outstanding executive contributions, some of whom, it was duly noted, had received advanced training in the West. At

---

63 The consolidation movement was carried out from top to bottom in two distinct stages, with each stage consisting of two (or more) phases. In the initial stage, Party committees and leading offices at the central, provincial, major municipal, and autonomous regional levels studied relevant documents and directives for three months (phase one) and then engaged in "examining and comparing" standards of organizational and individual behavior (phase two). Reportedly, some 960,000 Party cadres underwent examination during the latter phase of stage one. In stage two, which began in the winter of 1984–5, the movement was extended to some 13.5 million cadres in Party organs at the county, ordinary municipal, and local levels (including enterprises, research institutes, schools, and universities). In this second stage, the main tasks were to "unify thought" (*tongyi sixiang*), "correct work style" (*zhengdun zuofeng*), "strengthen discipline" (*jiaqiang jilu*), and "clean up organization" (*qingli zuzhi*). The ultimate phase involved the reregistration of Party members and the expulsion of those found guilty of serious attitudinal and behavioral impurities. Although some 3 million Party members had originally been slated for organizational discipline, official sources subsequently indicated that only about 30,000 to 40,000 people were expelled from the Party in the first two and a half years of the movement; of these, roughly 25 percent belonged to the ultra-leftist three kinds of people. The remainder had committed various non–Cultural Revolution-related offenses, most notably corruption, speculation, and profiteering. There was a marked increase in the frequency of expulsions beginning in mid-1985, following exposure of a rash of recent economic crimes. According to official statistics released in 1988, a total of 150,000 Party members were expelled for corruption between 1983 and 1987; if the earlier figures were correct, then the vast majority of these expulsions must have occurred after the middle of 1985. Sources on the Party rectification–consolidation movement include *FBIS*, 13 October 1983, K2–7; *SWB/FE* 7685 (3 July 1984), 7859 (26 January 1985), and 7868 (6 February 1985); *I&S* 20.8 (August 1984); *Liaowang* (hereafter, *LW*) 3 (14 January 1985); *ICM*, April 1985; and *BR* 28.10 (11 March 1985); *XH*, 11 August 1988; *Xue lilun*, April 1989.

64 On the changing emphasis of the consolidation campaign in this period, see *RMRB*, 15 and 20 April 1984. In August, the vice-chairman of the Party's CDIC, Bo Yibo (the man primarily responsible for supervising the Party's consolidation drive), argued that the elimination of leftist influences was an "essential prerequisite" for opening China to the outside world and for successfully adopting new technologies. See *SWB/FE* 7733 (28 August 1984).

65 See *RMRB*, 23 March 1984; Schram," 'Economics in command?' . . . ," 450.

the same time, veteran Party bureaucrats were chastised for obstructing the proper employment, promotion, and utilization of younger talent.[66]

Addressing the issue of generational change (and resistance thereto), Hu Yaobang pointed out, in an interview with Hong Kong journalists, that despite a concerted effort to encourage veteran cadres to retire, well over two-thirds of the members of the CCP's CC were over the age of sixty. "If a crisis exists," Hu averred, "this is it." Flatly declaring that it was a "natural law" for old cadres to retire, he vowed to fill the CC with younger people the following year.[67]

Speeding up the reforms: Economics takes command

In line with the revised goals of Party consolidation, the mass media in the summer of 1984 stressed the need to further develop and expand economic reforms and the open policy. In June, "Central document no. 1" was published, granting expanded rights of private economic activity and extended land-use contracts to individual peasant households.[68] In early July, it was announced that urban economic reform would commence in the autumn of the year, centering on the restructuring of state-owned enterprises, with a view toward increasing the operational autonomy, managerial responsibility, and profit incentives of state firms.[69] Also in early July, Beijing's newest architectural monument, the glitzy chrome-and-glass Great Wall Hotel, opened for business, a joint Sino-American venture that neatly symbolized Deng Xiaoping's commitment to modernization and the open door.

Throughout this period of accelerated reform and relaxation, the mass media played up China's efforts to attract and protect foreign investment; to refine and enforce China's newly enacted commercial laws and procedures; to encourage individual and collective entrepreneurship; to discourage "eating out of a common pot"; and to "smash the iron rice bowl" of guaranteed lifetime employment. Occasionally, the examples selected for favorable publicity in

---

66 The pointed references to Western training were intended as a slap at the spiritual pollutionists, who had been highly critical of Western influences. See, e.g., *RMRB*, 30 March 1984; also *Guangming ribao* (hereafter, *GMRB*), 16 March and 6 April 1984; *RMRB*, 25 March and 12–16 April 1984.

67 Hu's interview, which was conducted on 19 October 1984, is serialized in *MB*, 5, 6, and 8 December 1984; a translation appears in *ICM*, March 1985, 1–2. The quoted passages from the general secretary's statement were very similar to statements made by Deng Xiaoping at a meeting of the CAC, also held in October 1984 (*BR* 28.9 [4 March 1985], 15). In Hu Yaobang's interview, he provided several examples of third echelon cadres who had recently been elevated to responsible positions in the central Party and government apparatus. Among the newly promoted leaders singled out for special attention were Hu Qili, secretary of the Central Party Secretariat; Wang Zhaoguo, director of the CCP General Office; Hu Jintao, head of the Communist Youth League; Tian Jiyun, vice-premier of the State Council; and Li Peng, also a vice-premier.

68 *RMRB*, 12 June and 3 July 1984. For analysis, see Kenneth Lieberthal, "The political implications of document no. 1, 1984," *CQ* 101 (March 1985), 109–13.

69 *BR* 27.29 (16 July 1984), 9–10.

the official media raised some eyebrows. Under the headline "Prosperous girls attract husbands," for example, a major metropolitan newspaper approvingly recounted the story of a group of peasant spinsters from a poor village near Shanghai who suddenly become objects of intense matrimonial interest on the part of young men from a nearby factory after the women struck it rich as a result of adopting the new household responsibility system in agriculture.[70] Other articles sounded the praises of all manner of private enterprise, from short-order cooks and free-lance photographers to young girls who hired themselves out as personal maids and nannies;[71] still other articles celebrated the achievements of such "trail-blazing" reformers as the director of a collectively owned shirt factory in Zhejiang who had introduced variable piece rates, individualized bonuses, and other "common pot" – smashing productivity incentives among workers in his plant.[72] In the face of unbridled official enthusiasm for such innovations, the occasional voices of ideological dismay or uncertainty that were raised in the media were generally drowned out by a chorus of entrepreneurial affirmation.[73]

Also reflective of China's new mood of permissiveness was the reappearance, with official approval, of high-fashion Western clothing, including short, slitted skirts for women,[74] and the proliferation of certain risqué art forms that less than a year earlier would have stood condemned as spiritual pollution. *Beijing Review*, for example, ran on its inside back cover photos of two seminude female sculptures,[75] and the new international lounge of the Beijing Airport featured a wall-length mural depicting bare-breasted ethnic minority women frolicking in their native habitat. In the high tide of socio-economic experimentation and openness that swept through China in the summer of 1984, such things were possible.

Urban reform and the economic boom of 1984–5

Although restrictions on private entrepreneurship were greatly relaxed in the summer of 1984, reform in state-owned enterprises lagged noticeably.[76] The

---

70 *WHB* (Shanghai), cited in *BR* 27.29 (16 July 1984), 30.   71 *BR* 27.33 (13 August 1984), 31.

72 *BR* 27.29 (16 July 1984), 19–23. To motivate his workers, the factory director in question reportedly composed a song to reflect the pride of the factory's work force: "Work hard, hard, hard; we are the glorious shirtmakers! With good workmanship and novel designs, we dedicate our youth to making life beautiful."

73 Although it was periodically acknowledged that "some people" entertained doubts about the introduction of certain liberal economic innovations that ostensibly "eliminated the superiority of socialism" or "slid back from socialism to capitalism," such reservations were generally dismissed as misplaced or ill-informed. (See, e.g., ibid., 21.)

74 *BR* 27.33 (13 August 1984), 32.   75 *BR* 27.30 (23 July 1984).

76 Thomas Bernstein notes that although media reports of managerial innovation proliferated in this period, large numbers of state enterprises, indeed whole industrial sectors, appeared to be almost

growing disparity between the dynamic private and collective economy and the static public sector was addressed in the CC's long-awaited "Decision on reform of the economic structure," promulgated in late October. Among the many reforms called for in the new CC decision were a reduction in the scope of mandatory central planning for state enterprises (with a concurrent increase in flexible guidance planning); the introduction of a tax-on-profit system of microeconomic incentives (to replace the previous system of profit remittances); and an expansion of enterprise autonomy in such areas as supply and marketing, product mix, hiring and firing of staff, and allocation of retained profits. Also included was a call for the coupling of a gradual reform of China's irrational pricing system with the phasing out of costly and inefficient state subsidies in such areas as urban housing, energy supply, grain, and transportation. Such steps were deemed essential to the overall success of the reform program.[77]

The CC decision, which was loosely patterned after the Hungarian prototype of "market socialism," envisioned a mixed economy that would incorporate elements of both central planning and market regulation.[78] The state would continue to own the bulk of large and medium-sized enterprises and would continue to regulate the production and pricing of a number of strategic commodities; but the market mechanism would now be permitted to play an increasingly important (albeit supplemental) role in the pricing and allocation of nonstrategic goods and services, as well as in the allocation and remuneration of labor.[79] China's new "socialist commodity economy" would, in other words, permit the "bird" of protocapitalist market forces to fly with considerably more freedom than before within the newly enlarged "birdcage" of central planning.[80]

Bold and innovative in at least some of its implications, the urban reform program was slow to get off the mark after the CC plenum. Lack of elite consensus over, for instance, the proper sequences, priorities, and pacing of reform led to chronic delays in implementation. Substantial resistance was also encountered among workers and staff in many state enterprises, who were

entirely unaffected by such innovation. (Bernstein, "China in 1984: The year of Hong Kong," *AS* 25.1 [January 1985], 38.)

77 "Decision of the central committee of the CPC on reform of the economic structure," *BR* 27.44 (29 October 1984), III–XVI.
78 For analysis of the Hungarian influence on China's reforms, see Nina P. Halpern, "Learning from abroad: Chinese views of the East European economic experience, January 1977–June 1981," *Modern China* 1 (January 1985), 77–109.
79 For further analysis, see Christine Wong, "The second phase of economic reform in China," *Current History* 84.503 (September 1985), 260–63.
80 The birdcage analogy was first used by Chen Yun in the early 1980s. See David Bachman, "Differing visions of China's post-Mao economy: The ideas of Chen Yun, Deng Xiaoping, and Zhao Ziyang," *AS* 26.3 (March 1986), 297.

reluctant to give up the security of their iron rice bowl and common pot. For all these reasons, by the winter of 1984–5 the plan still had not been put into effect in most urban areas.[81]

Even in the absence of widespread implementation, the 1984 reform decision exerted a strong psychological impact on urban residents throughout the country. Fearing that imminent decontrol of prices and the reduction of state subsidies would lead to a runup of retail prices on vital consumer goods and services, nervous urbanites in many areas, including Shanghai, Beijing, and Guangzhou, rushed to withdraw money from the bank to stock up on essential commodities. With demand sharply up and retail inventories depleted, production units saw a golden opportunity to raise prices; with demand and prices both rising, output and profits increased, putting more money into circulation, which led to an even greater upsurge in consumer demand, which led to still further retail shortages. The result was the beginning of an inflationary spiral in which the *fear* of rising prices was mother to the *fact* – a classic self-fulfilling prophecy under capitalism.[82]

Coincidental with the mounting economic insecurity of late 1984, there occurred a sudden, sharp spurt in urban private business activity. For various reasons, including official government encouragement and the demonstration effect of private entrepreneurs who had grown prosperous without suffering adverse political consequences, large numbers of urbanites now embarked on the road of private business.[83]

Alongside the burgeoning army of petit-bourgeois *getihu* (individual households engaged in small-scale domestic trade), a wholly new category of upscale, quasi-private urban entrepreneurs now began to appear. These were the so-called *gaogan zidi*, children and other blood relatives of high-level cadres whose family connections gave them excellent financial and commercial contacts throughout the Party and state bureaucracies. Such people were strategically positioned to take full advantage of the government's liberalized commercial policies and credit controls, enabling them to set up new trading companies, secure business loans, and establish supply and marketing

---

81 On the implementation of the 1984 enterprise reforms and their implications for factory management, see Yves Chevrier, "Micropolitics and the factory director responsibility system, 1984–1987," in Deborah Davis and Ezra F. Vogel, eds., *Chinese society on the eve of Tiananmen*, 109–33.

82 The earliest account of this inflationary surge that I have come across appears in *Zhongguo zhichun* (China Spring), December 1984, in *ICM*, March 1985, 4–7.

83 The number of urban private businesses reportedly doubled in the last half of 1984 and then doubled again in 1985. Prominent among the groups drawn into private business in this period were unemployed youths, former Red Guards, ex-prisoners, laid-off workers from other enterprises, disabled people, moonlighting state employees, pensioners seeking to supplement their incomes, and others. See Thomas Gold, "Urban private business and China's reforms," in Baum, ed., *Reform and reaction* . . . ,90–2.

networks.[84] Within a matter of months, China's overprivileged *gaogan zidi* began to wheel and deal on a scale not seen since before the revolution.[85]

As a result of the confluence of these various reform-related developments, China's economy began to overheat seriously in the fall and winter of 1984–5.[86] The money supply increased by almost 40 percent in the last quarter of 1984 (compared with the corresponding quarter of the previous year), and industrial wages and bonuses rose 19 percent. Bank loans were also up a steep 29 percent, while foreign exchange reserves plummeted, the result of a wave of big-ticket foreign imports. With the rate of inflation approaching double digits in some Chinese cities for the first time since the early 1950s, consumer unrest now became a cause for concern. The potential gravity of the problem was conveyed in a comment made by a Chinese housewife to a visiting journalist early in 1985: "My mother says that ten years ago China was in chaos, but Mao kept prices stable. She says now China is stable, but prices are in chaos."[87]

The seriousness of such concerns was acknowledged by Zhao Ziyang in his report to the third session of the Sixth NPC in March 1985. Noting that the "temporary difficulties" of an overheated, unbalanced economy could not be ignored, Zhao admitted that a major source of difficulty lay in the fact that "we lack experience in restructuring an entire economy." Notwithstanding such inexperience, Zhao announced the government's intention to stay the course with respect to the main components of structural reform.[88]

As it turned out, inflation, a runaway money supply, and an upsurge in unregulated business activity were only the tip of a rather ominous economic iceberg. Just beneath the surface, another, potentially even more debilitating, side effect of China's hybrid structural reforms was beginning to make itself felt: an epidemic of brazen, high-stakes economic profiteering and corruption, much of it committed by *gaogan zidi*.

---

84 The appearance of a group of cadre-connected, quasi-private entrepreneurs, though new to the PRC, was by no means unprecedented in China. In late imperial and republican times, entrepreneurial success was often a function of one's personal or family ties to officialdom. See Albert Feuerwerker, *China's early industrialization: Sheng Hsuan-huai (1844–1916) and mandarin enterprise*. On the recrudescence of this phenomenon in the 1980s, see Dorothy Solinger, "Urban entrepreneurs and the state: The merger of state and society" (unpublished paper presented at the conference "State and society in China: The consequences of reform," Claremont-McKenna College, 16–17 February 1990).

85 The phenomenon of high-level cadres, their relatives, and their friends setting up trading companies was quite widespread. In February 1985, CDIC vice-chairman Bo Yibo claimed that in one province alone, Liaoning, more than 900 *gaogan*-affiliated companies were established between the summer of 1984 and the spring of 1985. See *I&S* 21.4 (April 1985), 1.

86 The following discussion draws on Richard Baum, "China in 1985: The greening of the revolution," *AS* 26.1 (January 1986), 31–53.

87 *Los Angeles Times* (hereafter, *LAT*), 4 February 1985.

88 Zhao's address appears in *BR* 28.16 (22 April 1985), III–XV.

Crime and corruption: The Achilles heel of reform

Due to their bloated administrative bureaucracies, chronic shortages of consumer goods, and informal networks of "back-door" clientelist ties, Leninist systems tend to spawn a relatively high degree of corruption.[89] In China, although economic crime and corruption were hardly unknown during the Maoist era, their severity was limited by the relatively small financial rewards and relatively high social and political costs involved.[90] Now, however, in the more permissive, "to-get-rich-is-glorious" environment of postreform China, the cost–benefit calculus changed dramatically; now there was a manifold increase in both the *incentives* to engage in corruption (in the form of substantially greater economic payoffs and diminished ethical constraints) and the *opportunities* to do so (presented by the rapid proliferation of deregulated, contract-based commercial exchanges). With the stakes thus raised and the transaction costs lowered, corruption and economic crime began to flourish.

One important new source of corruption in the postreform era was the hybrid nature of China's partially restructured economy. Writing in December 1984, a dissident Chinese intellectual foresaw with uncanny accuracy how a series of emerging gaps – in productivity, in pricing, and in performance – between the new market-regulated sectors of the economy and the old centrally planned sectors would inevitably give rise to a plethora of illicit commercial transactions. With scattered islands of free-market autonomy floating in a sea of socialist planning, the clear result, he predicted, would be a tremendous upsurge in economic malfeasance and back-doorism:

> Some of the reforms will have the effect of loosening the constraints on [smaller, nonstrategic] enterprises, leaving their management in the hands of workers and staff. The products of these enterprises will be regulated by the market mechanism. However, major enterprises such as . . . those dealing with steel, oil and electricity will still fall under the centrally planned economy. It can be predicted that the pace of their development will fall behind that of the [market-regulated] enterprises. . . . Hence, energy resources and certain raw materials which were already in short supply before [the advent of reform] will tend to be in even shorter supply afterwards. When there is not enough to go around, the [market-regulated] enterprises will use all kinds of methods (including bribery) to get hold of energy resources and raw

---

89 On the generic sources of clientelism and corruption in Leninist systems, see Kenneth Jowitt, "Soviet neotraditionalism: The political corruption of a Leninist regime," *Soviet Studies* 35.3 (July 1983), 275–97.
90 Under Mao, the Party's egalitarian, antibourgeois ethos made it extremely risky for anyone to engage in the conspicuous pursuit or consumption of wealth. What corruption did exist tended to be localized, unorganized, and limited in magnitude; much of it involved cadres extorting donations of various kinds, including sexual favors, from members of their work units. For a comparison of pre- and postreform patterns of corruption in China, see Connie Squires Meaney, "Market reform and disintegrative corruption in urban China," in Baum, ed., *Reform and reaction . . .* , 124–43.

materials destined for large enterprises under the state plan. The income of
the staff and workers in the large enterprises which are subject to guidance
planning will not be as high as those working in [market-regulated] enterprises. It will be difficult to avoid a situation wherein certain staff members
receive a "secondary salary" distributed in private by the [market-regulated]
enterprises, in order to bribe the units to open wide their "back doors." This
kind of unhealthy practice will increase and, if it does not attract notice, will
become ever more prevalent. . . . Economic crime will increase by leaps and
bounds.[91]

In other words (to use Chen Yun's birdcage analogy), once the bird of
market-driven economic activity was permitted freer flight, it would readily
exploit and enlarge back doors in its socialist cage, thereby undermining the
structural integrity of the entire system.[92]

In addition to structurally induced corruption, economic crime of a different
sort began to flourish in China's special economic zones and open coastal
cities in the winter and spring of 1984–5. In these enclaves of commercial
laissez-faire, a wave of speculation, smuggling, profiteering, and currency
manipulation by *gaogan zidi* and other quasi-private entrepreneurs resulted
in a series of major financial losses to the state. In one widely publicized
scandal, military cadres and their offspring in the duty-free port of Hainan
Island were arrested after having floated hard-currency bank loans and credits
in the amount of US$1.25 billion for the purpose of importing 89,000 Toyota
automobiles, 2.9 million television sets, 252,000 videocassette recorders, and
122,000 motorcycles, all destined for resale, at a high profit, on the domestic
market. As a result of this and other unauthorized transactions, China's foreign
exchange reserves plummeted by more than one-third, almost US$6 billion,
in the first six months of 1985.[93]

Responding to such developments, the Party's chief rectification overseer,
CDIC vice-chairman Bo Yibo, sounded a series of stern warnings in the
spring and summer of 1985 against Party members and cadres engaging in
improper commercial activities. Among the common practices cited were
establishment and operation of dummy companies (*pibao gongsi*; lit., "briefcase companies") for private profit; black market buying and selling of foreign

91 *Zhongguo zhichun*, December 1984, in *ICM*, March 1985, 4–7.
92 For analysis of the design flaws inherent in the CC's October 1984 blueprint for a hybrid "socialist
    commodity economy," see Jan Prybyla, "Why China's economic reforms fail," *AS* 29.11 (November
    1989), 1017–32.
93 Despite the subsequent arrest of the principal figures involved in the Hainan import scandal, it is
    not at all clear that any serious criminal acts were involved. The loans, foreign exchange transfers,
    import licenses, and commodity resale arrangements were all, strictly speaking, legal, though they
    were clearly not proper. This case illustrates how loopholes in reform laws and policies enabled
    unscrupulous profiteers (often *gaogan zidi*) to manipulate the system to their advantage. The Hainan
    scandal is documented in *JSND* 4 (1985) and *XH*, 31 July 1985. A collection of press reports on the
    upsurge in cadre corruption and economic crime in this period appears in *ICM*, June 1985, 10–17.

exchange certificates; unauthorized sale of lottery tickets and "bonus coupons"; distribution of money and goods under false pretexts; squandering of public funds on lavish feasts and gift giving; and the practice of nepotism and cronyism in personnel appointments and promotions. Bo Yibo attributed the rising incidence of such practices to a general decline in "Party spirit" (*dang jingshen*) among CCP members, many of whom allegedly "put money above everything else" and "seek personal gain by taking advantage of their authority."[94]

"What merits our grave concern," said Bo Yibo in October, "is that the principle of commodity exchange has permeated the political life of some party organs." Noting that indiscipline had become "very serious" in some Party organizations, he argued that a substantial number of CCP members and cadres were unqualified for membership. Calling such people "black sheep who have the appearance of party members," Bo stated that their behavior had infuriated the people, who "demand strongly that the party . . . and the people's courts take resolute action to punish" the offenders.[95]

Bo's demand for people's courts to play a stronger role in punishing corrupt Party members and *gaogan zidi* represented a major shift away from the CCP's traditional emphasis on punishment via internal Party discipline. Indeed, Bo Yibo's reference to mounting public fury over the lack of legal accountability of Party members proved highly sensitive within the Party.[96] Although a certain number of aberrant municipal, county, and provincial-level cadres and relatives of cadres were subsequently brought to trial and sentenced to prison terms for economic crimes, generally amid great fanfare, such cases generally involved extraordinarily blatant or heinous offenses. The vast majority of ordinary cases of cadre corruption, and cases involving people very high up in the leadership hierarchy, continued to be dealt with behind closed doors.[97]

94 Bo Yibo's various anticorruption commentaries appear in *SWB/FE* 7897 (12 March 1985), 7942 (4 May 1985), 7993 (3 July 1985), and 8085 (18 October 1985).
95 Ibid.
96 Beginning in 1984–5, the issue of corrupt *gaogan zidi* became a significant factor in factional politics within the Party. For example, Hu Yaobang reportedly raised the ire of several senior Party leaders, including Hu Qiaomu and Peng Zhen, by suggesting that their children should be investigated for corruption. During the Tiananmen demonstrations in May 1989, there were frequent references in wall posters and parade banners to Deng Xiaoping's son, Deng Pufang, who was widely reported to have enriched himself through a series of lucrative commercial transactions. Also in May 1989, Zhao Ziyang reportedly ran afoul of senior Party leaders when, in an attempt to shore up the Party's sagging public image, he volunteered to turn his own sons over to a special tribunal for criminal investigation. Zhao never had the chance to follow through with his offer; he was removed from power within a week.
97 The highest-level *gaogan zidi* to be judicially punished in this period was the daughter of Ye Fei, form[er] commander of the Chinese navy. In 1986 she was sentenced to seventeen years in prison for her [part in] the Hainan import scandal. Other relatives of high-level cadres, including the offspring of [Bo Yibo] and Hu Qiaomu, were reportedly investigated for corruption in this period but were s[pared] prosecution because of their ostensible "inexperience." On the protection of the ch[ildren of] cadres, see Stanley Rosen, "China in 1986: A year of consolidation," *AS* 27.1

Responding to strong calls for action to eliminate the spreading cancer of economic crime and corruption, the CDIC in 1985 shifted the main focus of its second-stage rectification drive. The first stage had stressed rooting out remnant Maoists, whateverists, and other assorted three kinds of people. Now, several months into the second stage (which had begun in the winter of 1984–5), the emphasis shifted to the elimination of a series of "new unhealthy tendencies" – tendencies that sprang not from remnant Cultural Revolution ultra-leftism, but from economic indiscipline, opportunism, and the pervasive "get rich quick" mentality that had begun to infect the country, and the Party, since the introduction of economic reform. With that shift, the sensitive directional indicators of the *fang–shou* cycle began to oscillate once more, moving back toward the reaffirmation of traditional, conservative values.

The battle over Marxism and capitalism

As it had in the past, the conservative ideological revival of early 1985 brought with it renewed expressions of concern for preserving the doctrinal integrity of Marxism. During the heyday of entrepreneurial liberalism in the fall of 1984, the position of orthodox Marxism had ostensibly been attenuated, among other things, by Deng Xiaoping's widely quoted statement to the effect that "a little capitalism isn't necessarily harmful."[98] By autumn's end, a mini-storm had erupted over the issue of whether (and how) Marxism could be creatively enriched to prevent it from becoming totally anachronistic and irrelevant to China's current needs.

The controversy began when the *People's Daily* declared, in a front-page commentary published on 7 December, that "since Marx has already been dead for 101 years . . . some of his assumptions are not necessarily appropriate." Calling the worship of individual words and sentences from Marxist texts "childish ignorance," the commentary said it was unrealistic to expect the works of Marx and Lenin, written in the nineteenth century, to "solve today's problems." A few days later, a Chinese government official went a bit further, asserting that "most people today don't care whether something is c˷˙ ˸r socialist. They just want their lives to improve. The details are ˙he theoreticians."[99] At this point a leading Party theoretician, ˙ed the fray and proclaimed bluntly: "There are no Marxist

˙istance to legal accountability for CCP members, see James D. Seymour,
" *AJCA* 21 (January 1989), 1–27.
nade at a meeting of the CAC in October 1984. See *New York Times*

†.

quotations for what we are doing now."[100] Reacting to such developments, a few foreign journalists were moved to speculate that Marxism had virtually been abandoned in China.[101]

In the event, such obituaries proved wishful thinking, In a rare editorial retraction, the *People's Daily* informed its readers that a mistake had been made in a key sentence of its 7 December commentary, and that the sentence in question should have stated that Marxist–Leninist works could not "solve *all of* today's problems."[102] In discussing the source of the "error," Chinese officials informed a group of foreign journalists that the original commentary had been flawed because it did "not sufficiently stress the continuing importance of Marxist principles."[103]

Mounting conservative pressures soon caused Deng Xiaoping to back away somewhat from his October assessment of the harmlessness of "a little capitalism." In a 1985 New Year's message to the Chinese people, Deng continued to defend his tolerance of a small amount of private enterprise on the grounds that without it, China would not be able "to catch up with the level of the developed countries within fifty years." But he now tempered such positive assessments with a candid acknowledgment that "some old comrades . . . can't bear [the idea that] after they fought all their lives for socialism, for communism, suddenly capitalism is coming back." In an attempt to mollify these old comrades, Deng ruled out the possibility of a wholesale departure from socialism, insisting that the "basic things will still be state-owned" in the twenty-first century.[104]

Deng's reassurance failed to stem the swelling ideological backlash, which was now being fueled by fresh reports of corruption, black marketeering, smuggling, and economic mismanagement. Such reports prompted Party conservatives to issue new allegations of moral degeneration.[105] Ever sensitive to such criticism, Deng continued to give ground. Speaking at a national science conference in March, he acknowledged that "some people are worried that China will turn capitalist. . . . We cannot say that they are worried for nothing."[106]

---

100 Quoted in ibid.

101 For example, soon after the 7 December *RMRB* commentary, the Associated Press sent out an "urgent" dispatch from Beijing under the headline "China abandons Marx." See also "Did Marx fall, or was he pushed?" *The Economist*, 15 December 1984.

102 *RMRB*, 8 December 1984 (emphasis added).

103 *NYT*, 11 December 1984. Reportedly, the offending sentence in the original commentary had been drawn directly from a talk given by Hu Yaobang at the end of November. See *ICM*, January 1985, 1–3.

104 *RMRB*, 1 January 1985.

105 See, e.g., *BR* 28.7 (13 February 1985), 4; *NYT*, 23 February and 31 March 1985.

106 *BR* 28.11 (18 March 1985), 15–16.

The attack on bourgeois liberalism

With the second stage of Party consolidation now focusing on the rectification of cadres afflicted with spiritual disorders of the get-rich-quick variety,
conservatives soon broadened their ideological offensive. One of their principal
targets was bourgeois liberalism in the mass media.

As on previous occasions, the lead role in the new offensive was played
by Deng Liqun Deng had reportedly been irritated by some recent liberal
comments on the subject of press freedom made by Hu Yaobang and two of his
key supporters, Hu Qili and Hu Jiwei.[107] At a meeting of the Party's Central
Secretariat in early February, Deng Liqun reportedly pressed Hu Yaobang to
reaffirm the party's traditional norms concerning obedience of the mass media
to the line, principles, and policies of the CCP. Bowing to pressure (some of
it presumably applied by Deng Xiaoping), Hu Yaobang conceded that the
proper role of the official media was to serve as "mouthpiece of the party,"
though he hastened to add that the media should also faithfully reflect the
views of the people.[108] At the same meeting, Hu gave even more ground to
Deng Liqun and the conservatives, calling on the mass media to stop being so
"gloomy" in their coverage of China's domestic situation. In general, he said,
"newspapers should devote eighty percent of their space to achievements and
the positive side, and only twenty percent to shortcomings and criticism."
Continuing his tactical retreat, Hu conceded that a recent proliferation of
unauthorized liberal tabloids (*xiaobao*) in several Chinese cities represented a
harmful tendency that should be "boycotted and opposed."[109]

Deng Liqun's hard-line literary policies resulted in renewed political pressure being brought to bear on China's critical intellectuals. In March 1985,
a serialized essay written by investigative journalist Liu Binyan, entitled "A
second kind of loyalty," was banned from publication, as was the tabloid that

107 In December 1984, at the Fourth Congress of the Chinese Writers' Association, Hu Qili had stressed
    that "literary creation must be free" and that journalists and writers must not be subject to political
    litmus tests or discrimination (*NYT*, 31 December 1984). At the same meeting, Hu Yaobang said
    that people should no longer talk about eliminating spiritual pollution and combating bourgeois
    liberalization. See *Baixing* (hereafter, *BX*) 138 (16 February 1987), 4. Hu Jiwei, who had been
    "reassigned" to work at the Educational and Cultural Committee of the NPC following his ouster from
    RMRB in late 1983, made a similar plea for creative freedom at a meeting of journalists and scholars
    held in Shanghai early in 1985. See *ZM* 91 (1 May 1985) in *ICM*, July 1985, 1–10.
108 *SWB/FE* 7927 (17 April 1985); see also *ZM* 91 (1 May 1985). As mentioned earlier, it was not unusual
    in China for the losers in a policy dispute to display their fidelity to the Party line by articulating the
    policy of the winners.
109 Ibid. At this point in Hu's talk, Deng Liqun reportedly interrupted the general secretary with a sharp
    dig at Hu's liberal supporters in the official media, pointing out that some of the tabloids in question
    had actually been set up, financed, and run by the Party's own newspapers. Presumably, Deng had
    in mind such underground journals as *Yecao* (Weeds), published in Guangzhou, which had run two
    articles highly critical of him, calling him, among other things, a "sycophantic yesman" who was out
    to "curry favor with Deng Xiaoping" (*Yecao*, February 1984, in *ICM*, October 1984, 9).

had featured it.[110] In this controversial essay, Liu disparaged the type of loyalty displayed by "obedient tools" of the Party who always agreed with their superiors and compulsively glorified the Party's line and policies. In place of such mindless obeisance, Liu proposed a higher standard of fealty: individual moral conscience and the courage to follow it. Among Party traditionalists, this theme did not prove popular. Nor did the ideas of writer Wang Ruowang, who, like Liu Binyan, had repeatedly asserted the primacy of the demands of individual conscience over the mandates of the state. Wang's works, too, were now banned from publication.[111]

Guerrilla warfare between Deng Liqun and Hu Yaobang continued for several months. In mid-April 1985, Deng (with the help of his patron, Hu Qiaomu) succeeded in embarrassing Hu Yaobang by arranging to have the full text of the general secretary's February remarks concerning restrictions on press freedom published in the *People's Daily* – without Hu's prior approval, while the general secretary was away on a visit to Australia and New Zealand.[112] Seeking to even the score, upon his return to China, Hu Yaobang gave a lengthy (and at times seemingly indiscreet) interview to a friendly Hong Kong journalist, Lu Keng. Responding to the interviewer's query about his adversarial relationship with Deng Liqun, Hu obliquely damned Deng with faint praise, noting that Deng was a man of great talent who should not be held solely responsible for all the shortcomings and mistakes in the Party's ideological work.[113]

Not to be outdone, Deng Liqun launched a broadside of his own, zeroing in once again on liberals in the mass media and their supporters in the Party hierarchy. In one statement, he noted with deep alarm that "some people" in the Party and the media treat as outmoded ideas such hallowed CCP traditions as plain living, sacrifice, and hard struggle. In another statement, he observed ruefully that under the onslaught of monetary transactions, China's "spiritual pillar" had been seriously eroded, to the point where "it has now become inadvisable to advocate . . . communist morality."[114] Deng's tactics apparently had a certain effect, for at the end of spring, third-echelon liberal Hu Qili, who only a few months earlier had championed total creative freedom for writers and artists, spoke out on the need to "criticise, educate and help" those misguided Party members who, "having lost their socialist and communist

110 *I&S* 23.5 (May 1987), 48–36. The first installment of "A second kind of loyalty" (*Di'erzhong zhongcheng*) appeared in the March 1985 issue of *Kaituo* (Opening Up). The issue was withdrawn from circulation, and subsequent installments were banned by the Beijing authorities.

111 See Kyna Rubin, "Keeper of the flame: Wang Ruowang as moral critic of the state," in Goldman et al., *China's intellectuals and the state . . . ,*" 249.

112 *BX*, 1 June 1985, in *SWB/FE* 7970 (6 June 1985).

113 Ibid; see also *ICM*, August 1985, 5–8.

114 *SWB/FE* 7973 (10 June 1985).

convictions and ideals, have even advocated Western 'democracy' and 'freedom' and advertised the bourgeoisie's liberal thinking."[115]

Notwithstanding Deng Liqun's heavy-handedness and Hu Qili's apparently softening spine, Hu Yaobang was able to enjoy the last laugh, at least for the moment: Early in the summer, without comment or explanation, Deng Liqun was removed from his position as director of the CC's propaganda department; named to replace him was Hu ally Zhu Houze, a strong advocate of creative freedom for artists and writers.[116]

The struggle over SEZs and the open policy

Central to the bubbling furor over bourgeois liberalism was mounting conservative disillusionment with the free-wheeling economic and social environment of China's fourteen open coastal cities and five special economic zones (SEZs), in particular the thriving South China township of Shenzhen, near the Hong Kong border. Shenzhen's close proximity to, and increasingly intimate financial and social contacts with, the largest capitalist entrepot in East Asia made it an especially tempting target for those who had serious questions about the nature and implications of China's wide-ranging reforms.

At the beginning of 1985, the Chinese press had been filled with favorable publicity concerning Shenzhen's "remarkable progress" as a model development zone.[117] But in early spring, new concerns were voiced over a rising tide of illicit commercial activities, including foreign exchange laundering, fraudulent bank loans, excessive wage and bonus payments to workers and managers, smuggling, gambling, prostitution, and pornography.[118] As spring turned to summer, the attack grew sharper. Party theoretician Hu Qiaomu, speaking during a tour of the Xiamen SEZ in late June, warned against giving preferential treatment to foreigners in the SEZs. Citing the disastrous experience of the Qing dynasty in granting economic concessions to foreign powers in the late nineteenth century, Hu cautioned against giving up Chinese rights to outside interests, and he insisted that "foreign investment enterprises are not concessions; their inordinate demands cannot be given tacit consent."[119] Later in the summer, the irrepressible Deng Liqun joined the chorus, stating that

---

115 *SWB/FE* 8005 (17 July 1985).
116 Kyodo News Service (Tokyo), 12 July 1985. At the rime, it was widely rumored (though never confirmed) that Deng Liqun's dismissal was related to his excessive criticism of Deng Xiaoping's open policy.
117 See, e.g., the five-part series "Reports from Shenzhen," in *BR* 27.47 (26 November 1984) through 28.6 (11 February 1985).
118 See, e.g., *FBIS*, 15 and 16 April and 15 July 1985; also *BR* 28.39 (30 September 1985), 5.
119 *SWB/FE* 7986 (25 June 1985).

all patriotic Chinese should "oppose the trend of worshipping things foreign and fawning on foreigners."[120]

The critics may have hoped to derail China's economic reforms by attacking them at their weakest link. Other major elements of the reform program, most notably the rural agricultural responsibility system, were less susceptible to challenge because of their visible contribution to the nation's economic growth and to the rising family incomes of the majority of China's 800 million rural dwellers. But the open policy was vulnerable to criticism on the highly sensitive issues of national autonomy and bourgeois corrosion. By pointing out the twin dangers of selling out the nation's sovereignty to foreigners and breathing too closely the toxic fumes of capitalism, conservatives could hope to cast sinister shadows on the propriety of the Zhao–Hu reform program.

Confronted with mounting economic difficulties and a rising conservative backlash, reformers began to give additional ground. Backing away from his earlier defense of the economic freedom and autonomy of the SEZs, Deng Xiaoping in early July declared that the SEZs were merely "an experiment" whose correctness "remains to be seen."[121] Concurrently, the Chinese government announced that ten of the fourteen coastal cities opened to foreign investors in the spring of 1984 would slow down the signing of new contracts with foreigners.[122]

But if Deng Xiaoping was willing to retreat a bit on the SEZs and open cities, he was clearly not prepared to backtrack on the general principles of his open policy. In October 1984 he had argued that the open policy was needed to overcome 300 years of impoverishment, backwardness, and ignorance caused by China's self-imposed isolation from the outside world.[123] Six months later, in the face of mounting furor over the spread of bourgeois corrosion along China's exposed eastern seaboard, Deng dug in his heels: "To open to the world is a fundamental policy for China," he asserted. "If there is to be any change in the policy, it will be that China's doors will be opened even wider."[124] Although the scope and limitations of the SEZ and open city experiments were thus negotiable, the open policy itself was not.

Reform of the PLA

In the midst of the swirling ideological currents of 1984–5, an important series of structural reforms was carried out affecting China's military establishment. Long considered a bastion of traditional Maoist thinking, the military high command had, since the late 1970s, stubbornly resisted implementing the

120 XH, 30 August 1985. For analysis of the Shenzhen experience, see ZM 94 (1 August 1985).
121 FBIS, 15 July 1985.   122 NYT, 4 August 1985.
123 NYT, 21 February 1985.   124 Quoted in BR 28.13 (1 April 1985), 15.

Third Plenum's reform agenda. Each time reformers had attempted to make inroads, military pressure had forced them to back off.[125] Frustrated by such intransigence, Deng Xiaoping had on at least one occasion referred to members of the PLA's senior officer corps as "undisciplined, arrogant, extravagant, and lazy";[126] and in a 1981 commentary on ideological problems within the army, Deng claimed that continued ultra-leftist factionalism had done great harm to the army's prestige and credibility.[127]

Following initiation of the Party rectification campaign in the late fall of 1983, the PLA was periodically criticized in the mass media for leftist tendencies.[128] When the rectification drive entered its second stage in the early winter of 1984–5, pressures on the PLA began to increase noticeably. Reformers now brought two main weapons to bear on the army: retirement and reorganization. In late December it was announced that forty senior general staff officers had opted to retire – the largest top-level group retirement in PLA history. In an interview that accompanied the announcement, Deng Xiaoping said that he "hoped to see more open-minded people in the army." Most of the retiring officers were over the age of sixty; several had served as section chiefs, equivalent to the rank of lieutenant general and above.[129]

This pruning of the general staff was followed, in early January 1985, by an announcement of substantial cutbacks in military budgets and manpower. PLA Chief of Staff Yang Dezhi, a Deng Xiaoping ally, explained the cuts as being vital to the success of the nation's overall modernizaton drive. In order to reduce military outlays and pave the way for the much-needed technological upgrading of the armed forces, Yang argued, it was necessary to streamline the PLA and reduce noncombatant personnel.[130]

In a bold reorganization measure, several hundred thousand PLA security troops were demobilized and reassigned to a state security force known as the "People's Armed Police." In a related move, the PLA Railway Corps, long known for its loyalty to Maoist ideas, was placed under civilian jurisdiction.

125 See Richard D. Nethercut, "Deng and the gun: Party–military relations in the People's Republic of China," AS 22.8 (August 1982), 691–704. For a somewhat different interpretation, which sees Deng as having asserted effective control over the army by the late 1970s, see Ellis Joffe, "Party and military in China: Professionalism in command?" POC, 32.5 (September–October 1983), 56–63.
126 Quoted in NYT, 6 March 1985.
127 Deng Xiaoping, "On opposing wrong ideological trends" (27 March 1981), in Selected works of Deng Xiaoping (1975–1982).
128 See, e.g., RMRB, 30 April, 20 May, and 9 October 1984; Jiefangjun bao (hereafter, JFJB), 8 and 18 May 1984. The antileftist criticisms followed the exposure of serious corruption in a PLA tank division under the command of leftist general Li Desheng. See Alastair I, Johnston, "Party rectification in the People's Liberation Army, 1983–87," CQ 112 (December 1987), 611 (n. 57).
129 JFJB, 22 December 1984; NYT, 30 December 1984 and 20 April 1985; Johnston, "Party rectification."
130 CD, 3 January 1985. China's military budget for 1984 was estimated at RMB 18 billion yuan (US$6.4 billion), down from 22 billion in 1979, the year of the Sino-Vietnamese border war. See NYT, 3 January 1985.

Finally, thousands of factories engaged in defense production were turned over to the manufacture of nonmilitary consumer goods such as motorcycles and electronic appliances.[131]

Predictably, many aging veterans of the PLA's earliest guerrilla struggles, who now staffed the upper reaches of the military hierarchy, were unmoved by the logic of such reforms. In their speeches, they now began to refer defensively to the importance of giving "careful consideration" to any changes that might undermine the nation's military preparedness. Ignoring such precautionary pleas, the reformers pushed on, with Deng Xiaoping's clear blessing. In a highly symbolic gesture laced with deep political overtones, it was announced that the streamlined PLA would soon be outfitted with new uniforms, complete with insignias of rank, which had been abolished at Mao Zedong's behest in 1965, on the eve of the Cultural Revolution.[132]

Shortly after the 1985 Lunar New Year, a number of additional military reorganization measures were introduced. In early March, it was announced that 47,000 officers, approximately 10 percent of the entire officer corps, would be retired before the end of 1986, with 20,000 to 30,000 additional officers slated for retirement by 1990. In disclosing this decision, the official *Xinhua* News Agency said that the officers to be demobilized had joined the PLA during the anti-Japanese and civil wars of the 1930s and 1940s. Most were said to have attained junior rank up to regimental level – the equivalent of major – or lower. To help mollify the new retirees, a program of improved military pensions and welfare benefits, including new housing, was instituted.[133]

In April, while on a visit to New Zealand, Hu Yaobang announced that within the next year the Chinese army would be subject to conventional force reductions totaling 1 million men, approximately 25 percent of the current troop level. The money saved was to be earmarked for the technological modernization of China's antiquated weapons systems and for upgrading the professional qualifications of the officer corps.[134]

In May, Hu Yaobang was asked by a Hong Kong journalist whether disgruntled military critics of reform, including controversial Northeast regional commander General Li Desheng (whom the interviewer characterized as "a nail that can't be pulled out"), might use troops under their command to resist further military cutbacks, including their own forced retirement. Hu responded that such a thing would be "absolutely impossible" and could "never occur in our party." Responding to a question about whether General

131 *NYT*, 20 April 1985.   132 Ibid.; *FBIS*, 14 January 1985.
133 *XH*, 5 March 1985; *NYT*, 6 March 1985.
134 *Reuters* (Wellington), 19 April 1985; *NYT*, 20 April 1985.

Li Desheng was untouchable, Hu answered cryptically: "Outsiders *think* he cannot be removed."[135]

In early June, the other shoe dropped. At a meeting of the Party's MAC, chaired by Deng Xiaoping, it was decided to "readjust" the regional command structure of the PLA, consolidating the eleven existing military regions into seven and pensioning off several superannuated regional commanders, including the "untouchable" general, Li Desheng. The *Xinhua* News Agency dispatch that announced the shakeup pointedly noted that younger, better-educated, and professionally more competent officers had been selected to succeed the retiring commanders. By the end of summer, the readjustment had resulted in a full 50 percent reduction in the number of senior officers in the seven newly consolidated regional commands and a 24 percent cut in the number of ranking officers at the PLA general staff headquarters and its political and logistics departments.[136]

The influence of the PLA was further reduced by a series of top-level CCP leadership changes carried out at the end of summer 1985. At the Twelfth CC's Fourth Plenum, held in mid-September, six veteran military leaders, including the redoubtable Li Desheng, retired from the Politburo, leaving only a token contingent of military figures to sit on the Party's highest decision-making body. To all intents and purposes, it seemed that the reformers had succeeded in bringing the PLA to heel.[137]

The third echelon arrives

The retirement of the six Politburo military veterans represented only a small fraction of a much larger turnover in party leadership that took place in September 1985. After three years of alternately persuading, cajoling, and demanding that elderly cadres step down in favor of younger blood, Deng

135 *BX*, 1 June 1985, in *SWB/FE* 7970 (6 June 1985). Verbal indiscretions such as this one reportedly brought rebukes from several of Hu Yaobang's senior colleagues. When Hu was dismissed from office in January 1987, one of the reasons given was his penchant for talking out of school, without CC authorization. See "The 'resignation' of Hu Yaobang."

136 *XH*, 11 June and 27 October 1985; *NYT*, 11 and 23 June 1985; *XH*, 27 October 1985; *LAT*, 28 October 1985. Many of the regional commanders and field officers who survived the readjustment had strong career ties to Deng Xiaoping through their common service in the PLA's Second Field Army. See Li Kwok Sing, "Deng Xiaoping and the 2nd field army," *China Review* (Hong Kong), January 1990, 40–1.

137 In addition to Li Desheng (sixty-nine), the other five military retirees were Marshals Ye Jianying (eighty-nine), Nie Rongzhen (eighty-six), and Xu Xiangqian (eighty-six) and Generals Wang Zhen (seventy-seven), Song Renqiong (seventy-six), and Wei Guoqing (seventy-two). To help ease the pain of retirement, all were appointed to the CAC. Among the handful of military leaders who remained on the Politburo were longtime Deng Xiaoping associates Yang Shangkun (seventy-eight) and Yang Dezhi (seventy-five). For a slightly different interpretation of these events, see *I&S* 21.12 (December 1985), 76–92.

Xiaoping's youth movement finally reached fruition.[138] Altogether, sixty-four full and alternate members of the CC announced their retirement at the Fourth Plenum. With three exceptions, all were over the age of sixty-seven, including forty-four septuagenarians and seven octogenarians. Also included were one member of the Politburo Standing Committee (PSC) (Ye Jianying), nine ordinary Politburo members, and twenty-six military men.[139] Seven superannuated Politburo members failed to retire at the September plenum: Deng Xiaoping, Chen Yun, Li Xiannian, Peng Zhen, Yang Shangkun, Hu Qiaomu, and Yang Dezhi.

Ye Jianying's resignation from the Politburo SC reduced that body's membership from six to five, creating a virtual deadlock between the committee's first-echelon traditionalists (Chen Yun and Li Xiannian) and its second-echelon liberals (Hu Yaobang and Zhao Ziyang) – with Deng Xiaoping as the crucial swing vote.[140]

To replace the retiring CC members, a special "national party conference" was convened on 18 September, immediately following adjournment of the Fourth Plenum.[141] Of the sixty-four new CC members and alternates selected at this conference, the overwhelming majority belonged to the third echelon. Seventy-six percent were college educated; their average age was just over fifty.[142]

---

138 In his October 1984 speech to recent retirees on the CAC, Deng had noted that "It is not easy to ask older comrades to give up their posts. But we must; and we must stay this course. If the old do not vacate their posts, . . . how can our cause thrive?" (BR 28.9 [4 March 1985], 15).

139 In addition to the aforementioned six military leaders, the civilian Politburo retirees were Deng Yingchao (eighty-four), Ulanfu (seventy-nine), and Zhang Tingfa (sixty-eight). It was widely rumored that among the many inducements offered to elderly Politburo members to ease their retirement was the appointment of their offspring or other relatives to high-level administrative or commercial positions. See I&S 21.12 (December 1985), 25, 67.

140 At the time of the Fourth Plenum, it was widely rumored that the conservative group had wanted to promote old comrade Peng Zhen to the SC to replace Ye Jianying, whereas Deng and Hu Yaobang had preferred to add third-echelon newcomer Hu Qili. According to these reports, neither side would budge, so no one was selected (see ibid., 23–4). According to reports widely circulated in Beijing in late 1985, Peng's prestige and popularity among the people of Beijing had been badly damaged by his involvement in a plan to raze a large residential neighborhood near the Great Hall of the People to build an expensive new municipal government complex.

141 The convening of a special Party conference represented another of Deng Xiaoping's many ad hoc improvisations. The Party's constitution stipulates that the CC is elected by the National Party Congress, but the Thirteenth Congress was not scheduled to meet for another two years. Not wanting to wait, Deng resorted to creative institution making. When asked why the business of replacing old leaders couldn't be put off until the Thirteenth Congress, Party spokesman Zhu Muzhi said, "We cannot wait two years. . . . By then some comrades' state of health might have changed. . . . It is better to make gradual changes now" (WHB, 19 September 1985).

142 XH, 22 September 1985. The movement to promote educated young people to leadership roles was also reflected in Party recruitment figures in the mid-1980s. From 1984 to 1987, the proportion of party members with at least a senior high school education rose from 17.8 to 28.5 percent; in the same period, almost a million college graduates were added to the Party roster. See Stanley Rosen, "The Chinese communist party and Chinese society: Popular attitudes toward party membership and the party's image," AJCA 24 (July 1990), tables 1 and 3 and passim.

At the Fifth Plenum of the Twelfth CC, held immediately following the national work conference, six newcomers were named to the Politburo, including two men tabbed by informed sources as likely successors to Premier Zhao and General-Secretary Hu, respectively. The first, Vice-Premier Li Peng (fifty-seven), was a Soviet-trained, Russian-speaking engineer with experience both in the electric power industry and as deputy finance minister. He was the adopted son of outgoing Politburo member Deng Yingchao and the late Premier Zhou Enlai. The second major Politburo newcomer, Central Secretariat member Hu Qili, (fifty-six), was a protégé of Hu Yaobang, under whose leadership he had previously toiled as a cadre in the Party's youth league.[143]

For all the third echelon's highly acclaimed advances, Party traditionalists nevertheless managed to avoid a clean sweep in the leadership changes of September 1985. In addition to the carryover of certain members of the Politburo old guard, conservatives won two other skirmishes: First, despite reported opposition from the Party's liberal wing, Deng Liqun was permitted to retain his seat on the Central Secretariat; second, the PLA high command refused to ratify Deng Xiaoping's choice of Hu Yaobang to succeed him as chairman of the Party's MAC.[144]

Reflecting the mixed outcome of the September 1985 Party meetings, Deng Xiaoping's closing address contained a strong, measured appeal to all factions to close ranks in pursuit of the twin objectives of reform and socialist spiritual civilization. Calling on "old comrades" to overcome dogmatic tendencies and "new comrades" to resist the temptations of bourgeois liberalization, which he now ominously equated with "taking the capitalist road," China's senior leader sought once more to chart a middle course between the Scylla of ultra-leftism and the Charybdis of spiritual pollution.[145]

Social contradictions intensify

For a variety of reasons, Deng's middle course became progressively harder to steer. Despite the senior leader's periodic pleas for unity and stability, a

143 Other new faces in the Politburo included vice-premier Tian Jiyun (fifty-six), a reform economist; former CCP organization department director Qiao Shi (sixty-one), who had reputedly had ties to Peng Zhen; and foreign minister Wu Xueqian (sixty-four). A sixth newcomer, vice-premier Yao Yilin (sixty-eight), a centrist with strong ties to Chen Yun, was promoted from alternate to full Politburo status. Members of the third echelon also gained five seats on the Party's Central Secretariat. In addition to Politburo appointees Li, Tian, and Qiao, the other newcomers were Wang Zhaoguo (forty-four), director of the Party's General Office, and Hao Jianxiu (fifty), a former cotton mill worker who had served briefly as a textile minister (and who was the only female promoted to a top Party post at the September Party meeting).

144 On military opposition to Hu Yaobang, see ZM 110 (1 December 1986), 6–8.

145 The complete text of Deng's address appears in *Dangde jiaoyu* (Party Education) (Tianjin) 5 (October 1985), 17–21; a partial translation, erroneously dated, appears in *ICM*, November 1985, 18.

series of reform-related stresses now began seriously to pull apart the social fabric of urban China. Three emergent social trends contributed to this over-all effect, comingling and ultimately synergizing to produce the beginnings of a serious urban crisis. The first was an incipient intellectual renaissance, partly inspired by China's rapidly expanding cultural contacts with the out-side world and facilitated by the July 1985 ouster of Deng Liqun from his post as Party propaganda chief. Under the stewardship of Deng's successor, Hu Yaobang associate Zhu Houze, and a newly appointed minister of cul-ture, the renowned writer Wang Meng, Chinese art and literature entered a new golden age of creative expression in the summer of 1985. The new era, which was to last for approximately sixteen months, witnessed a strong revival of pre–spiritual pollution campaign-era philosophical debates – for example, over socialist alienation, humanism, and the relevance of Marxist economic theory.[146] The period also witnessed a proliferation of new academic and pro-fessional societies; an outpouring of innovative theatrical, cinematic, artistic and literary works;[147] the birth of liberal newspapers such as the Shanghai *World Economic Herald (Shijie jingji daobao;*[148] and a resurgence of hard-hitting social commentary by such respected essayist-critics as Liu Binyan, Su Shaozhi, Wang Ruowang, and Fang Lizhi. Indeed, in many respects, it appeared that an incipient "civil society" might be emerging in China, one in which the opinions and attitudes of the creative and critical intelligentsia would play a significantly expanded role.[149]

The second major trend to emerge in 1985 was an increase in social mobi-lization among various newly articulate urban social groups and strata. With the fabric of daily life increasingly strained by the contradictions of partial reform, by frequent policy oscillations in the *fang–shou* cycle, by mounting inflation, economic corruption, and by a host of perceived inequities in the

---

146 In mid-1985, Wang Ruoshui published a refutation of criticisms leveled earlier by Hu Qiaomu against his theory of alienation under socialism. Ma Ding (pseud.) and Liu Zaifu were two other liberal scholars who figured prominently in the 1985–8 revival of earlier themes. An article by Ma, questioning the contemporary relevance of Marxist economic theory, appeared in *Gongren ribao* (Workers' Daily; hereafter, *GRRB*), 2 November 1985, and is analyzed in *ZM* 103 (1 May 1986). Liu's defense of a humanist approach to socialism appears in *ZM* 104 (1 June 1986), trans. in *FBIS*, 12 June 1986, W6–13.

147 The impact of the 1985–6 literary and artistic renaissance is discussed in Bei Dao, "Terugblik van een balling," in *Het Collectieve Geheugen: Over Literatuur En Geschiedenis*, 77ff.

148 On the role played by the *World Economic Herald* and other liberal media in the reform debates in this period, see Kate Wright, "The political fortunes of Shanghai's 'World economic herald,'" *AJCA* 23 (January 1990), 121–32; and Seth Faison, "The changing role of the Chinese media," in Tony Saich, ed., *The Chinese people's movement: Perspectives on spring 1989*, 144–62.

149 For analysis of the main intellectual currents of this period, see David A. Kelly, "The Chinese student movement of December 1986 and its intellectual antecedents," *AJCA* 17 (January 1987), 127–42. On the emergence of an incipient civil society in China, see Gold, "Party-state versus society." Key speeches and writings of Liu Binyan, Fang Lizhi, Wang Ruowang, and Su Shaozhi from this period are translated in *Chinese Law and Government* (hereafter, *CLG*) 21.2 (Summer 1988).

social distribution of the costs and benefits of reform, frustration, alienation, and envy began to mount. For the first time since the reforms were introduced in the winter of 1978–9, Chinese cities now began to witness significant social unrest.[150]

On the surface, the various urban disturbances that broke out in 1985 seemed random, spontaneous, and almost wholly unrelated. In May, a riot occurred at a Beijing soccer match, touched off when the local club was upset by a team of Hong Kong Chinese. Shortly thereafter, a group of 300 former Beijing residents who had been "sent down" (*xiaxiang*) to rural areas in Shanxi province in the last years of the Maoist era held a sit-in at the headquarters of the Beijing municipal government, demanding the right to return to their homes in the Chinese capital. In late May, a new round of price decontrols in Beijing triggered a wave of vocal complaints and letters to newspapers from nervous, angry consumers.[151]

Chinese students, too, grew more restive in 1985. Their unhappiness reportedly stemmed from multiple sources, including poor food and unhealthy dormitory conditions, low monthly stipends (averaging around RMB 22 yuan), rising living costs, and flagrant profiteering by *gaogan zidi*.[152] Toward the end of the summer, students began to show signs of social activism. On 18 September, the fifty-fourth anniversary of Japan's invasion of Manchuria, 1,000 college students in Beijing took to the streets to protest Japanese Prime Minister Nakasone's visit to a Shinto shrine honoring the militarists responsible for Japan's World War II invasion of China. One hundred demonstrators were arrested in what was reported to be the largest Chinese student protest in over a decade.[153] In November, a fresh wave of student disturbances occurred, this time openly protesting the recent Japanese "economic invasion." China's

150 On the relationship between economic reform and the social mobilization of urban discontent in this period, see Nina P. Halpern, "Economic reform, social mobilization, and democratization in post-Mao China," in Baum, ed., *Reform and reaction. . . . ,*" 38–59. On the dysfunctional social effects of partial reform, see Zweig, "Dilemmas of partial reform"; James T. Myers, "China: Modernization and 'unhealthy tendencies,'" *Comparative Politics* 21.2 (January 1989), 193–214; and James C. Hsiung, "Mainland China's paradox of partial reform: A postmortem on Tiananmen," *I&S* 26.6 (June 1990), 29–43.
151 See *ZM* 93 (1 July 1985); also *LW* 4 (21 January 1985).
152 For analysis of the sources of student unrest, see *Chaoliu yuekan* (Hong Kong) 1 (March 1987), 45–54; *Zhongbao* (hereafter, *ZB*), 31 December 1985; and *ICM*, February 1986, 4–6. The history of student protest in China is traced in Jeffrey N. Wasserstrom, "Student 'protests and the Chinese tradition, 1919–1989" in Saich, ed., *The Chinese people's movement . . .* , 3–24.
153 A collection of student posters from the 18 September demonstrations at Tiananmen Square is translated in *ICM*, January 1987, 3–6. Some of these posters alluded to mounting student resentment over a "new economic invasion" from Japan and called for a boycott of Japanese products; others criticized university authorities for trying to intimidate students by threatening to withhold job assignments after graduation; still others took a dim view of all authority, calling on the masses to rise up against "bureaucrats [who] make up rules and regulations whenever they please . . . [telling] us we can't march, . . . can't go to Tiananmen Square because they tell us not to."

top leaders were reported to be "deeply concerned" about the latent antigovernment, antireform overtones of the new demonstrations.[154]

On the occasion of Sino-African Friendship Day in the autumn of 1985, several hundred Chinese students at Tianjin University blockaded the school's canteen, shouting insults at African students gathered there concerning their alleged social and sexual misconduct.[155] In an unrelated incident, in late December 1,500 students at the Beijing Agricultural University occupied campus dormitories and staged a march in protest over the continued presence of PLA personnel on campus. At around the same time, 100 Uighur students demonstrated in Beijing in a protest against continuing Chinese nuclear weapons tests in Lop Nor, Xinjiang.[156]

In the relatively permissive urban climate of 1985–6, students (and others) could give vent to their frustrations and anxieties more openly than at any time since the winter of 1978–9. In one extraordinary incident, the angry father of a student arrested during the 18 September anti-Japanese demonstrations in Beijing staged a successful jailbreak, freeing his son from police custody.[157]

Despite bringing enhanced freedom of expression, China's increasingly permissive urban milieu was a distinctly mixed blessing. Although it contained the embryo of an emergent civil society, marked by incipient socioeconomic pluralism and the first stirrings of autonomous behavior on the part of newly emerging social forces, it also served to amplify all the various social cleavages and contradictions engendered in the process of incomplete reform. The result was a situation that was both highly stressful and increasingly volatile.

As early as mid-1985, public opinion polls began registering a slight downturn in popular enthusiasm for reform. In one eleven-city, sixteen-county survey taken in February, over 80 percent of the 2,400 urban respondents

154 On November 16, a Reuters dispatch, citing the Hong Kong journal *Zhengming*, reported that a CC directive had referred to recent student protests as potentially posing "the gravest challenge since the downfall of the 'gang of four.'" This tends to support Suzanne Pepper's assertion that the predominant cause of campus unrest in 1985 was student resentment of the negative consequences of the reforms, including China's opening to the outside world. See Suzanne Pepper, "Deng Xiaoping's political and economic reforms and the Chinese student protests," *Universities field staff international reports* 30 (1986).

155 Sporadic anti-African demonstrations continued for many months. In one incident, in late May 1986, 18 African students were besieged by 500 Chinese students at a dance, resulting in several injuries; two weeks later, a group of 200 African students demonstrated in Beijing against campus discrimination. A similar demonstration was held in January 1988, when 300 African students marched from the Beijing Language Institute to African embassies demanding protection. See *I&S* 25:2 (February 1989), 9–11. The largest and most violent of the campus-based racial disturbances took place in Nanjing in December 1988 (see "The gathering storm: Winter 1988–9").

156 *ZB*, 28 December 1985; *ICM*, February 1986.

157 The father, a high-ranking military officer, surrounded the Beijing public security bureau with troops, demanding that the authorities release his son, whom he claimed had been unlawfully arrested. When Deng Xiaoping capitulated to the angry officer, refusing to halt the jailbreak, students throughout Beijing reportedly began to feel emboldened, as they now perceived themselves to be safe from arbitrary arrest. See *ZM* 111 (1 January 1987), trans. in *FBIS*, 5 January 1987, K9–10. The incident is recounted in Benedict Stavis, *China's political reforms: An interim report*, 91.

queried reported a rise in their standard of living since the advent of reform; by July of the same year, however, a follow-up survey revealed that the proportion had declined to 70 percent, with a threefold increase (from 4.3 to almost 14 percent) in the number of people who indicated that their living standard had actually declined overall. Not surprisingly, those who experienced a decline in living standards were notably less enthusiastic about reform than those who felt themselves to be doing well. By early 1986, public enthusiasm for economic reform had further diminished- Now only 29 percent of urban residents surveyed felt that the reforms provided equal opportunity for all; by November of the same year, almost 75 percent of the people queried expressed dissatisfaction with rising inflation.[158]

Young people were especially sensitive to the complex, mounting pressures and stresses of reform. Surveys in 1986 revealed a youth culture that was becoming significantly more cynical, materialistic, and hedonistic – and considerably less idealistic – than that of preceding generations.[159] For many urbanites, young and old alike, perceptions of unequal opportunity fueled a mounting sense of resentment. As revealed in various opinion surveys of this period, urban residents were becoming more and more convinced that the costs and benefits of reform had been inequitably distributed. For example, pollsters frequently encountered the view that whereas *getihu* (individual entrepreneurs) could pass rising costs on to consumers, and whereas government cadres could use their authority and/or commercial contacts to buy and sell goods and materials acquired in the state sector for a handsome profit, ordinary people (including industrial workers, lower-level administrative staff, students, housewives, and intellectuals, *inter alia*) had no such options or opportunities available to them.[160] Partly reflecting the prevalence of such views, there were increasing reports of reform-related labor disturbances in the summer of 1986, including strikes, work slowdowns, and even occasional riots.[161]

The rising sense of popular malaise was also affected by the third major social trend of the mid-1980s – a new urban crime wave. After dropping

158 These and other related survey research data are analyzed in Bruce Reynolds, ed., *Reform in China: Challenges and chokes*, 59–63 and passim. On the nature and functions of survey research in the reform period, see Stanley Rosen, "The rise (and fall) of public opinion in post-Mao China," in Baum, ed., *Reform and reaction . . .* , 60–83.

159 See Stanley Rosen, "Youth and students in China before and after Tiananmen," in Winston Yang and Marcia Wagner, eds., *Tiananmen: China's struggle for democracy.*

160 Ibid. Disaffection with the inequitable effects of reform also began to rise in the countryside in this period. Most rural complaints appeared to center on the proliferation of illegal businesses, cadre corruption, discrimination against private households, and envy of "ten thousand yuan households." See *LW* 45 (11 November 1985); *ZB*, 18 December 1985; and *ICM*, February 1986, 7–13. For further analysis, see Jean C. Oi, "Partial market reform and corruption in rural china," in Baum, ed., *Reform and Reaction . . .* , 143–61.

161 *FEER*, 16 October 1986, 69–70.

sharply toward the end of 1983, the nation's crime rate began to creep up again in 1984. By 1985, crime and corruption were said to be increasing almost geometrically.[162] In response to the rising tide of lawlessness, 1 million new public security personnel were recruited in 1985;[163] the following year a nationwide crackdown on crime was initiated, with a reversion to earlier techniques of mass trials, heavy sentences, perfunctory appeals, and, in the most severe cases, immediate executions.[164] As before, the objective was to intimidate and deter potential lawbreakers through a demonstration effect of harsh and immediate punishment.[165]

Although these three emerging urban trends of 1985–6 – creative freedom for intellectuals, social mobilization of urban unrest, and rising crime – were not formally interconnected, they tended to cross over and mutually reinforce each other. With rising freedom of expression accompanied by rising crime rates, and higher food prices comingling with higher social frustrations, the resulting social chemistry was becoming volatile and more than a little worrisome to China's leaders.

Political reform redivivus: The summer of 1986

In part because of the perceived worsening of urban unrest and in part because of the growing political influence of the newly empowered third echelon, pressures for political reform began to increase again in the winter of 1985–6. In January, CASS published in its official journal a lengthy critique of China's system of government administration. Reporting on a National Conference on Administrative Reform, held in November 1985, the journal claimed that all earlier efforts to rationalize China's administrative structure had failed because they lacked a systemic viewpoint and paid inadequate attention to political reform as an essential prerequisite for successful economic reform. In order to remedy these failings, CASS analysts argued that it was necessary to do two main things: (1) completely separate the Party from economic decision

---

162 See, e.g., *ZM* 94 (August 1985); *Faxue* (Legal Studies) (Shanghai) 11 (November 1985) and 2 (February 1986); *XH*, 19 December 1985; *ICM*, November 1985, 25. See also Lawrence R. Sullivan, "Assault on the reforms: Conservative criticism of political and economic liberalization in China, 1985–86," *CQ* 114 (June 1988), 209–12.

163 *LW* 33 (19 August 1985). Many of these new police recruits were ex-servicemen demobilized in the army reorganization of 1984–5.

164 It was widely rumored (but never officially confirmed) that the new crackdown had been precipitated by. two incidents that occurred in the summer of 1986: the rape of a high-level Party official's daughter in Beijing and the armed robbery of a high cadre on the road from Beijing to the seaside resort of Beidaihe, neat Tianjin.

165 In an unusual exception to the normal rule of exempting *gaogan zidi* from severe legal punishment, it was reported that a distant relative of president Li Xiannian was executed in 1986. Li was said to have become furious with Hu Yaobang when the Party Secretariat refused to intervene with the courts to prevent the execution.

making and administration and (2) institute a civil service system for the recruitment, promotion, and dismissal of cadres.[166]

The CASS recommendations were favorably received (indeed, had originally been solicited) by technocratic cadres of the third echelon, whose political visibility had begun to increase noticeably following the Party conference of September 1985. Supported by Zhao Ziyang and Hu Yaobang, the third echelon's elevated status was reinforced in January 1986, when the CCP's ongoing rectification/anticorruption drive underwent yet another modification in orientation and leadership: A new "leading group" was now set up under third-echelon cadres Qiao Shi and Wang Zhaoguo for the purpose of monitoring improvements in the Party's work style. Henceforth, elderly CDIC watchdogs such as Chen Yun and Bo Yibo would have to share the rectification spotlight with these technocratic newcomers.[167]

The overall divergence in outlook between the revolutionary cadres of the first two echelons and the technocrats of the third echelon was striking. In analyzing the problems of economic crime and corruption, for example, younger leaders tended to stress the systemic, structural sources of aberrant behavior, arguing that institutional reform was a prerequisite for improved Party discipline and work style; by contrast, old guard conservatives tended to stress the moral and spiritual sources of behavioral malfeasance, arguing that it was individuals, not institutions, that required remolding.

By the spring of 1986, the technocrats had gained Deng Xiaoping's sympathetic ear. At a meeting of provincial governors in April, Deng repeated his August 1980 diagnosis of China's ossified and overbureaucratized leadership system.[168] At another April meeting, Deng pointed to the inseparability of economic and political reform, posing the rhetorical question, "What good is it to decentralize power [to enterprise managers] . . . if it is always being taken back, again [by Party committees]?" Two months later, at a Party meeting on 20 June, Deng suggested that much of the official racketeering recently uncovered in China was not merely coincidental or occasional but was the product of flaws in the basic system. Without taking action to reform the political system, he argued, it would be impossible to root out unhealthy tendencies in the Party.[169]

---

166 *Shehui kexue* (Social Sciences; hereafter, *SHKX*) 1 (1986), in *ICM*, July 1986, 15–20.

167 The new leading group was set up at a meeting attended by 8,000 Party cadres. Significantly, neither Deng Xiaoping, Chen Yun, nor Li Xiannian was present. Although it did not replace the conservative-dominated CDIC, the new body was given a broad mandate to make recommendations on a variety of issues affecting Party organization, discipline, and spirit. See *XH*, 10–11 January 1986; *FEER*, 23 and 30 January 1986; and Rosen, "China in 1986 . . .," 37.

168 See *WHB* (Hong Kong), July 21–2, 1986; also *ICM*, September 1986, 4–5. For analysis of Deng's 1980 proposals, see Schram," 'Economics in command'? . . ."

169 *ICM*, September 1986, 4–5.; see also Rosen, "China in 1986 . . .," 38. At the same meeting, Deng suggested that China's ruling Communist Party should be "subject to restrictions."

With Deng Xiaoping now ostensibly on board the political reform band-wagon, the mass media soon fell into line. Taking their lead (and much of their language) from Deng's 1980 treatise on leadership reform, the media now began to publish frequent articles criticizing such "feudal vestiges" as patri-archal authority, bureaucratic work styles, corrupt personal networks based on kinship, special cadre privileges, and a host of other "serious abuses in the political system."[170] Increasingly, newspapers and journals treated polit-ical reform as an essential guarantee against future abuses of power and an essential prerequisite for successful economic reform.[171]

In June, CASS political scientist Yan Jiaqi published a broad critique of the Chinese political system. In Yan's analysis (which closely paralleled Deng's 1980 report), the Chinese polity suffered from four main defects, all of which were traceable to the "overconcentration of power":

> (1) We have never defined the scope of functions, powers, and respon-sibilities of party organizations, as distinct from governmental organiza-tions. . . . Party organizations at all levels have, in practice, taken on matters which should have been handled by [executive] organs of state power. . . . (2) Not only does the party function in place of executive agencies, but the system of people's congresses has never functioned effectively. . . . (3) Pow-ers are overcentralized, so that the initiative of local authorities cannot be brought fully into play. . . . (4) We have never defined the scope of functions, powers, and responsibilities of governmental bodies as distinct from those of economic enterprises and social institutions. [Hence,] enter-prises and institutions became, in effect, subsidiary bodies of executive agencies. . . .[172]

Although Yan Jiaqi did not directly address the sensitive issue of political democratization, a handful of other liberal scholars did, albeit gingerly. This was uncharted territory, insofar as advocacy of anything other than "socialist democracy" (i.e., democracy under Party leadership) could be construed as contravening the four cardinal principles. Those writers who did broach the subject of democracy generally limited themselves to attacking safe, preap-proved targets, such as (conveniently unnamed) "some feudal patriarchs," who purportedly "never consult with subordinates" and "always arbitrarily impose their will on others." Such people, wrote social scientist Li Honglin

---

170 A useful collection of newspaper articles, essays, and documents pertaining to proposals for political reform in this period appears in CLG 20.1 (Spring 1987).

171 Many of the leading theoretical articles on political reform were now authored by CASS scholars. Among the most active reform theorists in this period were Yan Jiaqi, director of the CASS Institute of Political Science; Su Shaozhi, director of the CASS Institute of Marxism–Leninism–Mao Zedong Thought; and Li Honglin, director of the Fujia, provincial Social Science Academy. Party leaders active in the political reform movement included Hu Qili, Tian Jiyun, Wang Zhaoguo, Zhu Houze, and Yan Mingfu, director of the CC's United Front Work Department.

172 Yan's critique is translated in CLG 20.1 (Spring 1987).

in June, "tremble with fear whenever they hear the word 'democracy.'" They treat democracy as a "weapon used by subordinates and the masses against higher-ups and cadres, a force to weaken and shatter stability and unity, even something tantamount to anarchy." Worse yet, wrote Li, they "take any expression of different opinions as a sign of rebellion, and put any convenient political label upon those who voice them."[173]

The issue of the detrimental effects of political labeling and intimidation was taken up by vice-premier Wan Li in an address to a national conference on "soft sciences" in late July. Arguing that such "feudal practices" had caused great damage in the past, Wan proposed the adoption of legislation to protect people engaged in policy-oriented research from the threat of political pressure, intimidation, or recrimination.[174]

With few exceptions, the great majority of voices urging leadership reform within the Chinese political establishment in the spring and summer of 1986 were moderate, technocratic, and nonprovocative – that is, they advocated such things as enhanced administrative rationalization, freedom of expression, and legislative supervision within the existing framework of the Leninist "Party leadership" model, rather than proposing any radical innovations such as limited government, separation of powers, or multiparty competition. A few theoretical articles did speak approvingly of such devices as checks and balances (*zhi heng*), but only insofar as these might be applied *within* the CCP, not *between* the party and other institutions. Similarly, the American doctrine of three separate, coequal branches of government, although occasionally praised, for example, for having "prevented the restoration of feudal dictatorship" in the West,[175] was generally rejected as inappropriate for a socialist country such as China, since the doctrine had allegedly been invented "to protect the secure rule of the bourgeoisie."[176]

As reform expectations heightened in the summer of 1986, a flurry of organizational activity took place. In July, a conference on reform of the political structure was held at the Central Party School in Beijing. Attended by several hundred younger cadres from various party organs who had been sent by their senior leaders, the conference was addressed by the Party's liberal propaganda chief, Zhu Houze. According to those in attendance, Zhu urged the young cadres to study, clarify, and absorb relevant Western, non-Marxist

173 *Shijie jingji daobao* (hereafter, SJJJDB), 2 June 1986, trans. in *CLG* 20.1 (Spring 1987).
174 XH, 14 August 1986; *I&S* 22.9 (September 1986), 4–7. Wan's speech also offered a strong rationale for the political insulation of social science think tanks, which had already begun to appear in China by this time. See Rosen, "China in 1986 ...," 39–40.
175 *Faxue yanjiu* (Legal Studies) 10 (October 1986), trans. in *CLG* 20:1 (Spring 1987), 74–77.
176 *SHKX* 4 (1986), in *ICM*, November 1986, 1–4.

political ideas and institutions. Later, Deng Liqun would allege that "it was this conference that started a new upsurge in liberalism."[177]

Responding to Zhu Houze's call, a few reform theorists began to speak with bolder voices in the late summer of 1986. Yan Jiaqi, for example, now suggested that China should seriously study parliamentary forms of government, and Su Shaozhi recommended the introduction of political pluralism and multiparty competition.[178] Also in this period, Liu Binyan, Fang Lizhi, Wang Ruowang, and Yu Haocheng all began to intensify their ongoing criticisms of the Party's prevailing ideological ethos, characterized by blind obedience to authority, monistic interests, "forbidden zones," and intolerance toward creative intellectuals.[179]

Toward the end of the summer, the SC of the Politburo established a five-person "central discussion group for reform of the political structure." Made up of a cross section of leading Party reformers and traditionalists but pointedly excluding Hu Yaobang, the five-person group was instructed by Deng Xiaoping to "clarify the content of political restructuring, and work out the details."[180]

The question of "guiding principles"

Against this background of renewed organizational activity, party leaders gathered in August for their annual midsummer retreat at the seaside resort of Beidaihe, near Tianjin. The main topic on the agenda was how to understand the party's "guiding principles" in an age of societal transformation. Whereas Politburo reformers wanted to push ahead with new definitions and ideological orientation, conservatives balked at anything that might undermine the four cardinal principles, preferring instead to stress the struggle against bourgeois liberalization. In the estimation of people like Chen Yun, Li Xiannian, and Peng Zhen, pushing political reform too rapidly could easily undermine social stability; they remained largely unmoved by the argument that political reform was an essential precondition for successful economic reform.[181]

---

177 Feng Shengbao, "Preparations for the blueprint on political restructuring presented by Zhao Ziyang at the Thirteenth Party Congress" (unpublished paper presented to the Harvard University East Asia Colloquium, July 1990), 2.

178 ZM 108 (1 October 1986), 21, in FBIS, 19 September 1986, K20; Dagong bao (hereafter, DGB), 17 September 1986, in FBIS, 29 September 1986, K16.

179 For analysis of these developments, See Kelly, "The Chinese student movement . . . ," 135–38; and Stavis, China's political reforms . . . , 51–9.

180 Feng, "Preparations for the blueprint. . . ." The five members of the group were Zhao Ziyang, Hu Qili, Tian Jiyun, Bo Yibo, and Peng Chong.

181 On the Beidaihe meeting, see WHB (Hong Kong), 8 August 1986, in SWB/FE 8335 (12 August 1986).

388 THE POLITICS OF CHINA

With the two main factions deeply divided, no new ideological ground could be broken at the Beidaihe meeting. When the Twelfth CC's Sixth Plenum met in late September, China's leaders publicly papered over their differences, passing a highly ambivalent, middle-of-the-road resolution on "building a socialist society with an advanced culture and ideology." It was a convoluted document, filled with lofty and frequently self-contradictory moral generalities. For example, while exalting the four cardinal principles and condemning bourgeois liberalization, the resolution also stressed the importance of promoting intellectual freedom, democracy, socialist humanism, and learning from advanced capitalist countries.[182] Thus deadlocked, the Sixth Plenum postponed serious consideration of political reform for another year, until the Thirteenth Party Congress, scheduled to be held in 1987.

Despite the superficial blandness of the CC's resolution on guiding principles, a tense drama took place behind the scenes at the Sixth Plenum. Originally, Deng Xiaoping had decided not to raise the divisive issue of bourgeois liberalization at the plenum, for fear of alienating the Party's pro-reform wing. In the course of the meeting, however, he changed his mind; during debate over the Party's guiding principles, he delivered a strong condemnation of bourgeois liberalization. In his remarks, Deng alleged that the trend toward bourgeois liberalization, if allowed to continue, would "lead our present policies onto the capitalist road." He reminded reformers that it was not just a few diehard conservatives who opposed bourgeois liberalization: "I am the one," he admonished, "who has talked about it most often and most insistently."[183]

The reason for Deng's sudden intervention ostensibly lay in the fact that Hu Yaobang had failed to publicize adequately Deng's serious misgivings about liberalization. "Apparently my remarks had no effect," said Deng. "I understand they were never disseminated.... I haven't changed my mind about opposing spiritual pollution.... The struggle against bourgeois liberalization will last for at least twenty years."[184]

With the CC increasingly paralyzed by factional divisions, with political reform shelved for another year, and with Deng Xiaoping growing visibly impatient with Party liberals, the momentum of the reformers, built up over a period of several months, was now partially lost. Although activities of the

182 The text of the resolution appears in BR 29.40 (6 October 1986), I–VIII.
183 The text of Deng's address is in BR 30.26 (29 June 1987), 14; a slightly different version appears in CLG 21.1 (Spring 1988), 22–3.
184 BR 30.26, ibid.; I&S 23.6 (June 1987), 17–18. It is the context of Deng's remarks that strongly suggests his extreme personal displeasure with Hu Yaobang. Deng's reference to "not chang[ing] my mind about opposing spiritual pollution" appears to be a pointed reference to Hu Yaobang's December 1984 injunction to "no longer talk about spiritual pollution" (see footnote 107). Ironically, Deng's complaint about Hu Yaobang's lack of attention to his views was strongly reminiscent of Mao Zedong's famous 1965 complaint about Deng Xiaoping, in which the late chairman observed that Deng treated him "like an ancestral spirit at a funeral."

Standing Committee's five-person group on reform of the political structure continued apace, the prevailing atmosphere in Beijing began to change.[185] The optimism of summer now gave way to a growing pessimism as rumors began to spread that liberal ideas and values were about to be targeted for criticism once again.[186] The evidence was fragmentary but palpable: A second young cadres' conference on reform of the political structure, scheduled to be held at the Beijing Central Party School in early November, now had its venue changed suddenly, as the school's top officials, conservative generals Li Desheng and Wang Zhen, refused permission for the convocation to be held on school grounds; in similar fashion, the Chinese Air Force now withdrew its sponsorship from a reform-oriented journal, Lilun xinxi bao; shortly thereafter, a nationwide academic conference on political reform, scheduled to be held in Shanghai in late November, was abruptly canceled a few days before its scheduled opening, with no explanation offered.[187]

In midautumn, Party conservatives mounted an ideological counterattack against liberalism. The point man for the assault this time was Peng Zhen. In November, Peng indirectly criticized one of the key economic tenets of the reformers: the idea that it was perfectly acceptable for some people to get rich before others. Under socialism, he admonished, "people [should] get rich together."[188] Addressing a session of the NPC's SC toward the end of November, Peng turned his attention to politics, noting sarcastically that "Some people cherish bourgeois democracy. To these people, it seems that even the moon in the capitalist world is brighter than the sun in out society."[189] In a pointed rejoinder to liberals who had complained about the undemocratic nature of Party discipline, Peng gave the following definition of intra-Party democracy:

> We follow whatever ideas are correct. If there is no unanimity of views [after discussion], then the minority submits to the majority, the individual submits to the organization, the lower level submits to the higher level, and the entire country submits to the central government. . . . This is the essential content of our system of collective democracy.[190]

185 Feng, "Preparations for the blueprint . . ." The reform group's major activity in this period was to sponsor a series of academic panels and symposia on various aspects of political reform in preparation for drafting a comprehensive reform plan to be introduced at the Thirteenth Party Congress.

186 Some newspapers began to react apprehensively to this change in the political climate. On 1 November, for example, GMRB ran an editorial arguing that it should not be a cause for alarm that some people in China no longer saw Communism as the ultimate goal, See SWB/FE 8407 (4 November 1986).

187 Feng, "Preparations for the blueprint . . . ," 2–4.

188 RMRB, 15 January 1987; transl. in FBIS, 16 January 1987, K14.

189 Quoted in I&S 23.6 (June 1987), 17.

190 XH, 26 November 1986. Peng's definition of collective democracy was virtually identical to the classical Leninist concept of democratic centralism; as such, it differed substantially from the concept of socialist democracy widely advocated by reform leaders since 1978.

Thus did Party conservatives sharpen their polemical swords. With ideological battle lines drawn, the battle itself was not long in coming.

Fang Lizhi and the students

During the student demonstrations of autumn 1985, astrophysicist Fang Lizhi had made a series of controversial speeches on Chinese college campuses, including Peking University (Beida) and Zhejiang University. One of Fang's main themes had been to challenge Chinese students boldly to "break all barriers" that served to impede intellectual awareness and creativity. At Beida he had urged young people to take their future into their own hands, speaking passionately about the continued prevalence of corruption and patronage within the Party organization. Unlike most establishment critics, however, Fang Lizhi named names. He cited, for example, the case of Beijing Vice-Mayor Zhang Baifa, who had recently traveled to the United States as a member of an academic delegation attending a seminar on high-energy physics. "What was he doing there?" asked Fang. "This kind of free-loading is corrupt. . . . I don't care if it is Zhang Baifa, I'm going to stand here and say it."[191]

Almost a year after delivering these remarks, Fang Lizhi went on another multicampus speaking tour. By all accounts, his November 1986 talks were even more provocative than the earlier ones. Speaking at Shanghai's Jiaotong University on 6 November, Fang elaborated on the theme of breaking barriers. He now urged students to challenge authority and to demand democratic rights and freedoms, rather than waiting for them to be bestowed from above by the party:

> I really feel that now we should not be afraid of anybody. Some people do not dare to challenge our leaders; but I have found that if you challenge them, they dare not do anything against you. . . . For instance, last year J criticized Zhang Baifa by name. . . . Later he began to find fault with me. But he can no longer pick on anyone now. (Laughter from the audience) In August, I criticized Hu Qiaomu by name at a press conference, and he did not do anything against me. (Laughter from the audience) . . . This year I criticized leaders of the Politburo. (Laughter). . . . I insist on expressing my own opinion. . . .
>
> The core problem is: If China's reforms depend completely on the moves of our top leaders, China will not become a developed nation. . . . Democracy granted by leaders is not true democracy. (Applause) What is the meaning of democracy? Democracy means that each human being has his own rights and that human beings, each exercising his own rights, form our

---

191 Fang's speech appears in *ICM*, December 1986, 8–10.

society. Therefore, rights are in the hands of every citizen. They are not given by top leaders of the nation.[192]

Fang Lizhi reiterated these themes on other college campuses in the Shanghai area. On 18 November, at Tongji University, he delivered perhaps his most controversial statement: "I am here to tell you that the socialist movement, from Marx and Lenin to Stalin and Mao Zedong, has been a failure. . . . I think that complete Westernization is the only way to modernize." Everywhere Fang went, students were reportedly moved by his words; he rapidly became a campus hero.[193]

Party leaders, including many who supported political reform, were not so enthralled by Fang's rhetoric. On 30 November, Vice-Premier Wan Li paid a visit to Fang's home campus, the Chinese University of Science and Technology (CUST) in Hefei, where he delivered a thinly veiled warning, reminding Fang (who was vice-president of CUST) that university leaders had an obligation to implement the line, principles, and policies of the Party.[194] In an impromptu debate with Fang, the vice-premier failed to make any headway, either with the astrophysicist or with an informal audience of students. At one point, a visibly frustrated Wan Li reportedly said to Fang, "I have already granted you enough freedom and democracy." Thereupon Fang shot back "What do you mean, enough democracy'? It was the people who made you vice premier. It's not up to any single person to hand out democracy."[195]

Perhaps coincidentally, and perhaps not, when Chinese students began demonstrating in early December, the arc of political contagion paralleled rather closely (though not precisely) the itinerary of Fang's various lecture tours. Beginning at CUST in Hefei, protest spread to Jiaotong and Tongji in Shanghai before moving north to Beida. All along the arc of contagion, Chinese students began to break barriers.

Breaking barriers: December 1986

The movement began on 5 December, when several hundred students at CUST assembled to protest their exclusion both from the process of selecting the head of their local student union and from nominating candidates for the provincial people's congress.[196] Four days later, on the symbolic occasion of the

---

192 Fang's speech appears in *I&S* 23.4 (April 1987), 124–42.
193 Stavis (*China's political reforms* . . . , 92–5) gives a vivid account of these events.
194 *XH*, 3 December 1986, in *FBIS*, 23 December 1986, K18–19.
195 *South China Morning Post*, 12 January 1987; *ZM* 111 (1 January 1987).
196 Just days earlier, China's election law had been amended to make selection procedures for people's congress candidates more democratic; among other things, the new law specifies that more candidates must be nominated than the number of seats to be filled (*XH*, 15 November 1986); the text of the new election law appears in *FBIS*, 8 December 1986. The day before the protest, on 4 December,

fifty-first anniversary of the anti-Japanese student movement of 9 December 1935, some 2,000 to 3,000 CUST students marched through the streets of Hefei, criticizing the government, *inter alia*, for reneging on its promise of expanded electoral democracy. Embarrassed by the protest, authorities gave in to students' demands, postponing the provincial people's congress election. Smaller demonstrations also occurred on 9 December at a handful of college campuses in other cities, including Wuhan and Xian.[197]

When word of the success of the Hefei students reached other campuses, it served as a catalyst, amplifying local protest and creating a contagion effect. On 10 December, posters calling for democracy appeared at Jiaotong and Beida, among other universities. Small demonstrations also broke out on college campuses in Shandong, Shenzhen, and Kunming.

At Jiaotong and Beida, university authorities gave orders to remove posters; students at Jiaotong planned a march to protest the removal order. When Shanghai Mayor Jiang Zemin visited the campus on 18 December to try to cool down the students, pleading for unity and stability, he was heckled and repeatedly interrupted. At one point, a student provocatively asked Jiang Zemin whether he had been elected mayor by the citizens of Shanghai. Momentarily taken aback, the mayor asked for the student's name and department. Offended by this crude attempt at intimidation, a number of students in attendance leaped verbally to their classmate's defense.[198]

News of the Jiaotong confrontation spread quickly, and students at nearby Tongji and Fudan universities took to the streets on 19 December, angrily denouncing bureaucratism and demanding liberty and democracy. Congregating at Shanghai's Peoples Square, several thousand students demanded a meeting with the mayor. After a delay of several hours, during which time the movement began to dissipate, students marched to city hall, singing the *Internationale* en route. Eventually, Jiang Zemin sent a vice-mayor to meet with student representatives. The students presented four demands: (1) they wanted Mayor Jiang to address them personally; (2) they wanted their demonstration to be treated as legal and patriotic; (3) they wanted assurances against future

---

Fang Lishi reportedly told his students, "Democracy is not granted from the top down; it is won by individuals" (*BR* 29.8 [23 February 1987], 17–18).

197 According to eyewitnesses in these cities, the complaints of the demonstrators varied greatly and lacked coherent focus. Some students clamored for electoral democracy; others complained about the poor quality of campus food and living conditions (including the presence of rats in the dormitories); still others protested against inflation, corruption, rising tuition fees, and the elimination of automatic student aid. For analysis of the 1986 student demonstrations see Stavis, *China's political reform* . . . , 96–104; Julia Kwong, "The 1986 student demonstrations in China: A democratic movement?" *AS* 28.9 (September 1988), 970–85; Lowell Dittmer, "Reform, succession and the resurgence of Mainland China's old guard," *I&S* 24.1 (January 1988), 96–113; and *ICM*, January 1987, 2–6, and March 1987, 27–28.

198 *South China Morning Post*, 24 December 1986; Stavis, *China's political reforms* . . . , 97.

recriminations; and (4) they wanted newspapers to carry fair and accurate reports of the demonstration.[199]

The vice-mayor tried to convince the students to return to their campuses, offering buses to escort them. Undaunted, hundreds of protesters remained at city hall. At around 5:45 A.M. the next morning, police marched in and forceably removed the students, putting them in buses to be driven back to their campuses. A handful of students who refused to leave were detained briefly; a few were roughed up; one reportedly suffered a broken leg. Over the next few days, the protests of People's Square grew larger, now involving more than 10,000 people, including substantial numbers of nonstudents. According to eyewitnesses, the level of emotional excitement now surpassed anything seen in China since the Cultural Revolution.

In Nanjing, Tianjin, and Beijing, thousands of students demonstrated during the week of 22–26 December, some in support of the Shanghai students and some merely in response to the heightened excitement of the times. Altogether, tens of thousands of people, students and nonstudents alike, in seventeen cities, representing more than 150 colleges and universities (out of a total of around 1,000), participated in demonstrations in the last half of December 1986.[200]

The official media, which had previously ignored the demonstrations altogether, now sought to cool things down by publishing commentaries urging moderation and restraint. On 22 December, *Xinhua* publicized a statement by Tianjin's pro-reform mayor, Li Ruihuan, in which the mayor exhorted people in his city not to be unduly alarmed by the disturbances. "There is nothing extraordinary about such incidents," he said; "there is no reason for us to lose our composure." At the same time, the mayor cautioned students against being led astray by people who claimed that China's future lay in "complete Westernization." Such notions were entirely inappropriate, said Li Ruihuan, and must be resolutely opposed.[201] A few days later, the *People's Daily* ran an editorial urging Chinese students to have patience, arguing that democratization was a lengthy process that could not be realized overnight.[202] Meanwhile, municipal authorities in Beijing employed more direct, straightforward means of discouraging protest: On 26 December, they enacted new

199 These demands, as well as several other aspects of the December 1986 student movement, are of particular interest because of their striking similarity to events that transpired some twenty-eight months later, at the height of the 1989 Tiananmen Square demonstrations. See "Mourning becomes electric" and "The aftermath of 26 April: Public resentment deepens."

200 Estimates of total participation vary widely, from a low of around 20,000 (roughly 2 percent of China's total college population), as reported in the official *RMRB* (31 December 1986), to a high of over 75,000, representing a compilation of various foreign media estimates. The largest individual demonstrations were in Shanghai and Beijing, where some crowds (including both demonstrators and spectators) were estimated to have been as large as 30,000.

201 *XH*, 23 December 1986, in *ICM*, April 1987, 3–4. 202 *RMRB*, 25 December 1986.

regulations restricting the issuance of parade permits; this was followed by the arrest of a handful of demonstrators on charges ranging from disturbing the peace to incitement to riot.

Despite the occasional arrests and sporadic use of intimidation tactics by public security forces, the local authorities generally refrained from using excessive force to quell student protests. In the absence of inflammatory government behavior, popular passions began to subside, and the movement lost momentum; by early January 1987, a combination of winter weather and the natural dissipation of student energies served to dampen the protesters' fervor. Before returning to their classes, however, Beijing students engaged in one final act of symbolic political defiance: On 5 January they publicly burned copies of the *Beijing Daily*, official organ of the municipal government, which the students claimed had presented a grossly distorted view of their movement.

The empire strikes back

Throughout most of December, China's party leaders outwardly maintained their composure. Inwardly, however, many of them began to bridle.[203] Beijing's Mayor Chen Xitong and municipal Party chief Li Ximing were said to be particularly angry over the burning of the *Beijing Daily*, On 28 December, Party conservatives spoke out: Bo Yibo, Hu Qiaomu, and Deng Liqun all issued statements denouncing bourgeois democracy, which they said would destabilize the country and retard modernization. Two days later, Wang Zhen issued a similar statement, going so far as to suggest the possibility of using military force to put an end to student demonstrations.[204]

Now Deng Xiaoping entered the fray. On 30 December, in a meeting with Wan Li, Hu Qili, Li Peng, and the deputy state counselor for education, He Dongchang, Deng delivered a talk "On the problem of the present student disturbances." In his remarks, Deng leveled what was by far his most vitriolic attack to date against liberalism. Placing the blame for escalating student "turmoil" (*dongluan*) squarely on the shoulders of "leaders in [various] places who failed to take a firm attitude . . . toward bourgeois liberalization," Deng asserted that this was "not just a matter of one or two places, or one or two years'

203 Shanghai mayor Jiang Zemin, at a meeting of municipal cadres, roundly denounced the students of Jiaotong University for opposing the Party. Afterwards, he reportedly ordered that "not one word" of his remarks should be repeated outside of the meeting (*ZM* 111 [1 January 1987], in *ICM*, March 1987, 24–6).

204 *SWB/FE* 8464 (13 January 1987); *ZB*, February 1987, 26. Wang Zhen was reportedly criticized for his provocative remarks; subsequently he was demoted from his post as president of the Central Party School. See Feng, "Preparations for the blueprint . . . ," 8.

duration"; rather, it was a question of "failing to take a clear stand . . . over a period of several years."[205]

Lashing out at members of the liberal intelligentsia, whom he blamed for instigating the students, Deng named names and demanded punishment: "I have seen statements by Fang Lizhi," he said. "They are absolutely unlike anything a party member ought to say. What point is there in allowing him to remain in the party?" Of Wang Ruowang, Deng said: "[He] is a cunning rascal. I said a long time ago that we ought to expel him. Why haven't we done it?" Next, Deng denounced bourgeois democracy: "When we speak of democracy, we must not mean bourgeois democracy. We cannot set up such gimmicks as the division of powers between three branches of government. This causes great trouble." Alluding to the way dissidents were handled during the short-lived democracy movement of 1978–9, Deng said that "We cannot allow people who turn right and wrong around . . . to do as they please. Didn't we arrest Wei Jingsheng? . . . We arrested him and haven't let him go, yet China's image has not suffered the slightest damage." Praising the Polish government's handling of the Solidarity crisis in 1981, Deng said that the Polish leaders had showed "cool and Level-headed judgment. Their attitude was firm. . . . They resorted to martial law to bring the situation under control." For Deng, the lesson to be drawn was clear: "This proves," he said, "that you cannot succeed without recourse to methods of dictatorship."[206]

Arguing that it was generally advisable to "arrest as few as possible," Deng nevertheless asserted that a show of force was an indispensable tactic in dealing with unruly demonstrators. In a passage that ominously foreshadowed certain events of May and June 1989, Deng raised the question of how to deal with people who are determined to provoke a confrontation:

> [I]f they want to create a bloody incident, what can we do about it? . . . We do all we can to avoid bloodshed. If not even a single person dies, that is the best way. It is even preferable to allow our own people to be injured.[207] But the most important thing is to grasp the object of struggle. . . . If we do not take appropriate steps and measures, we will be unable to control this type of incident; if we pull back, we will encounter even more trouble later on. . . . Don't worry that foreigners will say we have ruined our

205 The main points of Deng's talk were later incorporated into the text of "Central document No. 1, 1987," promulgated on 6 January 1987. The text of this document, along with other related documents, appears in *CLG* 21.1 (Spring 1988), 18–21.

206 Ibid.

207 In a somewhat more strident translation of this same passage, the *South China Morning Post* of 12 January 1987, quotes Deng as saying: "We can afford to shed some blood. Just try as much as possible not to kill anyone." An official Chinese government translation of the same passage reads: "We should . . . do our best to avoid shedding blood, even if it means some of our own people get hurt" (BR 30.26 [29 June 1987], 15–16).

reputation. . . . We must show foreigners that the political situation in China is stable. . . . [208]

Such was senior leader Deng Xiaoping's prescription for dealing with the fire next time; for the moment, however, the students were quiescent, and the crisis went into remission.

The "resignation" of Hu Yaobang

The student demonstrations of December 1986 were the leading edge of a widening pattern of social unrest that began to affect urban China in the mid-1980s. Although demands for greater democracy comprised the broadest common denominator of student protest, such demands tended to be vague and unfocused, often masking a wide variety of underlying social stresses, grievances, and tensions. Some of these were preexisting, and others were reform-induced; all were subject to intensification in the swirling vortex of heightened expectations, loosened behavioral constraints, and accelerated social mobilization that characterized China in the mid-1980s.

If the students themselves were somewhat diffuse and unfocused in their demands and objectives, China's rebounding conservatives were not. They knew exactly what they wanted: the removal of Hu Yaobang. This was nothing new, of course; Chen Yun, Hu Qiaomu, and Deng Liqun (among others) had been visibly unhappy with Hu at least since 1982–3. Now, however, the conservatives had a powerful new weapon at their disposal, the wrath of Deng Xiaoping, and they used it with maximum effect. On 27 December, a delegation of seven conservative leaders visited Deng to request Hu Yaobang's dismissal, raising numerous allegations of misconduct.[209] Deng reportedly temporized: Having only recently expressed confidence in Hu's leadership to a group of foreign visitors, he could hardly fire the general secretary at this juncture without having it reflecting badly upon his own judgment.[210]

Meanwhile, the conservative backlash against the December "turmoil" was intensifying. On 6 January, following the public burning of copies of the *Beijing Daily*, the Politburo promulgated "Central document no. 1, 1987." It called on leading cadres in all organizations and at all levels to take an "unwavering stand" on the "front lines of the battle" to quell student

208 *CLG* 21.1 (Spring 1988).
209 BX 141 (1 April 1987), 3. The seven were Peng Zhen, Hu Qiaomu, Wang Zhen, Deng Liqun, Bo Yibo, Yang Shangkun, and Yu Qiuli.
210 On this point, see Parris Chang, "From Mao to Hua to Hu to Chao: Changes in the CCP leadership and its rule of the game, *I&S* 25.1 (January 1989), 66.

unrest, Those who violated the Party's injunction against supporting student turmoil would be dealt with "in accordance with Party rules and regulations"; where circumstances were serious, severe punishments would be meted out.[211] Three days later, it was unofficially reported that Fang Lizhi, Liu Binyan, and Wang Ruowang had been ordered expelled from the CCP.[212]

In the aftermath of the *Beijing Daily* incident, Deng Xiaoping made up his mind: Hu Yaobang had to go.[213] On 16 January, at an enlarged meeting of the Politburo, Hu was relieved of his duties as general secretary after reportedly having thrice rejected Deng Xiaoping's request that he resign. More than twenty people spoke out against Hu at the meeting, including some of his erstwhile supporters.[214]

The next day, the Politburo promulgated "Central document no. 3, 1987," cataloguing Hu's alleged misdeeds. Six separate charges were set out in the document: (1) Hu Yaobang had for several years resisted the Party's "entirely correct" efforts to combat spiritual pollution and bourgeois liberalization in the ideological sphere, thus contributing to an upsurge in liberal demands for "total Westernization," culminating in the student turmoil of December 1986;[215] (2) he had failed to provide correct leadership in the Party rectification–consolidation campaign, virtually ignoring the four cardinal principles and "only opposing the 'Left'" while "never opposing the Right"; (3) in economic work, he had overemphasized the need to stimulate and satisfy consumer demand, leading to undue acceleration in the rate of planned economic growth, making it impossible to adequately "lay the ideological groundwork" for rapid growth, and thus causing the economy to go "out of control"; (4) in political work, he frequently violated legal procedures and "repeatedly spoke out about government legislative work in a way that was not serious"; (5) in foreign affairs, he "said many things he should not have said"; and (6) he often disobeyed Party resolutions and frequently took the

211 The document appears in *ICM*, April 1987, 1–2.
212 Kyodo (Tokyo), 9 January 1987, *SWB/FE* 8462 (10 January 1987). The separate decisions to expel the three liberals were offically reported in *XH*, 14 January 1987; *XH*, 19 January 1987; and *RMRB*, 24 January 1987.
213 It has been reported that Deng ultimately decided to sack Hu Yaobang because Chen Yun persuaded him that Hu's leadership style risked splitting the Party and provoking the formation of autonomous labor unions (and strikes) among urban workers – a sort of Chinese Gdansk. See Wilson and Ji, "Leadership by 'lines' . . . ," 34.
214 *SWB/FE* 8467 (16 January 1987).
215 The document makes an explicit reference to the late U.S. Secretary of State John Foster Dulles, who once said that "the policy of the American government is to encourage liberalization in the Soviet Union and the countries of Eastern Europe," Apparently, Hu Yaobang was being judged guilty by association for having (unwittingly) advanced the aims of U.S. imperialism. Similar allegations, to the effect that China's liberal reformers were promoting Western schemes for the "peaceful evolution" of bourgeois democracy, later provided a significant part of the government's rationale for cracking down on student demonstrators in the spring of 1989.

initiative in expressing his own ideas "without authorization from the Central Committee."[216]

Central document no. 3 also contained a summary of Hu Yaobang's self-criticism. In it, he apologized for overstepping the bounds of his authority as general secretary, acknowledging that because he had occupied a leading position, his errors had caused "very grave damage" to the Party, the nation, and the people. He also acknowledged that his errors "were not isolated mistakes but a whole series of major errors involving political principles"; at the same time, however, he carefully avoided conceding the substance of the most damaging charges against him, that is, that his ideological laxity had fostered spiritual pollution and bourgeois liberalization, thereby bringing on student turmoil.[217] Despite Hu's failure to confess to specifics, those present at his self-criticism "expressed satisfaction" with his "feelings and attitude"; consequently, he was not expelled from the Party and was even permitted to retain his seat on the Politburo.[218]

Toward the end of Central document no. 3, a short passage was devoted to the question of how to avoid future recurrences of reckless behavior by Party leaders. Though it received scant attention at the time, this passage subsequently provided the rationale for allowing retired Party elders to override younger leaders in time of crisis: "The comrades who took part in the session all felt that, for the long term peace and order of our country, it would be a good idea if, while such older generation revolutionaries as Deng Xiaoping, Chen Yun, and Li Xiannian are still in good health, a system might be devised to control and supervise the leaders at the highest levels in Party and government."[219] Such a system was put in place later in the year, at the Thirteenth Party Congress; it was actively invoked during the next round of student "turmoils" in May–June 1989.

Combatting bourgeois liberalism

Despite the vehemence of the Party leadership's denunciation of bourgeois liberalization, the ensuing propaganda drive was considerably milder than its predecessor, the anti–spiritual pollution campaign of 1983. The reason was clear: Negative backlash from the earlier campaign had threatened to scare

216 The text of "Central document no. 3" appears in *ICM*, May 1987, 1–3. Of the six charges raised against Hu, the first two were the most serious, and the last three were quite vague and skeletal. The document was said to be based on a report delivered by Bo Yibo summarizing the proceedings of a top-level leadership meeting held in Beijing from 10 to 15 January.

217 Ibid., 2–3.

218 Peng Zhen would subsequently boast (obliquely) that he and his old comrades played an instrumental role in ousting Hu (*DGB* [Hong Kong], 9 April 1987). Hu later expressed his regret for having capitulated to conservative pressures to engage in self-criticism.

219 *ICM*, May 1987, 3.

off foreign investors and undermine Deng's reform program. To avoid repetition, the 1987 campaign was narrowly circumscribed from the outset. It was not to be a mass movement but was to be confined within the ranks of the Party apparatus; expulsions from the Party were to be relatively few, as were removals from office. Indeed, aside from Hu Yaobang, the only other top Party official actually sacked in the aftermath of the December 1986 student demonstrations was Zhu Houze.[220] Although there followed a clear tightening of press censorship and a blacklisting of certain liberal magazines and journalists in the late winter and spring of 1987, no large-scale police crackdown was launched against people who had supported the student demonstrations;[221] only a handful of alleged troublemakers, most of them nonstudents, were reportedly jailed for instigating the December turmoil.[222] Finally, the new campaign was carefully prevented from spilling over into an attack on

---

220 Zhu, who retained his Party membership, was replaced as Party propaganda chief by Wang Renzhi, the former deputy editor-in-chief of *Red Flag*. Among prominent liberal critics, only Fang Lizhi, Wang Ruowang, and Liu Binyan were expelled from the Party in the immediate aftermath of the student disturbances, although five other liberal intellectuals, including Su Shaozhi and reform economist Yu Guangyuan, were pressured to resign from the CCP during the summer of 1987. They were reportedly spared loss of Party membership through the personal intervention of retired PLA marshal Nie Rongzhen, who was a patron of one of the five targeted intellectuals, Song Changjiang. See *ICM*, December 1987, 34; and *China News Analysis* (Hong Kong) (hereafter, *CNA*) 1342 (1 September 1987), 4. In addition to CUST vice-president Fang Lizhi, a number of other leading academic administrators, including Fang's boss, CUST president Guan Weiyan, and the president and vice-president of the Chinese Academy of Sciences, Lu Jiaxi and Yan Dongsheng, were dismissed from their jobs early in 1987. Even after being expelled from the Party, Fang Lizhi and Liu Binyan were permitted to attend professional meetings in China; Liu, Wang Ruowang, Su Shaozhi, and others were later granted permission to travel abroad.

221 "Central document no. 4, 1987," released in March, called for removing people with persistent bourgeois liberal tendencies from leading posts on newspapers and periodicals. The document also said that "we have decided to suppress further publication of those newspapers and periodicals that have commited political mistakes or which contain material not on a high level," See *SWB/FE* 8512 (10 March 1987); *BX* 140 (16 March 1987); and *ICM*, May 1987, 3–5, 10. Most of the periodicals affected by this decision were smaller, lesser-known journals, such as the *Society News* (Shanghai), the *Special Economic Zone Workers' News* (Shenzhen), the *Youth Forum* (Hebei), and the *Science, Technology and Financial Report* (Anhui). The more notorious *World Economic Herald* of Shanghai was criticized but not shut down in this period. Among the liberal editors and journalists suspended from their posts in the winter and spring of 1987 were Liu Zaifu *at Literary Criticism* and Liu Xinwu of *People's Literature*, both of whom had actively participated in the 1986 critical debates on Marxist theory. Although political scientist Yan Jiaqi and his wife Gao Gao had their book, *A history of the decade of the Cultural Revolution*, banned from publication in 1986, this was apparently not directly related to their activities in support of bourgeois liberalization. Other prominent intellectuals criticized or blacklisted in this period included Wang Ruoshui, Hu Jiwei, Su Shaozhi, Yu Guangyuan, Li Honglin, Wu Zuguang, Wen Yuankai, Zhang Xianyang, Xu Liangying, Guo Luoji, and Ge Yang. For documentation, see *BX* 140, (16 March 1987); *JSND* 4 and 5 (1987); and Kelly, "The Chinese student movement. . . ."

222 In late January, a student at Tianjin University was arrested on a charge of having supplied classified information to a French journalist during the December student demonstrations (a charge strikingly similar to one leveled against Wei Jingsheng in 1979). In March, two nonstudents wre convicted of inciting riots on college campuses and were sentenced to prison terms of three and five years, respectively (*ICM*, May 1987, 30); and in May there was a report that another individual arrested during the December disturbances had been sent to prison for three years (Stavis, *China's political reforms . . .* , 123). There may well have been other criminal convictions, but they were not documented at the time.

economic reform and the open policy, both of which were consistently upheld, by reformers and conservatives alike, as entirely "necessary and correct."[223]

In a move intended to ensure a modicum of leadership continuity in the reform process, the Politburo unanimously selected Zhao Ziyang as acting general secretary of the CCP to replace Hu Yaobang.[224] One of Zhao's first acts in his new role was to reassure the country and the outside world that "China will not launch a political movement to oppose bourgeois liberalization. . . . The current work of opposing bourgeois liberalization will be strictly limited within the CCP and will be mainly carried out in the political and ideological fields. Nothing of the sort will be conducted in rural areas, while in enterprises and institutions the task will be handled in the form of study and self-education."[225]

Even Deng Liqun showed new and rather uncharacteristic restraint. In a February article aimed at a youthful audience, the erstwhile firebrand gently admonished China's young people to consider the harmful impact of recent student disturbances; he questioned the appropriateness of letting young people "do their own thing" and advocated stepping up political and ideological study in schools and universities.[226] But his tone was now schoolmasterly rather than strident, didactic rather than dogmatic. He could afford to be avuncular: He had won; Hu Yaobang was gone.

Notwithstanding Deng Liqun's patronizing tone, Chinese students and educators soon found themselves subject to tightened security measures, strengthened political loyalty tests, and intensified ideological indoctrination. Vice-Premier Li Peng set the tone for these changes in a February speech to a national educational work conference. While urging educators to "do our best to win the understanding and support of students," Li announced that all schools and universities in China would soon undergo a tightening of control in order to enforce rigorously the rules and regulations.[227]

---

223 The danger that the campaign against bourgeois liberalization might be used as a pretext by opponents of economic reform and the open policy to sabotage Deng's reform program was explicitly acknowledged in "Central document no. 4, 1987" (see ftn. 221), which "strictly prohibited" such pretexts and proscribed such devious tactics as "using the Left to criticize the Right." In calling for stricter controls to be exercised over the press, publishing companies, and various artistic media, document no. 4 added the important caveat that "no general housecleaning will be carried out," further stipulating that there should be "no sudden switching from Right to Left, no requiring permission for everything, and no interfering with the normal development of literature and art."

224 BR 30.4 (26 January 1987), 5. The "acting" designation was removed later in the year when Zhao's selection as general secretary was formally ratified at the Thirteenth Party Congress.

225 BR 30.5–6 (9 February 1987), 6–7. China's leaders were obviously concerned in this period about calming popular fears, both domestic and foreign, of a new ideological witch hunt. Thus, the same issue of Beijing Review that carried Zhao's reassuring message about "no political movement" also carried, on its inside front cover, a full-page color photo of a relaxed and smiling Deng Xiaoping, casually attired in Western-style sweater and open-necked sport shirt, playing bridge.

226 Zhongguo qingnian bao, 12 February 1987, in ICM, May 1987, 13–14.

227 Li Peng's address appears in XH, 16 February 1987; trans. in ICM, April 1987, 5–6.

Changes in the focus of the educational curriculum were also called for, centering on the need to readjust the content of liberal arts courses in order to promote the goal of "graduating young people with high ideals, moral character, culture, and discipline." Finally, the vice-premier announced that henceforth political character and "attitude toward the four cardinal principles and bourgeois liberalization" would be taken into consideration as major qualifications for students taking high school and college entrance examinations.[228]

Also, in February 1987, in a proposal designed to enable China's conservative "old comrades" to gain a modicum of added control over the actions of their successors, Bo Yibo called for a revival of the previously discarded "three-in-one" (san jiehe) leadership formula, combining "old, middle-aged, and young" leaders. Bo's call was echoed a month later by Vice-Premier Yao Yilin in a press conference with foreign journalists.[229]

With Hu Yaobang in disgrace, with liberalism in ill repute, and with elderly conservatives once again balking at the prospect of total retirement, Zhao Ziyang found himself operating on a rather short leash. Although he remained an important symbol of reform continuity and moderation, Zhao was forced to accommodate to the Party's prevailing antiliberal mood. His political report to the NPC in late March thus reflected a delicate balance between continued strong support for "total overall reform" of the economy and an equally firm denunciation of bourgeois liberalization. Blaming the December student demonstrations on "ideological confusion" sown as a result of the "erroneous trend" of bourgeois liberalization, Zhao now dutifully repeated Deng Xiaoping's warning of the previous December: "If bourgeois liberalization were allowed to spread unchecked . . . it would plunge our country into turmoil and make it impossible for us to proceed with our normal construction and reform programs."[230] Arguing that China must resolutely adhere to the four cardinal principles, Zhao flatly rejected the notions of "total Westernization" and "Americanized bourgeois liberal democracy," which were said to have exerted a "pernicious influence" on China's socialist modernization.[231] Trying his best to bridge the deep chasm that separated rival wings of the party, Zhao argued that there was no necessary antagonism between the four cardinal principles and the policies of structural reform and opening up to the outside world. "They are not mutually exclusive," he asserted;

228 Ibid., 6. See also XH, 2 February 1987.

229 DGB, 14 February and 29 March 1987. Yao Yilin was widely regarded as a protégé of Chen Yun.

230 Zhao's report appears in BR 30.16 (20 April 1987), III–XX.

231 A similar theme had been stressed by president Li Xiannian in a meeting with Japanese politicians on 3 March. On that occasion Li had said that it was "wishful thinking" for foreigners to expect China to go in for a market economy, capitalism, and total Westernization (RMRB, 4 March 1987).

"they complement and penetrate each other, forming an integral whole."[232] It was an assertion Zhao would later have intensely personal reason to reconsider.

Zhao Ziyang's ideological bow to Party conservatives was apparently part of a bargain struck early in the spring: In exchange for Zhao's denunciation of bourgeois liberalism and support for the four cardinal principles, the conservatives would halt their antireform, antiretirement backlash. The deal was brokered by Deng Xiaoping, who was said to be growing increasingly concerned, as in November 1983, over the excessive zeal displayed by conservatives in combatting liberalism.[233]

Whether or not the deal was struck in precisely these terms, a trade-off was very much in evidence in the spring of 1987, as condemnations of bourgeois liberalization subsided in intensity while talk of leadership rejuvenation and political structure reform correspondingly increased, with Deng's own voice now added to the pro-reform chorus.[234] Signalling the new *modus vivendi*, Peng Zhen gave a rare interview to foreign journalists in April, in which he indicated that he and several other old comrades, pointedly excluding Deng Xiaoping, would announce their retirement at the Thirteenth Party Congress.[235] Reform of China's political and administrative structures would resume, Peng predicted, but only within the framework of the four cardinal principles; in the reform process, emphasis would be placed on enhancing the administrative autonomy of urban enterprises and rural villages and increasing the supervisory functions of peoples congresses at all levels. It was a formula that strongly suggested moderation and compromise, if not long-term political viability.

Having gained some measure of policy leverage, Zhao Ziyang reportedly resisted pressure from Party conservatives to discipline severely political reformers such as Yan Jiaqi and Su Shaozhi. On the recommendation of his political secretary, Bao Tong, who claimed that Deng Liqun had fabricated

232 *BR* 30.16 (20 April 1987), XVI.
233 Ian Wilson and You Ji suggest that Deng decided to modulate the anti-bourgeois liberalization campaign at the urging of his son, Deng Pufang ("Leadership by 'lines' . . . ," 34–35). See also Stuart R. Schram, "China after the 13th congress," *CQ* 114 (June 1988), 180; and Tony Saich, "The thirteenth congress of the Chinese Communist Party: An agenda for reform?" *journal of Communist Studies* 4.2 (June 1988), 205.
234 In mid-March, Deng told the visiting governor-general of Canada that "at the Thirteenth Congress this year we shall discuss plans for reform of the political system." At around the same time, a new volume of Deng's collected writings was issued. Entitled *Fundamental issues in present-day China*, the book contained several of the senior leader's pre-December 1986 statements stressing the necessity of political reform. See *BR* 30.20 (18 May 1987), 14–17.
235 As for Deng Xiaoping, Peng said that "We should keep just him on the Standing Committee as an old timer, and let all the rest be relatively young." See *DGB*, 9 April 1987; and *BR* 30.17 (27 April 1987), 14–15. In the event, it was Yang Shangkun, not Deng Xiaoping, who remained on the new Politburo as the lone old-timer after the Thirteenth Congress, though he was not elevated to the SC.

evidence against Yan Jiaqi, Zhao now exonerated Yan of the charge of bourgeois liberalism.[236]

Meanwhile, Zhao and his five-person group (which by this time had been expanded to nineteen members) now resumed work on their blueprint for reform of the political structure. In March 1987, the group transmitted a letter to Deng Xiaoping outlining some "initial thoughts" on the problem of reform. After a few days, Deng returned the letter with the annotation, "the design is good."[237] In May, the first working draft of a plan was submitted for Deng's approval. The core of the plan was a proposal to separate Party and government, one of Deng's principal reform recommendations of August 1980. However, Zhao and his colleagues apparently went further toward circumscribing and balancing Party power than Deng had intended, for now the senior leader balked at Zhao's draft, pointing out sharply that the bourgeois system of checks and balances was "still being dished up in new form." The political structure reform group thereupon went back to the drawing board.[238] At least four more drafts were prepared between May and September, some of which were disseminated for debate and discussion. The final version, draft number seven, was approved at the Seventh Plenum of the Twelfth CC, which met in mid-October on the eve of the Thirteenth Party Congress.[239]

Throughout the summer, there was a great deal of speculation about the upcoming Thirteenth Congress. In June, Deng had confounded party old-timers, who wished to retain a share of power at the top, by announcing his intention to retire.[240] In August, at the annual leaders' meeting at Beidaihe, there were reports that Deng had agreed, after intense lobbying by Chen Yun and others, to approve the promotion of two second-echelon conservatives, Song Ping and Yao Yilin, to the Politburo and its SC, respectively, in order to compensate partially for the retirement of elderly veterans.[241] Later in the summer, the name of Deng Liqun was also floated as a conservative choice for a Politburo seat.

In late August, *Xinhua* revealed that the guiding document for political reform at the Thirteenth Congress would be Deng Xiaoping's recently rereleased 1980 essay "On the reform of the system of Party and state

236 *WHB* (Shanghai), 8 August 1989; Wilson and Ji, "Leadership by 'lines'. . . ." 35, n. 17.
237 Quoted in Michel Oksenberg, "China's 13th Party congress," *POC* 36:6 (November–December 1987). 15–16.
238 Feng, "Preparations for the blueprint. . . ." 7. Aside from the five original members of the political structure reform group, three other individuals who played a prominent role in shaping the draft reform proposals in this period were Zhao's political secretary, Bao Tong, who was also vice-minister of the State Commission on Economic Restructuring; political scientist Yan Jiaqi; and long-time reform advocate Liao Gailong, who was responsible for coordinating the theoretical recommendations made by the group's various study panels (ibid.).
239 Oksenberg, "China's 13th . . . ," 15–16.   240 *DGB*, 4 June 1987.
241 *I&S* 23.12 (December 1987), 96.

leadership."[242] Also at the end of August, Hu Qili indicated that "at least seven" members of the Politburo would resign at the Congress; Deng Xiaoping was not among them.[243] At around the same time, it was revealed that Vice-Premier Li Peng would soon be named to succeed Zhao Ziyang as premier, enabling Zhao to concentrate on his Party leadership duties.[244]

THIRD CYCLE: LIBERALIZATION AND REPRESSION

Toward reform and renewal: The Thirteenth Party Congress

The Thirteenth Party Congress met from 25 October to 1 November. As expected, two items dominated the agenda: leadership changes and Zhao Ziyang's reform blueprint. In both of these areas, the Congress appeared to represent a victory for the reformers.[245]

Fully half of the members of the old Politburo, ten out of twenty, announced their retirement at the Congress. Heading the list, unexpectedly, was Deng Xiaoping himself; the others were Chen Yun, Li Xiannian, Peng Zhen, Hu Qiaomu, Wang Zhen, Xi Zhongxun, Yu Qiuli, Yang Dezhi, and Fang Yi.[246] Among the Party's top leaders, only four Politburo members remained from the twenty elected at the Twelfth Party Congress in 1982: Yang Shangkun, Wan Li, Zhao Ziyang, and – somewhat surprisingly – Hu Yaobang, who easily gained reelection despite his recent disgrace. Yang Shangkun, at eighty, was by far the oldest member of the new Politburo; no one else was above the age of seventy-three.[247]

The new Politburo Standing Committee, headed by general secretary (no longer "acting") Zhao Ziyang, included Hu Qili, Li Peng, Qiao Shi, and Yao Yilin. Politburo newcomers included CCP Organization Department Director Song Ping (seventy), Shanghai Mayor Jiang Zemin (sixty-one), Beijing municipal Party secretary Li Ximing (sixty-one), Tianjin Mayor Li Ruihuan (fifty-three), and State Commissioner for Economic Restructuring Li Tieying

242 XH, 28 August 1987, in SWB/FE 8661 (1 September 1987).
243 SWB/FE 8676 (18 September 1987). The seven named included six elderly veterans (Chen Yun, Li Xiannian, Hu Qiaomu, Peng Zhen, Xi Zhongxun, and Fang Yi), as well as one relative newcomer to the Politburo, Ni Zhifu.
244 SWB/FE 8684 (28 September 1987).
245 The Thirteenth Congress is analyzed in Schram, "China after the 13th congress"; Saich, "The thirteenth congress. . . ."; Oksenberg, "China's 13th. . . ."; and I&S 23.12 (December 1987), 12–99.
246 Although both Peng Zhen and Hu Qili had previously indicated that Deng Xiaoping would not step down at the Thirteenth Congress, Deng's last-minute decision to retire was rumored to be part of a quid pro quo arranged at the insistence of Chen Yun, who reportedly refused to resign from the Standing Committee unless Deng joined him. See Saich, "The thirteenth congress . . .," 204.
247 Yang, a longtime Deng Xiaoping associate, was reportedly retained as the result of an agreement between Deng and Chen Yun that would permit both leaders to retire while still giving China's old-timers one set of eyes and ears on the Politburo.

(fifty-one). Former alternate Qin Jiwei (seventy-two) was now elevated to full Politburo membership, thereby becoming the lone career military figure on the new ruling body.[248] Arguably the most significant of all the Politburo selections, however, was the one that wasn't made – that is, Deng Liqun.

Most of the personnel changes made at the Thirteenth Congress had been agreed to in advance by Party leaders. Deng Liqun's nonselection came as a surprise, however. His exclusion was the result of new election procedures introduced at the Thirteenth Congress, reportedly at Zhao Ziyang's behest. To ensure a modicum of democratic competition, the new rules required that there be ten more nominees for the CC than the actual number of seats to be filled; the ten candidates receiving the least support in the first round of voting (which was to be conducted by secret ballot) would be dropped and would have their names added to a list of nominees for alternate CC membership. A second ballot would then be taken, and the sixteen lowest vote getters in this latter round would be dropped altogether.[249]

When this system was used for the first time at the Thirteenth Congress, the candidate who reportedly received the lowest number of votes in the first round of balloting was none other than Deng Liqun. Deng's electoral rebuff was doubly embarrassing insofar as the seventy-two-year-old firebrand had previously been tabbed by Party leaders (reportedly after some heavy arm twisting by Chen Yun) to replace the retiring Hu Qiaomu on the Politburo. After having been flatly rejected for CC election on the first ballot, however, Deng Liqun apparently chose to avoid the possibility of further humiliation; he now withdrew his name from the second ballot, thereby forfeiting his eligibility for selection to the Politburo.[250] In the wake of this rebuff, Chen Yun reportedly lobbied hard to have Deng Liqun's name added to the ballot for election to the SC of the CAC. Once again Deng failed to gain peer acceptance, however, as he reportedly received less than half of the votes cast by members of the CAC. Utterly rejected, Deng's humiliation at the Thirteenth Party Congress must have come as sweet revenge for Hu Yaobang, who, despite his recent fall from grace, received sufficient delegate support to be handily reelected to both the CC and its Politburo.[251]

As a result of revamped selection procedures adopted at the Thirteenth Congress, the new CC was considerably smaller, younger, and better-educated than its predecessor. Its size was reduced from 385 full and alternate members

248 As a result of these changes, the average age of Politburo members declined from seventy to sixty-four.

249 This procedure is described in Oksenberg, "China's 13th...."; see also Wilson and Ji, "Leadership by lines'...," 36.

250 Schram, "China after the 13th ...," 184; Oksenberg, "China's 13th ...," 16. Since the Politburo was a subcommittee of the CC, Politburo members had to be selected from among CC members.

251 Hu Yaobang's long-disgraced predecessor, Hua Guofeng, also received strong delegate support in the CC elections at the Thirteenth Congress.

to 285, a drop of more than 25 percent. Forty-two percent of the CC members and alternates were first-timers, and more than 70 percent were college trained; fifty-seven members were employed in high-technology fields. Only 20 percent of the members were over the age of sixty-one; almost half were fifty-five years of age or younger. Significantly, although military representation on the new Politburo remained low, the picture was somewhat more ambiguous on the full CC, where almost 20 percent of the members were PLA officers.[252]

Even more ambiguous was the relationship between the Party and the army. Prior to the Thirteenth Congress, Deng Xiaoping had made it clear that he wanted to resign from his post as chairman of the Party's powerful MAC, and that he wished to have Zhao Ziyang installed as his successor. PLA leaders were apparently unmoved by Deng's appeal, for they refused to agree to Zhao's selection; consequently, Deng was forced to retain the MAC chairmanship, the only Party post he did not relinquish at the Congress.[253] In deference to Deng's wishes, senior military leaders did consent to name Zhao as first vice-chairman of the MAC; at the same time, however, they insisted on installing Yang Shangkun as "permanent" vice-chairman and Yang's younger half-brother, Yang Baibing, as chief of the PLA's general political department. Through such arrangements, China's conservative senior military leaders hoped to ensure against the possibility of a "hostile takeover" of the MAC in the event of Deng Xiaoping's early death or disability.[254]

Yet another important safeguard against a possible hostile takeover was put into place at the Thirteenth Congress, though it went unreported for almost two years. In response to the expressed concerns of certain old comrades, voiced at the time of Hu Yaobang's ouster, over possible future recurrences of reckless Party leadership, it was now stipulated that henceforth the PSC would consult with Deng Xiaoping on all important political matters, and with Chen Yun on all important economic matters, before making any major decisions. In this way, China's outgoing elder statesmen would retain effective veto power over vital policy initiatives even after retiring from office. The irony of such an arrangement was considerable: In order to help effect a smooth transition to a more highly developed structure of formal, institutionalized political power, Chinas leaders were opening a back door to the reassertion of informal, highly personalized authority. It was, of course, precisely this arrangement that enabled China's old guard to reassert its policy-making prerogatives during the Tiananmen crisis of April–June 1989.[255]

252 *I&S* 23.12 (December 1987), 95ff.
253 Deng also retained his concurrent chairmanship of the governmental MAC.
254 In this respect, as with regard to his continued presence on the Party Politburo, Yang Shangkun's designated role on the MAC was to represent the interests of CAC old-timers.
255 The existence of such an arrangement, which had been anticipated by "Central document No. 1, 1987," was first confirmed in November 1987 in a speech by Zhao Ziyang to a plenary session of

Structural reform in the primary stage of socialism

If leadership change was one of the big stories of the Thirteenth Congress, a potentially even bigger story was the unveiling of Zhao Ziyang's long-awaited blueprint for structural reform. There were a number of significant doctrinal departures in Zhao's report to the Congress. These included a new basic Party line, identified as "one center and two basic points," and a novel, neo-Marxist ideological rationale for undertaking bold economic experiments, the theory of the "primary stage of socialism" (*shehuizhuyi de chuji jieduan*).[256]

"One center and two basic points"

As spelled out in Zhao's report, economic development was henceforth to be considered the "central task" of the present era, to be pursued by grasping simultaneously two "basic points": adherence to the four cardinal principles and persistence in the policy of reform and opening up to the outside world. What made this rather stylized formulation noteworthy was its explicit subordination of the four cardinal principles to the strategic requirements of economic development. "Whatever is conducive to the growth [of the productive forces]," said Zhao, "is in keeping with the fundamental interests of the people and is therefore needed by socialism and allowed to exist." Conversely, Zhao continued, "whatever is detrimental to this growth goes against scientific socialism and is therefore not allowed to exist."[257]

"The primary stage of socialism"

If Zhao's "whatever works" ethos did not explicitly give Chinese reformers *carte blanche* to try out anything they thought might spur economic growth and call it "socialism," then it certainly came very close. In support of this pragmatic ethos, Zhao invoked China's developmental backwardness. Harking back to the New Democratic era of the early 1950s, Zhao stated that "because our socialism has emerged from the womb of a semi-colonial, semi-feudal society, with the productive forces lagging far behind those of the developed capitalist countries, we are destined to go through a very long primary stage." In this

---

the CC. In the speech, Zhao said: "Comrade Xiaoping still has the power to convene our standing committees whenever he feels that it is necessary. When we have any major problems it is still to him that we should turn to seek instruction" (*ZM* 122 [December 1987], in *ICM*, January 1988, 9). The arrangement was publicly revealed in Zhao Ziyang's fateful meeting with Mikhail Gorbachev on 16 May 1989 (see the section "Waging Moral Warfare: Gorbachev, the Media, and the Hunger Strike"). Additional details concerning the arrangement were subsequently published in *ZM* 121 (1 November 1990).

256 Zhao's report appears in *BR* 30.45 (9–15 November 1987), I–XXVII.

257 Ibid., XXVI. After the Congress, Zhao Ziyang combined the two whatevers of this formulation into one single, complex whatever, thereby avoiding invidious comparison with the two whatevers promulgated by former Party Chairman Hua Guofeng. See *CNA* 1354 (15 February 1988), 4.

stage, said Zhao, China must use whatever means are available to catch up with the advanced capitalist countries. It would be "naive and Utopian," he argued, to believe that China could skip over this primary stage and proceed directly to mature socialism; indeed, such a Utopian belief comprised "the major cognitive root of Leftist mistakes."[258]

In the realm of economic strategy, Zhao's report went well beyond the party's cautious October 1984 "bigger birdcage" reform proposals, calling now for substantially stepped-up use of the free-market mechanism and for rapid expansion of the collective and privately owned sectors of the economy.[259] Under the slogan "The state regulates the market; the market guides the enterprise," Zhao urged the creation of private markets for "essential factors . . . such as funds, labor services, technology, information, and real estate." In another break from Marxist tradition, Zhao further indicated that "in the future, buyers of bonds will earn interest, and shareholders dividends; enterprise managers will receive additional income to compensate for bearing risks." New price reforms were also called for, to be introduced gradually and in conjunction with rising incomes, "so that actual living standards do not decline." The report further recommended the introduction of "new types of institutions for commodity circulation, foreign trade and banking, as well as networks of [autonomous] agencies to provide technology, information, and service." In an attempt to preempt conservative criticism that such radical economic innovations smacked strongly of capitalism, Zhao tersely asserted that the measures called for in his report "are not peculiar to capitalism."[260]

Political reform: Toward "neoauthoritarianism"

Turning next to the realm of politics, Zhao called political reform an "urgent matter," noting that the CC "believes it is high time to put reform of the political structure on the agenda for the whole party." Otherwise, he asserted, economic reform would be doomed to failure. Henceforth, the two were to be considered inseparable.

258 BR 30.45 (9–16 November 1987), III–IV. The term "primary stage of socialism" was first used in the CCP's 1981 Resolution on CPC history (1949–1981), 74. Su Shaozhi is widely credited with having popularized the term in 1986. Stuart Schram ("China after the 13th . . . ," 177–8) states that the term's immediate antecedent, "undeveloped socialism" (bufada de shehuizhuyi), was first coined in 1979; however, the present author recalls hearing the latter term used in discussions with faculty members from the Beida department of politics and law as early as September 1978.

259 In an interview on 29 October, Zhao predicted that within two or three years only 30 percent of China's economy would be subject to central planning (The Guardian, 30 October 1987, cited in Saich, "The thirteenth congress . . . ," 205).

260 BR 30.45 (9–16 November 1987), XI–XIV. Despite the overall progressive thrust of his report, Zhao did make some notable compromises with Party conservatives. For example, he backed away from advocating rapid price reform, and he upheld the vital importance of grain production, two major concerns of Chen Yun since 1985 (ibid., IX).

Zhao's specific proposals for political reform were more skeletal than substantive. Reiterating a basic theme initially raised in August 1980 by Deng Xiaoping and subsequently elaborated in 1986 by Yan Jiaqi, *inter alia*, Zhao argued that China's feudal heritage had created severe problems of overconcentrated power, bureaucratism, and feudalization of the political structure. To remedy these defects, Zhao called for reform in seven broad areas: (1) separating Party and government; (2) delegating state power and authority to lower levels; (3) reforming government bureaucracy; (4) reforming the personnel (cadre) system; (5) establishing a system of political dialogue and consultation between the Party and the people; (6) enhancing the supervisory roles of representative assemblies and mass organizations; and (7) strengthening the socialist legal system.[261]

Although few concrete measures for implementing reforms in these seven areas were elaborated in Zhao's report, some potentially far-reaching structural changes were suggested. For example, in proposing the gradual elimination of "party groups" (*dangzu*) in governmental organs at all levels, Zhao clearly sought to neutralize a major obstacle blocking the reformers' key goal of separating Party from government. In similar fashion, Zhao's recommendation that those CCP organs responsible for enforcing Party discipline (the CDICs) should no longer exercise exclusive jurisdiction over breaches of law by Party members represented a major departure from existing policy, insofar as it clearly implied that henceforth Party members ought not to be routinely shielded from criminal prosecution for their misdeeds.[262]

New also was Zhao Ziyang's call for a major overhaul of China's Leninist–Stalinist personnel system, the *nomenklatura*, and its replacement by a civil service system of impersonal, professionalized cadre recruitment and evaluation. Although campaigns to eliminate excessive bureaucratism had been frequent occurrences in China under both Mao and Deng, never before had a top Chinese leader called for such broad, sweeping civil service reform. If implemented, Zhao's proposal could have spelled the end of the CCP's traditional monopoly of control over the government's personnel staffing and review procedures.[263]

In a section of his report detailing suggestions for improving the quality of "mutual consultation and dialogue" between the government and the people, Zhao made yet another noteworthy departure from China's established political tradition. He implicitly rejected the conventional notion of "unified public opinion" under socialism, arguing that the government should be concerned with listening to and reflecting the divergent opinions and interests of its

---

261 Ibid., XV–XXI.   262 Ibid., XVI.
263 See John P. Burns, "Chinese civil service reform: The 13th party congress proposals," *CQ* 120 (December 1989), 739–70.

citizens. "Different groups of people may have different interests and views," he said; "they too need opportunities and channels for the exchange of ideas."[264]

In each of these respects, Zhao Ziyang's report broke significant new ground, albeit only in preliminary fashion and only on paper. Painfully short on programmatic details, the report nonetheless offered some tantalizing glimpses into the political philosophy and strategy of Deng Xiaoping's newly designated successor. Perhaps most important, the report revealed Zhao to be an advocate not of Western-style liberalism but of Chinese "neoauthoritarianism," a doctrine that stressed the need for strong, centralized technocratic leadership throughout the "primary stage of socialism." Insofar as modernization and structural reform were inherently turbulent and stressful processes, Zhao argued, there were inevitably "many factors making for instability." For this reason, he averred, the transition to democracy had to be undertaken "step by step in an orderly way." Explicitly rejecting bourgeois democracy – with its separation of powers, multiparty competition, and freedom of political expression – as unsuited to China's current conditions, Zhao invoked the memory of Cultural Revolution chaos (and, by implicit extension, the more recent memory of student turmoil) to bolster his argument for limiting popular political participation and free expression. "We shall never again," he warned, "allow the kind of 'great democracy' that undermines state law and social stability." In lieu of competitive political parties and elections, Zhao proposed to further refine and perfect the Party's existing institutions and mechanisms of "democratic consultation and mutual supervision."[265]

Although Zhao's composite vision for China's political development thus had a decidedly illiberal edge to it, it represented a significant break with the past. Falling far short of being a blueprint for bourgeois democratization, it nonetheless offered the first broad, tentative sketches of an emergent nontotalitarian Chinese political future, one that contained at least the seeds, if not yet the sprouts, of incipient pluralism. Viewed in this light, that is, as a transitional neoauthoritarian manifesto, Zhao Ziyang's report to the Thirteenth Party Congress was a most important – if not an obviously revolutionary – document.[266]

---

264 *BR* 30.45 (9–16 November), XIX. Zhao had made a similar appeal on the eve of the Thirteenth Congress, arguing that "Socialist society is not a monolith.... [S]pecial interests should not be overlooked. Conflicting interests should be reconciled." See *BR* 30.50 (14–20 December 1987), 16.

265 *BR* 30.45 (9–15 November 1987), VI, XV.

266 For elaboration of the concept of neoauthoritarianism, see note 4 and the sections "Political Reform: Toward 'Neoauthoritarianism'" and "Zhao's Neoauthoritarian Counteroffensive."

Consolidating the gains

In the aftermath of the October 1987 Party Congress, Zhao moved to consolidate his political gains. He first moved to reassert control over the Party's propaganda apparatus. Commenting that he "never read" the CC's principal ideological organ, *Red Flag (Hongqi)*, Zhao indicated his intention to disband the journal, which had long been a thorn in the side of Party reformers.[267] Alarmed, a group of old-timers from the CAC, led by Bo Yibo, along with the Party's propaganda chief, Wang Renzhi, reportedly requested that the journal be placed on probation rather than shut down. Undeterred, Zhao initiated a shakeup in the Party's propaganda apparatus. In December 1987, *Red Flag's* editor and deputy editor were quietly retired, as was the conservative deputy director of the CC propaganda department. A month later, propaganda chief Wang Renzhi was also squeezed out. In May 1988, it was officially announced that *Red Flag* would cease publication, to be replaced by a new journal with a significantly altered title: *Seeking Truth (Qiushi)*.[268]

Meanwhile, it was decided that the traditional ceremonial portraits of Marx, Engels, Lenin, and Stalin would no longer grace Tiananmen Square after the PRC's fortieth anniversary celebration of October 1989. As if for emphasis, two oversized statues of Mao Zedong were quietly hauled away from the Beida campus in the dark of night, following at least one unsuccessful attempt at on-the-spot demolition.

With the Party's pragmatic reform wing seemingly in control, a mood of elation spread among China's intellectuals. In November 1987, a symposium was convened in Beijing to discuss the outcome of the Thirteenth Party Congress. At the meeting, a number of prominent Chinese political scientists expressed their deep satisfaction with the results of the Congress:

> [Zhao Ziyang's] report directly or indirectly contains all the proposals we have advocated.[269]

> The theory [of] the primary stage of socialism is a great breakthrough.... Stepping off the path is not running away from the road;

267 The editors of *Red Flag* had been critical of Hu Yaobang and Zhao Ziyang's reform policies at the time of the 1983 anti-spiritual pollution campaign. Hu had reciprocated their dislike, claiming at one point that he found the magazine "boring." See *WHB* (Hong Kong), 24 December 1987; *CNA* 1351 (1 January 1988), 4.

268 These developments are documented in *I&S* 24.2 (February 1988), 1; *WHB* (Hong Kong), 28 April 1988; *RMRB*, 2 May 1988, 3; *CNA* 1360 (15 May 1988), 4; *Qiushi* (hereafter, *QS*) 1 (1 July 1988), 1, in JPRS Report: China (hereafter, JPRS) CAR-88-043 (4 August 1988). The new journal was placed under the jurisdiction of the Central Party School, rather than the CC's propaganda department, as before, thereby implicitly downgrading its status. For further analysis see Lowell Dittmer, "China in 1988: The dilemma of continuing reform," *AS* 29. 1 (January 1989), 13–15.

269 Tan Jian (research department chairman, CASS Institute of Political Science), in *WHB* (Hong Kong), 7–8 November 1987; trans. in *ICM*, January 1988, 2.

differing with those at the top is not rebellion; esteeming things foreign is not toadying to alien ways.[270]

This session of the party congress produced great results.... [It] went far beyond what was expected.... For the first time [it] elevated reform to the position of a major societal activity under socialism.[271]

The most wonderful accomplishment of this session ... was holding elections in which the number of candidates exceeded the number of positions.[272]

Not everyone shared the enthusiasm of these reform-oriented political scientists, however; indeed, some liberal critics of the regime were openly skeptical. Fang Lizhi, for example, reminded a Hong Kong interviewer that although Zhao Ziyang's report "was very moving to listen to," in his own time "Mao Zedong made speeches that were even better to listen to than this one. It's not enough just to read the speeches.... You also have to keep your eye on the concrete indicators."[273]

Signs of stress: The economy overheats

Not long after the Thirteenth Congress adjourned, the concrete indicators began to go sour. As during the previous reform-induced growth spurt of 1984–5, it was Chinas overheated, unbalanced economy that produced the early warning signs. Freed from some but not all of its traditional central planning constraints, the Chinese economy began to lurch out of control toward the end of 1987. The main problems were familiar enough: spiraling wage–price inflation, a runaway money supply, surging consumer demand, overinvestment in capital construction, rampant commercial speculation, and official profiteering. In a rather gloomy 1988 New Year's economic message, the government broke the bad news:

Inflation has become a problem.... People worry that unless price rises are checked, the benefit from the reform will be cancelled out.... Price rises point to economic instability, resulting mainly from excessive demand. Inordinate investment in capital construction, consumption outstripping production, and excessive money supply have remained uncorrected for a number of years....

Many enterprises have failed to comply with the state's rule that enterprises should spend 60 percent of their operating funds on production ... and have instead spent most of the money on welfare and bonuses, resulting in a further expansion of consumption funds.

---

270 Yu Haocheng (vice-chairman, Chinese Political Science Association), in ibid.
271 Gao Fang (professor of international politics, Beida), in ibid.
272 Ma Peiwen (chairman, Chinese Political Science Association), in ibid.
273 *BX* 155 (1 November 1987).

> Taking advantage of relaxed controls, some enterprises raised prices without authorization. Some . . . joined lawless retailers in speculation to disrupt the market and harm the consumers' interests.[274]

With many enterprises granting unauthorized wage and bonus increases to workers, large quantities of money were pumped into an already overheated economy. As consumer demand rose, output and prices also soared for certain luxury goods, such as automatic washing machines, color TVs, stereo sets, and refrigerators. By contrast, output of vital capital goods for the national economy remained relatively static.[275]

Government statistics confirmed the worsening situation of economic imbalance. In the winter of 1987–8, the money supply grew at twice the rate of economic output. Food prices on urban markets, which had increased more than 10 percent in 1987, continued their upward march: In the first quarter of 1988, prices for nonstaple foods rose by 24.2 percent, and fresh vegetable prices soared 48.7 percent. To deal with surging demand (and surging prices), the government reintroduced rationing for pork, eggs, and sugar.[276]

For the first time since the reforms began, there was a real drop in the purchasing power of substantial numbers of urban wage earners. In a 1987 survey of more than 2,300 residents in thirty-three Chinese cities, more than two-thirds indicated that their real income was falling. Rising prices were the number one source of worry for more than 70 percent of those sampled.[277] Reflecting such concerns, early in 1988 *Xinhua* reported that a married couple, each earning an average wage of 70–80 yuan per month, "cannot afford to raise a child in [Beijing]." Throughout the winter and early spring of 1988, a swelling flow of letters to the editors of China's major newspapers testified to the painful effects of inflation.

Searching for a viable economic strategy: The Seventh NPC

Against this background of declining urban economic health, the Seventh NPC convened in late March. The meeting was dominated by reformers of

274 *BR* 31.1 (4–10 January 1989), 4.
275 In Guangzhou municipality, it was reported that the purchasing power of urban residents rose 55.4 percent in the first quarter of 1988 compared to the same quarter in 1987. The highest spending growth was in the areas of appliance purchases and "treating friends to meals" (*Nanfang ribao*, 3 May 1988, in *ICM*, July 1988, 21). In the electronics industry, over 70 percent of total national output in the early winter of 1987–88 was accounted for by luxury goods such as television sets, radios, and stereos (*ICM*, January 1988, 26).
276 *WHB* (Hong Kong), 5 June 1988; *BR* 31.1 (4–10 January 1988), 4. The problem of rising prices is discussed in *XH*, 12, 14 January and 1 February 1988, in *ICM*, March 1988, 12–18; see also *JSND*, March 1988, 44–6.
277 *BR* 31,17 (12–18 September 1988), 29; *WHB* (Hong Kong), 4 September 1988; also John P. Burns, "China's governance: Political reform in a turbulent environment," *CQ* 119 (September 1989), 489.

various stripes. The Party's conservative wing, dealt a major blow at the Thirteenth Congress, was little in evidence, save for some largely ceremonial appointments and functions. Indeed, the demographic composition of the NPC suggested the extent of the third echelon's dramatic ascent to political maturity: More than 70 percent of the almost 3,000 delegates were first-timers; the average age of all delegates was only fifty-two; 56 percent had received postsecondary education. Generational change was equally striking on the NPC Standing Committee, where 64 percent of the 135 ordinary members had been elected for the first time. Only at the very top of the NPC hierarchy was there substantial leadership continuity, as eleven of the nineteen previous SC vice-chairmen were reelected. At the apex of the organization stood the newly elected NPC SC chairman, Wan Li. The choice of Wan, an ally of Zhao Ziyang, to replace the retiring Peng Zhen augured the likely development of a more open and democratic NPC work style.[278]

The delegates to the Seventh NPC did, in fact, display a considerably stronger inclination toward independence, spontaneity, and critical scrutiny of the government than their predecessors. In a secret ballot to elect a successor to retiring PRC President Li Xiannian, Deng Xiaoping's hand-picked candidate, Yang Shangkun, received an unprecedented 124 "no" votes and an additional 34 abstentions. In the contest for vice-president, there were even more nay-sayers, as the party leadership's choice, conservative Wang Zhen, received 212 negative votes and 77 abstentions – more than 10 percent of the total ballots cast.[279]

In addition to showing signs of incipient independence in the election of state leaders, NPC delegates engaged in a good deal of lively debate on government policies. Delegates held numerous small-group meetings, where they openly protested various social ills such as inflation, low pay for teachers, inequitable distribution of benefits from the coastal development strategy, and the forcible imposition of central policies in minority nationality areas such as Tibet.[280]

278 For useful accounts of the NPC proceedings, see *CNA* 1360 (15 May 1988), 1–10; *FEER*, 21 April 1988, 12–13; and Dittmer, "China in 1988 . . . ," 16–18.

279 The most frequent dissenting votes at the NPC were reportedly cast by delegates from Hong Kong, Macao, and China's coastal cities and provinces. One noncandidate for office, Hu Yaobang, received twenty-six write-in votes for the PRC presidency and twenty-three more for the vice-presidency. Aside from Wang Zhen, the only other leaders to draw more than a 10 percent negative vote at the Seventh NPC were SC candidate Chen Muhua, a female, who had unsuccessfully sought a Politburo seat at the Thirteenth Party Congress, and an eighty-nine-year-old man whom some delegates thought was too old to serve in an official capacity (*CNA* 1360 [15 May 1988], 3–4).

280 An opinion poll conducted among several hundred NPC delegates at the conclusion of the March 1988 NPC meeting revealed that a large number of people's deputies took seriously the notions of democratic "supervision" and "consultation" which had been the catchwords of Zhao Ziyang's neoauthoritarian proposals for democratic reform at the Thirteenth Party Congress. See Shi Tianjian, "Role culture and

Although the Seventh NPC thus displayed a new degree of openness and a new diversity of opinions, arguably its most critical function was to serve as a sounding board for the government's emerging strategy for the next stage of economic reform. Generally speaking, two competing approaches were advocated by policymakers: speed and caution. Zhao Ziyang favored the former; newly installed premier Li Peng preferred the latter.[281]

On the eve of the NPC, Zhao had outlined a bold, optimistic plan for further structural reform. At the Second Plenum of the Thirteenth CC meeting in mid-March, he spelled out his three main concerns: to further emancipate thinking, to deepen reform, and to stabilize the economy. Central to Zhao's plan was the further extension of decentralized responsibility systems in state-owned industrial enterprises, breaking once and for all the industrial workers' iron rice bowl and eliminating the common pot of collective benefits for enterprise cadres and staff personnel. Zhao also stressed the need gradually to enlarge the scope of price reforms and to expand further the coastal development strategy in order to give preferential incentives to export-oriented areas and enterprises that could succeed in attracting foreign investment and technology.[282]

The priorities outlined in Zhao's plan stood in subtle, if marked, contrast to Li Peng's priorities, adumbrated earlier in the year. Where Zhao stressed emancipating the mind, Li stressed cultivating socialist ethics; where Zhao called for a deepening of reforms to be followed by efforts to stabilize the economy, Li called for stability first, then – and only then – deepened reform. The word order was crucial, since the term "stabilize the economy" had become a euphemism for limiting the scope and pace of basic structural reforms.[283]

Li Peng's government work report to the Seventh NPC represented an effort to downplay differences within the leadership. It was a consensus-seeking document designed to minimize conflict and contention. Once again, however, Li's primary emphasis was on stabilization rather than emancipation, caution rather than boldness. Addressing himself to some of the key concerns of Party conservatives, Li stressed the need to increase grain production while simultaneously developing the country's basic industries and infrastructure – issues that were of perennial concern to central planners in command economies. On price reform, by contrast, the premier's report remained largely silent.[284]

political liberalism among deputies to the seventh National People's Congress, 1988" (paper presented at the annual meeting of the Association for Asian Studies, Washington, D.C., March 1989).

281 Li had been named acting premier by the NPC SC shortly after the Thirteenth Party Congress; his appointment was formally confirmed at the Seventh NPC.

282 Zhao's report to the Second Plenum is summarized in BR 31.13 (28 March–3 April 1988), 5–6. For Zhao's views on coastal development, see BR 31.5 (1–7 February 1988), 5.

283 Li's priorities are outlined in BR 31.2 (11–17 January 1988), 5.

284 Li's report appears in BR 31.17 (25 April–1 May 1988), 18–43; for an analysis, see I&S 24.6 (June 1988), 12–18.

In terms of new legislation, the most significant action taken at the Seventh NPC was final approval of a long-delayed law on enterprise reform. The new law, which had been bottled up for two years by the outgoing NPC SC chairman, Peng Zhen, had as its key provisions the separation of ownership from management (allowing state-owned enterprises greater autonomy, vis-à-vis their parent bodies, over management, contracts, and leasing arrangements) and the director responsibility system (giving enterprise managers legal authority to hire and fire workers, plan production, and allocate retained profits, free from interference by local Party secretaries). With the enterprise reform law enacted, the PRC's long-dormant bankruptcy law, approved in December 1986 but never implemented for lack of enterprise reform legislation, was now scheduled to take effect in three months. The bankruptcy law provided both a legal basis and a procedural framework for shutting down chronically unprofitable state-owned enterprises.[285]

Toward urban socioeconomic meltdown: The crisis of 1988

In the months following adjournment of the Seventh NPC, China's urban malaise, which had been deepening quietly throughout the winter, took a turn for the worse. As on previous occasions, students were the bellwether. In early April, students at Beida began to demonstrate again, first on campus and then moving to Tiananmen Square; the targets this time were rising living costs, meager student stipends, and an inadequate government education budget. Significantly, their protest coincided with the twelfth anniversary of the "April 5th incident" at Tiananmen Square.[286] In the first six months of 1988, seventy-seven colleges and universities in twenty-five cities were involved in direct or indirect protest demonstrations; in response, the central government decided to set up public security headquarters on many university campuses.[287]

Another focal point of rising urban discontent was the government's plan to privatize housing and to decontrol rents for urban dwellers, moves that would have the effect of forcing families to pay a larger share of their household income for rent at a time when food prices were already rising at an

---

285 The Seventh NPC also enacted constitutional amendments guaranteeing the legal status of private enterprises and delegating additional powers over rural land contracting to local governments. The latter amendment, which established a legal basis for long-term leasing and transfer of use rights, gave Chinese farmers greater control over land-use decisions, thus encouraging them to invest in land improvement. Finally, the NPC approved creation of a new province-level administrative unit, Hainan Island, which was granted the autonomous commercial status of a special economic zone (SEZ).

286 *FEER*, 21 April 1988, 13; *I&S* 24.7 (July 1988), 9–11. Initially, Beida administrators pleaded unsuccessfully with the students to halt their demonstrations; the protest ended peacefully after student petitions were delivered by an NPC delegate to the presidium of the NPC and to the CPPCC.

287 *WHB* (Hong Kong), reported in *FEER*, 3 November 1988, 23; also *ICM*, January 1989, 15–16.

alarming rate. Fearful of a consumer backlash, government officials in many areas began to provide temporary cost-of-living subsidies to renters, in the form of redeemable "housing certificates," to offset the costs of decontrol. Like so many other stopgap measures of the 1980s, however, the housing subsidies, once they were in place, tended to become permanent.[288]

As inflation worries deepened, labor problems also began to increase. Following enactment of the enterprise reform law, managers of state enterprises became seriously concerned, in most cases for the first time, with the need to increase profits and cut production costs. Given enhanced authority over enterprise operations, factories now began to reduce wages and lay off redundant workers;[289] first to go were recently hired contract workers, who lacked lifetime job security.[290] In the spring and early summer of 1988, 400,000 workers were laid off from 700 factories in Shenyang;[291] by August, Chinese officials had almost doubled their previous estimate of the 1988 urban unemployment rate – from 2 to 3.5 percent, representing over 4 million people. At around the same time, many enterprises were reported to be unable (or unwilling) to pay taxes. According to government estimates, fully 50 percent of all state and collectively owned enterprises failed to pay their due taxes in the first half of 1988; among private entrepreneurs the figure was even higher, officially put at 80 percent.[292] Enterprise failures were also up sharply, particularly in small towns and villages, with the majority of affected firms being collective and cooperatively owned ventures.[293]

With rural and small-town unemployment up, labor migration increased, as did urban vagrancy; in Beijing alone, almost half a million *youmin* (drifters)

---

288 On the impact (real and anticipated) of housing reform, see *BR* 31.46 (14–20 November 1988), 14–18; CAM. 1358 (15 April 1988), 1–9; and *FEER*, 26 May 1988, 72–3. For analysis, see Tony Saich. "Urban Society in China" (paper presented to the international colloquium on China, Saarbrucken, 3–7 July 1990), 4–12.

289 There were, at this time, reportedly between 20 and 30 million redundant or nonessential workers in state-owned Chinese factories. See *WHB* (Hong Kong), 4 July 1988; and *CNA* 1370 (15 October 1988), 1.

290 State-owned enterprises had started hiring new workers on fixed-term contracts in 1986 as a means of breaking the iron rice bowl and thereby strengthening productivity incentives. However, by 1988 only about 4 percent of the work force in state-owned enterprises were employed under such contracts. The figure rose to 10 percent by 1989 (Saich, "Urban society . . . ," 16).

291 *SWB/FE* 0234 (19 August 1988). Tens of thousands of contract workers were also laid off in industrial reorganization drives in Hunan, Hubei, Shandong, and Shanghai, among other places (*ICM*, December 1988, 28–9).

292 *RMRB*, 20 August 1988.

293 *JJRB*, 6 January 1988, 2, in *ICM*, April 1988, 14. Despite enactment of a bankruptcy law, in the absence of a national system of unemployment benefits or adequate job retraining programs there was a clear reluctance on the part of government officials to force closure of state-owned enterprises, Consequently, in the first two years of the law's operation, only a handful of state enterprises formally declared bankruptcy. However, a number of chronically unprofitable firms were either consolidated or sold off to collective and individual buyers. See Dorothy Solinger, "Capitalist measures with Chinese characteristics," *POC* 38.1 (January–February 1989), 22–3.

lived an illegal, and for the most part squalid, existence; for the first time since 1949, beggary was now widely observed in many Chinese cities.²⁹⁴

With the threat of layoffs and/or bankruptcy now looming over chronically unprofitable firms (which reportedly accounted for almost 20 percent of China's 6,000 largest state-owned enterprises), there was a rise in the incidence of labor unrest; in all, forty-nine industrial work stoppages were recorded in the first half of 1988.²⁹⁵ Given the magnitude of the economic dislocations, however, the number of strikes was quite low; the most commonly cited reason was that Party control of the trade unions made organized protest difficult at best.²⁹⁶

The nation's crime rate also registered a sharp increase in 1988. After going up 21 percent in 1987, "serious crime" rose by 34.8 percent in the first half of 1988.²⁹⁷ Profiteering and corruption by Party members and cadres were said to be particularly rampant.²⁹⁸ With official misconduct reportedly at an all-time high, one Communist-sponsored newspaper acknowledged a precipitous decline in public confidence in the integrity of the Communist Party:

> The decay of party discipline, bribery and corruption, covering up for friends and relatives, deceiving and taking advantage of good cadres and party members, open violations of the law . . . being covered up through "special connections" of various kinds . . . – all these types of flagrant misconduct have produced such harmful social results and led to such a deterioration of the party's image that the damage done is inestimable.²⁹⁹

It may or may not have helped the Party's tarnished image when it was revealed, in the summer of 1988, that between 1983 and 1987 the CCP had

294 *BR* 31.35 (29 August–4 September 1988), 29; *GRRB*, 5 June 1988; *Fazhi ribao* (Legal System Daily), 5 August 1988; *LW* 32 (8 August 1988), 12–13; *CNA* 1371 (1 November 1988), 2; Saich, "Urban society . . . ," 20–3.

295 See *LW* 36 (5 September 1988), 18–19, in *FBIS*, 14 September 1988, 36; *CNA* 1359 (1 May 1988), 1–8; and *ICM*, December 1988, 28–33; and *South China Morning Post*, 3 September 1988, in *FBIS*, 6 September 1988.

296 Saich, "Urban society . . . ," 16–17. Andrew Walder notes that even during the massive Tiananmen protests of spring 1989, worker self-organization was extremely limited, and was more an effect of the upheaval than a cause. See Andrew G. Walder, "The political sociology of the Beijing upheaval of 1989," *POC* 38.5 (September–October 1989), 35. Walder further suggests that the economic problems posed by inflation were not serious enough, in isolation from other factors, to lead to significant political unrest among industrial workers. See his "Urban industrial workers" (paper presented to the conference "State and society in China: The consequences of reform," Claremont-McKenna College, 16–17 February 1990), 8.

297 According to Chinese government statistics, over 2 million people were prosecuted for various criminal offenses in China from 1983 to 1987, with the majority of these being economic crimes *I&S* 24.6 [June 1988], 30).

298 In 1986, the Supreme People's Court handled over 77,000 serious cases of economic crime; the majority of these cases involved cadres. Between 1982 and 1986, more than 27 percent of the 11,000 people investigated for committing economic crimes in Beijing municipality were Party members (*FEER*, 16 June 1988, 22).

299 *DGB*, 12 April 1988, in *ICM*, June 1988, 1.

expelled more than 150,000 members, mostly for corruption, with an additional 500,000 members receiving lesser punishment for assorted varieties of malfeasance.[300] Notwithstanding this internal housecleaning, the *People's Daily* in May 1988 conceded that official corruption still had not been punished severely enough. Many in China would have agreed, since only 97 of the more than 650,000 party members disciplined from 1983 to 1987 – a miniscule 0.01 percent of the total – were cadres at or above the provincial level. Those near the top clearly remained substantially immune from punishment.[301]

The CCP, which once had prided itself on the integrity, spirit, and devotion of its members, now suffered greatly diminished popular prestige. In one nationwide survey involving more than 600,000 Chinese workers, taken after three years of party rectification, only 7 percent of the respondents believed that there had been a "clear change for the better" in Party spirit. Among more than twenty occupations rank-ordered according to public image by 1,700 respondents in a 1988 survey, basic-level cadres, government cadres, and Party cadres all ranked in the bottom third, a notch below railroad workers and a notch above tax collectors. In a 1988 survey involving 2,000 educated rural youths in Gansu province, only 6.1 percent of the young people expressed any interest in joining the Party.[302]

Students were among the most pessimistic of all groups surveyed about the CCP. After the 1986 student demonstrations, 92 percent of graduate students and 62 percent of undergraduates interviewed in a survey commissioned by the Beijing municipal Party committee saw the root causes of student unrest to be corrupt Party work style and/or lack of democracy. Fewer than 10 percent of the undergraduates surveyed said they were "very confident" that Party members' work styles would improve within the next few years.[303]

---

300 *XH*, 11 August 1988, in *FBIS*, 11 August 1988, 18. Another 25,000 were expelled in 1988.
301 The data are presented in Rosen, "The Chinese Communist Party . . . ," 83.
302 Survey data cited in ibid., 21, 49, 53.
303 Ibid., 28–9. As public cynicism mounted, open defiance of Party authority also increased. In a widely publicized incident that occurred in the town of Shekou, near the Hong Kong border, a meeting of young workers organized in January 1988 by the local branch of the Communist Youth League was addressed by three veteran Party propaganda cadres. When one of the cadres finished his talk (in which he praised the virtues and successes of the Party's current line and policies), a young worker stood up and told the propagandist to "stop delivering empty sermons and speak about substantial questions." Referring to the propagandist's criticism of people who think only about "reaping profits" and "driving foreign cars," the young worker asked, "What's wrong with that? . . . What is illegal about making money in modern China?" When one of the cadres pointedly asked the young man for his name, members of the audience rallied around the worker, subjecting the cadre to verbal abuse for his intimidation tactics. Such open disrespect for the Party and its cadres had been virtually unknown in China before the "opening up" of the 1980s. This particular incident, known as the "Shekou storm," was talked about in newspaper editorials and letters-to-the-editor columns for months afterward. See *CNA* 1374 (15 December 1988), 2–4; and *FEER*, 27 October 1988, 41.

With public confidence in the Party, the government, and the economy sagging badly in the late spring and summer of 1988, a significant rise in anomic crimes of violence was recorded. In May, 130 people were injured in a soccer riot in Sichuan; most of the rioters were youths, half were peasants, and many were unemployed.[304] According to Chinese legal sources, cases of first-degree murder, assault with injury, gang violence, armed robbery, and even dynamiting had all dramatically increased. In one province, almost 300 enterprise managers were physically assaulted in the first six months of 1988 – mostly for reasons of personal revenge. Organized gangs operating along roads, highways, and railway lines in several areas reportedly hijacked dozens of buses and trains, robbing passengers and stealing cargo.[305]

The rising incidence of lawlessness triggered a backlash of social protest. In December 1987, more than 1,000 students from Beijing's University of International Business and Trade marched in protest over the murder of a student in a campus store; six months later, in what was said to be the most serious threat to public order since the student disturbances of December 1986, 2,000 Beida students gathered in Tiananmen Square in early June 1988 to demand action from the government following the murder of a student by a gang of local hoodlums. Some of the protesters put up posters criticizing the Party and government leaders; others called for mass demonstrations against corruption and in support of human rights.[306] In July, the governor of Guangdong province, Ye Xuanping, strongly condemned a rising tide of juvenile crime after vandals defiled the memorial stele of his father, Ye Jianying, at a cemetery for revolutionary heroes.[307]

In this situation of mounting social anxiety and unrest, a television documentary broadcast in China in the summer of 1988 provided a focal point for questioning the nation's fundamental goals and values. The documentary, "Heshang" ("River Elegy"), used the slow-moving, heavily silted waters of the Yellow River – long known as "China's Sorrow" – as a metaphor for the unbroken cultural continuity and conservatism of Chinese civilization. The image of a stagnant, meandering Yellow River, unwashed by the dynamic, vibrant blue waters of the oceanic littoral, neatly symbolized the traditional isolationism and xenophobia of the Middle Kingdom. Painting a grim picture

---

304 Agence France Presse (Hong Kong), 30 May 1988.

305 *ICM*, November 1988, 4; *WHB* (Hong Kong), 13 September 1988, 14; *CNA* 1371 (1 November 1988), 2–3. In some areas, things got so bad that foreign researchers were issued travel advisories by their work units warning them to avoid traveling on interior roads and highways because of the increasing threat of banditry.

306 *I&S* 24.1 (January 1988), 162; *RMRB*, 8 June 1988; *SWB/FE* 0172 (8 June 1988); *FEER*, 16 June 1988, 18, and 21 July 1988, 19–21. Six people were subsequently arrested and tried for the murder of the Beida student.

307 *DGB* (Hong Kong), 6 August 1988. For additional documentation on social unrest in 1987–8, see Burns, "China's governance . . ."; and Lowell Dittmer, "China in 1988," 12–28.

of the enervating long-term effects of China's insular traditions and atavistic values, the authors of "River Elegy" were openly and severely critical of the dogmatic chauvinism inherent in classical Confucianism and revolutionary Maoism alike; by the same token, they were lavish in their praise of modern Western institutions and values.[308]

The six-part documentary was initially aired over Beijing's Central Television Station in mid-June, with several other provinces and municipalities rebroadcasting the series in quick succession. The Beijing telecast evoked a storm of excitement, as the station reportedly received more than 1,000 letters requesting that the series be rerun. It was even reported that a number of PLA generals and their wives took videotape copies of "River Elegy" to Beidaihe for summer vacation viewing.

Within the Party apparatus, the response was less enthusiastic; Wang Zhen was said to be livid. An informal discussion meeting was held at the Beijing Central Television Station, at which a number of speakers criticized the series for being anti-Party and antisocialist and for ostensibly advocating "total Westernization." Others defended the series as forthright and honest. After initially wavering, the Party's central propaganda department issued a notification that no further showings of "River Elegy" would be permitted, either at home or abroad.[309]

Conflict at the summit: Beidaihe, summer 1988

As China's urban malaise worsened in the first half of 1988, a debate raged among reform-oriented economists and their high-level political patrons in Beijing. At issue was whether to place primary stress on enterprise reform, price decontrol, or privatization of the economy.[310] Although Zhao Ziyang had been an early advocate of price reform, the inflationary spiral of 1984–5 had apparently convinced him of the need to give priority to enterprise reform.

---

308 Accounts of the "River Elegy" controversy appear in FEER, 1 September 1988, 40–3; ICM, January 1989, 1–10; and JPRS CAR-89–004 (11 January 1989), 6. See also Woei Lien Chong, "Present worries of Chinese democrats: Notes on Fang Lizhi, Liu Binyan, and the film 'River elegy,'" CI 3.4 (Spring 1989), 1–20.

309 JSND 11 (November 1988), 62–3, in I&S 25.6 (June 1989), 29–30. It was subsequently reported that Hu Qili, the Politburo Standing Committee member in charge of ideological work, had solicited various opinions about "River Elegy" before deciding to ban it, delaying his decision just long enough to permit the complete series to be shown (ICM, January 1989, 2).

310 The enterprise reform school was led by Beida economics professor Li Yining, an advisor to Zhao Ziyang. The price reform school was led by CASS economist Wu Jinglian. A leading figure in the privatization school was Chen Yizi, former director of the State Council's Institute for Reform of the Economic Structure, a pro-Zhao Ziyang think tank. On the economic debates of 1988, see Robert C. Hsu, "Economics and economists in post-Mao China," AS 28.12 (December 1988), 1225–8; and Gang Zou, "Debates on China's economic situation and reform strategies" (paper presented to the annual meeting of she Association for Asian Studies, Washington, D.C., March 1989).

Deng Xiaoping, on the other hand, was a belated convert to the camp of the
price reformers, apparently becoming convinced in the spring of 1988 that
China could withstand the anticipated transitional shock of a "big bang" in
price deregulation. Dragging a reportedly reluctant Zhao Ziyang along with
him, Deng claimed at the end of May that "We now have the requirements to
risk comprehensive wage and price reforms."[311] At a June Politburo meeting,
Deng pushed through a proposal for accelerated deregulation of prices, and
Zhao Ziyang dutifully instructed the CC's economic reform think tank to
prepare plans for a multiyear program of wage and price reforms.[312] At around
the same time, retail prices in urban markets were deregulated for four types
of nonstaple foods: meat, sugar, eggs, and vegetables. In July, cigarettes and
alcoholic beverages were added to the list of deregulated commodities. With
each new step toward deregulation, real or only rumored, consumer anxiety
mounted and retail demand surged as heightened fears of inflation fueled the
beginning of a new urban spending spree.[313]

Against this background of renewed market volatility, China's Party leaders
congregated at Beidaihe for their annual summer meeting. Discussions began
on 20 July amid unconfirmed rumors of intense top-level disagreement over
economic strategy. Rumors of conflict between Zhao Ziyang, who favored
radical decentralization of economic authority and rapid structural reform of
state-owned enterprises, and Li Peng, who favored a more cautious policy of
gradual, balanced reform, slow growth, and centralized economic authority,
became so thick that several top Party leaders, including Hu Qili, Qiao Shi,
and Zhao Ziyang himself, went out of their way to deny them in meetings
with foreign visitors.

Persisting reports of elite conflict were matched by new rumors of imminent, sweeping price decontrol. Fueled by reports out of Beidaihe that Deng
Xiaoping remained committed to price reform, a fresh wave of panic buying
broke out in several cities at the end of July as nervous consumers rushed to
stockpile everything from blankets and sewing machines to color TV sets and
refrigerators. In Harbin municipality, the city's largest department store sold
over RMB 1.1 million yuan worth of electrical appliances in the month of
July, 200 times its monthly average. To pay for these purchases, consumers
drew down their savings. In one three-day period, from 25 to 27 July, Harbin's
residents withdrew more than RMB 12 million yuan from local banks.[314] A

311 DGB (Hong Kong), 26 July 1988, in ICM, September 1988, 26.
312 Zhao reportedly asked for three different plans to be studied, with three different timetables for price
   reform: three years, five years, and eight years. He subsequently combined elements of the three- and
   five-year plans into a four-year "preliminary price rationalization program." See WHB (Hong Kong),
   30 July and 1 August 1988; and DGB, 26 July 1988, in ICM, September 1988, 26–8.
313 Ibid.; also I&S 24.9 (September 1988), 1–4; FEER, 26 May and 4 August 1988.
314 PEER, 22 and 29 September 1988.

similar run occurred in Guangzhou, where panicky consumers emptied their bank accounts to buy whatever they could in anticipation of imminent price hikes. To stem the outpouring of savings, China's banks announced substantial hikes in interest rates on long-term deposits; but even at the new rates of 10 to 13 percent, bank interest was considerably lower than the current rate of inflation, which unofficially exceeded 20 percent in midsummer.[315]

Sensitive to the new signals of alarm emanating from the urban economy, Deng began to back away from his previous support for a big push in price reform. According to reports out of Hong Kong, the unprecedented urban buying spree and bank run of late July and early August served to convince China's senior leader of the need to tighten the nation's money supply and delay further price deregulation.[316]

With Deng suddenly changing his mind, Zhao Ziyang was left holding the bag of responsibility for China's mounting economic instability. Pressed by senior Party conservatives to clarify the nature and extent of his confidence in Zhao's economic leadership, Deng Xiaoping now distanced himself from the general secretary, visibly backing off from his previous unequivocal endorsement of Zhao. "I won't vouch for anyone," he said; "if the situation continues to deteriorate, let the general secretary be held responsible." Shaken by Deng's withdrawal of support, Zhao reportedly fought back, challenging the rationale for the conservatives' emphasis on slow growth and economic stability. Taking aim squarely at Li Peng, he challenged the premier: "You always stress tightening money [supplies]," he said. "Who will be responsible if production declines?" To this Li Peng responded, "There is nothing wrong with slowing down development. It is time to pour cold water on an overheated economy." With Deng now standing aloof, Zhao reportedly threatened to resign: "All of you say that I have failed to do my work well. You come and do it. I don't want to do it any more."[317]

Lost amid all the commotion and recrimination over price deregulation was a rather dramatic irony: The consumer panic that served to precipitate Deng's sudden decision to reverse his position on price reform was initially sparked by

315 A number of Chinese media reports about rising consumer complaints in this period are translated in *ICM*, October 1988, 11–14, and November 1988, 14–20.

316 According to these reports, Deng personally decided to abort price reform after reading two reports from Zhao's think tank on China's foreign debt and the reform experience in Eastern Europe, respectively (see Wilson and Ji, "Leadership by lines'...," 35). True or not, there were certainly a number of alarming economic signals available to Deng at the time. For example, in the first half of 1988, total supply had grown by 17.2 percent while aggregate demand grew by 31.4 percent; also, by midyear 1988, urban subsidies were 59 percent higher than the corresponding figure for the previous year, and bonuses for urban staff and workers had registered a 36 percent increase in the same period.

317 *ZM* 131 (1 September 1988); *I&S* 24.10 (October 1988), 1, The 1988 Beidaihe debates are chronicled in *JSND* 9 (September 1989), 16–19; *ICM*, September 1988, 24–9; and Dittmer, "China in 1988...." 21–2.

rumors emanating directly from top Party leaders themselves. By all accounts, the 1988 Beidaihe meetings were unusually well-publicized, being punctuated periodically by media interviews, policy briefings, and receptions for foreign visitors. Such unprecedented elite openness and accessibility – reflections of a new Chinese commitment to *glasnost* – provided much of the grist for the PRC's hyperexcitable rumor mill. In this respect it was the Party's own top leadership, including Deng Xiaoping himself, who arguably bear much of the responsibility for precipitating the consumer panic of 1988.[318]

Zhao descends; Li Peng rises

Having at least indirectly started the panic, Party leaders now moved to end it. After weeks of discord, the Politburo in mid-August passed favorably on a "tentative plan for price and wage reforms." The plan represented a tactical victory for Li Peng's "economic stabilization" line insofar as it effectively delayed implementation of new price reforms while vaguely upholding, at least in principle, the ultimate goal of further decontrol.[319]

Having lost the policy initiative to Li Peng, and having lost Deng's personal endorsement as well, Zhao quickly fell from grace. In an interview with a foreign visitor in early September, the general secretary acknowledged that he no longer played a major role in economic policymakings Asked how much time he spent each day handling his various duties, he responded: "I do not directly deal with economic affairs but concentrate my efforts on research and investigation so that I can discuss major policy issues with my colleagues at party meetings." With Zhao's economic star deeply descending, Li Peng's correspondingly rose. Primary responsibility for economic policymaking now shifted from the Party CC, where Zhao was in charge, to the State Council, where Premier Li and his top economic adviser, Vice-Premier Yao Yilin, were able to dominate discussions of economic strategy.[320]

318 On the spate of media rumors that circulated during the 1988 Beidaihe meetings, see *DGB* (Hong Kong), 14 August 1988, in *ICM*, October 1988, 26–7. The fact that Party leaders were responsible for stimulating the rumor mill suggests the intriguing possibility that perhaps the pro-"stability" faction deliberately planted some of the wilder and more unsettling rumors precisely in order to trigger an adverse public reaction to proposed price reforms.
319 It was subsequently reported that the CAC had been instrumental in securing Li Peng's victory at Beidaihe, backing the premier in his policy confrontation with Zhao Ziyang. See Wilson and Ji, "Leadership by 'lines'. . . ," 37.
320 *FEER*, 22 September 1988, 70–1. Despite having lost confidence in Zhao's economic policies, Deng did not completely abandon his former protégé, as he had Zhao's predecessor, Hu Yaobang. In political and diplomatic affairs Zhao continued to be highly visible, presiding over important Party meetings, attending to public ceremonies, and meeting foreign heads of state. On one occasion, Deng obliquely defended Zhao's economic thinking, venturing the opinion that China's inflation was due primarily not to price reform but to lax economic management. See *I&S* 24.9 (September 1988), 4. Still, the damage was done, and Zhao Ziyang would never recover his lost stature.

With Li Peng seizing the initiative, a joint work conference of the Politburo and the State Council was held in mid-September; there Zhao came under heavy fire for his economic policies and was forced to make a self-criticism in which he acknowledged partial responsibility for China's economic difficulties. A week later, the Third Plenum of the Thirteenth CC was convened. Once again Zhao faced criticism; reportedly it was only the intervention of Deng Xiaoping that saved him from being dismissed.[321] The major action taken at the plenum was a decision to freeze consumer prices for two years. This and other related measures to tighten up the economy were said to be necessary to reduce total social demand, curb excessive capital construction, and check runaway inflation.[322]

Throughout the autumn of 1988, Li Peng and Yao Yilin moved further away from Zhao's accelerated reform agenda, back toward restabilization and a partial recentralization of economic decision making. What had initially been presented as a temporary respite from economic overheating thus took on the characteristic of a more long-range readjustment, one that favored a reduction of market controls and a reassertion of at least some of the prerogatives of central planning.[323] In early December, price controls were reimposed in Beijing on thirty-six categories of previously decontrolled goods, from beef and eggs to shoes, towels, television sets, and washing machines; fines of up to 10,000 yuan were to be levied against violators.

When local and provincial leaders balked at giving back some of their recently gained economic autonomy, Deng Xiaoping pointedly reminded them of their dependent status: "Since we can delegate power, we can also take it back any time we like."[324] In the event, however, Deng's boast proved at least partially hollow. Long after the Third Plenum had adjourned, provincial and local governments continued to issue their own laws and regulations, collect their own taxes, and provide their own incentive packages to lure business and investment away from other regions, all in defiance of central authority and all further contributing to China's emerging macroeconomic incoherence. In the view of an increasing number of observers, inside and outside China alike, Beijing had, by the autumn of 1988, lost the ability

321 *Jingbao* (Hong Kong) [hereafter, *JB*] 11 (November 1988), 20–3, trans. in JPRS CAR-89–007 (19 January 1989), 10–11.
322 *RMRB*, 27 September and 1 October 1988; *CNA* 1370 (15 October 1988), 4. Despite Zhao's evident fall from grace, he presented the political report to the Third Plenum. The text appears in *BR* 31.46 (14–20 November 1988), I–VIII.
323 Li Peng and Yao Yilin were also reportedly cool toward Zhao Ziyang's coastal development strategy, though they did not immediately act to reverse existing policy in this area. Zhao continued to speak out on behalf of the coastal strategy throughout the autumn of 1988.
324 *WHB* (Hong Kong), 11 October 1988, 1; *CNA* 1371 (1 November 1988), 4.

to regulate and control a considerable amount of provincial and local-level economic activity.[325]

As part of the attempt to bring China's runaway economy back under control, a new get-tough policy toward cadre-centered speculation and profiteering was initiated in the fall of 1988. Put in charge of the anticorruption drive was Politburo SC member Qiao Shi.[326] Targeted for special attention in the new campaign was the phenomenon of "bureaucratic racketeering" (*guandao*), the practice of high-level cadres and *gaogan zidi* using their official connections to bestow commercial favors on private trading companies with which they (or their family members) were affiliated. In his report to the Third Plenum, Zhao Ziyang had made a special plea to attack this problem: "It is necessary to . . . severely punish 'bureaucratic racketeers.' All [private] companies . . . must sever their links with party and government organizations. . . . Otherwise, their licenses will be revoked."[327] To help put teeth into this exhortation, the State Council in October issued new regulations stipulating that retired cadres above the county level were forbidden either to set up or to accept employment in commercial enterprises.

More than 360,000 trading companies had been set up in China between 1986 and 1988; although the majority of these were small in size and modest in scale (e.g., the so-called briefcase companies), a few had vast dimensions and resources, including the "Big Four Companies," CITIC, Kang Hua, Everbright, and China Economic Development Corporation.[328] Among the senior staff of these giant corporations were many former ministers, vice-mayors, and Party secretaries; although nominally private, these companies all enjoyed high-level official patronage. As China's officially approved "windows to the world," they also enjoyed quasi-monopolistic access to foreign customers, markets, and hard currency reserves.[329]

---

325 *FEER*, 27 October 1988, 38–42, and 8 December 1988, 60–1; *NYT*, 11 December 1988. On the causes, consequences, and political implications of diminishing central control over fiscal levers and resource allocations, see Barry Naughton, "The decline of central control over investment in post-Mao China," in David M. Lampton, ed., *Policy implementation in post-Mao China*, 51–80; Susan L. Shirk, "'Playing to the provinces': Deng Xiaoping's political strategy of economic reform," *SICC* 23.3/4 (Autumn–Winter 1990), 227–58; Christine Wong, "Central–local relations in an era of fiscal decline" (paper presented at the annual convention of the Association for Asian Studies, New Orleans, April 1991); and Barry Naughton, "Macroeconomic Obstacles to reform in China" (paper presented at the Southern California China Colloquium, UCLA, November 1990).

326 Qiao, a specialist in Party organization and security affairs, was reportedly the swing vote in the five-man Politburo SC: Zhao Ziyang and Hu Qili formed the SC's liberal wing, whereas Li Peng and Yao Yilin took a more conservative line. Qiao Shi's views on the need to tighten Party discipline and combat profiteering are presented in *RMRB*, 29 October 1988, trans. in *ICM*, February 1989, 2–3.

327 *BR* 31.46 (14–20 November 1988), II.   328 Kang Hua reportedly had more than 170 subsidiaries.

329 See *FEER*, 3 November 1988, 23–5, and 17 November 1988, 90–2. On the high-level patronage networks that served to protect and nurture private companies, see Solinger, "Urban entrepreneurs and the state. . . ."

It was this system of official patronage and protected market access that gave rise to the epidemic of *guandao* that beset China in the late 1980s. As observed in the Party's new theoretical journal, *Seeking Truth, guandao* was an "ulcer" growing out of the "sick system" of official corruption:

> With the deepening of reforms, we have been trying to separate the party from the government, the functions of the government from those of the enterprise, and administrative power from managerial power. Those who use their official posts to obtain profits for their own ends... lose no time in taking advantage of the transition between the old and new systems. They truly feel that if they miss the opportunity while they still have power, it will be too late. To transform power into currency is the card trick [performed by] *guandao*.
>
> If our old system breeds and covers up the corruption of some officials, the emergence of *guandao* is the ulcer that grows out of this sick system. Unless *guandao* is eliminated, there will not be any peace in China....
>
> ... What is peddled in the *guandao* is the party spirit of the members of the communist party and the conscience of society's public servants. If such commerce is not abolished, what will depreciate is not only the [money] in the hands of ordinary people, but their confidence in and support of the ruling party and government.[330]

Although the new antiracketeering drive was nominally directed at all firms engaged in speculation, profiteering, and currency manipulation, it was generally the smaller, less well-connected companies that bore the brunt of the government's get-tough policy. Only one of the major trading corporations, Kang Hua, was directly affected by the crackdown of autumn 1988; the vast majority of firms that got caught were much smaller in scale.[331] Despite an announcement by the CDIC in November that 330,000 Party cadres had been charged with racketeering-related crimes since 1983, there was a widespread popular perception that the really big fish had, as usual, been allowed to slip away.[332] The evident selectivity of the Party's antiracketeering drive was to become a major focus of public anger when China's unhappy students took to the streets once again in the spring of 1989.

---

330 *QS* 8 (16 October 1988), 46–7, in JPRS CAR-89-001 (3 January 1989), 41–2. For additional media accounts of the effects of *guandao*, see *ICM*, February 1989, 3–6.

331 Because Deng Xiaoping's son, Deng Pufang, had close connections with Kang Hua, this case was closely watched as a possible bellwether of government intentions with respect to cleaning up racketeering among the *gaogan zidi*. Although Deng Pufang subsequently severed his connection with Kang Hua, he was never punished.

332 In those cases where criminal charges had been brought against party cadres, trials were frequently postponed or delayed indefinitely. Aware of this problem, the Supreme People's Court issued a notice on 3 November requiring all courts to enforce the law vis-à-vis cadre profiteers "in the strictest possible fashion" and to "bring all [pending] cases to trial." See *ICM*, January 1989, 29–30.

Zhao's neoauthoritarian counteroffensive

In the autumn of 1988–9, Zhao Ziyang's supporters, seeking to restore their champion's badly tarnished image and to reverse his slip from power, began openly to promote the theory of neoauthoritarianism. Spearheaded by economist Chen Yizi and other leading members of various reform-oriented think tanks, and backed behind the scenes by key Zhao Ziyang political advisers Bao Tong and Yan Jiaqi, the neoauthoritarians raised a number of general proposals. Arguing that market forces alone could provide the dynamism necessary to reform the Chinese economy successfully, they proposed a wholesale dismantling of the bureaucratic apparatus of the command economy and a privatization of state-owned industrial and commercial property. This put them squarely at odds with the more cautious and conservative stability faction of Li Peng and Yao Yilin, who continued to assert the need for unified political and economic command under the people's democratic dictatorship. The conservatives' gradual, incremental approach to reform was doomed to failure, averred the neoauthoritarians, because the persistence of powerful bureaucratic vested interests served to block fundamental structural change. To overcome this obstacle and to get China started down the road toward genuine market reform, a clear separation between politics and economics was necessary. To effect such a clean break with China's Maoist–Stalinist past, strong political leadership, à la Mikhail Gorbachev, was necessary. This was precisely the role the neoauthoritarians sought to carve out for their patron, Zhao Ziyang. For the sake of reform, they argued, "there must be sufficient authoritative power to remove the obstacles formed by forces such as the vested interests in the old system." This, in turn, "requires a strong centralization of power in the political sphere. . . . What neoauthoritarianism emphasizes is not the political *system* but a [political] *leader*."[333]

Throughout the late fall and winter of 1988–9, reform-oriented journals such as the *Guangming ribao* and the *World Economic Herald* published a number of articles promoting neoauthoritarian theories and concepts. The common denominator of these articles was the call for strong political leadership to effect a withdrawal of the instruments of proletarian dictatorship from the economic sphere.[334] In their new emphasis on the need for a powerful central leader to effect needed structural reforms, the neoauthoritarians began to diverge markedly from their liberal-democratic counterparts, including Fang Lizhi,

---

333 Wu Jiaxiang, cited in Ma, "The rise and fall of neo-authoritarianism . . . ," 13–14 (emphasis added). Chinese proponents of neoauthoritarianism frequently cited Samuel P. Huntington's influential 1965 book, *Political order in changing societies*, as a key source for their ideas on the need for strong political leadership during the early stages of modernization.
334 See Petracca and Xiong, "The concept of Chinese neo-authoritarianism . . . ," 1106–11; and Ma, "The rise and fall of neo-authoritarianism . . . ," 8–13.

Yu Haocheng, Su Shaozhi, and Liu Binyan, who, throughout this period, continued to stress the urgent necessity of democratic political reforms. And although both groups shared a deep concern over the implications of Zhao Ziyang's recent loss of stature vis-à-vis Li Peng, the evident political Bonapartism of the neoauthoritarians put them increasingly at odds with China's liberal democrats.[335]

The gathering storm: Winter 1988–9

In the face of the neoauthoritarians' attempt to reverse Zhao Ziyang's political decline, Party conservatives in the autumn of 1988 stepped up their campaign to oust the general secretary. In November, Chen Yun issued the first of "eight opinions" on the subject of Zhao Ziyang's leadership. Chen was particularly unhappy about the general secretary's lack of firmness in dealing with bourgeois ideology. Complaining, among other things, that under Zhao "almost all proletarian ideological bridgeheads have been occupied by bourgeois ideologies," Chen asserted that "it is time for us to counterattack."[336]

Chen's concerns could hardly have been assuaged when, the following month, at a conference of reform-oriented intellectuals jointly sponsored by the CCP propaganda department and CASS to commemorate the tenth anniversary of the historic Third Plenum of the Eleventh CC, Su Shaozhi gave a bold speech attacking the campaigns against spiritual pollution and bourgeois liberalization. With several members of the SC of the Politburo in attendance, Su called for a reevaluation of two prominent victims of the earlier campaigns, Wang Ruoshui and Yu Guangyuan. Although he did not actually name those responsible for persecuting Wang and Yu, Su tacitly pointed the finger of accusation at Hu Qiaomu as the individual most responsible for "appropriating Marxist theory" as his "private preserve."[337]

Visibly disturbed by the tone and content of Su's remarks, the Party's top propaganda officials, Hu Qili and Wang Renzhi (who, ironically, had helped organize the decennial conference), now sought to prevent publication of his speech; their efforts were foiled when Su's talk was printed on 26 December in the unofficial Shanghai newspaper *World Economic Herald*, whose publisher, Qin Benli, was an outspoken proponent of accelerated structural reform. Two

---

335 The growing fissure between neoauthoritarians and democrats was later reflected in the emergence of strategic disputes among various student groups and leaders during the Tiananmen demonstrations, particularly in the critical period of escalating conflict from 13 May to 30 May, 1989. See footnote 372.

336 *JB* 1 (January 1989), 29; *I&S* 25.6 (June 1989), 30.

337 Although both Wang Ruoshui and Yu Guangyuan had been invited to attend the decennial reform conference, the two men boycotted the proceedings to protest the blacklisting of several of their colleagues, including Yan Jiaqi, who had been barred from participating. The proceedings of the conference are discussed in *JB* 137 (1988), 40–2, in JPRS-CAR-89-018 (1 March 1989), 12–16.

days later, a leading government-run newspaper ran the first of two editorials that contended, among other things, that "there is a need courageously to draw lessons" from "modern democratic forms" that "have developed under Western capitalism."[338]

In late December 1988 and early January 1989, a new series of racially motivated campus disturbances revealed the existence of intensified urban stresses and tensions. The incidents, which involved clashes between Chinese and African students at various college campuses, seemed to be more a product of China's increasingly strained socioeconomic conditions than of the country's shifting intellectual or ideological currents. On Christmas Eve 1988, a riot broke out at Hehai University in Nanjing when a group of male African students reportedly brought Chinese women to their dormitory, refusing to register them in accordance with school regulations. The Africans were accosted by a crowd of Chinese youths who hurled sexual epithets and other verbal abuse at them. In the ensuing melee, two Africans and eleven university employees were injured. For several days thereafter, the situation in Nanjing remained tense as armed security troops were called in to maintain order among the more than 5,000 Chinese students who took part in anti-African demonstrations. On 31 December, Chinese security police, using clubs, forcibly dispersed a group of over 100 African students who had barricaded themselves in a guest house in suburban Nanjing.[339]

The next day, New Year's Day 1989, a similar incident occurred at the Beijing Language Institute, hundreds of miles to the north. There an African student who had allegedly abused a Chinese woman was the object of an angry protest by several hundred Chinese students who put up wall posters and demanded punishment for the African. Two weeks later, African students at Zhejiang Agricultural University went on strike to protest against Chinese officials who charged that the Africans were carriers of the deadly AIDS virus.[340]

Although these incidents clearly involved elements of racism, there were other, nonracial undercurrents and overtones as well. The anti-African protests served to rekindle many of the chauvinistic, anti-foreign sentiments that had previously risen to the surface during the 1985 and 1986 campus demonstrations; such sentiments tended to be symptomatic of the intensified, reform-induced social tensions and emotional stresses that characterized urban China in the middle and late 1980s. From this perspective, it did not matter so much

338 *GMRB*, 29 and 31 December 1988. These events are analyzed in Lowell Dittmer, "The Tiananmen massacre," *POC* 38.5 (September–October 1989), 4; see also Wright, "The political fortunes of . . . ," and Faison, "The changing role . . . ," 149.
339 Even before this particular incident, Hehai University had a rather long history of racial tensions. See *I&S* 25.2 (February 1989), 9–11; and *ICM*, February 1989, 29.
340 *I&S* 25.2, (February 1989).

that the targets of student hostility in the winter of 1988–9 were Africans rather than Japanese (or even corrupt Chinese officials); what mattered was that many Chinese, and not just students, were feeling threatened by forces not subject to their control; stressed and confused, they lashed out at convenient, culturally preordained targets.[341]

In this situation of rising social volatility, the renewed activism of China's liberal intellectuals further stirred things up. In early December, on the occasion of the tenth anniversary of the opening of the Xidan democracy wall, a former activist in China's short-lived democracy movement of 1978–9, Ren Wanding, publicly released a four-page letter addressed to the United Nations Commission on Human Rights, Amnesty International, and the Hong Kong Commission for Human Rights requesting inquiries into the condition of democracy activists imprisoned since the spring of 1979.[342]

On 6 January 1989, Ren Wanding's request for an investigation into the condition of China's political prisoners was carried a step further by Fang Lizhi. In an open letter to Deng Xiaoping, copies of which were made available to the foreign press, Fang called for the release of *all* political prisoners in China, specifically mentioning Wei Jingsheng. Fang argued that 4 May 1989, the seventieth anniversary of China's historic May Fourth Incident, would provide a suitable symbolic occasion for such a general amnesty. In mid-February, two young Chinese writers, Bei Dao and Chen Jun, collected the signatures of thirty-three Chinese scholars and writers supporting Fang Lizhi's open letter and calling for an acceleration of political structure reform. A similar "letter of opinion," signed in early March by forty-two scholars and scientists, was sent to CCP leaders and to the SC of the NPC.[343]

Reenter the gerontocrats

As political pressure from liberal intellectuals increased, so did political counterpressure from conservative Party elders. After Chen Yun had delivered the first of his eight opinions about Zhao Ziyang's leadership, Bo Yibo circulated a "letter of appeal" protesting the December decennial conference at which Su Shaozhi had launched his attack on the anti–spiritual pollution and bourgeois liberalization campaigns. Bo charged that a number of "middle-aged intellectuals" were whipping up public opinion, undermining the four

341 For a slightly different interpretation of the anti-African riots of 1988, one that stresses elite manipulation of latent chauvinistic feelings among Chinese students, see Edward Friedman, "Permanent technological revolution and China's tortuous path to democratizing Leninism," in Baum, ed., *Reform and reaction . . .*, 162–82.
342 Ren himself had been arrested in April 1979 but was released in 1983. See *FEER*, 15 December 1989, 38–9.
343 *JB*, 10 April 1989, 22–3; *I&S* 25.3 (March 1989), 1, 4–6; *ZM*, 1 March 1989, 6–9. These events are analyzed in Chong, "Present worries . . .," 2–4; and Dittmer, "The Tiananmen massacre," 4–5.

cardinal principles, and encouraging bourgeois liberalism, and he characterized the tenth anniversary conference as an "attack on the party CC." Several
old-timers from the CAC, including Bo, Chen Yun, Li Xiannian, and Wang
Zhen, now began pressuring Deng Xiaoping to sack Zhao Ziyang for his "failure to do public opinion, ideological and theoretical work properly." At one
point during this process, Li Xiannian reportedly flew to Shanghai to consult
secretly with Deng about possible scenarios for Zhao's resignation.[344] According to one such scenario, Zhao would be required to make a self-criticism
for his errors and resign at the CC's Fourth Plenum, scheduled for March
1989. Deng is said to have refused, arguing that (1) one of his closest deputies
(Hu Yaobang) had already been deposed and (2) there was no one suitable to
replace Zhao. China's senior leader then decided that the question of whether
to replace Zhao would be put off at least until summer, after Deng's anticipated
summit meeting with Mikhail Gorbachev.[345]

Under pressure, and in danger of losing the last remaining shred of Deng
Xiaoping's confidence, Zhao now temporized. Though he refused to bow to
hard-line conservative demands either to submit his resignation or undergo
self-criticism, he nonetheless began to take a firmer stance toward liberal
intellectuals. Together with Hu Qili, Zhao summoned *World Economic Herald*
publisher Qin Benli to Beijing, where the journalist was reprimanded for
publishing Su Shaozhi's incendiary decennial speech; thereafter, Qin Benli
agreed to accept a six-month moratorium on publishing materials submitted
by any of the thirty-three signatories to the petition demanding amnesty for
Wei Jingsheng.[346] At around the same time, in a seminar for Party cadres,
Zhao Ziyang explained that the improvement of ideological and political work
within the Party was an "urgent concern" that would occupy 50 percent of
the Party's attention in the near future.

Despite such evident backpedaling, Zhao managed to retain at least some
freedom of maneuver. He did not, for example, move to have Su Shaozhi
expelled from the Party,[347] nor did he agree to transmit around the country Chen Yun's eight opinions of November-December 1988, as Chen had
insisted. And finally, in response to Bo Yibo's criticism, Zhao defended China's

344 *I&S* 25.3 (March 1989), 4–7; *ZM* 138 (1 April 1989), 6–9; Dittmer, "The Tiananmen massacre."
345 *ZM* 138 (1 April 1989); *South China Morning Post*, 22 March 1989; *I&S* 25.6 (June 1989), 20. Although
   the conservatives were unable to secure Zhao's ouster, they did manage to prevent him from exercising
   leadership over the Party's MAC, where Yang Shangkun, though nominally ranking below Zhao,
   remained the principal decision maker. Zhao reportedly had access to Yang's decisions only after they
   were made. See Wilson and Ji, "Leadership by 'lines' . . . ," 38.
346 *ZM* 137 (1 March 1989), 6–9. The Party's central propaganda department issued an order for the
   People's Daily nor to publish any articles written by Yan Jiaqi (who had signed the petition of the
   thirty-three) without prior approval from the CC (*I&S* 25.3 [March 1989], 7).
347 Instead, Su was reportedly advised by his boss, CASS president Hu Sheng, to go abroad for a while.

critical intellectuals by saying, "Intellectuals have their own understanding of problems. What is there to be surprised at?"[348]

In late February, Fang Lizhi inadvertently reentered the political arena. Newly elected U.S. President George Bush, paying a brief get-reacquainted visit to China in conjunction with his attendance at a state funeral for the deceased Japanese Emperor Hirohito, issued an invitation to Fang to attend a presidential banquet at Beijing's Great Wall Sheraton Hotel. Intended as a sign of strong American support for human rights in China, President Bush's gesture provoked an equally strong response from Chinese leaders: On the night of the banquet, 26 February, Fang's car was obstructed by Chinese police and prevented from reaching the hotel. Having missed the banquet, Fang later gave a press conference at which he sardonically quipped that the incident revealed the weakness of a Chinese leadership that "had to go to all this trouble" just to prevent one scholar from attending a banquet.[349]

Deng Xiaoping reportedly was not amused. Even Zhao Ziyang reacted with dismay, pointedly warning President Bush that any American meddling in China's internal politics could undermine the country's stability and thereby play into the hands of opponents of reform. A week after the Fang Lizhi incident, Zhao gave a speech at an enlarged Politburo meeting in which he attacked foreign critics of China's Tibetan policy.[350]

In this situation of mounting political tension, Hu Yaobang suddenly reentered the political arena. Returning to Beijing in early April from a sojourn in southern China, Hu registered to speak at an enlarged Politburo meeting convened to discuss problems in education. At the 8 April meeting, Hu delivered a passionate appeal for greater Party support of education. During the meeting, shortly after completing his remarks, the former general secretary collapsed, suffering from a massive heart attack. A week later, on 15 April, Hu Yaobang died of a myocardial infarction.

Mourning becomes electric

Even before Hu Yaobang died, rumors began circulating in Beijing to the effect that he had suffered his fatal heart attack while engaged in a heated debate

---

348 I&S 25.3 (March 1989), 5; ZM, 1 March 1989, 6–9; Dittmer, "The Tiananmen massacre," 5.

349 Washington Post, 28 February 1989; Chong, "Present worries . . . ," 3. Two other prominent critical intellectuals, Su Shaozhi and playwright Wu Zuguang, had also been invited to the presidential banquet; neither one was prevented by the authorities from attending.

350 The Economist (London), 4 March 1989, 67; Chong, "Present worries . . . ," 3; Asiaweek, 7 July 1989, 26–31. Since October 1987 there had been recurrent episodes of political unrest in Tibet. Chinese troops had been used to quell protests on at least three occasions. In the late winter of 1989, following the death of the Panchen Lama (Tibet's pro-Chinese religious leader), the situation worsened; a series of pro-independence demonstrations occurred from mid-February to early March, leading to the imposition of martial law on 7 March. Thereafter, there were reports that a number of Tibetan protesters were killed by Chinese troops. See I&S 25.4 (April 1989), 8–11.

with arch-nemesis Bo Yibo.[351] Whether true or not, the rumors added to the already powerful sense of frustration and alienation shared by many Chinese students, providing the catalytic spark that reignited the long-smoldering fuse of campus unrest.

One day after Hu's death, on 16 April, several hundred students from various Beijing universities marched to Tiananmen Square to place memorial wreaths at the foot of the Revolutionary Heroes' Monument.[352] Over the next several days, the ranks of the mourners swelled to tens of thousands. The first pro-democracy rallies also took place in this period, accompanied by demonstrations in front of the government's official Zhongnanhai residential compound, west of Tiananmen. At this stage, the movement was composed almost entirely of university students.[353]

On 18 April, the first autonomous student organization was set up at Beida. Not coincidentally, the first set of student demands, addressed to the NPC Standing Committee, appeared the following day. Among the seven points raised by the students, the most important were those calling for a "correct evaluation" of the merits and demerits of Hu Yaobang; rehabilitation of all people wrongly persecuted in the campaigns against spiritual pollution and bourgeois liberalization; publication of the salaries and income sources of all top Party and government leaders and their offspring; new legislation promoting freedom of the press and public expression; and substantially

---

351 *JB*, 10 May 1989, 2–6. A number of other rumors were also spread about the circumstances of Hu's fatal heart attack. See *CLG* 23.1 (Spring 1990), 56–7.

352 There is a rich symbolic tradition of politicized displays of mourning at the Heroes' Monument. The "Tiananmen incident" of April 1976 began as a mourning display in honor of the late premier Zhou Enlai; the democracy movement of winter 1978–9 similarly involved a strong mourning theme. Noting this connection, Lucian Pye has written that "Funeral rituals provide one of the few opportunities Chinese have for publicly displaying emotion. . . . In Chinese culture, public grieving can legitimize the expression of sentiments that are only vaguely related to any sense of personal loss." See Lucian W. Pye, "Tiananmen and Chinese political culture: The escalation of confrontation from moralizing to revenge," *AS* 30.4 (April 1990), 331–47.

353 There are numerous discrepancies in the various available accounts of the student movement of 1989, particularly with respect to such things as crowd sizes and specific dates of unofficial events (e.g., the founding of the Beijing Students' Autonomous Federation). In reconstructing the events and political dynamics of this period, I have sought wherever possible to reconcile conflicting accounts. In doing so, I have found the following sources particularly useful: Ruth Cremerius, Doris Fischer, and Peter Schier, eds., *Studentenprotest und repression in China, April–Juni 1989; analyse, chronologie, dokumente*; (1990); Stefan R. Landsberger, "The 1989 student demonstrations in Beijing: A chronology of events," *CI* 4.1 (Summer 1989), 37–56; Yi Mu and Mark V. Thompson, *Crisis at Tiananmen: Reform and reality in modern China*; "CND interview with Gao Xin," *China News Digest* (global edition; hereafter, *CND*), 7–8 April 1991; Tony Saich, "The rise and fall of the Beijing people's movement," *AJCA* 24 (July 1990), 181–208; Dittmer, "The Tiananmen massacre"; Walder, "The political sociology. . . ."; Andrew J. Nathan, "Chinese democracy in 1989: Continuity and change," all in *POC* 38.5 (September–October 1989), 17–29; Pye, "Tiananmen and. . . ."; Corinna-Barbara Francis, "The progress of protest in China," *AS* 29.9 (September 1989), 898–915; Frank Naming, "Learning how to protest," in Saich, ed., "The Chinese people's movement . . . ," 83–105; and two special issues of *CLG*, edited by James Tong, 23.1 (Spring 1990) and 23.2 (Summer 1990).

increased stipends, salaries, and budgets for students, teachers, and educational programs.[354]

On the night of 18–19 April, student demonstrators, numbering more than 10,000, repeatedly attempted to gain entry into Zhongnanhai, demanding to see Premier Li Peng. The students eventually clashed with soldiers guarding the compound, and several students were injured in a police charge. When the official police report failed to mention student casualties, and referred to demonstration leaders as "troublemakers" who had incited students to injure police officers, the students were handed a potent new weapon: martyrdom. It was a weapon they would use against the government with great effect in succeeding weeks.

Over the weekend of 21–2 April, crowds of people began arriving at Tiananmen for the official memorial service for Hu Yaobang. In anticipation of possible disorder, 2,000 uniformed soldiers and riot police were mobilized for duty in and around the Square.[355] Despite official warnings to clear the Square, in the early morning hours of 22 April 100,000 people gathered quietly for the funeral ceremony. At 10:00 A.M. the service began inside the Great Hall, accompanied by the broadcast of somber music throughout the Square. Although Zhao Ziyang in his eulogy praised Hu Yaobang as "a great Marxist," the general tone of the service was reserved and low-key. When Party and government leaders left the Hall at the conclusion of the service around 11:30 A.M., students chanted, "Dialogue, dialogue, we demand dialogue" and "Li Peng, come out!" After having reportedly been told that the government would grant their request for an audience with high-level officials, the students waited for a government spokesman to appear; by 1:30 P.M., when no government official had shown up, student leaders conducted a ceremonial remonstrance on the steps of the Great Hall, presenting their scrolled-up demands on hands and knees in the exaggerated, ritually stylized manner of an imperial petition. Believing they had been fooled by government leaders, students angrily surged forward toward the Great Hall, only to be pushed back by police; a few students were reportedly hit with police batons; many students broke down in tears. The drama of the moment was powerful; the feelings were intense.[356]

---

354 *CLG* 23.2 (Summer 1990), 17–18. With the exception of the relatively new demands for making public the incomes of top leaders and their children (a product of rising popular anger over *guandao*) and for "reversing verdicts" on bourgeois liberalization, the demands were virtually identical to those raised in previous student demonstrations in 1985 and 1986.

355 It was also reported that up to 20,000 troops from the PLA's 38th army, stationed in Baoding, north of Beijing, received orders to move to the capital.

356 These events are chronicled in *CLG* 23.2 (Summer 1990), 22–3. Chinese officials later claimed that no government spokesman had agreed to meet with students on the afternoon of 22 April – indeed, that none had even been asked to do so – and that protest leaders had invented the promise to

Responding to the escalating threat of student protest and martyrdom, the Politburo on 22 April held an urgent meeting at which it was decided (1) to terminate the official period of mourning for Hu Yaobang; (2) not to capitulate to student pressures to soften the original verdict on Hu; and (3) to reaffirm the correctness of the 1987 campaign against bourgeois liberalism.[357] The next day, Zhao Ziyang left for a scheduled week-long visit to Pyongyang, North Korea. With Zhao out of the country, Li Peng convened an emergency session of the remaining members of the Politburo Standing Committee (Li, Qiao Shi, Yao Yilin, and Hu Qili), plus Yang Shangkun, who served as Deng Xiaoping's personal emissary. At the meeting, the student protest was described, for the first time, as "turmoil" (*dongluan*), the same term Deng had used to characterize the student demonstrations of December 1986.

On 25 April, Li Peng and Yang Shangkun briefed Deng Xiaoping on the Standing Committee meeting and on the developing student protest situation. Deng's response, which included a sharp jab at Zhao Ziyang's memorial characterization of Hu Yaobang as "a great Marxist," was subsequently circulated among party cadres:

> Some people want to build up [Hu Yaobang] as "a great Marxist." . . . Even when I die they will not call me a great Marxist. Who do they think that turtle egg Yaobang was? . . . Hu Yaobang was irresolute and made concessions in combatting bourgeois liberalism. The drive against spiritual pollution lasted only a little over twenty days. If we had vigorously launched the drive, the ideological field would not have been . . . so tumultuous [as it is today]. . . . Some people crave nothing short of national chaos. . . . We must take a clear-cut stand and forceful measures to oppose and stop the turmoil. Don't be afraid of students, because we still have several million troops.[358]

Claiming that the demonstrations had been organized and led by troublemakers with ulterior motives who were engaged in a plot to overthrow China's socialist system, Deng once again warned (as he had done in December 1986) of the dangers of a Polish-style uprising: "Events in Poland prove that making concessions provides no solutions. The greater the concessions made by the government, the greater the opposition forces became."

Deng might well have been concerned, for a new and potentially troublesome element was now being added to the equation of student protest: working-class involvement. On 20 April, a newly formed (and somewhat obscure) "Beijing Workers' Federation" issued a public manifesto blaming "dictatorial bureaucrats" for social ills ranging from soaring inflation and a sharp drop in

---

whip up feelings of martyrdom and betrayal among the students. Although evidence on this point is inconclusive, such a scenario is not entirely implausible.

357 Reportedly, Wan Li disapproved of the Politburo's decision.

358 *JB*, 10 May 1989, 22–6; Pye, "Tiananmen and . . . ," 337.

urban living standards to "expropriating the minimal income of the people for their own use." The manifesto further exhorted the citizens of Beijing, specifically including police and firemen, to "stand on the side of the people and justice" and not become "tools of the people's enemies." "We the working class of Beijing," the manifesto concluded, "support the just struggle of the college students across the nation!"[359]

Between 22 and 25 April, students in several Chinese cities, organizing themselves into autonomous unions, launched protests of various types. In Shanghai, Tianjin, Nanjing, and Wuhan, as well as in Beijing, citywide boycotts of classes were initiated. In Beijing, a Students' Autonomous Federation (BSAF) was established on 26 April at a meeting attended by 2,000 students from ten universities.

For the most part, student protest in this period was relatively calm and orderly. In a few places, however, most notably the cities of Changsha and Xi'an, peaceful demonstration degenerated into anomic vandalism and rioting as nonstudent elements, including unemployed workers, drifters, and juvenile gang members, took advantage of student protest to stir up trouble, resulting in declarations of martial law in both cities.[360]

Faced with a seemingly contagious situation of expanding student protest, mounting worker unrest, and escalating anomic violence on the part of urban marginals, party leaders now toughened their stance. Basing themselves on Deng Xiaoping's uncompromising statement of 25 April, they drafted a hardline editorial for publication in the *People's Daily*. The editorial, published on 26 April, appeared under the page-one headline "It is necessary to take a clear-cut stand to oppose turmoil." The editorial echoed Deng's allegations about the unpatriotic motives of student leaders, claiming that the students demonstrations constituted an "act of hooliganism" that had been "incited by a very small number of people with evil motives."[361] On the same day, Shanghai Party Secretary Jiang Zemin announced the Party's decision to "reorganize" the Shanghai *World Economic Herald* and fire its editor, Qin Benli.[362]

359 CLG 23.2 (Summer 1990), 31. It is not clear how many workers were actually represented by this organization, though as a rule, Beijing's working class did not join the student-led movement in large numbers until after the government's failed attempt to impose martial law on 20 May, See Niming, "Learning how to protest . . . ," 84–6.
360 For a survey of provincial reactions to the Tiananmen demonstrations, see the special section in *AJCA* 24 (July 1990), 181–314.
361 The editorial had reportedly been assigned to Hu Qili to draft. When Hu attempted to soften the thrust of the commentary by describing the students' actions as "demonstrations," Deng reportedly crossed out the milder phrase and inserted the word "turmoil." See John H. Maier, "Tiananmen 1989: The view from Shanghai," *CI* 5.1 (Summer 1990), 5. Although Zhao Ziyang was out of the country on 26 April, and although he subsequently disavowed the hard line taken in the 26 April editorial, it was subsequently alleged (by Yang Shangkun) that Zhao had cabled his "complete support" of the editorial's contents from North Korea. See *CLG* 23. 1 (Spring 1990), 80.
362 Two days earlier, the *Herald* had published a plea for a postmortem reevaluation of Hu Yaobang's contributions; at the time of his firing, Qin Benli was preparing to publish a "full account" of Hu's 1987 dismissal. *See FEER*, 11 May 1989, 12.

The aftermath of 26 April: Public resentment deepens

If the *People's Daily* allegations were calculated to have a sobering, intimidating effect on student demonstrators and their nonstudent sympathizers, the calculation apparently backfired. As soon as the editorial was published, the BSAF seized the moral initiative, calling for immediate "patriotic" mass marches on Tiananmen in support of "socialist order" and in opposition to "bureaucracy, corruption, and special privilege."

The counterproductivity of the government's approach became evident almost immediately. On 27 April, the day following publication of the *People's Daily* editorial, the number of protesters marching to Tiananmen Square from Beijing's university quarter doubled over the previous day's total, involving up to 100,000 people; it was said to be the largest spontaneous demonstration to occur in the PRC since 1949. For the first time, large numbers of nonstudents marched alongside students; in addition, more than half a million Beijing residents lined the streets of the demonstration route, offering encouragement, food, and drink to the protesters. Arriving at Tiananmen to the accompaniment of approving crowds, the demonstrators broke through police lines positioned to obstruct their entrance to the Square; the police backed off without serious incident. Cognizant of government warnings concerning the possible use of the military to quell disorder, student organizers dispatched squads of monitors to maintain order and discipline within the ranks of the demonstrators.

After years of mounting socioeconomic stress, the cumulative pressures of a decade of uneven and incomplete reform now began to break through the restraining bonds of Party and government authority. Energized by the government's ineffectual attempt to intimidate them into submission, the students seized the initiative. Occupying the moral high ground, they made effective use of the weapons of irony, shame, and martyrdom. During their marches, for example, they regularly chanted orthodox socialist slogans, sang the *Internationale*, and carried ironic banners urging citizens to support the party's "correct" leadership. By the end of April, such devices had become part and parcel of the students' attempt to reverse the roles of hero and villain in the unfolding drama at Tiananmen, and thereby to shame and humiliate Party and government hard-liners in the eyes of the citizenry.[363]

Popular opposition to the government's heavy-handed tactics spread rapidly: A public opinion poll conducted by the psychology department of Beijing Normal University at the end of April indicated that a majority of inflation-averse, corruption-weary citizens in the nation's capital now

---

363 This point is emphasized by Pye, "Tiananmen and . . . ," 339–40, The students' tactics were quite clever insofar as it would have been extremely awkward for the authorities to arrest students demonstrating peacefully while singing the *Internationale* and chanting pro-socialist slogans.

supported the students.[364] Concerned over their tarnished image and reduced credibility, Party and government leaders sought ways to disarm a perilous situation. Their preferred responses varied considerably. For Beijing Party Secretary Li Ximing, the optimal solution was to get even tougher. He repeatedly threatened students with harsh reprisals and warned of the serious "unforeseen consequences" of a failure to terminate student demonstrations. At a high-level strategy session on 28 April, a group of younger, more reform-oriented Party leaders (including Zhao Ziyang's associates Bao Tong and Yan Mingfu) opposed Li Ximing's views, counseling against a government crackdown.

In a two-pronged attempt to deflect mounting public criticism and drive a wedge between different groups of Beijing students (i.e., divide and rule), government leaders now agreed to hold televised talks with representatives of the "official" student unions in Beijing but not with the Autonomous Federation. Having been refused the right to participate, the BSAF's newly elected president, Wu'er Kaixi, angrily withdrew from the proceedings. When the meeting was held on 29 April, State Council spokesman Yuan Mu pointed out that the target of the 26 April *People's Daily* editorial had not been the broad masses of patriotic student demonstrators, but rather a small group of "behind-the-scenes conspirators."[365] At the same meeting, State Education Commission spokesman He Dongchang reiterated the government's refusal to recognize the legality of the BSAF. Three days later, BSAF leaders delivered a twenty-four-hour ultimatum demanding government approval of their conditions for dialogue. The ultimatum was rejected by the government on 3 May. The following day, protest demonstrations reached a peak, as a crowd estimated at 150,000 people filled Tiananmen Square to mark the seventieth anniversary of the May Fourth movement.[366]

Returning from North Korea at the end of April, Zhao Ziyang traveled hurriedly to Beidaihe to confer with Deng Xiaoping and to convey his misgivings about the government's choice of tactics in dealing with rebellious students. Apparently taken by surprise by the strength of the popular backlash to the 26 April editorial, Deng agreed to allow Zhao to try a softer approach with the students, telling the general secretary: "The most important thing is to stabilize the situation. . . . [Once] the situation is stabilized, you may

364 This and other opinion surveys concerning public attitudes toward the student movement in April–May 1989 are reproduced in *CI* 4.1 (Summer 1989), 94–124.
365 *FEER*, 11 May 1989, 11–12.
366 Similar (though smaller) demonstrations occurred on 4 May in Shanghai, Changsha, Nanjing, Wuhan, Xi'an, Changchun, and Dalian. In Harbin and Shenyang, campus gates were locked to prevent students from marching. Altogether, demonstrations were reported in twenty cities, involving upward of 1 million people. According to official accounts, by the end of May, over 2.8 million students from 600 Chinese institutions of higher education in eighty cities joined demonstrations in support of the Beijing students (statistics cited in Rosen, "Chinese youth," 20).

carry out your plans; if they prove feasible [you may] disregard what I said [before]."[367]

In line with Deng's instructions, on 4 May Zhao Ziyang outlined a more conciliatory government response in remarks delivered to representatives of the Asian Development Bank, meeting in Beijing. Claiming that most of the protesters "are in no way opposed to our basic system; they only demand that we correct malpractices in our work," the general secretary declared that "the reasonable demands of the students must be met through democratic and legal means." "We must remain calm," he said, "we must employ reason and restraint."[368]

Zhao's conciliatory tone had the paradoxical effect of undermining the cohesion of the popular movement in a way that the government's previous hard line had failed to accomplish. For one thing, it prompted radical elements among the movement's leadership, whose sense of moral indignation was strong to begin with, to adopt an even more intransigent posture vis-à-vis the government; for another, in revealing the existence of a clear split among top Party leaders, Zhao's talk emboldened many previously inert social forces, including factory workers and journalists, to join in the movement to press for their own particular demands and interests, thereby both enlarging and diffusing the arena of protest. As a result, the movement's previous unity of purpose and outlook became increasingly strained.[369]

With students and nonstudents alike pursuing a plurality of diverse, often shifting agendas, some of which were rather murky, it became increasingly difficult to formulate a coherent strategy within the movement, and more difficult still for concerned Party leaders like Zhao Ziyang to respond effectively. With both government and students internally divided between hard- and soft-liners, the net result was a standoff, marked by immobility and stalemate.

Under these circumstances, the enthusiasm of many students began to ebb, and in the second week of May the number of demonstrators at the Square began to dwindle noticeably. Faced with the prospect of an imminent loss of critical mass, student leaders were hard pressed to sustain the momentum of their movement. At this critical juncture, a golden opportunity presented itself: the approaching visit of Soviet leader Mikhail Gorbachev, scheduled

367 MB, 26 May 1989; South China Morning Post, 29 May 1989.
368 RMRB, 5 May 1989; ZM 140 (1 June 1989), 6–10.
369 These effects are discussed in Saich, "The rise and fall . . . ," 190–3. In early May, core student demands centered on (a) retraction of the 26 April editorial (with apologies), (b) reevaluation of Hu Yaobang, and (c) government recognition of the BSAF. In addition to these core concerns, however, various groups of new participants raised other demands, including inter alia, demands for a reevaluation of bourgeois liberalization (raised by a group of nonstudent intellectuals), for publishing the salaries and benefits of top Party and government leaders and their offspring (raised by the newly organized Autonomous Workers' Federation, among others), and for enhanced freedom of the press (raised by a group of 500 journalists employed in Party-controlled newspapers).

for 15–18 May. As the date of Gorbachev's arrival approached, the eyes of the entire world would focus on Beijing. It was "manna from Moscow," a situation made to order for the students and their increasingly media-conscious leaders.

Waging moral warfare: Gorbachev, the media, and the hunger strike

On 13 May, with scores of international journalists and television cameras converging on Beijing to record the Sino-Soviet summit, protest leaders dramatically escalated their confrontation with Chinese authorities. Declaring their moral abhorrence of a government that callously labeled the patriotic actions of its loyal citizens as "turmoil," several hundred students began a sit-in and hunger strike in Tiananmen Square.[370] With the government unable to take strong countermeasures because of the presence of Gorbachev and the global mass media, the ranks of the hunger strikers soon swelled to over 35,000; large crowds of sympathetic onlookers also began to flock to the Square, forcing the Chinese authorities to reroute Gorbachev's motorcade and change the venue of the Soviet leader's scheduled press conference.

Originally conceived as a limited, symbolic protest, the hunger strike was so stunningly successful in generating favorable publicity for the student cause that movement leaders soon decided to fast "to the bitter end," or until the government capitulated to the movement's demands.[371] With an important foreign head of state in the Chinese capital, with a plethora of international television crews on hand to record the proceedings, and with public sympathy increasingly swinging over to their side, the students felt relatively safe from the threat of a government crackdown. The safer they felt, the more audacious and intransigent some of them became.[372]

By this time, the striking students and their supporters, now including people of all ages and from all walks of life, had taken effective control of Tiananmen and its immediate environs. Using sophisticated broadcasting

---

370 Two early declarations of the hunger strikers appear in *CLG* 23.2 (Summer 1990), 50–3.

371 At this point, there were only two core demands: (a) the government must enter into a dialogue "on the basis of equality" with a Dialogue Delegation (*duihua daibiaotuan*) made up of student representatives from various universities in Beijing; and (b) the government must "stop its name calling" and confirm the patriotic nature of the democracy movement (ibid., 52–3; Francis, "The progress of protest . . . ," 912).

372 On the eve of Gorbachev's visit, student leaders in the Square reportedly rejected overtures from Zhao Ziyang designed to bring about a settlement, contemptuously referring to Zhao's emissaries as "neoauthoritarians." In one of the more dramatic student manifestos of this period, a group of hunger strikers waxed eloquent about their chosen path of martyrdom: "Fathers and mothers! Don't grieve because we are hungry. Uncles and aunts! Don't mourn when we bid life good-bye. Our sole desire is that everyone live a better life . . . . Farewell, fellow students, take care! Remember, though we may be dead, our loyal hearts remain among the living. Farewell, sweethearts, take care! We hate to leave you but we must. . . . Our pledge, written at the cost of our lives, will surely illuminate the skies of our Republic" (*CLG* 23.2 (Summer 1990), 52).

equipment hooked up to loudspeakers in the Square, strike leaders could counteract government propaganda broadcasts and spread their own messages among the milling throngs. Mimeograph machines poured out a steady stream of handbills, policy statements, and other printed materials. Posters now went up in the Square (some written in English to attract foreign media attention) calling for the resignations of Li Peng and Deng Xiaoping. Unflattering cartoon caricatures of Chinese leaders were also in evidence.

In the face of polarizing attitudes on both sides, Zhao Ziyang persisted in trying to bring about a peaceful resolution. On 15 May he (along with Hu Qili) agreed to meet the demands of several hundred petitioning journalists to allow the mass media to report on the student demonstrations objectively, free from official censorship. The next day, at a meeting of the PSC, Zhao proposed among other things, to retract the 26 April editorial, publish the incomes and emoluments of top Party and government leaders, and set up an organization under the auspices of the NPC to investigate allegations of *guandao* among high officials and their offspring. The proposal was voted down by four to one; even Hu Qili, Zhao's erstwhile strongest supporter on the SC, now voted against him.[373]

The primary reason for Zhao's increasing isolation among his peers was clear: Deng Xiaoping had already made up his mind to get tough with the students. The growing popular support and self-assurance of the protest movement had confirmed the senior leader's presumption that further government concessions would bring not peace but the escalation of demands, leading to ultimate chaos, Gdansk-style. Under these circumstances, the hunger strike proved the last straw. On 16 May, Yang Shangkun, relaying Deng's views, instructed an enlarged meeting of the party's MAC to make preparations for assembling troops to impose military control in Beijing.[374]

Deng's loss of confidence in Zhao, and Zhao's consequent loss of influence over decisions affecting the handling of the student movement, were signaled to the world during a televised meeting between Zhao and Mikhail Gorbachev on 16 May. In this meeting, Zhao confirmed the existence of the secret protocol enacted at the Thirteenth Party Congress giving Deng Xiaoping the final say on all "important" policy matters. The next day Zhao, clearly on the defensive in his struggle against the gerontocrats of the CAC, who, by this time, had begun regularly to attend and speak out at all important leadership meetings, made one last attempt to bring about a peaceful resolution of the crisis.

373 FEER, 1 June 1989, 12–18. Later, Yang Shangkun would allege that not all of Zhao Ziyang's proposals had been rejected outright by the SC and that everyone "agreed" with at least two of his earlier suggestions, i.e., that problems should be solved "on the basis of democracy and law" and that a "check-up" should be made of all private business companies (CLG 23.1 (Spring 1990), 72).
374 ZM 140 (1 June 1989), 6–10. Unofficial accounts of these events, given by Yang Shangkun and Li Peng, appear in CLG 23.1 (Spring 1990), 69–87.

Sending a message to the hunger strikers in the Square (via Yan Mingfu) on behalf of the CC and the State Council, he formally acknowledged the "patriotic spirit" of the student movement and promised no reprisals if the students would terminate their strike. Although a clear majority of the young strikers reportedly favored accepting Zhao's offer, acceptance was blocked by a minority coalition of hard-line Beijing students and students from out of town.[375]

Later that same day, 17 May, Zhao attended an expanded meeting of the PSC, held in Deng Xiaoping's home. At the meetings which was attended by Yang Shangkun and several old comrades, including Chen Yun, Li Xiannian, Peng Zhen, and Wang Zhen, Zhao once again appealed for a retraction of the 26 April editorial. Deng refused, arguing that "We cannot retreat. One retreat will lead to another"; and he added, "Comrade Ziyang, your speech to the Asian Development Bank officials on 4 May became a turning point, because after that the students created more serious disturbances." Deng next proposed to implement martial law. The old comrades present agreed, saying that things had "gone far enough." Zhao strongly objected, informing Deng and the SC that he could no longer serve as general secretary. His resignation was rejected out of hand, whereupon the SC approved Deng's proposal to implement martial law at the conclusion of Gorbachev's visit. Acknowledging defeat, Zhao sought to wash his hands of responsibility for the consequences that might follow: "Let comrade Xiaoping make the final decision," he said.[376]

Although senior leaders had thus decided by 17 May to crack down on the student movement, there was considerable anxiety among the leadership (shared by conservatives and moderates alike) that some of the hunger strikers, weakened by exhaustion and lack of nourishment, might die in front of the world's television cameras, providing the student movement with instant martyrs and thereby setting off a massive antigovernment reaction.[377] Under these circumstances, the authorities made a number of hastily improvised last-ditch efforts to coax the students into calling off their strike and peacefully evacuating the Square.

375 The hard-line Beijing student faction was reportedly led by Chai Ling, who later gained notoriety by her harrowing escape from China in the aftermath of the 3 June crackdown. See Woei Lien Chong, "Petitioners, Popperians, and hunger strikers," in Saich, ed., The Chinese people's movement . . . , 115, 121. According to eyewitness accounts, Yan Mingfu worked hard in this period to convince student leaders that they should narrow their demands to two: retraction of the 26 April editorial and governmental recognition of the BSAF. Yan's efforts to achieve a compromise settlement were reportedly rejected by Deng Xiaoping, as well as by Chai Ling, however, and one participant subsequently noted that "There was no majority opinion in Tiananmen Square at that time. Everybody had his own ideas. Even if Deng had accepted those two points, it was still useless." See "CND interview with Gao Xin."

376 These events are described in CLG 23.1 (Spring 1990), 69–72; FEER, 8 June 1989, 14–18; and MB, 30 May 1989.

377 By this time, approximately 2,500 hunger strikers had reportedly been treated for dehydration and heat exhaustion at local hospitals and makeshift health stations around the Square.

At 5:00 A.M. on 18 May, members of the Politburo's Standing Committee paid a highly publicized "comfort visit" to a group of hospitalized hunger strikers. In the televised film footage of this visit, Zhao Ziyang, Li Peng, Qiao Shi, and Hu Qili (Yao Yilin was not present) displayed visible concern for the health and well-being of the frail, weakened youngsters, shaking hands with them and stopping to chat at their bedsides. The dominant image conveyed by the TV cameras was one of benevolent paternalism.[378] A second government initiative came later the same day in the form of a televised address by state counselor Li Tieying. Again adopting a paternalistic stance, Li sought to reassure the striking students. "Your country loves you," he said; and he implored the protesters to end their hunger strike: "Come back, students; come back!"[379]

By far the most important official initiative was a televised meeting on 18 May between Party and government officials, including Li Peng, Li Tieying, Chen Xitong, and Yan Mingfu, and leaders of the student hunger strike, represented by Wu'er Kaixi and Wang Dan, among others.[380] Wu'er, who had been rushed from the hospital to attend the meeting, was clothed in pajamas and bathrobe; looking pale and weak, he had an intravenous feeding device attached to his nose. At this remarkable meeting, Li Peng began by calmly striking a concerned, paternalistic posture; shortly thereafter, things began to deteriorate:

> *Li Peng:* Today we will discuss one issue: How to relieve the hunger strikers of their present plight. The party and government are most concerned about the health of the students. You are all young, the oldest among you is only twenty-two or twenty-three, younger than my youngest child. None of my children are engaged in *guandao*. . . .

378 The hospital visit is described in *SWB/FE* 0462 (20 May 1989). During the visit, Zhao Ziyang told one student: "The goal of the party and government is identical with that of the students; there is no fundamental conflict of interests. A variety of methods can be adopted to exchange views and resolve problems; don't adopt the method of a hunger strike. . . . You should look after your health." Talking with another bedridden student, Hu Qili counseled patience, saying that "Some problems cannot be solved immediately." When the student indicated that the Party needed to reestablish its credibility in order to restore people's confidence, Hu Qili responded, "We fully agree with you." The student continued: "If you want to have prestige, I think that those who practice *guandao* and those high-ranking officials involved should start taking action against their own sons."

379 Although some observers are inclined to regard the government's show of concern for the welfare of the hunger strikers at this point as a cynical charade designed to mask the fact that a decision to impose martial law had already been taken, I am inclined to believe that many (if not most) Chinese leaders were quite sincere in their attempt to engineer an eleventh-hour settlement of the hunger strike, albeit for their own reasons, which ranged from genuine concern for the students' welfare to fear of massive rebellion in the event of deaths among the hunger strikers.

380 A formal transcript of the meeting appears in *CLG* 23.2 (Summer 1990), 46–54. However, certain impromptu remarks and gestures made during and at the conclusion of the meeting are not included in this transcript.

Wu'er Kaixi: Excuse me for interrupting you, premier Li, but time is running short. We are sitting here comfortably while students outside are suffering from hunger. You just said that we should discuss only one issue. [Wu'er points his index finger at Premier Li] But the truth is, it was not you who invited us to talk, but we, all of us on Tiananmen Square, who invited you to talk. So we should be the ones to name the issues to be discussed. . . .

Wang Dan: . . . For the students to leave the Square and call off the hunger strike, our conditions must be met in full. . . . First, a positive affirmation of the current student movement as a democratic and patriotic movement, not a "turmoil." Second, a dialogue to be held as soon as possible. . . .

Yan Mingfu:. . . . We are very worried about how events will continue to develop. The only influence you can now exert is to decide to evacuate all hunger strikers. . . . The major issue concerning people now is the lives of the young hunger strikers; we must treasure their lives and take responsibility for them. . . .

Li Peng: . . . Neither the government nor the party Central Committee has ever said that the students are causing a turmoil.[381] We have consistently acknowledged your patriotic fervor. . . . However, events are not developing in conformity with your good intentions. . . . The fact is, social disorder has occurred in Beijing and is spreading to the whole country. The current situation . . . is out of control. . . . Anarchy has reigned in Beijing for the past several days. I have absolutely no intention of putting the blame on [individual student leaders], but the anarchy I have just described is a reality. The government of the People's Republic of China . . . cannot disregard such phenomena. . . .

Wu'er Kaixi: . . . *I want to repeat what I have just said: We don't want to be bogged down in discussions. Give an immediate response to our conditions, because the students in the Square are starving. If this is overruled, and we remain bogged down on this one question, then we will conclude that the government is not at all sincere in solving this problem. Then there will be no need for us representatives to stay here any longer.*

Wang Dan: If premier Li thinks that turmoil will ensue that will cause a bad impact on society, then I can declare on behalf of all the students that the government will be entirely to blame. . . .

At the conclusion of this remarkable confrontation, Wu'er Kaixi collapsed on the floor in a faint.[382] As the meeting adjourned, Li Peng rose and extended his hand toward the students in a gesture of apparent conciliation. When his outstretched hand was brushed aside, the premier was heard to remark: "You've

---

381 Strictly speaking, Li's point was correct, since it had been Deng Xiaoping and individual members of the PSC and the CAC who had used the term "turmoil"; though the term also appeared in the 26 April editorial, it had never been incorporated into official Party documents or directives.

382 Wu'er subsequently developed something of a reputation for "strategic fainting," a behavior he exhibited on more than one occasion in public appearances. See Joseph F. Kahn, "Better fed than red," *Esquire*, September 1990, 186–97.

gone too far." Visibly angered and struggling to maintain his composure, Li walked stiffly out of the room.

With Gorbachev departing from China on 18 May, and with the students refusing to terminate their hunger strike, the situation moved quickly toward a confrontation.[383] In the early morning hours of 19 May, Zhao Ziyang made one last attempt to head off a declaration of martial law. At a Politburo meeting, he offered to take full responsibility for the student protest and volunteered to turn his own sons over to a special tribunal that would be charged with investigating high-level *guandao*. His offer was refused, and an argument reportedly ensued between Zhao and Deng Xiaoping, during the course of which Zhao once again offered to resign. As before, Zhao's resignation was rejected, on the grounds that it would reveal a deep split within the leadership and would thus encourage the students to continue their strike.

At this point, Zhao left the meeting, ordered a car, and asked to be driven to Tiananmen Square; he was accompanied by a visibly nervous Li Peng. Arriving at the Square around the crack of dawn, Zhao addressed the student strikers through a hand-held amplifier. "We've come too late," he said, his voice heavy with emotion. "I'm sorry. You should criticize us and blame us. It is reasonable that you should do so." This was to be Zhao's last public act as general secretary. Thereafter, he returned home and refused all requests to see visitors, claiming illness. Within several hours of Zhao's visit to the Square, the first contingents of PLA troops began arriving at the outskirts of Beijing. Soldiers were also moved into position to take over radio, television, and newspaper facilities throughout the capital.

Martial law: The crackdown that failed

At midnight on Friday, 19 May, Li Peng told a nationally televised meeting of several thousand Party leaders, military officers, and Beijing municipal officials that a declaration of martial law had been approved for certain parts of Beijing, to take effect at 10:00 A.M. the next morning. Four members of the PSC and president Yang Shangkun were on stage during Li Peng's address; conspicuous by his absence was Zhao Ziyang.[384]

---

383 By this time, facing a near-certain government crackdown, a substantial majority of fasting students favored evacuation from the Square. However, because the hunger strikers had previously agreed to abide by the rule of "decision by consensus," this meant that a small, vocal minority could, and did, block a settlement of the strike. A similar situation of an intransigent minority overruling a large majority later prevented the occupation of Tiananmen Square from ending peacefully on 30 May, following construction of the Goddess of Democracy.

384 A few days later, Yang would allege that Zhao's nonattendance at the meeting of 19 May gave the students a feeling of hope that they had a high-level supporter, thus encouraging them to "stir up greater trouble" (*MB*, 29 May 1989).

By midday, 20 May, an estimated quarter of a million troops had taken up positions in and around Beijing. When military units moved into the city in truck convoys from the suburbs, huge crowds of Beijing citizens poured into the streets, erecting roadblocks and surrounding the military vehicles, preventing them from moving. Unarmed and apparently unprepared for such overwhelming popular resistance on the part of the Beijing *shimin* (urban residents), the soldiers were engulfed in a virtual sea of nay-saying humanity. The leadership's worst fears of a catalytic fusion of hitherto fragmented, atomized pockets of urban alienation and discontent into a single, coherent rebellion now began to come true.[385]

The scene, though intensely emotional, was generally nonviolent. No shots were fired, and relatively few physical scuffles took place. Indignant residents, offended by the government's attempts to impose martial law, lectured soldiers about the peaceful, patriotic aims of the movement. A number of soldiers were seen flashing the "V for Victory" sign to the crowds that surrounded their vehicles; a few held hand-written placards attesting to their support for human rights and democracy; most simply appeared bored or bewildered as they awaited further instructions from their equally bewildered officers.

Because nothing like this had ever happened in the PRC, neither the students nor the *shimin* knew quite what to make of the situation or how to react. For almost two days, reports of government ultimatums and rumors of an imminent military crackdown circulated in Beijing and other cities, creating a tense, anxious situation. A near-total government blackout on news concerning conditions in Beijing, imposed following the martial law declaration, made it difficult to obtain accurate information.[386]

Notwithstanding the paucity of reliable news, the wave of unsubstantiated rumors, or the palpably heightened anxieties of the urban populace, on 21 May approximately 1 million Beijing residents demonstrated against the

---

385 Some army units reportedly failed to respond to orders issued by the martial law command to enter the city: see footnote 394. Eyewitnesses variously estimate the total number of *shimin* who took part in the 20 May effort to stop the PLA from entering the city at between 1 and 2 million.

386 Despite the news blackout, urban residents along China's eastern seaboard were able to keep abreast of at least some of the latest developments in Beijing through Voice of America (VOA) short-wave radio transmissions, television satellite dishes, and telephone/telegraph contacts, inter alia. In Nanjing, for example, on 20–1 May young people with portable stereo "boom boxes," perched high in the branches of trees in the town square, played recorded tapes of hourly VOA news summaries for the benefit of large crowds of attentive listeners below. On 21–2 May, tourists in Shanghai were able to view the latest developments in and around Tiananmen Square from the comfort of their hotel rooms via a mysteriously unbroken satellite television link. On at least two occasions during that period, rumors swept through Shanghai that martial law troops were about to enter the city. Municipal authorities promptly denied the rumors and effectively calmed popular fears. On the effects of the 20 May martial law declaration on protest demonstrations in other Chinese cities, see *AJCA* 24 (July 1990), 226–7, 239–40, 251–2, 268–9, 287–8.

imposition of martial law.[387] The same day, the hunger strikers at Tiananmen Square terminated their nine-day fast in order to join forces with other urban groups and strata in the rapidly burgeoning movement of popular resistance.

Movement leaders now made active preparations to deal with a possible military assault on the Square. Makeshift roadblocks, set up on 19–20 May to prevent the entry of army vehicles into the city, were now hardened and reinforced; checkpoints were established by students along key thoroughfares, with coded identification required to pass in or out. "Flying Tiger" squads, composed of affluent young urban *getihu* on motorcycles, recruited their members to ride picket along the outer perimeter and to serve as messengers. Gifts of money, supplies, and equipment began to pour into Tiananmen from various places, including Hong Kong and Taiwan, as a semipermanent encampment was erected in the Square.[388] By this time the student movement had become, in effect, a state within a state, complete with its own communications center, security apparatus, housing, and sanitation departments.

As the first tense days under martial law passed with no sign of a government reaction, the ranks of the demonstrators continued to swell. Now whole factories and government work units openly displayed their solidarity with the students; banner-waving contingents representing CCP organs and youth groups, government ministries, official media agencies, CASS research institutes, university departments, factories, labor unions, hotels, and even public security agencies and law courts marched together in open support of what had become, by this time, an extremely broad-based urban coalition.[389]

While popular support for the movement swelled, opposition to the government's hard-line tactics increased among a number of respected active and retired leaders of the Chinese army and government. On 21 May, the only two living PLA field marshals, Nie Rongzhen and Xu Xiangqian, were seen on national television praising the patriotism of the student movement; the following day, it was reported that seven senior PLA generals had drafted a letter to Deng Xiaoping protesting the imposition of martial law and affirming the view that the PLA "belongs to the people" and "should under no

387 An equally massive demonstration took place in Hong Kong on 21 May, with approximately 1 million people parading in support of the Chinese students.

388 Financial support for the students in this period was also provided by the Stone Computer Company, a quasi-private enterprise whose president, Wan Runnan, reportedly donated US$25,000 in cash plus a great deal of electronic broadcasting equipment to the antigovernment forces.

389 Significantly, the one major occupational group not represented in the demonstrations in substantial numbers was the peasantry. By and large, China's peasants, particularly those living in the fertile valleys and deltas near the urban centers along China's eastern seaboard, had done quite well under Deng Xiaoping's agricultural and marketing reforms; consequently, most appeared relatively indifferent to the events unfolding in Beijing.

circumstances fire on the people." The letter was reportedly signed by 100 senior army officers.[390]

On the government side, a petition was circulated among members of the NPC Standing Committee on 22 May (reportedly at the initiative of Hu Jiwei, with logistical support from the Stone Computer Company) calling for a special session of the NPC SC to be convened for the express purpose of repealing martial law.[391] On the same day, NPC SC Chairman Wan Li, on a visit to the United States and Canada, criticized the decision to invoke martial law and declared his intention to "firmly protect the patriotic enthusiasm of the young people in China." The next day, he cut short his visit to North America and returned to China, citing health problems as the reason.

Meanwhile, in Beijing, orders were passed down to martial law troops on 22 May to withdraw to the city limits. The orders were generally carried out calmly and without incident.[392] Following the army's withdrawal, the students and their supporters were effectively in control of the heart of Beijing. To all outward appearances, "the people" had won.[393]

Circling the wagons: Deng prepares his response

Behind the scenes, things appeared quite differently. Shortly after ordering the imposition of martial law, Deng Xiaoping reportedly flew to Wuhan to line up the support of PLA regional forces. By 26 May, commanders of all seven military regions had publicly declared their support, with the Beijing regional commander the last, and apparently the most reluctant, to do so.[394] Meanwhile, on 22 May, the PSC, minus Zhao Ziyang, convened an enlarged

390 *FBIS*, 22 May 1989, 16. The letter's drafters were said to have included former defense minister Zhang Aiping, former PLA chief of staff Yang Dezhi, former naval commander Ye Fei, and generals Xiao Ke and Chen Zaidao.

391 Approximately 40 of the SC's 135 members reportedly signed the petition, well short of the majority needed to call a special session (*SWB/FE* 0466 [25 May 1989]). At the end of June, following the military crackdown at Tiananmen, several SC members who had signed the 22 May petition were subtly reprimanded by being excluded from receiving invitations to attend the next meeting of the committee.

392 There were at least two exceptions: on 23 May, at Liuliqiao and in the southwestern Beijing suburb of Fengtai, violence erupted when security forces assaulted citizens who had erected street barricades. Unofficial sources put the total number of people injured at forty.

393 Just before the troops were withdrawn, PSC security expert Qiao Shi had argued against such a move, warning that a troop pullback would have the effect of making the students "think they had won" the struggle (*CLG* 23.1 (Spring 1990), 77).

394 The reluctant deputy commander of the Beijing military region, General Yan Tongmao, was relieved of his duties shortly after the crackdown of 3–4 June. His boss, General Zhou Yibing, was subsequently transferred to another post. It was rumored at the time that General Zhou had a daughter among the student demonstrators at Tiananmen Square. Also disciplined for insubordination in this period was the commander of China's elite 38th army, General Xu Qinxian, who reportedly feigned illness to avoid ordering his troops to enforce martial law in Beijing. General Xu was arrested on 24 or 25 May and was subsequently court-martialed. See *FEER*, 8 June 1989, 16; 21 September 1989, 19–20; and 1 February 1990, 22.

meeting of the Politburo. At the meeting, Yang Shangkun, Li Peng, and Qiao Shi all gave reports reaffirming their support for the decision to impose martial law and criticizing Zhao Ziyang's handling of the situation between 29 April and 19 May. Of the various reports, Qiao Shi's was the most foreboding. "At present," said the Party's top security expert, "we will on the one hand use troops as a deterrent, and on the other find [a suitable] occasion to clear the Square.... The reason we have procrastinated [until now] is that we ... are trying to avoid bloodshed. But it won't do to [have the situation] drag on like this."[395]

Two days later, on 24 May, at yet another enlarged session of the Politburo, Zhao Ziyang's dismissal from the Politburo Standing Committee was approved; the reason given was Zhao's post facto withdrawal of support for the 26 April *People's Daily* editorial, an act that, according to Deng Xiaoping, had sown confusion within the party and split the party leadership into "two headquarters."[396]

With the general secretary now officially in disgrace, Yang Shangkun stepped up his criticism of Zhao's behavior at an emergency meeting of the Party's MAC, also held on 24 May.[397] In affirming the opinion of "chairman Deng"[398] that Zhao's actions following his return from North Korea had served to split the Party into two competing headquarters, Yang now compared the behavior of the Zhao-inspired Beijing students with the anarchistic behavior of China's Gang of Four–inspired Red Guards during the Cultural Revolution.[399] This was a serious charge, one that could, if upheld, result in Zhao's expulsion from the Party, or worse.

At the conclusion of his 24 May remarks to the MAC, Yang Shangkun spoke ominously about preparations for future military action:

> We can no longer retreat, but must launch an offensive. I want to tell you about this today so that you can prepare yourselves mentally. In particular, the army must be consolidated; this is of vital importance.... If any troops do not obey orders, I will punish those responsible according to military law.[400]

Also on 24 May, Wan Li, whose return from Canada had been widely expected to provide a strong boost for the students in Tiananmen Square, was whisked into seclusion by Party officials as soon as his plane touched

---

395 In their remarks of 22 May, both Yang Shangkun and Li Peng were rather mild and circumspect in their criticism of Zhao Ziyang's behavior, accusing him of "making mistakes" but avoiding the inflammatory rhetoric used to attack Hu Yaobang in 1987.
396 At this meeting, Hu Qili was said to have defended Zhao and opposed the martial law declaration of Li Peng.
397 Throughout the unfolding crisis of May–June 1989, Yang apparently functioned as Deng Xiaoping's alter ego, publicly articulating the private opinions of China's senior leader.
398 At the time, Deng's only remaining official posts were as chairman of the two MACs.
399 *CLG* 23.1 (Spring 1990), 80–1.   400 Ibid., 86–7.

down in Shanghai. When he emerged three days later, it was to announce his support for martial law, though he continued to describe the student movement as "patriotic." Taking a considerably darker view of things, Chen Yun, in a televised address on 26 May, indirectly implicated Zhao Ziyang in the conspiratorial activities of a "treacherous anti-party clique." The same day, six of Zhao's supporters, including Hu Qili, defense minister Qin Jiwei, and political reform adviser Bao Tong, were singled out for criticism by CAC conservatives at a leadership meeting.

Meanwhile, in Tiananmen Square, there was a noticeable attrition in the ranks of the encamped students. Although massive public demonstrations continued to be held almost daily, dwindling numbers of students living and sleeping on the Square bespoke the growing exhaustion of the student movement. On 27 May, exactly one week after the declaration of martial law, student leaders Wu'er Kaixi and Wang Dan proposed to end the occupation of the Square on 30 May with one final, massive demonstration and triumphal procession. As before, however, a minority coalition composed of out-of-towners and radical Beijing students, led by Chai Ling, objected to the evacuation proposal, blocking its adoption and binding the students to remain in the Square until 20 June, the date of the next scheduled meeting of the NPC SC.

At dusk on 29 May, with fewer than 10,000 protesters remaining in Tiananmen Square, a group of students from Beijing's Central Arts Academy began to construct a bamboo scaffolding in the northern quadrant of the Square, directly opposite the portrait of Mao Zedong that hangs atop the entrance to the Forbidden City. With the scaffolding completed, the students next assembled, from prefabricated sections brought to the Square on bicycle carts, a thirty-foot-high statue of a woman grasping a torch in her upstretched arms. Variously known as the "Goddess of Democracy" (*minzhu nushen*), the "Spirit of Democracy" (*minzhu jingshen*), and the "Goddess of Liberty" (*ziyou nushen*), the statue was completed in the early morning hours of 30 May.

Construction of the statue, like Mikhail Gorbachev's visit to Beijing two weeks earlier, served to inject new life and energy into the dwindling student movement. As many as 300,000 spectators flocked to Tiananmen Square on 30–31 May to see the white plaster-and-styrene Goddess standing eyeball to eyeball with Mao Zedong, torch defiantly raised. Whether or not mockery had been the conscious intent of the art students, it surely was the effect, as dozens of television cameras expertly framed the ironic, silent confrontation between Goddess and Chairman. The students, their flagging spirits revived, announced their determination to continue occupying the Square.

Two days earlier, on 28 May, student leaders had been informally warned that they would be subject to arrest as "agents" of Zhao Ziyang. Even as the Goddess was being assembled in the Square on the night of 29 May, the detentions began. Students were not the immediate targets; their allies, the radicalized *shimin*, were. First to be arrested were three members of the newly formed Beijing Autonomous Workers' Federation; later the same day, eleven members of the Flying Tigers motorcycle squad were jailed. The crackdown had begun.[401]

Clubs are trump: The June debacle

It is tempting to pinpoint the appearance of the Goddess of Democracy on 30 May as the final straw, or trigger, that brought the full, militarized wrath of Deng Xiaoping and the old comrades of the CAC down upon the heads of the audacious, libertarian students of Beijing and their newfound allies, the angry *shimin* of urban China. More likely, however, the decisive catalysts of the debacle that followed were, first, the rapid rise of a militant, autonomous workers' movement that was proclaiming its solidarity with the students in opposition to the regime, bringing ever closer to reality Deng's recurrent Polish nightmare;[402] and second, the progressive defection of substantial numbers of Party, government, and army leaders to the side of the students during the second half of May, lending critical weight and legitimacy to the antiregime fervor that was sweeping through the country's major urban centers. In short, China's leaders in early June acted to preempt what they viewed, not without reason, as a rapidly deteriorating and deeply threatening situation.[403]

Many things remain unclear about just what happened and why in the first week of June 1989. Two things ate clear, however. First, a substantial number of Beijing *shimin* died in the course of a brutal assault by fully armed, heavily armored units of the PLA in central Beijing on the evening of 3–4 June and in subsequent mopping-up operations: Best available estimates place the total number of dead at between 600 and 1,200, including at least 39 students and "several dozen" soldiers, with an additional 6,000 to 10,000 civilians

401 It is not particularly surprising that nonstudents should be the first to be arrested. China's political tradition confers an unusual degree of paternalistic tolerance upon students, rendering them relatively immune from harsh punishment; such latitude is not granted to other occupational groups, however, and especially not to workers. See, e.g., Robin Munro, "Who died in Beijing, and why?" *The Nation*, 11 June 1990.

402 By 1 June, autonomous workers' organizations had sprung up in most of China's major cities. In Beijing, membership in the Workers' Autonomous Federation increased rapidly following the 29 May arrest of three Federation members.

403 According to an internal Party investigation conducted after the crackdown of 3–4 June, more than 10,000 cadres from central-level Party and government departments took part in the May demonstrations (FBIS, 10 November 1989, 46–9). Unofficial estimates place the figure much higher – by several orders of magnitude. In light of events that subsequently unfolded in Eastern and Central Europe in the latter part of 1989, particularly in Romania, Chinese leaders' fears of being swept away in a burgeoning, out-of-control antigovernment rebellion may not have been so far off the mark as was originally supposed by many outside observers.

and soldiers injured. Second, there was no massacre of students in Tiananmen Square.[404]

The military crackdown was presaged, shortly after midnight on the morning of 3 June, by a puzzlingly ineffectual foray into Beijing by a column of several thousand unarmed and ostensibly ill-seasoned young PLA soldiers who had been sent jogging, double-time, sans officers, toward Tiananmen Square from the eastern suburbs of the city. After running for nearly two hours, the exhausted soldiers had their route blocked by a large crowd of people near the Beijing Hotel, east of the Square, at around 3.00 A.M. The hapless soldiers were surrounded and sternly lectured on the subject of civil-military amity by the irate *shimin*, who had been roused from their beds by reports of advancing troops. The soldiers, unarmed, weary, leaderless, and confused, were easily immobilized. Once again, as on 20 May, it seemed as though the people had won a major victory.[405]

This time, the victory was short-lived. On the afternoon of 3 June, thousands of PLA troops, unarmed but in battle dress, were disgorged from underground tunnels leading into the Great Hall of the People. Sent to clear Tiananmen Square, the troops were immediately surrounded by masses of *shimin* behind the Great Hall and prevented from reaching their destination. Though tempers were short and incidents of violence flared episodically, student monitors enforced discipline among the crowds, preventing any serious conflagration.

Such was not the case in other areas of Beijing. At around 2:00 P.M. in the afternoon, west of the Square on Chang'an dajie near Liubukou, loudspeakers blared out a directive from the martial law command headquarters, ordering the crowds to disperse immediately. Shortly thereafter, hundreds of soldiers and armed security forces rushed into the streets, firing tear gas shells and clubbing those unfortunate enough to get in their way. Similar incidents were reported from other areas of the city throughout the afternoon.

At 6:30 P.M., the Beijing municipal government and martial law headquarters issued an emergency notice warning Beijing residents not to go out

404 In the following discussion, I have relied on Munro, "Who died in Beijing...?"; "CND interview with Gao Xin"; Mu and Thompson, *Crisis al Tiananmen....*; and *Massacre in Beijing: China's struggle for democracy*. Other useful sources on the events of June 1989 include Amnesty International, *China: The massacre of June 1989 and its aftermath;* Michael Fathers and Andrew Higgins, *Tiananmen: The rape of Peking;* and Scott Simmie and Bob Nixon, *Tiananmen Square: An eyewitness account of the Chinese people's passionate quest for democracy.*
405 There is considerable controversy over the purpose of this curious foray. Some observers believe it was a deliberate provocation by the government, akin to throwing a lighted match into a gas tank, designed to precipitate a violent attack on the unarmed soldiers, which could then be used as a pretext for launching a violent crackdown on the students. Others have argued that the unarmed soldiers were to have been reunited with their weapons, which were being transported separately into the city on at least three unmarked buses, at Tiananmen Square. However, the buses (like the soldiers themselves) were intercepted and immobilized by crowds of *shimin* before they could reach the scheduled rendezvous point.

onto the streets or into the Square; violaters would be "responsible for their own fate." The message was broadcast repeatedly from 7:00 to 9:00 P.M. on government radio and television stations. At 10:00 P.M., troops massed on the outskirts of Beijing received their orders to proceed immediately to Tiananmen and to clear the Square by 6:00 A.M. the following day, 4 June.

The first known shooting of civilians occurred at around 10:30 P.M. on Chang'an Boulevard near Muxidi, a few miles west of Tiananmen, where a column of advancing troops, armed with assault rifles and machine guns and accompanied by tanks and armored personnel carriers (APCs), met a wall of nonviolent but unyielding *shimin*. Under orders to reach Tiananmen Square or face military discipline, which under the circumstances meant the strong likelihood of a firing squad, the soldiers first discharged their rifles into the air, hoping to frighten the crowds into dispersing. When the people did not yield, the soldiers gradually lowered their sights; eventually they began to fire into the crowd. At first paralyzed by dismay and disbelief, the crowd soon broke up. Many fled in panic; others stayed behind to care for the dead and wounded. Bullets flew in random, stray patterns, felling fleeing protesters and innocent bystanders alike.

Most of the killing took place between 10:30 P.M. and 2:30 A.M., as the scene at Muxidi was replayed, with minor variations, at other locations throughout the city. With armored PLA units continuing their relentless advance toward the Square, enraged *shimin* now began to fight back, using whatever materials were at hand, including rocks, bottles, Molotov cocktails, and an assortment of homemade knives and clubs. Jamming iron construction rods into the treads of army APCs, they succeeded in disabling a number of vehicles, several of which they then set afire; when the frightened APC crews tried to escape, some were set upon by the angry crowds and savagely beaten; a few were immolated, hanged, or even disemboweled; but a substantial number were escorted to safety by student monitors.

Although the Chinese government would subsequently charge "counter-revolutionary conspirators," "hooligans," and "rioters" with instigating the carnage of 3–4 June through acts of unprovoked violence against martial law forces, it was reasonably clear that such acts, which did in fact occur, were largely a consequence, rather than a cause, of the army's brutal assault on the *shimin* of Beijing. Even the government's vaunted "smoking gun," a crudely edited videotape showing civilians savagely attacking and torching army vehicles, turns out to have been recorded several hours *after* the initial slaughter of civilians had commenced at Muxidi.[406]

---

406 It has been suggested, but never proved, that on the morning after the assault on Tiananmen Square, the government deliberately allowed a number of army vehicles to stall or break down in the immediate vicinity of strategically placed video cameras precisely in order to precipitate, and then record, violent acts by enraged citizens.

The "Tiananmen massacre"

As the PLA pincer movement approached Tiananmen after midnight, the mood among students in the Square became increasingly tense. All around, tracer bullets could be seen cutting a path through the night sky, and staccato bursts of machine gun fire could be heard from all directions. But in Tiananmen Square itself, where an estimated 3,000 to 5,000 students now sat huddled close together on the three tiers and steps of the Heroes' Monument, no shots were fired.

Beginning around 1:30 A.M., an "emergency notice" was broadcast repeatedly over government loudspeakers around the Square, reporting that a "serious counterrevolutionary rebellion" had broken out and that "ruffians" were "savagely attacking" PLA units, setting military vehicles afire, kidnapping soldiers, and seizing army weapons. After having previously acted with "great restraint," the PLA would now have to "resolutely counterattack the counterrevolutionary rebellion," the notice proclaimed.

Moving in from three directions, soldiers sealed off the Square between 2:00 and 3:00 A.M. Almost all nonstudents, including the vast majority of journalists, had left the Square by this time.[407] The students who remained at the Heroes' Monument reportedly had in their possession at least two rifles and one machine gun, which was manned by a team of "pickets" (*jiuchadui*) and pointed in the general direction of PLA troops arrayed in front of the Great Hall of the People. According to one eyewitness account, the soldiers facing the students shouted, "We will not attack unless we are attacked first" (*ren bufan wo, wo bufan ren*).[408]

At this point a dispute arose between Chai Ling, who was in favor of allowing those students who wished to remain in the Square "to the end" to do so, and another group of strike leaders who wished to persuade the remaining few thousand students to evacuate peacefully before it was too late. The Chai Ling group, which controlled access to the loudspeaker system mounted high up on the Heroes' Monument, announced its intention to lead the students in singing a final, defiant rendition of the *Internationale* as the final moment of truth approached.

After considerable heated debate, the pro-evacuation group, led by Beijing Normal University lecturers Liu Xiaobo and Gao Xin, social scientist Zhou Duo, and the well-known Taiwanese pop singer Hou Dejian, managed to take control of the machine gun at the base of the Heroes' Monument, which they proceeded to dismantle, thereby averting a potentially disastrous

---

407 The withdrawal of foreign journalists in the early morning hours of 4 June helps to explain the dearth of reliable eyewitness reports describing the unfolding of subsequent events, including the army's recapture of Tiananmen Square and the students' eleventh-hour evacuation.

408 "CND interview with Gao Xin."

clash with the troops opposite. Their attempt to persuade the students to leave the Square suffered a setback, however, when the Chai Ling–controlled loudspeaker system suddenly went dead.

Some time after 3:00 A.M., Chai Ling left Tiananmen Square. At 4:00 A.M., all lights in the Square suddenly went out; for the few thousand students who remained huddled around the base of the Heroes' Monument, the moment of truth was seemingly at hand. According to eyewitness observers, a curious calm now descended upon the Heroes' Monument: It was the eye of the hurricane.

Meanwhile, the four pro-evacuation leaders, Liu Xiaobo, Gao Xin, Zhou Dou, and Hou Dejian, redoubled their efforts to avoid an imminent holocaust by negotiating a last-minute student withdrawal from the Square. Descending from the Heroes' Monument and hitching a ride with a passing ambulance, Zhou and Hou sought out the local commander of the PLA forces in Tiananmen Square. After some initial confusion, they managed to locate a PLA regimental commissar, who listened to their evacuation proposal. A few minutes later, the local commander arrived and approved the plan, which called for the students to file out of the Square toward the southeast. The students were promised safe conduct and a period of grace in which to leave.

At around 4:30 A.M. the lights in the Square went back on, and a sea of troops poured out of the Great Hall of the People. After taking up positions on the east side of the Square, the troops proceeded to shoot out the student loudspeakers atop the Heroes' Monument.[409] At this point, a representative of the Beijing Autonomous Workers" Federation urged the students to evacuate the Square immediately, before a bloodbath took place; his advice was seconded by Hou Dejian, who had hurriedly rejoined the students after completing his negotiations. Hou's pleas were countered, however, by another speaker who urged the students to "stand firm." After a brief period of uncertainty, punctuated by the sound of tank engines coming to life at the northern edge of the Square, a voice vote was taken; someone then announced that a "democratic decision" had been made to leave the Square.

The evacuation, which was calm and orderly, began shortly before 5:00 A.M. and lasted approximately half an hour. By 5:30 A.M., only a small handful of people remained at the Monument; by the time the first line of bayonet-wielding soldiers climbed the steps to reclaim the Monument a few minutes

---

409 It was apparently these bursts of gunfire, seen ricocheting off the top of the Monument, that triggered the subsequent rumors, spread by the mass media in Hong Kong and elsewhere, that soldiers had cold-bloodedly massacred rows of students sitting quietly at the base of the Monument. Wu'er Kaixi, who had himself left the Square shortly after midnight, would later claim that 200 students were killed in this early morning assault.

later, most of these stragglers had also left.[410] As dawn broke on Sunday, 4 June, Chinese tanks at the northern end of Tiananmen Square crushed the Goddess of Democracy.

After the storm

Sporadic, often apparently random shootings of civilians, including innocent bystanders and apartment dwellers, by martial law troops continued at various points around Beijing for several days after 4 June.[411] Although there were frequent rumors in this period of an impending civil war involving allegedly rebellious armored units of the PLA, no organized military mutiny occurred; there were, however, numerous reported cases of intra-PLA dissension and failure to carry out orders.[412]

On 6 June, Beijing Mayor Chen Xitong publicly congratulated the martial law forces on winning "initial victory" in the struggle to quell counterrevolutionary rebellion; at the same time, he cautioned that final victory would require a "long and complicated struggle."[413] On the same day, Fang Lizhi and his wife, Li Shuxian, whose names were about to be placed on a government arrest warrant, sought and received sanctuary inside the U.S. Embassy in Beijing. Also on 6 June, antigovernment demonstrations broke out in at least a dozen Chinese cities. The most serious incidents took place in Chengdu, where rioting by angry crowds led to a declaration of martial law, culminating in the shooting of scores of *shimin*, and in Shanghai, where antigovernment workers set fire to a train that had hurtled into a crowd of protesters, killing six and wounding at least six others.[414]

410 One eyewitness to these final moments at the Heroes' Monument was the Chinese scholar Yu Shuo, who later recounted her experience: "As I was talking to an [army] officer I suddenly realized that I was the last person left at the Monument. As I walked down the terrace . . . I saw that a soldier was about to pierce a bed with his bayonet. I saw two feet sticking out from it. . . . I rushed forward and dragged the feet. A boy fell down from the bed; he was not completely awake yet. He was the last student to leave the Square" (quoted in Munro, "Who died . . . ?"). An account by Gao Xin differs only marginally, on the question of who was the last to leave the Monument: "Chen Zheng might be the last one to leave. She and a friend from Hong Kong refused to leave, sat on a step of the Monument to the People's Heroes, and kept crying. A soldier stood on a higher step, ordered them to leave immediately, cursing and threatening. I ran to them and pushed them away" ("CND interview with Gao Xin").

411 On 7 June, the foreign diplomatic residential compound at Jianguomen, east of Tiananmen Square, was fired on by Chinese troops in an apparent attempt at intimidation.

412 See June Teufel Dreyer, "The People's Liberation Army and the power struggle of 1989," *POC* 38.5 (September–October 1989), 41–8.

413 On 6 June, State Council spokesman Yuan Mu held a press conference at which he presented the government's initial version of the events of 3–4 June. The text appears in *SWB/FE* 0476 (7 June 1989).

414 It was subsequently reported that between 30 and 300 people had been killed, and more than 1,000 others injured (including security forces), in the Chengdu violence, which continued for three days after 4 June. See Amnesty International, *China: The massacre* . . . , 58–67; and Karl Hutterer, "Eyewitness: The

The arrests began on 6 June; among the first group of pro-democracy activists to be detained by security forces were Ren Wanding and Liu Xiaobo. On 11 June, arrest warrants were issued for a number of student leaders, prominent Chinese intellectuals, and other outspoken supporters of human rights who stood accused of instigating or supporting the counterrevolutionary rebellion. Among the names appearing on government "most wanted" lists in this period were Fang Lizhi, Li Shuxian, Wu'er Kaixi, Wang Dan, Chai Ling, Bao Tong, Yu Haocheng, Yan Jiaqi, and Wan Runnan; arrest warrants were also issued for the outspoken coauthor and director of "River Elegy," Su Xiaokang, as well as for such inveterate human rights activists as economist Chen Ziming and newspaper editor Wang Juntao, both of whom had played prominent roles in earlier democratic protest movements.

On 7 June, China's highest prosecuting authority, the Supreme People's Procuratorate, issued an "emergency notice" to public security bureaus around the country, advising them not to be "hamstrung by details" in the detention and prosecution of hooligans and rebels. Over the next several days, large-scale detentions of suspected counterrevolutionaries were carried out in Beijing and elsewhere. Within two weeks, the number of officially reported arrests throughout the country reached 1,600, with unofficial estimates being many times higher.[415]

Chengdu massacre," *China Update* 1 (August 1989), 4–5. On the violence in Shanghai, see Maier, "Tiananmen 1989...."

415 The official figures generally included only people formally charged with committing rebellion-related crimes; unofficial figures, compiled by foreign human rights groups, tended to include along with those formally arrested a much larger number of people, generally reckoned in the tens of thousands, who were picked up and detained for questioning (often for twenty-four or forty-eight hours) before being released.

According to official sources, at least forty fugitive student leaders and dissident intellectuals managed to escape from China in the first several weeks after the 4 June crackdown (*RMRB*, 7 July 1989). Escapees included Wu'er Kaixi, Chai Ling, Yan Jiaqi, Gao Gao, Wan Runnan, and Su Xiaokang. In the weeks that followed, a number of other dissidents were arrested in China, including Bao Tong (who was accused of leaking information from Politburo meetings to the students in the Square), Yu Haocheng, Wang Dan, Chen Ziming, and Wang Juntao. Singer Hou Dejian, after spending ten weeks hiding out in the Australian embassy, returned to his Beijing residence in August 1989. After initially corroborating the government's claim that no students had been massacred in Tiananmen Square on 4 June, Hou later declared himself in opposition to the regime. At the end of May 1990, he, along with two of the others who had helped negotiate the 4 June evacuation of Tiananmen Square, Zhou Duo and Gao Xin, announced their intention to hold a press conference on the first anniversary of the Tiananmen crackdown in order to read an open letter to Chinese leaders demanding the release of all political prisoners, including the fourth member of their Tiananmen negotiating team, Liu Xiaobo. When the three dissidents were detained by security police before they could hold their press conference, Hou Dejian, a celebrity whose international fame made it difficult for the government to crack down on him with impunity, negotiated his second evacuation agreement with the authorities: In exchange for a government pledge not to arrest him or his two collaborators, Hou agreed to accept deportation to his native Taiwan. He was escorted out of the country toward the end of June, at around the same time that Chinese authorities were permitting Fang Lizhi and Li Shuxian to leave the U.S. embassy in Beijing for exile in England.

In the winter of 1991, at the height of the Persian Gulf crisis, thirty-one Chinese intellectuals, jailed in the aftermath of the Tiananmen crackdown, were tried, convicted; and sentenced to prison

As a deterrent to would-be counterrevolutionaries, in the last two weeks of June at least thirty-five people in five different cities, mostly workers, unemployed youths, and members of the urban "floating population," were hastily tried, sentenced, and publicly executed for various acts of violence committed during the uprising of early June. Contrary to widespread rumors, no students or intellectuals were among those sentenced to death for their role in the June disturbances.[416]

While the public security apparatus mobilized for a crackdown on "ruffians," "thugs," and other assorted counterrevolutionaries, Party and government leaders turned their attention to the delicate task of fashioning an intraelite consensus in support of the 3–4 June crackdown. With the leadership deeply divided by the events of the previous two months, this proved no mean feat.

Damage control: The center tightens its grip

First came the self-congratulations; then came the denials. On 6 June, the government officially complimented the martial law forces for their bravery, restraint, and self-discipline in the face of counterrevolutionary rebellion. A day later, the political commissar of the PLA's 27th army appeared on Chinese television to assert that not a single student had been killed by troops during the operation to clear Tiananmen Square.[417] Seeking to shift the focus of attention from the PLA's bloody assault on the *shimin* of Beijing to acts of

terms of varying lengths for assorted "counterrevolutionary crimes." Eighteen other dissidents had all formal charges against them dropped, and an additional forty-five were released from detention in lieu of formal charges being filed. Among the thirty-one convicted dissidents, some, including Liu Xiaobo, were credited for time already served and were released from custody after reportedly showing "sincere repentance" for their actions; Wang Dan, whose alleged crimes included "counterrevolutionary propaganda and incitement," reportedly showed repentance at his trial and was sentenced to four years in prison; Ren Wanding, remaining unrepentant throughout, was sentenced to seven years; Chen Ziming and Wang Juntao, who were defiant in protesting their innocence, were given the harshest sentences of all, thirteen years each, on charges of sedition. According to reports circulating in Beijing, the defense attorneys who represented Chen and Wang at their trials were subjected to considerable governmental harassment following the conclusion of the courtroom proceedings. See CND, 4 April 1991. For accounts of the trials of the Beijing democracy activists, see NYT, 27 January and 13 February 1991; Associated Press, 12 February 1991; and CND, 10 and 25 March 1991.

416 Among those executed were three young workers accused of setting fire to the Shanghai train that had plowed into a crowd of demonstrators on 6 June. By September 1990, Amnesty International had recorded the names of more than fifty people sentenced to death for crimes allegedly committed in connection with protests against the military crackdown of 3–4 June. See Amnesty International, *China: The massacre. . . .* , 54–8.

417 The distinction here was a rather fine one. Although the 27th army had been responsible for much of the bloodshed that occurred in the western part of Beijing, between Muxidi and Tiananmen Square, on the night of 3–4 June, neither it nor any other main force units of the PLA had actually gunned down students in the Square. There were some early reports of Chinese tanks crushing students in sleeping bags and tents on the Square, but these reports have generally been discounted due to lack of reliable eyewitness corroboration.

violence committed against the army by "ruffians"' and "rioters," he described
in detail a series of antimilitary atrocities. This was to become the pattern for
government self-justification in the weeks and months that followed, that is,
that the PLA's use of deadly force on 3–4 June was a "defensive" reaction forced
upon the martial law forces by the violent provocations of counterrevolutionary
conspirators.[418]

On 8 June, Premier Li Peng, accompanied by a somber and restrained
Wan Li, appeared on television to reaffirm the government's gratitude to
the martial law forces for their heroic role in restoring order in Beijing.[419]
The next day, 9 June, Deng Xiaoping appeared publicly for the first time in
several weeks. In a televised meeting attended by virtually the entire Chinese
civilian and military high commands, minus only Zhao Ziyang and Hu Qili,
Deng effusively praised the martial law forces for their bravery in nipping a
counterrevolutionary rebellion in the bud. Reflecting on the sources of China's
crisis, Deng defended his reform policies and argued that the rebellion had
been the inevitable result of Party leaders permitting the global climate of
bourgeois liberalization to spread unchecked within China:

> In recent days I have pondered these points.... Is there anything wrong
> with the basic concept of reform and openness? No. Without reform and
> openness how could we have what we have today? ... [Nor is] there anything
> wrong with the four cardinal principles. If there is anything amiss, it's
> that these principles haven't been thoroughly implemented; they haven't
> been used as the basic concept to educate the people the students, and
> educate all the cadres and party members. The crux of the current incident is
> basically a confrontation between the four cardinal principles and bourgeois
> liberalization.[420]

Toward the end of June, Party leaders convened an enlarged CC plenum.
Attended by almost 200 old-timers of the CAC, the Fourth Plenum formally removed Zhao Ziyang and Hu Qili from the Politburo and the Central
Secretariat.[421] Zhao stood accused of a series of "grave errors and mistakes,"
including "splitting the Party," and was stripped of all formal Party posts

---

418 The most detailed governmental account of the origins and development of the Tiananmen crisis was
contained in a 30 June speech by mayor Chen Xitong to the NPC SC. The text of Chen's speech appears
in *CQ* 120 (December 1989), 919–46.
419 The appearance of Wan Li, who did not speak, alongside Li Peng on this occasion was clearly designed
to demonstrate to the Chinese people (and more particularly to restive Party, government, and army
cadres throughout the country) that the top leadership had closed ranks, and that even those leaders
who had previously sympathized with the student protests had now gone over to the side of the
hard-liners.
420 Deng's speech is translated in *BR* 32.28 (10–16 July 1989), 14–17. See also *FEER*, 10 August 1989,
13.
421 The communiqué of the fourth plenum appears in CQ 119 (September 1989), 729–31; for analysis,
see David L. Shambaugh, "The fourth and fifth plenary sessions of the 13th CCP central committee,"
CQ 120 (December 1989), 852–62.

(though he was not expelled); his request to address the plenum in his own defense was turned down.[422] Hu Qili, in turn, was reprimanded for having supported the wrong side at the critical moment but was spared further disciplinary action. Two other erstwhile Zhao loyalists, Yan Mingfu and Rui Xingwen, were also dismissed from the Party's Central Secretariat.[423]

After securing the dismissal of Zhao and his key allies, the Fourth Plenum turned to the business of selecting a new general secretary, an exercise that should have been largely pro forma, insofar as Deng Xiaoping had already made known his personal choice for the post: Shanghai party secretary (and former mayor) Jiang Zemin. Despite having the advantage of Deng's support, however, Jiang barely managed to muster a majority of votes in the CC.[424] To round out the new party leadership group, two other newcomers were promoted from the ranks of the Politburo to join Jiang Zemin on the revamped SC: the veteran economic planner and Party organization department head, Song Ping, and the reformist ex-mayor of Tianjin, Li Ruihuan.[425]

At a meeting of the NPC Standing Committee, held at the end of June, Hu Jiwei's 22 May petition drive, urging an emergency meeting of the SC for the purpose of reversing Li Peng's martial law declaration, was severely criticized, and Hu himself was accused of complicity in a plot to further the aims of the "turmoil creators," including the aim of securing Li Peng's dismissal. In his defense, Hu insisted that the petition drive had been wholly "reasonable and legal," and he denied that his real motive had been to oust Li Peng.

---

422 At an earlier meeting of the Politburo, on 14 June, Zhao had steadfastly refused to acknowledge his culpability: "First, I did not make a mistake; second I still hold that the starting point of the student movement was good. They were patriotic" (*BX* 203 [1 November 1989], 19–22).

423 Other key Zhaoists removed from Party posts at the Fourth Plenum included Zhao's political adviser, Bao Tong (who had already been arrested); An Zhiwen, vice-minister of the State Commission for Reform of the Economic Structure; Wen Jiabao, head of the CC General Office; and Du Runsheng, director of the Rural Policy Research Center. On 23 June, the pro-Zhao director and the chief editor of *RMRB* were removed from their posts, ostensibly for "reasons of health." Soon afterward, minister of culture Wang Meng was also forced to resign.

424 As early as 31 May, Deng had indicated that Jiang Zemin would be the "core" (*hexin*) of the new Party leadership (*I&S* 26.3 [March 1990], 13). Evidently, Chen Yun had initially recommended Yao Yilin to replace Zhao Ziyang as general secretary, whereas Peng Zhen had favored Qiao Shi (Li Peng had reportedly been tainted as a result of his role in declaring, and later enforcing, martial law). Jiang Zemin, a compromise candidate, had been nominated by Li Xiannian. Deng's expression of support for Jiang was ostensibly based on four primary criteria: First, Jiang occupied a centrist position on the reform spectrum, i.e., he was committed both to economic reform and to the four cardinal principles; second, he was an outsider who was not beholden to Chen Yun or any other factional interests; third, he had taken a firm stand against bourgeois liberalism in the Shanghai media; and fourth, he had succeeded in defusing student protest in Shanghai without recourse to martial law or organized violence (*I&S* 25.7 [July 1989], 1–4). For analysis of Jiang Zemin's role in handling student protest in Shanghai, see Maier "Tiananmen 1989 . . . ," 3–6, and passim.

425 Li Peng, Qiao Shi, and Yao Yilin all remained on the new SC, thus raising its total membership from five to six. To replace the three dismissed members of the Central Secretariat (Zhao, Yan, and Rui), Li Ruihuan and Party General Office director Ding Guang'en were added to that body.

Hu's arguments were dismissed as "flawed" and "lacking justification."[426] On 3 July, premier Li sent the NPC Standing Committee a draft law on demonstrations, stipulating, among other things, that henceforth protesters would not be allowed to question the leadership of the CCP or undermine the nation's unity or stability in any way.

In the aftermath of the Fourth Plenum, China's elderly hard-liners sought to consolidate their gains. Calling Zhao Ziyang the "'root of evil'. . . who intended to reach his required goals through turmoil," Li Xiannian urged a new rectification drive to eliminate remnant pockets of Zhaoist influence within the Party. Wang Zhen charged Zhao with "surrendering to the bourgeoisie." Along similar lines, Peng Zhen accused Zhao of "working with hostile forces at home and abroad to overthrow the CCP and disrupt the socialist system." Official media sources now began to hold the former general secretary personally responsible for a wide variety of societal ills, including hyperinflation, social instability, and rampant official profiteering.[427]

In the face of strong conservative pressures to prosecute Zhao Ziyang, spearheaded by Chen Yun and supported by Li Peng and Yao Yilin, Deng Xiaoping refused to be drawn into an anti-Zhao vendetta. Counseling caution and restraint in the handling of Zhao's case, China's senior leader once again revealed his underlying concern for carefully counterbalancing *fang* and *shou*. "Let us not get tangled up in who is responsible for what right now," he said on 16 June; "Let those questions be raised two or three years from now."[428] Deng prevailed, and no formal charges were filed against Zhao; however, for the next several months the former general secretary remained confined to quarters, living in relative comfort at Hu Yaobang's former residence in Fuqiang Lane, Beijing.[429]

Although Deng's personal intervention enabled Zhao to avoid criminal prosecution, CAC old comrades nonetheless went forward with their attempt to root out remnant Zhaoists within the Party apparatus. At the end of June 1989, the CDIC, under Peng Zhen protégé Qiao Shi, launched a new rectification drive, in the course of which all Party members in Beijing and other cities were required to undergo investigation and reregistration in connection with their attitudes and behavior during the six weeks of turmoil. Notwithstanding its intended gravity, however, the new campaign was muted from the outset by a virtual conspiracy of silence on the part of leading cadres and

426 *RMRB*, 11 July 1989; *CQ* 120 (December 1989), 894–5.
427 *WHB*, 24 July 1989; *FEER*, 10 August 1989, 13; *SWB/FE* 0518 (26 July 1989). For a summary of the charges against Zhao in this period, see *CQ* 120 (September 1989), 900–1.
428 *WHB*, 28 June 1989.
429 In the spring of 1990, Deng reportedly gave the go-ahead for Zhao eventually to begin resuming some administrative responsibilities after first undergoing an extensive period of "investigation and research," *South China Morning Post*, 24 and 25 July 1990.

work unit heads, many of whom withheld from investigation teams the names of people in their units who had taken part in the April–May demonstrations. Frustrated by this evident lack of cadre enthusiasm for the new rectification campaign, Party conservatives in mid-July created a special investigatory body to facilitate the work of "ferreting out the guilty ones." As before, however, the severity of the Party's internal probe continued to be effectively softened by a combination of passive resistance and pro forma compliance on the part of large numbers of unit leaders.[430]

Disarming urban anger; The new anticorruption drive

Even as Party and government leaders circled their wagons in defense June crackdown, they came under intense pressure to confront the u problems that had given rise to the massive urban protests of Apr As early as 6 June, State Council spokesman Yuan Mu acknowled to (re-)open a dialogue between government and citizens on a socioeconomic and political issues. "Once the whole situation said, "the government will give much thought to proposal raised by the people of various circles, including the stud official profiteering, uprooting corruption, and promoting and earnestly accept suggestions from various quarters."[431] non: Xiaoping, in a speech on 16 June, explicitly linked . There confidence in the Party and government with the co policies with the need to deal forthrightly with the proble who engage

> We must perform certain acts to inspire satisfactie, particularly
> are two aspects to this: one is to pursue the
> more aggressively, and the other is to catch the Party
> in corruption. . . . If we fail to catch and pu confidence, the Party
> those inside the party, we run the risk of f drive in the summer of

In line with Deng's objective of reg the expulsion of hundreds belatedly launched a high-profile ant the Politburo decreed that all 1989. On 10 July, the *People's Dail* m engaging in private business of corrupt Party members; two w nger have access to imported cars *gaogan zidi* would henceforth be ovember 1989; and BX, 16 December 1989, in ibid., and that top Party officials wo National Public Radio, *Weekend Edition*, 10 March 1990. st-talking Party leaders turned out to be among chose most from harm.

430 See, e.g., *JB*, 10 November J989, in also recommended setting a public example by severely punishing
    19 December 1989; also Daniel So profiteers.
    Interestingly, some of the ostensib
    effective in shielding their subo
431 *SWB/FE* 0476 (7 June 1989).
432 *ICM*, September 1989, 3–5.
    one or two dozen high-level

and private supplies of food. At the same time, the Politburo ordered the breakup of the notorious Kang Hua Development Corporation.[433] A month later, the Chinese Auditing Administration imposed fines amounting to more than RMB 50 million yuan ($US 12.8 million) on five of China's largest quasi-private corporations: Kang Hua, CITIC, Everbright, China Economic Development Corporation, and China Rural Trust and Development Corporation. In September, the governor of Hainan province, Liang Xiang, was dismissed from his post on assorted charges of economic malfeasance, making him the highest-ranking official to be netted in the new anticorruption drive.[434]

The unquiet summer of 1989: "Neijin, Waisong"

By midsummer, a situation of uneasy calm, characterized as *"neijin, waisong"* ("internal tension, external tranquility"), had blanketed the nation's capital. Through an extraordinary assertion of personal authority and Party discipline, with strong backing from the so-called Yang family generals within the PLA, Deng Xiaoping had managed to weather the immediate crisis and the flow of high-level Party and military defections that threatened to China's Communist regime.[435] Yet the government's visible success in restoring public order was achieved at considerable cost. Whether measured by the severe loss of popular legitimacy in urban China, the further erosion of central authority over the provinces, the emergence of deep schisms within the Party, the paralysis of economic decision making, or the diplomatic and economic sanctions imposed upon China by foreign governments, banks, and aid agencies, the costs were staggering.[436]

[433] As noted, profits, of ... be deeply inv... for the Handicap... publishing erotic ... see "The politics of p... manuscript, n.a., n.d., 19...

[434] By April 1991, 72,000 CC... subjected to lesser forms of dis... bourgeois liberalism. No breakdo... See CND, 18 April 1991. On implen...

[435] It has been widely reported that Yang Shan... PLA "family" (including his half-brother, gene... to be high in the command structure of the 27... headed by Jiang Zemin, in exchange for a domi... military command structure. See *South China Morning* ...

[436] These negative effects are examined in Tony Saich, "... revolution from above," in Marta Dassù and Tony Saich, eds... dismay. See also Swaine, "China faces the 1990s...."; and Hsiu...

Deng Pufang had frequently been linked to the activities, and enormous ... to his links with Kang Hua, the younger Deng was reported to ... the Huaxia company, a subsidiary of the China Welfare Fund ... director) that in 1988 had been fined RMB 150,000 yuan for ... shady economic dealings of Deng and other *gaogan zidi*, ... The case of the *Taizidang* (Princes' party)" (unpublished ...

reportedly been expelled, and an additional 256,000 ... post-Tiananmen crackdown on official corruption and ... istics, e.g., by type of offense, was given, however. ... the 1989 anticorruption campaign, see Michael D. ... *OC* 39.3 (May–June 1990), 20–35. ... this full weight, and the weight of his extended ... bing, and at least two other relatives reputed ... p), behind Deng's new centrist coalition, ... in China's revamped post-Tiananmen ... uly 1990. ... m decade in China: The limits to ... reform decade in China: From hope to ... Mainland China's paradox...."

Despite the initiation of high-profile campaigns to "emulate Lei Feng"[437] and to improve the public image of the PLA (e.g., by having soldiers clear garbage from sidewalks, give haircuts to civilians, and help old folks to cross streets), the PLA's prestige and morale reportedly fell to an all-time low. According to a high-level PLA source, over 100 senior military officers had "breached discipline in a serious manner" during the struggle to crush the student-led rebellion in early June; an additional 1,400 PLA soldiers had "shed their weapons and run away" during the crackdown.[438]

Isolated sniper attacks against martial law troops reportedly continued throughout the summer of 1989. In late July a Chinese newspaper revealed an attempt by a Beijing resident to kill martial law troops by offering them a bucket of drinking water laced with poison.[439] In a highly unusual display of intraelite dissidence, the commander of the Twenty-Seventh Army, who was believed to have given the initial order for troops to open fire on civilians near Muxidi on the night of 3 June, was audibly hissed by an audience composed primarily of civilian cadres when he rose to address a propaganda conference in Beijing in August; obviously flustered, he angrily denied that his troops had slaughtered innocent civilians.

Deep divisions were also at play within the PLA. According to one oft-repeated (but subsequently discounted) rumor that swept through China in the summer of 1989, Yang Shangkun, in an attempted putsch, had placed four high-level PLA officials, including Defense Minister Qin Jiwei and three regional commanders, Beijing's Zhou Yibing, Guangzhou's Zhang Wannian, and Nanjing's Xiang Shouzhi, under house arrest. Although the rumor proved false, it nonetheless pointed up the existence of a serious schism within the military between forces supporting the June crackdown (reportedly led by the Yang family generals) and those opposing it (including Qin Jiwei and a number of military region and district commanders).[440]

---

437 Lei Feng was a young PLA recruit who died an accidental death in 1962. The "spirit of Lei Feng," characterized by unquestioning loyalty, self-sacrifice, and ceaseless devotion to duty, has recurrently been invoked by Chinese leaders in periods of severe ideological stress or flagging military morale.

438 These figures were revealed by the PLA's chief political commissar, Yang Baibing. The 111 officers charged with "breach of discipline" included 21 officers at or above the rank of divisional commander, 36 regimental or battalion commanders, and 54 company-level commanders (*South China Morning Post*, 28 December 1989). Subsequently, it was reported that between 1,500 and 3,000 army officers were required to undergo loyalty checks as a result of their questionable behavior during and after the June uprising (*The Observer* [London], 18 February 1990). On the role of the military during the May–June crisis and its aftermath, see Harlan Jencks, "Party authority and military power: Communist China's continuing crisis," *I&S* 26.7 (July 1990), 11–39; Dreyer, "The People's Liberation Army ...," 42–5; Wilson and Ji, "Leadership by 'lines'...," 38–43; and Swaine, "China faces the 1990s ...," 26–7, 32–4.

439 *JJRB*, 31 July 1989.

440 A wholesale reshuffle of PLA regional commanders took place in the spring of 1990, in the course of which six of the seven regional commanders and five of their seven chief political commissars were transferred or retired. Evidently, the "Yang-family generals" were the prime beneficiaries of the reshuffle. See *FEER*, 14 June 1990, 32; also Jencks, "Party authority and military power ...," 25–6.

Continuing student unrest was another prime source of concern to Party and government leaders throughout the summer of 1989. In an attempt to deal with the problem of student rebelliousness at its putative source, the government on 21 July announced a decision to cut back on new college enrollments in the humanities and social sciences for 1989–90 by a total of 30,000 students; two days later, several hundred Beida students spontaneously marched through the campus late at night to protest both the cutbacks and the crackdown; as they marched, they sang, with more than a slight hint of irony and sarcasm, the lyrics to a well-known revolutionary song: "Without the communist party, there would be no new China." When the song was finished, the students began to chant, with gleeful double entendre, the lyrics to an animated television commercial for a pesticide spray: "We are the mighty pests! We are the mighty pests! Oh, oh, here come the dreaded pest-killers; let's bug out of here!" Three weeks later, in mid-August, the tolerant, reform-minded president of Beida, Ding Shisun, was dismissed; concurrently, it was announced that the entire 1989 Beida freshman class, whose numbers had been cut back from 2,000 to only 800, would be required to undergo a year of military training before being permitted to attend regular classes.

In mid-August, Beijing Mayor Chen Xitong disclosed that previously announced plans to hold a military parade in Beijing on 1 October, the fortieth anniversary of the founding of the PRC, had officially been scrapped, At the same time, it was announced that Tiananmen Square, closed to the public since 4 June, would soon be reopened to selected tour groups "in an organized manner." Although the government now routinely asserted that everything was back to business as usual in the nation's capital, the continued presence of large numbers of uniformed, fully armed martial law troops in the heart of Beijing bespoke a different condition: *neijin, waisong*. As if to underscore that condition, at summer's end the authorities in Beijing intervened at the eleventh hour to cancel a performance of Verdi's *Requiem*, which was to have been presented on the Beida campus to commemorate the passing of 100 days since Tiananmen. In lieu of the canceled performance, Beida students held a candlelight vigil on school grounds. Though liberalization had given way to catastrophic repression in yet another revolution of the *fang–shou* cycle, the students' flickering candles appeared to bespeak a tremendous confidence that eventually there would be another round of letting go.

Epilogue: The end of an era?

In the aftermath of the Tiananmen crisis, the longer-term consequences of China's national trauma could only be guessed at. But when the PRC marked its fortieth anniversary on 1 October 1989, there were few congratulations and fewer smiles. Though legions of gaily outfitted dancers and a lavish display of fireworks brightened the appearance of Tiananmen Square, the mood in the nation's capital was anything but festive.

It was a far cry from 1 October 1949, when Mao Zedong had ascended the rostrum at Tiananmen to the sound of thunderous cheers, proclaiming triumphantly, "The Chinese people have stood up!" On that earlier occasion, there had been genuine popular elation and high hopes for China's future. Now, forty years later, the capital was under martial law, hope seemed strangely out of place, and elation was wholly absent as the nation's shoulders sagged visibly under the weight of the Tiananmen tragedy.

All great revolutions inspire millennarian visions; few ultimately deliver the goods. So it was with Mao's original revolution, which exhausted itself in the course of two grandiose, and ultimately hugely destructive, experiments in human social engineering: the Great Leap Forward and the Great Proletarian Cultural Revolution. Now, it seemed, Deng Xiaoping's "second Chinese revolution" had also reached a point of near-exhaustion, running out of fresh ideas and of people to implement them.

As the 1980s gave way to the 1990s, a cascading wave of bourgeois liberalization swept over the Soviet Union, Eastern Europe, and Central Europe, causing Communist regimes throughout the region to concede power. In Moscow, the original Bolshevik Party of V. I. Lenin formally accepted the principle of political pluralism, thereby relinquishing its seventy-two-year monopoly on power; in Warsaw, a rebellious union organizer was elected president; in Prague, a dissident playwright assumed the mantle of leadership; in Bucharest, the Communist army refused an order to fire upon its own people, and the dictator who gave the order was executed. Reacting to these events, a group of old comrades in Beijing, circling their wagons ever tighter, demanded renewed allegiance to the four cardinal principles and proposed, yet again, the name of their irrepressible paladin, Deng Liqun, for promotion to the CC Politburo. Under such circumstances, many Chinese citizens hunkered down for the long haul, taking what comfort they could from actuarial tables that suggested that the crusty old comrades of the CAC could not, despite their rumored periodic blood transfusions and Qigong breathing exercises, live forever.

CHAPTER 6

REACTION, RESURGENCE, AND SUCCESSION: CHINESE POLITICS SINCE TIANANMEN

JOSEPH FEWSMITH

Tiananmen shook the Chinese Communist Party (CCP) to its core. The charge leveled against former general secretary Zhao Ziyang was that "[a]t the critical juncture involving the life and death of the Party and state, he made the mistake of supporting turmoil and splitting the Party, and he bears unshirkable responsibility for the formation and development of the turmoil. The nature and consequences of his mistakes are very serious."[1] The issues the Party faced, however, ran far deeper than even this charge suggested. Tiananmen threw open a whole series of questions that had been simmering just below the surface for years.

The most fundamental of these was the nature of reform itself. Tiananmen, many Party leaders believed, was the inevitable denouement of the reform program that Zhao led and symbolized; more important, the content of that reform program was inextricably intertwined with Zhao's patron, senior leader Deng Xiaoping. The question raised by Tiananmen, then, was the nature of Deng's leadership and thus whether or not the Party should continue reform as Deng had defined it. Many believed it should not.

The question of the content of reform, or, in Chinese jargon, the political line,[2] was related to a number of state–society issues: the relations between the

---

1 "Zhongguo gongchandang di shisanju Zhongyang weiyuanhui di sice quanti huiyi gongbao" (Communiqué of the Fourth Plenary Session of the Thirteenth Central Committee of the CCP), in *Shisanda yilai zhongyao wenxian xuanbian, zhong* (Important documents since the Thirteenth Party Congress, vol. 2; hereafter, *Shisanda yilai*, 2), 544.

2 In the reform period, different conceptions of the scope, pace, and goal of reform grew up around Chen Yun, on the one hand, and Deng Xiaoping, on the other. Although Chen never challenged Deng's "core" status directly, he and his colleagues did develop a systematic critique of Deng's approach to reform. This critique was used in an effort to limit reform. The conservative critique of reform became the basis for criticizing a whole series of policies, and implicitly Deng's leadership, in the post-Tiananmen period. It thus seems appropriate to refer to this struggle as a "line" struggle, even though it remained implicit. For a discussion of the conflict between Chen and Deng, see Joseph Fewsmith, *Dilemmas of reform in China*. For a contrary interpretation, see Frederick C. Teiwes, "The paradoxical post-Mao transition: From obeying the leader to 'normal politics,'" *China Journal*, 34 (July 1995), 55–94.

central government and the localities; the rapidly changing social structure of Chinese society, including the emergence of a middle class; the growing independence of the intellectual elite; the rising expectations of society; and the very real fears of many people that reform might hurt rather than help their interests. In other words, reform had generated a range of profound social changes, and the question that had racked the Party for years was how it should respond to these changes. How should it channel, suppress, or incorporate the demands that increasingly emanated from this changing society?

Another broad area of questions generated by Tiananmen revolved around China's relations with the outside world. Deng Xiaoping himself raised this issue in his 9 June 1989 address to martial law troops. Deng declared the Tiananmen incident "the inevitable result of the domestic microclimate and the international macroclimate."[3] This sense that domestic upheavals were influenced (if not instigated) by outside forces raised the issue of readjusting China's relations with the outside world, particularly the United States. This issue has continued to intrude on Chinese domestic politics throughout the post-Tiananmen period as first East Europe and then the Soviet Union rejected communism, as relations with the United States have remained generally strained, and as closer ties with East Asia have suggested alternative development models.

In the seven years between Tiananmen and Deng's fading from the political scene, Chinese politics were driven by deep divisions among the elite, uncertainty about how to respond to the changing forces of society, a rapidly changing international environment, and finally, the emergence of a new generation to take the place of the founders of the People's Republic of China (PRC). In June 1989 a shaken and divided Party leadership tried to begin the process of reconstituting itself while sorting out how its domestic and foreign policies should or should not be changed. Looming over these initial efforts was the shadow of former general secretary Zhao Ziyang, who quickly became a foil for critics of reform.

THE QUESTION OF ZHAO

The question of how to deal with Zhao Ziyang was inevitably linked with the question of Deng Xiaoping's leadership, not just because Zhao's selection first as premier and then as general secretary now seemed to reflect poorly on Deng Xiaoping's judgment, but because Zhao had been implementing a

---

3 Deng Xiaoping, "Zai jiejian shoudu xieyan budui junyishang ganbu shi de jianghua" (Talk on receiving martial law cadres at the army level and above in the capital), in *Deng Xiaoping wenxuan* (Selected works of Deng Xiaoping), 3.302.

political-cum-economic line long supported by Deng.[4] Deng clearly recognized that dismissing a second successor (following former general secretary Hu Yaobang's ouster in January 1987) would raise doubts about his own judgment, and he was determined to salvage as much advantage as he could by denying the fruits of victory to the winners.

Four days before the crackdown and more than three weeks before the Party's Central Committee would meet to confirm changes in the leadership, Deng Xiaoping met with Premier Li Peng and Politburo Standing Committee (PSC) member Yao Yilin to tell them that Jiang Zemin, then CCP secretary of Shanghai, would be plucked from relative obscurity to become the "core" of the third generation of CPC leadership.[5] In explaining his decision, Deng almost contemptuously told Li and Yao, "The people see reality. If we put up a front so that people feel that it is an ossified leadership, a conservative leadership, or if the people believe that it is a mediocre leadership that cannot reflect the future of China, then there will be constant trouble and there will never be a peaceful day." He also tried to forestall an all-out attack on Zhao's policies (and himself) by declaring that "the political report of the Thirteenth Party Congress was passed by the representatives of the Party to the congress; not even one character must be changed."[6]

When Deng met with leaders of martial law troops on 9 June, he declared that the line of "one center and two basic points" (economic development was the center, and reform and opening to the outside world on the one hand and opposition to "bourgeois liberalization" on the other were the two basic points), which had been adopted at the Thirteenth Party Congress in 1987, was correct and that reform and opening up must be pursued even more vigorously.[7] Moreover, a week before the Fourth Plenum convened, Deng urged the Party to avoid destructive ideological struggles: "If at this time we open up some sort of discussion on ideology, such as a discussion

4 One can draw distinctions between Zhao and Deng, but the similarities predominate. Overall, Zhao appears to have been closer to Deng on more issues than was Hu Yaobang. Although Zhao was more open-minded in his response to the Tiananmen demonstrations than Deng, Zhao was hardly a liberal. It was, after all, Zhao who sponsored discussions on the "new authoritarianism." The Thirteenth Party Congress, which clearly bears Zhao's imprint, was strongly supported by Deng. On economic issues, Deng was in some sense the more radical, or at least the more impatient, as suggested by his 1988 advocacy of rapid price reform. Certainly in the eyes of Zhao's and Deng's critics, the similarities were far greater than the differences.

5 In his 31 May talk to Li Peng and Yao Yilin, Deng defined three "generations" of leadership: the first was led by Mao Zedong, the second by himself, and the third by Jiang Zemin. See Deng Xiaoping, "Zucheng yige shixing gaige de you xiwang de lingdao jiti" (Organizing a reformist, hopeful leadership collective), in *Deng Xiaoping wenxuan*, 3.298–9.

6 Ibid., 296–301.

7 Deng, "Zai jiejian shoudu xieyan budui junyishang ganbu shi de jianghua," 3.302–8. Of course, Deng coupled his declaration of reform and opening up with the need to uphold the four cardinal principles and to increase ideological and political education.

regarding markets and planning, then not only would bringing up this sort of issue be disadvantageous to stability but it would cause us to miss an opportunity."[8]

The Fourth Plenary Session of the Thirteenth Central Committee, which convened on 23–4 June 1989 following a three-day enlarged Politburo meeting, confirmed Deng's decision to name Jiang Zemin as general secretary and added him, veteran planner Song Ping, and Tianjin mayor Li Ruihuan to the PSC. Li Ruihuan and Ding Guan'gen, Deng's bridge partner, were added to the Secretariat in partial replacement of Zhao associates Hu Qili, Rui Xingwen, and Yan Mingfu, who were removed. On the critical question of Zhao, however, the plenum could not come to a final resolution. Having judged Zhao's actions harshly, the conclave nevertheless could only declare that the party would "continue to investigate his problem."[9]

The plenum's failure to conclude Zhao's case reflected the depth of division within the Party. Obviously, some within the Party wanted to pursue the issue of Zhao's guilt, perhaps even to the point of criminal prosecution, a course that would have had profound implications for Deng Xiaoping and the continuation of reform. For instance, Yuan Mu, the hard-line spokesman for the State Council and protégé of Premier Li Peng, stated that Zhao's case would be handled "in accordance with the criterion based on law," suggesting the possibility of legal prosecution.[10] Some Party elders were blunter. PRC president Li Xiannian allegedly called Zhao the "root cause of the riots and rebellion," while Party elder Peng Zhen accused Zhao of "attempting to topple the Communist Party and wreaking havoc with the socialist system in coordination with hostile powers at home and abroad."[11]

In fact, during the campaign against "bourgeois liberalization" that was unleashed following Tiananmen, it was impossible to separate criticism of Zhao Ziyang from issues of ideology and Party line, and there is every indication that hard liners within the Party wished to press such issues with an eye to curtailing Deng's authority and returning the Party to the more limited notion of reform that had prevailed in the late 1970s and early 1980s. In his 1989 National Day (1 October) address, Jiang Zemin asserted that there were two types of reform: one that upheld the four cardinal principles and another that was based on "bourgeois liberalization." The question, Jiang said, was

8 Deng Xiaoping, "Disandai lingdao jiti de dangwu zhi ji" (Urgent tasks of the third generation leadership collective), in *Deng Xiaoping wenxuan*, 3.312.
9 "Zhongguo gongchandang di shisanju Zhongyang weiyuanhui di sice quanti huiyi gongbao," 2.543–6.
10 Xinhua, trans. in *FBIS Daily Report: China* (hereafter, *FBIS-Chi*), 12 July 1989, 25.
11 [Zeng Bin] Tseng Pin, "Party struggle exposed by senior statesmen themselves; meanwhile, the new leading group is trying hard to build new image," *JB*, 145 (10 August 1989), trans. in *FBIS-Chi*, 10 August 1989, 14. See also *WHB* (Hong Kong), 24 July 1989.

whether the socialist orientation would be up-held.[12] In posing the question in this way, Jiang raised the issue that would dominate Chinese politics for much of the next two years: What was socialist and what was capitalist?

By the same reasoning, if Zhao had advocated a reform that was based on "bourgeois liberalization" and hence was capitalist in nature, then Zhao's mistake would not have been a simple error of implementation (one hand firm and the other lax, as Deng put it) but an error of line. Although the Party, in the interest of putting ideological battles behind it at the beginning of the reform era, had ceased to describe intra-Party conflicts as "line struggles," the notion of political line and hence of line struggle remained very much a part of Party life at the elite level. For instance, in a talk to a national meeting of organization department heads, Song Ping implicitly criticized Zhao for making line errors. For Song, Tiananmen was the inevitable outcome of a trend of bourgeois liberalization that extended back to Democracy Wall in 1978, had never been effectively opposed, and had resulted in such "absurd theories" (*miaolun*) as the "criterion of productive forces." The theory of productive forces, a phrase used (frequently by critics) to describe the view that anything that improves the economy is *ipso facto* socialist, was voiced prominently in an article by Zhao Ziyang that appeared in the *People's Daily (Renmin ribao)* in February 1988,[13] but Song's reference was clearly to Deng Xiaoping as well. It was, after all, Deng who had always asserted that "it doesn't matter what color the cat, the one that catches the mouse is a good cat."[14] This trend of bourgeois liberalization, Song asserted, went against the Marxist political line set by the Third Plenum in 1978, and Tiananmen was the "bitter fruit of violating this [Marxist] *line*."[15]

12 Jiang Zemin, "Zai qingzhu Zhonghua renmin gongheguo chengli sishi zhounian dahuishang de jianghua" (Talk celebrating the fortieth anniversary of the establishment of the PRC), in *Shisanda yilai*, 2.618. Deng had opened the way for this line of analysis in his 31 May talk with Li Peng and Yao Yilin. In that talk, Deng said that the "center of their [in reference to Zhao Ziyang and others] so-called 'reform' is capitalization. The reform I talk about is different." See "Zucheng yige shixing gaige de you xiwang de lingdao jiti," 3.297.
13 Zhao Ziyang, "Further emancipate the mind and further liberate the productive forces," *RMRB*, 8 February 1988, trans. in *FBIS-Chi*, 8 February 1988, 12–14.
14 In the aftermath of Deng's trip to the South in early 1992, a propaganda book put out to hype Deng's thought was unabashed in its touting of Deng's "criterion of productive forces." See Yu Xiguang and Li Langdong, eds., *Dachao xinqi: Deng Xiaoping nanxun qianqian houhou* (A great tide rising: Before and after Deng Xiaoping's southern sojourn).
15 Song Ping, "Zai quanguo zuzhi buzhang huiyi shang de jianghua" (Talk to a national meeting of organization department heads), in *Shisanda yilai*, 2.568–9, 574 (emphasis added). Contrast Song's emphasis on political loyalty with Li Ruihuan's statement that "[i]n assessing a leading cadre, his accomplishments in government are primary." See *Nanfang ribao*, 28 October 1989, trans. in *FBIS-Chi*, 6 November 1989, 22. See also Chen Yun's "six points," conveyed to the Central Advisory Commission in November 1991. The third point reads, "Marxists must admit that there are line struggles within the party, which is part of normal party life, and it is necessary to actively launch inner-Party criticism and self-criticism." [Luo Bing] Lo Ping and [Li Zejing] Li Tzu-ching, "Chen Yun raises six points of view to criticize Deng Xiaoping," *ZM*, 171 (1 January 1992), 18–19, trans. in *FBIS-Chi*, 3 January 1992, 22–3.

DENG'S STRATEGY

In the wake of the Tiananmen debacle and confronted by an outpouring of ideological vitriol from hard liners presenting themselves as true Marxists who had been attacked and suppressed by Zhao and his allies, Deng's strategy could only be the relatively passive one of emphasizing stability, promoting economic development, and relaxing the ideological atmosphere. In a talk with leaders on the eve of the Fourth Plenum, Deng urged that the Party not dissipate its energies in ideological disputes and called for "doing some things to satisfy the people."[16] In response, the State Council in July passed a resolution on resolving problems the people were concerned about, on restricting the activities of leading cadres' families, and on reorganizing suspect companies.[17] Similarly, Li Ruihuan, the former carpenter whom Deng had put in charge of ideology, made an effort to relax the ideological atmosphere in the summer by calling for a campaign against pornography.[18] It was a clever ploy that left conservatives nonplussed. After all, pornography was associated with Western influences, but it hardly raised the central ideological issues that conservatives wished to pursue. In September, Li asked in a sharply worded interview with the PRC-owned Hong Kong paper *Dagong bao*, "Why do we always have to go to excess?" Berating conservative ideologues, Li said, "We must not use dogmatic and rigid methods to criticize bourgeois liberalization."[19]

Deng also harped on the issue of stability (eventually coining the phrase "Stability overrides everything" [*wending yadao yiqie*])[20] and emphasized the continuity of reform and opening up. Deng had successfully employed similar tactics in 1987 after he had unceremoniously dumped General Secretary Hu Yaobang. In 1989, however, the situation was vastly different. First, the depth of Party division created by Tiananmen was far greater than at the time of Hu Yaobang's ouster. Second, Deng's prestige within the Party was also greatly diminished by Tiananmen and the disgrace of Zhao. Chen Yun had summed up the feelings of many conservatives when he had accused Deng of being

16 Deng, "Disandai lingdao jiti de dangwu zhi ji."
17 "Zhonggong Zhongyang, Guowuyuan guanyu jinqi zuo jijian qunzhong guanxin de shi de jueding" (Decision of the CCP Central Committee and State Council regarding doing a few things of concern to the masses in the present period), in *Shisanda yilai*, 2.555–7.
18 The campaign started on 11 July 1989, when the Press and Publications Administration issued a circular on rectifying the cultural market. Over the summer, Li spoke on the issue of pornography many times. See, for instance, Beijing television service, 24 August 1989, trans. in *FBIS-Chi*, 25 August 1989, 15–16.
19 "Li Ruihuan meets with Hong Kong journalists," *DGB*, 20 September 1989, trans. in *FBIS-Chi*, 20 September 1989, 10–12.
20 Deng apparently first used this phrase in his 31 October 1989 talk with Richard Nixon. See Deng Xiaoping, "Jiesu yanjun de ZhongMei guanxi yao you Meiguo caiqu zhudong" (Resolving the serious situation in Sino-U.S. relations requires that the U.S. take the initiative), in *Deng Xiaoping wenxuan*, 3–331.

rightist in his economic policies and leftist in his use of the military.[21] Deng could no longer dominate Chinas policy agenda.

Finally, the international situation made Deng's task much more difficult. On the one hand, China's relations with the West, particularly the United States, were strained badly by China's crackdown and the subsequent imposition of sanctions. Deng's room for maneuvering was extremely limited. On the other hand, the unraveling of communism in Eastern Europe made the threat of "peaceful evolution" very real to China's leaders and added weight to conservatives' contention that China should assert ideological leadership on issues of international socialism. Deng rejected such urgings, successfully arguing that China's leaders should "coolly observe, keep our feet steady, and react soberly." Whatever happened in the world, Deng said, China should concentrate on economic development.[22]

THE CONSERVATIVE CHALLENGE

As Deng and Li Ruihuan tried to cool the ideological atmosphere and refocus the Party's attention on reform and opening up, conservatives were determined to press their advantage. With the suppression of the protest movement in Beijing and elsewhere and the ouster of Zhao Ziyang, conservatives seized the opportunity to criticize Zhao's economic leadership and impose their own interpretation of economic reform. This effort began with the editing of Deng Xiaoping's remarks. In Deng's 9 June talk, he was quoted as referring to the "integration of planned economy and market regulation."[23] This expression restored the preferred usage of conservatives, which they had been able to impose during the 1981–2 retreat from more market-oriented reforms.[24] As later revealed, Deng had originally called for the integration of the "planned economy and the market economy," thus putting the two economic types on the same plane. Before his remarks were published in the *People's Daily*, however, conservatives had edited them to fit their agenda.[25]

In November 1989, Chen Yun's economic thought was restored as orthodoxy by the Fifth Plenary Session of the Thirteenth Central Committee. The "CCP Central Committee decision on furthering improvement and rectification and deepening reform" (frequently referred to as "the thirty-nine points") that was adopted by the plenum laid out a systematic, albeit implicit, critique

21 Richard Baum, *Burying Mao: Chinese politics in the age of Deng Xiaoping*, 319.
22 Deng Xiaoping, "Gaige kaifang zhengce wending, Zhongguo dayou xiwang" (If China's policy of reform and opening up remains stable, there is great hope for China), in *Deng Xiaoping wenxuan*, 3.321.
23 Deng, "Zai jiejian shoudu xieyan budui junyishang ganbu shi de jianghua," 306.
24 Fewsmith, *Dilemmas of reform in China*, ch. 3.   25 Baum, *Burying Mao*, 294.

of Zhao's management of the economy. That decision, like much commentary in the months after Tiananmen, intimated the implicit line struggle that had existed within the Party by suggesting that the economy had begun to go awry in 1984 – when the decision on the reform of the economic structure was adopted. Since that time, the Fifth Plenum decision declared, economic policy had ignored China's "national strength" (guoli – a famous Chen Yun thesis), allowing aggregate demand to "far, far" exceed aggregate supply, had upset the balance between industry and agriculture, had ignored basic industries, and had dispersed financial resources too widely, thus eroding the state's ability to exercise macroeconomic control. These problems, the decision declared, constituted a "mortal wound" (zhimingshang) to the economy.[26]

In his speech to the plenum, Jiang Zemin declared that the "greatest lesson" to be derived from the PRC's economic past was that the country must not "depart from its national conditions, exceed its national strength, be anxious for success, or have great ups and downs."[27] These were all well-known theses of Chen Yun, so Jiang's endorsement of Chen Yun's thought over Deng's line of reform and opening up was apparent.

Just as Party conservatives rejected Deng's economic line, they spurned efforts to reduce ideological tensions. As suggested above, their rejection of Deng's efforts to reduce tensions was based not only on the depth of division within the Party but also on the collapse of socialism in East Europe.[28]

On 15 December, Wang Renzhi, head of the Propaganda Department, launched a blistering attack on bourgeois liberalization in a talk to a Party-building class. In direct opposition to Deng's theses that economic development would promote social stability and that ideological debates should be put off, or better, not taken up, Wang argued that stability could be built only on the basis of Marxist ideology. Only in this way, Wang argued, could economic work be carried out without deviating from the socialist orientation. Wang, in effect, reinterpreted Deng's slogan "Stability overrides everything," a phrase coined to relax ideological tension, as a clarion call for making ideological struggle the basis of future stability. Lest anyone think that the time had come to relax the campaign against bourgeois liberalization, Wang declared,

---

26 "Zhonggong Zhongyang guanyu jinyibu zhili zhengdun he shenhua gaige de jueding (zheyao)" (CCP Central Committee decision on furthering improvement and rectification and deepening reform [outline]), in Shisanda yilai, 2.680–708. All these charges were part of the conservative critique of reform that had been ongoing at least since 1984.

27 Jiang Zemin, "Zai dang de shisanju wuzhong quanhui shang de jianghua" (Talk to the Fifth Plenary Session of the Thirteenth CCP Central Committee), in Shisanda yilai, 2.711.

28 Some within the Party argued that the implementation of reform in East Europe had led to the collapse of communism there, while others argued that communism collapsed because the planned economy had continued to prevail in those countries. Wu Jinglian, Jihua jingji haishi shichang jingji (Planned economy or market economy), 41.

"We have only just started" to clarify ideological errors and "The logic of struggle is cruel and merciless."[29]

Wang's speech was followed by a full-page article in the *People's Daily* praising the notorious "Zhuozhuo meeting" of 1987. At that meeting, conservative Party leaders, concerned that Zhao and others would blunt the campaign against bourgeois liberalization that unfolded in the wake of Hu Yaobang's ouster, tried to breathe new fire into the movement. It was after that meeting, and perhaps because of it, that Deng authorized Zhao's famous 13 May 1987 speech closing off the campaign against bourgeois liberalization and preparing the political atmosphere for the Thirteenth Party Congress in the fall. Now, in the wake of Zhao's ouster, conservative writer Chen Daixi, under the pseudonym "Yi Ren," accused Zhao of using "all kinds of dirty tricks with the most malicious motives" to suppress the Zhuozhuo meeting.[30] Obviously, Chen, as well as other conservative writers at the time, were aware that Deng had fully supported the stoppage of the 1987 campaign and they were determined to prevent him from doing so again.

REINFORCING STATE PLANNING

The strength of the conservative wing of the Party in the winter of 1989–90 was indicated not only by the directness of the challenge to Deng's ideological authority but also by a major effort to restore at least a significant measure of state planning to the economy. For years, conservatives had complained that reform had directed investment into small-scale, less efficient industries (mostly township and village enterprises – TVEs) that competed with large and medium-sized state-owned industries for scarce energy, transportation, and raw materials. As a result, basic energy and material sectors were drained of investment capital while transportation and energy supplies were always strained by the demand. Moreover, reform strategy had led to a regional bias as TVEs along the east coast grew and developed while industry and living standards in the interior lagged behind.

A major effort to strengthen the "pillars" of the economy, as the large and medium-sized state-owned industries were called, came in late 1989 when Li Peng announced that a State Council Production Commission (*guowuyuan shengchan weiyuanhui*) was being established to "promptly resolve major

29 Wang Renzhi, "Guanyu fandui zechan jieji ziyouhua" (On opposing bourgeois liberalization), *RMRB*, 22 February 1990. See also the harsh speech Wang delivered to *Qiushi* staffers in August, "Lilun gongzuo mianlin de xin qingquang he dangqian de zhuyao tenwu" (The new situation confronting theoretical work and the primary task at the moment), *Xuexi, yanjiu, cankao*, 11 (1990), 8–17.
30 Yi Ren, "Zhuozhuo huiyi de qianqian houhou" (Before and after the Zhuozhuo meeting), *RMRB*, 14 February 1990.

problems regarding production."[31] The new commission, which was headed by Ye Qing, a specialist in the coal industry, incorporated offices that had once belonged to the State Economic Commission (SEC).[32] Instead of resurrecting the SEC, which had often acted as an advocate of industry interests and had often clashed with the more conservative State Planning Commission (SPC), the new State Council Production Commission was clearly intended to be subordinate to the SPC. The idea behind the establishment of the State Production Commission was apparently to coordinate more effectively the functions of planning and plan implementation through a newly established "double-guarantee" system to be administered by the Production Commission, which would, in turn, be overseen by the SPC. The double-guarantee system was intended, on the one hand, to guarantee the supply of the necessary raw materials and funds to important state-owned enterprises and, on the other hand, to guarantee enterprises' delivery of profits, taxes, and output to the state.[33] The double-guarantee system was initially imposed on 50 major enterprises in Northeast China and then extended to cover 234 of China's largest enterprises.

The establishment of the Production Commission and the implementation of the double-guarantee system was a clear victory for the conservative wing of the Party and especially for Li Peng, who would have a chance to try out his policies for strengthening socialist management. The victory for Li Peng was underscored by the appointment of Zou Jiahua, Li's close colleague of many years, as head of the SPC in December 1989 (replacing the conservative planner Yao Yilin).

RENEWED DEBATE OVER THE DIRECTION OF THE ECONOMY

In the weeks and months after Tiananmen, there was virtually no debate over the course of the economy, at least in the major newspapers. In fact, most economic commentaries carried by the *People's Daily* and *Guangming ribao* in those early months were written by unknown reporters or economists. It was only after the Party's Fifth Plenum in November 1989 that the *People's Daily* began running serious economic views again: a number of well-known economists, including Ma Hong, Zhang Zhuoyuan, Li Chengrui, and Wang Jiye, all argued, in measured, academic terms, the case for the Fifth Plenum's

---

31 *Hong Kong Standard*, 18 December 1989; and *JJDB*, 50 (18 December 1989), trans. in *FBIS-Chi*, 20 December 1989, 22–3.

32 *JJDB*, 50 (18 December 1989), trans. in *FBIS-Chi*, 20 December 1989, 22–3.

33 *Jinrong shibao*, 30 January 1990, trans. in *FBIS-Chi*, 14 February 1990, 24–5.

call for continuing retrenchment.[34] At the same time, more liberal economists began to suggest that the policy of reform and readjustment had already achieved the major goal of controlling inflation and was beginning to hurt economic development by excessively reducing demand. The emergence of this debate over retrenchment policies marked the first time in nearly half a year that a tone of rational discussion had entered the press.

This trend continued the following spring with Li Peng's address to the National People's Congress (NPC) in March 1990. Although Li was uncompromising on the need to continue "improvement and rectification," the name given to the retrenchment policies adopted in the fall of 1988, he called for finding a means of successfully "integrating" planning and market regulation.[35] This talk inaugurated a public discussion on the topic – the third such discussion in the history of the PRO The previous two rounds of discussion, however, had taken place in the wake of economic difficulties in 1959 and 1979 and had been intended to justify an expansion of market forces. In contrast, this new discussion was intended to justify integration on the basis of planning. But at least an opening for rational discourse on the economy had been created.

Even as Li Peng was seeking to define and defend a policy that would recentralize the economy and reimpose a significant degree of planning, economic trends were revealing just how wrong conservative views of the economy were. As Naughton has argued, China's economy in 1989 was far healthier than the conservatives' declaration of profound economic crisis would allow.[36] The harsh restrictions on credit and investment were so successful in reducing demand that by September 1989 consumer prices were actually falling – though China's planners, calculating inflation on a year-to-year rather than month-to-month basis, were unaware of this dramatic turnaround.[37] Even calculating on a year-to-year basis, inflation in the first half of 1990 was only 3.2 percent, making it apparent to everyone that the urgency that had generated the retrenchment policies had passed. Meanwhile, the profitability of large state firms – the very sector conservative policies had been designed

---

34 See Ma Hong, "Have a correct understanding of the economic situation, continue to do a good job in economic improvement and rectification," *RMRB*, 17 November 1989, trans. in *FBIS-Chi*, 5 December 1989, 37–9; Zhang Zhuoyuan, "Promoting economic rectification by deepening reform," *RMRB*, 27 November 1989, trans. in *FBIS-Chi*, 7 December 1989, 28–31; Li Chengrui, "Some thoughts on sustained, steady, and coordinated development," *RMRB*, 20 November 1989, trans. in *FBIS-Chi*, 12 December 1989, 32–4; and Wang Jiye, "Several questions on achieving overall balance and restructuring," *RMRB*, 8 December 1989, trans. in *FBIS-Chi*, 19 January 1990, 30–3.

35 Li Peng, "Wei woguo zhengzhi jingji he shehui de jinyibu wending fazhan er fendou" (Struggle to take another step for the stable development of China's politics, economics, and society), in *Shisanda yilai*, 2.948–94.

36 Barry Naughton, *Growing out of the plan: Chinese economic reform, 1978–1983*, 275.

37 Ibid., 281, 347 n. 2.

to shore up – was collapsing. In 1990, profits of in-budget state firms fell 57 percent.[38] At the same time, inventory stocks shot up, enterprise losses jumped 89 percent over the same period the previous year, and the retail sales of commodities fell 1.9 percent.[39] The difficulties in the state-owned sector would force the government to pump an additional 270 billion yuan of loans into that sector in 1990 on top of the 126 billion yuan of loans issued in the fourth quarter of 1989.[40]

The combination of subsiding inflationary fears and stagnating industrial production brought renewed calls to revive reform, although it is surprising how slowly such calls were heeded given the debacle produced by conservative control of the economy. In May and June of 1990 some leaders solicited input from economists by questioning whether China's economy had come out of the economic trough.[41] This request stirred a new round of economic debate, and in the summer the Economic Situation Group of the Chinese Academy of Social Sciences (CASS), headed by Liu Guoguang, proposed that the "weight" of reform be increased.[42] This proposal by no means rejected the austerity program adopted in 1988 (indeed, Liu had been one of the authors of that program), but it did emphasize that improvement and rectification were intended to bring about an atmosphere conducive to a market-oriented reform rather than a reinstitution of the planned economy.

CENTER–PROVINCIAL CONFLICT OVER THE EIGHTH
FIVE-YEAR PLAN

One of the conservatives' biggest complaints about Zhao's management of the economy was that the strategy of decentralization pursued in the 1980s was leading to Beijing's loss of economic, and perhaps political, control over the provinces. Conservative instincts were to recentralize by exercising more direct control over the economy. This was the route mapped out by the draft of the Eighth Five-Year Plan as it neared completion in the summer of 1990. As Zou Jiahua, vice-premier and head of the SPC (the organization with primary responsibility for drafting the plan), put it, "The integration

---

38 Ibid., 284–5.
39 [He Dexu] Ho Te-hsu, "China has crossed the nadir of the valley but is still climbing up from the trough: Liu Guoguang talks about the current economic situation in China," *JJDB*, 38–9 (1 October 1990), 12–13, trans. in *FBIS-Chi*, 12 October 1990, 27–30.
40 Wu, *Jihua jingji haishi shichang jingji*, 12–13.
41 Ibid., 14. Wu does not specify which leaders raised this issue.
42 Ibid., 25; "Promote stability through reform, achieve development through this stability: Basic concepts of development and reform based on 'seeking progress through stability' in the 1990s," *JJYJ*, 7 (20 July 1990), 3–19.

of central planning and market regulation is a basic principle" of economic policy making, but "the two do not have equal status. Central planning is of primary importance. Market regulation is supplementary."[43]

The difference between this concept of planning and the provincial interest in continuing existing patterns of reform came to a head at the September 1990 Economic Work Conference. Two issues were central to the conflict. One was an evaluation of reform. Whereas Li Peng insisted that reform had led to various "dislocations" in the economy, the provinces insisted that reform be affirmed and written into the Eighth Five-Year Plan. The other issue concerned the financial interests of the provinces. The central government wanted to replace the local financial contract system, under which the provinces were responsible only for delivering a specified sum to Beijing, with a "dual tax system" that would designate clearly which taxes would go to the central government and which to the localities. Led by Ye Xuanping, governor of Guangdong, Zhu Rongji, CCP secretary and mayor of Shanghai, and Zhao Zhihao, governor of Shandong, the provinces virtually rebelled against the authority of the central government.[44]

The September work conference is often taken as a symbol of the growing independence of the provinces, and to a certain extent it was. Over the years, reform had allowed the provinces to accumulate considerable resources, primarily in the form of extrabudgetary revenues, which freed them from dependence on the central government. Provincial authorities went to elaborate lengths to nurture – and conceal – such funds, and they would not willingly yield their economic interests.

There was, however, another important aspect of this provincial "rebellion," namely that the central government was itself divided, with some political leaders and organizations sympathizing with the provinces. The most important of these was none other than Deng Xiaoping, who feared that the conservative agenda being pushed by Li Peng would negate the contributions of reform (and therefore of Deng Xiaoping) and would lead to lower growth rates. Throughout the 1980s, Deng had emerged as the champion of higher growth rates, not only because the economic achievements of China would reflect favorably on his own leadership and place in history but also because he believed that as the economy developed, political and social conflicts would be more easily resolved, thus reducing the possibility that major conflicts could lead to another cultural revolution.[45] Thus, on the eve of the Economic

43 *JJDB*, 5 November 1990, as cited in Willy Lam, *China after Deng Xiaoping*, 56.
44 Baum, *Burying Mao*, 326–8.
45 A third reason to support higher growth rates was that a greater percentage of the growth would necessarily occur outside the scope of the plan and thus limit the capacity of such conservative bureaucratic organs as the SPC to control and restrict reform.

Work Conference, Deng sent Yang Shangkun to talk to such provincial leaders as Zhu Rongji and Ye Xuanping, letting them know that they had Deng's support in their opposition to Li Peng.[46]

SINO-U.S. RELATIONS

A significant part of reformers' efforts to regain the initiative in 1990 lay in their improving Sino-U.S. relations. In his speech to martial law troops on 9 June, Deng Xiaoping laid the foundation for the campaign against "peaceful evolution" when he declared that the 4 June "storm" had been an inevitable product of the "international macroclimate" and the domestic "microclimate."[47] A week later, Deng was more explicit, saying that "[t]he entire imperialist Western world plans to make all socialist countries discard the socialist road and then bring them under the control of international monopoly capital and onto the capitalist road." and that if China did not uphold socialism, it would be turned into an appendage of the capitalist countries.[48] Moreover, in his October 1989 talk with former president Richard Nixon, Deng charged that the "United States was too deeply involved" in the student movement.[49]

Conservative leaders, deeply suspicious of the United States, were, on the basis of Deng's comments, able to whip up a campaign against "peaceful evolution." Such conservatives charged that the United States, having failed to contain and overthrow socialism in the 1950s and 1960s, had pinned its hope on the third or fourth generation of Chinese, who might be susceptible to Western influences and thus bring about change from within. These officials argued in the summer of 1989 that China should reorient its foreign policy away from the West to build stronger ties with the remaining socialist states and the Third World.[50]

Although these advocates did not carry the day, their views certainly influenced China's top leadership. In Jiang Zemin's 1 October 1989 speech marking the fortieth anniversary of the founding of the PRC, which was accorded the sort of press treatment reserved for only the most authoritative addresses, the Party general secretary charged that "international reactionary forces have never given up their fundamental stance of enmity toward and [desire to] overthrow the socialist system."[51]

---

46 Gao Xin and He Pin, *Zhu Rongji zhuan* (Biography of Zhu Rongji), 212.
47 Deng, "Zai jiejian shoudu xieyan budui junyishang ganbu shi de jianghua," 302.
48 Deng, "Disandai lingdao jiti de dangwu zhi ji," 310.
49 Deng, "Jiesu yanjun de ZhongMei guanxi yao you Meiguo caiqu zhudong," 331.
50 Harry Harding, *The fragile relationship: The United Stales and China since 1972*, 236.
51 Jiang, "Zai qingzhu Zhonghua renmin gongheguo chengli sishi zhounian dahui shang de jianghua," 631.

THE POLITICS OF CHINA

Although conservatives were never able to bring about a fundamental reorientation of Chinese foreign policy, they certainly were able to constrain the Chinese government's capacity to take initiatives that might have improved relations. Thus, as Deng told Nixon, "The United States can take a few initiatives; China cannot take the initiative."[52]

The United States responded to Deng's advice by sending Deputy Secretary of State Lawrence Eagleburger and National Security Adviser Brent Scowcroft to Beijing in December 1989. The timing of the trip, it turned out, was not good. The collapse of socialism in East Europe was provoking new debate in Beijing and bringing about an upswing in conservative influence. Thus, China was able to make only minor concessions in return for the visit. It was not until June 1990 that Fang Lizhi, the Chinese astrophysicist who had taken refuge in the U.S. Embassy in Beijing after the 4 June crackdown, was finally permitted to leave the country. Fang's release came too late to be viewed as much of a concession by many in the U.S. Congress and the press, but it did begin to ease the tensions in Sino-U.S. relations. In late 1990, ties improved again with Chinese Foreign Minister Qian Qichen's visit to the United States, which culminated in a meeting with President Bush. After the meeting, Qian declared that the visit would "help open vast vistas for bilateral relations."[53]

DENG'S MOVE TO REVIVE REFORM

By late 1990, Deng seemed visibly distraught by China's situation and his own inability to reassert his leadership. Whereas the communiqué adopted by the party's Seventh Plenum in December 1990 "highly evaluated" China's "tremendous achievements" in reform and opening up, it nevertheless went on to stress the "integration of the planned economy with market *regulation*" and to repeat such staples of Chen Yun's economic thought as calling for "sustained, stable and coordinated" economic development and "acting according to one's capability" (*liangli erxing*).[54]

Such limited endorsement of Deng's views apparently left the patriarch frustrated. "Nobody is listening to me now," Deng allegedly complained. "If such a state of affairs continues, I have no choice but to go to Shanghai to issue my articles there."[55] So saying, Deng traveled to the east coast metropolis

---

52 Deng, "Jiesu yanjun de ZhongMei guanxi yao you Meiguo caiqu zhudong," 332.
53 Beijing radio, 1 December 1990, trans. in *FBIS-Chi*, 3 December 1990, 6–7.
54 "Zhongguo gongchandang di shisanju Zhongyang weiyuanhui di qice quanti huiyi gongbao" (Communiqué of the Seventh Plenary Session of the Thirteenth CCP Central Committee), in *Shisanda yilai*, 2.1420–6, emphasis added. The phrase *liangli erxing* was used widely in the 1980–1 period as Chen Yun's influence increased and as various retrenchment measures were adopted.
55 Cited in [Liu Bi] Liu Pi, "Deng Xiaoping launches 'northern expedition' to emancipate mind; Beijing, Shanghai, and other provinces and municipalities 'respond' by opening wider to the outside world," *JB*, 166 (10 May 1991), trans. in *FBIS-Chi*, 6 May 1991, 26–9.

and proceeded to give a number of talks intended to rekindle reform. In his talks, Deng declared that market and planning were both economic "methods" (rather than distinguishing characteristics of capitalism and socialism, respectively) and argued that whatever promoted the socialist economy was socialist. The Hong Kong press quickly dubbed Deng's comments his "new cat thesis" (because of the idea that anything that promotes production is socialist) after his famous aphorism from the 1960s that the color of the cat does not matter.

The gist of Deng's talks in Shanghai was summarized in four commentaries carried in the Shanghai Party paper, *Jiefang ribao (Liberation Daily)*, under the pen name "Huangfu Ping." Their writing and publication were overseen by Deng's daughter Deng Nan and Shanghai Party secretary Zhu Rongji.[56] Using language not heard since the heyday of reform in the late 1980s, the commentaries excoriated "ossified thinking" and repeatedly called for a new wave of "emancipating the mind." For instance, one article declared that China would "miss a good opportunity" if it got bogged down in worrying about whether something was capitalist or socialist,[57] while another quoted Deng as saying that capitalist society was "very bold in discovering and using talented people" and urging the promotion of a large number of "sensible persons."[58]

RESPONSE FROM THE PROVINCES

It did not take long for several of China's provincial leaders to respond to Deng's initiative. On 11 March 1990, Guangdong's Party secretary Lin Ruo, who had close ties to Zhao Ziyang, published an article in the Guangdong Party paper *Nanfang ribao (Southern Daily)* and a shorter, somewhat watered-down version in the *People's Daily*. Lin pointedly attributed the rapid growth that Guangdong had enjoyed over the previous decade to the implementation of market-oriented policies. Similarly, Tan Shaowen, the Party secretary of Tianjin, declared that "it was because of the reform and opening up that we conducted that we withstood the severe tests of the changes in the international situation, the political storms in the country, and numerous difficulties."

56 Huangfu Ping is homophonous with the characters for "Commentary from Shanghai." The four commentaries were published on 15 February, 2 March, 22 March, and 12 April 1991. The writers of Huangfu Ping articles were Zhou Ruijin, Ling He, and Shi Zhihong. See [Wei Yongzheng] Wei Yung-cheng, "Reveal the mystery of Huangfu Ping." According to Gao Xin and He Pin, the galleys of each article were personally approved by Deng's daughter, Deng Nan. See *Zhu Rongji zhuan*, 218.
57 Huangfu Ping, "The consciousness of expanding opening needs to be strengthened," *Jiefang ribao*, 22 March 1991, trans. in *FBIS-Chi*, 1 April 1991, 39–41.
58 Huangfu Ping, "Reform and opening require a large number of cadres with both morals and talents," *Jiefang ribao*, 12 April 1991, trans. in *FBIS-Chi*, 17 April 1991, 61–3.

In good Dengist fashion, Tan argued that "[e]conomic stability is the foundation of political and social stability."[59]

At the same time, Hebei governor Cheng Weigao sharply criticized planners
in Beijing who had recentralized authority over the economy and demanded
that central policies regarding enterprise autonomy be enforced and the Enterprise Law (passed in 1988 but never really put into effect) be implemented.[60]
Jiangxi governor Wu Guanzheng likewise called on his colleagues to "emancipate the mind" and "increase the weight of reform."[61]

Most surprising of all was the call from Beijing mayor Chen Xitong to
"emancipate the mind." One of the most conservative of China's high officials
and a hard liner who actively encouraged the use of force in suppressing
the 1989 protest movement, Chen was nevertheless a close follower of Deng
and responded to his call. Criticizing "ossified thinking," Chen gave explicit
support to Deng's "new cat thesis."[62] In contrast, Beijing Party secretary Li
Ximing, who would be ousted for his conspicuous resistance to Deng's policies
following the patriarch's 1992 trip to Shenzhen, avoided the use of similar
reformist rhetoric.

CAMPAIGN TO PROMOTE SCIENCE AND TECHNOLOGY

Even as Deng traveled to Shanghai to launch his "Northern Expedition," the
dramatic outcome of the Gulf War was forcing the Chinese leadership to
reassess the impact of science and technology – and by implication that of
ideology – in the contemporary world. This reassessment, which apparently
began as early as March 1991,[63] reached its peak in May when Deng Xiaoping's
office wrote and forwarded to the *People's Daily* an article reviving many of the
themes associated with the discussions on the new technological revolution
that had been used by Zhao Ziyang and others in the 1983–4 period to turn
back the campaign against "spiritual pollution."[64] That the Gulf War had a
direct impact on this campaign was evident from Jiang Zemin's statement

59 Tan Shaowen, "Emancipate the mind, seek truth from facts, be united as one, and do solid work,"
   Tianjin ribao, 17 April 1991, trans. in *FBIS-Chi*, 18 June 1991, 62–8. Tan's speech was given to the
   municipal party's Fifth Plenary Session in January but not publicized until after the fourth Huangfu
   Ping commentary.
60 Cheng Weigao, "Further emancipate the mind and renew the concept, and accelerate the pace of reform
   and development," *Hebei ribao*, 18 April 1991, trans. in *FBIS-Chi*, 7 June 1991, 60–8.
61 "Increase weight of reform, promote economic development: Speech delivered by Wu Guanzheng at
   the provincial structural reform work conference," *Jiangxi ribao*, 4 May 1991, trans. in *FBIS-Chi*, 12
   June 1991, 45–9.
62 *Banyuetan*, 25 March 1991. See also Chen's call for emancipating the mind at a meeting of the Beijing
   municipal government, *Beijing ribao*, 8 March 1991.
63 In an internal address, Li Peng elevated science and technology to first place in the four modernizations
   (up from their normal third-place listing). *WHB* (Hong Kong), 10 March 1991.
64 *XH*, 2 May 1991, trans. in *FBIS-Chi*, 3 May 1991, 23–6.

that the performance of high-tech weapons in that war had prompted him to stress the importance of science and technology.[65]

ENTRY OF ZHU RONGJI INTO THE LEADERSHIP

One major success for Deng in the spring of 1991 was the elevation of Zhu Rongji to the position of vice-premier during the annual session of the NPC – though his promotion was balanced by the simultaneous selection of the conservative Zou Jiahua as a vice-premier.[66] Zhu has elicited intense interest from domestic and foreign observers alike because he is unique in Chinese politics. Named a rightist in 1957, Zhu has nevertheless risen to the inner circles of power; moreover, he has firm ideas on economic reform and the personality to push them against strong opposition. That Deng would reach out to such a person suggests his need and determination to counterbalance the conservative bureaucrats who had come to dominate the top of the system in the wake of Tiananmen.

Like Li Ruihuan in Tianjin, Zhu seems to have drawn Deng's interest by his skillful handling of the 1989 demonstrations in Shanghai. Despite pressure, Zhu rejected calls to declare martial law in the city, opting instead for organizing worker pickets to restore order. After the violent suppression of protesters in Beijing, Zhu became famous for his remark that "the facts will eventually be made clear."[67] But Zhu was no liberal. When a train accident led an inflamed crowd to beat the driver and set fire to the train, Zhu oversaw the arrest, conviction, and execution of three people within eight days.[68]

When Zhu first came to Beijing as vice-premier, Li Peng apparently declined to assign him a portfolio. Three months later, under pressure from Deng, Li finally allowed Zhu to take over the State Council Production Commission, the name of which was changed to State Council Production Office (*guowuyuan shengchan bangongshi*), which had failed in its initial task to oversee the double-guarantee system and had instead contributed to a ballooning of triangular debts among enterprises.[69] Zhu was also assigned the task of clearing up triangular debts, a job that had clearly not been completed by Zou Jiahua, Li

---

65 This acknowledgment, however, did not stop Jiang from saying in his Party Day speech that men, not weapons, were the most important thing in war.

66 After the NPC meeting, there were five vice-premiers: Yao Yilin, Tian Jiyun, Wu Xueqian, Zou Jiahua, and Zhu Rongji. Yao was a member of PSC, and Tian and Wu were members of the Politburo. Zou was a full member of the Central Committee, but Zhu was only an alternate member. It was highly unusual for an alternate member of the Central Committee to be promoted to vice-premier.

67 Ibid., 170.   68 Ibid., 173–8.

69 Triangular debts were debts that accrued between suppliers, producers, and buyers as enterprises, subject to mandatory plans, sent materials or finished products to others, but received little or no payment in return.

Peng's old protégé, who had been given the task in 1990.[70] Putting Zhu in charge of the State Council Production Office and clearing up triangular debts marked an obvious policy failure for Li Peng, Zou Jiahua, and Ye Qing, and it gave Zhu a chance to develop a bureaucratic apparatus.

Zhu quickly recruited his former associates from the old SEC, including former vice-chairmen Zhang Yanning and Zhao Weichen, who were made deputy directors of the new Production Office. The roles of Zhu and the Production Office were further enhanced in May 1993 when the office was expanded and reorganized as the State Economic and Trade Commission. The new office had a bureaucratic standing equivalent to that of the SPC, and effectively hollowed out the latter organization by taking over day-to-day management of the economy, leaving the SPC to deal with the macroeconomy.[71] Moreover, Zhu was successful, at least temporarily, in reducing the problem of triangular debts. In June 1991, such inter-enterprise debts had amounted to some 300 billion yuan; about two-thirds of that was cleared by the end of 1992.[72] Zhu's successes would eventually enable him to enter the PSC at the Fourteenth Party Congress in late 1992.

CONSERVATIVE RESPONSE

Deng's offensive from the fall of 1990 through the spring of 1991 would prove to be a trial run for his efforts of the following year, but in 1991 he came up short. He had indeed used provincial officials to undermine the draft of the Eighth Five-Year Plan and then to publicize and promote his own thought, and he had laid the basis for a later breakthrough by promoting Zhu Rongji and giving him an institutional base from which to rival Li Peng. But conservative opposition remained fierce. Despite Li Ruihuan's formal position as head of the Ideological Leading Small Group, conservatives had since 1989 dominated the top reaches of the Propaganda and Organization Departments as well as economic policy making.[73] They would not give up without a fight.

---

70 The Leading Group for the Resolution of Triangular Debt was established in March 1990 with Zou Jiahua in charge. At that time, triangular debt amounted to more than 100 billion yuan (up from 32 billion yuan in 1988). Despite a State Council circular setting a four-month deadline for the clearing of such debt and despite state expenditures of about 160 billion yuan to clear such debt, by the end of 1990 enterprise indebtedness was nearing 150 billion yuan. *CD*, 6 July 1991.
71 Gao and He, *Zhu rongji zhuan*, 242–56.
72 *XH*, 25 December 1992, trans. in *FBIS-Chi*, 28 December 1992, 36–9.
73 Defiance of Li Ruihuan's leadership of ideological work was evident not only from the speeches of such leaders as Wang Renzhi and Song Ping and from Gao Di's management of the *People's Daily* but also from such specific statements as Wang Renzhi's December 1989 comment that the campaign against pornography, championed by Li, "certainly cannot replace opposing bourgeois liberalization." See *RMRB*, 23 December 1989.

This opposition was led by the father–son combination of Chen Yun and Chen Yuan, the deputy governor of the People's Bank of China. Even as Deng carried his message to Shanghai, Chen Yun was quoted in the *People's Daily* as saying, "As leading cadres, we must pay attention to exchanging views with others, especially those who hold views opposite from our own" – a remark that implicitly criticized Deng for his failure to consult his colleagues.[74] At almost the same time, in December 1990, Chen Yuan presented a paper excoriating the decline in central authority that had resulted from a decade and more of devolving economic power. Chen called for a "new centralization" to deal with the emergence of "feudal lords" and the "disintegration of macrocontrol."[75] Then, in May 1991, Chen Yun presented Shanghai leaders with a rhymed couplet that enjoined them to "not simply follow what superiors or books say" but to "act only according to reality."[76]

If Chen in his reminders to Deng was gentle, almost obscure, others were willing to be much more direct. A sharp attack on the Huangfu Ping commentaries, and hence on Deng, came in the form of a Commentator article in the conservative journal *Dangdai sichao* (*Contemporary Trends*), which was excerpted shortly thereafter in the *People's Daily*. Reviving themes raised by Song Ping and Wang Renzhi the previous year, the commentary warned that those in favor of "bourgeois liberalization" remained "resolute" and that "we must be soberly aware that the liberalized trend of thought and political influence, which was once a major trend, will not disappear because we have won a victory in quelling the rebellion, but will again stubbornly manifest itself in a new form, spar with us, and attack us."[77]

A TROUGH IN THE ROAD TO REFORM

With the publication of the *People's Daily's* excerpt of the article from *Dangdai sichao* and other attacks on the themes raised by the Huangfu Ping commentaries, reformers fell quiet. Four explanations for this sudden setback seem possible.

The first is that in the spring of 1991 Deng simply lacked the political strength to reinstate his vision of reform. Such an explanation assumes not only that Deng failed to win over (or intimidate) his opponents, but also that

---

74 *RMRB*, 18 January 1991.
75 Chen Yuan, "Wo guo jingji de shenceng wend he xuanze (gangyao)" (China's deep-seated economic problems and choices [outline]), *JJYJ*, 4 (April 1991), 18–9. Joseph Fewsmith, "Neoconservatism and the end of the Dengist era," *AS*, 35.7 (July 1995), 635–51. On Chen Yuan, see He Pin and Gao Xin, *Zhonggong "taizi dang"* ("Princelings" of the CCP), 97–124.
76 *XH*, 15 May 1991, trans. in *FBIS-Chi*, 17 May 1991, 22.
77 "Why must we unremittingly oppose bourgeois liberalization?" *RMRB*, 24 April 1991, 5, trans. in *FBIS-Chi*, 26 April 1991, 18–21.

he failed to win the support of the "silent majority" of Party elders who seem to move to one side or the other in periods of political conflict, thereby shifting the political center of gravity. Second, and more plausibly, one can assume that Deng, faced with opposition and uncertainty, yielded once again, as he had apparently done several times over the preceding two years, biding his time until a more opportune moment arose to renew his assault. This explanation assumes that Deng possessed the power necessary to prevail (which he would demonstrate a year later), but that he believed the cost in terms of Party unity outweighed the importance of prevailing at that time. Third, the situation in the Soviet Union, namely Gorbachev's turn to the right, which culminated in cracking down on the Baltic republics in January 1991, may have bolstered conservatives in Beijing, who were likely to have seen such a shift as a sign that the Soviet Union, too, was finally backing away from radical reform.[78] Fourth, the swift U.S. victory in the Gulf War, which apparently caught China off guard, may very well have renewed fears in Beijing that the world was becoming unipolar and that the United States would apply new pressures on China. Such a concern would most likely have reinforced the tendency among Party leaders to hunker down, assess the situation, and avoid divisive conflicts.

In the event, with the publication of Jiang Zemin's speech on the seventieth anniversary of the CCP on 1 July 1991, it became clear that reform was, once again, on hold. Jiang's speech linked domestic class struggle to international class struggle, emphasizing that "the ideological area is an important arena for the struggle between peaceful evolution and anti-peaceful evolution."[79] Despite bows in a reformist direction, Jiang's speech clearly reflected conservative control over the overall ideological and policy agenda. More important, any reformist sentiments conveyed by Jiang's speech were soon played down as the Party responded to renewed liberalization in the Soviet Union by circling the wagons even more tightly.

In late July 1991, the Soviet Communist Party (CPSU) surrendered its monopoly on political power and moved its ideological stance toward democratic socialism. This shift caused obvious anxieties in China and prompted conservatives to take an even harder line. In particular, a 16 August

---

78 It should be noted that by mid-April to late April, just as the *People's Daily* was reprinting the *Dangdai sichao* article, Gorbachev was once again turning toward radical reform – which also scared conservatives into taking a harder line. Though it seems inconsistent, it can be argued that Chinese conservatives reacted to both a tightening up and a political relaxation in the Soviet Union by calling for heightening ideological orthodoxy in China. They would see in the former confirmation of the need to prevent reform from getting out of control and in the latter a hostile foreign environment that would necessitate a reassertion of socialist values at home.

79 Jiang Zemin, "Zai qingzhu Zhongguo gongchandang chengli qishi zhounian dahuishang de jianghua" (Talk celebrating the seventieth anniversary of the founding of the CCP), in *Shisanda yila*, 3.1627–60. The quotes are from 1647, 1640, 1646, 1639, and 1638, respectively.

Commentator article in the *People's Daily* put an even more conservative spin on Jiang's CCP anniversary speech, calling for building a "great wall of steel against peaceful evolution" in order to protect the country from "hostile forces" at home and abroad. If such hostile forces won, the Commentator article warned, it would be a "retrogression of history and a catastrophe for the people."[80]

THE SOVIET COUP

Given the reaction of Chinese hard liners to what they regarded as the downward spiral of events in the Soviet Union, it is no wonder that they could barely contain their glee when they heard the news of the conservative coup d'état launched on 19 August. China's ambassador congratulated the perpetrators of the coup, and conservative elder Wang Zhen, then in Xinjiang, called on China's party leaders "never to deviate" from Marxism–Leninism–Mao Zedong Thought and to "fight to the death" for communism. Jiang Zemin reportedly hailed the coup in a speech to a Politburo meeting, and the gist of his remarks were disseminated in a secret document entitled "The victory of the Soviet people is a victory for the Chinese people."[81] Apparently a variety of meetings of leftists were called to consider their response.

The ebullient mood did not last long. When the coup collapsed after only three days, Chinese leaders were despondent. Even Deng worried that if Yeltsin banished the CPSU, China would be the only major state practicing socialism. "Then what shall we do?" he reportedly asked.[82]

What the abortive coup in the Soviet Union did was to pose in the starkest possible terms the fundamental question of the period: Should the CCP try to preserve its own rule by emphasizing ideology and socialist values, or should it try to win popular support and strengthen the nation through continued economic reform? Leftists in the Party clearly wanted to take the former route. Chen Yun, in a scarcely veiled attack on newly promoted Vice-Premier Zhu Rongji, reputedly warned against allowing a "Yeltsin-like figure" to emerge in China.[83]

80 "Build up a great wall of steel against peaceful evolution," *RMRB* Commentator, 16 August 1991, trans. in *FBIS-Chi*, 19 August 1991, 27–8.
81 Xinjiang television, 24 August 1991, trans. in *FBIS-Chi*, 27 August 1991, 28–9; *RMRB*, 29 August 1991. While in Xinjiang, Wang gave a number of fiery speeches. See, for instance, Xinjiang television, 21 August 1991, trans. in *FBIS-Chi*, 22 August 1991, 20. The *People's Daily* account of Wang's trip deleted most of Wang's harshest language, including his vow to "fight to the death." On Jiang Zemin's reaction, see James Miles, *The legacy of Tiananmen: China in disarray*, 71.
82 *South China Morning Post*, 26 August 1991.
83 Ibid., 4 September 1991; Baum, *Burying Mao*, 333. Note *WHB*'s reference to Yeltsin as a "dangerous" person in its examination of the abortive coup. See *WHB* (Hong Kong), 23 August 1991, trans. in *FBIS-Chi*, 27 August 1991, 8–9.

If Deng was initially despondent over events in the Soviet Union, he did not stay that way for long. Reacting quickly to conservatives' efforts to assert themselves following the Soviet coup, Deng intervened to insist on speeding up reform and opening up. As a PRC-affiliated Hong Kong magazine later put it, "Deng played a crucial role in preventing China from incorrectly summing up the experiences of the Soviet coup and in rendering the 'leftist' forces in the party unable to use the opportunity to expand their influence."[84]

Internationally, Deng reiterated his call for caution, saying that China should "tackle calmly, observe coolly, and pay good attention to our own national affairs."[85] Domestically, he inaugurated a determined campaign to reassert his own leadership and to put his understanding of reform back in the center. That campaign would last from the time of the abortive Soviet coup until the convening of the Fourteenth Party Congress in October 1992.

The first public sign that political winds were shifting came on 1 September when the Xinhua News Service transmitted the text of an editorial to be run the following day by the *People's Daily*. The editorial contained some of the most reformist language to be used since the previous spring, and did so in a more authoritative context. However, the first sentence contradicted and effectively negated the rest of the editorial. It read, "While carrying out reform and opening up to the outside world, we must ask ourselves whether we are practicing socialism or capitalism, and we must uphold the socialist orientation." Seven hours after this editorial was transmitted, Xinhua released a new version in which the first sentence was changed dramatically to read, "While carrying out reform and opening up to the outside world, we must firmly adhere to the socialist course and uphold the dominant role of public ownership."[86] The critical question of whether a reform was "socialist" or "capitalist" had been cut.

It turned out that the second version was actually the editorial as originally approved, but before transmission Gao Di, director of the *People's Daily*.[87]

---

84 Sun Hong, "Anecdotes about Deng Xiaoping's political career and family life," *JB*, 11 (5 November 1993), 26–31, trans. in *FBIS-Chi*, 18 November 1993, 34–9.

85 [He Yuan] Ho Yuen, "CCP's 'five adherences' and 'five oppositions' to prevent peaceful evolution," *MB*, 29 August 1991, trans. in *FBIS-Chi*, 29 August 1991, 23–5.

86 Both statements were released by Xinhua on 1 September 1991, the first at 0723 GMT and the second at 1456 GMT. See *FBIS-Chi*, 2 September 1991.

87 In the early 1980s, the editor in chief was the highest-ranking official of the *People's Daily*. In the wake of the 1983 campaign against spiritual pollution, a separate post of director was created to allow Hu Jiwei, criticized during that campaign, to take up a "second line" position. Nevertheless, as director, Hu was able to exercise considerable influence over the paper, as evidenced by the replacement of Hu by the open-minded Qin Chuan as editor in chief. Thus, well before Tiananmen the director had become the effective head of the *People's Daily*, although the distinction between director and editor in chief continued. After the Tiananmen crackdown, Gao Di was named director (replacing Qian Liren), and Shao Huazi became editor in chief (replacing Tan Wenrui). In December 1992, Shao replaced Gao as director, and Fan Jingyi became editor in chief.

rewrote the first sentence to insert the conservative's pet thesis. This change was spotted, and at Deng's behest Li Ruihuan ordered that the offending sentence be removed. Thus, the editorial that appeared in the *People's Daily* on 2 September differed from what listeners had heard on the radio the evening before. Deng angrily declared that the *"People's Daily* wants to comprehensively criticize Deng Xiaoping."[88]

This incident not only underscores the deadly serious nature of "documentary politics" in the PRC, it also makes clear that reformers were responding quickly to evolving events in the Soviet Union by restoring the push that had stalled the previous spring.[89] Just how difficult that task would be was indicated by an article by former Organization Department head Chen Yeping that appeared in the *People's Daily* on 1 September. Taking the unusual step of criticizing former general secretary Zhao Ziyang by name (attacks by name having generally died out more than a year earlier), Chen accused him of advocating "productivity as the criterion for selecting cadres" – essentially what the Huangfu Ping commentaries had called for the previous spring – and claimed that his "erroneous viewpoint still has some effect in the cadre work of some regions and departments."[90]

Reformers responded almost immediately. In late September, Deng instructed Jiang Zemin and Yang Shangkun to persevere in reform and opening up,[91] and Yang subsequently gave a ringing endorsement of reform on the eightieth anniversary of the 1911 Revolution. Reform was, he said, a part of the historical effort to revive and develop China that had begun with Sun Yat-sen.[92] More important in terms of the immediate political debate, Yang declared unequivocally that *"all* other work must be subordinate to and serve" economic construction and that the party must not allow its "attention to be diverted or turned away" from economic construction.[93]

Despite such clear signals from Deng and his supporters, conservatives continued to resist. During his November visit to Shanghai, Li Peng could not

88 Gao and He, *Zhu Rongji zhuan*, 231–2.
89 Guoguang Wu, "Documentary politics: Hypotheses, process, and case studies," in Carol Lee Hamrin and Suisheng Zhao, eds., *Decision-making in Deng's China: Perspectives from insiders*, 24–38.
90 Chen Yeping, "Have both political integrity, ability, stress political ability: On criteria for selecting cadres," *RMRB*, 1 September 1991, trans. in *FBIS-Chi*, 6 September 1991, 26–31.
91 Cited in Baum, *Burying Mao*, 334.
92 In its stress on patriotism and the assessment that economic development was the common goal of all Chinese, communist or not, Yang's speech echoed the 1986 Third Plenum resolution on building socialist civilization. That resolution played down the importance of communist ideology in favor of a "common ideal" to which all patriotic Chinese could subscribe. See "Resolution of the Central Committee of the Communist Party of China on the guiding principles for building a socialist society with advanced culture and ideology," *XH*, 28 September 1986, trans. in *FBIS-Chi*, 29 September 1986, K2–13.
93 Yang Shangkun, "Zai Xinghai geming bashi zhounian dahui shang de jianghua" (Speech at the meeting to commemorate the eightieth anniversary of the Xinghai Revolution), in *Shisanda yilai*, 3.1713–19. Emphasis added.

resist telling Zhu Rongji, who had overseen the compilation of the Huangfu Ping articles, that "[t]he influence of the 'Huangfu Ping' articles was terrible. It caused the unified thinking that the center had expended a great deal of effort to bring about to become chaotic again."[94]

On 23 October, the *People's Daily* published a hard-hitting article by the leftist ideologue Deng Liqun, which declared that class struggle was more acute than at any time since the founding of the PRC. An editor's note said that "the harsh reality of struggle has made clear to us that pragmatism can make a breach for peaceful evolution."[95] The term "pragmatism" seemed a clear allusion to the policies of Deng Xiaoping.

At the meeting of the Central Advisory Commission (CAC) convened on 29 November, party elder Bo Yibo conveyed six points raised by Chen Yun that stressed strengthening party organization, the threat of peaceful evolution posed by the United States, and the danger posed by overzealous efforts to speed up economic development.[96]

In late November, Deng Xiaoping urged the leadership to improve relations with the United States by not raising the issue of peaceful evolution so frequently and by compromising with the United States on human rights issues. On hearing Deng's suggestion, Party elder Wang Zhen apparently flew into a rage, declaring that Deng's policies were leading the country down the road to capitalism.[97] At the time, as Wang Zhen's outburst showed, the Party remained deeply divided over the danger posed by "peaceful evolution." In September, Propaganda Department head Wang Renzhi and others had organized an "anti-peaceful evolution" study group at the Central Party School which warned that peaceful evolution could be boosted by "pragmatists" in the leadership. Conservatives participating in the group denounced Li Ruihuan as "a person who wants to be Gorbachev" and called Qiao Shi a "fence sitter."[98]

DENG'S "SOUTHERN TOUR"

On 19 January, almost eight years to the day since Deng's first visit to Shenzhen inaugurated a new push in opening China to the outside world, Deng once again set foot in the Special Economic Zone (SEZ). Accompanied by Yang Shangkun and other officials, Deng spent the next several days touring

94 Quoted in Gao and He, *Zhu Rongji zhuan*, 232.
95 [Jing Wen] Ching Wen, "Abnormal atmosphere in *Renmin ribao*," *JB*, 178 (5 May 1992), 46–7, trans. in *FBIS-Chi*, 18 May 1992, 22.
96 [Luo] and Li, "Chen Yun raises six points of view to criticize Deng Xiaoping."
97 *South China Morning Post*, 1 January 1992, 2 January 1992; Baum, *Burying Mao*, 336.
98 *Dangdai* 14 (15 May 1992), 21–2, trans. in *FBIS-Chi*, 21 May 1992, 18–20.

Shenzhen and then the Zhuhai SEZ, talking about the importance of reform and blasting his opponents as he went.

Perhaps the most critical point in his talks was his contention that without the ten years of reform and opening up, the CCP would not have survived an upheaval such as the Party had faced in the spring of 1989. This judgment was Deng's response to his opponents' contention that reform had led to the Tiananmen incident and would lead to the downfall of the CCP, just as it had to that of the CPSU and the various Communist parties of East Europe.

In order to defend his vision of reform against his critics' arguments, Deng reiterated the theoretically unsophisticated but ultimately effective argument that he had put forth in Shanghai the previous year, namely that planning and markets, far from being distinguishing characteristics of socialism and capitalism, were simply economic "methods" possessed by both types of systems. Moreover, Deng hit back directly at the numerous derogatory criticisms of the so-called criterion of productive forces made over the previous two years. In the baldest statement of that thesis since Zhao Ziyang had championed it on the front page of the *People's Daily* four years before, Deng declared that socialism could be defined in terms of the three "advantages": whether or not something was advantageous to the development of socialist productive forces, advantageous to increasing the comprehensive strength of a socialist nation, and advantageous to raising the people's standard of living."[99]

Deng blasted his cautious colleagues with one of Mao's most famous metaphors. He urged them not to act like "women with bound feet"; reform had to be bolder and the pace of development faster. "For a large, developing country like ours," Deng said, "the economic growth rate must be a bit faster; it cannot always be calm and steady." Underscoring his implicit but pointed criticism of Chen Yun's thought, Deng declared, "We must pay attention to the steady and coordinated development of the economy, but being steady and coordinated is relative, not absolute." He then called on Guangdong to catch up to the "four small dragons" (South Korea, Taiwan, Singapore, and Hong Kong) in twenty years.[100]

The most eye-catching passages in Deng's talks, however, were his blunt criticisms of the "Left." In sharp contrast to the constant criticism of bourgeois liberalization and peaceful evolution over the preceding two years, Deng pointed out that the main danger to the Party lay on the "Left." "The Right can bury socialism, the 'Left' can also bury socialism," declared the patriarch.[101]

---

99 Deng Xiaoping, "Zai Wuchang, Shenzhen, Zhuhai dengdi de tanhua yaodian" (Essential points from talks in Wuchang, Shenzhen, Zhuhai, and Shanghai), in *Deng Xiaoping wenxuan*, 3.372.
100 Ibid., 3.377.   101 Ibid., 3.370–83.

Not mincing words, Deng directly criticized a number of conservative leaders, though in the version later circulated in the Party and included in Deng's *Selected Works* these remarks were deleted.

THE STRUGGLE FOR DOMINANCE

Initially, the PRC media did not report Deng's trip and the CCP did not relay his comments internally. The obvious resistance to publicizing the trip and the subsequent process of yielding partially while continuing to resist reflect the ambiguity of authority relations at the highest level of the CCP in the early 1990s. To use Deng's evocative terminology, Deng, like Mao before him, had been the "core" of the Party since the Third Plenary Session of the Eleventh Central Committee in December 1978. The term "core" reflects a series of formal and informal power arrangements through which the supreme leader maintains and wields power; it evokes the image of a spider at the center of a web.[102]

Deng began to shed his formal authority by stepping down from the PSC at the Thirteenth Party Congress in September 1987 and then yielding leadership over the party's Central Military Commission (CMC) to Jiang Zemin in September 1989. Deng, however, seems to have been unwilling to shed all vestiges of formal authority and rule solely through informal politics. Thus, the Thirteenth Party Congress passed a secret resolution to refer all major decisions to Deng Xiaoping as the "helmsman" of the Party.[103] The authority conferred by this resolution, however, appears to have been ambiguous; "helmsman" was not a formal position and it was not clear whether Deng's wishes still had to be obeyed in the same way as before his retirement. With the Tiananmen incident, Deng's prestige within the Party plummeted, weakening his ability to exercise informal authority. The conservatives' strategy in the three years following that incident appears to have been one of hamstringing Deng's capacity to exercise authority but not to challenge directly his "core" position. The intention was to turn Deng into the titular leader of the Party, much as Liu Shaoqi and Deng himself might have hoped to do to Mao in the early 1960s.

As the struggle for dominance in the spring of 1992 would show, Deng had (or had regained) enough authority to force nominal compliance with his wishes but not enough to subdue opposition immediately. Unlike in the spring of 1991, when Deng had backed off a decisive confrontation with

---

102 Tang Tsou, "Chinese politics at the top: Factionalism or informal politics? Balance-of-power politics or a game to win all?" *China Journal*, 34 (July 1995), 95–156.

103 Beijing television, 16 May 1989, trans. in *FBIS-Chi*, 16 May 1989, 28; *RMRB*, 17 May 1989, trans. in *FBIS-Chi*, 17 May 1989, 16.

his opponents, in 1992, with the Fourteenth Party Congress looming on the horizon, Deng was determined to raise the stakes to the level of a contest for party leadership. In such a contest, the advantages of being "core," ambiguous as they were, would eventually secure victory for Deng – but his opponents would not yield without staunch resistance.

A turning point in this struggle for dominance – the first of several – came when a Politburo meeting on 12 February 1992, under obvious pressure from Deng, decided to relay the content of Deng's talks orally to cadres at and above the ministerial, provincial, and army ranks.[104] This limited dissemination of Deng's views reflected a pattern that would hold throughout most of the spring, namely yielding to direct pressure from Deng (thereby sidestepping direct confrontation) but doing so only as little as possible (in the hope that Deng would yield to resistance).

In the face of this passive resistance, Dengist forces used local media to step up the pressure on Beijing's still silent official media. Finally, the *People's Daily* began to yield to the pressure. On 22 February, it published an authoritative editorial, presumably reflecting the Politburo meeting ten days earlier, that called for strengthening reform. In contrast to the emphasis on slow and steady economic growth that had dominated press coverage in recent months, the *People's Daily* now declared that "the fundamental point for upholding socialism is developing the economy as fast as possible."[105] Two days later, a second editorial urged people to "be more daring in carrying out reform" and cited Deng's dictum "Practice is the sole criterion of truth."[106]

Despite the publication of the two editorials, Beijing's media remained silent about Deng's trip to the South, an indication of the deep opposition within the Party to Deng and his views. Indeed, Deng's opponents took active measures to resist his new offensive. Deng Liqun made his own trip to the South, visiting the cities of Wuhan and Xining, where he declared, 'There is the core of economic work but also another core of fighting peaceful evolution and waging class struggle. And sometimes, the campaign against peaceful evolution is more important."[107] Chen Yun himself presided over a meeting of the CAC held in Beijing on 17 February at which he declared that

104 Suisheng Zhao, "Deng Xiaoping's southern tour: Elite politics in post-Tiananmen China," *AS* 33.8 (August 1993), 751.
105 "Adhere better to taking economic construction as the center," *RMRB* editorial, 22 February 1992, trans. in *FBIS-Chi*, 24 February 1992, 40–1. The editorial made clear its criticism of "leftists" within the Party by pointing out the "catastrophes" caused in the past by "taking class struggle as the key link."
106 "Be more daring in carrying out reform," *RMRB* editorial, 24 February 1992, trans. in *FBIS-Chi*, 24 February 1992, 41–2.
107 *South China Morning Post*, 11 May 1992.

the only way for the CCP to avoid a CPSU-style collapse was to emphasize communist ideology and strengthen Party building. Thirty-five senior leaders at the meeting drafted a strong letter to Deng demanding that communist ideology continue to be propagated and that the Party strongly maintain its opposition to peaceful evolution.[108]

It was not until 1 March that Deng's remarks were officially disseminated within the Party in the form of Central Document No. 2, but even this action did not squelch opposition. Not only did the propaganda system limit circulation of the document,[109] Party elder Song Renqiong declared that he could not detect any leftist tendencies, while Gao Di, the director of the *People's Daily*, declared defiantly, "We have already published two or three comments, and that is enough for the moment. No more articles will be published."[110]

In the midst of this acrimonious dispute, an enlarged meeting of the Politburo was convened on 10–12 March. Yang Shangkun, Deng's close associate and permanent vice-chairman of the CMC, led the charge by demanding that the body endorse Deng's view of economic work at the center. Jiang Zemin offered a self-criticism for his laxity in promoting reform and opening up and echoed Yang's views.[111] Politburo member and NPC chairman Wan Li also strongly endorsed Deng's views, and PSC member Qiao Shi argued pointedly that the leadership of the Party remained hindered by leftist ideology, which interfered with the effective implementation of the Party's principles and policies. In opposition, PSC member Yao Yilin argued that Deng's comments on guarding against leftism referred to the economic field; there were no indications of leftism in other fields. Yao's comments were echoed by Song Ping, also a member of the PSC.[112]

The outcome favored Deng. The communiqué issued by the Politburo meeting endorsed the "necessity" of upholding the "one center" of economic development and called on the Party to "accelerate the pace of reform and opening to the outside world." Moreover, it affirmed Deng's thesis that the main danger the Party faced was leftism.[113] Accordingly, China's central media finally publicized Deng's trip. On 31 March, the *People's Daily* reprinted a long, detailed account of Deng's activities in Shenzhen entitled, "East wind

108 Zhao, "Deng Xiaoping's southern tour," 754.

109 *MB*, 7 March 1992, trans. in *FBIS-Chi*, 9 March 1992, 26–7.

110 [Ling Xuejun] Ling Hsueh-chun, "Wang Zhen and Li Xiannian set themselves up against Deng," *ZM*, 175 (1 May 1992), 14–15, trans. in *FBIS-Chi*, 12 May 1992, 26; and [Jing] Ching, "Abnormal atmosphere in *Renmin ribao*," 21.

111 *XH*, 11 March 1992; Baum, *Burying Mao*, 347.

112 [Ren Huiwen] Jen Hui-wen, "Political bureau argues over 'preventing leftism,'" *Xinbao*, 14 April 1992, 6, trans. in *FBIS-Chi*, 17 April 1992, 28–9.

113 Zhao, "Deng Xiaoping's southern tour," 752.

brings spring all around: On-the-spot report on Comrade Deng Xiaoping in Shenzhen."[114]

Despite this important endorsement, the meeting nevertheless decided to delete a reference to guarding against leftism from the draft of Li Peng's Government Work Report to the upcoming session of the NPC on the grounds that it would be inappropriate to include any reference to differences of opinion in a government (as opposed to party) work report.[115] A fusillade of criticism from the floor, clearly abetted by NPC chairman Wan Li, forced the premier to add a warning to his report that the main danger lay on the left – as well as to make 149 other major and minor changes.

The enormous stakes involved and Deng's willingness to use any and all methods to carry the day were clearly revealed at the NPC meeting when Yang Baibing, vice-chairman of the CMC, declared that the People's Liberation Army (PLA) would "escort and protect" (*baojia huhang*) reform.[116] Over the ensuing months, four delegations of senior PLA officers visited the Shenzhen SEZ to demonstrate their support for reform and opening up, and the army newspaper, the *Liberation Army Daily*, repeatedly ran articles in support of reform.[117] The effort to professionalize and depoliticize the military, which had suffered badly from the use of the military to crush the 1989 movement, was again thwarted. It became clear that military backing was the ultimate support for Deng's rule, and trying to secure that support would soon become central to Jiang Zemin in his quest to become "core" of the Party in reality as well as in name.

THE CONTINUING DEBATE

The March 1992 Politburo meeting and the subsequent NPC session marked important, if not unambiguous, victories for Deng. The battle over reform

---

114 *RMRB*, 31 March 1992, trans. in *FBIS-Chi*, 1 April 1992 (supplement), 7–15. The article had originally appeared in the *Shenzhen tequ bao* (Shenzhen special economic zone daily) on 26 March. By reprinting the article, the *People's Daily* demonstrated its desire to stay at arm's length from the content.

115 [Ren] Jen, "Political bureau argues over 'preventing leftism.'"

116 XH, 23 March 1992. Note that the *JFJB* editorial hailing the close of the NPC prominently played the theme of "protecting and escorting" reform. See "Make fresh contributions on 'protecting and escorting' reform, opening up, and economic development: Warmly congratulating conclusion of the Fifth Sessions of the Seventh National People's Congress and Seventh Chinese People's Political Consultative Conference," *JFJB*, 4 April 1992, trans. in *FBIS-Chi*, 21 April 1992, 36–7.

117 The first group of PLA leaders visited Shenzhen in late February, the fourth group in early June. See *WHB* (Hong Kong), 16 April 1992, 2, trans. in *FBIS-Chi*, 16 April 1992, 38; XH, 19 May 1992, trans. in *FBIS-Chi*, 21 May 1992, 31–2; *Xinwanbao*, 11 June 1992, 2, trans. in *FBIS-Chi*, 16 June 1992, 32–3. On *JFJB*'s support for reform, see, for instance, Shi Bonian and Liu Fang, "Unswervingly implement the party's basic line," *JFJB*, 18 March 1992, trans. in *FBIS-Chi*, 15 April 1992, 44–7; He Yijun, Jiang Bin, and Wang Jianwei, "Speed up pace of reform, opening up," *JFJB*, 25 March 1992, trans. in *FBIS-Chi*, 22 April 1992, 30–3; and Lan Zhongping, "Why do we say that special economic zones are socialist rather than capitalist in nature?" *JFJB*, trans. in *FBIS-Chi*, 11 June 1992, 25–6.

continued. On 8 April members of the CAC held a meeting to draft a letter to the Central Committee, which was subsequently forwarded on the 14th. The letter warned against the tendency to "completely negate" the theories of Marxism–Leninism–Mao Zedong Thought and declared, in direct opposition to Deng's comments in Shenzhen, that "the biggest danger is the rightist' tendency and bourgeois liberalization in the last 10 years."[118]

Shortly thereafter, on 14 April, the *People's Daily* ran a long article by Li Peng confidant Yuan Mu, head of the State Council Research Office, which did to Deng what Deng had previously done to Mao, namely reinterpret the leader's thought by insisting that it be viewed "comprehensively." For instance, while endorsing Deng's view about the importance of guarding against the Left, Yuan went on to stress the need to maintain "vigilance against bourgeois liberalization" in order to prevent the sort of "evolution" experienced by East Europe and the Soviet Union."[119]

In response, Deng's supporters rallied. On 6 April, Qiao Shi derided "some leading comrades" who only feigned compliance with the line of reform and opening up. Such people, Qiao urged, should step down from power.[120] Similarly, during his 16–22 April tour of Shanxi Province, Qiao touted Dengist themes, calling for an "ideological leap" in people's awareness of the need for reform.[121] On 13 April, Gong Yuzhi, former deputy head of the Propaganda Department and a longtime supporter of Deng, gave a talk called "Emancipating thought, emancipating productive forces" at the Central Party School. This talk marked an important signal to intellectuals and opened the way to harsher attacks on leftism.[122]

In late April, Vice-Premier Tian Jiyun went to the Central Party School, where he lambasted leftists for having "basically repudiated all the most fundamental and substantial elements that we have upheld since reform and opening up." In a barb apparently directed at General Secretary Jiang Zemin, Tian declared, "To do away with leftist' influence, one must particularly guard against those who bend with the wind, the political acrobats who readily vacillate in attitude." Using a parody rare in Chinese politics, Tian told his

118 [Yue Shan] Yueh Shan, "Central Advisory Commission submits letter to CCP Central Committee opposing 'rightist' tendency," *ZM*, 175 (1 May 1992), 13–14, trans. in *FBIS-Chi*, 30 April 1992, 15–16.
119 Yuan Mu, "Firmly, accurately, and comprehensively implement the party's basic line: Preface to 'Guidance for studying the government work report to the fifth session of the Seventh NPC,'" *RMRB*, 14 April 1992, trans. in *FBIS-Chi*, 16 April 1992, 20–3.
120 Lin Wu, "Deng's faction unmasks face of 'ultraleftists,'" *ZM*, 175 (1 May 1992), 17–18, trans. in *FBIS-Chi*, 12 May 1992, 27–8.
121 *XH*, 22 April 1992, trans. in *FBIS-Chi*, 23 April 1992, 11–12.
122 Gong Yuzhi, "Emancipate our minds, liberate productive forces: Studying Comrade Deng Xiaoping's important talks," *WHB* (Shanghai), 15 April 1992, trans. in *FBIS-Chi*, 20 April 1992, 25–8. See also *Dangdai*, 14 (15 May 1992), 21–2, trans. *in FBIS-Chi*, 21 May 1992, 18–20.

listeners that leftists should go to a "special leftist zone" in which there would be total state planning, supplies would be rationed, and people could line up for food and other consumer items.[123] Soon pirated copies of Tian's talk were being sold on the streets of Beijing.

Deng's demonstration that he would not back off this time, underscored by the mobilization of the army on his behalf, stirred Chen Yun to make some concessions. Appearing in Shanghai on the eve of Labor Day, the Party elder encouraged leaders there to "emancipate their minds" and "take bold steps." Chen, who had opposed the establishment of SEZs in 1978–9 and especially opposed the establishment of one in Shanghai, was now quoted as saying, "I very much favor the development and opening of Pudong!"[124] Apparently Chen also said, "Shanghai should sum up experiences of its own and should not mechanically follow the example of Shenzhen," but this was not reported by the media.[125]

Despite Chen's partial concession in Shanghai, Deng Xiaoping obviously remained frustrated by the lack of meaningful response from the leadership. On 22 May, Deng showed up at Capital Iron and Steel (usually referred to as Shougang) and listened to Zhou Guanwu, the longtime leader of the model enterprise and allegedly Deng's personal friend, report on the enterprise's reform experience. Deng complained that many leaders were "merely going through the motions" of supporting reform and that they were in danger of losing their jobs.[126] Just as important, Deng signaled his strong support for Zhu Rongji, whom he had sponsored to become vice-premier in March 1991. Zhu, Deng said, is "quite capable" in economics.[127]

Deng's criticism of China's leadership finally stirred Jiang Zemin to action. On 9 June, the general secretary followed in the wake of Qiao Shi and Tian Jiyun and gave a major speech at the Central Party School. Jiang finally openly endorsed the view that the "primary focus must be guarding against the 'Left.'" Quoting liberally from Deng's talks in Shenzhen, Jiang now argued

123 *South China Morning Post*, 7 May 1992; "Summary of Tian Jiyun's speech before Party school," *BX*, 266 (16 June 1992), 4–5, trans. in *FBIS-Chi*, 18 June 1992, 16–18; Baum, *Burying Mao*, 353.
124 *XH*, 1 May 1992, trans. in *FBIS-Chi*, 1 May 1992, 18–19.
125 [Ren Huiwen] Jen Hut-wen, "There is something behind Chen Yun's declaration of his position," *Xinbao*, 12 May 1992, trans. in *FBIS-Chi*, 13 May 1992, 21–2. According to Baum, Chen's supporters later accused Shanghai city officials of distorting Chen's comments. See *Burying Mao*, 449 n. 63.
126 Deng's comments were reported by Hong Kong media in May but were not publicized by PRC media until early July when Shanghai's *Jiefang ribao* finally broke the long silence. *MB*, 28 May 1992, trans. in *FBIS-Chi*, 28 May 1992, 15; *South China Morning Post*, 28 May 1992; and Agence France Presse, 7 July 1992. The following month, Deng followed up his trip to Shougang with a trip to the Northeast. See *South China Morning Post*, 24 June 1992.
127 [Yan Shenzun] Yen Shen-tsun, "Deng Xiaoping's talk during his inspection of Shoudu Iron and Steel Complex," *Guangjiaojing*, 238 (16 July 1992), 6–7, trans. in *FBIS-Chi*, 17 July 1992, 7–8.

that reform was like "steering a boat against the current. We will be driven back if we do not forge ahead."[128]

Reform was given new momentum in late May with the circulation of Document No. 4, "The CPC Central Committee's opinions on expediting reform, opening wider to the outside world, and working to raise the economy to a new level in a better and quicker way." The document, apparently drafted under the auspices of Zhu Rongji, marked a major new stage in China's policy of opening to the outside by declaring that five major inland cities along the Yangtze and nine border trade cities would be opened and that the thirty capitals of China's provinces and regions and municipalities would enjoy the same preferential treatment and policies as the SEZs. Moreover, the document stated formally what Deng had said in January, namely that Guangdong was to catch up with the four small dragons in twenty years.[129]

The more open political atmosphere of the spring encouraged long-silenced liberal intellectuals once again to raise their voices in protest against leftism. A collection of essays by such famous intellectuals as former minister of culture Wang Meng, former editor in chief of the *People's Daily* Hu Jiwei, and former editor of the *Science and Technology Daily* Sun Changjiang created a storm when it was published under the title *Historical trends*.[130] The book's sharp criticism of leftism quickly brought the wrath of the Propaganda Department, which banned the book.[131] Shortly after the book's publication, Yuan Hongbing, the law lecturer from Beijing University who had edited the book, presided over a gathering of more than 100 well-known intellectuals in Beijing. Such people as Wang Ruoshui, the former deputy editor of the *People's Daily*, and Wu Zuguang, the famous playwright who had been expelled from the Party in 1987, addressed the forum.[132] In the months that followed, other books denouncing leftism came off the press.[133]

The renewed activities of such liberal intellectuals was certainly grist for the leftists' mill. Shortly after the forum in Beijing, Deng Liqun launched

128 *XH*, 14 June 1992, trans. in *FBIS-Chi*, 15 June 1992, 23–6. Jiang's speech was the occasion of the *People's Daily's* first authoritative comment on reform since February. See "New stage of China's reform and opening to the outside world," *RMRB* editorial, 9 June 1992, trans. in *FBIS-Chi*, 9 June 1992, 17–18.
129 [Xia Yu] Hsia Yu, "Beijing's intense popular interest in CPC Document No. 4," *DGB*, 12 June 1992, trans. in *FBIS-Chi*, 12 June 1992, 17–18; "The CCP issues Document No. 4, fully expounding expansion of opening up," *DGB*, 18 June 1992, trans. in *FBIS-Chi*, 18 June 1992, 19–20.
130 Yuan Hongbing, *Lishi chaoliu* (Historical trends).
131 [Lu Mingsheng] Lu Ming-sheng, "Inside story of how *Historical trends* was banned," *ZM*, 177 (1 July 1992), 33–4, trans. in *FBIS-Chi*, 7 July 1992, 19–21.
132 *MB*, 15 June 1992, trans. in *FBIS-Chi*, 15 June 1992, 26–7.
133 See Zhao Shilin, ed., *Fang "zuo" beiwanglu* (Memorandum on opposing "leftism"); Wen Jin, ed., *Zhongguo "zuo" huo* (China's "leftist" peril); and Yuan Yongsong and Wang Junwei, eds., *Zuoqing ershinian, 1957–1976* (Twenty years of leftism, 1957–1976).

a new attack. In an internal speech at the Office for the Research of Party History, Deng called for "extra vigilance over the recent rise in rightist tendencies."[134]

Many intellectuals had taken heart from Deng Xiaoping's trip to the South and his harsh denunciations of the Left. They hoped that at last the patriarch would deal a fatal blow to such leftist leaders as Deng Liqun, Wang Renzhi, and Gao Di. Deng's calculus, however, remained different from that of the intellectuals. His goals were twofold. First, he wanted to reassert his dominance in the Party. His southern tour, his harsh rhetoric, and his willingness to use the military in an intra-Party struggle demonstrated his determination, while the Fourteenth Party Congress's enshrinement of Deng's thought would signal his success. Second, however, Deng sought a path that might ensure stability after his passing, and the terrible intra-Party struggles that Tiananmen and the ensuing changes in the international environment had set off demonstrated just how precarious that goal was. In 1988 Deng had endorsed the concept of neoauthoritarianism – the idea that the authority of the state could be used to build a strong economy and stable society à la the authoritarian regimes on China's periphery. During his trip to the South, Deng praised the example of Singapore. And during his visit to Shougang, he signaled that he had found his tool for building such a society: Zhu Rongji.

Thus, the Fourteenth Party Congress that convened in October 1992 sought to do two seemingly contradictory things: establish clear dominance over Chen Yun and deny the fruits of victory to the "bourgeois liberals" within the Party.

THE FOURTEENTH PARTY CONGRESS

Deng's efforts over the preceding year and more, starting with his early 1991 trip to Shanghai and building momentum following the abortive coup in the Soviet Union and with his trip to Shenzhen, finally culminated in October 1992 with the adoption by the Fourteenth Party Congress of the most liberal economic document in CCP history. Whereas a year earlier Deng Liqun had been calling reform and opening up the source of peaceful evolution,[135] the Fourteenth Party Congress report declared that "the most clear-cut characteristic of the new historical period is reform and opening up" and that the "new revolution" inaugurated by Deng was "aimed at

---

134 *South China Morning Post*, 24 June 1992. See also Meng Lin, "Deng Liqun reaffirms disapproval of phrase 'Deng Xiaoping thought,'" *JB*, 180 (5 July 1992), 42, trans. in *FBIS-Chi*, 6 July 1992, 28–9.

135 Baum, *Burying Mao*, 334.

fundamentally changing the economic structure rather than patching it up."
Underlining the profound changes called for by Deng's revolution, the political report endorsed the creation of a "socialist *market* economic system" as
the goal of reform, thereby advancing a major step beyond the 1984 thesis of
building a "socialist planned commodity economy" – which had itself been
controversial.[136]

Moreover, the political report endorsed the important theses of Deng Xiaoping's southern tour, including his statement that planning and market were
merely economic "means" for regulating the economy, his proposition that
the 1978 Third Plenum line should be pursued for a hundred years, and –
most important – his assertion that it was necessary "mainly to guard
against 'leftist' tendencies within the Party, particularly among the leading
cadres."[137]

The Fourteenth Party Congress was certainly a personal victory for Deng.
Whereas his policies had been under nearly constant attack since 1989 and
Chen Yun's economic thought had been repeatedly written into speeches
and policy documents, the Fourteenth Party Congress lauded Deng for his
"tremendous political courage in opening up new paths in socialist construction and a tremendous theoretical courage in opening up a new realm in
Marxism." No other plenum or congress report in the reform era had been so
personal or so laudatory. Rhetorically at least, Deng's status became comparable to, if not higher than, that of Mao.

Personnel changes at the Fourteenth Party Congress supported the policies
Deng favored to some extent. Conservative leaders Yao Yilin and Song Ping
were removed from the PSC, and Zhu Rongji, Liu Huaqing, a senior military
modernizer who was also promoted to the position of vice-chairman of the
CMC, and Hu Jintao, a fifty-one-year-old former China Youth League cadre
and former Party secretary of Tibet, were added. The conservative Li Ximing,
targeted by Deng during his southern tour, was removed from the Politburo
and subsequently replaced as Beijing Party secretary by Chen Xitong, who
had responded loyally to Deng's "emancipate the mind" campaign in 1991,
despite his hard-line stance during the 1989 protest movement. Overall, the
number of full Politburo members was increased to twenty from fourteen as
a number of provincial and younger leaders joined the august body while
several elders retired (Yang Shangkun, Wan Li, Qin Jiwei, Wu Xueqian, and
Yang Rudai).[138] Moreover, the CAC, of which Chen Yun was the head and

---

136 "Political report" to the Fourteenth Party Congress, Beijing television, trans. in *FBIS-Chi*, 13 October
     1992, 23–43. Quotes taken from pages 25 and 24, respectively. Emphasis added.
137 Ibid., 29.
138 Joseph Fewsmith, "Reform, resistance, and the politics of succession," in William A. Joseph, ed., *China
     briefing, 1994*, 8–11.

which had long served as a bastion of conservative opposition to Deng, was abolished.

While these changes reflected a major change in China's top-level policy-making body, Deng stopped short of a fundamental overhaul. In particular, Deng was determined to prevent supporters of former general secretary Zhao Ziyang from moving into the highest positions. Thus, Vice-Premier Tian Jiyun, a protégé of Zhao who had pushed Deng's themes with such devastating effectiveness the previous spring, was denied a PSC seat. Moreover, such Zhao associates as Hu Qili and Yan Mingfu, partially rehabilitated in June 1991, did not rejoin the Politburo and Secretariat, respectively, as some had hoped and expected.[139]

Most important, the changes stopped short of affecting the so-called Jiang-Li structure at the top of the system. Many had expected Zhu Rongji or Tian Jiyun to be elevated to the second slot, in line to succeed Li Peng as premier at the NPC meeting the following spring. Perhaps such predictions cum hopes were unrealistic. In restructuring the leadership, Deng carefully maintained a balance between reformers and conservatives. As the well-known writer Bai Hua put it, "It was as though he [Deng] were afraid that once the leftists had been wiped out, the [factional] balance would be upset and another wave of 'bourgeois liberalization' would set in."[140] The point of such balancing was to shore up the authority of Deng's third choice to succeed him, Jiang Zemin, though, as we shall see, it remains less than clear that Jiang remains committed to upholding Deng's legacy.

Deng did at least two things that bolstered Jiang. First and foremost, on the eve of the Fourteenth Party Congress, Deng decided to oust Yang Baibing, who had led the PLA to "escort reform" the previous spring, as vice-chairman of the powerful CMC. In so doing, Deng undercut the authority of his longtime confidant and supporter, Yang Shangkun, who is Yang Baibing's elder half-brother. Deng took this step in part because much of the professional military establishment (as opposed to the political commissars) resented Yang Baibing for his lack of professional military experience and because his rise was widely believed to be attributable to the influence of his older sibling. In addition, Yang Baibing stirred resentment in the military by promoting his own loyalists, and he undercut Jiang Zemin by conferring major promotions himself instead of deferring to Jiang as head of the CMC. Following Yang's ouster, some three hundred high-level officers were retired or rotated. While

139 Former PSC member Hu Qili, purged for his support of Zhao during the 1989 demonstrations, was appointed vice-minister of the Ministry of the Machine-Building and Electronics Industry. Yan Mingfu, former member of the Secretariat and head of the party's United Front Work Department, was appointed a vice-minister of civil affairs. A third Zhao associate, Rui Xingwen, was named vice-minister of the SPC at the same time. XH, 1 June 1993, trans. in FBIS-Chi, 4 June 1991, 30.
140 Quoted in Lam, China after Deng Xiaoping, 171.

many of these changes can be attributed to normal rotation, it seems clear that several protégé of the Yang brothers were removed from critical positions.

To replace the Yangs, Deng turned to the elderly (seventy-seven in 1992) Liu Huaqing, who was given a PSC seat and named vice-chairman of the CMC, and Zhang Zhen (seventy-nine in 1992), who was named second vice-chairman of the CMC. The surprise elevation of Liu and Zhang certainly underscored a renewed professionalism in the PLA (Liu is one of the leading modernizers in the PLA, particularly of the navy, which he led for many years, and Zhang was commandant of the National Defense University), but their promotion also highlighted the impossibility of turning over the leadership of the military to a younger generation, even as the age of the country's civilian leaders continued to fall.

In addition to shoring up Jiang's authority by shaking up the military hierarchy, Deng limited his purge of leftists. Although Li Ximing was removed from the Politburo and from his position as secretary of the Beijing Municipal CCP Committee and Gao Di was removed as director of the *People's Daily*, many leftists remained in influential positions.

BACK TO THE MIDDLE

The effort to strike a new balance was apparent in the aftermath of the Fourteenth Party Congress. Whereas Deng's new reform push had dominated Chinese politics since his trip to Shenzhen at the beginning of the year, shortly after the congress closed China's leaders began to warn liberal intellectuals not to go too far. In late November Jiang Zemin warned cadres to exercise caution in criticizing Marxism–Leninism–Mao Zedong Thought, saying that their viewpoints represented "the most updated reflection of class struggle inside society and inside the party in a certain realm." As the political atmosphere became more conservative, Yao Yilin, who had stepped down from the PSC at the Fourteenth Party Congress, sharply criticized economic czar Zhu Rongji first at a State Council meeting and then at a conference for Politburo members and state councilors. Yao argued that capital investment had exceeded the plan by too much (38 percent), that bank credits had likewise greatly exceeded the plan (120 percent), and that debt chains and stockpiles were again building up. Zhu reportedly defended himself by arguing that although there were problems with the economy, it was not "overheated."[141] Nevertheless, both

141 [Zheng Delin] Cheng Te-lin, "Yao Yilin launches attack against Zhu Rongji, Tian *Jiyun*," *JB*, 1 (5 January 1993), 44–5, trans. in *FBIS-Chi*, 22 January 1993, 46–7; [Ren Huiwen] Jen Hui-wen, "Deng Xiaoping urges conservatives not to make a fuss," *Xinbao*, 1 January 1993, trans. in *FBIS-Chi*, 4 January 1993, 43–4; and [Chen Jianbing] Chen Chien-ping, "Zhu Rongji urges paying attention to negative effects of reform," *WHB* (Hong Kong), 13 January 1993, trans. in *FBIS-Chi*, 15 January 1993, 27–8.

Jiang Zemin and Li Peng warned at the year-end National Planning Conference and National Economic Conference against the "overheated economy."[142]

This renewed attack on rapid economic growth prompted the patriarch to intervene again. For the third year in a row, Deng reappeared in Shanghai to encourage high growth and reform. This time, Deng was quoted as saying, "I hope you will not lose the current opportunities. Opportunities for great development are rare in China."[143] Immediately China's media began to explain why China's economy was not overheated, despite the opinion of many economists that it was.

Deng's intervention and the subsequent media campaign were apparently intended not only to keep up reform momentum in general but also specifically to influence the NPC meeting scheduled for March. In early March the Second Plenary Session of the Fourteenth Central Committee met to consider policy before the NPC and endorsed Deng's view that "at present and throughout the 1990s, the favorable domestic and international opportunities should be grasped to speed up the pace of reform, opening up, and the modernization drive." On the basis of this optimistic assessment, the plenum endorsed an upward revision of the annual growth target set by the Eighth Five-Year Plan (1991–5) from 6 percent to 8–9 percent.[144]

Following this plenum resolution, Li Peng and his drafting team had to go back to work on the text of the Government Work Report, much as Li had been forced to revise the text of the previous year's work report. According to the PRC-owned Hong Kong paper *Wenweibao*, the work report was revised to reflect "more positively, more comprehensively, and more accurately" the guiding principles of the Fourteenth Party Congress – an admission of just how far the initial draft had deviated from Deng's policies. The revised version of the work report highlighted the essence of Deng's talk in Shanghai, namely that it was necessary to "grasp the opportunity, because there will not be many big opportunities for China."[145]

THE EIGHTH NATIONAL PEOPLE'S CONGRESS

The first session of the Eighth NPC, which convened in March 1993, marked both a passing of generations and a change of political strategy. In the opening session, longtime Deng loyalist Wan Li, who had perhaps done more than anyone else to shepherd and nurture the early rural reforms, declared that the

142 *XH*, 27 December 1992, trans. in *FBIS-Chi*, 28 December 1992, 34–6.
143 Central television, 22 January 1993, trans. in *FBIS-Chi*, 22 January 1993, 20–1.
144 *XH*, 7 March 1993, in *FBIS-Chi*, 8 March 1993, 13–14.
145 "Major revisions to the government work report," *WHB* (Hong Kong), 16 March 1993, trans. in *FBIS-Chi*, 16 March 1993, 23–4.

session would take "Comrade Deng Xiaoping's theory on building socialism with Chinese characteristics" as its guide and would "vigorously push ahead reform, opening up, and the modernization drive." Having said this, Wan turned the gavel over to his successor, Qiao Shi, and embraced him before leaving the hall.[146]

The appointment of Qiao Shi as head of the NPC not only upgraded the legislative body – in the reform era it had not previously been headed by a PSC member – but also marked the abandonment of Deng's long-term strategy of separating party and government. At least since his famous 1980 speech "On the reform of the Party and state leadership system," Deng had championed the separation of Party and state as a way of making state administration more efficient and the Party less intrusive.[147] This effort had culminated in Zhao Ziyang's proposal at the Thirteenth Party Congress to establish a civil service system and to remove Party groups (*dangzu*) from government organs. Apparently taking account of both the collapse of the Soviet Union, which Chinese analysts attributed in part to efforts to separate Party and state, and of similar but more limited efforts in China, Deng finally abandoned his former reform strategy and decided that only by having top Party leaders manage leading government posts could the Party's leadership be guaranteed.

The NPC also formally appointed Jiang Zemin as president of the PRC, replacing Yang Shangkun and making Jiang the first person to hold concurrently the top three posts in the Party, military, and state apparatus since the ill-starred Hua Guofeng – to whom Jiang has frequently been compared.[148] The NPC also reappointed Li Peng as premier, but 210 votes were cast against him, 120 delegates abstained, and 1 vote was cast for Zhao Ziyang. The concurrent session of the Chinese People's Political Consultative Conference (CPPCC) named fourth-ranking PSC member Li Ruihuan as its head. Thus, the top four members of the Politburo held all the leading positions in the government as well.[149]

The most important outcome of the NPC session, however, was the diminution of the authority of the SPC. The SPC, frequently referred to as the "little State Council," had traditionally been the nerve center of China's planned

146 XH, 14 March 1993, in FBIS-Chi, 15 March 1993, 19.
147 Deng Xiaoping, "Dang he guojia lingdao zhidu de gaige" (On the reform of the Party and state leadership system), in Deng Xiaoping wenxuan (1975–1982), 280–302.
148 Hua Guofeng was Party chairman from the time of Mao's death in 1976 to 1980, when he was replaced by Hu Yaobang. The position of Party chairman was subsequently abolished (by the Party constitution of 1982), making the position of general secretary the top post in the Party.
149 Joseph Fewsmith, "Notes on the first session of the Eighth National People's Congress," Journal of Contemporary China, 3 (Summer 1993), 81–6.

economy. In the Dengist period, it had always been headed by loyal support-ers of Chen Yun and was a bastion of conservative economic thought. When Zou Jiahua, a longtime protégé of Li Peng, was appointed to head the SPC in 1989 and subsequently was made a vice-premier in 1991, this trend was confirmed.

In March 1993, however, Chen Jinhua, a former vice-mayor of Shanghai (in the late 1970s and early 1980s) and general manager of the China Petrochem-ical Corporation (1983–90), was appointed to replace Zou Jiahua as head of the SPC. Although a member of the Central Committee, Chen was neither a member of the Politburo, much less its Standing Committee (as Yao Yilin had been), nor a vice-premier (as Zou Jiahua had been). This diminution in the status of the SPC would presage the emergence of the State Economic and Trade Commission, established in May 1993, as China's most authoritative economic policy-making body and made its head, Vice-Premier Zhu Rongji, even more powerful.

Zhu's role as economic czar was unexpectedly reinforced when Li Peng suffered a heart attack on or about 25 April. Li, Zhu's primary rival for control over the economy, disappeared from public sight for two months before he emerged for two brief appearances in mid-June and then disappeared for another two months. Although there seems little doubt that the premier was seriously ill in at least the early part of this period, his problems appear to have been political as well. After all, no one had done more on the economic front than Li Peng to shore up the old planned economy and to oppose Deng's new push for reform – as his need to revise his work reports to the NPC in 1992 and 1993 showed.

ZHU RONGJI AND THE ECONOMY

Zhu's control over economic management was greatly enhanced in June 1993. Jiang Zemin presided over a "Central Financial and Banking Work Confer-ence" at which Zhu presented a sixteen-point proposal aimed at restoring economic order and reducing inflationary pressures. Zhu's proposals were sharply opposed by Li Guixian, a longtime protégé of Li Peng and head of the People's Bank of China. The showdown resulted in Li's ouster and Zhu's installation as concurrent head of the central bank.[150]

With Zou Jiahua demoted from leadership of the SPC and with Li Peng sidelined, Zhu Rongji's control over China's economy became nearly total.

---

150 [Ren Huiwen] Jen Hui-wen, "Different views within the CCP on the banking crisis," *Xinbao*, 9 July 1993, trans. in *FBIS-Chi*, 12 July 1993, 41–2.

Zhu was named to head a newly established leading group for reform of the financial, taxation, and banking structures, a position he added to his already powerful posting as deputy head of the Central Finance and Economics Leading Group.[151] Moreover, Zhu quickly brought in a number of his trusted aides to help him manage the economy. For instance, Dai Xianglong, president of the Shanghai-based Bank of Communications, and Zhu Xiaohua, vice-president of the Shanghai Branch of the Bank of China, were named vice-governors of the People's Bank of China, and a number of economists associated with market-oriented economist Wu Jinglian, who had been a prominent adviser to Zhao Ziyang, were brought in as advisers.[152]

The sixteen-point plan that Zhu had presented at the June meeting and was subsequently issued as a Central Committee circular (Document No. 6) marked the inauguration of a new round of austerity and the beginning of a long, new effort to combine reform of the economy with a redefinition of the relations between Beijing and the provinces.

Zhu has often been referred to as "China's Gorbachev" by the Western press (and by his domestic enemies as well), but there is little in his economic thinking, much less political position, to suggest that he either desires or can play such a role in China. Indeed, Zhu has engaged in considerable jousting with China's reform-minded economists.[153] Zhu's approach to economic reform and political control appears modeled after that of Park Chung-hee or Lee Kuan Yew, favoring strong state control combined with a marketized economy. On the one hand, he favors strong actions to move the economy away from the old planned economy, while on the other hand, he is inclined to use the "visible hand" to try to guide this process from the top. Unlike many of the reformers associated with Zhao Ziyang, who were willing to devolve much decision-making authority to lower levels, Zhu clearly believes that too much authority (and too many fiscal resources) have slipped out of Beijing's control. Drawing heavily on the experiences of the East Asian developmental state, this approach is often referred to as "neoauthoritarian."

---

151 Jiang Zemin was the head of this group, though there is little indication that he involved himself in the details of economic management. Li Peng was the other deputy head of the group.

152 Wang Qishan, then vice-president (and now president) of the Construction Bank of China and son-in-law of Yao Yilin, was also named a vice-governor of the People's Bank of China, perhaps in an effort to allay conservative opposition. Chen Yun's son, Chen Yuan, was the fourth vice-governor of the bank. On Wu Jinglian's economic thought, see Fewsmith, *Dilemmas of reform in China*, 161–6.

153 For instance, in October 1993, a number of liberal economists voiced concerns that Zhu's austerity program would lead to a retreat from reform. See *Zhongguo xinwen she*, 25 October 1993, trans. in *FBIS-Chi*, 29 October 1993, 38–9. In turn, Zhu has criticized some Chinese textbooks that "blindly worship" Western laissez-faire economics. See *Zhongguo tongxun she*, 2 December 1994, trans. in *FBIS-Chi*, 2 December 1994, 24–5. On Zhu's willingness to use administrative measures alongside market forces, see his speech, "Should the government intervene in the market and regulate prices in a socialist market economy?" *Jiage lilun yu shijian*, 10 (October 1993), 1–5, trans. in *FBIS-Chi*, 10 January 1995.

This approach was reflected in Zhu's campaign against speculation and inflation in the summer and fall of 1993. As control over the money supply was loosened in 1992 in response to Deng's call for faster economic growth, speculation and corruption mushroomed. The teal estate market took off, and by the end of 1992 there were more than 12,000 real estate companies, a 2.4-fold increase over the year before.[154] At the same time, local areas continued to open up "developmental zones" in the hope of attracting foreign capital and to take advantage of loopholes in the financial regulations. By the end of 1992, there were said to be some 8,000 development zones.[155]

These speculative markets quickly drew large sums of money from the hinterland, exacerbating the problem of IOUs being given to peasants for the grain they grew. According to one report, at least Rmb 57 billion had been diverted through interbank loans to the coastal areas, where it was used to speculate in real estate and the stock market. The result was a "bubble economy" that could "vanish without warning."[156] In an effort to curb such speculative activity and bring the economy under control, Zhu ordered banks to recall loans that had not been issued according to regulations and mandated a 20 percent cut in government spending.[157]

THE THIRD PLENUM

The Third Plenary Session of the Fourteenth Central Committee, which was convened in Beijing on 11–14 November 1993, took up the task of translating the Fourteenth Party Congress's goal of building a "socialist market economy" into a concrete program of reform. The crux of the plenum decision lay in its promises, on the one hand, to reform the macroeconomic system by building the financial, tax, and monetary systems necessary to manage the economy through economic means, and, on the other hand, to reform the microeconomy by building "socialist modern enterprises." This proposed reform of China's enterprise system was apparently the hottest area of contention in the discussions leading up to the Third Plenum because it involved the issue of ownership, and ownership reform was inextricably bound up with both ideological issues and vested interests. Nevertheless, the Third Plenum decision

---

154 *XH*, 21 May 1993, trans. in *FBIS-Chi*, 21 May 1993, 28–9. See also Zhu Jianhong and Jiang Yaping, "Development and standardization are necessary: Perspective of real estate business," *RMRB*, 11 May 1993, trans. in *FBIS-Chi*, 24 May 1993, 56–7.
155 Xiang Jingquan, "Review and prospects of China's economic development," *GMRB*, trans. in *FBIS-Chi*, 19 March 1993, 48–50.
156 "Central authorities urge banks to draw bank loans and stop promoting the bubble economy," *DGB*, 1 July 1993, trans. in *FBIS-Chi*, 1 July 1993, 31–2.
157 [Chen Jianbing] Chen Chien-ping, "The CCP Central Committee announces 16 measures," *WHB* (Hong Kong), 3 July 1993, trans. in *FBIS-Chi*, 7 July 1993, 12–13.

specified that the property rights of socialist modern enterprises should be
clarified and that enterprises would be entitled to manage their assets independently, would be responsible for profits and losses, and would maintain
and increase the net worth of the enterprises.[158]

What was not specified by the decision was how property rights would be
allocated and how state interests were to be protected. The decision was not
intended to take the state out of the business of owning enterprises; after all,
it specified that the "public ownership system" would remain the "foundation
of the socialist market economy." But the decision moved further in the
direction of ownership reform than had seemed possible only a year before –
or even in the heyday of reform in the late 1980s. In an internal speech on the
eve of the plenum, Jiang Zemin went so far as to declare that the dominance
of the public ownership system meant only that public ownership had to
remain dominant in national terms; individual localities and industries need
not be subject to this requirement.[159] Perhaps the most important aspect of
the plenum decision on enterprise reform was the promise that all enterprises,
"especially" the state-owned sector, would compete equally and "without
discrimination" on the market.[160] In other words, state-owned enterprises
were to be "pushed onto the market" – a dramatic difference in official policy
from the period following Tiananmen during which discrimination between
types of ownership was taken as distinguishing socialist reform from bourgeois
liberalization.

In order to implement this decision, the Third Plenum called for a major
reform of the banking system and an overhaul of the tax system. The People's
Bank of China was, at long last, to be turned into a genuine central bank
that would "implement monetary policies independently."[161] Guo Shuqing,
a close adviser to Zhu Rongji and head of the Comprehensive Section of the
State Commission for Economic Restructuring, declared that the People's
Bank should be as independent as the Federal Reserve or Bundesbank.[162]
At the same time, "policy banks" would be set up to deal with enterprises and economic sectors as well as capital construction projects that
were important to the state and/or in the red. In this way, the problems of
deficit enterprises could be separated out from the overall management of the
economy.

158 "Decision of the CCP Central Committee on some issues concerning the establishment of a socialist
     market economic structure" (hereafter, "Establishment of a socialist market structure"), RMRB, 17
     November 1993, trans. in FBIS-Chi, 17 November 1993, 23.
159 [Ji Wenge] Chi Wei-ke, "Three new moves on the eve of the Third Plenary Session of the CPC Central
     Committee; Deng makes new comments on macrocontrol," JB, 12 (5 December 1993), 30–4, trans.
     in FBIS-Chi, 8 December 1993, 18–22.
160 "Establishment of a socialist market structure," 25.   161 Ibid., 28.
162 South China Sunday Morning Post, 14 November 1993.

REFORMING THE TAX SYSTEM

For both economic and political reasons, the Third Plenum also endorsed a major change in China's tax system. Economically it made sense to implement a uniform tax rate across all forms of enterprises; it would, after all, provide a financial underpinning to the nondiscrimination between state-owned and other enterprises called for by the plenum decision. But it was the political logic that was more compelling. Central government revenues as a proportion of GNP and as a proportion of all government revenues had fallen steadily throughout the reform period. The share of total state revenues in GNP had fallen monotonously from 31.2 percent in 1978 to 16.2 percent in 1993, and Beijing's portion of overall state revenues had fallen from 57 percent in 1981 to 33 percent in 1993.[163] Moreover, due largely to the mismanagement of the economy by conservatives in the 1989–90 period, state-owned enterprises could no longer serve as financial supports for the central budget. Long the milch cows of the central government, such enterprises, after subtracting their losses, repayments to banks, and retained profits, contributed no profit to the state budget after 1990.[164] New sources of revenue had to be found.

The basic reason for the decrease of central revenues with respect to overall government revenues was that in order to stimulate local "enthusiasm" for production at the beginning of the reform era, China had adopted a fiscal system popularly known as "eating in separate kitchens" (*fenzao chifan*), the essence of which was to stimulate local interest in developing the economy and collecting taxes by giving localities a fiscal interest. Later, the country adopted the fiscal contracting responsibility system, which basically allowed localities (and some industrial sectors) to pay either a set amount or a certain percentage of revenue to the center (and keep the rest).

These fiscal arrangements had in many ways achieved exactly what they were supposed to do – arouse the enthusiasm of the localities for promoting economic development. Indeed, much of the economic success China has enjoyed in the reform period has come about precisely because fiscal arrangements gave local governments a stake in developing their local economies. As Jean Oi put it, economic development in China came about because China "got the taxes wrong."[165]

Although China's tax system was critical for providing incentives for economic development, it also had a number of side effects that were less

163 Jae Ho Chung, "Central–provincial relations," in Lo Chi Kin, Suzanne Pepper, and Tsui Kai Yuen, eds., *China review, 1995*, 3.7.
164 Naughton, *Growing out of the plan*, 286.
165 Jean Oi, *Rural China takes off: Incentives for industrialization*.

benevolent. In particular, the system allowed localities to develop large sources of "extrabudgetary" revenues – revenues that did not have to be passed on to the central government – which local governments could allocate to develop, and protect, local industry. Extrabudgetary revenues increased very quickly over the course of reform, from a mere Rmb 34.7 billion in 1978 to 385 billion in 1992. Put another way, extrabudgetary funds rose from only 31 percent of budgetary revenues in 1978 to 98 percent in 1992. It was the amassing of this pot of extrabudgetary revenue that allowed China's localities to ride out the austere economic policies imposed during the period of "improvement and rectification." Despite central policies that were manifestly opposed to the TVE sector, most localities were able to protect their local industries and in many areas these industries continued to grow rapidly despite central proscriptions.[166]

The fiscal contracting system that had been so generous to local government led to Beijing's relative decline in revenue. Conservatives had long railed against the loss of central power implied by these figures; indeed, a major goal of the "improvement and rectification" policy was to reverse these trends. Nevertheless, in December 1990 the Seventh Plenum, in part to alleviate the tense central–provincial relationship, which had been reflected in the Economic Work Conference the previous September, promised to leave the tax structure unchanged during the course of the Eighth Five-Year Plan (1991–5).

The continuing erosion of the central government's fiscal position – including annual budget deficits, inflationary pressures, and growing tax evasion (estimated to be around 100 billion yuan in the early 1990s) – caused the issue of tax reform to be revisited. Perhaps more important, as he demonstrated repeatedly, Zhu Rongji was as much a statist as he was a marketeer. Zhu's objective, as reflected in the Third Plenum decision and other measures, was to use the power of the state to rationalize and marketize the economic system.

Thus, the Third Plenum declared that the fiscal contracting system would be replaced by the tax-sharing system (*fenshuizhi*). Under the new system, the consolidated commercial–industrial tax would be divided into a business tax (which would be retained by the localities) and a product circulation tax (which would be shared between the localities and the central government). At the same time, other shared taxes, including a value-added tax, were to be imposed. Under the new system, and consistent with the government's goal of "pushing state-owned enterprises onto the market," all enterprises would be taxed at the same 33 percent rate.[167]

166 Ibid.   167 Chung, "Central–provincial relations," 5.9–12.

The goal of this tax system was to raise the proportion of budgetary revenues in the national income from the current 16 percent to 25 percent in the short run and 35 percent over the longer term, and to raise the central share of budget revenues from the present 33 percent to 50 percent in the short run and more than 65 percent in the long run.[168]

This effort to recentralize fiscal control was predictably resisted by the provinces. Before the plenum, Zhu Rongji made forays to sixteen provinces and municipalities in an effort to strong-arm them into compliance. In some cases his discussions were extremely acrimonious. Jiangsu provincial Party secretary Shen Daren was a particularly outspoken critic of the tax reform, and Zhu Rongji apparently chose to make an example of him by having him removed from office. But other provincial officials, particularly from coastal provinces, were equally opposed, believing the tax reform to be a scheme to "rob from the rich to aid the poor." Officials from Guangdong and Fujian were critical of the reform, as were, for different reasons, leaders of Yunnan and Guizhou.[169] At the 1994 meeting of the NPC, nearly one-quarter of the delegates either voted against or abstained during the vote on the new budgetary law.[170]

The other major change that came out of the Third Plenum was the decision to end the use of foreign exchange certificates and to unify foreign exchange rates in a bid to move toward free convertibility of the renminbi. Under the new system, export firms are supposed to sell all of their foreign exchange earnings to thirteen banks and then purchase whatever amount of foreign currency they need with renminbi. Like the other measures adopted at the Third Plenum, this change appeared to be an effort to boost central authority even as it moved China more fully toward a market economy.[171]

TOWARD SUCCESSION

By late 1994, at least two things had begun to impinge on China's political situation. First and foremost, after many ups and downs and a constant stream of rumors, it finally seemed certain that Deng's physical ability to oversee affairs of state had finally given out. In particular, around December 1994 to January 1995, Deng apparently hung between life and death. His daughter, who goes by the name Xiao Rong, declared in an unusual interview with *The New York Times* in January 1995 that her father's health was declining

---

168 Ibid., 3.12.
169 Guizhou and Yunnan were opposed because the tax reform would take much of the revenues those provinces earned from their production of cigarettes and liquor. See ibid., 3.14.
170 Ibid., 3.15.   171 Ibid., 3.24.

"day by day."[172] Indeed, by the time of the interview, Deng had not appeared in public since the previous January, and the release of a photograph of a very old looking Deng sitting and enjoying the fireworks on National Day (1 October) 1993 underscored the fact that it would not be long before the patriarch finally "went to join the Premier" (as Deng had once put it).[173] Even reports that Deng's health had remarkably improved in the summer of 1995 could not dispell the impression that he no longer controlled political developments.

Second, Zhu Rongji's bold effort to move China firmly onto the path of a market economy had clearly stalled. Inflationary pressures remained strong throughout 1994, and hopes of pushing state-owned enterprises onto the market were checked by the very real fear of social disorder that a large number of unemployed workers might bring about.

Under these circumstances, Jiang Zemin began to adopt a more cautious course of economic reform while moving vigorously to prove that he was the successor in fact as well as in name. As already noted, Jiang was successful at the time of the Fourteenth Party Congress in gaining Deng's support against the Yang brothers. Another round of military rotations was launched in 1993–4 that resulted in the movement of nearly a thousand additional officers.[174] At the same time, Jiang made obvious efforts to cultivate the support of the army and to promote his own followers. In June 1993, he personally promoted nineteen senior officers to the rank of general, and he also moved a number of trusted officers into sensitive positions, although not always successfully. In particular, Jiang replaced Yang Dezhong, the head of the sensitive Central Guard Bureau, with You Kexi, a military associate from Shanghai. He also appointed as head of the People's Armed Police Force (PAP) Ba Zhongtan, who had served as head of the Shanghai garrison, but Ba was subsequently forced to step down after a PAP security guard killed NPC vice-chairman Li Peiyao.[175]

In the fall of 1994, as Deng's health declined, Jiang dropped economic issues from the agenda of the forthcoming Fourth Plenum in order to concentrate on Party-building issues. As a result, the "Decision of the Central Committee of the Communist Party of China concerning some major issues on strengthening Party building," adopted by the plenum in October, stressed strengthening

172 *The New York Times*, 13 January 1995. Xiao Rong later claimed that she had been misquoted. See Jean Philippe Beja, The year of the dog: In the shadow of the ailing patriarch," in Lo, Pepper, and Tsui, eds., *China review, 1995*, 1.8–10.
173 Deng reportedly spoke to some leaders about the upcoming Fourth Plenum on 9 October 1994. See *ZM*, 205 (1 November 1994), 6–8, trans. in *FBIS-Chi*, 4 November 1994, 15–17.
174 Lam, *China after Deng Xiaoping*, 213–16.
175 On the appointments of You and Ba, see R. N. Schiele, "Jiang's men move out of the shadows," *Eastern Express*, 27 December 1994, in *FBIS-Chi*, 27 December 1994, 27–9. On Ba's dismissal, see Tony Walker, "Security chief's sacking seen as rebuff for Jiang," *Financial Times*, 27 February 1996, 6.

"democratic centralism," which emphasizes the subordination of lower levels to higher levels, the part to the whole, and everything to the party center.[176]

The plenum proved to be an important victory for Jiang Zemin. The *People's Daily* noted that "the second-generation central leading collective has been successfully relieved by its third-generation central leading collective" – a point reiterated by Li Peng during his November trip to Korea and again by Jiang Zemin a few days later during his trip to Malaysia.[177] Not only did the "Decision" reaffirm Jiang's position as the "core" of the leadership, it also promoted three of his protégés to the center. Huang Ju, mayor of Shanghai, was promoted to the Politburo, while Wu Bangguo, Party secretary of Shanghai and a member of the Politburo, and Jiang Chunyun, Party secretary of Shandong province, were added to the Party Secretariat.

The promotion of Wu Bangguo and Jiang Chunyun served not only to shore up Jiang Zemin's personal support at the center but also to diminish the authority of Zhu Rongji, a potential rival. With the reforms Zhu had spearheaded at the 1993 Third Plenum slowed, Jiang now began parceling out bits of Zhu's portfolio. Wu Bangguo was named deputy head of the Central Finance and Economic Leading Group (replacing, Li Peng) and thus would share leadership of that critical body with Zhu, under the general supervision of Jiang, who remained head of the group. More important, Wu was placed in charge of the reform of state-owned enterprises, which was designated as the focus of economic reform in 1995. At the same time, Jiang Chunyun was given the task of overseeing agriculture, another task for which Zhu Rongji had previously been responsible.

Year-end economic meetings made it evident that Jiang intended to steer a slow, steady course, preferring to shore up inefficient state-owned enterprises rather than push them onto the market as Zhu had tried to do the year before. Jiang Zemin and other conservative leaders were afraid that biting the bullet, as Zhu had urged the year before, would erode the authority of the Party and government and undermine what remained of socialist ideology. As Premier Li Peng put it, "Without solid state-owned enterprises, there will be no socialist China."[178] Hence, reform in 1995 concentrated on the selection of a hundred state-owned enterprises for pilot projects in the creation of a modern "corporate" form – as if China has not carried out hundreds of pilot projects over the past decade and more. At the same time, leaders vowed to

---

176 "Decision of the Central Committee of the Communist Party of China concerning some major issues on strengthening Party building," *XH*, 6 October 1994, in *FBIS-Chi*, 6 October 1994, 13–22.

177 [Xu Simin] Hsu Szu-min, "On the political situation in post-Deng China," *JB*, 210 (5 January 1994), 26–9, trans. in *FBIS-Chi*, 30 January 1994, 13–17.

178 "Forward: Explosive economic growth raises warning signal," *JSND*, 10 (1 October 1993), 58–9, trans. in *FBIS-Chi*, 11 January 1994, 49–50.

control inflation, though they promised not to repeat the "hard landing" of the 1988–91 austerity program.

Even as Jiang tried to reinforce his personal strength through the strategic promotion of protégés, to rein in centrifugal tendencies by reemphasizing democratic centralism, and to steer a course of "stability and unity" by curbing inflation and slowing the pace of economic reform, he also made a dramatic bid to win public support by finally swatting some tigers in the ongoing campaign against corruption. Public anger at Party corruption had fed the 1989 protest movement as well as the subsequent "Mao craze" that surfaced in late 1989 and the early 1990s, but corruption had been difficult to tackle because of the political clout protecting some of the worst offenders. Hu Yaobang discovered this in 1986 when his hard-hitting campaign against corruption aroused the anger of Party elders and contributed to his own downfall the following January.

The Party had launched a campaign against corruption in the immediate aftermath of Tiananmen, but that had faded away like its predecessors. Finally, in the summer of 1993, amid evidence that corruption was spreading uncontrollably, the Party launched another campaign. For the first year, this campaign seemed to go pretty much as its predecessors had – catching many flies but few tigers.[179] In the winter of 1994–5, however, the campaign shifted into high gear. The first major casualty was Yan Jianhong, the wife of former Guizhou provincial Party secretary Liu Zhengwei, who was executed in January for taking advantage of her connections in order to embezzle and misappropriate millions of yuan.[180]

Then in February 1995, Zhou Beifang was arrested. Zhou, the head of Shougang (Capital Iron and Steel) International in Hong Kong, is the son of Zhou Guanwu, who was then not only head of the model enterprise Shougang but was well connected to such senior leaders as Wan Li, Peng Zhen, and Deng Xiaoping himself. The following day, the elder Zhou retired as head of Shougang. In addition, Deng Xiaoping's son, Deng Zhifang, who was a manager with Shougang International, was apparently detained and questioned with regard to the case, though no charges were filed against him.[181]

179 The slow pace of the campaign against corruption in 1993 might be attributable to Deng Xiaoping's apparent statement during an inspection trip around Beijing on 31 October that year that the campaign should not be allowed to undermine the "reform enthusiasm" of cadres and citizens. See *South China Morning Post*, 30 November 1993. This comment makes it all the clearer that Jiang Zemin's stepping up of the campaign in late 1994 really was intended to distance himself from his erstwhile patron – as his actions against protégés of Deng would strongly suggest.

180 "Crimes behind the power: Analyzing the serious crimes committed by Yan Jianhong," *RMRB*, 14 January 1995, trans. in *FBIS-Chi*, 24 January 1995, 29–31.

181 Zhang Weiguo, "Chen Xitong an yu quanli douzheng" (The Chen Xitong case and the struggle for power), *Beijing zhi chun*, 30 (November 1995), 30–2.

At the same time, an ongoing investigation into corruption in Beijing Municipality apparently resulted in the detention of some sixty cadres in the city, including the secretaries of Party chief Chen Xitong and Mayor Li Qiyan. Then in early April, Vice-Mayor Wang Baosen, who had been implicated by the investigation, committed suicide. The upheaval in the city came to a climax in late April when CCP secretary Chen Xitong, a member of the Politburo and ally of Deng Xiaoping, was removed from office and subsequently placed under investigation. At the Party's Fifth Plenary Session in September 1995, Chen was officially removed as a member of the Politburo – the highest-ranking official accused of corruption in PRC history.[182]

With the removal of Chen Xitong, it seemed apparent that the effort to strengthen "democratic centralism," the campaign against corruption, and the power struggle among the leadership had come together. In a single stroke, Jiang Zemin moved against one of the most entrenched local leaders in the country, made a bid for popular support in the campaign against corruption, and acted against powerful people who might oppose him in the future, including the Deng family and Party elder Wan Li (Wan was a longtime supporter of Shougang and, as a former vice-mayor of Beijing, had close ties to the city's leadership).

In the fall of 1995, Jiang Zemin made another move to establish himself as the real leader of China. At the Fifth Plenary Session of the Fourteenth Central Committee in October, Jiang gave a major speech outlining twelve critical relationships that the Party and government must deal with in the coming years. Overall, it was a speech that called for development and marketization on the one hand and for stability and enhancing state capabilities on the other. The speech was obviously intended to present Jiang as a thoughtful leader, cognizant of the difficulties facing China and reasonable in his approach to problems. It was, in short, an agenda-setting speech intended to lay the foundation for Jiang Zemin's leadership.[183]

But even as Jiang has moved to shore up his position as the core of the leadership, others have staked out rival issues and bases of power. The leader who seems to have the greatest likelihood of challenging Jiang for power, or at least restraining Jiang's core status, is Qiao Shi. When Qiao took over as head of the NPC in March 1993, he was stripped of his other positions as head of the powerful Central Political and Legal Commission and as head of the Central Party School. But Qiao appears to continue to have much influence in the security apparatus that he built his career in. Ren Jianxin, who replaced

182 "Communiqué of the Fifth Plenary Session of the Fourteenth Central Committee of the CCP," XH, 28 September 1995, in FBIS-Chi, 28 September 1995, 15–17.

183 Jiang Zemin, "Correctly handle some major relationships in the socialist modernization drive," XH, 8 October 1995, trans. in FBIS-Chi, 10 October 1995, 29–36.

Qiao as head of the Legal Affairs Leading Group, had been promoted by Qiao, and Wei Jianxing, who became head of the Comprehensive Group on Social Order and subsequently replaced Chen Xitong as Beijing Party secretary, likewise appears to have strong ties to Qiao.[184] Meanwhile, Qiao has turned the NPC into a real base of support, much as Peng Zhen, who headed that body from 1981 to 1988, had used it as a base from which to oppose reform.

Qiao, who was Jiang Zemin's superior in the Shanghai underground during the revolution, has frequently challenged Jiang by being out in front of him on reform issues. As noted earlier, he beat the drums for Deng's reform campaign in the spring of 1992 long before Jiang Zemin came out in support of it. Stressing institution building and the rule of law, Qiao declared in his inaugural speech to the NPC, "Democracy must be institutionalized and codified into laws so that this system and its laws will not change with a change in leadership, nor with changes in their viewpoints and attention."[185] In January 1995, even as Jiang Zemin was stressing democratic centralism and the role of the core, Qiao chose to stress political reform and democratization.[186] At the same time that Qiao has stepped up the pace of legislation and incorporated greater expertise into its formulation, he has also given greater weight to provincial initiative and to the speed of economic reform than have Jiang Zemin and Li Peng.[187]

Aiding Qiao in this effort has been Tian Jiyun, the Politburo member whose withering criticism of leftism in April 1992 may have cost him a seat on the PSC. During the March 1995 session of the NPC, Tian listened sympathetically to Guangdong delegates, who complained that China's rulers were not allowing the NPC to function as the "highest administrative organ" as called for by the constitution. The day after this raucous meeting, 36 percent of NPC delegates either abstained or voted against Jiang Chunyun, Jiang Zemin's handpicked nominee as vice-premier. Never had China's legislature registered such a large protest.[188]

TOWARD THE POST-DENG ERA

Tiananmen marked an upheaval along three interrelated fault lines: between conservatives and reformers within the Party leadership, between the Party – state on the one hand and the emerging forces of society on the other,

184 Gao Xin and He Pin, "Tightrope act of Wei Jianxing," *Dangdai*, 23 (15 February 1993), 42–5, trans. in *FBIS-Chi*, 24 February 1993, 24–6.
185 *XH*, 31 March 1993, trans. in *FBIS-Chi*, 1 April 1993, 23.
186 *XH*, 5 January 1995, trans. in *FBIS-Chi*, 6 January 1995, 11–13.
187 See, for instance, *XH*, 13 October 1994, trans. in *FBIS-Chi*, 20 October 1994, 35–7.
188 *South China Morning Post*, 17 March 1995.

and between China and the outside world, particularly the United States. Whereas Deng continued to insist that reform and opening up could continue as before (indeed, "even faster"), conservatives viewed the course of reform as championed by Deng as the source of the trouble in 1989. In their view, reform had to be redefined (or, more accurately, returned to its pre-1984 meaning), the development of relations with the outside world slowed down, and domestic controls tightened through a renewed emphasis on ideology and the "dictatorship of the proletariat." It took a full three years for Deng to emerge triumphant in this implicit "struggle between two lines."

This struggle between the conservative wing of the party, led by Chen Yun, and the reform wing, led by Deng Xiaoping, was a continuation and intensification of what had gone on between them for most of the decade preceding Tiananmen. But if that struggle was pursued with deadly earnestness, it was nevertheless fated to fade into history not only with the deaths of Chen Yun (in April 1995) and, inevitably, of Deng but also with the impossibility of restoring anything that resembled the old planned economy. So even as the struggle between the titans of the older generation played itself out, a new contest for the soul of China began to emerge more clearly.

The contours of a new political dynamic are now being shaped by generational change on the one hand and the emergence of a dynamic, diverse, and assertive society on the other. China's economic dynamism has been long apparent. In 1995, China's GDP reached 5.77 trillion yuan (about $660 billion at the official exchange rate and about $1.6 billion when calculated according to purchasing price parity), an increase of 10.2 percent over the GDP for 1994, which was, in turn, 11.8 percent above that for 1993. As China's economy has expanded rapidly, it has also diversified and become increasingly internationalized. In 1992, China's rural industrial sector for the first time accounted for more than 50 percent of China's industrial production, and, as noted earlier, China's provinces have developed unprecedented fiscal autonomy. In 1995, China's total imports and exports topped $280 billion, and in the same year China employed over $38 billion in foreign iinvestment.[189]

Because of the various ways in which collective and private businesses are intertwined, it is difficult to estimate the size of China's private sector or interpret its significance. By the early 1990s, official statistics revealed 120,000 private enterprises with more than 2 million workers. That is in addition to the 23 million individual households (*getihu*) throughout the

189 State Statistical Bureau, "Intensify reform, accelerate structural adjustments, promote healthy development of the national economy; Economic situation in 1995 and outlook for 1996," *RMRB*, 1 March 1996, trans. in *FBIS-Chi*, 4 April 1996, 32–8; and *Zhongguo xinwen she*, 23 January 1996, trans. in *FBIS-Chi*, 24 January 1996, 40.

country.[190] The nonstate sector (which contains but is not limited to the private economy) was given a major boost by Document No. 4 of 1992, which permitted Party units and cadres to operate businesses. Bo Xicheng, the son of Party elder Bo Yibo, aroused popular interest when he left his position as head of the Beijing Tourism Bureau to start a hotel management company. His "plunge into the sea" (*xia hai*) of commerce led the way for a tidal wave of cadre offspring (usually referred to as "princelings") to join the nonstate economy. Of course, given their links with state-owned enterprises, government ministries, and high-level leaders, these princelings helped bring about an amalgam of public and private concerns (perhaps not unlike the "crony capitalism" of Indonesia and the Philippines) – as well as an unprecedented wave of corruption.

This entrepreneurial sector seems destined to play an increasingly important role in China's society and politics. Even before the latest group of nonstate enterprises was established, market-oriented businesses were finding allies at the state as well as the local level. An important example of this came in 1989 when central planners seemed determined to trim back the TVE sector. The interests of China's TVEs were defended not only by the localities that had an economic, social, and political interest in the livelihood of their residents but also by some state bureaucracies. For instance, the Ministry of Agriculture emerged as a leading advocate for the TVEs, and one of its newspapers, the *Township and Village Enterprise News* (*Xiangzhen qiye bao*), repeatedly emphasized the importance of TVEs for the rural as well as national economies. Other bureaucracies, such as the Ministry of Personnel and Labor, likewise voiced support for TVEs. The ensuing alliance of central bureaucracies and local governments goes a long way to explain why the plans of conservative leaders were blunted and then reversed.[191]

Increasingly the link between the entrepreneurial economy and the state at various levels appears to be more organized. For instance, in late 1993 the All-China Federation of Industry and Commerce was transformed into the China Non-Governmental Chamber of Commerce, whose charter was to "provide guidance" for the nonstate sector. It seems likely that that and other organizations will defend their constituents' interests as well as channel and curtail their activities. This trend suggests that China could evolve into a corporatist system.[192]

190 Susan Young, *Private business and economic reform in China*.
191 Dali Yang, *Catastrophe and reform in China*, ch. 9.
192 China's traditional organic conception of the state–society relationship resonates with many strains of corporatist thought, and certain forms of corporatist organization were implemented in the Nationalist period. See Joseph Fewsmith, *Party, state, and local elites in republican China*. On contemporary trends in a corporatist direction, see Jonathan Unger and Anita Chan, "China, corporatism, and the East Asian model," *AJCA*, 33 (January 1995), 29–53.

As the economy has grown more complex and less statist, China's intellectuals have similarly become more independent of the regime and more critical in their thinking. Whereas Chinese intellectuals in the communist era have generally expressed dissent both cautiously and through personal links with like-minded party officials (and have paid dearly even for such limited expressions of opinion), they have in recent years increasingly moved, like much of the economy, out of the state orbit.[193] The obvious failures of CCP rule, the collapse of communist rule in East Europe and the dismemberment of the Soviet Union, and the crushing of expression at Tiananmen have all contributed to the declining persuasiveness, indeed the bankruptcy, of Marxist thought. The ensuing ideological vacuum has set off a search for meaning unprecedented since the May Fourth era, leading some intellectuals to return to traditional thought, others to look to the West, and still others to explore Eastern models.

Moreover, this search for ideological meaning has taken place at a time when the role of intellectuals in Chinese society has been undergoing a profound change. The commercialization of Chinese society, on the one hand, and the bureaucratization of the Chinese state, on the other, have left Chinese intellectuals far less able to play their traditional role of social conscience. To the dismay of some, Chinese intellectuals are themselves jumping into the sea of commerce, taking up unfamiliar jobs as writers for popular ("middlebrow") literature and soap operas.[194] Whether these trends will ultimately force the Chinese state to be more responsive to an articulate population or simply contribute to the marginalization of intellectuals in Chinese politics remains to be seen.

At the same time, China's ruling elite is no longer composed of the battle-hardened, mostly ill-educated cadres who fought the revolution and have ruled the country for nearly half a century. Their successors are generally technocrats and bureaucrats, people who might look for practical solutions and be more inclined to usher in a politics of compromise than their more ideologically driven elders.[195]

The political history of Chinese politics since Tiananmen and the economic, social, and intellectual trends outlined in this chapter suggest an enormously fluid situation that could evolve in a number of directions in the post-Deng era.

It should be apparent just how deeply Tiananmen traumatized the Party, setting off the most serious intra-Party struggle for control of ideology and

193 Merle Goldman, *Sowing the seeds of democracy in China.*
194 Jianying Zha, *China pop.*
195 Hong-yung Lee, *From revolutionary cadres to party technocrats in socialist China.*

policy since the Dengist coalition came to power in 1978. These struggles were, of course, continuations of positions that had been well staked out in the years before Tiananmen, and thus had contributed to the making of that tragedy, but the recriminations set off by Tiananmen and the subsequent collapse of communism in East Europe substantially increased tensions within the Party and weakened Deng Xiaoping's core position. Although such tensions eased with Deng's victory at the Fourteenth Party Congress and with the passing of several conservative leaders (CPPCC deputy secretary Wang Renzhong in March 1992, former president and CPPCC chairman Li Xiannian in June 1992, former Mao secretary Hu Qiaomu in September 1992, and Chen Yun in April 1995), the obvious debates within the Party among such leaders as Jiang Zemin, Zhu Rongji, and Qiao Shi make it apparent that neither leadership nor policy agenda has yet been established.

Indeed, the generation that is taking over leadership in China is characterized by its lack of revolutionary legitimacy, its technocratic training, its relatively narrow career paths, its bureaucratic route to power, and its general weakness, both individually and collectively.

The greatest handicap this generation faces in its efforts to establish its leadership and build the sort of institutions that China will need as it moves into the twenty-first century is its lack of revolutionary legitimacy. Although the role of the revolutionary elders remains palpable, their grip is weakening and political leadership, for better or for worse, will fall to the first nonrevolutionary generation of leaders in the history of the PRC. If they can establish their authority, they may be less ideological and less conflictual than their elders, but establishing their authority will not be easy. They lack legitimacy not only in the eyes of society, but in the eyes of their colleagues. There is, in short, no particular reason why leaders of similar age and experience, not to mention those who are older, will defer to people like Jiang Zemin and Li Peng.[196] Moreover, the new generation of leaders cannot count on institutional authority to bolster their leadership. Thus, they will pay a price for the most unfortunate legacy of the Mao and Deng eras, namely the failure to build sound and credible institutions.

This generation is also typified by its technical and bureaucratic backgrounds. Much of this successor generation has been trained as engineers. Jiang Zemin spent most of his career in electrical engineering, and Li Peng built his in the hydroelectric power industry, climbing the ladder of specialized bureaucratic systems step by step.

---

196 The unnamed son of "one of China's most famous military leaders" was quoted in *The New York Times* on 15 December 1995 as saying that if Jiang Zemin did not stand up for Chinese sovereignty, he "could be changed. It would not be a big thing. We have a collective leadership."

These career paths underscore other major differences between this successor generation and its revolutionary elders. People of Deng Xiaoping's generation were largely political generalists. There were very few who did not participate in a whole range of military, political, organizational, and ideological affairs. The revolutionary elders were also supremely self-confident people. They had engaged in one of history's great revolutionary struggles, "overturning heaven and earth" in their quest to create a new order. Both Mao and Deng had the confidence to launch bold experiments, believing that whatever happened they would be able to maintain control.

In contrast, the leaders of the third generation are products of that new order. They have risen, usually slowly and step by step, through a system that allows little imagination and creativity and demands great obedience to and respect for higher-ups and elders. They give little indication of being bold and innovative people.

These generational characteristics, combined with the divisions within the leadership outlined earler, as well as the problems the Party faces as an institution, its relations with the military, its loss of legitimacy, and the tense relations between the central government and the localities make it possible, as some predict, that the Party will collapse.[197] Indeed, there are plenty of smoldering conflicts in society that could burst into view and challenge the Party's hold on power. Public anger at official corruption appears to be rising once again, peasant anger at local officials has repeatedly boiled over into major and minor confrontations, closing of bankrupt state-owned enterprises could result in large-scale worker layoffs, and the growth of crime and drug-related gangs could all challenge the social and political order. Given the tensions within the Party and the passing of the generation that made the revolution, it is certainly possible that a repetition of the sort of social movement that took place in 1989 could irrevocably divide the Party and bring about its collapse.

However, many of these same developments could, if handled skillfully, facilitate a relatively smooth transition to the post-Deng era. As already suggested, China's nonstate economy has gained a degree of representation either through state agencies that support the interests of nonstate enterprises or through new associations that are set up at least in part to control these new social forces. One can imagine that such organizations could work with more reform-minded people within the regime to establish a more institutionalized, law-based order. With the growth of market forces, the state might have no

---

197 See the following articles by Roderick MacFarquhar in *The New York Review of Books:* "The end of the Chinese revolution" (20 July 1989), 8–10; "The anatomy of collapse" (26 September 1991), 5–9; and "Deng's last campaign" (17 December 1992), 22–8. See also the pessimistic portrait of contemporary China in Miles, *The legacy of Tiananmen.*

choice but to adapt to the new reality and evolve along the lines of China's neighbors by becoming a "developmental state."[198]

Although current socioeconomic trends may engender a more open, law-based society, it is also possible that current developments could well drive the political system in a more authoritarian direction. Indeed, the very success of reform threatens not only to overwhelm the old planned economy but also to drown the state-owned sector in the process, thereby arousing a counterreaction to defend the state-owned sector at all costs. Traditionally, the defense of the state-owned economy has fallen to conservatives, who have argued in Marxist–Leninist terms about the importance of public ownership and the superiority of planning. In recent years, however, a new breed of neoconservatives has emerged on the scene to argue the same case in different terms. Instead of stressing public ownership in ideological terms, neoconservatives argue in practical terms that state-owned industries support the state and that the state can exercise macroeconomic control only if it can control the "heights of the economy." In short, the state-owned economy is a matter of political control, not of realizing communism. Traditional conservatives were true believers; neoconservatives are pragmatists, albeit authoritarian ones.[199]

Similarly, the decentralization that has been the *sine qua non* of reform has come under attack from neoauthoritarians and neoconservatives alike. Both believe that the economic and political autonomy of the localities threatens the state's ability to exercise macroeconomic and political control over the nation and thus impairs the formulation and implementation of national policy. Decentralization has been accompanied by growing regional inequalities as the areas along China's "gold coast" have begun to take part in the East Asian miracle while hinterland areas remain very much a part of the Third World.

Perhaps of greatest popular salience is the number of peasants who migrate from the rural areas to the cities, which has now reached some 20 million a year. The spectacular growth of rural incomes that typified the early part of reform began to slow in the mid-1980s. As the terms of trade began to tilt increasingly in favor of the cities and as the impediments to migration began to disappear, an increasing number of peasants began seeking work, temporary or permanent, in the cities. In recent years, this flood of migrant workers has begun to overwhelm urban resources and to accelerate urban crime. The result has been intense urban hostility toward these newcomers,

198 This is the scenario projected by William Overholt in his *The rise of China: How economic reform is creating a new superpower.*
199 Fewsmith, "Neoconservatism and the end of the Dengist era."

and demands that national and local authorities take measures to stem the tide.[200]

Urban resentment of the influx of peasants from the countryside was one of the central issues explored (and exploited) in 1994's surprise best-seller, *Looking at China through the third eye*. The book argues that rural reforms have threatened the future stability of China by releasing peasants from their existence of semistarvation and bondage to the commune and by raising their expectations. Once the peasants filled their bellies, the book contends, they continuously raised new demands – and have begun leaving the land in order to fulfill their hopes. The result has been an immense floating population, which has led to urban crime and constitutes a "living volcano" threatening the stability of Chinese society and state.[201]

Neoconservatives, such as the author of *The third eye*, argue that reform is now careening out of control, with the result that social dissolution and class conflict have emerged and are likely to culminate in a social explosion.[202] In order to arrest such trends, neoconservatives call for a restoration of central authority, frequently invoking the need for a unifying ideology. Indeed, Jiang Zemin himself recognized such a need when he commented that while the first generation of communist leaders (led by Mao) created the theory of revolutionary socialism and the second generation (led by Deng) developed the theory of building socialism with Chinese characteristics, the third generation (of which Jiang is supposedly the core) has not yet put its ideological stamp on Chinese politics.[203] Indeed, one can read Jiang's speech to the 1995 Fifth Plenum, discussed earlier, as a bid to define such a vision.

THE LEGACY OF DENG XIAOPING

It is beyond question that Deng Xiaoping has done more than any other figure in modern Chinese history to realize the century-old dream of attaining wealth and power. With the not insignificant exceptions of a short war with Vietnam in 1979 and the Tiananmen crackdown in 1989, the eighteen years during which Deng has presided over China's affairs has marked the longest stretch of domestic and foreign tranquillity in China's modern history. When Deng came to power in 1978, per capita peasant income was a mere 132 yuan

200 Dorothy Solinger, "China's urban transients in the transition from socialism and the collapse of the communist 'urban public goods regime,' " *Comparative Politics* (January 1995), 127–46; and idem, "China's transients and the state: A form of civil society?" *Politics and Society*, 21.1 (March 1993), 91–122.

201 Luo yi ning ge er, *Disanzhi yanjing kan Zhongguo* (Looking at China through the third eye; hereafter, *The third eye*), 28, 60–3. Joseph Fewsmith, "Review of *Looking at China through the third eye*," *Journal of Contemporary China*, 7 (Fall 1994), 100–4.

202 *The third eye*, 178. 203 *Hong Kong Standard*, 8 April 1995.

($66 at the then-prevailing exchange rate), and fully one-quarter of China's rural population had a per capita income of less than 50 yuan. The urban population fared better, with an average per capita income of 383 yuan, but workers' salaries had actually been falling – by some 19 percent – since the beginning of the Cultural Revolution. In 1995 rural income had risen to 1,578 yuan, and urban income to 3,893 yuan.[204]

The statistics, of course, tell only part of the story, and in many ways the less significant part of the story. The transformation of Chinese society over those eighteen years has been no less startling – and far more benevolent – than the changes in Chinese society over which Mao Zedong presided. Politically, the beginning of the Dengist era was marked by the slogans "Seek truth from facts" and "Practice is the sole criterion of truth." It was nothing less than an effort to save the Party and the country from the man who had done more than any other to lead the Party to victory only to convulse it and the nation it ruled in turmoil.

Deng sought to "refunctionalize" the ideology of the Party by moving away from the radical, dysfunctional ideology of Mao and to ensure party control by upholding the four cardinal principles.[205] In contrast to the Cultural Revolution's struggle between two lines, Deng sought to carve out a middle course by struggling against both fronts (Left and Right).[206] But as many have pointed out, steering a middle course has been difficult; reform has unleashed many forces that threaten to overturn the institutions that freed them.[207]

As this chapter and Richard Baum's contribution (Chapter 5) show, the conflicts generated in the reform period have been both within the Party and between the Party–state and society; moreover, these different axes of conflict have interacted as different elements within the Party have adopted different stances vis-à-vis the pressures emanating from society.

Deng's greatest failing, as many have pointed out, has been his unwillingness or inability to address these pressures and conflicts adequately. This has been a failure not only to incorporate new demands into the system but, even more important, to address fundamental flaws in China's political system, flaws that are not limited to post-1949 politics. The central problem that Chinese politics must deal with is the assumption that political power is unified, monistic, and indivisible.[208] Instead of political conflicts being resolved through bargaining and compromise, they become part of a game to

204 *Zhongguo tongji zheyao*, 1995, 51; and State Statistical Bureau, "Intensify reform."
205 The term "refunctionalize" is from Peter Ludz, *Changing party elites in East Germany*.
206 Tang Tsou, "Political change and reform: The middle course," in Tang Tsou, ed., *The cultural revolution and post-Mao reforms: A historical perspective*, 219–58.
207 Gordon White, *Riding the tiger: The politics of economic reform in post-Mao China*.
208 Tang Tsou, "The Tiananmen tragedy," in Brantly Womack, ed., *Contemporary Chinese politics in historical perspective*, 265–327.

"win all."[209] In an earlier period, this underlying dynamic led to the split in the CCP leadership and ultimately to the Cultural Revolution. In the early reform period, Deng appeared to begin to address this political problematic by deemphasizing the role of ideology; what was or was not "socialist" would be decided not through polemics but rather through practice. This strategy reflected Deng's own impatience with ideological disputation, resonated with a long-suffering society's desire to return to normal patterns of life, and served to build a broad coalition within a Party shattered by a decade of turmoil.

Deng's understanding of the flaws within the Party and his apparent desire to address them, as reflected in his landmark 1980 speech, "On the reform of the Party and state leadership system," were ultimately submerged by the constraints of the political system itself as Deng fell back on long-standing patterns of political behavior to rule China.[210] Differences of opinion within the Party were not reconciled through a politics of compromise but rather became tectonic forces whose shifts would slowly undermine the Party's surface calm. Fault lines within the Party clearly deepened following the 1984 adoption of the "Decision on the reform of the economic structure" as Deng moved decisively away from the limited notion of economic reform championed by Chen Yun in the early years of reform. The constant barrage of conservative criticism that accompanied Zhao Ziyang's largely successful effort to transform China's economic system reflected the clashing of these subterranean forces, forces that would shift violently in the spring of 1989 and result in the deep fissures within the Party that are chronicled in this chapter.

Deng merged victorious in this his final struggle, but it is evident from his struggle to regain ascendancy that the rules of political conflict remain largely unchanged in China. Thus, it is evident that Deng has not bequeathed a fundamentally transformed political system – either with regard to intra-Party conflict or between the Party–state and society – to go along with the transformed economic system that he has wrought. Thus, the question that remains as we assess Deng's legacy is whether he has created conditions that will allow the next generation of leaders to tackle the problems of China's political system that he himself did not resolve. From the vantage point of the present it appears that he has not. Deng accomplished many things in his eighteen years at the top of the political system; alas, institution building was not one of them.

209 The most elegant presentation of this thesis is Tsou, "Chinese politics at the top."
210 Lucian W. Pye, "An introductory profile: Deng Xiaoping and China's political culture," *CQ*, 135 (September 1993), 413–43.

CHAPTER 7

DILEMMAS OF GLOBALIZATION
AND GOVERNANCE

ALICE MILLER

As the prospect of Deng Xiaoping's passing loomed in 1995, there were considerable grounds for skepticism that the pace and scale of change that China had witnessed since he launched the reform era in 1978 would continue. In China's still partially reformed economy, Beijing had yet to transform the sagging state-owned industries – a project begun in 1984 – nor had it secured the legal foundations of the fast-growing private sector in its broader political economy. The PRC was emerging as a major player in world trade, yet it remained outside the newly established World Trade Organization (WTO) system, despite a major push by Beijing to join in 1994.

Internationally, in the wake of the Cold War, Beijing's stature in international politics continued to be dimmed by its suppression of the Tiananmen demonstrations in 1989, reinforced by what the international community perceived to be its belligerent conduct in the 1995–6 Taiwan Strait confrontation. In addition, Beijing had to maneuver in international politics in the shadow of American global power, wielded by an American president who had declared his commitment to "enlarging democracy" in the world and who held Beijing diplomatically at a disdainful distance.

Politically, anticipation of the passing of Deng Xiaoping, the architect of China's transformation after 1978, invited uncertainty about stability among the leadership and about continuity of the policies he had pursued. Despite leaving his last official post – as chairman of the PRC Central Military Commission – in March 1990, Deng had continued to engage in politics and policy in retirement, most famously in his "southern tour" intervention on behalf of renewed economic reform in early 1992. In 1994, however, his personal office and staff were disbanded, marking the end of his political life, and television footage of a wizened and weak Deng watching National Day fireworks on 1 October 1995 gave an unmistakable public signal that his passing could not be far off.

Meanwhile, Party General Secretary Jiang Zemin had only begun to consolidate his position among a top leadership that continued to divide and contend over how to govern in a post-Tiananmen domestic and international setting. Finally, as the previous chapter concludes, it was not at all clear that Deng had succeeded in stabilizing leadership politics by means of an institutionalized collective leadership that simultaneously constrained factional conflict and personal ambitions within established norms and routines, as well as harnessed the expertise and experience necessary to guide an increasingly complex economy and govern a correspondingly diverse society.

As the People's Republic approached its sixtieth anniversary in the fall of 2009, however, the uncertainties about China's prospects in the mid-1990s had evaporated. The PRC's economy, society, and politics had evolved well beyond what they had been only a decade and a half earlier. In many ways, China in 2009 was as different from the China in 1995 as China in 1995 differed from where it was at the beginning of the reform era in the late 1970s. From 1995 to 2009, China's economy sustained the nearly 10 percent average annual growth rate of the preceding decade and a half of reform. Its state-owned industrial sector had been transformed through a series of wrenching reforms in the late 1990s, giving way to a diverse landscape of state-owned pillar industries and enterprise groups, public corporations, and private and foreign businesses. Meanwhile, according to World Bank statistics, by 2006 China's manufacturing sector surged to nearly 50 percent of the PRC's gross domestic product while the share of agriculture declined to slightly less than 12 percent.

During the first decade of the twenty-first century, the PRC emerged as a manufacturing hub in the international economy, second in manufacturing output only to the United States. Beijing joined the WTO in December 2001, and in doing so joined the club of key policy makers for the organization. China ranked among the top three traders in the international economy and by 2010 had amassed US$2.4 trillion in foreign exchange reserves. During the same decade, flows of foreign investment, which took off in 1992, continued to pour into China and remained a major driver of domestic economic growth.

This accelerating scale of international engagement reflected a deliberate decision by China's leadership in the mid-1990s to adapt to trends of globalization. It also meant that the PRC, which had been virtually excluded from the world economy in the early 1970s, was increasingly dependent on it. According to World Bank figures, the degree of China's interdependence with the world economy – measured as the proportion of its exports and imports to its overall GDP – was more than 70 percent in 2006; by comparison, the ratios for the United States and Japan were slightly more than 25 percent, for Russia about 55 percent, and for India slightly less than 50 percent.

The political significance of all these economic developments was, first of all, that China's leaders had a much more complex economy to manage. Across the decade and a half since the mid-1990s, Chinese leaders have worked energetically to fashion the legal framework, regulatory regimes, and fiscal and monetary tools to govern a more broadly market-based economy. Second, the scale of China's interdependence with the world economy meant that foreign interests were much more entangled in China's domestic politics and many of China's own domestic constituencies had a much greater stake in the fortunes of the international economy. The once-sharp boundary that segregated China's foreign relations from its domestic politics was now perforated by the interlocking interests and resulting mutual vulnerabilities brought about by China's rise in the world economy. The reality of this interdependence registered with force in late 2008, when the crisis in the American financial system triggered a downturn in the world economy and produced the most difficult domestic economic recession in China in more than a decade.

The economic changes of the period also stimulated comparable changes in Chinese society. An increasingly developed economy spawned an increasingly diverse and complex society. In 2001, a widely publicized analysis by the Institute of Sociology of the Chinese Academy of Social Sciences (CASS) proposed a new breakdown of Chinese society into ten "strata" (*jieceng*). This analysis incorporated new managerial, private entrepreneurial, technical, professional, clerical, and service elements into China's social structure, alongside the industrial workers, peasants, and (sometimes) intellectuals who figured in the traditional "class" (*jieji*) analysis of society before the onset of the reform era. Underscoring the impact of the changing social realities brought about by two decades of market-driven reform on traditional Marxist-Leninist ideological frameworks, one commentary noted that the new analysis of Chinese society reflected the necessity of classifying social divisions "based on profession" in place of the pre-reform approach "on the basis of political status, residence registration, and administrative affiliation."[1]

China's sustained economic growth during this period was manifest in rising prosperity among at least some in Chinese society. In 1978, real per capita income in China had been US$200. In 1995, it had reached just under US$800, but by 2008 it had soared to US$2,330.[2] Anecdotally, in the early 1980s, at the beginning of the reform era, young urban couples hoped to acquire "three revolving things" – bicycles, wristwatches, and a sewing

1 Ru Xin, Lu Xueyi, and Li Peilin, 2002 *nian: Zhongguo shehui xingshi fenxi yu yuce*; Lu Pipi, "Ten Strata of Chinese Society," *BR*, 45.12 (21 March 2002), 22–3.
2 United States Department of Agriculture Economic Research Service, "Historical Gross Domestic Product (GDP) Per Capita and Growth Rates of GDP Per Capita, 1969–2009," 2 November 2009, at www.ers.usda.gov/Data/.../HistoricalRealPerCapitaIncomeValues.xls.

machine to make their own clothes. By the end of the 1980s, they hoped to acquire a stove, a washing machine, and a VCR. By 1995, middle-class urban Chinese were just beginning to contemplate buying personal automobiles. By 2009, cars clogged China's major cities. In 1995 Beijing had only three ring roads to facilitate travel in and around the city. In September 2009, Beijing announced the opening of its sixth ring road.

Prosperity, however, did not spread evenly across Chinese society. Income disparities between urban and rural citizens and among urban classes that were already polarizing society in the mid-1990s became even more severe during the decade and a half that followed. By 2006, in the context of official apprehension over the growing frequency of "mass incidents," Chinese economists noted with alarm that a standard measure of income inequality – the Gini coefficient – had reached crisis levels. Meanwhile, despite centrally directed efforts to "enliven" China's western regions and to "revive" the ageing industrial rust belt in the northeast, regional disparities persisted, sustaining an uneven pattern of development across the country.

Chinese society was also increasingly wired. In 1997, China had a total of 620,000 Internet accounts. By January 2009, there were 298 million Internet users, and Internet cafés were ubiquitous in both large and small cities. At the end of 2008, China's Internet featured 107 million blogs. In 1995, China counted 3.7 million cell phone users. As of March 2009, it had 670 million, with the advantage of third-generation communications technology. Traditional media flourished as well. At the beginning of the reform era in 1978, the PRC had a total of 186 newspapers in circulation; by 1995 there were 1,049. It took only until 2003 to add another 1,000. In 1978 Chinese book publishers offered slightly fewer than 15,000 new titles; by 1995, 101,381 new titles were published and in 2003 the number soared to 190,391 new titles. By 2003, China had more than 9,000 periodicals in circulation, roughly 1,500 more than in 1995.[3]

These developments in communications and publishing facilitated the advances in economic modernization and growth that China had witnessed since the mid-1990s. They also abetted the rise of a more vigorous public opinion in Chinese society with which the Chinese leadership had to engage. These new media enabled the emergence of a new corps of public intellectuals whose perspectives ranged across a broad spectrum of independent and critical political outlooks.[4] They also facilitated the expression of clashing strands of Chinese nationalism that enflamed larger public reaction to perceived international slights and domestic events. The new information and communications

3 National Bureau of Statistics, *China statistical yearbook 2004*, 846.
4 The emergence of these public intellectuals is traced and assessed succinctly in Fewsmith, *China since Tiananmen*, 2nd ed.

technology aided public agitation and mobilization on behalf of social and political issues, prompting protest demonstrations and sometimes violent "mass incidents." In the spring of 2005, Internet blogs and petitions helped kindle violent anti-Japanese protests in many Chinese cities over a bid by Tokyo for a seat on the United Nations Security Council and other issues. In June 2007, text messaging facilitated successful public protests in Xiamen over the construction of a new chemical factory. In June 2008, China's Internet circumvented censorship in the official media by circulating firsthand accounts and photographs of a public riot that burned official buildings and vehicles in Weng'an, Guizhou, over alleged police abuse and the murder of a schoolgirl.

Politically, all of these trends in China's economy and society posed new problems of governance that the Chinese political leadership had to address. The foremost focus of politics since the mid-1990s, therefore, has been the problem of improving the communist regime's ability to adapt to the new challenges of governing a rapidly changing economy and society. This concern was evident in the effort to co-opt the rising entrepreneurial, technical, and professional elites produced by the advances of the reform era into the Chinese Communist Party (CCP) – the thrust of General Secretary Jiang Zemin's "three represents" innovation of 2000. It was also reflected in General Secretary Hu Jintao's initiatives calling for a more balanced approach to economic development – his "scientific development concept" advanced in 2003 – and for the creation of a "socialist harmonious society" thereafter. It also was the focus of a highly authoritative Central Committee resolution on improving the CCP's "governing capacity" in 2004 and a subsequent campaign to enhance the CCP's "advanced nature" in 2005.

This focus helped motivate the incremental institutionalization of politics that has been visible since the late 1990s. Leadership politics after the mid-1990s enjoyed a relative stability, continuity, and predictability that surpassed any previous period in PRC politics. This occurred despite the uncertainties provoked by the imminent passing of Deng Xiaoping and the generation of veteran revolutionaries who had dominated politics in the first two decades of the reform era and in the face of the new challenges posed by China's evolving economy and society.

In part, the problems of governing an increasingly globally interdependent and market-driven economy and a correspondingly more complex and sophisticated society required a politics of expertise. For this reason, since the beginning of the reform era, both Deng Xiaoping and Chen Yun stressed recruitment and promotion of cadres who were not only politically principled but also "younger, better educated, and professionally competent."[5] Because

---

5 In his landmark 18 August 1980 speech, "On the reform of the system of Party and state leadership," Deng first raised this requirement, citing Chen Yun's views, that the Party should recruit and promote

of this emphasis, as Deng's generation of veteran revolutionaries died off in the 1990s, they were replaced at the top by new leaders – first a "third generation" around Jiang Zemin and later a "fourth generation" around Hu Jintao – who were promoted in significant part because they possessed professional expertise and administrative experience demonstrated by implementing the policies of reform. Increasingly, appointment to the CCP Politburo and its Standing Committee no longer was allotted simply on the basis of political connections to powerful leaders and their factions, but also on the basis of informed decision-making abilities. Borrowing Richard Lowenthal's terminology, the CCP leadership transitioned from the "revolutionary" leaders of Mao's day – committed to the transformation of Chinese society according to egalitarian communist ideals – to "post-revolutionary" leaders competent to govern a rapidly modernizing economy and society.[6]

The demands of effective governance also required a politics of consensus at the top. As China grew more powerful and wealthy as a consequence of the policies of the reform era, much more was at stake politically for the increasingly complex array of interests and constituencies that constituted China's changing political order. In that regard, the vagaries of strongman politics in the PRC's past provided a powerful negative example of the costs to national progress incurred by excessive concentration of power, unconstrained factional infighting, and the attendant twists in policy. The experience of the leadership division during the 1989 Tiananmen crisis also underscored the necessity of sustaining a public façade of leadership unanimity. From the beginning of the reforms, Deng Xiaoping stressed the need for collective leadership decision making, for orderly political processes and predictable routines, and for stable and durable institutions. Despite the evident lapses in the politics of the 1980s, these processes began to take hold visibly in the 1990s.

What emerged across the late Jiang and Hu Jintao periods, therefore, was an oligarchic politics of collective leadership. Although Jiang Zemin enjoyed special prominence as a "core leader" in leadership politics during his tenure as the CCP's top leader, Hu Jintao had none of these trappings, even after he assumed the last of Jiang's posts in 2005. Nor were any of the ideological innovations promulgated during Hu's leadership described as the product of

---

cadres who are "younger, better educated, and professionally competent." In a speech to a central work conference on 25 December 1980, Deng added that cadres must also be "revolutionary." [Deng Xiaoping], *Selected works of Deng Xiaoping, 1975–1982*, 308, 342. The Central Committee work report delivered by Hu Yaobang at the Twelfth Party Congress in September 1982 ratified these views, requiring that the Party promote cadres who are "revolutionary, younger, better educated, and professionally competent" (*geminghua, nianqinghua, zhishihua, zhuanyehua*), henceforth referred to as the "four changes" (*sihua*) in Party recruitment work.

6 Richard Lowenthal, "Development and utopia in communist policy," 33–116; and Richard Lowenthal, "The post-revolutionary phase in Russia and China," *SICC*, 13.3 (Autumn 1983), 91–101.

his personal invention, in contrast to the attention given to the supposed theoretical contributions of Jiang Zemin, and to those of Deng Xiaoping and Mao Zedong before him. Instead, even though Hu was clearly in charge, his stature in the leadership collective seemed purposefully and consistently advertised simply as *primus inter pares*. In short, the rules of elite politics seemed to be changing in response to the changing economy and society. No doubt, leadership conflict and factional competition continued in the Hu era, but they now appeared circumscribed by still informal but increasingly binding norms and by pressures for a politics of consensus.

As the People's Republic turned sixty, the communist regime celebrated the achievements of its leadership. But it also faced new and seemingly intractable challenges in governing a country that was changing in often dramatic and surprising ways. Therefore, the foremost question was whether the CCP could continue to adapt sufficiently to meet its challenges and sustain its power.

TOWARD THE FIFTEENTH PARTY CONGRESS

Anticipation of an upcoming Party congress typically heats up the political atmosphere as much as two years in advance. In the case of the Fifteenth Party Congress, expected to convene in 1997, several major issues figured in the preparations. Foremost among them were the reform of China's 370,000 state enterprises and an expected transition in leadership generations.

As the previous chapter observed, the CCP's Fourteenth Congress in 1992 laid the ideological foundation for the fundamental transformation of China's economic structure by declaring that the goal of reform was the creation of a "socialist market economy."[7] The Congress's endorsement of this turn of phrase reflected Deng Xiaoping's decisive defense of the place of markets in a socialist economy during his "southern tour" preceding the Party congress, and it altered the previously authoritative characterization of China's political economy as a "socialist commodity economy." The latter term had been adopted in the CCP's landmark decision on reform of the industrial economy in 1984 and had implicitly confirmed the role of markets in a socialist economy by revising the traditional ideological characterization of China's political economy as a "socialist product economy." The distinction implicit between these terms pertained fundamentally to the role of state planning: a planned economy produces "products" (*chanpin*), whereas "commodities" (*shangpin*) are produced for markets. The endorsement by the Fourteenth Congress of the

---

7 Jiang Zemin, "Accelerating reform and opening-up," report to the 14th CCP Congress, 12 October 1992, *BR*, 35.43 (26 October-1 November 1992), 18–19.

goal of a "socialist market economy" therefore capped more than a decade of intense intra-Party debate over the role of planning versus markets and over the future of the state-enterprise system in the Chinese economy.

The implications for state-enterprise reform of these ideological revisions at the 1992 Party congress emerged clearly a year later at the Fourteenth Central Committee's Third Plenum, convened in November 1993. The plenum adopted a sweeping fifty-point "Decision on Some Issues Concerning Establishment of a Socialist Market Economic Structure." The decision called for "changing the operating mechanism of state-owned enterprises and establishing a modern enterprise system" through the authorization of diverse forms of state, corporate, collective, and private modes of ownership and operation. It also called for steps to alter the state's traditional role in guiding the economy through direct bureaucratic command in favor of indirect fiscal and monetary levers, laying out complementary reforms in the banking, fiscal, and foreign trade systems, and it authorized compensatory steps to create a social security system to replace the former social welfare functions of the state-owned enterprise system.

Progress toward these goals stalled, however, in the face of a new surge of inflation in 1993–4 that rivaled the soaring rates of 1988. Premier Li Peng and other conservative Party leaders had sought in the fall of 1988 to redress that episode of overheating in the economy with a three-year program of economic retrenchment, an effort that helped stir public anxieties leading to the Tiananmen demonstrations in 1989. This time, with Li Peng sidelined by illness, Vice Premier Zhu Rongji led a three-year effort to prepare the way for the Third Plenum enterprise reforms by cooling inflation and recentralizing fiscal and monetary authority that had devolved to the provinces.

The effort to restore price stability limited the steps toward reform to pilot projects to implement a "modern enterprise system" in selected cities and other trial measures. Perhaps the most significant step during this period was the establishment of a legal foundation for transforming the state-owned enterprise system. The Company Law, which was adopted by the National People's Congress (NPC) Standing Committee on 29 December 1993 and came into force on 1 July 1994, provided for procedures to create corporations, authorized in principle by the 1993 Third Plenum, stipulating that corporatized enterprises could sell public shares as a means to raise capital. In May and June 1995, Jiang Zemin toured state-owned enterprises in the heavy industrial centers of Shanghai and Manchuria, making widely publicized comments on the necessity of enterprise reform. In September 1995, the Fourteenth Central Committee's Fifth Plenum adopted guidelines for drafting the Ninth Five-Year Plan that stipulated establishing a "modern enterprise system" based on the approach of "invigorating the large enterprises and liberalizing the small enterprises" – often rendered as "grasping the large and letting go of the small" (*zhuada fangxiao*) – through techniques of merger and bankruptcy by the end of the century.[8]

Under Vice Premier Zhu Rongji's strong-arm tactics, inflation fell from 25 percent at the end of 1994 to roughly 15 percent at the end of 1995 and to 6.1 percent at the end of 1996, while China's economy grew at a rate of 9.7 percent in 1996.[9] The 1996 convocation of the annual central conference on economic work, held on 21–24 November, declared that "after three years of hard work," Beijing had "effectively brought inflation under control while maintaining rapid economic growth." The conference called on state-owned enterprises to "accelerate their reform" in the coming year under the general guideline of "improving large enterprises and handling smaller ones with flexibility." In his work report to the NPC session the following March, Premier Li Peng proclaimed victory over inflation and specified that Beijing would concentrate on "rejuvenating" 1,000 large state-owned enterprises through infusion of credit and merger into competitive enterprise groups, while sloughing off most of China's small state-owned enterprises through merger or bankruptcy.[10] Finally, in mid-April 1997, the State Council publicized a circular that spelled out in unprecedented detail the steps to transform state-owned enterprises, including provisions for the dissolution of their assets and for assistance to laid-off workers and the establishment of a National Leading Group for Merger, Bankruptcy, and Worker Re-Employment under Zhu Rongji's favored instrument, the State Economic and Trade Commission.[11]

Opposition to Reform

As the Jiang leadership prepared to transform the PRC's state-owned enterprises – the very core of the socialist economic order built in the 1950s – into enterprise groups, publicly owned corporations, and private firms that would operate in a market economy increasingly open to foreign competition, political opposition arose from several quarters in 1995. The most visible attacks came from the "ten-thousand-character memorials" linked to Deng Liqun, the

8 "Proposal of the Central Committee of the Communist Party of China for formulating the ninth five-year plan (1996–2000) for national economic and social development and the long-term target for 2010," adopted 28 September 1995, *XH*, 4 October 1995, available in *SWB*, 7 October 1995.

9 National Bureau of Statistics, "Zhonghua renmin gongheguo guojia tongjiju guanyu 1996 nian guomin jingji he shehui fazhan de tongji tongbao" (Statistical communiqué on socio-economic development in 1996), 4 April 1997, available at http://www.stats.gov.cn/tjgb/ndtjgb/qgndtjgb/t20020331_15391. htm (accessed 9 August 2010); Barry Naughton, *The Chinese economy: Transitions and growth*, 442–4; Avery Goldstein, "China in 1996: Achievement, assertiveness and anxiety," *AS*, 37.1 (January 1997), 30.

10 Li Peng, "Report on the work of the government," 1 March 1997, *BR*, 40.13 (31 March – 6 April 1997), I-XVI.

11 *XH*, 19 April 1997.

former Party ideologue and propaganda czar who was unceremoniously voted off the Party Central Committee at the 1987 Thirteenth Congress, and from journals strongly associated with the Party's ideological left.

Four "ten-thousand-character memorials" circulated in internal Party channels from the fall of 1995 to the convocation of the Fifteenth CCP Congress in September 1997. The "ten-thousand-character memorial" vehicle of political dissent dates back to the eleventh century, when the reformer Wang Anshi presented ideas of reform to a conservative-dominated court under the Northern Song emperor Renzong in 1058.[12] The same vehicle was used in 1895 by Kang Youwei, Liang Qichao, and some 600 other candidates sitting for the metropolitan (jinshi) examination to protest the humiliating Treaty of Shimonoseki ending the Sino-Japanese War.[13] And although Peng Dehuai did not call his July 1959 letter to Mao Zedong during the Lushan meetings on problems during the Great Leap Forward a "ten-thousand-character memorial," it has been sometimes referred to as such in the post-Mao era.[14] Though none of the four "memorials" that circulated in the two years preceding the Fifteenth Party Congress were ten-thousand characters in length – they were in fact considerably longer – reference to them as "ten-thousand-character memorials" conveyed a connotation of principled protest in a time of national crisis.[15]

The first "ten-thousand-character memorial" criticizing the impending state-owned enterprise reforms appeared in the spring of 1995 under the title "Several Factors Influencing Our Country's National Security." The text focused on the implications for both Chinese socialism and for the CCP regime of the rise of a new bourgeoisie in China attending the decline of the state-enterprise system and the proliferation of private forms of ownership since the beginning of the economic reforms. The second, titled "A Preliminary Investigation of the Domestic and External Circumstances and the Principal Threats to Our Country's National Security in the Next Ten to Twenty Years," began circulating in the fall of 1995. It argued that China's march toward a market-driven economy played into the hands of Western forces bent on a program of regime change through "peaceful evolution" and warned that as a

---

12 For background on Wang's memorial and its impact, see Frederick W. Mote, *Imperial China–900–1800*, 139ff.

13 On Kang's "ten-thousand-character memorial," see Immanuel C.Y. Hsu, *The rise of modern China*, 6th ed., 366–7.

14 For background on Peng's letter, see page 105 in this volume. The text of Peng's letter is available in [Peng Dehuai], *Peng Dehuai zishu*, 281–7. A firsthand account of the Lushan meetings and of Peng's letter by Mao's secretary is Li Rui's memoir, *Lushan huiyi shilu*, 121–34.

15 The texts of the first three "memorials" are collected in Shi Liaozi, ed., *Beijing dixia wanyanshu* (The Beijing underground's ten-thousand-character memorials). Excerpts are included in the 1998 partisan book published in the wake of the Fifteenth Party Congress by Ma Licheng and Ling Zhijun, *Jiaofeng: Dangdai Zhongguo sanci sixiang jiefang shilu* (Crossed swords: A veritable record of contemporary China's three liberations of thought), 242–51, 276–80, 312–16, and 351–2. For background, see Joseph Fewsmith, *China since Tiananmen*, 2nd ed., 176–7 and 194–5.

consequence China faced the prospect of political dissolution paralleling the fall of socialism in the USSR and the Eastern European bloc.

Themes echoing those laid out in the first two "memorials" were forcefully elaborated during the same period in a steady stream of attacks on the pending reform of the state-owned enterprise system that poured forth from three left-wing journals. These were *Pursuit of Truth* (*Zhenli de zhuiqiu*), *Mainstream* (*Zhongliu*), and *Contemporary Trends* (*Dangdai sichao*), all of which were authorized to publish in the immediate wake of the 1989 Tiananmen crisis and whose first issues appeared in 1990. The articles dwelled on several ideologically driven themes to defend the central place of state-owned enterprises in a socialist economy and to assert the overriding commitment of the CCP in upholding the interests of the workers. For example, an article in the first 1996 issue of *Contemporary Trends* warned that as China moved toward a "modern enterprise system," views "belittling the working class" were taking hold, including the judgment that "labor is a commodity in a socialist market economy," that "dictatorial management" of enterprises by "industrialists" and shareholders is appropriate, and that Party organizations within enterprises should be abolished.[16] An article in *Pursuit of Truth* warned that the CCP's rank-and-file membership was being "eroded" by three waves of "corrupting Western bourgeois ideas and values" as China's economy diversified its forms of enterprise ownership: namely, the erosion of the concept of public ownership by the concept of private ownership; the erosion of communist values by the value of "money above everything"; and the erosion of the communist principle of collectivism by bourgeois individualism.[17]

Other articles in 1996 argued that Western theories of economics – and especially Friedrich von Hayek's neo-liberal theories – were steadily displacing the Marxist-Leninist political economy in China.[18] Several articles warned that the transition to a "socialist market economy" was permitting foreign corporations to invade and dominate China's markets at the expense of longstanding brands produced indigenously by state-owned enterprises. If China did not defend the place of its state-owned enterprises in Chinese markets, one article predicted, China would again become a "colonial economy."[19]

16 Li Yonghai, "Gongren jieji de lingdao diwei burong dongyao" (The leading role of the working class must not be shaken), *Dangdai sichao*, 1 (1996), 18–24.
17 Zheng Zhibiao, "Shilun shehuizhuyi shichang jingji tiaojianxia de dangnei zhuyao maodun" (A tentative discussion of the principal contradiction within the Party under conditions of a socialist market economy), *Zhenli de zhuiqiu*, 1 (1996), 20–3.
18 Liu Rixin, "Xifang jingjixue yu woguo jingji tizhi gaige" (Western economics and economic reform in our country), and Zhou Guangchun, "Xin ziyouzhuyi jingjixue zai woguo de shiji yingxiang" (The real influence of neo-liberal economics in our country), *Zhenli de zhuiqiu*, 6 (1996), 2–6 and 6–8 respectively.
19 Zhou Guangchun, "Waishang jiajin qiangzhan woguo shichang" (Foreign businesses are intensifying their race to control our country's markets), *Zhenli de zhuiqiu*, 2 (1996), 26–7.

Many articles predicted that as China's economy and society changed, the ultimate consequence would be regime change. The object lesson, of course, was the fate of the Soviet Union under Mikhail Gorbachev's *perestroika*. Several articles traced the reasons for the collapse of the USSR in 1991 to the failure by Gorbachev and the Communist Party of the Soviet Union (CPSU) leadership to sustain a clear direction in favor of the fundamentals of socialism in the attempt to reform the Soviet economy and to their consequent loss of public support. "The painful lessons of the upheavals in the Soviet Union and Eastern Europe tell us, by negative example, the consequences of burying our heads in economic tasks and not discussing ideals and beliefs and not considering political direction," one article concluded. This failure played into the hands of "adversaries" at home and abroad who "do not show their cards all at once but first lay down some vague and misleading concepts to revise Marxist viewpoints bit by bit." "As soon as the masses follow their lead down the path and transform their outlook," the author warned, they "bring socialism to political and economic collapse and replace it with capitalism."[20]

The third and fourth "ten-thousand-character memorials" circulated in late 1996 and early 1997, as Jiang and the Party leadership began in earnest to prepare for the Fifteenth CCP Congress to be convened in the fall of 1997. The third, entitled "Several Theoretical and Policy Issues Regarding Upholding the Dominant Position of Public Ownership," first appeared in October 1996 and in revised form in December with an alternative title in *Contemporary Trends*.[21] It took extensive issue with including public share-holding corporations within the definition of public ownership. It further argued that China's large, medium, and small state-owned enterprises should be maintained as "a unified and comprehensive system" and that "grasping the large while letting go of the small" amounted to privatization of a huge part of the public sector. Even though the state-owned sector faced tough circumstances, it warned, "if public ownership loses its dominant position, there will be serious class polarization, the entire working class will be reduced to mere wage labor, the CCP will lose the economic basis of its rule, state governance will degenerate, the ideals of socialism will dissolve, the spiritual pillar of socialism will collapse, and the country as a whole will change its socialist character and become an appendage of international capitalism."[22] The fourth "memorial," circulated in early 1997 under the title "The Trend

20 Zhou Hao, "Zhengzhi de hexin: Zhengzhi fangxiang he zhengzhi lichang" (The core of politics–Political direction and political stance), *Zhenli de zhuiqiu*, 3 (1996), 7–11, slightly modified trans. from that in *FBIS*, FTS19960301000003.
21 Special Commentator, "Yi gongyouzhi wei zhuti jiben biaozhi ji zenmeyang cai neng jianchi gong-youzhi de zhuti diwei" (Public ownership as the basic characteristic and how to uphold the central position of public ownership), *Dangdai sichao*, 4 (1996), 2–17.
22 Trans. modified from *FBIS*, FTS19970519001420.

and Characteristics of Bourgeois Liberalization since 1992," attacked a wave of anti-socialist liberalizing ideas in theoretical, economic, legal, and cultural sectors.

As sharp and as visible as these attacks on the effort to build a "modern enterprise system" were, by the mid-1990s the ideological left was increasingly a spent force. Jiang and the top leadership nevertheless could not afford to ignore the attacks because they gave impetus to resistance to enterprise reform from more substantial quarters. If the plan to "grasp the large enterprises and let go of the small" were to proceed, an estimated 15 million surplus workers would lose their jobs, creating a potential for serious urban unrest. In addition, China's state-owned enterprises supported an increasing number of retirees – the total had grown from 22 million in 1990 to 28 million in 1994 – and the reform made no provisions for them. Compounding the complexity of the reform, many state-owned enterprises provided schools, living arrangements, and medical institutions for their employees, and dissolution of the sponsoring enterprises would mean dissolution of all these welfare provisions.[23] The scale of dislocation in the lives of the 120 million workers in the state-owned sector invited powerful resistance to the pending enterprise reforms.

In addition, there was as yet no authoritative guidance on the disposition of the assets of bankrupt enterprises. The 1986 Enterprise Bankruptcy Law, whose adoption on a trial basis by the NPC was achieved only after bruising legislative battles and which had come into effect in 1988, made no clear provisions for the disposal of assets and their distribution among creditors. Revision of the 1986 law to address these issues began in 1993, soon after adoption of the Third Plenum's fifty-point decision on creating a "modern enterprise system." By October 1996, a draft revision was submitted for review to the NPC Standing Committee and was expected to pass by the end of the year. By the end of 1997, however, it still awaited approval, and in his report on the work of the NPC Standing Committee to the Ninth National People's Congress in March 1998, Tian Jiyun acknowledged that the revised bankruptcy law and related legislation on state-owned assets had failed to pass because of "failure to reach consensus by all parties concerned."[24] Ultimately, a new enterprise bankruptcy law was adopted by the NPC in 2006.

Finally, uncertainties in relations with the United States and Japan clouded the international context and thus raised doubts about whether the moment was appropriate to press ahead with wrenching enterprise reforms at home.

23 "Zhongguo jingji gaige renzhong daoyuan" (China's economic reform is a heavy responsibility), *Jingji cankao bao*, 16 December 1997, 4, trans. in *FBIS*, FTS19980203000476.

24 Huang Zhiling, "New law to better guide bankruptcy," *China Daily*, 18 June 1996, 4; Sun Shangwu, "Economy forces NPC to revise some laws," *China Daily*, 1 November 1997, 1; and Tian Jiyun, "Report on the work of the NPC Standing Committee," *XH*, 22 March 1998, available in *SWB*, 26 March 1998.

During most of its first term in office, the Clinton administration, reflecting the president's disdain for China's human rights record, had held Beijing at some distance. Clinton met with Jiang Zemin several times in multilateral contexts – at APEC and UN sessions – but there had been no bilateral summit in either capital. Similarly, although Secretary of State Warren Christopher met several times with his PRC counterpart Qian Qichen in multilateral settings, there had been only two bilateral exchanges during Clinton's first term – Qian's 1993 visit to Washington and Christopher's frustrating visit to Beijing in March 1994 to attempt to get the Chinese to meet the human rights conditions that Clinton had imposed in 1993 to enable him to save face and renew China's most favored nation trade status. In addition, Beijing had made a major push in 1993–4 to complete the required bilateral trade agreements in time to allow it to accede to the new World Trade Organization with the completion of the Uruguay Round in 1994. The failure of Beijing and Washington to negotiate a bilateral accord impeded comparable agreements with the EU and Japan, and thus Beijing's ambitions of becoming a founding member of the WTO were dashed. Finally, the 1995–6 Taiwan Strait crisis, prompted by the last-minute decision of the Clinton administration to grant a visa to ROC President Lee Teng-hui to visit his alma mater Cornell University, culminated in PLA missile firings into waters off Taiwan's major ports of Kaohsiung (Gaoxiong) and Keelung (Jilong) and added military tensions to an already troubled relationship.

The Renewed Push for Enterprise Reform

By mid-1996, however, several factors compelled, or at least favored, moving ahead with enterprise reform. One was that enterprise losses, already severe, were worsening. In the early 1990s, 30 percent of state-owned enterprises were losing money. By 1995 the proportion reached 40 percent, and in the first half of 1996 the figure was 43 percent. In addition, total enterprise profits were slipping into the red. As late as 1994, net enterprise profits totaled RMB 90 billion; by mid-1996, however, state-owned enterprises were operating at a net loss of RMB 13 billion.[25]

In addition, relations with the United States took a turn for the better in the second half of 1996. The Taiwan Strait crisis convinced the Clinton administration of the need for a new approach to relations with Beijing. Following the Beijing visit of National Security Adviser Anthony Lake, arrangements were made for an official visit to Washington by Jiang Zemin and an official visit to Beijing by Vice President Al Gore, followed by an official visit by President

---

25 "Zhongguo jingji gaige renzhong daoyuan."

Clinton. With the favorable turn in U.S. relations, prospects brightened for a renewed effort for PRC entry into the WTO.

Finally, by the end of 1995, all of the retired elder leaders who held conservative views with regard to reform of the state-owned sector had passed from the scene. Hu Qiaomu and Li Xiannian died in 1992, and Wang Zhen died in 1993. Former executive vice premier and Politburo Standing Committee (PSC) member Yao Yilin died in December 1994, and Chen Yun, one of the architects of the state-owned sector in the early 1950s, died in April 1995. Chen, Li, and Yao, along with Premier Li Peng, had played critical roles in the landmark political defeat of the wage and price reforms proposed in the spring of 1988 by Deng Xiaoping and advanced by then General Secretary Zhao Ziyang. Instead, they imposed a three-year program of economic retrenchment to bring surging inflation under control later that fall.[26] With these leaders gone, a major political obstacle to enterprise reform was removed, leaving Li Peng isolated as the champion of the state-owned enterprise sector.

In late 1995, Jiang had already begun to blunt attacks from the Party's ideological left, while also preempting criticism from the right. In late September and again in early November, Jiang made speeches that emphasized the need for Party leaders at provincial levels and above to "talk politics" (jiang zhengzhi).[27] By "talking politics," he explained in his September speech, he meant in particular paying attention to "political direction, political stand, political outlook, political discipline, political discrimination, and political acuity." In addition, in early January in a speech at the National Conference on Propaganda, Jiang stressed the need to "discriminate between Marxism and anti-Marxism, between developing a socialist economy with a dominant public sector and coexisting diverse ownership forms and privatization, between socialist democracy and Western parliamentary democracy, between dialectical materialism and idealist metaphysics, between socialist ideology and corrupt ideas of feudalism and capitalism, between studying advanced Western things and worshiping Western things and fawning on foreign things," and so forth. The thrust of these talks was to rally consensus around the leadership's reform line and to blunt criticisms from both the left and the right.

In March 1996, Jiang renewed these themes in separate speeches to assembled Party members and People's Liberation Army (PLA) delegates attending

26 See pp. 424–9 in this volume.

27 Jiang Zemin, "Lingdao ganbu yiding yao jiang zhengzhi" (Leading cadres must talk politics), excerpt of a speech delivered to a group session during the Fifth Plenum on 27 September 1995, in *Jiang Zemin wenxuan*, 1.455–9; and Jiang Zemin, "Jiang xuexi, jiang zhengzhi, jiang zhengqi" (Talking study, talking politics, and talking upright trends), excerpt of a talk given while inspecting work in Beijing on 8 November 1995, in *Shisida zhongyao wenxian xuanbian*, 2.1559–62. Neither talk was publicized at the time of delivery, but the 27 September talk was eventually released by *XH* on 17 January 1996.

the Fourth Session of the Eighth NPC.[28] This time, a wave of elaborating commentary followed in a coordinated response to the criticism from the left in particular. On 15 March, the PLA General Political Department issued a circular mandating study throughout the army of Jiang's remarks to the PLA delegates. The PLA newspaper *Liberation Army Daily* on 1 April began a series of eight commentator articles on the various areas in which Jiang had called for discrimination. These articles rebutted criticism from both the left and the right, but on balance the focus was on the left.

For broader Party audiences, *People's Daily* on 1 April carried a long commentary under the authoritative byline "Ren Zhongping" – a homophone for "important *People's Daily* commentary" – on Jiang's September 1995 talk at the Fifth Plenum, "Leading Cadres Must Talk Politics." Underscoring the necessity of a correct political orientation based on practice and in an evident rejoinder in particular to the left, the commentary declared that "stressing the need to talk politics and emphasizing that economic construction must have a political guarantee does not mean returning to the beaten path of 'armchair politics' or 'allowing politics to override everything else.'"[29] On 1 June, Jiang's September 1996 talk was published in book form, together with fifteen commentaries from *Liberation Army Daily*, including the eight published in April and early May, for study within the broader Party ranks.

Finally, *People's Daily* capped the wave of countercriticism on 6 June by publishing a long article on the need to "draw a clear line between Marxism and anti-Marxism" by Xing Bensi.[30] Xing, as vice president of the Central Party School under Hu Jintao and previously director of the Institute of Philosophy of the Academy of Social Sciences, had a long-established reputation as a liberal interpreter of Marxism-Leninism as it applied to contemporary Chinese purposes and undoubtedly wrote at the behest of Hu and Jiang. Repeating words that Jiang had used in his talks, Xing began by declaring that China was at a "crucial moment" in the progress of reform. Sounding a hallmark

28 Jiang Zemin, "Guanyu jiang zhengzhi" (On talking politics), excerpt of a talk delivered to Party member delegates to the Fourth Session of the Eighth NPC and Eighth CPPCC, 3 March 1996, in *Shisida yilai zhongyang wenxian xuanbian*, 2:1743–9 and *Jiang Zemin wenxuan*, 1.514–17; and Jiang Zemin, "President Jiang reaffirms China's stance on Taiwan, stresses army building," talk to PLA delegates attending the Second Plenary Session of the Fourth Session of the NPC, CCTV, 11 March 1996, *SWB*, 12 March 1996.

29 Ren Zhongping, "Wei jingji jianshe he shehui fazhan tigong qiang you li de zhengzhi baozheng – Xuexi Jiang Zemin tongzhi 'Lingdao ganbu yiding yao jiang zhengzhi' de jianghua" (A powerful political guarantee for economic construction and social development – Studying Comrade Jiang Zemin's speech "Leading cadres must pay attention to politics"), *RMRB*, 1 April 1996, 1,3, trans. in *SWB*, 4 April 1996.

30 Xing Bensi, "Jianchi Makesizhuyi budongyao – Huaqing Makesizhuyi yu fan-Makesizhuyi de jiexian" (Never waver in upholding Marxism – Drawing a clear demarcation line between Marxism and anti-Marxism), *RMRB*, 6 June 1996, 9, trans. in *SWB*, 27 June 1996.

theme of the liberal reformers, he argued that the only way forward was to continue to "develop Marxism" as Deng Xiaoping had done in pioneering "socialism with Chinese characteristics" and that Marxism should not be made into rigid "dogma." Throughout the article, Xing took both the ideological left and opportunistic right to task on the still-sensitive issues of ownership, disparities in remuneration, and a planned economy versus market economy in building a "modern enterprise system." At the end, Xing concluded, "we must resolutely comply with the decisions of the central authorities" on these issues.

In October 1996, the Fourteenth Central Committee held its Sixth Plenum. In addition to adopting a long decision on "building socialist spiritual civilization," the plenum passed a resolution scheduling the Party's Fifteenth Congress for the latter half of 1997. With that, preparations began in earnest to draft the political report for Jiang Zemin to present to the congress that would stake out the same middle course evident in the wave of countercriticism the preceding spring.

Preparing for the Party Congress in the Shadow of Deng's Passing

Four months later, on 19 February 1997, Deng Xiaoping died. In contrast to Hua Guofeng's decision contravening Mao's preferences in 1976, Jiang Zemin followed Deng's wishes, as conveyed in a letter from his family, and had Deng's remains cremated and his ashes scattered at sea. At the official memorial service on 25 February, an openly weeping Jiang Zemin delivered the eulogy, describing Deng – in terms equaling the evaluation of Mao Zedong in the CCP's 1981 Resolution on Party History – as "a great Marxist, a great proletarian revolutionary, statesman, military strategist and diplomat, and a long-tested fighter, the chief architect of China's reforms, opening up, and modernization drive, and the founder of the theory of building socialism with Chinese characteristics." In reviewing Deng's impact on the CCP's post-Mao course, Jiang credited Deng with resolving the question of "what socialism is and how to build it." Jiang specified as enduring contributions to the Party Deng's judgment that China was at "the initial stage of socialism," his formulation of "socialism with Chinese characteristics," his recognition of the role of markets under socialism, his 1987 linkage of the "one center" of economic development with the "two points" of "reform and opening up," and the "four cardinal principles" as the fundamental strategy of the CCP. With regard to Party politics, Jiang saluted Deng's pressing for an end to "lifetime tenure" for Party leaders and the precedent he set by retiring from his leadership posts, thereby "creating full conditions for and playing a crucial role in the smooth transition from the second generation central collective leadership to the new central collective leadership, ensuring stability in the Party and state."[31]

By this time, the process of drafting the report on the work of the Fourteenth Central Committee that Jiang would deliver at the Fifteenth Party Congress was well under way. After the October 1996 plenum put the congress on the Party agenda, Jiang Zemin met with the drafting team in December to lay out the general themes that the work report should address. Over the following ten months, the PSC reviewed successive drafts three times. In July 1997, a draft was circulated for review and comment within Party channels and through the United Front Work Department to the "democratic" parties and associations under the Chinese People's Political Consultative Conference (CPPCC).[32]

Midway through the drafting process, Jiang gave a long speech at the Central Party School on 29 May that previewed several major themes of the congress work report and that bluntly rebutted the attacks of the Party's left wing over the preceding months.[33] First, Jiang pledged that the Party would "unswervingly uphold the banner of Deng Xiaoping Theory," which he characterized as "the Marxism of contemporary China" because it had "for the first time in a relatively systematic way" answered "the basic theoretical questions of what is socialism and how to build socialism" in China. Hence, adopting the jargon of Party liberals in a clear counter to the left's criticism, Jiang declared that Marxism must be "developed" in practice. "It is meaningless," he stated, "to talk about Marxism independent of the realities of a country" and "to study Marxism in an isolated and static way," and so to seek answers to contemporary issues "from a few isolated words and phrases in Marxist works." Second, Jiang set the stage for the congress's ratification of the ideological legitimacy of the pending state-owned enterprise reforms by reaffirming the judgment that China is and for a long time would remain at "the initial stage of socialism." This assessment first appeared at the Sixth Plenum of the Eleventh Party Congress in the 1981 Resolution on Party History and was the hallmark theme of the strongly reformist 1987 Thirteenth Party Congress. It was reaffirmed as an essential element of "socialism with Chinese characteristics" at the 1992 Fourteenth Party Congress. It remained, according to Jiang, "the basic starting point for us to formulate our lines, principles, and policies." In another rebuke to the left's charge that under his leadership the Party was "giving up the basic system of socialism," Jiang stated that "practice proves that these doings of ours, instead of deviating from socialism, are dedicated to

---

31 [Jiang Zemin], "Zai Deng Xiaoping tongzhi zhuidao dahuishang Jiang Zemin tongzhi zhi daoci" (Comrade Jiang Zemin's memorial meeting eulogy for Comrade Deng Xiaoping), delivered 25 February 1997, *RMRB*, 26 February 1997, 1ff.

32 *XH*, 25 September 1997.

33 Long excerpts were published in *Renmin ribao*, 30 May 1997, and in *BR*, 40.34 (25–31 August 1997), 10–13. The speech is not included in Jiang's official collection *Jiang Zemin wenxuan*.

building socialism in a down to earth manner." Third, Jiang renewed the call set down at the 1993 Third Plenum to build a "fairly complete socialist market economy" and to "perfect an ownership structure with public ownership as the main body" and concurrent development of diverse ownership forms through creation of a "modern enterprise system."

In subsequent months, articles and interviews in the press elaborating on the themes of Jiang's 29 May speech amplified the coordinated effort to build momentum in anticipation of the congress. On 15 July, for example, the State Economic and Trade Commission newspaper *Economic Daily (Jingji ribao)* published a front-page article by Li Junru, the deputy director of the Theory Bureau of the Party Propaganda Department and director of the Deng Xiaoping Theory Research Center of the Shanghai Academy of Social Sciences. Li underscored the importance of Jiang's assessment that China is at the "initial stage of socialism" and will remain so for a long time to come. Li defended the legitimacy of this judgment by tracing its lineage back to Deng Xiaoping, and he directly linked the necessity of renewing attention to it to controversy over the effort to transform the state-owned enterprise sector.[34] In the first of a weekly series of interviews in the State Council's Development Research Center newspaper *China Economic Times (Zhongguo jingji shibao)*, Xing Bensi recounted how the left had attempted to use Jiang Zemin's call to "stress politics" to criticize Deng Xiaoping's emphasis on economic development "in order to set third generation leaders against second generation leaders," and he underscored that in this critical stage of reform the main priority must be to guard against "leftism."[35]

On 5 August, *China Economic Times* published an interview with reform economist Wu Jinglian, sometimes referred to as "Market Wu," in which Wu chided the Party left's "superstitious" insistence that socialism requires predominance of state ownership in the economy as the residue of erroneous Stalinist political-economy views and as having been proven false by the failures of the Soviet bloc economies.[36] Finally, on 12 August *China Economic Times* published an interview with Li Junru, who described Jiang's Central Party School speech as inaugurating a "third ideological emancipation." Where the first such emancipation of thought – the 1978 debate on "practice as the sole criterion for testing truth" – had established the path toward "socialism

34 Li Junru, "Yiqie cong shehuizhuyi chuji jieduan de shiji chufa" (Proceed in all cases from the reality of the initial stage of socialism), *JJRB*, 15 July 1997, 1 and 3, trans. in *FBIS*, FTS19971006000205.

35 Xing Bensi, "Chongfen renshi chuji jieduan, jianjue fang 'zuo'" (Gain a full understanding of the primary stage and resolutely prevent leftism), *Zhongguo jingji shibao*, 29 July 1997, 1, trans. in *SWB*, 31 July 1997.

36 Wu Jinglian, "Shehuizhuyi jiben tezheng shi shehui gongzheng + shichang jingji" (The basic characteristics of socialism – Social justice plus market economy), *Zhongguo jingji shibao*, 5 August 1997, 1, trans. in *FBIS*, FTS19971016000355.

with Chinese characteristics," and the second – during Deng Xiaoping's 1992 tour of Guangdong and Shanghai – had clarified the role of markets under socialism, Jiang's speech made clear the relationship between state, public, and private ownership under socialism.[37]

In addition to the tide of press commentary countering left-wing criticism of the pending enterprise reforms, two notable books contributed to the effort. One, entitled *Heart-to-Heart Talks with the General Secretary* and published in October 1996, reprinted Jiang Zemin's speech at the September 1995 Fifth Plenum detailing the twelve "great relationships" and carried a preface by Liu Ji, vice president of the Academy of Social Sciences and an associate of Jiang Zemin from his Shanghai days. Liu's preface explained that the book represented the distillation of views of several young researchers associated with the Academy's Center for the Humanities and Social Sciences by Young Scholars at a three-day meeting to study Jiang's plenum speech. The book thus incorporated a separate chapter on each of the "great relationships" and was a thoroughgoing apology on behalf of renewed reform. Indeed, one of the chapters carried the title "Reform Reform Reform – China Has No Other Path."[38]

The other book, *A Critical Moment – Contemporary China's 27 Problems That Urgently Await Solution*, published in April 1997, also carried a preface by Liu Ji. Picking up on Jiang Zemin's enjoinder in speeches that China's modernization had reached a "critical moment," Liu explained that reform had reached the point of a "qualitative leap." If this leap could not be made, then the project of China's socialist modernization would fail. Out of that recognition, a group of mostly young CASS specialists had come together to produce the book's twenty-seven chapters, each detailing a problem – ranging from international strategy to state-owned enterprise reform to environmental degradation to cultural crisis – that China must address urgently. "History has already shown and will more and more prove," Liu concluded, "that 1997 is a critical year in China's destiny."[39]

The Fourteenth Central Committee's Seventh Plenum convened on 6–9 September 1997 and scheduled the Fifteenth Party Congress to open on 12 September. It amended and approved the draft work report, by then having undergone repeated revision and approval by the Politburo, to be delivered by Jiang on behalf of the Central Committee, and it approved draft amendments to the Party Constitution to be taken up by the Party congress. Finally, it endorsed the Party Central Discipline Inspection Commission's investigation

37 Li Junru, "Di sanci sixiang jiefang: Chongpo xing 'gong' xing 'si' de sixiang yihuo" (The third ideological reform—Clarification of ideas about public and private ownership), *Zhongguo jingji shibao*, 12 August 1997, 1, trans. in *FBIS*, FTS19971101000220.

38 Weng Jieming et al., eds., *Yu zongshuji tanxin* (Heart-to-Heart Talks with the General Secretary).

39 Xu Ming, ed., *Guanjian shike: Dangdai Zhongguo jidai jiejue de 27ge wenti* (A Critical Moment – Contemporary China's 27 Problems That Urgently Await Solution).

report on Chen Xitong, who had already been removed from the Politburo at the Fifth Plenum in September 1995, preparing the way for his subsequent criminal prosecution on corruption charges.[40]

THE FIFTEENTH CCP CONGRESS – JIANG CONSOLIDATES POWER

The Fifteenth Congress, which convened in Beijing on 12–18 September 1997, put an authoritative capstone on the long debate over how to transform the state-owned sector of the Chinese economy. It also consolidated the power and stature of Jiang Zemin in Chinese leadership politics, ending his eight-year struggle to secure his position at the top. In addition, Deng Xiaoping's death the previous February – once again demonstrating his astute political acumen in departing from the scene only after his more conservative peers had already died off – meant that the Jiang leadership emerging from the Party congress was the first "post-liberation" leadership to govern the PRC. From that perspective alone, the Fifteenth Party Congress marked a fundamental turning point. Henceforth, China's politics would be guided by leaders whose experience and credentials were entirely different from those of the professional communist revolutionaries who had established the People's Republic and who had dominated politics and policies for more than four decades.

Laying out the ideological foundation for the impending transformation of the state-owned enterprise system, the long report on the work of the Fourteenth Central Committee delivered by Jiang Zemin on the opening day pronounced the "main theme" of the congress to be "holding high the great banner of Deng Xiaoping Theory."[41] Only Deng Xiaoping Theory, Jiang declared, "can settle issues concerning the future and destiny of socialism" in China and provides the means of "emancipating thought and seeking truth from facts." Thus, it "not only inherits the achievements of predecessors but also breaks with outmoded conventions on the basis of new practice." Deng Xiaoping Theory had demonstrated this at "critical historical junctures" – first, in the 1978 debate over "taking practice as the sole criterion for testing truth," which broke the hold of Mao's Cultural Revolution "class struggle" doctrine on Party ideology, and, second, in Deng's 1992 talks during his tour of Guangdong and Shanghai, which asserted the legitimacy of market economics under socialism. Deng Xiaoping Theory would settle issues on the future and destiny of socialism again at present, when the Party was "faced

---

40 "Communiqué of the Seventh Plenary Session of the 14th CCP Central Committee," *XH*, 9 September 1997, available in *SWB*, 10 September 1997.
41 Jiang Zemin, "Hold high the great banner of Deng Xiaoping theory for an all-round advancement of the cause of building socialism with Chinese characteristics into the 21st century," delivered on 12 September 1997, *BR*, 40.40 (6–12 October 1997), 10–33.

with many hard issues we have never met before" and must again "emancipate thought" to address the question of "what socialism is and how to build it." Reinforcing the authority of this reformist interpretation, the Party congress amended the CCP Constitution, placing "Deng Xiaoping Theory" alongside Mao Zedong Thought as a "guide to action."

The work report devoted a long section to the Party's "basic line" during the "initial stage of socialism." "One of the basic reasons for the achievements of reform, opening up and the modernization drive over the past two decades," Jiang declared, "is that we corrected the erroneous concepts and policies transcending the initial stage of socialism and rejected the erroneous proposition that we should give up the basic system of socialism." "The key to resolving various contradictions, dispelling doubts and understanding why we must carry out the existing line and policies and not any other line and policies," he went on, "lies in our unified and correct understanding of the basic conditions in China today in the initial stage of socialism." In that regard, he concluded, "we should maintain vigilance against the 'Right' tendencies, but primarily against the 'Left.'"

The work report then spelled out the implications of these ideological disquisitions for enterprise reform. Addressing the sensitive topic of ownership and what constitutes "socialism," the report reaffirmed the longstanding line that the "public sector" must remain "dominant" in a socialist economy. But it expanded what it called "the full meaning" of the public sector to include not only enterprises owned by the state and collectively (as stipulated in a traditional definition), but also "elements owned by the state and by collectives in the sector of mixed ownership." That is to say, the public sector also includes state and collectively owned shares in the various publicly traded corporations sanctioned by the 1993 Third Plenum's fifty-point decision on economic reform. As to whether such corporations in essence are public or private, the report argued, "the key lies in who holds the controlling share." "If the state or collective holds the controlling share, it obviously shows the characteristics of public ownership." The bottom line, the report concluded, is that "even if the state-owned sector accounts for a smaller proportion of the economy, this will not affect the socialist nature of our country."

The work report thereafter renewed the call made at the 1993 plenum to create a "modern enterprise system" and affirmed the plan to "grasp the large and let go of the small" in transforming the state-owned sector, mandating completion of the transformation by 2000. With the necessity to downsize transformed enterprises and to declare bankruptcy on others, "it will be hard to avoid fluidity of personnel and layoffs." Such "temporary difficulties for some of the workers," it continued, are nevertheless "conducive to economic development, thus conforming to the long-term interests of the working class." Sounding more like the neo-classically inclined editorial writers of the *Wall Street Journal* or the *Economist* than the authoritative consensus of the leadership of a proletarian workers' party, the report urged Chinese workers to "change their ideas about employment and improve their quality to meet the new requirements of reform and development" as the state-owned sector adapted to the hard realities of the market.

The Post-Deng Party Leadership

The Party congress concluded on 18 September, and its First Plenum on 19 September elected the Fifteenth Central Committee. Turnover among the full Central Committee members – 57 percent – was significant, exceeded in the post-Mao period only by the turnover at the 1987 Thirteenth Party Congress, which completed the wave of retirements of revolutionary Party members that had begun in 1985.[42] With very few exceptions, almost all of the 193 members of the new Central Committee were under the age of sixty-five. The Party congress had been preceded by an extensive shake-up of provincial leaders in nearly all of China's thirty-one provincial-level units, replacing twenty-nine provincial Party chiefs and twenty-seven governors. The new Fifteenth Central Committee included thirty provincial Party secretaries, twenty-six governors, and twelve out of fourteen military region commanders and political commissars among its members, all of whom were expected to remain in their posts for some time after the congress. It included only thirty of the current forty-one ministers, portending a major shake-up of the State Council at the Ninth NPC scheduled for the following spring.

As reflected in the appointments to Party leadership bodies at the First Plenum of the Fifteenth Central Committee on 19 September, turnover on the Politburo was more modest, although nonetheless significant, both in terms of an emergent institutionalization of leadership succession procedures and an enhancement of the power of Jiang Zemin, who retained his posts as Party general secretary and chairman of the Central Military Commission. Four of the nineteen full members and one of the two alternates of the outgoing Politburo retired, while the new Politburo was expanded to twenty-two, and two alternates, including eight new members.[43] The two leaders who retired

---

42 For a comparative analysis of successive Central Committees, see Li Cheng, and Lynn White, "The Fifteenth Central Committee of the Chinese Communist Party," *AS*, 38.3 (March 1998), 231–64, especially 241ff.

43 A total of twenty members and two alternates were appointed to the 14th Central Committee Politburo in 1992, but Tianjin Party Secretary Tan Shaowen died in February 1993, six months after the Fourteenth Congress, and Chen Xitong was removed in 1995. Shanghai Party chief Huang Ju was added in 1994.

from the seven-member PSC were replaced by two who were promoted from the Politburo.

Incipient institutionalization of leadership succession processes was evident in the fact that all leaders serving on the outgoing Politburo who were age seventy or older, save Jiang Zemin, retired. In his landmark 1980 speech "On the Reform of the System of Party and State Leadership," Deng Xiaoping had argued strongly for an end to leaders serving indefinitely in leadership posts, but he noted that the leadership had debated but deferred the issue of explicit retirement ages for Politburo members. The 1982 PRC Constitution specified limits for the posts of NPC chairman and premier to two five-year terms, and the 1982 CCP Constitution stipulated that Party leaders are "not entitled to lifelong tenure," although it stopped short of prescribing formal term limits for the top leadership posts. On that basis, in subsequent years retirement norms were established for Party and state officials at various levels, including provincial Party secretaries, governors, members of the Central Committee departments, and State Council ministers. Mandatory retirement ages were set in 1988 and again in 1994 for military officers according to rank and service on the Central Military Commission, in PLA headquarters departments, and in the seven military regions. In this context, the retirement of Politburo members according to an age criterion indicated that norms for retirement, although not publicized, were finally taking hold at the top level.

The impact of applying these norms at the congress was revealed poignantly in the fate of Qiao Shi, the third-ranking PSC member and chairman of the NPC. Qiao was widely seen by foreign observers to be a rival of Jiang Zemin and a proponent of liberalizing reforms, especially with regard to "using law to govern the country" (yi fa zhiguo), in opposition to the more authoritarian notion of "using law to regulate the country" (yi fa zhiguo). If he was such a rival, he was also a collaborator insofar as the NPC under his leadership turned out scores of new laws to lay a legal foundation for the market-oriented reforms, including the 1993 Company Law. Whatever the truth of these conjectures, Qiao's future by the time of the Party congress rested on reconciliation of the emerging succession norms. On the one hand, Qiao was eligible by the PRC Constitution to serve a second term as NPC chairman. On the other, at seventy-three, he should retire from the Politburo and its Standing Committee if retirement at age seventy or older were to be upheld. In the end, his retirement served both to reinforce the Politburo retirement norm and to remove a political rival to Jiang. By some accounts Jiang's exception from the norm of retirement at age seventy resulted from the timely intervention of Party elder Bo Yibo, who broke a deadlock within the Politburo over leadership retirement by proposing that all leaders age seventy or older retire – except for Jiang, whose continued tenure was necessary for "Party unity" during the period of transition.[44]

The rankings of the members of the new PSC implied that Li Peng, having served two five-year terms as premier, would replace Qiao as NPC chairman at the Ninth NPC. Zhu Rongji, who had served as executive vice premier and who had led the struggle to rein in the 1993–4 wave of inflation and to reassert central authority over policy areas ceded to provincial leaders, would replace Li as premier. The resulting line-up – with the conservative Li Peng replacing liberalizing Qiao Shi as NPC chairman and the liberalizing Zhu Rongji replacing the conservative Li as premier, and with Jiang between the two – would preserve the balance that had prevailed before the congress and that likely reflected a deliberate design by Deng Xiaoping since the early 1980s to balance the posts of NPC chairman and premier.[45]

Jiang Zemin emerged from the Fifteenth Party Congress in an improved position. The retirement of Qiao Shi eliminated a rival on the Standing Committee. The retirement from the Central Military Commission of Liu Huaqing and Zhang Zhen in favor of Zhang Wannian and Chi Haotian indicated Jiang's improved relationship with the PLA brass. Among the Politburo members, Jia Qinglin, newly appointed as Beijing Party secretary, and perhaps Li Changchun, who had been Party secretary of Henan at the time of the congress but who would become Party chief in Guangdong the following spring, in addition to Jiang Chunyun, Huang Ju, and Wu Bangguo, could be counted among Jiang's "Shanghai Gang." Finally, there was the appointment of Jiang's personal secretary and chief of staff, Zeng Qinghong, to the Secretariat and as an alternate member of the Politburo. In 1989, on assuming the post of general secretary, Jiang had brought Zeng with him from Shanghai, where Zeng had been chief of his personal staff, and appointed him deputy director of the Party General Office. In 1993, Zeng replaced Wen Jiabao as director of the office. Because the General Office manages the entire array of leadership logistical functions – from maintaining communications and paper flows among the leadership to managing office space, living quarters, travel arrangements, and security for leaders – the ability to place one's own crony as its director was a key step in the consolidation of the general secretary's power. Zeng's appointment as a member of the Politburo and the Secretariat thus reinforced this consolidation and also affirmed Zeng's rise as Jiang's agent

---

44 On Bo's intervention, see Richard Baum, "The Fifteenth National Party Congress: Jiang takes command?" *CQ*,153 (March 1998), 150–1, and Joseph Fewsmith, *China since Tiananmen*, 2nd ed., 201.

45 Thus, from 1983 to 1987, conservative Peng Zhen served as NPC chairman while liberalizing Zhao Ziyang served as premier, and from 1988 to 1993 liberal Wan Li served as NPC chairman while conservative Li Peng was premier.

in politics at the top, as confirmed in his appointment as head of the Party Organization Department two years later.

Hu Jintao, reappointed concurrently as executive secretary of the Secretariat, moved up from seventh to fifth on the PSC. His subsequent appointments as PRC vice president at the Ninth NPC in March 1998 and as vice chairman of the Central Military Commission at the Fourth Plenum of the Fifteenth Central Committee in September 1999 strongly suggested that he was being groomed to succeed Jiang as paramount leader in the next round of top leadership changes at the Sixteenth Party Congress in 2002. Also noteworthy in this regard was the addition of Wen Jiabao to the Politburo. Since 1992, Wen had served on the Secretariat as the secretary in charge of the economy, working with Li Peng and especially Zhu Rongji. His appointment as a Politburo member and, at the Ninth NPC, as vice premier suggested that he was one of two men being groomed to possibly succeed Zhu Rongji as premier. The other was Wu Bangguo, who had been appointed to the Politburo in 1992 while serving as Shanghai Party boss and had been brought to Beijing in 1994 by Jiang Zemin and added to the Secretariat. At the Fifteenth Party Congress, Wu was reappointed to the Politburo, but not to the Secretariat, and was made a vice premier. From 1994 to 1997, there appeared to be a division of labor on the Secretariat between Wu Bangguo and Wen Jiabao, with Wen managing implementation of financial affairs and Wu managing enterprise reform, an arrangement that persisted after 1997. In 1997 both Wen and Wu were fifty-six years of age, indicating that either one could succeed as premier in 2003 and be eligible for two five-year terms before retiring under the age-seventy norm.

Overall, the Politburo leadership appointed in 1997 marked a watershed transition from the two generations of Party veterans who had led the CCP to victory in 1949 and who had dominated PRC politics for more than four decades to a new generation of leaders who had little or no direct experience of the pre-1949 struggle. In contrast to the credentials of past CCP leaders as professional revolutionaries who had created the PRC, the new leaders were promoted primarily because they suited the criteria Deng Xiaoping had deliberately sought – leaders who were younger, better-educated, and technically proficient and thus were better equipped to guide a country undergoing rapid modernization. The leaders of the Fifteenth Central Committee Politburo around Jiang Zemin might be described as both "post-Liberation" – having risen to power during the PRC – and "post-revolutionary" – suited to the pursuit of modernization and administration rather than to social transformation through pursuit of "class struggle."

These qualifications are immediately apparent in a comparison of the collective attributes of the twenty-four members of the Fifteenth Central Committee

Politburo with the twenty-five members of the Twelfth Central Committee Politburo appointed in 1982, when Deng Xiaoping was consolidating his power during the early years of the reform era. First, on average the members of Jiang's Politburo were nearly a decade younger at appointment than those on the 1982 Politburo – sixty-three years old versus seventy-three among the Deng group. Second, directly following the turnover of successive generations, most of the 1997 Politburo members (fourteen of twenty-four) had begun their Party careers after the 1949 revolution; the remaining ten had joined the Party in the 1940s. The 1982 Politburo counted twenty-three of twenty-five members who had joined the Party before the 1935–6 Long March – a status equivalent to that of the "old Bolsheviks" in the Soviet leadership – and sixteen of those had joined the Party in the period from its founding in 1921 through the end of the First United Front in 1927.

Third, the Jiang leadership was far better educated than the 1982 leadership centered around Deng Xiaoping. None of the twenty-five members in the Deng leadership held university degrees, although two (Hu Qiaomu and Liao Chengzhi) had studied two years at university level, two others (Xu Xiangqian and Nie Rongzhen) had studied at the Whampoa Military Academy, and Nie had studied engineering for two years at the Université de Travail in Charleroi, Belgium, as well as at a military academy in Moscow, and two more (Ulanfu and Yang Shangkun) had studied at Sun Yat-sen University in Moscow. By contrast, seventeen members of the Jiang Politburo held university degrees. Among the seventeen, fourteen held engineering degrees, two held technical degrees, and one (Li Lanqing) held a degree in enterprise management.

Fourth, the Politburo leaders around Jiang Zemin were strongly associated with the coastal regions. Thirteen hailed from the coastal provinces of Shandong, Jiangsu, Zhejiang, Fujian, and Guangdong and the two provincial-level coastal cities of Tianjin and Shanghai. Four others (Zhu Rongji, Wu Bangguo, Jia Qinglin, and Zeng Qinghong) had risen to national politics after serving long periods in the coastal provinces during the heyday of the economic reforms in the 1980s and early 1990s. Therefore, seventeen of the twenty-four members of the 1997 Politburo had a strong association with the coastal backbone of the reform era. By contrast, only six of the twenty-five members of the 1982 leadership hailed from the coastal provinces, and most of the remainder came from Deng's home province of Sichuan and from provinces in the Party's former Central-South Bureau, with a sprinkling of Shanxi leaders.

Finally, the 1997 Politburo was a thoroughly civilian leadership. Among its twenty-four members, only the two professional military leaders – Zhang Wannian and Chi Haotian, who both had fought in the Civil War and in Korea – had firsthand military experience and had served in the PLA or military-related institutions over their careers. The remaining twenty-two, including Jiang Zemin, had no military experience. By contrast, twenty of the twenty-five members of the 1982 Politburo had significant military experience by way of past leadership or combat roles in the war against Japan and the Civil War, and among those, seven, including Deng Xiaoping, had followed military careers or played significant military roles after 1949.

The significance of this leadership transition is difficult to overstate. For the most part, the leaders around Jiang were educated and began their political careers in the 1950s, and they had endured the Cultural Revolution rather than profiting from it. Their rise to power began with the demise of Mao Zedong's "revolutionary" politics and the advance of Deng Xiaoping's reforms in the 1980s. By education and experience, they shared a technocratic outlook, preferring a pragmatic, problem-solving approach to China's modernization agenda rather than seeing themselves as heroic social revolutionaries. And, unprecedentedly, they were a strongly civilian leadership, presiding over a country in which security had long been the foremost national priority and a Party in which the military had long been a primary base of political power.

JIANG ZEMIN AND THE DILEMMAS OF GLOBALIZATION

The Fifteenth Party Congress endorsement of the program to transform the state-owned enterprise system into a "modern enterprise system" meant that the effort to implement the approach of "grasping the large and letting go of the small" could proceed in earnest. The Ninth NPC, which convened the following spring, launched a sweeping reorganization of the State Council to facilitate the complementary goals of "separating government and enterprise." These steps and others – such as the call at the Third Plenum in 1998 to address the "three rural issues" and in 2000 to spur development of China's west – accompanied renewed efforts to gain admission to the WTO.

Taken together, such efforts reflected a decision on the part of the Chinese leadership to accommodate rather than resist the impact of globalization on China. Jiang Zemin's remarks to the Hong Kong delegation attending the Ninth NPC reflect this decision:

> One of the things we have learned is this: We must have a comprehensive and correct understanding of the issue of economic "globalization." Economic "globalization" is an objective trend of economic development of the world. No one can avoid this trend. The key to this issue is that we should treat "globalization" dialectically. . . . We should be bold in and good at participating in international economic cooperation and competition under the condition of this economic "globalization" trend. We should learn how to seek profits and avoid damages. On one hand, we should fully utilize the opportunities and favorable conditions it provides to accelerate our development.

On the other hand, we should be fully aware and prevent in timely fashion unfavorable factors and risks it might bring about.[46]

Jiang's remarks followed increasingly frequent PRC-media discussions – provoked by the 1997 Asian financial crisis – about the implications for China of globalization. These included new criticisms of the impending enterprise reforms in left-wing journals such as *Pursuit of Truth* and *Contemporary Trends*, which argued that joining the WTO would open China's economy to foreign investment and domination by multinational corporations and thus return the country to foreign subjugation. As debate in the press over the implications of globalization continued into 1998, the leadership's line on the issue consolidated along the themes expressed by Jiang at the NPC session and became a standard element in authoritative pronouncements.[47]

The post-Party congress efforts at enterprise reform and to join the WTO thus played out in a context of uncertainty about trends in the world economy and concerns about social and political instability at home. These stemmed not only from the massive worker lay-offs entailed by enterprise reform and from the uncertainties of the 1997 Asian financial crisis, but also from the social and political consequences of globalization in an increasingly open China – a mercurial popular nationalism, the emergence of an increasingly contentious arena of public commentary, new avenues of official corruption, and the use of the new media for agitation and protest.

The Ninth National People's Congress

The Ninth NPC, which convened on 5–19 March 1998, put forward the most extensive reform of the State Council and its associated ministries and agencies since the 1983 reorganization under Zhao Ziyang. The 1983 Sixth, 1988 Seventh, and 1993 Eighth NPCs had introduced successive reforms of the State Council, together with corresponding changes in lower-level government institutions, but those efforts had relatively little impact on basic problems of coordination, overstaffing, and overlapping functions. Indeed, as then-Premier Li Peng commented in explaining pending State Council changes in his report to the 1993 Eighth NPC, the two previous reorganizations in 1983 and 1988, despite their goal of streamlining, left the State Council even larger than before.[48]

---

46 "China: Jiang Zemin, HK Deputies Mull Work Report," *XH*, 9 March 1998, available in *FBIS*, CHI-98-069.

47 See, for example, "Chinese president on diplomatic work," *XH*, 28 August 1998, available in *SWB/Asia Pacific*, 28 August 1998.

48 Li Peng, "Report on the work of the government," delivered at the Eighth NPC, 15 March 1993, *BR*, 36.15 (12–18 April 1993), I–XVI.

The 1993 reforms reduced the number of State Council ministries, commissions, and agencies from eighty-six to fifty-nine – including forty-one ministries and commissions – and they sought to reduce the number of employees of those institutions by 25 percent. The 1998 State Council reforms further reduced the number of ministries and commissions to twenty-nine and sought a reduction in staff by half – in 1998 numbering 47,000 against an authorized level of 31,000.[49]

The overarching purpose of the 1998 government reform was to break the longstanding linkages between State Council ministries and their corresponding industrial bureaus in provincial and local governments on the one hand and the state-owned enterprises they administered on the other. Therefore, the most significant changes were made in the industrial ministries, such as those supervising the coal, machine-building, chemical, and metallurgy industries, which thereafter became policy-planning bureaus under a revamped State Economic and Trade Commission. Several others – such as the ministries of Posts and Telecommunications – were merged and lost their supervisory roles. The state-owned enterprises once managed by these ministries were regrouped as independent enterprise groups. Finally, complementing the hiving off of the social welfare functions from the state-owned enterprises under the reforms, the Ministry of Labor, becoming the Ministry of Labor and Social Security, was expanded to incorporate social insurance functions that were previously spread across several ministries.

The roles of the three major state commissions involved in the economy were also recast. The State Economic and Trade Commission emerged as the preeminent industrial and trade policy body in the State Council. The State Planning Commission, once one of the most powerful bureaucracies in the PRC political order before the reform era, was downgraded to a reduced planning and forecasting role. The State Commission for Restructuring the Economy was elevated to a staff office directly managed by Premier Zhu Rongji to implement the transformation of the state-owned enterprise system. These changes effectively resurrected the roles and priorities of these bodies in the 1980s, when Zhao Ziyang served as premier, and overturned the roles they played after 1988 under Premier Li Peng. Zhao had created the State Commission for Restructuring the Economy in 1982 and had presided over it personally. Li Peng relegated it to a lower-ranking role and downgraded the State Economic Commission to a State Production Commission in 1990. This was consistent with his own conservative views and in step with the program of economic retrenchment that was authorized in the fall of 1988 and formalized

---

49 The details of and rationale for the State Council reforms were spelled out in the report to the Ninth NPC by Luo Gan; [Luo Gan], "State Councillor Luo Gan sets out structure for government streamlining," 6 March 1998, *DGB*, 7 March 1998, B1-B2, trans. in *SWB*, 13 March 1998.

in the thirty-nine-point Central Committee decision of 1989. When Zhu Rongji was elevated from his post as Shanghai mayor to Beijing in 1991, he was made director of the reduced State Production Commission. Finally, in the State Council reorganization of 1993, the State Production Commission was again upgraded and its purview expanded as the State Economic and Trade Commission, with Zhu protégé Wang Zhongyu as director.

As these institutional changes and the plans to transform the state-owned enterprise sector took hold over the next three years, China's industrial sector was transformed and the planned-economy order built in the 1950s gave way to a new landscape of state corporations and independent enterprise groups, publicly held companies, foreign-invested firms, and a range of other formats. The new order was incomplete, to be sure. In particular, it still lacked an adequately reformed banking and financial sector that established an independent central bank and that broke the pattern of government-directed lending by the People's Bank to failing state-owned enterprises, although new steps in that direction were announced by Zhu Rongji at the Ninth NPC.[50] Also, new institutions were needed to manage the array of assets the state would own in the economy in the wake of the reforms, a gap filled in 2003 with the creation of the State Assets Supervision and Administration Commission (SASAC) and parallel bodies at provincial and local levels in 2004 and 2005.[51] Nevertheless, the late 1990s reform of state-owned enterprises brought about fundamental changes that would better position the Chinese economy for entry into the WTO and for the deeper integration into the world economy that followed. In turn, the complementary push to join the WTO gave Jiang and Zhu added leverage to press the urgency of enterprise reform on resistant government bureaucrats and enterprise managers, warning that the onset of foreign competition would decimate inefficient enterprises unless they were reformed.

The Push for WTO Membership

The replacement of Li Peng as premier by Zhu Rongji at the Ninth NPC made possible a renewed push by Beijing to negotiate accession to the WTO. By all appearances, Li as premier had resisted the concerted but ultimately failed effort to negotiate accession in the early 1990s, prior to the creation of the WTO in 1995, which Jiang Zemin and perhaps Zhu supported. The appointment of Li Lanqing, who had long experience in China's foreign trade ministry,

---

50 On these steps and Zhu Rongji's efforts at financial centralization leading up to them, see Victor C. Shih, *Factions and finance in China*, 161–78.

51 On the establishment of the SASAC, see Barry Naughton, *The Chinese economy*, 316–19; Barry Naughton, "The State Asset Commission: A powerful new government body," *China Leadership Monitor*, 8 (Fall 2003); and Barry Naughton, "SASAC rising," *China Leadership Monitor*, 14 (Spring 2005).

as PSC member at the Fifteenth Party Congress and as executive vice premier at the Ninth NPC, also strengthened the push for WTO accession. The key to this goal lay in securing a bilateral accession accord with Washington; with that in hand, agreements with Europe and Japan, which deferred their conclusion of bilateral negotiations with Beijing pending an American accord, would follow. But, as previously discussed, Beijing's relations with Washington during President Clinton's first term were uncertain, both because of the president's own views on China after the Tiananmen crackdown and because of antagonistic views of China in Congress.

Zhu's appointment as premier, however, came in the midst of an upturn in U.S.–China relations, manifested by Jiang Zemin's official visit to Washington in October 1997, immediately after the Fifteenth Party Congress, and by Vice President Al Gore's visit to Beijing in March 1998, immediately after the Ninth NPC. A visit by Clinton was scheduled for the following June, the first by a sitting American president since President George H.W. Bush's visit in February 1989. In that context, Chinese leaders began to signal their interest in pushing forward on a bilateral accord on WTO accession. Movement was slowed, however, by political wrangling over a range of issues in both Washington and Beijing. Significant progress toward an agreement was not apparent until early 1999, following two letters from President Clinton – in November 1998 and February 1999 – to Jiang Zemin on the issue of accession and following visits to Beijing by Federal Reserve Chairman Alan Greenspan in January 1999 and United States Trade Representative negotiator Charlene Barshevsky in early March. These efforts culminated in the 6–10 April visit to Washington by Zhu, in expectation of a bilateral accession accord.[52]

These expectations were severely disappointed. By the time Zhu arrived in Washington, allegations of Chinese espionage at the U.S. nuclear research laboratory in Los Alamos darkened an atmosphere already clouded by Congressional Cox Committee investigations of unauthorized transfers of missile-guidance technology in 1999, by charges of illicit Chinese contributions to President Clinton's 1996 reelection campaign, and by continued pressures over Chinese human rights practices.[53] Already beset by longstanding opposition

---

52 For an authoritative account from an American perspective of Zhu Rongji's Washington visit and its aftermath through the November 1999 U.S.-PRC accord on WTO accession, see Robert L. Suettinger, *Beyond Tiananmen*, 358–88. For an analysis of Beijing's perspective, see Joseph Fewsmith, "China and the WTO: The politics behind the agreement," *NBR Analysis*, 10.5 (December 1999), 23–39. For a fascinating but unconfirmed account of the Chinese leadership's handling of these events, see Zong Hairen [pseud.], *Zhu Rongji zai 1999* (Zhu Rongji in 1999), 25–43 and 71–99.

53 The Los Alamos espionage story was broken by the *New York Times* on 5 March 1999 in a "special report" by James Risen and Jeff Gerth, "Breach at Los Alamos: China stole nuclear secrets for bombs, U.S. aides say." For a later *Times* account casting doubt on the original story, see William J. Broad, "Spies vs. sweat: The debate over China's nuclear advance," *NYT*, 7 September 1999. For the *Times'* self-criticism, see "The *Times* and Wen Ho Lee," *NYT*, 26 September 2000.

to China's entry into the WTO from right-wing Republicans and left-wing Democrats and from textile producers, trade unions, and other interests, Clinton, on the advice of his domestic policy advisers, walked away from an agreement that, from Beijing's perspective, had made major concessions to Washington. Zhu left Washington with a major embarrassment and without an agreement.

Facing immediate criticism from the American business community engaged in China, Clinton quickly changed his mind and sought to reopen the talks. But by then, because of his failure to conclude an agreement, Zhu faced ferocious criticism, made worse soon thereafter by the bombing of the PRC embassy in Belgrade on 7 May by NATO forces operating in the Kosovo War, killing three Chinese and triggering outrage and nationalistic demonstrations outside the U.S. embassy in Beijing. In this context of outraged popular opinion, Zhu and, less directly, Jiang were put in a defensive position, not only with regard to WTO accession, but also across the board. In May and June, leadership differences were apparent in the appearance in the press of contrasting reactions to the Belgrade bombing. On the one hand, public statements by Vice President Hu Jintao on 9 May and by Jiang Zemin on 13 May and six successive *People's Daily* editorials counseled "turning our tremendous righteous indignation . . . and our great patriotic enthusiasm into a powerful propelling force, being of one heart and one mind, and working arduously to constantly increase the economic strength, the national defense strength, and the national cohesion of our country." On the other hand, over the same period, three "Observer" articles – a rarely used byline that conveys a significant but not consensus view among the leadership – excoriated the Belgrade bombing as the point of departure for a broad-gauged assault on American "hegemonism," using vituperative language on a scale not seen since the late Mao era.[54] Thereafter, new tensions in cross-Strait relations complicated the leadership's agenda, when ROC President Lee Teng-hui remarked to *Deutsche Welle* correspondents on 9 July that Taipei and Beijing had "a

54 "Full text of Vice-President Hu Jintao's speech on NATO attack," *XH*, 9 May 1999, available in *SWB/Asia Pacific*, 9 May 1999; and "Jiang Zemin speech at ceremony to welcome back embassy staff members from Yugoslavia," *XH*, 13 May 1999, available in *SWB/Asia Pacific*, 17 May 1999. The six *RMRB* editorials appeared on 21, 25, and 28 May and 2, 3, and 8 June 1999. The three "Observer" articles are: "Shi rendaozhuyi, haishi baquanzhuyi?" (Humanitarianism or hegemonism?), *RMRB*, 17 May 1999, trans. in *SWB/Asia Pacific*, 17 May 1999; "Lun Meiguo baquanzhuyi de xin fazhan" (On the new development of American hegemonism), *RMRB*, 27 May 1999, trans. in *SWB*, 29 May 1999; and "Fengquan dangjin baquanzhuyi zhao yi zhao lishi zhe mian jingzi" (Contemporary hegemonism should take a look in the mirror of history), *RMRB*, 22 June 1999, trans. in *SWB* 25 June 1999. Joseph Fewsmith argues plausibly that the "Observer" articles attacking American "hegemonism" were authorized by Jiang to demonstrate to his critics that he could be as harsh on Washington as they were. (See Fewsmith, "China and the WTO: The politics behind the agreement," 34–6, and Joseph Fewsmith, *China since Tiananmen*, 2nd ed., 220.) Either way, there was clearly contention among the top leadership on these issues.

special state-to-state relationship," effectively challenging the PRC's "one China principle."

By the fall, however, Jiang and Zhu were renewing the push to transform the state-owned enterprise system as launched at the Fifteenth Party Congress and the Ninth NPC. Through the summer and early fall, Jiang gave a series of talks during local inspection tours reaffirming the importance of the reforms.[55] Thereafter, at the 19–22 September 1999 Fourth Plenum, the leadership endorsed a new decision on aspects of the advancing enterprise reform program. The reforms have reached "a crucial stage," the plenum communiqué advised, urging that "in the midst of fierce global competition at the turn of the century, no time can be lost in pushing forward the restructuring and development of state-owned enterprises."[56]

Thereafter, Beijing became more receptive to Clinton administration entreaties to complete negotiation of a U.S.–PRC bilateral accord on WTO accession that included a personal pitch by Clinton in a meeting with Jiang at the Auckland APEC meeting in September. After four days of marathon negotiations in mid-November, U.S. and Chinese negotiators reached agreement. Following conclusion of bilateral accords with the other WTO members, including Japan and Europe, Beijing joined the WTO on 11 December 2001. With that, the politics of China's integration into the world economy – of adapting to globalization – had crossed a watershed.

The Emergence of Public Opinion

The struggle in the late 1990s over the future of the economic reforms and Beijing's accession to the WTO took place in a domestic political setting that in fundamental ways was different from that in preceding periods. Most notably, the Jiang leadership began in the mid-1990s to tolerate – within bounds – public expression of views that departed from the regime's line on issues of the day. The roots of this shift go back to the 1980s, when an expanding space for public expression followed naturally from the loosening of state controls over society since the beginning of the reform era. In part, the broadening of public discourse on political issues reflected the rapid proliferation of think tanks and the role of researchers in the broader policy process since the 1970s. Promoted as the application of the "soft sciences"

55 Jiang Zemin, "Jianding xinxin, shenhua gaige, kaichuang gongyouzhi fazhan de xin jumian" (Strengthen confidence, deepen reform, and create a new situation in the development of state-owned enterprises), speech delivered at the Dalian forum on enterprise reform, 12 August 1999, in *Shiwuda yilai zhongyao wenxian xuanbian*, 2.916–32; Editorial, "General Secretary Jiang Zemin on the reform of state-owned enterprise," *Liaowang*, 36 (6 September 1999), 2–8, trans. in *FBIS*, FTS19990920000076.
56 "Decision of the Central Committee of the Chinese Communist Party (CCP) on major issues concerning reform and development," *XH*, 26 September 1999, available in *SWB/Asia Pacific*, 27 September 1999.

(*ruan kexue*) to policy making, the use of think-tank researchers and specialists to supply feasibility studies, cost-benefit analyses, background analyses, and summaries of policy options made the political process more consultative.[57] As the Party leadership debated fundamental issues of reform, research institutions had incentives to publish their researchers' views as a way to expand their influence, and Party leaders found it useful to have expert research and opinion published that supported their views. In addition, state subsidies to PRC media declined in the early 1980s, and consequently newspapers and publishing houses faced an increasing need to make money to survive. Under pressures of commercialization, publishers sought to offer books, magazines, articles, and other products that could satisfy a broader readership, and the previously rigid controls on what could be published were relaxed.[58] Finally, the Party recognized the utility both of a degree of transparency with regard to its own activities and of liberalizing public access to information and ideas that might serve the broader project of China's modernization. All of these factors combined to produce a proliferation of media and a widening of intellectual, cultural, and entertainment content in the 1980s, worlds apart from that in the preceding decades.

The Tiananmen crisis and the ensuing suppression of political and intellectual discourse slowed this evolution but did not halt it. By the mid-1990s, the Party leadership appeared to sanction a leap in what could be expressed in print. A flood of new publications emerged that were startling in their range and surprising in the degree of criticism and "permitted dissent" they conveyed.[59] By the late 1990s, new electronic media were beginning to take hold, including widespread availability of cell phones and the onset of the Internet revolution, supplementing the growth of television since the early 1980s. Taken together, these developments provided the infrastructure for the advent of public opinion, a new reality that the leadership had to take into account, manage, and manipulate.[60]

57 The landmark discussion of this development in the 1980s was Wan Li's speech to a national symposium on soft science research on 31 July 1986, entitled "The democratization of policy decision-making and the adoption of scientific methods are vital parts of the reform of the political system," reported in *XH*, 31 July 1986, available in *SWB*, 4 August 1986. At that time, leadership deliberation over the building of the Three Gorges dam was frequently cited as benefiting from the "soft sciences" approach.

58 For a thorough analysis of these developments, see Zhao Yuezhi, *Media, market, and democracy in China*.

59 The term "permitted dissent" is purloined from Dina Spechler, whose penetrating study of the role of the journal *Novy Mir* in providing a platform for airing the views of the Soviet intelligentsia and in contributing to the rise of a "genuine public opinion" during the post-Stalin "thaw" in the USSR offers apt parallels. See *Permitted dissent in the USSR*, xv–xxi.

60 A path-breaking assessment of the emergence of the role of public opinion during this period is Joseph Fewsmith and Stanley Rosen, "The domestic context of Chinese foreign policy: Does 'public opinion' matter?" in David M. Lampton, ed., *The making of Chinese foreign and security policy in the era of reform*, 151–87.

The leadership's reasons for sanctioning this development are not entirely clear. In part, it may simply have served the leadership's political needs. As China moved into a post-Deng era after 1994 and at a time when significant leadership differences existed over issues such as enterprise reform and policy toward the United States, Jiang Zemin did not have the stature of Deng as paramount leader to regulate and referee elite politics. In addition, the leadership may have calculated that with the final dismantling of the command economic order in favor of a principally market-driven system, China's political order needed new corresponding mechanisms for establishing consensus among its growing and increasingly diverse constituencies. Finally, the move also may have followed directly from the consequences anticipated from China's integration into the globalizing world economy.

The resulting public discourse featured a startlingly diverse spectrum of viewpoints, controversies, and voices. These included the views of establishment intellectuals, associated with major think tanks and university research centers, who, as earlier, put forward views in service to or directed at ongoing leadership debates. This type of advocacy is exemplified by the attacks of the "old Left" on the Jiang leadership's efforts to build a "modern enterprise system" published in left-wing journals such as *Pursuit of Truth* and by the reprise by intellectuals associated with the Central Party School and other institutions, such as Xing Bensi and Li Junru. Also typical of this kind of advocacy was a controversial book published in March 1998 as the Ninth NPC convened by two *People's Daily* writers, Ma Licheng and Ling Zhijun. Entitled *Crossed Swords* and published in the "China's Problems" series with a preface by Jiang Zemin crony Liu Ji, the book depicted the revision of what defines a socialist economy ratified at the Fifteenth Party Congress as a "liberation of thinking" that "smashed the cult of ownership" in the same way that the 1978 debate over "practice as the sole criterion of truth" "smashed the cult of personality" and Deng Xiaoping's 1992 tour of south China "smashed the cult of the planned economy."[61] Incorporating long extracts of the previously unpublished "ten-thousand-character memorials," the book put forward a scathing attack on the "old Left" opposition to the enterprise reforms ratified at the Fifteenth Party Congress and the Ninth NPC.

What was new in the late 1990s' public discourse was the publication of views by writers and "public intellectuals" who had no institutional connection to the establishment and, as often as not, directed their writings to broader popular audiences. These included "New Left" writers such as Wang Hui, who criticized the unexamined modernism and inherently Western liberal outlook of many intellectuals in the 1980s. There also emerged nationalistic works

---

61 Ma Licheng and Ling Zhijun, *Jiaofeng*, 424.

such as Wang Shan's 1994 book *Looking at China Through a Third Eye*, which lamented the consequences of the Deng reforms on the authority of the CCP and on society, and the 1996 polemic *China Can Say No!*, which called on China to stand up more forcefully to alleged American efforts to "contain," or to put a brake on, China's rising power. There were also populist writings, such as He Qinglian's *The Pitfalls of Modernization*, that railed against the social inequities that the reforms had fostered.[62] These views frequently prompted responses from establishment intellectuals, such as the 1998 rejoinder to *China Can Say No!* by Shen Jiru, *China Should Not Be 'Mr. No' – Issues in Contemporary Chinese International Strategy*, yet another book published in the "China's Problems" series and with a preface by Liu Ji.[63] Remarkably, even issues in foreign policy – a realm strictly controlled in the past – could be debated.[64]

Finding the Limits of Dissent

The emergence of this vigorous, free-for-all-but-sanctioned discourse in China's media made it difficult to locate the boundary between permitted debate and proscribed dissent. In a period of regime concern about social dislocations resulting from economic reform and globalization, however, that post-Tiananmen injunctions against political agitation remained in force was nevertheless clear. Protest activities on the occasion of the Beijing visits of President Clinton and UK Prime Minister Blair in June and July 1998 were shut down. Efforts by Democracy Wall dissident Xu Wenli and others to register an opposition political party – the China Democracy Party – in the fall of 1998 were suppressed, and Xu, Wang Youcai, and Qin Yongmin were arrested and sentenced to prison terms of thirteen, eleven, and twelve years, respectively.

The most spectacular public agitation was the mobilization of thousands of members of the syncretic *qigong*-based religious movement Falungong (Wheel of Dharma Discipline) outside the gateway into Zhongnanhai, the leadership's work compound on the west side of the old Forbidden City. The Falungong movement emerged in the early 1990s as part of the religious awakening that the Dengist retreat from society had tolerated.[65] Its founder Li Hongzhi

62 A useful survey and assessment of the intellectual debate emerging in this period is Joseph Fewsmith, *China since Tiananmen*, 2nd ed. See also Wang Hui's two essays "The 1989 social movement and the historical roots of China's neoliberalism" and "Contemporary Chinese thought and the question of modernity," translated and with a helpful "Introduction" by Theodore Huters, in Wang Hui, *China's new order*. See also Zheng Yongnian, *Globalization and state transformation in China*, 162–86.
63 Shen Jiru, Zhongguo budang "Bu Xiansheng" (China should not be Mr. No).
64 H. Lyman Miller and Liu Xiaohong, "The foreign policy outlook of China's 'third generation' elite," in David M. Lampton, ed., *The making of Chinese foreign and security policy*, 146–7.
65 On the emergence and suppression of Falungong, see David Ownby, *Falungong and the future of China*. On the emergence of *qigong* generally, see Nancy N. Chen, "Urban spaces and experiences of *qigong*," in Deborah S. Davis et al., eds., *Urban spaces in contemporary China*, 347–61.

drew on elements from Buddhism and Daoism to create a series of exercises that practitioners believed would induce spiritual enlightenment and physical health. After 1992, Li began attracting followers as a spiritual healer, selling books and tapes of lectures on his teachings, before moving to New York City in 1995 to build an international movement but also perhaps to evade anticipated trouble with the authorities. As it did for other *qigong* sects, the CCP regime tolerated the Falungong sect as it grew. But in 1996 Party criticisms of growing "superstitions" in society began to target Falungong, and the Party Propaganda Department banned publication of the movement's books.

In April 1998, Falungong followers in Tianjin protested criticism of their beliefs as superstition by the conservative quantum theorist He Zuoxiu in a Tianjin social sciences journal.[66] Thereafter, using cell phones to coordinate their mobilization, roughly 10,000 protesters assembled outside Zhongnanhai in Beijing on 25 April. The protest at the seat of power in Beijing – the largest protest since 1989 – caught the Party leadership completely by surprise. After subsequent discovery of the breadth of the movement's followers – including some in the public security apparatus and the PLA – the Ministry of Civil Affairs banned the Falungong organization on 22 July. A Central Committee circular the same day banned the practice of Falungong among members of the CCP.[67] A ruthless suppression movement followed to root out followers of the movement, leading to the death of several thousand adherents and imprisonment of several tens of thousands.[68]

Although from the regime's perspective adherents of the China Democracy Party and the Falungong had crossed a threshold and so provoked the crackdowns, the line between tolerated expression and suppression was not always easy to discern. Popular demonstrations of nationalism, in particular, at times were promoted, at other times manipulated, and sometimes suppressed. In the summer of 1996, after Japanese citizens built a lighthouse on one of the Senkakus (which – as the Diaoyutai – are claimed by Beijing), nationalistic protests broke out in Taiwan and Hong Kong but were suppressed in the PRC because at the time Beijing was working to improve its relations with Tokyo. After NATO forces bombed the PRC embassy in Belgrade in May 1999, furious popular protesters surrounded the American embassy in Beijing. Public security and PLA forces blocked the protestors from entering the embassy

---

66 An analysis of He Zuoxiu's politics may be found in H. Lyman Miller, "Xu Liangying and He Zuoxiu: Divergent responses to physics and politics in the post-Mao period," *Historical studies in the physical and biological sciences*, 30, Part I (1999), 89–114.

67 *XH*, 22 July 1998.

68 Estimates of the numbers killed and imprisoned as a result of the campaign to suppress the Falungong vary, from those of PRC official sources on the low side to those of the Falungong on the high side. For assessments, see Human Rights Watch, "Dangerous meditation: China's campaign against Falungong," January 2002; and David Ownby, *Falungong and the future of China*, 15–16 and 161–4.

grounds, but they simply stood by as the protestors threw rocks and broke embassy windows. After four days, the demonstrations miraculously stopped. When, on 13 July 2001, the International Olympic Committee selected Beijing to host the 2008 Olympic Games, 400,000 people spontaneously flooded Tiananmen Square in Beijing, joined by Jiang Zemin and other members of the leadership, to celebrate a moment of national triumph.[69]

In this context, in an effort to adapt to the potential offered by the new media to mobilize popular agitation and protest, the State Council in October 2000 adopted the PRC's first regulations on managing Internet and telecommunications services. Article 15 of the Internet regulations prohibited service providers from "producing, reproducing, releasing or disseminating" information in nine categories, including information that "endangers national security," that "instigates ethnic hatred or discrimination," that "preaches evil cults or feudalistic and superstitious beliefs," or that "disseminates rumors, disturbs social order, or undermines social stability." Article 57 of the new telecommunications regulations incorporated identical stipulations.[70]

Globalization and Corruption

The PRC's advancing engagement with the world economy also stimulated a new phase in the evolution of corruption in China.[71] Corruption had been an integral part of the command economy before the reform era, as exchange of favors through personal connections was often the grease necessary to make the intrinsically inefficient and bureaucratized system work. The onset of the market-based reforms brought new types of corruption as the forms of ownership shifted from state-owned to public to private and as commercialization took hold. Party cadres who formerly presided over agricultural collectives in the countryside found new opportunities as rural brokers, and Party cadres in the cities often were best placed to take advantage of the opportunities of arbitrage in the partially reformed dual-price system of the 1980s and early 1990s.

The "opening" (*kaifang*) element of the reform policies also established the context for corrupt engagement in the world economy. This appeared to achieve a mammoth scale in the late 1990s push to accommodate globalization, judging by the series of smuggling cases brought to light in those years.

69 *XH*, 13 July 2001.
70 State Council, "Hulianwang xinxi fuwu guanli banfa" (Measures for managing Internet information services), Order No. 292, 25 September 2000, available at http://www.chinaculture.org/library/2008–02/06/content_23369.htm (accessed 9 August 2010); Ministry of Information Industry, "Telecommunications regulations of the People's Republic of China," 25 September 2000, at http://tradeinservices.mofcom.gov.cn/en/b/2000–09-25/18619.shtml (accessed 9 August 2010).
71 For a general discussion of the roots of corruption in China's evolving economic system, see Wu Jinglian, *Understanding and interpreting Chinese economic reform*, 391–8.

Perhaps the most spectacular of these was the Yuanhua Corporation case in Xiamen, the special economic zone in Fujian facing Taiwan. Exposed in 1999 and described by Zhu Rongji as the biggest smuggling prosecution in PRC history, between 1996 and early 1999 Yuanhua smuggled 4.5 million tons of oil, 3 million cases of cigarettes, more than 3,000 luxury automobiles, and large volumes of electronics, textiles, and other goods, totaling RMB 53 billion in value and evading RMB 30 billion in customs duties.[72] The Yuanhua network included more than 300 local, provincial, and even national officials, including a vice minister of public security.[73] Trials in the fall of 2000 convicted more than 80, including a dozen who were executed. Yuanhua's founder Lai Changxing fled to Canada and fought extradition back to China. The case resulted in a shake-up in the Fujian provincial Party and government and for a time threatened to implicate Politburo member Jia Qinglin, a Jiang Zemin crony and former Fujian Party secretary, and his wife.[74]

Concerns over corruption also motivated the July 1998 Central Military Commission (CMC) decision to order the PLA to divest of joint-venture business operations. The PLA had been encouraged to engage in such ventures in the late 1980s, in addition to foreign arms sales and other activities, to supplement state budget funding, for the PLA modernization effort that had begun in 1985. By 1997, Jiang Zemin and Zhu Rongji were increasingly alarmed at the impact both on military professionalism and discipline and in terms of lost customs revenue of PLA involvement in corruption and smuggling. Therefore, at a 22 July 1998 CMC meeting Jiang Zemin ordered the PLA to disengage from the business relationships it had built over the preceding decade. The degree to which this order has been complied with is uncertain at best.[75]

The "Three Represents"

Finally, the CCP moved to accommodate the impact of the late 1990s reforms on Chinese society. On 25 February 2000 in Guangdong – in the course of an inspection visit that recalled Deng Xiaoping's landmark "southern tour" in early 1992 – Jiang Zemin put forward a new formulation regarding the mission and nature of the CCP that soon was encapsulated as the "three represents." "The reason why our Party has won the people's support," Jiang declared, "is that our Party, as the vanguard of the working class, has always represented

---

72 XH, 25 July 2001.   73 XH, 5 September 2001.

74 Guangzhou ribao, 25 January 2000, trans. in FBIS, FTS20000126000372.

75 James Mulvenon, Soldiers of fortune; James Mulvenon, "To get rich is unprofessional: Chinese military corruption in the Jiang era," China Leadership Monitor, 6 (Spring 2003); and James Mulvenon, "So crooked they have to screw their pants on: New trends in Chinese military corruption," China Leadership Monitor, 19 (Fall 2006).

the demands of the development of the advanced social forces of production in China, represented the direction of the development of advanced culture in China, and represented the fundamental interests of the broad masses of people in China."[76]

Over the next three months, a well-coordinated media campaign underscored the significance of the new formulation. On 7 March, Jiang repeated the formulation in remarks to the assembled Shanghai delegation to the annual NPC session in Beijing.[77] While the NPC was in session, on 4, 7, and 9 March *People's Daily* ran successive commentator articles – an authoritative vehicle – on each of the three "represents." On 17 March, *Xinhua* publicized a commentator article from a forthcoming issue of the Party journal *Seeking Truth (Qiushi)*, which declared that "the scientific summation and formulation of the 'three represents' is Comrade Jiang Zemin's creative application and development of Marxist theory on Party-building in the new era" and that the "'three represents' has enriched the treasure house of Marxism-Leninism-Mao Zedong Thought and Deng Xiaoping Theory."[78] On 23 March, *People's Daily* published a long exegesis of the ideological roots of Jiang Zemin's "important expositions" on the "three represents" by the Deng Xiaoping Theory Research Center, a Jiang think tank at the PLA's foremost military academy, the National Defense University.[79]

On 14 May, Jiang delivered a long speech to a forum on Party building in Shanghai that elaborated on the reasons for and implications of the "three represents" for the CCP. "Under the new historic conditions," Jiang stated, "extensive and profound changes have taken place in China's social life, and the diversification of various socioeconomic components, organizational forms, distribution of interests, and forms of employment will develop further." These developments, he went on, underscore the priority of linking Party building with the creation of a "modern enterprise system," especially in "non-public" enterprises.[80] Concurrently, circulars issued by the CCP

76 Jiang Zemin, "Zai xin de lishi tiaojianxia geng haode zuodao 'sange daibiao,'" (Carry out the "three represents" better under the situation of the new historical conditions), 25 February 2000, in *Jiang Zemin wenxuan*, 3.1–5. A partial English translation is available in *FBIS*, CPP20000225000113.

77 *XH*, 7 March 2000.

78 Editorial, "Jiaqiang xinshiqi dangde jianshe de genben zhidao sixiang: Xuexi Jiang Zemin zai Guangdong kaocha gongzuo shi de zhongyao jianghua" (Strengthen the basic leading thought of Party construction in the new period: Study Jiang Zemin's important speech during an inspection of Guangdong), *Qiushi*, 6 (2000), 7–9, trans. in *FBIS*, CPP20000317000143.

79 "Yongyuan liyu bubai zhidi de fabao: Xuexi Jiang Zemin tongzhi guanyu 'sange daibiao' de zhongyao lunshu" (A magic weapon for always establishing ourselves in an unassailable position: Studying Comrade Jiang Zemin's important expositions on the "three represents"), *RMRB*, 23 March 2000, 9, trans. in *FBIS*, CPP20000323000048.

80 Jiang Zemin, "Shizhong zuodao 'sange daibiao' shi women dangde lidang zhi ben, zhizheng zhi ji, liliang zhi yuan" (From beginning to end make the "three represents" the foundation of our Party, the source of the ruling Party, and the origin of its strength), 14 May 2000, in *Jiang Zemin wenxuan*, 3.6–33. Also transmitted by *XH*, 15 May 2000, available in *FBIS*, CPP20000515000070.

Central Organs Work Committee, the Party Central Discipline Inspection Commission, the Ministry of Supervision, and the PLA General Political Department called on Party members under their purview to study Jiang's "important expositions" on the "three represents."[81] On 18 May, *People's Daily* carried a long assessment of the significance of the "three represents" by Zheng Bijian, personal secretary to Hu Jintao and the executive vice president of the Central Party School. Jiang's "three represents" formulation, Zheng stated, is "the most concentrated scientific reply" to the question raised in the section on Party building in the work report delivered to the Fifteenth Party Congress of "what kind of Party to build and how to build it." "If we shut our eyes and stop up our ears, stand still and refuse to make progress, and are utterly ignorant of the developments and changes in the advanced forces of production" brought about by globalization and the reforms, Zheng warned, "it will be out of the question for us to be able to lead the people in promoting the liberation and development of the advanced forces of production, and we may even be knocked down by the continuing advances of the era." Finally, Zheng argued, the laying off of state-owned enterprise workers in the effort to create a "modern enterprise system" does not mean that China's "working class" has lost its "advanced nature," nor does it mean that the working class is no longer the "class basis" of the CCP.[82] A 22 May *People's Daily* editorial – ordinarily the foremost vehicle of authoritative commentary – underscored the leadership consensus behind the "three represents" concept, describing it as "a brilliant theoretical conclusion made by the Party Central Committee with Comrade Jiang Zemin as the core."[83]

The introduction of the "three represents" formulation followed directly from the leadership's determination over the preceding several years to transform the state-owned and collective economy into a "modern enterprise system" and from its decision to accommodate rather than resist integration with a globalizing international economy. Like the dissolution of the collective economy in favor of household-based contract agriculture in the rural areas two decades earlier, the dismantling of the state-owned enterprise system dissolved CCP roots in large sectors of the urban industrial economy. In addition, the concurrent rise of newly legitimate forms of economic organization – public share-holding corporations, private enterprises, and foreign-funded ventures – and of new professions associated with the advanced economy fostered new elites in society with whom the Party had no formal connections.

---

81 *XH*, 18 and 19 May 2000.

82 Zheng Bijian, "'Sange daibiao' zhongyao lunshu yu mianxiang ershiyi shiji de Zhongguo gongchandang" (An important exposition of the "three represents" and the CCP's keeping step with the 21st century), *RMRB*, 18 May 2000, modified trans. in *FBIS*, CPP20000518000074.

83 Editorial, "Quanmian jiaqiang dangde jianshe de weida gangling" (Comprehensively strengthen the great program of Party building), *RMRB*, 22 May 2000.

Such elites, some commentaries warned, had the resources and skills to constitute a challenge to the political order if their political interests could not be accommodated.

Jiang Zemin's "three represents" thus reflected the Party leadership's decision to pursue a strategy of political co-option with regard to the entrepreneurial, managerial, technical, and professional elites who were emerging in Chinese society as a consequence of the economic reforms. The formulation was naturally controversial because it raised inevitable questions about the Party's "class basis." Was the CCP still a vanguard "proletarian" party if it presided over the dissolution of state-owned enterprises – formerly the core of the socialist system in China – and abandoned millions of laid-off workers to the uncertainties of unemployment in a market-driven economic order? Could a party that claimed the working class as its basis recruit corporation executives, private entrepreneurs, lawyers, scientists, technicians, and intellectuals into its ranks in the name of "representing the advanced forces of production" without increasingly resembling a "bourgeois" party? Recruiting private entrepreneurs had been debated in the 1980s and ultimately rejected in 1989.[84] The logic of the "three represents" bore an unmistakable resemblance to the declaration incorporated into the Soviet Communist Party's 1961 program that it was a "party of the whole people" – a party not just of the Soviet working class but of the entire Soviet people, among whom fundamental conflicts of interests (and so "class struggle") no longer existed. For the "old Left," who clung to long-held orthodox views of the CCP's "class nature" and remembered the 1960s polemics with Moscow over this issue, the "three represents" was anathema.

In the midst of continuing controversy over the implications of the "three represents" direction, Jiang Zemin delivered a long speech on 1 July 2001, marking the eightieth anniversary of the CCP's founding. The speech was more than a recitation of Jiang's personal views; it had been vetted by the Politburo and its Standing Committee and so reflected a consensus view of the top leadership. The speech put forward a highly authoritative and systematic defense of the "three represents" as the concept guiding CCP development in China's evolving social and economic order. "To meet the requirements of the 'three represents,'" Jiang stated, "we must uphold the Party's nature as the vanguard of the working class and make sure it remains advanced. At the same time, in light of economic development and social progress, we must constantly consolidate the class foundation of the Party, expand its popular support, and increase its social influence." Noting that China's "social strata" (*shehui jiceng*) have evolved and that as a consequence of the reforms "many

---

84 On the history of CCP debates on this issue, see Bruce J. Dickson, *Wealth into power*, 66–83.

people move from one ownership sector to another," the Party's recruitment criteria needed to be adjusted accordingly. Specifically:

> The main criteria to admit a person into the Party are whether he or she works wholeheartedly for the implementation of the Party's line and program and meets the requirements for Party membership. The basic components and backbone of the Party are workers, peasants, intellectuals, soldiers, and cadres. At the same time, it is also necessary to accept those outstanding elements from other sectors of society who subscribe to the Party's program and constitution, work for the Party's line and program wholeheartedly, and prove to meet the requirements for Party membership through a long period of tests.[85]

In the wake of the speech, the Party Organization Department prepared to resume admission of private entrepreneurs, stalled since 1989, into the Party.

However, Jiang's Party-anniversary speech did not end the controversy over the "three represents" and its implications for Party recruitment.[86] In late July, yet another "ten-thousand-character memorial" was circulated, this one signed by Deng Liqun, Yuan Mu, and other remnants of the "old Left." Offering Party membership to private business people, the text stated, violated the Party Constitution and standing Party regulations, opened the way for the transformation of the Party through "peaceful evolution" as advocated by the capitalist West and as witnessed in the collapse of the USSR, and spelled the end of the Party by means of fragmentation. In changing the Party's recruitment policy and pressing the "three represents," the text charged, Jiang Zemin personally violated Party procedures, "set himself above the Party," and was promoting his own "personality cult" in concert with his Shanghai cronies who constitute a "new gang of four."[87] By that time, however, the Party leadership was beginning preparations to convene the Sixteenth CCP Congress, which the Sixth Plenum that convened on 24–26 September scheduled for the second half of 2002.[88] In that context, the leadership was no longer willing to tolerate the vituperation of the left as it had while preparing for the Fifteenth Congress in 1997. In August, publication of two of the three left-wing journals – *Pursuit of Truth* and *Mainstream* – ceased.

---

85 Jiang Zemin, "Qingzhu Zhongguo gongchandang chengli bashi zhounian dahuishang de jianghua" (Speech commemorating the 80th anniversary of the founding of the CCP), 1 July 2001, in *Jiang Zemin wenxuan*, 3.264–99, modified trans. by *XH*, 1 July 2001, available in *SWB/Asia Pacific*, 2 July 2001.
86 For a solid review of controversy attending Jiang's 1 July speech, see Joseph Fewsmith, "Rethinking the role of the CCP: Explicating Jiang Zemin's Party anniversary speech," *China Leadership Monitor*, 2 (Spring 2002).
87 Text trans. in *FBIS*, CPP20010802000183, from the *RMRB* Web site, 28 July 2001.
88 "Communiqué of the 15th Central Committee Sixth Plenum," *XH*, 26 September 2001.

TRANSITION TO THE "FOURTH GENERATION" LEADERSHIP

The Sixteenth CCP Congress, which convened on 8–14 November 2002, together with the Tenth NPC, which met 5–18 March 2003, brought about the first orderly, planned transfer of power in PRC history from a retiring top leader to a younger man deliberately prepared to succeed. The Party and people's congresses also saw a sweeping turnover of the broader top leadership in which "third generation" leaders around Jiang Zemin gave way to younger "fourth generation" leaders. In turn, the transition created a new group of "third generation" retired elders who could be expected to continue to have influence on politics and policy. The new leaders appointed to the Party Politburo largely shared the technocratic attributes of the members appointed in 1992 and 1997.

The turnover of leaders on the Politburo and its Standing Committee reported at the Sixteenth Central Committee's First Plenum on 15 November 2002 was sweeping. Of the twenty-one full members of the outgoing Fifteenth Central Committee Politburo, thirteen retired. Among these, six of the seven members of the outgoing Standing Committee retired, including General Secretary Jiang Zemin, NPC Chairman Li Peng, Premier Zhu Rongji, and CPPCC Chairman Li Ruihuan, leaving Hu Jintao as the only continuing member. Eleven of the thirteen retiring Politburo members had passed the presumed retirement norm of seventy years old. The other two – Li Ruihuan, at age sixty-eight, and Li Tieying, at age sixty-six – were not required by that norm to retire.

All seven of the Politburo members who did not retire from the outgoing Politburo were elevated onto the new PSC. In addition, Zeng Qinghong was promoted from alternate member on the outgoing Politburo to membership on the PSC, expanding that body's membership from seven to nine. Fifteen new full members – including former alternate member Wu Yi – were appointed to the Politburo, and Party General Office Director Wang Gang was added as an alternate, bringing the total Politburo membership to twenty-five. Six of the seven members of the Party Secretariat were replaced, with Zeng Qinghong as the only holdover.

The Tenth NPC the following spring saw a comparable turnover in state institutions. Former Vice Premier Wen Jiabao replaced Zhu Rongji as premier, and former Vice Premier Wu Bangguo became chairman of the NPC Standing Committee, replacing Li Peng. All four vice premiers and all five state councilors retired in favor of new leaders. Eighteen of the twenty-eight ministers of the State Council were new. Finally, at the Tenth CPPCC session, which met concurrently with the NPC, Jia Qinglin replaced Li Ruihuan as chairman.

Change in the Central Committee was substantial but somewhat less dramatic than the transition in the top leadership. Fifty-four percent of the 198 full members of the Sixteenth Central Committee and 72 percent of the 158 alternates were new, for an overall change of 61 percent for the combined membership – an average turnover when compared to Party central committees since 1987.[89]

On the eleven-member Party and state CMCs, two of the three vice chairmen and four of the seven members retired. Only three new members were added, but this low turnover obscures the fact that the three men had already been promoted to the CMC at the 1999 Fourth Plenum in anticipation of the retirements at the Sixteenth Congress. In September 2004, at the Fourth Plenum of the Sixteenth Central Committee, CMC membership was expanded to include the commanders of the three specialized forces of the PLA (the Navy, Air Force, and Second Artillery strategic command).

The Dynamics of Succession

As dramatic as the turnover in central Party and state institutions was, however, the focus of attention at home and abroad was on the transfer of power at the very top from Jiang Zemin to Hu Jintao. Leading up to the Party congress, speculation about the looming succession surged in the Hong Kong and Western press over whether Jiang would retire completely (*quantui*), retire partially (*bantui*), or not retire at all (*butui*). Numerous accounts had Jiang bargaining his retirement in exchange for high placement of his cronies in the forthcoming leadership. Praise for his leadership of the PLA was interpreted alternatively as evidence that the military was pressing for his continued tenure as CMC chairman or as a salute for his service over the preceding thirteen years.

In the event, Jiang retired in three steps over the three-year period from 2002 to 2005. At the Sixteenth Party Congress, he retired as Party general secretary in favor of Hu Jintao. At the Tenth NPC the following March, he was succeeded as PRC president by Hu. And at the Fourth Plenum of the Sixteenth Central Committee in September 2004 and the third session of the 10th NPC in March 2005, Jiang ceded his posts as chairman of the CCP and PRC Central Military Commissions, respectively, to Hu. This orderly transfer of power through retirement of a longstanding paramount leader in favor of a younger man deliberately prepared to succeed him was, in the light of past failures, a watershed moment in PRC political history and, more generally, in the history of major communist states.

---

89 Li Cheng, and Lynn White, "The Sixteenth Central Committee of the Chinese Communist Party: Hu gets what?" *AS*, 43.4 (July-August 2003), 560.

This staggered transfer of top leadership posts from Jiang to Hu was taken by many Chinese and foreign observers as evidence that Jiang was resisting long-established succession arrangements and seeking to hang on to power. In the end, according to this view, Jiang did retire but had to be pushed, first from the top Party post and, two years later, from the top military posts. In addition, Jiang succeeded in bargaining his stepping down as Party chief and, four months later, as head of state in exchange for promotion of several of his cronies onto the expanded PSC. By this count, the new Party chief Hu Jintao and Wen Jiabao, Zhu Rongji's successor as premier, sat on a PSC that included one political protégé of Li Peng, Luo Gan, and six of Jiang Zemin – Wu Bangguo, Jia Qinglin, Zeng Qinghong, Huang Ju, Wu Guanzheng, and Li Changchun.[90]

As persuasive as this analysis may be, it is noteworthy, first, that the staggered transfer of power from Jiang to Hu followed precedents set by Deng Xiaoping's retirement between 1987 and 1990 and, second, that the expansion of the PSC from seven to nine members appeared to reflect an elaboration of that body's operating structure and relations to the broader Party apparatus. In that light, the expansion of the Standing Committee may not have been merely a stacking of that body with Jiang cronies to ensure his influence after he retired from the post of Party general secretary. Although not apparent until Jiang retired from his posts as Party and state CMC chairman in September 2004 and March 2005, the staggering of his retirement from his Party and military positions matched precisely the staggered retirement of Deng Xiaoping's retirement from the PSC at the Thirteenth CCP Congress in 1987 and then from his posts as Party and state CMC chairman in November 1989 and March 1990, respectively.[91] In addition, Hu Jintao's staggered assumption of the top Party, state, and military posts over the 2002–5 period was preceded by his promotion as Jiang's deputy as head of state and on the CMC according to the same staggered sequence. Thus, following his reappointment as executive secretary of the Party Secretariat at the Fifteenth Party Congress in 1997, Hu was appointed PRC vice president the following spring at the Ninth NPC and Party and state CMC vice chairman at the Party Fourth Plenum in September 1999 and at the Third Session of the Ninth NPC in March 1999, respectively. Both the match of Jiang's staggered retirement from his posts with the precedent set by Deng Xiaoping's retirement and the corresponding staggered promotion of Hu Jintao into state and Party posts

---

90 See, for example, the skillful analysis along these lines by Joseph Fewsmith, "The Sixteenth National Party Congress: The succession that didn't happen," *CQ*, 173 (March 2003), 1–16.

91 The relevance of the Deng precedent was noted at the time by the Hong Kong communist newspaper *WHB*, "Jiang's control of the military is conducive to smooth transition," 16 November 2002, trans. in *FBIS*, CPP20021116000016.

directly under Jiang Zemin invite the conclusion that retirement in successive steps by Jiang over the 2002–5 period was a deliberate plan of several years' standing.

With regard to the expansion of the PSC, the assignment of policy roles at the new Politburo's first meeting after the Party congress made clear a strengthened direct supervisory role of the Standing Committee in the day-to-day operations of the political system. The division of policy labor among the new PSC members was as follows:

Hu Jintao	CCP general secretary; PRC president; director, Central Committee (CC) Foreign Affairs and Taiwan Affairs Leading Small Groups
Wu Bangguo	NPC chairman
Wen Jiabao	State Council premier; director, CC Finance and Economy Leading Small Group
Jia Qinglin	CPPCC chairman
Zeng Qinghong	Executive secretary, Secretariat
Huang Ju	Executive vice premier
Wu Guanzheng	Central Discipline Inspection Commission chairman
Li Changchun	Director, CC Propaganda and Ideology Leading Small Group
Luo Gan	Director, CC Politics and Law Committee

The division of policy labor among the 1997 PSC members of the Fifteenth Central Committee had featured the same cluster of supervisory roles among the first seven members of the 2002 PSC under Hu. From a functional perspective, the expansion of the PSC from seven to nine members was achieved by the addition of Luo Gan as director of the leading small group in charge of domestic security (a post he assumed in 1998) and of Li Changchun as director of the propaganda system.[92] Notably, the same nine-member division of policy labor was continued on the Seventeenth Central Committee PSC appointed in 2007. (See the section "The Seventeenth Party Congress and Hu's Power" below for more on this point.)

The significance of this expansion of policy supervisory roles appears to reflect an effort to consolidate the Standing Committee's position both as the decision-making and operational core of the leadership. The addition of the security and propaganda arenas rounded out representation on the Standing Committee of the broad policy arenas needed to enable that body as a collective oligarchy to make informed decisions on all major issues that might confront the central leadership on a day-to-day basis. At the same time, it facilitated the Standing Committee's ability to supervise and monitor implementation of policies once they were decided through the relevant leading small groups and the Party Secretariat. The consolidation of the Standing Committee's roles

92 For a listing and analysis of the Central Committee's leading small groups since their inception in 1958, see Alice L. Miller, "The CCP Central Committee's leading small groups," *China Leadership Monitor*, 26 (Fall 2008).

carried with it the implication of a reduced role for the broader Politburo, which henceforth appeared largely to ratify and consolidate decisions made by the Standing Committee.

In the light of the foregoing, the staggered transfer of power from Jiang Zemin to Hu Jintao over the years from 2002 to 2005 and the expansion of the PSC may be explained by longstanding succession arrangements made on the basis of precedent and by revisions in the Party's leadership structure and processes. It may well be that Jiang attempted to use his pending retirement to bargain for promotion of his political allies. But in the end, his retirement proceeded according to precedents set by Deng Xiaoping, and the Party leadership decision-making processes appeared to have been revised at the Sixteenth Party Congress.

Another Technocratic Leadership

As a group, the Politburo under Hu Jintao's leadership that emerged from the First Plenum of the Sixteenth Central Committee the day after the Party congress closed shared and even extended attributes of the Politburo appointed in 1997 after the Fifteenth Party Congress under Jiang's leadership that it succeeded. The average age on appointment of the members of the 1997 Jiang Politburo was 63; the average age of the members of the 2002 Hu Politburo was 60. Among the twenty-four members of the 1997 Politburo, seventeen had university educations, fourteen of whom were engineers and another two held degrees in scientific fields. Among the twenty-five members of the 2002 Hu Politburo, twenty-two had university degrees. Seventeen were engineers and one (Wen Jiabao) held a degree in geology. Most members of the 1997 Jiang Politburo had joined the CCP in the 1950s; most members of the Hu Politburo had joined the Party in the early to mid-1960s on the eve of the Cultural Revolution, and so the beginning of their careers had been disrupted or deferred by the turmoil of that period.

Whereas the 1997 Politburo had a strong orientation toward the coastal provinces that were the vanguard of the economic reforms – with seventeen members either hailing from that region or having served there for long portions of their careers – the Hu Politburo membership incorporated a more balanced regional representation, with only eleven from the coastal provinces. Finally, like the 1997 Politburo, the 2002 Politburo was thoroughly civilian. Except for the two PLA leaders serving on the Politburo, only two others – Zeng Qinghong and Chen Liangyu, both of whom had served brief tours as military technicians in the 1960s – had some military experience; the remaining twenty-one members had none at all. Also like the 1997 Jiang Politburo, the new Hu Politburo shared the same "post-liberation, post-revolutionary" attributes that, as noted above, Deng Xiaoping had sought to promote in the CCP leadership since the early 1980s.

HU JINTAO AND THE POLITICS OF GOVERNANCE

The long report on the work of the Fifteenth Central Committee that Jiang Zemin delivered to the Sixteenth Party Congress ratified the leadership consensus behind the major initiatives that he had pressed since 1997 – most notably the "three represents" formulation and its implications for Party recruitment. The report described the "three represents" as "the crystallization of the Party's collective wisdom and a guiding ideology the Party must follow for a long time to come."[93] On that basis, the "important thinking of the three represents" was written into the CCP Constitution's preamble, together with Mao Zedong Thought and Deng Xiaoping Theory, as the Party's "guiding ideology," but without specific accreditation to Jiang. Calling on the Party to "consolidate its class base by expanding its mass base," the report also called on the Party to "unite with the people of all social strata," including those who had emerged as a consequence of the reforms, specifying "entrepreneurs and technical personnel employed by non-public scientific and technological enterprises, managerial and technical staff employed by foreign-funded enterprises, the self-employed, private entrepreneurs, employees in intermediary organizations, and freelance professionals." It charged further that "it is improper to judge whether people are politically progressive or backward by whether they own property or how much property they own." Rather, they should be assessed according to "their political awareness, state of consciousness and performance, by how they have acquired and used their property, and by how they have contributed to the cause of building socialism with Chinese characteristics." The report stipulated that the Party should continue to recruit members "mainly" from among the workers, peasants, military, and intellectuals, but added that "we should make a point" of recruiting from among those "in the forefront of work and production" and from among "prominent intellectuals and young people," as well as from among the "advanced elements of other social strata."

Accordingly, the preamble to the Party Constitution was revised to declare that the CCP is "the vanguard both of the Chinese working class and of the Chinese people and the Chinese nation," as well as "the core of leadership for the cause of socialism with Chinese characteristics and represents the development trend of China's advanced forces of production, the orientation of China's advanced culture, and the fundamental interests of the overwhelming

---

93 Jiang Zemin, "Build a well-off society in an all-round way and create a new situation in building socialism with Chinese characteristics," text of report delivered to China's 16th National Party Congress, 8 November 2002, *SWB*, 8 November 2002.

majority of the Chinese people."[94] The Party Constitution had previously stated that the CCP is "the vanguard of the Chinese working class, the faithful representative of the interests of the people of all nationalities in China, and the core of leadership of China's socialist enterprise."[95] Chapter I of the new Party Constitution was revised to stipulate that application for Party membership was open to "any Chinese worker, peasant, member of the armed forces, intellectual, or any advanced element of other social strata."

The work report to the Sixteenth Party Congress also broadly reaffirmed the emphases on economic growth and technology that had flourished under Jiang's leadership in the 1990s. In its opening paragraphs, it noted that "trends toward multipolarization and globalization" and the advance of science and technology were continuing to develop, and so "the competition in comprehensive national strength" was "becoming increasingly fierce." "Given this pressing situation," Jiang declared, "we must move forward or we shall fall behind." Although reaffirming that China remains at the "initial stage of socialism," Jiang's report called on the Party to build a "well-off society" (xiaokang shehui) and to quadruple China's 2000 GDP by the year 2020.

Given the guidelines of the congress report and Jiang's considerable residual strength after retirement, it might have been expected that the new general secretary Hu Jintao was in a weak position to launch new political and policy initiatives. Nevertheless, Hu and Wen Jiabao immediately began new and distinctive political directions and policy emphases that played out over the next five years in two broad areas. One was to broaden the concept of "development" beyond the Jiang era's single-minded pursuit of economic growth to redress some of the social and economic consequences of development. These efforts proceeded under the new rubric of "people-centered" governance and included several new formulations, including adoption of a "scientific development concept" and an effort to build "a new socialist countryside." The second focus was on Party reform and problems of governance, embodied in calls to enhance the capabilities of the CCP as a "ruling party" based on its "advanced nature," to improve "intra-Party democracy," transparency and accountability in the Party's operations, and to realize a "socialist harmonious society." Many of these themes were not completely new. In some instances, they drew on initiatives begun in the late Jiang years; others were foreshadowed in formulations in the work report to the Sixteenth Party Congress. But taken together, they reflected the priorities of the new leadership.

94 "Constitution of the Communist Party of China," amended and adopted by the 16th National Congress of the CPC on 14 November 2002, in *Documents of the 16th National Congress of the Communist Party of China*, 76–114.

95 "Constitution of the Communist Party of China," partially revised by the 15th National Congress of the Communist Party of China and adopted on 18 September 1997, in *Selected Documents of the 15th CPC National Congress*, 59–88.

Setting a New Agenda

That Hu had new priorities to add to the agenda set down at the Sixteenth Party Congress was apparent immediately. The day after the new Politburo was appointed at the First Plenum of the Sixteenth Central Committee on 15 November, *Xinhua* publicized an account of a Politburo meeting that inaugurated a Party-wide campaign to study the congress Party documents.[96] Over the next month and a half, *Xinhua* reported on the deliberations of three more Politburo meetings; and over the next five years, until the Seventeenth CCP Congress was convened in October 2007, *Xinhua* reported a total of fifty-six meetings of the Politburo. For most of CCP history since 1949, meetings of the Politburo were not reported on a current basis. The exception was the period under Zhao Ziyang's leadership as general secretary from late 1987 through the Tiananmen crisis in 1989. The routine reporting of Politburo meetings under Hu's leadership thus marked a resumption of practices inaugurated by Zhao in the wake of the reformist Thirteenth CCP Congress in 1987.

Moreover, *Xinhua* also began occasionally to report on a current basis meetings of the PSC, a practice that was nearly without precedent before the Hu era.[97] Finally, the Politburo began holding regular "study sessions" that were routinely reported by *Xinhua*. Most sessions were held immediately after a Politburo meeting, and they addressed major topics of foreign, economic, or social policy, first listening to lectures by academics and think-tank experts and then listening to summary comments by Hu on the Politburo's discussions of the topic. The first of these study sessions was held on 26 December 2002 to study the 1982 PRC Constitution as the basis for "using law to govern the country" (*yi fa zhiguo*). Over the five years down to the Seventeenth Party Congress in 2007, forty-four such study sessions were held. Study sessions had been an informal, although not routinely publicized, practice during the tenures of Hu Yaobang and Zhao Ziyang, thus their resumption marked a return to practices of that era.

These steps to introduce a modicum of publicity to previously highly secretive processes of the Party's top leadership were followed by new steps toward transparency in the name of accountability at other levels of the Party and state.[98] These included regular reports to Central Committee plenums by Hu

---

96 *XH*, 16 November 2002.
97 The single exception was a 2 February 2002 *Xinhua* account of a PSC presided over by Jiang Zemin to discuss poverty relief efforts on the eve of the Spring Festival holiday.
98 Hu's brief discussion of the rationale for these steps may be found in his report to the Second Plenum of the Sixteenth Central Committee in February 2003; "Guanyu zhongyang de gongzuo" (On the work of the Central Committee), 26 February 2003, in *Shiliuda yilai zhongyao wenxian xuanbian* (Selected important documents since the Sixteenth Party Congress), 1.152–3. For the General Office notice directing publicity on meetings of the Politburo and other bodies, see "Zhonggong zhongyang bangongting yinfa 'Guanyu jinyibu gaijin huiyi he lingdao tongzhi huodong xinwen baodao de yijian'

Jintao on the work of the Politburo that intended to underscore the accountability of the Politburo to the Central Committee.[99] In subsequent months, it
was announced that Party congresses in some provinces and some lower levels
would begin convening annual sessions (rather than once every five years) to
hear reports on the work of Party committees.[100] Following the Tenth NPC
in March 2003, the media also began more extensive reporting on meetings of
the State Council Executive Committee under Premier Wen Jiabao. In the fall
of 2003, the State Council Information Office held classes to train spokesper-
sons for central and provincial Party and state institutions.[101] By 2005,
many central and provincial Party and state institutions had Web sites that
regularly disseminated information on their staffing, operations, and business.

The push for greater transparency gained additional but unexpected
momentum from the crisis created by the spread of severe acute respiratory
syndrome (SARS). This highly contagious disease was discovered in Guangdong in November 2002 and spread rapidly to several major cities, including
Beijing and Hong Kong. The emerging epidemic created both uncertainty
about the disease's impact on domestic economic and social stability and foreign consternation at Beijing's failure to publicize an epidemic of international
dimensions, resulting in a ban on travel to Beijing by the WHO. In that context, Wen Jiabao presided over a State Council meeting on 2 April 2003 that,
assured by the Ministry of Public Health, concluded that the epidemic was
under control and that there were limited cases of the disease. This judgment
was belied a week later by statements to the foreign press by Jiang Yanyong,
a retired military doctor with direct knowledge of SARS cases in three PLA
hospitals.[102] Central and PLA officials, if not others higher up, clearly had
been suppressing information about the spread of the disease.

Finally, on 17 April, *Xinhua* reported a PSC meeting convened by Hu Jintao
that ordered immediate steps to contain the spread of the disease and warned
that "delayed or deceptive reports are impermissible."[103] Three days later,
both the minister of public health (a Jiang Zemin appointee) and the mayor of
Beijing (a Hu Jintao crony) were removed from office for their handling of the
epidemic. Over the next several weeks, Hu and Wen moved decisively, sacking
more than a hundred central and provincial officials, touring hospital wards,

de tongzhi" (Central Committee General Office notice distributing the "Opinions on improving
reporting on meetings and activities of leading comrades"), in ibid., 1:285–6.
99 These reports were not publicized on a current basis, even though plenum communiqués routinely
mentioned Hu delivering them; portions are available in *Shiliuda yilai zhongyao wenxian xuanbian*
(Selected important documents since the Sixteenth Party Congress) and *Shiqida yilai zhongyao wenxian
xuanbian* (Selected important documents since the Seventeenth Party Congress).
100 *WHB*, 27 August 2003, trans. in *FBIS*, CPP20030827000091.
101 *XH*, 22 September and 3 November 2003.
102 Allen T. Cheng et al., "WHO seeks full probe on virus," *South China Morning Post*, 10 April 2003.
103 *XH*, 17 April 2003.

imposing restrictions on public travel, pledging cooperation with the WHO, and authorizing daily counts of new cases of the disease in the media, all in what Hu called a "people's war" against its spread. By 24 June, the WHO lifted its ban on travel to Beijing. The belated transparency given the SARS episode in the end promoted more open treatment in PRC media to events that previously had been suppressed, such as natural disasters and major accidents.

The other new emphasis introduced by Hu Jintao – on what later were called "people-centered" policies that redressed the plight of those disadvantaged or left behind by the economic reforms of recent years – also emerged soon after the Seventeenth Party Congress. On 5–6 December 2002, Hu led nearly the entire membership of the Secretariat to visit Xibaipo, a Hebei town that had been the seat of CCP headquarters on the eve of its move into Beijing in March 1949. In that context, Mao Zedong had convened the Second Plenum of the Seventh Central Committee and delivered a speech enjoining the Party that was about to assume national power to maintain its tradition of "plain living and hard struggle," to resist corruption by privilege and status, and to strive to serve the people. At Xibaipo, Hu Jintao declared that the CCP faced a comparable challenge in undertaking the effort to build a "well-off society" and in implementing the "three represents." He charged his colleagues in the new leadership to adhere to the "two musts" put forth by Mao in 1949 – to "remain modest, prudent, and free from rashness" and to "preserve the style of plain living and hard struggle."[104]

In pitching these themes at Xibaipo, Hu was cautious in stressing their continuity not only with Mao but also Deng Xiaoping and Jiang Zemin (who had also visited Xibaipo in 1991), and thus not as an oblique criticism of Jiang. The coordinated media blitz that followed the visit to Xibaipo, including authoritative comment in *People's Daily* and subsequent repetition of the "two musts" by the rest of the leadership, indicated that the enunciation of these themes reflected broader leadership endorsement of the initiative. On 12 December, *Xinhua* publicized a PSC meeting that discussed approaches to aiding the poor, and over the next several weeks and during the Spring Festival holiday, the media reported that Hu, Wen, and the rest of the Politburo had paid visits to the urban and rural poor, unemployed workers, and impoverished PLA veterans to express sympathy over their plight.

Other steps along these lines followed, the most striking of which was the cancellation of the leadership's annual summer retreat to the seaside resort of Beidaihe. Nearly every year since 1953, the Party leadership had retired to Beidaihe to escape the heat and dust of Beijing in July and August and to

---

104 *XH*, 7 December 2002, available in *FBIS*, CPP20021207000055.

discuss the coming year's issues.[105] These retreats had been particularly important in the final stages of preparing for the convocation of Party congresses,
as was the case in 2002 when Beidaihe provided the setting for the ongoing
bargaining over the leadership line-up to be appointed at the Sixteenth Party
Congress. In July 2003, however, the Hong Kong communist newspaper *Wen
Wei Po* disclosed that henceforth the Party leadership would discontinue the
annual Beidaihe retreat to foster "a new image of the Party and government as
enlightened, open, approachable, and pragmatic."[106] Instead, Beidaihe would
be used "on behalf of the Central Committee and State Council" to reward
meritorious service to China's modernization, exemplified by the reception
by PSC member Zeng Qinghong on 29 July to 7 August 2003 for medical personnel and scientists who had worked to suppress the SARS epidemic
the previous spring.[107] Although in subsequent years the independent Hong
Kong China-watching press and foreign observers speculated annually about
a resumption of leadership retreats at Beidaihe, the evidence each year since
2003 indicated otherwise.[108]

The Scientific Development Concept

The emphasis accorded to the themes of "plain living and hard struggle" and
to "people-centered" policies may easily be attributed to the personal outlook
and experiences of Hu Jintao and Wen Jiabao. Before they rose to prominence
in national politics in the 1990s, both men spent long portions of their early
careers in Gansu, one of China's poorest provinces, and Hu served as Party chief
in both Guizhou and Tibet. These personal predilections, however, should not
overshadow the longer roots of these themes. The theme of "plain living and
hard struggle," as discussed earlier in "Setting a New Agenda," reflected a long
Party tradition that Hu chose to play up at Xibaipo, and the "people-centered"
theme had been the subject of intellectual and Party contemplation since at
least the 1980s. In addition, Hu had been careful to press these themes in
terms of continuity with the leadership of his predecessor Jiang Zemin.

The Hu leadership's promotion of a "scientific development concept"
(*kexue fazhan guan*) in the fall of 2003, however, marked a new ideological
departure.[109] In enunciating it, Hu Jintao nevertheless followed the classical pattern of putting forth a new formulation, employed, for example, by

105 Occasionally – in 1959, 1961, and 1970 – the leadership instead retired to the Jiangxi resort of Lushan.
106 *WHB*, 18 July 2003, trans. in *FBIS*, CPP20030718000062.
107 *XH*, 13 August 2003, available in *FBIS*, CPP20030813000147.
108 See Alice L. Miller, "Beijing prepares to convene the 17th Party Congress," *China Leadership Monitor*,
    22 (Fall 2007), 2–4.
109 For an analysis of the emergence of this concept, see Joseph Fewsmith, "Promoting the scientific
    development concept," *China Leadership Monitor*, 11 (Summer 2004).

Jiang Zemin in launching the "three represents" concept in early 2000. In remarks made during an inspection tour of Jiangxi – including Ruijin, site of Mao Zedong's rural Soviet base area in the late 1920s and early 1930s – Hu introduced the "scientific development concept" for the first time:

> It is necessary to adopt a scientific development concept of coordinated, all-round, and sustainable development, actively explore a new development path that conforms to reality, further improve the socialist market structure, combine intensified efforts to readjust structure with the cultivation of new economic growth points, combine the promotion of urban development with the promotion of rural development, combine efforts to bring into play the role of science and technology with efforts to bring into play the advantages of human resources, combine the development of the economy with the protection of resources and environment, combine opening up to the outside world with opening up other parts of the country, and strive to take a civilized development path characterized by the development of production, a well-off life, and a good ecological environment.[110]

In early October, on the eve of the Third Plenum, Hu again raised the concept during a tour of Hunan.[111]

The Third Plenum of the Sixteenth Central Committee, convened in Beijing on 11–14 October 2003, adopted a long "Decision on Several Issues Related to Perfecting the Socialist Market Economic System" that did not cite the "scientific development concept" explicitly, but clearly used the concept to frame its policy recommendations. The "Decision" thus stipulated the need for "overall planning" in five areas, each of which correlated directly to issues that the single-minded pursuit of economic growth had exacerbated and that the "scientific development concept" sought to address. These areas included the widening gap between urban and rural development; the uneven development among China's regions, particularly between the coastal provinces and the interior; the focus on economic development with little regard for its attendant social requirements and implications; the all-out pursuit of economic growth without regard for its environmental consequences; and the imbalance between export-driven growth and domestic consumption. The watchword of the new "overall planning" approach reflected in the "Decision" resonated strongly with Hu's phrasing of the "scientific development concept": "to steadfastly take people as the basis, to establish a concept of all-round, coordinated, and sustainable development, and to promote all-round economic, social, and human development."[112] Although the plenum decision did not explicitly

110 *XH*, 2 September 2003, available in *FBIS*, CPP20030902000029.
111 *XH*, 4 October 2003.
112 "Zhonggong zhongyang guanyu wanshan shehuizhuyi shichang jingji tizhi ruogan wenti de jueding" (CCP Central Committee decision on several issues related to perfecting the socialist market economic system), in *Shiliuda yilai zhongyao wenxian xuanbian*, 1.464–82.

cite Hu Jintao's formulation, he did elaborate on it explicitly in his talk to the plenum, which was not publicized at the time.[113]

In the wake of the plenum, the "scientific development concept" received authoritative endorsement in the Party newspaper *People's Daily*, confirming that the formulation now enjoyed consensus support among the broader leadership. This was also evident when the Politburo met on 24 November 2003, according to a *Xinhua* account that day, to review plans for economic work in 2004 on the basis of the "scientific development concept," to be presented to the annual central conference on economic work.[114] Over the next several months, the leaders in nearly uniform lock step repeated the "scientific development concept" formulation in their public remarks. In February, a "special study course" on "implanting and implementing the scientific development concept" was held in Beijing for ministerial and provincial-level leaders, at which Wen Jiabao delivered a long speech elaborating on the significance of the concept.[115] On 23 February 2004, the Politburo again endorsed the concept and the "people-centered" approach in reviewing arrangements for the Second Session of the Tenth NPC. Wen Jiabao's report on the work of the State Council to the NPC session on 16 March was framed in terms of the "scientific development concept" and the five areas of overall planning, now described as the "five balanced aspects."[116]

The emergence of the "scientific development concept" has been depicted in Chinese media as reflecting the CCP's maturing appreciation of the need for "overall planning" in developing a socialist market economy from several points of departure. Typically, an account by *Xinhua* on 9 November 2004 on the drafting of the plenum decision described it as a successor to the decision on economic reform adopted at the Third Plenum of the Fourteenth Central Committee in 1993 that launched the effort to create a "modern enterprise system." That effort produced side-effects and "new contradictions" – "uneven development between urban and rural areas, a lack of a fully developed system of property rights, market disorder, and an incomplete transformation of government functions" – that now were sharpened by complementary pressures of economic globalization and entry into the WTO. In addition, the group that drafted the decision was set up in the midst of the SARS crisis, which, according to the *Xinhua* account, "made us realize the existence of problems

113 Hu Jintao, "Shuli he luoshi kexue fazhan guan" (Implant and implement the scientific development concept), 14 October 2003, in *Shiliuda yilai zhongyao wenxian xuanbian*, 1: 483–4.
114 *XH*, 24 November 2003.
115 Wen Jiabao, "Tigao renshi, tongyi sixiang, laogu shuli he renzhen luoshi kexue fazhan guan" (Raise awareness, unify thinking, and firmly implant and conscientiously implement the scientific development concept), 21 February 2004, in *Shiliuda yilai zhongyao wenxian xuanbian*, 1.755–6, trans. in *SWB*, 23 February 2005.
116 Wen Jiabao, "Report to the 2nd session of the 10th NPC," delivered on 16 March 2004, *XH*, 16 March 2004, trans. in *FBIS*, CPP20040316000088.

of coordinating between economic and social development and between urban and rural development" and thus "the extreme importance of establishing and implementing a 'scientific development concept' calling for comprehensive, coordinated and sustainable development."[117] From a political perspective, however, the "scientific development concept" was the first major innovation of the Hu leadership and its first distinguishing policy departure from the Jiang era.

Building a "Socialist Harmonious Society"

The Hu leadership's broadening of economic reform to encompass its social and environmental consequences, encapsulated in the "scientific development concept" formulation, emerged in a setting of persistent and sharpening concern about social stability and political unrest. In the rural areas, stagnating incomes among peasant families resulted from the fall in prices for agricultural goods in the late 1990s, thus widening the disparity of incomes with people in the urban economy. As local government services withered, local officials imposed a bewildering array of taxes and fees on peasant households to augment local administrative budgets, and, with increasing frequency in collusion with developers, they forced peasants off their farms by buying out their land contracts at low rates of compensation, leaving peasant families without a livelihood. The flow of rural workers coming from the countryside to the cities in hopes of work and a higher living standard began to create a sizable "floating population" in the 1980s, but by the late 1990s the rate of migration was escalating.[118] In the cities, workers left unemployed and laid-off from the reform of the state-owned enterprise system in the late 1990s faced uncertain futures, despite government efforts to set up employment centers to assist them in finding new work. Meanwhile, with the dissolution of the state-owned sector's welfare functions, many urban residents were left to fend for themselves with regard to retirement, education for their children, and health care. In China's "autonomous regions" where large populations of ethnic minorities reside, longstanding disaffection and unrest festered over a broad range of economic, cultural and religious, and nationalistic tensions.

The leadership's concerns over social stability were thus not without foundation. Authoritative discussions elaborating the "scientific development

117 Sun Chengbin, and Zhao Cheng, "Chui xiang jingji tizhi gaige de xin haojiao – Zhonggong zhongyang guanyu wanshan shehuizhuyi shichang jingji tizhi ruogan wenti de jueding qicao gongzuo jishi" (Sounding a new clarion call to reform the economic system – An account of the process of drafting the CCP Central Committee decision on several issues in perfecting the socialist market economic system), *Dangde shenghuo*, 11 (2003), 16–19, trans. in *FBIS*, CPP20031109000025.
118 The figures are estimated to be 70 million in 1988, 100 million in 1997, and 200 million by 2008. Kam Wing Chan, "Internal labour migration in China: Trends, geographical distribution and policies," UN Population Division, UN/POP/EGM-URB/2008/05, 3 January 2008.

concept" in early 2005 noted that per capita GDP in China had reached US$1,000 and could be expected to rise to US$3,000 by 2020 if the goal of establishing a "well-off society" was achieved. This transition, these analyses warned, meant that China had entered a critical period of opportunity but also of potential danger. In the latter case, "the polarization between rich and poor grows, the jobless population increases, the urban-rural and interregional disparities widen, social conflicts intensify, the ecological environment deteriorates, and so on, leading to long-term stagnation in economic and social development and even social upheaval and retrogression."[119] In addition, official statistics in the mid-2000s published in the media pointed to the growing number of "mass incidents," increasing tenfold from 8,700 in 1993 to 87,000 in 2005. Although what exactly counted as a "mass incident" is not entirely clear, there was no doubt about the overall trend. In addition, articles by social scientists in the media warned about the dangers of widening income disparities, not only between urban and rural citizens but also, as some Chinese became very rich, among residents of the cities. An article by Vice Minister of Finance Lou Jiwei in the Central Party School newspaper *Study Times* in June 2006 noted that the Gini coefficient – a scale of income inequality in society – had reached 0.46, a level that portended serious social instability and that raised major issues of "social justice" and "fairness."[120]

These perceptions of social instability in part led Beijing to attempt to redress its causes. In December 2005, for example, a set of Central Committee-State Council "opinions" circulated as Central Document No.1 of 2006 that called for the creation of a "new socialist countryside," seeking to alleviate what had been called the "three rural issues" (*sannong*) since the 1998 Third Plenum decision on agriculture. The document called for new subsidies and price supports for agricultural products to help offset sagging peasant incomes, enhanced government support for rural infrastructure and services, and strengthened protection of land-use rights against official-entrepreneurial predation. Also, the document called for the abolition of the agricultural tax, which Premier Wen Jiabao announced outright at the NPC session two months later.[121]

119 Wen Jiabao, "Tigao renshi, tongyi sixiang, laogu shuli he renzhen luoshi kexue fazhan guan." See also Ren Zhongping, "Zai gan yige ershi nian: Lun woguo gaige fazhan de guanjian shike" (Do it for another 20 years: On the crucial period in China's reforms and development), *RMRB*, 12 July 2004, 1,2, trans. in OSC, CPP20040712000083.
120 Lou Jiwei, "Guanyu xiaolu, gongping, gongzheng xianghu de ruogan sikao" (Some thoughts on the relationship between efficiency, fairness, and justice), *Xuexi shibao*, 19 June 2006, 1–5, trans. in OSC, CPP20060713442001.
121 "Zhonggong zhongyang, Guowuyuan guanyu tuijin shehuizhuyi xin nongcun jianshe de ruogan yijian" (Some opinions of the Central Committee and State Council for advancing the establishment of a new socialist countryside), 31 December 2005, in *Shiliuda yilai zhongyao wenxian xuanbian*, 3.139–55. For an English translation, see OSC, CPP20060221045001.

Although attempting to alleviate social tensions through new policy pitches, the regime at the same time displayed no inclination to tolerate agitation and dissent. In some cases, local officials responded to local unrest and agitation – some of which their own actions had provoked – with forceful suppression, and in some of these cases, central authorities in Beijing could intervene, chastening misdeeds of local officialdom in provoking mass protests and presenting itself as the agent of reform on behalf of the people. But, reminded of the potential for social unrest to provoke political upheaval exhibited by the "color revolutions" in the former Soviet republics of Georgia in 2003, Ukraine in 2004, and in Kyrgyzstan in 2005, the central leadership showed no hesitation to deploy force when it believed that prudence recommended it, as in the case of unrest in Tibet in March 2008 and in Xinjiang in July 2009. And to further constrain the use of electronic media to spark social unrest, in September 2005 the State Council Information Office and Ministry of Industry and Information issued new regulations on the Internet, including proscriptions against content that "instigates illegal assembly, association, processions or demonstrations" or "organizes people to disturb social order" and against content circulated "in the name of illegal civil society organizations."[122]

In this context, the Sixth Plenum of the Sixteenth Central Committee met on 8–11 October 2006 to adopt a long resolution on "building a socialist harmonious society." Jiang Zemin's work report to the Sixteenth Party Congress in November 2002 had set "social harmony" as a priority. But the goal of building a "socialist harmonious society" was first put forward in authoritative Party statements only in the fall of 2004, in the Central Committee resolution on improving the CCP's ability to govern adopted at the Fourth Plenum in September that year. Thereafter, Hu Jintao set down the elements of a "socialist harmonious society" in a major speech at the Central Party School in February 2005. The goal was incorporated into the "proposals" for compiling the Eleventh Five-Year Plan adopted at the Fifth Plenum in October 2005. On 4 March 2006, during a meeting with delegates to the CPPCC, Hu laid out eight standards of "honor and disgrace" as the foundation of a civic ethics to be incorporated into the "socialist harmonious society." These standards were further elaborated upon by an authoritative set of "opinions" formulated by the Central Committee's Committee for Guiding the Building of Socialist Spiritual Civilization.[123]

---

122 State Council Information Office and the Ministry of Information Industry, "Rules on the management of Internet news information services," 25 September 2005; available at http://www.cecc.gov/pages/virtualAcad/index.phpd?showsingle=24396 (accessed 9 August 2010).
123 *XH*, 23 May 2006.

The long resolution adopted at the Sixth Plenum on "major issues concerning the building of a socialist harmonious society" thus culminated a two-year effort under the Hu leadership to lay out a programmatic Party response to the daunting array of social tensions that had sharpened as a consequence of the economic reforms set in motion in the late 1990s. Setting out a series of priorities in Party work spanning the years until 2020, the resolution aimed at addressing several issues that figured prominently in the maintenance of social stability and political order. These included an endorsement of steps to provide adequate social services and legal processes in rural areas, under the rubric of "building a new socialist countryside," to stem incidents of rural disaffection and unrest; a call to redress imbalances in regional development after two decades of emphasis on rapid economic growth in China's coastal regions by directing accelerated central revenue transfers to the central and western provinces; renewed emphasis on expanding education and a new focus on ensuring access to educational opportunities in China's less-developed regions through enhanced central allocations of resources; reconstruction of China's medical and public-health services that had been debilitated by the dissolution of the formerly state-owned and collective work-unit economy; and enhanced attention to the environmental impact of economic development. The object of these efforts, according to the resolution, was to create "a socialist society that is democratic and law-based, fair and just, trustworthy and friendly, full of vigor and vitality, secure and orderly, and in which man and nature are in harmony."[124]

Some observers have seen in the resolution's focus on the goal of "social harmony" and in the values enshrined in Hu Jintao's "eight honors and disgraces" a resurrection of elements of Confucian tradition in Chinese political discourse. There is no denying that the emphasis on harmony in Chinese society directly contradicts the preoccupation with "class struggle" during the Mao era. But the ideological lineage of the "socialist harmonious society" concept and of the values Hu was promoting seem much more akin to the idea of a "party of the whole people" advanced in the 1961 Party program of the CPSU and the values associated with it than to the values of traditional Confucianism. Not surprisingly, PRC media commentary in the wake of the plenum dissociated the "socialist harmonious society" idea from both traditions.[125]

---

124 "Zhonggong zhongyang guanyu goujian shehuizhuyi hexie shehui ruogan zhongda wenti de jueding" (Resolution of the CCP Central Committee on major issues concerning the building of a socialist harmonious society), 14 October 2003, in *Shiliuda yilai zhongyao wenxian xuanbian*, 3.648–71, trans. in OSC, CPP20061018707007.

125 On this point, see Alice L. Miller, "Hu Jintao and the Sixth Plenum," *China Leadership Monitor*, 20 (Winter 2007).

Building the Party's Governing Capacity

Hu Jintao's efforts early in his tenure as general secretary to introduce a modicum of transparency into the Party's decision making and operations were followed by several steps intended, in the jargon of the day, to enhance the CCP's "governing capacity" as a "ruling party." These efforts proceeded from the call in Jiang Zemin's report to the Sixteenth CCP Congress in 2002 for steps to "improve the Party's style of leadership and governance," including a "scientific and democratic" approach to leadership decision making, changes in Party procedure to reinforce collective leadership and "democratic" processes, greater accountability to law and to the governed, and curbs on corruption. As in the case of the enhanced transparency to leadership meetings that began immediately after the Party congress, some of these efforts traced their origins to the aborted political reform agenda of the 1987 Thirteenth CCP Congress under Zhao Ziyang's leadership. Such efforts were given added impetus, however, by the new problems of governance of a society and economy that had been significantly transformed since the late 1990s and by the leadership's perceptions of the fate of political parties in other countries – in the USSR and Mexico, for example – facing social and political upheaval.

These considerations motivated a steady stream of new Party regulations and directives, including most notably the "CCP Regulations for Inner-Party Supervision," disseminated for trial implementation in February 2004.[126] These and other steps were reinforced by a lengthy "Decision on Enhancing the Party's Ability to Govern," adopted at the Fourth Plenum convened in Beijing on 16–19 September 2004, which in general terms authorized Party efforts on a number of fronts. As spelled out more explicitly in plenum commentary, these included further trial implementation of "permanent tenure" for Party congresses, by which Party congresses at various levels would meet in annual session – or, when necessary, in ad hoc session – to review the work of their subordinate decision-making bodies and extend or deny them a vote of confidence, making the Party congress at each level "the Party's supreme organ of power." Also authorized were steps already encompassed in the "Regulations on Inner-Party Supervision" to enhance the autonomy of and give teeth to the Party's discipline inspection commissions so that they would be able more effectively to root out abuses of power by leaders and the networks of corruption that comprise the "family kingdoms" of "power-grabbing" top leaders.[127] The decision also called for new, broadened voting procedures to appoint and promote Party officials and reinforce collective decision making.

---

126 "(Trial) CPC regulations on inner-party supervision," *XH*, 17 February 2004, available in *SWB*, 19 February 2004.

127 *DGB*, 14 July 2004; *WHB*, 26 August 2004.

Finally, the plenum decision authorized a Party-wide campaign to promote the "advanced nature" of Party members that had commenced in January 2005 and that proceeded in three stages over an eighteen-month period.

Many of the efforts to reform the CCP proceeded on a trial basis at lower levels of the Party, with the implication that they would eventually be extended to Party institutions at the central levels. How soon such efforts will begin to affect leadership politics at the center is not clear. But among the steps to advance "inner-Party democratic reform" of leadership selection mechanisms, perhaps the most intriguing was the use of a straw poll to nominate candidates for the Politburo to be elected at the First Plenum of the Seventeenth CCP Congress. According to a report transmitted only after the congress, on 25 June 2007 Hu Jintao had presided over a meeting of some 400 members and alternates of the Sixteenth Central Committee and "relevant responsible comrades" who voted on a "recommendation ballot" of nearly 200 names. This procedure of "democratic recommendation" (*minzhu tuicun*) produced a short list of names that subsequently the Politburo and its Standing Committee took into consideration when compiling the final list of candidates to be submitted to the Seventeenth Congress. *Xinhua* heralded the straw-poll procedure as providing "experience in perfecting the mechanism for selecting Party and state leaders and promoting the institutionalization, standardization, and proceduralization (*zhiduhua, guifanhua, chengxuhua*) for the replacement of high-level Party and state veterans with younger ones" and having "great significance for further developing inner-Party democracy and perfecting the inner-Party democratic system."[128]

THE SEVENTEENTH CCP CONGRESS AND AFTER

The convocation of the Seventeenth CCP Congress on 15–21 October 2007 and the leadership appointments made at the First Plenum the day after the congress closed afforded the opportunity to assess how much Hu Jintao was able to gain ratification of the policy initiatives that he had pressed for during his first term as Party top leader and to assess how much he had been able to consolidate his power as China's paramount leader. On both counts, Hu had come a long way. The Party congress was important in other respects as well, most notably in taking steps to prepare for the leadership succession in 2012.

<hr>

128 Liu Xiyang, Liu Gang, and Sun Chengbin, "Weile dang he guojia xingwang fada changzhi jiu'an: Dangde xinyijie zhongyang lingdao jigou chansheng jilu" (Shouldering the great trust of the Party and the people: An account of the birth of the new CCP Central Committee and its Commission for Discipline Inspection), *XH*, 21 October 2007, available in *SWB/Asia Pacific*, 24 October 2007.

The months following the Party congress were filled with anticipation of Beijing's hosting of the Olympic Games in August 2008, a moment of anticipated triumph symbolizing, from Beijing's perspective, China's successful engagement in the world after a century and a half of trials and humiliation, paralleling the significance for Japan of the 1964 games in Tokyo and for South Korea of the 1988 games in Seoul. Soon after the conclusion of the Beijing games, however, the regime faced a new challenge arising from China's deep engagement with the world economy. In the fall of 2008, the major downturn in the world economy triggered by the burst bubble in the American financial system threatened severe cutbacks in China's export-led economy, portending slowing economic growth and attendant unemployment and potential social unrest and political agitation. An adroitly managed injection of stimulus funding into the domestic economy in early November 2008 blunted the impact of the sagging world economic trends, however, and by the following summer Beijing appeared confident of its ability to weather the crisis as it looked forward to celebrating the sixtieth anniversary of the PRC.

The Seventeenth Party Congress and Hu's Power

Change in the top leadership at the Seventeenth Party Congress was markedly less dramatic in scale than that at the Sixteenth Congress in 2002, which had seen a turnover of leadership generations. This time, only four of the nine members of the PSC retired and were replaced by four new members. Where fifteen of the twenty-five members of the broader Politburo were new in 2002, only nine of the twenty-five were added in 2007. All of those retiring at the congress had reached the age of sixty-eight or older, and so the retirement norm implemented at the Sixteenth Party Congress in 2002 continued to hold. Changes in the membership of the Party Secretariat and CMC were also more limited than in 2002.

Furthermore, there was strong continuity in the attributes shared by the members of the new Party leadership. The average age of the members of the new Politburo was sixty-three on appointment, slightly older than the average of sixty for members of the 2002 Politburo – not a surprising result given that the congress was midway between the anticipated ten-year tenure for leaders appointed in 2002. By regional origin, the new Politburo membership was somewhat more evenly balanced. Only ten leaders hailed from the coastal provinces, whereas fifteen were from the central provinces and none were from the western regions.

The new Politburo furthered the trend of the 1990s by electing leaders who held university degrees. Among the new Politburo's twenty-five members, twenty-three had university degrees, compared to twenty-two who held university degrees on the 2002 Politburo. For the first time, the new Politburo included a smaller proportion of "technocratic" leaders – those with university degrees in engineering or the hard sciences. The 1997 Politburo had counted sixteen of seventeen degree-holders in these fields, including fourteen engineers, whereas the 2002 Politburo had counted seventeen engineers and one geologist among its twenty-two degree-holders. Among the twenty-three degree-holders on the new Politburo, only eleven were engineers and two were in the hard sciences or mathematics. The remaining ten degree-holders included four economists, one political scientist, and three in the humanities. Finally, for the first time the new Politburo included several holders of advanced degrees. Three members – Xi Jinping, Li Yuanchao, and Liu Yandong – had law degrees, Li Keqiang a doctorate in economics, and two members had master's degrees.

With regard to military experience, twenty-two of the Politburo's twenty-five members had none, either through service in the PLA or through work in the military bureaucracies. The three exceptions included two professional military men concurrently serving in high military posts and, significantly, Xi Jinping. In summary, the new Politburo leadership extended trends evident in leadership attributes over the past two decades. It was the best-educated leadership in PRC history, less thoroughly technocratic, and still starkly civilian in experience.

From an institutional perspective, the size of the PSC remained at nine members, reinforcing the impression that the expansion of that body in 2002 was intended in part to support an enhanced role in the structure of central leadership organs. The roles of the new Standing Committee members closely followed the pattern of work assignments in the 2002 body:

Hu Jintao	CCP general secretary; PRC president; director, Central Committee (CC) Foreign Affairs and Taiwan Affairs Leading Small Groups
Wu Bangguo	NPC chairman
Wen Jiabao	State Council premier; director, CC Finance and Economy Leading Small Group
Jia Qinglin	CPPCC chairman
Li Changchun	Director, CC Propaganda and Ideology Leading Small Group
Xi Jinping	Executive secretary, Secretariat
Li Keqiang	Executive vice premier
He Guoqiang	Central Discipline Inspection Commission chairman
Zhou Yongkang	Director, CC Politics and Law Committee

That Hu Jintao managed to consolidate his power within the top leadership was evident for several reasons. For one, the "Shanghai Gang" – leaders promoted into the leadership by Jiang Zemin – was significantly diminished by the leadership changes at the congress. Foremost among these changes was the retirement from the PSC of Zeng Qinghong, Jiang's closest crony in the leadership, having reached the age of sixty-eight. In addition, Shanghai Party chief Chen Liangyu had already been removed from power in Shanghai and from the Politburo on charges of corruption in 2006, reportedly with Jiang Zemin's acquiescence. By some accounts, Chen had vocally resisted efforts by Wen Jiabao to rein in investment and so may have aroused the ire of both Wen and Hu, perhaps making him already a marked man. His removal for corruption also immediately brought to mind the removal on corruption charges of Beijing Party chief Chen Xitong in 1995, an event that aided Jiang Zemin's efforts to consolidate his power leading up to the Fifteenth Party Congress. It seems likely that Chen Liangyu was targeted for removal ahead of the Seventeenth Congress. In any case, his fall abetted the dissolution of the "Shanghai Gang," as did the death of PSC member Huang Ju in June 2007. Most of the adherents of the Jiang group remaining in the leadership, such as PSC member Jia Qinglin and Politburo member Liu Qi, appeared to be weak figures and no obstacle to Hu's power.

Complementing the decline of the "Shanghai Gang" was Hu's ability to promote his own allies on to the Politburo. These included Li Keqiang on the PSC, as well as Organization Department director Li Yuanchao, Guangdong Party chief Wang Yang, and former United Front Work Department director Liu Yandong on to the larger Politburo. All of these leaders shared associations with Hu going back to his leadership of the Communist Youth League in the early 1980s. In addition, Hu managed to install his personal chief of staff Ling Jihua as director of the Party General Office. Placing his own ally in charge of this body was critical to the power of the Party general secretary so as to steer the leadership in directions to his liking. Jiang Zemin had placed his own man – his chief of staff Zeng Qinghong – in this key post in 1993.

Hu also established a surer hold over the Party *nomenklatura* with the appointment of his ally Li Yuanchao as Organization Department director immediately after the Seventeenth Party Congress. The Party's appointment process has traditionally been managed by a trio composed of the general secretary, the executive secretary of the Secretariat, and the director of the Organization Department, who would facilitate the process in nominating personnel changes sanctioned by the Politburo and its Standing Committee. During Hu's first term as general secretary, the process was thus managed by Hu, Zeng Qinghong, and former Organization Department chief He Guo-qiang – a line-up that Hu likely could not unilaterally dominate. The new line-up would bring Hu together with Xi Jinping and his ally Li Yuanchao. In this trio, Xi, as presumptive successor, would have an incentive to work with Hu.

Finally, the hallmark theme of Hu Jintao's first term as general secretary – the "scientific development concept" – was written into the preamble of the

Party Constitution. The "scientific development concept," the constitution now declared, "is a scientific theory that is in the same line as Marxism-Leninism, Mao Zedong Thought, Deng Xiaoping Theory, and the important thought of Three Represents and keeps up with the times" and so "an important guiding principle for China's economic and social development and a major strategic thought that must be upheld and applied in developing socialism with Chinese characteristics." Embedding this formulation in the Party's foundational document added to its authority in subsequent leadership policy making and reflected a signal achievement by Hu.

Although Hu gained a stronger hand in leadership decision making in key areas owing to the Party congress, it is also notable that his authority was not comparably elevated. One of the remarkable developments of Hu's first term as the Party's top leader was that the trappings of paramount leadership previously accorded to Deng Xiaoping and, after Deng, Jiang Zemin, were not extended to Hu. During his tenure as general secretary, Jiang was routinely referred to in PRC media as "the core" of the "Fifteenth Central Committee leadership collective," but Hu Jintao after 2002 was not accorded such stature and was instead referred to consistently by an alternative formulation that suggested that Hu was simply *primus inter pares* in the Politburo. Thus, the media consistently referred only to "the Sixteenth Central Committee leadership collective with Comrade Hu Jintao as general secretary." In addition, throughout Hu's first term as the Party's top leader, none of the ideological departures of the era during Hu's leadership – "people-centered" governance, the effort to develop a "new socialist countryside," building a "socialist harmonious society," and promoting a "scientific development concept" with respect to economic growth – were hailed as the contribution of Hu's individual genius or as his sole intellectual property. Instead, they were advertised as products of the collective leadership.

This failure before the Seventeenth Congress to accord Hu Jintao the trappings of paramount power might be explained on the grounds that he had not yet consolidated sufficient power as the Party's top leader. Alternatively, the formulations according Hu status only as first among equals in the leadership and the attribution of theoretical advances to the broader collective leadership rather than to Hu alone might be interpreted as consistent with a new political dynamic of collective leadership that played down the role of the general secretary. The persistence of the trappings of collective leadership rather than those of Hu's dominant power in the wake of the Seventeenth Party Congress, even as Hu strengthened his actual power in the leadership at the congress, underscores that the latter interpretation is likely correct.

The image of collective leadership in an oligarchy of Party leaders is reinforced by two other observations – the apparent balancing of institutional constituencies on the Politburo and the limited representation on that body by the PLA. Aside from the placement of the heads of the major hierarchies on the Standing Committee – the Party general secretary, the NPC chairman and the premier, and the chairman of the CPPCC – the number of leaders working concurrently in the Party apparatus, in state institutions, and in the provinces has been closely balanced, evidently to inhibit the ability of any single bloc – or the general secretary – from dominating the body. An abiding concern to constrain the power of the general secretary may also be the reason why PLA representation on the Politburo since 1997 has been limited to two members.

Preparing for Succession

The elevation of Xi Jinping and Li Keqiang on to the PSC – neither had previously served on the Politburo – appeared to prepare both men to succeed to the top in 2012 and 2013. Both the rank of Xi and Li on the Standing Committee and their respective work assignments after the Party congress indicate that Xi was being prepared to replace Hu Jintao as Party chief at the Eighteenth CCP Congress in 2012 and that Li was being groomed to succeed Wen Jiabao as premier.

Speculation and rumors about who might emerge as Hu's successor flourished preceding the Party congress, with many observers predicting in favor of one of Hu's cronies – Li Keqiang or Li Yuanchao, in particular. A number of factors likely favored Xi's selection as Hu's prospective successor. He was the son of Xi Zhongxun, a prominent veteran communist revolutionary and longtime supporter of Deng Xiaoping, and so a "princeling" – a person of reliable communist bloodlines. His education combined a degree in chemical engineering from China's top engineering school, Qinghua University, with postgraduate study in Marxist theory and a law degree. He had extensive provincial experience, having risen through the ranks to the top of Fujian's Party and government hierarchy over the years 1985–2002, followed by five years' experience as governor and then Party secretary of Zhejiang and a brief six-month stint as Party chief of Shanghai. By all accounts, he had a clean record without blemish of corruption in his years in the provinces. He was fifty-four years old on appointment to the PSC at the Seventeenth Party Congress, and so would be fifty-nine upon succession to Hu Jintao as Party general secretary in 2012 – thus eligible for two five-year terms before retirement. Alone among the new Politburo members he had important military experience, having served, according to his official biography, three years as "an active duty officer" in the CMC General Office, giving him firsthand acquaintance with the top-level processes of Party-military relations. He was neither a protégé of Jiang's "Shanghai Gang" nor of Hu Jintao, thus satisfying a critical element in oligarchic politics – that the reigning paramount leader not dictate his own successor. Finally, he had a glamorous wife – the folksinger Peng Liyuan.

The array of posts that Xi was given alongside his placement on the PSC also suggested that he was being groomed to succeed Hu. Replicating the pattern of Hu's appointments during his rise to power in the 1990s, Xi was made executive secretary of the Secretariat at the First Plenum of the Seventeenth Central Committee on 22 October, and in December he was made president of the Central Party School. At the Eleventh NPC in March 2008, Xi was also appointed PRC vice president. These appointments together suggested that the same pattern of staggered appointments to key posts in Hu's rise was being used to prepare Xi to succeed Hu Jintao in 2012.

However, the Fourth Plenum of the Seventeenth Central Committee on 15–18 September 2009 raised momentary doubts about this succession scenario. Based on the pattern of appointments given Hu, Xi might have been expected to be appointed vice chairman of the CMC, placing him directly beneath Hu on that body and preparing him to succeed to leadership over the military, perhaps in 2014. The Fourth Plenum, however, made no such appointment, raising speculations that the succession arrangements were unraveling, perhaps by Hu himself so as to replace Xi as his successor with Li Keqiang. Nevertheless, the work assignments of neither Xi nor Li were altered in the wake of the plenum. Xi continued to run the Party apparatus on Hu's behalf, whereas Li continued to work exclusively in the State Council as Wen Jiabao's apparent understudy. It is possible, therefore, that the leadership intends that Xi will succeed Hu in 2012 but according to different procedures – possibly as a model of the "democratic" selection procedures employed in June 2007 prior to the Seventeenth Congress.[129] On that score, only time will tell.

THE PEOPLE'S REPUBLIC AT SIXTY

China celebrated the sixtieth anniversary of the People's Republic on 1 October 2009 with an enormous parade in Beijing testifying to the progress the country had made since 1949. China was indeed worlds apart from the place it had been when the PRC was founded, far different from the country when Mao Zedong died in 1976, and also different from what it was in 1997 when Deng Xiaoping died. Uncertainties abounded, but China in 2009 was far richer and much stronger than at any point in its modern history.

China's political order was also perceptibly different from what it had been only fifteen years earlier. The transformation of China's economy in the

129 On these issues, see Alice L. Miller, "The case of Xi Jinping and the mysterious succession," *China Leadership Monitor*, 30 (Fall 2009), and "The preparation of Li Keqiang," ibid., 31 (Winter 2010).

late 1990s and China's embrace of a globalizing world had resulted in a more complex market-based economy, a more pluralistic society, and an increasingly wired and sophisticated populace, raising problems of governance that the CCP had never previously faced. In its effort to become a "ruling party," the CCP, numbering seventy-seven million members, had been transformed in the process. No longer a strictly "worker-peasant-soldier" proletarian party, it had become by 2009, judging by the statistics on the educational credentials and professional backgrounds of its membership, a party that Mao Zedong likely would have considered "bourgeois." Certainly, the degree of income disparities resulting from, if not encouraged by, Party policy since the late 1990s and the Party's still-controversial vision of a "socialist harmonious society" would have given the chairman pause.

The political order in 2009 was also far more institutionalized than it had been in 1995. The foundations of this transformation were laid in the early 1980s by Deng Xiaoping, who regarded the restoration of organizational authority and institutional routine essential both to guide China's modern-ization and to inhibit a recurrence of the disastrous unpredictability of the emphasis on "revolutionary" spontaneity of the late Mao era. Since the 1980s, the processes of politics were more clearly routinized, as Party congresses, Central Committee plenums, NPC sessions, and State Council meetings, and the corresponding events at lower levels, met on schedules prescribed by the Party and state constitutions. These processes in turn generated institutional routines in subordinate bureaucracies that were required to draft budgets, draft plans and proposals, and gather information and statistics. Over time, the political system appeared more reliably stable and thus more predictable.

The institutionalization of politics also transformed the acutely sensitive question of succession. Formal term limits on government posts prescribed during the Deng era and internally set norms for turnover in Party leadership positions beneath the very top of the political system were visibly in force throughout the late 1990s and on through the following decade. Promotion and retirement criteria for PLA officers set down in the late 1980s and refined in 1994 produced both a routinized turnover of leadership generations in the military and a more professionalized officer corps. At the top, the evident adherence to the age limit of sixty-eight at the 2002 and 2007 Party congresses suggested that the politics of succession, although perhaps still evolving, was well along the road to institutionalization. Finally, the delivery in 2002 of an orderly and planned retirement of the paramount leader in favor of a younger man prepared to succeed to the top position of the political system was an achievement without precedent in PRC history or, for that matter, in the history of the former Soviet Union. As of 2009, the Party leadership appeared to be working to accomplish the same in 2012.

Across the Hu period, the leadership appeared to be operating much more clearly as an oligarchy. The absence of the trappings of paramount leadership attached to Hu Jintao, who has never been described as the leadership's "core leader," and the fastidious ascription of the Hu era's ideological innovations – including the signature formulation of a "scientific development concept" – to the leadership as a whole bespoke a deliberate effort to reduce the stature of the Party general secretary and to recast him as only first among equals. In addition, the complexity of the governing challenges the Party addressed since the late 1990s encouraged making bureaucratic representation and technical and administrative expertise an increasingly important criterion for membership on the Politburo. This did not mean that leaders no longer formed factions and coalitions, advocated distinctive policy viewpoints, or struggled for power. It seems increasingly apparent, however, that they did so within the hierarchies of an increasingly institutionalized political system.

Finally, civil-military relations crossed a watershed during the Jiang and Hu eras. Jiang Zemin was the first thoroughly civilian leader to assume command of the military in a century of militarized politics in China. Beginning with Yuan Shikai's leadership of the Republic established in 1912, through Chiang Kai-shek's re-creation of the Republic in Nanjing in 1928, and through Mao Zedong's and Deng Xiaoping's leadership of the PRC, China's leaders have either been professional military men or revolutionary veterans with extensive military-command experience. Jiang Zemin's appointment as chairman of both the Party and state CMCs after Deng retired from those positions in 1989 and 1990 – a remarkable step only months after the Tiananmen crisis and amid concerns about PLA responsiveness to the political leadership – and Hu Jintao's appointment to those posts in 2004 and 2005 broke that pattern.

Together, all of these changes have strengthened the political system. But whether they are sufficient to enable the CCP to remain in power is an open question. The regime's hold on power is constantly challenged by a rapidly evolving economy, an increasingly restive society, and a turbulent and globalized international order in which Beijing is a more important player. As both the Jiang and Hu leaderships observed repeatedly since the 1990s, the CCP cannot afford to stand still. In addition, as Aristotle observed, oligarchy is a difficult politics to sustain. Stable collective leadership requires a constant effort to resist attempts by any single leader – and especially the general secretary – to establish a paramount position of dominance over the other members of the leadership collective and, at the same time, attempts by any leader to fracture the collective by reaching out to outside constituencies. Finally, although absolute command of civilian authority over the military has been in place for two decades, it has also never been tested in times of crisis.

For all of these reasons, projecting China's political trajectory is a treacherous undertaking. And so from the perspective of 2009, the leadership watching the spectacular parade atop the Tiananmen rostrum had reason to be both confident and apprehensive.

APPENDIX: LEADERS AND MEETINGS

Party leaders, 1992–2010

Fourteenth CCP Congress (12–18 October 1992)

Politburo Standing Committee

Jiang Zemin*, Li Peng, Qiao Shi, Li Ruihuan, Zhu Rongji, Liu Huaqing, Hu Jintao

Full members

(stroke order): Ding Guan'gen, Tian Jiyun, Zhu Rongji, Qiao Shi, Liu Huaqing, Jiang Zemin, Li Peng, Li Lanqing, Li Tieying, Li Ruihuan, Yang Baibing, Wu Bangguo, Zou Jiahua, Chen Xitong++, Hu Jintao, Jiang Chunyun, Qian Qichen, Wei Jianxing, Xie Fei, Tan Shaowen+

*General Secretary
Huang Ju, added September 28, 1994 at the Fourth Plenum
+Deceased February 3, 1993
++Dismissed September 28, 1995 at the Fifth Plenum

Alternate members

Wen Jiabao, Wang Hanbin

Fifteenth CCP Congress (12–18 September 1997)

Politburo Standing Committee

Jiang Zemin*, Li Peng, Zhu Rongji, Li Ruihuan, Hu Jintao, Wei Jianxing, Li Lanqing

*General Secretary

Full members:

(stroke order): Ding Guan'gen, Tian Jiyun, Li Changchun, Li Tieying, Li Ruihuan, Wu Bangguo, Wu Guanzheng, Chi Haotian, Zhang Wannian, Luo Gan, Jiang Chunyun, Jia Qinglin, Qian Qichen, Huang Ju, Wen Jiabao, Xie Fei+

+Deceased October 27, 1999

Alternate members

Zeng Qinghong, Wu Yi (f)

Sixteenth CCP Congress (8–14 November 2002)

Politburo Standing Committee

Hu Jintao*, Wu Bangguo, Wen Jiabao, Jia Qinglin, Zeng Qinghong, Huang Ju+, Wu Guanzheng, Li Changchun, Luo Gan

*General Secretary

+Deceased June 2, 2007

Full members:

(stroke order): Wang Lequan, Wang Zhaoguo, Hui Liangyu, Liu Qi, Liu Yunshan, Wu Yi (f), Zhang Lichang, Zhang Dejiang, Chen Liangyu+, Zhou Yongkang, Yu Zhengsheng, He Guoqiang, Guo Boxiong, Cao Gangchuan, Zeng Peiyan

+Suspended 2006

Alternate member

Wang Gang

Seventeenth CCP Congress (15–21 October 2007)

Politburo Standing Committee

Hu Jintao*, Wu Bangguo, Wen Jiabao, Jia Qinglin, Li Changchun, Xi Jinping, Li Keqiang, He Guoqiang, Zhou Yongkang

*General Secretary

Full members

(stroke order): Wang Gang, Wang Lequan, Wang Zhaoguo, Wang Qishan, Hui Liangyu, Liu Qi, Liu Yunshan, Liu Yandong (f), Li Yuanchao, Wang Yang, Zhang Gaoli, Zhang Dejiang, Yu Zhengsheng, Xu Caihou, Guo Boxiong, Bo Xilai

State leaders, 1998–2010

Ninth NPC (5–19 March 1998)
  Head of State: **JIANG ZEMIN**
  Vice Head of State: **HU JINTAO**
  Chairman, NPC: **LI PENG**
  State Council Premier: **ZHU RONGJI**
  Vice Premiers: **LI LANQING, Qian Qichen, Wu Bangguo Wen Jiabao**
  (boldface and capitals indicate members of PSC at time of appointment)
  (boldface indicates members of the Politburo at time of appointment)

Tenth NPC (5–18 March 2003)
  Head of State: **HU JINTAO**
  Vice Head of State : **ZENG QINGHONG**
  Chairman, NPC: **WU BANGGUO**
  State Council Premier: **WEN JIABAO**
  Vice Premiers: **HUANG JU+, Wu Yi (f), Zeng Peiyan, Hui Liangyu**
  + Deceased June 2, 2007
  (boldface and capitals indicate members of PSC at time of appointment)
  (boldface indicates members of the Politburo at time of appointment)

Eleventh NPC (3–18 March 2008)
  Head of State: **HU JINTAO**
  Vice Head of State: **XI JINPING**
  Chairman, NPC: **WU BANGGUO**
  State Council Premier: **WEN JIABAO**
  Vice Premiers: **Li Keqiang, Hui Liangyu, Zhang Dejiang, Wang Qishan**
  (boldface and capitals indicate members of PSC at time of appointment)
  (boldface indicates members of the Politburo at time of appointment)

High-level Party Meetings, 1992–2010

CCP Fourteenth National Congress, Beijing	12–18 Oct. 1992
First Plenum	19 Oct. 1992
Second Plenum	5–7 Mar. 1993

Third Plenum — 11–14 Nov. 1993
Fourth Plenum — 25–28 Sept. 1994
Fifth Plenum — 25–28 Sept. 1995
Sixth Plenum — 7–10 Oct. 1996
Seventh Plenum — 6–9 Sept. 1997

CCP Fifteenth National Congress, Beijing — 12–18 Sept. 1997
First Plenum — 19 Sept. 1997
Second Plenum — 25–26 Feb. 1998
Third Plenum — 12–14 Oct. 1998
Fourth Plenum — 19–22 Sept. 1999
Fifth Plenum — 9–11 Oct. 2000
Sixth Plenum — 24–26 Sept. 2001
Seventh Plenum — 3–5 Nov. 2002

CCP Sixteenth National Congress, Beijing — 8–14 Nov. 2002
First Plenum — 15 Nov. 2002
Second Plenum — 24–26 Feb. 2003
Third Plenum — 11–14 Oct. 2003
Fourth Plenum — 16–19 Sept. 2004
Fifth Plenum — 8–11 Oct. 2005
Sixth Plenum — 8–11 Oct. 2006
Seventh Plenum — 9–12 Oct. 2007

CCP Seventeenth National Congress, Beijing — 15–21 Oct. 2007
First Plenum — 22 Oct. 2007
Second Plenum — 25–27 Feb. 2008
Third Plenum — 9–12 Oct. 2008
Fourth Plenum — 15–18 Sept. 2009
Fifth Plenum — 15–18 Oct. 2010

REFERENCES

"Adhere better to taking economic construction as the center." *RMRB* editorial, 22 February 1992, trans. in *FBIS Daily Report: China*, 24 February 1992, 40–1.

Agence France Presse. Press service.

"Agricultural cooperativization in communist China." *CB*, 373 (20 January 1956), 1–31.

Ahn, Byung-joon. *Chinese politics and the Cultural Revolution: Dynamics of policy processes.* Seattle, Wash. and London: University of Washington Press, 1976.

AJCA. Australian Journal of Chinese Affairs.

Amnesty International. *China: The massacre of June 1989 and its aftermath.* London: 1990.

Amnesty International. *China: Violations of human rights.* London: 1984.

[An Ziwen] An Tzu-wen. "Training the people's civil servants." *PC*, 1 January 1953, 8–11.

AS. Asian Survey.

Ashbrook, Arthur G., Jr. "China: Economic modernization and long-term performance," in U.S. Congress [97th], Joint Economic Committee, *China under the Four Modernizations*, 1.99–118.

Asian Survey: A monthly review of contemporary Asian affairs. Bimonthly. Berkeley: Institute of East Asian Studies, University of California Press, 1961–. Cited as *AS.*

Asiaweek. Weekly. Hong Kong: Asiaweek Ltd., 1975–2001.

Associated Press. News service.

Australian Journal of Chinese Affairs, The. Semiannual. Canberra: Contemporary China Centre, Australian National University, 1979–1995. Cited as *AJCA.*

Bachman, David. "Differing visions of China's post-Mao economy: The ideas of Chen Yun, Deng Xiaoping, and Zhao Ziyang." *AS*, 26.3 (March 1986), 292–321.

[*Baixing*] Pai-hsing. Monthly. Hong Kong: 1981–. Cited as *BX.*

Bao Ruo-wang (Jean Pasqualini), and Chelminski, Rudolph. *Prisoner of Mao.* New York: Coward, McCann, 1973.

Barnett, A. Doak. *Communist China: The early years, 1949–55.* New York: Praeger, 1964.

Barnett, A. Doak, with Ezra Vogel. *Cadres, bureaucracy and political power in communist China*. New York: Columbia University Press, 1967.

Bastid, Marianne. "Economic necessity and political ideals in educational reform during the Cultural Revolution." *CQ*, 42 (April–June 1970), 16–45.

Baum, Richard. *Burying Mao: Chinese politics in the age of Deng Xiaoping*. Princeton, N.J.: Princeton University Press, 1994.

Baum, Richard. "China: Year of the mangoes." *AS*, 9.1 (January 1969), 1–17.

Baum, Richard. "China in 1985: The greening of the revolution." *AS*, 26.1 (January 1986), 30–53.

Baum, Richard. "The Cultural Revolution in the countryside: Anatomy of a limited rebellion," in Thomas W. Robinson, ed., *The Cultural Revolution in China*, 367–476.

Baum, Richard. "Elite behavior under conditions of stress: The lesson of the 'Tang-ch'üan p'ai' in the Cultural Revolution," in Robert A. Scalapino, ed., *Elites in the People's Republic of China*, 540–74.

Baum, Richard. "The Fifteenth National Party Congress: Jiang takes command? *CQ*, 153 (March 1998), 141–56.

Baum, Richard. "Modernization and legal reform in post-Mao China: The rebirth of socialist legality." *SICC*, 19.2 (Summer 1986), 69–103.

Baum, Richard. "The perils of partial reform," in Richard Baum, ed., *Reform and reaction*, 1–17.

Baum, Richard. *Prelude to revolution: Mao, the Party, and the peasant question, 1962–66*. New York: Columbia University Press, 1975.

Baum, Richard, ed. *Reform and reaction in post-Mao China: The road to Tiananmen*. New York and London: Routledge, Chapman and Hall, 1991.

"Be more daring in carrying out reform." *RMRB* editorial, 24 February 1992, trans. in *FBIS Daily Report: China*, 24 February. 1992, 41–2.

Bei Dao. "Terugblik van een balling," in *Het Collective Geheugen: Over Literatuur En Geschiedenis*, 77–84.

Beijing Review. Cited as *BR*. See *Peking Review*.

Beijing wanbao (Beijing Evening News). Daily. Beijing.

Béja, Jean-Philippe. "The year of the dog: In the shadow of the ailing patriarch," in Lo Chi Kin, Suzanne Pepper, and Tsui Kai Yuen, eds., *China review, 1995*, ch. 1.

Bennett, Gordon A. *China's Eighth, Ninth, and Tenth Congresses, Constitutions, and Central Committees: An institutional overview and comparison*. Occasional Paper, no. 1. Austin: Center for Asian Studies, University of Texas, 1978.

Bennett, Gordon A., and Montaperto, Ronald N. *Red Guard: The political biography of Dai Hsiao-ai*. New York: Anchor Books, 1972; Garden City, N.Y.: Doubleday, 1971.

Bernstein, Thomas P. "China in 1984: The year of Hong Kong." *AS*, 25.1 (January 1985), 33–50.

Bernstein, Thomas P. *Up to the mountains and down to the villages: The transfer of youth from urban to rural China*. New Haven, Conn.: Yale University Press, 1977.

Binder, Leonard et al., contribs. *Crises and sequences in political development*. Studies in Political Development, no. 7. Princeton, N.J.: Princeton University Press, 1971.

Blecher, Marc J., and White, Gordon. *Micropolitics in contemporary China: A technical unit during and after the Cultural Revolution.* White Plains, N.Y.: M. E. Sharpe, 1979.

Bonavia, David. *Verdict in Peking: The trial of the Gang of Four.* New York: Putnam; London: Burnett Books, 1984.

BR. Beijing Review.

Bridgham, Philip. "The fall of Lin Piao." *CQ*, 55 (July–September 1973), 427–49.

Bridgham, Philip. "Mao's Cultural Revolution: The struggle to consolidate power." *CQ*, 41 (January–March 1970), 1–25.

Bridgham, Philip. "Mao's Cultural Revolution: The struggle to seize power." *CQ*, 34 (April–June 1968), 6–37.

British Broadcasting Corporation. *Summary of world broadcasts. Part 3: The far east.* Caversham Park, Reading: British Broadcasting Corporation, 1939–. Cited as *SWB/FE.*

Broad, William J. "Spies vs. sweat: The debate over China's nuclear advance." *NYT*, 7 September 1999.

"Build up a great wall of steel against peaceful evolution." *RMRB* Commentator, 16 August 1991, trans. in *FBIS Daily Report: China*, 19 August 1991, 27–8.

Bujin de sinian (Inexhaustible memories). Beijing: Zhongyang wenxian, 1987.

Burns, John P. "China's governance: Political reform in a turbulent environment." *CQ*, 119 (September 1989), 481–518.

Burns, John P. "Chinese civil service reform: The Thirteenth Party Congress proposals. *CQ*, 120 (December 1989), 739–70.

Burton, Barry. "The Cultural Revolution's ultraleft conspiracy: The 'May 16 Group.'" *AS*, 11.11 (November 1971), 1029–53.

Butterfield, Fox. *China: Alive in the bitter sea.* New York: Bantam Books, 1983; New York: Times Books, 1982.

BX. Baixing.

Cambridge History of China, The (CHOC). Vol. 1. *The Ch'in and Han empires, 221 B.C.–A.D. 220,* ed. Denis Twitchett and Michael Loewe (1986). Vol. 3. *Sui and T'ang China, 589–906, Part 1,* ed. Denis Twitchett (1979). Vol. 7. *The Ming Dynasty, 1368–1644, Part 1,* ed. Frederick W. Mote and Denis Twitchett (1988). Vol. 10. *Late Ch'ing 1800–1911, Part 1,* ed. John K. Fairbank (1978). Vol. 11. *Late Ch'ing 1800–1911, Part 2,* ed. John K. Fairbank and Kwang-Ching Liu (1980). Vol. 12. *Republican China 1912–1949, Part 1,* ed. John K. Fairbank (1983). Vol. 13. *Republican China 1912–1949, Part 2,* ed. John K. Fairbank and Albert Feuerwerker (1986). Vol. 14. *The People's Republic, Part 1: The emergence of revolutionary China 1949–1965,* ed. Roderick MacFarquhar and John K. Fairbank (1987). Vol. 15. *The People's Republic, Part 2: Revolutions within the Chinese revolution 1966–1982,* ed. Roderick MacFarquhar and John K. Fairbank (1991). Cambridge: Cambridge University Press.

Carrère d'Encausse, Hélène, and Schram, Stuart Reynolds, comps. *Marxism and Asia: An introduction with readings.* London: Allen Lane, Penguin Press, 1969.

CB. See U.S. Consulate General, *Current Background.*

CCP. *Resolution on CPC history (1949–81).* Beijing: FLP, 1981.

CCP CC Documents Research Office. Zhonggong zhongyang wenxian yanjiushi.

CCP CC Party History Research Office. Zhonggong zhongyang dangshi yanjiushi.

"CCP Central Committee's notification of the question of propagandizing and reporting on the struggle to seize power," 19 February 1967, in "Collection of documents."

CCP. Chinese Communist Party. Zhongguo gongchandang.

CCP documents of the Great Proletarian Cultural Revolution, 1966–1967. See Union Research Institute.

"The CCP issues Document No. 4, fully expounding expansion of opening up." DGB, 18 June 1992, trans. in FBIS Daily Report: China, 18 June 1992, 19–20.

CD. China Daily.

"Central authorities urge banks to draw bank loans and stop promoting the bubble economy." DGB, 1 July 1993, trans. in FBIS Daily Report: China, 1 July 1993, 31–2.

Chan, Anita. "Images of China's social structure: The changing perspectives of Canton students." World Politics, 34.3 (April 1982), 295–323.

Chan Kam Wing. "Internal labour migration in China: Trends, geographical distribution and policies." UN Population Division, UN/POP/EGM-URB/2008/05, 3 January 2008.

Chang, Parris H. "From Mao to Hua to Hu to Chao: Changes in the CCP leadership and its rule of the game." I&S, 25.1 (January 1989), 56–72.

Chang, Parris H. Power and policy in China. University Park: Pennsylvania State University Press, 1978 [1975].

Chang, Parris H. "Provincial Party leaders' strategies for survival during the Cultural Revolution," in Robert A. Scalapino, ed., Elites in the People's Republic of China, 501–39.

Chaoliu yuekan. Monthly. Hong Kong: 1987–92.

Ch'en, Jerome, ed. Mao. Englewood Cliffs, N.J.: Prentice-Hall, 1969.

Ch'en, Jerome, ed. Mao papers: Anthology and bibliography. London: Oxford University Press, 1970.

[Chen Jianbing] Chen Chien-ping. "The CCP Central Committee announces 16 measures." WHB (Hong Kong), 3 July 1993, trans. in FBIS Daily Report: China, 7 July 1993, 12–13.

[Chen Jianbing] Chen Chien-ping. "Zhu Rongji urges paying attention to negative effects of reform." WHB (Hong Kong), 13 January 1993, trans. in FBIS Daily Report: China, 15 January 1993, 27–8.

Chen, Nancy N. "Urban spaces and experiences of qigong," in Deborah S. Davis et al., eds., Urban spaces in Contemporary China, 347–61.

Chen Shihui. "Guanyu fandui Gao Gang, Rao Shushi fandang yinmo huodong de wenti" (Questions concerning opposition to the anti-Party conspiratorial activities of Gao Gang and Rao Shushi). In Jiaoxue cankao, xia.

Chen Yeping. "Have both political integrity, ability, stress political ability: On criteria for selecting cadres." RMRB, 1 September 1991, trans. in FBIS Daily Report: China, 6 September 1991, 26–31.

Chen Yuan. "Woguo jingji de shenceng wenti he xuanze (gangyao)" (China's deep-seated economic problems and choices [outline]). JJYJ, 4 (April 1991), 18–26.

[Chen Yun]. *Chen Yun wenxuan (1956–1985)* (Selected works of Chen Yun). Beijing: Renmin, 1986.

Chen Zaidao. "Wuhan 'qierling shijian' shimo" (The beginning to end of the "July 20th incident" in Wuhan). *Gemingshi ziliao*, 2 (September 1981), 7–45.

Cheng, Allen et al. "WHO seeks full probe on virus." *South China Morning Post*, 10 April 2003.

Cheng Weigao. "Further emancipate the mind and renew the concept, and accelerate the pace of reform and development." *Hebei ribao*, 18 April 1991, trans. in *FBIS Daily Report: China*, 7 June 1991, 60–8.

Chevrier, Yves. "Micropolitics and the factory director responsibility system, 1984–1987," in Deborah Davis and Ezra F. Vogel, eds., *Chinese society on the eve of Tiananmen*, 109–33.

Chi Hsin. *The case of the Gang of Four*. Hong Kong: Cosmos Books, 1977.

Chien Yu-shen. *China's fading revolution: Army dissent and military divisions, 1961–68*. Hong Kong: Centre of Contemporary Chinese Studies, 1969.

"China: Jiang Zemin, HK deputies mull work report." *XH*, 9 March 1998, available in *FBIS*, CHI-98-069.

China Daily. Beijing: 1981–. [Printed and distributed in Beijing, Hong Kong, New York, et al.] Cited as *CD*.

China Information. Quarterly. Leiden: Documentation and Research Center for Contemporary China, 1986–. Cited as *CI*.

China Journal. Semiannual. Canberra: Contemporary China Centre, Australian National University, 1995–.

China Leadership Monitor. Quarterly (online). Stanford: Hoover Institution, 2002–.

China News Analysis. Fortnightly. Hong Kong: 1953–82; 1984–98. [1953–82 issues published by Fr. Ladany.] Cited as *CNA*.

China News Digest (Global News). Daily. Internet Electronic Edition: CND-INFO. LIBRARY. UTA. EDU. Cited as *CND*.

China Quarterly, The. Quarterly. London: Congress for Cultural Freedom (Paris), 1960–8; Contemporary China Institute, School of Oriental and African Studies, 1968–. Cited as *CQ*.

China Review. Monthly. Hong Kong. 1988–90.

China Update. Irregular. Cambridge, Mass.: China Scholars Coordinating Committee, Fairbank Center, Harvard University, 1989–90.

Chinese communist internal politics and foreign policy: Reviews on reference materials concerning education. Taipei: Institute of International Relations, 1974.

Chinese Law and Government: A journal of translations. Quarterly. Armonk, N.Y.: M. E. Sharpe, 1968–. Cited as *CLG*.

Chinese Literature. Monthly. Beijing: FLP, 1951–2000.

"Chinese president on diplomatic work." *XH*, 28 August 1998, available in *SWB/Asia Pacific*, 28 August 1998.

Chinese Sociology and Anthropology: A journal of translations. Quarterly. Armonk, N.Y.: M. E. Sharpe, 1968–.

Chinese statistical yearbook. See *Zhongguo tongji nianjian*.

Chinese Studies in History: A journal of translations. Quarterly. Armonk, N.Y: M. E. Sharpe, 1967–. [Formerly *Chinese Studies in History and Philosophy.*]

CHOC. Cambridge history of China, The.

Chong, Woei Lien. "Petitioners, Popperians, and hunger strikers," in Tony Saich, ed., *The Chinese people's movement*, 106–25.

Chong, Woei Lien. "Present worries of Chinese democrats: Notes on Fang Lizhi, Liu Binyan, and the film 'River Elegy.'" *CI*, 3.4 (Spring 1989), 1–20.

Chow Ching-wen. *Ten years of storm: The true story of the communist regime in China.* Westport, Conn.: Greenwood Press, 1960.

Christman, Henry M. *See* Lenin, Vladimir Il'ich.

Chung, Jae Ho. "Central–provincial relations," in Lo Chi Kan, Suzanne Pepper, and Tsui Kai Yuen, eds., *China review, 1995*, ch. 3.

CI. China Information.

"Circular of [the] Central Committee of [the] CCP [on the Cultural Revolution]," 16 May 1966, in "Collection of documents concerning the Great Proletarian Cultural Revolution."

CLG. Chinese Law and Government.

CNA. China News Analysis.

CND. China News Digest.

"CND Interview with Gao Xin." *CND*, 7–8 April 1991.

Cohen, Jerome A. *The criminal process in the People's Republic of China, 1949–63: An introduction.* Cambridge, Mass.: Harvard University Press, 1968.

"Collection of documents concerning the Great Proletarian Cultural Revolution." *CB*, 852 (6 May 1968).

"Communiqué of the 15th Central Committee Sixth Plenum." *XH*, 26 September 2001.

"Communiqué of the Fifth Plenary Session of the Fourteenth Central Committee of the CCP." *XH, in FBIS Daily Report; China*, 28 September 1995, 15–17.

"Communiqué of the Seventh Plenary Session of the 14th CCP Central Committee." *XH*, 9 September 1997, available in *SWB*, 10 September 1997.

Communist Affairs: Documents and analyses. Quarterly. Guilford, Surrey: Butterworth Scientific, 1982–4.

Communist China 1955–1959: Policy documents with analysis. With a foreword by Robert R. Bowie and John K. Fairbank. Cambridge, Mass.: Harvard University Press, 1965.

Comparative Politics. Quarterly. New York: Political Science Program, City University of New York, 1968–.

"Constitution of the Communist Party of China." *BR*, 25.38 (20 September 1982), 14–16.

"Constitution of the Communist Party of China," amended and adopted by the 16th National Congress of the CPC on 14 November 2002, in *Documents of the 16th National Congress of the Communist Party of China*, 76–114.

"Constitution of the Communist Party of China," partially revised by the 15th National Party Congress of the Communist Party of China and adopted on 18 September 1997, in *Selected Documents of the 15th CPC National Congress*, 59–88.

CQ. China Quarterly, The.

Cremerius, Ruth, Fischer, Doris, and Schier, Peter, eds. *Studentenprotest und repression in China, April–Juni 1989: Analyse, chronologie, dokumente.* Hamburg: Institut für Asienkunde, 1990.

"Crimes behind the power: Analyzing the serious crimes committed by Yan Jianhong." *RMRB*, 14 January 1995, trans. in *FBIS Daily Report: China*, 24 January 1995, 29–31.

Current Background. See U.S. Consulate General.

Current History. 9/year (monthly except June, July, and August). Philadelphia: Current History, Inc., 1914–.

Dagong bao ("L'Impartial"). Hong Kong. Cited as *DGB*.

Dangdai (Contemporary). Monthly. Hong Kong, 1991–5.

Dangdai sichao (Contemporary Trends). Bimonthly. Beijing: 1990–2004.

Dangde jiaoyu (Party education). Tianjin.

Dangde shenghuo (Party Life). Semi-monthly. Harbin: Zhonggong Heilongjiang shengwei, 1959–.

Dangshi huiyi baogao ji (Collected reports from the Conference on Party History). Quanguo dangshi ziliao zhengji gongzuo huiyi he jinian Zhongguo gongchandang liushi zhounian xueshu taolun hui mishu chu (Secretariat of the National Work Conference on Collecting Party History Materials and the Academic Conference in Commemoration of the Sixtieth Anniversary of the Chinese Communist Party), eds. Beijing: Zhonggong zhongyang dangxiao, 1982.

Dangshi tongxun (Party history newsletter). Bimonthly 1980–4; Monthly 1984–8. Beijing.

Dangshi yanjiu (Research on Party history). Beijing: Zhonggong zhongyang dangxiao, 1980–7. Also see *Zhonggong dangshi yanjiu.*

Dassu, Marta, and Saich, Tony, eds. *The reform decade in China: From hope to dismay.* London: Kegan, Paul International, 1990.

Daubier, Jean. *A history of the Chinese Cultural Revolution.* Trans. Richard Seaver. Preface by Han Suyin. New York: Vintage Books, 1974.

Davis, Deborah, and Vogel, Ezra F., eds. *Chinese society on the eve of Tiananmen.* Cambridge, Mass.: Council on East Asian Studies, Harvard University, 1990.

Davis, Deborah S. et al., eds. *Urban spaces in contemporary China: The potential for autonomy and community in post-Mao China.* New York: Cambridge University Press and Washington, D.C.: Woodrow Wilson Center Press, 1995.

"The debate on the neo-authoritarianism." *Chinese Sociology and Anthropology*, 23.2 (Winter 1990–1), 3–93.

"Decision of the CCP Central Committee . . . on resolute support for the revolutionary masses of the left," 23 January 1967, in "Collection of documents concerning the Great Proletarian Cultural Revolution."

"Decision of the CCP Central Committee on some issues concerning the establishment of a socialist market economic structure." *RMRB*, 17 November 1993, trans. in *FBIS Daily Report: China*, 17 November 1993, 22–35.

"Decision of the Central Committee of the Chinese Communist Party concerning the Great Proletarian Cultural Revolution," in "Collection of documents concerning the Great Proletarian Cultural Revolution."

"Decision of the Central Committee of the Chinese Communist Party (CCP) on major issues concerning reform and development." *XH*, 26 September 1999, available in *SWB/Asia Pacific*, 27 September 1999.

"Decision of the Central Committee of the Communist Party of China concerning some major issues on strengthening Party building." *XH*, 6 October 1994, in *FBIS Daily Report: China*, 6 October 1994, 13–22.

"Decision of the Central Committee of the Communist Party of China on reform of the economic structure," 20 October 1984. *BR*, 27.44 (29 October 1984), I–XVI.

Deng Liqun. *Xiang Chen Yun tongzhi xuexi zuo jingji gongzuo* (Study how to do economic work from Comrade Chen Yun). Beijing: Zhonggong zhongyang dangxiao, 1981.

Deng Liqun. "Xuexi 'Guanyu jianguo yilai dangde ruogan lishi wenti de jueyi' de wenti he huida" (Questions and answers in studying the "Resolution on certain historical questions since the founding of the state"), in *Dangshi huiyi baogao ji*, 74–174.

Deng Xiaoping. "Answers to the Italian journalist Oriana Fallaci," in *Selected works of Deng Xiaoping (1975–1982)*, 326–34.

Deng Xiaoping. "Dang he guojia lingdao zhidu de gaige" (On the reform of the Party and state leadership system), in *Deng Xiaoping wenxuan (1975–1982)*, 280–302.

[Deng Xiaoping]. *Deng Xiaoping wenxuan 1975–1982*. (Selected works of Deng Xiaoping). Beijing: Renmin, 1983.

[Deng Xiaoping]. *Deng Xiaoping wenxuan* (Selected works of Deng Xiaoping), vol. 3. Beijing: Renmin, 1993.

Deng Xiaoping. "Disandai lingdao jiti de dangwu zhi ji" (Urgent tasks of the third generation leadership collective), in *Deng Xiaoping wenxuan*, 3.309–14.

Deng Xiaoping. *Fundamental issues in present-day China*. Beijing: FLP, 1987.

Deng Xiaoping. "Gaige kaifang zhengce wending, Zhongguo dayou xiwang" (If China's policy of reform and opening up remains stable, there is great hope for China), in *Deng Xiaoping wenxuan*, 3.315–21.

Deng Xiaoping. "Jiesu yanjun de ZhongMei guanxi yao you Meiguo caiqu zhudong" (Resolving the serious situation in Sino-U.S. relations requires that the U.S. take the initiative), in *Deng Xiaoping wenxuan*, 3.330–3.

Deng Xiaoping. "On opposing wrong ideological tendencies" (27 March 1981), in *Selected works of Deng Xiaoping (1975–1982)*, 356–9.

Deng Xiaoping. "On the reform of the system of Party and state leadership," in *Selected works of Deng Xiaoping (1975–1982)*, 302–25.

[Deng Xiaoping] Teng Hsiao-ping. "Report on the revision of the constitution of the Communist Party of China" (16 September 1956). *Eighth National Congress of the Communist Party of China*. I. 169–228. Beijing: FLP, 1956.

[Deng Xiaoping]. *Selected works of Deng Xiaoping (1975–1982)*. Beijing: FLP, 1984.

Deng Xiaoping. "Uphold the four cardinal principles," in *Selected works of Deng Xiaoping (1975–1982)*, 166–91.

Deng Xiaoping. "Zai jiejian shoudu jieyan budui junyishang ganbu shi de jianghua" (Talk on receiving martial law cadres at the army level and above in the capital), in *Deng Xiaoping wenxuan*, 3.302–8.

Deng Xiaoping. "Zai Wuchang, Shenzhen, Zhuhai dengdi de tanhua yaodian" (Essential points from talks in Wuchang, Shenzhen, Zhuhai, and Shanghai), in *Deng Xiaoping wenxuan*, 3.370–83.

Deng Xiaoping. "Zucheng yige shixing gaige de you xiwang de lingdao jiti" (Organizing a reformist, hopeful leadership collective), in *Deng Xiaoping wenxuan*, 3.296–301.

"Deng Xiaoping's visit to special zones shows China is more open." *WHB* (Hong Kong), editorial, 28 January 1992, trans. in *FBIS Daily Report: China*, 28 January 1992, 23–4.

Deng Zihui. "Zai quanguo disanci nongcun gongzuo huiyi shang de kaimu ci" (Inaugural speech at the third national rural work conference). *Dangshi yanjiu* 2.1 (1981), 2–9.

DGB. Dagong bao.

Diao, Richard K. "The impact of the Cultural Revolution on China's economic elite." *CQ*, 42 (April–June 1970), 65–87.

Dickson, Bruce J. *Wealth into power: The Communist Party's embrace of China's private sector*. New York: Cambridge University Press, 2008.

"Did Marx fall, or was he pushed?" *The Economist*, 15 December 1984.

Dittmer, Lowell. "Bases of power in Chinese politics: A theory and an analysis of the fall of the 'Gang of Four.'" *World Politics*, 31.1 (October 1978), 26–60.

Dittmer, Lowell. "China in 1988: The continuing dilemma of socialist reform." *AS*, 29.1 (January 1989), 12–28.

Dittmer, Lowell. "China in 1989: The crisis of incomplete reform." *AS*, 30.1 (January 1990), 25–41.

Dittmer, Lowell. *Liu Shao-ch'i and the Chinese Cultural Revolution: The politics of mass criticism*. Berkeley: University of California Press, 1974.

Dittmer, Lowell. "Patterns of elite strife and succession in Chinese politics." *CQ*, 123 (September 1990), 405–30.

Dittmer, Lowell. "Reform, succession and the resurgence of mainland China's old guard." *I&S*, 24.1 (January 1988), 96–113.

Dittmer, Lowell. "The Tiananmen massacre." *POC*, 38.5 (September–October 1989), 2–15.

Dittmer, Lowell. "The 12th congress of the Chinese Communist Party." *CQ*, 93 (March 1983), 108–24.

Djilas, Milovan. *The new class: An analysis of the communist system*. New York: Praeger, 1957.

Documents of the Chinese Communist Party Central Committee, September 1956–April 1969. See Union Research Institute.

Documents of the Thirteenth National Congress of the Communist Party of China (1987). Beijing: FLP, 1987.

Documents of the 16th National Congress of the Communist Party of China. Beijing: FLP, 2002.

Domes, Jürgen. "The Cultural Revolution and the army." *AS*, 8.5 (May 1968), 349–63.

Domes, Jürgen. *The government and politics of the PRC: A time of transition*. Boulder, Colo.: Westview Press, 1985.

Domes, Jürgen. *The internal politics of China, 1949–1972*. Trans. Rudiger Machetzki. New York: Praeger; London: C. Hurst, 1973.

Domes, Jürgen. "The role of the military in the formation of revolutionary committees, 1967–68." *CQ*, 44 (October–December 1970), 112–45.

Doolin, Dennis J., trans. *Communist China: The politics of student opposition*. Stanford, Calif.: Hoover Institution, 1964.

Dreyer, June Teufel. "The People's Liberation Army and the power struggle of 1989." *POC*, 38.5 (September–October 1989), 41–8.

"East wind brings spring all around: On-the-spot report on Comrade Deng Xiaoping in Shenzhen." *RMRB*, 31 March 1992, trans. in *FBIS Daily Report: China*, 1 April 1992 (supplement), 7–15.

Eastman, Lloyd E. *The abortive revolution: China under Nationalist rule, 1927–1937*. Cambridge, Mass.: Harvard University Press, 1974.

Economist, The. Weekly. London: Economist Newspaper Ltd., 1843–.

Editorial. "General Secretary Jiang Zemin on the reform of state-owned enterprise." *Liaowang*, 36 (6 September 1999), 2–8, trans. in *FBIS*, FTS19990920000076.

Editorial. "Jiaqiang xinshiqi dangde jianshe de genben zhidao sixiang: Xuexi Jiang Zemin zai Guangdong kaocha gongzuo shi de zhongyao jianghua" (Strengthen the basic leading thought of Party construction in the new period: Study Jiang Zemin's important speech during an inspection of Guangdong). *Qiushi*, 7 (2000), 7–9, trans. in *FBIS*, CPP20000317000143.

Editorial. "Quanmian jiaqiang dangde jianshe de weida gangling" (Comprehensively strengthen the great program of Party building). *RMRB*, 22 May 2000.

Edwards, R. Randle, Henkin, Louis, and Nathan, Andrew J. *Human rights in contemporary China*. New York: Columbia University Press, 1986.

Eighth National Congress of the Communist Party of China. Vol. I: *Documents*. Vol. II: *Speeches*. Beijing: FLP, 1956.

Eleventh National Congress of the Communist Party of China (documents). Beijing: FLP, 1977.

Esquire. Monthly. Chicago: Esquire, Inc., 1933–.

Etzioni, Amitai, ed. *Complex organizations: A sociological reader*. New York: Holt, Rinehart and Winston, 1969 [1961].

Faison, Seth. "The changing role of the Chinese media," in Tony Saich, ed., *The Chinese people's movement*, 145–63.

Fan, K., ed. *Mao Tse-tung and Lin Piao: Post-revolutionary writings*. Garden City, N.Y.: Anchor Books, 1972.

Fan Shuo. "The tempestuous October: A chronicle of the complete collapse of the 'Gang of Four.'" *Yangcheng wanbao*, 10 February 1989, trans. in *FBIS Daily Report: China*, 14 February 1989, 16–22.

Fang, Percy Jucheng, and Fang, Lucy Guinong J. *Zhou Enlai: A profile*. Beijing: FLP, 1986.

Fang Weizhong, ed. *Zhonghua renmin gongheguo jingji dashiji (1949–1980)* (A record of the major economic events of the PRC [1949–1980]). Beijing: Zhongguo shehui kexue, 1984.

Far Eastern Economic Review. Weekly. Hong Kong: Far Eastern Economic Review Ltd., 1946–2004. Dec. 2004–Dec. 2009, 10/yr. Cited as *FEER*.

Fathers, Michael, and Higgins, Andrew. *Tiananmen: The rape of Peking*. London: Doubleday, 1989.

Faxue. Shanghai: Shanghai faxue hui, 1957–.

Faxue yanjiu (Legal studies). Bimonthly. Beijing: Zhongguo shehui kexue, 1979–.

FBIS. Foreign Broadcast Information Service.

FEER. Far Eastern Economic Review.

Feng Shengbao. "Preparations for the blueprint on political restructuring presented by Zhao Ziyang at the Thirteenth Party Congress." Unpublished paper presented to the Harvard University East Asia Colloquium, July 1990.

Feuerwerker, Albert. *China's early industrialization: Sheng Hsuan-huai (1844–1916) and mandarin enterprise*. Cambridge, Mass.: Harvard University Press, 1958.

Fewsmith, Joseph. "China and the WTO: The politics behind the agreement." *NBR Analysis*, 10.5 (December 1999), 23–39.

Fewsmith, Joseph. *China since Tiananmen: From Deng Xiaoping to Hu Jintao*. 2nd ed. New York: Cambridge University Press, 2008.

Fewsmith, Joseph. *Dilemmas of reform in China: Political conflict and economic debate*. Armonk, N.Y.: M. E. Sharpe, 1994.

Fewsmith, Joseph. "Neoconservatism and the end of the Dengist era." *AS*, 35.7 (July 1995), 635–51.

Fewsmith, Joseph. "Notes on the first session of the Eighth National People's Congress." *Journal of Contemporary China*, 3 (Summer 1993), 81–6.

Fewsmith, Joseph. *Party, state, and local elites in Republican China*. Honolulu: University of Hawaii Press, 1985.

Fewsmith, Joseph. "Promoting the scientific development concept." *China Leadership Monitor*, 11 (Summer 2004).

Fewsmith, Joseph. "Reform, resistance, and the politics of succession," in William A. Joseph, ed., *China briefing, 1994*, 7–34.

Fewsmith, Joseph. "Rethinking the role of the CCP: Explicating Jiang Zemin's Party anniversary speech." *China Leadership Monitor*, 2 (Spring 2002).

Fewsmith, Joseph. "Review of *Looking at China through the third eye*." *Journal of Contemporary China*, 7 (Fall 1994), 100–4.

Fewsmith, Joseph. "The Sixteenth National Party Congress: The succession that didn't happen." *CQ*, 173 (March 2003), 1–16.

Fewsmith, Joseph, and Rosen, Stanley. "The domestic context of Chinese foreign policy: Does 'public opinion' matter?" in David M. Lampton, ed., *The making of Chinese foreign and security policy in the era of reform*, 151–87.

Field, Robert Michael, McGlynn, Kathleen M., and Abnett, William B. "Political conflict and industrial growth in China: 1965–1977," in U.S. Congress [95th], Joint Economic Committee, *The Chinese economy post-Mao*, 1.239–83.

Fifth session of the Fifth National People's Congress (main documents). Beijing: FLP, 1983.

Foreign Broadcast Information Service. Washington, D.C.: U.S. Department of Commerce, 1941–. Cited as *FBIS*. The *Daily Report* of this agency has appeared in sections designated for specific regions, but the names of these regions have been changed from time to time in a manner that makes it difficult to construct a precise genealogy. These designations have been used at various times: Asia and Pacific, China, Communist China, East Asia, Eastern Europe, Far East, People's Republic of China, USSR, USSR and Eastern Europe. *FBIS* is discussed in *CHOC*, 14.557 et passim.

Foreign Languages Press. Cited as FLP.

"Forward: Explosive economic growth raises warning signal." *JSND*, 10 (1 October 1993), 58–9, trans. in *FBIS Daily Report: China*, 11 January 1994, 49–50.

Francis, Corinna-Barbara. "The progress of protest in China." *AS*, 29.9 (September 1989), 898–915.

Fraser, John. *The Chinese: Portrait of a people*. London: Fontana/Collins, 1982; New York: Summit Books, 1980.

Friedman, Edward. "Permanent technological revolution and China's tortuous path to democratizing Leninism," in Richard Baum, ed., *Reform and reaction*, 162–82.

"Full text of Vice-President Hu Jintao's speech on NATO attack." *XH*, 9 May 1999, available in *SWB/Asia Pacific*, 9 May 1999.

Gang Zou. "Debates on China's economic situation and reform strategies." Paper presented to the annual meeting of the Association for Asian Studies, Washington, D.C., March 1989.

Gao Gao, and Yan Jiaqi. *"Wenhua da geming" shinian shi, 1966–1976* (A history of the ten years of the "Great Cultural Revolution," 1966–1976). Tianjin: Renmin, 1986.

Gao Xin, and He Pin. "Tightrope act of Wei Jianxing." *Dangdai*, 23 (15 February 1993), 42–5, trans. in *FBIS Daily Report: China*, 24 February 1993, 24–6.

Gao Xin, and He Pin. *Zhu Rongji zhuan* (Biography of Zhu Rongji). Hong Kong: Xinxinwen, 1993.

Gardner, John. *Chinese politics and the succession to Mao*. London: Macmillan, 1982.

Gardner, John. "Educated youth and urban–rural inequalities, 1958–66," in John Wilson Lewis, ed., *The city in communist China*, 235–86.

Garside, Roger. *Coming alive! China after Mao*. New York: McGraw-Hill; London: Andre Deutsch, 1981.

Geming shichao (A transcript of revolutionary poems). 2 vols. Beijing: Dier waiyu xueyuan, 1977.

Gemingshi ziliao (Reference materials of revolutionary history). Quarterly. Shanghai: 1986–9.

Gittings, John. "Army–Party relations in the light of the Cultural Revolution," in John Wilson Lewis, ed., *Party leadership and revolutionary power in China*, 373–403.

Gittings, John. "The Chinese army's role in the Cultural Revolution." *Pacific Affairs*, 39.3–4 (Fall–Winter 1966–7), 269–89.

Gittings, John. "The 'Learn from the army' campaign." *CQ*, 18 (April–June 1964), 153–9.

Gittings, John. *The role of the Chinese army*. London and New York: Oxford University Press, 1967.

GMRB. Guangming ribao.

Gold, Thomas B. "'Just in time!' China battles spiritual pollution on the eve of 1984." *AS*, 24.9 (September 1984), 947–74.

Gold, Thomas B. "Party–state versus society in China," in Joyce K. Kallgren, ed., *Building a nation-state*, 125–52.

Gold, Thomas B. "Urban private business and China's reforms," in Richard Baum, ed., *Reform and reaction*, 84–103.

Goldman, Merle. *China's intellectuals: Advise and dissent.* Cambridge, Mass.: Harvard University Press, 1981.

Goldman, Merle. *Sowing the seeds of democracy in China.* Cambridge, Mass.: Harvard University Press, 1994.

Goldman, Merle, with Cheek, Timothy, and Hamrin, Carol Lee, eds. *China's intellectuals and the state: In search of a new relationship.* Cambridge, Mass.: Council on East Asian Studies, Harvard University, 1987.

Goldstein, Avery. "China in 1996: Achievement, assertiveness and anxiety." *AS*, 37.1 (January 1997), 29–42.

Gong Yuzhi. "Emancipate our minds, liberate productive forces: Studying Comrade Deng Xiaoping's important talks." *WHB* (Shanghai), 15 April 1992, trans. in *FBIS Daily Report: China*, 20 April 1992, 25–8.

Gongren ribao (Workers' daily). Beijing: 15 July 1949 (suspended 1 April 1967, resumed 6 October 1978–). Cited as *GRRB*.

Goodman, David S. G. *Beijing street voices: The poetry and politics of China's democracy movement.* London and Boston: Marion Boyars, 1981.

Gray, Jack, and Cavendish, Patrick. *Chinese communism in crisis: Maoism and the Cultural Revolution.* New York: Praeger, 1968.

"The Great Proletarian Cultural Revolution: A record of major events – September 1965 to December 1966." JPRS, 42,349 *Translations on Communist China: Political and Sociological Information*, 25 August 1967.

A great trial in Chinese history: The trial of the Lin Biao and Jiang Qing counterrevolutionary cliques, Nov. 1980–Jan. 1981. Beijing: New World Press, 1981.

GRRB. Gongren ribao.

Guangming ribao (Enlightenment daily). Beijing: 1949–. Cited as *GMRB*.

"Guanyu Guomindang zaoyao wumie de dengzai suowei 'Wu Hao Qishi' wenti de wenjian" (Document on the problems of the Guomindang maliciously concocting and publishing the so-called 'Wu Hao notice'). *Dangshi yanjiu*, 1.1 (1980), 8.

<<*Guanyu jianguo yilai dangde ruogan lishi wenti de jueyi*>> *zhushi ben (xiuding).* (Revised annotated edition of the Resolution on certain questions in the history of our party since the founding of the state). Beijing: Renmin, 1985.

Guo Moruo. *Moruo shici xuan* (Selected poems of [Guo] Moruo). Beijing: Renmin wenxue, 1977.

Guo Moruo. "On seeing 'The monkey subdues the demon.'" *Chinese Literature*, 4 (1976), 44.

Guo Moruo. "Three poems." *Chinese Literature*, 1 (1972), 50–2.

Gurtov, Melvin. "The foreign ministry and foreign affairs in the Chinese Cultural Revolution," in Thomas W. Robinson, ed., *The Cultural Revolution in China*, 313–66.

Halpern, Nina P. "Economic reform, social mobilization, and democratization in post-Mao China," in Richard Baum, ed., *Reform and reaction*, 38–59.

Halpern, Nina P. "Learning from abroad: Chinese views of the East European economic experience, January 1977–June 1981." *Modern China*, 1 (1985), 77–109.

Hamrin, Carol Lee. *China and the challenge of the future: Changing political patterns.* Boulder, Colo.: Westview Press, 1990.

Hamrin, Carol Lee, and Cheek, Timothy, eds. *China's establishment intellectuals.* Armonk, N.Y.: M. E. Sharpe, 1986.

Hamrin, Carol Lee, and Zhao, Suisheng, eds. *Decision-making in Deng's China: Perspectives from insiders.* Armonk, N.Y.: M. E. Sharpe, 1995.

Hao Mengbi, and Duan Haoran, eds. *Zhongguo gongchandang liushi nian, xia* (Sixty years of the Chinese Communist Party, part 2). Beijing: Jiefangjun, 1984.

Harding, Harry. *China's second revolution: Reform after Mao.* Washington, D.C.: Brookings Institution, 1987.

Harding, Harry. *The fragile relationship: The United States and China since 1972.* Washington, D.C.: Brookings Institution, 1992.

Harding, Harry. "From China, with disdain: New trends in the study of China." *AS*, 22.10 (October 1982), 934–58.

Harding, Harry. *Organizing China: The problem of bureaucracy, 1949–1976.* Stanford, Calif.: Stanford University Press, 1981.

Harding, Harry. "Reappraising the Cultural Revolution." *The Wilson Quarterly*, 4.4 (Autumn 1980), 132–41.

Harding, Harry, and Gurtov, Melvin. *The purge of Lo Jui-ch'ing: The politics of Chinese strategic planning.* Santa Monica, Calif.: The RAND Corporation, R-548-PR, February 1971.

Hartford, Kathleen. "Socialist agriculture is dead; long live socialist agriculture! Organizational transformations in rural China," in Elizabeth J. Perry and Christine Wong, eds., *The political economy of reform in post-Mao China*, 31–61.

[He Dexu] Ho Te-hsu. "China has crossed the nadir of the valley but is still climbing up from the trough: Liu Guoguang talks about the current economic situation in China." *JJDB*, 38.9 (1 October 1990), 12–13, trans. in *FBIS Daily Report: China*, 12 October 1990, 27–30.

He Pin, and Gao Xin. *Zhonggong "taizi dang"* ("Princelings" of the CCP). Hong Kong: Shibao, 1992.

He Yijun, Jiang Bin, and Wang Jianwei. "Speed up pace of reform, opening up." *JFJB*, 25 March 1992, trans. in *FBIS Daily Report: China*, 22 April 1992, 30–3.

[He Yuan] Ho Yuen. "CCP's five adherences' and 'five oppositions' to prevent peaceful evolution." *MB*, 29 August 1991, trans. in *FBIS Daily Report: China*, 29 August 1991, 23–5.

Het Collectieve Geheugen: Over Literatuur En Geschiedenis. Amsterdam: DeBalie/Novib, 1990.

Hinton, Harold C., ed. *The People's Republic of China, 1949–1979: A documentary survey.* 5 vols. Wilmington, Del.: Scholarly Resources, Inc., 1980.

Historical Studies in the Physical and Biological Sciences. Semi-annual. Berkeley: 1971–.

History Writing Group of the CCP Kwangtung Provincial Committee. "The ghost of Empress Lü and Chiang Ch'ing's empress dream." *Chinese Studies in History*, 12.1 (Fall 1978), 37–54.

Hongqi (Red flag). Beijing: 1958–88. Cited as *HQ*.

Howe, Christopher, ed. *Shanghai: Revolution and development in an Asian metropolis.* Cambridge: Cambridge University Press, 1981.

HQ. Hongqi.

Hsiung, James C. "Mainland China's paradox of partial reform: A postmortem on Tienanmen." *I&S*, 26.6 (June 1990), 29–43.

Hsu, Immanuel C.Y. *The rise of modern China.* 6ᵗʰ ed. New York: Oxford University Press, 2000.

Hsu, Robert C. "Economics and economists in post-Mao China." *AS*, 28.12 (December 1988), 1211–28.

Hu Hua. *Zhongguo shehuizhuyi geming he jianshe shi jiangyi* (Teaching materials on the history of China's socialist revolution and construction). Beijing: Zhongguo renmin daxue, 1985.

Hu Jintao. "Guanyu zhongyang de gongzuo" (On the work of the Central Committee), 26 February 2003, in *Shiliuda yilai zhongyao wenxian xuanbian* (Selected important documents since the 16ᵗʰ Party Congress), 1.149–53.

Hu Jintao. "Shuli he luoshi kexue fazhan guan" (Implant and implement the scientific development concept), 14 October 2003, in *Shiliuda yilai zhongyao wenxian xuanbian*, 1.483–4.

Hu Yaobang. "Lilun gongzuo wuxu hui yinyan" (Introduction to theoretical work conference), in *Zhonggong shiyijie sanzhong quanhui yilai zhongyang shouyao jianghua ji wenjian xuanbian, 2.* 48–63.

Huainian Zhou Enlai (Longing for Zhou Enlai). Beijing: Renmin, 1986.

Huang Zhiling. "New law to better guide bankruptcy." *China Daily*, 18 June 1996, 4.

Huangfu Ping. "The consciousness of expanding opening needs to be strengthened." *Jiefang ribao*, 22 March 1991, trans. in *FBIS Daily Report: China*, 1 April 1991, 39–41.

Huangfu Ping. "Reform and opening require a large number of cadres with both morals and talents." *Jiefang ribao*, 12 April 1991, trans. in *FBIS Daily Report: China*, 17 April 1991, 61–3.

Huaqiao ribao (China daily news). New York: 1940–89.

Human Rights Watch. "Dangerous meditation: China's campaign against Falungong," January 2002; available at http://www.hrw.org/en/reports/2002/02/07/dangerous-meditation (accessed 3 August 2010).

Hunter, Neale. *Shanghai journal: An eyewitness account of the Cultural Revolution.* New York: Praeger, 1969; Boston: Beacon Press, 1971.

Huntington, Samuel. *Political order in changing societies.* New Haven, Conn.: Yale University Press, 1968.

Hutterer, Karl. "Eyewitness: The Chengdu massacre." *China Update*, 1 (August 1989), 4–5.

IS. Issues & Studies.

ICM. Inside China Mainland.

"Increase weight of reform, promote economic development: Speech delivered by Wu Guanzheng at the provincial structural reform work conference." *Jiangxi ribao*, 4 May 1991, trans. in *FBIS Daily Report: China*, 12 June 1991, 45–9.

Inside China Mainland. Monthly. Taipei: Institute of Current China Studies, 1979–99. Cited as *ICM*.

Issues & Studies. Monthly. Taipei: Institute of International Relations, 1964–98; Bimonthly, 1999–2001; Quarterly, 2002–. Cited *as IS*.

JB. Jingbao.

Jencks, Harlan. "Party authority and military power: Communist China's continuing crisis." *IS*, 26.7 (July 1990), 11–39.

JFJB. Jiefangjun bao.

[Ji Weige] Chi Wei-ke. "Three new moves on the eve of the Third Plenary Session of the CCP Central Committee; Deng makes new comments on macrocontrol." *JB*, 12 (5 December 1993), 30–4, trans. in *FBIS Daily Report: China*, 8 December 1993, 18–22.

Jiang Zemin. "Accelerating reform and opening-up," report to the 14th CCP Congress, 12 October 1992. *BR*, 35.43 (26 October–1 November 1992), 9–32.

Jiang Zemin. "Build a well-off society in an all-round way and create a new situation in building socialism with Chinese characteristics," text of report delivered to China's 16th National Party Congress, 8 November 2002, *SWB*, 8 November 2002.

Jiang Zemin. "Correctly handle some major relationships in the socialist modernization drive." *XH*, 8 October 1995, trans. in *FBIS Daily Report: China*, 10 October 1995, 29–36.

Jiang Zemin. "Guanyu jiang zhengzhi" (On talking politics), excerpt of a talk delivered to Party member delegates to the Fourth Session of the Eighth NPC and Eighth CPPCC, 3 March 1996, in *Shisida yilai zhongyang wenxian xuanbian*, 2.1743–9.

Jiang Zemin. "Hold high the great banner of Deng Xiaoping theory for an all-round advancement of the cause of building socialism with Chinese characteristics into the 21st century," delivered on 12 September 1997. *BR*, 40.40 (6–12 October 1997), 10–33.

Jiang Zemin. "Jianding xinxin, shenhua gaige, kaichuang gongyouzhi fazhan de xin jumian" (Strengthen confidence, deepen reform, and create a new situation in the development of state-owned enterprises), speech delivered at the Dalian forum on enterprise reform, 12 August 1999, in *Shiwuda yilai zhongyao wenxian xuanbian*, 2.916–32.

Jiang Zemin. "Jiang xuexi, jiang zhengzhi, jiang zhengqi" (Talking study, talking politics, and talking upright trends), excerpt of a talk given while inspecting work in Beijing on 8 November 1995, in *Shisida yilai zhongyao wenxian xuanbian*, 2.1559–62.

[Jiang Zemin]. *Jiang Zemin wenxuan* (Selected writings of Jiang Zemin). Beijing: Renmin, 2006.

Jiang Zemin. "Lingdao ganbu yiding yao jiang zhengzhi" (Leading cadres must talk politics), excerpt of a speech delivered to a group session during the Fifth Plenum on 27 September 1995, in *Jiang Zemin wenxuan*, 1.455–9.

[Jiang Zemin]. "President Jiang reaffirms China's stance on Taiwan, stresses army building," talk to PLA delegates attending the Second Plenary Session [of the Fourth Session] of the NPC, CCTV, 11 March 1996, *SWB*, 12 March 1996.

Jiang Zemin. "Qingzhu Zhongguo gongchandang chengli bashi zhounian dahui-shang de jianghua" (Speech commemorating the 80th anniversary of the founding of the CCP), 1 July 2001, in *Jiang Zemin wenxuan*, 3.264–99, modified trans. by XH, 1 July 2001, available in FBIS, CPP20010701000035.

Jiang Zemin. "Shizhong zuodao 'sange daibiao' shi women dangde lidang zhi ben, zhizheng zhi ji, liliang zhi yuan" (From beginning to end make the "three repre-sents" the foundation of our Party, the source of the ruling Party, and the origin of its strength), 14 May 2000, in *Jiang Zemin wenxuan*, 3.6–33.

Jiang Zemin. "Zai dangde shisanju wuzhong quanhui shang de jianghua" (Talk to the Fifth Plenary Session of the Thirteenth CCP Central Committee), in *Shisanda yilai*, 2.709–20.

[Jiang Zemin]. "Zai Deng Xiaoping tongzhi zhuidao dahuishang Jiang Zemin tongzhi zhi daoci" (Comrade Jiang Zemin's memorial meeting eulogy for Comrade Deng Xiaoping), delivered 25 February 1997. *RMRB*, 26 February 1997, 1ff.

Jiang Zemin. "Zai qingzhu Zhongguo gongchandang chengli qishi zhounian dahui-shang de jianghua" (Talk celebrating the seventieth anniversary of the founding of the CCP), in *Shisanda yilai*, 3.1627–60.

Jiang Zemin. "Zai qingzhu Zhonghua renmin gongheguo chengli sishi zhounian dahuishang de jianghua" (Talk celebrating the fortieth anniversary of the estab-lishment of the PRC), in *Shisanda yilai*, 2.609–35.

Jiang Zemin. "Zai xin de lishi tiaojianxia geng haode zuodao 'sange daibiao'" (Carry out the "three represents" better under the situation of the new historical condi-tions), 25 February 2000, in *Jiang Zemin wenxuan*, 3.1–5.

"Jiang Zemin speech at ceremony to welcome back embassy staff members from Yugoslavia." XH, 13 May 1999, available in *SWB/Asia Pacific*, 17 May 1999.

"Jiang's control of the military is conducive to smooth transition," 16 November 2002, *WHB*, trans. in FBIS, CPP20021116000016.

Jiaoxue cankao: Quanguo dangxiao xitong Zhonggong dangshi xueshu taolun hui, shang, xia (Reference for teaching and study: Central Party School system's academic conference on CCP history, vols. 1 and 2). N.P.: Zhonggong Anhui shengwei dangxiao, December 1980. Cited as *Jiaoxue cankao, xia*.

Jiefangjun bao (Liberation Army news). 1956–. Cited as *JFJB*.

Jin Chunming. "'Wenhua da geming' de shinian" (The decade of the "Great Cultural Revolution"), in Zhonggong dangshi yanjiu hui, ed., *Xuexi lishi jueyi zhuanji*, 144–69.

[Jing Wen] Ching Wen. "Abnormal atmosphere in *Renmin ribao.*" *JB*, 178 (5 May 1992), 46–7, trans. in *FBIS Daily Report: China*, 18 May 1992, 22.

Jingbao [Ching Pao]. Monthly. Hong Kong. 1977–. Cited as *JB*.

Jingji cankao bao (Economic information daily). Beijing: Xinhua, 1991–.

Jingji daobao (Economic reporter). Weekly. Hong Kong: 1947–. Cited as *JJDB*.

Jingji ribao (Economic daily). Beijing: 1955–. Cited as *JJRB*.

Jingji yanjiu (Economic studies). Bimonthly, 1995–7; monthly, 1958–66, 1978–. Beijing. Cited as *JJYJ*.

Jiushi niandai (The nineties). Monthly. Hong Kong: 1984–98. From 1970 to 1983, titled *Qishi niandai* (The seventies). Cited as *JSND*.

JJDB. Jingji daobao.

JJRB. Jingji ribao.

JJYJ. Jingji yanjiu.

Joffe, Ellis. "The Chinese army under Lin Piao: Prelude to political intervention," in John M. H. Lindbeck, ed., *China: Management of a revolutionary society*, 343–74.

Joffe, Ellis. *Party and army: Professionalism and political control in the Chinese officer corps, 1949–1964.* Cambridge, Mass.: East Asian Research Center, Harvard University, 1965.

Joffe, Ellis. "Party and military in China: Professionalism in command?" *POC*, 32.5 (September–October 1983), 48–63.

Johnston, Alastair I. "Party rectification in the People's Liberation Army, 1983–87." *CQ*, 112 (December 1987), 591–630.

Johnson, Chalmers, ed. *Change in communist systems.* Stanford, Calif.: Stanford University Press, 1970.

Joint Economic Committee. *See* United States Congress.

Joint Publications Research Service (JPRS). Washington, D.C.: U.S. Government. Various series. See Peter Berton and Eugene Wu, *Contemporary China: A research guide.* Stanford, Calif.: Stanford University Press, 1967, 409–30, and M. Oksenberg summary in *CHOC*, 14.557–8. Includes regional, worldwide, and topical translations and reports. Published periodically. The following items are cited in footnotes:

Joint Publications Research Service. *China Area Report (CAR).* 1987–94.

Joint Publications Research Service. *Miscellany of Mao Tse-tung Thought. See* [Mao Zedong] Mao Tse-tung. *Miscellany . . .*

Joint Publications Research Service. *Translations on communist China: Political and sociological information.* 1962–8.

Joseph, William A. *The critique of ultra-leftism in China, 1958–1981.* Stanford, Calif.: Stanford University Press, 1984.

Joseph, William A., ed. *China briefing, 1994.* Boulder, Colo.: Westview Press, 1994.

Journal of Asian Studies. Quarterly. Ann Arbor: Association for Asian Studies, University of Michigan, 1956–. Cited as *JAS*.

Journal of Communist Studies. Quarterly. London: Frank Cass, 1985–93.

Jowitt, Kenneth. "Soviet neotraditionalism: The political corruption of a Leninist regime." *Soviet Studies*, 35.3 (July 1983), 275–97.

JPRS. *See* Joint Publications Research Service.

JSND. Jiushi niandai.

Kahn, Joseph F. "Better fed than red." *Esquire*, September 1990, 186–97.

Kaituo. Bimonthly. Beijing: Gongren, 1985.

Kallgren, Joyce K., ed. *Building a nation-state: China at forty years*. China Research Monograph, no. 37. Berkeley: Institute of East Asian Studies, University of California, 1990.

Kau, Michael Y. M. [Ying-mao], ed. *The Lin Piao affair: Power politics and military coup*. White Plains, N.Y.: International Arts and Sciences Press, 1975.

Kau, Yi-maw [Ying-mao]. "Governmental bureaucracy and cadres in urban China under communist rule, 1949–1965." Ph.D. dissertation, Cornell University, 1968.

Kau, Ying-mao. "The case against Lin Piao." *CLG*, 5.3–4 (Fall-Winter 1972–73), 3–30.

Kelly, David A. "The Chinese student movement of December 1986 and its intellectual antecedents." *AJCA*, 17 (January 1987), 127–42.

Kelly, David A. "The emergence of humanism: Wang Ruoshui and the critique of socialist alienation," in Merle Goldman, with Timothy Cheek and Carol Lee Hamrin, eds., *China's intellectuals and the state*, 159–82.

Kessler, Lawrence D. *K'ang-hsi and the consolidation of Ch'ing rule, 1661–1684*. Chicago: University of Chicago Press, 1976.

Khrushchev remembers: The last testament. Trans. and ed. Strobe Talbott, with detailed commentary and notes by Edward Crankshaw. Boston: Little, Brown, 1974; New York: Bantam, 1976.

Kissinger, Henry. *White House years*. Boston: Little, Brown, 1979.

Klein, Donald W., and Clark, Anne B. *Biographic dictionary of Chinese communism, 1921–1965*. 2 vols. Cambridge, Mass.: Harvard University Press, 1971.

Klein, Donald W., and Hager, Lois B. "The Ninth Central Committee." *CQ*, 45 (January–March 1971), 37–56.

Kraus, Richard. "Bai Hua: The political authority of a writer," in Carol Lee Hamrin and Timothy Cheek, eds., *China's establishment intellectuals*, 201–11.

Kuan, H. C. "New departures in China's constitution." *SICC*, 17.1 (Spring 1984), 53–68.

Kuhn, Philip A. *Rebellion and its enemies in late imperial China: Militarization and social structure, 1796–1864*. Cambridge, Mass.: Harvard University Press, 1980 [1970].

Kwong, Julia. "The 1986 student demonstrations in China: A democratic movement?" *AS*, 28.9 (September 1988), 970–85.

Kyodo. News service.

Ladany, Laszlo. *The Communist Party of China and Marxism, 1921–1985: A self-portrait*. Stanford, Calif.: Hoover Institution Press. 1988.

Lam, Willy Wo-lap. *China after Deng Xiaoping*. New York: Wiley, 1995.

Lampton, David M. *The politics of medicine in China: The policy process, 1949–1977*. Boulder, Colo.: Westview Press, 1977.

Lampton, David M., ed. *The making of Chinese foreign and security policy in the era of reform.* Stanford, Calif.: Stanford University Press, 2001.

Lampton, David M., ed. *Policy implementation in post-Mao China.* Berkeley: University of California Press, 1987 [1985].

Lan Zhongping. "Why do we say that special economic zones are socialist rather than capitalist in nature?" *JFJB*, 22 May 1992, trans. in *FBIS Daily Report: China*, 11 June 1992, 25–6.

Landsberger, Stefan R. "The 1989 student demonstrations in Beijing: A chronology of events." *CI*, 4.1 (Summer 1989), 37–63.

LAT. Los Angeles Times.

Latham, Richard J. "The implications of rural reforms for grass-roots cadres," in Elizabeth J. Perry and Christine Wong, eds., *The political economy of reform in post-Mao China*, 157–73.

Lee, Hong Yong. "China's 12th Central Committee." *AS*, 23.6 (June 1983), 673–91.

Lee, Hong Yung. *From revolutionary cadres to party technocrats in socialist China.* Berkeley: University of California Press, 1991.

Lee, Hong Yung. *The politics of the Chinese Cultural Revolution: A case study.* Berkeley: University of California Press, 1978.

Lenin, Vladimir I. "The state and revolution," in Henry M. Christman, ed., *Essential works of Lenin.* New York: Bantam Books, 1966, 271–364.

Lewis, John Wilson. *Chinese Communist Party leadership and the succession to Mao Tse-tung: An appraisal of tensions.* Washington, D.C.: Policy Research Study, U.S. Department of State, January 1964.

Lewis, John Wilson, ed. *The city in communist China.* Stanford, Calif.: Stanford University Press, 1971.

Lewis, John Wilson, ed. *Party leadership and revolutionary power in China.* Cambridge: Cambridge University Press, 1970.

Li Cheng, and White, Lynn. "The Fifteenth Central Committee of the Chinese Communist Party: Full-fledged technocratic leadership with partial control by Jiang Zemin." *AS*, 38.3 (March 1998), 231–64.

Li Cheng, and White, Lynn. "The Sixteenth Central Committee of the Chinese Communist Party: Hu gets what?" *AS*, 43.4 (July–August 2003), 553–97.

Li Chengrui. "Some thoughts on sustained, steady, and coordinated development." *RMRB*, 20 November 1989, trans. in *FBIS Daily Report: China*, 12 December 1989, 32–4.

Li Hong Kuan. "Ode to the constitution," in David S. G. Goodman, *Beijing street voices: The poetry and politics of China's democracy movement*, 70.

Li Junru. "Di sanci sixiang jiefang: Chongpo xing 'gong' xing 'si' de sixiang yihuo" (The third ideological reform – Clarification of ideas about public and private ownership). *Zhongguo jingji shibao*, 12 August 1997, 1, trans. in *FBIS*, FTS19971101000220.

Li Junru. "Yiqie cong shehuizhuyi chuji jieduan de shiji chufa" (Proceed in all cases from the reality of the initial stage of socialism). *JJRB*, 15 July 1997, 1 and 3, trans. in *FBIS*, FTS19971006000205.

Li Kwok Sing. "Deng Xiaoping and the 2nd field army." *China Review*, 3.1 (January 1990), 40–2.

Li Peng. "Report on the work of the government," delivered at the Eighth NPC, 15 March 1993. *BR*, 36.15 (12–18 April 1993), I–XVI.

Li Peng. "Report on the work of the government," 1 March 1997. *BR*, 40.13 (31 March–6 April 1997), I–XVI.

Li Peng. "Wei woguo zhengzhi jingji he shehui de jinyibu wending fazhan er fendou" (Struggle to take another step for the stable development of China's politics, economics, and society), in *Shisanda yilai*, 2.948–94.

Li Rui. *Lushan huiyi shilu* (A veritable record of the Lushan meetings). Beijing: Chunqiu, 1989.

"Li Ruihuan meets with Hong Kong journalists." *DGB*, 20 September 1989, trans. in *FBIS Daily Report: China*, 20 September 1989, 10–12.

Li Yonghai. "Gongren jieji de lingdao diwei burong dongyao" (The leading role of the working class must not be shaken). *Dangdai sichao*, 1 (1996), 18–24.

Liang Heng, and Shapiro, Judith. *Son of the revolution*. New York: Knopf, 1983; New York: Vintage, 1984.

[Liao Gailong] Liao Kai-lung. "Historical experiences and our road of development (October 25, 1980)." *I&S*, 17.10 (October 1981), 65–94; 17.11 (November 1981), 81–110.

Liaowang (Outlook weekly). Weekly. Beijing: 1981–. Cited as *LW*.

Liberation Army News. See *Jiefangjun bao*.

Lieberthal, Kenneth. "The political implications of document no. 1, 1984." *CQ*, 101 (March 1985), 109–13.

Lieberthal, Kenneth. *A research guide to central Party and government meetings in China 1949–1975*. Foreword by Michel Oksenberg. Michigan Papers in Chinese Studies, Special Number. White Plains, N.Y.: International Arts and Sciences Press, 1976.

Lieberthal, Kenneth, and Dickson, Bruce J. *A research guide to central Party and government meetings in China 1949–1986*. Armonk, N.Y.: M. E. Sharpe, 1989.

Lieberthal, Kenneth, with the assistance of James Tong and Sai-cheung Yeung. *Central documents and Politburo politics in China*. Ann Arbor: Center for Chinese Studies, University of Michigan, 1978.

Lifton, Robert Jay. *Revolutionary immortality: Mao Tse-tung and the Chinese Cultural Revolution*. New York: Vintage, 1968.

[Lin Biao] Lin Piao. "Long live the victory of People's War!" *PR*, 8.36 (3 September 1965), 9–30. Also Beijing: FLP, 1965.

"Lin Doudou who lives in the shadow of history." *Huaqiao ribao*, 14–16 June 1988.

Lin Wu. "Deng's faction unmasks face of 'ultraleftists.'" *ZM*, 175 (1 May 1992), 17–18, trans. in *FBIS Daily Report; China*, 12 May 1992, 27–8.

Lindbeck, John M. H., ed. *China: Management of a revolutionary society*. Seattle: University of Washington Press, 1971.

Ling, Ken. *The revenge of heaven: Journal of a young Chinese*. Trans. Miriam London and Lee Ta-ling. New York: Putnam, 1972.

[Ling Xuejun] Ling Hsueh-chun. "Wang Zhen and Li Xiannian set themselves up against Deng." *ZM*, 175 (1 May 1992), 14–15, trans. in *FBIS Daily Report: China*, 12 May 1992, 26.

Lishi jiangyi. See Sun Dunfan et al., eds. *Zhongguo gongchandang lishi jiangyi*.

[Liu Bi] Liu Pi. "Deng Xiaoping launches 'northern expedition' to emancipate mind; Beijing, Shanghai, and other provinces and municipalities 'respond' by opening wider to the outside world." *JB*, 166 (10 May 1991), 24–7, trans. in *FBIS Daily Report: China*, 6 May 1991, 26–9.

Liu Binyan. "Di'erzhong zhongcheng" (A second kind of loyalty). *Kaituo*, March 1985.

Liu Rixin. "Xifang jingjixue yu woguo jingji tizhi gaige" (Western economics and economic reform in our country). *Zhenli de zhuiqiu*, 6 (1996), 2–6.

[Liu Shaoqi]. *Collected works of Liu Shao-ch'i, 1945–1957*. Hong Kong: URI, 1969.

Liu Xiyang, Liu Gang, and Sun Chengbin. "Weile dang he guojia xingwang fada changzhi jiu'an: Dangde xinyijie zhongyang lingdao jigou chansheng jilu" (Shouldering the great trust of the Party and the people: An account of the birth of the new CCP Central Committee and its Commission for Discipline Inspection). *XH*, 21 October 2007, available in *SWB/Asia Pacific*, 24 October 2007.

Lo Chi Kin, Suzanne Pepper, and Tsui Kai Yuen, eds. *China review, 1995*. Hong Kong: Chinese University Press, 1995.

Los Angeles Times. Daily. Los Angeles: Times Mirror Co., 4 December 1881–. Cited as *LAT*.

Lotta, Raymond, ed. *And Mao makes 5: Mao Tse-tung's last great battle*. Chicago: Banner Press, 1978.

Lou Jiwei. "Guanyu xiaolu, gongping, gongzheng xianghu de ruogan sikao" (Some thoughts on the relationship between efficiency, fairness, and justice). *Xuexi shibao*, 19 June 2006, 1–5, trans. in OSC, CPP20060713442001.

Lowenthal, Richard. "Development and utopia in communist policy," in Chalmers Johnson, ed., *Change in communist systems*, 33–116.

Lowenthal, Richard. "The post-revolutionary phase in Russia and China." *SICC*, 13.3 (Autumn 1983), 91–101.

[Lu Mingsheng] Lu Ming-Sheng. "Inside story of how *Historical trends* was banned." *ZM*, 177 (July 1, 1992), 33–4, trans. in *FBIS Daily Report: China*, 7 July 1992, 19–21.

Lu Pipi. "Ten strata of Chinese society." *BR*, 45.12 (21 March 2002), 22–3.

Ludz, Peter. *Changing Party elites in East Germany*. Cambridge, Mass.: MIT Press, 1972.

[Luo Bing] Lo Ping, and [Li Zejing] Li Tzu-ching. "Chen Yun raises six points of view to criticize Deng Xiaoping." *ZM*, 171 (1 January 1992), 18–19, trans. in *FBIS Daily Report: China*, 3 January 1992, 22–3.

[Luo Gan]. "State Councillor Luo Gan sets out structure for government streamlining," 6 March 1998. *DGB*, 7 March 1998, B1–B2, trans. in *SWB*, 13 March 1998.

[Luo Ruiqing] Lo Jui-ching. "Commemorate the victory over German fascism! Carry the struggle against U.S. imperialism through to the end!" *HQ*, 5 (1965), in *PR*, 8.20 (14 May 1965), 7–15.

[Luo Ruiqing] Lo Jui-ching. "The people defeated Japanese fascism and they can certainly defeat U.S. imperialism too." NCNA, 4 September 1965, in *CB*, 770 (14 September 1965), 1–12.

Luo yi ning ge er [pseud.]. *Disanzhi yanjing kan Zhongguo* (Looking at China through the third eye). Taiyuan: Shanxi, 1994.

LW. Liaowang.

Ma Hong. "Have a correct understanding of the economic situation, continue to do a good job in economic improvement and rectification." *RMRB*, 17 November 1989, trans. in *FBIS Daily Report: China*, 5 December 1989, 37–9.

Ma Licheng, and Ling Zhijun. *Jiaofeng: Dangdai Zhongguo sanci sixiang jiefang shilu* (Crossed swords: A veritable record of contemporary China's three liberations of thought). Beijing: Jinri Zhongguo, 1998.

Ma Shu Yun. "The rise and fall of neo-authoritarianism in China." *CI*, 5.3 (Winter 1990–1), 1–18.

MacFarquhar, Roderick. "The anatomy of collapse." *The New York Review of Books*, 38.9 (26 September 1991), 5–9.

MacFarquhar, Roderick. "Aspects of the CCP's Eighth Congress (first session)." University Seminar on Modern East Asia: China, Columbia University, 19 February 1969.

MacFarquhar, Roderick. "Deng's last campaign." *The New York Review of Books*, 39.12 (17 December 1992), 22–8.

MacFarquhar, Roderick. "The end of the Chinese revolution." *The New York Review of Books*, 36.7 (20 July 1989), 8–10.

MacFarquhar, Roderick. *The origins of the Cultural Revolution, 1: Contradictions among the people 1956–1957*. London: Oxford University Press; New York: Columbia University Press, 1974.

MacFarquhar, Roderick. *The origins of the Cultural Revolution, 2: The Great Leap Forward 1958–1960*. London: Oxford University Press; New York: Columbia University Press, 1983.

MacFarquhar, Roderick. "Passing the baton in Beijing." *The New York Review of Books*, 35.2 (18 February 1988), 21–2.

Mackerras, Colin. "'Party consolidation' and the attack of 'spiritual pollution.'" *AJCA*, 11 (January 1984), 175–85.

Maier, John H. "Tian'anmen 1989: The view from Shanghai." *CI*, 5.1 (Summer 1990), 1–13.

Major, John S., ed. *China briefing, 1985*. Boulder, Colo.: Westview Press, 1987 [1986].

"Major revisions to the government work report." *WHB* (Hong Kong), 16 March 1993, trans. in *FBIS Daily Report; China*, 16 March 1993, 23–4.

"Make fresh contributions on 'protecting and escorting' reform, opening up, and economic development: Warmly congratulating conclusion of the Fifth Sessions of the Seventh National People's Congress and Seventh Chinese People's Political Consultative Conference." *JFJB*, 4 April 1992, trans. in *FBIS Daily Report: China*, 21 April 1992, 36–7.

Mao. *SW*. *See* [Mao Zedong] Mao Tse-tung. *Selected Works of Mao Tse-tung*.

[Mao Zedong] Mao Tse-tung. *Miscellany of Mao Tse-tung Thought (1949–1968)*. 2 vols. Arlington, Va.: JPRS, Nos. 61269–1 and –2, 20 February 1974. [Trans. of materials from *Mao Zedong sixiang wansui*.]

[Mao Zedong] Mao Tse-tung. "Opening address at the Eighth National Congress of the Communist Party of China" (15 September 1956). *Eighth National Congress of the Communist Party of China*. I. 5–11.

[Mao Zedong]. *Selected works of Mao Tse-tung* [English trans.]. Beijing: FLP, vols. 1–3, 1965; vol. 4, 1961; vol. 5, 1977. Cited as Mao. *SW*. For the Chinese ed., *see* Mao Zedong, *Xuanji*.

Mao Zedong. *Xuanji* (Selected works). Beijing: Renmin, vols. 1–4, 1960; vol. 5, 1977.

Mao Zedong. "Zai Shanghai shi gejie renshi huiyi shang de jianghua" (Speech at the conference of all circles in Shanghai Municipality) (8 July 1957). *Wansui* (1969), 109–21.

Mao Zedong. "Zai Zhonggong zhongyang zhaokai de guanyu zhishi fenzi wenti huiyi shang de jianghua." (Speech at the conference on the question of intellectuals convened by the CCP Central Committee) (20 January 1956). *Wansui* (1969), 28–34.

Mao Zedong sixiang wansui (Long live Mao Zedong Thought). N.p.: n.p., 1969. Cited as *Wansui* (1969).

Massacre in Beijing: China's struggle for democracy. New York: Warner Books, 1989.

Materials Group of the Party History Teaching and Research Office of the CCP Central Party School. *See Zhongguo gongchandang lici zhongyao huiyi ji*.

Maxwell, Neville. "The Chinese account of the 1969 fighting at Chenpao." *CQ*, 56 (October–December, 1973), 730–9.

MB. *Mingbao*.

Meaney, Connie Squires. "Market reform and disintegrative corruption in urban China," in Richard Baum, ed., *Reform and reaction*, 124–42.

Meng Lin. "Deng Liqun reaffirms disapproval of phrase 'Deng Xiaoping thought.'" *JB*, 180 (5 July 1992), 42, trans. in *FBIS Daily Report: China*, 6 July 1992, 28–9.

Miles, James. *The legacy of Tiananmen: China in disarray*. Ann Arbor: University of Michigan Press, 1996.

Miller, Alice L. "Beijing prepares to convene the 17th Party Congress." *China Leadership Monitor*, 22 (Fall 2007).

Miller, Alice L. "The case of Xi Jinping and the mysterious succession." *China Leadership Monitor*, 30 (Fall 2009).

Miller, Alice L. "The CCP Central Committee's leading small groups." *China Leadership Monitor*, 26 (Fall 2008).

Miller, Alice L. "Hu Jintao and the Sixth Plenum." *China Leadership Monitor*, 20 (Winter 2007).

Miller, Alice L. "The preparation of Li Keqiang." *China Leadership Monitor*, 31 (Winter 2010).

Miller, H. Lyman. "Xu Liangying and He Zuoxiu: Divergent responses to physics and politics in the post-Mao period." *Historical Studies in the Physical and Biological Sciences*, 30, pt. I (1999), 89–114.

Miller, H. Lyman, and Liu Xiaohong. "The foreign policy outlook of China's 'third generation' elite," in David M. Lampton, ed., *The making of Chinese foreign and security policy*, 123–50.

Mills, William deB. "Generational change in China." *POC*, 32.6 (November–December 1983), 16–35.

Mingbao. Monthly. Hong Kong: 1968–. Cited as *MB*.

Ministry of Information Industry. "Telecommunications regulations of the People's Republic of China." 25 September 2000; available at http://tradeinservices.mofcom.gov.cn/en/b/2000-09-25/18619.shtml (accessed 9 August 2010).

Miscellany of Mao Tse-tung Thought. See Mao Zedong.

Modern China: An international quarterly of history and social science. Quarterly. Newbury Park, Calif.: Sage, 1975–.

Mote, Frederick W. *Imperial China – 900–1800*. Cambridge, Mass.: Harvard University Press, 1999.

Mulvenon, James. "So crooked they have to screw their pants on: New trends in Chinese military corruption." *China Leadership Monitor*, 19 (Fall 2006).

Mulvenon, James. *Soldiers of fortune: The rise and fall of the Chinese military business complex, 1978–1998*. Armonk, N.Y.: M.E. Sharpe, 2001.

Mulvenon, James. "To get rich is unprofessional: Chinese military corruption in the Jiang era." *China Leadership Monitor*, 6 (Spring 2003).

Munro, Donald J. "Egalitarian ideal and educational fact in communist China," in John M. H. Lindbeck, ed., *China: Management of a revolutionary society*, 256–301.

Munro, Robin. "Who died in Beijing, and why?" *The Nation*, 11 June 1990, 811–22.

Myers, James T. "China: Modernization and 'unhealthy tendencies.'" *Comparative Politics*, 21.2 (January 1989), 193–214.

Nakajima, Mineo. "The Kao Kang affair and Sino-Soviet relations." *Review*. Tokyo: Japanese Institute of International Affairs, March 1977.

Nathan, Andrew J. "Chinese democracy in 1989: Continuity and change." *POC*, 38.5 (September–October 1989), 16–29.

Nation, The. Weekly. New York: Nation Enterprises, 1865–.

National Bureau of Statistics. *China statistical yearbook 2004*. Beijing: China Statistics Press, 2004.

National Bureau of Statistics. "Zhonghua renmin gongheguo guojia tongjiju guanyu 1996 nian guomin jingji he shehui fazhan de tongji tongbao" (Statistical communiqué on socio-economic development in 1996), 4 April 1997; available at http://www.stats.gov.cn/tjgb/ndtjgb/qgndtjgb/t20020331_15391.htm (accessed 9 August 2010).

Naughton, Barry. *The Chinese economy: Transitions and growth*. Cambridge, Mass.: The MIT Press, 2007.

Naughton, Barry. "The decline of central control over investment in post-Mao China," in David Lampion, ed., *Policy implementation in post-Mao China*.

Naughton, Barry. *Growing out of the plan: Chinese economic reform, 1978–1983*. Cambridge: Cambridge University Press, 1995.

Naughton, Barry. "Macroeconomic obstacles to reform in China." Paper presented at the Southern California China Colloquium, UCLA, November 1990.

Naughton, Barry. "SASAC rising." *China Leadership Monitor*, 14 (Spring 2005).

Naughton, Barry. "The State Asset Commission: A powerful new government body." *China Leadership Monitor*, 8 (Fall 2003).

NBR Analysis. Irregular. Seattle: 1990–.

NCNA. New China News Agency.

Nelsen, Harvey W. *The Chinese military system: An organizational study of the Chinese People's Liberation Army*. Boulder, Colo.: Westview Press, 1981 [1977].

Nelsen, Harvey W. "Military bureaucracy in the Cultural Revolution." *AS*, 14.4 (April 1974), 372–95.

Nelsen, Harvey W. "Military forces in the Cultural Revolution." *CQ*, 51 (July–September 1972), 444–74.

Nethercut, Richard D. "Deng and the gun: Party–military relations in the People's Republic of China." *AS*, 22.8 (August 1982), 691–704.

New China News Agency. (*Xinhua she*). Cited as NCNA. See *Xinhua tongxun she*.

"New stage of China's reform and opening to the outside world." *RMRB* editorial, 9 June 1992, trans. in *FBIS Daily Report: China*, 9 June 1992, 17–18.

New York Review of Books, The. 21/yr. New York: NYRB, 1963–.

New York Times, The. Daily. New York: 13 September 1857–. Cited as *NYT*.

[Nie Rongzhen] *Nie Rongzhen huiyi lu* (Memoirs of Nie Rongzhen). 3 vols. Beijing: Jiefangjun, 1983, 1984.

Niming, Frank. "Learning how to protest," in Tony Saich, ed., *The Chinese people's movement*, 83–105.

NMRB. Nongmin ribao.

Nongmin ribao. Daily. Beijing. Cited as *NMRB*.

"Nothing is hard in this world if you dare to scale the heights." *RMRB, HQ, JFJB* joint editorial, 1 January 1976. Trans. in "Quarterly chronicle and documentation." *CQ*, 66 (June 1976), 411–16.

NYT. New York Times.

Observer, The. Daily. London. 1791–.

Observer. "Fengquan dangjin baquanzhuyi zhao yi zhao lishi zhe mian jingzi" (Contemporary hegemonism should take a look in the mirror of history). *RMRB*, 22 June 1999, trans. in *SWB*, 25 June 1999.

Observer. "Lun Meiguo baquanzhuyi de xin fazhan" (On the new development of American hegemonism). *RMRB*, 27 May 1999, trans. in *SWB*, 29 May 1999.

Observer. "Shi rendaozhuyi, haishi baquanzhuyi?" (Humanitarianism or hegemonism?). *RMRB*, 17 May 1999, trans. in *SWB/Asia Pacific*, 17 May 1999.

Oi, Jean C. "Partial market reform and corruption in rural China," in Richard Baum, ed., *Reform and reaction*, 143–61.

Oi, Jean. *Rural China takes off: Incentives for industrialization*. Berkeley: University of California Press, 1999.

Oi, Jean C. *State and peasant in contemporary China: The political economy of village government*. Berkeley: University of California Press, 1989.

Oksenberg, Michel. "China's 13th Party Congress." *POC*, 36.6 (November–December 1987), 1–17.

Oksenberg, Michel. "The exit pattern from Chinese politics and its implications." *CQ*, 67 (September 1976), 501–18.

Oksenberg, Michel, and Yeung Sai-cheung. "Hua Kuo-feng's pre–Cultural Revolution Hunan years, 1949–1966: The making of a political generalist." *CQ*, 69 (March 1977), 3–53.

OSC. Open Source Center. Washington, DC: 2005–. (Formerly Foreign Broadcast Information Center [*FBIS*], 1941–.)

Overholt, William. *The rise of China: How economic reform is creating a new superpower.* New York: W. W. Norton, 1993.

Ownby, David. *Falungong and the future of China.* New York: Oxford University Press, 2008.

Pacific Affairs: An international review of Asia and the Pacific. Quarterly. Vancouver, B.C.: 1926–. Vols. 1–33 published by the Institute of Pacific Relations. Vols. 34 to the present published by the University of British Columbia, Vancouver.

Parish, William L. "Factions in Chinese military politics." *CQ*, 56 (October–December 1973), 667–99.

PC. People's China.

Peking Review. Beijing: 1958–. Cited as *PR*. (From January 1979, *Beijing Review*.)

Peng Dehuai. *Memoirs of a Chinese marshal: The autobiographical notes of Peng Dehuai (1898–1974).* Trans. Zheng Longpu; English text edited by Sara Grimes. Beijing: FLP, 1984.

Peng Dehuai. *Peng Dehuai zishu* (Peng Dehuai's own account). Beijing: Renmin, 1981. Translated as *Memoirs of a Chinese marshal.* Beijing: FLP, 1984.

Peng Zhen. "Report on the draft of a revised constitution of the PRC." *BR*, 25.50 (13 December 1982), 9–20.

People's China. Semimonthly. Beijing: 1950–7. Cited as *PC*.

People's Daily. See *Renmin ribao*.

Pepper, Suzanne. *Civil war in China: The political struggle, 1943–1949.* Berkeley: University of California Press, 1978.

Pepper, Suzanne. "Deng Xiaoping's political and economic reforms and the Chinese student protests." *Universities Field Staff International Reports*, 30 (1986).

Perry, Elizabeth J. "Social ferment: Grumbling amidst growth," in John S. Major, ed., *China briefing, 1985*, 39–52.

Perry, Elizabeth J., and Wong, Christine, eds. *The political economy of reform in post-Mao China.* Cambridge, Mass.: Council on East Asian Studies, Harvard University, 1985.

Petracca, Mark, and Xiong, Mong. "The concept of Chinese neo-authoritarianism: An exploration and democratic critique." *AS*, 30.11 (November 1990), 1099–1117.

POC. Problems of Communism.

Polemic on the general line of the international communist movement, The. Beijing: FLP, 1965.

"Political report" to the Fourteenth Party Congress. Beijing television, trans. in *FBIS Daily Report: China*, 13 October 1992, 23–43.

"The politics of prerogatives in China: The case of the *Taizidang* (Princes' party)." Unpublished manuscript, 1990.

Powell, Ralph I. "Commissars in the economy: The 'Learn from the PLA' movement in China." *AS*, 5.3 (March 1965), 125–38.

PR. Peking Review.

Problems of Communism. Bimonthly. United States Information Agency. Washington, D.C.: U.S. Government Printing Office, 1952–1992. Cited as *POC*.

"Promote stability through reform, achieve development through this stability: Basic concepts of development and reform based on 'seeking progress through stability' in the 1990s." *JJYJ*, 7 (20 July 1990), 3–19.

"Proposal of the Central Committee of the Communist Party of China for formulating the ninth five-year plan (1996–2000) for national economic and social development and the long-term target for 2010," adopted 28 September 1995. *XH*, 4 October 1995, available in *SWB*, 7 October 1995.

Prybyla, Jan. "Why China's economic reforms fail." *AS*, 29.11 (November 1989), 1017–32.

Pusey, James R. *Wu Han: Attacking the present through the past.* Cambridge, Mass.: East Asian Research Center, Harvard University, 1969.

Pye, Lucian W. "An introductory profile: Deng Xiaoping and China's political culture." *CQ*, 135 (September 1993), 413–43.

Pye, Lucian W. "Tiananmen and Chinese political culture: The escalation of confrontation from moralizing to revenge." *AS*, 30.4 (April 1990), 331–47.

Qiang Yuangan, and Lin Bangguang. "Shilun yi jiu wu wu nian dangnei guanyu nongye hezuohua wenti de zhenglun" (A discussion of the debate within the Party in 1955 concerning the issue of agricultural cooperativization). *Dangshi yanjiu*, 2.1 (1981), 10–17.

Qishi niandai (The seventies). Monthly. Hong Kong: 1970–1983. Cited as *QSND*. In 1984, title changed to *Jiushi niandai* (The nineties). Cited as *JSND*.

Qiu Zhizhuo. "Deng Xiaoping zai 1969–1972" (Deng Xiaoping in 1969–1972). *Xinhua wenzhai*, 4 (April 1988), 133–55.

Qiushi (Seeking Truth). 24/yr. Beijing: July 1988–. Cited as *QS*.

QS. Qiushi.

QSND. Qishi niandai.

Quanguo dangshi ziliao. . . . See *Dangshi huiyi baogao ji.*

"Quarterly chronicle and documentation." *CQ* in each issue.

Red Flag. See *Hongqi.*

[Ren Huiwen] Jen Hui-wen. "Deng Xiaoping urges conservatives not to make a fuss." *Xinbao*, 1 January 1993, trans. in *FBIS Daily Report: China*, 4 January 1993, 43–4.

[Ren Huiwen] Jen Hui-wen. "Different views within the CCP on the banking crisis." *Xinbao*, 9 July 1993, trans. in *FBIS Daily Report: China*, 12 July 1993, 41–2.

[Ren Huiwen] Jen Hui-wen. "Political Bureau argues over 'preventing leftism.'" *Xinbao*, 14 April 1992, trans. in *FBIS Daily Report: China*, 17 April 1992, 28–9.

[Ren Huiwen] Jen Hui-wen. "There is something behind Chen Yun's declaration of his position," *Xinbao*, 12 May 1992, trans. in *FBIS Daily Report: China*, 13 May 1992, 21–2.

Ren Zhongping. "Wei jingji jianshe he shehui fazhan tigong qiang you li de zhengzhi baozheng – Xuexi Jiang Zemin tongzhi 'Lingdao ganbu yiding yao jiang zhengzhi' de jianghua" (A powerful political guarantee for economic construction and social development – Studying Comrade Jiang Zemin's speech "Leading cadres must pay attention to politics"). *RMRB*, 1 April 1996, 1,3, trans. in *SWB*, 4 April 1996.

Ren Zhongping. "Zai gan yige ershi nian: Lun woguo gaige fazhan de guanjian shike" (Do it for another 20 years: On the crucial period in China's reforms and development). *RMRB*, 12 July 2004, 1, 2, trans. in OSC, CPP20040712000083.

Renmin ribao (People's Daily). Beijing: 1946–. Cited as *RMRB*.

"Reports from Shenzhen." *BR*, 27.47–28.6 (26 November 1984–11 February 1985).

Research Office of the Supreme People's Court. See *Zhonghua renmin gongheguo.* . . .

"Resolution of the Central Committee of the Communist Party of China on the guiding principles for building a socialist society with advanced culture and ideology." *XH*, 28 September 1986, trans. in *FBIS Daily Report: China*, 29 September 1986, K2–13.

Resolution on certain questions in the history of our Party since the founding of the People's Republic of China [27 June 1981]. NCNA, 30 June 1981; *FBIS Daily Report: China*, 1 July 1981, K1–38; published as *Resolution on CPC History (1949–1981)*. Beijing: FLP, 1981.

Reuters. News service.

Review of Socialist Law. Quarterly. Leiden: 1975–91.

Reynolds, Bruce, ed. *Chinese economic policy*. New York: Paragon House, 1989.

Reynolds, Bruce I., ed. and intro. *Reform in China: Challenges and choices*. Chinese Economic System Reform Research Institute, Beijing. Armonk, N.Y.: M. E. Sharpe, 1987.

Risen, James, and Gerth, Jeff. "Breach at Los Alamos: China stole nuclear secrets for bombs, U.S. aides say." *NYT*, 5 March 1999.

RMRB. Renmin ribao.

Robinson, Thomas W. "Chou En-lai and the Cultural Revolution," in Thomas W. Robinson, ed., *The Cultural Revolution in China*, 165–312.

Robinson, Thomas W. "The Wuhan incident: Local strife and provincial rebellion during the Cultural Revolution." *CQ*, 47 (July–September 1971), 413–38.

Robinson, Thomas W., ed. *The Cultural Revolution in China*. Berkeley: University of California Press, 1971.

Rosen, Stanley. "China in 1986: A year of consolidation." *AS*, 27.1 (January 1987), 35–55.

Rosen, Stanley. "The Chinese Communist Party and Chinese society: Popular attitudes toward Party membership and the Party's image." *AJCA*, 24 (July 1990), 51–92.

Rosen, Stanley. *Red Guard factionalism and the Cultural Revolution in Guangzhou (Canton)*. Boulder, Colo.: Westview Press, 1982.

Rosen, Stanley. "The rise (and fall) of public opinion in post-Mao China," in Richard Baum, ed., *Reform and reaction*, 60–83.

Rosen, Stanley. "Youth and students in China before and after Tiananmen," in Winston Yang and Marcia Wagner, eds., *Tiananmen: China's struggle for democracy*, 203–27.

Ru Xin, Lu Xueyi, and Li Peilin. 2002 *nian: Zhongguo shehui xingshi fenxi yu yuce* (2002: Analysis and prospects for China's social situation). Beijing: Shehui kexue wenxian, 2002.

Rubin, Kyna. "Keeper of the flame: Wang Ruowang as moral critic of the state," in Merle Goldman, with Timothy Cheek and Carol Lee Hamrin, eds., *China's intellectuals and the state*, 233–50.

Saich, Tony. "The fourth constitution of the People's Republic of China." *Review of Socialist Law*, 9.2 (1983), 113–24.

Saich, Tony. "Party consolidation and spiritual pollution in the People's Republic of China." *Communist Affairs*, 3.3 (July 1984), 283–9.

Saich, Tony. "The People's Republic of China," in W. B. Simons and S. White, eds., *The party statutes of the communist world*, 83–113.

Saich, Tony. "The reform decade in China: The limits to revolution from above," in Marta Dassu and Tony Saich, eds., *The reform decade in China*, 10–73.

Saich, Tony. "The rise and fall of the Beijing people's movement," *AJCA*, 24 (July 1990), 181–208.

Saich, Tony. "The Thirteenth Congress of the Chinese Communist Party: An agenda for reform?" *Journal of Communist Studies*, 4.2 (June 1988).

Saich, Tony. "Urban society in China." Paper presented to the International Colloquium on China, Saarbrucken, 1990.

Saich, Tony, ed. *The Chinese people's movement: Perspectives on spring 1989*. Armonk, N.Y.: M. E. Sharpe, 1990.

Scalapino, Robert A. "The transition in Chinese Party leadership: A comparison of the Eighth and Ninth Central Committees," in Robert A. Scalapino, ed., *Elites in the People's Republic of China*, 67–148.

Scalapino, Robert A., ed. *Elites in the People's Republic of China*. Seattle: University of Washington Press, 1972.

Schiele, R.N. "Jiang's men move out of the shadows." *Eastern Express*, 27 December 1994.

Schram, Stuart. "China after the 13th Congress." *CQ*, 114 (June 1988), 177–97.

Schram, Stuart [R.]. "'Economics in command?' Ideology and policy since the Third Plenum, 1978–1984." *CQ*, 99 (September 1984), 417–61.

Schram, Stuart R. "From the 'Great Union of the Popular Masses' to the 'Great Alliance.'" *CQ*, 49 (January–March 1972), 88–105.

Schram, Stuart R. *The political thought of Mao Tse-tung*. New York: Praeger, 1969 [1963].

Schram, Stuart R., ed. *Authority, participation and cultural change in China*. Cambridge: Cambridge University Press, 1973.

Schram, Stuart R., ed. *Chairman Mao talks to the people. See* Schram, Stuart R., ed., *Mao Tse-tung unrehearsed.*

Schram, Stuart R., ed. *Mao Tse-tung unrehearsed: Talks and letters, 1956–71*. Middlesex, Eng.: Penguin Books, 1974. Published in the United States as *Chairman Mao talks to the people: Talks and letters, 1956–1971*. New York: Pantheon, 1975.

Schurmann, Franz H. *Ideology and organization in communist China*. Berkeley and Los Angeles: University of California Press, 1968 [1966].

SCMM. See U.S. Consulate General (Hong Kong). *Selections from China Mainland Magazines.*

SCMP. See U.S. Consulate General (Hong Kong). *Survey from China Mainland Press.*

Selected Documents of the 15th CPC National Congress. Beijing: New Star, 1997.

Selected Studies on Marxism. Irregular. Beijing: Institute of Marxism-Leninism and Mao Zedong Thought, 1981–7.

Seybolt, Peter J., ed. *Revolutionary education in China: Documents and commentary.* White Plains, N.Y.: International Arts and Sciences Press, 1973.

Seymour, James D. "Cadre accountability to the law." *AJCA,* 21 (January 1989), 1–27.

Shambaugh, David L. "The fourth and fifth plenary sessions of the 13th CCP Central Committee." *CQ,* 120 (December 1989), 852–62.

Shao Huaze. "Guanyu 'wenhua da geming' de jige wenti" (On several questions concerning the "Great Cultural Revolution"), in *Dangshi huiyi baogao ji,* 337–92. *Shehui kexue.* Cited as *SHKX.*

Shen Jiru. *Zhongguo budang "Bu Xiansheng": Dangdai Zhongguo de guoji zhanlüe wenti* (China should not be Mr. No: Issues in contemporary Chinese international strategy). Beijing: Jinri Zhongguo, 1998.

Shi Bonian, and Liu Fan. "Unswervingly implement the Party's basic line." *JFJB,* 18 March 1992, trans. in *FBIS Daily Report: China,* 15 April 1992, 44–7.

Shi Jingtang et al., eds. *Zhongguo nongye hezuohua yundong shiliao* (Historical materials on China's cooperatization movement). Beijing: Sanlian shudian, 1957.

Shi Liaozi, ed. *Beijing dixia wanyanshu* (The Beijing underground's ten-thousand-character memorials). Hong Kong: Mingjing, 1997.

Shi Tianjian. "Role culture and political liberalism among deputies to the Seventh National People's Congress, 1988." Paper presented to annual meeting of AAS. Washington, D.C., 1989.

Shih, Victor C. *Factions and finance in China: Elite conflict and inflation.* New York: Cambridge University Press, 2008.

Shijie jingji daobao (World economic herald). Weekly. Shanghai: 1980–9. Cited as *SJJJDB.*

Shiliuda yilai zhongyao wenxian xuanbian (Selected important documents since the Sixteenth CCP Congress), ed. Zhonggong zhongyang wenxian yanjiushi (CCP CC Documents Research Office). 3 vols. Beijing: Zhongyang wenxian, 2005, 2006, 2008.

Shiqida yilai zhongyao wenxian xuanbian (Selected important documents since the Seventeenth CCP Congress), ed. Zhonggong zhongyang wenxian yanjiushi (CCP CC Documents Research Office). Beijing: Zhongyang wenxian, 2009.

Shirk, Susan L. "Playing to the provinces: Deng Xiaoping's political strategy of economic reform." *SICC,* 23.3/4 (Autumn–Winter 1990), 227–58.

Shirk, Susan. *The political logic of economic reform.* Berkeley: University of California Press, 1993.

Shisanda yilai zhongyao wenxian xuanbian, zhong, xia (Important documents since the Thirteenth Party Congress, vols. 2 and 3). Beijing: Renmin, 1991. Cited as *Shisanda yilai,* 2 and 3.

Shisida yilai zhongyang wenxian xuanbian (Selected important documents since the Fourteenth CCP Congress), ed. Zhonggong zhongyang wenxian yanjiushi (CCP CC Documents Research Office). 3 vols. Beijing: Renmin, 1996, 1997, 1999.

Shiwuda yilai zhongyao wenxian xuanbian (Selected important documents since the Fifteenth CCP Congress), ed. Zhonggong zhongyang wenxian yanjiushi (CCP CC Documents Research Office). 3 vols. Beijing: Renmin, 2000, 2001, 2003.

SHKX. Shehui kexue.

SICC. Studies in Comparative Communism.

Sicular, Terry. "Rural marketing and exchange in the wake of recent reforms," in Elizabeth J. Perry and Christine Wong, eds., *The political economy of reform in post-Mao China*, 83–109.

Simmie, Scott, and Nixon, Bob. *Tiananmen Square; An eyewitness account of the Chinese people's passionate quest for democracy*. Seattle: University of Washington Press, 1989.

Simons, W. B., and White, S., eds. *The party statutes of the communist world*. The Hague: Martinus Nijhoff, 1984.

SJJJDB. Shijie jingji daobao.

Skinner, G. William. "Marketing and social structure in rural China." *JAS*, Part I, 24.1 (November 1964), 3–43; Part II, 24.2 (February 1965), 195–228; Part III, 24.3 (May 1965), 363–99.

Skinner, G. William, and Winckler, Edwin A. "Compliance succession in rural communist China: A cyclical theory," in Amitai Etzioni, ed., *Complex organizations*, 410–38.

Snow, Edgar. *The long revolution*. New York: Vintage Books; London: Hutchinson, 1973.

Socialist Upsurge in China's Countryside. Beijing: FLP, 1957.

Solinger, Dorothy. "Capitalist measures with Chinese characteristics." *POC*, 38.1 (January–February 1989), 19–33.

Solinger, Dorothy. "China's transients and the state: A form of civil society?" *Politics and society*, 21.1 (March 1993), 91–122.

Solinger, Dorothy. "China's urban transients in the transition from socialism and the collapse of the communist 'urban public goods regime.'" *Comparative Politics*, 27.2 (January 1995), 127–46.

Solinger, Dorothy. "Urban entrepreneurs and the state: The merger of state and society." Unpublished paper presented at the Conference on State and Society in China, Claremont-McKenna College, 16–17 February 1990.

Solomon, Richard. *Mao's revolution and the Chinese political culture*. Berkeley: University of California Press, 1971.

Song Ping. "Zai quanguo zuzhi buzhang huiyi shang de jianghua" (Talk to a national meeting of Organization Department heads). In *Shisanda yilai*, 2.566–77.

South China Morning Post. Daily. Hong Kong. 1903–.

Soviet Studies. Quarterly. Glasgow: University of Glasgow, 1949–92.

Spechler, Dina. *Permitted dissent in the USSR: Novy Mir and the Soviet Regime*. New York: Praeger, 1982.

Special Commentator. "Yi gongyouzhi wei zhuti jiben biaozhi ji zenmeyang cai neng jianchi gongyouzhi de zhuti diwei" (Public ownership as the basic characteristic and how to uphold the central position of public ownership). *Dangdai sichao*, 4 (1996), 2–17.

Starr, John Bryan. "Revolution in retrospect: The Paris Commune through Chinese eyes." *CQ*, 49 (January–March 1972), 106–25.

State Council. "Hulianwang xinxi fuwu guanli banfa" (Measures for managing Internet information services), Order No. 292, 25 September 2000; available at http://www.chinaculture.org/library/2008–02/06/content_23369.htm

State Council Information Office, and the Ministry of Information Industry. "Rules on the management of Internet news information services," 25 September 2005; available at http://www.cecc.gov/pages/virtualAcad/index.phpd?showsingle=24396 (accessed 9 August 2010).

State Statistical Bureau. See *Zhongguo tongji nianjian*.

State Statistical Bureau. "Intensify reform, accelerate structural adjustments, promote healthy development of the national economy: Economic situation in 1995 and outlook for 1996." *RMRB*, 1 March 1996, trans. in *FBIS Daily Report: China*, 4 April 1996, 32–8.

State Statistical Bureau. *Statistical yearbook of China, 1984*. Hong Kong: Economic Information & Agency, 1984.

Stavis, Benedict. *China's political reforms: An interim report*. New York: Praeger, 1988.

Stavis, Benedict. *The politics of agricultural mechanization in China*. Ithaca, N.Y.: Cornell University Press, 1978.

Studies in Comparative Communism. Quarterly. Los Angeles: School of International Relations, University of Southern California, 1968–71; Oxford: 1971–92. Cited as *SICC*.

Su Shaozhi. "Develop Marxism under contemporary conditions." *Selected Studies on Marxism*, 2 (February 1983), 1–39.

Suettinger, Robert L. *Beyond Tiananmen: The politics of U.S.-China relations, 1989–2000*. Washington, D.C.: Brookings Institution, 2003.

Sullivan, Lawrence R. "Assault on the reforms: Conservative criticism of political and economic liberalization in China, 1985–86." *CQ*, 114 (June 1988), 198–22.

"Summary of the Forum on the Work in Literature and Art in the Armed Forces with which Comrade Lin Piao entrusted Comrade Chiang Ch'ing." *PR*, 10.23 (2 June 1967), 10–16.

"Summary of Tian Jiyun's speech before Party school." *BX*, 266 (16 June 1992), 4–5, trans. in *FBIS Daily Report: China*, 18 June 1992, 16–18.

Summary of World Broadcasts. Daily and weekly reports. Caversham Park, Reading: British Broadcasting Corporation, Monitoring Service, 1939–. Cited as *SWB/FE*.

Sun Chengbin, and Zhao Cheng. "Chui xiang jingji tizhi gaige de xin haojiao – Zhonggong zhongyang guanyu wanshan shehuizhuyi shichang jingji tizhi ruogan wenti de jueding qicao gongzuo jishi" (Sounding a new clarion call to reform the economic system – An account of the process of drafting the CCP Central

Committee decision on several issues in perfecting the socialist market economic system). *Dangde shenghuo*, 11 (2003), 16–19, trans. in *FBIS*, CPP20031109000025.

Sun Dunfan et al., eds. *Zhongguo gongchandang lishi jiangyi* (Teaching materials on the history of the Chinese Communist Party). 2 vols. Ji'nan: Shandong renmin, 1983. Cited as *Lishi jiangyi*.

Sun Hong. "Anecdotes about Deng Xiaoping's political career and family life." *JB*, 11 (5 November 1993), 26–31, trans. in *FBIS Daily Report: China*, 18 November 1993, 34–9.

Sun Shangwu. "Economy forces NPC to revise some laws." *China Daily*, 1 November 1997, 1.

Swaine, Michael D. "China faces the 1990s: A system in crisis." *POC*, 39.3 (May–June 1990), 20–35.

SWB/FE. Summary of World Broadcasts/Far East.

Tan Shaowen. "Emancipate the mind, seek truth from facts, be united as one, and do solid work." *Tianjin ribao*, 17 April 1991, trans. in *FBIS Daily Report: China*, 18 June 1991, 62–8.

[Tan Zheng] T'an Cheng. "Speech by Comrade T'an Cheng" (18 September 1956). *Eighth National Congress of the Communist Party of China.* 2. 259–78.

Tan Zongji. "Lin Biao fangeming jituan de jueqi jiqi fumie" (The sudden rise of the Lin Biao counterrevolutionary clique and its destruction), in *Jiaoxue cankao, xia*, 38–57.

Tanjug. Press service. Yugoslavia.

Teaching and Research Office for CCP History of the [PLA] Political Academy. See *Zhongguo gongchandang liushi nian dashi jianjie*.

Teiwes, Frederick C. *Leadership, legitimacy and conflict in China: From a charismatic Mao to the politics of succession.* Armonk, N.Y.: M. E. Sharpe, 1984.

Teiwes, Frederick C. "The paradoxical post-Mao transition: From obeying the leader to 'normal politics.'" *China Journal*, 34 (July 1995), 55–94.

Teiwes, Frederick C. *Politics and purges in China: Rectification and the decline of Party norms 1950–65.* White Plains, N.Y.: M. E. Sharpe, 1979.

Teiwes, Frederick C. *Provincial leadership in China: The Cultural Revolution and its aftermath.* Ithaca, N.Y.: China–Japan Program, Cornell University, 1974.

Tenth National Congress of the Communist Party of China (documents), The. Beijing: FLP, 1973.

Terrill, Ross. *Mao: A biography.* New York: Harper Colophon Books, 1981.

Terrill, Ross. *The white-boned demon: A biography of Madame Mao Zedong.* New York: William Morrow, 1984.

Tian Jiyun. "Report on the work of the NPC Standing Committee." *XH*, 22 March 1998, available in *SWB*, 26 March 1998.

"The *Times* and Wen Ho Lee." *NYT*, 26 September 2000.

Ting Wang. *Chairman Hua: Leader of the Chinese communists.* Montreal: McGill–Queen's University Press, 1980.

[Ting] Ding Wang. *Wang Hongwen, Zhang Chunqiao pingzhuan (Biographies of Wang Hongwen and Zhang Chunqiao).* Hong Kong: Mingbao yuekan, 1977.

Tong Huaizhou [pseud.], ed. *Tiananmen shiwen ji* (Poems from the Gate of Heavenly Peace). Beijing: Renmin wenxue, 1978.

Tong, James, ed. *Chinese Law and Government*, 23.1 (Spring 1990) and 23.2 (Summer 1990).

"(Trial) CPC regulations on inner-Party supervision." *XH*, 17 February 2004, available in *SWB*, 19 February 2004.

Tsou, Tang. "Chinese politics at the top: Factionalism or informal politics? Balance-of-power politics or a game to win all?" *China Journal*, 34 (July 1995), 95–156.

Tsou, Tang. "Political change and reform: The middle course," in Tang Tsou, ed., *The Cultural Revolution and post-Mao reforms*, 219–58.

Tsou, Tang. "The Tiananmen tragedy," in Brantly Womack, ed., *Contemporary Chinese politics in historical perspective*, 265–327.

Tsou, Tang, ed. *The Cultural Revolution and post-Mao reforms: A historical perspective*. Chicago: University of Chicago Press, 1986.

Twelfth National Congress of the CPC (September 1982). Beijing: FLP, 1982.

Unger, Jonathan, and Chan, Anita. "China, corporatism, and the East Asian model." *AJCA*, 33 (January 1995), 29–53.

Union Research Institute [URI]. *The case of Peng Teh-huai*, 1959–1968. Hong Kong: URI, 1968.

Union Research Institute [URI]. *CCP documents of the Great Proletarian Cultural Revolution, 1966–1967*. Hong Kong: URI, 1968.

Union Research Institute [URI]. *Documents of the Chinese Communist Party Central Committee, September 1956–April 1969*. Hong Kong: URI, 1971.

United States. Department of Agriculture. Economic Research Service. "Historical Gross Domestic Product (GDP) Per Capita and Growth Rates of GDP Per Capita, 1969–2009," 2 November 2009; available at www.ers.usda.gov/Data/.../HistoricalRealPerCapitaIncomeValues.xls.

United States Congress [95th]. Joint Economic Committee. *The Chinese economy post-Mao*. Vol. 1: *Policy and performance*. Washington, D.C.: U.S. Government Printing Office, 1978.

United States Congress [97th]. Joint Economic Committee. *China under the four modernizations*. 2 vols. Washington, D.C.: U.S. Government Printing Office, 1982.

Universities Fieldstaff International Reports.

Urban, George, ed. and intro. *The miracles of Chairman Mao: A compendium of devotional literature, 1966–1970*. London: Tom Stacey, 1971.

URI. Union Research Institute. Hong Kong.

U.S. Consulate General. Hong Kong. *Current Background*. Weekly (approx.). 1950–77. Cited as *CB*.

U.S. Consulate General. Hong Kong. *Extracts from China Mainland Magazines*, 1955–60. Cited as *ECMM*. Title changed to *Selections from China Mainland Magazines*, 1960–77.

U.S. Consulate General. Hong Kong. *Selections from China Mainland Magazines*, 1960–77. Cited as *SCMM*. Formerly *Extracts from China Mainland Magazines*.

U.S. Consulate General. Hong Kong. *Survey of China Mainland Press.* Daily (approx.). 1950–77. Cited as *SCMP.*

U.S. Consulate General. Hong Kong. *Survey of China Mainland Press, Supplement.* 1960–73.

van Ginneken, Jaap. *The rise and fall of Lin Piao.* Harmondsworth: Penguin Books, 1976.

Walder, Andrew G. *Chang Ch'un-ch'iao and Shanghai's January Revolution.* Ann Arbor: Center for Chinese Studies, University of Michigan, 1978.

Walder, Andrew G. "The political sociology of the Beijing upheaval of 1989." *POC,* 38.5 (September–October 1989), 30–40.

Walder, Andrew G. "Urban Industrial Workers." Paper presented to the Conference on State and Society in China, Claremont-McKenna College, 16–17 February 1990.

Walker, Kenneth R. "Collectivisation in retrospect: The 'socialist high tide' of autumn 1955–spring 1956." *CQ,* 26 (April–June 1966), 1–43.

Walker, Tony. "Security chief's sacking seen as rebuff for Jiang." *Financial Times,* 27 February 1996, 6.

Wan Li. "The democratization of policy decision-making and the adoption of scientific methods are vital parts of the reform of the political system," reported in *XH,* 31 July 1986, available in *SWB,* 4 August 1986.

Wang Hui. *China's new order: Society, politics, and economy in transition,* trans. Theodore Huters. Cambridge, Mass.: Harvard University Press, 2003.

Wang Hui. "Contemporary Chinese thought and the question of modernity," in Wang Hui, *China's new order,* 139–87.

Wang Hui. "The 1989 social movement and the historical roots of China's neoliberalism," in Wang Hui, *China's new order,* 41–137.

Wang Jiye. "Several questions on achieving overall balance and restructuring." *RMRB,* 8 December 1989, trans. in *FBIS Daily Report: China,* 19 January 1990, 30–3.

Wang Lingshu. "Ji Dengkui on Mao Zedong." *LW,* overseas edition, 6–13 February 1989, trans. in *FBIS Daily Report: China,* 14 February 1989, 22–26.

Wang Nianyi. *1949–1989 nian de Zhongguo: Da dongluan de niandai* (China from 1949–1989: A decade of great upheaval). Zhengzhou: Henan renmin, 1988.

Wang Nianyi. "'Wenhua dageming' cuowu fazhan mai luo" (Analysis of the development of the errors of the "Great Cultural Revolution"). *Dangshi tongxun,* October 1986.

Wang Renzhi. "Guanyu fandui zichan jieji ziyouhua" (On opposing bourgeois liberalization). *RMRB,* 22 February 1990.

Wang Renzhi. "Lilun gongzuo mianlin de xin qingkuang he dangqian de zhuyao renwu" (The new situation confronting theoretical work and the primary task at the moment). *Xuexi, yanjiu, cankao,* 11 (1990), 8–17.

Wang Ruoshui. "Cong pi 'zuo' daoxiang fanyou de yici geren jingli" (The experience of one individual of the reversal from criticizing "leftism" to opposing rightism). *Huaqiao ribao,* 12–21 March 1989.

Wang Ruoshui. "In defense of humanism." *WHB,* 17 January 1983, 4.

Wansui (1969). See *Mao Zedong sixiang wansui.*

Washington Post, The. Daily. Washington, D.C.: The Washington Post Co., 1877–.

Wasserstrom, Jeffrey N. "Student protests and the Chinese tradition," in Tony Saich, ed., *The Chinese people's movement*, 3–24.

[Wei Yongzheng] Wei Yung-cheng. "Reveal the mystery of Huangfu Ping." *DGB*, 7 October 1992, and 8 October 1992, trans. in *FBIS Daily Report: China*, 16 October 1992, 18–21.

Wen Jiabao. "Report to the 2nd session of the 10th NPC," delivered on 16 March 2004. *XH*, 16 March 2004, trans. in *FBIS*, CPP20040316000088.

Wen Jiabao. "Tigao renshi, tongyi sixiang, laogu shuli he renzhen luoshi kexue fazhan guan" (Raise awareness, unify thinking, and firmly implant and conscientiously implement the scientific development concept), 21 February 2004, in *Shiliuda yilai zhongyao wenxian xuanbian*, 1.755–76, trans. in *SWB*, 23 February 2005.

Wen Jin, ed. *Zhongguo "zuo" huo (China's 'leftist' peril)*. [Beijing]: Chaohua, 1993.

Weng Jieming, Zhang Ximing, Zhang Qiang, and Qu Kemin, eds. *Yu zongshuji tanxin* (Heart-to-heart talks with the general secretary). Beijing: Zhongguo shehui kexue, 1996.

[*Wenhui bao*] Wen-hui Pao (Wenhui daily). Shanghai: 1938–. Cited as *WHB*.

WHB. Wenhui bao.

White, Gordon. *Riding the tiger: The politics of economic reform in post-Mao China*. Stanford, Calif.: Stanford University Press, 1993.

Whitson, William W., with Huang Chen-hsia. *The Chinese high command: A history of communist military politics, 1927–71*. New York: Praeger, 1973.

"Why must we unremittingly oppose bourgeois liberalization?" *RMRB*, 24 April 1991, trans. in *FBIS Daily Report: China*, 26 April 1991, 18–21.

Wilson, Ian, and Ji, You. "Leadership by 'lines': China's unresolved succession." *POC*, 39.1 (January–February 1990), 28–44.

Wilson Quarterly. 5/yr. Washington, D.C.: Woodrow Wilson International Center for Scholars, 1976–.

Witke, Roxane. *Comrade Chiang Ch'ing*. Boston: Little, Brown, 1977.

Womack, Brantly, ed. *Contemporary Chinese politics in historical perspective*. Cambridge: Cambridge University Press, 1991.

Wong, Christine. "Central–local relations in an era of fiscal decline." Paper presented at the annual meeting of the Association for Asian Studies, New Orleans, April 1991.

Wong, Christine. "The second phase of economic reform in China." *Current History*, 84.503 (September 1985), 260–3.

World Economic Herald. See *Shijie jingji daobao*.

World Politics: A quarterly journal of international relations. Quarterly. Princeton, N.J.: Center of International Studies, Princeton University Press, 1948–.

Wright, Kate. "The political fortunes of Shanghai's 'World Economic Herald.'" *AJCA*, 23 (January 1990), 121–32.

Wu, Guoguang. "Documentary politics: Hypotheses, process, and case studies," in Carol Lee Hamrin and Suisheng Zhao, eds., *Decision-making in Deng's China: Perspectives from insiders*, 24–38.

Wu Jinglian. *Jihua jingji haishi shichang jingji* (Planned economy or market economy). Beijing: Zhongguo jingji, 1993.

Wu Jinglian. "Shehuizhuyi jiben tezheng shi shehui gongzheng + shichang jingji" (The basic characteristics of socialism – Social justice plus market economy). *Zhongguo jingji shibao*, 5 August 1997, 1, trans. in *FBIS*, FTS19971016000355.

Wu Jinglian. *Understanding and interpreting Chinese economic reform*. Singapore: Thompson, 2005.

Wylie, Raymond F. *The emergence of Maoism: Mao Tse-tung, Ch'en Po-ta and the search for Chinese theory, 1935–1945*. Stanford, Calif.: Stanford University Press, 1980.

XH. *Xinhua {tongxun she}*.

[Xia Yu] Hsia Yu. "Beijing's intense popular interest in CPC Document No. 4." *DGB*, 12 June 1992, trans. in *FBIS Daily Report: China*, 12 June 1992, 17–18.

Xiang Jingquan. "Review and prospects of China's economic development." *GMRB*, 23 February 1993, trans. in *FBIS Daily Report: China*, 19 March 1993, 48–50.

Xiao Lan, ed. *The Tiananmen poems*. Beijing: FLP, 1979.

Xing Bensi. "Chongfen renshi chuji jieduan, jianjue fang 'zuo'" (Gain a full understanding of the primary stage and resolutely prevent "leftism"). *Zhongguo jingji shibao*, 29 July 1997, 1, trans. in *SWB*, 31 July 1997.

Xing Bensi. "Jianchi Makesizhuyi budongyao – Huaqing Makesizhuyi yu fan-Makesizhuyi de jiexian" (Never waver in upholding Marxism – Drawing a clear line of demarcation between Marxism and anti-Marxism). *RMRB*, 6 June 1996, 9, trans. in *SWB*, 27 June 1996.

Xinhua {tongxun she} (New China News Agency). Cited as *XH*.

Xinhua wenzhai (New China digest). Monthly. Beijing: 1981–.

Xu Ming, ed. *Guanjian shike: Dangdai Zhongguo jidai jiejue de 27 ge wenti* (A critical moment: Contemporary China's 27 problems that urgently await solution). Beijing: Jinri Zhongguo, 1997.

[Xu Simin] Hsu Szu-min. "On the political situation in post-Deng China." *JB*, 210 (5 January 1994), 26–9, trans. in *FBIS Daily Report: China*, 30 January 1994, 13–17.

Xue lilun. Monthly. Harbin: 1981?–.

Xue Yesheng, ed. *Ye Jianying guanghui de yisheng* (Ye Jianying's glorious life). Beijing: Jiefangjun, 1987.

Xuexi shibao. Bimonthly. Beijing: Zhonggong zhongyang dangxiao, 2002–.

Yahuda, Michael. "Kremlinology and the Chinese strategic debate, 1965–66." *CQ*, 49 (January–March 1972), 32–75.

Yan Fangming, and Wang Yaping. "Qishi niandai chuqi woguo jingji jianshe de maojin jiqi tiaozheng" (The blind advance in our national economic construction in the early 1970s and its correction). *Dangshi yanjiu*, 5 (1985), 55–60.

Yan Jingtang. "Zhongyang junwei yange gaikuang" (Survey of the evolution of the Central Military Commission), in Zhu Chengjia, ed., *Zhonggong dangshi yanjiu lunwen xuan, xia*, 567–87.

[Yan Shencun] Yen Shen-tsun. "Deng Xiaoping's talk during his inspection of Shoudu Iron and Steel Complex." *Guangjiaojing*, 238 (16 July 1992), 6–7, trans. in *FBIS Daily Report: China*, 17 July 1992, 7–8.

Yang, Dali. *Catastrophe and reform in China*. Stanford, Calif.: Stanford University Press, 1996.

Yang Guoyu et al., eds. *Liu Deng da jun zhengzhanji* (A record of the great military campaigns of Liu [Bocheng] and Deng [Xiaoping]). 3 vols. Kunming: Yunnan renmin, 1984.

Yang Shangkun. "Zai Xinghai geming bashi zhounian dahui shang de jianghua." (Speech at the meeting to commemorate the eightieth anniversary of the Xinghai revolution), in *Shisanda yilai*, 3.1713–19.

Yang, Winston, and Wagner, Marcia, eds. *Tiananmen: China's struggle for democracy*. Baltimore: University of Maryland School of Law, 1990.

·*Yangcheng wanbao* (Yangcheng evening news). Daily. Guangzhou; 1957–1966; 1980–.

Yao Ming-le. *The conspiracy and death of Lin Biao*, Trans. with an introduction by Stanley Karnow. New York: Knopf, 1983. Published in Britain as *The Conspiracy and murder of Mao's heir*. London: Collins, 1983.

[Yao Wenyuan] Yao Wen-yuan. "On the new historical play *Dismissal of Hai Jui*," *WHB*, 10 November 1965. Reprinted in *RMRB*, 30 November 1965; *CB*, 783 (21 March 1966), 1–18.

[Yao Wenyuan] Yao Wen-yuan. *On the social basis of the Lin Piao anti-Party clique*. Beijing: FLP, 1975. Also in Raymond Lotta, ed., *And Mao makes* 5, 196–208.

Yi Mu, and Thompson, Mark V. *Crisis at Tiananmen: Reform and reality in modern China*. San Francisco: China Books and Periodicals, 1989.

Yi Ren. "Zhuozhuo huiyi de qianqian houhou" (Before and after the Zhuozhuo meeting). *RMRB*, 14 February 1990.

"Yingsi lu" bianji xiaozu. *Yingsi lu: Huainian Ye Jianying* (A record of contemplation: Remembering Ye Jianying). Beijing: Renmin, 1987. Cited as *Yingsi lu*.

Yomiuri Shinbun. Daily. Tokyo: 1912–.

"Yongyuan liyu bubai zhidi de fabao: Xuexi Jiang Zemin tongzhi guanyu 'sange daibiao' de zhongyao lunshu" (A magic weapon for always establishing ourselves in an unassailable position: Studying Comrade Jiang Zemin's important expositions on the "three represents"). *RMRB*, 23 March 2000, 9, trans. in *FBIS*, CPP20000323000048.

Young, Susan. *Private business and economic reform in China*. Armonk, N.Y.: M. E. Sharpe, 1995.

Yu Nan. "Zhou Zongli chuzhi '9.13' Lin Biao pantao shijian de yixie qingkuang" (Some of the circumstances regarding Premier Zhou's management of the 13 September incident when Lin Biao committed treachery and fled). *Dangshi yanjiu*, 3 (1981), 59.

Yu Xiguang, and Li Langdong, eds. *Dachao xinqi: Deng Xiaoping nanxun qianqian houhou* (A great tide rising: Before and after Deng Xiaoping's southern sojourn). Beijing: Xinhua shudian, 1992.

Yuan Hongbing, ed. *Lishi de chaoliu* (Historical trends). Beijing: Chinese People's University Press, 1992.

Yuan Mu. "Firmly, accurately, and comprehensively implement the Party's basic line: Preface to 'Guidance for studying the government work report to the Fifth Session of the Seventh NPC.'" *RMRB*, 14 April 1992, trans. in *FBIS Daily Report: China*, 16 April 1992, 20–3.

Yuan Ssu. "Bankruptcy of Empress Lü's dream." *Chinese Studies in History*, 12.2 (Winter 1978–9), 66–73.

Yuan Yongsong, and Wang Junwei, eds. *Zuoqing ershinian, 1957–1976* (Twenty years of leftism, 1957–1976). Beijing: Nongcun duwu, 1993.

Yue Daiyun, and Wakeman, Carolyn. *To the storm: The odyssey of a revolutionary Chinese woman*. Berkeley: University of California Press, 1985.

[Yue Shan] Yueh Shan. "Central Advisory Commission submits letter to CCP Central Committee opposing 'rightist' tendency." *ZM*, 175 (1 May 1992), 13–14, trans. in *FBIS Daily Report: China*, 30 April 1992, 15–16.

ZB. Zhongbao.

[Zeng Bin] Tseng Pin. "Party struggle exposed by senior statesmen themselves; meanwhile, the new leading group is trying hard to build new image." *JB*, 145 (10 August 1989), trans. in *FBIS Daily Report: China*, 10 August 1989, 14.

Zha, Jianying. *China pop*. New York: The New Press, 1995.

[Zhang Chunqiao] Chang Ch'un-ch'iao. "On exercising all-round dictatorship over the bourgeoisie," in Raymond Lotta, ed., *And Mao makes 5*, 209–20.

Zhang Weiguo. "Chen Xitong an yu quanli douzheng" (The Chen Xitong case and the struggle for power). *Beijing zhi chun*, 30 (November 1995), 30–2.

Zhang Yufeng. "Anecdotes of Mao Zedong and Zhou Enlai in their later years." *GMRB*, 26 December 1988–6 January 1989, trans. in *FBIS Daily Report: China*, 27 January 1989, 16–19 and 31 January 1989, 30–37.

Zhang Yunsheng. *Maojiawan jishi: Lin Biao mishu huiyi lu* (An on-the-spot report on Maojiawan: The memoirs of Lin Biao's secretary). Beijing: Chunqiu, 1988.

Zhang Zhuoyuan. "Promoting economic rectification by deepening reform." *RMRB*, 27 November 1989, trans. in *FBIS Daily Report: China*, 7 December 1989, 28–31.

Zhao Shilin, ed. *Fang "zuo" beiwanglu* (Memorandum on opposing "leftism"). Taiyuan: Shuhai, 1992.

Zhao, Suisheng. "Deng Xiaoping's southern tour: Elite politics in post-Tiananmen China." *AS*, 33.8 (August 1993), 739–56.

Zhao Yuezhi. *Media, market, and democracy in China: Between the Party line and the bottom line*. Urbana: University of Illinois Press, 1998.

Zhao Ziyang. "Further emancipate the mind and further liberate the productive forces." *RMRB*, 8 February 1988, trans. in *FBIS Daily Report: China*, 8 February 1988, 12–14.

Zhao Ziyang. "Report on the work of the government." *BR*, 26.25 (4 July 1983), XVIII–XIX.

Zheng Bijian. "'Sange daibiao' zhongyao lunshu yu mianxiang ershiyi shiji de Zhongguo gongchandang" (An important exposition of the "three represents" and the CCP's keeping step with the 21st century). *RMRB*, 18 May 2000, modified trans. in *FBIS*, CPP20000518000074.

[Zheng Delin] Cheng Delin. "Yao Yilin launches attack against Zhu Rongji, Tian Jiyun." *JB*, 1 (5 January 1993), 44–5, trans. in *FBIS Daily Report: China*, 22 January 1993, 46–7.

Zheng Yongnian. *Globalization and state transformation in China*. New York: Cambridge University Press, 2004.

Zheng Zhibiao. "Shilun shehuizhuyi shichang jingji tiaojianxia de dangnei zhuyao maodun" (A tentative discussion of the principal contradiction within the Party under conditions of a socialist market economy). *Zhenli de zhuiqiu*, 1 (1996), 20–3.

Zhengming (Contention). Monthly. Hong Kong: 1977–. Cited as *ZM*.

Zhenli de zhuiqiu (Pursuit of truth). Monthly. Beijing: 1990–2001.

Zhong Kan. *Kang Sheng pingzhuan* (A critical biography of Kang Sheng). Beijing: Hongqi, 1982.

Zhongbao. Daily. New York: 1982–7.

Zhonggong dangshi dashi nianbiao (A chronological table of major events in the history of the Chinese Communist Party). Zhonggong zhongyang dangshi yanjiushi, ed. Beijing: Renmin, 1987.

Zhonggong dangshi yanjiu (Research into the history of the CCP). Bimonthly. Beijing: Zhonggong zhongyang dangxiao, 1988–. Replaced *Dangshi yanjiu*.

Zhonggong dangshi yanjiu hui (Research Society on the History of the Chinese Communist Party), ed. *Xuexi lishi jueyi zhuanji* (Special publication on studying the resolution on history). Beijing: Zhonggong zhongyang dangxiao, 1982.

Zhonggong shiyijie sanzhong quanhui yilai zhongyang shouyao jianghua ji wenjian xuanbian (Compilation of selected major central speeches and documents since the Third Plenum of the Eleventh Central Committee). 2 vols. Taipei: Chung-Kung yen-chiu tsa-chih-she, 1983.

"Zhonggong zhongyang bangongting yinfa 'Guanyu jinyibu gaijin huiyi he lingdao tongzhi huodong xinwen baodao de yijian' de tongzhi" (Central Committee General Office notice on distributing the "Opinions on improving reporting on meetings and activities of leading comrades"), 5 April 2003, in *Shiliuda yilai zhongyao wenxian xuanbian*, 1.285–6.

Zhonggong zhongyang dangxiao nianjian, 1984 (CCP Central Party School yearbook, 1984). Beijing: Zhonggong zhongyang dangxiao, 1985.

"Zhonggong zhongyang guanyu goujian shehuizhuyi hexie shehui ruogan zhongda wenti de jueding" (Resolution of the CCP Central Committee on major issues concerning the building of a socialist harmonious society), 11 October 2006, in *Shiliuda yilai zhongyao wenxian xuanbian*, 3.648–71, trans. in *SWB/Asia Pacific*, 27 October 2006.

"Zhonggong zhongyang guanyu jinyibu zhili zhengdun he shenhua gaige de jue-ding (zhaiyao)" (CCP Central Committee decision on furthering improvement and rectification and deepening reform [abstract]), in *Shisanda yilai*, 2.680–708.

"Zhonggong zhongyang guanyu wanshan shehuizhuyi shichang jingji tizhi ruogan wenti de jueding" (CCP Central Committee decision on several issues related to perfecting the socialist market economic system), 14 October 2003, in *Shiliuda yilai zhongyao wenxian xuanbian*, 1.464–82.

"Zhonggong zhongyang, Guowuyuan guanyu jinqi zuo jijian qunzhong guanxin de shi de jueding" (Decision of the CCP Central Committee and State Council regarding doing a few things of concern to the masses in the present period), in *Shisanda yilai*, 2.555–7.

"Zhonggong zhongyang, Guowuyuan guanyu tuijin shehuizhuyi xin nongcun jianshe de ruogan yijian" (Some opinions of the Central Committee and State Council for advancing the establishment of a new socialist countryside), 31 December 2005, in *Shiliuda yilai zhongyao wenxian xuanbian*, 3.139–55, trans. in OSC, CPP20060221045001.

Zhongguo gongchandang. Chinese Communist Party.

Zhongguo gongchandang di jiuci quanguo daibiao da hui (Huace) (Ninth Congress of the Chinese Communist Party [pictorial volume]). Hong Kong: Sanlian shudian, 1969.

"Zhongguo gongchandang di shisanjie Zhongyang weiyuanhui diqice quanti huiyi gongbao" (Communiqué of the Seventh Plenary Session of the Thirteenth CCP Cental Committee), in *Shisanda yilai*, 2.1420–6.

"Zhongguo gongchandang di shisanjie Zhongyang weiyuanhui disice quanti huiyi gongbao" (Communiqué of the Fourth Plenary Session of the Thirteenth Central Committee of the CCP), in *Shisanda yilai*, 2.543–6.

Zhongguo gongchandang lici zhongyao huiyi ji (Collection of various important conferences of the CCP). Zhonggong zhongyang dangxiao dangshi jiaoyanshi ziliao zu, ed. Shanghai: Renmin, vol. 1, 1982; vol. 2, 1983.

Zhongguo gongchandang liushinian dashi jianjie (A summary of the principal events in the 60 years of the Chinese Communist Party). Zhengzhi xueyuan Zhonggong dangshi jiaoyanshi. Cited as Teaching and Research Office for CCP History of the [PLA] Political Academy, *Zhongguo gongchandang.* . . . Beijing: Guofang daxue, 1985.

"Zhongguo jingji gaige renzhong daoyuan" (China's economic reform is a heavy responsibility). *Jingji cankao bao*, 16 December 1997, 4, trans. in *FBIS*, FTS19980203000476.

Zhongguo qingnian bao (China youth news). 3/week. Beijing.

Zhongguo renmin jiefangjun jiangshuai minglu (The names and records of marshals and generals of the Chinese People's Liberation Army). Xinghuo liaoyuan bianjibu (A single spark can start a prairie fire editorial department). Beijing: Jiefangjun, vol. 1, 1986; vol. 2, 1987; vol. 3, 1987.

Zhongguo tongji nianjian, 1981 (Statistical yearbook of China, 1981). Zhonghua renmin gongheguo guojia tongji ju, ed. Beijing: Zhongguo tongji nianjian, 1982.

Zhongguo tongji nianjian, 1983 (Statistical yearbook of China, 1983). Zhonghua renmin gongheguo guojia tongji ju, ed. Beijing: Zhongguo tongji nianjian, 1983.

Zhongguo tongji zhaiyao, 1995 (Abstracts on Chinese statistics, 1995). Beijing: Zhongguo tongji, 1995.

Zhongguo zhichun (China spring). Monthly. New York: 1982–.

Zhonghua renmin fayuan tebie fating shenpan Lin Biao Jiang Qing fangeming jituan an zhufan jishi (A record of the trial by the Special Tribunal of the PRC's Supreme People's Court of the principal criminals of the Lin Biao and Jiang Qing counter-revolutionary cliques). Zui gao renmin fayuan yanjiushi (Research Office, Supreme People's Court), ed. Beijing: Falü, 1982.

Zhonghua renmin gongheguo diwujie quanguo renmin daibiao dahui disanci huiyi wenjian (Documents of the Third Session of the 5th NPC of the PRC). Beijing: Renmin, 1980.

Zhongliu. Monthly. Beijing: Guangming ribao, 1990–2002.

Zhou Enlai. See *Zhou zongli. . . .*

[Zhou Enlai]. *Selected works of Zhou Enlai.* Vol. 1. Beijing: FLP, 1981.

Zhou Enlai shuxin xuanji (Zhou Enlai's selected letters). Beijing: Zhongyang wenxian, 1988.

Zhou Guangchun. "Waishang jiajin qiangzhan woguo shichang" (Foreign businesses are intensifying their race to control our country's market). *Zhenli de zhuiqiu,* 2 (1996), 26–7.

Zhou Guangchun. "Xin ziyouzhuyi jingjixue zai woguo de shiji yingxiang" (The real influence of neo-liberal economics in our country). *Zhenli de zhuiqiu,* 6 (1996), 6–8.

Zhou Hao. "Zhengzhi de hexin: Zhengzhi fangxiang he zhengzhi lichang" (The core of politics: Political direction and political stance). *Zhenli de zhuiqiu,* 3 (1996), 7–11, slightly modified trans. from that in *FBIS,* FTS19960301000003.

Zhou Ming, ed. *Lishi zai zheli chensi: 1966–1976 nian jishi* (History is reflected here: A record of the years 1966–1976). Vols. 1–3, Beijing: Huaxia, 1986; vols. 4–6, Taiyuan: Beiyue, 1989.

Zhou Yang. "Inquiry into some theoretical problems of Marxism." *RMRB,* 16 March 1983, 4–5.

Zhou zongli shengping dashiji (Major events in the life of Premier Zhou). Chengdu: Sichuan renmin, 1986.

Zhu Chengjia, ed. *Zhonggong dangshi yanjiu lunwen xuan, xia* (Selection of research papers on the history of the CCP, vol. 3). Changsha: Hunan renmin, 1984.

Zhu Jianhong, and Jiang Yaping. "Development and standardization are necessary: Perspective of real estate business." *RMRB,* 11 May 1993, trans. in *FBIS Daily Report: China,* 24 May 1993, 56–7.

Zhu Rongji. "Should the government intervene in the market, and regulate prices in a socialist market economy?" *Jiage lilun yu shijian,* 10 (October 1993), 1–5, trans. in *FBIS Daily Report: China,* 10 January 1995, 68–72.

Zhushi ben. See *Guanyu jianguo yilai . . .*

ZM. Zhengming.

Zong Hairen [pseud.]. *Zhu Rongji zai 1999* (Zhu Rongji in 1999). Hong Kong: Mingjing, 2001.

Zweig, David. *Agrarian radicalism in China, 1968–1981.* Cambridge, Mass.: Harvard University Press, 1989.

Zweig, David. "Dilemmas of partial reform," in Bruce Reynolds, ed., *Chinese economic policy,* 13–40.

Zweig, David. "Strategies of policy implementation: Policy 'winds' and brigade accounting in rural China, 1966–1978." *World Politics,* 37.2 (January 1985), 26–93.

INDEX

Afro-Asian Conference, 128
Agricultural Producers' Cooperatives (APCs),
  58–65, 69, 72
Agricultural reforms
  cooperativization, 13, 57–65, 60n46, 61n48
  Cultural Revolution, 151–152, 158–159,
    238–239
  Deng Xiaoping, 332–333
  Deng Xiaoping's policies, 291–292
  post-Tiananmen, 515
  tax abolishment, 586
  Third Plenum/Eleventh CC, 318
All-China Federation of Trade Unions, 56
Anshan Iron and Steel Works, 109
Anti-pornography campaign, 473, 486n73
Anti-Rightist Campaign, 81–85, 94–96, 99, 231
Anti-Right Opportunist Campaign, 104
An Ziwen, 48, 49, 461n423

Bai Hua, 330, 348, 348n25
Bankruptcy reforms, 540. *See also* Economic
  reforms
Bao Tong
  arrest of, 458, 458n415
  bourgeois liberalization role, 403n238
  criticism of by PSC, 451
  political reform role (neoauthoritarianism),
    428–429
  purge of, 461n423
  student protest role, 439
Barshevsky, Charlene, 559
Baum, Richard, 238
Ba Zhongtan, 514
Beidaihe Conference, Liu-Deng program,
    121–125, 121n20, 122n22, 132, 136
Beida-Qinghua Two Schools Big Criticism Group
  "Two Schools," 284

Beijing Students' Autonomous Federation (BSAF),
  437–439, 440n369, 443n375
Beijing Workers' Federation, 436–437, 456
Blair, Anthony, 564
Bonaparte, Napoleon, 1n1, 2n5
Bourgeois liberalization
  Bo Yibo role, 401, 431–432
  CCP criticism of, *fang-shou* cycle, 388,
    388n184, 394–395, 398–404,
    399nn220–222, 400n223, 400n225,
    402nn233–235, 403n238
  democracy movement, 431
  Deng Liqun role, 400, 402–403
  Deng Xiaoping role, 388, 388n184, 394–395,
    402, 402nn233–235, 403
  globalization, governance issues, 539–540
  Liao Gailong role, 403n238
  Li Peng role, 400–401
  Peng Zhen role, 402, 402n235
  People's Daily articles, 487
  post-Tiananmen criticism of, 471–473,
    475–476
  Wang Renzhi criticism of, 475–476
  Yan Jiaqi role, 403n238
  Yao Yilin role, 401
  Zhao Ziyang role, 401–403, 403n238
  Zhuozhuo meeting, 476
Bo Xicheng, 520
Bo Yibo
  anticorruption drive role, 384, 384n167
  bourgeois liberalization role, 401, 431–432
  Chen Yun's desire for justice for, 316
  crime, corruption policies, 366–367
  dismissal of, 226, 316
  economic reform claims by, 364n85
  Gao-Rao affair role, 49
  Hongqi (Red Flag) support by, 411

Bo Yibo (*cont.*)
  Mao's policies in support of, 55
  rectification campaign role, 354, 384, 384n167
  reform policies generally, 492
  student movement response, 394
  taxation policy, 42, 48, 87
Bridgham, Philip, 255
Bukharin, Nikolai, 94
Bush, George H. W., 559
Bush, George W., 433, 433n349, 482

Cao Diqiu, 188–189, 191, 198
Cao Yiou, 171
Capital Iron and Steel (Shougang), 499, 516
Castro, Fidel, 1n1
Central Advisory Commission (CAC), 340,
  343–344, 343n9, 502–503
Central Discipline Inspection Commission
  (CDIC), 343n9, 354
Central Military Commission, 331
Central Party Secretariat office, 344–345
Chai Ling, 455–456, 458, 458n415
Charles I, 1n1
Charles II, 1n1, 2n5
Chen Boda
  Beidaihe Conference role, 122
  Cultural Revolution role, 157, 161, 172, 187,
    192, 197, 207
  dismissal of, 260, 263–265, 264n69
  516 Group purge role, 215
  as Lin Bao ally, 256–260, 257n41
  as Mao ally, 90
  Ninth Party Congress role, 225n136
  promotion to Politburo alternate, 176
  relationship with Wang Dongxing, 259
  relationship with Wang Hongwen, 259
Cheng Weigao, 484
Chen Jinhua, 507
Chen Li, 207, 209
Chen Liangyu, 593
Chen Muhua, 414n279
Chen Xilian
  dismissal of, 322, 323
  as MAC head, 296, 296n198
  as political ally, 297
  power, position of, 274
  promotion of, 277
Chen Xitong
  arrest of, 517
  criminal prosecution of, 547–548
  criticism of economic policies by, 484
  hunger strike role, 444
  promotion to Politburo, 502

removal from Politburo, 517
Tiananmen Square role, 457, 466
Chen Yi, 213, 214, 224, 276
Chen Yizi, 428–429
Chen Yonggui, 283, 322
Chen Yuan
  criticism of Deng Xiaoping by, 487
  as People's Bank of China vice president,
    508n152
  on Soviet Union abortive coup, 489
Chen Yun
  anticorruption drive role, 384, 384n167
  APC setup by, 61, 62
  background, 2, 14
  Beidaihe Conference role, 122
  criticism of Deng Xiaoping by, 487, 495–496
  criticism of Hua Guofeng by, 310
  criticism of Zhao Ziyang by, 429, 432, 451
  death of, 519, 522, 542
  Gao-Rao affair role, 49–51
  Great Leap Forward role, 90, 93–94, 99–100,
    102
  guiding principles policy, 387
  Hu Yaobang resignation role, 396
  Liu-Deng program role, 114–115
  Mao's policies in support of, 55
  martial law declaration role, 451
  modern sector transformation, 58–60, 65–67
  opposing rash advance program, 69–70, 74
  promotion to Politburo, 76, 317
  publication of essays by, 126
  rectification campaign role, 354, 384, 384n167
  reform policies generally (the thirty-nine
    points), 474–475, 499, 519
  refusal to retire, 377
  relationship with Deng Xiaoping, 468n2
  retirement of, 404
  Seven Thousand Cadres Conference (1962), 117,
    119
  Soviet model adaptations, 71
  spiritual pollution attack role, 354, 359
  support for Yao Yilin, 461n424
  Third Plenum/Eleventh CC role, 316–317
  Twelfth Party Congress role, 343
  Thirteen Party Congress role, 405, 406
Chen Zaidao, 210, 212, 252
Chen Ziming, 458, 458n415
Chiang Kai-shek, 250
Chi Haotian, 552
China Can Say No!, 564
China Economic Development Corporation,
  426–427, 464
China Economic Times (Zhongguo jingji shibao), 546

China Rural Trust and Development Corporation, 464
China Should Not Be 'Mr. No' – Issues in Contemporary Chinese International Strategy, 564
Chinese Communist Party (CCP)
  achievements of, 6
  admission criteria, 570–571
  bourgeois liberalization role (*See* Bourgeois liberalization)
  Chairman role, 118
  collapse of authority, 178–190
  collective leadership image, 594–595
  consolidation movement, 352–357, 354n45, 355nn47–48, 356n51, 356n54
  consolidation–rectification campaign, 358–360, 359n63 (*See also* Rectification campaigns)
  Constitution, 226, 254–255, 281, 344, 577–578, 593–594
  crime, corruption in, 418–419, 418n298
  Cultural Revolution role (*See* Cultural Revolution)
  Deng Xiaoping's reform program, 332–336, 332nn323–324, 335nn333–334
  divisions, factionalization post-Tiananmen, 472, 472n15, 475, 494–501, 519, 521–522
  fang–shou cycle role (*See Fang–shou* cycle)
  Fifteenth Party Congress (*See* Fifteenth Party Congress)
  First (General) Secretary role, 118
  Fourteenth Party Congress, 495, 501–504, 534–535
  governing capacity development, 589–590
  Great Leap Forward role (*See* Great Leap Forward)
  intellectuals, double hundred policy towards, 350, 350n30
  January Revolution, 190–197, 207
  leadership split in, 119, 123, 144–146, 494–497
  line struggles within, 290, 290n168
  militarization of politics, 247–252, 247n4, 248n5, 250n16, 251n19
  military representation on, 227
  Ninth Party Congress, 150, 222, 225–228, 225n136, 257–261, 261n59
  Party leaders, qualifications of, 532–533
  perceptions of Mao in, 326
  post-Eleventh Congress membership, 313
  post-Ninth Congress members, April 1969, 249
  public criticism of, 319–322, 419, 419n303
  Qin Benli dismissal role, 437
  reaction to Red Guards, 183–185
  reconstruction of, post-Cultural Revolution, 221–223, 253–254
  role of, Peng Zhen on, 330–331
  Seventeenth Congress, 590–595
  Sixteenth Central Committee, Sixth Plenum, 587–588
  Sixteenth Central Committee, Third Plenum, 583
  Sixteenth Congress, 572–577
  Sixteenth Congress work report, 577–578
  social humanism support by, 349–350
  succession dynamics, 573–576
  summer retreat cancellation, 581–582
  Tenth Party Congress, 281–283
  Thirteenth Congress, 402nn234–235, 403–406, 404n246, 405n251, 406n255, 471, 506
  "three represents," 567–571, 577
  Twelfth Party Congress, 342–345, 343n9, 344n12
  Vietnam War policy, 128–130
  Zhao Ziyang case handling by, 469–472, 470nn4–5, 472nn12–15
Chinese People's Political Consultative Conference (CPPCC), 27
Chi Qun, 284, 285, 294
Christopher, Warren, 541
CITIC, 426–427, 464
Clinton, William J., 541–542, 559–561, 564
Common Program, 28–30, 51
Communist Party of Indonesia (PKI), 128
Confucius, 283–285, 283n137
Consolidation, reconstruction (1949–52)
  administrative regions, 31
  armed resistance, 22
  career line development, 24
  CCP attitudes, strategies, 24–26, 37, 38
  CCP inadequacies, shortages, 23–24
  Common Program, 28–30, 51
  counterrevolutionary suppression, 33, 37–40, 38n25
  democratic dictatorship, 27–29
  establishment of control, 21–25
  FIve Antis Campaign (rural), 37–41, 38n25, 65
  gradualism policy, 27–29
  labor issues, policies, 24–26
  landlord land redistribution, 35–37, 36n24
  land reforms, 32, 33–37, 36n24
  military rule, 29–30
  modernization, 30
  new liberated areas, 21–22, 35
  Northeast region role, 33
  old liberated areas, 21

Consolidation, reconstruction (1949–52) (cont.)
  overview, 19–21
  parochialism, 20
  Party member recruitment, 23
  peasant associations, 34–35, 36
  political achievements, 37
  power transfers, 32
  private sector control, 26–27, 41
  production restoration, 26
  program implementation, 32–33
  provision of services, 25–26
  reassurance policy, 20–21
  regional authority, 30–33
  taxation, 34
  Three Antis Campaign, 33, 37–41, 38n25, 65
  united front strategy, 27–29
  urban mass movements, 37–41, 38nn25–26
  urban reconstruction, 22–24
  worker retention, recruitment, 24–25, 40
Constitution, 226, 254–255, 281, 344, 577–578,
  593–594
Contemporary Trends (Dangdai sichao), 437, 538,
  539, 556
Counterrevolutionary campaigns. See also
  Rectification campaigns
  consolidation, reconstruction (1949–52), 33,
    37–40, 38n25
  socialist construction, transformation (1953–6),
    61–63, 65
  Tiananmen Square (See Tiananmen Square)
Crime, corruption
  anticorruption drives, fang-shou cycle, 384,
    384n167, 463–464, 464nn433–434
  anticorruption drives, post-Tiananmen,
    516–517, 516n179
  anti-pornography campaign, 473, 486n73
  Bo Yibo anticorruption drive role, 384,
    384n167
  in CCP, 418–419, 418n298
  Chen Yun anticorruption drive role, 384,
    384n167
  economic reforms, 365–368, 365n90, 366n93,
    367nn96–97
  fang-shou cycle generally, 365–368, 365n90,
    366n93, 367nn96–97, 382–384,
    383nn164–165, 384n167, 418–420,
    418n298, 426–427, 426n326,
    427nn331–332
  globalization, governance issues, 566–567
  Hu Yaobang policies, 367n96, 516
  People's Daily coverage, 419, 463
  Qiao Shi anticorruption drive role, 384,
    384n167

Wang Zhaogao anticorruption role, 384,
  384n167
Zhao Ziyang policies, 367n96
A Critical Moment – Contemporary China's 27
  Problems That Urgently Await Solution, 547
Cromwell, Oliver, 1n3, 3n6
Cromwell, Richard, 2n5
Crossed Swords, 563
Cuban revolution, 1n1
Cultural policy
  Cultural Revolution, 152–153, 156–158, 161,
    164–168, 239–240
  Jiang Qing, 130–136, 239, 294n192
Cultural Revolution
  agriculture, industry, health reforms, 151–152,
    158–159, 238–239
  anti-revisionism campaign, 161, 171–174
  balance of power shifts, 202–204, 227–228
  cadre rank divisions preceding, 138
  coalition groups, 124–125
  collapse of authority, 178–190, 242
  consequences of, 227–228, 236–245
  crisis emergence, 160–161
  criticism of, 204–209, 315–317, 326–328
  cultural policy, 152–153, 156–158, 161,
    164–168, 239–240
  Cultural Revolution Group role, 169–170, 174,
    186, 187, 191, 199–200, 202, 207–208,
    213–215, 235, 256–257
  deaths attributed to, 242
  decentralization of power, 227
  Deng Xiaoping's Resolution, 327–328, 330
  deportations, 181
  disillusionment process, 243–244
  economic reforms, 151–152, 159, 238–239
  education reforms, 151–152, 158–159,
    171–174, 176, 239–240
  Eleventh Plenum, 174–178, 182, 183, 185,
    192, 204–205, 247, 247n4
  February Adverse Current, 204–209, 213–214,
    224, 227, 235
  "February Outline" document, 166–167, 171
  Fifty Days Campaign, 171–174, 176, 178,
    182
  516 Group purge, 204, 212–215
  Five-Man Group, 164–168
  Forum (February) Summary, 167–168
  fragmentation of power, 228, 242–243
  goals of, 111, 177, 192, 246–247
  government reorganizations during, 170, 172,
    179, 240–241
  industry reforms, 151–152, 159–160, 238–239
  intellectual policy, 164–168, 239–240

January Revolution (seizure of power),
   190–197, 207, 278
labor reforms, 171–175, 189–190
leaders, trial of, 326
"Learn from the PLA" Campaign, 156
Mao's power base, 153–154
mass base, 158–160, 233–234
military control committees, 196
Million Heroes, 211, 212
Ninth Party Congress, 150, 222, 225–228,
   225n136, 257
origins of, 91–92, 110, 138, 230–237, 261
overview, 147–150, 228–230
Paris Commune model, 194–195, 205
Party's role generally, 234–236
people's communes, 194–196, 205, 238
Politburo meeting, May, 168–170
political conflict sources, 151–153
political department formation, 156
political system reconstruction (See Political
   system reconstruction, post-Cultural
   Revolution)
Propaganda Department, 164–168, 172, 188,
   192
provincial authority collapse, 188–190
radical intellectuals role, 156–158, 192, 197
Red Guards role in (See Red Guards)
revisionism, Mao's concerns with, 152–153
revisionism critique by, 144–145
revolutionary committees, 196, 202–204, 217,
   220–221, 253, 253n28
Shanghai Commune, 195, 205
Sixteen Point Decision, 177–178, 182
strategy, 147–150, 177, 214, 232–233,
   236–237
three-in-one combinations, 193–203
university administration reorganization,
   171–175
worker-peasant system, 159–160
Workers' Headquarters, 188–189, 191, 210
work teams (rectification campaign), 171–175
Wuhan Incident, 204, 209–212

Dai Xianglong, 508
Dalai Lama, 103
Dangdai sichao (Contemporary Trends), 437, 538,
   539, 556
"Decision on Several Issues Related to Perfecting
   the Socialist Market Economic System," 583
Democracy movement, fang-shou cycle, 385–386,
   388, 390–396, 392n197, 431. See also
   Tiananmen Square
Democracy Wall, 319–322

Deng Liqun
   bourgeois liberalization role, 400, 402–403
   Central Secretariat seat, 378
   economic reform policy, 495
   Hu Yaobang resignation role, 396
   liberal intellectual policy, 500–501
   Marxism-capitalism debate role, 370–372,
      370n109
   People's Daily class struggle article by, 492
   political reforms, fang-shou cycle, 387
   promotion to Politburo, 467
   special economic zone policy, 372–373
   spiritual pollution attack role, 355, 356, 357
   student movement response, 394
   ten-thousand-character memorials, 536–540,
      537n15, 563, 571
   Thirteen Party Congress role, 405
   "three represents" article, 571
Deng Nan, 483
Deng Pufang
   economic pursuits of, 367n96, 427n331,
      464n433
   spiritual pollution campaign role, 356n54
Deng Tuo, 117, 168
Deng Xiaoping
   ability of, 311, 523
   background, 1–2, 3n7, 14
   bourgeois liberalization role, 388, 388n184,
      394–395, 402, 402nn233–235, 403
   center-provinicial conflict role, 480–481
   criticism of Hu Yaobang by, 436
   Cultural Revolution role, 168, 171–174, 176,
      178, 182, 187–189, 198, 235
   death of, 528, 544–548
   Democracy Wall, 319–322
   diminishment of influence, 473–474
   dismissal of, 227
   Eleventh Congress role, 312–313
   fall, Gang of Four affair, 293–296, 302, 310
   fang-shou cycle role (See Fang-shou cycle)
   Fifty Days Campaign, 171–174, 176, 178, 182
   four cardinal principles, 338, 347, 470n7
   Gang of Four arrest role, 303–304
   Gao-Rao affair role, 49–51
   Great Leap Forward role, 90–92, 99–100, 101
   group identities as source of friction in, 11–12
   health issues, 513–514
   Hua Guofeng fall role, 322–325, 323n299
   humanism/spiritual pollution, combating,
      352–354, 354n45
   hunger strike resolution role, 443, 443n375
   Hu Yaobang resignation role, 396–397
   Jiang Zemin support by, 461, 461n424

Deng Xiaoping (*cont.*)
  Later Ten Points, 136–137
  leadership, post-Gang of Four, 289–294,
    289n165
  legacy, 4, 525–527
  Liu-Deng program (*See* Liu-Deng program)
  new cat thesis, 483, 484
  on Party member recruitment, 23
  Party/state separation, 506
  policies generally, 470n4
  political reforms, *fang–shou* cycle, 384–385
  promotion of, 7, 50, 75
  public criticism of, 205, 208
  rectification campaign role, 141–142
  reform program generally, 4, 332–336,
    332nn323–324, 335nn333–334, 470,
    470n7, 472n12
  reforms, post-Tiananmen (*See* Reforms,
    post-Tiananmen)
  refusal to retire, 377, 377n138
  rehabilitation of, 276–277, 287–289,
    310
  reinstatement of, 312
  relationship with Chen Yun, 468n2
  relationship with Li Xiannian, 311
  relationship with Luo Ruiqing, 316
  relationship with Mao, 7, 50, 75, 111, 151,
    289n165, 292–293, 325
  relationship with Ye Jianying, 311, 316, 330
  resignation of, 442
  retirement of, 403, 404, 404n246, 574
  return, post-Gang of Four, 286–289
  on seeking truth from facts, 315–316
  on Sino-U.S. relations, 481, 482
  special economic zone policy, 373
  spiritual pollution campaign role, 356–357,
    356n54
  student movement response, 394–396,
    395n207
  as successor of Mao, 325–329
  support of Hua Guofeng by, 311–312
  Third Plenum/Eleventh CC role, 314–318,
    317n279
  Thirteen Party Congress role, 406
  Tiananmen Square justification by, 460
  Zhaoist influence rectification drive, 462
  Zhao Ziyang as implied criticism of, 470–472
  as Zhou Enlai's successor, 295
Deng Xiaoping's Resolution, 327–328, 330
Deng Xiaoping Theory, 545, 548–549, 568, 577,
  594
Deng Yingchao, 298, 317, 377n139
Deng Zhifang, 516

Deng Zihui
  APC setup by, 61–63
  Beidaihe Conference role, 124
  exclusion from Politburo, 75
  land reform criticism by, 36
Ding Guan'gen, 461n425, 471
Ding Sheng, 306
Ding Shisun, 466
Discipline Inspection Commission, 317
Dittmer, Lowell, 158
Djilas, Milovan, 304
Domes, Jürgen, 201, 324n304
Dong Biwu, 276, 281
Du Runsheng, 461n423

Eagleburger, Lawrence, 482
Economic Daily (*Jingji ribao*), 546
Economic reforms. *See also* Industry reforms
  bankruptcy reforms, 540
  Company Law, 535
  crime, corruption, 365–368, 365n90, 366n93,
    367nn96–97
  Cultural Revolution, 151–152, 158–159,
    238–239
  democratic centralism, 514–515, 517
  Deng Xiaoping, 290–291, 333–334, 340
  entrepreneurism, 519–520
  fang–shou cycle, 360–364, 361nn72–76,
    363n83, 364nn84–85, 407, 412–416,
    413n275, 421–427, 421n310, 422n312,
    423n316, 424n318, 425n323
  globalization, governance issues, 534–547,
    555–556
  Hu Yaobang policy, 358, 358n60
  modern enterprise system, 535–547, 561, 563,
    569
  People's Daily coverage, 477–478, 483
  post-Tiananmen, 477–479, 482–484, 492–494,
    504–505, 507–510, 508nn151–153,
    514–516, 519–520
  price control, 340, 341, 362, 415, 421–427,
    421n310, 422n312, 423n316, 424n318,
    535
  retrenchment, 477–478, 535, 542
  state-owned enterprises, 514–516, 529,
    535–540, 558, 561
  Third Plenum/Eleventh CC, 318
  Zhao Ziyang policy, 358, 358n60
Education reforms
  Cultural Revolution, 151–152, 158–159,
    171–174, 176, 239–240
  Deng Xiaoping, 294, 334
  Great Leap Forward, 73, 158–159

socialist construction, transformation (1953–6), 73

Eight Articles on Literature and Art, 114, 115

Eighth Party Congress
Great Leap Forward role, 93, 97, 100
origin of, 47
overview, 74–77
Party military representation, 227

English Protectorate revolution longevity, 1n1, 1n3, 2n5, 3n6

Enlightenment Society, 320

Enterprise Bankruptcy Law, 540

Enterprise Law, 484

Entrepreneurism, 519–520. See also Economic reforms

Everbright, 426–427, 464

Falungong movement, 564–565, 565n68

Fang Lizhi
amnesty, call for, 431
arrest of, 458
criticism of Zhao Zhang by, 412
expulsion from Party of, 399n220
political reforms, fang-shou cycle, 387, 428–429, 433
release of, 481
U.S. embassy sanctuary for, 457
youth movement role, 390–391, 395

Fang-shou cycle
anticorruption drives, 384, 384n167, 463–464, 464nn433–434
Beijing Students' Autonomous Federation (BSAF), 437–439, 440n369, 443n375
bourgeois liberalization (See Bourgeois liberalization)
Central document no. 1, 360, 396, 406n255
Central document no. 3, 397–398, 398n216
Central document no. 4, 399n221, 400n223
Central Party Secretariat office, 344–345
coastal strategy, 425n323
consolidation–rectification campaign, 358–360, 359n63
crime, corruption (See Crime, corruption)
democracy movement, 385–386, 388, 390–396, 392n197, 431
economic reforms, 360–364, 361nn72–76, 363n83, 364nn84–85, 407, 412–416, 413n275, 421–427, 421n310, 422n312, 423n316, 424n318, 425n323
guiding principles question, 387–390, 388n184, 389n190, 389nn185–186
housing privatization, 416–417, 417n288
human rights, 431, 433

intellectual renaissance effects, 379, 379n146
labor reforms, urban demonstrations against, 417–418, 417nn289–293, 418n296
leftism revival, 357–358, 358nn60–62
martial law declarations, 437, 437n360, 443, 445nn390–393, 446–452, 446n384, 447nn385–386, 448nn387–389, 470
martyrdom as weapon, 435, 441–446, 441nn371–372, 442n373, 443n375, 444nn378–379, 445nn381–382
Marxism-capitalism debate, 368–372, 370nn107–109
neijin, waisong, 464–466, 464n435
neoauthoritarianism, 408–410, 414n280, 415, 428–429, 429n335
overview, 337–342, 466–467
PLA reform, 373–376
political reforms, 383–387, 384n167, 385n171, 386n174, 431–433, 432nn345–346, 433nn349–350, 463–464
popular support for reforms, 381–382, 382n160
price control, 421–424, 421n310, 422n312, 423n316
primary stage of socialism, 407–408, 408nn258–260
racism, 430–431
Seventh NPC, 413–416, 414nn279–280, 416n285
socialist spiritual civilization, 345–357
social mobilization, 379–380, 380n153
special economic zones (SEZs), open policy debate, 372–373
structural reforms, 407, 415
student movement (See Student movement)
Thirteenth Congress, 402nn234–235, 403–406, 404n246, 405n251, 406n255, 471, 506
Twelfth CC Sixth Plenum, 388
Twelfth Party Congress, 342–345, 343n9, 344n12
urban discontent (1988), 416–421, 416n286, 417nn288–293, 418n296, 419n303, 420n305, 421nn308–310
working-class demonstrations, 436–437
youth movement, 359–360, 376–378, 377nn138–142, 378n143, 390–394, 391n196, 392n197, 393nn199–200

Fang Yi, 404

Fan Jingyi, 490n87

February Adverse Current, 204–209, 213–214, 224, 227, 235

"February Outline" document, 166–167, 171

Fewsmith, Joseph, 560n64, 564n62
Fifteenth Party Congress
  economic reforms, 529, 535–540
  enterprise reform, 541–544
  Fourteenth Central Committee, Seventh
    Plenum, 547–548
  Fourteenth Central Committee report, 545,
    547
  media coverage of, 546
  opposition to reform, 536–541
  overview, 548–550
  preparations for generally, 534–536
  ten-thousand-character memorials, 536–540,
    537n15, 563, 571
Fifty Days Campaign, 171–174, 176, 178,
  182
Five Antis Campaign
  rural, 37–41, 38n25, 65
  urban, 137, 137n38
"Five balanced aspects," 584
516 Group purge, 204, 212–215
Five-Man Group, 134, 164–168
Five-Year Plan (First)
  agricultural cooperativization, 57–65, 60n46,
    61n48, 92–93
  agricultural production, 67, 93
  differences between PRC and Soviet cases, 93
  factory Party committees within, 55
  labor reforms, 55
  limitations of, 92–93
  Mao's views of, 127
  modern sector transformation, 58–60, 65–67
  overview, 2–3, 41–45
  Soviet Union as model for, 17
  stratification of Chinese society, 96
Five-Year Plan (Second), 71, 74, 76–77
Five Year Plan (Eighth), 479–481
Five Year Plan (Ninth), 535–536
Former Ten Points, 136, 176
Forum (February) Summary, 167–168
Fraser, John, 320
French Revolution, 1n1, 2n5, 3n6
Fu Chongbi, 216

Gang of Four. See also specific individuals
  arrest of, 304–307, 305nn238–240, 307n250
  Deng Xiaoping's fall, 293–296, 302, 310
  Deng Xiaoping's leadership, 289–294,
    289n165
  Deng Xiaoping's return, 286–289
  Mao's death, 303–304, 303n231
  military coup preparations, 306–307
  Nanjing incident, 298, 300, 317

Pi Lin, pi Kong, 283–286, 283n137, 285n145,
  290
  as scapegoat, 326
  strategy of, 296–298
  succession issue, 275–279
  Tenth Party Congress, 281–283
  Tiananmen incident, 298–303, 299n209,
    301n216, 310, 316–317, 319
  Zhou Enlai anti-leftist offensive, 279–280,
    279n122, 280n127
Gao Di, 490–491, 490n87
Gao Gang
  background, 46, 251
  incident described, 45–51, 50n39, 106
  independent kingdom establishment by, 33
  influences of, 44
  purge of, 7, 11, 45
  relationship with Mao, 47
  relationship with Soviet Union, 48–49
Gao Gao, 458n415
Gao Xin, 455–456, 457n410, 458n415
Globalization, governance issues
  bankruptcy reforms, 540
  bourgeois liberalization, 539–540
  Central Document No.1, 586
  collective leadership politics, 533–534
  corruption, 566–567
  Deng Xiaoping Theory, 545, 548–549, 568,
    577, 594
  dissent, limitations on, 564–566, 565n68, 587
  economic reforms, 534–547, 555–556
  economics of, 528–530
  effects on prosperity, 530–531
  effects on social structure, 530–531
  Enterprise Bankruptcy Law, 540
  Falungong movement, 564–565, 565n68
  human rights, 541
  international relations, 528, 540–542
  Internet access, 531–532, 566, 587
  newspapers, publishing, 531
  Ninth NPC, 555–558
  overview, 528–530, 555–556
  ownership reforms, 539, 544
  Party leaders, qualifications of, 532–533
  political reforms, 538–539, 542–544
  public agitation, mobilization, 531–532
  public opinion emergence (permitted dissent),
    561–564, 562nn57–60
  scientific development concept, 582–585,
    593–594
  socialist modernization, 545–550
  social stability, 585–588
  "three represents," 567–571, 577

transparency, accountability trends in, 579–581
World Trade Organization membership,
528–529, 555, 558–561, 559n53, 560n54
Gold, Thomas, 354n45
Gong Yuzhi, 498
Gorbachev, Mikhail, 1n1, 2n5, 440–441,
441n372, 446, 488, 488n78, 539. *See also*
Soviet Union
Gore, Al, 541, 559
Government Work Report (Li Peng), 505
Great Leap Forward
Anti-Right Opportunist Campaign, 104
consequences, failures of, 110–113
education reforms, 73, 158–159
effect on Mao's status, 111–112
Great Proletarian Cultual Revolution
(*See* Cultural Revolution)
limitation of Mao's role in, 96–97
Liu-Deng recovery program, 113–114
Liu Shaoqi's views of, 142
Lushan Conference (1959), 103–110, 108n11,
131, 208, 251, 537
Mao's adjustments to, 102, 109
Mao's views of, 127, 142
mass mobilization policy, 94–96, 142
modern sector transformation, 65–67
origins of, 92–97
overview, 4, 87–92, 148
People's Communes, 95–96, 95n2, 99, 109,
113, 115–116
PLA modernization, 73
politics of, 99–103
review, investigation of, 116–121
second, 109–110, 110n15
statistical system dismantling, 96, 98
strategy, 88, 98–99
tensions among leadership, 88–92
Great Proletarian Cultual Revolution. *See* Cultural
Revolution
Greenspan, Alan, 559
Guan Feng, 133, 157, 213
Guangming ribao, 477–478
Gulf of Tonkin incident, 130
Gulf War, 484–485, 488
Gu Mu, 207
Guo Moruo, 283

Hainan import scandal, 366, 366n93, 367n97
Harding, Harry, 136
Hat Rui dismissed from office (Wu Han), 134–135,
164–168, 235
Health care reforms, Cultural Revolution,
151–152, 158–159, 238–239

Heart-to-Heart Talks with the General Secretary,
547
He Dongchang, 439
He Long, 188, 201, 205
He Qinglian, 564
"Heshang" ("River Elegy"), 420–421, 421n309
He Zizhen, 131
Higher Party School, 133
Historical trends, 500
Hongqi (Red Flag)
anticrime campaign, 351–352, 352n36
ceasing of publication by, 215, 411
class struggle coverage, 351
January Revolution, 193–195
Party oversight of, 264
pi Lin, pi Kong coverage, 284
revisionism, 213
Hou Dejian, 456, 458n415
Hua Guofeng
criticism of, 297–298
as Cultural Revolution beneficiary, 278, 283
Deng Xiaoping support of, 311–312
Eleventh Congress role, 312
establishment of power base by, 309–310,
310n254
fall of, 322–325, 323n299, 324n303
Gang of Four arrest role, 303–306, 307,
323–324
Mao cult preservation, 309–310
notification duties of, 294
political allies of, 296
praise of Cultural Revolution by, 229
promotion of, 109, 278, 302, 308
public criticism of, 310–311
Ten-Year Plan generally, 313–314, 318
Third Plenum/Eleventh CC role, 314–318
Tiananmen incident role, 300
two whatevers, 310–312, 315–317, 324
Ye Jianying criticism of, 310–311, 324,
324n303
as Zhou Enlai's successor, 295–296, 296n197
Huangfu Ping, 483, 483n56, 487. *See also* Deng
Xiaoping
Huang Hua, 323
Huang Ju, 515, 552, 574
Huang Yongsheng
coup involvement, 262, 266
criticism of by Zhou Enlai, 264
promotion of, 322–323
purge of, 273
Red Guard criticism of, 213
relationship with Lin Biao, 216, 258
Hu Feng, 68

Hu Fuming ("Practice is the sole criterion for testing truth"), 315, 315nn266–268
Hu Jintao
    agenda, 579–582
    authority of, 594
    on Belgrade bombing, 560, 560n64
    collective leadership image, 594–595
    consolidation of power by, 592–595
    economic policies generally, 532, 561
    "five balanced aspects," 584
    governing capacity development, 589–590
    leadership status of, 533–534, 553
    legacy, 4
    "people-centered" policies, 581, 584
    policies generally, 577–578
    promotion to Politburo, 502
    scientific development concept, 582–585, 593–594
    social stability, 585–588
    succession dynamics, 573–576, 595–596
    summer retreat cancellation, 581–582
    transparency, accountability trends, 579–581
Hu Jiwei
    criticism of leftism by, 500
    dismissal of, 357
    martial law repeal, 449, 449nn390–391, 461
    Marxism-capitalism debate role, 370, 370n107
    in People's Daily hierarchy, 490n87
    PSC criticism of, 461–462
    public criticism of, 356
Humanism/spiritual pollution, combating, 352–354, 354n45. See also Spiritual pollution campaign
Human rights
    globalization, governance issues, 541
    political reforms relating to, 431, 433
    violations in Tibet, 433n350
Human Rights Alliance, 320
Hundred Flowers movement, 13, 54, 77–81, 83, 94
Hundred Regiments campaign, 100, 250n16
Hu Qiaomu
    alienation theory debate role, 379n146
    criticism of by Fang Lizhi, 390
    criticism of by Su Shaozhi, 429
    death of, 522, 542
    economic pursuits of, 367n96
    education of, 554
    Hat Rui dismissed from office (Wu Han), 134
    Hu Yaobang resignation role, 396
    Marxism-capitalism debate role, 371
    refusal to retire, 377
    relationship with Zhou Yang, 356n51

    retirement of, 404, 405
    special economic zone policy, 372
    student movement response, 394
Hu Qili
    banning of "River Elegy" by, 421n309
    criticism of by PSC, 451, 461
    denial of Politburo seat to, 503, 503n139
    hunger strike resolution role, 442, 444, 444n378
    martial law declarations, 437, 437n360
    Marxism-capitalism debate role, 370–372, 370n107
    price control policy, 422
    promotion to Politburo, 378
    removal from Politburo, 471
    Su Shaozhi reform speech, 432
    Su Shaozhi's speech publication, 429
    Thirteen Party Congress role, 404
Hu Yaobang
    crime, corruption policies, 367n96, 516
    death of, 341, 433
    as Deng Xiaoping's successor, 339, 378
    economic reform policy, 358, 358n60
    legitimacy of as successor, 328
    Marxism-capitalism debate role, 370–372, 370n107
    memorial service demonstrations, 433–436, 434nn352–353, 435nn354–356
    in PLA reform under Deng Xiaoping, 375–376, 376nn135–137
    political reforms, fang–shou cycle, 384
    promotion to Politburo, 317, 378
    reelection of, 404
    reevaluation of, 434, 437n362, 440n369
    relationship with Deng Liqun, 355
    relationship with Deng Xiaoping, 470n4
    resignation of, 396–398, 397n215, 397n218, 398nn216–218, 437n362
    self-criticism, 398, 398n218
    Seventh NPC role, 414n279
    spiritual pollution campaign role, 356–357
    Thirteen Party Congress role, 405
    on unjust treatment of population, 238
    youth movement role, 360, 360n67

Industry reforms. See also Economic reforms
    Cultural Revolution, 151–152, 159–160, 238–239
    Deng Xiaoping, 333–334
Institute of Philosophy and Social Science, Chinese Academy of Sciences, 157
Intellectuals
    Anti-Rightist Campaign, 81–85, 94–96, 99

criticism of leftism by, 500, 501
Cultural Revolution policy toward, 164–168,
239–240
Cultural Revolution role, 156–158, 192, 197
democracy movement, 431
double hundred policy towards, 350, 350n30
Hundred Flowers movement, 13, 54, 77–81,
83, 94
intellectual policy, post-Tiananmen, 521
Jiang-Kang vilification of, 132–135
Lu Dingyi policy, 69, 151
public opinion emergence (permitted dissent)
role, 563–564
renaissance effects, *fang-shou* cycle, 379,
379n146
as target of PLA criticism, 330
Zhao Ziyang's defense of, 432–433
Internet access, 531–532, 566, 587

January Revolution, 190–197, 207, 278
Jiang Chunyun, 515, 518, 552
Jiang Qing
arrest of, 307, 307n250
barring from power of, 286–287
Beidaihe Conference role, 122, 123
criticism of by Mao, 287
criticism of Deng Xiaoping's policies by,
291–292
cultural reform by, 130–136, 239, 294n192
Cultural Revolution role, 152–153, 156–158,
161, 169, 172, 192, 197, 202, 212, 239, 326
516 Group purge role, 214
Gang of Four arrest role, 305, 306
Great Leap Forward role, 90–92
Lin Bao purge role, 265
Lushan Conference (1959), 131
as Mao ally, 90
Pi Lin, pi Kong, 283–286, 283n137
public perceptions of, 300
relationship with Kang Sheng, 132–136
relationship with Lin Biao, 130–132, 257, 259
relationship with Wang Hongwen, 286
succession issue role, 276
Tiananmen incident role, 300
Wuhan Incident role, 211
Yang Chengwu purge role, 216
Zhou Enlai anti-leftist offensive, 279–280,
279n122, 280n127
Jiang Zemin
background, 522
consolidation of leadership by, 548–550
Deng Xiaoping's eulogy, 544–545
on development of Marxism, 545–546

legacy, 4
political strategy, 497, 515–517, 540, 563
as PRC president, 506, 506n148
public ownership system, 510
Qin Benli dismissal role, 437
reform lectures by, 499–500
reform policies generally, 471–472, 475, 488,
514–516, 542–543, 561
relationship with Zhou Rongjii, 515
on science, technology reforms, 484–485
self-criticism by, 496
on Sino-U.S. relations, 481
student protest role, 392–394, 394n203
succession dynamics, 573–576
support of by Deng Xiaoping, 461, 461n424,
503–504, 514
Thirteen Party Congress role, 404
"three represents," 532, 567–571, 577
twelve critical relationships speech, 517
WTO membership role, 559–561, 560n64
as Zhao Ziyang's replacement, 461, 461n424,
470–471
Jia Qinglin, 552, 567, 572, 574
Ji Dengkui, 264, 265, 277, 296, 322, 323
Jiefang ribao (Liberation Daily), 483
Jingji ribao (Economic Daily), 546

Kang Hua Development Corporation, 426–427,
427n331, 464, 464n433
Kang Sheng
Beidaihe Conference role, 122
Chen Yun's criticism of, 316
control of police by, 56n44
Cultural Revolution role, 145, 161, 166, 172,
174, 192, 197, 199, 207
decentralization role, 72
exclusion from Politburo, 75, 132
Great Leap Forward role, 90–92
Lin Bao purge role, 265
as Mao ally, 90, 111
nine polemics, 140
Pi Lin, pi Kong role, 285
promotion to Politburo alternate, 176
as radical, 281
relationship with Jiang Qing, 132–136
relationship with Peng Zhen, 135, 135n36
succession issue role, 276
Kang Youwei, 537
Ke Qingshi
Cultural Revolution role, 157
economic reforms support by, 120
labor reforms support by, 102
relationship with Jiang Qing, 132, 133

Khrushchev, Nikita. *See also* Soviet Union
  criticism of communes by, 105
  denunciation of Stalin by, 74, 325–326
  relationship with Peng Dehuai, 104, 105
  support of Mao by, 101
  withdrawal of support by, 110–111, 139–141,
      139n40, 141n42
Kissinger, Henry, 263
Korean War
  as impetus for modernization, 30, 36, 38–39
  Mao's handling of, 13, 13n6, 38
  Peng Dehuai's role in, 100
Kosovo War, 560
Kuai Dafu, 174, 188, 208, 217, 235
Ku Lian (Bai Hua), 348, 348n25

Labor reforms
  Cultural Revolution, 171–175, 189–190
  Deng Xiaoping's policies, 290–291
  Five-Year Plan (First), 55
  mutual aid teams (MATs), 57–58, 63
  peasant associations, 34–35, 36
  urban demonstrations against, *fang-shou* cycle,
      417–418, 417nn289–293, 418n296
  wages, 421–424, 421n310, 422n312,
      423n316
  worker-peasant system, 159–160
  worker retention, recruitment, 24–25, 40
Lai Changxing, 567
Land reforms. *See also* Ownership reforms
  consolidation, reconstruction (1949–52), 32,
      33–37, 36n24
  Deng Xiaoping, 332–333
  landlord land redistribution, 35–37, 36n24
  Third Plenum/Eleventh CC, 318
Later Ten Points, 136–137
Leading Group for the Resolution of Triangular
      Debt, 486n70
"Learn from the PLA" Campaign, 156
Lee Teng-hui, 541
Lei Feng, 465, 465n437
Lenin, Vladimir Illyich, 3n9, 29, 467
Liang Qichao, 537
Liang Xiang, 464
Liao Chengzhi, 343n9, 554
Liao Gailong, 403n238
Liao Luyan, 62
Liberation Army News/Liberation Army Daily
  bourgeois liberalization, 330
  Cultural Revolution criticism, 315, 316
  pi Lin, pi Kong coverage, 284
  reform articles, 497
  reform coverage, 543

Liberation Daily (Jiefang ribao), 483
Li Changchun, 552, 574
Li Chengrui, 477–478
Li Desheng
  as Cultural Revolution beneficiary, 277
  as Politburo member, 274, 282
  political reform role, *fang-shou* cycle, 389
  relationship with Hu Yaobang, 375–376
Lifton, Robert, 143
Li Fuchun
  attempted purge of, 224
  on economic development, 44
  February Adverse Current role, 207
  516 Group criticism of, 214
  Mao's policies in support of, 55
  policy papers. post-GLF, 114
  promotion to Politburo, 76
Li Guixian, 507
Li Hongzhi, 564–565
Li Jingquan, 102, 283
Li Junru, 546
Li Keqiang, 593, 595
Li Lanqing, 554, 558–559
Li Lisan, 56–57
Lin Biao. *See also* People's Liberation Army (PLA)
  attempted coup (571), 265–269, 266n76,
      269n85
  Beidaihe Conference role, 122
  Cultural Revolution role, 150, 152–156,
      160–164, 168–170, 175, 183, 186–187,
      197, 201–202, 205, 236
  death, legacy of, 273–275, 275n110
  defiance of Mao by, 254–260
  fall of, 252–274
  foreign policy, post-Cultural Revolution,
      260–263
  Gao-Rao affair role, 49, 50
  Great Leap Forward role, 90–92
  health issues, 162, 255–256, 255n35
  as Mao's successor, 135–136, 138–139, 139n39,
      150, 176, 226, 236, 247, 247n4
  Ninth Party Congress role, 225, 225n136, 257
  Order No. 1, 262
  Pi Lin, pi Kong, 283–286, 283n137
  PLA reform by, 125–128, 152–156
  political strategy of, 130, 255, 258–261,
      258n46
  promotion of, 101, 104, 106–109
  purge of, 201, 263–265
  relationship with Chen Boda, 215
  relationship with Jiang Qing, 130–132, 257,
      259
  relationship with Luo Ruiqing, 128, 162–163

relationship with Mao, 90, 101, 106, 117, 129–130, 202, 226, 251–252, 256–260, 258n46, 263–265
relationship with Peng Dehuai, 113, 129
relationship with Zhou Enlai, 255
as scapegoat, 326
13 September Incident, 269–273
Twelfth Plenum role, 224
Vietnam War policy, 129
Yang Chengwu purge role, 216
Ling Zhijun, 563
Lin Jie, 157, 213
Lin Liguo, 265–273
Lin Liheng, 270–271, 270n92
Lin Ruo, 483
Li Peiyao, 514
Li Peng
background, 522
bourgeois liberalization role, 400–401
coastal strategy, 425n323
criticism of Zhao Ziyang by, 450n395, 470
economic policies generally, 478, 480, 535
Government Work Report, 505
health problems of, 507
hunger strike resolution role, 444–446, 445n381, 450
as NPC chairman, 552
political reform role (neoauthoritarianism), 428–429
price control policy, 423
promotion to Politburo, 378
promotion to premier, 404, 506
reform policies generally, 491–492
replacement of, 572
resignation of, 442, 515
Seventh NPC role, 415
Thirteen Party Congress role, 404
Tiananmen Square justification by, 460, 460n419
on Zhao Ziyang case, 471
Li Qiyan, 517
Li Rui, 359–360
Li Ruihuan, 471, 486n73
anti-pornography campaign, 473, 486n73
promotion to Politburo, 461, 461n425
replacement of, 572
student protest role, 393
Thirteen Party Congress role, 404
Li Shuxian, 457, 458
Li Tieying, 404–405, 444
Little red book. See Quotations from Chairman Mao Zedong

Liu Binyan
expulsion from Party of, 399n220
Marxism-capitalism debate role, 370–371
political reform role (neoauthoritarianism), 428–429
political reforms, fang–shou cycle, 387
Liu Bocheng, 276
Liu-Deng program
Beidaihe Conference, 121–125, 121n20, 122n22, 132, 136
Chen Yun analysis, 119–120, 120n18
commune decentralization, 113
economic policy, 113
GLF recovery, 113–114
policy group development, 114–116, 115n17
policy papers, 114, 115
Seven Thousand Cadres Conference (1962), 116–121, 129
Tenth Plenum, 121–125, 121n20, 122n22, 132, 136
Xilou Conference, 119–120, 120n18
Liu Guoguang, 479
Liu Huaqing, 502, 504, 552
Liu Ji, 547, 563, 564
Liu Lantao, 176
Liu Qi, 593
Liu Shaoqi
APC setup by, 61
attempted ousting of (See Gao Gang)
background, 3n7, 14
on class struggle, 42
Cultural Revolution role, 145, 156, 161, 168, 171–174, 187–189, 198
demotion of, 176, 185
dismissal of, 224, 274
Great Leap Forward role, 90–92, 99–100
group identity as source of friction, 11–12
land reform criticism by, 36
Liu-Deng program (See Liu-Deng program)
opposition to succession of, 90
provision of services policies, 26
public criticism of, 205, 208, 224
rectification campaigns role, 80, 137–138, 141–143
rehabilitation of, 323, 330
relationship with Mao, 47, 75, 100, 161
succession of Mao by, 105, 236
Liu Xiaobo, 455–456, 458
Liu Yandong, 593
Liu Zaifu, 379n146
Liu Zhengwei, 516
Liu Zhidan, 132
Li Weixin, 266

Li Xiannian
  attempted purge of, 224
  Beidaihe Conference role, 124
  criticism of Cultural Revolution by, 207
  criticism of Gang of Four by, 290
  criticism of Hua Guofeng by, 310–311
  criticism of Zhao Ziyang by, 432
  death of, 522, 542
  execution of, 383n165
  516 Group criticism of, 214
  Gang of Four arrest role, 306, 307
  guiding principles policy, 387
  Mao's policies in support of, 55
  nomination of Jiang Zemin by, 461n424
  policy papers. post-GLF, 114
  promotion to Politburo, 76
  refusal to retire, 377
  relationship with Deng Xiaoping, 311
  retirement of, 404, 414
  succession issue role, 276, 308, 325
  Twelfth Party Congress role, 343
  Zhaoist influence rectification drive, 462
  on Zhao Ziyang case, 471
  as Zhou Enlai's successor, 295
Li Ximing
  criticism of economic policies by, 484
  removal from Politburo, 502
  student protest role, 439
  Thirteen Party Congress role, 404
Li Xuefeng, 73, 176
Li Yuanchao, 593, 595
Li Zuopeng
  coup involvement, 266
  role in Lin Biao's political strategy, 216, 255,
    258
  self-criticism, 264
  13 September Incident role, 271
  Wuhan Incident role, 211
Long Marchers, 10
Looking at China through the third eye, 525, 564
Louis XVI execution, 111
Lowenthal, Richard, 533
Lu Dingyi
  conspiracy accusations against, 168–170
  Cultural Revolution role, 134, 135, 165
  dismissal of, 176, 198
  intellectual policy, 69, 151
  public criticism of, 188
Lu Keng, 371
Luo Gan, 574
Luo Ronghuan, 128–129
Luo Ruiqing
  background, 145, 162

  conspiracy accusations against, 168–170
  control of police by, 56
  Cultural Revolution role, 160–164
  dismissal of, 176, 198, 235
  promotion to PLA chief of staff, 109
  public criticism of, 188, 205
  relationship with Deng Xiaoping, 316
  relationship with Lin Biao, 128, 162–163
  Lushan Conference (1959), 103–110, 108n11,
    131, 208, 251, 537

MacFarquhar, R., 104, 278n118, 354n45,
    434n353, 444n379
Ma Ding, 379n146
Ma Hong, 477–478
Mainstream (Zhongliu), 538, 571
Ma Licheng, 563
Malraux, André, 143
Mao Yuanxin, 293, 301, 302, 306, 307, 307n250
Mao Zedong
  ability of, 523
  on agrarian reform, 34
  agricultural cooperativization policy, 13, 57–65,
    60n46, 61n48
  anticipations of expansion by, 23
  Anti-Rightist Campaign, 81–85, 94–96, 99
  attempted assassination of, 265–269, 266n76,
    269n85
  background, 3n7
  changes to internal criticism policy, 108
  collectivization policy, 13
  on the Common Program, 28
  consolidation, reconstruction (1949–52) (See
    Consolidation, reconstruction (1949–52))
  crime, corruption under, 365n90
  criticism of Soviet Union by, 91
  Cultural Revolution role (See Cultural
    Revolution)
  death of, 303–304, 303n231, 304n235
  democratic centralism adherence, 14–15, 14n7
  elite solidarity enhancement by, 13–14
  fifty character policy, 253
  Gao-Rao affair role, 48, 50, 51
  Great Leap Forward (See Great Leap Forward)
  health issues, 292–293
  Hundred Flowers movement, 13, 54, 77–81, 83
  legacy, 143–146
  Lushan Conference (1959), 103–110, 108n11,
    131
  on mass organizations, 43
  on military rule, 30
  modern sector transformation, 58–60, 65–67
  nine polemics, 140

policy impacts of, 15
policy papers, post-GLF, 114
rectification campaigns, 136–146,
    141nn42–44
relationship with Deng Xiaoping, 7, 50, 75,
    111, 151, 289n165, 292–293, 325
relationship with Lin Biao, 90, 101, 106, 117,
    129–130, 202, 226, 251–252, 256–260,
    258n46, 263–265
relationship with Peng Dehuai, 11, 89, 100,
    104, 113, 251
retirement, succession, 75
on the Revised Later Ten Points, 138
role of generally, 12–16, 12n5, 13n6, 14n7
Seven Thousand Cadres Conference (1962),
    116–121
Socialist Education Campaign, 4
Soviet model adaptations (1956–7), 67–74
Soviet model of socialism under, 3–4, 3n9, 6n2,
    16–19, 39, 45, 52–55, 67–72, 139, 250
Ten great relationships, 70–71, 84
13 September Incident, 269–273
Tiananmen incident, 298–303, 299n209,
    301n216
unity of leadership under, 7–16, 7n3, 75, 88
Mao Zedong Thought. See Quotations from
    Chairman Mao Zedong
Martial law declarations, 437, 437n360, 443,
    445nn390–393, 446–452, 446n384,
    447nn385–386, 448nn387–389, 470
Martyrdom as weapon, 435, 441–446,
    441nn371–372, 442n373, 443n375,
    444nn378–379, 445nn381–382
Militarization of politics, 247–252, 247n4,
    248n5, 250n16, 251n19
Military Affairs Commission (MAC)
    Chinese Communist Party role in, 330–331
    civilian control of, 332
    Lin Biao's policies, 125–126
    Nie Rongzhen MAC directive, Red Guard
        arrests, 206
    parallel governmental, 340
Military Control Commissions, 29, 30
Million Heroes, 211, 212
Ming dynasty, 251n19
Municipal Propaganda Department,
    157
Mutual aid teams (MATs), 57–58, 63
Mu Xin, 213

Nanchang uprising, 10
Nanfang ribao (Southern Daily), 483
Nanjing incident, 298, 300, 317

National People's Congress
    constitutional backing of, 347
    economic reforms, 535
    Eighth NPC, 505–507, 543
    elections 1953–4, 44
    Fourth NPC, 254–255
    Great Leap Forward role, 109
    martial law repeal, 449, 449nn390–391
    Ninth NPC, 555–558
    Seventh NPC, 413–416, 414nn279–280,
        416n285
    Sixth NPC, 350–352, 351n34, 364
    State Council reforms, 556–557
    Tenth, 572
Naughton, Barry, 478
Neoauthoritarianism
    fang-shou cycle, 408–410, 414n280, 415,
        428–429, 429n335
    generally, 341, 508–509
    Politburo members role in, 428–429
New Democratic Youth League, 43
Nie Rongzhen
    attempted purge of, 201, 216, 224
    Cultural Revolution criticism by, 207
    education of, 554
    Gang of Four, plotting against, 303–304
    MAC directive, Red Guard arrests, 206
    political alliances, 399n220
    promotion to Politburo, 176
    relationship with Lin Biao, 210, 216
    retirement of, 376n137
    Twelfth Party Congress role, 343n9
Nie Yuanzi, 133, 171–174, 189
Nixon, Richard, 481, 482
Novak, Robert, 320

Oi, Jean, 511
Olympic Games 2008, 566, 591
Opium War (first), 248
Opposing rash advance program, 69–70, 74, 85
Organic Law, 51
Outside world relations (Sino-U.S. relations), 469,
    474, 481–482, 492
Ownership reforms. See also Land reforms
    globalization, 539, 544
    landlord land redistribution, 35–37, 36n24
    post-Tiananmen, 509–510
    socialist construction, transformation (1953–6),
        63–64

Pan Fusheng, 184
Peaceful evolution policy, 474, 481, 488–489,
    492–493, 495–496, 501

Peng Dehuai. *See also* People's Liberation Army
    (PLA)
    Chen Yun's desire for justice for, 316
    fate of, 108–109, 109n13
    Gao-Rao affair role, 49, 50
    Great Leap Forward role, 99–101
    Hai Rui dismissed from office (Wu Han), 134–135,
        164–168
    Hundred Regiments campaign, 100, 250n16
    Lushan Conference role, 104–108, 108n11,
        113, 251, 537
    PLA modernization by, 76–77, 154
    purge of, 89, 129
    rehabilitation of, 113, 116, 118, 124, 134
    relationship with Khrushchev, 104, 105
    relationship with Mao, 11, 89, 100, 104, 113,
        251
    ten-thousand-character memorial, 537
Peng Zhen
    bourgeois liberalization role, 402, 402n235
    on Chinese Communist Party role, 330–331
    conspiracy accusations against, 168–170
    control of police by, 56
    criticism of Zhao Ziyang by, 462
    Cultural Revolution role, 145, 151, 164–168
    dismissal of, 176, 198, 205
    economic pursuits of, 367n96
    Gao-Rao affair role, 49
    guiding principles policy, 387
    Hu Yaobang resignation role, 398n218
    Later Ten Points, 136–137
    Luo Ruiqing affair role, 164
    modern sector transformation role, 66
    Party rectification role, 80
    policy papers. post-GLF, 114
    political reform role, *fang-shou* cycle, 389
    public criticism of, 188, 205, 235
    refusal to retire, 377, 377n140
    relationship with Kang Sheng, 135,
        135n36
    retirement of, 402, 404
    return to Politburo, 322
    Seventh NPC role, 416
    Seven Thousand Cadres Conference (1962),
        117–118
    spiritual pollution attack role, 354, 359
    Twelfth Party Congress role, 343n9
People's Armed Police, 374, 514
People's Bank of China, 508, 508n152, 510, 558
People's Communes
    Cultural Revolution role, 194–196, 205, 238
    Great Leap Forward role, 95–96, 95n2, 99, 109,
        113, 115–116

Sixty Articles on, 115–116
People's Daily. See also Hu Jiwei; Wang Ruoshui
    Belgrade bombing coverage, 560
    bourgeois liberalization articles, 487
    censorship of, 280, 280n127, 371, 432n346,
        490–491
    Central Document No. 2 publication, 496
    Chen Yun's criticism of Deng Xiaoping, 487
    class struggle coverage, 292
    corruption coverage, 419, 463
    criticism of Li Riuhan by, 486n73
    Cultural Revolution criticism, 315, 316
    Deng Liqun class struggle article, 492
    double hundred policy, 349–350, 350n30
    economic coverage by, 477–478, 483
    Hai Rui dismissed from office (Wu Han), 165
    Mao's criticism of, 79
    on Marxist–Leninist works, 368–369
    Party oversight of, 264
    post-Tiananmen reform coverage, 490–492,
        490n87, 495, 515
    reform coverage, 358, 368–369, 543
    on science, technology, 484
    scientific development concept, 584
    Shenzhen trip coverage, 495–497, 497n114
    spiritual pollution campaign role, 356, 357,
        490n87
    student demonstration coverage, 393, 437, 438,
        450
    "three represents" coverage, 568, 569
    Yuan Mu article on Deng Xiaoping, 498
    Zhou Enlai memorial incident, 302
People's Liberation Army (PLA). *See also* Lin Biao;
    Peng Dehuai
    business venture divestiture, 567
    control of civilian population by, 126–127
    Cultural Revolution role, 150, 153–156, 161,
        163, 169, 190–197, 199–203
    Deng's legitimacy with, 2, 326
    Deng Xiaoping's policies toward, 290,
        326–332, 340, 373–376
    divisions in, 465, 465n440
    early land reforms role, 34
    fang-shou cycle reforms, 373–376
    516 Group purge role, 204, 212–215
    founding, 10
    Great Leap Forward role, 91
    as Mao's power base, 250–251, 250n16
    Mao's vision of, 250
    martial law response, 447–449,
        447nn385–386, 449nn393–394
    militia's role in, 154–155
    as model organization, 91, 127, 155–156

modernization of, 73, 75–77, 125–128,
154–155
morale lifting of, post-GLF, 114
prestige, morale in, 465, 465n438
provincial secretariats, 253–254
purge of, 192
rank abolishment in, 127–128, 375
rank reinstatement in, 375
reform of under Lin Biao, 125–128, 152–156
reform under Deng Xiaoping, 375–376,
376nn135–137
seizure of power by, 199–202
Tiananmen Square (*See* Tiananmen Square)
Wuhan Incident, 204, 209–212
People's Republic of China (PRC)
decollectivization in, 3, 3n8
group identities as source of friction in, 10–12
leadership polarization in, 11
military control, 2, 2n5
modernization success in, 10
nationalism in, 3–4, 3n9
personality friction among elite in, 11
readiness to rule, 2–3
revolutionary high tide, length/impact of, 3,
3n6
revolutionary leadership longevity, 1–2, 1n3,
6–7, 6n2
sixtieth anniversary, 596–599
unity of leadership in, 7–16, 7n3
Permitted dissent (public opinion emergence),
561–564, 562nn57–60
Pi Lin, pi Kong, 283–286, 283n137, 285n145,
290
The Pitfalls of Modernization, 564
PLA Railway Corps, 374
Politburo Standing Committee (PSC). *See also*
specific individual members
collective leadership image, 594–595
education levels within, 554, 576–577,
591–592
enlargement of, 281
Fifteenth Central Committee, 550–555,
550n43
hunger strike resolution role, 443–444,
443n375, 444n378, 444n379
Hu Yaobang resignation role, 396–398,
397n215, 397n218, 398nn216–218
leadership posts term limitations, 551
longevity, purging of by Mao, 1–2, 2n4
martial law declarations, 437, 437n360, 443,
445nn390–393, 446–452, 446n384,
447nn385–386, 448nn387–389
membership of, 1969–1973, 281–282

membership of, post-Zhou Enlai, 297
post-Eleventh Congress membership, 313
Seventeenth Committee, 591–592
succession issue role, 276, 308
Tiananmen Square strategy, 449–452,
450nn395–397, 455
transparency, accountability trends in, 579–581
Zhaoist influence rectification drive, 462–463
Political reforms
fang-shou cycle, 383–387, 384n167, 385n171,
386n174, 431–433, 432nn345–346,
433nn349–350, 463–464
human rights, 431, 433
neoauthoritarianism (*See* Neoauthoritarianism)
post-Tiananmen generally, 468–469, 468n2,
519–521
Political system reconstruction, post-Cultural
Revolution
CCP reconstruction, 221–223
central leadership selection, 226–227
Democracy Wall, 319–322
foreign policy (Sino-American contacts),
260–263
Fourth National People's Congress, 254–255
Mao's strategy, 219–223
Ninth CC Second Plenum, 257–260, 258n46
Ninth Party Congress, 150, 222, 225–228,
225n136, 257–261, 261n59
overview, 218–219
Party constitution, 226, 254–255, 281, 344,
577–578, 593–594
PLA role in, 220
revolutionary committees, 220–221
state chairmanship proposal, 254–260
state structure, 254–260
Tenth Party Congress, 281–283
Third Plenum/Eleventh CC, 314–318,
317n279
Twelfth Plenum, 223–225
Zhou Enlai anti-leftist offensive, 279–280,
279n122, 280n127
Politics, militarization of, 247–252, 247n4,
248n5, 250n16, 251n19
"Practice is the sole criterion for testing truth"
(Hu Fuming), 315, 315nn266–268
PRC Belgrade embassy bombing, 560
Property rights. *See* Ownership reforms
Public opinion emergence (permitted dissent),
561–564, 562nn57–60
Pursuit of Truth (*Zhenli de zhuiqiu*), 538, 556, 563,
571

Qian Liren, 490n87

Qian Qichen, 482, 541
Qiao Shi
    antiracketeering drive, 426, 426n326
    criticism of Yuan Mu by, 498
    hunger strike resolution role, 444, 449n393,
        450
    on leftism in CCP, 496
    as NPC head, 506
    political strategy, Party leadership, 517–518
    price control policy, 422
    rectification/anticorruption drive role, 384,
        384n167
    reform policies generally, 518
    retirement of, 551–552
    Thirteen Party Congress role, 404
    Zhaoist influence rectification drive, 462–463
Qi Benyu, 133, 157, 165, 216
Qin Benli
    dismissal of, 437
    Hu Yaobang's dismissal, 437n362
    Su Shaozhi reform speech, 432
Qing dynasty, 248, 250
Qinghua University, 217, 284
Qing Ming Festival, 298–300, 299n209
Qin Jiwei
    criticism of by PSC, 451
    retirement of, 502
    Thirteen Party Congress role, 405
Qin Shihuangdi, 283, 283n137, 285, 301n216
Qin Yongmin, 564
Qiu Huizuo
    coup involvement, 266
    purge of, 273
    relationship with Lin Biao, 216, 258
    self-criticism of, 264
Quotations from Chairman Mao Zedong (little red
        book, Mao Zedong Thought)
    as basis for constitutional reform, 347n23
    Deng Xiaoping's support of, 312, 321, 327,
        334
    Lin Biao's use of, 114, 115, 126, 129–130, 132,
        251–252

Rao Shushi. See also Gao Gang
    background, 46
    purge of, 7, 11
    support of Gao by, 48
Rectification campaigns
    Bo Yibo role, 354, 384, 384n167
    CCP consolidation, 358–360, 359n63
    Chen Yun role, 354, 384, 384n167
    Cultural Revolution work teams, 171–175
    Deng Xiaoping role, 141–142

fang-shou cycle, 358–360, 359n63
    Liu Shaoqi role, 80, 137–138, 141–143
    Mao Zedong, 136–146, 141nn42–44
    Qiao Shi role, 384, 384n167
    socialist construction, transformation (1953–6),
        77–81, 79n67
    Wang Guangmei role, 137, 174
    Wang Zhaogao role, 384, 384n167
    Zhaoist influence, 462–463
    Zhou Enlai role, 145–146
Red Army. See People's Liberation Army (PLA)
Red Guards
    brutality by, 181, 184
    Cultural Revolution role generally, 178–183,
        198, 199
    demobilization of, 217–218
    deportations by, 181
    factionalism within, 181–182, 242
    516 Group purge role, 204, 212–215
    ink bottle test, 180–181
    January Revolution, 190–197, 207
    legacy, 238–239
    limitation of powers of, 206–207, 214
    Maoist support of, 179, 186–188, 252
    Mao Zedong Thought (little red book), 154
    as opportunity, 182, 229
    origins of, 160, 179
    overview, 149–150
    Party establishment reaction to, 183–185
Reforms, post-Tiananmen
    agriculture, 515
    anticorruption drive, 516–517, 516n179
    anti-pornography campaign, 473, 486n73
    banking system, 510
    center-provinicial conflict, 479–481
    Central Document No. 2, 496
    conservative policy, 474–476, 475n28,
        486–487, 491–492, 519
    Deng Xiaoping's strategy, 473–474, 473n18,
        482–483, 490–494, 491n92, 501
    Document No. 4, 500
    Document No. 6, 508
    dominance struggle, 494–497
    double-guarantee system, 477
    economic, 477–479, 482–484, 492–494,
        504–505, 507–510, 508nn151–153,
        514–516, 519–520
    Eighth NPC, 505–507, 543
    Five Year Plan (Eighth), 479–481
    Fourteenth Central Committee, Third Plenary
        Session, 509–510
    Fourteenth Party Congress, 495, 501–504,
        534–535